Index of American Periodical Verse: 1993

Rafael Catalá

and

James D. Anderson

assisted by

Martha Park Sollberger

The Scarecrow Press, Inc.
Lanham, Md., & London

SCARECROW PRESS, INC.

Published in the United States of America
by Scarecrow Press, Inc.
4720 Boston Way
Lanham, Maryland 20706

4 Pleydell Gardens, Folkestone
Kent CT20 2DN, England

ISBN 0–8108–3066–3 (cloth : alk. paper)

⊖™ The paper used in this publication meets the minimum requirements of
American National Standard for Information Sciences—Permanence of
Paper for Printed Library Materials, ANSI Z39.48–1964.
Manufactured in the United States of America.

Contents

Preface   v

Introduction   vii

Abbreviations   xi

Periodicals Added   xii

Periodicals Deleted   xiii

Periodicals Indexed, Arranged by Acronym   1

Alphabetical List of Journals Indexed   23

The Author Index   29

The Title Index   521

About the Authors   669

Preface

This twenty-third annual volume of the *Index* was produced with the cooperation of 298 participating periodicals from Canada, the United States, and the Caribbean. More than 7,300 entries for individual poets and translators are included, with more than 20,000 entries for individual poems. A separate index provides access by title or first line.

The importance of the *Index* grows as its necessity becomes more apparent in circles of contemporary poetry research. The increasing demand for inclusion corroborates this fact. The *Index* constitutes an objective measure of poetry in North America, recording not only the publication of our own poets in Canada, the U.S., and the Caribbean, but also those from other lands and cultures and from other times. Of course, the *Index*'s primary purpose is to show what poems have been published by particular poets, what poems have been translated by particular translators, and who wrote poems with particular titles or first lines. But taken together, the *Index* reveals trends and influences: the ebb and flow of particular poets, as well as the influence of cultures of other lands and times as represented by their poets published in North American journals.

James D. Anderson has made a major contribution to the *Index* by designing and refining computer programs that greatly facilitate the indexing process, proof-reading and error-checking, control of cross-references and consistency in names, sorting, formatting, and typesetting. To him also goes credit for managing relations with participating journals and for seeing that indexing gets done in a timely and accurate manner. Also, I want to express my sincere appreciation to Martha Park Sollberger, librarian *emerita*, for her valuable assistance.

Rafael Catalá
Co-Editor

Introduction

Scope

The *Index of American Periodical Verse* indexes poems published in a broad cross-section of poetry, literary, scholarly, popular, general, and "little" magazines, journals, and reviews published in the United States, Canada, and the Caribbean. These periodicals are listed in the "Periodicals Indexed" section, together with names of editors, addresses, issues indexed in this volume, and subscription information. Selection of periodicals to index is the responsibility of the editors, based on recommendations of poets, librarians, literary scholars, and publishers. Publishers participate by supplying copies of all issues to the editors. Criteria for inclusion include the quality of poems, their presentation and the status or reputation of poets. Within these very broad and subjective guidelines, the editors attempt to include a cross-section of periodicals by type of publisher and publication, place of publication, language, and type of poetry. Periodicals published outside of North America are included only if they have North American editors.

Compilation

Citation data are compiled using the WordStar word-processing program, version 4, on a 286 MS/DOS computer. "Shorthand" macro programs are used to repeat author headings for multiple poems by the same poet, create translator entries from author entries for translated poems, and transform complex author names into cross-reference entries. Sorting is done by "IOTA Big Sort," a fast program for sorting very large files written by Fred A. Rowley. Title entries are extracted from the original author entries. Sorted and formatted entries are transferred to a Macintosh computer with laser printer for typesetting and page formatting using Microsoft Word™ and PageMaker™ programs.

Persons interested in the precise details of compilation, including the computer programs used for error-checking, sorting, and formatting, should write to the editors at P.O. Box 38, New Brunswick, NJ 08903-0038. The *Indexes* for 1982 through 1993 are available from the editors on micro-computer disks.

Names and Cross-References

Because many poets have compound surnames and surnames containing various prefixes, we recognize the need for systematic provision of cross-references from alternative forms of surname to the form chosen for entry in the *Index*. We have included cross-references whenever the form used for entry does not fall under the last part or element of the name. In addition, many poets publish under different forms of the same name, for example, with or without a middle initial. When poets are known to use different forms of the same name, alternative forms may be indicated using the format authorized by the *Anglo-American Cataloguing Rules*, Second Edition. For example:

WHEATLEY, Pat (Patience)

This heading indicates that this poet has poems published under two forms of name: Pat Wheatley and Patience Wheatley.

When two or more different names refer to the same poet, one name will be chosen, with "see" references to the chosen name from other names. When it is not possible to determine with assurance whether a single poet is using variant forms of name or different poets have similar names, both names will be used. In such cases, "see also" references may be added to headings to remind users to check the variant name forms that might possibly refer to the same poet.

Format and Arrangement of Entries

The basic format and style of the *Index* remain unchanged. Poets are arranged alphabetically first by surname, then by forenames. In creating this alphabetical sequence, we have adopted principles of alphanumeric arrangement adopted in 1980 by the American Library Association and the Library of Congress. Names are arranged on the basis of their spelling, rather than their pronunciation, so that, for example, names beginning with "Mac" and "Mc" are placed in separate sections. Similarly, a space has a consistent arrangement value, coming before all numerals or letters. Therefore, similar compound and prefixed surnames are often separated by some distance, as illustrated in the following examples. Note that "De BOLT" precedes "DeBEVOISE" by a considerable number of entries.

De ANGELIS	Van BRUNT
De BOLT	Van DUYN
De GRAVELLES	Van HALTEREN
De LOACH	Van TOORN
De PALCHI	Van TROYER
De RONSARD	Van WERT
De VAUL	Van WINCKEL
DEAL	VANCE
DeBEVOISE	Vander DOES
DeFOE	VANDERBEEK
DEGUY	VanDEVENTER
Del VECCHIO	
DeLISLE	
DeMOTT	
DENNISON	
DER-HOVANESSIAN	
DESY	
DeYOUNG	

Abbreviations are also arranged on the basis of spelling, rather than pronunciation or meaning, so that "ST. JOHN" is *not* arranged as "SAINT JOHN," but as "S+T+space+JOHN." Punctuation (including apostrophes and accents), signs, and symbols (other than alphabetic letters and numerals) are not considered, but a hyphen is arranged as if it were a space. Initial articles ("a," "an," "the" and their equivalents in other languages) are ignored in titles of poems and in names of corporate bodies, but they are considered in the arrangement of names of persons and places (e.g., La RUE, El Paso). Numerals, including Roman numerals, are arranged in numerical order preceding alphabetical letters rather than as if they were spelled out.

Under each poet's name, poems are arranged alphanumerically by title or, if there is no title, by first line. Poems with only "Untitled" printed as if it were the title are entered as "Untitled" plus the first line of the poem. In the title index, two entries are provided, one under "Untitled" plus the first line, and one directly under the first line. Numbered poems are handled in the same way. Under poets, initial numbers are treated as the first part of titles, and they are so entered. In the title index, they are entered both under their initial numbers and under the part following the number, if any.

Poem titles and first lines are placed within quotation marks. All significant words of titles are capitalized, but in first lines, only the first word and proper nouns are capitalized. Incomplete excerpts from larger works are followed by the note "Excerpt" or "Excerpts," or, if they are presented as complete sections, by "Selection" or "Selections." The title, first line, or number of excerpts or selections may follow if given in the publication. For example:

WALCOTT, Derek
  "Midsummer" (Selections: XXXIV-XXXVI). [Agni] (18) 83, p. 5-7.

WEBB, Phyllis
  "The Vision Tree" (Selection: "I Daniel"). [PoetryCR] (5:2) Wint 83-84, p. 11.

WAINWRIGHT, Jeffrey
  "Heart's Desire" (Excerpt: "Some Propositions and Part of a Narrative"). [Agni] (18) 83, p. 37.

WATTEN, Barret
  "One Half" (Excerpts). [ParisR] (24:86) Wint 82, p. 112-113.

If an excerpt is treated as a complete "sub-work," it receives an independent entry, with reference to the larger work in a note. For example:

ANDERSON, Jack
  "Magnets" (from "The Clouds of That Country"). [PoNow] (7:2, #38) 83, p. 23.

Notes about dedications, joint authors, translators, and sources follow the title, enclosed in parentheses. A poem with more than one author is entered under each author. Likewise, a translated poem is entered under each translator, as well as its author(s). Each entry includes the names of all authors and all translators. Multiple authors or translators are indicated by the abbreviation "w.," standing for "with." Translators are indicated by the abbreviation "tr. by," standing for "translated by," and original authors are indicated by the abbreviation "tr. of," standing for "translation of." For example:

AGGESTAM, Rolf
"Old Basho" (tr. by Erland Anderson and Lars Nordström). [NewRena] (16) Spr 83, p. 25.

ANDERSON, Erland
"Old Basho" (tr. of Rolf Aggestam, w. Lars Nordström). [NewRena] (16) Spr 83, p. 25.

NORDSTRÖM, Lars
"Old Basho" (tr. of Rolf Aggestam, w. Erland Anderson). [NewRena] (16) Spr 83, p. 25.

The periodical citation includes an abbreviation standing for the periodical title, followed by volume and issue numbers, date, and page number(s). The periodical abbreviation is enclosed in square brackets. An alphabetical list of these periodical abbreviations is included at the front of the volume, followed by the full periodical titles, names of editors, addresses, the numbers of the issues indexed for this volume of the *Index*, and subscription information. A separate list of indexed periodicals is arranged by full periodical title, with a reference to the abbreviated title. Volume and issue numbers are included within parentheses, for example, (16:5) stands for volume 16, number 5; (21) refers to issue or volume 21 for a periodical that uses only one numerical sequence. Dates are given using abbreviations for months and seasons. Year of publication is indicated by the last two digits of the year, for example, 92. Please see the separate list of abbreviations at the front of the volume.

Compiling this year's *Index* has been an adventure into the wealth and variety of poetry published in U. S., Caribbean, and Canadian periodicals as well as the intricacies of bringing this richness together and organizing it into a consistent index. The world of poetry publication is a dynamic one, with new periodicals appearing, older periodicals declining, dying, reviving, and thriving. This year saw the loss of seven periodicals and the addition of sixteen new ones. Two other periodicals that had been dropped were reinstated. Both deleted and newly added periodicals are listed at the front of the volume. Keeping up with these changes is a big job, and we solicit our readers' suggestions as to periodicals that should be included in future volumes of the *Index*, and also, periodicals that could be dropped. Editors who would like their periodicals considered for inclusion in future volumes should send sample issues to:

Rafael Catalá, Editor
Index of American Periodical Verse
P.O. Box 38
New Brunswick, NJ 08903-0038

Although indexing is indispensable for the organization of any literature, so that particular works can be found when needed and scholarship and research facilitated, it is a tedious business. I know that we have made mistakes. We solicit your corrections and suggestions, which you may send to me at the above address.

James D. Anderson
Co-Editor

Abbreviations

dir., dirs.	director, directors
Dept.	Department
ed., eds.	editor, editors
(for.)	price for foreign countries
(ind.)	price for individuals
(inst.)	price for institutions
(lib.)	price for libraries
NS	new series
p.	page, pages
po. ed.	poetry editor
pub.	publisher
(stud.)	price for students
tr. by	translated by
tr. of	translation of
U.	University
w.	with

Months

Ja	January	Jl	July
F	February	Ag	August
Mr	March	S	September
Ap	April	O	October
My	May	N	November
Je	June	D	December

Seasons

Aut	Autumn	Spr	Spring
Wint	Winter	Sum	Summer

Years

89	1989	92	1992
90	1990	93	1993
91	1991	94	1994

Periodicals Added

Periodical acronyms are followed by titles. Full information may be found in the list of periodicals indexed.

AlabamaLR: ALABAMA LITERARY REVIEW

AmerLC: AMERICAN LETTERS & COMMENTARY

Arshile: ARSHILE: A Magazine of the Arts

BlackBread: BLACK BREAD

Border: BORDERLANDS: Texas Poetry Review

CaribbeanW: THE CARIBBEAN WRITER

Drumvoices: DRUMVOICES: A Confluence of Literary, Cultural & Vision Arts

Gaia: GAIA: A Journal of Literature & Environmental Arts

GlobalCR: GLOBAL CITY REVIEW

HarvardR: HARVARD REVIEW

IllinoisR: THE ILLINOIS REVIEW

ProseP: THE PROSE POEM: An International Journal,

Rosebud: ROSEBUD: For People Who Enjoy Writing

Trasimagen: TRASIMAGEN: Revista Latinoamericana de Literatura y Arte

Tricycle: TRICYCLE: The Buddhist Review

XavierR: XAVIER REVIEW

In addition, the following two journals, which had been dropped in 1992, were reinstated in 1993:

ApalQ: APALACHEE QUARTERLY

CuadP: CUADERNOS DE POÉTICA

Periodicals Deleted

Mildred: MILDRED, Ellen Biss, Kathryn Poppino, eds., 961 Birchwood Lane, Schenectady, NY 12309. No 1992 or 1993 issues received. Letters not answered.

Notus: NOTUS: New Writing, Pat Smith, ed., 2420 Walter Dr., Ann Arbor, MI 48103. No 1992 or 1993 issues received. Letters not answered.

Pig: PIG IRON, Jim Villani, Naton Leslie, eds., Pig Iron Press, P.O. Box 237, Youngstown, OH 44501. No 1992 or 1993 issues received. Letters not answered.

Rohwedder: ROHWEDDER: International Journal of Literature & Art, Nancy Antell, Angela Dawn Baldanado, Robert Dassanowsky-Harris, Hans Jurgen Schacht, eds., P.O. Box 29490, Los Angeles, CA 90029. No 1993 issues received. Mail returned by post office.

Sidewalks: SIDEWALKS: An Anthology of Poetry, Short Prose, & Art, Tom Heie, ed., P.O. Box 321, Champlin, MN 55316. No 1992 or 1993 issues received. Letters not answered.

ThRiPo: THREE RIVERS POETRY JOURNAL, Gerald Costanzo, Jim Daniels, ed., Three Rivers Press, P.O. Box 21, Carnegie-Mellon U., Pittsburgh, PA 15213. Nos. 39/40, indexed in the 1992 volume, was "the final issue."

Tribe: TRIBE: An American Gay Journal, Bernard Rabb, ed., Columbia Publishing Co., 234 E. 25th St., Baltimore, MD 21218. No 1992 or 1993 issues received. Letters not answered.

Periodicals Indexed

Arranged by acronym, with names of editors, addresses, issues indexed, and subscription information. New titles added to the *Index* in 1993 are marked with an asterisk (*).

13thMoon: 13TH MOON : A Feminist Literary Magazine, Judith Emlyn Johnson, ed., Katie Yates, Emily Novak, Jen Spungin, po. eds., Dept. of English, State U. of NY, Albany, NY 12222. Issues indexed: (11:1/2, 12:1/2). Subscriptions: $10/1 vol., $18/2 vols., $26/3 vols; Back issues: $6.50-$10/vol.

Abraxas: ABRAXAS, Ingrid Swanberg, ed., 2518 Gregory St., Madison, WI 53711. Issues indexed: No 1992 issues published -- No. 42 expected in Fall 93, but not yet received. Subscriptions: $12/4 issues; Single issue: $3; Double issues: $6.

Aerial: AERIAL, Rod Smith, ed., P.O. Box 25642, Washington, DC 20007. Issues indexed: No 1992 or 1993 issues received. Subscriptions: $20/3 issues; Single issue: $7.50; Double issues: $15.

AfAmRev: AFRICAN AMERICAN REVIEW, Division on Black American Literature and Culture, Modern Language Association, Joe Weixlmann, ed., Dept. of English, Indiana State U., Terre Haute, IN 47809. Issues indexed: (27:1-4). Subscriptions: $24/yr. (ind.), $44/yr. (inst.), $31/yr. (for.), $51/yr. (for. inst.). Single issue: $10, $12 (for.).

Agni: AGNI, Askold Melnyczuk, ed., Creative Writing Program, Boston U., 236 Bay State Rd., Boston, MA 02115. Issues indexed: (37-38). Subscriptions: $12/yr. (2 issues), $23/2 yrs., $34/3 yrs.; $24/yr. (inst.); plus $4/yr. (for.); Single issue: $7.

*AlabamaLR: ALABAMA LITERARY REVIEW, Theron Montgomery, ed., Ed Hicks, po. ed., Smith 253, Troy State Univ., Troy, AL 36082. Issues indexed: (7:1-2). Subscriptions: $10/yr. (2 issues); Single issue: $5.

Amelia: AMELIA, Frederick A. Raborg, Jr., ed., 329 "E" St., Bakersfield, CA 93304. Issues indexed: 21; No. 18 never received. Subscriptions: $25/yr. (4 issues), $48/2 yrs., $70/3 yrs.; $27/yr., $52/2 yrs., $76/3 yrs. (Canada, Mexico); $41/yr., $80/2 yrs., $118/3 yrs. (for. air mail); Single issue: $7.95, $8.50 (Canada & Mexico); $12 (for. air mail).

Americas: THE AMERICAS REVIEW, A Review of Hispanic Literature and Art of the USA, Nicolás Kanellos, ed.& pub., U. of Houston, Houston, TX 77204-2090. Issues indexed: (21:1-2, 3/4). Subscriptions: $15/yr. (ind.), $20/yr. (inst.); Single and back issues: $5; Double issues. $10.

*AmerLC: AMERICAN LETTERS & COMMENTARY, Jeanne Beaumont, Anna Rabinowitz, eds., 850 Park Ave, Suite 5-B, New York, NY 10021. Issues indexed: (5). Subscriptions: $5/yr. (1 issue).

AmerPoR: THE AMERICAN POETRY REVIEW, Stephen Berg, David Bonanno, Arthur Vogelsang, eds., 1721 Walnut St., Philadelphia, PA 19103. Issues indexed: (22:1-6). Subscriptions: $14/yr., $25/2 yrs., $35/3 yrs.; $17/yr., $31/2 yrs., $44/3 yr. (for.); classroom rate $7/yr. per student; Single issue: $3. PA residents add 6% sales tax; Philadelphia residents, 7%.

AmerS: THE AMERICAN SCHOLAR, Joseph Epstein, ed., The Phi Beta Kappa Society, 1811 Q St. NW, Washington, DC 20009. Issues indexed: (62:1-4). Subscriptions: $21/yr., $38/2 yrs., $57/3 yrs.; $25/yr., $46/2 yrs., $69/3 yrs. (inst.); plus $3/yr. (for.); Single issue: $5.75; $7 (inst.).

AmerV: THE AMERICAN VOICE, Frederick Smock, eds., The Kentucky Foundation for
Women, Inc., 332 West Broadway, Suite 1215, Louisville, KY 40202. Issues indexed:
(30-32). Subscriptions: $15/yr. (3 issues); Back issues: $5; Single issue: $5.

AnotherCM: ANOTHER CHICAGO MAGAZINE, Barry Silesky, ed. & pub., 3709 N.
Kenmore, Chicago, IL 60613. Issues indexed: (25-26). Subscriptions: $15/yr., $60/5
yrs., $199.95/lifetime; Single issue: $8.

Antaeus: ANTAEUS, Daniel Halpern, ed., The Ecco Press, 100 W. Broad St., Hopewell, NJ
08525. Issues indexed: (70-71/72). Subscriptions: $36/4 issues (2 yrs.), plus $1.50/issue
(for. surface mail) or $4.50/issue (for. airmail); Single issue: $10 ($12.99 Canada);
Double issues: $15 ($18.99 Canada).

AnthNEW: THE ANTHOLOGY OF NEW ENGLAND WRITERS, Frank Anthony, ed., New
England Writers/Vermont Poets Association, P.O. Box 483, Windsor, VT 05089. Issues
indexed: (5). Single isse: $3.

AntigR: THE ANTIGONISH REVIEW, George Sanderson, ed., Box 5000, St. Francis Xavier
U., Antigonish, Nova Scotia B2G 2W5 Canada. Issues indexed: (92, 93/94, 95).
Subscriptions: $18/4 issues; Single issue: $5.

AntR: THE ANTIOCH REVIEW, Robert S. Fogarty, ed., David St. John, po. ed., P.O. Box
148, Yellow Springs, OH 45387-9910. Issues indexed: (51:1/2-4). Subscriptions: $30/yr.
(4 issues), $53/2 yrs., $75/3 yrs. (ind.); $42/yr., $74/2 yrs., $105/3 yrs. (inst.); plus $9/yr.
(for.); Single issue: $5.50. Subscription address: P.O. Box 626, Dayton, OH 45459-0626.

ApalQ: APALACHEE QUARTERLY, Barbara Hamby, Pam Ball, Bruce Boehrer, Paul
McCall, Mary Jane Ryals, Ann Turkle, eds., P.O. Box 20106, Tallahassee, FL 32316.
Issues indexed: (35, 36/37, 38-39). Subscriptions: $15/yr. (2 issues, ind.), $20/yr. (inst.),
$30/yr. (for.); Single issue: $5; Double issues: $10.

Arc: ARC, John Barton, Nadine McInnis, eds., P.O. Box 7368, Ottawa, Ont. K1L 8E4 Canada.
Issues indexed: (30-31). Subscriptions: $18/4 issues (2 years, Canada); $22/yr. (USA &
for.); Single issue: $6 (Canada), $7 (USA & for.); Back issues: $2-$3.

Archae: ARCHAE, Alan Davis Drake, ed., 10 Troilus, Old Bridge, NJ 08857-2724. Issues
indexed: No 1993 issues received. Subscriptions: $13/yr. (2 issues); $17/yr. (for.); Single
issue: $7, $9 (for.).

Areíto: AREITO, Andrés Gómez, Director, P.O. Box 44-1803, Miami, FL 33144. Issues
indexed: Segunda Epoca (4:13-14). Subscriptions: $12/yr. (ind.), $20/yr. (inst.), $18/yr.
(for. ind.), $30/yr. (for. inst.).

Arion: ARION: A Journal of Humanities and the Classics, Herbert Golder, ed., 10 Lenox St.,
Brookline, MA 02146. Issues indexed: (2:2/3). Subscriptions: $19/yr. (3 issues, ind.),
$35/yr. (inst.), $12/yr. (students), plus $3/yr. (for.); Single issue, $7; Back issues, $8.
Subscription address: Arion, c/o Office of Scholarly Publications, Boston U., 985
Commonwealth Ave., Boston, MA 02215.

*Arshile: ARSHILE: A Magazine of the Arts, Mark Salerno, ed., P.O. Box 3749, Los Angeles,
CA 90078. Issues indexed: (1-2). Subscriptions: $18/2 issues, $36/4 issues (ind.); $24/2
issues, $48/4 issues (inst.); single issue: $10 plus $2.50 shipping and handling.

Art&Und: ART & UNDERSTANDING: The Journal of Literature and Art About AIDS, David
Waggoner, ed., Suite 205, 25 Monroe St., Albany, NY 12210. Issues indexed: (2:1-4).
Subscriptions: $22/yr. (6 issues), $32/yr. (Canada), $42/yr. (elsewhere); Back issues: $5
plus $1 postage and handling; Single issue: $3.95, $4.95 (Canada).

ArtfulD: ARTFUL DODGE, Daniel Bourne, ed., Dept. of English, College of Wooster,
Wooster, OH 44691. Issues indexed: (24/25); numbers 22/23 were indexed in the 1992
volume, not "23/23". Subscriptions: $10/2 double issues (ind.), $16/2 double issues
(inst.); Single issue: $5.

Ascent: ASCENT, Audrey Curley, Mark Costello, Paul Friedman, Rocco Fumento, Philip Graham, Carol LeSeure, Jerry Mirskin, Nancy Roberts, George Scouffas, Jean Thompson, Michael Van Walleghen, Kirsten Wasson, eds., P.O. Box 967, Urbana, IL 61801. Issues indexed: (17:2-3, 18:1). Subscriptions: $6/yr. (3 issues), $12/2 yrs.; $5/yr. (for.); Single issue: $2 (bookstore), $3 (mail).

Asylum: ASYLUM, Greg Boyd, ed., P.O. Box 6203, Santa Maria, CA 93456. Issues indexed: (8:1/4). Subscriptions: $10/yr. (1 annual issue, ind.).

Atlantic: THE ATLANTIC, William Whitworth, ed., Peter Davison, po. ed., 745 Boylston St., Boston, MA 02116-2603. Issues indexed: (271:1-6, 272:1-6). Subscriptions: $17.94/yr., $29.95/2 yrs., $39.95/3 yrs., plus $8/yr. (Canada), $12/yr. (for.); Single issue: $2.95, $3.50 (Canada). Subscription address: Atlantic Subscription Processing Center, Box 52661, Boulder, CO 80322.

Avec: AVEC: A Journal of Writing, Cydney Chadwick, ed., P.O. Box 1059, Penngrove, CA 94951. Issues indexed: (6:1). Subscriptions: $12/2 issues, $22/4 issues; $15/issue (inst.); Single issue: $7.50.

BambooR: BAMBOO RIDGE: The Hawaii Writers' Quarterly, Eric Chock, Darrell H. Y Lum, eds., P.O. Box 61781, Honolulu, HI 96839-1781. Issues indexed: (57-58/59). Subscriptions: $16/yr. (4 issues); Single issue, $5; Double issues: $8.

BellArk: BELLOWING ARK, Robert R. Ward, ed., P.O. Box 45637, Seattle, WA 98145. Issues indexed: (9:1-6). Subscriptions: $15/yr. (6 issues), $24/2 yrs.; Single issue: $3.

BellR: THE BELLINGHAM REVIEW, Knute Skinner, ed., 1007 Queen St., Bellingham, WA 98226. Issues indexed: (16:1/2, #33/34). Subscriptions: $5/yr. (2 issues), $9.50/2 yrs., $12.50/3 yrs.; plus $1/yr. (for.); through agencies, $6/yr.; Single issue: $2.50; double issue: $5.

BelPoJ: THE BELOIT POETRY JOURNAL, Marion K. Stocking, ed., RR 2, Box 154, Ellsworth, ME 04605. Issues indexed: (43:3-4, 44:1-2). Subscriptions: $12/yr. (4 issues, ind.), $33/3 yrs.; $18/yr., $49.50/3 yrs. (inst.); plus $3.20/yr. (Canada), $3.70/yr. (for.); Single issue: $4.

BilingR: THE BILINGUAL REVIEW / LA REVISTA BILINGÜE, Gary D. Keller, ed., Hispanic Research Center, Arizona State U., Tempe, AZ 85287-2702. Issues indexed: (18:1). Subscriptions: $16/yr., $30/2 yrs., $42/3 yrs. (ind.); $28/yr. (inst.).

BlackALF: BLACK AMERICAN LITERATURE FORUM see AfAmRev: AFRICAN AMERICAN REVIEW (title change).

BlackBR: BLACK BEAR REVIEW, Ave Jeanne, po. ed., 1916 Lincoln St., Croydon, PA 19021. Issues indexed: (17). Subscriptions: $10/yr. (2 issues); Single issue: $5; $7 (for.).

*BlackBread: BLACK BREAD, Jessica Lowenthal, Sianne Ngai, eds., 46 Preston St., #2, Providence, RI 02906. Issues indexed: (3). Subscriptions: $10/2 issues; Single issue: $5.

BlackWR: BLACK WARRIOR REVIEW, Leigh Ann Sackrider, ed., Timothy Geiger, po. ed., U. of Alabama, P.O. Box 2936, Tuscaloosa, AL 35486-2936. Issues indexed: (19:1-2, 20:1); Vol. 19, number 1-2 indexed from photocopies. Subscriptions: $11/yr. (ind.), $17/yr. (inst.); plus $5/yr. (for.); Single issue: $6, plus $3 (for.).

Blueline: BLUELINE, Alan Steinberg, ed., Stephanie Coyne DeGhett, po. ed., English Dept., Potsdam College, SUNY, Potsdam, NY 13676. Issues indexed: (14). Single issue: $6.

Bogg: BOGG, John Elsberg, ed., 422 N. Cleveland St., Arlington, VA 22201. Issues indexed: (66), including "Reviews" supplement. Subscriptions: $12/3 issues; Single issue: $4.50.

Bomb: BOMB MAGAZINE, Betsy Sussler, ed. & pub., Roland Legiardi-Laura, po. ed., New Art Publications, P.O. Box 2003, Canal Station, New York, NY 10013. Issues indexed: (43-45); Numbers 35, 37-42 not received. Subscriptions: $18/yr. (4 issues). $32/2 yrs.; $28/yr. (for.); Single issue: $4.

*Border: BORDERLANDS: Texas Poetry Review, Dorothy Barnett, Lynn Gilbert, eds., P.O. Box 49818, Austin, TX 78765. Issues indexed: (2). Subscriptions: $14/yr. (ind.), $16/yr. (inst.); Single issue: $7.50 (ind.), $8.50 (inst.).

BostonR: BOSTON REVIEW, Joshua Cohen, ed., Kim Cooper, po. ed., 33 Harrison Ave., Boston, MA 02111. Issues indexed: (18:1-2, 3/4, 5-6). Subscriptions: $15/yr., $30/2 yrs. (ind.); $18/yr., $36/2 yrs. (inst.); plus $6/yr. (Canada, Mexico); plus $12/yr. (for.); Single issue: $4.

Boulevard: BOULEVARD, Richard Burgin, ed., Drexel U., P.O. Box 30386, Philadelphia, PA 19103. Issues indexed: (8:1, 8:2/3, #22, 23/24). Subscriptions: $12/3 issues, $20/6 issues, $25/9 issues; Single issue: $6; make checks payable to Opojaz, Inc.

BrooklynR: BROOKLYN REVIEW, Serena Siegfried, Michael Gates, Giles Scott, Tim Gerken, Lori Horowitz, po. eds., Joan Larkin, faculty advisor, English Dept., Brooklyn College, Brooklyn, NY 11210. Issues indexed: (10). Single issue: $5.

Caliban: CALIBAN, Lawrence R. Smith, ed., P.O. Box 561, Laguna Beach, CA 92652. Issues indexed: (12-13). Subscriptions: $14/yr. (2 issues), $26/2 yrs. (ind.); $24/yr. (inst.); plus $2/yr. (for.); Single issue: $8.

Callaloo: CALLALOO: A Journal of African-American and African Arts and Letters, Charles H. Rowell, ed., Dept. of English, Wilson Hall, U. of Virginia, Charlottesville, VA 22903. Issues indexed: (16:1-4). Subscriptions: $25/yr. (ind.), $50/yr. (inst.); plus $6.05 (Canada, Mexico); plus $17.85 (outside North America, airfreight); Subscription address: The Johns Hopkins University Press, Journals Publishing Division, 2715 N. Charles St., Baltimore, MD 21218-4319.

CalQ: CALIFORNIA QUARTERLY, Jack Hicks, ed., Kristin Steege, po. ed., 159 Titus Hall, U. of California, Davis, CA 95616. Publication suspended indefinitely "due to California state budget cuts."

Calyx: CALYX: A Journal of Art and Literature by Women, Margarita Donnelly, Managing ed., P.O. Box B, Corvallis, OR 97339-0539. Issues indexed: (14:3, 15:1). Subscriptions: $18/yr. (3 issues), $32/2 yrs., $42/3 yrs.; $22.50/yr. (inst.); $30/yr. (ind. Canada); $36/yr. (ind. for.); $15/yr. (ind. low income); Single issue: $8 plus $1.25 postage.

CanLit: CANADIAN LITERATURE, W. H. New, ed., U. of British Columbia, 2029 West Mall, Vancouver, BC, V6T 1Z2 Canada. Issues indexed: (136-137, 138/139). Subscriptions: $30/yr. (ind.), $45/yr. (inst.) plus $10/yr. outside Canada; Single issue: $15.

CapeR: THE CAPE ROCK, Harvey Hecht, ed., Southeast Missouri State U., Cape Girardeau, MO 63701. Issues indexed: (28:1-2). Subscriptions: $5/yr. (2 issues); Single issue: $3.

CapilR: THE CAPILANO REVIEW, Robert Sherrin, ed., 2055 Purcell Way, North Vancouver, B.C. V7J 3H5 Canada. Issues indexed: (Series 2:10-11). Subscriptions: $25/yr., $45/2 yrs. (ind.); $30/yr. (inst.); Single issue: $9.

*CaribbeanW: THE CARIBBEAN WRITER, David Edgecombe, Erika J. Waters, Roberta Q. Knowles, ed. board, Research Publications Center, University of the Virgin Islands, RR 2, Box 10,000, Kingshill, St. Croix, VI 00850. Issues indexed: (7). Subscriptions: $18/2 yrs. (2 issues).

CarolQ: CAROLINA QUARTERLY, Amber Vogel, ed., Julia Stockton, po. ed., Greenlaw Hall CB#3520, U. of North Carolina, Chapel Hill, NC 27599-3520. Issues indexed: (45:2-3, 46:1). Subscriptions: $10/yr. (3 issues, ind.), $12/yr. (inst.); Single issue: $5.

CentR: THE CENTENNIAL REVIEW, R. K. Meiners, ed., College of Arts and Letters, 312 Linton Hall, Michigan State U., East Lansing, MI 48824-1044. Issues indexed: (37:1-3). Subscriptions: $12/yr. (3 issues), $18/2 yrs., plus $4.50/yr. (for.); Single issue: $6.

CentralP: CENTRAL PARK, Stephen-Paul Martin, Eve Ensler, Stacey Schrader, eds., Box 1446, New York, NY 10023. Issues indexed: (22). Subscriptions: $15/yr., 2 issues (ind.), $20/yr. (inst.); Single issue: $7.50 (ind), $9 (inst).

ChamLR: CHAMINADE LITERARY REVIEW, Loretta Petrie, ed., Chaminade U. of Honolulu, 3140 Waialae Ave., Honolulu, HI 96816. Issues indexed: No 1993 issues received. Subscriptions: $10/yr. (2 issues); $18/2 yrs.; plus $2 (for.).; Single issue: $5.

ChangingM: CHANGING MEN: Issues in Gender, Sex and Politics, Rick Cote, Michael Biernbaum, eds., 306 N. Brooks St., Madison, WI 53715; Bob Vance, po. ed., 1024 Emmet St., Petosky, MI 49770. Issues indexed: (25-26). Subscriptions: $24/4 issues, $40/4 issues (inst.); $16/4 issues (limited income); $27/4 issues (Canada & Mexico); $40/4 issues (for., air mail); Single issue: $6.

CharR: THE CHARITON REVIEW, Jim Barnes, ed., Northeast Missouri State U., Kirksville, MO 63501. Issues indexed: (19:1-2). Subscriptions: $9/2 issues; Single issue: $5.

ChatR: THE CHATTAHOOCHEE REVIEW: The DeKalb College Literary Quarterly, Lamar York, ed., Collie Owens, po. ed., 2101 Womack Road, Dunwoody, GA 30338-4497. Issues indexed: (13:2-4, 14:1). Subscriptions: $15/yr. (4 issues), $25/2 yrs.; Single issue: $4.

Chelsea: CHELSEA, Sonia Raiziss, ed., P.O. Box 5880, Grand Central Station, New York, NY 10163. Issues indexed: (54-55). Subscriptions: $11/yr. (2 issues or 1 double issue), $20/2 yrs.; $14/yr., $27/2 yrs. (for.); Single issue: $6, $7 (for.).

ChiR: CHICAGO REVIEW, David Nicholls, ed., Angela Sorby, po. ed., Division of Humanities, University of Chicago, 5801 South Kenwood, Chicago, IL 60637. Issues indexed: (38:4, 39:1-3/4). Subscriptions: $15/yr. (ind.); $35/yr. (inst.); plus $5/yr. (for.); Single issue: $5; Double issue: $7.

ChironR: CHIRON REVIEW, Michael Hathaway, ed., 522 E. South Ave., St. John, KS 67576-2212. Issues indexed: (12:1-3, 12:4/13:1, #34-37/38). Subscriptions: $10/yr. (4 issues); $20/yr. (for.); $24/yr. (inst.); Single issue: $3; $6. (for.).

ChrC: THE CHRISTIAN CENTURY, James M. Wall, ed., 407 S. Dearborn St., Chicago, IL 60605-1150. Issues indexed: (110:1-37). Subscriptions: $32/yr.; Single issue: $1.75.

CimR: CIMARRON REVIEW, Gordon Weaver, ed., Thomas Reiter, Jeff Kersh, Sally Shigley, Sharon Gerald, po. eds., 205 Morrill Hall, Oklahoma State U., Stillwater, OK 74078-0135. Issues indexed: (102-105). Subscriptions: $12/yr., $15 (Canada); $30/3 yrs., $40 (Canada); plus $2.50/yr. (for.); Single issue: $3.

CinPR: CINCINNATI POETRY REVIEW, Jeff Hillard, ed., Cincinnati Writers' Project, College of Mt. St. Joseph, 5701 Delhi Rd., Cincinnati, OH 45233. Issues indexed: (24). Subscriptions: $9/4 issues; Single issue: $3; Sample copies: $2.

CityLR: CITY LIGHTS REVIEW, Nancy J. Peters, ed., Lawrence Ferlinghetti, pub., City Lights Books, 261 Columbus Ave., San Francisco, CA 94133. Issues indexed: No 1993 issues received. Single issue: $11.95.

ClockR: CLOCKWATCH REVIEW: A Journal of the Arts, James Plath, ed., Dept. of English, Illinois Wesleyan Univ., Bloomington, IL 61702-2900. Issues indexed: (8:1/2). Subscriptions: $8/yr. (2 issues); Single issue: $4; Double issues: $8.

CoalC: COAL CITY REVIEW, Brian Daldorph, Sandra Tompson, eds., 1324 Connecticut, Lawrence, KS 66044. Issues indexed: (6-7). Subscriptions: $6/2 issues; Single issue: $4.

ColEng: COLLEGE ENGLISH, National Council of Teachers of English, Louise Z. Smith, ed., Helene Davis, Thomas Hurley, po. eds., Dept. of English, UMass-Boston, Boston, MA 02125. Issues indexed: (55:1-8). Subscriptions: $40/yr. (ind.), $50/yr. (inst.), plus $6/yr. (for.); Single issue: $6.25; Subscription address: NCTE, 1111 W. Kenyon Rd., Urbana, IL 61801-1096.

ColR: COLORADO REVIEW, David Milofsky, ed., Jorie Graham, po. ed., Dept. of English, Colorado State U., Fort Collins, CO 80523. Issues indexed: (NS 20:1-2). Subscriptions: $15/yr. (2 issues), $28/2 yrs.; $25/yr. (inst.); plus $6/yr. (for.); Single issue: $8. Subscription address: University Press of Colorado, P.O. Box 849, Niwot, CO 80544.

Colum: COLUMBIA: A Magazine of Poetry & Prose, Darlene Gold, Joshua Sinel, eds., Christina Thompson, Heather Winterer, po. eds., Graduate Writing Division, 404 Dodge Hall, Columbia Univ., New York, NY 10027. Issues indexed: (20); Nos. 18 and 19 not received. Subscriptions: $7/1 issue, $13/2 issues, $18/3 issues.

Comm: COMMONWEAL, Margaret O'Brien Steinfels, ed., Rosemary Deen, po. ed., 15 Dutch St., New York, NY 10038. Issues indexed: (120:1-22). Subscriptions: $39/yr., $41/yr. (Canada), $44/yr. (for.); $67/2 yrs., $71/2 yrs. (Canada), $77/2 yrs. (for.), plus $35/yr. or $44/yr for international airmail; Single issue: $2.

Confr: CONFRONTATION, Martin Tucker, ed., English Dept., C. W. Post Campus of Long Island U., Brookville, NY 11548. Issues indexed: (51). Subscriptions: $10/yr., $20/2 yrs., $30/3 yrs.; plus $5/yr. (for.).; Single issue: $7.

Conjunc: CONJUNCTIONS: Bi-Annual Volumes of New Writing, Bard College, Bradford Morrow, ed., 33 W. 9th St., New York, NY 10011. Issues indexed: (20-21). Subscriptions: Bard College, Annandale-on-Hudson, NY 12504; $18/yr. (2 issues), $32/2 yrs. (ind.); $25/yr., $40/2 yrs. (inst., for.); Back and single issues: $10.

ConnPR: THE CONNECTICUT POETRY REVIEW, J. Claire White, James Wm. Chichetto, eds., P.O. Box 3783, Amity Station, New Haven, CT 06525. Issues indexed: (12:1). Single issue: $3 (including postage).

Conscience: CONSCIENCE: A Newsjournal of Prochoice Catholic Opinion, Maggie Hume, ed, Andrew Merton, po. ed., Catholics for a Free Choice, 1436 U St. NW, Washington, DC 20009-3997. Issues indexed: (14:1-4). Subscriptions: $10/yr.; Single issue: $3.50; Back issues: $1-3.

Contact: CONTACT II: A Poetry Review, Maurice Kenny, J. G. Gosciak, eds., P.O. Box 451, Bowling Green, New York, NY 10004. Issues indexed: (11:65/66/67). "Final issue."

ContextS: CONTEXT SOUTH, David Breeden, po. ed., pub., Box 4504, Schreiner College, 2100 Memorial Blvd., Kerrville, TX 78028-5697. Issues indexed: (3:1). Subscriptions: $10/3 issues.

CrabCR: CRAB CREEK REVIEW, Linda Clifton, ed., 4462 Whitman Ave. N., Seattle WA 98103. Issues indexed: No 1993 issues received. Subscriptions: $10/3 issues.

Crazy: CRAZYHORSE, Zabelle Stodola, managing ed., Ralph Burns, po. ed., Dept. of English, U. of Arkansas, 2801 S. University, Little Rock, AR 72204. Issues indexed: (44-45). Subscriptions: $10/yr. (2 issues), $18/2 yrs., $27/3 yrs. Single issue: $5.

CreamCR: CREAM CITY REVIEW, Sandra Nelson, ed., Paul August, Cynthia Belmont, Aedan Hanley, po. eds., English Dept., U. of Wisconsin, P.O. Box 413, Milwaukee, WI 53201. Issues indexed: (17:1-2). Subscriptions: $10/yr. (2 issues), $14/2 yrs.; Single issue: $6; Sample & back issues: $4.50.

CrossCur: CROSSCURRENTS, Linda Brown Michelson, ed., 2200 Glastonbury Road, Westlake Village, CA 91361. Issues indexed: No 1993 issues received. Subscriptions: $18/yr. (4 issues), $25/2 yrs., $30/3 yrs.; Single issue: $6.

Crucible: CRUCIBLE, Terrence L. Grimes, ed., Barton College, College Station, Wilson, NC 27893. Issues indexed: (29). Subscriptions: $5/yr. (1 issue), $10/2 yrs; Back issues: $5.

CuadP: CUADERNOS DE POÉTICA, Diógenes Céspedes, Director, Apartado Postal 1736, Santo Domingo, Dominican Republic; US Editor: Rafael Catalá, P.O. Box 38, New Brunswick, NJ 08903. Issues indexed: (7:21). Subscriptions: America & Europe, $25/yr. (ind.), $30/yr. (inst.); Africa, Asia & Oceania, $30/yr. (ind.), $40/yr. (inst.).

CumbPR: CUMBERLAND POETRY REVIEW, Ingram Bloch, Bob Darrell, Sherry Bevins Darrell, Malcolm Glass, Jeanne Gore, Laurence Lerner, Alison Touster-Reed, Eva Touster, Brad Young, eds., Poetics, Inc., P.O. Box 120128, Acklen Station, Nashville, TN 37212. Issues indexed: (12:2, 13:1). Subscriptions: $14/yr, $26/2 yrs. (ind.); $17/yr., $31/2 yrs. (inst.); $23/yr., $37/2 yrs. (for.); Single issue: $7; $10 (for.).

CutB: CUTBANK, Judy Blunt, Bob Hackett, eds., Matt Yurdana, po. ed., Jocelyn Siler, faculty advisor, Dept. of English, U. of Montana, Missoula, MT 59812. Issues indexed: (39-40). Subscriptions: $12/yr., $22/2 yrs.; Single issue: $6.95-9.95; Sample copies: $4.

Dandel: DANDELION, Barbara Kermode-Scott, managing ed., Deborah Miller, Allan Serafino, po eds., Alexandra Centre, 922 - 9th Ave., S.E., Calgary, Alberta T2G 0S4 Canada. Issues indexed: (20:1). Subscriptions: $10/yr. (2 issues), $18/2 yrs.; $15/yr. (inst.); Single issue: $6.

DenQ: DENVER QUARTERLY, Donald Revell, ed., U. of Denver, Denver, CO 80208. Issues indexed: (27:3-4, 28:1-2). Subscriptions: $15/yr., $28/2 yrs.; $18/yr. (inst.); plus $1/yr. (for.); Single issue: $5.

Descant: DESCANT, Karen Mulhallen, ed., P.O. Box 314, Station P, Toronto, Ontario M5S 2S8 Canada. Issues indexed: (24:2-3, #81-82). Subscriptions: $22.47/yr., $40.66/2 yrs., $58.85/3 yrs. (ind.); $31.03/yr., $62.06/2 yrs., $88.81/3 yrs. (inst.); plus $6/yr. (for.); Single issue: $13.91.

DogRR: DOG RIVER REVIEW, Laurence F. Hawkins, ed., Trout Creek Press, 5976 Billings Road, Parkdale, OR 97041-9610. Issues indexed: (12:1-2, #23-24). Subscriptions: $7/yr. (2 issues); Single issue: $3.50; Sample copy: $2.50.

*Drumvoices: DRUMVOICES: A Confluence of Literary, Cultural & Vision Arts, Eugene B. Redmond, ed., English Dept., Southern Illinois U. at Edwardsville in collaboration with the Eugene B. Redmond Writers Club of East St. Louis, Dept. of English, Box 1431, SIUE, Edwardsville, IL 62026-1431. Issues indexed: (1:1/2, 2:1/2, 3:1/2). Subscriptions: $10/yr. (2 issues); Single issues: $6.

DustyD: DUSTY DOG, John Pierce, ed. & pub., 1904-A Gladden, Gallup, NM 87301. Issues indexed: 2 chapbooks (Brian Daldorph, Simon Perchik). Single chapbook: $5.95.

Elf: ELF: Eclectic Literary Forum, C. K. Erbes, ed., P. O. Box 392, Tonawanda, NY 14150. Issues indexed: (3:1-4). Subscriptions: $16/yr. (4 issues), $32/yr. (inst.), plus $8/yr. (for.); Single issue: $5.50.

EmeraldCR: EMERALD COAST REVIEW: West Florida Authors and Artists, Ellen G. Peppler, Charmaine Wellington, eds., West Florida Literary Federation, P.O. Box 1644, Pensacola, FL 32597-1644. Issues indexed: No 1992 or 1993 issues received. Single issue: $9.95.

EngJ: ENGLISH JOURNAL, National Council of Teachers of English, Ben F. Nelms, ed., 200 Norman Hall, U. of Florida, Gainesville, FL 32611; Paul Janeczko, po. ed., P.O. Box 1079, Gray, ME 04039. Issues indexed: (82:1-8). Subscriptions: $40/yr. (ind.), $50/yr. (inst.), plus $6/yr. (for.); Single issue: $6.25; Subscription address: 1111 W. Kenyon Rd., Urbana, IL 61801-1096.

Epiphany: EPIPHANY: A Journal of Literature, Gordon Grice, Bob Zordani, eds., P.O. Box 2699, University of Arkansas, Fayetteville, AR 72701. Issues indexed: (4:2-3); 4:1 not received. Subscriptions: $10/yr., $20 (for.); Single Copies: $5, $6 (for.).

Epoch: EPOCH, Michael Koch, ed., Burlin Barr, po., ed., 251 Goldwin Smith Hall, Cornell U., Ithaca, NY 14853-3201. Issues indexed: (42:1-3). Subscriptions: $11/yr.; $15/yr. (for).; Single issue: $5

Event: EVENT: The Douglas College Review, Dale Zieroth, ed., Gillian Harding-Russell, po. ed., Douglas College, P.O. Box 2503, New Westminster, B.C. V3L 5B2 Canada. Issues indexed: (22:1-3); volume 21, nos. 1-3 were indexed in the 1992 volume, not "20:1-3" as stated; volume 20, nos. 1-3 were indexed in the 1991 volume. Subscriptions: $15/yr. + $1.05 GST, $25/2 yrs. + $1.75 GST; Single issue: $6.

EvergreenC: THE EVERGREEN CHRONICLES: A Journal of Gay and Lesbian Literature, Greta Gaard, M. Kiesow Moore, Mark Reschke, eds., P.O. Box 8939, Minneapolis, MN 55408-0936. Issues indexed: (8:1-2). Subscriptions: $15/yr. (2 issues), $28/2 yrs.; $18/yr. (for.); $20/yr. (inst.); Single issue: $7.95.

Eyeball: EYEBALL, Jabari Asim, ed., First Civilizations Inc., P.O. Box 8135, St. Louis, MO 63108. Issues indexed: (2). Subscriptions: $7/yr. (2 issues), $14/2 yrs., $21/3 yrs; $28/yr., $56/2 yrs., $82/3 yrs. (for.); Single issue: $3.50.

Farm: FARMER'S MARKET, Jean C. Lee, John E. Hughes, Lisa Ress, Romayne Rubinas, Tracey Winbigler, eds., Midwest Farmer's Market, Inc., P.O. Box 1272, Galesburg, IL 61402. Issues indexed: (10:1-2). Subscriptions: $10/yr. (2 issues); Single issue: $6.

Field: FIELD: Contemporary Poetry and Poetics, Stuart Friebert, David Young, eds., Rice Hall, Oberlin College, Oberlin, OH 44074. Issues indexed: (48-49). Subscriptions: $12/yr., $20/2 yrs.; Single issue: $6; Back issues: $12.

FloridaR: THE FLORIDA REVIEW, Russell Kesler, ed., Dept. of English, U. of Central Florida, Orlando, FL 32816. Issues indexed: (19:1). Subscriptions: $7/yr., $11/2 yrs.; Single issue: $4.50.

Footwork: FOOTWORK: The Paterson Literary Review, Maria Mazziotti Gillan, ed., Passaic County Community College, 1 College Blvd., Paterson, NJ 07505-1179. Issues indexed: (23) 1993. Subscriptions: $10/issue.

FourQ: FOUR QUARTERS, John J. Keenan, ed., La Salle U., 1900 W. Olney, Philadelphia, PA 19141. Issues indexed: (7:1-2). Subscriptions: $8/yr. (2 issues), $13/2 yrs.; Single issue: $4.

FreeL: FREE LUNCH: A Poetry Journal, Free Lunch Arts Alliance, Ron Offen, ed., P.O. Box 7647, Laguna Niguel, CA 92607-7647. Issues indexed: (11-12). Subscriptions: Free to all serious poets in the U.S.A.; $12/3 issues; $15/3 issues (for.); Single issue: $5, $6 (for.).

*Gaia: GAIA: A Journal of Literature & Environmental Arts, Robert S. King, ed., Whistle Press, Inc., P.O. Box 709, Winterville, GA 30683. Issues indexed: (1/2, 3). Subscriptions: $9/4 issues, $16/8 issues; plus $4/4 issues (for.); Single issue: $4; Double issue: $6.

GeoR: GEORGIA REVIEW, Stanley W. Lindberg, ed., U. of Georgia, Athens, GA 30602. Issues indexed: (47:1-4). Subscriptions: $18/yr., $30/2 yrs., plus $5/yr. (for.); Single issue: $7; Back issues: $7.

GettyR: GETTYSBURG REVIEW, Peter Stitt, ed., Gettysburg College, Gettysburg, PA 17325-1491. Issues indexed: (6:1-4). Subscriptions: $15/yr., $27/2 yrs., $36/3 yrs., plus $5/yr. (for.); Single issue: $7.

*GlobalCR: GLOBAL CITY REVIEW, Linsey Abrams, E. M. Broner, eds., Simon H. Rifkind Center for the Humanities, City College of New York, 138th & Convent Ave, York, NY 10031. Issues indexed: (1-2). Subscriptions: $12/yr. (2 issues); $20/2 yrs.; $15/yr., $25/2 yrs. (inst.); $17/yr., $30/2 yrs. (for.); Single issue: $6.

GrahamHR: GRAHAM HOUSE REVIEW, Peter Balakian, Bruce Smith, eds., Colgate U. Press, Box 5000, Colgate U., Hamilton, NY 13346; Issues indexed: (17). Subscriptions: $15/2 yrs. (2 issues); Single issue: $7.50.

Grain: GRAIN, Saskatchewan Writers Guild, Geoffrey Ursell, ed., Elizabeth Philips, interim ed., Judith Krause, po. ed., Box 1154, Regina, Saskatchewan S4P 3B4 Canada. Issues indexed: (21:1-3). Subscriptions: $19.95+$1.40 GST/yr., $34.95+$2.45 GST/2 yrs., plus $4/yr. (U.S.), plus $6/yr. (for.); Single issue: $6.95.

GrandS: GRAND STREET, Jean Stein, ed., Erik Rieselbach, po. ed., 131 Varick St. #906, New York, NY 10013. Issues indexed: (11:4, 12:1-3, #44-47). Subscriptions: $30/yr. (4 issues), $40/yr. (for.); Single issue: $10, $12.99 (Canada); Subscription address: Dept. GRS, PO Box 3000, Denville, NJ 07834.

GreenMR: GREEN MOUNTAINS REVIEW, Neil Shepard, ed. & po. ed., Johnson State College, Johnson, VT 05656. Issues indexed: (NS 6:1-2). Subscriptions: $12/yr. (2 issues); Single issue: $6.

GreensboroR: THE GREENSBORO REVIEW, Jim Clark, ed., Julie Funderburk, po. ed., Dept. of English, U. of North Carolina, Greensboro, NC 27412. Issues indexed: (54-55). Subscriptions: $8/yr. (2 issues), $20/3 yrs.; Single issue: $4.

Gypsy: GYPSY, Belinda Subraman, S. Ramnath, eds, 10708 Gay Brewer Dr., El Paso, TX 79935. Issues indexed: (20). Subscriptions: $14/yr. (2 issues); Single issue: $7.

HampSPR: THE HAMPDEN-SYDNEY POETRY REVIEW, Tom O'Grady, ed., P.O. Box 126, Hampden-Sydney, VA 23943. Issues indexed: Winter 1993. Subscriptions: $5/single issue; 1990 Anthology, $12.95.

HangL: HANGING LOOSE, Robert Hershon, Dick Lourie, Mark Pawlak, Ron Schreiber, eds., 231 Wyckoff St., Brooklyn, NY 11217. Issues indexed: (62-63). Subscriptions: $12.50/3 issues, $24/6 issues, $35/9 issues (ind.); $15/3 issues, $30/6 issues, $45/9 issues (inst.); $22/3 issues, $42/6 issues, $62/9 issues (for.); Sample issue: $5 plus $1.50 postage and handling.

Harp: HARPER'S MAGAZINE, Lewis H. Lapham, ed., 666 Broadway, New York, NY 10012. Issues indexed: (286:1712-1717, 287:1718-1723). Subscriptions: $18/yr., plus $2/yr. (USA possessions, Canada), plus $20/yr. (for.); Single issue: $2.95; Subscription address: P.O. Box 7511, Red Oak, IA 51591-0511.

HarvardA: THE HARVARD ADVOCATE, Bernie Meyler, Managing ed., Niko Canner, po. ed., 21 South St., Cambridge, MA 02138. Issues indexed: (127:2-4, 128:1); 127:4 (Sum 93) appears to be incorrectly numbered 128:4. Subscriptions: $15/yr. (ind.), $17/yr. (inst.), $20/yr. (for.); Single issue: $4.

*HarvardR: HARVARD REVIEW, Stratis Haviaras, ed., Poetry Room, Harvard College Library, Cambridge, MA 02138. Issues indexed: (3-5). Subscriptions: $12/yr. (2 issues); $18/yr. (for.); Single issue: $8.

HawaiiR: HAWAI'I REVIEW, Tamara Moan, ed., Alan Aoki, Annie Fanning, po. eds., Dept. of English, U. of Hawai'i, 1733 Donaghho Rd., Honolulu, HI 96822. Issues indexed: (16:3, 17:1-3, #36-39). Subscriptions: $15/yr. (3 issues), $25/2 yrs.; Single issue: $5.

HayF: HAYDEN'S FERRY REVIEW, Salima Keegan, Managing ed., Ruth Ellen Kocher, Jan Selving, po. eds., Box 871502, Arizona State U., Tempe, AZ 85287-1502. Issues indexed: (12-13). Subscriptions: $10/yr. (2 issues), $18/2 yrs.; $13/yr., $26/2 yrs. (inst.); Single issue: $5 plus $1 postage.

HeavenB: HEAVEN BONE, Steven Hirsch, ed., pub., P.O. Box 486, Chester, NY 10918. Issues indexed: (10). Subscriptions: $16.95/4 issues; Single issue: $6.

Hellas: HELLAS: A Journal of Poetry and the Humanities, Gerald Harnett, ed., The Aldine Press, Ltd., 304 S. Tyson Ave., Glenside, PA 19038. Issues indexed: (4:1-2). Subscriptions: $14/yr. (2 issues), $24/2 yrs.; plus $4/yr. (for.); Single issue: $7.50.

HighP: HIGH PLAINS LITERARY REVIEW, Robert O. Greer, Jr., ed., Joy Harjo, po. ed., 180 Adams St., Suite 250, Denver, CO 80206. Issues indexed: (8:1-3). Subscriptions: $20/yr. (3 issues), $38/2 yrs., plus $5/yr. (for.); Single issue: $7.

HiramPoR: HIRAM POETRY REVIEW, English Dept., Hiram College, Hale Chatfield & Carol Donley, eds., P.O. Box 162, Hiram, OH 44234. Issues indexed: (53/54). Subscriptions: $8/yr. (2 issues); $20/3 yrs. (ind.); Single issue: $4.

HolCrit: THE HOLLINS CRITIC, John Rees Moore, ed., Hollins College, VA 24020. Issues indexed: (30:1-5). Subscriptions: $6/yr. (5 issues); $7.50/yr. (for.).

HopewellR: HOPEWELL REVIEW: New Work by Indiana's Best Writers, Michael Wilkerson, ed., Arts Indiana, Inc., The Majestic Building, 47 S. Pennsylvania St., Suite 701, Indianapolis, IN 46204-3622. Issues indexed: (5). Single issue: $6.95; Back issues: $2.50-$4.95 plus $2.50 shipping.

Hudson: THE HUDSON REVIEW, Paula Deitz, Frederick Morgan, eds., 684 Park Ave., New York, NY 10021. Issues indexed: (45:4, 46:1-3). Subscriptions: $24/yr., $46/2 yrs., $68/3 yrs., plus $4/yr. (for.); Single issue: $7.

*IllinoisR: THE ILLINOIS REVIEW, Illinois Writers, Inc., Jim Elledge, ed., 4240/Dept. of English, Illinois State U., Normal, IL 61790-4240. Issues indexed: (1:1). Subscriptions: $10/yr. (2 issues), $18/yr. (inst.), $15/yr. (prepaid inst.).; Single issue: $6.

IndR: INDIANA REVIEW, Gretchen Knapp, ed., Talvikki Ansel, Khaled Mattawa, po. eds., Indiana U., 316 N. Jordan Ave., Bloomington, IN 47405. Issues indexed: (16:1-2). Subscriptions: $12/2 issues, $15/2 issues (inst.); $22/4 issues (ind.), $25/4 issues (inst.); plus $5/2 issues (for.). Single issue: $7.

Interim: INTERIM, A. Wilber Stevens, ed., Dept. of English, U. of Nevada, 4505 Maryland Parkway, Box 455011, Las Vegas, NV 89154-5011. Issues indexed: (12:1-2). Subscriptions: $8/yr. (2 issues), $13/2 yrs., $16/3 yrs. (ind.); $14/yr. (lib.), $16/yr. (for.); Single issue: $5, $8 (for.).

InterPR: INTERNATIONAL POETRY REVIEW, Mark Smith-Soto, ed., Dept. of Romance Languages, U. of North Carolina, Greensboro, NC 27412-5001. Issues indexed: (19:1-2). Subscriptions: $10/yr. (2 issues, ind.), $15/yr. (inst.); Plus $2/yr. (for.); Single issue: $5.

Inti: INTI: Revista de Literatura Hispánica, Roger B. Carmosino, ed., Dept. of Modern Languages, Providence College, Providence, RI 02918. Issues indexed: (37-38). Subscriptions: $25/yr. (2 issues, ind.), $45/yr. (inst.); Single issue: $20, $35 (double issues).

Iowa: IOWA REVIEW, David Hamilton, ed., 308 EPB, U. of Iowa, Iowa City, IA 52242. Issues indexed: (23:1-3). Subscriptions: $18/yr. (3 issues, ind.), $20/yr. (inst.), plus $3/yr. (for.); Single issue: $6.95.

Jacaranda: THE JACARANDA REVIEW, Bruce Kijewski, Katherine Swiggart, eds., Gregory Castle, po. ed., Dept. of English, U. of California, Los Angeles, CA 90024. Issues indexed: No 1993 issues received. Subscriptions: $10/yr. (2 issues, ind.), $14/yr. (inst.); Sample issues: $6.

JamesWR: THE JAMES WHITE REVIEW, A Gay Men's Literary Journal, Phil Willkie, pub., Clif Mayhood, po. ed., P.O. Box 3356, Butler Quarter Station, Minneapolis, MN 55403. Issues indexed: (10:2-4, 11:1). Subscriptions: $12/yr., $20/2 yrs.; $14/yr. (Canada); $17/yr. (other for.); Single issue: $3; Back issues: $1 (for minimum order of $10).

JlNJPo: THE JOURNAL OF NEW JERSEY POETS, Sander Zulauf, ed., Center for Teaching Excellence, County College of Morris, 214 Center Grove Rd., Randolph, NJ 07869-2086. Issues indexed: (15:1-2). Subscriptions: $7/yr. (2 issues), $12/2 yrs.; Single issue: $4.

Journal: THE JOURNAL, Kathy Fagan, Michelle Herman, eds., The Ohio State U., Dept. of English, 164 W. 17th Ave., Columbus, OH 43210. Issues indexed: (17:1-2). Subscriptions: $8/yr. (2 issues), $16/2 yrs., $24/3 yrs.; Single issue: $5.

Kaleid: KALEIDOSCOPE, International Magazine of Literature, Fine Arts, and Disability, Darshan Perusek, ed., Chris Hewitt, po. ed. (51 W. 86th ST., #404, New York, NY 10024), United Disability Services, 326 Locust St., Akron, OH 44302. Issues indexed: (26-27). Subscriptions: $9/yr. (2 issues, ind.), $14/yr. (inst.), plus $5/yr. (Canada); plus $8/yr. (other for.); Single issue: $4.50, $7 (for.); Sample issue: $4. Also available on audio cassette.

Kalliope: KALLIOPE: A Journal of Women's Art, Mary Sue Koeppel, ed., Florida Community College at Jacksonville, 3939 Roosevelt Blvd., Jacksonville, FL 32205. Issues indexed: (15:2-3). Subscriptions: $12.50/1 yr. (3 issues), $22/2 yrs. (ind.); $20/yr. (inst.); plus $6/yr. (for.); free to women in prison; Single issue: $7, plus $2 (for.), $3 (for., double issue); Back issues: $4-8.

KenR: KENYON REVIEW, Marilyn Hacker, ed., Kenyon College, Gambier, OH 43022. Issues indexed: (NS 15:1-4). Subscriptions: Kenyon Review, P.O. Box 8062, Syracuse, NY 13217; $22/yr., $40/2 yrs., $60/3 yrs. (ind.); $24/yr. (inst.); plus $8 (for.); Single issue: $7, including postage; Back issues: $10.

Lactuca: LACTUCA, Mike Selender, ed., P.O. Box 621, Suffern, NY 10901. Issues indexed: (17). Subscriptions: $10/3 issues, $13/3 issues (for.), $17/6 issues, $23/6 issues (for.); Single issue: $4, plus $2 (for.).

LaurelR: LAUREL REVIEW, Craig Goad, David Slater, William Trowbridge, eds., GreenTower Press, Dept. of English, Northwest Missouri State U., Maryville, MO 64468. Issues indexed: (27:1-2). Subscriptions: $8/yr. (2 issues), $14/2 yrs.; $11/yr., $20/2 yrs. (for.); Single issue: $5; Back issues: $4.50.

Light: LIGHT: A Quarterly of Humorous, Occasional, Ephemeral & Light Verse, John Mella, ed., Box 7500, Chicago, IL 60680. Issues indexed: (5-8). Subscriptions: $12/yr. (4 issues), $22/2 yrs.; $18/yr. (for.); Single issue: $4; Back issues: $3.

LindLM: LINDEN LANE MAGAZINE, Belkis Cuza Malé, ed., P.O. Box 2384, Princeton, NJ 08543-2384. Issues indexed: (12:1, 2/4). Subscriptions: $12/yr. (ind.), $22/yr. (inst.), $22/yr. (Latin America, Europe); Single issue: $2.

LitR: THE LITERARY REVIEW: An International Journal of Contemporary Writing, Walter Cummins, ed., Fairleigh Dickinson U., 285 Madison Ave., Madison, NJ 07940. Issues indexed: (36:2-4, 37:1). Subscriptions: $18/yr., $21/yr. (for.); $30/2 yrs., $36/2 yrs. (for.); Single issue: $5, $6 (for.).

LouisL : LOUISIANA LITERATURE: A Review of Literature and Humanities, David C. Hanson, ed., Dept. of English, SLU-792, Southeastern Louisiana Univ., Box 792, Hammond, LA 70402. Issues indexed: (10:1-2). Subscriptions: $10/yr. (2 issues, ind.); $12.50/yr. (inst.); plus $5/yr. (Canada), plus $10/yr. (other for.).

LullwaterR: LULLWATER REVIEW, Daniel A. Atkins, ed., Box 22036, Emory U., Atlanta, GA 30322. Issues indexed: (4:2). Subscriptions: $12/yr. (2 issues), plus $3 (for.); Single issue: $5.

Luz: LUZ: En Arte y Literatura, Verónica Miranda, Directora/Editora, Luz Bilingual Publishing, P.O. Box 571062, Tarzana, CA 91357-1062. Issues indexed: (3-5). Subscriptions: $25/yr. (3 issues); $35/yr. (for.); Single issue: $14 plus $1.50 postage (U.S.A.), $3 (for.).

MalR: THE MALAHAT REVIEW, U. of Victoria, Derk Wynand, ed., P.O. Box 1700, Victoria, BC, Canada V8W 2Y2. Issues indexed: (102-105). Subscriptions: $18 plus $1.26 GST/yr. (4 issues), $32 plus $2.24 GST/2 yrs.; $20/yr. US Funds (U.S.); Single issue: $7.

ManhatPR: MANHATTAN POETRY REVIEW, Elaine Reiman-Fenton, ed., P.O. Box 8207, New York, NY 10150-1917. Issues indexed: (14). Single issues: $7.50, plus $5 per item (for.).

ManhatR: THE MANHATTAN REVIEW, Philip Fried, ed., 440 Riverside Dr., #45, New York, NY 10027. (7:1). Subscriptions: $10/2 issues (ind.), $14/2 issues (inst.), plus $3/issue (outside USA & Canada); Back issues: $5 (ind.), $7 (inst); include 6" x 9" envelope and $1.45 for postage.

Manoa: MANOA: A Pacific Journal of International Writing, Robert Shapard, Frank Stewart, eds., Frank Stewart, po. ed., English Dept., U. of Hawaii, Honolulu, HI 96822. Issues indexed: (5:1-2). Subscriptions: $18/yr. (2 issues), $32/2 yrs. (ind.); $22/yr., $40/2 yrs. (inst.); $21/yr., $38/2 yrs. (for. ind.); $26/yr., $47/2 yrs. (for. inst.); plus $12/yr. (for. airmail); Single issue: $12. Subscription address: Univ. of Hawaii Press, 2840 Kolowalu St., Honolulu, HI 96822.

MassR: THE MASSACHUSETTS REVIEW, Jules Chametzky, Mary Heath, Paul Jenkins, eds., Anne Halley, Paul Jenkins, po. eds., Memorial Hall, U. of Massachusetts, Amherst, MA 01003. Issues indexed: (33:4, 34:1-4). Subscriptions: $15/yr. (4 issues, ind.), $20/yr. (lib.), $25/yr. (for.); Single issue: $5.

Mester: MESTER, Carmela Zanelli, ed., Dept. of Spanish and Portuguese, U. of California, Los Angeles, CA 90024-1532. Issues indexed: (22:1). Subscriptions: $18/yr. (2 issues, ind.), $30/yr. (inst.), $12/yr. (stud.), $24/yr. (Latin America), plus $5/yr. outside U.S., Canada, Mexico.

MichQR: MICHIGAN QUARTERLY REVIEW, Laurence Goldstein, ed., 3032 Rackham Bldg., U. of Michigan, Ann Arbor, MI 48109. Issues indexed: (32:1-4). Subscriptions: $18/yr., $36/2 yrs. (ind.), $20/yr. (inst.); Single issue: $5-$8; Back issues: $2.50.

MidAR: MID-AMERICAN REVIEW, Robert Early, George Looney, eds., Doug Martin, Edward A. Dougherty, po. eds., 106 Hanna Hall, Dept. of English, Bowling Green State U., Bowling Green, OH 43403. Issues indexed: (14:1). Subscriptions: $12/yr. (2 issues), $20/2 yrs., $28/3 yrs; Single issue: $7; Sample issue: $5.

MidwQ: THE MIDWEST QUARTERLY: A Journal of Contemporary Thought, James B. M. Schick, ed., Stephen E. Meats, po. ed., Pittsburg State U., Pittsburg, KS 66762-5889. Issues indexed: (34:2-4, 35:1). Subscriptions: $10/yr. plus $3 (for.); Single issue: $3.

MinnR: THE MINNESOTA REVIEW, Jeffrey Williams, ed, Dept. of English, East Carolina Univ., Greenville, NC 27858-4353. Issues Indexed: (NS 40). Subscriptions: $10/yr. (2 issues); $20/yr. (inst.), plus $5/yr. (for.); Single issue: $7.50; Back issues: $4.50.

MissouriR: THE MISSOURI REVIEW, Speer Morgan, ed., College of Arts & Science, 1507 Hillcrest Hall, U. of Missouri, Columbia, MO 65211. Issues indexed: (16:1-3). Subscriptions: $15/yr. (3 issues), $27/2 yrs., $36/3 yrs.; Single issue: $6.

MissR: MISSISSIPPI REVIEW, Frederick Barthelme, ed., The Center for Writers, U. of Southern Mississippi, Southern Station, Box 5144, Hattiesburg, MS 39406-5144. Issues indexed: (21:1/2-3; 22:1/2). Subscriptions: $15/yr. (2 issues), $28/2 yrs., $40/3 yrs., plus $2/yr. (for.); Single issue: $8-$12.

MoodySI: MOODY STREET IRREGULARS: A Jack Kerouac Newsletter, Joy Walsh, Nan Pine eds., P.O. Box 157, Clarence Center, NY 14032. Issues indexed: No 1993 issues received. Subscriptions: $10/4 single, 2 double issues (ind.), $15/4 single, 2 double issues (lib.); Single issue: $3, double issues: $5.

Nat: THE NATION, Richard Lingeman, ed., Grace Schulman, po. ed., 72 Fifth Ave., New York, NY 10011. Issues indexed: (256:1-25, 257:1-21). Subscriptions: $48/yr., $80/2 yrs., plus $18/yr. (for.); Single issue: $2.25, $2.75 (Canada); Back issues: $4, $5 (for.). Send subscription correspondence to: P.O. Box 10763, Des Moines, IA 50340-0763.

NegC: NEGATIVE CAPABILITY, Sue Walker, ed., 62 Ridgelawn Dr. East, Mobile, AL 36608. Issues indexed: No 1993 issues received. Subscriptions: $15/yr. (3 issues, ind.), $20/yr. (inst., for.); Single issue: $5.

NewAW: NEW AMERICAN WRITING, Maxine Chernoff, Paul Hoover, eds., OINK! Press, 2920 West Pratt, Chicago, IL 60645. Issues indexed: (11). Subscriptions: $18/3 issues; $24/3 issues (inst.); plus $7/3 issues (for.); Single issue: $7.

NewDeltaR: NEW DELTA REVIEW, Janet Wondra, ed., Ethan Gilsdorf, po. ed., James Gordon Bennett, faculty advisor, Creative Writing Program, English Dept., Louisiana State U., Baton Rouge, LA 70803-5001. Issues indexed: No 1993 issues received. Subscriptions: $7/yr. (2 issues); Single issue: $4.

NewEngR: NEW ENGLAND REVIEW, Middlebury Series, T. R. Hummer, ed, Middlebury College, Middlebury, VT 05753. Issues indexed: (15:1-4). Subscriptions: $20/yr. (4 issues), $37/2 yrs., $55/3 yrs. (ind.); $35/yr., $65/2 yrs., $96/3 yrs. (lib., inst.); plus $10/yr. (for. surface) or $20/yr. (for. airmail); Single issue: $7, $9 (for. surface), $10 (for. airmail); subscription address: University Press of New England, 23 S. Main St., Hanover, NH 03755-2048.

NewL: NEW LETTERS, James McKinley, ed., U. of Missouri-Kansas City, 5100 Rockhill Rd., Kansas City, MO 64110. Issues indexed: (59:2-4, 60:1). Subscriptions: $17/yr. (4 issues), $28/2 yrs., $55/5 yrs. (ind.); $20/yr., $34/2 yrs., $65/5 yrs. (lib.); Single issue: $5,$6 (Canada).

NewMyths: NEW MYTHS, Robert Mooney, ed., State U. of New York, P.O. Box 6000, Binghamton, NY 13902-6000. Issues indexed: No 1993 issues received. Subscriptions: $12/yr. (2 issues), $20/2 yrs. (ind.); $15/yr., $25/2 yrs. (libs.); Single issue: $7.

NewOR: NEW ORLEANS REVIEW, John Biguenet, John Mosier, eds., Box 195, Loyola U., New Orleans, LA 70118. Issues indexed: (19:1-3/4); "The New Orleans Review will be on sabbatical during the 1993 calendar year." Subscriptions: $25/yr. (ind.), $30/yr. (inst.), $35/yr. (for.); Single issue: $9.

NewRena: THE NEW RENAISSANCE, Louise T. Reynolds, ed., James E. A. Woodbury, po. ed., 9 Heath Road, Arlington, MA 02174. Issues indexed: (8:3, #26). Subscriptions: $19.50/3 issues, $37.50/6 issues; $21/3 issues, $39/3 issues (Canada); $23/3 issues, $41/6 issues (other for.); Single issue: $9, $9.50 (for.).

NewRep: THE NEW REPUBLIC, Andrew Sullivan, ed., Mary Jo Salter, po. ed., 1220 19th St. NW, Washington, DC 20036. Issues indexed: (208:1/2-26, 209:1-26). Subscriptions: $69.97/yr., $84.97/yr. (Canada), $99.97/yr. (elsewhere). Back issues: $3.50. Single issue: $2.95. Subscription Service Dept., The New Republic, P.O. Box 602, Mount Morris, IL 61054.

NewYorker: THE NEW YORKER, Pamela Maffei McCarthy, managing ed., 20 W. 43rd St., New York, NY 10036. Issues indexed: (68:47-52, 69:1-44). Subscriptions: $32/yr., $52/2 yrs.; $65.27/yr. (Canada); $76/yr. (other for.); Single issue: $1.95; Subscription correspondence to: Box 56447, Boulder, CO 80322.

NewYorkQ: THE NEW YORK QUARTERLY, William Packard, ed., P.O. Box 693, Old Chelsea Station, New York, NY 10113. Issues indexed: (50-52). Subscriptions: $15/yr., $30/2 yrs., $45/3 yrs.; $25/yr. (lib.); plus $5/yr. (for.); Single issue: $6; subscription address: 302 Neville Hall, U. of Maine, Orono, ME 04469.

NewYRB: THE NEW YORK REVIEW OF BOOKS, Robert B. Silvers, Barbara Epstein, eds., 250 W. 57th St., New York, NY 10107. Issues indexed: (40:1/2-21). Subscriptions: $45/yr.; Single issue: $2.95, $3.75 (Canada); NY Review of Books, P.O. Box 420384, Palm Coast, FL 32142-0384.

Nimrod: NIMROD, Francine Ringold, ed., Manly Johnson, po. ed., Arts and Humanities Council of Tulsa, 2210 S. Main St., Tulsa, OK 74114. Issues indexed: (36:2, 37:1). Subscriptions: $11.50/yr. (2 issues), $21/2 yrs., $30.50/3 yrs.; plus $3/yr. (for.); Single issue: $6.95.

Noctiluca: NOCTILUCA: An International Magazine of Poetry, Judy Katz-Levine, ed., 10 Hillshire Ln., Norwood, MA 02062-3009. Issues indexed: No 1993 issues published. Subscriptions: $10/3 issues.

NoAmR: THE NORTH AMERICAN REVIEW, Robley Wilson, ed., Peter Cooley, po. ed., U. of Northern Iowa, Cedar Falls, IA 50614-0516. Issues indexed: (278:1-6). Subscriptions: $18/yr., $22/yr. (Canada, Latin America), $24/yr. (elsewhere); Single issue: $4, $5 (Canada).

NoCarLR: NORTH CAROLINA LITERARY REVIEW, Alex Albright, ed., English Dept., East Carolina U., Greenville, NC 27858-4353. Issues indexed: (1:2). Subscriptions: $15/yr. (2 issues), $28/2 yrs.; plus $5/yr. (for.); Single issues: $9.50.

NoDaQ: NORTH DAKOTA QUARTERLY, Robert W. Lewis, ed., Jay Meek, po. ed., U. of North Dakota, Grand Forks, ND 58202-7209. Issues indexed: (61:1-4). Subscriptions: $20/yr., $24/yr. (inst.); $23/yr. (for. ind.), $28/yr. (for. inst.); Single issue: $5 (ind.), $7 (for.); Special issues: $10, $12 (for.).

Northeast: NORTHEAST, John Judson, ed., Juniper Press, 1310 Shorewood Dr., La Crosse, WI 54601. Issues indexed: (Ser. 5:8-9). Subscriptions: $33 (2 issues, including books and gifts of the press, ind.), $38 (inst.); Single issue: $4.

NorthStoneR: THE NORTH STONE REVIEW, James Naiden, ed., D Station, Box 14098, Minneapolis, MN 55414. Issues indexed: (11). Subscriptions: $15/yr. (2 issues); Single issue: $8.

NowestR: NORTHWEST REVIEW, John Witte, ed. & po. ed., 369 PLC, U. of Oregon, Eugene, OR 97403. Issues indexed: (31:1-3). Subscriptions: $14/yr. (3 issues), $26/2 yrs., $35/3 yrs.; $12/yr., $22/2 yrs. (stud.); plus $2/yr. (for.); Single issue: $5.

Nuez: LA NUEZ: Revista Internacional de Arte y Literatura, Rafael Bordao, ed., P.O. Box 023617, Brooklyn, NY 11202. Issues indexed: No 1993 issues published. Subscriptions: $12/yr. (ind.), $15/yr. (inst.), $18/yr. (for.).

Obs: OBSIDIAN II: Black Literature in Review, Gerald Barrax, ed. & po. ed., Dept. of English, Box 8105, North Carolina State U., Raleigh, NC 27695-8105. Issues indexed: (8:1-2). Subscriptions: $12/yr. (2 issues), $20/2 yrs.; $13/yr. (Canada), $15/yr. (other for.); Single issue: $5; Double issues: $10.

OhioR: THE OHIO REVIEW, Wayne Dodd, ed., Ellis Hall, Ohio U., Athens, OH 45701-2979. Issues indexed: (49-50). Subscriptions: $16/yr. (3 issues), $40/3 yrs.; Single issue: $6.

Ometeca: OMETECA: Ciencia y Literatura, Science & Literature, Ciência e literatura, Rafael Catalá, ed., P.O. Box 38, New Brunswick, NJ 08903-0038. Issues Indexed: No 1993 issues published. Subscriptions: $20/yr. (2 issues) (ind.), $35/yr. (inst.) (USA, Canada, Mexico); $33/yr. (elsewhere).

OnTheBus: ONTHEBUS: A New Literary Magazine, Jack Grapes, ed., Bombshelter Press, 6421-1/2 Orange St., Los Angeles, CA 90048. Issues indexed: (5:2, 6:1, #12-13). Subscriptions: $28/3 issues (ind.), $33/3 issues (inst.); Single issue: $11, plus $1 postage; Double issue: $13.50 plus $1.50 postage.

OntR: ONTARIO REVIEW, Raymond J. Smith, ed., 9 Honey Brook Dr., Princeton, NJ 08540. Issues indexed: (38-39). Subscriptions: $10/yr. (2 issues), $18/2 yrs., $24/3 yrs., plus $2/yr. (for.); Single issue: $4.95.

Os: OSIRIS, Andrea Moorhead, ed., P.O. Box 297, Deerfield, MA 01342. Issues indexed: (36-37). Subscriptions: $10/2 issues; Single issue: $5.

Outbr: OUTERBRIDGE, Charlotte Alexander, ed., English Dept. (A323), College of Staten Island (CUNY), 2800 Victory Blvd., Staten Island, NY 10314. Issues indexed: (24). Subscriptions: $5/yr. (1 issue).

OxfordM: OXFORD MAGAZINE, Constance Pierce, editorial advisor, Dept. of English, Bachelor Hall, Miami U., Oxford, OH 45056. Issues indexed: (9:1). Single issue: $5.

PacificR: THE PACIFIC REVIEW: A Magazine of Poetry and Prose, Judith Hawkins, ed., James Brown, faculty ed., Derek McKown, po. ed., Dept. of English, California State U., 5500 University Parkway, San Bernardino, CA 92407-2397. Issues indexed: (11). Subscriptions: $6.50/yr. (1 issue), $12/2 yrs.; Back issues: $2.50.

Paint: PAINTBRUSH: A Journal of Poetry, Translations, and Letters, Ben Bennani, ed., Northeast Missouri State U., Kirksville, MO 63501. Issues indexed: (19:38, 20:39/40). Subscriptions: $9/yr. (2 issues, ind.), $12/yr. (inst.); Single & back issues: $7.

PaintedB: PAINTED BRIDE QUARTERLY, Teresa Leo, ed., Painted Bride Arts Center, 230 Vine St., Philadelphia, PA 19106. Issues indexed: (49, 50/51, 52). Subscriptions: $16/yr. (4 issues), $28/2 yrs., $20/yr. (lib, inst.); Single issue: $5. Distributed free to inmates.

PaintedHR: PAINTED HILLS REVIEW, Michael Ishii, Kara D. Kosmatka, eds., 2950 Portage Bay West #411, Davis, CA 95616. Issues indexed: (8-10). Subscriptions: $10/3 issues, $18/6 issues (USA & Canada); $14/3 issues, $24/6 issues (other for.); Single issue: $3.50.

ParisR: THE PARIS REVIEW, George A. Plimpton, Peter Matthiessen, Donald Hall, Robert B. Silvers, Blair Fuller, Maxine Groffsky, Jeanne McCulloch, James Linville, eds., Richard Howard, po. ed., Box S, 541 East 72nd St., New York, NY 10021. Issues indexed: (35:126-129). Subscriptions: $34/4 issues, plus $7/4 issues (for.); Single issue: $7; Subscription address: 45-39 171st Place, Flushing, NY 11358.

Parting: PARTING GIFTS, Robert Bixby, ed. & pub., March Street Press, 3413 Wilshire Dr., Greensboro, NC 27408-2923. Issues indexed: (6:1-2). Subscriptions: $5/yr. (2 issues), $9/2 yrs., $13/3 yrs.; Single issue: $3.

PartR: PARTISAN REVIEW, William Phillips, ed., Boston U., 236 Bay State Rd., Boston, MA 02215. Issues indexed: (60:1-4). Subscriptions: $18/yr. (4 issues), $33/2 yrs., $47/3 yrs.; $21/yr., $36/2 yrs. (for.); $28/yr. (inst.); Single issue: $5-$8, plus $1.50 per issue postage and handling.

PassN: PASSAGES NORTH, Michael Barrett, ed., Conrad Hilberry, po. ed., Kalamazoo
   College, 1200 Academy St., Kalamazoo, MI 49006-3295. Issues indexed: (14:1-2).
   Subscriptions: $10/yr., $18/2 yrs; Single issue: $5.

Pearl: PEARL, Joan Jobe Smith, Marilyn Johnson, Barbara Hauk, eds., 3030 E. 2nd St., Long
   Beach, CA 90803. Issues indexed: (17-19). Subscriptions: $15/yr. (3 issues, ind.); $20/yr.
   (lib.); $30/yr. (patrons); Single issue: $6-$7.

Pembroke: PEMBROKE MAGAZINE, Shelby Stephenson, ed., Box 60, Pembroke State U.,
   Pembroke, NC 28372. Issues indexed: (25). Subscriptions: $5/issue (USA, Canada,
   Mexico), $5.50/issue (other for.).

PennR: THE PENNSYLVANIA REVIEW, Ed Ochester, executive ed., Leasa Burton, po. ed.,
   526 Cathedral of Learning, U. of Pittsburgh, Pittsburgh, PA 15260. Issues indexed: (5:2).
   Subscriptions: $10/yr. (2 issues), $18/2 yrs.; Single issue: $6.

Pequod: PEQUOD, Mark Rudman, ed., Dept. of English, Room 200, New York U., 19
   University Place, New York, NY 10003. Issues indexed: (35-36). Subscriptions: $12/yr.
   (2 issues), $20/2 yrs. (ind.); $18/yr., $34/2 yrs. (inst).; plus $3/yr. (for.); Single issue:
   $7.50-$10.

PikeF: THE PIKESTAFF FORUM, Robert D. Sutherland, James R. Scrimgeour, eds./pubs.,
   P.O. Box 127, Normal, IL 61761. Issues indexed: (11). Subscriptions: $12/6 issues;
   Single issue: $3.

Plain: PLAINSONGS, Dwight Marsh, ed., Dept. of English, Hastings College, Hastings, NE
   68902. Issues indexed: (13:2-3, 14:1). Subscriptions: $9/yr. (3 issues).

Ploughs: PLOUGHSHARES, DeWitt Henry, executive director, David Daniel, po. ed.,
   Emerson College, 100 Beacon St., Boston, MA 02116-1596. Issues indexed: (19:1, 2/3,
   4). Subscriptions: $19/yr., $36/2 yrs. (ind.); $24/yr. (for. ind.); $22/yr. (inst.), $27/yr. (for.
   inst.). Single issue: $8.95.

Poem: POEM, Huntsville Literary Association, Nancy Frey Dillard, ed., c/o English Dept., U.
   of Alabama, Huntsville, AL 35899. Issues indexed: (69-70). Subscriptions: $10/yr.; Back
   issues: $5; Subscription address: Huntsville Literary Association, P.O. Box 919,
   Huntsville, AL 35804.

PoetC: POET AND CRITIC, Neal Bowers, ed., 203 Ross Hall, Iowa State U., Ames, IA 50011.
   Issues indexed: (24:2-3, 25:1); 24:1, indexed in the 1992 volume, was listed as 23:1 in
   error. Subscriptions: Iowa State U. Press, South State St., Ames, IA 50010, $18/yr. (3
   issues), $21/yr. (for.); $46/3 yrs, $55/3 yrs. (for.); Single issue: $8.

PoetL: POET LORE, Philip K. Jason, executive ed., The Writer's Center, 4508 Walsh St.,
   Bethesda, MD 20815. Issues Indexed: (88:1-4). Subscriptions: $10/yr. (Writer's Center
   members); $15/yr. (ind.); $24/yr. (inst.), plus $5/yr. (for.); Single issue: $4.50, plus $1
   postage and handling; Samples: $4.

Poetry: POETRY, Joseph Parisi, ed., 60 W. Walton St., Chicago, IL 60610. Issues indexed:
   (161:4-6, 162:1-6, 163:1-3). Subscriptions: $25/yr. (ind.); $31/yr. (for.); $27/yr. (inst.);
   $33/yr. (for. inst.); Single issue: $2.50 plus $1 postage; Back issues: $3 plus $1 postage.

PoetryC: POETRY CANADA, Barry Dempster, po. ed., P.O. Box 1061, Kingston, Ont. K7L
   4Y5 Canada. Issues indexed: (13:2-4, 14:1). Subscriptions: $17.12/4 issues (ind.);
   $34.24/4 issues (inst.); Back issues: $5; Single issue: $4.75, Double issue: $7.95.

PoetryE: POETRY EAST, Richard Jones, ed., Dept. of English, 802 W. Belden Ave., DePaul
   Univ., Chicago, IL 60614. Issues indexed: (35-36). Subscriptions: $12/yr.; Single issue:
   $7.

PoetryNW: POETRY NORTHWEST, David Wagoner, ed., U. of Washington, 4045 Brooklyn
   Ave. NE, Seattle, WA 98105. Issues indexed: (34:1-4). Subscriptions: $10/yr., $12/yr.
   (for.); Single issue: $3, $3.50 (for.).

PoetryUSA: POETRY USA, Jack Foley, ed., 2569 Maxwell Ave., Oakland, CA 94601. Issues indexed: (25/26). Subscriptions: $10/4 issues; Single issue: $1; Double issue: $2.

PottPort: THE POTTERSFIELD PORTFOLIO, Joe Blades, Margaret McLeod, managing eds., Wild East Publishing Co-operative Ltd., 151 Ryan Court, Fredericton, NB, Canada E3A 2Y9. Issues indexed: (15:1). Subscriptions: $12/yr. (2 issues, ind.), $15/yr. (inst.); $9/yr. (students), $15/yr. (USA, for.); Single issue: $6.

PraF: PRAIRIE FIRE: A Canadian Magazine of New Writing, Andris Taskans, ed., Méira Cook, Catherine Hunter, po. eds., 423-100 Arthur St., Winnipeg, Manitoba R3B 1H3 Canada. Issues indexed: (14:1-4, #62-65). Subscriptions: $24/yr., $44/2 yrs. (ind.); $32/yr. (inst.), plus $4 (USA), plus $6 (for.); Single issue: $8.95-10.95.

PraS: PRAIRIE SCHOONER, Hilda Raz, ed., 201 Andrews Hall, U. of Nebraska, Lincoln, NE 68588-0334. Issues indexed: (67:1-4). Subscriptions: $20/yr., $35/2 yrs., $46/3 yrs. (ind.); $22/yr. (lib.); Single issue: $6.45

Prima: PRIMAVERA, Arlene Zide, Ruth Young, Lisa Grayson, William Falloon, Martha Ann Selby, Kathleen Kuiper, eds., Box 37-7547, Chicago, IL 60637. Issues indexed: (16/17). Single issue: $9; Back issues: $5.

*ProseP: THE PROSE POEM: An International Journal, Peter Johnson, ed., English Dept., Providence College, Providence, RI 02918. Issues indexed: (1-2). Subscriptions: $8/annual issue.

Quarry: QUARRY, Steven Heighton, ed., P.O. Box 1061, Kingston, Ontario K7L 4Y5 Canada. Issues indexed: (42:1-3). Subscriptions: $22.47/yr. (4 issues), $39.85/2 yrs. (8 issues); Single issue: $5.95.

QRL: QUARTERLY REVIEW OF LITERATURE, T. & R. Weiss, eds., 26 Haslet Ave., Princeton, NJ 08540. Issues indexed: (Poetry series 12, vol. 32/33: "50th Anniversary Anthology"). Subscriptions: $20/2 volumes (paper), $20/volume (cloth, inst.).

QW: QUARTERLY WEST, Jeffrey Vasseur, M. L. Williams, eds., Craig A. Arnold, Sally Thomas, po. eds., 317 Olpin Union, U. of Utah, Salt Lake City, UT 84112. Issues indexed: (37). Subscriptions: $11/yr. (2 issues), $20/2 yrs.; $16/yr., $30/2 yrs. (for.); Single issue: $6.50.

RagMag: RAG MAG, Beverly Voldseth, ed. & pub., Black Hat Press, Box 12, 508 2nd Ave., Goodhue, MN 55027. Issues indexed: (11:1-2). Subscriptions: $10/yr. (2 issues), $15/yr. (inst.); Single issue: $6.

Raritan: RARITAN: A Quarterly Review, Richard Poirier, ed., Rutgers U., 31 Mine St., New Brunswick, NJ 08903. Issues indexed: (12:3-4, 13:1-2). Subscriptions: $16/yr., $26/2 yrs. (ind.); $20/yr., $30/2 yrs. (inst.); plus $5.50/yr (for.); Single issue: $5; Back issues: $6.

RedBass: RED BASS, Jay Murphy, ed., 105 W. 28th St., 3rd floor, New York, NY 10001. Issues indexed: (16). Subscriptions: $20/2 issues (ind.), $35 (inst., for.); Single issue: $8.50; Back issues: $5.

RiverC: RIVER CITY, Sharon Bryan, ed., Dept. of English, Memphis State U., Memphis, TN 38152. Issues indexed: (13:1-2, 14:1). Subscriptions: $9/yr. (ind., 2 issues), $10/yr. (inst).; Single issue: $5.

RiverS: RIVER STYX, Lee Fournier, ed., 3207 Washington Ave., St. Louis, MO 63103. Issues indexed: (37-39). Subscriptions: $20/3 issues, $38/6 issues; Single issue: $7.

*Rosebud: ROSEBUD: For People Who Enjoy Writing, Roderick Clark, ed., P.O. Box 459, Cambridge, WI 53523. Issues indexed: (1:1). Subscriptions: $12/2 years (4 issues), plus $7 (for.); Single copy: $5 plus $2.40 postage; Subscription address: Beth Swan, 4218 Barnett St., Madison, WI 53704.

Salm: SALMAGUNDI: A Quarterly of the Humanities and Social Sciences, Robert Boyers, ed., Skidmore College, Saratoga Springs, NY 12866. Issues indexed: (97, 98/99, 100). Subscriptions: $15/yr., $25/2 yrs. (ind.); $22/yr., $37/2 yrs. (inst.); plus $10/yr. (for.); Sample issues: $6; Single issue: $7.

17   Periodicals Indexed

SenR: SENECA REVIEW, Deborah Tall, ed., Hobart and William Smith Colleges, Geneva, NY 14456. Issues indexed: (23:1/2). Subscriptions: $8/yr. (2 issues), $15/2 yrs.; Single issue: $5.

Sequoia: SEQUOIA: Stanford Literary Magazine, Carlos Rodriguez, managing ed., Ruth Porritt, Carlos Rodriguez, po. eds., Storke Publications Building, Stanford U., Stanford, CA 94305. Issues indexed: (34/35). Subscriptions: $10/yr. (1 issue), $12/yr. (for.).

SewanR: THE SEWANEE REVIEW, George Core, ed., U. of the South, Sewanee, TN 37383-1000. Issues indexed: (101:1-4). Subscriptions: $16/yr., $28/2 yrs., $40/3 yrs. (ind.); $20/yr., $38/2 yrs., $55/3 yrs. (inst.); plus $5/yr. (for.); Single issue: $5.75; Back issues: $8.

ShadowP: SHADOW PLAY, Jan Bender, ed., 99 Reynolds Rd., Grand Isle, VT 05458. Issues indexed: No 1993 issues published; No. 4 published in 1994. Single issue: $3.

Shen: SHENANDOAH: The Washington and Lee University Review, Dabney Stuart, ed., Box 722, Lexington, VA 24450. Issues indexed: (43:1-4). Subscriptions: $11/yr., $18/2 yrs., $25/3 yrs.; $14/yr., $24/2 yrs., $33/3 yrs. (for.); Single issue: $3.50; Back issues: $6.

Shiny: SHINY: The Magazine of the Future, Michael Friedman, ed. & pub., 39 E. 12th St., Suite 603, New York, NY 10003. Manuscripts to Kim Rosenfield, associate ed., 52 MacDougal St., Apt. 1C, New York, NY 10012. Issues indexed: No 1993 issues received. Subscriptions: $28/4 issues; Single issue: $5, double issue: $10.

SilverFR: SILVERFISH REVIEW, Rodger Moody, ed., P.O. Box 3541, Eugene, OR 97403. Issues indexed: (24). Subscriptions: $12/3 issues (ind.), $15/3 issues (inst.), Single issue: $4-5.

SingHM: SING HEAVENLY MUSE!: Women's Poetry and Prose, Ruth Berman, Joline Gitis, Karen Karsten, Carol Masters, Sue Ann Martinson, Corinna Nelson, Rafael Tilton, Linda Webster, eds, P.O. Box 13320, Minneapolis, MN 55414. Issues indexed: No issues published in 1993; no. 21 published in 1994. Subscriptions: $14/2 issues, $19/3 issues, $36/6 issues (ind.); $21/3 issues, $40/6 issues (inst.); $16/3 issues (low income); Single issue: $7 plus $2 postage and handling.

SinW: SINISTER WISDOM: A Journal for the Lesbian Imagination in the Arts and Politics, Elana Dykewomon, ed. & pub., P.O. Box 3252, Berkeley, CA 94703. Issues indexed: (49-51). Subscriptions: $17/yr. (4 issues), $30/2 yrs. (ind.); $30/yr. (inst.); $22/yr. (for.); $8-15/yr. (hardship); Free on request to women in prisons and mental institutions; Single issue: $5.

SlipS: SLIPSTREAM, Robert Borgatti, Livio Farallo, Dan Sicoli, eds., P.O. Box 2071, Niagara Falls, NY 14301. Issues indexed: (13). Subscriptions: $8.50/2 issues; Single issue: $5.

SmPd: THE SMALL POND MAGAZINE OF LITERATURE, Napoleon St. Cyr, ed., pub., P.O. Box 664, Stratford, CT 06497. Issues indexed: (30:1-3, #87-89). Subscriptions: $8/yr. (3 issues), $15/2 yrs., $22/3 yrs., plus $1.50/yr. (for.); Single issue: $3; Random back issues, $2.50.

SnailPR: THE SNAIL'S PACE REVIEW: A Biannual Little Magazine of Contemporary Poetry, Ken Denberg, Darby Penney, eds., RR 2 Box 363 Brownell Rd., Cambridge, NY 12816. Issues indexed: (3:1). Subscriptions: $7/yr. (ind.), $12/yr. (inst.); Single issue: $4.

Sonora: SONORA REVIEW, Elizabeth Taggart, ed, Chalon Emmons, Jami Macarty, po. eds., Dept. of English, U. of Arizona, Tucson, AZ 85721. Issues indexed: (24/25, 26). Subscriptions: $10/yr. (2 issues); Single issue: $5.

SoCaR: SOUTH CAROLINA REVIEW, Richard J. Calhoun, executive ed., Dept. of English, Clemson U., Strode Tower, Box 341503, Clemson, SC 29634-1503. Issues indexed: (25:2, 26:1). Subscriptions: $7/yr., $13/2 yrs. (USA, Canada, Mexico); $8.75/yr., $16.25/2 yrs. (inst.); plus $1.50/yr. (other for.); Back issues: $5.

SoCoast: SOUTH COAST POETRY JOURNAL, John J. Brugaletta, ed., English Dept., California State U., Fullerton, CA 92634. Issues indexed: (14-15). Subscriptions: $10/yr. (2 issues), $18/2 yrs. (ind.); $12/yr. (inst.); Single issue: $6.

SoDakR: SOUTH DAKOTA REVIEW, John R. Milton, ed., Dept. of English, U. of South Dakota, Box 111, U. Exchange, Vermillion, SD 57069. Issues indexed: (31:1-4). Subscriptions: $15/yr., $25/2 yrs. (USA, Canada); plus $1/yr. elsewhere; Single issue: $5.

SouthernHR: SOUTHERN HUMANITIES REVIEW, Dan R. Latimer, R. T. Smith, eds., 9088 Haley Center, Auburn U., AL 36849. Issues indexed: (27:1-4). Subscriptions: $15/yr.; Single issue: $5.

SouthernPR: SOUTHERN POETRY REVIEW, Lucinda Grey, Ken McLaurin, eds., English Dept., U. of North Carolina, Charlotte, NC 28223. Issues indexed: (33:1-2). Subscriptions: $8 yr.

SouthernR: SOUTHERN REVIEW, James Olney, Dave Smith, eds., Louisiana State U., 43 Allen Hall, Baton Rouge, LA 70803-5005. Issues indexed: (29:1-4). Subscriptions: $18/yr., $32/2 yrs., $45/3 yrs.; $35/yr., $55/2 yrs., $80/3 yrs. (inst.); Single issue: $5, $10 (inst.).

SouthwR: SOUTHWEST REVIEW, Willard Spiegelman, ed., Southern Methodist U., Dallas, TX 75275. Issues indexed: (78:1-4). Subscriptions: $20/yr., $35/2 yrs., $50/3 yrs. (ind.); $25/yr. (inst.); Single issue: $5.

Sparrow: SPARROW, Felix Stefanile, Selma Stefanile, eds. & pubs., 103 Waldron St., West Lafayette, IN 47906. Issues indexed: (60). Single issue: $5, $7.50 (libs., inst.), $10 (for.).

Spirit: THE SPIRIT THAT MOVES US, Morty Sklar, ed., pub., P.O. Box 820, Jackson Heights, NY 11372. Issues indexed: No 1992 or 1993 issues published; #12 expected in 1994.

SpiritSH: SPIRIT: A Magazine of Poetry, David Rogers, ed., Dept. of English, Seton Hall U., South Orange, NJ 07079. Issues indexed: (58). Subscriptions: $4/yr. (1 issue).

Spitball: SPITBALL: The Literary Baseball Magazine, Mike Shannon, pub. & ed., William J. McGill, po. ed., 6224 Collegevue Pl., Cincinnati, OH 45224. Issues indexed: (43-45). Subscriptions: $16/yr. (4 issues); $22/yr. (Canada, U.S. funds); Single issue: $5.

SpoonR: THE SPOON RIVER POETRY REVIEW (formerly Spoon River Quarterly), Lucia Cordell Getsi, ed., English Dept., 4240 Illinois State U., Normal, IL 61790-4240. Issues indexed: (18:1-2). Subscriptions: $12/yr. (2 issues); $15/yr. (inst.); Single issue: $6.

Stand: STAND MAGAZINE, Daniel Schenker, Amanda Kay, RR 2 Box 122-B, Lacey's Spring, AL 35754. Issues indexed: (34:2-4, 35:1). Subscriptions: $25/yr., $46/2 yrs.; $22/yr. (students, unwaged); Single issue: $7; U.S.A. distributor: Anton J. Mikovsky, 50 E. 42nd St. Ste. 1809, New York, NY 10017.

Sulfur: SULFUR: A Literary Bi-Annual of the Whole Art, Clayton Eshleman, ed., English Dept., Eastern Michigan U., Ypsilanti, MI 48197. Issues indexed: (13:1-2, #32-33). Subscriptions: $13/2 issues (ind.), $19/2 issues (inst.), plus $4 (for.) or $10 (for. airmail postage); Single issue: $8.

Sun: SUN: A Magazine of Ideas, Sy Safransky, ed., 107 N. Roberson St., Chapel Hill, NC 27516. Issues indexed: (205-216). Subscriptions: $30/yr., $50/2 yrs., $125/5 yrs., $250/10 yrs., $1,000 lifetime, plus $10/yr. (for.). The Sun, Subscription Service, P.O. Box 6706, Syracuse, NY 13217.

SycamoreR: SYCAMORE REVIEW, Linda Haynes, ed., Kim Karaff, Scott Pierce, po. eds., Dept. of English, Heavilon Hall, Purdue U., West Lafayette, IN 47907. Issues indexed: (5:1-2). Subscriptions: $9/yr., $18/2 yrs.; Single issue: $5.

Talisman: TALISMAN: A Journal of Contemporary Poetry and Poetics, Edward Foster, ed., Box 1117, Hoboken, NJ 07030. Issues indexed: (10-11). Subscriptions: $9/yr. (2 issues); $13/yr. (inst.); plus $2/yr. (for.); Single issue: $5.

TampaR: TAMPA REVIEW: Literary Journal of the University of Tampa, Richard Mathews, ed., Donald Morrill, Kathryn Van Spanckeren, po. eds., Box 19F, U. of Tampa, 401 W. Kennedy Blvd., Tampa, FL 33606-1490. Issues indexed: (6-7). entry. Subscriptions: $10/yr. (2 issues); plus $4/yr. (for.); Single issue: $5.95.

TarRP: TAR RIVER POETRY, Peter Makuck, ed., Dept. of English, General Classroom Bldg., East Carolina U., Greenville, NC 27858-4353. Issues indexed: (32:2, 33:1). Subscriptions: $10/yr (2 issues), $18/2 yrs.; Single issue: $4.50.

TexasR: TEXAS REVIEW, Paul Ruffin, ed., Division of English and Foreign Languages, Sam Houston State U., Huntsville, TX 77341. Issues indexed: (14:1/2-3/4). Subscriptions: $10/yr., $18/2 yrs., $26/3 yrs.; $10.50/yr. (Canada), $11/yr. (for.); Single issue: $5.

Thirteenth Moon: *See* 13thMoon *at beginning of file.*

Thrpny: THE THREEPENNY REVIEW, Wendy Lesser, ed., pub., P.O. Box 9131, Berkeley, CA 94709. Issues indexed: (52-55). Subscriptions: $12/yr., $20/2 yrs., $24/yr. (for.); Single issue: $3.

TickleAce: TICKLEACE: A Journal of Literary and Visual Art, Susan Ingersoll, Lawrence Mathews, Bruce Porter, Michael Winter, eds., P.O. Box 5353, St. John's, NF, A1C 5W2 Canada. Issues indexed: (22-26). Subscriptions: $11/yr. (2 issues), $13/yr. (inst.), plus $4/yr. (for.); Single issue: $6.

Trans: TRANSLATION, The Journal of Literary Translation, Frank MacShane, Lori M. Carlson, eds., The Translation Center, 412 Dodge Hall, Columbia U., New York, NY 10027. Issues indexed: (28); No. 27 not received. Subscriptions: $18/yr. (2 issues), $34/2 yrs.; Single issue: $9.

*Trasimagen: TRASIMAGEN: Revista Latinoamericana de Literatura y Arte, Lillian Haddock, directora; Lillian Haddock, Jose Luis Colon-Santiago, eds., P.O. Box 2581, Stuyvesant Station, New York, NY 10009. Issues indexed: (1:1). Subscriptions: $20/yr. (2 issues); $24/yr. (inst.); $30/yr. (for.); Single issue: $10.

*Tricycle: TRICYCLE: The Buddhist Review, Helen Tworkov, ed., The Buddhist Ray, Inc., 163 W. 22nd St., New York, NY 10011. Issues indexed: (2:3-4, 3:1-2). Subscriptions: $20/yr. (4 issues), $38/2 yrs., $57/3 yrs., plus $5/yr. (for. surface mail), $15/yr. (for. airmail); Single copy: 6. Subscription address: Dept. TRI, P.O. Box 3000, Denville, NJ 07834-9897.

TriQ: TRIQUARTERLY, Reginald Gibbons, ed., Northwestern U., 2020 Ridge Ave., Evanston, IL 60208. Issues indexed: (87-89). Subscriptions: $20/yr. (3 issues), $36/2 yrs., $500/life (ind.); $26/yr., $44/2 yrs., $300/life (inst.), plus $4/yr. (for.); Single issue: cost varies; Sample copies: $4.

Turnstile: TURNSTILE, Daniel Bial, Lindsey Crittenden, Meghan Daum, Ann Biester Deane, Vira DeFilippo, Twisne Fan, Ann McKay Farrell, Kit Haines, Marian Lizzi, Mitchell Nauffts, George Witte, eds., 175 Fifth Avenue, Suite 2348, New York, NY 10010. Issues indexed: (4:1-2). Subscriptions: $12/2 issues, $22/4 issues; Single issue: $6.50.

US1: US 1 WORKSHEETS, Irene Willis, coordinating ed., Rebekah Nicholson, Mark Scott, po eds., US 1 Poets' Cooperative, P.O. Box 1, Ringoes, NJ 08551-0001. Issues indexed: (28/29). Subscriptions: $10/2 double issues; Single (double) issue: $6.

Verse: VERSE, Henry Hart, U. S. ed., Dept. of English, College of William and Mary, Williamsburg, VA 23185. Issues indexed: (10:1-3). Subscriptions: $15/yr. (3 issues), $21/yr. (libraries); Single issue: $5.

VirQR: THE VIRGINIA QUARTERLY REVIEW: A National Journal of Literature and Discussion, Staige D. Blackford, ed., Gregory Orr, po. consultant, One West Range, Charlottesville, VA 22903. Issues indexed: (69:1-4). Subscriptions: $15/yr., $22/2 yrs., $30/3 yrs. (ind.); $22/yr., $30/2 yrs., $50/3 yrs. (inst.); plus $3/yr. (for.); Single issue: $5.

Vis: VISIONS INTERNATIONAL, Bradley R. Strahan, po. ed., pub., Black Buzzard Press, 1110 Seaton Lane, Falls Church, VA 22046. Issues indexed: (41-43). Subscriptions: $14/yr. (3 issues), $27/2 yrs. (ind.); $42/3 yrs. (lib).; Single issue: $5.

WashR: WASHINGTON REVIEW, Clarissa K. Wittenberg, ed., P.O. Box 50132, Washington, DC 20091-0132. Issues indexed: (18:5-6; 19:1-4). Subscriptions: $12/yr. (6 issues), $20/2 yrs.; Single issue: $3.

WeberS: WEBER STUDIES: An Interdisciplinary Humanities Journal, Neila C. Seshachari, ed., Weber State U., Ogden, UT 84408-1214. Issues indexed: (10:1-3). Subscriptions: $10/yr. (3 issues), $20/yr. (inst.); plus actual extra postage costs per year (for.); Back issues: $7; Single issue: $5.

WebR: WEBSTER REVIEW, Nancy Schapiro, Robert Boyd, Greg Marshall, eds., English Dept., SLCC-Meramec, 11333 Big Bend Rd., St. Louis, MO 63122. Issues indexed: (17). Subscriptions: $5/yr. (1 issue).

WestB: WEST BRANCH: a twice-yearly magazine of poetry and fiction, Karl Patten, Robert Love Taylor, eds., Bucknell Hall, Bucknell U., Lewisburg, PA 17837. Issues indexed: (31/32, 33). Subscriptions: $7/yr. (2 issues), $11/2 yrs.; Single issue: $4, double issue: $7.

WestCL: WEST COAST LINE: A Journal of Contemporary Writing and Criticism, Roy Miki, ed., 2027 East Academic Annex, Simon Fraser U., Burnaby, B.C. V5A 1S6 Canada. Issues indexed: (27:1-3, #10-12). Subscriptions: $20/yr. (ind., 3 issues), $30/yr. (inst.); Single issue: $10.

WestHR: WESTERN HUMANITIES REVIEW, Barry Weller, ed., Richard Howard, po. ed., U. of Utah, Salt Lake City, UT 84112. Issues indexed: (47:1-4); all issues have 1991 copyright date, surely in error! Subscriptions: $20/yr. (4 issues, ind.), $26/yr. (inst.); Single issue: $6.

WilliamMR: THE WILLIAM AND MARY REVIEW, Stacy Payne, ed., Adrien Ardoin, Lauren Butcher, po. eds., College of William and Mary, P.O. Box 8795, Williamsburg, VA 23187. Issues indexed: (31). Subscriptions: $4.50/single issue, plus $1.50 (for.); Single issue: $5.

WillowR: WILLOW REVIEW, Paulette Roeske, Larry Starzec, Joy Wideburg, eds., College of Lake County, 19351 W. Washington St., Grayslake, IL 60030. Issues indexed: (20). Subscriptions: $11/3 issues, $18/5 issues; Single issue: $4.

WillowS: WILLOW SPRINGS, Nance Van Winckel, ed., Laurel Darrow, po. ed., Eastern Washington U., MS-1, Cheney, WA 99004. Issues Indexed: (31-33); both number 31 and 33 are labeled "Winter 1993".. Subscriptions: $8/yr. (2 issues), $15/2 yrs.; Single issue: $4.50.

Wind: WIND, Steven R. Cope, Charlie G. Hughes, eds., P.O. Box 24548, Lexington, KY 40524. Issues indexed: (23:72). Subscriptions: $10/yr. (2 issues, ind.), $12/yr. (inst.), $14/yr. (for.); Single issue: $5.50; Back issues: $3.50.

WindO: THE WINDLESS ORCHARD, Robert Novak, ed., English Dept., Indiana-Purdue U., Fort Wayne, IN 46805. Issues indexed: (57). Subscriptions: $10/3 issues; Single issue: $4.

Witness: WITNESS, Peter Stine, ed., Oakland Community College, Orchard Ridge Campus, 27055 Orchard Lake Road, Farmington Hills, MI 48334. Issues indexed: 7:1-2. Subscriptions: $12/yr. (2 issues), $22/2 yrs.; $18/yr., $34/2 yrs. (inst.); plus $4/yr. (for.); Single copies: $7.

WorldL: WORLD LETTER, Jon Cone, ed., 2726 E. Court St., Iowa City, IA 52245. Issues indexed: (4). Subscriptions: $9/2 issues (U.S.), $12/2 issues (Canada); Single issue: $5 (U.S.), $7 (Canada).

WorldO: WORLD ORDER, Firuz Kazemzadeh, Betty J. Fisher, Howard Garey, Robert H. Stockman, James D. Stokes, eds., Herbert Woodward Martin, po. consultant, National Spiritual Assembly of the Bahá'ís of the United States, 415 Linden Ave., Wilmette, IL 60091. Issues indexed: (25:1-2). Subscriptions: $10/yr. (4 issues), $18/2 yrs.; $15/yr., $28/2 yrs. (for.); $20/yr., $38/2 yrs. (for. airmail); Single issue: $3.

WormR: THE WORMWOOD REVIEW, Marvin Malone, ed., P.O. Box 4698, Stockton, CA 95204-0698. Issues indexed: (33:1-4; #129-132). Subscriptions: $8/4 issues (ind.), $10/4 issues (inst.); $24/4 issues (patrons); Single issue: $4; Back issues: $4.

Writ: WRIT, Roger Greenwald, ed., Innis College, U. of Toronto, 2 Sussex Ave., Toronto, Canada M5S 1J5. Issues indexed: (25). Subscriptions: $18/2 issues (ind.), $20/2 issues (inst.); same amount in U.S. funds outside Canada; Back issues: $10-20.

Writer: THE WRITER, Sylvia K. Burack, ed., pub., 120 Boylston St., Boston, MA 02116-4615. Issues indexed: (106:1-12). Subscriptions: $27/yr., $50/2 yrs., $74/3 yrs.; plus $8/yr. (for.); $10/5 issues for new subscribers; Single issue: $2.25.

WritersF: WRITERS' FORUM, Alexander Blackburn, ed., Victoria McCabe, po ed., P.O. Box 7150, U. of Colorado, Colorado Springs, CO 80933-7150. Issues indexed: (19). Subscriptions: $8.95/yr. (1 issue) plus $1.05 postage and handling; Back issue sample: $5.95 plus $1.05 postage and handling. Subscription address: University Press of Colorado, P.O. Box 849, Niwot, CO 80544.

*XavierR: XAVIER REVIEW, Thomas Bonner, Jr., ed., Box 110C, Xavier U. of Louisiana, New Orleans, LA 70125. Issues indexed: (13:1-2). Subscriptions: $10/yr. (2 issues, ind.), $15/yr. (inst.).

YaleR: THE YALE REVIEW, J. D. McClatchy, ed., P.O. Box 1902A, Yale Station, New Haven, CT 06520. Issues indexed: (81:1-4). Subscriptions: $21.50/yr., $38.50/2 yrs., $60/3 yrs. (ind.); $32.50/yr., $60/2 yrs., $87/3 yrs. (for. ind.); $43.50/yr. (inst.), $48.50/yr. (for. inst.); Single issues: $7, $14.50 (inst.), $10.50 (for. ind.), $15.50 (for. inst.).

YellowS: YELLOW SILK, Journal of Erotic Arts, Lily Pond, ed., pub., P.O. Box 6374, Albany, CA 94706. Issues indexed: (42-43). Subscriptions: $30/yr. (4 issues, ind.), $38/yr. (lib., inst.), plus $8/yr. (for. surface) or $22/yr. (for. air). Single issue: $7.50.

Zyzzyva: ZYZZYVA: The Last Word, West Coast Writers & Artists, Howard Junker, ed, 41 Sutter St., Suite 1400, San Francisco, CA 94104. Issues indexed: (9:1-4, #33-36). Subscriptions: $28/yr. (4 issues), $48/2 yrs. (ind.); $36/yr. (inst.); $48/yr. (for.); Single issue: $10.

Alphabetical List of Journals Indexed, with Acronyms

13th Moon: A Feminist Literary Magazine : 13th Moon

Abraxas : Abraxas
Aerial : Aerial
African American Review : AfAmRev
Agni : Agni
Alabama Literary Review : AlabamaLR
Amelia : Amelia
American Letters & Commentary : AmerLC
The American Poetry Review : AmerPoR
The American Scholar : AmerS
The American Voice : AmerV
The Americas Review: A Review of Hispanic Literature and Art of the USA :
    Americas
Another Chicago Magazine : AnotherCM
Antaeus : Antaeus
The Anthology of New England Writers : AnthNEW
The Antigonish Review : AntigR
The Antioch Review : AntR
Apalachee Quarterly : ApalQ
Arc : Arc
Archae : Archae
Areíto : Areíto
Arion: A Journal of Humanities and the Classics : Arion
Arshile: A Magazine of the Arts : Arshile
Art & Understanding: The Journal of Literature and Art About AIDS : Art&Und
Artful Dodge : ArtfulD
Arts Indiana Literary Supplement: *See* Hopewell Review *(title change)*
Ascent : Ascent
Asylum : Asylum
The Atlantic : Atlantic
Avec: A Journal of Writing : Avec

Bamboo Ridge: The Hawaii Writers' Quarterly : BambooR
The Bellingham Review : BellR
Bellowing Ark : BellArk
The Beloit Poetry Journal : BelPoJ
The Bilingual Review / La Revista Bilingüe : BilingR
Black American Literature Forum: *See* African American Review *(title change)*
Black Bear Review : BlackBR
Black Bread : BlackBread
Black Warrior Review : BlackWR
Blueline : Blueline
Bogg : Bogg
Bomb Magazine : Bomb
Borderlands: Texas Poetry Review : Border
Boston Review : BostonR
Boulevard : Boulevard
Brooklyn Review : BrooklynR

Caliban : Caliban
California Quarterly : CalQ
Callaloo: A Journal of African-American and African Arts and Letters :
    Callaloo

Calyx: A Journal of Art and Literature by Women : Calyx
Canadian Literature : CanLit
The Cape Rock : CapeR
The Capilano Review : CapilR
The Caribbean Writer : CaribbeanW
Carolina Quarterly : CarolQ
The Centennial Review : CentR
Central Park : CentralP
Chaminade Literary Review : ChamLR
Changing Men: Issues in Gender, Sex and Politics : ChangingM
The Chariton Review : CharR
The Chattahoochee Review: The DeKalb College Literary Quarterly : ChatR
Chelsea : Chelsea
Chicago Review : ChiR
Chiron Review : ChironR
The Christian Century : ChrC
Cimarron Review : CimR
Cincinnati Poetry Review : CinPR
City Lights Review : CityLR
Clockwatch Review: A Journal of the Arts : ClockR
Coal City Review : CoalC
College English : ColEng
Colorado Review : ColR
Columbia: A Magazine of Poetry & Prose : Colum
Commonweal : Comm
Confrontation : Confr
Conjunctions : Conjunc
The Connecticut Poetry Review : ConnPR
Conscience: A Newsjournal of Prochoice Catholic Opinion : Conscience
Contact II : Contact
Context South : ContextS
Crab Creek Review : CrabCR
Crazyhorse : Crazy
Cream City Review : CreamCR
Crosscurrents : CrossCur
Crucible : Crucible
Cuadernos de Poética : CuadP
Cumberland Poetry Review : CumbPR
Cutbank : CutB

Dandelion : Dandel
Denver Quarterly : DenQ
Descant : Descant
Dog River Review : DogRR
Drumvoices: A Confluence of Literary, Cultural & Vision Arts : Drumvoices
Dusty Dog : DustyD

Elf: Eclectic Literary Forum : Elf
Emerald Coast Review: West Florida Authors and Artists : EmeraldCR
English Journal : EngJ
Epiphany: A Journal of Literature : Epiphany:
Epoch : Epoch
Event: The Douglas College Review : Event
The Evergreen Chronicles: A Journal of Gay & Lesbian Literature : EvergreenC
Eyeball

Farmer's Market : Farm
Field: Contemporary Poetry and Poetics : Field
The Florida Review : FloridaR
Footwork: The Paterson Literary Review : Footwork
Four Quarters : FourQ
Free Lunch: A Poetry Journal : FreeL

Gaia: A Journal of Literature & Environmental Arts : Gaia
Georgia Review : GeoR
Gettysburg Review : GettyR

Global City Review : GlobalCR
Graham House Review : GrahamHR
Grain : Grain
Grand Street : GrandS
Green Mountains Review : GreenMR
The Greensboro Review : GreensboroR
Gypsy : Gypsy

The Hampden-Sydney Poetry Review : HampSPR
Hanging Loose : HangL
Harper's Magazine : Harp
The Harvard Advocate : HarvardA
Harvard Review : HarvardR
Hawaii Review : HawaiiR
Hayden's Ferry Review : HayF
Heaven Bone : HeavenB
Hellas: A Journal of Poetry and the Humanities : Hellas
High Plains Literary Review : HighP
Hiram Poetry Review : HiramPoR
The Hollins Critic : HolCrit
Hopewell Review: New Work by Indiana's Best Writers : HopewellR
The Hudson Review : Hudson

The Illinois Review : IllinoisR
Indiana Review : IndR
Interim : Interim
International Poetry Review : InterPR
Inti: Revista de Literatura Hispánica : Inti
Iowa Review : Iowa

The Jacaranda Review : Jacaranda
The James White Review: A Gay Men's Literary Journal : JamesWR
The Journal : Journal
The Journal of New Jersey Poets : JlNJPo

Kaleidoscope: International Magazine of Literature, Fine Arts, and Disability :
        Kaleid
Kalliope: A Journal of Women's Art : Kalliope
Kenyon Review : KenR

Lactuca : Lactuca
Laurel Review : LaurelR
Light: A Quarterly of Humorous, Occasional, Ephemeral & Light Verse : Light
Linden Lane Magazine : LindLM
The Literary Review: An International Journal of contemporary Writing : LitR
Louisiana Literature: A Review of Literature and Humanities : LouisL
Lullwater Review : LullwaterR
Luz: En Arte y Literatura : Luz

The Malahat Review : MalR
Manhattan Poetry Review : ManhatPR
The Manhattan Review : ManhatR
Manoa: A Pacific Journal of International Writing : Manoa
The Massachusetts Review : MassR
Memphis State Review: *See* River City *(title change)*
Mester : Mester
Michigan Quarterly Review : MichQR
Mid-American Review : MidAR
The Midwest Quarterly: A Journal of Contemporary Thought : MidwQ
The Minnesota Review : MinnR
Mississippi Review : MissR
The Missouri Review : MissouriR
Moody Street Irregulars: A Jack Kerouac Newsletter : MoodySI
Mss : *superseded by* New Myths

The Nation : Nat
Negative Capability : NegC
New American Writing : NewAW
New Delta Review : NewDeltaR
New England Review : NewEngR
New Letters : NewL
New Myths : NewMyths
New Orleans Review : NewOR
The New Renaissance : NewRena
The New Republic : NewRep
The New York Quarterly : NewYorkQ
The New York Review of Books : NewYRB
The New Yorker : NewYorker
Nimrod : Nimrod
Noctiluca: An International Magazine of Poetry : Noctiluca
The North American Review : NoAmR
North Carolina Literary Review : NoCarLR
North Dakota Quarterly : NoDaQ
The North Stone Review : NorthStoneR
Northeast : Northeast
Northwest Review : NowestR
La Nuez: Revista Internacional de Arte y Literatura : Nuez

Obsidian II: Black Literature in Review : Obs
The Ohio Review : OhioR
Ometeca: Ciencia y Literatura, Science & Literature : Ometeca
Ontario Review : OntR
OnTheBus: A New Literary Magazine : OnTheBus
Osiris : Os
Outerbridge : Outbr
Oxford Magazine : OxfordM

Pacific Review: A Magazine of Poetry and Prose : PacificR
Paintbrush: A Journal of Poetry, Translations, and Letters : Paint
Painted Bride Quarterly : PaintedB
Painted Hills Review : PaintedHR
The Paris Review : ParisR
Parting Gifts : Parting
Partisan Review : PartR
Passages North : PassN
Pearl : Pearl
Pembroke Magazine : Pembroke
The Pennsylvania Review : PennR
Pequod : Pequod
The Pikestaff Forum : PikeF
Plainsongs : Plain
Ploughshares : Ploughs
Poem : Poem
Poet And Critic : PoetC
Poet Lore : PoetL
Poetry : Poetry
Poetry Canada : PoetryC
Poetry East : PoetryE
Poetry Northwest : PoetryNW
Poetry USA : PoetryUSA
The Pottersfield Portfolio : PottPort
Prairie Fire: A Canadian Magazine of New Writing : PraF
Prairie Schooner : PraS
Primavera : Prima
The Prose Poem: An International Journal : ProseP

Quarry : Quarry
Quarterly Review of Literature : QRL
Quarterly West : QW

Rag Mag : RagMag
Raritan: A Quarterly Review : Raritan
Red Bass : RedBass
River City : RiverC
River Styx : RiverS
Rosebud: For People Who Enjoy Writing : Rosebud

Salmagundi: A Quarterly of the Humanities and Social Sciences : Salm
Seneca Review : SenR
Sequoia: Stanford Literary Magazine : Sequoia
The Sewanee Review : SewanR
Shadow Play : ShadowP
Shenandoah: The Washington and Lee University Review : Shen
Shiny: The Magazine of the Future : Shiny
Silverfish Review : SilverFR
Sing Heavenly Muse!: Women's Poetry and Prose : SingHM
Sinister Wisdom: A Journal for the Lesbian Imagination in the Arts and Politics
     : SinW
Slipstream : SlipS
The Small Pond Magazine of Literature : SmPd
The Snail's Pace Review: A Biannual Little Magazine of Contemporary Poetry :
     SnailPR
Sonora Review : Sonora
South Carolina Review : SoCaR
South Coast Poetry Journal : SoCoast
South Dakota Review : SoDakR
Southern Humanities Review : SouthernHR
Southern Poetry Review : SouthernPR
Southern Review : SouthernR
Southwest Review : SouthwR
Sparrow : Sparrow
Spirit : SpiritSH
The Spirit That Moves Us : Spirit
Spitball: The Literary Baseball Magazine : Spitball
The Spoon River Poetry Review (*formerly* The Spoon River Quarterly) :
     SpoonR
Stand Magazine : Stand
Sulfur: A Literary Bi-annual of the Whole Art : Sulfur
Sun: A Magazine of Ideas : Sun
Sycamore Review : SycamoreR

Talisman: A Journal of Contemporary Poetry & Poetics : Talisman
Tampa Review: Literary Journal of the University of Tampa : TampaR
Tar River Poetry : TarRP
Texas Review : TexasR
Thirteenth Moon: *See* 13th Moon (*at beginning of list*)
The Threepenny Review : Thrpny
TickleAce: A Journal of Literary and Visual Art : TickleAce
Translation: The Journal of Literary Translation : Translation
Trasimagen: Revista Latinoamericana de Literatura y Arte : Trasimagen
Tricycle: The Buddhist Review : Tricycle
Triquarterly : TriQ
Turnstile : Turnstile

US 1 Worksheets : US1

Verse : Verse
The Virginia Quarterly Review: A National Journal of Literature and Discussion
     : VirQR
Visions International : Vis

Washington Review : Wash
Weber Studies: An Interdisciplinary Humanities Journal : WeberS
Webster Review : WebR
West Branch: A twice-yearly magazine of poetry and fiction : WestB

West Coast Line: A Journal of Contemporary Writing and Criticism (*formerly* West Coast Review) : WestCL
Western Humanities Review : WestHR
The William and Mary Review : WilliamMR
Willow Review : WillowR
Willow Springs : WillowS
Wind : Wind
The Windless Orchard : WindO
Witness : Witness
World Letter : WorldL
World Order : WorldO
The Wormwood Review : WormR
Writ : Writ
The Writer : Writer
Writers' Forum : WritersF

Xavier Review : XavierR

The Yale Review : YaleR
Yellow Silk: Journal of Erotic Arts : YellowS

Zyzzyva: The Last Word, West Coast Writers and Artists : Zyzzyva

The Author Index

1. AARNES, William
   "Home for Christmas." [PoetC] (24:2) Wint 93, p. 36.
   "Parade." [Wind] (23:72) 93, p. 1-2.
   "Prudence." [PoetC] (24:2) Wint 93, p. 34.
   "They Work Indoors." [Interim] (12:2) Fall-Wint 93, p. 10.
   "Wind." [PoetC] (24:2) Wint 93, p. 35.
   "Worship." [HiramPoR] (53/54) Fall 92-Sum 93, p. 11-12.
2. ABBAS, Azra
   "After You Come" (tr. by C. M. Naim). [Prima] (16/17) 93, p. 83.
   "Bitch" (tr. by C. M. Naim). [Prima] (16/17) 93, p. 84-85.
3. ABBEY, L. M.
   "The Little Goat — Jean-Bertrand Aristide." [IndR] (16:2) Fall 93, p. 161-163.
4. ABBOTT, Anthony S.
   "Carrot Colored Words" (For Kappa and Jay). [Pembroke] (25) 93, p. 12.
   "Words Are the Only Fingers of the Soul." [Crucible] (29) Fall 93, p. 39-40.
5. ABBS, Peter
   "Artemesia Gentileschi Speaks." [TarRP] (32:2) Spr 93, p. 2.
   "The Melancholic Speaks." [Stand] (34:3) Sum 93, p. 52.
   "Prologue." [TarRP] (32:2) Spr 93, p. 1.
   "Stanley Spencer's Beatitude." [TarRP] (32:2) Spr 93, p. 2.
6. ABINADER, Elmaz
   "Arabic Music." [Footwork] (23) 93, p. 19.
   "Letters from Home" (To my father). [Footwork] (23) 93, p. 18-19.
   "Living with Opposition." [Footwork] (23) 93, p. 19-20.
7. ABLEY, Mark
   "Expecting." [MalR] (105) Wint 93, p. 60-63.
   "In a Desert." [MalR] (105) Wint 93, p. 59.
8. ABRAHAMS, Lionel
   "A Professional Dying." [BostonR] (18:3/4) Je-Ag 93, p. 32.
   "Words for Ruth Miller." [BostonR] (18:3/4) Je-Ag 93, p. 32.
9. ABRAMS, Bill
   "Old Desires." [Interim] (12:2) Fall-Wint 93, p. 12-13.
10. ABSE, Dannie
   "Between 3 and 4 A.M." [QRL] (12:32/33) 93, p. 3-5.
   "A Doctor's Register." [QRL] (12:32/33) 93, p. 6.
   "In the National Gallery." [QRL] (12:32/33) 93, p. 1.
   "Meurig Dafydd to His Mistress." [QRL] (12:32/33) 93, p. 2.
   "On the Evening Road." [QRL] (12:32/33) 93, p. 5-6.
   "Shmelke" (for A.B.). [QRL] (12:32/33) 93, p. 2-3.
   "Some Blood." [QRL] (12:32/33) 93, p. 7-8.
11. ABU-SABA, Elias G.
   "Beirut" (tr. of Munif Mousa). [InterPR] (19:1) Spr 93, p. 20-21.
   "Lamentation" (tr. of Munif Mousa). [InterPR] (19:1) Spr 93, p. 22-25.
   "To a Nipple." [InterPR] (19:2) Fall 93, p. 74.
12. ACKERMAN, Stephen
   "Insomnia Asylum." [PartR] (60:3) Sum 93, p. 430-431.
13. ACKLAND, Joan
   "Carnal Pursuits." [Nimrod] (36:2) Spr-Sum 93, p. 101.
   "Cattle Country." [Nimrod] (36:2) Spr-Sum 93, p. 102.
   "Gretchen at the Wheel." [Nimrod] (36:2) Spr-Sum 93, p. 104.
   "Maundy Thursday." [Nimrod] (36:2) Spr-Sum 93, p. 103.
14. ADAM, Rosemary
   "I Don't Have My Homework, Cause My Uncle Ate It." [EngJ] (82:4) Ap 93, p. 96.
15. ADAMOUR, Beth
   "Cutting Down a Tree Still Alive." [InterPR] (19:2) Fall 93, p. 70.
16. ADAMS, Chris
   "The Garden." [FourQ] (7:2) Fall 93, p. 24.

17. ADAMS, Cyd
 "Barter." [Poem] (69) My 93, p. 13.
 "Communion." [Poem] (69) My 93, p. 14.
18. ADAMS, Elizabeth
 "Red Sea" (To J.D.). [CharR] (19:2) Fall 93, p. 134-135.
 "Trilobites." [SoDakR] (31:3) Fall 93, p. 55-56.
19. ADAMS, Jeanette
 "Commandments." [Drumvoices] (2:1/2) Fall-Wint 92-93, p. 70-71.
 "Girlfriend's Got It Goin' On" (for Terry McMillan). [Drumvoices] (2:1/2) Fall-Wint
 92-93, p. 71-72.
20. ADAMS, Jefferson
 "For John Berryman." [HayF] (12) Spr-Sum 93, p. 92.
 "Pisces in Flight." [HayF] (12) Spr-Sum 93, p. 91.
 "Returning From the Home of a Friend Along South Mountain Drive." [Caliban] (12)
 93, p. 152.
 "What Praise Escapes the Night." [AntR] (51:3) Sum 93, p. 378.
21. ADAMS, Maureen
 "Gatherings" (Episodes of Work). [Agni] (37) 93, p. 107-110.
 "Hunt in Couples." [Agni] (37) 93, p. 111-112.
22. ADAMS, Monica
 "Creche." [Footwork] (23) 93, p. 111.
23. ADAMSON, Eve
 "Darwin and Five Gauchos." [AntR] (51:2) Spr 93, p. 236.
24. ADAMSON, Gil
 "My Wife Suffers From Excitability." [Caliban] (12) 93, p. 155.
25. ADAMSON, Robert
 "Outside of Delacroix" (for Barret Reid). [Stand] (35:1) Wint 93-94, p. 60-61.
 "Waving to Hart Crane." [Stand] (35:1) Wint 93-94, p. 60.
26. ADCOCK, Betty
 "Four from the Spider." [GettyR] (6:4) Aut 93, p. 605.
 "The Mind" (after Dr. Oliver Sacks). [Shen] (43:3) Fall 93, p. 64.
 "Poem for Dizzy" (Written after discovering that no poem in *The Anthology of Jazz
 Poetry* is written to or for or about Dizzy Gillespie). [TarRP] (33:1) Fall 93, p.
 34-35.
 "To a Young Feminist Who Wants to Be Free." [Shen] (43:3) Fall 93, p. 60-61.
 "Valentine at Fifty." [GeoR] (47:2) Sum 93, p. 301.
 "Voyages." [TarRP] (33:1) Fall 93, p. 33-34.
 "Writing Poems Late." [Shen] (43:3) Fall 93, p. 62-63.
27. ADCOCK, Fleur
 "The Pilgrim Fathers." [Verse] (10:2) Sum 93, p. 7.
 "Willow Creek." [Verse] (10:2) Sum 93, p. 7-8.
28. ADDONIZIO, Kim
 "Conversation in Woodside." [Thrpny] (54) Sum 93, p. 25.
 "In Brooklyn." [OnTheBus] (5:2, #12) Sum-Fall 93, p. 31.
 "Last Call." [NowestR] (31:1) 93, p. 69.
 "Late Round." [Sun] (213) S 93, p. 16.
29. ADELL, Tim
 "News and the Rut." [CharR] (19:1) Spr 93, p. 103-104.
30. ADISA, Opal Palmer
 "The Desperate Series I." [Obs] (8:2) Fall-Wint 93, p. 89-91.
 "Development." [Obs] (8:2) Fall-Wint 93, p. 88-89.
ADORNO, Pedro López
 See LOPEZ ADORNO, Pedro
31. AETHRIDGE
 "Transformations." [OnTheBus] (6:1, #13) Wint 93-Spr 94, p. 35.
 "Unholy Desire — It Depends." [OnTheBus] (6:1, #13) Wint 93-Spr 94, p. 36.
32. AFRIKA, Tatamkulu
 "Night-Light." [BostonR] (18:3/4) Je-Ag 93, p. 33.
33. AGARWAL, Bina
 "Mother's Milk." [KenR] (NS 15:3) Sum 93, p. 90-91.
34. AGGEN, Gail
 "Mother's Breasts." [CoalC] (7) Apr 93, p. 1.
35. AGOOS, Julie
 "Brain Damage." [Pequod] (35) 93, p. 79-89.
36. AGOSTINO, Paul
 "Carnage." [ChironR] (12:4/13:1, #37/38) Wint 93-Spr 94, p. 18.

"Fleeing Walden Pond, Italy." [Bogg] (66) Wint 92-93, p. 18.
"How Can I Whine?" [WormR] (33:1, #129) 93, p. 37-38.
"Job." [WormR] (33:1, #129) 93, p. 39.
"Maybe If." [WormR] (33:1, #129) 93, p. 40.
"On Line at the Supermarket, Wandering Through Entertainment and Fashion
  Magazines." [ChironR] (12:2, #35) Sum 93, p. 16.
"Rear-View Mirror." [WormR] (33:1, #129) 93, p. 38.
"The Sins of the Father, the Sins of the Sons, and the Sins of the Nephew." [ChironR]
  (12:2, #35) Sum 93, p. 16.
37. AGRAFIOTIS, Demosthenes
"The Chinese Notebook" (Selections, tr. by the author and Theo Dorgan, Tony Curtis,
  Pat Boran, and Kate Newman). [Sulfur] (32) Spr 93, p. 206-212.
AGUDELO, Dario Jaramillo
  See JARAMILLO AGUDELO, Dario
38. AGUERO, Kathleen
"Driving." [HangL] (62) 93, p. 5.
39. AGÜEROS, Jack
"Psalm for Modernization." [BostonR] (18:3/4) Je-Ag 93, p. 41.
"Psalm for Modernization" (Corrected reprint). [BostonR] (18:5) O-N 93, p. 23.
"Psalms for the New Catechism, #17." [BostonR] (18:3/4) Je-Ag 93, p. 41.
"Psalms for the New Catechism, #17" (Corrected reprint). [BostonR] (18:5) O-N 93, p.
  23.
"Sonnet for Jorge Soto, Painter, b. 1947, New York, d. 1987, Vermont." [BostonR]
  (18:3/4) Je-Ag 93, p. 41.
"Sonnet for Jorge Soto, Painter, b. 1947, New York, d. 1987, Vermont" (Corrected
  reprint). [BostonR] (18:5) O-N 93, p. 23.
"Sonnet for Miss Beausoleil." [BostonR] (18:3/4) Je-Ag 93, p. 41.
"Sonnet for Miss Beausoleil" (Corrected reprint). [BostonR] (18:5) O-N 93, p. 23.
"Sonnet for Raymond Castro." [BostonR] (18:3/4) Je-Ag 93, p. 41.
"Sonnet for Raymond Castro" (Corrected reprint). [BostonR] (18:5) O-N 93, p. 23.
"Sonnet: Tompkins Square Park, October 18th, 1989, 5:45 pm." [BostonR] (18:3/4) Je -
  Ag 93, p. 41.
"Sonnet: Tompkins Square Park, October 18th, 1989, 5:45 pm" (Corrected reprint).
  [BostonR] (18:5) O-N 93, p. 23.
AGUILAR, O. L. Chavarria
  See CHAVARRIA-AGUILAR, O. L.
40. AGUILAR-CARIN~O, Maria Luisa B.
"Farewell." [Bomb] (45) Fall 93, p. 79.
"Vendor of Sweets." [Bomb] (45) Fall 93, p. 79.
41. AGZIGIAN, Zan
"Alita." [YellowS] (42) Wint-Spr 93, p. 21.
42. AH, Wu
"Couldn't Get Flatter" (tr. by Denis Mair). [ChiR] (39:3/4) 93, p. 297.
43. AHO, Margaret
"Climacteric." [Kalliope] (15:2) 93, p. 27.
"Figs." [Kalliope] (15:2) 93, p. 26.
"On the Blue Wire." [BelPoJ] (44:1) Fall 93, p. 36.
"Pause at 47." [Kalliope] (15:2) 93, p. 28.
"Two Burns." [BelPoJ] (44:1) Fall 93, p. 38-40.
"When Did the Dream Scrotum Darken." [BelPoJ] (44:1) Fall 93, p. 37.
44. AHR, Katherine
"Night Piece." [SpiritSH] (58) 93, p. 8.
"Woman Bathing" (after Mary Cassatt). [SpiritSH] (58) 93, p. 9.
45. AI
"The Director: Hoover, Edgar J." [OnTheBus] (5:2, #12) Sum-Fall 93, p. 32-35.
"Hoover Trismegistus." [OnTheBus] (6:1, #13) Wint 93-Spr 94, p. 37-39.
"Life Story" (For Father Ritter and Other Priests Accused of Sexual Abuse). [Agni]
  (38) 93, p. 200-206.
46. AI, Qing
"The Diver" (in Chinese and English, tr. by Li Xi-jian and Gordon Osing). [PikeF] (11)
  Fall 93, p. 15.
47. AIELLO, Mark
"Fence" (2nd Prize, 7th Annual Contest). [SoCoast] (14) Ja 93, p. 50-51.
48. AIKEN, Chris
"Place Between Us" (Poets of High School Age). [HangL] (62) 93, p. 76.

49. AIKEN, William
 "A Dog's Death." [PoetryNW] (34:3) Aut 93, p. 39.
 "Few Understand." [HampSPR] Wint 93, p. 29.
 "Landfall." [Elf] (3:4) Wint 93, p. 39.
50. AINSWORTH, Alan
 "Breath." [NewEngR] (15:2) Spr 93, p. 109-110.
 "Nothing But Ourselves." [WestHR] (47:2) Sum 93, p. 103-105.
51. AISENBERG, Nadya
 "Hunger Moon." [HarvardR] (5) Fall 93, p. 130.
 "Out to Tea." [HarvardR] (3) Wint 93, p. 131.
52. AIZENBERG, Mikhail
 "This wood is bordered by dust and rot" (tr. by J. Kates). [HarvardR] (3) Wint 93, p.
 155.
 "Untitled: Lightbulbs catch fire. The rooms are full" (in Russian and English, tr. by Jim
 Kates). [RiverS] (39) 93, p. 48-49.
 "Untitled: Take this smudged snapshot for a sign" (in Russian and English, tr. by Jim
 Kates). [RiverS] (39) 93, p. 46-47.
53. AIZPURIETE, Amanda
 "This Eventide Seems Spilt" (tr. by Inguna Jansone). [CimR] (104) Jl 93, p. 31-38.
AKEMI, Nakamura
 See NAKAMURA, Akemi
54. AKMAKJIAN, Alan P.
 "The Great Green Lion." [OnTheBus] (6:1, #13) Wint 93-Spr 94, p. 40.
 "Keeping Up with the Jones'." [OnTheBus] (6:1, #13) Wint 93-Spr 94, p. 40.
 "Montagnard Sax Player." [BlackBR] (17) Sum-Fall 93, p. 31.
 "New Americans in San Jose" (The Montagnards, Vietnam's mountain people).
 [BlackBR] (17) Sum-Fall 93, p. 32.
 "New Christian's Church, Columbia, SC." [WormR] (33:3, #131), 93, p. 131.
 "New York September in Snow." [WormR] (33:3, #131), 93, p. 131.
 "Two Montagnard Boys." [BlackBR] (17) Sum-Fall 93, p. 32.
 "Upon Hearing of the Death of Y-Bham Enuol, a 'Fulro' Leader." [BlackBR] (17)
 Sum-Fall 93, p. 33.
 "Willie Two Hats Shot Down During a 7-Eleven Robbery Dies." [OnTheBus] (6:1,
 #13) Wint 93-Spr 94, p. 40.
55. AKUA (Carol F. Bebelle)
 "Song of Joy." [AfAmRev] (27:1) Spr 93, p. 127.
56. Al-HAMMARH, Abu 'Amir ibn (Al-HAMMARA, Abu Amir Ben, 12th c.)
 "Insomnio" (Spanish tr. by Emilio García Gómes). [Luz] (5) N 93, p. 15.
 "Insomnia" (tr. by Cola Franzen). [Luz] (5) N 93, p. 15.
57. AL-TABBAN, Levi Ibn
 "An Exchange Between Levi Ibn Al-Tabban and Yehuda Halevi" (tr. by Ammiel
 Alcalay). [Sulfur] (33) Fall 93, p. 198.
58. ALABAU, Magali
 "Hermana" (Fragmento/Fragment, in Spanish and English, tr. by Anne Twitty). [Luz]
 (4) My 93, p. 40-47.
 "To Be a Deserter" (tr. by Anne Twitty). [AmerV] (31) 93, p. 120.
ALAN of Lille
 See INSULIS, Alanus de (Alan of Lille)
59. ALBAN, Laureano
 "Geografía Invisible de América" (Selections: 2 poems, in Spanish and English, tr. by
 Frederick Fornoff). [Luz] (4) My 93, p. 9-24.
 "Itinerario del Sueño" (from "Herencia del Otoño"). [Luz] (5) N 93, p. 48.
 "Itinerary of Sleep" (from "Autumn's Legacy," tr. by Frederick Fornoff). [Luz] (5) N
 93, p. 49.
60. ALBERGOTTI, Mary
 "Hometown." [SouthernPR] (33:2) Fall 93, p. 54.
61. ALBERT, Jordi
 "Catalan Morning" (tr. by the author). [Os] (37) Wint 93, p. 27.
 "Matinada Catalana." [Os] (37) Wint 93, p. 26.
62. ALBERTI, Rafael
 "Adieu, Chimères, Idéals, Erreurs" (— Rimbaud. Tr. by Linda Scheer, w. Brian
 Swann). [QRL] (12:32/33) 93, p. 11-13.
 "The Eyes of the Bull" (tr. by Cecilia C. Lee and Laura Higgins). [LitR] (36:3) Spr 93,
 p. 356.
 "Prado Museum" (tr. by Linda Scheer, w. Brian Swann). [QRL] (12:32/33) 93, p. 8-11.

"This Everlasting Evening" (tr. by Cecilia C. Lee and Laura Higgins). [LitR] (36:3) Spr 93, p. 357.
63. ALBERTO, Eliseo
"Juego de Manos." [Areíto] (4:14) O 93, inside back cover.
"Talismán." [Areíto] (4:14) O 93, inside front cover.
64. ALBIZZI, Niccolò degli
"Prolonged Sonnet: When the Troops Were Returning from Milan" (tr. by Dante Gabriel Rossetti). [SoCoast] (15) Je 93, p. 61.
"Sonetto Prolungato: Quando la Gente Tornava da Milano." [SoCoast] (15) Je 93, p. 60.
65. ALBRECHT, Laura
"To Plant." [WindO] (57) Fall 93, p. 29.
66. ALCALA, Carlos
"News Item." [Light] (7) Aut 93, p. 15.
"Point of Ordure, or, Two Questions, but Just One Answer." [Light] (6) Sum 93, p. 12.
67. ALCALAY, Ammiel
"Axiom" (tr. of Yehuda Halevi). [Sulfur] (33) Fall 93, p. 194-195.
"Before Departure" (tr. of Yehuda Halevi). [Sulfur] (33) Fall 93, p. 194.
"An Exchange Between Levi Ibn Al-Tabban and Yehuda Halevi" (tr. of Yehuda Halevi). [Sulfur] (33) Fall 93, p. 198.
"Love Poem" (tr. of Yehuda Halevi). [Sulfur] (33) Fall 93, p. 195.
"Love Song" (tr. of Yehuda Halevi). [Sulfur] (33) Fall 93, p. 197.
"Poem in Parts" (tr. of Yehuda Halevi). [Sulfur] (33) Fall 93, p. 196-197.
68. ALCOSSER, Sandra
"The Intimacy of the Song Inverse to the Dull Lores." [MichQR] (32:3) Sum 93, p. 457-458.
"Like Leonardo, Like a Dog." [CutB] (40) Spr 93, p. 211-212.
"Throughout the Duration of a Pulse a Heart Changes Form." [CutB] (40) Spr 93, p. 213-214.
69. ALDRIDGE, Richard
"Chickens." [HiramPoR] (53/54) Fall 92-Sum 93, p. 13-14.
"No But About It." [BelPoJ] (43:4) Sum 93, p. 23.
70. ALEGRIA, Claribel
"Packing My Bags." [NewL] (59:4) 93, p. 23-25.
71. ALENIER, Karren L.
"A Ceremony" (for Marilyn & Allen). [Footwork] (23) 93, p. 88.
72. ALESHIRE, Joan
"Cheek to Cheek." [QRL] (12:32/33) 93, p. 15-16.
"The Children" (from Giovanni di Paolo's "Raising of Lazarus," Walters Art Gallery, Baltimore). [QRL] (12:32/33) 93, p. 18-19.
"Full Flower Moon." [QRL] (12:32/33) 93, p. 14.
"Into History" (to my daughter). [QRL] (12:32/33) 93, p. 16-18.
"Use." [QRL] (12:32/33) 93, p. 19-21.
73. ALEXANDER, Elizabeth
"Aspirin." [WilliamMR] (31) 93, p. 76.
"At Seventeen." [YellowS] (43) Fall 93, p. 21.
"Cleaning Out Your Apartment." [WilliamMR] (31) 93, p. 7.
"The Dark Room: an Invocation." [Callaloo] (16:3) Sum 93, p. 554-555.
"Equinox." [Poetry] (162:6) S 93, p. 313.
"Four Rounds from 'Narrative: Ali'" (6, 8, 10-11). [Agni] (37) 93, p. 92-95.
"French." [YellowS] (43) Fall 93, p. 21.
"Fugue" (for E.S.S.). [WilliamMR] (31) 93, p. 52.
"Josephine Baker: Two Poems." [KenR] (NS 15:2) Spr 93, p. 144-145.
"Manhattan Elegy." [Poetry] (162:6) S 93, p. 314.
"Sonnet: This morning I wished (once) to be a quiet." [YellowS] (43) Fall 93, p. 21.
74. ALEXANDER, Hannah
"Eve Alone." [Parting] (6:2) Wint 93, p. 10-11.
75. ALEXANDER, M.
"Depuis." [HeavenB] (10) Wint-Spr 93, p. 4.
"Ever Since." [HeavenB] (10) Wint-Spr 93, p. 4.
"Hellespont." [HeavenB] (10) Wint-Spr 93, p. 23.
76. ALEXANDER, Margaret Walker
"Dedication" (For Collins Chapel and Abundant Living Center). [Drumvoices] (1:1/2) Fall-Wint 91-92, p. 115-117.
77. ALEXANDER, Marlene
"Anniversary Waltz." [OnTheBus] (6:1, #13) Wint 93-Spr 94, p. 41-42.

"Unraveling." [OnTheBus] (5:2, #12) Sum-Fall 93, p. 36-37.
78. ALEXANDER, Pamela
"Fogbow." [Field] (49) Fall 93, p. 61.
"Fortune." [Field] (49) Fall 93, p. 60.
"Souvenir." [Field] (49) Fall 93, p. 62-63.
79. ALEXANDER, Will
"Albania & the Death of Enver Hoxha." [Sulfur] (32) Spr 93, p. 229-233.
"Explosive Decibel Journeys" (for Javier García Sánchez). [Sulfur] (32) Spr 93, p. 239-242.
"The Final Poltergeist of Pompeii." [Talisman] (11) Fall 93, p. 199-201.
"The Psychotropic Squalls." [Sulfur] (32) Spr 93, p. 237-238.
"Song of Occult Solar Riddles." [WashR] (19:4) D 93-Ja 94, p. 10-11.
"The Stratospheric Canticles" (excerpt). [Sulfur] (32) Spr 93, p. 243-251.
"The Water Dog." [Sulfur] (32) Spr 93, p. 234-236.
80. ALEXIE, Sherman
"Apologies." [HangL] (62) 93, p. 6-8.
"Breakfast with Seymour." [Lactuca] (17) Apr 93, p. 23.
"Dreaming Anna Mae." [BelPoJ] (43:3) Spr 93, p. 22-23.
"How Lester FallsApart Came to Believe in Magic After He Tripped Over a Beer Bottle . . . ." [HangL] (62) 93, p. 9.
"The Native American Savings & Loan." [Lactuca] (17) Apr 93, p. 23.
"A Reservation Table of the Elements." [Caliban] (13) 93, p. 33-36.
"Robert DeNiro." [Caliban] (13) 93, p. 37.
"Seven Love Songs Which Include the Collected History of the United States of America" (for Kari). [HangL] (62) 93, p. 13-17.
"Sign Language." [BelPoJ] (43:3) Spr 93, p. 19-21.
"Sundays, Too." [Lactuca] (17) Apr 93, p. 24.
"Supply & Demand." [HangL] (62) 93, p. 10.
"Tiny Treaties." [HangL] (62) 93, p. 11-12.
ALFONSO, Antonio d'
  See D'ALFONSO, Antonio
81. ALFORD, Andrew
"Making Room (for a Friend From Italy, Who Only Knew the Half of It)." [Footwork] (23) 93, p. 133.
82. ALICE, M. S.
"I get enough." [Bogg] (66) Wint 92-93, p. 62.
ALIRE SAENZ, Benjamin
  See SAENZ, Benjamin Alire
83. ALKALAY-GUT, Karen
"Concentration" (at a concert). [RagMag] (11:1) 93, p. 86.
"Licks." [RagMag] (11:1) 93, p. 84-85.
"Sympathy for the Devil" (Tel Aviv, February 1991). [RagMag] (11:1) 93, p. 83.
84. ALLARDT, Linda
"Stuck." [BelPoJ] (44:2) Wint 93-94, p. 25.
85. ALLEGRA, Donna
"The Women Always Wave the Flags." [SinW] (51) Wint 93-94, p. 97.
86. ALLEN, Annette
"My Grandmother's Name." [GreensboroR] (55) Wint 93-94, p. 52.
"The Reach." [SouthernPR] (33:2) Fall 93, p. 58-59.
"A Runner's Quarrel." [SouthernPR] (33:2) Fall 93, p. 59-60.
87. ALLEN, Barbara
"Donne." [Sequoia] (34/35) 92-93, p. 93-94.
88. ALLEN, Barton
"Wet Rocks." [Wind] (23:72) 93, p. 2.
89. ALLEN, Blair H.
"Good Kind Souls, May 2, 1992." [Gypsy] (20) Sum 93, p. 53.
90. ALLEN, Dick
"Blanket Weather." [AmerS] (62:1) Wint 93, p. 51-52.
"M.F.A." (for Sarah Collings). [GettyR] (6:1) Wint 93, p. 122-123.
"A Short History of the Vietnam War Years." [GettyR] (6:1) Wint 93, p. 120-121.
"Three A.M." [GettyR] (6:1) Wint 93, p. 119.
91. ALLEN, Gilbert
"The Age of Nostalgia." [Gaia] (1/2) Ap-Jl 93, p. 29.
"Los Alamos, 1945." [Sequoia] (34/35) 92-93, p. 56.
"Harmony." [Border] (2) Spr 93, p. 1.
"Threadleaf" (Acer Palmatum). [Wind] (23:72) 93, p. 3-4.

"Trouble, Maybe." [Gaia] (1/2) Ap-Jl 93, p. 29.
92. ALLEN, Heather
"Dream Cycle." [Poetry] (162:5) Ag 93, p. 279-280.
93. ALLEN, James
"Farcical Eye." [Elf] (3:1) Spr 93, p. 25.
94. ALLEN, Jed
"Interrogation" (for two voices taped). [HayF] (12) Spr-Sum 93, p. 50-53.
95. ALLEN, Jeffrey Renard
"Shadowboxing" (for Harriet Tubman). [Obs] (8:1) Spr-Sum 93, p. 80-83.
"Undervoicing" (for Sarah Vaughn, dead at 66). [Obs] (8:1) Spr-Sum 93, p. 77-79.
"With It" (for Miles Davis). [Obs] (8:1) Spr-Sum 93, p. 79-80.
96. ALLEN, Joseph R.
"An Autumnal Prayer to Tu Fu" (tr. of Yang Mu). [ChiR] (39:3/4) 93, p. 302.
"Found by the Pool" (tr. of Lo Ch'ing). [ChiR] (39:3/4) 93, p. 301.
97. ALLEN, Paul
"Judy." [PoetC] (25:1) Fall 93, p. 20.
"Miss Rose Chisolm. Lois Day. Miss Rose Chisolm and Lois Day !" [LaurelR] (27:1)
Wint 93, p. 88-89.
"Tattoo #47, 'Happy Dragon'." [NoAmR] (278:5) S-O 93, p. 31.
98. ALLEN, Paula Gunn
"Quién Es Que Anda?" [ChiR] (39:3/4) 93, p. 24-26.
99. ALLEN, Sheri Foley
"Matreshka." [Gaia] (1/2) Ap-Jl 93, p. 12.
100. ALLEN, Stephánia
"XXX. By the number thirty-eight bus down Dostojevsky Lane" (tr. of Brano Hochel,
w. James Sutherland-Smith). [OxfordM] (9:1) Spr-Sum 93, p. 48-49.
"Bequest (to Other Thieves)" (tr. of Karol Chmel, w. James Sutherland-Smith).
[OxfordM] (9:1) Spr-Sum 93, p. 116.
"Between Us" (tr. of Ján Strasser, w. James Sutherland-Smith). [OxfordM] (9:1) Spr-
Sum 93, p. 27.
"By the Way" (tr. of Ján Strasser, w. James Sutherland-Smith). [OxfordM] (9:1) Spr-
Sum 93, p. 27.
"Contents of a Fever" (tr. of Ivan Laucík, w. James Sutherland-Smith). [OxfordM]
(9:1) Spr-Sum 93, p. 105.
"The Hour of Misrepresentation" (tr. of Ján Strasser, w. James Sutherland-Smith).
[OxfordM] (9:1) Spr-Sum 93, p. 26.
"I've Seen God Only Twice" (tr. of Brano Hochel, w. James Sutherland-Smith).
[OxfordM] (9:1) Spr-Sum 93, p. 47-48.
"Micro-stories" (5 selections, tr. of Brano Hochel, w. James Sutherland-Smith).
[OxfordM] (9:1) Spr-Sum 93, p. 49-50.
"Mist" (tr. of Ján Buzássy, w. James Sutherland-Smith). [OxfordM] (9:1) Spr-Sum
93, p. 26.
"Skepticism" (tr. of Karol Chmel, w. James Sutherland-Smith). [OxfordM] (9:1) Spr-
Sum 93, p. 116.
"Skin Is Wrapping for Bones" (tr. of Ivan Kolenic, w. James Sutherland-Smith).
[OxfordM] (9:1) Spr-Sum 93, p. 116-117.
"Verses" (tr. of Karol Chmel, w. James Sutherland-Smith). [OxfordM] (9:1) Spr-Sum
93, p. 115-116.
"While Unity Lasts" (tr. of Ivan Strpka, w. James Sutherland-Smith). [OxfordM]
(9:1) Spr-Sum 93, p. 107.
101. ALLEN, William
"On Photographs of War" (5 poems with photographs). [Chelsea] (54) 93, p. p. 101 -
111.
" The Bacchae on the Docks at Tenth Street" (for David Wojnarowicz, 1954-1992).
[MinnR] (NS 40) Spr-Sum 93, p. 19-20.
102. ALLENDORF, Karen
"A Pat on the Back." [QW] (37) Sum-Fall 93, p. 209-210.
103. ALLEY, Rick
"Exemplary Life Above Ground." [WillowS] (32) Sum 93, p. 59.
104. ALLINSON, Nancy
"Mid-West Scorcher." [PoetL] (88:4) Wint 93-94, p. 20.
105. ALLPORT, S. K.
"Some Impulsive Ideas." [ChatR] (13:3) Spr 93, p. 62.
106. ALLRED, Joanne
"Demeter to the Academic." [QW] (37) Sum-Fall 93, p. 87-89.
"Mercy." [QW] (37) Sum-Fall 93, p. 86.

"The Story Aunt Beth Told." [WritersF] (19) 93, p. 104.
107. ALLYN, Jerri
"Cups and Saucers." [Kaleid] (26) Wint-Spr 93, p. 15-16.
"Dance Coo." [Kaleid] (26) Wint-Spr 93, p. 18-19.
"Heart Grab." [Kaleid] (26) Wint-Spr 93, p. 19-20.
"Latina Cultura." [Kaleid] (26) Wint-Spr 93, p. 16-17.
"One Good Hand." [Kaleid] (26) Wint-Spr 93, p. 16.
"The One in the Other Place." [Kaleid] (26) Wint-Spr 93, p. 14.
"Theo Didn't Smoke." [Kaleid] (26) Wint-Spr 93, p. 17-18.
108. ALMON, Bert
"The Clematis Seminar." [CanLit] (136) Spr 93, p. 22-23.
"February Walk Near False Creek Mouth." [CanLit] (136) Spr 93, p. 58.
"Lloyd Byrd's Women." [SlipS] (13) 93, p. 6.
"Painting Is the Lightning Art." [CanLit] (136) Spr 93, p. 21-22.
"The Pursuit of Learning." [Light] (6) Sum 93, p. 13.
109. ALMON, Margaret
"Nightshift." [CreamCR] (17:2) Fall 93, p. 130.
"Saturday Morning." [CreamCR] (17:2) Fall 93, p. 131.
110. ALPAUGH, David
"Impromptu Meeting in the Falklands." [Asylum] (8) 93, p. 107-108.
"On the Raritan, 1959." [Footwork] (23) 93, p. 111.
111. ALSOP, Jaimes
"The Evidence of Miracles" (from a line by Robert Bly). [Sun] (206) F 93, p. 27.
112. ALTMAN, Klim
"The Eye and the Heart" (tr. from the Persian). [PoetryUSA] (25/26) 93, p. 54.
113. ALVAREZ, Julia
"Anatomy Lesson." [Chelsea] (55) 93, p. 9-12.
114. ALVAREZ-KOKI, Francisco
"Circunferencia de la Palabra" (Selections: 3 poems). [Luz] (3) Ja 93, p. 28-29.
"Circunferencia del Recuerdo" (from "Sombra de Luna"). [Luz] (5) N 93, p. 28, 30.
"The Encircling Memory" (from "Sombra de Luna," tr. by Angela McEwan). [Luz]
      (5) N 93, p. 29, 31.
AMATO, Michael d'
      See D'AMATO, Michael
115. AMATUZIO, Anna
"Two Seated Women." [BambooR] (57) Wint 93, p. 153-154.
116. AMELIA, William
"Rejected, Not Quite." [Light] (5) Spr 93, p. 37.
117. AMICHAI, Yehuda
"Autumn Rain in Tel Aviv" (tr. by Chana Bloch). [Trans] (28) Spr 93, p. 108.
"A Flock of Sheep Near the Airport" (tr. by Chana Bloch). [Trans] (28) Spr 93, p.
      107.
"In the Middle of This Century" (tr. by Assia Guttman). [QRL] (12:32/33) 93, p. 367
      368.
"Like Our Bodies' Imprint" (tr. by Assia Guttman). [QRL] (12:32/33) 93, p. 368.
118. AMIRKHANIAN, Charles
"Empty Cage" (for John in passing). [PoetryUSA] (25/26) 93, p. 29.
119. AMIRTHANAYAGAM, Indran
"Elephant Meditation." [GrahamHR] (17) Fall 93, p. 112-113.
"Under the Tent." [GrahamHR] (17) Fall 93, p. 114-116.
120. AMISON, Les
"Mr. Washington." [PoetryUSA] (25/26) 93, p. 54.
121. AMMONS, A. R.
"Alligator Holes Down Along About Old Dock." [NoCarLR] (1:2) Spr 93, p. 228.
"Blues in the Valley." [Hudson] (46:1) Spr 93, p. 170.
"The Constant." [QRL] (12:32/33) 93, p. 369-370.
"The Crystal Tree." [ParisR] (35:127) Sum 93, p. 36-37.
"Death and Silhouettes." [ParisR] (35:127) Sum 93, p. 35.
"For Emily Wilson from a Newcomer." [Chelsea] (55) 93, p. 13.
"For My Beloved Son." [Hudson] (46:1) Spr 93, p. 172.
"Glass." [QRL] (12:32/33) 93, p. 368-369.
"The Land of the Knobble-Jobble Tree." [GrandS] (12:1, #45) 93, p. 68-69.
"A Little Thing Like That." [Chelsea] (55) 93, p. 14-15.
"The Many Ways Not Supreme." [Chelsea] (55) 93, p. 14.
"Modes aginst Too Much." [ParisR] (35:127) Sum 93, p. 34.
"Moving Figures." [TarRP] (33:1) Fall 93, p. 44.

37

"Opinion's Pinions." [HarvardR] (5) Fall 93, p. 27-28.
"Period." [Colum] (20) Sum 93, p. 26-27.
"Prisons There and Not." [TarRP] (33:1) Fall 93, p. 44-46.
"The Sale Sale." [Hudson] (46:1) Spr 93, p. 169-170.
"Turning Things Out Good." [Hudson] (46:1) Spr 93, p. 171.
AMORES de PAGELLA, Angela Blanco
    See BLANCO AMORES de PAGELLA, Angela
122. AMOSS, Lindsay S.
    "Giacometti." [AmerPoR] (22:6) N-D 93, p. 32.
123. AMTZIS, Wayne
    "Sky" (tr. of Manjul). [WebR] (17) Fall 93, p. 16.
AN, Yue
    See YUE, An
124. ANANIA, Michael
    "As in a Pourtract" (For Denise Levertov). [IllinoisR] (1:1) Fall 93, p. 55-56.
    "November or Else: An Ode." [ApalQ] (36/37) 91, p. 67-70.
125. ANDELORA, Miller
    "Distillation, February." [PoetryNW] (34:1) Spr 93, p. 21-22.
126. ANDERS, Stefan
    "Less than One-Sixth Gravity." [FreeL] (12) Sum 93, p. 28.
127. ANDERSEN, Astrid Hjertenaes
    "Black Spruce" (tr. by Aina Gerner-Mathisen and Suzanne Bachner). [MassR] (34:4)
        Wint 93-94, p. 503.
    "Double Image" (tr. by Suzanne Bachner and Aina Gener-Mathisen). [Vis] (43) 93, p.
        42.
    "Image" (tr. by Suzanne Bachner and Aina Gener-Mathisen). [Vis] (43) 93, p. 42.
    "Impressions from the Legends about The Twelve Constellations" (tr. by Aina
        Gerner-Mattisen and Suzanne Bachner). [NewYorkQ] (52) 93, p. 51-54.
    "Winter sine Anno" (tr. by Aina Gerner-Mathisen and Suzanne Bachner). [WillowS]
        (33) Wint 93, p. 20-21.
128. ANDERSON, Alice
    "Girl Cadaver." [Agni] (37) 93, p. 105-106.
    "The Problem." [NewYorkQ] (51) 93, p. 90.
129. ANDERSON, Beth
    "Blue Screen." [13thMoon] (12:1/2) 93-94, p. 5-6.
    "Pulse and Terrace." [BlackBread] (3) 93, p. 20-24.
    "Views." [BlackBread] (3) 93, p. 25-28.
130. ANDERSON, Doug
    "History Lesson." [ClockR] (8:1/2) 93, p. 102.
    "Judgment" (Near Hoi Anh, 1967). [VirQR] (69:3) Sum 93, p. 506.
    "North of Tam Ky, 1967." [VirQR] (69:3) Sum 93, p. 507.
    "Turning Fifty." [VirQR] (69:3) Sum 93, p. 508.
131. ANDERSON, Jack
    "How It Goes in This Family." [AnotherCM] (25) Spr 93, p. 5-6.
    "Leather Bar." [HangL] (62) 93, p. 18.
    "My Mother Growing Old." [ProseP] (2) 93, p. 6.
    "The Somnambulists' Hotel." [ProseP] (1) 92, p. 10-11.
132. ANDERSON, Kathleen
    "Focal Point" (Honorable Mention, 7th Annual Contest). [SoCoast] (15) Je 93, p. 8-9.
133. ANDERSON, Kemmer
    "Negev Anatomy." [ChrC] (110:18) 2-9 Je 93, p. 599.
134. ANDERSON, Kirk
    "Looking through my skylight" (from "El silencio del Viento," tr. of Juan Miguel
        Asensi). [Luz] (5) N 93, p. 32.
135. ANDERSON, Linda
    "Santa Claus." [Stand] (34:2) Spr 93, p. 50.
136. ANDERSON, Lori
    "She Must Be Giant." [PassN] (14:2) Wint 93, p. 7.
137. ANDERSON, Maggie
    "Closed Mill." [PennR] (5:2) 93, p. 7-9.
    "Marginal." [PennR] (5:2) 93, p. 10.
    "Ontological." [PennR] (5:2) 93, p. 11.
138. ANDERSON, Robert
    "Dear Miss Ross." [CreamCR] (17:1) Spr 93, p. 54.
139. ANDERSON, Scott
    "Carpentry." [BostonR] (18:1) Ja-F 93, p. 12.

38

"Rubberneck" (for Nick Regan). [Agni] (38) 93, p. 188.
140. ANDERSON, Susan
    "The Cougar." [Caliban] (13) 93, p. 54.
    "That Damn Painted Cave." [Caliban] (13) 93, p. 55.
141. ANDERSON, Teresa
    "Dream Train." [Footwork] (23) 93, p. 21-22.
    "Kneading Bread" (for Denis, on a day when there is no money). [Footwork] (23) 93, p. 22.
    "Lament for Marguerite." [Footwork] (23) 93, p. 23.
    "Llanto para Margarita." [Footwork] (23) 93, p. 23.
    "Picking Persimmons" (near Guthrie, Oklahoma). [Footwork] (23) 93, p. 23.
    "Powerhouse Mechanic, 1920" (For Alexander and Guy and all our grandfathers). [Footwork] (23) 93, p. 24.
    "So Many Roads." [Footwork] (23) 93, p. 24.
142. ANDERSON-JONES, Teruko
    "Bringing in the Horses." [CanLit] (138/139) Fall-Wint 93, p. 33.
143. ANDRADE, Eugenio de
    "Almost Nothing" (tr. by Alexis Levitin). [WebR] (17) Fall 93, p. 17.
    "Body" (tr. by Alexis Levitin). [QRL] (12:32/33) 93, p. 22.
    "Cante Jondo" (tr. by Alexis Levitin). [Epiphany] (4:2) Ap 93, p. 114.
    "A Casa." [Nimrod] (37:1) Fall-Wint 93, p. 97.
    "Cicade." [Nimrod] (37:1) Fall-Wint 93, p. 97.
    "City" (tr. by Alexis Levitin). [Nimrod] (37:1) Fall-Wint 93, p. 96.
    "Despertar." [Os] (36) Spr 93, p. 14.
    "Early in the Morning" (tr. by Alexis Levitin). [QRL] (12:32/33) 93, p. 21.
    "Epitaph" (tr. by Alexis Levitin). [Epiphany] (4:2) Ap 93, p. 113.
    "Eros Thanatos" (tr. by Alexis Levitin). [Epiphany] (4:2) Ap 93, p. 115.
    "Even in Ruins" (tr. by Alexis Levitin). [QRL] (12:32/33) 93, p. 21.
    "Heart of Day" (tr. by Alexis Levitin). [TampaR] (7) Fall 93, p. 41.
    "Hoarse Song" (tr. by Alexis Levitin). [Epiphany] (4:2) Ap 93, p. 112.
    "The House" (tr. by Alexis Levitin). [Nimrod] (37:1) Fall-Wint 93, p. 96.
    "Instances" (tr. by Alexis Levitin). [SenR] (23:1/2) Wint 93, p. 155.
    "Introdução as Canto." [Os] (36) Spr 93, p. 12.
    "Introduction to the Song" (tr. by Alexis Levitin). [Os] (36) Spr 93, p. 13.
    "Lágrima." [Os] (36) Spr 93, p. 10.
    "The Little Persian" (tr. by Alexis Levitin). [Nimrod] (37:1) Fall-Wint 93, p. 98.
    "Nocturne for Two Voices" (tr. by Alexis Levitin). [HolCrit] (30:3) Je 93, p. 15.
    "O Pequeno Persa." [Nimrod] (37:1) Fall-Wint 93, p. 98.
    "The Patio Light" (tr. by Alexis Levitin). [QRL] (12:32/33) 93, p. 22.
    "Peaches" (tr. by Alexis Levitin). [QRL] (12:32/33) 93, p. 22.
    "Receding Surf" (tr. by Alexis Levitin). [QRL] (12:32/33) 93, p. 22.
    "Sound" (tr. by Alexis Levitin). [WebR] (17) Fall 93, p. 17.
    "Tear" (tr. by Alexis Levitin). [Os] (36) Spr 93, p. 11.
    "To Waken" (tr. by Alexis Levitin). [Os] (36) Spr 93, p. 15.
    "What Morning Does He Wish for Still" (tr. by Alexis Levitin). [SenR] (23:1/2) Wint 93, p. 156.
ANDRADE, Jorge Carrera
    See CARRERA ANDRADE, Jorge
144. ANDRE, Jean
    "Mythonomy." [Elf] (3:3) Fall 93, p. 28-29.
    "Newsboy, Skid Road." [Elf] (3:3) Fall 93, p. 29.
ANDRESEN, Sophia de Mello Breyner
    See BREYNER, Sophia de Mello
145. ANDREU, Blanca
    "From a Child of the Provinces Who Wound Up Livng in a Chagall" (Excerpt, tr. by Michael L. Johnson). [LitR] (36:3) Spr 93, p. 358.
146. ANDREWS, Bruce
    "The f in soft-pedal." [HangL] (63) 93, p. 5.
    "Fixed Stars 2" (from Lip Service). [WestCL] (27:3, #12) Wint 93-94, p. 37-40.
147. ANDREWS, Claudia Emerson
    "Prodigal." [SouthernPR] (33:2) Fall 93, p. 20-21.
148. ANDREWS, Dolph
    "Letter Home from North of Saigon — 1972." [Parting] (6:2) Wint 93, p. 28.
    "Signposts." [Parting] (6:2) Wint 93, p. 6.
149. ANDREWS, Michael
    "Between a Pig and a Baby." [OnTheBus] (5:2, #12) Sum-Fall 93, p. 40-43.

"Buying Balloons — November 27, 1970." [WormR] (33:4, #132) 93, p. 179-180.
"Coffin Lumber." |OnTheBus] (6:1, #13) Wint 93-Spr 94, p. 44-45.
"The Dragon Lady and the Nun, 1960." [OnTheBus] (6:1, #13) Wint 93-Spr 94, p. 49-50.
"The Ends of the Earth." [OnTheBus] (5:2, #12) Sum-Fall 93, p. 38-39.
"The Gecko and the Beanie Weanies." [OnTheBus] (6:1, #13) Wint 93-Spr 94, p. 47 - 48.
"Life Insurance Is Not the Answer." [OnTheBus] (6:1, #13) Wint 93-Spr 94, p. 45 - 46.
"The Old Hand." [OnTheBus] (5:2, #12) Sum-Fall 93, p. 40.
"The Root Canal." [WormR] (33:4, #132) 93, p. 177-179.
"A Significant Poet." [OnTheBus] (6:1, #13) Wint 93-Spr 94, p. 43-44.
"To the Reader From the Heart of the Moment." [OnTheBus] (6:1, #13) Wint 93-Spr 94, p. 50.
"A White Rose in a Blizzard." [Event] (22:2) Sum 93, p. 30-31.
"Women Are People Too." [ChatR] (13:2) Wint 93, p. 8.
150. ANDREWS, Nin
    "Confessions of a Nude." [Boulevard] (8:2/3, #23/24) Fall 93, p. 188.
    "The End of the Affair." [SpoonR] (18:1) Wint-Spr 93, p. 52-53.
    "Man-Thing." [CreamCR] (17:2) Fall 93, p. 156.
    "Notes on the Orgasm." [Chelsea] (55) 93, p. 17-18.
    "Orange." [SpoonR] (18:2) Sum-Fall 93, p. 90.
    "Pants." [Chelsea] (55) 93, p. 16.
    "Poem: All for once I melt to like it." [Chelsea] (55) 93, p. 16.
    "Selected Orgasms." [YellowS] (43) Fall 93, p. 5-6.
    "The Silence." [SpoonR] (18:2) Sum-Fall 93, p. 91.
    "Zip Codes." [CreamCR] (17:2) Fall 93, p. 157.
151. ANDREWS, Tom
    "Ars Poetica." [Witness] (7:1) 93, p. 167.
    "At Burt Lake." [Witness] (7:1) 93, p. 165.
    "Cinema Vérité: Jacques Derrida and God's Tsimtsum." [Field] (48) Spr 93, p. 36.
    "Cinema Vérité: The Death of Alfred, Lord Tennyson." [Field] (48) Spr 93, p. 34.
    "Cinema Vérité: William Makepeace Thackeray Follows His Bliss." [Field] (48) Spr 93, p. 35.
    "Reading Frank O'Hara in the Hospital." [Witness] (7:1) 93, p. 166.
    "Transparent Things." [SycamoreR] (5:2) Sum 93, p. 49.
    "A Visit to the Cathedral." [Witness] (7:1) 93, p. 167.
152. ANDROLA, Ron
    "Space of No Moment." [Bogg] (66) Wint 92-93, p. 33.
153. ANGEL, George
    "Septic." [Caliban] (12) 93, p. 182.
154. ANGELINE, Mary
    "Due Direction." [Arshile] (1) Spr 93, p. 57.
    "Extravagant." [Avec] (6:1) 93, p. 30-33.
    "Inside Passage" (Excerpts). [Arshile] (1) Spr 93, p. 48-56.
    "That It All Might Have You." [Arshile] (1) Spr 93, p. 58.
155. ANGELO, David
    "Do You Know Where Your Children Are?" (At the World Fireworks Finals, coinciding with the International Gay Games, Vancouver, BC). [Footwork] (23) 93, p. 132-133.
    "Do You Remember" (Mother's Day Reflections 1990). [Footwork] (23) 93, p. 132.
    "Heartspace." [Footwork] (23) 93, p. 133.
    "I Know Love." [Footwork] (23) 93, p. 132-133.
    "In the Rainbows." [Footwork] (23) 93, p. 133.
ANGELO, Mary d'
    See D'ANGELO, Mary
156. ANGELOU, Maya
    "Our Grandmothers." [Drumvoices] (1:1/2) Fall-Wint 91-92, p. 119-122.
157. ANKNEY, Rick
    "Timepieces." [PennR] (5:2) 93, p. 40.
ANNA, Lynette (Dueck) d'
    See D'ANNA, Lynette (Dueck)
158. ANONYMOUS
    "Corrido de Chavez Garcia." [BilingR] (18:1) Ja-Ap 93, p. 9-10.
    "The Metamorphosis of the Indigenous." [Stand] (35:1) Wint 93-94, p. 58-59.

ANONYMOUS

    "Poem of the Cid" (Selections, tr. by Paul Blackburn). [Sulfur] (33) Fall 93, p. 175 -
        184.
    "Some Amatory Epigrams from the Greek Anthology" (tr. by James Laughlin).
        [Sulfur] (33) Fall 93, p. 50-53.
    "Somebody Stole George Washington's False Teeth." [EngJ] (82:8) D 93, p. 83.
159. ANONYMOUS (9th century)
    "In the long evening" (in romanized Japanese and English, tr. by Sam Hamill).
        [Pequod] (36) 93, p. 15.
    "Now I go to live" (in romanized Japanese and English, tr. by Sam Hamill). [Pequod]
        (36) 93, p. 16.
160. ANONYMOUS (12-13th century)
    "Ur-Valentine?" (tr. by Karl Shapiro based on the literal tr. from the Middle-High
        German by Sopie Wilkins). [Sparrow] (60) Sum 93, p. 20.
ANONYMOUS (El Cid)
    See EL CID (Anonymous)
161. ANONYMOUS (Jamaica, 1793)
    "Tajo, tajo, tajo! tajo, my mackey massa!" (work-song recorded by J.B. Moreton in
        Jamaica, 1793). [WestCL] (27:1, #10) Spr 93, p. 52.
162. ANONYMOUS (Korean Sijo)
    "¿Cuándo se hizo el vino?" (Spanish tr. by William Martínez Jr.). [Luz] (4) My 93, p.
        56.
    "En la montaña con agua clara hago casa de hierbas junto a la roca" (Spanish tr. by
        William Martínez Jr.). [Luz] (4) My 93, p. 56.
    "El pino solitario junto al río es fuerte y recto" (Spanish tr. by William Martínez Jr.).
        [Luz] (4) My 93, p. 56.
163. ANONYMOUS (panhandler)
    "Homeless Veteran" (seen on cardboard sign). [PoetryUSA] (25/26) 93, p. 52.
164. ANONYMOUS (rural Greece)
    "A Daughter from the Grave" (tr. by Minas Savvas). [HawaiiR] (17:1, #37) Spr 93, p.
        117.
165. ANONYMOUS (Tiananmen Square, Spring 1989)
    "Mad Woman" (tr. by Mike O'Connor). [ChiR] (39:3/4) 93, p. 284-286.
    "Tonight Martial Law Was Imposed" (tr. by Mike O'Connor). [ChiR] (39:3/4) 93, p.
        286-287.
    "Words for Xn" (tr. by Mike O'Connor). [ChiR] (39:3/4) 93, p. 287.
166. ANONYMOUS (Yiddish poem)
    "Ghetto Song" (tr. by Aaron Kramer). [Vis] (41) 93, p. 12.
167. ANONYMOUS (Yunnan Yi)
    "Cutting the New Year's Firewood" (tr. by Mark Bender). [ChiR] (39:3/4) 93, p. 256 -
        257.
168. ANSAY, A. Manette
    "After One Year in Exeter, New Hampshire." [GreensboroR] (55) Wint 93-94, p. 70.
    "Blue Hill Fair." [HayF] (13) Fall-Wint 93, p. 77.
    "Communion" (Greensboro Review Literary Award Poem). [GreensboroR] (55) Wint
        93-94, p. 68-69.
    "Lullaby" (for a.j.a., 1904-1991). [NowestR] (31:2) 93, p. 104-106.
    "Overtime." [ChatR] (14:1) Fall 93, p. 59.
169. ANSEL, Talvikki
    "Conversation with the Sun Bittern." [PoetryE] (36) Fall 93, p. 23.
    "Filaments." [Iowa] (23:3) Fall 93, p. 68-69.
    "Fishing." [Iowa] (23:3) Fall 93, p. 69-70.
    "Flemish Beauty." [PoetryE] (36) Fall 93, p. 24-25.
170. ANSTETT, Aaron
    "Blur of Atoms." [Sonora] (26) Fall 93, p. 21.
    "Claw." [Shen] (43:1) Spr 93, p. 42.
    "One Small Angel." [Interim] (12:1) Spr-Sum 93, p. 42.
    "Over the Transom." [Interim] (12:1) Spr-Sum 93, p. 41.
    "Running the Stunt Over." [Shen] (43:1) Spr 93, p. 43.
    "Slow Learners." [Shen] (43:1) Spr 93, p. 41.
    "Starts Out a Mouse." [Pearl] (17) Spr 93, p. 12.
171. ANTIN, David
    "The Theory and Practice of Postmodernism: A Manifesto." [Conjunc] (21) 93, p.
        335-343.
172. ANTLER
    "Blow as Deep as You Want to Blow" (—Jack Kerouac). [ChironR] (12:4/13:1,
        #37/38) Wint 93-Spr 94, p. 19.

"Blowjob Bonnet vs. War Bonnet." [ChironR] (12:4/13:1, #37/38) Wint 93-Spr 94, p. 19.
"Blowjob Mantra." [PennR] (5:2) 93, p. 44-47.
"Childfoot Visitation." [Sun] (207) Mr 93, p. 32.
"Dream." [NewYorkQ] (52) 93, p. 31.
"Ejaculation." [Sun] (205) Ja 93, p. 11.
"Factory Sacrifice." [GreenMR] (NS 6:1) Wint-Spr 93, p. 87.
"First Step From the Playpen." [ChironR] (12:4/13:1, #37/38) Wint 93-Spr 94, p. 6-7.
"First Step from the Playpen." [NewYorkQ] (51) 93, p. 48-51.
"Follow Orders." [HeavenB] (10) Wint-Spr 93, p. 47-50.
"Laying On of Hands Vs. Laying On of Ears." [ChironR] (12:4/13:1, #37/38) Wint 93-Spr 94, p. 7.
"On My Way to Lake Michigan Sunrise on the Milwaukee Lakefront Breakwater." [PennR] (5:2) 93, p. 48.
"The Puberty of Smell." [Sun] (216) D 93, p. 22-23.
"The Reason We Work So Hard." [Sun] (212) Ag 93, p. 19.
"Sweet-Talk." [NewYorkQ] (50) 93, p. 46-47.
"Warcry vs. Blowjobcry." [ChironR] (12:4/13:1, #37/38) Wint 93-Spr 94, p. 19.
173. ANTOSOVA, Svatava
"The Ace" (tr. by Ellen Rosenbaum). [OxfordM] (9:1) Spr-Sum 93, p. 44-46.
"Farewell Letter" (tr. by Ellen Rosenbaum). [OxfordM] (9:1) Spr-Sum 93, p. 46-47.
174. APONICK, Kathleen
"In the Bindery" (at the site of Riverside Press). [SenR] (23:1/2) Wint 93, p. 97-98.
175. APOTHEKER, Alison M.
"Hitching a Ride with Gold Miners in the Yukon." [CreamCR] (17:1) Spr 93, p. 24-25.
"The Lightning Photographer." [GreensboroR] (55) Wint 93-94, p. 3.
"Planting Trees for the Walamut Paper Company." [LouisL] (10:1) Spr 93, p. 53-54.
176. APPLEBAUM, David
"Returning to the Nest." [Comm] (120:20) 19 N 93, p. 12.
177. APPLEWHITE, James
"The Bulldozer's Syntax." [NoCarLR] (1:2) Spr 93, p. 43.
"Cemetery Hickory." [NoCarLR] (1:2) Spr 93, p. 47.
"Faith in Flight." [NoCarLR] (1:2) Spr 93, p. 47.
"Grits." [NoCarLR] (1:2) Spr 93, p. 45.
"The Light's Beginning." [NoCarLR] (1:2) Spr 93, p. 46.
"Post-War Days." [NoCarLR] (1:2) Spr 93, p. 44.
"The Quilt She Started." [NoCarLR] (1:2) Spr 93, p. 42.
"What You Don't See Is There." [PoetC] (24:2) Wint 93, p. 39.
178. ARANA, Rubi
"Las Heridas del Hudson." [LindLM] (12:2/4) Ap-D 93, p. 13.
"Huellas Rituales." [LindLM] (12:2/4) Ap-D 93, p. 12-13.
179. ARCE, John
"Help Me!" [Americas] (21:2) Sum 93, p. 65.
"Outcast." [Americas] (21:2) Sum 93, p. 65.
180. ARCHER, Nuala
"Eloquent Lingo." [CreamCR] (17:1) Spr 93, p. 279.
"Time for Zinnias." [Confr] (51) Sum 93, p. 263.
181. ARENAS, Marion
"Beechey Island." [Nimrod] (37:1) Fall-Wint 93, p. 107-108.
"The Bone Room." [Nimrod] (37:1) Fall-Wint 93, p. 105-106.
"The Children at the Shelter." [NewYorkQ] (52) 93, p. 78.
"Music Class, P.S. 158." [Footwork] (23) 93, p. 106.
"The Painting." [WestB] (33) 93, p. 26-27.
182. ARENAS, Rosa Maria
"Experiment." [SycamoreR] (5:1) Wint 93, p. 26-27.
"The Shaman Talks to the Documentary Crew." [SycamoreR] (5:1) Wint 93, p. 24-25.
183. ARENYS, Teresa
"Mediterrània" (tr. by Adela Robles Salz). [Iowa] (23:2) Spr-Sum 93, p. 8.
184. ARGABRITE, Angie
"Their Wedding Picture." [TarRP] (32:2) Spr 93, p. 25.
185. ARGENTARIUS, Marcus
"Some Amatory Epigrams from the Greek Anthology" (tr. by James Laughlin). [Sulfur] (33) Fall 93, p. 51.

186. ARGÜELLES, Ivan
    "[Blues for Ron Dellums]" (from "Paronomasia"). [PoetryUSA] (25/26) 93, p. 42-43.
    "Chicano, Canto 0 8: Fangs of my puto." [PoetryUSA] (25/26) 93, p. 39-41.
    "From Canto the Eighth, 'That' *Goddess*." [PoetryUSA] (25/26) 93, p. 23.
    "A History of Hellas" (for sarah). [SilverFR] (24) Wint 93, p. 24-25.
    "Il Poemetto." [PoetryUSA] (25/26) 93, p. 10.
    "Shaking It Out of the Orient." [YellowS] (42) Wint-Spr 93, p. 31.
187. ARGUETA, Manlio
    "Mama" (tr. by Dan Bellm and Stacey Ross). [KenR] (NS 15:3) Sum 93, p. 94-95.
188. ARGYLE, Gisela
    "About the Clocks" (tr. of Ulrich Grasnick). [PoetryC] (13:2) 93, p. 22.
    "And the Toy Boat Is Ready to Go" (tr. of Christiane Grosz). [PoetryC] (13:2) 93, p. 22.
    "Elderberry-Blossom" (tr. of Johannes Bobrowski). [PoetryC] (13:2) 93, p. 23.
    "Expectation" (tr. of Hanns Cibulka). [PoetryC] (13:2) 93, p. 21.
    "Happy Conspiracy" (tr. of Volker Braun). [PoetryC] (13:2) 93, p. 20.
    "Madrigal" (tr. of Hanns Cibulka). [PoetryC] (13:2) 93, p. 21.
    "Metabolism" (Hieronymous Bosch. Tr. of Paul Wiens). [PoetryC] (13:2) 93, p. 23.
    "Who Knows Who She Was" (tr. of Peter Gosse). [PoetryC] (13:2) 93, p. 23.
    "The Words" (tr. of John Erpenbeck). [PoetryC] (13:2) 93, p. 21.
    "Your Three Wishes" (tr. of Christiane Grosz). [PoetryC] (13:2) 93, p. 22.
189. ARIDJIS, Homero
    "Diary Without Dates, VIII" (tr. by George McWhirter). [Chelsea] (54) 93, p. 22-24.
    "Greek Things" (tr. by George McWhirter). [PoetryC] (13:4) 93, p. 20.
    "Hernan Cortes Sails" (tr. by George McWhirter). [Chelsea] (54) 93, p. 25.
    "The House of Hernan Cortes, Antigua, Veracruz" (tr. by George McWhirter).
        [Chelsea] (54) 93, p. 25.
    "Lunar Variations" (tr. by George McWhirter). [PoetryC] (13:4) 93, p. 20.
    "These Are the Sleeping Conditions" (tr. by George McWhirter). [MalR] (102) Spr
        93, p. 72-73.
190. ARJONILLA, Christian
    "Cérémonie" (extraits de *Cérémonies et autres chants de guerre*). [Os] (37) Wint 93,
        p. 17-19.
191. ARKÉ
    "The Young Wilde." [Light] (8) Wint 93, p. 10.
192. ARMANTROUT, Rae
    "My Problem." [Zyzzyva] (9:3) Fall 93, p. 42-43.
    "Native." [Conjunc] (20) 93, p. 40-41.
    "Normal Heights." [Conjunc] (20) 93, p. 39-40.
    "Spans." [Conjunc] (20) 93, p. 41-42.
    "States." [Avec] (6:1) 93, p. 3.
    "A Story." [Avec] (6:1) 93, p. 2.
    "The Work." [Avec] (6:1) 93, p. 4.
193. ARMER, Sondra Audin
    "How to Live Forever." [ApalQ] (39) 93, p. 31-32.
    "Sometimes a Snake Is Just a Snake." [Light] (8) Wint 93, p. 18.
194. ARMITAGE-KAWAJI, Ken
    "Palimpsests" (for Heidi, by way of an english teacher bored by feminism).
        [PaintedB] (52) 93, p. 40-41.
195. ARMSTRONG, Denise Stair
    "Pieta in Black, II, The Bearer." [CaribbeanW] (7) 93, p. 33-34.
196. ARMSTRONG, Glen
    "Copperhead." [PaintedB] (49) 93, p. 6.
    "Racists." [FreeL] (11) Wint 93, p. 24.
197. ARMSTRONG, Jeannette C.
    "Permanent Grooves." [Contact] (11:65/66/67) Spr 93, p. 61.
    "Red Trails." [Contact] (11:65/66/67) Spr 93, p. 61.
198. ARNETT, Carlen
    "From Bakersfield." [MassR] (34:4) Wint 93-94, p. 576.
199. ARNOLD, Anita
    "The Other Woman." [CapeR] (28:1) Spr 93, p. 18.
200. ARNOLD, Craig Anthony
    "Hermit Crab" (for Sue and Wally). [NewRep] (209:17) 25 O 93, p. 41.
    "Sainte-Chapelle." [NewRep] (208:10) 8 Mr 93, p. 41.
201. ARNOLD, Edwin
    "The Light of Asia" (Excerpt from Book 7). [Tricycle] (3:2) Wint 93, p. 11-12.

ARPINO, Tony d'
   See D'ARPINO, Tony
202. ARRIETA, Marcia
   "You Will Never Know Me." [Plain] (13:3) Spr 93, p. 10.
203. ARRIVI, Franciso
   "Canticle for a Memory" (tr. by Clementine Rabassa). [Luz] (4) My 93, p. 33.
   "Cantico para un Recuerdo." [Luz] (4) My 93, p. 32.
   "City Without Me" (tr. by Clementine Rabassa). [Luz] (4) My 93, p. 35.
   "Ciudad sin Ti." [Luz] (4) My 93, p. 34.
   "Sobre Adoquines." [Luz] (4) My 93, p. 36.
   "Upon Cobblestones" (tr. by Clementine Rabassa). [Luz] (4) My 93, p. 37.
204. ARROWSMITH, William
   "The Arno at Rovezzano" (tr. of Eugenio Montale). [Pequod] (36) 93, p. 22.
   "Götterdämmerung" (tr. of Eugenio Montale). [Pequod] (36) 93, p. 17.
   "In Smoke" (tr. of Eugenio Montale). [Pequod] (36) 93, p. 18.
   "Late at Night" (tr. of Eugenio Montale). [Pequod] (36) 93, p. 21.
   "Men Who Turn Back" (tr. of Eugenio Montale). [Pequod] (36) 93, p. 23.
   "Nothing Serious" (tr. of Eugenio Montale). [Pequod] (36) 93, p. 19.
   "Time and Times" (tr. of Eugenio Montale). [Pequod] (36) 93, p. 20.
205. ARROYO, Diana
   "Teacher." [Americas] (21:2) Sum 93, p. 66.
206. ARROYO, Rane
   "The Amateur Matador." [Art&Und] (2:4) O-N 93, p. 13.
   "Chapter One from the Book of Lamentations." [Contact] (11:65/66/67) Spr 93, p. 41.
   "Feeling Old in New Chinatown." [Callaloo] (16:3) Sum 93, p. 630.
   "I'm Bridges Away." [Contact] (11:65/66/67) Spr 93, p. 41.
   "Juan Angel." [KenR] (NS 15:1) Wint 93, p. 20-22.
   "The Lonely Latin Lover." [US1] (28/29) 93, p. 4.
   "Los Angeles: Two Chapters from the Sex Manual of Lamentations." [Art&Und]
      (2:4) O-N 93, p. 12.
   "Monsters." [Confr] (51) Sum 93, p. 226.
   "On the Chastity of Henry James." [Confr] (51) Sum 93, p. 227.
   "Ralph." [Callaloo] (16:3) Sum 93, p. 632.
   "The Red Bed" (Special Feature: Chapbook Contest. 12 poems). [Sonora] (24/25)
      Spr 93, p. 73-95.
   "Rodeo of Blood." [Caliban] (12) 93, p. 58.
   "Silver." [Caliban] (12) 93, p. 57.
   "Worldly Embraces." [Callaloo] (16:3) Sum 93, p. 631.
207. ARTHUR, Chris
   "Antecedents." [AntigR] (93-94) Spr-Sum 93, p. 22-23.
   "Atiq." [AntigR] (93-94) Spr-Sum 93, p. 20-21.
208. ARTHURS, Pat
   "Docile in Dublin." [SenR] (23:1/2) Wint 93, p. 183.
   "Templemore Talking." [SenR] (23:1/2) Wint 93, p. 184.
209. THE ARTIST & HOMELESS COLLABORATIVE
   "Summer in New York" (by Doris, Judy, Lucy L.,Suzan, Hazel, Julie, Aida, Gertie,
      Mamie, Lois, Suzie). [GlobalCR] (2) Fall 93, p. 28-29.
210. AS-SABAH, Sabah
   "Invocation." [Eyeball] (2) 93, p. 34.
   "So Let's Get One Thing Straight, Sweetness." [Eyeball] (2) 93, p. 35.
211. ASEKOFF, L. S. (Lou S.)
   "Black Spring." [AmerPoR] (22:4) Jl-Ag 93, p. 6.
   "Blue Flower." [AmerPoR] (22:4) Jl-Ag 93, p. 5.
   "Crowdoll" (for Douglas Culhane). [AmerPoR] (22:4) Jl-Ag 93, p. 3.
   "Cygnus Olor." [AmerPoR] (22:4) Jl-Ag 93, p. 6.
   "Flowers by the Sea" (For Fairfield Porter). [Poetry] (161:6) Mr 93, p. 325.
   "Hôtel de la Rêve" (for Joseph Cornell). [AmerPoR] (22:4) Jl-Ag 93, p. 4.
   "In the Place of the Absence of Desire." [AmerPoR] (22:4) Jl-Ag 93, p. 5.
   "Loom" (for Paul Auster, in memory of George Oppen). [BrooklynR] (10) 93, p. 90 -
      91.
   "The Master, 1941." [AmerPoR] (22:4) Jl-Ag 93, p. 4.
   "North Star." [AmerPoR] (22:4) Jl-Ag 93, p. 3.
   "Pilot." [AmerPoR] (22:4) Jl-Ag 93, p. 5.
   "The Prisoner" (for Amnesty International). [AmerPoR] (22:4) Jl-Ag 93, p. 7.
   "Sharktalk." [AmerPoR] (22:4) Jl-Ag 93, p. 7.
   "Starwork." [AmerPoR] (22:4) Jl-Ag 93, p. 3.

"Thule." [Poetry] (163:3) D 93, p. 139.
"Tierra del Uomo." [AmerPoR] (22:4) Jl-Ag 93, p. 6.
"The White Narcissus." [AmerPoR] (22:4) Jl-Ag 93, p. 7.
212. ASENSI, Juan Miguel
"En mi buhardilla" (from "El silencio del Viento"). [Luz] (5) N 93, p. 32.
"Looking through my skylight" (from "El silencio del Viento," tr. by Kirk Anderson). [Luz] (5) N 93, p. 32.
213. ASHANTI, Baron James
"All Blues" (for Miles Dewey Davis). [Drumvoices] (2:1/2) Fall-Wint 92-93, p. 206 - 208.
214. ASHBERY, John
"About to Move." [GrandS] (12:3, #47) Fall 93, p. 218-219.
"American Nocturne" (tr. of Pierre Martory). [AmerPoR] (22:5) S-O 93, p. 10-11.
"And the Stars Were Shining." [Conjunc] (21) 93, p. 64-80.
"The Archipelago." [AmerPoR] (22:1) Ja-F 93, p. 4.
"The Art of Speeding." [BlackWR] (19:1) Fall-Wint 92, p. 27-28.
"Between Her and Me" (tr. of Pierre Martory). [AmerPoR] (22:5) S-O 93, p. 11.
"Coming and Going" (tr. of Pierre Martory). [Poetry] (162:3) Je 93, p. 133.
"Coventry." [NewYorker] (69:34) 18 O 93, p. 74.
"Dinosaur Country." [HarvardR] (3) Wint 93, p. 24.
"Dune" (tr. of Pierre Martory). [AmerPoR] (22:5) S-O 93, p. 8.
"Elegy: Adieu near those fields that smoke disembowels" (tr. of Pierre Martory). [Poetry] (162:3) Je 93, p. 135.
"Falls to the Floor, Comes to the Door." [AmerPoR] (22:1) Ja-F 93, p. 3.
"The Friendly City." [NewYorker] (69:12) 10 My 93, p. 60.
"From Here On" (tr. of Pierre Martory). [AmerPoR] (22:5) S-O 93, p. 9.
"Ghost Riders of the Moon." [NewYorker] (69:42) 13 D 93, p. 110.
"Glazunoviana." [QRL] (12:32/33) 93, p. 372.
"The Great Bridge Game of Life." [PaintedB] (50/51) 93, p. 19.
"Gummed Reinforcements." [AmerPoR] (22:1) Ja-F 93, p. 3.
"Hotel Dauphin." [QRL] (12:32/33) 93, p. 372-373.
"Ice Cream in America." [NewYorker] (69:28) 6 S 93, p. 96.
"Just What's There." [ColR] (20:1) Spr 93, p. 34-35.
"The Landscape Is Behind the Door" (tr. of Pierre Martory). [AmerPoR] (22:5) S-O 93, p. 10.
"The Landscapist" (tr. of Pierre Martory). [AmerPoR] (22:5) S-O 93, p. 9.
"Leeward." [Poetry] (162:3) Je 93, p. 130.
"Light Turnouts." [Art&Und] (2:3) Special Edition 93, p. 10.
"The Lounge." [ColR] (20:1) Spr 93, p. 36-37.
"Ma Chandelle Est Morte" (tr. of Pierre Martory). [AmerPoR] (22:5) S-O 93, p. 8.
"Myrtle." [NewYorker] (69:4) 15 Mr 93, p. 92.
"The New York Times, Sunday, October 25, 1953" (w. Kenneth Koch). [Chelsea] (55) 93, p. 23-31.
"A Night on the Dead Sea" (tr. of Pierre Martory). [AmerPoR] (22:5) S-O 93, p. 11.
"On a White Horse." [Chelsea] (55) 93, p. 19.
"Passing the Frontier" (tr. of Pierre Martory). [Poetry] (162:3) Je 93, p. 132.
"Pathless Wanderings." [GrandS] (12:3, #47) Fall 93, p. 220-221.
"Poem: How do you say tomorrow in this country?" (tr. of Pierre Martory). [AmerPoR] (22:5) S-O 93, p. 8.
"A Postcard to Popeye" (w. Kenneth Koch). [Chelsea] (55) 93, p. 21-22.
"Strange Things Happen at Night." [Poetry] (162:3) Je 93, p. 131.
"Tahiti Trot." [Poetry] (162:3) Je 93, p. 129.
"A Waltz Dream." [NewYRB] (40:15) 23 S 93, p. 10.
"Weather and Turtles." [NewYRB] (40:20) 2 D 93, p. 15.
"What I Say, Perhaps, Isn't True" (tr. of Pierre Martory). [AmerPoR] (22:5) S-O 93, p. 11.
"Wine" (tr. of Pierre Martory). [Poetry] (162:3) Je 93, p. 134.
215. ASHER, Mark
"Class Exercise." [BelPoJ] (44:1) Fall 93, p. 13-16.
216. ASHLEY, Marie
"Leavings." [PassN] (14:2) Wint 93, p. 54.
217. ASHLEY, Renée
"Arethusa, Deep." [HarvardR] (4) Spr 93, p. 121.
"(Five) Untitled Poems: Rain." [SouthernPR] (33:2) Fall 93, p. 44-46.
"Lost Dogs." [SouthernPR] (33:2) Fall 93, p. 42-44.
"That Fall: Icarus in the Exurbs." [AmerV] (30) 93, p. 64.

45

"The Various Reasons of Light." [KenR] (NS 15:4) Fall 93, p. 106-110.
218. ASIM, Jabari
"The Place Where You Live" (Selections: 4 poems). [Drumvoices] (2:1/2) Fall-Wint
92-93, p. 194-195.
219. ASKEW, Ana Y.
"Searching for Arrowheads." [Blueline] (14) 93, p. 51.
220. ASPEN
"Loving Song." [SinW] (50) Sum-Fall 93, p. 98.
"Muscle Fetish." [SinW] (50) Sum-Fall 93, p. 96-97.
221. ASSIS, Luiza
"Our Wombs" (tr. by the author). [Vis] (43) 93, p. 44.
222. ASTELL, Ann
"Marian Sonnet" (#1 and #10). [Sparrow] (60) Sum 93, p. 44.
223. ATASHI, Manuchehr
"Songs of Fire" (tr. by Ali Zarrin). [Vis] (43) 93, p. 43.
224. ATENCIA, María Victoria
"Blindman's Bluff" (tr. by Cecilia C. Lee and Laura Higgins). [LitR] (36:3) Spr 93, p.
359.
"Martha and Mary" (tr. by Cecilia C. Lee and Laura Higgins). [LitR] (36:3) Spr 93, p.
360.
"With the Table Ready" (tr. by Cecilia C. Lee and Laura Higgins). [LitR] (36:3) Spr
93, p. 360.
225. ATHEY, David
"After Mourning." [BellArk] (9:6) N-D 93, p. 1.
"Bliss." [BellArk] (9:6) N-D 93, p. 1.
"Fishing Minnesota." [SoDakR] (31:3) Fall 93, p. 57.
"Revelation." [HampSPR] Wint 93, p. 46.
226. ATHY, Deborah
"Crow." [MidwQ] (35:1) Aut 93, p. 31.
"Omega Farms." [MidwQ] (35:1) Aut 93, p. 32-33.
"Snake Pit." [MidwQ] (35:1) Aut 93, p. 34.
227. ATKINS, C. E. (Christine E.)
"Confessions." [SinW] (51) Wint 93-94, p. 82.
"Lust." [EvergreenC] (8:1) Spr-Sum 93, p. 16.
"Snake." [SinW] (51) Wint 93-94, p. 37.
228. ATKINS, Cynthia
"Weird Sisters." [SenR] (23:1/2) Wint 93, p. 106-107.
"Woman in Bathtub." [CreamCR] (17:1) Spr 93, p. 72-73.
229. ATKINS, Gail
"The Dead Fox." [SoCoast] (15) Je 93, p. 48-49.
230. ATKINS, Kathleen
"Eurydice Spoke to Orpheus Mostly in Prose." [GeoR] (47:4) Wint 93, p. 680-681.
231. ATKINSON, Michael
"Airfield." [LitR] (36:2) Wint 93, p. 144-145.
"Awakening." [Sequoia] (34/35) 92-93, p. 81.
"Barfight." [Footwork] (23) 93, p. 90-91.
"Cleavage." [Footwork] (23) 93, p. 90.
"The Holy Bloom." [CimR] (105) O 93, p. 86.
"'Manhunter' (1986)." [ArtfulD] (24/25) 93, p. 112.
"Night of the Octopus." [NewL] (59:3) 93, p. 75.
"On the 9 Train, Downtown." [Thrpny] (55) Fall 93, p. 13.
"Outskirts of the Kingdom." [SouthernPR] (33:1) Spr 93, p. 14-15.
"The Ravens at the Tower of London." [Turnstile] (4:1) 93, p. 20.
"String Up Your Idiot Kings." [HiramPoR] (53/54) Fall 92-Sum 93, p. 15-16.
"Sunrise Highway." [GreenMR] (NS 6:2) Sum-Fall 93, p. 120.
"The Tattooed Woman in Heaven's Flower Shop." [MichQR] (32:3) Sum 93, p. 455 -
456.
"We All Knew Garbo Would One Day Die." [PikeF] (11) Fall 93, p. 9.
"Words Written Thinking of Being Near the Surface of Water." [PikeF] (11) Fall 93,
p. 13.
232. ATLIN, Gary
"The Death of the Spectator." [PoetC] (25:1) Fall 93, p. 31.
"Mantidae." [AntigR] (92) Wint 93, p. 23.
"The Poetry Room." [AntigR] (92) Wint 93, p. 21.
"Soft Money." [AntigR] (92) Wint 93, p. 22.
"The Teacher in Her Dress of Woe." [AntigR] (92) Wint 93, p. 20.

ATSUKO, Kato
 See KATO, Atsuko
ATSUSUKE, Tanaka
 See TANAKA, Atsusuke
233. ATTANASIO, Daniela
 "The Care of Things" (2 excerpts, tr. by Kathleen Fraser and Alberto Rossatti).
 [13thMoon] (11:1/2) 93, p. 206-207.
234. ATWOOD, Margaret
 "Monet's Olympia." [Ploughs] (19:4) Wint 93-94, p. 83-84.
235. AUBERT, Alvin
 "Like Miles Said." [Drumvoices] (2:1/2) Fall-Wint 92-93, p. 209.
236. AUDEN, W. H.
 "Humpty Dumpty" (previously unpublished, written at the age of 19). [YaleR] (81:4)
 O 93, p. 21-23.
237. AUDIBERTI, Jacques
 "Held Over" (tr. by Dennis Barone). [WashR] (19:2) Ag-S 93, p. 15.
 "La Souffrance." [WashR] (19:2) Ag-S 93, p. 14-15.
238. AUER, Benedict
 "Hauling in the Net." [NewRena] (8:3, #26) Spr 93, p. 89.
 "My Pagan Baby." [NewRena] (8:3, #26) Spr 93, p. 90.
239. AUFDERHEIDE, Charles
 "Two Nursery Rhymes." [Asylum] (8) 93, p. 19.
240. AUGUST, Edmund
 "Hands and Fathers." [Footwork] (23) 93, p. 79-81.
 "Roling Off." [GreensboroR] (54) Sum 93, p. 97-98.
 "Selma." [HiramPoR] (53/54) Fall 92-Sum 93, p. 17-18.
 "With Heavenly Fire." [CreamCR] (17:1) Spr 93, p. 56-57.
241. AUGUST, Paul Scot
 "Bluegrass" (after a photograph by Ralph Eugene Meatyard). [CreamCR] (17:1) Spr
 93, p. 10.
242. AUSTIN, Annemarie
 "Cut-Outs." [Verse] (10:1) Spr 93, p. 100.
243. AUSTIN, Bob
 "Catch & Release." [ChironR] (12:4/13:1, #37/38) Wint 93-Spr 94, p. 33.
 "News from the Maze Stone." [ChironR] (12:4/13:1, #37/38) Wint 93-Spr 94, p. 33.
244. AUSTIN, David (Dave)
 "Elegy for the Eastern League." [JINJPo] (15:2) Aut 93, p. 39-40.
 "First Day Morning, Haddonfield Meeting." [JINJPo] (15:2) Aut 93, p. 36-38.
 "Tattoos." [Footwork] (23) 93, p. 105.
245. AUSTIN, Jerry
 "Tell Me How Old I Am" (— E.B.). [BellArk] (9:4) Jl-Ag 93, p. 22.
246. AUSTIN, Penelope
 "Unless You Think." [TampaR] (6) Spr 93, p. 24.
247. AUTREY, Ken
 "Climbing to the Cemetery." [ChatR] (13:2) Wint 93, p. 6.
 "Heat Wave." [ChatR] (13:4) Sum 93, p. 53-54.
 "One Wave." [Poem] (70) N 93, p. 16.
 "Outpost." [Poem] (70) N 93, p. 17.
248. AVAKIAN, Arevshad
 "Earth" (tr. by Diana Der-Hovanessian). [Vis] (43) 93, p. 6-7.
249. AVERILL-SAVINO, Kelly Ann
 "Ovoviviparous." [CreamCR] (17:1) Spr 93, p. 67-69.
250. AVERY, Brian C.
 "Counting Coyotes to Stay Awake." [PoetL] (88:1) Spr 93, p. 44.
 "Waiting for the Breath of God." [ColEng] (55:5) S 93, p. 539.
251. AVIANUS
 "The Greedy Man and the Envious Man" (tr. by David R. Slavitt). [GrandS] (12:1,
 #45) 93, p. 216.
 "The Hunter and the Tiger" (tr. by David R. Slavitt). [GrandS] (12:1, #45) 93, p. 215.
 "The Wolf and the Kid" (tr. by David R. Slavitt). [GrandS] (12:1, #45) 93, p. 217.
AVIENUS
 See AVIANUS
AVILA, Leonora de
 See De AVILA, Leonora
252. AVILA, Ricardo
 "Homo / Latino." [ChangingM] (26) Sum-Fall 93, p. 23.

253. AVIS, Nick
   "Bending with the Wind" (Excerpt). [TickleAce] (26) Fall-Wint 93, p. 105.
   "Her Silence." [TickleAce] (26) Fall-Wint 93, p. 104.
254. AWAD, Joseph
   "Imagining Cavafy." [CharR] (19:1) Spr 93, p. 100.
   "Magnitudes." [Vis] (41) 93, p. 20.
   "Two Dolphins." [CharR] (19:1) Spr 93, p. 101.
255. AXELROD, David
   "Nightshade Preserves." [GreenMR] (NS 6:2) Sum-Fall 93, p. 92-93.
256. AXINN, Donald Everett
   "The Mondrians." [Confr] (51) Sum 93, p. 261-262.
257. AYALON, Leah
   "A Closed Place" (tr. by Gabriel Levin). [Trans] (28) Spr 93, p. 83-84.
   "Second Woman and Insecurity" (tr. by Gabriel Levin). [Trans] (28) Spr 93, p. 85.
258. AYGI, Gennady
   "Salute — To Singing" (Selections from 36 variations on themes from Chuvash and
      Tatar folksongs, tr. by Peter France). [Verse] (10:2) Sum 93, p. 86-87.
259. AYRES, Noreen
   "For Men." [YellowS] (43) Fall 93, p. 19.
   "Let Me." [YellowS] (43) Fall 93, p. 18.
   "Outlets." [YellowS] (43) Fall 93, p. 18.
260. AZRAEL, Mary
   "Joan Herself." [ChatR] (14:1) Fall 93, p. 67.
261. AZZOPARDI, Mario
   "Twilight" (tr. by Oliver Friggieri). [Vis] (43) 93, p. 40.
262. AZZOUNI, Jody
   "Well, Son, We Could Always Throw the Pigskin Around." [HiramPoR] (53/54) Fall
      92-Sum 93, p. 19-20.
263. BA, Bulinbuhe
   "Natural Beauty" (in Chinese and English, tr. by Li Xi-jian and Gordon Osing).
      [PikeF] (11) Fall 93, p. 15.
264. BAATZ, Ronald
   "After Dinner." [Pearl] (17) Spr 93, p. 48.
   "Dry Toast." [WormR] (33:1, #129) 93, p. 7.
   "From Rock to Rock." [WormR] (33:3, #131), 93, p. 114.
   "Hanging from a maple branch." [WormR] (33:1, #129) 93, p. 5.
   "Helpless Fishes." [WormR] (33:1, #129) 93, p. 6.
   "I Have Stopped Talking about the Ants." [WormR] (33:3, #131), 93, p. 115-116.
   "In the Kitchen of the Bungalow." [YellowS] (43) Fall 93, p. 25.
   "My Prize Possession." [WormR] (33:3, #131), 93, p. 117-118.
   "On What to Do with My Ashes." [WormR] (33:1, #129) 93, p. 9.
   "Our Town." [WormR] (33:3, #131), 93, p. 116-117.
   "Sermon to the Birds." [WormR] (33:1, #129) 93, p. 8.
   "Sleepless." [WormR] (33:1, #129) 93, p. 5.
265. BAATZ, Tricia Holland
   "Water, Air, Fire, Earth" (The Pablo Neruda Prize for Poetry: First Prize). [Nimrod]
      (37:1) Fall-Wint 93, p. 15-19.
266. BABSTOCK, Ken
   "The Bone Carriage Answers." [AntigR] (93-94) Spr-Sum 93, p. 62.
   "The Idea as Mollusk, or The Shadow of Fruit." [AntigR] (93-94) Spr-Sum 93, p. 63.
   "The Mind Addresses Its Bone Carriage." [AntigR] (93-94) Spr-Sum 93, p. 61.
267. BACHAR, Greg
   "Inside a Ring." [HawaiiR] (17:2, #38) Spr 93, p. 1.
268. BACHARACH, Deborah
   "What She Can Control." [BellArk] (9:4) Jl-Ag 93, p. 23.
269. BACHE-SNYDER, Kaye
   "The Chicken Business." [Plain] (14:1) Fall 93, p. 24.
270. BACHELOR, Rhonda
   "The Monsoon Hour" (for Sujata Bhatt). [Arc] (31) Aut 93, p. 79.
271. BACHHUBER, Daniel
   "Rembrandt's Lucretia." [SouthernPR] (33:1) Spr 93, p. 35-37.
272. BACHMAN, Merle
   "Suspect Retrievals." [Talisman] (11) Fall 93, p. 136-137.
273. BACHMANN, Ingeborg
   "Im Gewitter der Rosen." [Sulfur] (32) Spr 93, p. 165.
   "In the Storm of Roses" (tr. by Marjorie Perloff). [Sulfur] (32) Spr 93, p. 165.

48

BACHMANN

"Schatten Rosen Schatten." [Sulfur] (32) Spr 93, p. 166.
"Shadow Roses Shadow" (tr. by Marjorie Perloff). [Sulfur] (32) Spr 93, p. 167.
274. BACHNER, Suzanne
"Black Spruce" (tr. of Astrid Hjertenaes Andersen, w. Aina Gerner-Mathisen).
[MassR] (34:4) Wint 93-94, p. 503.
"Double Image" (tr. of Astrid Hjertenaes Andersen, w. Aina Gener-Mathisen). [Vis]
(43) 93, p. 42.
"Image" (tr. of Astrid Hjertenaes Andersen, w. Aina Gener-Mathisen). [Vis] (43) 93,
p. 42.
"Impressions from the Legends about The Twelve Constellations" (tr. of Astrid
Hjertenaes Andersen, w. Aina Gerner-Mattisen). [NewYorkQ] (52) 93, p. 51-
54.
"Winter sine Anno" (tr. of Astrid Hjertenaes Andersen, w. Aina Gerner-Mathisen).
[WillowS] (33) Wint 93, p. 20-21.
275. BAER, Tom
"Wild Iris and Tiger Lily." [WormR] (33:1, #129) 93, p. 17.
"Witness." [WormR] (33:1, #129) 93, p. 17.
276. BAER, William
"Christmas Night in Charleston Harbor." [Hellas] (4:2) Fall 93, p. 111.
"Hospital." [HopewellR] (5) 93, p. 51.
BAEZ, Edith María Baez
See BAEZ BAEZ, Edith María
277. BAEZ BAEZ, Edith María
"Encuentro." [13thMoon] (12:1/2) 93-94, p. 103.
"Fantasmas." [13thMoon] (12:1/2) 93-94, p. 107.
"Lorelei." [13thMoon] (12:1/2) 93-94, p. 104-106.
"Poema de la Lluvia." [13thMoon] (12:1/2) 93-94, p. 110-111.
"Tristeza." [13thMoon] (12:1/2) 93-94, p. 108-109.
278. BAGGETT, Rebecca
"An American Primitive: Before the Fall." [13thMoon] (12:1/2) 93-94, p. 7.
"Apology" (for my mother-in-law). [Confr] (51) Sum 93, p. 224-225.
"Illiterate" (for Emma). [CentR] (37:3) Fall 93, p. 522.
"Move." [CentR] (37:3) Fall 93, p. 523.
"Tree, Salt, Sea." [GreensboroR] (55) Wint 93-94, p. 71-72.
279. BAGRYANA, Elisaveta
"Fall" (tr. by Yuri Vidov Karageorge). [CimR] (102) Ja 93, p. 20.
"Horizons" (tr. by Yuri Vidov Karageorge). [CimR] (102) Ja 93, p. 18.
"Paris" (tr. by Yuri Vidov Karageorge). [CimR] (102) Ja 93, p. 19-20.
280. BAI, Hua
"Secret Talking" (in Chinese and English, tr. by Li Xi-jian and Gordon Osing).
[PikeF] (11) Fall 93, p. 15.
281. BAI, Juyi (772-846)
"Lao-Tzu" (tr. by Arthur Waley). [NewYorkQ] (51) 93, p. 98.
282. BAILEY, Clay
"Adding Water to Your Specimen May Cause You to Test Positive." [ChironR]
(12:1, #34) Spr 93, p. 13.
"Foxes Have Holes." [Pearl] (17) Spr 93, p. 91.
283. BAILEY, D. R. Shackleton
"Epigrams" (tr. of Martial). [GrandS] (12:2, #46) Sum 93, p. 119-124.
284. BAILEY, Jan
"Communion." [Ploughs] (19:1) Spr 93, p. 122-123.
"Custody." [WillowS] (32) Sum 93, p. 58.
285. BAILEY, Mary Elizabeth
"Hitchhiking." [ColEng] (55:4) Ap 93, p. 432.
"The Vine." [ColEng] (55:4) Ap 93, p. 433.
286. BAILEY, Tisha
"Curved cardboard applicator." [WashR] (18:5) F-Mr 93, p. 5.
"Grey, creamy slate." [WashR] (18:5) F-Mr 93, p. 5.
"Road of Remembrance." [WashR] (18:5) F-Mr 93, p. 5.
"Untitled: Contradiction over and over, rolling limbs flailing." [WashR] (18:5) F-Mr
93, p. 16.
287. BAIN, Frederika
"Birthright." [HawaiiR] (16:3, #36) Wint 93, p. 103.
"The Girl Who Taught Time to Fly." [HawaiiR] (16:3, #36) Wint 93, p. 96.
288. BAKER, David
"Divorce." [DenQ] (27:3) Wint 93, p. 5.

"Echo for an Anniversary" (Chapbook: 8 poems). [BlackWR] (19:1) Fall-Wint 92, p. 67-82.
"Holding Katherine." [Poetry] (161:6) Mr 93, p. 330.
"Lightning at Night." [SouthernR] (29:2) Spr, Ap 93, p. 293.
"The Park, the Bells, the Lovers." [DenQ] (27:3) Wint 93, p. 6-7.
"The Truth about Small Towns." [Poetry] (161:6) Mr 93, p. 329.
"Windchime." [SouthernR] (29:2) Spr, Ap 93, p. 294.
289. BAKER, Dean
"Troubador." [Wind] (23:72) 93, p. 15.
"Unborn Child to Its Parents." [Wind] (23:72) 93, p. 15.
290. BAKER, Donald W.
"Responsibilities" (from the sequence: 5). [LaurelR] (27:1) Wint 93, p. 36-37.
291. BAKER, June Frankland
"In Memory" (Clara Eppinger Morrill, 1889-1981). [HiramPoR] (53/54) Fall 92-Sum 93, p. 22.
"Long-Distance Poem." [HiramPoR] (53/54) Fall 92-Sum 93, p. 21.
"Receiving a Videotape of My 36th-Year High School Reunion." [WebR] (17) Fall 93, p. 112.
"Spelunking at Brown's Cave." [Blueline] (14) 93, p. 57.
"Yesterday Morning." [WebR] (17) Fall 93, p. 113.
292. BAKER, Lori
"A Little Open Space." [ProseP] (2) 93, p. 7.
293. BAKER, S. D.
"Santa Ana River Sequence." [Caliban] (12) 93, p. 96-98.
294. BAKHT, Baidar
"Black Letters of Insensitivity" (tr. of W. A. Shaheen, w. Leslie Lavigne). [CanLit] (136) Spr 93, p. 99-100.
"I'm Mad Because of You" (tr. of W. A. Shaheen, w. Leslie Lavigne). [CanLit] (136) Spr 93, p. 100.
"The Sound of Grief" (tr. of W. A. Shaheen, w. Leslie Lavigne). [CanLit] (136) Spr 93, p. 99.
295. BAKKEN, Christopher
"The Traverse." [GettyR] (6:3) Sum 93, p. 542-543.
296. BAKOWSKI, Peter
"Around at Our Place." [HangL] (62) 93, p. 19.
"Bee." [FreeL] (11) Wint 93, p. 6.
"The Jaws of Factory (Graveyard Shift)." [Lactuca] (17) Apr 93, p. 2-5.
"The Little Old Ladies of Camden Town." [Pearl] (19) Fall-Wint 93, p. 52.
"The Old Men with Canes Know." [Vis] (42) 93, p. 12.
"Surgery." [Event] (22:3) Wint 93-94, p. 72-73.
"These Heart Hammers, These Small Xylophone Joys." [FreeL] (12) Sum 93, p. 30.
"The Tramps of Shepherd's Bush." [Gypsy] (20) Sum 93, p. 23-24.
"What Is a Man?" (for Primo Levi). [Vis] (41) 93, p. 38.
"Whatever Hidden Drummers." [Amelia] (7:2, #21) 93, p. 105.
297. BALABAN, John
"Passing Through Albuquerque." [PaintedB] (50/51) 93, p. 22.
298. BALAKIAN, Peter
"After the Survivors Are Gone." [PoetryE] (36) Fall 93, p. 133.
"First Communion." [Boulevard] (8:2/3, #23/24) Fall 93, p. 48.
299. BALANTIC, France
"At the Crossroads" (tr. by Frank F. Bulvic). [NoDaQ] (61:1) Wint 93, p. 30.
"Autumn Fires" (tr. by Frank F. Bulvic). [NoDaQ] (61:1) Wint 93, p. 29.
"The Evening is Red" (tr. by Frank F. Bulvic). [NoDaQ] (61:1) Wint 93, p. 30.
"The Marked Ones" (tr. by Frank F. Bulvic). [NoDaQ] (61:1) Wint 93, p. 28.
"A Mouth Filled with Earth" (tr. by Frank F. Bulvic). [NoDaQ] (61:1) Wint 93, p. 29.
"The Whiteness of Death" (tr. by Frank F. Bulvic). [NoDaQ] (61:1) Wint 93, p. 28.
300. BALAZ, Joe
"Catch da Bone." [HawaiiR] (17:1, #37) Spr 93, p. 42-43.
301. BALAZS, Mary
"Inside St. Paul's." [Crucible] (29) Fall 93, p. 31.
302. BALBIERIUS, Alis
"XXX: How lonely the spirit of Erich Fromm." [CimR] (104) Jl 93, p. 22.
"The Garden God" (tr. by Jolanta Vitkuaskaite, w. Bradley R. Strahan). [Vis] (43) 93, p. 38.
"The Nemunas River Today." [CimR] (104) Jl 93, p. 22.

50

BALBO

303. BALBO, Ned
   "An Autumn Evening" (for Karl Rock, tr. of Georg Trakl). [Verse] (10:2) Sum 93, p.
      65.
   "Dream of Evil" (tr. of Georg Trakl). [Verse] (10:2) Sum 93, p. 65.
   "Film Noir." [ApalQ] (39) 93, p. 61-62.
   "That Night." [ApalQ] (39) 93, p. 63.
304. BALDERSTON, Jean
   "Emily Dickinson: A Clerihew." [Light] (6) Sum 93, p. 19.
   "Force of Wind Table: Land Criterion" (Cf. Bird Observatory, Fair Isle, Shetland,
      Scotland). [WormR] (33:1, #129) 93, p. 4-5.
   "Force of Wind Table: Sea Criterion" (Cf. Bird Observatory, Fair Isle, Shetland,
      Scotland). [WormR] (33:1, #129) 93, p. 3-4.
   "Snake Date." [Light] (5) Spr 93, p. 15.
305. BALDWIN, Barbara
   "Interview with the Patient in 302." [LullwaterR] (4:2) Spr-Sum 93, p. 108.
   "Subtropical Fruit." [Plain] (13:2) Wint 93, p. 7.
306. BALE, James
   "The Blue God." [BellArk] (9:1) Ja-F 93, p. 21.
307. BALK, Christianne
   "The Road to Marshfield Lake." [Pequod] (35) 93, p. 90-96.
   "You Say You Love How Unexpected, Open Fields." [WillowS] (32) Sum 93, p. 16 -
      17.
308. BALL, Angela
   "Chassé." [Stand] (34:3) Sum 93, p. 66.
   "Counter." [PraS] (67:1) Spr 93, p. 86-87.
   "The Man in a Shell" (for Anton Chekhov). [Field] (48) Spr 93, p. 33.
   "No One by That Name." [PraS] (67:1) Spr 93, p. 85-86.
   "Nora: Part One." [CreamCR] (17:2) Fall 93, p. 166-167.
   "Nora: Part Three." [CreamCR] (17:2) Fall 93, p. 168-169.
   "The Nothing Above the Water." [Field] (48) Spr 93, p. 32.
   "The Rainy Night" (tr. of Xi Murong, w. Jianging Zheng). [MidAR] (14:1) 93, p. 46.
   "World-Famous Sex Acts." [DenQ] (27:3) Wint 93, p. 8-9.
309. BALL, Joseph (Joseph H.)
   "Autobiographical Notes." [WebR] (17) Fall 93, p. 49-50.
   "The Last Five Minutes of Of Mice and Men." [EngJ] (82:4) Ap 93, p. 96.
310. BALL, Roger
   "Dry Dream." [CoalC] (7) Apr 93, p. 5.
   "Fall." [CoalC] (7) Apr 93, p. 21.
311. BALL, Sally
   "Cook's Desire." [PoetryE] (36) Fall 93, p. 27.
312. BALLOU, Emily
   "Poem for Corn Moon Sister: What I Learned Among Women." [SinW] (50) Sum -
      Fall 93, p. 108-109.
313. BALOGH, Jennifer E.
   "The Photo Exhibit* Will Be Closed Today" (*"Executive Order 9066"). [Parting]
      (6:2) Wint 93, p. 8-9.
314. BALOIAN
   "Fingerprints." [Sonora] (26) Fall 93, p. 73.
   "Kingdom Come." [AntR] (51:2) Spr 93, p. 241.
BALTATZI, Adamandia (Adamantia García)
   See GARCIA-BALTATZI, Adamantia
315. BALUNER, Laurie
   "The Agnostic Returns to Town." [ColEng] (55:2) F 93, p. 208.
316. BANANI, Sheila
   "I Can Imagine the Earth." [WorldO] (25:2) Wint 93-94, p. 38.
   "Physics in the Family." [WorldO] (25:2) Wint 93-94, p. 38.
   "The Sound of Gabriel's Wings." [WorldO] (25:2) Wint 93-94, p. 34.
317. BANDY, J. W.
   "A Marine's Last Leave" (December, 1990, San Diego). [MidAR] (14:1) 93, p. 145 -
      147.
318. BANERJEE, Paramita
   "Another Spring, Darkness" (tr. of Anuradha Mahapatra, w. Carolyne Wright).
      [AmerPoR] (22:4) Jl-Ag 93, p. 22.
   "Biography" (tr. of Anuradha Mahapatra, w. Carolyne Wright). [MidAR] (14:1) 93,
      p. 99.

51

BANERJEE

"The Child's Saying" (tr. of Nabaneeta Dev Sen, w. Carolyne Wright and the author).
[HawaiiR] (17:1, #37) Spr 93, p. 91.
"City Nocturne" (tr. of Anuradha Mahapatra, w. Carolyne Wright). [AmerPoR] (22:4)
Jl-Ag 93, p. 22.
"Friend" (tr. of Anuradha Mahapatra, w. Carolyne Wright). [AmerPoR] (22:4) Jl-Ag
93, p. 23.
"Impatient" (tr. of Anuradha Mahapatra, w. Carolyne Wright). [AmerPoR] (22:4) Jl -
Ag 93, p. 21.
"The Monster" (tr. of Anuradha Mahapatra, w. Carolyne Wright). [AmerPoR] (22:4)
Jl-Ag 93, p. 22.
"Mosquito Net" (tr. of Nabaneeta Dev Sen, w. Nandana Dev Sen, Carolyne Wright
and the author). [AmerPoR] (22:4) Jl-Ag 93, p. 25.
"Night Reader" (tr. of Anuradha Mahapatra, w. Carolyne Wright). [AmerPoR] (22:4)
Jl-Ag 93, p. 23.
"Pyre Tender" (tr. of Anuradha Mahapatra, w. Carolyne Wright and the author).
[HawaiiR] (17:1, #37) Spr 93, p. 220.
"Tamboura" (tr. of Anuradha Mahapatra, w. Carolyne Wright). [MidAR] (14:1) 93, p.
100-101.
"The Temple" (tr. of Nabaneeta Dev Sen, w. Carolyne Wright and the author).
[HawaiiR] (17:1, #37) Spr 93, p. 89.
"This Night Train" (tr. of Gita Chattopadhyay, w. Carolyne Wright). [Prima] (16/17)
93, p. 82.
"Thou Art Durga" (tr. of Gita Chattopadhyay, w. Carolyne Wright). [Prima] (16/17)
93, p. 81.
"You (II.)" (tr. of Anuradha Mahapatra, w. Carolyne Wright). [AmerPoR] (22:4) Jl -
Ag 93, p. 22.
BANERJEE, Swapna Mitra
See MITRA-BANERJEE, Swapna
319. BANGGO, Kathy Dee Kaleokealoha Kaloloahilani
"No Mindless Digging" (For Jeff). [HawaiiR] (17:1, #37) Spr 93, p. 11-13.
"Thirst" (for Kekuhaupi'o). [HawaiiR] (17:3, #39) Fall 93, p. 4.
320. BANKS, Kym
"Lareina Silenciosa" (from "Families, Streets and Dreams," a poetry/photography
event by 3rd grade students, Whittier Elementary, Tulsa). [Nimrod] (37:1)
Fall-Wint 93, p. 85.
"Silent Lareina" (from "Families, Streets and Dreams," a poetry/photography event
by 3rd grade students, Whittier Elementary, Tulsa). [Nimrod] (37:1) Fall-Wint
93, p. 85.
321. BANNER, Vera
"Tents." [Border] (2) Spr 93, p. 2-3.
322. BANNISTER, Ellen
"Taxidermy." [Caliban] (12) 93, p. 40-41.
"Timid Family." [Agni] (37) 93, p. 66.
323. BANUS, Maria
"Your Name" (tr. by Diana Der-Hovanessian and the author). [Vis] (42) 93, p. 32-33.
BAR, Ann La
See LaBAR, Ann
324. BARAKA, Amiri
"The Heir of the Dog." [Drumvoices] (1:1/2) Fall-Wint 91-92, p. 128.
"Sin Soars." [NewL] (59:3) 93, p. 5-13.
"Weimar II" (a drama). [Arshile] (2) 93, p. 93-131.
325. BARAN, Marcin
"Sosnowiec Is Like a Woman" (tr. by Ewa Horodyska). [Stand] (34:3) Sum 93, p. 17.
"Sosnowiec Is Like a Woman" (tr. by Ewa Horodyska). [Verse] (10:2) Sum 93, p. 41.
326. BARAN, Susan
"Bracelet" (for Skylar). [Chelsea] (55) 93, p. 32-33.
327. BARANCZAK, Stanislaw
"Brueghel's Two Monkeys" (tr. of Wislawa Szymborska, w. Clare Cavanagh).
[NewYorker] (69:5) 22 Mr 93, p. 61.
"Cat in an Empty Apartment" (tr. of Wislawa Szymborska, w. Clare Cavanagh).
[NewYRB] (40:17) 21 O 93, p. 42.
"Conversation with a Stone" (tr. of Wislawa Szymborska, w. Clare Cavanagh).
[ManhatR] (7:1) Fall 93, p. 79-80.
"The End and the Beginning" (tr. of Wislawa Szymborska, w. Clare Cavanagh).
[NewRep] (208:3) 18 Ja 93, p. 40.

"In Heraclitus's River" (tr. of Wislawa Szymborska, w. Clare Cavanagh). [Agni] (38) 93, p. 107.
"No Title Required" (tr. of Wislawa Szymborska, w. Clare Cavanagh). [ManhatR] (7:1) Fall 93, p. 81-82.
"A Paleolithic Fertility Fetish" (tr. of Wislawa Szymborska, w. Clare Cavanagh). [ManhatR] (7:1) Fall 93, p. 78.
"Parting with a View" (tr. of Wislawa Szymborska, w. Clare Cavanagh). [TriQ] (89) Wint 93-94, p. 178-179.
"Reality Demands" (tr. of Wislawa Szymborska, w. Clare Cavanagh). [NewYorker] (69:2) 1 Mr 93, p. 86-87.
328. BARANOW, Joan
"Colposcopy." [US1] (28/29) 93, p. 15.
"Lily, Crystal, Mirror." [SpoonR] (18:2) Sum-Fall 93, p. 41-42.
"What It's Like." [US1] (28/29) 93, p. 8.
329. BARATTA, Edward
"Faith." [HarvardR] (3) Wint 93, p. 134.
"Me." [MassR] (34:4) Wint 93-94, p. 592.
"Places, Everyone." [ArtfulD] (24/25) 93, p. 46.
330. BARBA, Yliana
"A Quien Escribo Yo." [LindLM] (12:2/4) Ap-D 93, p. 8.
"Odas IV al Caminante." [LindLM] (12:2/4) Ap-D 93, p. 8.
"La Palabra, Meditacion Conceptual." [LindLM] (12:2/4) Ap-D 93, p. 8.
"Vengo con el Sudor de Mis Manos" (Sobre un tema de León Felipe. Para Manuel Díaz Martínez). [LindLM] (12:2/4) Ap-D 93, p. 8.
331. BARBARESE, J. T.
"Eclipse." [PaintedB] (50/51) 93, p. 116.
332. BARBER, Connie
"Dog Days." [Nimrod] (36:2) Spr-Sum 93, p. 48.
"The Land of the Lemon Trees" (A Prose/Poem). [Nimrod] (36:2) Spr-Sum 93, p. 51 - 54.
"My Father on Paper." [Nimrod] (36:2) Spr-Sum 93, p. 49.
333. BARBER, David
"Autumnal Primer." [NewRep] (208:22) 31 My 93, p. 44.
"Dawn of the Atom" (St. George, Utah, 1953). [GrahamHR] (17) Fall 93, p. 51-52.
"Dürer's Rhinoceros" (1515). [ParisR] (35:129) Wint 93, p. 183-184.
334. BARBER, Jennifer
"Summer As a Large, Reclining Nude." [Poetry] (162:4) Jl 93, p. 193.
335. BARCLAY, Heather Haas
"Little Remains of Sparta." [Dandel] (20:1) 93, p. 43.
336. BARD, Karen S.
"Craven Images." [PoetryE] (36) Fall 93, p. 13.
"Drought." [PoetryE] (36) Fall 93, p. 10.
"Faith." [PoetryE] (36) Fall 93, p. 11.
"Night Kitchen." [PoetryE] (36) Fall 93, p. 12.
337. BARDEN, Louise
"Catching Turtles." [ChatR] (13:3) Spr 93, p. 25.
"July, I-77." [ChatR] (13:3) Spr 93, p. 26.
"More News from the Front" (February 1991, For Curt). [ChatR] (13:3) Spr 93, p. 29.
"River Travel." [ChatR] (13:3) Spr 93, p. 27-28.
"Tea Leaves." [SoCoast] (14) Ja 93, p. 52.
338. BAREA, Michael
"A Furtive Life" (tr. of Gabriel Ferrater). [Vis] (43) 93, p. 9.
"My Reader" (tr. of Gabriel Ferrater). [Vis] (43) 93, p. 9.
339. BARGEN, Walter
"Chain of Being." [CapeR] (28:1) Spr 93, p. 13.
"Chinese Boxes." [SpoonR] (18:1) Wint-Spr 93, p. 92-93.
"The Itch and Scratch of Earth — for Rod Tullis (1960-93)." [SpoonR] (18:2) Sum - Fall 93, p. 118-120.
"Jellyfish." [CharR] (19:2) Fall 93, p. 114.
"Lush Survivor." [PoetC] (25:1) Fall 93, p. 32.
"Newton Revisited." [Farm] (10:2) Fall-Wint 93-94, p. 95.
"Sorting Snapshots." [CapeR] (28:1) Spr 93, p. 12.
340. BARGER, Rose
"Cindy." [WashR] (18:5) F-Mr 93, p. 16.
341. BARGOWSKI, John D., Sr.
"The Ashes." [JlNJPo] (15:2) Aut 93, p. 7-8.

"Fourth of July." [JlNJPo] (15:2) Aut 93, p. 6.
"Rita." [SlipS] (13) 93, p. 93.
"Stickball." [JlNJPo] (15:2) Aut 93, p. 5.
"Three Printers Eating Lunch." [SmPd] (30:2, #88) Spr 93, p. 37-38.
342. BARKAN, Stanley H.
"Behind His Eyes" (for David Gershator). [Footwork] (23) 93, p. 44-45.
"Grandfather." [Footwork] (23) 93, p. 43.
"Two Grandmas." [Footwork] (23) 93, p. 44.
"Uncle Moe." [Footwork] (23) 93, p. 43-44.
343. BARKER, Ann S.
"Exploring the Dark." [CumbPR]] (13:1) Fall 93, p. 80.
"Thaw in the Bracken." [CumbPR]] (13:1) Fall 93, p. 79.
344. BARKER, David
"After the Big Earth-." [WormR] (33:4, #132) 93, p. 168.
"Bats." [WormR] (33:4, #132) 93, p. 170-171.
"Black and Blind." [WormR] (33:4, #132) 93, p. 168.
"Blame It on Jack." [WormR] (33:4, #132) 93, p. 170.
"Dog Days of the Empire." [WormR] (33:4, #132) 93, p. 169.
"The Queen of Sheba Restaurant." [WormR] (33:4, #132) 93, p. 167.
"Time to Change the Furnace Filter." [WormR] (33:4, #132) 93, p. 170.
345. BARKER, Helene
"The Barn's Blue Light." [Poem] (69) My 93, p. 20.
"The Hour Before Dawn." [Poem] (69) My 93, p. 21.
"Night Pushing In." [IndR] (16:1) Spr 93, p. 151.
"Shipshewana." [SycamoreR] (5:2) Sum 93, p. 59-60.
"That Domestic Circle." [SycamoreR] (5:2) Sum 93, p. 57-58.
346. BARKER, Lucile
"Sonnet III." [RagMag] (11:1) 93, p. 42.
347. BARKER, Wendy
"Color Analysis." [Poetry] (162:5) Ag 93, p. 259.
"Of Mice and Men." [AmerS] (62:1) Wint 93, p. 78-80.
"Taking a Language." [Poetry] (162:5) Ag 93, p. 257-258.
348. BARKS, Coleman
"Some Orange Juice." [PaintedB] (50/51) 93, p. 105.
349. BARNES, Dick
"James Joyce" (tr. of Jorge Luis Borges, w. Robert Mezey). [ArtfulD] (24/25) 93, p. 41.
"Junín" (tr. of Jorge Luis Borges). [ArtfulD] (24/25) 93, p. 43.
"Truco" (tr. of Jorge Luis Borges, w. Robert Mezey). [ArtfulD] (24/25) 93, p. 44.
350. BARNES, Jim
"Fall in the Tuileries." [LaurelR] (27:2) Sum 93, p. 100.
"Finding Oscar Wilde." [GreenMR] (NS 6:1) Wint-Spr 93, p. 82.
"Interlude." [TexasR] (14:3/4) Fall-Wint 93, p. 72.
"Lamentation and Farewell" (leaving Paris, 1992). [NewL] (60:1) 93, p. 73.
"Place des Vosges." [GreenMR] (NS 6:1) Wint-Spr 93, p. 83.
"Shakespeare & Co." [WestB] (33) 93, p. 73.
"Up from the Metro into Fire." [GreenMR] (NS 6:1) Wint-Spr 93, p. 84.
351. BARNES, Kate
"Elizabeth and Sally." [BelPoJ] (44:1) Fall 93, p. 20-21.
"Imaginining It." [HarvardR] (5) Fall 93, p. 160.
352. BARNES, Kim
"Dust." [CimR] (104) Jl 93, p. 152-153.
"My Mother Bakes Pies for the Clearwater Cafe." [CimR] (104) Jl 93, p. 153.
"The Strong Swimmer." [CutB] (40) Spr 93, p. 215-216.
353. BARNES, Mike
"Natalie." [Event] (22:3) Wint 93-94, p. 74.
354. BARNES, R. G.
"Allusion to the Death of Colonel Francisco Borges (1833-74)" (tr. of Jorge Luis Borges, w. Robert Mezey). [NowestR] (31:3) 93, p. 59.
"Limits" (tr. of Jorge Luis Borges, w. Robert Mezey). [Poetry] (162:3) Je 93, p. 157-158.
"On Forgetting a Dream" (To Viviana Aguilar, tr. of Jorge Luis Borges, w. Robert Mezey). [NowestR] (31:3) 93, p. 60.
"Written in a Copy of the Geste of Beowulf" (tr. of Jorge Luis Borges). [Poetry] (162:3) Je 93, p. 159.

355. BARNES, Richard
    "Brunanburh, 937 A.D." (tr. of Jorge Luis Borges). [MissouriR] (16:3) 93, p. 31.
    "To a Coin" (tr. of Jorge Luis Borges). [MissouriR] (16:3) 93, p. 30.
356. BARNES, Tim
    "Botany and Memory." [SilverFR] (24) Wint 93, p. 26-27.
357. BARNETT, Ruth Anderson
    "Class Reunion" (from "The Stripper in the Mojave"). [BelPoJ] (44:1) Fall 93, p. 41.
    "Vacation Bible School." [ChatR] (14:1) Fall 93, p. 62-63.
358. BARNEY, Anne
    "The Cesarian." [ChironR] (12:4/13:1, #37/38) Wint 93-Spr 94, p. 35.
359. BARNEY, William D.
    "Clerihew: 'Dear, dear me,' purred Priscilla." [Light] (8) Wint 93, p. 15.
    "Clerihew: Despite a very large hernia, which hung down." [Light] (5) Spr 93, p. 26.
    "Clerihew: 'Good Heavens!' cried Galileo." [Light] (6) Sum 93, p. 19.
    "Clerihew: 'The State,' said Louis Fourteen." [Light] (8) Wint 93, p. 11.
360. BARNIE, John
    "2 A.M." [PoetryC] (14:1) 93, p. 23.
    "Heroes." [PoetryC] (14:1) 93, p. 22.
    "Inhuman." [PoetryC] (14:1) 93, p. 22.
    "Knocking at This Door." [PoetryC] (14:1) 93, p. 22.
    "Mother." [PoetryC] (14:1) 93, p. 23.
    "The Shrike." [PoetryC] (14:1) 93, p. 23.
    "Untitled: The one lapwing wheeling away from me." [PoetryC] (14:1) 93, p. 22.
    "Untitled: Two hercules swung down low over the marsh then on to the estuary."
        [PoetryC] (14:1) 93, p. 23.
361. BARNSTONE, Aliki
    "Blue Room, Blue Horse." [ArtfulD] (24/25) 93, p. 102-103.
    "Brothers." [GrahamHR] (17) Fall 93, p. 35.
    "A Declining Neighborhood." [Agni] (38) 93, p. 77-78.
362. BARNSTONE, Tony
    "Birds Sing in the Ravine" (tr. of Wang Wei, w. Willis Barnstone and Xu Haixin).
        [AmerPoR] (22:2) Mr-Ap 93, p. 45.
    "Black Gold" (tr. of Tang Yaping, w. Newton Liu). [ChiR] (39:3/4) 93, p. 295.
    "Deer Park" (tr. of Wang Wei, w. Willis Barnstone and Xu Haixin). [AmerPoR]
        (22:2) Mr-Ap 93, p. 46.
    "I Am" (tr. of Jorge Luis Borges). [LitR] (36:2) Wint 93, p. 143.
    "In Memory of Angelica" (tr. of Jorge Luis Borges). [LitR] (36:2) Wint 93, p. 143.
    "Love" (tr. of Xi Murong, w. Newton Liu). [ChiR] (39:3/4) 93, p. 305.
    "New Discovery" (tr. of Zhang Zhen, w. Newton Liu). [ChiR] (39:3/4) 93, p. 294.
    "Return to Wang River" (tr. of Wang Wei, w. Willis Barnstone and Xu Haixin).
        [AmerPoR] (22:2) Mr-Ap 93, p. 46.
    "Solar Tide" (from the poem cycle "Nuorilang," tr. of Yang Lian, w. Newton Liu).
        [ChiR] (39:3/4) 93, p. 290-291.
    "To Robinson Jeffers" (tr. of Bei Ling, w. Xi Chuan). [ChiR] (39:3/4) 93, p. 298.
    "Vineyard" (tr. of Mang Ke, w. Willis Barnstone and Gu Zhongxing). [ChiR] (39:3/4)
        93, p. 289.
    "Violence." [Agni] (38) 93, p. 75.
    "You Asked About My Life. I Send You, Pei Di, These Lines" (tr. of Wang Wei, w.
        Willis Barnstone and Xu Haixin). [AmerPoR] (22:2) Mr-Ap 93, p. 46.
363. BARNSTONE, Willis
    "The Aviator's Restaurant." [ArtfulD] (24/25) 93, p. 56.
    "Birds Sing in the Ravine" (tr. of Wang Wei, w. Tony Barnstone and Xu Haixin).
        [AmerPoR] (22:2) Mr-Ap 93, p. 45.
    "Deer Park" (tr. of Wang Wei, w. Tony Barnstone and Xu Haixin). [AmerPoR] (22:2)
        Mr-Ap 93, p. 46.
    "Homeless." [Agni] (38) 93, p. 19.
    "Return to Wang River" (tr. of Wang Wei, w. Tony Barnstone and Xu Haixin).
        [AmerPoR] (22:2) Mr-Ap 93, p. 46.
    "Vineyard" (tr. of Mang Ke, w. Tony Barnstone and Gu Zhongxing). [ChiR] (39:3/4)
        93, p. 289.
    "You Asked About My Life. I Send You, Pei Di, These Lines" (tr. of Wang Wei, w.
        Tony Barnstone and Xu Haixin). [AmerPoR] (22:2) Mr-Ap 93, p. 46.
364. BAROLINI, Helen
    "Xenia" (1964-1966 — in memory of the poet's wife, tr. of Eugenio Montale). [QRL]
        (12:32/33) 93, p. 474-475.

365. BARON, Henry
   "Conversation" (tr. of Tiny Mulder). [Vis] (43) 93, p. 20.
   "Words" (tr. of Tiny Mulder). [Vis] (43) 93, p. 20.
366. BARON, Suze
   "The Cross" (from "Diacoute," tr. of Felix Morisseau-Leroy). [NewYorkQ] (51) 93,
      p. 76-77.
367. BARONE, Dennis
   "Held Over" (tr. of Jacques Audiberti). [WashR] (19:2) Ag-S 93, p. 15.
   "Law and Order" (tr. of Francis Ponge). [WashR] (19:2) Ag-S 93, p. 14.
   "Let's Play." [Talisman] (10) Spr 93, p. 99.
   "Not Again" (tr. of Henri Michaux). [WashR] (19:2) Ag-S 93, p. 15.
   "Shoot-Up" (tr. of Charles Baudelaire). [WashR] (19:2) Ag-S 93, p. 14.
368. BAROT, Rick
   "Between Grief and Nothing." [GeoR] (47:4) Wint 93, p. 678-679.
369. BARR, Burlin
   "Tremendous Mood Swings." [GrandS] (12:2, #46) Sum 93, p. 229-231.
370. BARR, Tina
   "Between the House and the Sky." [PaintedB] (50/51) 93, p. 86.
371. BARRERA VALVERDE, Alfonso
   "Canción del Sencillo Amor." [InterPR] (19:2) Fall 93, p. 8, 10.
   "Death of the Woodcutter" (tr. by H. J. Van Peenen). [InterPR] (19:2) Fall 93, p. 15,
      17.
   "An Introduction" (tr. by H. J. Van Peenen). [InterPR] (19:2) Fall 93, p. 13.
   "Meditación sobre el Desconocido." [InterPR] (19:2) Fall 93, p. 4, 6.
   "Meditation on the Unknown" (tr. by H. J. Van Peenen). [InterPR] (19:2) Fall 93, p.
      5, 7.
   "Muerte del Leñador." [InterPR] (19:2) Fall 93, p. 14, 16.
   "Presentación." [InterPR] (19:2) Fall 93, p. 12.
   "A Song of Simple Love" (tr. by H. J. Van Peenen). [InterPR] (19:2) Fall 93, p. 9, 11.
372. BARRESI, Dorothy
   "Called Up: Tinker to Evers to Chance." [Agni] (37) 93, p. 298-299.
   "Surfing as Meditation" (for Phil). [MichQR] (32:2) Spr 93, p. 206-208.
373. BARRETT, Chuck
   "Waiting for Heraclitis." [BlackBR] (17) Sum-Fall 93, p. 16.
374. BARRETT, Ed
   "Vermont House." [Agni] (37) 93, p. 214-217.
375. BARRETT, Nick
   "The Story of Two People Picking Zucchini" (for my grandfather). [CreamCR] (17:1)
      Spr 93, p. 4-5.
   "Voices." [PaintedB] (49) 93, p. 10-14.
376. BARRINGER, Margaret
   "Small Inns and Lodges." [Agni] (38) 93, p. 79.
377. BARRINGTON, Judith
   "Four Reasons for Destroying a Spider's Web" (A Meditation during the Gulf War).
      [KenR] (NS 15:3) Sum 93, p. 53-54.
378. BARROWS, Anita
   "Exiles" (Inspired by the work of the Russian sculptor Julia Segal). [QRL] (12:32/33)
      93, p. 23-26.
   "Impression" (tr. of Edith Bruck). [13thMoon] (11:1/2) 93, p. 207.
   "Quelques Leçons des Tenebres." [QRL] (12:32/33) 93, p. 26-31.
   "Survivors" (tr. of Edith Bruck). [13thMoon] (11:1/2) 93, p. 206.
379. BARRY, Sandra
   "In Memory of Abner Troop" (died 1872, 42 years of age). [AntigR] (93-94) Spr -
      Sum 93, p. 104-105.
   "Ruby's House." [AntigR] (93-94) Spr-Sum 93, p. 103.
380. BARTKOWECH, R.
   "Why There Is a Talking Sea Lion at the New England Aquarium." [Outbr] (24) 93,
      p. 110-111.
381. BARTLETT, Brian
   "An Eagle above Mt. Hunger" (a Canadian in Vermont). [TickleAce] (25) Spr-Sum
      93, p. 200.
   "Hutterite Twins Tropical." [TickleAce] (24) Fall-Wint 92, p. 13.
   "An Imp Tale." [PoetryC] (14:1) 93, p. 25.
   "A Landlord Tale." [PoetryC] (14:1) 93, p. 25.
   "Two Circuses." [TickleAce] (24) Fall-Wint 92, p. 14-15.

382. BARTLEY, Jackie
"Confirmation." [WestB] (31/32) 93, p. 106-107.
"The Curator's Lecture on Birds." [Outbr] (24) 93, p. 92.
"Divining." [WestB] (31/32) 93, p. 103.
"Learning to Make a Good Confession." [WestB] (31/32) 93, p. 105.
"Secrets." [WestB] (31/32) 93, p. 104.
"Sounds of the Sun." [Outbr] (24) 93, p. 91.
383. BARTON, Bruce
"1968." [WillowS] (31) Wint 93, p. 77.
384. BARTON, Christine C.
"Mama Ken" (for father). [WilliamMR] (31) 93, p. 37.
385. BARTON, David
"Dust." [QRL] (12:32/33) 93, p. 35-36.
"Elocution Lessons." [QRL] (12:32/33) 93, p. 36-37.
"Gilbert White Street." [QRL] (12:32/33) 93, p. 32-33.
"Palm Sunday, Palm Springs." [QRL] (12:32/33) 93, p. 34-35.
"Place Clichy." [QRL] (12:32/33) 93, p. 33-34.
386. BARTON, John
"Destinations, Leaving the Map." [AmerV] (31) 93, p. 65-66.
"Last Contact." [PoetL] (88:3) Fall 93, p. 15-17.
"Lift." [TickleAce] (26) Fall-Wint 93, p. 36-37.
"Road, River, Snake." [TickleAce] (26) Fall-Wint 93, p. 34-35.
"West Then East." [Grain] (21:3) Fall 93, p. 55-56.
"Yarn." [AntigR] (92) Wint 93, p. 111-112.
387. BASCOM, Tim
"Cicada Song." [ChrC] (110:19) 16-23 Je 93, p. 636.
388. BASHAM, Kate
"Figure / Ground." [EvergreenC] (8:2) Sum-Fall 93, p. 29.
"Stepped Leader." [EvergreenC] (8:2) Sum-Fall 93, p. 27-28.
389. BASHEVA, Miriana
"The fast train? The express?" (tr. by Lisa Sapinkopf, w. Georgi Belev). [Agni] (37) 93, p. 259.
"It Was War" (tr. by Lisa Sapinkopf and Georgi Belev). [Paint] (19:38) Aut 92, p. 73.
390. BASHO, Matsuo
"Seized with a disease." [ChiR] (39:3/4) 93, p. 59.
391. BASINSKI, Michael
"A Form of the Tell-Tale Heart by Edgar Allan Poe and Michael Basinski." [PoetryUSA] (25/26) 93, p. 32.
"Odalisque 1." [PoetryUSA] (25/26) 93, p. 10.
"Odalisque 2." [PoetryUSA] (25/26) 93, p. 11.
"Odalisque 3." [PoetryUSA] (25/26) 93, p. 12.
"Odalisque 4." [PoetryUSA] (25/26) 93, p. 12.
392. BASKETT, Franz K.
"The Example of the Cat." [Pearl] (19) Fall-Wint 93, p. 52.
"Sermon for the Comfort of the Masses." [Epiphany] (4:2) Ap 93, p. 109-110.
"Talk." [Epiphany] (4:2) Ap 93, p. 111.
393. BASNEY, Lionel
"By the Grand Trunk Line." [Shen] (43:1) Spr 93, p. 26.
"Sound Going Out." [Shen] (43:1) Spr 93, p. 27.
394. BATEMAN, Claire
"Pluck." [GeoR] (47:2) Sum 93, p. 250.
395. BATES, Robert L.
"On Entering the Supermarket." [Light] (7) Aut 93, p. 11.
396. BATHANTI, Joseph
"On the Banks of the Chattahoochee." [Crucible] (29) Fall 93, p. 29.
"The Toy Warehouse" (Third Place, Annual Poetry Contest). [PaintedB] (49) 93, p. 42-44.
397. BATKI, John
"Christmas, Nineteen-fifties" (tr. of Miklós Mészöly). [HarvardR] (3) Wint 93, p. 49.
398. BATTAGLIA, J.
"Columb—I-AD." [Footwork] (23) 93, p. 131.
"Einstein Looking Down." [Footwork] (23) 93, p. 130.
"Imagoes." [Footwork] (23) 93, p. 129.
"Monticello 4 July 1826." [Footwork] (23) 93, p. 130.
"Near." [Footwork] (23) 93, p. 131.
"Not Praying." [Footwork] (23) 93, p. 129-130.

57

BATTAGLIA

"Reunion." [Footwork] (23) 93, p. 130.
"Tel Aviv, 1993." [Footwork] (23) 93, p. 130.
"Woman in the Ermine Dress." [Footwork] (23) 93, p. 131.
399. BATTERSBY, J. T.
"Adieu." [Bogg] (66) Wint 92-93, p. 54.
400. BATTIN, Wendy
"At the Synchrotron Lab." [MassR] (34:1) Spr 93, p. 100-101.
"Four." [SouthwR] (78:3) Sum 93, p. 384.
"Who Flies, Who Swims." [GeoR] (47:4) Wint 93, p. 666.
401. BATTRAM, Michael R.
"Embarrassments." [Pearl] (17) Spr 93, p. 47.
402. BATTSON, Jill
"Degrazzia." [AntigR] (93-94) Spr-Sum 93, p. 137-138.
"Delongpre." [CapeR] (28:2) Fall 93, p. 26.
403. BAUDELAIRE, Charles (Pierre Charles)
"Correspondences" (Les Fleurs du Mal, tr. by Richard Howard). [HarvardR] (5) Fall
93, p. 140.
"Enivrey-Vous." [WashR] (19:2) Ag-S 93, p. 14.
"Shoot-Up" (tr. by Dennis Barone). [WashR] (19:2) Ag-S 93, p. 14.
"The Swan" (tr. by Rachel Hadas). [Pequod] (35) 93, p. 66-67.
404. BAUER, Ann
"The Fiction Writer." [PoetC] (25:1) Fall 93, p. 29-30.
405. BAUER, Erika
"Afternoon Meeting with an Angel." [DenQ] (27:4) Spr 93, p. 17.
406. BAUER, Grace
"Note from the Imaginary Daughter." [ApalQ] (36/37) 91, p. 74.
"She Marvels at His Face." [TampaR] (6) Spr 93, p. 67.
407. BAUER, Tricia
"Hearts." [Calyx] (14:3) Sum 93, p. 14-15.
408. BAUM, Diane
"Big Dick." [ChangingM] (26) Sum-Fall 93, p. 45.
409. BAUMEL, Judith
"Custard of the Pawpaw." [NewRep] (209:2) 12 Jl 93, p. 38.
"Einstein's Curse." [DenQ] (27:4) Spr 93, p. 32.
"The Park of the Monsters" (At the gardens of Vicino Orsino. to A. on his unfaithful
wife). [Agni] (38) 93, p. 64-67.
410. BAUMGARTNER, Howard G.
"Pantyhose." [Sparrow] (60) Sum 93, p. 46.
411. BAUMGARTNER, Willima
"Dream Memorial." [EngJ] (82:2) F 93, p. 91.
412. BAUSCH, Victor H.
"What They Wanted." [Footwork] (23) 93, p. 134.
413. BAUTISTA, Pablo Tapay
"Come." [Bomb] (43) Spr 93, p. 74-75.
BAW, Dominique La
See LaBAW, Dominique
414. BAYER, Deanne
"For the Love of Living Things" (In Memory of Molly La Rue). [Plain] (13:3) Spr 93,
p. 33.
"Night Watch." [Elf] (3:1) Spr 93, p. 30-31.
415. BEAKE, Fred
"For My Brother at a Dark Time." [Stand] (34:2) Spr 93, p. 75.
416. BEAL, Robert Stephen
"Hungarian Trouble." [Gypsy] (20) Sum 93, p. 66.
BEAR, Ray Young (Ray A. Young)
See YOUNG BEAR, Ray (Ray A.)
BÉARN, Roger du
See Du BÉARN, Roger
417. BEASLEY, Bruce
"Advent: Snow Incantation." [Journal] (17:2) Fall-Wint 93, p. 87-88.
"Arcana Mundi." [Journal] (17:2) Fall-Wint 93, p. 89.
"The Conceiving." [Hudson] (46:3) Aut 93, p. 492-495.
"Consolation." [Poetry] (161:5) F 93, p. 251-253.
"Doxology." [Journal] (17:2) Fall-Wint 93, p. 96-98.
"Going Home to Georgia." [Hudson] (46:1) Spr 93, p. 179-181.
"Longing." [Journal] (17:2) Fall-Wint 93, p. 94-95.

"Noli Me Tangere." [Journal] (17:2) Fall-Wint 93, p. 90-93.
"Red Reed." [Field] (49) Fall 93, p. 43-44.
418. BEASLEY JR.
"Free at Last." [PoetryUSA] (25/26) 93, p. 55.
419. BEATTY, Christy
"What of This Jesus." [Lactuca] (17) Apr 93, p. 33.
420. BEATTY, Jan
"Did You Think I Never Thought About It?" [QW] (37) Sum-Fall 93, p. 108-109.
421. BEATTY, Paul
"That's Not in My Job Description." [Agni] (37) 93, p. 38-43.
422. BEAUMONT, Jeanne
"Female Navigation (1818)." [AntR] (51:2) Spr 93, p. 246-247.
"The First Red Place." [AntR] (51:2) Spr 93, p. 245.
"Lullaby." [SouthernHR] (27:2) Spr 93, p. 119.
"No Surprises." [SouthernHR] (27:1) Wint 93, p. 44-45.
"Proxy." [PoetryNW] (34:4) Wint 93-94, p. 20-21.
"St. One." [Boulevard] (8:2/3, #23/24) Fall 93, p. 91-92.
"Two Bowls." [Poetry] (163:1) O 93, p. 27.
BEBELLE, Carol F.
    See AKUA (Carol F. Bebelle)
423. BECK, Art
"#13. Magus" (tr. of Luxorius). [PassN] (14:1) Sum 93, p. 29.
"#27. Well, Fame, the Painting Is" (tr. of Luxorius). [PassN] (14:1) Sum 93, p. 31.
"#90. Hilderic's Palace" (tr. of Luxorius). [PassN] (14:1) Sum 93, p. 31.
"Cemetery Strike." [PaintedB] (50/51) 93, p. 110.
424. BECKER, Robin
"Bicycle Days." [GlobalCR] (2) Fall 93, p. 107-109.
"Family Romance." [TampaR] (7) Fall 93, p. 33-34.
"Meeting the Gaze of the Great Horned Owl." [BostonR] (18:3/4) Je-Ag 93, p. 8.
"My Grandmother's Crystal Ball." [GlobalCR] (1) Spr 93, p. 116-117.
"Solar." [TampaR] (7) Fall 93, p. 49.
"We Thought of Each Other as Food" (After David Shapiro). [HarvardR] (5) Fall 93,
    p. 157.
425. BECKER, Therese
"Above the White Sheet." [PoetryE] (36) Fall 93, p. 128-129.
"The Same Material." [PoetryE] (36) Fall 93, p. 126.
"To a Small Light" (for Matthew). [PoetryE] (36) Fall 93, p. 127.
"Under the Overpass." [PoetryE] (36) Fall 93, p. 130-131.
426. BECKOVIC, Matija
"False Tracks" (tr. by Peter Russell). [NoDaQ] (61:1) Wint 93, p. 31.
"A Lament for Myself" (A Fragment, tr. by Peter Russell). [NoDaQ] (61:1) Wint 93,
    p. 33.
"Matija Beckovic" (tr. by Peter Russell). [NoDaQ] (61:1) Wint 93, p. 32.
427. BEDDOW, Jeff
"Crabs" (w. James Naiden). [NorthStoneR] (11) 93, p. 168-169.
428. BEDELL, Jack B.
"In the Marsh." [WestB] (31/32) 93, p. 150-151.
"Marsh House at Pointe au Chenes." [WestB] (31/32) 93, p. 151-152.
429. BEDICHEK, Don
"An Angel's Time." [Poem] (70) N 93, p. 43.
"Miles from Anywhere Usual." [Poem] (70) N 93, p. 44.
430. BEDIENT, Cal
"Modern Love." [AntR] (51:1) Wint 93, p. 85.
431. BEECHHOLD, Henry F.
"A Time in February." [US1] (28/29) 93, p. 7.
432. BEGLEY, T.
"Sea Blouse Open" (Selections: 2 poems, w. Olga Broumas). [Sonora] (26) Fall 93, p.
    44-45.
"Sophia and True" (Selections: 3 poems, w. Olga Broumas). [Sonora] (26) Fall 93, p.
    46-48.
"Your Sacred Idiot with Me" (Selections: 2 poems, w. Olga Broumas). [Sonora] (26)
    Fall 93, p. 49-50.
433. BEHM, Richard
"A Fat Man Makes History at Mabel's Cafe." [Farm] (10:2) Fall-Wint 93-94, p. 77.
"Walking on Worms." [PoetL] (88:3) Fall 93, p. 29.

59

434. BEHN, Robin
"30 Windsor." [Crazy] (44) Spr 93, p. 62-63.
"The Pit." [SpoonR] (18:1) Wint-Spr 93, p. 19-23.
435. BEHRENDT, Stephen C.
"The Dull Lecture." [PraS] (67:3) Fall 93, p. 42-43.
"Jaffrey Center Cemetery." [PraS] (67:3) Fall 93, p. 38.
"Mt. Moriah Dawn." [PraS] (67:3) Fall 93, p. 41-42.
"Persephone in Nebraska." [SouthernR] (29:1) Wint, Ja 93, p. 173-174.
"The Ruts of the Oregon Trail." [Hudson] (46:2) Sum 93, p. 351.
"Snow Geese." [PraS] (67:3) Fall 93, p. 39-40.
"Welcome Back." [Hudson] (46:2) Sum 93, p. 352.
"Wreckage." [PraS] (67:3) Fall 93, p. 40-41.
436. BEI, Dao
"Andante Cantabile" (tr. by Donald Finkel and Xueliang Chen). [SenR] (23:1/2) Wint
93, p. 158-159.
"Bridge" tr. by Donald Finkel and Xueliang Chen). [DenQ] (28:1) Sum 93, p. 24.
"Commercial" (tr. by Donald Finkel and Xueliang Chen). [SenR] (23:1/2) Wint 93, p.
157.
"Deserted City" (tr. by Donald Finkel and Xueliang Chen). [ManhatR] (7:1) Fall 93,
p. 51.
"Guide to Summer" (tr. by Donald Finkel and Xueliang Chen). [SenR] (23:1/2) Wint
93, p. 160.
"Hurried Night" (tr. by Donald Finkel and Xueliang Chen). [SenR] (23:1/2) Wint 93,
p. 161.
"Loyalty" (tr. by Donald Finkel and Xueliang Chen). [ManhatR] (7:1) Fall 93, p. 49.
"Night Patrol" (tr. by Donald Finkel and Xueliang Chen). [ManhatR] (7:1) Fall 93, p.
50.
"Notes of an Afternoon" (tr. by Donald Finkel and Xueliang Chen). [ManhatR] (7:1)
Fall 93, p. 52.
"On Eternity" (tr. by Donald Finkel and Xueliang Chen). [ManhatR] (7:1) Fall 93, p.
55.
"Portrait" (tr. by Donald Finkel and Xueliang Chen). [SenR] (23:1/2) Wint 93, p. 162.
"Requiem" (for the victims of June Fourth, tr. by Bonnie S. McDougall and Chen
Maiping). [ChiR] (39:3/4) 93, p. 288.
"Scenery" (tr. by Donald Finkel and Xueliang Chen). [ManhatR] (7:1) Fall 93, p. 54.
"Sower" (tr. by Donald Finkel and Xueliang Chen). [SenR] (23:1/2) Wint 93, p. 163.
"Untitled: At the front, defending the mother tongue" (tr. by Donald Finkel and
Xueliang Chen). [ManhatR] (7:1) Fall 93, p. 53.
"Variations" (tr. by Donald Finkel and Xueliang Chen). [ManhatR] (7:1) Fall 93, p.
48.
437. BEI, Ling
"To Robinson Jeffers" (tr. by Tony Barnstone and Xi Chuan). [ChiR] (39:3/4) 93, p.
298.
438. BEISSEL, Henry
"San Miguel Sketchbook" (5 poems). [PoetryC] (13:4) 93, p. 4-5.
439. BEJERANO, Maya
"Word Processing" (1-4, tr. by Gabriel Levin). [Trans] (28) Spr 93, p. 66-69.
440. BELATTHAKANI
"Abandoning his house" (Songs from the Theragatha: Songs of the Buddhist Monks,
circa 450 B.C.E.). [Tricycle] (2:3) Spr 93, p. 39.
441. BELDEN, Rick
"Doorway." [SlipS] (13) 93, p. 15.
"Penguins." [SlipS] (13) 93, p. 15-16.
442. BELEV, Georgi
"Beacon" (In memory of Danila Stoyanova, tr. of Vladimir Levchev, w. Lisa
Sapinkopf). [Paint] (19:38) Aut 92, p. 62.
"Birth" (tr. by Lisa Sapinkopf, w. the author). [Stand] (34:3) Sum 93, p. 63.
"Blue Pond at Berkovitsa" (To Tsvetana, tr. of Vladimir Levchev, w. Lisa
Sapinkopf). [Paint] (19:38) Aut 92, p. 63.
"Business Trip" (in Bulgarian and English, tr. by Lisa Sapinkopf, w. the author).
[SouthernHR] (27:3) Sum 93, p. 246-247.
"Evaporations" (tr. of Ani Ilkov, w. Lisa Sapinkopf). [Paint] (19:38) Aut 92, p. 65.
"The fast train? The express?" (tr. of Miriana Basheva, w. Lisa Sapinkopf). [Agni]
(37) 93, p. 259.
"Garden with Stone Wall and Quince Trees" (tr. by Lisa Sapinkopf). [Vis] (41) 93, p.
6.

"Gates" (tr. of Georgi Borisov, w. Lisa Sapinkopf). [Paint] (19:38) Aut 92, p. 58.
"Give the snow a good interrogation!" (tr. by Lisa Sapinkopf). [GreenMR] (NS 6:1)
    Wint-Spr 93, p. 157.
"Green and Gold" (tr. of Ani Ilkov, w. Lisa Sapinkopf). [Paint] (19:38) Aut 92, p. 64.
"The Horse" (tr. of Georgi Borisov, w. Lisa Sapinkopf). [Paint] (19:38) Aut 92, p. 59.
"If the Silence Should Suddenly Return" (tr. of Ekaterina Iosifova, w. Lisa
    Sapinkopf). [Paint] (19:38) Aut 92, p. 70-71.
"If there were a sun to see you" (in Bulgarian and English, tr. by Lisa Sapinkopf, w.
    the author). [SouthernHR] (27:3) Sum 93, p. 248.
"Interior with Faded Colors" (tr. of Blaga Dimitrova, w. Lisa Sapinkopf). [Paint]
    (19:38) Aut 92, p. 69.
"It Was War" (tr. of Miriana Basheva, w. Lisa Sapinkopf). [Paint] (19:38) Aut 92, p.
    73.
"It's time — farewell to irony!" (tr. by Lisa Sapinkopf and the author). [HarvardR] (3)
    Wint 93, p. 170.
"Mice" (tr. of Alexander Gerov, w. Lisa Sapinkopf). [Agni] (37) 93, p. 258.
"Moth" (tr. by Lisa Sapinkopf, w. the author). [PennR] (5:2) 93, p. 38.
"Riverbend" (tr. of Marin Georgiev, w. Lisa Sapinkopf). [Paint] (19:38) Aut 92, p.
    57.
"Seduced and Abandoned" (tr. of Radoi Ralin, w. Lisa Sapinkopf). [Agni] (37) 93, p.
    262-263.
"Seventh Heaven Can Be Seen at First Glance" (tr. of Nikolai Kanchev, w. Lisa
    Sapinkopf). [Agni] (37) 93, p. 261.
"Silence" (tr. of Marin Georgiev, w. Lisa Sapinkopf). [Paint] (19:38) Aut 92, p. 56.
"The Soul" (tr. of Nedelcho Ganev, w. Lisa Sapinkopf). [Agni] (37) 93, p. 260.
"Still Life" (tr. of Georgi Rupchev, w. Lisa Sapinkopf). [Agni] (37) 93, p. 264.
"These Things from Words" (tr. of Ivan Metodiev, w. Lisa Sapinkopf). [Paint]
    (19:38) Aut 92, p. 60.
"This Crow" (tr. of Ivan Metodiev, w. Lisa Sapinkopf). [Paint] (19:38) Aut 92, p. 61.
"Three mares" (tr. of Danila Stoyanova, w. Lisa Sapinkopf). [Vis] (41) 93, p. 6.
"The Tree" (tr. by Lisa Sapinkopf, w. the author). [PennR] (5:2) 93, p. 37.
"Vision" (tr. by Lisa Sapinkopf and the author). [Paint] (19:38) Aut 92, p. 66.
"Vulnerability" (tr. of Fedya Filkova, w. Lisa Sapinkopf). [Paint] (19:38) Aut 92, p.
    72.
"Wedding Song" (tr. by Lisa Sapinkopf, w. the author). [PennR] (5:2) 93, p. 39.
"Who Cares for the Blind Stork" (tr. of Blaga Dimitrova, w. Lisa Sapinkopf). [Paint]
    (19:38) Aut 92, p. 68.
"Zoo" (tr. by Lisa Sapinkopf and the author). [Paint] (19:38) Aut 92, p. 67.
443. BELIEU, Erin
    "The Man Who Tried to Rape You." [Journal] (17:2) Fall-Wint 93, p. 19-20.
    "Rondeau at the Train Stop." [AntR] (51:3) Sum 93, p. 372.
    "A Sleeping Man Must Be Awakened to Be Killed." [Journal] (17:2) Fall-Wint 93, p.
        21-22.
444. BELIN, Mel
    "Early March in the Park." [CapeR] (28:2) Fall 93, p. 49.
445. BELITT, Ben
    "1966: The Stone Mason's Funeral." [QRL] (12:32/33) 93, p. 373-376.
446. BELL, Chana
    "All the Noise of the World." [OnTheBus] (6:1, #13) Wint 93-Spr 94, p. 53.
447. BELL, Jason Scott
    "Contributor's Notes." [Harp] (286:1712) Ja 93, p. 36.
448. BELL, Marvin
    "The Book of the Dead Man" (Selections: #4, #18). [NoAmR] (278:6) N-D 93, p. 26 -
        27.
    "The Book of the Dead Man" (Selections: #6, #13, #26). [Iowa] (23:3) Fall 93, p.
        132-136.
    "The Book of the Dead Man" (Selections: #9, #20, #30). [HarvardR] (5) Fall 93, p. 8 -
        13.
    "The Book of the Dead Man" (Selections: #15-17)." [MassR] (34:3) Aut 93, p. 327 -
        331.
    "The Book of the Dead Man" (Selections: #21, 25, 29, 31). [NewEngR] (15:4) Fall
        93, p. 98-103.
    "The Book of the Dead Man (#23)." [GeoR] (47:3) Fall 93, p. 452-453.
    "The Book of the Dead Man (#27)." [Poetry] (163:2) N 93, p. 90-91.
    "The Book of the Dead Man (#28)." [DenQ] (28:2) Fall 93, p. 4-5.
    "The Book of the Dead Man (#33)." [Poetry] (163:2) N 93, p. 92-93.

61

"Cryptic Version of Ecstasy." [GettyR] (6:2) Spr 93, p. 321.
"Dream Journals." [VirQR] (69:1) Wint 93, p. 97-98.
"Ecstasy." [GettyR] (6:2) Spr 93, p. 318-320.
"The Hen." [Atlantic] (271:5) My 93, p. 90.
"To Logan in the Grave." [PaintedB] (50/51) 93, p. 112.
449. BELLA
"Kings Road Cafe." [Pearl] (17) Spr 93, p. 45.
BELLAY, Joachim du
See Du BELLAY, Joachim
450. BELLEFEUILLE, Norman de
"Rien d'Autre Que le Tonnerre" (à Doug Jones). [WestCL] (27:3, #12) Wint 93-94, p.
54-55.
451. BELLEN, Martine
"Four Kinds of Water." [Conjunc] (20) 93, p. 34-38.
"Renga" (w. Elaine Equi and Melanie Neilson). [Conjunc] (21) 93, p. 263-268.
452. BELLM, Dan
"Buried Treasure." [Thrpny] (53) Spr 93, p. 29.
"Mama" (tr. of Manlio Argueta, w. Stacey Ross). [KenR] (NS 15:3) Sum 93, p. 94 -
95.
"Silence" (In memoriam John Cage). [Poetry] (163:1) O 93, p. 15.
453. BELTON, Ellen
"Threesome." [13thMoon] (11:1/2) 93, p. 6-7.
454. BEN-LEV, Dina
"Driving." [Field] (48) Spr 93, p. 25-27.
"The Enemy." [PoetL] (88:4) Wint 93-94, p. 26.
"In My Insomnia I Was Advised." [PoetL] (88:4) Wint 93-94, p. 27.
"The Orange Armchair" (for Henry McMonagle, 1939-1991). [Sun] (215) N 93, p.
17.
"Tending." [Sun] (216) D 93, p. 29.
455. BENBOW, Margaret
"The Champion: Neighborhood Tale." [SpoonR] (18:1) Wint-Spr 93, p. 115-116.
"How to Tell a Bird of Prey." [PraS] (67:1) Spr 93, p. 125.
"Interview owith Carmela." [PraS] (67:1) Spr 93, p. 124-125.
"Violencia." [SpoonR] (18:1) Wint-Spr 93, p. 117.
456. BENDER, Mark
"Cutting the New Year's Firewood" (tr. of anonymous Yunnan Yi traditional poem).
[ChiR] (39:3/4) 93, p. 256-257.
457. BENDIS, Debra Kortmeier
"Living Past Mozart." [ChrC] (110:12) 14 Apr 93, p. 404.
458. BENEDIKT, Michael
"Approach to a View in Perspective" (tr. of Max Jacob). [QRL] (12:32/33) 93, p. 445.
"Hat" (tr. of Max Jacob). [QRL] (12:32/33) 93, p. 444-445.
"Of 'Turning Away from the World'" (In Memory, Stéphane Mallarmé, and The
Others). [Agni] (38) 93, p. 187.
"Some Feelings" (after Larry Rivers). [QRL] (12:32/33) 93, p. 376.
"The Toymaker Gloomy But Then Again Sometimes Happy." [ProseP] (2) 93, p. 8-9.
459. BENEVENTO, Joe
"Dream of Maria Abruzzino." [Footwork] (23) 93, p. 93.
"Walking Around Walden Pond" (September 4, 1987). [Elf] (3:3) Fall 93, p. 38.
460. BENFEY, Christopher
"The Absent Father." [Pequod] (36) 93, p. 73.
"First Metaphor." [Pequod] (36) 93, p. 74.
461. BENITEZ, Luis
"Arte Poetica (One More)" (from "Fractal," tr. by Ricardo Carrizo). [Luz] (5) N 93, p.
19.
"Arte Poetica, Otra" (from "Fractal"). [Luz] (5) N 93, p. 18.
"Una Avispa Cruzo el Himen de la Ventana." [Luz] (4) My 93, p. 52.
"Caracol de Sueño sobre una Cosa Que Mata" (from "Fractal"). [Luz] (5) N 93, p. 52.
"Comentario sobre un Crimen Pasional Concretado en 1949." [Luz] (4) My 93, p. 54.
"Ella Respira la Sombra." [Luz] (4) My 93, p. 53.
"Snail of Sleep over a Killing Thing" (from "Fractal," tr. by Ricardo Carrizo). [Luz]
(5) N 93, p. 53.
462. BENJAMIN, Walter
"Sonnet 52: In every beauty lies some hidden sorrow" (tr. by Mary Maxwell).
[Pequod] (35) 93, p. 70.

463. BENKA, Jen
    "Symbol of Sound." [SinW] (51) Wint 93-94, p. 75.
    "Tracing." [SinW] (50) Sum-Fall 93, p. 105-107.
464. BENN, Gottfried
    "Quaternary" (tr. by Teresa Iverson). [PartR] (60:3) Sum 93, p. 425-426.
465. BENNANI, Ben
    "Caffeine." [RiverS] (37) 93, p. 80.
    "Primal Sympathy." [RiverS] (37) 93, p. 81.
466. BENNETT, Bruce
    "After School." [TarRP] (32:2) Spr 93, p. 8.
    "Authorized Version." [HarvardR] (5) Fall 93, p. 74.
    "Close Reading." [TarRP] (32:2) Spr 93, p. 9.
    "David Ignatow Examines His Motives." [TarRP] (32:2) Spr 93, p. 48.
    "The Garden." [TarRP] (32:2) Spr 93, p. 47.
    "Love in Venice." [Light] (5) Spr 93, p. 16.
    "Rear View." [Light] (8) Wint 93, p. 12.
    "Retribution." [HarvardR] (3) Wint 93, p. 113.
    "Round and around it bobs and drifts." [HarvardR] (3) Wint 93, p. 113.
    "Solo." [Light] (8) Wint 93, p. 15.
    "This Dance." [LaurelR] (27:2) Sum 93, p. 59.
    "To a Formal Poet." [HarvardR] (5) Fall 93, p. 157.
    "Upstate." [TarRP] (32:2) Spr 93, p. 47.
467. BENNETT, Charles
    "The Hare." [Stand] (35:1) Wint 93-94, p. 63.
468. BENNETT, John
    "Beachcombing." [Nimrod] (36:2) Spr-Sum 93, p. 13-14.
469. BENNETT, John (John M.)
    "A Bushwalk." [Nimrod] (36:2) Spr-Sum 93, p. 110-112.
    "Capertee." [Nimrod] (36:2) Spr-Sum 93, p. 4-5.
    "Dam Division." [Caliban] (12) 93, p. 172.
    "Dressed to Spill." [Caliban] (12) 93, p. 173.
    "Extract from Antarctica." [Stand] (34:2) Spr 93, p. 8.
    "A Poem: Her skin is like a crumpled paper" (Slovakia, spring 1990). [Stand] (34:2)
        Spr 93, p. 9.
    "Sat 'n Lied." [Caliban] (12) 93, p. 174.
    "Underlying Ideologist" (Based on John W. Bennett's *Human Ecology as Human
        Behavior*, 1993). [Caliban] (13) 93, p. 84.
    "The Wolgan Valley." [Nimrod] (36:2) Spr-Sum 93, p. 1-3.
470. BENSE, Robert
    "Hard Words." [WebR] (17) Fall 93, p. 119.
    "Labyrinth." [WebR] (17) Fall 93, p. 120.
    "Last of the Guelder Roses." [WebR] (17) Fall 93, p. 119.
471. BENSEN, Robert
    "Abode" (tr. of Alvaro Mutis, w. Timothy J. Keating). [HarvardR] (4) Spr 93, p. 136.
    "Three Images" (tr. of Alvaro Mutis, w. Timothy J. Keating). [HarvardR] (4) Spr 93,
        p. 137.
472. BENSKO, John
    "The Cave Diver." [NewL] (60:1) 93, p. 79-80.
    "Crabbing." [Iowa] (23:3) Fall 93, p. 147.
    "Eastpoint, Bill's Grocery, and Love." [NewL] (60:1) 93, p. 76-77.
    "Escaping Eden." [Iowa] (23:3) Fall 93, p. 143-145.
    "The Terrorist." [PoetryNW] (34:3) Aut 93, p. 32-33.
    "The Waterman's Children." [Iowa] (23:3) Fall 93, p. 146.
    "The Window Man." [NewL] (60:1) 93, p. 78-79.
473. BENSON, Robert
    "The Bronze Slave" (for Earl Lovelace. Robert Penn Warren Poetry Prize Winner,
        First Prize). [CumbPR]] (13:1) Fall 93, p. 1.
    "The Time of Wind." [CumbPR]] (13:1) Fall 93, p. 2-3.
474. BENTLEY, Beth
    "In the Intense Latitudes" (For Nelson 1918-1990). [PassN] (14:2) Wint 93, p. 9-11.
475. BENTLEY, Laura Treacy
    "Topography." [SmPd] (30:3, #89) Fall 93, p. 7-8.
476. BENTLEY, Nelson
    "The Moosead" (An epic fragment in five books: Book Four). [BellArk] (9:6) N-D
        93, p. 15-22.

63

"The Moosead" (An epic fragment in five books: Book One. Illustrations by Erin Peterson Donovan.). [BellArk] (9:3) My-Je 93, p. 15-18.
"The Moosead" (An epic fragment in five books: Book Three). [BellArk] (9:5) S-O 93, p. 15-20.
"The Moosead" (An epic fragment in five books: Book Two). [BellArk] (9:4) Jl-Ag 93, p. 15-19.
477. BENTLEY, Roy
"The Morning After the Running of the 116th Kentucky Derby." [Journal] (17:2) Fall-Wint 93, p. 74.
478. BENTTINEN, Ted
"Ice and Sun." [LitR] (37:1) Fall 93, p. 56.
"Sanctus." [SouthernHR] (27:3) Sum 93, p. 267.
"Totem." [Paint] (19:38) Aut 92, p. 44.
479. BENWARE, Todd M.
"The Weight Guesser." [Plain] (13:2) Wint 93, p. 28.
480. BERBEROVA, Nina
"Dialogue Before Death (1983)" (tr. by Diana Der-Hovanessian, w. Marsbed Hablanian). [Agni] (38) 93, p. 106.
481. BERESFORD, Anne
"Willow" (taken from the Russian by Valentin Berestov). [Stand] (34:2) Spr 93, p. 12.
482. BERESTOV, Valentin
"Willow" (tr. by Anne Beresford). [Stand] (34:2) Spr 93, p. 12.
483. BERG, Nancy
"Blue Train Rant." [SouthernPR] (33:2) Fall 93, p. 36-38.
"I Could Have Danced All Night If I Hadn't Spontaneously Combusted." [Footwork] (23) 93, p. 86-87.
"Kaua'i" (With gratitude to the creators of the *Kumulipo*, an ancient Hawaiian creation chant). [HawaiiR] (17:3, #39) Fall 93, p. 1-3.
"Opthamology" [sic]. [SouthernPR] (33:2) Fall 93, p. 35-36.
484. BERG, Stephen
"Burning." [DenQ] (27:3) Wint 93, p. 10-11.
"On This Side of the River." [PoetryE] (35) Spr 93, p. 96, 113.
"Shaving" (2 selections). [DenQ] (28:2) Fall 93, p. 6-8.
485. BERGAMINO, Gina
"Baby Poems." [NewYorkQ] (50) 93, p. 64.
"Everybody's Baby." [NewYorkQ] (51) 93, p. 53.
486. BERGER, Bruce
"The Brave Siesta." [Light] (8) Wint 93, p. 9.
"Cat Martha Watches CNN." [Light] (7) Aut 93, p. 8.
"Don't Ask." [Poetry] (162:1) Ap 93, p. 13.
"Enigma Variations." [Poetry] (162:1) Ap 93, p. 12.
"Opus 28, the Preludes." [Poetry] (162:1) Ap 93, p. 11.
487. BERGER, Jacqueline
"Grandfather." [Agni] (37) 93, p. 70.
488. BERGER, L. R.
"Blue Mountain Autumn." [Blueline] (14) 93, p. 10.
"Elegy." [Blueline] (14) 93, p. 9.
489. BERGER, Linda-Ruth
"The Upstaging of a Coastal Sunset." [BelPoJ] (44:1) Fall 93, p. 5.
490. BERGER, Suzanne E.
"The House of the Body." [HarvardR] (5) Fall 93, p. 71.
491. BERGMAN, David
"Benny." [ParisR] (35:127) Sum 93, p. 129-130.
"The Guide of Tiresias." [ParisR] (35:127) Sum 93, p. 128.
"Teh Care and Treatment of Pain" (In Memory of Allen Barnett). [Art&Und] (2:3) Special Edition 93, p. 7.
492. BERGMAN, Denise
"Photo: The Dump." [Contact] (11:65/66/67) Spr 93, p. 23.
493. BERGMAN, Susan
"Fire." [PraS] (67:3) Fall 93, p. 90-91.
"Sight." [PraS] (67:3) Fall 93, p. 91-92.
"Water." [PraS] (67:3) Fall 93, p. 93-94.
"Wind." [PraS] (67:3) Fall 93, p. 89-90.
494. BERKE, Judith
"Hook." [MassR] (34:4) Wint 93-94, p. 590.

64

"Hotel Beach / After the Hurricane." [ParisR] (35:127) Sum 93, p. 134.
"In Which Nothing Is As It Seems: Vizcaya." [ParisR] (35:127) Sum 93, p. 135-136.
"The Names." [MassR] (33:4) Wint 92-93, p. 580.
"Quetzalcoatl." [MassR] (34:4) Wint 93-94, p. 591.
"Which Do You Prefer." [NewL] (59:3) 93, p. 89.
495. BERLAND, Dinah
"Milk Glass." [Ploughs] (19:1) Spr 93, p. 170.
"Ninth Month." [Pearl] (17) Spr 93, p. 96.
"The Poet Has No Privacy." [HayF] (12) Spr-Sum 93, p. 67.
"Your Secret Life." [YellowS] (43) Fall 93, p. 24.
496. BERLANDT, Herman
"Communication." [PoetryUSA] (25/26) 93, p. 43.
497. BERLIN, Jason
"Intimations of Snowlight in Autumn" (for Derek Walcott). [HarvardA] (127:2) Wint
     93, p. 8.
498. BERLIND, Bruce
"Before a Rendezvous" (tr. of Gyorgy Petri, w. Mária Körösy). [ConnPR] (12:1) 93,
     p. 6.
"Bell Inscription" (Ars Poetica, tr. of Sándor Kányádi, w. Mária Körösy). [WillowS]
     (33) Wint 93, p. 23.
"Canto" (tr. of Ottó Orbán, w. Mária Körösy). [CharR] (19:2) Fall 93, p. 144-145.
"Comparison" (tr. of Agnes Nemes Nagy). [AmerPoR] (22:1) Ja-F 93, p. 7.
"Crisis" (tr. of Gyorgy Petri, w. Mária Körösy). [ConnPR] (12:1) 93, p. 5.
"Five Verse Memoirs" (Selection: "4. Chopcock"). [Agni] (37) 93, p. 296-297.
"The Geyser" (tr. of Agnes Nemes Nagy). [AmerPoR] (22:1) Ja-F 93, p. 5-6.
"How Many" (tr. of Imre Oravecz, w. Mária Körösy). [ProseP] (1) 92, p. 65.
"I Remember Clearly" (tr. of Imre Oravecz, w. Mária Körösy). [ProseP] (1) 92, p. 66 -
     67.
"It Happened in the Afternoon" (tr. of Imre Oravecz). [ProseP] (2) 93, p. 72-73.
"Mane and Skull" (a fragment, tr. of Sándor Kányádi, w. Mária Körösy). [WillowS]
     (33) Wint 93, p. 22.
"Minneapolis Intersection" (a topographical poem, to Ken Bales, tr. of Ottó Orbán, w.
     Mária Körösy). [CharR] (19:2) Fall 93, p. 140-141.
"Now Then" (tr. of Imre Oravecz). [ProseP] (2) 93, p. 74-75.
"Oklahoma Gold" (tr. of Ottó Orbán, w. Mária Körösy). [CharR] (19:2) Fall 93, p.
     142-143.
"On My Fifty-First Birthday in Minneapolis" (tr. of Ottó Orbán, w. Mária Körösy).
     [CharR] (19:2) Fall 93, p. 147.
"September, 1972" (2 selections, tr. of Imre Oravecz). [Talisman] (11) Fall 93, p.
     266-267.
"September, 1972" (3 selections, tr. of Imre Oravecz). [Talisman] (10) Spr 93, p. 79 -
     81.
"The Sleeping Horsemen" (tr. of Agnes Nemes Nagy). [AmerPoR] (22:1) Ja-F 93, p.
     6.
"Snow" (Eyewitness News, Channel Five, Minneapolis-St. Paul, tr. of Ottó Orbán, w.
     Mária Körösy). [CharR] (19:2) Fall 93, p. 140.
"Statues" (tr. of Agnes Nemes Nagy). [AmerPoR] (22:1) Ja-F 93, p. 5.
"Stopgap Arrangement" (tr. of Gyorgy Petri, w. Mária Körösy). [ConnPR] (12:1) 93,
     p. 9.
"Successful Effort" (tr. of Gyula Illyés, w. Mária Körösy). [ProseP] (1) 92, p. 43.
"Sunday in a Small American Town" (tr. of Ottó Orbán, w. Mária Körösy). [CharR]
     (19:2) Fall 93, p. 146.
"Thus I Registered" (tr. of Gyorgy Petri, w. Mária Körösy). [ConnPR] (12:1) 93, p.
     10.
"To Kornis" (tr. of Gyorgy Petri, w. Mária Körösy). [ConnPR] (12:1) 93, p. 11.
"Today, Accidentally" (tr. of Imre Oravecz). [BostonR] (18:1) Ja-F 93, p. 25.
"Trees" (tr. of Agnes Nemes Nagy). [AmerPoR] (22:1) Ja-F 93, p. 6-7.
"University Commencement" ("The National Weather Service has issued a tornado
     warning," tr. of Ottó Orbán, w. Mária Körösy). [CharR] (19:2) Fall 93, p. 147.
499. BERLINER, Nancy
"The Terrible Fear." [NewYorkQ] (52) 93, p. 77.
500. BERMAN, Ruth
"Camera Obscurant." [SoDakR] (31:3) Fall 93, p. 139.
501. BERNATH, James
"Mylady Lives Unto the World." [Plain] (13:3) Spr 93, p. 31.

502. BERNHARD, J.
    "E. W. Burns Shoe Salesman." [BellArk] (9:5) S-O 93, p. 14.
    "Motorcycle Nightmare." [BellArk] (9:5) S-O 93, p. 14.
    "Three Weeks Back from Saigon." [BellArk] (9:5) S-O 93, p. 14.
503. BERNSTEIN, Charles
    "Almost There." [RiverS] (39) 93, p. 2.
    "Dark City." [Avec] (6:1) 93, p. 5-10.
    "Emma's Nursery Rimes." [WashR] (19:1) Je-Jl 93, p. 12.
    "Nickey, Turn Off the Lights." [RiverS] (39) 93, p. 3.
504. BERNSTEIN, Kim
    "Even still perception moves." [Talisman] (10) Spr 93, p. 141.
505. BERNSTEIN, Laura
    "Insomnia After Moving." [PoetryNW] (34:3) Aut 93, p. 19-20.
    "Sorting Papers Before Leaving." [PoetryNW] (34:3) Aut 93, p. 17-18.
    "To Those Who Fear Explosions." [BlackWR] (19:2) Spr-Sum 93, p. 127-128.
    "Transfer." [PoetryNW] (34:3) Aut 93, p. 18-19.
    "We're All Angels Under the Skin." [PoetryNW] (34:4) Wint 93-94, p. 42-43.
    "What I Missed When I Left Before Summer." [PoetryNW] (34:4) Wint 93-94, p. 42.
    "What You Remember About Natural Disasters." [PoetryNW] (34:3) Aut 93, p. 20 -
       21.
506. BERNSTEIN, Richard
    "Sea Wolves." [AnthNEW] (5) 93, p. 14.
507. BEROLD, Robert
    "Two Meditations on Chuang Tsu." [BostonR] (18:3/4) Je-Ag 93, p. 33.
508. BERRIAN, Joyce
    "Lifestory #3." [Footwork] (23) 93, p. 109.
    "Out in the Barn." [Footwork] (23) 93, p. 109.
509. BERRIGAN, Edmund
    "Midnight." [HangL] (62) 93, p. 20.
    "Storyline." [HangL] (62) 93, p. 20.
510. BERRY, D. C.
    "Ball" (for Em and Daryl). [XavierR] (13:1) Spr 93, p. 75.
    "Betty's Birthday." [CimR] (104) Jl 93, p. 151.
    "Hog Myth." [CimR] (104) Jl 93, p. 150.
    "Mother" (for my sister). [PoetC] (24:2) Wint 93, p. 8.
    "Students." [PoetC] (24:2) Wint 93, p. 7.
    "Wishbone." [SouthernR] (29:4) Aut, O 93, p. 720.
511. BERRY, Jake
    "After Observing American Bureaucracy 10.91." [HeavenB] (10) Wint-Spr 93, p. 44.
    "Can I speak" (from Brambu Drezi). [PoetryUSA] (25/26) 93, p. 26.
    "Ear   virus I (character) • (dementia)Ivirus" (from Brambu Drezi). [PoetryUSA]
       (25/26) 93, p. 10.
    "Election Year." [HeavenB] (10) Wint-Spr 93, p. 3.
    "Essay: Empire Poets" (for Jack Foley and Michael McClure). [HeavenB] (10) Wint -
       Spr 93, p. 56-57.
    "Facing the Leopard" (from Brambu Drezi). [PoetryUSA] (25/26) 93, p. 13.
    "House of the Sun." [PoetryUSA] (25/26) 93, p. 12.
    "Imago . . . to let bloods divide" (from Brambu Drezi). [PoetryUSA] (25/26) 93, p.
       11.
    "It moves and you're standing a stone" (from Brambu Drezi). [PoetryUSA] (25/26)
       93, p. 23.
    "KI som nah, Can speak" (from Brambu Drezi). [PoetryUSA] (25/26) 93, p. 11.
    "Redding fur" (from Brambu Drezi). [PoetryUSA] (25/26) 93, p. 15.
    "There are snakes in the water" (from Brambu Drezi). [PoetryUSA] (25/26) 93, p. 16.
    "Tunnel." [HeavenB] (10) Wint-Spr 93, p. 44.
512. BERRY, Mary
    "Beach Post Office." [Pearl] (19) Fall-Wint 93, p. 73.
513. BERRY, Paul
    "Golden Moments of English Verse" (Excerpt). [Bogg] (66) Wint 92-93, p. 16.
514. BERRY, Roger
    "Last August" (Honorable Mention, 7th Annual Contest). [SoCoast] (15) Je 93, p. 3.
515. BERRY, Wendell
    "The Farm." [Hudson] (46:1) Spr 93, p. 123-134.
516. BERRYMAN, John
    "Message." [AmerPoR] (22:5) S-O 93, p. 29.

517. BERSSENBRUGGE, Mei-mei
"Combustion." [NewAW] (11) Sum-Fall 93, p. 63-64.
"Pollen." [Conjunc] (20) 93, p. 135-139.
"Sphericity." [GrandS] (11:4, #44) 93, p. 174-175.
"Value." [NewEngR] (15:3) Sum 93, p. 7-9.
518. BERTIN, Kate
"Expectations." [Amelia] (7:2, #21) 93, p. 84.
519. BERTO, Al
"Hermitage" (tr. by Richard Zimler). [JamesWR] (11:1) Fall 93, p. 18.
"A Return to Simple Stories" (tr. by Richard Zimler). [JamesWR] (11:1) Fall 93, p. 20.
520. BERTO, T.
"Shawnee National Forest." [CanLit] (137) Sum 93, p. 49-50.
521. BERTOLINO, James
"The Body Holographic." [QRL] (12:32/33) 93, p. 43.
"The Flying Dwarf." [QRL] (12:32/33) 93, p. 37.
"Indra's Falls." [QRL] (12:32/33) 93, p. 40-41.
"The Landscape." [PaintedB] (50/51) 93, p. 43.
"Lines to Restore Van Gogh's Ear." [QRL] (12:32/33) 93, p. 38.
"Metabolism: A Letter." [QRL] (12:32/33) 93, p. 39.
"Octopus." [Gypsy] (20) Sum 93, p. 19.
"Paranormal Boot Camp." [OnTheBus] (6:1, #13) Wint 93-Spr 94, p. 54.
"Rescue: A Letter." [QRL] (12:32/33) 93, p. 40.
"Second Coming." [QRL] (12:32/33) 93, p. 43-44.
"See Willow." [QRL] (12:32/33) 93, p. 41-42.
"Snail River." [QRL] (12:32/33) 93, p. 42.
"A Wedding Toast." [QRL] (12:32/33) 93, p. 39.
522. BERTOLUCCI, Attilio
"April for B—" (tr. by Charles Tomlinson). [TriQ] (88) Fall 93, p. 25.
"Fires in November" (tr. by Charles Tomlinson). [TriQ] (88) Fall 93, p. 24.
"October" (tr. by Charles Tomlinson). [TriQ] (88) Fall 93, p. 26.
"To Giuseppe in October" (tr. by Charles Tomlinson). [TriQ] (88) Fall 93, p. 28.
"To His Mother Whose Name Was Maria" (tr. by Charles Tomlinson). [TriQ] (88) Fall 93, p. 27.
523. BERTON, Melissa
"Temperamental" (recipient of The Hellas Award, 1993). [Hellas] (4:2) Fall 93, p. 53.
524. BERZINS, Uldis
"First Snow" (tr. by Ingus Josts). [CimR] (104) Jl 93, p. 39.
"Moralizing Prose" (tr. by Ingus Josts). [CimR] (104) Jl 93, p. 39.
525. BESKIN, Lisa
"Cronos and His Children" (for Freud and Melanie Klein). [NewYorkQ] (51) 93, p. 78.
526. BESS, Robert
"105 Degrees." [Light] (5) Spr 93, p. 21.
527. BETHANIS, Peter
"Barn." [Blueline] (14) 93, p. 36.
"Fishing with Uncle." [Blueline] (14) 93, p. 37.
"The Kitchen Table." [Blueline] (14) 93, p. 38.
528. BETTRIDGE, Michael G.
"Night Light" (A Plainsongs Award Poem). [Plain] (13:2) Wint 93, p. 5.
529. BEVERIDGE, Robert P.
"Redhead." [Bogg] (66) Wint 92-93, p. 46.
530. BEYER, Lynne
"Air." [GrandS] (12:2, #46) Sum 93, p. 214.
"Krishnamurti's Journal." [GrandS] (12:2, #46) Sum 93, p. 213.
"More Humans." [AnotherCM] (25) Spr 93, p. 9.
"Naked." [AnotherCM] (25) Spr 93, p. 7.
"Spin." [Talisman] (11) Fall 93, p. 253.
"Surrender." [Talisman] (11) Fall 93, p. 254.
"Symmetrical." [AnotherCM] (25) Spr 93, p. 8.
531. BHARATA
"Come Nandaka, let's give the lion's roar" (Songs from the Theragatha: Songs of the Buddhist Monks, circa 450 B.C.E.). [Tricycle] (2:3) Spr 93, p. 39.
532. BHASIN, Mohit
"Hooked Bait." [Callaloo] (16:2) Spr 93, p. 325.

67

533. BIANCO, Adriana
   "Poemas Recurrentes / Si Puedes Quémate, Oh Baby / Poemas Californianos"
      (Selection: IX). [Luz] (5) N 93, p. 71.
534. BIBLE. O.T. Song of Songs
   "Lyrics from the Song of Songs" (tr. by Ariel and Chana Bloch). [Iowa] (23:1) Wint
      93, p. 1-4.
   "Song of Songs" (Selections: 5:2-8, 2:4-7, tr. by Ariel and Chana Bloch). [Poetry]
      (163:2) N 93, p. 83-84.
535. BIEHL, Michael
   "Kansas 1888." [GrahamHR] (17) Fall 93, p. 46.
   "Saint Beethoven." [GrahamHR] (17) Fall 93, p. 45.
   "Senior Tax Accountant at Star Field, Inc." [GrahamHR] (17) Fall 93, p. 44.
536. BIELE, Joelle
   "The Feast of Saint Joseph." [IndR] (16:2) Fall 93, p. 32-34.
   "When Kingship Descended from Heaven." [PoetryNW] (34:4) Wint 93-94, p. 3-8.
   "White Herons." [IndR] (16:2) Fall 93, p. 28-29.
   "Whitemarsh Graveyard." [IndR] (16:2) Fall 93, p. 30-31.
537. BIEN, Jeff
   "Almost Spring." [PoetryC] (13:2) 93, p. 7.
   "Buttons." [AntigR] (95) Aut 93, p. 18.
   "The Language of Rilke." [PoetryC] (13:2) 93, p. 6.
   "Parenthetic." [PoetryC] (13:2) 93, p. 6.
   "Rooms." [PoetryC] (13:2) 93, p. 7.
   "Ropes." [AntigR] (95) Aut 93, p. 16-17.
538. BIENEN, Leslie
   "Icarus." [CreamCR] (17:1) Spr 93, p. 15.
   "Night Landing in a Light Rain." [PaintedB] (49) 93, p. 7.
539. BIENKOWSKI, Brian
   "Picture in the Attic." [JlNJPo] (15:2) Aut 93, p. 14-15.
540. BIENVENU, Roberta
   "Early Spring." [OhioR] (50) 93, p. 104.
   "The Green Car." [OhioR] (50) 93, p. 105.
541. BIERDS, Linda
   "The Fish." [NewYorker] (69:21) 12 Jl 93, p. 47.
542. BIERON, Tomek
   "Germany, Bavaria" (tr. of Krzysztof Koehler). [Verse] (10:2) Sum 93, p. 40.
   "Manoeuvres" (tr. of Wojciech Wilczyk). [Verse] (10:2) Sum 93, p. 37.
   "Translation from the Chinese" (tr. of Wojciech Wilczyk). [Verse] (10:2) Sum 93, p.
      37.
543. BIESPIEL, David
   "On Earth As It Is in Heaven." [Journal] (17:1) Spr-Sum 93, p. 66-69.
544. BIGGINS, Michael
   "Occurrence" (tr. of Edvard Kocbek). [GrandS] (11:4, #44) 93, p. 203.
   "A Plea" (tr. of Edvard Kocbek). [GrandS] (11:4, #44) 93, p. 204-205.
545. BILGERE, George
   "The Going." [TarRP] (33:1) Fall 93, p. 48.
   "Open House." [TarRP] (33:1) Fall 93, p. 49.
   "Reunion." [Shen] (43:4) Wint 93, p. 80.
   "Sunday Night." [LitR] (37:1) Fall 93, p. 72.
   "Tryst." [Shen] (43:4) Wint 93, p. 79.
   "Zones of Embarkation." [IndR] (16:1) Spr 93, p. 131.
546. BILL, Jim
   "According to Legend." [SlipS] (13) 93, p. 32.
   "Double Crossers." [HampSPR] Wint 93, p. 74.
   "Fool Thoughts." [HiramPoR] (53/54) Fall 92-Sum 93, p. 23.
   "Mr. Cleaver Explains a Contemporary Poet to the Beave." [CapeR] (28:2) Fall 93, p.
      19.
   "Unto You a Cube Is Given." [Plain] (14:1) Fall 93, p. 13.
547. BILLINGS, Philip
   "Holding Out" (Carrie Stober). [WestB] (31/32) 93, p. 91-93.
   "The Old Stories, the Red Peppers" (Nellie Bernarda). [WestB] (31/32) 93, p. 81-90.
548. BILODEAU, Otis
   "Errata" (tr. of Juan Gelman). [MassR] (33:4) Wint 92-93, p. 614-615.
   "Lament for the Death of Parsifal Hoolig" (tr. of Juan Gelman). [MassR] (33:4) Wint
      92-93, p. 612-613.

"Lament for the Nape of Tom Steward's Neck" (tr. of Juan Gelman). [MassR] (33:4) Wint 92-93, p. 613-614.
549. BILYEU, Jody
"Downtown, Lindberg's, Featuring the Belairs." [CimR] (103) Ap 93, p. 98-99.
"Four Coffees." [LouisL] (10:1) Spr 93, p. 57-59.
BINH, Dang The
See DANG, The Binh
550. BIRCHARD, Guy
"The Efficacy of Anything." [WestCL] (27:2, #11) Fall 93, p. 10.
"The Favour of 40 Years." [WestCL] (27:2, #11) Fall 93, p. 12.
"Guy's Boast." [WestCL] (27:2, #11) Fall 93, p. 7.
"A Matter of Indifference." [WestCL] (27:2, #11) Fall 93, p. 11.
"Standing Wave Standing Sill." [WestCL] (27:2, #11) Fall 93, p. 8.
"They Polka'd Till His Shoe Broke." [WestCL] (27:2, #11) Fall 93, p. 9.
551. BIRDSEY, Tal
"At Quarry Hill Cemetery, an Angel." [CapeR] (28:1) Spr 93, p. 40.
552. BISHOP, Elizabeth
"For M. M." (suggested by a poem of Pablo Neruda). [QRL] (12:32/33) 93, p. 379 - 380.
553. BISHOP, Suzette
"But When She Gets to Her Dream Place" (Selection: Section II). [13thMoon] (12:1/2) 93-94, p. 8-9.
554. BISHOP, Wendy
"Built to Commemorate an Indian Burial Ground." [EngJ] (82:8) D 93, p. 83.
"Myrtle Brocee Amends *The Klondike Nugget* from Heaven." [ApalQ] (36/37) 91, p. 87-88.
"The Romantic Subway." [ApalQ] (36/37) 91, p. 89-90.
555. BITA, Lili
"Clytemnestras" (tr. by Robert Zaller). [AmerPoR] (22:3) My-Je 93, p. 43.
"The Debut" (tr. by Robert Zaller). [AmerPoR] (22:3) My-Je 93, p. 43.
"Today" (tr. by Robert Zaller). [AmerPoR] (22:3) My-Je 93, p. 43.
BITEK, Okot p'
See p'BITEK, Okot
556. BITTING, Dotty E.
"The Slush Pile." [Writer] (106:10) O 93, p. 2.
557. BLACK, Ayanna
"A Pretty Baby Girl in a da Nursery" (from *No Contingencies*). [WestCL] (27:1, #10) Spr 93, p. 54.
558. BLACK, Candace
"Royal Poinciana." [Conscience] (14:4) Wint 93-94, p. 8.
559. BLACK, D. M.
"The Bumble Bee." [Verse] (10:2) Sum 93, p. 6.
560. BLACK, David
"The Old Man Talks About, Among Other Things, Fireflies." [BellArk] (9:3) My-Je 93, p. 19.
561. BLACK, R. D.
"Bastille Day." [CapeR] (28:1) Spr 93, p. 49.
562. BLACK, Ralph W.
"Ghosting" (from "Firefighter's Testimonial"). [Nimrod] (37:1) Fall-Wint 93, p. 69.
BLACK, Sophie Cabot
See CABOT-BLACK, Sophie
563. BLACKARD, John A.
"The Easter Bunny Talks." [Crucible] (29) Fall 93, p. 32-34.
564. BLACKBIRD, Kat Snider
"Coven Poems" (13 poems). [MidwQ] (34:4) Sum 93, p. 416-421.
"Great Blue Heron Poems" (5 poems). [MidwQ] (34:4) Sum 93, p. 422-525.
565. BLACKBURN, Charles F., Jr.
"Saul's House." [Crucible] (29) Fall 93, p. 21-23.
566. BLACKBURN, Paul
"Poem of the Cid" (Selections, tr. of the anonymous poem "El Cid"). [Sulfur] (33) Fall 93, p. 175-184.
567. BLACKHAWK, Terry
"Waterworks." [ColEng] (55:1) Ja 93, p. 77-78.
568. BLACKWOMON, Julie
"Late Anger in a Cathedral." [SinW] (50) Sum-Fall 93, p. 73-74.

BLADE, Razor
See RAZOR BLADE
569. BLAIR FARNHAM
"E.J. Bellocq: Storyville Portraits, 1912." [BelPoJ] (43:3) Spr 93, p. 34-35.
570. BLAKE, Penny
"Desert Storm's Unknown Soldier." [AnthNEW] (5) 93, p. 13.
571. BLAKE, Rosemary
"For a Friend Who Died Three Days Before His Letter Came." [AntigR] (95) Aut 93,
p. 10.
"Nights." [AntigR] (95) Aut 93, p. 9.
"Sans Souci." [AntigR] (95) Aut 93, p. 8.
"Wintering." [AntigR] (95) Aut 93, p. 7.
572. BLAKE, Sarah
"On Snow Mountain." [Thrpny] (54) Sum 93, p. 17.
BLANC, Diane Le
See LeBLANC, Diane
573. BLANCHARD, Len
"Beach Sight." [Gaia] (1/2) Ap-Jl 93, p. 35-36.
"Crossing Big Cypress." [BellArk] (9:5) S-O 93, p. 6.
"Love's Vocabulary." [JamesWR] (11:1) Fall 93, p. 22.
574. BLANCHFIELD, Brian
"Early Morning Mire with Betty" (Second Place, Annual Poetry Contest). [PaintedB]
(49) 93, p. 41.
575. BLANCO, Alberto
"Why So Many Forms" (tr. by John Oliver Simon). [Agni] (38) 93, p. 4.
576. BLANCO AMORES de PAGELLA, Angela
"Un Soneto a lo Inalcanzable." [Luz] (5) N 93, p. 76.
577. BLAND, Celia
"White Lungs." [PoetL] (88:3) Fall 93, p. 19-20.
578. BLAND, James
"Five Verses." [Agni] (37) 93, p. 69.
"On African-American Aesthetics." [Ploughs] (19:4) Wint 93-94, p. 144.
579. BLANDIANA, Anna
"Pieta" (tr. by Adam Sorkin and Ioana Ieronim). [Vis] (41) 93, p. 39.
580. BLASING, Randy
"Cardiogram." [Poetry] (162:6) S 93, p. 334.
"Man of Letters." [Poetry] (162:6) S 93, p. 333.
581. BLATNER, Barbara
"Letter." [13thMoon] (11:1/2) 93, p. 8.
582. BLAUNER, Laurie
"The Children of Gravity" (for T.A.). [ColEng] (55:2) F 93, p. 207.
"Growing Ordinary." [PoetryNW] (34:3) Aut 93, p. 47.
"In One Version of the Shape of Things to Come." [OnTheBus] (5:2, #12) Sum-Fall
93, p. 44.
"Life in the Movies." [OnTheBus] (5:2, #12) Sum-Fall 93, p. 44.
"Matisse in the Company of Strangers." [Poetry] (161:6) Mr 93, p. 324.
"Two Views of a Beautiful Woman in the Same Mirror." [PoetryNW] (34:3) Aut 93,
p. 46-47.
"Where the Stars Disintegrate." [NewRep] (209:8/9) 23-30 Ag 93, p. 44.
583. BLAYLOCK, Robin
"Mi Gato de Copo de Nieve" (from "Families, Streets and Dreams," a
poetry/photography event by 3rd grade students, Whittier Elementary, Tulsa).
[Nimrod] (37:1) Fall-Wint 93, p. 86.
"My Cat Snowflake" (from "Families, Streets and Dreams," a poetry/photography
event by 3rd grade students, Whittier Elementary, Tulsa). [Nimrod] (37:1)
Fall-Wint 93, p. 86.
584. BLAZEK, Douglas
"A Real Event" (for Alta). [PaintedB] (50/51) 93, p. 44.
585. BLEHERT, Dean
"Bogged in Ogden." [Light] (5) Spr 93, p. 24.
"How Grimly They Bare It." [Light] (8) Wint 93, p. 14.
"Innocence." [Bogg] (66) Wint 92-93, p. 39.
586. BLEOCA, Liviu
"Seven Lean Cows" (tr. of Aurel Rau, w. Adam J. Sorkin). [LullwaterR] (4:2) Spr -
Sum 93, p. 12.
"Sign" (tr. of Aurel Rau, w. Adam J. Sorkin). [LullwaterR] (4:2) Spr-Sum 93, p. 123.

587. BLETSOE, Elisabeth
    "Rose and Amelie." [CoalC] (7) Apr 93, p. 44.
588. BLEVINS-CHURCH, Adrian
    "Kissing Faulkner." [ContextS] (3:1) 93, p. 25-26.
589. BLINN, Denise Berkshire
    "Prairie Boy Waltz." [PraF] (14:3) Aut 93, p. 22.
590. BLOCH, Ariel
    "Lyrics from the Song of Songs" (tr. of Bible. O.T. Song of Songs, w. Chana Bloch).
        [Iowa] (23:1) Wint 93, p. 1-4.
    "Song of Songs" (Selections: 5:2-8, 2:4-7, tr. of Bible. O.T., w. Chana Bloch).
        [Poetry] (163:2) N 93, p. 83-84.
591. BLOCH, Chana
    "Autumn Rain in Tel Aviv" (tr. of Yehuda Amichai). [Trans] (28) Spr 93, p. 108.
    "A Flock of Sheep Near the Airport" (tr. of Yehuda Amichai). [Trans] (28) Spr 93, p.
        107.
    "Lyrics from the Song of Songs" (tr. of Bible. O.T. Song of Songs, w. Ariel Bloch).
        [Iowa] (23:1) Wint 93, p. 1-4.
    "Song of Songs" (Selections: 5:2-8, 2:4-7, tr. of Bible. O.T., w. Ariel Bloch). [Poetry]
        (163:2) N 93, p. 83-84.
592. BLOCK, Jonathan
    "Gouldsboro Bay." [Bogg] (66) Wint 92-93, p. 18.
593. BLOCK, Laurie
    "The Consolation of Small Engines." [TickleAce] (23) Spr-Sum 92, p. 40-41.
594. BLOK, Alexander
    "Snow Wine" (tr. by Stephen Unsino). [TampaR] (6) Spr 93, p. 41.
595. BLOMAIN, Karen
    "First Night." [PaintedB] (49) 93, p. 20-21.
    "The Molly D. Mine." [PaintedB] (50/51) 93, p. 95.
    "Moving." [Sun] (205) Ja 93, p. 19.
596. BLONSTEIN, Anne
    "Herbstzeitlose." [Stand] (34:3) Sum 93, p. 12.
597. BLOOM, Barbara
    "Reading Your Poem on Miracles." [NorthStoneR] (11) 93, p. 129.
598. BLOOM, Ronna
    "Maybe You're with Me." [Writ] (25) 93, p. 29-30.
    "The Meeting of the Weather." [Writ] (25) 93, p. 26.
    "What a Kick Feels Like." [Writ] (25) 93, p. 27-28.
599. BLOOMFIELD, Maureen
    "Y W H." [WestHR] (47:4) Wint 93, p. 356.
600. BLOUNT, Chriscinthia
    "Her Favorite Color" (tr. by Antonio Cruz). [Footwork] (23) 93, p. 161.
    "Su Color Preferido." [Footwork] (23) 93, p. 161.
601. BLOYD, Rebekah
    "Dragon Bay." [CinPR] (24) Spr 93, p. 43-45.
602. BLUE, Jane
    "The Bee Man." [ProseP] (1) 92, p. 12.
603. BLUE CLOUD, Peter
    "Backward Dancer." [Contact] (11:65/66/67) Spr 93, p. 38-40.
604. BLY, Robert
    "Blessings on the Stomach, the Body's Inner Furnace." [MichQR] (32:4) Fall 93, p.
        597.
    "Dolly." [PaintedB] (50/51) 93, p. 78.
    "A Dream of William Carlos Williams." [AmerPoR] (22:4) Jl-Ag 93, p. 33.
    "The Exhausted Bug" (for my father). [AmerPoR] (22:4) Jl-Ag 93, p. 33.
    "The Gaiety of Form." [AmerPoR] (22:1) Ja-F 93, p. 12.
    "Holes in Our Speech." [Agni] (38) 93, p. 18.
    "My Father's Neck." [AmerPoR] (22:1) Ja-F 93, p. 12.
    "On the Oregon Coast" (for William Stafford). [AmerPoR] (22:4) Jl-Ag 93, p. 34.
    "An Open Rose." [ProseP] (2) 93, p. 13.
    "Poem for the Revival of the Democratic Party." [Nat] (256:6) 15 F 93, p. 210.
    "Poems on the Voyage." [QRL] (12:32/33) 93, p. 381-384.
    "Two Men Swimming." [HarvardR] (3) Wint 93, p. 47-48.
    "Two Ramages for Old Masters." [AmerPoR] (22:4) Jl-Ag 93, p. 33.
    "Warning to the Reader." [ProseP] (1) 92, p. 9.
BO, Zhang Xiao
    See ZHANG, Xiao Bo

71

BOARDMAN

BOARDMAN, Paul Harris
See HARRIS-BOARDMAN, Paul
605. BOBROWSKI, Johannes
"Elderberry-Blossom" (tr. by Gisela Argyle). [PoetryC] (13:2) 93, p. 23.
"Pruzzian Elegy" (tr. by Ruth and Matthew Mead). [QRL] (12:32/33) 93, p. 384-386.
606. BOCK, Kristin
"Eve As a Paperdoll." [NewYorkQ] (51) 93, p. 89.
607. BODENHEIM, Maxwell
"Fantasy" (From "The Sardonic Arm." The Free Lunch Reprise Series). [FreeL] (11)
Wint 93, p. 8-10.
608. BODUNDE, Charles
"Herald." [SpoonR] (18:2) Sum-Fall 93, p. 92-94.
"Passage." [SpoonR] (18:2) Sum-Fall 93, p. 95-96.
609. BOE, Deborah
"Country and Western." [HangL] (62) 93, p. 21.
"Reading by Christmas Light." [HangL] (62) 93, p. 22.
610. BOEKE, Wanda
"Canto" (tr. of Petr Mikes, w. the author). [OxfordM] (9:1) Spr-Sum 93, p. 115.
"I'm tortured" (tr. of Petr Mikes, w. the author). [OxfordM] (9:1) Spr-Sum 93, p. 113.
"A Lost Street" (tr. of Petr Mikes, w. the author). [OxfordM] (9:1) Spr-Sum 93, p.
114.
"The Memory of the Wound III" (tr. of Petr Mikes, w. the author). [OxfordM] (9:1)
Spr-Sum 93, p. 114.
"Parable" (tr. of Petr Mikes, w. the author). [OxfordM] (9:1) Spr-Sum 93, p. 113.
"The space of my sleep" (tr. of Petr Mikes, w. the author). [OxfordM] (9:1) Spr-Sum
93, p. 114.
"To Ross and His Children" (tr. of Petr Mikes, w. the author). [OxfordM] (9:1) Spr-
Sum 93, p. 113-114.
"To William Blake" (tr. of Petr Mikes, w. the author). [OxfordM] (9:1) Spr-Sum 93,
p. 115.
611. BOES, Don
"July Funeral." [HayF] (13) Fall-Wint 93, p. 43.
"Spark." [HayF] (13) Fall-Wint 93, p. 44.
612. BOGEN, Don
"La Clairière." [Poetry] (162:2) My 93, p. 83.
"Musée." [Poetry] (162:2) My 93, p. 84.
613. BOGEN, Laurel Ann
"Journal Entry from an Empty Hand." [ChironR] (12:4/13:1, #37/38) Wint 93-Spr 94,
p. 43.
"Prologue: The Waldorf Astoria" (Family Album, New York, August 1963: "Or, The
Good Life As We Knew It"). [Pearl] (17) Spr 93, p. 18.
614. BOGGAN, Larry
"Hoatzin" (Opisthocomos hoatzin of the order Galliformes). [WebR] (17) Fall 93, p.
79-80.
"Roadside Flowers." [WebR] (17) Fall 93, p. 80.
615. BOGGIS, Jay
"Geography Lesson." [Agni] (38) 93, p. 116.
616. BOGIN, Magda
"Trilce" (Selections: I-III, IX-XI, XIII, XV, tr. of César Vallejo). [MassR] (34:2) Sum
93, p. 185-192.
617. BOGIN, Nina
"Lappland: Ammarnäs." [Poetry] (162:2) My 93, p. 93-94.
"Two Poems" (For my father). [Poetry] (162:2) My 93, p. 94-95.
618. BOGOTCH, Hal
"Bagpipe Dream." [OnTheBus] (6:1, #13) Wint 93-Spr 94, p. 55.
619. BOHANAN, Audrey
"Sad Cabin." [VirQR] (69:2) Spr 93, p. 259-260.
620. BOISSEAU, Michelle
"The Anatomy Theater at Padua" (title page, *De Humani Corporis Fabrica*, 1547).
[SouthernR] (29:2) Spr, Ap 93, p. 295-296.
"At the Stillborn Grave." [CreamCR] (17:2) Fall 93, p. 103.
"Black Mulberry." [GreenMR] (NS 6:2) Sum-Fall 93, p. 122-123.
"Cold Harbor." [Crazy] (44) Spr 93, p. 12-15.
"The Cry." [CreamCR] (17:2) Fall 93, p. 104-105.
"Family Formicidae." [Crazy] (44) Spr 93, p. 16-17.
"Fog." [GreenMR] (NS 6:2) Sum-Fall 93, p. 121.

72

BOISSEAU

"Forerunner." [Crazy] (44) Spr 93, p. 10-11.
"Gratia Plena." [CreamCR] (17:2) Fall 93, p. 106.
621. BÖK, Christian
"Crystals." [CapilR] (2:10) Spr 93, p. 41.
"Diamonds" (Selections: 1-6). [CapilR] (2:10) Spr 93, p. 42-47.
622. BOLAND, Eavan
"The Death of Reason." [Atlantic] (272:3) S 93, p. 51.
"In Which the Ancient History I Learn Is Not My Own." [Poetry] (161:4) Ja 93, p. 218-220.
"The Parcel." [NewRep] (208:20) 17 My 93, p. 46.
"The Pomegranate." [NewYorker] (69:35) 25 O 93, p. 78.
623. BOLDUC, David A.
"The Reality." [ChangingM] (26) Sum-Fall 93, p. 71.
624. BOLLS, Imogene
"Coyote Wind." [AntR] (51:4) Fall 93, p. 567.
"Memorizing the Mountain" (Taos, New Mexico. For Frank Waters). [WritersF] (19) 93, p. 4.
"Recognition." [WritersF] (19) 93, p. 5.
625. BOLSTER, Stephanie
"Alice, Waiting." [PraS] (67:4) Wint 93, p. 31.
"Alice's Right Foot, Esq." [PoetryC] (13:4) 93, p. 16.
"Balsamroot, Paintbrush and Lomatium on a Slope." [PraS] (67:4) Wint 93, p. 28.
"Birthday Presence." [AntigR] (95) Aut 93, p. 24.
"Crows." [AntigR] (95) Aut 93, p. 19.
"Daphnia." [PraS] (67:4) Wint 93, p. 30.
"Excuses 2." [PraF] (14:4) Wint 93-94, p. 54-55.
"The Foreground Is All Flowers" (After the painting, "A Basket of Summer Flowers in a Wooded Landscape," by Emma Thomsen, 1820-1897). [AntigR] (95) Aut 93, p. 25.
"Legends." [AntigR] (95) Aut 93, p. 22.
"The Night Becomes You." [AntigR] (95) Aut 93, p. 20-21.
"Queen of Hearts." [PraS] (67:4) Wint 93, p. 27.
"The Serpentine Is a Lovely Lake and There Is a Drowned Forest at the Bottom of It" (from a painting by Arthur Rackham, 1867-1939). [AntigR] (95) Aut 93, p. 23.
"Symbolic Logic." [PoetryC] (13:4) 93, p. 16.
"They Annotated Alice." [PoetryC] (13:4) 93, p. 16.
"Transformations." [MalR] (105) Wint 93, p. 90.
"Visitor from Overseas." [PoetryC] (13:4) 93, p. 16.
"Wall/paper" (for Charlotte Perkins Gilman, d. 1935). [PraS] (67:4) Wint 93, p. 29.
"Whose Eyes." [MalR] (105) Wint 93, p. 89.
626. BOLSTRIDGE, Alice
"Song of Mary, Leaking." [Kalliope] (15:2) 93, p. 24-25.
627. BOLT, Thomas
"Dark Ice." [Bomb] (45) Fall 93, p. 88-95.
628. BOLTON, Joe
"South Boulevard." [ApalQ] (36/37) 91, p. 65-66.
629. BOLZ, Jody
"Sombra de la Familia." [IndR] (16:1) Spr 93, p. 118-119.
BOMBARD, Joan La
See LaBOMBARD, Joan
630. BOMMARITO, Angela
"Summer View with Metronome." [Sonora] (26) Fall 93, p. 29-30.
631. BONAFFINI, Luigi
"Cain" (tr. of Giovanni Cerri). [Vis] (43) 93, p. 29.
"There Was a Time" (tr. of Achille Serrao). [Vis] (43) 93, p. 29.
"You see him come, always" (tr. of Achille Serrao). [Vis] (43) 93, p. 30.
632. BOND, Bruce
"Broken Circle." [WestHR] (47:2) Sum 93, p. 163.
"Caravaggio: The Supper at Emmaus." [QRL] (12:32/33) 93, p. 44-45.
"Cardinal." [QRL] (12:32/33) 93, p. 45.
"Cardinal." [Shen] (43:2) Sum 93, p. 104.
"Documentary." [ParisR] (35:128) Fall 93, p. 139-140.
"Elegiac Stanzas." [QRL] (12:32/33) 93, p. 45-46.
"The Last Great Flood." [QRL] (12:32/33) 93, p. 53.
"Legacy." [QRL] (12:32/33) 93, p. 46-48.

73

"Margin of Need." [QRL] (12:32/33) 93, p. 48-49.
"Naked Eye." [ParisR] (35:128) Fall 93, p. 140-141.
"North, 1991." [QRL] (12:32/33) 93, p. 49-50.
"On Certainty." [QRL] (12:32/33) 93, p. 50-51.
"Open Throat." [Thrpny] (55) Fall 93, p. 22.
"The Possible." [QRL] (12:32/33) 93, p. 51-52.
"The Possible." [Shen] (43:2) Sum 93, p. 105.
"Radiography." [WestHR] (47:3) Fall 93, p. 252-255.
"Taps." [Poetry] (161:6) Mr 93, p. 337.
"Taps." [QRL] (12:32/33) 93, p. 52-53.
633. BOND, Cynthia
"Reclamation." [Ascent] (18:1) Fall 93, p. 12.
"What You Want Means What You Can Afford." [Ascent] (18:1) Fall 93, p. 13.
634. BONDAR, Alanna F.
"I squashed a beetle walking across my carpet." [TickleAce] (26) Fall-Wint 93, p.
103.
635. BONDS, Diane
"The Life of the Body" (Edward Hopper's *People in the Sun*, 1960). [GeoR] (47:2)
Sum 93, p. 317-318.
"Together" (Edward Hopper's *Nighthawks*, 1942). [GeoR] (47:2) Sum 93, p. 315-
316.
BONGIORNO, Marylou Tibaldo
See TIBALDO-BONGIORNO, Marylou
636. BONNEFOY, Yves
"The Apples" (From "Début et fin de la neige," tr. by Lisa Sapinkopf). [GreenMR]
(NS 6:1) Wint-Spr 93, p. 156.
"Dedham, Seen from Langham" (Title of several paintings by Constable. Tr. by Lisa
Sapinkopf). [QRL] (12:32/33) 93, p. 58-61.
"The Dream's Restlessness" (tr. by Lisa Sapinkopf). [QRL] (12:32/33) 93, p. 56-58.
"The Farewell" (tr. by Lisa Sapinkopf). [QRL] (12:32/33) 93, p. 62-63.
"Fleeting Snow on scarf" (From "Début et fin de la neige," tr. by Lisa Sapinkopf).
[GreenMR] (NS 6:1) Wint-Spr 93, p. 155.
"Snowflakes" (From "Début et fin de la neige," tr. by Lisa Sapinkopf). [GreenMR]
(NS 6:1) Wint-Spr 93, p. 154.
"A Summer's Night" (tr. by Lisa Sapinkopf). [QRL] (12:32/33) 93, p. 54-55.
"The Swiftness of the Clouds" (tr. by Lisa Sapinkopf). [QRL] (12:32/33) 93, p. 61 -
62.
637. BOOKER, Stephen Todd
"Tripwire to a Halo." [Sonora] (24/25) Spr 93, p. 140-141.
638. BOOR, Paul J.
"Geese." [Blueline] (14) 93, p. 76.
639. BOOTH, Philip
"All-Night Radio." [DenQ] (27:4) Spr 93, p. 31.
"Linesquall." [YaleR] (81:2) Ap 93, p. 27.
"March Again." [Poetry] (161:6) Mr 93, p. 313.
"November Sun." [Poetry] (163:2) N 93, p. 72-73.
"Outlook." [Poetry] (161:6) Mr 93, p. 314.
"Pairs." [Atlantic] (271:4) Ap 93, p. 99.
"Sixty-Three." [OhioR] (50) 93, p. 58-59.
640. BORAN, Pat
"The Chinese Notebook" (Selections, tr. of Demosthenes Agrafiotis, w. the author,
Theo Dorgan, Tony Curtis, and Kate Newman). [Sulfur] (32) Spr 93, p. 206-
212.
641. BORDAO, Rafael
"Las Heridas del Hudson." [Trasimagen] (1:1) Otoño-Invierno 93, p. 41.
"Los Secretos Mas Blancos." [Trasimagen] (1:1) Otoño-Invierno 93, p. 41.
642. BORG, Shannon
"Catching Cold from a Lover." [PoetryNW] (34:3) Aut 93, p. 29.
"Hitchhiking Past the Drive-In." [PoetryNW] (34:3) Aut 93, p. 28-29.
"Returning to Town in Summer." [PoetryNW] (34:3) Aut 93, p. 27-28.
643. BORGES, Jorge Luis
"1891" (tr. by Robert Mezey). [ArtfulD] (24/25) 93, p. 45.
"Absence" (tr. by Robert Mezey, w. Naomi Mezey). [SenR] (23:1/2) Wint 93, p. 120.
"Allusion to the Death of Colonel Francisco Borges (1833-74)" (tr. by Robert Mezey
and R. G. Barnes). [NowestR] (31:3) 93, p. 59.
"Brunanburh, 937 A.D." (tr. by Richard Barnes). [MissouriR] (16:3) 93, p. 31.

"Buenos Aires" (tr. by Robert Mezey). [MissouriR] (16:3) 93, p. 32.
"A Compass" (tr. by Robert Mezey). [Poetry] (162:3) Je 93, p. 158.
"I Am" (tr. by Tony Barnstone). [LitR] (36:2) Wint 93, p. 143.
"In Memory of Angelica" (tr. by Tony Barnstone). [LitR] (36:2) Wint 93, p. 143.
"James Joyce" (tr. by Dick Barnes and Robert Mezey). [ArtfulD] (24/25) 93, p. 41.
"Junín" (tr. by Dick Barnes). [ArtfulD] (24/25) 93, p. 43.
"Limits" (tr. by R. G. Barnes and Robert Mezey). [Poetry] (162:3) Je 93, p. 157-158.
"The Night They Held a Wake on the Southside" (To Letizia Alvarez de Toledo, tr. by Robert Mezey). [MissouriR] (16:3) 93, p. 26-27.
"Of Which Nothing Is Known" (tr. by Robert Mezey). [SenR] (23:1/2) Wint 93, p. 124.
"On Forgetting a Dream" (To Viviana Aguilar, tr. by Robert Mezey and R. G. Barnes). [NowestR] (31:3) 93, p. 60.
"The Other Tiger" (tr. by Robert Mezey). [MissouriR] (16:3) 93, p. 28-29.
"Poem about Quantity" (tr. by Robert Mezey). [NewYRB] (40:12) 24 Je 93, p. 35.
"Religio Medici, 1643" (tr. by Robert Mezey). [SenR] (23:1/2) Wint 93, p. 119.
"Sleep" (tr. by Robert Mezey). [Poetry] (162:3) Je 93, p. 159.
"The Tango" (tr. by Robert Mezey). [SenR] (23:1/2) Wint 93, p. 121-123.
"Texas (2)" (tr. by Robert Mezey). [ArtfulD] (24/25) 93, p. 42.
"Things That Might Have Been" (tr. by Alastair Reid). [NewEngR] (15:1) Wint 93, p. 101.
"To a Coin" (tr. by Richard Barnes). [MissouriR] (16:3) 93, p. 30.
"To the One Reading Me" (tr. by Robert Mezey). [MissouriR] (16:3) 93, p. 25.
"Truco" (tr. by Dick Barnes and Robert Mezey). [ArtfulD] (24/25) 93, p. 44.
"Written in a Copy of the Geste of Beowulf" (tr. by R. G. Barnes). [Poetry] (162:3) Je 93, p. 159.
644. BORGES, Millicent C.
"Winter League Baseball." [Spitball] (45) Fall 93, p. 31.
645. BORICH, Barrie
"The Last Night That Stirred." [13thMoon] (11:1/2) 93, p. 17-18.
"Space" (On January 28, 1986 people across the United States watched on television as the Space Shuttle Challenger exploded. [13thMoon] (11:1/2) 93, p. 11.
"Too Fast for the Eye to Hold." [13thMoon] (11:1/2) 93, p. 15-16.
"The Watchers." [13thMoon] (11:1/2) 93, p. 9-10.
646. BORINSKY, Alicia
"Farewell Song for the Author" (tr. by Cola Franzen). [WorldL] (4) 93, p. 18.
"The Separation" (tr. by Cola Franzen). [WorldL] (4) 93, p. 19.
"Summer" (tr. by Cola Franzen). [WorldL] (4) 93, p. 18.
647. BORISOV, Georgi
"Gates" (tr. by Lisa Sapinkopf and Georgi Belev). [Paint] (19:38) Aut 92, p. 58.
"The Horse" (tr. by Lisa Sapinkopf and Georgi Belev). [Paint] (19:38) Aut 92, p. 59.
648. BORKHUIS, Charles
"Hypnogogic Sonnets" (Selections: IX-XI). [Caliban] (12) 93, p. 184-185.
"Instability." [Talisman] (11) Fall 93, p. 213-214.
"The Lighting Process." [Witness] (7:1) 93, p. 180.
"Severed Moon." [Talisman] (10) Spr 93, p. 153-154.
"Sky of Thorns." [HeavenB] (10) Wint-Spr 93, p. 9.
"This." [Asylum] (8) 93, p. 59.
649. BORKOVEC, Vera
"Dedication (A.M.P.)" (tr. of Jaroslav Seifert). [Vis] (43) 93, p. 15.
"Halley's Comet" (tr. of Jaroslav Seifert). [Vis] (43) 93, p. 13.
"The Weight of the Earth" (tr. of Jaroslav Seifert). [Vis] (43) 93, p. 14.
650. BORN, Anne
"The Great Alvar, Öland, Sweden." [CimR] (103) Ap 93, p. 82.
"I Talk About You" (tr. of Henrik Nordbrandt). [Verse] (10:1) Spr 93, p. 97.
651. BORNSTEIN, Judith
"My Woman" (tr. of Penelope Boutos). [Vis] (43) 93, p. 23.
"Note" (for Maria Varela). [Gypsy] (20) Sum 93, p. 18.
"Old Red" (tr. of Penelope Boutos). [Vis] (43) 93, p. 23.
652. BORRUS, Beth
"Adeline Stephen." [13thMoon] (12:1/2) 93-94, p. 10.
653. BORSON, Roo
"A Brightly Lit Ship" (w. Kim Maltman and Andy Patton in the collaborative writing group "Pain-not-Bread"). [PoetryC] (13:4) 93, p. 9.

75

"Chipmunks Enter the World of Don McKay and Jan Zwicky" (w. Kim Maltman and
    Andy Patton in the collaborative writing group "Pain-not-Bread"). [PoetryC]
    (13:4) 93, p. 9.
"Early Music." [MalR] (102) Spr 93, p. 53.
"George Bowering." [MalR] (102) Spr 93, p. 52.
"Hello Desire." [PraS] (67:4) Wint 93, p. 101-102.
"Introduction to the Introduction to Wang Wei" (w. Kim Maltman and Andy Patton.
    Winner of the 1993 Long Poem Prize). [MalR] (103) Sum 93, p. 16-27.
"Lying in Bed Reading Robert Gray." [MalR] (102) Spr 93, p. 54.
"Moon Tub." [PraS] (67:4) Wint 93, p. 101.
"Picnic Forest Crater Rhyme." [MalR] (102) Spr 93, p. 55-56.
"Pruner Speculates on Oscar Night" (w. Kim Maltman and Andy Patton in the
    collaborative writing group "Pain-not-Bread"). [PoetryC] (13:4) 93, p. 8.
"Spain." [Arc] (30) Spr 93, p. 19.
"Spring Light." [Arc] (30) Spr 93, p. 18.
"Thinking Clearly." [Arc] (30) Spr 93, p. 17.
"You Leave the City." [PraS] (67:4) Wint 93, p. 102.
654. BORUCH, Marianne
    "Ash Wednesday" (For Leonora Woodman). [Poetry] (161:5) F 93, p. 254.
    "At School." [Iowa] (23:2) Spr-Sum 93, p. 95-96.
    "At the Y." [Field] (48) Spr 93, p. 6-7.
    "The Bog." [SouthernR] (29:2) Spr, Ap 93, p. 304-305.
    "The Crickets." [Iowa] (23:2) Spr-Sum 93, p. 98.
    "Geese." [Iowa] (23:2) Spr-Sum 93, p. 96.
    "The Kingdom." [VirQR] (69:2) Spr 93, p. 263-264.
    "On Sorrow." [Iowa] (23:2) Spr-Sum 93, p. 97.
    "Then." [VirQR] (69:2) Spr 93, p. 265.
    "Total Eclipse." [GeoR] (47:1) Spr 93, p. 98-99.
    "Town Pool." [DenQ] (27:3) Wint 93, p. 12-13.
    "Tree." [DenQ] (27:3) Wint 93, p. 14.
    "Walking Home." [Field] (48) Spr 93, p. 5.
655. BOSCH, Daniel
    "The Crucible." [HarvardR] (4) Spr 93, p. 150.
656. BOSCHERT, Timothy
    "Love Song After Chet Baker." [Caliban] (12) 93, p. 145-146.
    "To Hernandez." [Caliban] (12) 93, p. 147.
657. BOSQUET, Alain
    "An Atheist's Creed" (10 selections, tr. by Edouard Roditi). [WorldL] (4) 93, p. 6-10.
658. BOSS, Laura
    "Sadie and Laura." [Footwork] (23) 93, p. 25.
659. BOSSELAAR, Laure-Anne
    "Days of Rules." [DenQ] (27:4) Spr 93, p. 48-49.
    "In Pocatello." [BellR] (16:1/2) Spr-Fall 93, p. 32.
660. BOTKIN, Nancy
    "Signs of Life." [PoetryE] (36) Fall 93, p. 137.
661. BOTTOMS, David
    "A Daughter's Fever." [Poetry] (163:1) O 93, p. 22.
662. BOUCHARD, Louise
    "Grand Jour." [WestCL] (27:3, #12) Wint 93-94, p. 65-67.
BOUCHET, André du
    See Du BOUCHET, André
663. BOULETTE, Linda
    "Islas de Canarias." [13thMoon] (11:1/2) 93, p. 19-20.
664. BOULTER, Joanna
    "The Hopelessness of the Co-op Butcher." [Stand] (34:4) Aut 93, p. 31.
665. BOURNE, Daniel
    "Alms" (tr. of Tomasz Jastrun). [Confr] (51) Sum 93, p. 239.
    "Beside the Road" (15th Anniversary Contest Winner, 1st Place — Poetry). [IndR]
        (16:1) Spr 93, p. 3.
    "I peak around the corner, ask" (tr. of Mira Kus). [RiverS] (38) 93, p. 66.
    "Intersection" (tr. of Tomasz Jastrun). [Witness] (7:1) 93, p. 132.
    "Love" (tr. of Mira Kus). [RiverS] (38) 93, p. 67.
    "Monuments" (tr. of Tomasz Jastrun). [Confr] (51) Sum 93, p. 238.
    "Nota Bene." [IndR] (16:1) Spr 93, p. 4.
    "Now or Never." [IndR] (16:1) Spr 93, p. 5.
    "Sleeplessness" (tr. of Tomasz Jastrun). [Confr] (51) Sum 93, p. 237.

"The State of Wyoming." [LitR] (36:2) Wint 93, p. 150.
"Tending One's Garden" (tr. of Tomasz Jastrun). [Witness] (7:1) 93, p. 132.
"Untitled: Night, the mountains, a storm. The shelter packed with people" (tr. of
    Bronislaw Maj). [CharR] (19:2) Fall 93, p. 91.
"Untitled: Not at once did you grasp the message" (tr. of Bronislaw Maj). [CharR]
    (19:2) Fall 93, p. 89.
"Untitled: Through the weight of this uneasy summer's air" (tr. of Bronislaw Maj).
    [CharR] (19:2) Fall 93, p. 90.
"Untitled: Weighed down by his bags, gray whiskers on his chin" (tr. of Bronislaw
    Maj). [CharR] (19:2) Fall 93, p. 91.
"Untitled: Whenever he described to me this park, this pathway" (tr. of Bronislaw
    Maj). [CharR] (19:2) Fall 93, p. 90.
"Untitled: Who will bear witness to these times" (tr. of Bronislaw Maj). [CharR]
    (19:2) Fall 93, p. 92.
666. BOURNE, Lesley-Anne
    "At the Window." [Event] (22:1) Spr 93, p. 54-55.
667. BOURQUE, Darrell
    "Putting William to Sleep." [XavierR] (13:2) Fall 93, p. 75.
    "Washing Clothes." [XavierR] (13:2) Fall 93, p. 74.
668. BOURSAULT, Edme
    "The Crayfish and Her Daughter" (tr. by Norman R. Shapiro). [Hudson] (45:4) Wint
        93, p. 680.
    "L'Ecrevisse et Sa Fille." [Hudson] (45:4) Wint 93, p. 680.
669. BOUTOS, Penelope
    "My Woman" (tr. by Judith Bornstein). [Vis] (43) 93, p. 23.
    "Old Red" (tr. by Judith Bornstein). [Vis] (43) 93, p. 23.
670. BOUVARD, Marguerite
    "Above the Mountains." [QRL] (12:32/33) 93, p. 68-69.
    "Back Road, Amherst Virginia." [SouthernHR] (27:1) Wint 93, p. 59.
    "Empire." [QRL] (12:32/33) 93, p. 66-67.
    "In Argentina" (For Juanita). [LitR] (36:2) Wint 93, p. 146.
    "In Argentina" (for Juanita). [QRL] (12:32/33) 93, p. 64-65.
    "Josefa's Dream." [QRL] (12:32/33) 93, p. 65.
    "The Mothers Say No." [QRL] (12:32/33) 93, p. 63-64.
    "My Life on a Distant Planet." [QRL] (12:32/33) 93, p. 69-70.
    "She Has Become an Older Woman." [QRL] (12:32/33) 93, p. 67-68.
    "A White Shawl." [QRL] (12:32/33) 93, p. 66.
671. BOUZANE, Lillian
    "The baby always gets heavier." [TickleAce] (26) Fall-Wint 93, p. 68.
    "Slow down the stair-way." [TickleAce] (26) Fall-Wint 93, p. 67.
672. BOWDAN, Janet
    "Climate." [ChiR] (39:2) 93, p. 97.
    "Kiss." [HawaiiR] (17:2, #38) Spr 93, p. 85.
    "Opera in a Closed Car." [AmerPoR] (22:2) Mr-Ap 93, p. 39.
    "Professing That." [AmerPoR] (22:2) Mr-Ap 93, p. 39.
    "That Hearing a Slide Projector." [AmerPoR] (22:2) Mr-Ap 93, p. 39.
673. BOWDEN, Michael
    "Hunter's Moon." [HayF] (13) Fall-Wint 93, p. 83.
    "Night River." [ProseP] (2) 93, p. 15.
    "Shrine." [HayF] (13) Fall-Wint 93, p. 82.
    "Yellow Weeds." [ProseP] (2) 93, p. 14.
674. BOWEN, Kevin
    "The Children's Tet." [BostonR] (18:2) Mr-Ap 93, p. 30.
    "Gelatin Factory." [Agni] (37) 93, p. 294-295.
    "Graves at Quang Tri" (Truong Son Cemetery, 1987). [PoetL] (88:4) Wint 93-94, p.
        43-44.
    "Peasant Fare: At the Museum of Fine Arts." [TriQ] (89) Wint 93-94, p. 200-201.
    "River Music." [BostonR] (18:2) Mr-Ap 93, p. 30.
    "Roses." [TarRP] (32:2) Spr 93, p. 18.
BOWENS, Eunice Knight
    See KNIGHT-BOWENS, Eunice
675. BOWERS, Cathy Smith
    "Groceries." [SouthernR] (29:3) Sum, Jl 93, p. 598-599.
    "The Scar." [SouthernR] (29:3) Sum, Jl 93, p. 599-600.
    "Sponges." [SouthernR] (29:3) Sum, Jl 93, p. 596-597.
    "Territorial." [SouthernR] (29:3) Sum, Jl 93, p. 597-598.

"You Can't Drive the Same Truck Twice." [GeoR] (47:3) Fall 93, p. 500.
676. BOWERS, Cherie
"Fingers in Popcorn." [SinW] (49) Spr-Sum 93, p. 54.
677. BOWERS, Edgar
"John." [Poetry] (161:4) Ja 93, p. 205-206.
678. BOWERS, Neal
"Applied Science." [Poetry] (162:6) S 93, p. 340.
"The Center." [Poetry] (162:6) S 93, p. 338.
"Changes" (5 poems). [SewanR] (101:3) Jl-S, Sum 93, p. 309-313.
"Death Sentence." [Hudson] (46:2) Sum 93, p. 355-356.
"Divestments." [Poetry] (162:2) My 93, p. 76.
"An Early Garden." [SewanR] (101:1) Ja-Mr, Wint 93, p. 29.
"The Following Word." [TarRP] (33:1) Fall 93, p. 36-37.
"Jackhammer in the Bakery." [CarolQ] (45:2) Wint 93, p. 26.
"Keeping Time" (for Nancy). [Shen] (43:4) Wint 93, p. 35.
"Last" (For Nancy). [Poetry] (162:2) My 93, p. 77.
"The Pain of Relativity." [SewanR] (101:1) Ja-Mr, Wint 93, p. 31.
"The Pledge." [CarolQ] (45:2) Wint 93, p. 25.
"RSVP." [LaurelR] (27:1) Wint 93, p. 3.
"Small Town Story." [MichQR] (32:1) Wint 93, p. 135.
"Some Friends." [Shen] (43:4) Wint 93, p. 36.
"Some Music, Then." [TarRP] (33:1) Fall 93, p. 36.
"Special Effects." [Poetry] (162:6) S 93, p. 339.
"Staking Tomatoes, I Think of Angels." [SewanR] (101:1) Ja-Mr, Wint 93, p. 30.
679. BOWLES, Brad
"I Liked Ike." [CapeR] (28:1) Spr 93, p. 5.
"Yardwork." [Footwork] (23) 93, p. 120.
680. BOWLES, Ka
"Dream Child." [CapeR] (28:2) Fall 93, p. 11.
"The Holly Bush." [CapeR] (28:2) Fall 93, p. 12.
681. BOWLING, Tim
"Great Blue Heron." [PoetryC] (14:1) 93, p. 16.
"Greeting the New Year in Vancouver." [PoetryC] (14:1) 93, p. 16.
"Half-Time at a Nephew's Soccer Game." [PoetryC] (14:1) 93, p. 16.
682. BOWMAN, Catherine (Cathy)
"The Lights of Marfa." [KenR] (NS 15:1) Wint 93, p. 93-94.
"Meat and Secrets." [RiverS] (38) 93, p. 3-4.
"Mr. X." [Chelsea] (55) 93, p. 34-35.
683. BOWRING, George
"Facing the Music" (An Audiobiographical Record). [Light] (7) Aut 93, p. 11.
684. BOYCE, Scott
"Sometimes the Land Can Be Shaken from Its Thin-lipped Silence." [Event] (22:3) Wint 93-94, p. 67.
"The Two Worlds." [Event] (22:3) Wint 93-94, p. 66.
685. BOYD, Gerry
"A Disease Becoming the Hero." [US1] (28/29) 93, p. 17.
686. BOYD, Greg
"Bee-Keeping." [Caliban] (12) 93, p. 56.
"The End." [Caliban] (12) 93, p. 55.
"The Sick King" (for Eric). [Caliban] (12) 93, p. 54.
"The Witch." [Caliban] (12) 93, p. 53.
687. BOYD, Melba Joyce
"Epitaph for Etheridge Knight." [Eyeball] (2) 93, p. 33.
"The Manifestation of Civilization." [Drumvoices] (3:1/2) Fall-Wint 93-94, p. 105 - 108.
688. BOYD, Robert
"Graffiti." [HampSPR] Wint 93, p. 42.
689. BOYKIN, Becky
"Senior Speicals" (Young Writers, age 17). [PikeF] (11) Fall 93, p. 19.
690. BOYLE, Kevin
"The Consumers." [PassN] (14:1) Sum 93, p. 34-35.
"Love Poem." [GreensboroR] (54) Sum 93, p. 82.
691. BOYNE, Daniel J.
"Having Read Hawthorne." [NewRena] (8:3, #26) Spr 93, p. 102.
"More Than Hemingway." [NewRena] (8:3, #26) Spr 93, p. 103.

692. BOZANIC, Nick
"The Academy." [PassN] (14:2) Wint 93, p. 18.
"Outing." [PassN] (14:2) Wint 93, p. 19-20.
"Pavane." [Manoa] (5:2) Wint 93, p. 91-92.
"Self-Portrait as Winter." [Manoa] (5:2) Wint 93, p. 92.
693. BOZDECHOVA, Ivana
"Everyday Occurrence" (tr. by Ewald Osers). [OxfordM] (9:1) Spr-Sum 93, p. 83-84.
694. BRACKENBURY, Alison
"Entrenched." [Verse] (10:1) Spr 93, p. 31.
"Talk." [Stand] (34:2) Spr 93, p. 48.
695. BRACKER, Jonathan
"On a Navy Ship at Sea: For Inspection." [JamesWR] (10:2) Wint 93, p. 17.
696. BRACKETT, Catherine
"Ride." [BrooklynR] (10) 93, p. 92-93.
697. BRADBURY, Steve
"The Understanding" (tr. of Yuan Ch'iung-ch'iung). [MidAR] (14:1) 93, p. 15.
698. BRADDOCK, Anne Vann
"Lavery Hill." [Lactuca] (17) Apr 93, p. 40.
699. BRADLEY, Ardyth
"When I Say the Moon Is a Boat." [Parting] (6:2) Wint 93, p. 4.
700. BRADLEY, George
"The Fire Fetched Down." [ParisR] (35:126) Spr 93, p. 134-135.
"Nanosecond." [ParisR] (35:126) Spr 93, p. 135-136.
701. BRADLEY, Jerry
"Imagine." [Border] (2) Spr 93, p. 4.
702. BRADLEY, John
"The Accident." [ProseP] (1) 92, p. 14.
"Crimes Against the Future." [ProseP] (2) 93, p. 16.
"The Perfection of War." [Sonora] (26) Fall 93, p. 65-66.
"Siamese Twins, Rio de Janeiro, 1907." [HayF] (12) Spr-Sum 93, p. 54.
"A Story of Hair." [Caliban] (12) 93, p. 132-134.
"There Is a World: Lee Harvey Oswald and the Seduction of History." [HayF] (12)
    Spr-Sum 93, p. 55.
"Yellow Grass." [ProseP] (1) 92, p. 13.
703. BRADLEY, Lawrence
"The Deerhunter." [SenR] (23:1/2) Wint 93, p. 114-115.
BRADLEY, Martha Carlson
    See CARLSON-BRADLEY, Martha
704. BRADY, Philip
"The Cornice of the Skull." [PoetryNW] (34:3) Aut 93, p. 42-43.
705. BRADY, Robert
"Flowers" (tr. of Toshiko Hirata, w. Odagawa Kazuko). [ChiR] (39:3/4) 93, p. 214-
    215.
706. BRAID, Kate
"Dreaming Houses." [PoetryC] (13:4) 93, p. 6.
"He Calls Me." [PoetryC] (13:4) 93, p. 6.
"Notes to Myself: Ten Lessons on Dying." [PoetryC] (13:4) 93, p. 6.
BRAKEMAN, Diane Seuss
    See SEUSS-BRAKEMAN, Diane
707. BRAND, Alice G.
"Writers in Winter." [Footwork] (23) 93, p. 134.
708. BRANDI, John
"Kathmandu, A Canto." [RiverS] (39) 93, p. 4-9.
709. BRANDON, Sherry
"Virgin Tributaries." [BellArk] (9:3) My-Je 93, p. 12-13.
710. BRANDON, Toneisha
"Sullen B." [Sequoia] (34/35) 92-93, p. 33.
711. BRANDT, Anthony
"Abraham" (For Kate). [Boulevard] (8:2/3, #23/24) Fall 93, p. 198.
712. BRANDT, Di
"this it it! i've found it at last! nirvana, the Elysian fields, heaven." [PraS] (67:4) Wint
    93, p. 32.
713. BRANNEN, Jonathan
"F Stop." [HeavenB] (10) Wint-Spr 93, p. 42.
"One Who Has Yet to Sleep with the Moon." [HeavenB] (10) Wint-Spr 93, p. 42.

714. BRANSON, Branley Allan
"Oklahoma Prairie Fire." [SycamoreR] (5:1) Wint 93, p. 47-50.
715. BRASCHI, Giannina
"And Now" (tr. by Tess O'Dwyer). [LitR] (36:2) Wint 93, p. 148.
"Eggs are months and days too" (tr. by Tess O'Dwyer). [Trasimagen] (1:1) Otoño -
Invierno 93, p. 35.
"Empire of Dreams" (Excerpt, tr. by Tess O'Dwyer). [Agni] (37) 93, p. 250.
"Esto es distinto." [Trasimagen] (1:1) Otoño-Invierno 93, p. 34.
"Huevos son los meses y también los días." [Trasimagen] (1:1) Otoño-Invierno 93, p.
34.
"I Am the Shepherd of Water" (tr. by Tess O'Dwyer). [LitR] (36:2) Wint 93, p. 149.
"It wasn't fire" (from "El Imperio de los sueños," tr. by Tess O'Dwyer). [Luz] (5) N
93, p. 21.
"El mundo es una bola de billar." [Trasimagen] (1:1) Otoño-Invierno 93, p. 34.
"El mundo es una casa de muñecas." [Trasimagen] (1:1) Otoño-Invierno 93, p. 34.
"El mundo está en blanco." [Trasimagen] (1:1) Otoño-Invierno 93, p. 34.
"No fue el fuego" (from "El Imperio de los sueños"). [Luz] (5) N 93, p. 20.
"On the Top Floor of the Empire State" (tr. by Tess O'Dwyer). [LitR] (36:2) Wint 93,
p. 148.
"This is different" (tr. by Tess O'Dwyer). [Trasimagen] (1:1) Otoño-Invierno 93, p.
35.
"The world is a billiard ball" (tr. by Tess O'Dwyer). [Trasimagen] (1:1) Otoño -
Invierno 93, p. 35.
"The world is a doll house" (tr. by Tess O'Dwyer). [Trasimagen] (1:1) Otoño -
Invierno 93, p. 35.
"The world is blank" (tr. by Tess O'Dwyer). [Trasimagen] (1:1) Otoño-Invierno 93, p.
35.
716. BRASS, Deborah
"Love Poem for My Grandfather." [AmerPoR] (22:5) S-O 93, p. 7.
"Nocturne." [AmerPoR] (22:5) S-O 93, p. 7.
"Sappho." [AmerPoR] (22:5) S-O 93, p. 7.
"Tonight." [AmerPoR] (22:5) S-O 93, p. 7.
"Untitled: The wall needs paper or a painting." [AmerPoR] (22:5) S-O 93, p. 7.
717. BRAUN, Henry
"The Grackles." [PaintedB] (50/51) 93, p. 16.
718. BRAUN, Volker
"Happy Conspiracy" (tr. by Gisela Argyle). [PoetryC] (13:2) 93, p. 20.
719. BRAVERMAN, Kate
"Falling in October #3." [OnTheBus] (5:2, #12) Sum-Fall 93, p. 45.
"Falling in October #4 (Possession Landscape)." [OnTheBus] (6:1, #13) Wint 93-Spr
94, p. 58-59.
720. BRAVERMAN, Melanie
"Effigy." [13thMoon] (11:1/2) 93, p. 21.
721. BRAXTON, Charlie R.
"South Central Olympics." [Eyeball] (2) 93, p. 12.
"Visions" (The Second Coming). [Eyeball] (2) 93, p. 12.
BREAUX, Quo Vadis Gex
    See GEX-BREAUX, Quo Vadis
722. BREBNER, Diana
"The Golden Lotus" (after a painting by Mary Pratt. 4 selections). [Quarry] (42:1) 93,
p. 115-118.
"Real Life, Still Life." [Event] (22:1) Spr 93, p. 24.
"Three Paintings by Mary Pratt." [Event] (22:1) Spr 93, p. 20-22.
"Virtual Reality." [Event] (22:1) Spr 93, p. 23.
BREBNER, Diane
    See BREBNER, Diana
723. BREEDEN, David
"Awful Coffee." [ContextS] (3:1) 93, p. 54.
"Opinion Poll." [Border] (2) Spr 93, p. 5-6.
"Silver Poplars." [PikeF] (11) Fall 93, p. 28.
724. BREHM, John
"Like Children." [PoetryNW] (34:4) Wint 93-94, p. 30-31.
"Passage." [Poetry] (162:6) S 93, p. 347.
"A Returning." [LitR] (37:1) Fall 93, p. 74-75.
"Tell Us." [PoetryNW] (34:4) Wint 93-94, p. 31.

725. BREINER, Laurence
     "Figure and Ground, or, Art Up to Its Neck in History." [Agni] (38) 93, p. 103-104.
BRENDAN-BROWN, Sean
     See BROWN, Sean (Sean Brendan)
726. BRENNAN, Matthew
     "The Beauty of Illness: A Family Vacation up in Michigan." [Footwork] (23) 93, p. 117.
     "A Prelude to Dawn Light." [Footwork] (23) 93, p. 117.
727. BRENNAN, Scott
     "Crossing Georgia." [CharR] (19:1) Spr 93, p. 88.
728. BRESKIN, David
     "Shatter Glass / Kristallnacht" (for Kurt Stern). [NewAW] (11) Sum-Fall 93, p. 85-86.
729. BRETON, André
     "Intérieur." [RiverS] (39) 93, p. 58.
     "Interior" (tr. by Christopher Merrill). [RiverS] (39) 93, p. 59.
730. BRETT, Peter
     "Conrad." [DogRR] (12:1, #23) Spr-Sum 93, p. 35.
     "The Maestro of Meadows." [DogRR] (12:1, #23) Spr-Sum 93, p. 34.
     "Onion." [DogRR] (12:2, #24) Fall-Wint 93, p. 44.
731. BRETT, Ralph
     "Punk Rock." [ChironR] (12:4/13:1, #37/38) Wint 93-Spr 94, p. 27.
732. BREWER, Gay
     "This Unnamed Town." [ArtfulD] (24/25) 93, p. 114.
733. BREWER, Kenneth W.
     "The House." [Plain] (13:3) Spr 93, p. 38.
734. BREWSTER, Elizabeth
     "For Krishna's Sake." [PraF] (14:4) Wint 93-94, p. 65.
     "November Bus Ride Between Prairie Cities." [PraF] (14:4) Wint 93-94, p. 64-65.
     "Pathfinders." [PraF] (14:4) Wint 93-94, p. 63.
     "Poems for Seven Decades" (Selections: 8 poems). [PraS] (67:4) Wint 93, p. 51-57.
735. BREWSTER, Reggie W.
     "Not About the Ocean." [SinW] (51) Wint 93-94, p. 65.
736. BREYNER, Sophia de Mello
     "Delphic" (Pt. IV, tr. by Lisa Sapinkopf). [HarvardR] (4) Spr 93, p. 149.
     "I'm Listening" (tr. by Lisa Sapinkopf). [Sun] (209) My 93, p. 15.
     "The Little Square" (tr. by Lisa Sapinkopf). [Sun] (207) Mr 93, p. 19.
     "Part VI From Gypsy Christ" (tr. by Lisa Sapinkopf). [Sun] (209) My 93, p. 15.
BREYNER ANDRESEN, Sophia de Mello
     See BREYNER, Sophia de Mello
737. BREZINA, Roger G.
     "Childless Myth." [Amelia] (7:2, #21) 93, p. 72.
738. BRICKHOUSE, Robert
     "Starlings." [SouthernPR] (33:1) Spr 93, p. 67-68.
739. BRIDGERS, Bennett
     "The Wicked Queen." [13thMoon] (12:1/2) 93-94, p. 11.
740. BRIDGERS, Jane Bennett
     "The Explosion." [MassR] (33:4) Wint 92-93, p. 501-504.
741. BRIDGES, William
     "Don't Wory." [Light] (6) Sum 93, p. 8.
     "From a Cheap Hotel at the Edge of the Known World." [HopewellR] (5) 93, p. 70.
742. BRIDGFORD, Kim
     "The Accident." [Pearl] (19) Fall-Wint 93, p. 49.
     "Blue Gone to Black." [SpoonR] (18:1) Wint-Spr 93, p. 7.
     "Gobbling." [LaurelR] (27:2) Sum 93, p. 22-23.
     "Green." [SmPd] (30:3, #89) Fall 93, p. 27.
     "Letters." [HiramPoR] (53/54) Fall 92-Sum 93, p. 24-25.
     "Medusa." [Ascent] (17:3) Spr 93, p. 7.
     "Seeing Things." [LaurelR] (27:2) Sum 93, p. 23-25.
     "Silky." [WestB] (31/32) 93, p. 7.
     "Stirrings." [SpoonR] (18:1) Wint-Spr 93, p. 10-11.
     "The Story of the Past." [WestB] (31/32) 93, p. 5-6.
     "When There's Pause." [SpoonR] (18:1) Wint-Spr 93, p. 8-9.
743. BRIGGS, Kenny
     "Degrees of Gray at Northside" (w. Brian Di Salvatore and Lora Jansson). [CutB] (40) Spr 93, p. 101-102.

81

744. BRIGHT, Kimberly J.
    "Caffeine Ode." [Gypsy] (20) Sum 93, p. 9.
745. BRIGHT, Susan
    "Do Not Forget in Peace Times." [Border] (2) Spr 93, p. 7-8.
    "Tower." [13thMoon] (11:1/2) 93, p. 22.
746. BRINES, Francisco
    "The Triumph of Idleness" (tr. by Michael L. Johnson). [LitR] (36:3) Spr 93, p. 361.
747. BRINT, Armand
    "A Neighborhood Kid." [Vis] (41) 93, p. 31.
748. BRISTER, J. G.
    "Faulkner in Hollywood." [NewYorkQ] (52) 93, p. 66.
749. BROADHEAD, Susan
    "At Night in Late Fall." [NorthStoneR] (11) 93, p. 10.
    "The Morning After the Election" (November 7, 1984). [NorthStoneR] (11) 93, p. 7 - 8.
    "A Northern Setting." [NorthStoneR] (11) 93, p. 11.
    "Speed." [NorthStoneR] (11) 93, p. 9.
    "Spoonbridge and Cherry" (On the occasion of the dedication of the Minneapolis Sculpture Garden, Sept. 1988). [NorthStoneR] (11) 93, p. 12-13.
750. BROCK, Garrett
    "The Messiah & the Bag Lady." [ChangingM] (26) Sum-Fall 93, p. 39.
    "On an Island on an A Train." [EvergreenC] (8:2) Sum-Fall 93, p. 42-43.
751. BROCK, Geoffrey
    "God Appears to the Atheist." [Hellas] (4:2) Fall 93, p. 109.
752. BROCK-BROIDO, Lucie
    "And Wylde for to Hold." [ParisR] (35:128) Fall 93, p. 210-211.
    "A Brief History of Asylum." [Agni] (38) 93, p. 15-16.
    "Elective Mutes." [NewEngR] (15:1) Wint 93, p. 102-106.
    "I Dont Know Who It Is, That Sings, Nor Did I, Would I Tell." [Agni] (38) 93, p. 14.
    "The Interrupted Life." [Agni] (38) 93, p. 13.
    "Prescient." [Boulevard] (8:1, #22) Spr 93, p. 55.
    "Rome Beauty." [HarvardR] (4) Spr 93, p. 15.
753. BROCKI, A. C.
    "Insight." [Poem] (70) N 93, p. 27.
    "Private Enterprise." [Poem] (70) N 93, p. 26.
754. BROCKWAY, James
    "Le Balcon." [Stand] (34:3) Sum 93, p. 65.
755. BRODIE, Harold
    "Denver." [PoetL] (88:3) Fall 93, p. 42.
    "My Sinister." [PoetL] (88:3) Fall 93, p. 42-43.
756. BRODSKY, Joseph
    "Achilles, Penthesilea" (tr. of Zbigniew Herbert). [NewYRB] (40:17) 21 O 93, p. 22.
    "Daedalus in Sicily" (tr. by the author). [NewYRB] (40:16) 7 O 93, p. 14.
    "Lullaby" (tr. by the author). [NewYorker] (69:43) 20 D 93, p. 104.
    "New Life" (tr. by David MacFadyen and the author). [NewYorker] (69:10) 26 Ap 93, p. 86-87.
    "Polonaise: A Variation" (To Z.K.). [Salm] (97) Wint 93, p. 154-156.
    "To Urania." [Salm] (97) Wint 93, p. 165.
757. BRODSKY, Louis Daniel
    "An Accompaniment to the Rain." [LitR] (37:1) Fall 93, p. 95.
    "Miss Emily." [SoCarR] (25:2) Spr 93, p. 123.
    "My Holocaust Flowers." [AlabamaLR] (7:1) 93, p. 36-37.
    "Second Comings" (For Jerry Call). [FourQ] (7:2) Fall 93, p. 25.
    "Staying Afloat." [SmPd] (30:1, #87) Wint 93, p. 23.
    "The Thorough Earth." [CapeR] (28:1) Spr 93, p. 10-11.
758. BRODY, Benjamin
    "Saint Petersburg Daze." [Light] (6) Sum 93, p. 14.
759. BRODY, Deborah
    "Infidelity." [LaurelR] (27:2) Sum 93, p. 37.
760. BRODY, Polly
    "From Second Mesa" (For Deborah — Novitiate). [SpoonR] (18:2) Sum-Fall 93, p. 32-33.
761. BROGAN, Patricia Burke
    "Cell." [SenR] (23:1/2) Wint 93, p. 67.
    "Miracle." [SenR] (23:1/2) Wint 93, p. 66.

BROIDO, Lucie Brock
    See BROCK-BROIDO, Lucie
762. BROIDY, Steve
    "February." [MidwQ] (34:2) Wint 93, p. 207.
763. BROMIGE, David
    "A Cast of Tens" (Selections: 3 poems). [Avec] (6:1) 93, p. 14-21.
    "The Harbor-Master of Hong Kong" (Selections: 2 poems). [Avec] (6:1) 93, p. 11-13.
764. BROMLEY, Anne (Anne C.)
    "The Art of Gratitude." [PraS] (67:3) Fall 93, p. 46-47.
    "Broken Shells." [PraS] (67:3) Fall 93, p. 48-49.
    "Dolls." [SouthernPR] (33:1) Spr 93, p. 57-58.
    "Fire Begets Village." [PraS] (67:3) Fall 93, p. 47-48.
    "Leaving Autumn." [ColEng] (55:6) O 93, p. 645.
    "The Nighthawk Sanskritist." [PraS] (67:3) Fall 93, p. 50-51.
765. BRONDY, Michele
    "Looks Like the Day Will Take Its Time" (tr. of Jacques Rancourt). [Vis] (42) 93, p.
        9.
766. BRONK, William
    "The Mild Day" (10 selections). [Talisman] (10) Spr 93, p. 6-15.
    "Short Walk." [Arshile] (2) 93, p. 9.
    "Story Time." [Arshile] (2) 93, p. 12.
    "Verbal." [Arshile] (2) 93, p. 11.
    "Who's There." [Arshile] (2) 93, p. 10.
767. BROOKNER, Edward
    "Hickok and the Sign." [Arshile] (1) Spr 93, p. 68.
    "Invocation" (for M.S.). [Arshile] (1) Spr 93, p. 67.
    "On a Country Walk Hayden Explains to Count Apponyi the First Movement of His
        D Major Quartet." [Arshile] (1) Spr 93, p. 69-70.
    "Song." [Arshile] (1) Spr 93, p. 71.
    "William Wyncherly." [Arshile] (1) Spr 93, p. 66.
768. BROOKS, Carellin
    "River." [SinW] (51) Wint 93-94, p. 62-63.
769. BROOKS, Gwendolyn
    "The Coora Flower" (Tinsel Marie). [NewYorkQ] (51) 93, p. 28.
    "I Am a Black." [NewYorkQ] (51) 93, p. 27.
    "Malcolm X" (For Dudley Randall). [Drumvoices] (2:1/2) Fall-Wint 92-93, p. 210.
    "Nineteen Cows in a Slow Line Walking." [NewYorkQ] (51) 93, p. 24.
    "Religion." [NewYorkQ] (51) 93, p. 26.
    "Sadie and Maud" (illustrated by Oriole Farb Feshbach). [MassR] (34:2) Sum 93, p.
        242-243.
    "To an Old Black Woman, Homeless and Indistinct." [Drumvoices] (2:1/2) Fall-Wint
        92-93, p. 120-121.
    "Uncle Seagram." [NewYorkQ] (51) 93, p. 25.
    "A Welcome Song for Laini Nzinga." [Art&Und] (2:3) Special Edition 93, p. 11.
770. BROOKS, Randy
    "Haiku" (3 poems). [Northeast] (5:9) Wint 93-94, p. 22.
771. BROUGHTON, Irv
    "The House of Roots" (after a photograph by Jerry Uelsmann, for Jerry). [CimR]
        (102) Ja 93, p. 75.
    "The Houseparaders" (for Callie). [CimR] (102) Ja 93, p. 75-76.
    "Making Movies" (for Gerry Cook). [CimR] (102) Ja 93, p. 73-74.
772. BROUGHTON, James
    "Uncle Nestor's Last Birthday Cake." [HangL] (62) 93, p. 5.
773. BROUGHTON, T. Alan
    "Death as a Cloudless Day." [PraS] (67:3) Fall 93, p. 53-54.
    "Forges at Conshohocken." [VirQR] (69:4) Aut 93, p. 655.
    "On This Side of the Canvas." [PraS] (67:3) Fall 93, p. 53.
    "Preparing the Way." [PraS] (67:3) Fall 93, p. 51-52.
    "Refuge." [PraS] (67:3) Fall 93, p. 54-55.
    "Somewhere in America." [BlackWR] (19:1) Fall-Wint 92, p. 106.
774. BROUMAS, Olga
    "Sea Blouse Open" (Selections: 2 poems, w. T. Begley). [Sonora] (26) Fall 93, p. 44 -
        45.
    "Sophia and True" (Selections: 3 poems, w. T. Begley). [Sonora] (26) Fall 93, p. 46 -
        48.

"Your Sacred Idiot with Me" (Selections: 2 poems, w. T. Begley). [Sonora] (26) Fall
93, p. 49-50.
BROUX, Peggy de
See De BROUX, Peggy
775. BROWDER, Clifford
"On Reading Certain Contemporaries." [SoCoast] (15) Je 93, p. 18.
776. BROWER, Brock
"Never criticize a man." [Footwork] (23) 93, p. 160.
777. BROWN, Abbie Howard
"Body Fascists." [Footwork] (23) 93, p. 104.
778. BROWN, Allan
"Ad Libitum." [Quarry] (42:3) 93, p. 52.
"Mirrors." [Quarry] (42:3) 93, p. 51.
"The Past Is Not History" (— Helen Tsiriotakis). [Quarry] (42:3) 93, p. 50.
779. BROWN, Andrea Carter
"The Los Angeles at Lankershim." [GettyR] (6:3) Sum 93, p. 454.
"Die Goldene Zeit" (after an anonymous print). [GettyR] (6:3) Sum 93, p. 455.
"Wit's End." [GettyR] (6:3) Sum 93, p. 456.
780. BROWN, Bill
"Bath." [WindO] (57) Fall 93, p. 26.
"Charms" (a confusion of particle physics and you). [SouthernPR] (33:1) Spr 93, p. 6 -
7.
"Charms" (a confusion of particle physics and you). [SouthernPR] (33:2) Fall 93, p.
9.
"Mounding Potatoes." [SouthernPR] (33:1) Spr 93, p. 5-6.
"On a Park Bench in Heaven." [PikeF] (11) Fall 93, p. 32.
"Strangers." [WindO] (57) Fall 93, p. 10-11.
781. BROWN, Celia
"The Darkest Leaves." [Vis] (42) 93, p. 20.
782. BROWN, Clarence
"1920" (tr. of Osip Mandelstam, w. W. S. Merwin). [QRL] (12:32/33) 93, p. 463.
"1933" (tr. of Osip Mandelstam, w. W. S. Merwin). [QRL] (12:32/33) 93, p. 463.
783. BROWN, Cory
"Blanch Wilcox Brown." [Light] (5) Spr 93, p. 20.
"High Court." [Farm] (10:1) Spr-Sum 93, p. 100.
"Isotropic Mist." [WestB] (31/32) 93, p. 139.
"Love Poem." [Light] (5) Spr 93, p. 15.
"Requiem." [Pembroke] (25) 93, p. 92-93.
"Rhetoric of Senses." [Farm] (10:2) Fall-Wint 93-94, p. 96-97.
"Snowing." [WestB] (31/32) 93, p. 138-139.
"To See Far." [Pembroke] (25) 93, p. 90-91.
"Too." [ChatR] (13:2) Wint 93, p. 1.
784. BROWN, Glen
"Briar Rose Defunct." [Pearl] (17) Spr 93, p. 60.
"Briar Rose Defunct." [SpoonR] (18:1) Wint-Spr 93, p. 15-16.
"Día de los Muertos." [WillowR] (20) Spr 93, p. 40-41.
"Epitaph for a Transsexual Dead of AIDS." [WillowR] (20) Spr 93, p. 43.
"In the Cross Hairs." [WillowR] (20) Spr 93, p. 42.
"Just Before Ovulation." [SlipS] (13) 93, p. 33.
"Math Class is Tough" (—Barbie). [SoCoast] (15) Je 93, p. 44.
"Red Riding Hood Buys Term Life." [SpoonR] (18:1) Wint-Spr 93, p. 17.
"Riding Rapunzel." [Pearl] (17) Spr 93, p. 61.
785. BROWN, Janet Elizabeth
"My Parents." [Parting] (6:1) Sum 93, p. 56.
786. BROWN, Jessica
"My Days" (Young Writers, age 9). [PikeF] (11) Fall 93, p. 19.
787. BROWN, Joyce S.
"Second Birth" (for Andrew Schenck, January 7, 1941-February 19, 1992). [AmerS]
(62:4) Aut 93, p. 590.
788. BROWN, Kurt
"The Corn Palace." [DenQ] (27:4) Spr 93, p. 100-101.
789. BROWN, Lee Ann
"Double Triolet" (w. Lisa Jarnot). [BlackBread] (3) 93, p. 72.
"Gerard for Unction." [13thMoon] (12:1/2) 93-94, p. 12.
790. BROWN, Mary M.
"Abiding." [ChrC] (110:35) 8 D 93, p. 1238.

"Close Call." [ChrC] (110:14) 28 Apr 93, p. 446.
791. BROWN, Peter
"For Darwin or the Reverend." [AnotherCM] (26) Fall 93, p. 5.
792. BROWN, Robert
"Cicada of Space" (tr. of Jean Tardieu). [PoetL] (88:1) Spr 93, p. 51.
"Lord Vulture Lady Pelican" (tr. of Jean Tardieu). [PoetL] (88:1) Spr 93, p. 52.
793. BROWN, Sean (Sean Brendan)
"By the Coat Rack." [WillowR] (20) Spr 93, p. 13.
"Cherries at Kajikawa." [WillowR] (20) Spr 93, p. 12.
"A Destroyed Paris Theater." [CoalC] (7) Apr 93, p. 10.
"Him — (Slash) Her." [AntigR] (92) Wint 93, p. 10.
"Prayer for Vicente." [CoalC] (7) Apr 93, p. 9.
"Rotten Cloth." [DogRR] (12:2, #24) Fall-Wint 93, p. 3.
794. BROWN, Steven Ford
"Cemetery in Colliure" (tr. of Angel Gonzalez). [QW] (37) Sum-Fall 93, p. 90-91.
"Erudites on Campus" (tr. of Angel González, w. Gutierrez Revuelta). [HarvardR] (3)
    Wint 93, p. 142.
"Love Poem." [PaintedB] (50/51) 93, p. 108.
"Residential Zone" (tr. of Angel Gonzalez). [QW] (37) Sum-Fall 93, p. 92-93.
795. BROWN, Susan E.
"Transformations." [BelPoJ] (43:4) Sum 93, p. 18-19.
796. BROWN-DAVIDSON, Terri
"The Painter at Yaddo." [HeavenB] (10) Wint-Spr 93, p. 29.
797. BROWNE, Laynie
"Caddy Tales Retold" (Excerpts). [13thMoon] (12:1/2) 93-94, p. 13-15.
"From a Picture Book." [BlackBread] (3) 93, p. 10-13.
"Pollen Memory" (6 selections). [Talisman] (10) Spr 93, p. 74-75.
"The Results of the Accidents of Conquest." [BlackBread] (3) 93, p. 6-9.
798. BROWNE, Michael Dennis
"Dream at the Death of James Wright." [GettyR] (6:2) Spr 93, p. 314.
799. BROWNING, Elizabeth Barrett
"Aurora Leigh" (Selection: Fifth Book, II. 199-222). [SoCoast] (15) Je 93, p. 65.
800. BROWNING, Preston
"Mr. Jefferson on 63rd Street (Chicago's South Side)" (for Fred Stern, in memoriam).
    [PikeF] (11) Fall 93, p. 3.
801. BRUCE, Debra
"Outside." [NoAmR] (278:6) N-D 93, p. 9.
"What Mother's Weather." [IllinoisR] (1:1) Fall 93, p. 23.
802. BRUCHAC, Joseph
"Broken Glass." [PaintedB] (50/51) 93, p. 41.
"The Dancing Boys." [GreenMR] (NS 6:1) Wint-Spr 93, p. 78-79.
"In the Little House at Sunset." [TarRP] (32:2) Spr 93, p. 28.
"Lady's Slippers by Deer Pond." [TarRP] (32:2) Spr 93, p. 29.
"Maple Sap." [GreenMR] (NS 6:1) Wint-Spr 93, p. 80-81.
"Reading in Fredonia." [PaintedB] (50/51) 93, p. 41.
"Splitting Wood on My 48th Brithday." [TarRP] (32:2) Spr 93, p. 30.
803. BRUCK, Edith
"Impression" (tr. by Anita Barrows). [13thMoon] (11:1/2) 93, p. 207.
"Survivors" (tr. by Anita Barrows). [13thMoon] (11:1/2) 93, p. 206.
804. BRUCK, Julie
"The Goldfish." [MalR] (104) Fall 93, p. 40-41.
"Summer on Rewind." [MalR] (104) Fall 93, p. 38-39.
805. BRUGALETTA, John J.
"Wedding." [Hellas] (4:2) Fall 93, p. 106.
806. BRUGNARO, Ferruccio
"Basta con Questa Atroce Guerra." [Arshile] (2) 93, p. 58.
"Enough with This Horible War" (tr. by Jack Hirschman). [Arshile] (2) 93, p. 59.
807. BRUNK, Juanita
"Bleeding Heart." [PoetL] (88:2) Sum 93, p. 26.
"Carrot." [PoetL] (88:2) Sum 93, p. 26.
"Heartbreak." [PoetL] (88:2) Sum 93, p. 27.
808. BRUNNER, Ernst
"A Dog's Bark Away, Where the Cigar" (tr. by Anselm Hollo). [ManhatR] (7:1) Fall
    93, p. 13.
"Prime the Wall That You Pass" (tr. by Anselm Hollo). [ManhatR] (7:1) Fall 93, p.
    12.

BRUNO, Michael la (Michael C. la)
See LaBRUNO, Michael (Carmen Michael)
809. BRUNTON, Alan
"Corona" (Selections: 1-10). [WestCL] (27:2, #11) Fall 93, p. 63-66.
810. BRUSH, Thomas
"A Gift." [Poetry] (162:6) S 93, p. 325.
"New & Used, 1964." [PoetryNW] (34:1) Spr 93, p. 16-17.
811. BRUTUS, Dennis
"Isla Negra: for Neruda." [Eyeball] (2) 93, p. 39.
812. BRYAN, Sharon
"Foretelling." [TarRP] (33:1) Fall 93, p. 40-41.
"Subjunctive." [TarRP] (33:1) Fall 93, p. 39-40.
"Trimmings." [SouthernR] (29:2) Spr, Ap 93, p. 274-275.
"Unhinged." [TarRP] (33:1) Fall 93, p. 38.
"Wrappings." [SouthernR] (29:2) Spr, Ap 93, p. 274.
813. BRYNER, Jeanne
"Delivery Men." [Plain] (13:2) Wint 93, p. 24.
"Under a Funeral Canopy in Rockingham, N.C." (for Chris Llewellyn and all those
who study ashes). [BlackWR] (19:1) Fall-Wint 92, p. 160-161.
814. BUCHANAN, C. J.
"The Mind Blows up the Moon." [Nimrod] (37:1) Fall-Wint 93, p. 109.
815. BUCHANAN, Carl
"How a Sunset Works" (for Jonathan Holden). [MidwQ] (34:2) Wint 93, p. 208.
816. BUCHANAN, Carl J.
"Ridiculous the Waste." [ColEng] (55:6) O 93, p. 648.
817. BUCHANAN, Mary Ann
"November." [Footwork] (23) 93, p. 106.
818. BUCHMAN, Ruth
"The Woman Next Door." [AntR] (51:2) Spr 93, p. 233.
819. BUCHSBAUM, Betty
"Kagami." [Kalliope] (15:3) 93, p. 30-31.
820. BUCK, Dan
"Edges." [Plain] (13:3) Spr 93, p. 8.
821. BUCKAWAY, C. M.
"Prairie Scene." [Bogg] (66) Wint 92-93, p. 21.
822. BUCKHOLTS, Claudia
"Lament." [ConnPR] (12:1) 93, p. 16.
823. BUCKLEY, B. J.
"Mad Alyce in October." [CumbPR]] (13:1) Fall 93, p. 24-26.
824. BUCKLEY, Christopher
"After Another War." [Hudson] (45:4) Wint 93, p. 617-618.
"Days of Black and White." [BlackWR] (19:1) Fall-Wint 92, p. 119-121.
"Going Home." [Crazy] (44) Spr 93, p. 69-70.
825. BUCKNER, Sally
"Notice." [ChrC] (110:14) 28 Apr 93, p. 458.
826. BUDBILL, David
"The Father and the Son." [Sun] (207) Mr 93, p. 22.
"He Sleeps." [Sun] (207) Mr 93, p. 23.
"I Shout Into the Phone." [Sun] (207) Mr 93, p. 23.
827. BUDDINGH, Mary E.
"Perching in the Midst" (Lucille Sandberg Haiku Award, 2nd honorable mention).
[Amelia] (7:2, #21) 93, p. 40.
828. BUDEK, Michael H.
"Goodbye to Yorkshire." [SpiritSH] (58) 93, p. 35.
829. BUDENZ, Julia
"Equipoise." [HarvardR] (4) Spr 93, p. 15.
"Exile" (from "The Gardens of Flora Baum" — a poem in five books). [Crazy] (45)
Wint 93, p. 86-121.
"Umbra" (Excerpt). [CreamCR] (17:1) Spr 93, p. 96-98.
830. BUDY, Andrea Hollander
"Women at Fifty" (after Donald Justice). [GeoR] (47:2) Sum 93, p. 302.
831. BUECHELE, Michael
"Bundle of Strawberries." [NewYorkQ] (50) 93, p. 52-53.
832. BUENG, E. Eng
"For in Her Heart Wounds Are Driven Most Deepest." [Plain] (13:3) Spr 93, p. 6.

"Untitled: Out here the evening soughed" (for Gabriel). [HawaiiR] (17:3, #39) Fall 93, p. 12.
833. BUFFAM, Suzanne
"Drive Thru." [PraF] (14:3) Aut 93, p. 12-13.
834. BUFFINGTON, Marcia
"Brothers." [MidAR] (14:1) 93, p. 150-151.
835. BUFFINGTON, Robert
"Modern Love." [SewanR] (101:1) Ja-Mr, Wint 93, p. 32.
836. BUGEJA, Michael (Michael J.)
"The Abandonment of the Body." [SpoonR] (18:1) Wint-Spr 93, p. 44.
"After Oz" (for Margaret Hamilton). [PoetC] (24:3) Spr 93, p. 40-43.
"Another Day in Valhalla." [SouthernHR] (27:1) Wint 93, p. 46.
"The Entomologist." [TriQ] (88) Fall 93, p. 88-90.
"Flashforward: Global Warming" (for Diane). [TarRP] (33:1) Fall 93, p. 55-56.
"Marionettes" (tr. of Rainer Maria Rilke). [SoCoast] (15) Je 93, p. 40-41.
"New Age." [Hellas] (4:2) Fall 93, p. 57.
"Pomp and Circumstance." [SpoonR] (18:1) Wint-Spr 93, p. 45-47.
"The Revisionist: On Noah's Ark." [GeoR] (47:4) Wint 93, p. 760.
837. BUHROW, B. J. (Bonnie)
"Also Lawyers." [CapeR] (28:1) Spr 93, p. 36.
"America." [OnTheBus] (6:1, #13) Wint 93-Spr 94, p. 60.
"Bachelor Party." [HiramPoR] (53/54) Fall 92-Sum 93, p. 26.
838. BUKOWSKI, Charles
"Ah, Look!" [NewYorkQ] (50) 93, p. 33-34.
"All My Friends." [SlipS] (13) 93, p. 19-20.
"Alone." [NewYorkQ] (52) 93, p. 36-37.
"And the Fish with the Yellow Eyes and the Green Tail Fins Leaped into the Volcano." [ChironR] (12:2, #35) Sum 93, p. 17.
"Bedtime Story." [WorldL] (4) 93, p. 14.
"Black and White Hell." [SlipS] (13) 93, p. 25-29.
"The Bully." [Zyzzyva] (9:1) Spr 93, p. 101-103.
"Burning, Burning." [NewYorkQ] (50) 93, p. 36-37.
"Chicken Giblets." [NewYorkQ] (51) 93, p. 34-36.
"The Condition Book." [WormR] (33:4, #132) 93, p. 213.
"Confessions of a Freak." [ChironR] (12:4/13:1, #37/38) Wint 93-Spr 94, p. 2.
"A Conversation Not to Remember." [Boulevard] (8:1, #22) Spr 93, p. 115-116.
"Dear Mr. Chinaski." [WormR] (33:3, #131), 93, p. 156-157.
"Depression Kid." [MidwQ] (34:2) Wint 93, p. 209-211.
"Fingernails, Nostrils, Shoelaces." [Poetry] (162:6) S 93, p. 341-342.
"For the Lady Who Hates It." [ChironR] (12:2, #35) Sum 93, p. 17.
"Friend of the Family." [NewYorkQ] (51) 93, p. 33.
"The Game." [NewYorkQ] (52) 93, p. 34-35.
"The Great Escape." [Zyzzyva] (9:1) Spr 93, p. 99-100.
"An Introduction to Greatness." [NewYorkQ] (50) 93, p. 35.
"It's a Drag Just Breathing Through My Nostrils All Day Long." [NewYorkQ] (51) 93, p. 30-31.
"Last Call." [Asylum] (8) 93, p. 97-101.
"The Laughing Heart." [PraS] (67:3) Fall 93, p. 168.
"The Mail." [OnTheBus] (6:1, #13) Wint 93-Spr 94, p. 25-29.
"Meeting the Famous at the Turf Club." [NewYorkQ] (51) 93, p. 32.
"A New War." [PraS] (67:3) Fall 93, p. 167.
"No Win." [SlipS] (13) 93, p. 21.
"Not Much Singing." [AmerPoR] (22:3) My-Je 93, p. 46.
"A Not So Good Night in the San Pedro of the World." [Poetry] (162:6) S 93, p. 342.
"A Note Upon the Masses." [Pearl] (19) Fall-Wint 93, p. 83.
"Notice." [WorldL] (4) 93, p. 17.
"Now." [PaintedB] (50/51) 93, p. 118-119.
"Now." [SlipS] (13) 93, p. 20.
"Now Ezra." [Bogg] (66) Wint 92-93, p. 30.
"The Old Literary Chitchat." [WorldL] (4) 93, p. 15-16.
"On Being 20." [WormR] (33:1, #129) 93, p. 45.
"Our Curious Position." [WormR] (33:3, #131), 93, p. 157-158.
"Out of Place." [WormR] (33:1, #129) 93, p. 44-45.
"P.O. Box 11946, Fresno, Calif. 90731." [WormR] (33:1, #129) 93, p. 46.
"Piss." [PaintedB] (52) 93, p. 26-27.
"Screwed within the Universe." [WorldL] (4) 93, p. 11-13.

87

"She Goes for the Spin-Off." [WormR] (33:3, #131), 93, p. 158-159.
"Slow Starter." [SlipS] (13) 93, p. 22-23.
"The Suicide Kid." [OnTheBus] (6:1, #13) Wint 93-Spr 94, p. 30-31.
"Total Madness." [OnTheBus] (5:2, #12) Sum-Fall 93, p. 21-28.
"Upon Splitting with the Last Woman." [WormR] (33:4, #132) 93, p. 211-212.
"Voice Out of the Void." [WormR] (33:4, #132) 93, p. 212-213.
BULINBUHE, Ba
    See BA, Bulinbuhe
839. BULL, Arthur
    "Fingertips." [TickleAce] (25) Spr-Sum 93, p. 209.
    "Making a Rubbing." [PottPort] (15:1) Spr-Sum 93, p. 45-46.
    "Something Almost Always Drops into Place." [TickleAce] (25) Spr-Sum 93, p. 208.
    "Tree Planting." [PottPort] (15:1) Spr-Sum 93, p. 47.
840. BULLINGTON, Mary Boxley
    "Forbidden Pictures." [InterPR] (19:1) Spr 93, p. 71-73.
    "On Empty Air the Orchid Feeds." [InterPR] (19:1) Spr 93, p. 74.
    "T-Square." [InterPR] (19:1) Spr 93, p. 69-70.
841. BULLOCK, Marnie
    "Doing the Right Thing." [AntR] (51:1) Wint 93, p. 90.
    "Sons of God, Daughters of Men." [PraS] (67:3) Fall 93, p. 95-96.
    "Violent Mercy." [PraS] (67:3) Fall 93, p. 96-97.
    "Women's Center Crisis Line." [PraS] (67:3) Fall 93, p. 94-95.
842. BULMER, April
    "Elizabeth, Mother of John the Baptist." [Arc] (31) Aut 93, p. 66.
    "Woman With the Flow of Blood." [Arc] (31) Aut 93, p. 67.
843. BULVIC, Frank F.
    "At the Crossroads" (tr. of France Balantic). [NoDaQ] (61:1) Wint 93, p. 30.
    "Autumn Fires" (tr. of France Balantic). [NoDaQ] (61:1) Wint 93, p. 29.
    "The Evening is Red" (tr. of France Balantic). [NoDaQ] (61:1) Wint 93, p. 30.
    "The Marked Ones" (tr. of France Balantic). [NoDaQ] (61:1) Wint 93, p. 28.
    "A Mouth Filled with Earth" (tr. of France Balantic). [NoDaQ] (61:1) Wint 93, p. 29.
    "The Whiteness of Death" (tr. of France Balantic). [NoDaQ] (61:1) Wint 93, p. 28.
844. BUNDY, Allen
    "Airborne" (Honorable Mention, 7th Annual Contest). [SoCoast] (15) Je 93, p. 10.
845. BURBRIDGE, Nick
    "Neighbours." [Stand] (34:4) Aut 93, p. 29.
846. BURDEN, Jean
    "Guardian Angels." [AmerS] (62:4) Aut 93, p. 580.
847. BURK, Ronnie
    "Genesis." [Caliban] (13) 93, p. 39.
    "The Hanged Man" (to Montana Houston). [Caliban] (13) 93, p. 38.
    "Mineral Life." [Caliban] (13) 93, p. 38.
    "Wednesdays." [Caliban] (13) 93, p. 39.
848. BURKARD, Michael
    "Books Fall from Love." [Epoch] (42:2) 93, p. 210-211.
    "The Bridge." [AmerPoR] (22:1) Ja-F 93, p. 13.
    "Entire Dilemma." [AmerPoR] (22:1) Ja-F 93, p. 13.
    "Living for Two." [DenQ] (27:3) Wint 93, p. 17.
    "On the Footfalls' Side." [AmerPoR] (22:1) Ja-F 93, p. 14.
    "Pennsylvania Collection Agency." [Epoch] (42:2) 93, p. 208-209.
    "Rivers on Fire." [DenQ] (27:3) Wint 93, p. 15-16.
    "The Spellers." [Epoch] (42:2) 93, p. 212-213.
    "Stalin." [AmerPoR] (22:4) Jl-Ag 93, p. 20.
    "The Summer." [Epoch] (42:2) 93, p. 206-207.
    "The Tenderness." [AmerPoR] (22:4) Jl-Ag 93, p. 20.
    "You: My Friend, My." [NoAmR] (278:1) Ja-F 93, p. 47.
849. BURKART, Erika
    "Participation" (tr. by Ellen and Ernest H. von Nardroff). [LitR] (36:4) Sum 93, p.
        550.
    "Partizipation." [LitR] (36:4) Sum 93, p. 551.
850. BURKE, Cate
    "After Marriage." [13thMoon] (11:1/2) 93, p. 23.
851. BURKE, Daniel
    "Teacher's Valediction." [FourQ] (7:1) Spr 93, p. 45.
852. BURKE, Marianne
    "Sweet Briar." [PassN] (14:2) Wint 93, p. 30.

"Vigil." [NewYorker] (69:26) 16 Ag 93, p. 58.
853. BURKE, Michael
"The Apostates Stop for a Phosphate." [PraS] (67:1) Spr 93, p. 111-112.
854. BURKE, Stephen
"Not Dodging." [Spitball] (43) Spr 93, p. 9.
855. BURNHAM, Deborah
"Albino." [PaintedB] (50/51) 93, p. 63.
"Born of Water and the Spirit." [WestB] (33) 93, p. 77.
"Forgetting." [Poetry] (161:4) Ja 93, p. 193.
"Steam." [ArtfulD] (24/25) 93, p. 127.
"Stone Soup." [WestB] (33) 93, p. 76-77.
"When the Unimaginable Becomes Easy." [Poetry] (161:4) Ja 93, p. 192.
856. BURNS, Cullen Bailey
"Sight Words." [Sonora] (26) Fall 93, p. 27-28.
857. BURNS, Elizabeth
"The Women Who Lived in Byron's Body." [13thMoon] (12:1/2) 93-94, p. 16.
858. BURNS, Gerald
"Atalanta in Cleveland." [GrandS] (11:4, #44) 93, p. 206-207.
"The Exorcism." [Talisman] (10) Spr 93, p. 160-161.
"Ing Poem for Sheila Murphy." [Boulevard] (8:1, #22) Spr 93, p. 164-165.
"Keats and Coleridge." [Talisman] (11) Fall 93, p. 244-246.
"Nature Poem." [NewAW] (11) Sum-Fall 93, p. 65-67.
"Poetry and Sleep." [AnotherCM] (25) Spr 93, p. 10-14.
"Superstar." [AmerPoR] (22:5) S-O 93, p. 20.
"Words Fail Me." [AnotherCM] (25) Spr 93, p. 15-16.
"Worm Casts" (for Vanessa Renwick). [Talisman] (10) Spr 93, p. 162.
859. BURNS, Heather
"The Last Image." [SouthernPR] (33:2) Fall 93, p. 54-55.
860. BURNS, Michael
"Hunting Wildflowers." [LaurelR] (27:2) Sum 93, p. 35-36.
"Speaking Mexican" (picking cotten with migrant workers near Egypt, Arkansas,
1961). [SouthernR] (29:2) Spr, Ap 93, p. 312.
"Store Boy." [LaurelR] (27:2) Sum 93, p. 36.
"The Urban Stream." [LaurelR] (27:2) Sum 93, p. 34-35.
861. BURNS, Ralph
"First Flight." [TriQ] (88) Fall 93, p. 82.
"For My Wife, on Our Son's Third Birthday." [TriQ] (88) Fall 93, p. 83.
"In the Bathroom Mirror." [GettyR] (6:3) Sum 93, p. 453.
"The Man Who Patched the Floor." [OhioR] (50) 93, p. 66-67.
"Two Birds." [OhioR] (50) 93, p. 68-69.
862. BURNS, Richard
"Analects" (Selections: 1-2, 24, 27, 31, 33-34, 48, 50, 82, 87, 91, 96, tr. of Vito
Markovic, w. Vera Radojevic). [NoDaQ] (61:1) Wint 93, p. 108-109.
"Anticipation" (tr. of Desanka Maksimovic, w. Jasna B. Misic). [NoDaQ] (61:1) Wint
93, p. 105.
"Anticipation" (tr. of Desanka Maksimovic, w. Jasna B. Misic). [NoDaQ] (61:1) Wint
93, p. 105.
"Between Bed and Table" (tr. of Duska Vrhovac, w. Vera Radojevic). [NoDaQ]
(61:1) Wint 93, p. 208.
"Daily Lament" (tr. of Tin Ujevic, w. Dasa Maric). [NoDaQ] (61:1) Wint 93, p. 188 -
189.
"Dinner by Candlelight" (tr. of Aleksandar Petrov). [NoDaQ] (61:1) Wint 93, p. 125 -
126.
"Dugout" (I-III, tr. of Duska Vrhovac, w. Vera Radojevic). [NoDaQ] (61:1) Wint 93,
p. 206-207.
"Frailty" (tr. of Tin Ujevic, w. Dasa Maric). [NoDaQ] (61:1) Wint 93, p. 191.
"Heavenly Firebird" (tr. of Aleksandar Petrov). [NoDaQ] (61:1) Wint 93, p. 126-128.
"I Have No More Time" (tr. of Desanka Maksimovic, w. Jasna B. Misic). [NoDaQ]
(61:1) Wint 93, p. 104.
"It Doesn't Matter Why" (tr. of Duska Vrhovac, w. Vera Radojevic). [NoDaQ] (61:1)
Wint 93, p. 208.
"The Necklace" (Selections: XXXII, XXV, XXXI, tr. of Tin Ujevic, w. Dasa Maric).
[NoDaQ] (61:1) Wint 93, p. 190-191.
"Nobody Knows" (tr. of Desanka Maksimovic, w. Jasna B. Misic). [NoDaQ] (61:1)
Wint 93, p. 105.

89

BURNS

"Poems from Hana (1939)" (tr. of Oskar Davico, w. Dasa Maric). [NoDaQ] (61:1)
Wint 93, p. 55-57.
"Poetry Visits an Old Lady" (tr. of Aleksandar Petrov). [NoDaQ] (61:1) Wint 93, p.
124-125.
"Poets" (tr. of A. B. Simic, w. Dasa Maric). [NoDaQ] (61:1) Wint 93, p. 174.
"Prayer" (tr. of Blaze Koneski, w. Dragana Marinkovic). [NoDaQ] (61:1) Wint 93, p.
98.
"Ring-a-by" (tr. of Duska Vrhovac, w. Vera Radojevic). [NoDaQ] (61:1) Wint 93, p.
207.
"Song of a Survivor" (for Oskar Davico). [NoDaQ] (61:1) Wint 93, p. 34-35.
"Speak Softly" (tr. of Desanka Maksimovic, w. Jasna B. Misic). [NoDaQ] (61:1)
Wint 93, p. 105.
"Star on High" (tr. of Tin Ujevic, w. Dasa Maric). [NoDaQ] (61:1) Wint 93, p. 192.
"Visitation" (tr. of Duska Vrhovac, w. Vera Radojevic). [NoDaQ] (61:1) Wint 93, p.
205.
863. BURNSIDE, John
"Dundee." [Verse] (10:1) Spr 93, p. 64.
"Form." [Verse] (10:1) Spr 93, p. 64.
"Home Farm." [Stand] (34:4) Aut 93, p. 64.
"Kissing the Mirror." [Verse] (10:1) Spr 93, p. 64.
"Lapsed." [Verse] (10:3) Wint 93, p. 96.
"A Merchant's House, West Friesland." [Verse] (10:3) Wint 93, p. 95.
"Occaisonal Poem" (for Charity Graepel, aged 2 months). [Verse] (10:3) Wint 93, p.
95.
"Stockholm Syndrome." [Verse] (10:3) Wint 93, p. 96-97.
864. BURRIS, Sidney
"Doing Lucretius." [IllinoisR] (1:1) Fall 93, p. 42-43.
"A Realm of Probability." [Poetry] (162:3) Je 93, p. 142.
865. BURROWS, E. G.
"Angels Among Us." [QRL] (12:32/33) 93, p. 71-73.
"At Home Within." [QRL] (12:32/33) 93, p. 74-75.
"Bog Life, Lake and Outlet." [Gaia] (1/2) Ap-Jl 93, p. 49.
"Dust." [Gaia] (1/2) Ap-Jl 93, p. 48-49.
"Elsewhere." [QRL] (12:32/33) 93, p. 77-78.
"The Honey Tree Cut Down for Firewood." [Wind] (23:72) 93, p. 10.
"Limits." [QRL] (12:32/33) 93, p. 74.
"The Market." [QRL] (12:32/33) 93, p. 76.
"Music Becoming Stone." [QRL] (12:32/33) 93, p. 71.
"Road Kill." [QRL] (12:32/33) 93, p. 76-77.
"The Wilderness." [QRL] (12:32/33) 93, p. 78-79.
866. BURRS, Mick
"The Tape of Silence." [PraF] (14:2) Sum 93, p. 14.
"To the Spirit of My Father I Address This Poem." [PraF] (14:2) Sum 93, p. 15.
BURSAC, Ellen Elias
See ELIAS-BURSAC, Ellen
867. BURSK, Christopher (Chris)
"Chief Never Weary." [QRL] (12:32/33) 93, p. 79-84.
"Impotence." [Sun] (214) O 93, p. 29.
"The Riot Police." [QRL] (12:32/33) 93, p. 85-89.
"Signaling" (for my son). [PaintedB] (50/51) 93, p. 49.
868. BURSKY, Rick
"Waiting for the Phone." [Plain] (13:2) Wint 93, p. 9.
869. BURT, Kathryn
"Everything Changes to Beauty." [Farm] (10:1) Spr-Sum 93, p. 48.
870. BUSCH, Trent
"The Box." [MidwQ] (34:2) Wint 93, p. 212.
"The Dime." [Verse] (10:3) Wint 93, p. 104-105.
"Dora Ann." [Manoa] (5:1) Sum 93, p. 24.
"The Orchard." [ClockR] (8:1/2) 93, p. 136-137.
"Summer Storm." [NowestR] (31:2) 93, p. 103.
"The Sweetness of Frenzy." [Manoa] (5:1) Sum 93, p. 25.
"Turner Cassity in Atlanta? I Thought He Was in Chicago." [CharR] (19:2) Fall 93,
p. 105.
871. BUSH, Rebecca
"She Likes the Pace of Insects." [13thMoon] (12:1/2) 93-94, p. 17.

90

872. BUSH, Stacy
   "Enchantment." [AmerPoR] (22:2) Mr-Ap 93, p. 44.
873. BUSHYEAGER, Peter
   "A person learns your name." [PaintedB] (50/51) 93, p. 97.
874. BUSTINZA, Ishmael
   " *Seguidillas* to Santiago, Born in Denton" (tr. of Jesús Díaz García, w. Leslie Palmer). [InterPR] (19:2) Fall 93, p. 29.
875. BUTCHER, Grace
   "Anything You Decide Changes Your Life." [HiramPoR] (53/54) Fall 92-Sum 93, p. 97-98.
876. BUTKA, Brenda
   "Amaryllis." [CumbPR] (12:2) Spr 93, p. 12-13.
877. BUTLER, Lynne Burris
   "Lucy Z." [ProseP] (2) 93, p. 17.
878. BUTLER, Robert Olen
   "She and I." [Conjunc] (21) 93, p. 344.
879. BUTLIN, Ron
   "Beginnings of the Ice Age." [Verse] (10:1) Spr 93, p. 62.
880. BUTOR, Michel
   "A Bride Abattue" (pour Vladimir Velickovic). [Os] (37) Wint 93, p. 22-23.
   "L'Opticien d'Argus" (pour Fernando Arrabal). [Os] (37) Wint 93, p. 20.
881. BUTSON, B. C. (Barry)
   "Anonymous." [PraF] (14:1) Spr 93, p. 115-116.
   "The Babysitter's Loss." [AntigR] (95) Aut 93, p. 39.
   "Girl in the Doorway." [EngJ] (82:5) S 93, p. 105.
   "Those Men Who Go Thump in the Night." [AntigR] (95) Aut 93, p. 38.
   "Wife." [Sun] (214) O 93, p. 7.
   "Working Man Fashion." [CanLit] (137) Sum 93, p. 50.
882. BUTTACI, Salvatore M. (Salvatore Amico M.)
   "Not About May Roses." [Plain] (13:2) Wint 93, p. 29.
   "What I Have Remembered." [Writer] (106:6) Je 93, p. 19.
883. BUTTERS, Christopher
   "Here." [SlipS] (13) 93, p. 9-10.
884. BUTTERWORTH, D. S.
   "In This Room." [WillowS] (32) Sum 93, p. 57.
885. BUTTIGIEG, Anton
   "Two Singers" (tr. by Oliver Friggieri). [Vis] (43) 93, p. 41.
886. BUTTS, W. E.
   "Remembering What Was Said." [PoetC] (24:3) Spr 93, p. 32.
887. BUZASSY, Ján
   "Mist" (tr. by Stephánia Allen and James Sutherland-Smith). [OxfordM] (9:1) Spr - Sum 93, p. 26.
888. BYARS, Anne
   "Yellow Insanity." [NorthStoneR] (11) 93, p. 112.
889. BYRKIT, Rebecca
   "The Only Dance There Is." [NewEngR] (15:2) Spr 93, p. 111-112.
890. BYRNE, Edward
   "April Snow." [AlabamaLR] (7:2) 93, p. 48-49.
891. BYRNE, Elena Karina
   "Every Definitive in July." [AntR] (51:2) Spr 93, p. 250.
892. BYRNE, Mairead
   "Commercial Street." [SenR] (23:1/2) Wint 93, p. 42.
   "Hunting." [SenR] (23:1/2) Wint 93, p. 43-44.
C RA
   See McGUIRT, C. Ra
893. CABA, Scarlet
   "Nightmare." [Americas] (21:2) Sum 93, p. 68.
   "Stress." [Americas] (21:2) Sum 93, p. 67.
894. CABALLERO-ROBB, Maria Elena
   "The Aging Saboteur Remembers the Majestic." [AntR] (51:1) Wint 93, p. 78-79.
   "The Lachrymose Marie d'Oignie." [PassN] (14:2) Wint 93, p. 8.
CABAN, David Cortes
   See CORTES-CABAN, David
895. CABANISS, Thomas
   "Of Rings and Roses." [SouthernPR] (33:1) Spr 93, p. 38.

896. CABLE, Gerald
   "Camp Job" (Kodiac [sic] Island, Alaska, 1983). [WillowS] (31) Wint 93, p. 85.
897. CABOT-BLACK, Sophie
   "21st of February" (tr. of Ana Cristina Cesar). [GrahamHR] (17) Fall 93, p. 101.
   "Among the Divided Lilies" (ICU Waiting Room, New York 1984). [Agni] (37) 93,
      p. 45-47.
   "Because Now." [Boulevard] (8:1, #22) Spr 93, p. 54.
   "Bedside" (tr. of Ana Cristina Cesar). [GrahamHR] (17) Fall 93, p. 98.
   "Midnight, June 16th" (tr. of Ana Cristina Cesar). [GrahamHR] (17) Fall 93, p. 99.
   "Overdose." [PartR] (60:3) Sum 93, p. 427-428.
   "Untitled: It is for you I write, hypocrite" (tr. of Ana Cristina Cesar). [GrahamHR]
      (17) Fall 93, p. 102.
   "Untitled: Nothing disguises the rush for love" (tr. of Ana Cristina Cesar).
      [GrahamHR] (17) Fall 93, p. 100.
   "Your Mouth Near My House." [Agni] (37) 93, p. 44.
898. CADDY, David
   "The Village Claws to Its Feet." [ChironR] (12:1, #34) Spr 93, p. 41.
899. CADNUM, Michael
   "Black Widow." [PikeF] (11) Fall 93, p. 5.
   "Burning the Garden." [CinPR] (24) Spr 93, p. 38-39.
   "The Changeling." [PikeF] (11) Fall 93, p. 29.
   "Dawn Heat." [GreenMR] (NS 6:2) Sum-Fall 93, p. 85.
   "The Eye." [LitR] (36:2) Wint 93, p. 158.
   "Flying over a River." [Comm] (120:16) 24 S 93, p. 18.
   "Genie." [PikeF] (11) Fall 93, p. 32.
   "Here There Is Only One Season." [GreenMR] (NS 6:2) Sum-Fall 93, p. 84.
   "Summer Pneumonia." [SlipS] (13) 93, p. 36.
   "Tomato Worms." [SouthernPR] (33:1) Spr 93, p. 66-67.
   "The Tongue." [LitR] (36:2) Wint 93, p. 159.
900. CAFAGNA, Marcus
   "Blood Rain." [LaurelR] (27:1) Wint 93, p. 38-39.
   "Reading Sex." [HarvardR] (4) Spr 93, p. 131.
   "Something Faithful." [Agni] (37) 93, p. 67.
   "The Way He Breaks." [Agni] (37) 93, p. 68.
901. CAGE, John
   "Forgive Me" (for Elfriede Fischinger). [GrandS] (12:1, #45) 93, p. 129.
902. CAGEN, Penny
   "Lament for Anne" (for Anne Krosby, 1957-1993). [Calyx] (15:1) Wint 93-94, p.
      114.
903. CAINE, Shulamith Wechter
   "The Long Slide." [Hellas] (4:1) Spr 93, p. 61.
904. CAIRNS, Scott
   "Advent." [Journal] (17:2) Fall-Wint 93, p. 7.
   "And Also from the Son" (qui ex Patre filioque). [ParisR] (35:128) Fall 93, p. 260.
   "Inscription." [ParisR] (35:128) Fall 93, p. 259.
   "Mortuary Art." [ParisR] (35:128) Fall 93, p. 261-262.
905. CALDER, Alison
   "I Tried to Write a Letter of Longing and Loss." [PraF] (14:3) Aut 93, p. 22.
906. CALHOUN, Quincy
   "Time's Up." [Americas] (21:2) Sum 93, p. 72-73.
907. CALISCH, Richard
   "Morning Song with Smoke." [CapeR] (28:2) Fall 93, p. 27.
   "The Watcher." [WillowR] (20) Spr 93, p. 22.
908. CALL, Jennifer
   "The Anatomy of Nostalgia." [LullwaterR] (4:2) Spr-Sum 93, p. 65.
   "Another Dream of Paleography" (for my mother). [CapeR] (28:2) Fall 93, p. 18.
   "The Story of Bones." [LullwaterR] (4:2) Spr-Sum 93, p. 18.
   "Vanishing Point." [CapeR] (28:2) Fall 93, p. 17.
909. CALLAN, Anne M.
   "All Souls' Day." [Poem] (70) N 93, p. 34-35.
   "Elegance." [Poem] (70) N 93, p. 37.
   "Having Spoken Only Once." [Poem] (70) N 93, p. 36.
910. CALLIN, Richard
   "Callin's Second Daughter" (for my mother). [SpoonR] (18:2) Sum-Fall 93, p. 45-48.
911. CAMERON, Lorna
   "Ecology." [PraF] (14:2) Sum 93, p. 21.

"Inquest." [PraF] (14:2) Sum 93, p. 20.
912. CAMMER, Les
"Come Here." [WormR] (33:1, #129) 93, p. 17.
"Have a good day." [WormR] (33:1, #129) 93, p. 18.
"Hot Green Pepper." [WormR] (33:1, #129) 93, p. 17.
"Malaiseville." [WormR] (33:3, #131), 93, p. 132.
"Radio Lady." [WormR] (33:3, #131), 93, p. 132.
913. CAMPBELL, Barbara
"Desire." [Epiphany] (4:3) Jl 93, p. 198.
914. CAMPBELL, Clinton B.
"Our Town." [JINJPo] (15:1) Spr 93, p. 30-31.
915. CAMPBELL, John R.
"Pastoral." [Poetry] (161:5) F 93, p. 278.
"Pornography." [Poetry] (161:5) F 93, p. 279.
916. CAMPBELL, Mary B.
"Are Sin Disease and Death Real?" (Chapbook: 17 poems. For George Starbuck:
      Bard, Birder, Blessed Mentor, Benevolent Inventor). [BlackWR] (19:2) Spr-
      Sum 93, p. 85-105.
917. CAMPBELL, Rick
"The Breathers, St. Mark's Lighthouse." [ChatR] (13:3) Spr 93, p. 13.
"The Dead." [Border] (2) Spr 93, p. 10.
"Leaving Home, Pittsburgh, 1966." [ApalQ] (38) 92, p. 78-79.
"Letter to Kathy from a Frigate at Sea." [ApalQ] (38) 92, p. 76-77.
"Orange Nights, Cold Stars." [ChatR] (13:3) Spr 93, p. 15-16.
"Pralines, Mt. Dora, a Bookmark." [ChatR] (13:3) Spr 93, p. 17.
"Sea Gull, Singer Island" (1/1/73). [ChatR] (13:3) Spr 93, p. 14.
918. CAMPBELL, Susan Maxwell
"The Concièrge Arrives in Heaven." [ChrC] (110:24) 25 Ag-1 S 93, p. 822.
"Sunday Night." [ChrC] (110:10) 24-31 Mr 93, p. 325.
919. CAMPERT, Remco
"Lullaby for a Bebop Baby." [Vis] (41) 93, p. 21.
920. CAMPIGLIO, Stephen
"Les Valeurs Personnelles." [Asylum] (8) 93, p. 111.
921. CAMPION, Dan
"Cold Spell." [Border] (2) Spr 93, p. 11.
"Englit." [Interim] (12:1) Spr-Sum 93, p. 23.
"Hyperbole." [Ascent] (17:3) Spr 93, p. 59.
"June 1st." [Light] (7) Aut 93, p. 8.
"Keeping Books." [Interim] (12:1) Spr-Sum 93, p. 24.
"The Magi." [Light] (8) Wint 93, p. 8.
"Salt." [Gaia] (3) O 93, p. 6.
"Scale." [Ascent] (17:3) Spr 93, p. 59.
"Vigil." [Gaia] (3) O 93, p. 6.
922. CAMPION, Thomas
"Now winter nights enlarge the number of their houres" (with music). [Light] (8)
      Wint 93, p. 24.
923. CAMPO, Rafael
"Age 5 Born with AIDS." [ParisR] (35:127) Sum 93, p. 213.
"Allegory." [KenR] (NS 15:4) Fall 93, p. 101-102.
"Anatomy Lesson." [PraS] (67:3) Fall 93, p. 65-66.
"Café Pamplona." [ParisR] (35:127) Sum 93, p. 212.
"Camino Real." [PartR] (60:3) Sum 93, p. 423-424.
"Cuban Poetry." [PraS] (67:3) Fall 93, p. 67.
"The Decline of the Spanish Empire." [PraS] (67:3) Fall 93, p. 66.
"The Distant Moon." [KenR] (NS 15:4) Fall 93, p. 104-105.
"DNA, or, the Legend of My Grandfather." [KenR] (NS 15:4) Fall 93, p. 103-104.
"The Doctor." [KenR] (NS 15:4) Fall 93, p. 103.
"Illness." [KenR] (NS 15:4) Fall 93, p. 102-103.
"Jorge Wrote This Poem." [JamesWR] (11:1) Fall 93, p. 17.
"An Obsession with Curlers." [Thrpny] (53) Spr 93, p. 22.
"Technology and Medicine." [KenR] (NS 15:4) Fall 93, p. 102.
"We Wear Each Other's Levis." [JamesWR] (11:1) Fall 93, p. 17.
924. CANAN, Janine
"Clarity." [Kalliope] (15:3) 93, p. 5.
"The Passage." [Kalliope] (15:3) 93, p. 6.
"What Woman Wants." [Kalliope] (15:3) 93, p. 7.

925. CANFIELD, Martha (Martha L.)
   "Raíz Absurda." [Luz] (5) N 93, p. 66-67.
   "Vigilia." [Luz] (5) N 93, p. 23.
926. CANNELLA, Wendy Anne
   "Afterlife" (The Free Lunch Mentor Series. Stephen Dunn Introduces). [FreeL] (12)
      Sum 93, p. 16.
   "What to Do When You Can't Control Anything" (The Free Lunch Mentor Series.
      Stephen Dunn Introduces). [FreeL] (12) Sum 93, p. 17.
   "White City" (The Free Lunch Mentor Series. Stephen Dunn Introduces). [FreeL]
      (12) Sum 93, p. 18-19.
927. CANNER, Niko
   "Ludwig Wittgenstein, 1946." [SpoonR] (18:1) Wint-Spr 93, p. 54.
   "What They've Let Me See." [Sequoia] (34/35) 92-93, p. 34.
   "Wittgenstein in the Trenches, 1916." [HarvardA] (127:2) Wint 93, p. 15.
928. CANNON, Harold C.
   "The Deaths of Poets." [Light] (6) Sum 93, p. 9.
929. CANNON, Maureen
   "Stair Case." [Light] (5) Spr 93, p. 10.
   "Suburban Sheik." [Light] (8) Wint 93, p. 19.
930. CANNON, Melissa
   "The Fertile Imagination." [Bogg] (66) Wint 92-93, p. 32.
931. CANNON, Moya
   "Arctic Tern." [SenR] (23:1/2) Wint 93, p. 28.
   "Scríob." [SenR] (23:1/2) Wint 93, p. 27.
   "Shards." [SenR] (23:1/2) Wint 93, p. 29.
932. CANTALUPO, Charles
   "Columbia, the Dove" (Excerpts). [Talisman] (11) Fall 93, p. 289-292.
933. CANTON y CANTON, Juan José
   "Tantas veces sonar, ¡tantas veces!" [LindLM] (12:2/4) Ap-D 93, p. 23.
934. CANTWELL, Kevin
   "Dora." [WestHR] (47:1) Spr 93, p. 55.
   "Madonna in Rome." [WestHR] (47:1) Spr 93, p. 57.
   "Prisoners Stealing Plums." [WestHR] (47:1) Spr 93, p. 56.
935. CAPELLO, Phyllis
   "My Father's Landscape." [Footwork] (23) 93, p. 177.
   "A Night's Sleep." [Footwork] (23) 93, p. 177.
936. CAPES, Andrea
   "A Civil Marriage." [Verse] (10:1) Spr 93, p. 78.
937. CAPITO
   "Some Amatory Epigrams from the Greek Anthology" (tr. by James Laughlin).
      [Sulfur] (33) Fall 93, p. 52.
938. CAPPELUTI, Jo-Anne
   "Response." [Journal] (17:1) Spr-Sum 93, p. 63.
939. CAPRON, Richard
   "Fallen Apples." [Footwork] (23) 93, p. 135.
CARBEAU, Mitchell Les
   See LesCARBEAU, Mitchell
940. CARBO, Nick
   "Land of the Morning." [GreenMR] (NS 6:1) Wint-Spr 93, p. 143-144.
941. CARDENAS, Rene
   "A Lesson in Sex." [PaintedHR] (9) Spr 93, p. 5.
942. CAREY, Barbara
   "Fear that the Bough." [MalR] (103) Sum 93, p. 54.
   "A Gap in the Streaming." [AmerV] (30) 93, p. 9.
   "The Ground of Events." [AmerV] (31) 93, p. 9-10.
   "In the Locked Room." [AmerV] (32) 93, p. 69.
   "The Struggle to Accept." [MalR] (103) Sum 93, p. 55.
943. CAREY, Michael
   "Archaeology" (for Gil Gee). [JINJPo] (15:1) Spr 93, p. 36-37.
   "By the Rising Waters" (for Sharon and Toby Parriott). [OnTheBus] (5:2, #12) Sum -
      Fall 93, p. 46.
   "Dead Wood." [PoetC] (24:3) Spr 93, p. 8-9.
   "Getting Ready to Spray Beans." [WebR] (17) Fall 93, p. 118.
   "Insistent" (For Sue and Ray Meylor). [WebR] (17) Fall 93, p. 116-117.
   "The Last Song of the Reluctant Landlord." [JINJPo] (15:1) Spr 93, p. 34-35.
   "The Loess Hills." [PoetC] (24:3) Spr 93, p. 6-7.

944. CAREY, Tom
    "Desire." [NewAW] (11) Sum-Fall 93, p. 101.
945. CARIAGA, Catalina
    "Saturn." [OnTheBus] (5:2, #12) Sum-Fall 93, p. 47.
CARIÑO, Maria Luisa B. Aguilar
    See AGUILAR-CARIÑO, Maria Luisa B.
946. CARIS, Jane
    "The Closet." [Pembroke] (25) 93, p. 103.
947. CARLILE, Henry
    "1953." [TarRP] (33:1) Fall 93, p. 42.
    "Her Things." [TarRP] (33:1) Fall 93, p. 42.
    "Ugly Money." [Poetry] (162:4) Jl 93, p. 219.
948. CARLIN, Mike
    "Where Are the Boyscouts When You Need Them?" [Pearl] (19) Fall-Wint 93, p. 22.
    "White Bread" (December. A mother writes to her son). [Pearl] (19) Fall-Wint 93, p. 23.
949. CARLIN, Vuyelwa
    "Darksmith." [FourQ] (7:2) Fall 93, p. 35.
    "Demeter's Lament for Her Coré." [Iowa] (23:1) Wint 93, p. 64-65.
    "Silver." [Iowa] (23:1) Wint 93, p. 63-64.
950. CARLISLE, Olga
    "Three Prayers for the First Forty Days of the Dead" (tr. of Essenin, w. W. S. Merwin). [QRL] (12:32/33) 93, p. 411-413.
951. CARLISLE, S. E.
    "Monk." [HarvardR] (5) Fall 93, p. 149.
952. CARLOS, Edward
    "Little Eva's Creation upon Her Death." [HampSPR] Wint 93, p. 19.
953. CARLSEN, Ioanna
    "A Week Before Christmas." [Poetry] (163:3) D 93, p. 144-145.
CARLSEN, Ivana Rangel
    See RANGEL-CARLSEN, Ivana
954. CARLSON, Barbara Siegel
    "King Richard's Faire." [PraS] (67:1) Spr 93, p. 83-84.
955. CARLSON, Thomas C.
    "The End of the History Lesson (Professor Guillaume)" (tr. of Virgil Mazilescu, w. Dumitru Radu Popa). [WillowS] (32) Sum 93, p. 25.
    "Guillaume's Song" (tr. of Vigil Mazilescu, w. Dumitru Radu Popa). [InterPR] (19:2) Fall 93, p. 59.
    "Not a monument have I raised in your soul" (tr. of Vigil Mazilescu, w. Dumitru Radu Popa). [InterPR] (19:2) Fall 93, p. 53.
    "Opinions About Guillaume" (tr. of Virgil Mazilescu, w. Dumitru Radu Popa). [WillowS] (32) Sum 93, p. 24.
    "Second Fairy Tale for Stefana" (tr. of Vigil Mazilescu, w. Dumitru Radu Popa). [InterPR] (19:2) Fall 93, p. 57.
    "Sleep My Love" (tr. of Vigil Mazilescu, w. Dumitru Radu Popa). [InterPR] (19:2) Fall 93, p. 61.
    "You Will Hear Once More: Be My Heart" (tr. of Vigil Mazilescu, w. Dumitru Radu Popa). [InterPR] (19:2) Fall 93, p. 55.
956. CARLSON-BRADLEY, Martha
    "Invitation to the Dance." [PoetryE] (36) Fall 93, p. 31.
    "Outing in October." [PoetryE] (36) Fall 93, p. 32.
957. CARNECI, Magda
    "An Immense Hand" (tr. by Adam Sorkin, w. the author). [Vis] (43) 93, p. 49.
958. CARNEY, Rob
    "Giant Steps." [Epiphany] (4:2) Ap 93, p. 123-124.
    "Reincarnation of a Love Bird" (Jazz at the Boathouse)." [Epiphany] (4:2) Ap 93, p. 125-134.
    "Softly, William, Softly." [BellArk] (9:1) Ja-F 93, p. 5.
    "Softly, William, Softly" (corrected reprint). [BellArk] (9:2) Mr-Ap 93, p. 13.
    "Syeeda's Song Flute." [BellArk] (9:6) N-D 93, p. 13.
    "Syeeda's Song Flute" (thanks to Anthony Richmond). [BellArk] (9:1) Ja-F 93, p. 14.
    "Vill-ah-nelling: thrivin' on a Riff." [BellArk] (9:4) Jl-Ag 93, p. 11.
959. CARPENTER, Bogdana
    "The Death of Lev" (tr. of Zbigniew Herbert, w. John Carpenter). [NewYorker] (69:4) 15 Mr 93, p. 78.

960. CARPENTER, Carol
"Musical Staff." [HawaiiR] (17:2, #38) Spr 93, p. 53.
961. CARPENTER, Jill
"This Is Not a Letter." [AntigR] (93-94) Spr-Sum 93, p. 158-159.
962. CARPENTER, John
"The Death of Lev" (tr. of Zbigniew Herbert, w. Bogdana Carpenter). [NewYorker]
(69:4) 15 Mr 93, p. 78.
963. CARPENTER, Lucas
"Connoisseur of Consciousness." [HampSPR] Wint 93, p. 71-72.
"Dada Nada Rama." [ChatR] (14:1) Fall 93, p. 69.
"In Kandinsky's Korner." [SoCoast] (15) Je 93, p. 22-23.
"Sitting on the Front Porch of Andalusia." [HampSPR] Wint 93, p. 70-71.
964. CARPENTER, William
"Girl Writing a Letter." [Iowa] (23:2) Spr-Sum 93, p. 102-103.
965. CARPER, Thomas
"A Bar in the Islands." [FreeL] (12) Sum 93, p. 7.
"From Nature." [Sparrow] (60) Sum 93, p. 52.
"A Late Rembrandt Self-Portrait." [Sparrow] (60) Sum 93, p. 52.
"Regrets" (I and II, tr. of Joachim du Bellay). [Sparrow] (60) Sum 93, p. 53-54.
"The Traveler's Story." [FreeL] (12) Sum 93, p. 7.
966. CARR, Nora J.
"Heart Throbs" (Young Writers, age 7). [PikeF] (11) Fall 93, p. 18.
967. CARR, Richard
"Sarah: Her Sibling in the Woods." [Plain] (13:2) Wint 93, p. 8.
968. CARR, Sally
"Trying to Sleep, Corsica." [Stand] (35:1) Wint 93-94, p. 62.
969. CARRANZA, Andrés "El Gato Rebelde"
"Cruisin the Boulevard." [BilingR] (18:1) Ja-Ap 93, p. 59.
"Ganga Slanga." [BilingR] (18:1) Ja-Ap 93, p. 58-59.
970. CARRARA, David
"Here and Back Again." [Talisman] (11) Fall 93, p. 270.
"Transfigured Fall" (tr. of George Trakl). [Talisman] (11) Fall 93, p. 212.
971. CARRERA, Margarita
"Encierro." [InterPR] (19:1) Spr 93, p. 16, 18.
"Solitary" (tr. by Leilani Wright). [InterPR] (19:1) Spr 93, p. 17, 19.
972. CARRERA ANDRADE, Jorge
"Nothing Is Ours" (tr. by Muna Lee). [QRL] (12:32/33) 93, p. 370-371.
973. CARRIER, Warren
"An Artist in Winter." [QRL] (12:32/33) 93, p. 91-92.
"Desert Places." [QRL] (12:32/33) 93, p. 90-91.
"Driving North" (for Paul Engle). [QRL] (12:32/33) 93, p. 91.
"The House." [QRL] (12:32/33) 93, p. 93.
"Island." [QRL] (12:32/33) 93, p. 90.
"Letter to Nobody." [QRL] (12:32/33) 93, p. 92.
"The Old Guy." [QRL] (12:32/33) 93, p. 92.
"Sleep." [QRL] (12:32/33) 93, p. 89-90.
"Stone Creek." [QRL] (12:32/33) 93, p. 93.
"You Ask Me a Question." [QRL] (12:32/33) 93, p. 89.
974. CARRILLO, Albino
"Moving Expenses." [AntR] (51:3) Sum 93, p. 374.
975. CARRINO, Michael
"The Dancer." [SycamoreR] (5:2) Sum 93, p. 77-78.
"Les Orangers" (A painting of the artist's brother and cousin in his garden — Gustave
Caillebotte, 1878). [GreenMR] (NS 6:2) Sum-Fall 93, p. 113-114.
"Wind, Santa Anna." [GreenMR] (NS 6:2) Sum-Fall 93, p. 115.
976. CARRIZO, Ricardo
"Arte Poetica (One More)" (from "Fractal," tr. of Luis Benítez). [Luz] (5) N 93, p. 19.
"Snail of Sleep over a Killing Thing" (from "Fractal," tr. of Luis Benítez). [Luz] (5) N
93, p. 53.
977. CARROLL, Anu
"Stuck." [HawaiiR] (17:3, #39) Fall 93, p. 99.
978. CARROLL, Lewis
"The Sea." [Light] (5) Spr 93, p. 30.
979. CARRUTH, Hayden
"Alteration." [Hudson] (46:1) Spr 93, p. 176.
"Another." [Nat] (257:5) 9-16 Ag 93, p. 186.

"The Camps." [KenR] (NS 15:4) Fall 93, p. 1-7.
"The Curtain." [Ploughs] (19:4) Wint 93-94, p. 50-51.
"Ecstasy." [KenR] (NS 15:4) Fall 93, p. 7.
"Endnote." [Poetry] (163:2) N 93, p. 89.
"Eternity Blues." [NewEngR] (15:1) Wint 93, p. 107-108.
"The Far-Removed Mountain Men." [QRL] (12:32/33) 93, p. 386-387.
"February Morning." [Ploughs] (19:4) Wint 93-94, p. 52-53.
"Five-Thirty A.M." [Hudson] (46:1) Spr 93, p. 173.
"Flying into St. Louis." [Hudson] (46:1) Spr 93, p. 173-174.
"Folk Song: On the Road Again." [OntR] (39) Fall-Wint 93-94, p. 60-61.
"Forty-Five." [AmerPoR] (22:1) Ja-F 93, p. 15.
"Graves." [BostonR] (18:5) O-N 93, p. 33.
"Hymn to Artemis." [QRL] (12:32/33) 93, p. 387-388.
"Old Poem Found on a Scrap of Paper: Penultimate Supplication." [GettyR] (6:3)
    Sum 93, p. 392.
"Particularity." [Boulevard] (8:1, #22) Spr 93, p. 48.
"Quality of Wine." [AmerPoR] (22:1) Ja-F 93, p. 15.
"Resorts." [AmerPoR] (22:1) Ja-F 93, p. 15.
"Surrealism" (for Charlie S.). [KenR] (NS 15:4) Fall 93, p. 8.
"Swept." [OntR] (39) Fall-Wint 93-94, p. 61.
"This Morning" (after Wang Wei). [Interim] (12:2) Fall-Wint 93, p. 3.
"Waterloo." [KenR] (NS 15:4) Fall 93, p. 9.
"Wife Poem." [Hudson] (46:1) Spr 93, p. 175.
"The Woodcut on the Cover of Robert Frost's *Complete Poems*." [Hudson] (46:1) Spr
    93, p. 176.
CARRUTH, Joe-Anne McLaughlin
    See McLAUGHLIN-CARRUTH, Joe-Anne
980. CARSON, Anne
    "Mimnermos and the Motions of Hedonism." [QRL] (12:32/33) 93, p. 97-101.
    "The Mimnermos Interviews" (I-III). [QRL] (12:32/33) 93, p. 101-104.
    "Mimnermos: the Brainsex Paintings" (A Translation of the Fragments of
        Mimnermos of Kolophon). [QRL] (12:32/33) 93, p. 94-96.
    "The Truth About God: Seventeen Poems." [AmerPoR] (22:1) Ja-F 93, p. 16-19.
981. CARTER, Andrea
    "Catch of the Day." [CapeR] (28:1) Spr 93, p. 2-3.
    "Will and Football." [Outbr] (24) 93, p. 86-87.
982. CARTER, Anne Babson
    "Cobb's Barns." [Nat] (256:21) 31 My 93, p. 746.
    "Miss Siegel's Boardinghouse." [WestHR] (47:4) Wint 93, p. 408-411.
    "Three Russias in One April." [WestHR] (47:4) Wint 93, p. 403-407.
983. CARTER, Ellin
    "Delusions of Starting Over." [Kalliope] (15:3) 93, p. 11.
    "Newsbreak." [ProseP] (2) 93, p. 18.
    "Steps." [ProseP] (2) 93, p. 19.
984. CARTER, Faye
    "Tomboy." [Wind] (23:72) 93, p. 5.
985. CARTER, Jared
    "Cistern." [CinPR] (24) Spr 93, p. 19.
    "Phosphorescence." [Iowa] (23:1) Wint 93, p. 62.
    "Spirea." [Iowa] (23:1) Wint 93, p. 57-61.
    "Visit" (First Place, Poetry Award). [NewL] (59:2) 93, p. 5-7.
986. CARTER, Laton
    "The Cats." [WormR] (33:3, #131), 93, p. 107.
    "The Names." [WormR] (33:3, #131), 93, p. 106.
987. CARTER, Nancy Corson
    "Partners." [AmerPoR] (22:6) N-D 93, p. 32.
CARTERET, Mark de
    See DeCARTERET, Mark
988. CARTWRIGHT, Keith
    "Black Rhythms of Peru" (tr. of Nicomedes Santa Cruz). [XavierR] (13:2) Fall 93, p.
        27-28.
    "Green China Tea." [Shen] (43:3) Fall 93, p. 23-25.
989. CARVER, Raymond
    "Alcohol." [NewEngR] (15:1) Wint 93, p. 109-110.
990. CASCELLA, Anna
    "Places" (tr. by Diane Lunde). [13thMoon] (11:1/2) 93, p. 208-209.

991. CASELLA, Paul J.
"Food and Lumber." [CutB] (39) Wint 93, p. 9-10.
992. CASELLA, R. Rantes
"At the Cafe Barbar." [OnTheBus] (5:2, #12) Sum-Fall 93, p. 48-49.
993. CASEY, Crysta
"Heart Clinic" (Selections: 6 poems). [BellArk] (9:6) N-D 93, p. 5.
"Highline Evaluation Treatment Center." [BellArk] (9:3) My-Je 93, p. 5.
"Source." [BellArk] (9:4) Jl-Ag 93, p. 8.
"The Voice." [BellArk] (9:1) Ja-F 93, p. 12.
994. CASEY, John Albert
"Barrens." [CarolQ] (46:1) Fall 93, p. 18.
"God's Blood." [CarolQ] (46:1) Fall 93, p. 16-17.
"Gravitas" (after Chekhov's "Gusev"). [CarolQ] (46:1) Fall 93, p. 15.
"Heron." [CarolQ] (46:1) Fall 93, p. 19.
995. CASEY, Kevin E.
"Who Do We Have Here?" [BlackWR] (19:1) Fall-Wint 92, p. 172.
996. CASH, Eric
"The Acid Rumor." [NewYorkQ] (50) 93, p. 65.
"Christmas Cards." [WormR] (33:3, #131), 93, p. 119.
"Continuing Ed." [WormR] (33:3, #131), 93, p. 119-120.
"The F.B.I. Involvement Rumor." [NewYorkQ] (50) 93, p. 67.
"The Kenya Rumor." [NewYorkQ] (50) 93, p. 66.
"Liquid Diet." [WormR] (33:3, #131), 93, p. 120.
"A Matter of Posturing." [WormR] (33:3, #131), 93, p. 119.
997. CASSELLS, Cyrus
"Coyote Seduces a Statue." [Ploughs] (19:1) Spr 93, p. 23-24.
"Marathon" (for Melvin Dixon. In Memoriam, 1950-1992). [KenR] (NS 15:4) Fall 93, p. 74.
"The Toss." [BostonR] (18:6) D 93-Ja 94, p. 27.
998. CASSELMAN, Barry
"An Age with Sunspots." [AmerPoR] (22:3) My-Je 93, p. 48.
"Deliveries." [NorthStoneR] (11) 93, p. 15.
"Gelatin Maps." [NorthStoneR] (11) 93, p. 16-17.
"Gravity Debris Resonating." [NorthStoneR] (11) 93, p. 14-15.
"Intimacy Joint Ventures." [AnotherCM] (26) Fall 93, p. 6-7.
999. CASSIDY, J. E.
"Blue Blood." [Footwork] (23) 93, p. 118.
"My Mother's Cowboy." [Footwork] (23) 93, p. 118.
1000. CASSIDY, John
"Looking Around." [Stand] (34:2) Spr 93, p. 49.
1001. CASSITY, Turner
"Horizons and Myopia." [Poetry] (162:5) Ag 93, p. 266-267.
"Red Rust in the Sunset." [Poetry] (162:5) Ag 93, p. 265.
1002. CASTANON, Ana
"I Am at Vons." [EvergreenC] (8:1) Spr-Sum 93, p. 6-7.
"Stick People." [EvergreenC] (8:1) Spr-Sum 93, p. 8.
1003. CASTILLO, Amelia del
"Géminis Deshabitado." [LindLM] (12:1) Mr 93, p. 25.
1004. CASTILLO, Arnulfo
"Corrido de Ines Chavez Garcia." [BilingR] (18:1) Ja-Ap 93, p. 5-6.
1005. CASTILLO, Sandra M.
"The Contra." [ApalQ] (38) 92, p. 49-50.
"Unearthing the Remains." [ApalQ] (38) 92, p. 47-48.
1006. CASTLEBERRY, R. T.
"33 3/4." [Vis] (42) 93, p. 26.
"Redemption's Wilderness." [Parting] (6:2) Wint 93, p. 5-6.
1007. CASTLEBURY, John
"Point Blank." [TickleAce] (25) Spr-Sum 93, p. 181-182.
1008. CASTRO, Adrian
"Music & Guaracha When Stories Sound Too Tall." [BilingR] (18:1) Ja-Ap 93, p. 53-55.
1009. CASTRO, Jan Garden
"Full Moon." [NewL] (59:4) 93, p. 99.
1010. CASTRO, Luisa
"It's Basic" (tr. by Deborah L. Owen). [LitR] (36:3) Spr 93, p. 362-364.

1011. CASTRO, Michael
"Xmas, 1991." [Drumvoices] (2:1/2) Fall-Wint 92-93, p. 38-39.
1012. CATACALOS, Rosemary
"The History of Abuse, a Language Poem." [ColR] (20:2) Fall 93, p. 81-83.
"Morning Geography" (for Naomi Shihab Nye). [ColR] (20:2) Fall 93, p. 79-80.
1013. CATALA, Rafael
"Los Dos Caminos." [Trasimagen] (1:1) Otoño-Invierno 93, p. 29.
"Holograma." [Trasimagen] (1:1) Otoño-Invierno 93, p. 30.
"La Pareja." [Trasimagen] (1:1) Otoño-Invierno 93, p. 31.
"Teatro de Sinonimos" (Del Libro: Teatro de Sinonimos — Realidad Aparte,
Corrales, Nuevo México). [Trasimagen] (1:1) Otoño-Invierno 93, p. 28.
1014. CATHERWOOD, Michael
"In the Big City." [BlackWR] (19:1) Fall-Wint 92, p. 170-171.
1015. CATLIN, Alan
"Lab Rats." [DogRR] (12:1, #23) Spr-Sum 93, p. 26-27.
"Spaces." [SlipS] (13) 93, p. 113-117.
1016. CATULLUS
"Fair Exchange" (tr. by Jack Flavin). [SpoonR] (18:1) Wint-Spr 93, p. 42.
"Letter to Flavius" (tr. by Jack Flavin). [ApalQ] (35) 90, p. 49.
"Poem After Sappho" (tr. by Jack Flavin). [ApalQ] (35) 90, p. 51.
"A Selection of Epigrams" (by Catullus, et al., tr. by Jack Flavin). [SpoonR] (18:1)
Wint-Spr 93, p. 41.
"Suffenus" (tr. by Jack Flavin). [ApalQ] (35) 90, p. 50.
1017. CAUDILL, Carla
"What He Knows." [Blueline] (14) 93, p. 19.
1018. CAULFIELD, Carlota
"Anonimo (Siglo XV)" (from "Polvo de Angel"). [Luz] (5) N 93, p. 68.
"Anonymous (Fifteenth Century)" (from "Angel Dust," tr. by Carol Maier). [Luz]
(5) N 93, p. 69.
"Zazen" (from "Polvo de Angel," in Spanish and English, tr. by Carol Maier). [Luz]
(5) N 93, p. 40.
1019. CAVAFY, Constantine (C. P., Constantine P.)
"Nero's Respite" (tr. by Edmund Keeley and Philip Sherrard). [QRL] (12:32/33) 93,
p. 390.
"Of Painting" (tr. by James Stone). [DenQ] (28:1) Sum 93, p. 25.
"One of Their Gods" (tr. by Edmund Keeley and Philip Sherrard). [QRL] (12:32/33)
93, p. 389.
"Waiting for the Barbarians" (tr. by Edmund Keeley and Philip Sherrard). [QRL]
(12:32/33) 93, p. 388-389.
"Walls" (tr. by James Stone). [DenQ] (28:1) Sum 93, p. 25.
1020. CAVALIERI, Grace
"The Perfect Day" (for Ken). [Footwork] (23) 93, p. 215.
1021. CAVALLO, Mildred
"One Tuesday in June." [NewYorkQ] (51) 93, p. 80.
1022. CAVANAGH, Clare
"Brueghel's Two Monkeys" (tr. of Wislawa Szymborska, w. Stanislaw Baranczak).
[NewYorker] (69:5) 22 Mr 93, p. 61.
"Cat in an Empty Apartment" (tr. of Wislawa Szymborska, w. Stanislaw
Baranczak). [NewYRB] (40:17) 21 O 93, p. 42.
"Conversation with a Stone" (tr. of Wislawa Szymborska, w. Stanislaw Baranczak).
[ManhatR] (7:1) Fall 93, p. 79-80.
"The End and the Beginning" (tr. of Wislawa Szymborska, w. Stanislaw Baranczak).
[NewRep] (208:3) 18 Ja 93, p. 40.
"In Heraclitus's River" (tr. of Wislawa Szymborska, w. Stanislaw Baranczak).
[Agni] (38) 93, p. 107.
"No Title Required" (tr. of Wislawa Szymborska, w. Stanislaw Baranczak).
[ManhatR] (7:1) Fall 93, p. 81-82.
"A Paleolithic Fertility Fetish" (tr. of Wislawa Szymborska, w. Stanislaw
Baranczak). [ManhatR] (7:1) Fall 93, p. 78.
"Parting with a View" (tr. of Wislawa Szymborska, w. Stanislaw Baranczak). [TriQ]
(89) Wint 93-94, p. 178-179.
"Reality Demands" (tr. of Wislawa Szymborska, w. Stanislaw Baranczak).
[NewYorker] (69:2) 1 Mr 93, p. 86-87.
1023. CAVANAUGH, William
"California Cycles." [HopewellR] (5) 93, p. 95.
"Killing Time." [HopewellR] (5) 93, p. 49.

CAYATTE, McNeal
    See CHAKULA CHA JUA (McNeal Cayatte)
1024. CAYLOR, Duane K.
    "Backwater." [MidwQ] (34:2) Wint 93, p. 213.
    "Nancy: After Her Bath." [Hellas] (4:2) Fall 93, p. 72.
    "Oranges." [Hellas] (4:2) Fall 93, p. 70.
    "The Way of Geese." [Hellas] (4:2) Fall 93, p. 73.
    "Yellow-eyed Grackle." [Hellas] (4:2) Fall 93, p. 71.
1025. CECIL, Richard
    "Adult Education." [Crazy] (44) Spr 93, p. 18-20.
    "American Parnassas." [Crazy] (44) Spr 93, p. 24-26.
    "Angel Sighted from Airliner!" [NoDaQ] (61:4) Fall 93, p. 67-68.
    "Charlie Chan Solves Another Murder." [HopewellR] (5) 93, p. 50-51.
    "Eighth Grade Science at Blessed Sacrament." [SycamoreR] (5:2) Sum 93, p. 73-74.
    "February 29." [HopewellR] (5) 93, p. 37-38.
    "Front Porch Visiting." [Crazy] (44) Spr 93, p. 21-23.
1026. CELAN, Paul
    "Alchemical" (tr. by Michael Hamburger). [QRL] (12:32/33) 93, p. 391-392.
    "Leap-Centuries" (tr. by Michael Hamburger). [QRL] (12:32/33) 93, p. 390-391.
    "Love Song" (tr. by Stavros Deligiorgis). [WorldL] (4) 93, p. 23.
    "Tenebrae" (in German and English, tr. by John Felstiner). [TriQ] (87) Spr-Sum 93,
        p. 196-197.
1027. CENTOLELLA, Thomas
    "Perfecta." [HayF] (12) Spr-Sum 93, p. 93-95.
1028. CERNUDA, Luis
    "Dark Afternoon" (tr. by Eddie Flintoff). [InterPR] (19:2) Fall 93, p. 23.
    "The Garden" (tr. by Eddie Flintoff). [InterPR] (19:2) Fall 93, p. 19, 21.
    "Jardín." [InterPR] (19:2) Fall 93, p. 18, 20.
    "Tarde Oscura." [InterPR] (19:2) Fall 93, p. 22.
1029. CERRI, Giovanni
    "Cain" (tr. by Luigi Bonaffini). [Vis] (43) 93, p. 29.
1030. CERRUTO, Lauren
    "Glen Ridge, NJ." [Footwork] (23) 93, p. 135-136.
1031. CERVANTES, Lorna Dee
    "On Speaking to the Dead." [ColR] (20:2) Fall 93, p. 181.
1032. CERVO, Nathan
    "Chardin and the New Filoque." [SpiritSH] (58) 93, p. 33-34.
    "Entelechy Just Happens." [SpiritSH] (58) 93, p. 32.
1033. CESAR, Ana Cristina
    "21st of February" (tr. by Sopie Cabot-Black). [GrahamHR] (17) Fall 93, p. 101.
    "Bedside" (tr. by Sopie Cabot-Black). [GrahamHR] (17) Fall 93, p. 98.
    "Midnight, June 16th" (tr. by Sopie Cabot-Black). [GrahamHR] (17) Fall 93, p. 99.
    "Untitled: It is for you I write, hypocrite" (tr. by Sopie Cabot-Black). [GrahamHR]
        (17) Fall 93, p. 102.
    "Untitled: Nothing disguises the rush for love" (tr. by Sopie Cabot-Black).
        [GrahamHR] (17) Fall 93, p. 100.
CHA JUA, CHAKULA (McNeal Cayatte)
    See CHAKULA CHA JUA (McNeal Cayatte)
1034. CHABEREK, Ed
    "An Anxious Dream." [Asylum] (8) 93, p. 120.
    "It's Time." [Plain] (13:3) Spr 93, p. 27.
    "Like in the Mirror." [Plain] (14:1) Fall 93, p. 27.
    "Reflecting" (tr. of Roberts Muks, w. Guna Kupcs Chaberek). [GrahamHR] (17)
        Fall 93, p. 43.
1035. CHABEREK, Guna Kupcs
    "1,980th Christmas" (tr. of Roberts Muks). [GrahamHR] (17) Fall 93, p. 42.
    "A Brief Meeting" (tr. of Roberts Muks). [Lactuca] (17) Apr 93, p. 36.
    "Leaping Over My Shadow" (tr. of Roberts Muks). [Lactuca] (17) Apr 93, p. 37.
    "More About Crocodiles" (tr. of Roberts Muks). [Lactuca] (17) Apr 93, p. 35.
    "Reflecting" (tr. of Roberts Muks, w. Ed Chaberek). [GrahamHR] (17) Fall 93, p.
        43.
    "To Bakchus" (tr. of Roberts Muks). [Lactuca] (17) Apr 93, p. 34.
1036. CHADBOURNE, Kate
    "Cables." [BelPoJ] (44:2) Wint 93-94, p. 32-33.
1037. CHAKULA CHA JUA (McNeal Cayatte)
    "Poem for Mildred, Wherever You Are." [AfAmRev] (27:1) Spr 93, p. 139-141.

CHALLANDER, Craig
    See CHALLENDER, Craig
1038. CHALLENDER, Craig
    "Dancing on Water." [BellArk] (9:2) Mr-Ap 93, p. 12.
    "The Journey." [CinPR] (24) Spr 93, p. 13.
    "Ted." [BellArk] (9:2) Mr-Ap 93, p. 25.
1039. CHALMER, Judith
    "Dolls and Rags." [PoetC] (24:3) Spr 93, p. 56-57.
    "Green River Reservoir." [SenR] (23:1/2) Wint 93, p. 117-118.
1040. CHAMBERS, Antonia
    "One World, Two Voices." [AmerPoR] (22:3) My-Je 93, p. 15.
1041. CHAMBERS, George
    "A Little Request" (w. Raymond Federman). [ProseP] (2) 93, p. 21.
    "The Princess and the Frog" (w. Raymond Federman). [ProseP] (2) 93, p. 20.
1042. CHAMOPOULOS, Penny
    "Summer evening rain." [Amelia] (7:2, #21) 93, p. 61.
1043. CHANDLER, Tom
    "Footage of Hitler." [Pembroke] (25) 93, p. 114.
    "Mazilli's Breakfast." [SycamoreR] (5:1) Wint 93, p. 55.
    "Nolan Ryan." [GrahamHR] (17) Fall 93, p. 82.
    "Ruth Briggs." [Pembroke] (25) 93, p. 113.
    "Shoveling Coal." [Pembroke] (25) 93, p. 112.
    "True Tales of Synchronicity." [Pembroke] (25) 93, p. 115.
    "Unsigned Confession." [Pembroke] (25) 93, p. 113.
1044. CHANDONNET, Ann Fox
    "Iris Is Last" (For Shem Pete, 1896?-1989, whom *USA Today* called "the last of his
        people"). [Gaia] (3) O 93, p. 37-38.
1045. CHANDRA, G. S. Sharat
    "The Absent." [GrahamHR] (17) Fall 93, p. 16.
    "Anniversary of a Drowning." [GrahamHR] (17) Fall 93, p. 17.
    "The Grail." [GrahamHR] (17) Fall 93, p. 13.
    "Islands." [PoetC] (24:2) Wint 93, p. 29-30.
    "The Muse." [GrahamHR] (17) Fall 93, p. 14.
    "Re-Entering the Past." [NewL] (59:3) 93, p. 85.
    "Road to Dhaka." [NoAmR] (278:1) Ja-F 93, p. 31.
    "Tailgating America Astride the Holy Cow." [NewL] (59:3) 93, p. 84.
    "Twilight in Bombay." [NewL] (59:3) 93, p. 86-87.
    "Two Women." [GrahamHR] (17) Fall 93, p. 15.
CHANG, Soo Ko
    See KO, Chang Soo
1046. CHANG, Victoria M.
    "The Day My Aunt Married a White Man." [HawaiiR] (17:1, #37) Spr 93, p. 98.
    "Mahjong Party: Chinatown, New York City." [HawaiiR] (17:1, #37) Spr 93, p. 97.
    "With the Communist Radio Buzz Behind: Leaving Beijing." [HawaiiR] (17:1, #37)
        Spr 93, p. 96.
1047. CHAO
    "An Anecdote of the Double Ninth Festival." [CharR] (19:2) Fall 93, p. 88.
    "Consecration." [CharR] (19:2) Fall 93, p. 87.
    "The Great Wall." [CharR] (19:2) Fall 93, p. 87.
    "The Pinwheel of Fortune — Double Ninth Festival." [CharR] (19:2) Fall 93, p. 88.
1048. CHAPEN, Skip
    "Cleaning the Gutters." [ChangingM] (26) Sum-Fall 93, p. 13.
1049. CHAPMAN, Freida
    "In My Vase." [13thMoon] (12:1/2) 93-94, p. 18.
1050. CHAPMAN, I. M.
    "A Spoon in Words, or, How Many Fathoms Deep." [Poem] (70) N 93, p. 40-41.
1051. CHAPMAN, Michael J.
    "Electric Heart." [JamesWR] (10:2) Wint 93, p. 7.
1052. CHAPMAN, Robin S.
    "The Jo-Al Beauty Shoppe." [SouthernR] (29:3) Sum, Jl 93, p. 589-590.
    "Valentines." [Northeast] (5:9) Wint 93-94, p. 15-16.
1053. CHAPMAN, Sean B.
    "Wounds." [LaurelR] (27:2) Sum 93, p. 85.
1054. CHAPPAZ, Maurice
    "Office des Morts." [LitR] (36:4) Sum 93, p. 531.
    "Service for the Dead" (tr. by Richard Kopp). [LitR] (36:4) Sum 93, p. 530.

1055. CHAPPELL, Fred
   "Literary Critic." [HarvardR] (5) Fall 93, p. 198.
   "Nettle." [HarvardR] (5) Fall 93, p. 198.
   "No Defense." [HarvardR] (5) Fall 93, p. 198.
   "Sex Manual." [HarvardR] (5) Fall 93, p. 199.
   "Upon a Confessional Poet." [HarvardR] (5) Fall 93, p. 198.
   "The Voices." [TarRP] (33:1) Fall 93, p. 37.
1056. CHAR, René
   "The Damaged Crop" (tr. by Charles Guenther). [QRL] (12:32/33) 93, p. 392-393.
   "Fascinating Four" (tr. by Charles Guenther). [QRL] (12:32/33) 93, p. 393.
1057. CHARITY, Nadine A.
   "Intersection." [LouisL] (10:2) Fall 93, p. 59-60.
1058. CHARLES, David
   "The Balding Animal Lover." [OnTheBus] (6:1, #13) Wint 93-Spr 94, p. 62-63.
   "Seven Horses." [OnTheBus] (6:1, #13) Wint 93-Spr 94, p. 62.
   "Silent Night." [OnTheBus] (6:1, #13) Wint 93-Spr 94, p. 63-65.
   "Those Hours." [OnTheBus] (6:1, #13) Wint 93-Spr 94, p. 61.
1059. CHARMAN, Janet
   "Found Language." [WestCL] (27:2, #11) Fall 93, p. 60-62.
1060. CHARTIER, Bill
   "Poem of My Skin." [BambooR] (57) Wint 93, p. 155.
1061. CHARTKOFF, Zachary
   "Still Born." [ChangingM] (25) Wint-Spr 93, p. 17.
1062. CHASE, Alfonso
   "Aniversario" (from "Entre el Ojo y la Noche"). [Luz] (5) N 93, p. 45-46.
1063. CHASE, Naomi Feigelson
   "Seascape with House and Stars." [HarvardR] (5) Fall 93, p. 168.
   "Since You Insisted on a Modern Love Poem." [SoCoast] (14) Ja 93, p. 12-13.
   "Waiting for the Messiah in Somerville, Mass." [SoCoast] (14) Ja 93, p. 10-11.
1064. CHATFIELD, Hale
   "Composition: Vox." [HiramPoR] (53/54) Fall 92-Sum 93, p. 99-100.
1065. CHATTERJEE, Enaksi
   "Curse" (tr. of Kabita Sinha, w. Carolyne Wright). [AmerPoR] (22:4) Jl-Ag 93, p.
      27.
   "Departure" (tr. of Kabita Sinha, w. Carolyne Wright). [AmerPoR] (22:4) Jl-Ag 93,
      p. 26.
   "Last Meeting" (tr. of Kabita Sinha, w. Carolyne Wright). [AmerPoR] (22:4) Jl-Ag
      93, p. 26.
   "Party" (tr. of Kabita Sinha, w. Carolyne Wright). [AmerPoR] (22:4) Jl-Ag 93, p.
      27.
   "Waterfall" (tr. of Kabita Sinha, w. Carolyne Wright). [AmerPoR] (22:4) Jl-Ag 93,
      p. 26.
1066. CHATTOPADHYAY, Gita
   "This Night Train" (tr. by Paramita Banerjee and Carolyne Wright). [Prima] (16/17)
      93, p. 82.
   "Thou Art Durga" (tr. by Paramita Banerjee and Carolyne Wright). [Prima] (16/17)
      93, p. 81.
1067. CHAUDHURY, Kirti
   "Welcoming All Comers" (tr. by Arlene Zide). [Vis] (43) 93, p. 26.
1068. CHAUSS, Harry
   "For a Friend" (for Carol). [QW] (37) Sum-Fall 93, p. 207.
1069. CHAVARRIA-AGUILAR, O. L.
   "Siberia." [Light] (7) Aut 93, p. 19.
1070. CHAVEZ, Daniel
   "The Darkness." [Sequoia] (34/35) 92-93, p. 32.
1071. CHAVIANO, Daína
   "Hijas de Mab." [LindLM] (12:1) Mr 93, p. 5.
   "Oyá." [LindLM] (12:1) Mr 93, p. 5.
   "Reencarnación." [LindLM] (12:1) Mr 93, p. 5.
1072. CHELIUS, Joseph A.
   "You, on Settlement Day." [FourQ] (7:2) Fall 93, p. 46.
1073. CHEN, Jingrong
   "Doves" (November 18, 1947, Shanghai, tr. by Emily Yau). [ConnPR] (12:1) 93, p.
      13.
   "Flowers, Trees, Clouds" (Fall 1981, Beijing, tr. by Emily Yau). [ConnPR] (12:1)
      93, p. 12.

CHEN

1074. CHEN, Lisa
"Redemption." [Thrpny] (54) Sum 93, p. 21.
1075. CHEN, Maiping
"Requiem" (for the victims of June Fourth, tr. of Bei Dao, w. Bonnie S.
McDougall). [ChiR] (39:3/4) 93, p. 288.
1076. CHEN, Xueliang
"Andante Cantabile" (tr. of Bei Dao, w. Donald Finkel). [SenR] (23:1/2) Wint 93, p.
158-159.
"Bridge" tr. of Bei Dao, w. Donald Finkel). [DenQ] (28:1) Sum 93, p. 24.
"Commercial" (tr. of Bei Dao, w. Donald Finkel). [SenR] (23:1/2) Wint 93, p. 157.
"Deserted City" (tr. of Bei Dao, w. Donald Finkel). [ManhatR] (7:1) Fall 93, p. 51.
"Guide to Summer" (tr. of Bei Dao, w. Donald Finkel). [SenR] (23:1/2) Wint 93, p.
160.
"Hurried Night" (tr. of Bei Dao, w. Donald Finkel). [SenR] (23:1/2) Wint 93, p. 161.
"Loyalty" (tr. of Bei Dao, w. Donald Finkel). [ManhatR] (7:1) Fall 93, p. 49.
"Night Patrol" (tr. of Bei Dao, w. Donald Finkel). [ManhatR] (7:1) Fall 93, p. 50.
"Notes of an Afternoon" (tr. of Bei Dao, w. Donald Finkel). [ManhatR] (7:1) Fall
93, p. 52.
"On Eternity" (tr. of Bei Dao, w. Donald Finkel). [ManhatR] (7:1) Fall 93, p. 55.
"Portrait" (tr. of Bei Dao, w. Donald Finkel). [SenR] (23:1/2) Wint 93, p. 162.
"Scenery" (tr. of Bei Dao, w. Donald Finkel). [ManhatR] (7:1) Fall 93, p. 54.
"Sower" (tr. of Bei Dao, w. Donald Finkel). [SenR] (23:1/2) Wint 93, p. 163.
"Untitled: At the front, defending the mother tongue" (tr. of Bei Dao, w. Donald
Finkel). [ManhatR] (7:1) Fall 93, p. 53.
"Variations" (tr. of Bei Dao, w. Donald Finkel). [ManhatR] (7:1) Fall 93, p. 48.
1077. CHEN, Yanbing
"Gate of Virtue and Victory (De Sheng Men)" (tr. of Gu Cheng, w. John
Rosenwald). [ChiR] (39:3/4) 93, p. 292.
CHEN, Yuan
See YUAN, Chen
CHENG, Gu
See GU, Cheng
1078. CHENOWETH, Okey
"A List of Prayers and a Gift." [Footwork] (23) 93, p. 64.
"An Old Woman Remembers." [Footwork] (23) 93, p. 65.
"On a Young Man Packing Groceries." [Footwork] (23) 93, p. 64.
"Supermen." [Footwork] (23) 93, p. 65.
"To the Children." [Footwork] (23) 93, p. 64.
1079. CHERKOVSKI, Neeli (Neelie)
"Gilgamesh: A Lament." [OnTheBus] (6:1, #13) Wint 93-Spr 94, p. 66-67.
"Historical Notes." [Talisman] (11) Fall 93, p. 163-165.
1080. CHERRY, Kelly
"Byrd's Survey of the Boundary: An Abridgment" (Drawn from *The History of the
Dividing Line Betwixt Virginia and North Carolina, Run in the Year of Our
Lord, 1728*). [Parting] (6:2) Wint 93, p. 12-15.
"Divorce in Wellfleet, Massachusetts." [Parting] (6:2) Wint 93, p. 19.
"How We Are Taken" (Lines written while thinking of my recently deceased parents
and what they are missing). [Hellas] (4:2) Fall 93, p. 110.
"I Loved You Once But Then I Was Not I." [IllinoisR] (1:1) Fall 93, p. 13.
"Listening to Oneself." [HarvardR] (3) Wint 93, p. 30.
"Street Cleaning in November." [Parting] (6:2) Wint 93, p. 21.
"Thin Black Man with Wife and Child in the Polonia Restaurant, New York, 1970."
[Parting] (6:1) Sum 93, p. 49.
1081. CHESAK, Laura
"The Call" (tr. of Soledad Santamaría). [InterPR] (19:2) Fall 93, p. 27.
1082. CHESS, Richard
"At Seven Months." [Sun] (214) O 93, p. 33.
"The Eve of Rosh Hashanah, 500 Years after the Inquisition." [LouisL] (10:2) Fall
93, p. 34-35.
"From a Prayer for the Bride." [Sun] (210) Je 93, p. 38.
"The Good Jew." [OnTheBus] (5:2, #12) Sum-Fall 93, p. 50.
"Holocaust Day." [LouisL] (10:2) Fall 93, p. 33.
"The Rabbi's Wife." [AmerV] (30) 93, p. 18.
"The Rest of the Year." [ColEng] (55:5) S 93, p. 536-537.
"Survivors." [MassR] (34:3) Aut 93, p. 392.

1083. CHI, Emily Exner
"This Way Out." [AmerS] (62:3) Sum 93, p. 421-422.
CHI, Ishioka
    See ISHIOKA, Chi
1084. CHI, K'ang (223-262)
"Taoist Song" (tr. by Arthur Waley). [NewYorkQ] (51) 93, p. 98.
CHIAO, Meng
    See MENG, Chiao
1085. CHIARILLI, Anthony L.
"Master of Winds." [CapeR] (28:2) Fall 93, p. 47.
1086. CHICOINE, Bob
"The Wrecking of Old Comiskey." [Spitball] (44) Sum 93, p. 36-59.
1087. CHIFU, Gabriel
"31 August 1986, 12:28 A.M. (Earthquake Time)" (tr. by Adam Sorkin and Taina Dutescu-Coliban). [IndR] (16:2) Fall 93, p. 82.
"Drawing Close" (tr. by Adam Sorkin and Taina Dutescu-Coliban). [IndR] (16:2) Fall 93, p. 84.
"Stubborn" (tr. by Adam Sorkin and Taina Dutescu-Coliban). [IndR] (16:2) Fall 93, p. 83.
1088. CHILCOTE, S. M.
"In This Old Fastness." [TickleAce] (23) Spr-Sum 92, p. 92.
1089. CHILDISH, Billy
"T.V." [Bogg] (66) Wint 92-93, p. 46.
1090. CHIN, Curtis
"Oranges." [PoetL] (88:1) Spr 93, p. 22.
1091. CHIN, David
"Bluebird." [Footwork] (23) 93, p. 48-49.
CH'ING, Lo
    See LO, Ch'ing
1092. CHINITZ, Helen Stevens
"Caboose." [SouthernPR] (33:1) Spr 93, p. 70-72.
1093. CHIPASULA, Frank
"The Dance Has Entered the Streets" (for the dead in Nairobi and Blantyre). [Paint] (20:39/40) Spr-Aut 93, p. 237-238.
"Singing Like Parrots" (from *Whispers in the Wings*, 1991). [Paint] (20:39/40) Spr-Aut 93, p. 233-234.
"The Water of Light." [Paint] (20:39/40) Spr-Aut 93, p. 235-236.
1094. CHISHOLM, Stephen
"The Strike Out King." [Pearl] (19) Fall-Wint 93, p. 67.
1095. CHITWOOD, Michael
"Assistant." [Thrpny] (55) Fall 93, p. 15.
"Basement Barber." [Poetry] (162:1) Ap 93, p. 32.
"Fossil." [Shen] (43:2) Sum 93, p. 25.
"Heft of the Afternoon." [ProseP] (1) 92, p. 15.
"Looking for Blues." [Thrpny] (52) Wint 93, p. 9.
"Lovers." [ProseP] (1) 92, p. 16.
"The Quick." [PraS] (67:1) Spr 93, p. 112-113.
"Sugar." [CreamCR] (17:1) Spr 93, p. 55.
"The Truth." [OhioR] (50) 93, p. 106-107.
"Watching My Father Look at *Playboy*." [AnotherCM] (25) Spr 93, p. 22.
CH'IUNG-CH'IUNG, Yuan
    See YUAN, Ch'iung-ch'iung
CHIWAN, Choi
    See CHOI, Chiwan
1096. CHMEL, Karol
"Bequest (to Other Thieves)" (tr. by Stephánia Allen and James Sutherland-Smith). [OxfordM] (9:1) Spr-Sum 93, p. 116.
"Skepticism" (tr. by Stephánia Allen and James Sutherland-Smith). [OxfordM] (9:1) Spr-Sum 93, p. 116.
"Verses" (tr. by Stephánia Allen and James Sutherland-Smith). [OxfordM] (9:1) Spr-Sum 93, p. 115-116.
1097. CHOCK, Eric
"In the Garden of the Tantalus Museum." [MidAR] (14:1) 93, p. 104-105.
1098. CHOE, Wolhee
"Like a Leaf" (tr. of Hyon-Jong Chong, w. Peter Fusco). [WebR] (17) Fall 93, p. 25.

1099. CHOI, Chiwan
"Breath Becomes Life." [OnTheBus] (6:1, #13) Wint 93-Spr 94, p. 68-74.
1100. CHOI, Kathleen T.
"Shark Bait." [HawaiiR] (17:1, #37) Spr 93, p. 41.
1101. CHONG, Hyônjong (Hyon-Jong)
"Like a Leaf" (tr. by Wolhee Choe and Peter Fusco). [WebR] (17) Fall 93, p. 25.
"Things That Float in the Air" (tr. by Edward W. Poitras). [ChiR] (39:3/4) 93, p. 246-247.
CHONGJU, So
   See SO, Chongju
1102. CHORLTON, David
"Castilian Lightning." [PoetL] (88:4) Wint 93-94, p. 31.
"Connections." [WebR] (17) Fall 93, p. 48.
"Full Moon." [Outbr] (24) 93, p. 21.
"Kien-Wu in a Nocturnal Storm." [DogRR] (12:1, #23) Spr-Sum 93, p. 55.
"The Living Land" (for Gary Fry). [SlipS] (13) 93, p. 40.
"Madera." [Outbr] (24) 93, p. 22-23.
"The New Peace." [InterPR] (19:1) Spr 93, p. 91.
"The Sick Man's House." [PoetL] (88:4) Wint 93-94, p. 30.
"Wedding in a Lost Republic." [FreeL] (12) Sum 93, p. 10.
"A Winter Marriage." [Parting] (6:2) Wint 93, p. 2.
1103. CHOU, Ping
"Missing You" (tr. of Shu Ting). [ChiR] (39:3/4) 93, p. 293.
"Walt Whitman: 'Whispers of Heavenly Death Murmur'd I Hear!'" [ChiR] (39:3/4) 93, p. 299-300.
1104. CHOULIARAS, Yiorgos
"The Ball of Yarn" (tr. by David Mason and the author). [Os] (36) Spr 93, p. 24.
"Classic Outlines" (tr. by the author). [HangL] (63) 93, p. 6.
"The Day Arrives" (tr. by the author and David Mason). [HangL] (63) 93, p. 7.
"Demetrius Phalereus" (Historical Poem, tr. by David Mason and the author).
   [Poetry] (162:3) Je 93, p. 137.
"Job" (tr. by the author). [HangL] (63) 93, p. 6.
"Occupied City" (tr. by David Mason and the author). [Poetry] (162:3) Je 93, p. 137.
"Odysseus at Home" (tr. of Homer, w. David Mason). [CumbPR]] (13:1) Fall 93, p. 27.
"Of the Sea" (3 poems, 1-3, tr. by David Mason and the author). [HarvardR] (3) Wint 93, p. 147.
"Refugees" (from *Fast Food Classics*, Athens, 1992, tr. by David Mason and the author). [Os] (36) Spr 93, p. 25.
"Regarding the Investment of the Ship Owner Mr. Andreas Embeirkos in a Blast Furnace (March 1935)" (tr. by the author and David Mason). [HangL] (63) 93, p. 6.
"The Saint" (tr. by the author and David Mason). [HangL] (63) 93, p. 7.
"The Signals" (tr. by David Mason and the author). [Poetry] (162:3) Je 93, p. 136.
"What Obstructs Literature" (tr. by the author and David Mason). [HangL] (63) 93, p. 7.
1105. CHOYCE, Lesley
"Allen Ginsberg on the Citadel: Halifax, 1986." [JlNJPo] (15:2) Aut 93, p. 30-31.
"Legend." [JlNJPo] (15:2) Aut 93, p. 28.
"My Father, Shaking Pepper." [JlNJPo] (15:2) Aut 93, p. 27.
"On the Road: New Brunswick." [JlNJPo] (15:2) Aut 93, p. 26.
"The Range." [JlNJPo] (15:2) Aut 93, p. 29.
1106. CHRISTGAU, John
"Cultivating by Tractor Light." [CreamCR] (17:1) Spr 93, p. 20.
"Sailing the Stone Boat." [CreamCR] (17:1) Spr 93, p. 21.
1107. CHRISTIANSON, Kate
"Noodles, Snakes and Mothers." [BellR] (16:1/2) Spr-Fall 93, p. 29.
1108. CHRISTIANSON, Kiel
"Melting." [CapeR] (28:1) Spr 93, p. 7.
1109. CHRISTIE, A. V.
"Coin." [Iowa] (23:3) Fall 93, p. 166.
"Eye Brooch." [Iowa] (23:3) Fall 93, p. 167.
"Glyph." [Iowa] (23:3) Fall 93, p. 166.
"In My Dream." [IndR] (16:1) Spr 93, p. 177.
"Landscape." [Iowa] (23:3) Fall 93, p. 167.
"Legend." [IndR] (16:1) Spr 93, p. 178-179.

"Nine Skies." [IndR] (16:1) Spr 93, p. 175-176.
"Rumor" (For J.M.). [SouthernPR] (33:2) Fall 93, p. 28-30.
"Surround." [IndR] (16:1) Spr 93, p. 173-174.
1110. CHRISTINA, Martha
"Impossibilities." [CapeR] (28:1) Spr 93, p. 28-29.
"Progressive Relaxation." [CapeR] (28:1) Spr 93, p. 30.
"When It Happens." [ChiR] (39:1) 93, p. 76.
1111. CHRISTOPHER, G. B.
"The Butterfly Hotline." [CumbPR]] (13:1) Fall 93, p. 29.
"Folly Bridge." [CumbPR]] (13:1) Fall 93, p. 31.
"The High Street." [CumbPR]] (13:1) Fall 93, p. 30.
1112. CHRISTOPHER, Nicholas
"5°." [NewYorker] (68:52) 15 F 93, p. 54.
"5°" (Selections: 1-6). [ParisR] (35:127) Sum 93, p. 194-200.
"Bees." [OntR] (39) Fall-Wint 93-94, p. 64-65.
"Cornelia Street, 6. A.M." [OntR] (39) Fall-Wint 93-94, p. 62-63.
"Far from Home." [OntR] (39) Fall-Wint 93-94, p. 63-64.
"Funeral Parlor, Trieste." [NewRep] (209:12/13) 20-27 S 93, p. 54.
"The Hotel Miramar." [NewRep] (209:25) 20 D 93, p. 44.
"The Hyperboreans." [ParisR] (35:129) Wint 93, p. 82-83.
"The Quiñero Sisters, 1968." [NewYorker] (69:29) 13 S 93, p. 80.
"Railroad Bridge." [OntR] (39) Fall-Wint 93-94, p. 63.
"Terminus." [ParisR] (35:129) Wint 93, p. 79-81.
"The Voyage of the *Moonlight*." [Nat] (256:13) 5 Ap 93, p. 456.
1113. CHRISTY, Ana
"Suburbia." [FreeL] (12) Sum 93, p. 12.
CHU-YI, Po
See BAI, Juyi
CHUAN, Xi
See XI, Chuan
1114. CHUBBS, Boyd
"By a Dublin Cathedral." [TickleAce] (26) Fall-Wint 93, p. 43.
"Jane, Remember These Men and Women." [TickleAce] (24) Fall-Wint 92, p. 114.
1115. CHUNG, Gong-chae
"Poetry Is Wine" (tr. by Chang Soo Ko). [Vis] (43) 93, p. 32.
CHURCH, Adrian Blevins
See BLEVINS-CHURCH, Adrian
1116. CHUTE, Robert M.
"Late Winter." [LitR] (37:1) Fall 93, p. 58.
"Rummage Sale, East Baldwin, Maine." [HiramPoR] (53/54) Fall 92-Sum 93, p. 27.
1117. CHYTILOVA, Lenka
"The Match" (tr. by Ellen Rosenbaum). [OxfordM] (9:1) Spr-Sum 93, p. 28.
"A Night out of Goethe" (tr. by Ellen Rosenbaum). [OxfordM] (9:1) Spr-Sum 93, p. 28.
1118. CIBULKA, Hanns
"Expectation" (tr. by Gisela Argyle). [PoetryC] (13:2) 93, p. 21.
"Madrigal" (tr. by Gisela Argyle). [PoetryC] (13:2) 93, p. 21.
CID (Anonymous)
See EL CID (Anonymous)
1119. CIHLAR, Jim
"The Boy Who Lives in the Backyard." [Plain] (13:3) Spr 93, p. 26.
"To Execute." [Plain] (13:2) Wint 93, p. 14.
"Walking Home." [MidwQ] (35:1) Aut 93, p. 35.
1120. CINGOLINI, Charles
"Fear II." [CoalC] (7) Apr 93, p. 27.
"Trees V." [CoalC] (7) Apr 93, p. 27.
1121. CIRINO, Leonard (Leonard J.)
"Corpus Domini." [ContextS] (3:1) 93, p. 4.
"A Kind of Grace." [Epiphany] (4:2) Ap 93, p. 86.
"Return." [Epiphany] (4:2) Ap 93, p. 87.
1122. CITINO, David
"Bathing Lenin." [CreamCR] (17:1) Spr 93, p. 94-95.
"Bread." [CentR] (37:3) Fall 93, p. 520-521.
"Clown Fish." [NewL] (59:3) 93, p. 81.
"Daisy." [SoDakR] (31:2) Sum 93, p. 170-172.
"The Hermit." [CinPR] (24) Spr 93, p. 76.

"Labor Day." [OnTheBus] (5:2, #12) Sum-Fall 93, p. 51-52.
"Letter from the Shaman: The Rite of Fertility" (after an Aborigine song). [FreeL] (11) Wint 93, p. 30-31.
"A Modern History of California." [Agni] (37) 93, p. 212-213.
"My Father Shaves with Occam's Razor." [Poetry] (162:5) Ag 93, p. 261.
"Sister Mary Appassionata Explicates a Graffito for the Eighth Grade Boys." [WestB] (33) 93, p. 46-47.
"Sister Mary Appassionata on the Nature of the Hero." [LaurelR] (27:1) Wint 93, p. 56-57.
"Sister Mary Appassionata to the Editor of *The Columbus Dispatch*." [CimR] (102) Ja 93, p. 89-90.
"Thefts from Italian Churches Reach All-time High." [TarRP] (32:2) Spr 93, p. 24 - 25.
"Walking by the Lion's Den Adult Theater and Bookstore, Sister Mary Appassionata Experiences the Stigmata." [CreamCR] (17:1) Spr 93, p. 92-93.
"With the Visiting Writer." [CentR] (37:3) Fall 93, p. 518-519.
"Yes They Had No Tomatoes." [HolCrit] (30:4) O 93, p. 19.
1123. CLAIR, Maxine
    "In the Backyard." [Prima] (16/17) 93, p. 54-55.
1124. CLAMPITT, Amy
    "Discovery." [NewYorker] (69:8) 12 Ap 93, p. 84.
    "Discovery" (for Katherine Jackson). [Verse] (10:3) Wint 93, p. 84-85.
    "Hispaniola." [Verse] (10:3) Wint 93, p. 15-16.
    "The Horned Rampion." [NewRep] (208:4) 25 Ja 93, p. 42.
    "Keats at Chichester." [NewEngR] (15:1) Wint 93, p. 111-113.
    "Matoaka" (commissioned by the College of William and Mary to commemorate the College's Tercentenary). [WilliamMR] (31) 93, p. 54-62.
    "Matoaka" (for the tercentenary of The College of William and Mary." [Verse] (10:3) Wint 93, p. 9-14.
    "Sed de Correr." [YaleR] (81:1) Ja 93, p. 61-65.
    "Shorebirds in Seasonal Plumage Observed Through Binoculars." [PartR] (60:1) Wint 93, p. 90-91.
    "Thinking Bed." [Verse] (10:3) Wint 93, p. 17.
1125. CLAMURRO, William H.
    "From the Magic Mountain." [CharR] (19:2) Fall 93, p. 123.
1126. CLARK, Dan
    "Creating Multitudes, Repeating." [BelPoJ] (44:1) Fall 93, p. 6-7.
    "Monday Mornings on Vacation." [BellArk] (9:3) My-Je 93, p. 13.
1127. CLARK, Elizabeth B.
    "Motivations of the Day" (tr. of Mario Rivero). [ApalQ] (36/37) 91, p. 58-60.
    "Psalm" (tr. of Mario Rivero). [ApalQ] (36/37) 91, p. 61.
1128. CLARK, Joan
    "Night Feeding." [Dandel] (20:1) 93, p. 28.
1129. CLARK, John Livingstone
    "Erotic Thoughts As the World Prepares for War." [Grain] (21:2) Sum 93, p. 37.
    "How Elvis Would Have Wept for the Children of Baghdad." [Grain] (21:2) Sum 93, p. 35.
    "January 23, 1991." [Grain] (21:2) Sum 93, p. 36.
1130. CLARK, Mary
    "Pantyhose." [Ploughs] (19:1) Spr 93, p. 164-165.
    "Parking." [Ploughs] (19:1) Spr 93, p. 163.
1131. CLARK, Merodie Martineau
    "The Man with Delicate Feet." [Elf] (3:4) Wint 93, p. 38.
1132. CLARK, Nancy L.
    "Passing Through Air." [Bogg] (66) Wint 92-93, p. 20.
1133. CLARK, Naomi
    "After The Circus at Santa Maria del Mar." [QRL] (12:32/33) 93, p. 107-108.
    "The Call." [QRL] (12:32/33) 93, p. 106-107.
    "In Fire Season: Suite for Sitar and Tabla." [PraS] (67:1) Spr 93, p. 116-118.
    "In Fire Season: Suite for Sitar and Tabla." [QRL] (12:32/33) 93, p. 108-111.
    "Listening to a Flute Above Deer Creek Canyon." [QRL] (12:32/33) 93, p. 111-112.
    "Lucy's Story: Marigolds" (for Lucy, who changed her name, her life). [QRL] (12:32/33) 93, p. 112-114.
    "Making Do." [PraS] (67:1) Spr 93, p. 114-115.
    "Moving North." [PraS] (67:1) Spr 93, p. 114.
    "Moving North." [QRL] (12:32/33) 93, p. 104-105.

"Waking in Intensive Care." [QRL] (12:32/33) 93, p. 106.
"The Witch's Tit." [QRL] (12:32/33) 93, p. 105.
1134. CLARK, Rod (Roderick)
"Hamm's Beer Mobile." [Rosebud] (1:1) Wint 93, p. 17.
1135. CLARK, Tom
"Cross-Currents" (February-March 1819). [AmerPoR] (22:6) N-D 93, p. 16.
"Debut" (Vale of Health, Hampstead, Fall 1816). [AmerPoR] (22:6) N-D 93, p. 15.
"From CODA: Echo & Variations" (XII). [AmerPoR] (22:6) N-D 93, p. 17.
"Hieroglyph" (February 1820). [AmerPoR] (22:6) N-D 93, p. 17.
"Imagination" (Leaving Guy's Hospital, November 1816). [AmerPoR] (22:6) N-D
93, p. 14.
"Inside the Marvelsphere." [Arshile] (1) Spr 93, p. 31.
"Junkets on a Sad Planet: A Poetic Novel Based on the Life of John Keats"
(Selections: 3 poems). [Arshile] (1) Spr 93, p. 32-34.
"Pegasus Jockey." [AmerPoR] (22:6) N-D 93, p. 14.
"Possession." [AmerPoR] (22:6) N-D 93, p. 14.
"Premonitory" (Teignmouth, Spring 1818). [AmerPoR] (22:6) N-D 93, p. 15.
"Quietness" (1810)." [AmerPoR] (22:6) N-D 93, p. 14.
"Romance." [AmerPoR] (22:6) N-D 93, p. 14.
"The Summer Triangle" (1819). [AmerPoR] (22:6) N-D 93, p. 16.
"Voyeurism" (Winchester, January 1819). [AmerPoR] (22:6) N-D 93, p. 16.
1136. CLARKE, Ian
"Poem: My breath is small game for the night wind" (For Frances). [CarolQ] (45:3)
Sum 93, p. 10.
1137. CLARKE, J. P.
"Parenthood." [Verse] (10:1) Spr 93, p. 81.
1138. CLARY, Killarney
"At first, I couldn't open the door." [AmerPoR] (22:4) Jl-Ag 93, p. 8.
"A bruise, from purple to yellow." [AmerPoR] (22:4) Jl-Ag 93, p. 8.
"I am going home now, Mama." [AmerPoR] (22:4) Jl-Ag 93, p. 8.
"I can't make her into a child." [AmerPoR] (22:4) Jl-Ag 93, p. 8.
"I told her in case she was dying." [AmerPoR] (22:4) Jl-Ag 93, p. 8.
"If I pause for an instant this afternoon." [AmerPoR] (22:4) Jl-Ag 93, p. 8.
"I've known for years I would be the one to find her." [AmerPoR] (22:4) Jl-Ag 93, p.
8.
"Prose Poem: He will come to cause mischief." [Arshile] (2) 93, p. 13.
"Prose Poem: If I can, I'll read birds." [Arshile] (2) 93, p. 15.
"Prose Poem: Restless before the canary." [Arshile] (2) 93, p. 14.
"Prose Poem: Why can't I tell you I want you to press your thick fingers." [Arshile]
(2) 93, p. 16.
"There will be other falls." [AmerPoR] (22:4) Jl-Ag 93, p. 8.
1139. CLAUSEN, Christopher
"Four Carolina Elegies" (In memory of Paul Chernin, M.D., 1942-1974). [CarolQ]
(45:3) Sum 93, 45th Anniversary section, p. 22-25.
1140. CLAUSEN, Jan
"636 11th" (In memory of Jean Millar). [KenR] (NS 15:1) Wint 93, p. 6-16.
1141. CLAUSER, Grant
"At a Farm in Dutch County." [Blueline] (14) 93, p. 56.
"For the Absence of Home." [Caliban] (13) 93, p. 106-107.
1142. CLEARY, Suzanne
"Last Poem for Gary Eddy." [PoetryNW] (34:2) Sum 93, p. 5-7.
"Study" (for Dolores, Pam, Laura). [GeoR] (47:3) Fall 93, p. 481-482.
1143. CLEAVELAND, Ruzha
"Heavenly Flower" (tr. of Josip Osti, w. Boris Novak). [WebR] (17) Fall 93, p. 29.
"Rose Garden" (tr. of Josip Osti, w. Boris Novak). [WebR] (17) Fall 93, p. 29.
"The Stake Stabbing the Tongue Has Sprouted Leaves" (tr. of Josip Osti, w. Boris
Novak). [WebR] (17) Fall 93, p. 29.
"Suddenly Everyone Beheld an Empty Sky" (tr. of Josip Osti, w. Boris Novak).
[WebR] (17) Fall 93, p. 28.
"Vanilla's Fragrance, Peppermint's Scent" (tr. of Josip Osti, w. Boris Novak).
[WebR] (17) Fall 93, p. 28.
1144. CLEMENTS, Brian
"Fashion." [Caliban] (12) 93, p. 154.
1145. CLEMENTS, Susan
"My Father Opened Doors for Women." [NoDaQ] (61:3) Sum 93, p. 34-36.
"Slow Dance in Kitchen." [NoDaQ] (61:3) Sum 93, p. 37.

1146. CLEVE, Emerald
"An Azure Shadowed Room." [SpiritSH] (58) 93, p. 16.
"Children in a Storm." [SpiritSH] (58) 93, p. 15.
"Untitled: Leave now all stale lack-luster." [SpiritSH] (58) 93, p. 15.
1147. CLEVER, Bertolt
"Sweet Razor, My Editor." [NewRena] (8:3, #26) Spr 93, p. 77-78.
"The TV Responsible." [NewRena] (8:3, #26) Spr 93, p. 79-80.
1148. CLEWELL, David
"Goodbye Note to Debbie Fuller: Pass It On." [MissouriR] (16:1) 93, p. 39-41.
"Holding On." [RiverS] (37) 93, p. 6-7.
"In Case of Rapture." [MissouriR] (16:1) 93, p. 45-47.
"Lessons in Another Language." [MissouriR] (16:1) 93, p. 42-44.
"What Some People Won't Do." [GeoR] (47:4) Wint 93, p. 773-774.
1149. CLIFTON, Lucille
"Each morning i pull myself out of despair." [KenR] (NS 15:1) Wint 93, p. 134.
"The Earth Is a Living Thing." [AmerPoR] (22:1) Ja-F 93, p. 20.
"Here Yet Be Dragons." [AmerPoR] (22:1) Ja-F 93, p. 21.
"January 1991." [AmerPoR] (22:1) Ja-F 93, p. 20.
"Leda 3" (a personal note, re: visitations). [KenR] (NS 15:1) Wint 93, p. 134.
"Night Vision." [AmerPoR] (22:1) Ja-F 93, p. 21.
"The rough weight of it." [KenR] (NS 15:1) Wint 93, p. 135.
"She Lived." [AmerPoR] (22:1) Ja-F 93, p. 21.
"Thel." [AmerPoR] (22:1) Ja-F 93, p. 21.
"Them and Us." [KenR] (NS 15:1) Wint 93, p. 135.
"The Women You Are Accustomed To." [AmerPoR] (22:1) Ja-F 93, p. 21.
"Won't you celebrate with me." [AmerPoR] (22:1) Ja-F 93, p. 20.
1150. CLINTON, DeWitt
"Bathing My Father." [LouisL] (10:1) Spr 93, p. 29-30.
"On the Way to Churchcamp, Mother Meets the Devil." [LouisL] (10:1) Spr 93, p. 31-32.
1151. CLINTON, Michelle T.
"I'm Dating." [OnTheBus] (5:2, #12) Sum-Fall 93, p. 53.
"Options for Girls: Patience & Loathing." [KenR] (NS 15:1) Wint 93, p. 39-40.
"Tantrum Girl Responds to Death." [KenR] (NS 15:1) Wint 93, p. 37-38.
1152. CLOUD, Kelly
"Cul-de-sac." [Poem] (69) My 93, p. 2-3.
"In August." [Poem] (69) My 93, p. 6.
"Stealing Blackberries." [Poem] (69) My 93, p. 5.
"Undertow." [Poem] (69) My 93, p. 4.
CLOUD, Peter Blue
See BLUE CLOUD, Peter
1153. CLOVER, Joshua
"Modern Language Association Annual (Near Mission Dolores)." [Zyzzyva] (9:3) Fall 93, p. 89.
"Totenbuch." [Sonora] (24/25) Spr 93, p. 107-108.
"Wreckage." [BlackWR] (19:1) Fall-Wint 92, p. 29-30.
1154. CLUTE, Mitchell
"Deep Winter." [CinPR] (24) Spr 93, p. 63.
"The Good Host's Song." [BlackWR] (19:1) Fall-Wint 92, p. 107.
1155. CLUTINGER, Thomas H.
"Light a Middle Way." [Border] (2) Spr 93, p. 12.
1156. CLYMAN, Shep
"Eternity Suffers from Distemper." [Ploughs] (19:1) Spr 93, p. 171-172.
1157. COATES, Chris
"So, So Long." [RiverS] (38) 93, p. 71.
1158. COCHRAN, Leonard
"Puppet Show." [SpiritSH] (58) 93, p. 7.
"Puppet to Puppeteer." [SpiritSH] (58) 93, p. 7.
1159. COCHRANE, Mark
"Bowen Island." [MalR] (103) Sum 93, p. 69.
"Cutting Promises." [PoetryC] (13:2) 93, p. 28.
"Day/Care" (for Devon Cochrane Parkin). [PoetryC] (13:2) 93, p. 28.
"Flatcar." [PoetryC] (13:2) 93, p. 28.
1160. COCHRANE, Shirley
"Entering Beijing." [InterPR] (19:1) Spr 93, p. 64-66.

109

1161. COCHRANE, Shirley G.
"Tattooed Man" (to Charles Salter, Jr., with appreciation). [PoetL] (88:1) Spr 93, p. 32.
1162. CODRESCU, Andrei
"The Differences." [PaintedB] (50/51) 93, p. 74-75.
1163. CODY, J. C.
"Watching for Tlaloc to Cool the Sun" (Amelia Native American Poetry Award). [Amelia] (7:2, #21) 93, p. 63.
1164. COEN, Kathy S.
"Born Free." [Nat] (256:5) 8 F 93, p. 172.
"The Quill." [CimR] (103) Ap 93, p. 93.
COEUR, Jo Le
See LeCOEUR, Jo
1165. COFER, Judith Ortiz
"Orar: To Pray." [CreamCR] (17:1) Spr 93, p. 66.
"The Woman Who Was Left at the Altar." [AmerV] (32) 93, p. 86.
1166. COFFEY, Kathy
"Holy Saturday." [ChrC] (110:11) 7 Apr 93, p. 365.
1167. COFFMAN, Lisa
"Beaded Tongue and Groove." [SouthernR] (29:1) Wint, Ja 93, p. 175.
"Likely." [SouthernR] (29:1) Wint, Ja 93, p. 176.
1168. COFRANCESCO, Joan
"Blocked Writer" (to Terry Stokes). [SinW] (50) Sum-Fall 93, p. 45.
"Lovers and Spoons." [Kalliope] (15:3) 93, p. 10.
1169. COGSWELL, Fred
"The Ballade of Dead Ladies" (After the French of François Villon). [AntigR] (92) Wint 93, p. 107.
"Disclaimer." [AntigR] (92) Wint 93, p. 108.
"José Carreras." [CanLit] (136) Spr 93, p. 23.
"Pavan: the Four Elements." [PottPort] (15:1) Spr-Sum 93, p. 44.
"The Same, Yet Not the Same." [PottPort] (15:1) Spr-Sum 93, p. 43.
"When We Discovered." [PottPort] (15:1) Spr-Sum 93, p. 43.
1170. COGSWELL, Kelly Jean
"Chronic Blues." [SinW] (49) Spr-Sum 93, p. 73.
1171. COGSWELL, Victoria
"Her Children, Leaping in the Atmosphere." [Poem] (69) My 93, p. 52.
"Treasures." [Poem] (69) My 93, p. 51.
1172. COHEE, Marcia
"Expecting Summer." [FreeL] (11) Wint 93, p. 32.
"Forcing the Muse to Stay Up All Night." [Gaia] (1/2) Ap-Jl 93, p. 2.
1173. COHEN, Bruce
"Hitting a Skunk at 60 Miles Per Hour." [TriQ] (87) Spr-Sum 93, p. 187-189.
1174. COHEN, Carole
"Appalling." [CapeR] (28:1) Spr 93, p. 46.
"New Woman in an Old Familiar Shoe." [CapeR] (28:1) Spr 93, p. 45.
"Paperweight." [CapeR] (28:2) Fall 93, p. 1.
1175. COHEN, Elizabeth
"Hard Sell." [NowestR] (31:1) 93, p. 59.
"The Ribs." [NowestR] (31:1) 93, p. 57-58.
1176. COHEN, Ira
"Elephant Dream." [Caliban] (12) 93, p. 116.
"For George Whitman & Wm. Shakespeare." [Caliban] (12) 93, p. 117.
"Ransom Note for Brion Gysin." [Caliban] (12) 93, p. 115.
1177. COHEN, Marc
"Schumann's Piano Concerto in A Minor." [Chelsea] (55) 93, p. 36.
1178. COHEN, Marion
"Childhood." [PaintedB] (50/51) 93, p. 91.
1179. COHEN, Philip
"The Miracel of Transubstantiation." [Poetry] (162:3) Je 93, p. 140.
1180. COHEN, Sascha Benjamin
"A Passing Thought on a Clear Night." [BellArk] (9:1) Ja-F 93, p. 14.
"Sightings of a UFO." [BellArk] (9:1) Ja-F 93, p. 21.
"Spirulae: Crossroads." [BellArk] (9:5) S-O 93, p. 6.
1181. COKE, A. A. Hedge
"The Change." [Caliban] (12) 93, p. 70-74.
"Darkening Light." [13thMoon] (12:1/2) 93-94, p. 19-21.

1182. COKINOS, Christopher
   "The Stars in November." [BellR] (16:1/2) Spr-Fall 93, p. 104.
1183. COLBURN, Charles
   "More Poetry." [Writer] (106:1) Ja 93, p. 2.
1184. COLBURN, Don
   "Days." [Plain] (14:1) Fall 93, p. 21.
   "Given." [VirQR] (69:3) Sum 93, p. 505.
   "The Luxury of Distance." [VirQR] (69:3) Sum 93, p. 506.
   "News." [Plain] (14:1) Fall 93, p. 21.
   "Timberline." [Plain] (14:1) Fall 93, p. 21.
   "Wildflowers" (Discovery-The Nation '93 Prizewinning Poet). [Nat] (256:17) 3 My
      93, p. 603.
   "Wrecking Ball." [CimR] (103) Ap 93, p. 94-95.
1185. COLBURN, John
   "It's Always Night." [RagMag] (11:2) 93, p. 77.
1186. COLDWELL, J. W.
   "Malcolm and the Fish." [Bogg] (66) Wint 92-93, p. 55-56.
1187. COLE, Henri
   "The Christological Year" (on my birthday). [ParisR] (35:126) Spr 93, p. 56-57.
   "The Housekeeper and the Handyman." [OhioR] (50) 93, p. 70-71.
   "Katrina's Bedroom." [PraS] (67:1) Spr 93, p. 43-44.
   "The Minimum Circus" (for Mary Doyle Springer). [YaleR] (81:2) Ap 93, p. 74-75.
   "Palette." [PraS] (67:1) Spr 93, p. 42.
   "Sacrament." [ParisR] (35:126) Spr 93, p. 58.
   "The Silver Cuffs." [Boulevard] (8:1, #22) Spr 93, p. 133.
   "Torso." [WestHR] (47:4) Wint 93, p. 370.
   "The World." [ParisR] (35:126) Spr 93, p. 59.
   "You Come When I Call You." [NewYorker] (69:21) 12 Jl 93, p. 54.
1188. COLE, Mike
   "Faith." [AntR] (51:1) Wint 93, p. 80.
   "Induction Center '71." [LaurelR] (27:2) Sum 93, p. 56-57.
   "King Snake." [LaurelR] (27:2) Sum 93, p. 57.
1189. COLE, Norma
   "The Comforts of a Bench" (Excerpts, tr. of Anne Portugal). [Avec] (6:1) 93, p. 103 -
      106.
   "Probation." [Avec] (6:1) 93, p. 76-84.
   "Rosetta" (Excerpts). [Sulfur] (32) Spr 93, p. 128-134.
1190. COLE, Peter
   "The Earthquake (1047)" (tr. of Samuel Ben Yosef Halevi Hanagrid, a/k/a Isma'il
      Ibn Nagrela). [Sulfur] (33) Fall 93, p. 191-193.
   "The Miracle at Sea" (tr. of Samuel Ben Yosef Halevi Hanagrid, a/k/a Isma'il Ibn
      Nagrela). [Sulfur] (33) Fall 93, p. 186-190.
1191. COLE, Robert
   "Leftovers." [Bogg] (66) Wint 92-93, p. 38.
1192. COLE, William (William Rossa)
   "A-driftin' down the Allagash" (A Watery Tribute to the Master). [Light] (5) Spr 93,
      p. 30.
   "As we were sailing off Bizerte." [Light] (5) Spr 93, p. 30.
   "In Stratford Town upon the Avon." [Light] (8) Wint 93, p. 23.
   "Salty Bore." [Light] (8) Wint 93, p. 10.
   "When I was a young man on the Ganges banks." [Light] (7) Aut 93, p. 24.
1193. COLEMAN, Anita
   "What Amelia Taught Me." [HopewellR] (5) 93, p. 81.
1194. COLEMAN, Earl
   "Deer Hunting." [Hellas] (4:1) Spr 93, p. 24.
   "A Fearful Symmetry." [Hellas] (4:2) Fall 93, p. 65.
   "Rigor." [CapeR] (28:2) Fall 93, p. 30.
1195. COLEMAN, Horace
   "Untitled: I like to go see those old blues players." [Obs] (8:2) Fall-Wint 93, p. 92.
   "Untitled: Sometimes I'll be drinking by myself." [Obs] (8:2) Fall-Wint 93, p. 92.
1196. COLEMAN, Wanda
   "African Sleeping Sickness." [Iowa] (23:3) Fall 93, p. 110.
   "Strayhorn." [RiverS] (37) 93, p. 62.
   "Talk about the Money." [RiverS] (37) 93, p. 61.
1197. COLES, Don
   "Aschenbach in Venice." [Quarry] (42:2) 93, p. 90-92.

111

COLES

"Gone Out Is Part of Sanity" (for Ivor Gurney, 1890-1937). [Arc] (30) Spr 93, p. 12 - 13.
"Knights of the Round Table." [Arc] (30) Spr 93, p. 10-11.
"Our Photos of the Children." [Arc] (30) Spr 93, p. 5-9.
1198. COLES, Katharine
"Elegy for a Dog Larger Than Life." [Poetry] (163:3) D 93, p. 141-143.
1199. COLES, R.
"Foreigner." [Obs] (8:2) Fall-Wint 93, p. 94-95.
"Reunion." [Obs] (8:2) Fall-Wint 93, p. 93.
"Silence Equals Death." [Obs] (8:2) Fall-Wint 93, p. 94.
"Urban Sketch." [Obs] (8:2) Fall-Wint 93, p. 93-94.
COLIBAN, Taina Dutescu
See DUTESCU-COLIBAN, Taina
1200. COLINAS, Antonio
"The City Is Dead" (tr. by Michael L. Johnson). [LitR] (36:3) Spr 93, p. 367.
"Night beyond the Night" (Excerpt, tr. by Michael L. Johnson). [LitR] (36:3) Spr 93, p. 366.
"The Path Blocked by Woods" (tr. by Michael L. Johnson). [LitR] (36:3) Spr 93, p. 365-366.
1201. COLKER, Larry
"Faust." [OnTheBus] (6:1, #13) Wint 93-Spr 94, p. 75.
COLLADO, Alfredo Villanueva
See VILLANUEVA-COLLADO, Alfredo
1202. COLLIER, Michael
"Bread Route." [SouthernR] (29:4) Aut, O 93, p. 721-722.
"Pictures Drawn by Atomic Bomb Survivors." [GettyR] (6:4) Aut 93, p. 594-595.
"The Rancher." [BostonR] (18:5) O-N 93, p. 9.
"The Welder." [DenQ] (28:1) Sum 93, p. 26-27.
1203. COLLIER, Phyllis K.
"At 78, Marge Goes River Rafting." [CumbPR]] (13:1) Fall 93, p. 82-83.
"Report on the Mothers." [CumbPR] (12:2) Spr 93, p. 32-33.
1204. COLLINS, Billy
"Apologizing to the Bees." [ChiR] (39:1) 93, p. 28.
"Budapest." [WestB] (33) 93, p. 62.
"Cheers." [Poetry] (161:6) Mr 93, p. 318-319.
"The End of the World." [Poetry] (161:6) Mr 93, p. 315-316.
"Horizon." [WestB] (33) 93, p. 63.
"Nightclub." [Crazy] (44) Spr 93, p. 52-53.
"On Turning Ten." [ParisR] (35:129) Wint 93, p. 229-230.
"Osso Buco." [Poetry] (162:5) Ag 93, p. 272-273.
"Pin-Up." [Poetry] (161:6) Mr 93, p. 316-317.
"Reading in a Hammock." [ChiR] (39:1) 93, p. 29-30.
"Shadow." [Chelsea] (55) 93, p. 37.
"Soap Opera Life: Its Relentlessness." [FreeL] (11) Wint 93, p. 20.
"The Sonneteer." [AmerS] (62:4) Aut 93, p. 589.
"Thesaurus." [Poetry] (161:4) Ja 93, p. 195-196.
"Wedding Anniversary." [Boulevard] (8:2/3, #23/24) Fall 93, p. 205.
"While Eating a Pear." [Poetry] (162:5) Ag 93, p. 274.
1205. COLLINS, Caroline
"Gretel." [SouthernPR] (33:2) Fall 93, p. 16-17.
1206. COLLINS, Loretta
"Justine Has a Few Words for the Marquis de Sade." [BlackWR] (19:2) Spr-Sum 93, p. 51-53.
1207. COLLINS, Martha
"Cloud-Play for Four Hands." [Field] (49) Fall 93, p. 39-41.
"Discourse." [Field] (49) Fall 93, p. 37.
"Down the Road." [PartR] (60:1) Wint 93, p. 100-101.
"Fall" (tr. of Richard Exner). [SnailPR] (3:1) Fall-Wint 93, p. 16-17.
"Forest for the Trees." [Field] (49) Fall 93, p. 38.
"Mass." [HarvardR] (3) Wint 93, p. 101-102.
"More." [Agni] (37) 93, p. 204.
"Nothing Doing." [Field] (49) Fall 93, p. 42.
"Valyermo, St. Andrew's" (winter evening, after Complin. Tr. of Richard Exner). [GrahamHR] (17) Fall 93, p. 76.
1208. COLLINS, Michael
"On the Rue Git-le-Coeur: Mirage #9." [Callaloo] (16:2) Spr 93, p. 322-323.

"To Pope Formosus." [Callaloo] (16:2) Spr 93, p. 320-321.
1209. COLLINS, Robert
"The Counterfeiter's Confession." [Plain] (14:1) Fall 93, p. 29.
1210. COLLINS, Terry
"Frank" (In Memory of Frank Heffernan 1924-1991). [AntigR] (95) Aut 93, p. 40 - 43.
1211. COLON-SANTIAGO, Jose Luis
"Mi Amado." [Trasimagen] (1:1) Otoño-Invierno 93, p. 26-27.
1212. COLONNESE, Michael
"The Territory." [PaintedB] (52) 93, p. 7.
1213. COLTEN, Joel
"Yesterday my sense of adventure." [PaintedB] (50/51) 93, p. 53.
1214. COLWELL, Anne
"Voice on the Train Out of Grand Central." [MidwQ] (35:1) Aut 93, p. 36-37.
1215. COMANESCU, Denisa
"Anamorphosis" (tr. by Adam J. Sorkin and Angela Jianu). [Kalliope] (15:2) 93, p. 18.
"Atlas" (tr. by Adam J. Sorkin and Angela Jianu). [Kalliope] (15:2) 93, p. 16.
"Impoverished Land" (tr. by Adam J. Sorkin and Angela Jianu). [Kalliope] (15:2) 93, p. 16.
"Leaving Port" (tr. by Adam J. Sorkin and Angela Jianu). [Kalliope] (15:2) 93, p. 16.
"Unforgiving Joy" (tr. by Adam J. Sorkin and Angela Jianu). [Kalliope] (15:2) 93, p. 17.
1216. COMAR, Martin
"The Case for Martha." [Sparrow] (60) Sum 93, p. 45.
1217. COMBS, Kimberly
"Sophistry." [GrahamHR] (17) Fall 93, p. 77.
1218. COMPANIOTTE, John
"Burial at Sea." [Poetry] (161:4) Ja 93, p. 202.
"Words I've Lost Forever." [Poetry] (161:4) Ja 93, p. 201.
1219. COMPTON, Cathleen
"Christmas Eve at the Chula Vista Marina." [SouthernR] (29:2) Spr, Ap 93, p. 313.
1220. COMPTON, Diane
"Something." [Verse] (10:1) Spr 93, p. 29-30.
"Talking." [Verse] (10:1) Spr 93, p. 30-31.
1221. COMPTON, Terry
"Fourteen Hours to Loredo." [IndR] (16:2) Fall 93, p. 154-155.
1222. CONARD, M. T.
"Infatuation." [Eyeball] (2) 93, p. 29.
"Roma." [Eyeball] (2) 93, p. 29.
1223. CONAWAY, Frank
"Coming Back." [PoetC] (24:2) Wint 93, p. 22.
1224. CONE, Jon
"The Adopted." [WorldL] (4) 93, p. 48.
"Letter to Robert Lax of Patmos, Greece." [WorldL] (4) 93, p. 48.
"Song." [WorldL] (4) 93, p. 47.
"Two Songs." [WorldL] (4) 93, p. 47.
1225. CONELLY, William
"A Summons." [Light] (8) Wint 93, p. 19.
"To a Faddist." [Light] (5) Spr 93, p. 13.
1226. CONN, Jan
"After a Late Latin Dinner at the Centro Español." [Event] (22:3) Wint 93-94, p. 57.
"After Reading Charles Dickens' Biography by Peter Ackroyd in Southern Florida." [Arc] (30) Spr 93, p. 22.
"El Amparo." [Arc] (30) Spr 93, p. 23.
"At 7 AM the River" (for Gina Aeschbacher). [MalR] (104) Fall 93, p. 55-57.
"Beyond Las Nieves." [Arc] (30) Spr 93, p. 21.
"Black Ibises." [Event] (22:3) Wint 93-94, p. 58-59.
"The Darker Blue Inside." [MalR] (104) Fall 93, p. 58-60.
"The Empire of Snow" (for Ellen Moore and Scott Harrison). [Arc] (30) Spr 93, p. 24.
"A Field, a Lily, a Great White Egret." [Quarry] (42:2) 93, p. 134-135.
"Letter to My Mother on the Anniversary of Her Suicide." [MalR] (104) Fall 93, p. 61.
"The Sky Over the Seno de Reloncavi." [Quarry] (42:2) 93, p. 132-133.

113

"Trop de Vert." [Event] (22:3) Wint 93-94, p. 62.
"La Virgen de la Paz." [Event] (22:3) Wint 93-94, p. 60-61.
1227. CONNELLAN, Leo
  "Tomorrow." [NewYorkQ] (50) 93, p. 38-39.
  "With Eberhart at Occom." [AnthNEW] (5) 93, p. 6.
1228. CONNELLY, Joseph F.
  "Riddle: I resist the sadness of daily drudge." [Light] (7) Aut 93, p. 13.
1229. CONNELLY, Karen
  "Teeth of Garlic." [Stand] (34:3) Sum 93, p. 14-16.
1230. CONNOLLY, Geraldine
  "The Unexplained Territories." [WestB] (31/32) 93, p. 152-153.
1231. CONNOLLY, J. F.
  "Telling My Sister How I Taught a Lesson on Child Abuse." [EngJ] (82:5) S 93, p.
    105.
1232. CONOLEY, Gillian
  "Adultery." [AntR] (51:1) Wint 93, p. 81.
  "Heroes, Saints, and Neighbors." [AntR] (51:1) Wint 93, p. 82-83.
  "Nocturne." [DenQ] (27:4) Spr 93, p. 51-52.
1233. CONOVER, Carl
  "After the Cicadas." [PoetL] (88:3) Fall 93, p. 53.
  "A Tour of the Tomb of Guiliano De' Medici" (Michelangelo Sculpture, San
    Lorenzo, Florence). [SoCarR] (25:2) Spr 93, p. 120-122.
1234. CONQUEST, Fax
  "Stop Me Before I Hurt Again." [NewYorkQ] (51) 93, p. 79.
1235. CONRAD, C. A.
  "(for Linda)." [Pearl] (19) Fall-Wint 93, p. 68.
  "(for Tiger)." [Pearl] (19) Fall-Wint 93, p. 68.
1236. CONSTANTINE, David
  "Master and Man." [NewRep] (208:17) 26 Ap 93, p. 44.
  "Piers." [Stand] (34:2) Spr 93, p. 7.
1237. CONTENT, Rob
  "Little Falls." [HayF] (13) Fall-Wint 93, p. 79.
  "The Open Season." [HayF] (13) Fall-Wint 93, p. 78.
1238. CONTI, Edmund
  "Aftermath." [Light] (6) Sum 93, p. 20.
  "Albert Einstein Explains Relativity Once and For All." [ChironR] (12:4/13:1,
    #37/38) Wint 93-Spr 94, p. 27.
  "Another Cat with Too Many Lives." [Light] (6) Sum 93, p. 10.
  "Divine Scripture." [DogRR] (12:2, #24) Fall-Wint 93, p. 10.
  "Gnashing." [Light] (5) Spr 93, p. 24.
  "Going Nowhere, Fast." [Bogg] (66) Wint 92-93, p. 33.
  "Gross National Product." [ChironR] (12:4/13:1, #37/38) Wint 93-Spr 94, p. 27.
  "Hey, Buddy." [ChironR] (12:4/13:1, #37/38) Wint 93-Spr 94, p. 27.
  "I Write Short Poems." [ChironR] (12:4/13:1, #37/38) Wint 93-Spr 94, p. 27.
  "Morning in Greece." [DogRR] (12:2, #24) Fall-Wint 93, p. 10.
  "Sailing on the broad Pacific." [Light] (6) Sum 93, p. 22.
  "Sailing on the Zuider Zee." [Light] (8) Wint 93, p. 23.
  "Sailing one day on the Black Sea." [Light] (7) Aut 93, p. 24.
  "Sleeping on the River Styx" (Third Prize, First Annual River Rhyme Competition).
    [Light] (5) Spr 93, p. 29.
  "Trade Off." [DogRR] (12:2, #24) Fall-Wint 93, p. 10.
1239. COOK, Albert
  "Human Wrecks Whose Years." [DenQ] (27:4) Spr 93, p. 50.
1240. COOK, Justine
  "Before Persephone." [NewYorker] (69:41) 6 D 93, p. 58.
1241. COOK, Méira
  "All Day." [PoetryC] (14:1) 93, p. 24.
  "The Greenest Eye." [PraF] (14:3) Aut 93, p. 23.
  "Toward a Catalogue of Falling." [PoetryC] (14:1) 93, p. 24.
1242. COOK, R. L.
  "Invocation." [DogRR] (12:2, #24) Fall-Wint 93, p. 51.
1243. COOKE, Robert (Robert P.)
  "Home on Highland Ridge." [WritersF] (19) 93, p. 134-135.
  "Just Visiting." [SycamoreR] (5:1) Wint 93, p. 54.
1244. COOKE, Thomas
  "One Rose." [Agni] (37) 93, p. 89.

"The Walk." [ProseP] (2) 93, p. 22.
1245. COOLEY, Dennis
"From Love in a Dry Land." [WestCL] (27:3, #12) Wint 93-94, p. 7-16.
1246. COOLEY, Nicole
"Diane Arbus, New York." [Field] (49) Fall 93, p. 52-54.
"Letter from the Arizona Women's Prison." [SouthernPR] (33:1) Spr 93, p. 62-63.
"Undine." [Poetry] (163:2) N 93, p. 87.
1247. COOLEY, Peter
"At the Special Olympics." [Crazy] (44) Spr 93, p. 57.
"Body of Night." [SouthernR] (29:1) Wint, Ja 93, p. 179.
"Coincidental Music." [SouthernPR] (33:2) Fall 93, p. 8.
"The Crow." [Crazy] (44) Spr 93, p. 61.
"Messengers." [Poetry] (163:3) D 93, p. 146.
"Psalm Before Sleep." [Poetry] (162:1) Ap 93, p. 35.
"The Return." [Crazy] (44) Spr 93, p. 58-60.
"Rites of Passage." [SouthernR] (29:1) Wint, Ja 93, p. 180.
1248. COOLIDGE, Clark
"City in Regard" (Selections). [Sulfur] (32) Spr 93, p. 75-94.
"One Thing Seen in an Other Space Burst." [Arshile] (2) 93, p. 44-45.
"Some Thing Seen in Some Other Space." [Arshile] (2) 93, p. 41-43.
1249. COOPER, David
"So." [LitR] (37:1) Fall 93, p. 16.
1250. COOPER, Gwen
"Curse of the Cusp-Born." [LullwaterR] (4:2) Spr-Sum 93, p. 97.
1251. COOPER, James
"Serving Time in Wichita." [IndR] (16:2) Fall 93, p. 164.
1252. COOPER, Jane
"For the Recorder of Suicides." [Pequod] (35) 93, p. 203.
1253. COOPER, Kent
"Recent Discoveries." [Footwork] (23) 93, p. 107.
1254. COOPER, Laura
"Love Canal." [WashR] (18:5) F-Mr 93, p. 8.
"Scenes from the Black Hole." [WashR] (18:5) F-Mr 93, p. 17.
1255. COOPER, Lisa
"Heaven Holds Forth a Land Mover Most of All." [Sonora] (24/25) Spr 93, p. 67-70.
"Procession." [Talisman] (11) Fall 93, p. 255-256.
1256. COOPER, Patricia
"Windfall." [SouthernPR] (33:1) Spr 93, p. 12.
1257. COOPER-FRATRIK, Julie
"August 6, 1989." [MinnR] (NS 40) Spr-Sum 93, p. 21.
1258. COOPERMAN, Matthew
"The Walking Sun." [ChiR] (39:1) 93, p. 99-101.
1259. COOPERMAN, Robert
"At the Babe Ruth Museum." [SlipS] (13) 93, p. 10.
"By the Score." [SoDakR] (31:3) Fall 93, p. 145.
"Captain Trelawny Embellishes upon the Death of Byron." [ApalQ] (36/37) 91, p. 62-63.
"Cement Running Shoes: Baton Rouge, Louisiana." [WebR] (17) Fall 93, p. 103.
"Charles Dilke Comments on the Engagement between John Keats and Fanny Brawne." [Interim] (12:1) Spr-Sum 93, p. 22.
"Condolences." [HiramPoR] (53/54) Fall 92-Sum 93, p. 28.
"Daniel Boone in Retirement in Femme Osage, Missouri." [ChatR] (14:1) Fall 93, p. 64-65.
"Drusilla, After Writing Her Third Letter to Her Exiled Husband, Ovid." [Parting] (6:2) Wint 93, p. 27-28.
"Dusk: December 10, 1991." [ChironR] (12:3, #36) Aut 93, p. 18.
"Family Fight." [Plain] (13:3) Spr 93, p. 25.
"For Robert Briscoe, the First Jewish Mayor of Dublin." [AntigR] (92) Wint 93, p. 121-122.
"The Fourth of July." [HampSPR] Wint 93, p. 35.
"The General Compares His Late Wife to His Daughter." [CentR] (37:3) Fall 93, p. 538-539.
"The General's Daughter Remembers Her Mother." [ChironR] (12:3, #36) Aut 93, p. 18.
"The General's Opposite Number." [ChironR] (12:3, #36) Aut 93, p. 19.
"Homer Speaks of Penelope." [PikeF] (11) Fall 93, p. 24.

115

"Imprints." [ApalQ] (39) 93, p. 59-60.
"In Perfect Harmony." [SoDakR] (31:3) Fall 93, p. 146.
"Incident on the Second Floor." [Gypsy] (20) Sum 93, p. 32.
"Isaac Taub Finds His Vocation as Rabbi: Czechoslovakia, 1791." [Plain] (14:1)
    Fall 93, p. 30.
"John Sprockett Finds Shelter for Himself and Sophia Starling from a Sudden
    Snowstrom, Colorado Territory, 1873." [PassN] (14:2) Wint 93, p. 5.
"Judah P. Benjamin in Exile in London, 1865." [LouisL] (10:2) Fall 93, p. 19-20.
"Keats Rants About Having Been Poisoned, Rome, December, 1820." [DogRR]
    (12:1, #23) Spr-Sum 93, p. 29-30.
"Like a Diver." [Plain] (13:2) Wint 93, p. 30.
"The Necklace." [SoDakR] (31:3) Fall 93, p. 143-144.
"On Watching Stanley Kubrick's Spartacus Again." [ChironR] (12:3, #36) Aut 93,
    p. 19.
"Portrait of a Gentleman with His Horse and Groom" (by Adraien Van Nieulandt,
    1624, The Walters Art Gallery). [SoCoast] (15) Je 93, p. 45.
"Refugee." [SoDakR] (31:3) Fall 93, p. 142.
"Roland of Nantes, Forced to Bring His Wife and Daughter on the Second Crusade."
    [ChironR] (12:3, #36) Aut 93, p. 19.
"Something to Agree On." [HampSPR] Wint 93, p. 34.
"To Make It Big." [ChironR] (12:3, #36) Aut 93, p. 19.
"The Touch of Lizard's Skin." [SnailPR] (3:1) Fall-Wint 93, p. 19.
"Yusuf-al-Durr Recalls the First Crusade, While Preparing for the Second."
    [DogRR] (12:1, #23) Spr-Sum 93, p. 28.
1260. COOPRIDER, Rebecca
    "Lester and Martha." [AntigR] (93-94) Spr-Sum 93, p. 139-140.
1261. COPE, Dave
    "Friday Afternoon Before Labor Day." [HeavenB] (10) Wint-Spr 93, p. 21.
    "Three Together Sat on the Shore." [HeavenB] (10) Wint-Spr 93, p. 45.
1262. COPE, Steven R.
    "Once in a Blue Moon." [LitR] (37:1) Fall 93, p. 59.
    "Red Orphan." [HolCrit] (30:2) Ap 93, p. 15.
1263. COPE, Wendy
    "An Argument with Wordsworth." [Light] (7) Aut 93, p. 27.
    "Bloody Men." [Light] (7) Aut 93, p. 27.
    "A Green Song" (to sing at the bottle-bank). [Light] (7) Aut 93, p. 27.
    "I Worry." [Light] (7) Aut 93, p. 27.
    "Loss." [Light] (7) Aut 93, p. 27.
    "Postcard Poem" (should be sung to the hymn-tune "Aurelia — The Church's One
        Foundation"). [Light] (6) Sum 93, p. 8.
    "Where Do You Get Your Ideas From?" [Light] (5) Spr 93, p. 8.
1264. COPELAND, Cynthia
    "Do You Know Where Your Daughter Is?" [PassN] (14:1) Sum 93, p. 33.
    "Public School." [PassN] (14:1) Sum 93, p. 32.
1265. COPELAND, Helen M.
    "Life Is Risky, Life Is Grand." [Light] (5) Spr 93, p. 7.
1266. COPELAND, R. F.
    "The Last Belle of St. Joe's." [JamesWR] (10:4) Sum 93, p. 15.
    "Manly Mantra Melody." [JamesWR] (10:4) Sum 93, p. 15.
    "The Quiet Chambers." [JamesWR] (10:4) Sum 93, p. 15.
    "Say Adieu." [JamesWR] (11:1) Fall 93, p. 21.
1267. COPENHAVER, Rebecca
    "Youth's Temple." [SmPd] (30:1, #87) Wint 93, p. 19.
1268. COPIOLI, Rosita
    "Gypsophila" (to L. Anceschi, tr. by Renata Treitel). [SnailPR] (3:1) Fall-Wint 93,
        p. 4.
    "The weather is fair, but to not quiver is an unravelling of all yesses" (tr. by Renata
        Treitel). [SnailPR] (3:1) Fall-Wint 93, p. 5.
1269. CORBETT, William
    "Bowl of Progresso Minestrone." [Arshile] (1) Spr 93, p. 61-62.
    "Homefires." [Talisman] (11) Fall 93, p. 36.
    "Walking Basil." [Talisman] (11) Fall 93, p. 35.
1270. CORDING, Robert
    "Cardinal." [TarRP] (32:2) Spr 93, p. 27.
    "The Cup." [Poetry] (162:6) S 93, p. 326.
    "The Feeder." [BostonR] (18:2) Mr-Ap 93, p. 27.

"A History." [BostonR] (18:2) Mr-Ap 93, p. 27.
"The Mouth of Grief." [BostonR] (18:2) Mr-Ap 93, p. 27.
"September Night." [BostonR] (18:2) Mr-Ap 93, p. 27.
"Zûni Fetish." [BostonR] (18:2) Mr-Ap 93, p. 27.
1271. COREY, Chet
    "Love at Midlife." [Plain] (13:3) Spr 93, p. 25.
1272. CORKERY, Caleb
    "Bellies." [BrooklynR] (10) 93, p. 70-71.
1273. CORLEY, William J.
    "Bosnia's Christian Soldiers." [PoetryUSA] (25/26) 93, p. 54.
CORMACK, Karen Mac
    See Mac CORMACK, Karen
1274. CORMAN, Cid
    "Bull Shot." [WestCL] (27:2, #11) Fall 93, p. 136-137.
    "The Idea of Poetry." [WestCL] (27:2, #11) Fall 93, p. 138.
    "Just Asking." [WestCL] (27:2, #11) Fall 93, p. 138.
    "September" (tr. of Gottfried Genn, w. Edgar Lohner). [QRL] (12:32/33) 93, p. 377 -
        378.
1275. CORN, Alfred
    "Balanchine's Western Symphony." [NewRep] (209:20) 15 N 93, p. 38.
    "The Shouters." [Nat] (256:16) 26 Ap 93, p. 564.
1276. CORNISH, Sam
    "When McCorkle Is Working on the Rail." [Ploughs] (19:1) Spr 93, p. 104-106.
1277. CORNITIUS, Susan Hall
    "Mermaid." [EngJ] (82:8) D 93, p. 82.
1278. CORPI, Lucha
    "On Being Alone: Berkeley 1969" (tr. by Catherine Rodríguez-Nieto). [ColR] (20:2)
        Fall 93, p. 49-51.
    "Soledades: Berkeley 1969." [ColR] (20:2) Fall 93, p. 46-48.
1279. CORR, Michael
    "Nami no Kokoro, Heart of the Wave Temple." [ChiR] (39:3/4) 93, p. 221-222.
CORRETJER, Zoé Jiménez
    See JIMENEZ CORRETJER, Zoé
1280. CORRIE, Daniel
    "Job's Punishment." [DenQ] (27:3) Wint 93, p. 18-19.
1281. CORTES-CABAN, David
    "Una Hora Antes" (3 poemas del Libro: Una Hora Antes). [Trasimagen] (1:1)
        Otoño-Invierno 93, p. 36.
1282. CORTESE, Christina
    "Skinhead Heaven" (Poets of High School Age). [HangL] (62) 93, p. 77.
    "Thrashing" (Poets of High School Age). [HangL] (62) 93, p. 77.
1283. CORY, Cynthia Jay (Cynie)
    "American Sky." [AmerPoR] (22:3) My-Je 93, p. 47.
    "The Importance of Angels." [AmerPoR] (22:3) My-Je 93, p. 47.
    "Montana Prenuptials." [AmerPoR] (22:3) My-Je 93, p. 48.
    "The Paradise Diary" (Excerpts). [Pequod] (36) 93, p. 75-76.
    "Sequel." [AmerPoR] (22:3) My-Je 93, p. 48.
    "Sudden Light." [AmerPoR] (22:3) My-Je 93, p. 47.
    "There Is a Thing Called." [WillowS] (31) Wint 93, p. 83.
1284. CORY, Jim
    "Carousel." [JamesWR] (11:1) Fall 93, p. 17.
    "Crossing the Street in the Rain." [PaintedB] (50/51) 93, p. 82.
    "Three 1-Line Poems." [WormR] (33:3, #131), 93, p. 120.
    "W.C.W." [WormR] (33:3, #131), 93, p. 121.
1285. COSEM, Michel
    "Etait-ce le monde et l'arc-en-ciel." [Os] (37) Wint 93, p. 14.
    "Jardins intérieurs." [Os] (37) Wint 93, p. 15.
    "J'ouvre cette orange." [Os] (37) Wint 93, p. 14.
    "Miracle et re^ve." [Os] (37) Wint 93, p. 16.
1286. COSIER, Tony
    "New Year Meditation" (for George Johnston). [EngJ] (82:3) Mr 93, p. 93.
    "Wild Strawberries." [Blueline] (14) 93, p. 17.
1287. COSTANZA, Natalie J.
    "Swing." [CimR] (102) Ja 93, p. 88.
1288. COSTANZO, Gerald
    "The Old Neighborhood." [NoDaQ] (61:2) Spr 93, p. 202-203.

117

"Runyonesque" (for Mark Shelton). [Light] (7) Aut 93, p. 9.
1289. COSTANZO, Mike
"Oscar." [ChironR] (12:3, #36) Aut 93, p. 27.
1290. COSTEA, Luciana
"The Convicted" (tr. of Marin Sorescu, w. W.D. Snodgrass & Dona Rosu). [Salm] (98/99) Spr-Sum 93, p. 81.
"Fortress" (tr. of Marin Sorescu, w. W.D. Snodgrass & Dona Rosu). [Salm] (98/99) Spr-Sum 93, p. 82.
"Frames" (tr. of Marin Sorescu, w. W.D. Snodgrass & Dona Rosu). [Salm] (98/99) Spr-Sum 93, p. 83.
1291. COSTELLO, Thomas F.
"Bunched in My Fist Like September." [Footwork] (23) 93, p. 164.
"Excused by the First Thing in His Mind." [Footwork] (23) 93, p. 164-165.
"Mutiny." [Footwork] (23) 93, p. 165.
1292. COSTOPOULOS, Olga
"Cactus Documentary." [Dandel] (20:1) 93, p. 48.
"Crocus." [Dandel] (20:1) 93, p. 49.
"Daughters of Wisdom." [AntigR] (93-94) Spr-Sum 93, p. 148-150.
"Nuisance Grounds." [AntigR] (93-94) Spr-Sum 93, p. 151-152.
"Pieces of Eight." [AntigR] (93-94) Spr-Sum 93, p. 147.
1293. COTTLE, Katherine
"Wedding Morning, September 1970." [GreensboroR] (55) Wint 93-94, p. 73-74.
1294. COULEHAN, Jack
"Anniversary" (The Knitted Glove, 1991). [Kaleid] (26) Wint-Spr 93, p. 49.
"Breathing." [Wind] (23:72) 93, p. 6.
"Easter Morning" (for Heather). [Wind] (23:72) 93, p. 6.
"Medicine Stone" (The Knitted Glove, 1991). [Kaleid] (26) Wint-Spr 93, p. 23.
"Shall Inherit." [SoCoast] (14) Ja 93, p. 49.
"The Sorrow of the World" (Journal of the American Medical Association, volume 262, p. 2018). [Kaleid] (26) Wint-Spr 93, p. 43.
"White Flower, White Flower" (The Knitted Glove, 1991). [Kaleid] (26) Wint-Spr 93, p. 47.
1295. COULIARAS, Yiorgos
"The Grapes" (tr. by David Mason and the author). [HarvardR] (5) Fall 93, p. 172.
1296. COULTER, Carol
"Predictions." [Wind] (23:72) 93, p. 7.
1297. COULTER, Page P.
"A Father's Deafness Late in Life." [SpoonR] (18:1) Wint-Spr 93, p. 35.
"Focus." [SpoonR] (18:1) Wint-Spr 93, p. 34.
"Walking to the Pond." [SpoonR] (18:1) Wint-Spr 93, p. 33.
COURCY, Lynne Hugo de
See DeCOURCY, Lynne Hugo
1298. COURSEN, H. R.
"Andriaen Adriaensz." [HolCrit] (30:3) Je 93, p. 17.
1299. COUTEAU, Robert
"Edda, Will You Walk with Me Tonight?" [Footwork] (23) 93, p. 97.
"Your Picture on the Wall." [Footwork] (23) 93, p. 97-98.
1300. COUTO, Nancy Vieira
"The Epistemology of Rescue." [ProseP] (2) 93, p. 23-24.
1301. COUTURIER, John
"Survival." [BrooklynR] (10) 93, p. 67.
"Unity." [Plain] (13:3) Spr 93, p. 11.
1302. COVEY, Patricia
"Estella Thinks of Pip." [LullwaterR] (4:2) Spr-Sum 93, p. 70.
"Metaphysics." [NewYorkQ] (52) 93, p. 50.
"Nancy Drew on the Azalea Path." [LitR] (37:1) Fall 93, p. 36-37.
"The Perfect Couple." [NewYorkQ] (50) 93, p. 72-73.
"Something Dark." [LullwaterR] (4:2) Spr-Sum 93, p. 42.
1303. COWING, Sue
"On Your Fiftieth Birthday." [CreamCR] (17:2) Fall 93, p. 133.
1304. COX, Mark
"The Blindness Desired." [AmerPoR] (22:1) Ja-F 93, p. 26.
1305. COX, Wayne
"Alone and Silent" (tr. of Miquel Martí i Pol, w. Lourdes Manyé i Martí). [WillowS] (31) Wint 93, p. 80.

"The Aprenticeship of Solitude" (tr. of Miquel Marti i Pol, w. Lourdes Manyé i
Martí). [ClockR] (8:1/2) 93, p. 23.
"Metamorphosis III" (tr. of Miquel Marti i Pol, w. Lourdes Manyé i Martí).
[ClockR] (8:1/2) 93, p. 25.
"This Future" (tr. of Miquel Martí i Pol, w. Lourdes Manyé i Martí). [WillowS] (31)
Wint 93, p. 80.
"Ultimate Metamorphosis" (tr. of Miquel Marti i Pol, w. Lourdes Manyé i Martí).
[ClockR] (8:1/2) 93, p. 27.
"White on White" (tr. of Miquel Martí i Pol, w. Lourdes Manyé i Martí). [WillowS]
(31) Wint 93, p. 79.
CRABBE, Chris Wallace
See WALLACE-CRABBE, Chris
1306. CRAIG, David
"May 21-26 'The Holy Innocents Will Not Be Little Children in Heaven . . . .'"
[HiramPoR] (53/54) Fall 92-Sum 93, p. 29.
"May 27 Ascension: 'I always see the good side of things. . . .'" [HiramPoR]
(53/54) Fall 92-Sum 93, p. 30.
1307. CRAIG, Kelly
"Octopi." [RiverS] (37) 93, p. 60.
1308. CRAIG, M. Earl
"Some Lilac from My Mother" (Winner, The Richard Hugo Memorial Poetry
Award). [CutB] (39) Wint 93, p. 41-42.
1309. CRAIG, Richard
"My Zulu Warrior." [Pearl] (17) Spr 93, p. 100.
"Welcome Home." [HawaiiR] (17:1, #37) Spr 93, p. 156-157.
"What I Used to Think About, Looking Out the Window As a Little Kid." [Pearl]
(19) Fall-Wint 93, p. 58.
1310. CRAIGE, Betty Jean
"The Art of Going Mad" (tr. of Manuel Mantero). [LitR] (36:3) Spr 93, p. 378-379.
"This Splendor" (tr. of Manuel Mantero). [LitR] (36:3) Spr 93, p. 378.
"To Kronos, or Words from a Drunk" (tr. of Manuel Mantero). [LitR] (36:3) Spr 93,
p. 377-378.
1311. CRAIGHILL,Virginia Ottley
"A Bad Day for Possums." [ChatR] (13:4) Sum 93, p. 55.
"Cinderella after the Ball." [ChatR] (13:4) Sum 93, p. 56.
1312. CRAM, David
"Story Lines." [Light] (6) Sum 93, p. 13.
"That Will Do Nicely." [Light] (5) Spr 93, p. 17.
1313. CRAMER, Steven
"The Anniversary." [ParisR] (35:129) Wint 93, p. 231-232.
"The Ghost in the Wedding Photograph." [ColR] (20:1) Spr 93, p. 88-89.
"Hundreds of Paired and Spinning Seeds." [TriQ] (89) Wint 93-94, p. 206-207.
"Landlocked." [IndR] (16:2) Fall 93, p. 6.
"The Long Haul." [TriQ] (89) Wint 93-94, p. 208.
1314. CRANDALL, Jeff
"The False Morel's Formula." [CutB] (39) Wint 93, p. 7-8.
1315. CRANFIELD, Steve
"Give Me Back My Man" (in memoriam Ricky Wilson). [Art&Und] (2:3) Special
Edition 93, p. 10.
1316. CRASNARU, Daniela
"Efficiency, Ecstasy" (tr. by Adam J. Sorkin). [AntigR] (93-94) Spr-Sum 93, p. 227.
"Under the Lens" (tr. by Adam J. Sorkin). [AntigR] (93-94) Spr-Sum 93, p. 228.
1317. CRATE, Joan
"Flight." [PoetryC] (14:1) 93, p. 11.
"Their Honeymoon Trip." [PoetryC] (14:1) 93, p. 11.
1318. CRAWFORD, Neta C.
"Sound of My Voice." [SinW] (51) Wint 93-94, p. 98.
"Thoughts of the Wise Men." [SinW] (50) Sum-Fall 93, p. 60-61.
1319. CREAGER, Alfred L.
"Winter Still Life." [ChrC] (110:7) 3 Mr 93, p. 229.
1320. CREED, Carolyn
"Wild Strawberry Walkabout." [Dandel] (20:1) 93, p. 61.
1321. CREELEY, Robert
"Billboards." [Arshile] (1) Spr 93, p. 43-45.
"Credo." [Conjunc] (21) 93, p. 288-290.
"Echo." [AmerPoR] (22:2) Mr-Ap 93, p. 24.

119

"For J.L." [PaintedB] (50/51) 93, p. 61.
"Parade." [AmerPoR] (22:2) Mr-Ap 93, p. 24.
"Parts" (w. Susan Rothenberg). [Conjunc] (20) 93, p. 87-103.
"The Place." [AmerPoR] (22:2) Mr-Ap 93, p. 23.
"The Road." [AmerPoR] (22:2) Mr-Ap 93, p. 24.
"Roman Sketchbook." [Ploughs] (19:4) Wint 93-94, p. 162-169.
"This House." [AmerPoR] (22:2) Mr-Ap 93, p. 23.
"Time." [AmerPoR] (22:2) Mr-Ap 93, p. 24.
1322. CREVEL, Maghiel van
    "Diminuendo" (from the cycle "For My Unborn Son," Dutch tr. of Song Lin, tr. into
        English by Ko Kooman). [GreenMR] (NS 6:2) Sum-Fall 93, p. 144.
    "Paul Celan in the Seine" (from the cycle "For My Unborn Son," Dutch tr. of Song
        Lin, tr. into English by Ko Kooman). [GreenMR] (NS 6:2) Sum-Fall 93, p.
        145.
1323. CREW, Louie
    "Welfare Diet." [ContextS] (3:1) 93, p. 39.
1324. CREWS, Judson
    "All Your Jabber of All Those People — Big." [Pearl] (19) Fall-Wint 93, p. 13.
    "The Crooked Waters of the River Might Spell." [Pearl] (17) Spr 93, p. 68.
    "How Often I Used Silence to Mask Anger." [ChironR] (12:1, #34) Spr 93, p. 11.
    "I Am Not As Philosophical About." [FreeL] (12) Sum 93, p. 9.
    "I Parked That Damn Girl's Cadillac." [ChironR] (12:1, #34) Spr 93, p. 11.
    "If I Have Not Trashed My Dearest Treasures." [ChironR] (12:1, #34) Spr 93, p. 11.
    "The Montage of All Varied Things — I Have." [RagMag] (11:1) 93, p. 41.
    "Our Lives Teach Us Who We Are." [ChironR] (12:1, #34) Spr 93, p. 11.
    "She Had a Lot of Tinsel But Her Stems." [Pearl] (19) Fall-Wint 93, p. 13.
    "Some Wonder Why I Need Fantasy Women, or." [ChironR] (12:1, #34) Spr 93, p.
        11.
    "Tell Me of the Hells You Went Through." [ChironR] (12:1, #34) Spr 93, p. 11.
    "Was I Ever Welcomed? To the Womb." [Pearl] (17) Spr 93, p. 68.
    "When It Is Over, When It Has Gotten to Be." [RagMag] (11:1) 93, p. 40.
    "Who Am I, Among These, She Asked, a One-Time Lover." [FreeL] (11) Wint 93,
        p. 22.
1325. CREWS, Mary
    "Sunday Afternoon at Aunt Maud's." [Crucible] (29) Fall 93, p. 17.
1326. CREWS, Richard
    "The Unremembered Future." [CumbPR]] (13:1) Fall 93, p. 91-92.
1327. CRILL, Hildred
    "A Room of One's Own." [CreamCR] (17:2) Fall 93, p. 108-109.
1328. CRIST-EVANS, Craig
    "Winter on La Veta Pass" (for Jim Evans). [AlabamaLR] (7:2) 93, p. 18-19.
1329. CROCKETT, Andy
    "First Hand." [PaintedHR] (8) Wint 93, p. 10.
    "From Laramie." [PaintedHR] (8) Wint 93, p. 8-9.
1330. CRONIN, Patrick
    "Passing" (in "1961-1991: Passing Through Fenway Park"). [Spitball] (43) Spr 93,
        p. 65-66.
1331. CRONWALL, Brian
    "Two Lovers." [EvergreenC] (8:1) Spr-Sum 93, p. 68.
1332. CROOKER, Barbara
    "Emily Dickinson's Answerphone." [Light] (7) Aut 93, p. 15.
    "Gardening in a Dry Year." [PaintedB] (50/51) 93, p. 128.
    "The Stone." [FourQ] (7:2) Fall 93, p. 36.
    "Walking about in Monet's Gardens at Giverny." [WestB] (33) 93, p. 25.
1333. CROSBIE, Lynn
    "Jesus the Low Rider." [Quarry] (42:2) 93, p. 115-116.
    "Little Stabs at Happiness." [Quarry] (42:2) 93, p. 112-114.
1334. CROSBY, Robbie
    "Forfeit." [JamesWR] (10:2) Wint 93, p. 16.
1335. CROSS, Elizabeth
    "The Death of All Authority." [DenQ] (27:3) Wint 93, p. 20.
1336. CROSS, William
    "Born" (tr. of Richard Exner). [LitR] (36:2) Wint 93, p. 162.
    "Boucher in the Grand Palais (Thirteen Fragments About Nakedness)" (tr. of
        Richard Exner). [Chelsea] (54) 93, p. 30-33.
    "Light, Near Perth" (tr. of Richard Exner). [Vis] (41) 93, p. 43.

"The Onset of Winter" (tr. of Richard Exner). [LitR] (36:2) Wint 93, p. 163.
"Question" (tr. of Richard Exner). [Chelsea] (54) 93, p. 33.
"Trains" (tr. of Richard Exner). [Chelsea] (54) 93, p. 34.
1337. CROW, Mary
"Ethnic Disturbances." [GreenMR] (NS 6:1) Wint-Spr 93, p. 91-93.
"Fire and Water." [GreenMR] (NS 6:1) Wint-Spr 93, p. 88-89.
"Last Campfire." [Contact] (11:65/66/67) Spr 93, p. 44-45.
"Lost Steps." [Contact] (11:65/66/67) Spr 93, p. 45.
"Luminous Path." [GreenMR] (NS 6:1) Wint-Spr 93, p. 90.
"Personal Stamp" (tr. of Olga Orozco). [SenR] (23:1/2) Wint 93, p. 132-133.
"Somber Cantata" (tr. of Olga Orozco). [SenR] (23:1/2) Wint 93, p. 136-138.
"To Make a Talisman" (tr. of Olga Orozco). [SenR] (23:1/2) Wint 93, p. 134-135.
1338. CROWE, Anna
"Skating out of the House" (after Interior with a Lady Playing at the Virginal, by
Emanuel de Witte). [Stand] (34:4) Aut 93, p. 32.
1339. CROWE, Chris
"Slipper Sex." [HawaiiR] (17:1, #37) Spr 93, p. 135.
1340. CROWELL, Doug
"Bamboo Shoots in Asia." [SnailPR] (3:1) Fall-Wint 93, p. 12-13.
1341. CROWN, Kathleen
"Necklace: Rich Pink Corona Round a Flashing Yellow Heart." [Calyx] (15:1) Wint
93-94, p. 42-45.
1342. CROZIER, Lorna
"The Game." [PraS] (67:4) Wint 93, p. 34-35.
"Going Back." [MalR] (104) Fall 93, p. 36.
"Island." [PraS] (67:4) Wint 93, p. 36.
"Learning to Read." [PraS] (67:4) Wint 93, p. 33-34.
"What Is Invisible." [MalR] (104) Fall 93, p. 37.
"When the Birds Spoke Greek." [MalR] (104) Fall 93, p. 34-35.
1343. CRUMMEY, Michael
"Atrocities." [AntigR] (95) Aut 93, p. 59.
"Balcony Poem #7." [TickleAce] (24) Fall-Wint 92, p. 8-9.
"A Day in the Life." [TickleAce] (24) Fall-Wint 92, p. 10-11.
"Driving, Highway 15." [TickleAce] (23) Spr-Sum 92, p. 14.
"The House They Lived In" (Competition Winner, 2nd). [TickleAce] (25) Spr-Sum
93, p. 120-125.
"In China." [TickleAce] (24) Fall-Wint 92, p. 7.
"Insomniac Trains." [TickleAce] (23) Spr-Sum 92, p. 15-16.
"Leaving Guatemala" (for Americo). [AntigR] (95) Aut 93, p. 57.
"Lessons" (for I.M.). [AntigR] (95) Aut 93, p. 56.
"News form Home: Burning Water." [TickleAce] (25) Spr-Sum 93, p. 185.
"On Frost's The Gift Outright." [TickleAce] (25) Spr-Sum 93, p. 186.
"Ski Hill." [Arc] (31) Aut 93, p. 80-82.
"Small Animals." [TickleAce] (23) Spr-Sum 92, p. 17-18.
"Structural Adjustment: An Introduction." [AntigR] (95) Aut 93, p. 58.
1344. CRUNK, Tony
"Eden." [VirQR] (69:1) Wint 93, p. 85-86.
"Leaving." [VirQR] (69:1) Wint 93, p. 86-87.
1345. CRUZ, Antonio
"Her Favorite Color" (tr. of Chriscinthia Blount). [Footwork] (23) 93, p. 161.
1346. CRYER, James
"A Traveler Seeks to Send This to Chou Chung Yang" (tr. of Hsü Wei). [InterPR]
(19:1) Spr 93, p. 60-61.
"What We Made a Long While Back a Certain Acquaintance Wishes Me to Do
Again" (tr. of Hsü Wei). [InterPR] (19:1) Spr 93, p. 58-59.
1347. CSIFFARY, Sylvia
"The Dissected Bird" (tr. of Bela Marko). [Vis] (41) 93, p. 8.
1348. CSOORI, Sandor
"Courtyard at Home, Before Autumn" (tr. by Len Roberts). [Chelsea] (54) 93, p. 28 -
29.
1349. CUENCA, Luis Alberto de
"The Flight into Egypt" (tr. by Cecilia C. Lee and Laura Higgins). [LitR] (36:3) Spr
93, p. 368.
"Julia" (tr. by Cecilia C. Lee and Laura Higgins). [LitR] (36:3) Spr 93, p. 368.
1350. CULVER, Irene
"But She Had Dropped Her Crown." [BellArk] (9:1) Ja-F 93, p. 9.

"The Cure." [BellArk] (9:3) My-Je 93, p. 8.
"Mija." [BellArk] (9:1) Ja-F 93, p. 12.
"The Newcomers." [BellArk] (9:3) My-Je 93, p. 22.
"Preconcieved" [sic] [BellArk] (9:1) Ja-F 93, p. 21.
"Puissant." [BellArk] (9:3) My-Je 93, p. 22.
"The Tall Women." [BellArk] (9:3) My-Je 93, p. 22.
"The Vulcan's Mirror." [BellArk] (9:3) My-Je 93, p. 22.
"Walking on Hollister Avenue After the Rain." [BellArk] (9:2) Mr-Ap 93, p. 6.
1351. CUMMING, Tim
"Down There." [Verse] (10:2) Sum 93, p. 93.
"Instant Sleep." [Verse] (10:2) Sum 93, p. 94.
1352. CUMMINGS, Darcy
"Still Life: Shipyard, September, 1950." [PaintedB] (50/51) 93, p. 101.
1353. CUMMINGS, E. E.
"1. quick i the death of thing." [QRL] (12:32/33) 93, p. 395.
"4. where's Jack Was." [QRL] (12:32/33) 93, p. 395-396.
"Five Poems" (Excerpt: "here's s"). [QRL] (12:32/33) 93, p. 396.
"Poem: of all the blessings which to man kind progress doth impart." [QRL]
    (12:32/33) 93, p. 394.
1354. CUMMINS, James
"Sestina." [ParisR] (35:126) Spr 93, p. 137-138.
1355. CUNNINGHAM, Mark
"The Fleet." [Asylum] (8) 93, p. 136.
"The Legs." [WormR] (33:4, #132) 93, p. 164-165.
"The Positions." [Asylum] (8) 93, p. 23.
"The Right Hand." [WormR] (33:4, #132) 93, p. 164.
"Umberto Boccioni." [WormR] (33:4, #132) 93, p. 165.
"Walking." [WormR] (33:4, #132) 93, p. 163-164.
1356. CURBELO, Silvia
"Janis Joplin." [Calyx] (15:1) Wint 93-94, p. 40-41.
1357. CURNOW, Wystan
"The Talk of Sailing." [WestCL] (27:2, #11) Fall 93, p. 54-57.
1358. CURRIER, Jameson
"Bloomsbury Remembered." [Art&Und] (2:1) Ja-F 93, p. 7.
1359. CURRY, Elizabeth R.
"Clytemnestra" (from The Book of Unspeakable Knives)." [Plain] (13:2) Wint 93, p.
    31.
"Harvest." [Gaia] (1/2) Ap-Jl 93, p. 33.
"I Loved It, Your Pain." [Confr] (51) Sum 93, p. 248.
1360. CURRY, M. Granville
"Rowboat." [Pequod] (36) 93, p. 77-79.
1361. CURTIS, Craig
"Today's Visit." [CreamCR] (17:1) Spr 93, p. 40-41.
"Womb Tidings." [CreamCR] (17:1) Spr 93, p. 42.
1362. CURTIS, Dana
"Breakfast in the Orchard." [Epiphany] (4:3) Jl 93, p. 162.
"The Carnivore under Glass." [Nimrod] (37:1) Fall-Wint 93, p. 111.
"Dancing with Luis Buñuel." [Nimrod] (37:1) Fall-Wint 93, p. 110.
"Double Feature." [OnTheBus] (6:1, #13) Wint 93-Spr 94, p. 76-77.
"The Flood." [Epiphany] (4:3) Jl 93, p. 163.
"Murder: Three Dreams." [OnTheBus] (5:2, #12) Sum-Fall 93, p. 54.
"The World Enters." [HayF] (13) Fall-Wint 93, p. 98.
1363. CURTIS, Simon
"Home Thoughts from the Kimberleys, WA." [Verse] (10:2) Sum 93, p. 97.
1364. CURTIS, Tony
"The Chinese Notebook" (Selections, tr. of Demosthenes Agrafiotis, w. the author,
    Theo Dorgan, Pat Boran, and Kate Newman). [Sulfur] (32) Spr 93, p. 206-
    212.
1365. CURZON, David
"Home" (Australia). [WestHR] (47:4) Wint 93, p. 340.
"A Mythical Creature" (for Jeffrey Fiskin). [WestHR] (47:4) Wint 93, p. 341.
1366. CUSHING, James
"Blues in the Night." [ProseP] (1) 92, p. 17.
"Cheek to Cheek." [LullwaterR] (4:2) Spr-Sum 93, p. 71.
"Everything Happens to Me." [Pearl] (19) Fall-Wint 93, p. 55.
"I Hear Music." [JamesWR] (10:3) Spr 93, p. 4.

"Send in the Clowns." [PoetL] (88:3) Fall 93, p. 31-32.
"Taking a Chance on Love." [JamesWR] (10:3) Spr 93, p. 4.
1367. CUTAJAR, Paul
"Potatoes." [SoCoast] (14) Ja 93, p. 42-43.
1368. CZEKANOWICZ, Anna
"I See the Future" (tr. by David Malcolm and Georgia Scott). [Prima] (16/17) 93, p. 31.
1369. CZURY, Craig
"Against the Black Wind." [ApalQ] (39) 93, p. 43.
"August 5." [ProseP] (2) 93, p. 25.
"Burning Culm" (for Franz Kline). [ApalQ] (39) 93, p. 41-42.
"Legend." [PaintedB] (50/51) 93, p. 122.
"Physics." [ProseP] (1) 92, p. 18.
D., H.
See H. D.
1370. DABBE, Vijaya
"The Windows" (tr. by Arlene Zide). [Vis] (43) 93, p. 31.
1371. DACEY, Philip
"The Art of Improvisation" (Beginning Acting, 101 — for Bill Hezlep). [ClockR] (8:1/2) 93, p. 4-5.
"The Book" (for Douglas Johnson). [NorthStoneR] (11) 93, p. 141.
"The Couple on the Roof" (for Beret and Emmett). [NorthStoneR] (11) 93, p. 143.
"A Divorced Father Takes His Two Small Children to McDonald's for Breakfast on Easter Morning." [SnailPR] (3:1) Fall-Wint 93, p. 15.
"Golf Crazed Women." [Journal] (17:1) Spr-Sum 93, p. 29-30.
"The Killing Poem." [Farm] (10:1) Spr-Sum 93, p. 126-127.
"The New Love Poem." [PaintedB] (50/51) 93, p. 12.
"Post" (for Layle Silbert). [CoalC] (7) Apr 93, p. 21.
"Reading While Driving." [NorthStoneR] (11) 93, p. 142.
"Teaching Three Essay Classes in a Row." [GreensboroR] (54) Sum 93, p. 116-117.
"Walt Whitman's Sunday with the Insane." [TexasR] (14:1/2) Spr-Sum 93, p. 92-93.
"The Web." [NorthStoneR] (11) 93, p. 144.
1372. DaGAMA, Steven
"Festive Snow." [YellowS] (42) Wint-Spr 93, p. 21.
1373. DAGOLD, Raphael
"Radio Tuning." [IndR] (16:2) Fall 93, p. 176-177.
1374. DAICHES, David
"Cherub." [Stand] (35:1) Wint 93-94, p. 10.
1375. DAIGON, Ruth
"Dachau." [CreamCR] (17:1) Spr 93, p. 77.
"Driftwood Days." [Footwork] (23) 93, p. 32.
"A Miracle." [Plain] (14:1) Fall 93, p. 25.
"Night Songs." [PoetC] (24:3) Spr 93, p. 35.
"Not Yet Visible." [ContextS] (3:1) 93, p. 27.
"Priority Mail for My Sons." [Vis] (42) 93, p. 21.
"With Apologies to a Hitchhiker." [CumbPR] (12:2) Spr 93, p. 35.
1376. DAILEY, Joel
"Continuous Present." [Arshile] (2) 93, p. 27.
1377. DAILY, Suan
"Poem No. 8: On this journey, nothing we already know" (from "The angel's wing, the landscape's calligraphy"). [PaintedB] (50/51) 93, p. 18.
1378. DALDORPH, Brian
"Adultery." [FreeL] (11) Wint 93, p. 11.
"Norita Eldodt Meets Josef Mengele, Alias 'Dr. Fritz Fischer,' in Bariloches, a Resort in the Foothills of the Andes, March 1960." [Parting] (6:2) Wint 93, p. 31.
"On TWA Flight 720, June 1990." [Bogg] (66) Wint 92-93, p. 23.
"Poet." [ContextS] (3:1) 93, p. 41.
"Shadowing Mengele: Holocaust Poems" (chapbook). [DustyD] 93, 24 p.
1379. DALE, David
"Impressions." [DogRR] (12:2, #24) Fall-Wint 93, p. 36.
1380. DALEY, Michael
"After That." [TampaR] (7) Fall 93, p. 26-27.
"Black Lid." [Manoa] (5:2) Wint 93, p. 27.
"Dunlins." [Manoa] (5:2) Wint 93, p. 28.

1381. D'ALFONSO, Antonio
"The Loss of a Culture." [Footwork] (23) 93, p. 21.
1382. DALIBARD, Jill
"After You Died." [AntigR] (92) Wint 93, p. 51-52.
1383. DALTON, Mary
"And Their Voices a River." [TickleAce] (26) Fall-Wint 93, p. 33.
"Bachelor Brothers." [TickleAce] (25) Spr-Sum 93, p. 63.
"The Book of Kells." [TickleAce] (23) Spr-Sum 92, p. 11.
"By the Shore." [TickleAce] (23) Spr-Sum 92, p. 7.
"Four and Forty, the Same Wave Cresting." [TickleAce] (25) Spr-Sum 93, p. 68.
"Humphrey Gilbert, Going Down." [TickleAce] (25) Spr-Sum 93, p. 62.
"Il Dolce Stil Novo." [TickleAce] (25) Spr-Sum 93, p. 64-65.
"In Mist, in Fire." [TickleAce] (23) Spr-Sum 92, p. 12.
"Pitcher Plant, Bog Pluto." [TickleAce] (26) Fall-Wint 93, p. 33.
"Say *Partridgeberry*." [TickleAce] (25) Spr-Sum 93, p. 66.
"Thirteen Ways of Looking at a Memo." [TickleAce] (23) Spr-Sum 92, p. 9-10.
"Where the Scars." [TickleAce] (25) Spr-Sum 93, p. 67.
"White Musk." [TickleAce] (23) Spr-Sum 92, p. 11.
"Winter Garden." [TickleAce] (23) Spr-Sum 92, p. 8.
"Woundings Past Weather." [TickleAce] (26) Fall-Wint 93, p. 32.
1384. DALY, Brian
"Chipping Some Teeth." [Pearl] (17) Spr 93, p. 79.
1385. DALY, Catherine
"Journeys on the Highway." [Footwork] (23) 93, p. 118.
"Kupec Family Reunion." [LullwaterR] (4:2) Spr-Sum 93, p. 34.
"Only This Is Manageable." [LullwaterR] (4:2) Spr-Sum 93, p. 39.
1386. DALY, Chris
"Ice." [ChironR] (12:4/13:1, #37/38) Wint 93-Spr 94, p. 34.
"Woody n Me." [ChironR] (12:4/13:1, #37/38) Wint 93-Spr 94, p. 34.
1387. DALY, Daniel
"This Morning a Strange Bird." [PoetL] (88:3) Fall 93, p. 27.
1388. D'AMATO, Michael
"The Sad Disruptions." [Gypsy] (20) Sum 93, p. 31.
1389. DAME, Enid
"Lilith, I Don't Cut My Grass." [AmerV] (32) 93, p. 34-35.
1390. DAMERON, Chip
"Unbrick the Night." [Elf] (3:1) Spr 93, p. 34.
1391. DAMIEN, Peter-Marc
"Zinnias" (for Clyde Howell). [JamesWR] (10:2) Wint 93, p. 17.
1392. DANA, Robert
"After After." [HighP] (8:3) Wint 93, p. 91-92.
"Anniversary" (For Liz). [Poetry] (162:5) Ag 93, p. 260.
"Here and Now." [HighP] (8:3) Wint 93, p. 93-94.
"Orphan Spring." [HighP] (8:3) Wint 93, p. 67.
"What I Did." [HighP] (8:3) Wint 93, p. 95-96.
"Wildebeest." [GeoR] (47:1) Spr 93, p. 15-21.
1393. DANFORD, Douglas
"A merchant who lives on the Tyne." [Light] (7) Aut 93, p. 24.
1394. DANG, The Binh
"The Prison Poems of Ho Chi Minh" (Selections, Photographs by Larry Towell, tr.
of Ho Chi Minh). [Quarry] (42:1) 93, p. 69-84.
1395. D'ANGELO, Mary
"Dance Lessons" (For Elmer). [CapeR] (28:1) Spr 93, p. 50.
"Fragments" (A Plainsongs Award Poem). [Plain] (13:2) Wint 93, p. 21.
"She-Wolf." [Plain] (13:3) Spr 93, p. 20.
"Slipping Away." [Plain] (14:1) Fall 93, p. 33.
1396. DANIEL, John
"Darwinian." [NorthStoneR] (11) 93, p. 24.
"The Dressmaker." [NorthStoneR] (11) 93, p. 22.
"Landscape for a Yorkshire Woman." [NorthStoneR] (11) 93, p. 23.
"Package Empire" (In the 6th century the Romans retreated to Ravello in the
mountains near Naples). [NorthStoneR] (11) 93, p. 25.
"To My Mother." [Poetry] (162:6) S 93, p. 318.
"The Visit: November 22, 1990." [NorthStoneR] (11) 93, p. 26-27.
1397. DANIELS, Barbara
"After the Quarrel." [JINJPo] (15:2) Aut 93, p. 20.

"The Bear." [FourQ] (7:1) Spr 93, p. 22.
"During the Prelude." [Footwork] (23) 93, p. 126.
1398. DANIELS, Carl M.
"Dick Cavett." [ChironR] (12:3, #36) Aut 93, p. 21.
"Garden Tour, Autumn." [WormR] (33:4, #132) 93, p. 165-166.
"Heaven." [WormR] (33:4, #132) 93, p. 166.
"Touchers." [ChironR] (12:3, #36) Aut 93, p. 21.
1399. DANIELS, Jim
"Blue Donuts." [WestB] (33) 93, p. 78.
"How." [Manoa] (5:2) Wint 93, p. 113-115.
"I slept with the Singing Nun." [PoetL] (88:1) Spr 93, p. 29-30.
"Keeping the Books." [HawaiiR] (16:3, #36) Wint 93, p. 85-86.
"My Two Aunts." [SycamoreR] (5:1) Wint 93, p. 59-61.
"Penny Candy." [NoDaQ] (61:4) Fall 93, p. 69-71.
"President Declares Cute Day." [PennR] (5:2) 93, p. 4-6.
"Skull and Crossbones." [LaurelR] (27:2) Sum 93, p. 71-73.
"War Dancing." [PoetL] (88:1) Spr 93, p. 31.
"Wrapping Bread." [PaintedB] (50/51) 93, p. 36.
1400. DANIELS, Lee
"A Line." [WebR] (17) Fall 93, p. 111.
1401. DANIELS, Peter
"A Clockwork Uncle." [JamesWR] (10:2) Wint 93, p. 4.
"Editorial." [Art&Und] (2:2) My-Je 93, p. 8.
"Family." [Verse] (10:2) Sum 93, p. 64.
"Wall Street." [Art&Und] (2:2) My-Je 93, p. 8.
1402. DANISON, Tracy
"With His Things." [MalR] (103) Sum 93, p. 73.
1403. D'ANNA, Lynette (Dueck)
"Cheap Lights Cheap." [Grain] (21:1) Spr 93, p. 79.
1404. DANQUAH, Meri Nana-Ama
"Prayers, Wishes and Other Impossibilities." [Eyeball] (2) 93, p. 11.
"White People." [OnTheBus] (5:2, #12) Sum-Fall 93, p. 55-56.
1405. DANSON, Elizabeth
"Unleaving." [US1] (28/29) 93, p. 28.
1406. DANTE (Dante Alighieri)
"Canto XV" (tr. by Robert Pinsky). [Thrpny] (54) Sum 93, p. 19.
"In Hell with Virg and Dan" (Canto XVII, tr. by Carolyn Kizer). [13thMoon]
(12:1/2) 93-94, p. 38-41.
"In the First Circle" (A Translation of the *Inferno*, Canto IV, by Robert Pinsky).
[NewEngR] (15:4) Fall 93, p. 55-61.
"Inferno: Canto V (Paolo and Francesca)" (tr. by Robert Pinsky). [AmerPoR] (22:1)
Ja-F 93, p. 57-59.
"Inferno" (Canto VII, tr. by Robert Pinsky). [Salm] (98/99) Spr-Sum 93, p. 37-41.
"Inferno, Canto XIII: The Wood of the Suicides" (tr. by Robert Pinsky). [BostonR]
(18:1) Ja-F 93, p. 19-21.
"Inferno" (Canto XVI-XVII, tr. by Robert Pinsky). [Poetry] (162:3) Je 93, p. 143 -
151.
"Inferno, Canto XXII: Among the Malebranche" (tr. by Robert Pinsky). [TriQ] (89)
Wint 93-94, p. 221-230.
"Purgatorio, Canto II" (Excerpt, tr. by W. S. Merwin). [OhioR] (50) 93, p. 11-15.
"Purgatorio" (Canto V, tr. by W. S. Merwin). [Poetry] (162:3) Je 93, p. 152-156.
"La Vita Nuova" (Selection: Chapter XXIII: "Donna pietosa." In Italian and English,
tr. by Andrew Frisardi). [CumbPR]] (13:1) Fall 93, p. 42-43.
"La Vita Nuova" (Selection: Chapter XXVI: "Tanto gentile e tanto." In Italian and
English, tr. by Andrew Frisardi). [CumbPR]] (13:1) Fall 93, p. 44-45.
"La Vita Nuova" (Selection: Chapter XLI: "Oltre la spera." In Italian and English, tr.
by Andrew Frisardi). [CumbPR]] (13:1) Fall 93, p. 46-47.
DAO, Bei
See BEI, Dao
1407. DAOUD, Marcia L.
"Little One of Bangladesh." [WorldO] (25:2) Wint 93-94, p. 59.
"Wounded Knee." [WorldO] (25:2) Wint 93-94, p. 58.
1408. DAOUST, Jean-Paul
"Le Chant des Serpents." [WestCL] (27:3, #12) Wint 93-94, p. 71-73.
"Décadence." [WestCL] (27:3, #12) Wint 93-94, p. 70.
"L'Enfant sur le Toit." [WestCL] (27:3, #12) Wint 93-94, p. 68.

"Guillotine." [WestCL] (27:3, #12) Wint 93-94, p. 69.
1409. DARIO, Ruben
   "Snail-Shell" (tr. by Henry M. Walker). [Asylum] (8) 93, p. 136.
1410. DARJES, Shelley
   "Between Stations." [MalR] (104) Fall 93, p. 80.
1411. DARLING, Charles W.
   "The High-School Band Director Conducts 'The Grand Canyon Suite'." [CimR]
      (105) O 93, p. 82-83.
   "Stick-Figures" (on a drawing by J.D., age five). [BlackWR] (20:1) Fall-Wint 93, p.
      63-64.
   "Willow Ware." [SycamoreR] (5:2) Sum 93, p. 39-40.
1412. DARLING, Robert
   "The Campers." [Blueline] (14) 93, p. 54-55.
   "The Maze." [Sparrow] (60) Sum 93, p. 31.
   "A Portrait from the Renaissance." [Sparrow] (60) Sum 93, p. 30.
   "The Search." [SoCoast] (15) Je 93, p. 58.
   "The Sermon of St. Franics." [Sparrow] (60) Sum 93, p. 30.
   "Vingt-et-un." [Sparrow] (60) Sum 93, p. 31.
1413. DARLINGTON, Tenaya
   "Riverbed." [WindO] (57) Fall 93, p. 21-23.
1414. DARNLEY, April
   "So We Hear" (for Dennis Cooley. With the Sisler High School Grade 10 I.B.
      English Class). [PraF] (14:3) Aut 93, p. 34-35.
1415. D'ARPINO, Tony
   "The Sequel to *Moby Dick*." [ProseP] (1) 92, p. 19.
1416. DARR, Ann
   "Night on the Seine." [PoetL] (88:1) Spr 93, p. 48.
1417. DARROUGH, Tiffany
   "T.V., Ghosts, and Poets Past." [AlabamaLR] (7:1) 93, p. 50-53.
1418. DARROW, Laurel
   "The Orchardist." [SouthernPR] (33:2) Fall 93, p. 12-13.
1419. DARWIN, Erasmus
   "The Temple of Nature" (2 excerpts). [Sulfur] (33) Fall 93, p. 67-72.
1420. DASSANOWSKY-HARRIS, Robert
   "For the Man Who Knows He Is the Father of His Country and Will Not Be Named
      Here." [OnTheBus] (5:2, #12) Sum-Fall 93, p. 57.
   "Fragments after Robert Browning" (tr. of Alexander Lernet-Holenia). [WebR] (17)
      Fall 93, p. 27.
   "Mutiny" (tr. of Alexander Lernet-Holenia). [WebR] (17) Fall 93, p. 26.
1421. DATCHER, Michael
   "Flying into Birmingham." [Eyeball] (2) 93, p. 9.
   "Flying into Memphis." [Eyeball] (2) 93, p. 9-10.
1422. DATTA, Jyotirmoy
   "The Boy" (tr. of Anuradha Mahapatra, w. Carolyne Wright). [MidAR] (14:1) 93, p.
      98.
1423. DAUER, Lesley
   "Falling." [Poetry] (162:2) My 93, p. 69.
1424. DAUGHERTY, Sarah
   "Quintessence." [ChironR] (12:3, #36) Aut 93, p. 31.
1425. DAUMAL, René
   "After" (tr. by Jordan Jones). [Asylum] (8) 93, p. 84.
   "Coldly" (tr. by Jordan Jones). [Asylum] (8) 93, p. 81-82.
   "Disillusion" (tr. by Jordan Jones). [Asylum] (8) 93, p. 82.
   "No More" (tr. by Jordan Jones). [Asylum] (8) 93, p. 85-86.
   "Prefatory Nymph" (tr. by Jordan Jones). [Asylum] (8) 93, p. 81.
   "To Nothingness" (tr. by Jordan Jones). [Asylum] (8) 93, p. 83-84.
1426. DAUNT, Jonathan
   "Fleas on the Space Shuttle Challenger." [AntigR] (92) Wint 93, p. 115-117.
   "Mother Earth." [SouthernPR] (33:1) Spr 93, p. 58-59.
   "The School." [BelPoJ] (44:1) Fall 93, p. 8-12.
1427. DAVICO, Oskar
   "Poems from Hana (1939)" (tr. by Richard Burns and Dasa Maric). [NoDaQ] (61:1)
      Wint 93, p. 55-57.
1428. DAVID, Almitra
   "Early." [AmerV] (31) 93, p. 42.
   "Pension." [AmerV] (31) 93, p. 43-44.

DAVID

"Poem to My Hungry Daughter." [BelPoJ] (43:4) Sum 93, p. 26-30.
"Skylight." [PaintedB] (50/51) 93, p. 26-27.
1429. DAVID, Nat
"Amazing Journey." [Footwork] (23) 93, p. 42-43.
1430. DAVIDSON, Cynthia
"Union." [AnotherCM] (26) Fall 93, p. 8.
1431. DAVIDSON, Daniel
"Bureaucrat, My Love" (Excerpt). [Talisman] (10) Spr 93, p. 142-145.
1432. DAVIDSON, Michael
"The Arcades" (Selections: 5 poems). [Avec] (6:1) 93, p. 46-48.
1433. DAVIDSON, Phebe
"Bulbs." [Vis] (42) 93, p. 38-39.
"Elegy for the Living." [JINJPo] (15:1) Spr 93, p. 17.
"Home." [JINJPo] (15:1) Spr 93, p. 16.
"How Mountains Crumble." [US1] (28/29) 93, p. 18.
"Lately She Has Been Dreaming." [ColEng] (55:6) O 93, p. 649.
"That Empty Place." [PoetryE] (36) Fall 93, p. 108-109.
DAVIDSON, Terri Brown
   See BROWN-DAVIDSON, Terri
1434. DAVIE, Donald
"First Epistle to Eva Hesse." [QRL] (12:32/33) 93, p. 397-403.
1435. DAVIES, Lynn
"After the Storm." [TickleAce] (26) Fall-Wint 93, p. 44.
"There Are Two Stills." [TickleAce] (26) Fall-Wint 93, p. 45.
1436. DAVIES, Robert A.
"Walt Whitman, AIDS Worker." [EvergreenC] (8:1) Spr-Sum 93, p. 76.
1437. DAVIGNON, Richard
"Cole Porter Variation." [Bogg] (66) Wint 92-93, p. 43.
"Elvis is Dead, Bubba." [HolCrit] (30:3) Je 93, p. 19.
"Mrs. Johnson." [HolCrit] (30:4) O 93, p. 18.
"Mrs. Johnson" (A Newark, New Jersey substitute teacher was arrested after
   practicing voodoo on her 7th grade class). [ChironR] (12:4/13:1, #37/38)
   Wint 93-Spr 94, p. 31.
"Neon Leon." [DogRR] (12:1, #23) Spr-Sum 93, p. 27.
1438. DAVIS, Adam Brooke
"First of March" (for Paulie). [CapeR] (28:1) Spr 93, p. 44.
1439. DAVIS, Andra
"Come Back from the Dead" (for an ex-lover on drugs). [Lactuca] (17) Apr 93, p. 7.
1440. DAVIS, Angela J.
"Blue Window." [CreamCR] (17:2) Fall 93, p. 150.
"The Great Taming Force." [Sequoia] (34/35) 92-93, p. 36.
1441. DAVIS, Brangien
"Winter." [CreamCR] (17:1) Spr 93, p. 35.
1442. DAVIS, Carol Ann
"Reprinted by Permission of Architectural Digest." [GettyR] (6:4) Aut 93, p. 684.
"The Search." [GettyR] (6:4) Aut 93, p. 683.
"Tips from My Father." [GettyR] (6:4) Aut 93, p. 685.
1443. DAVIS, Christopher
"Commencement Ode." [Agni] (37) 93, p. 73.
"A Costume Straitjacket's Black Sleeve in Armoire Shadows." [Agni] (37) 93, p. 74 -
   76.
"If You Love Something, Let It Go." [Agni] (37) 93, p. 71-72.
1444. DAVIS, Dick
"Into Care." [Thrpny] (53) Spr 93, p. 16.
1445. DAVIS, Ellen
"One Thing." [HarvardR] (3) Wint 93, p. 63.
1446. DAVIS, Heather
"After the King's Cross Fire." [Sonora] (24/25) Spr 93, p. 106.
"Watermusic." [PoetL] (88:2) Sum 93, p. 12.
1447. DAVIS, John
"Day One." [PennR] (5:2) 93, p. 42-43.
"How to Fire a Forklift Driver." [SycamoreR] (5:1) Wint 93, p. 58.
"Labor Day Nap." [BelPoJ] (43:4) Sum 93, p. 24.
"Schoolteacher Raking Crimson Leaves." [BelPoJ] (43:4) Sum 93, p. 25.
"Thursday, Across from My Work Station." [LullwaterR] (4:2) Spr-Sum 93, p. 43.

1448. DAVIS, Jon
"The Bait." [ProseP] (1) 92, p. 24-25.
"Blues." [ProseP] (1) 92, p. 22-23.
"The Frogs." [ProseP] (1) 92, p. 26.
"In History, I." [ProseP] (2) 93, p. 26.
"In History, II." [ProseP] (2) 93, p. 27.
"In the Sorry Part." [HarvardR] (5) Fall 93, p. 163.
"Relativity." [ProseP] (1) 92, p. 20-21.
1449. DAVIS, Jordan
"Hidden Poem." [Talisman] (10) Spr 93, p. 170.
"Jinx" (The Free Lunch Mentor Series. Kenneth Koch Introduces). [FreeL] (11)
Wint 93, p. 16-17.
"The Whole Time" (The Free Lunch Mentor Series. Kenneth Koch Introduces).
[FreeL] (11) Wint 93, p. 17-18.
1450. DAVIS, Lisa
"Elegy for Maurice Bishop" (tr. of Nancy Morejón). [Drumvoices] (3:1/2) Fall-Wint
93-94, p. 79-81.
"The Nightingale and Death" (tr. of Nancy Morejón). [Drumvoices] (3:1/2) Fall -
Wint 93-94, p. 76-77.
"A Simple Truth" (from a construction worker, my friend, tr. of Nancy Morejón).
[Drumvoices] (3:1/2) Fall-Wint 93-94, p. 82.
1451. DAVIS, Lloyd
"To Donald Davidson in Heaven (southern Section)." [SoCarR] (26:1) Fall 93, p.
111-112.
1452. DAVIS, Lyn
"Riding What Life Handed Her." [CapeR] (28:2) Fall 93, p. 31.
1453. DAVIS, Margo
"Stars." [LouisL] (10:2) Fall 93, p. 63-64.
1454. DAVIS, Melody
"Homecoming Dinner, Dr. Elizabeth Riefsynder, 1914." [BelPoJ] (44:2) Wint 93 -
94, p. 16-17.
"January 16, 1991, Owls's Head Park, False Spring." [BrooklynR] (10) 93, p. 3.
1455. DAVIS, Owen
"Let Them Move." [Os] (37) Wint 93, p. 3-7.
1456. DAVIS, Susan
"Hired Man." [Shen] (43:1) Spr 93, p. 24.
"Speaking." [Shen] (43:1) Spr 93, p. 25.
1457. DAVIS, Tito Antonio
"Butch Queen Strolling through the Bathhouse." [JamesWR] (10:4) Sum 93, p. 18.
1458. DAVIS, William Virgil
"The Fields." [PoetL] (88:3) Fall 93, p. 5.
"Frames." [GreenMR] (NS 6:2) Sum-Fall 93, p. 94.
"In the Wasteland" (tr. of Georg Trakl). [Paint] (19:38) Aut 92, p. 54.
"The Island." [CentR] (37:3) Fall 93, p. 548-549.
"The Levitator." [HiramPoR] (53/54) Fall 92-Sum 93, p. 31-32.
"The Mystery of Winter." [Border] (2) Spr 93, p. 14.
"Plum." [PaintedB] (50/51) 93, p. 85.
"Summer Celestial." [Shen] (43:2) Sum 93, p. 20.
"The Visit" (Puckberg am Schneeberg). [Shen] (43:2) Sum 93, p. 21.
"A Winter Evening" (tr. of Georg Trakl). [Paint] (19:38) Aut 92, p. 55.
1459. DAVISON, Peter
"The History of Uncle Botolph, or My Sainted Aunt" (An occasional Ode, written in
1989, for the dinner that first welcomed female members to a Boston club).
[Light] (6) Sum 93, p. 18.
1460. DAVISON, Scott
"Old Discipline" (tr. of Cesare Pavese). [CimR] (104) Jl 93, p. 139.
"Other Times" (tr. of Cesare Pavese). [CimR] (104) Jl 93, p. 141-142.
"Poetical" (tr. of Cesare Pavese). [ChiR] (38:4) 93, p. 151-152.
"Sad Wine" (tr. of Cesare Pavese). [CimR] (104) Jl 93, p. 140-141.
1461. DAVTIAN, Vahakn
"Enough to Make Him Howl" (tr. by Diana Der-Hovanessian). [Vis] (43) 93, p. 6.
1462. DAWE, Tom
"Daedalus." [TickleAce] (24) Fall-Wint 92, p. 18-20.
"Edwardians (Old Photograph)." [TickleAce] (24) Fall-Wint 92, p. 17.
"Methodists." [TickleAce] (24) Fall-Wint 92, p. 21.

1463. DAWES, Kwame
"Grace." [Callaloo] (16:3) Sum 93, p. 589.
"Progeny of Air." [Callaloo] (16:3) Sum 93, p. 585-588.
1464. DAWES, Stacey
"Never Say Goodbye." [13thMoon] (12:1/2) 93-94, p. 120.
"Tracks." [13thMoon] (12:1/2) 93-94, p. 118-119.
1465. DAWSON, Amy
"Mr. Doodle Man" (Young Writers, age 17). [PikeF] (11) Fall 93, p. 20.
1466. DAWSON, Mark
"Reading in the Poetry Journals." [PikeF] (11) Fall 93, p. 32.
"School Building." [PikeF] (11) Fall 93, p. 32.
1467. DAY, Meara
"Nocturne." [LullwaterR] (4:2) Spr-Sum 93, p. 58.
1468. DAYRIT, Joy T.
"Antique." [Bomb] (45) Fall 93, p. 80.
"Untitled: If all I'd leave you be a poem." [Bomb] (45) Fall 93, p. 80.
1469. DAYTON, Irene
"Two Studies." [NorthStoneR] (11) 93, p. 45.
De . . .
See also names beginning with "De" without the following space, filed below in
their alphabetic positions, e.g., DeFOE.
De ANDRADE, Eugenio
See ANDRADE, Eugenio de
1470. De AVILA, Leonora
"Deranged in the Marina Pacifica Lucky's" (with apologies to Allen Ginsberg).
[Pearl] (17) Spr 93, p. 88-89.
De BELLEFEUILLE, Norman
See BELLEFEUILLE, Norman de
1471. De BROUX, Peggy
"Shooting the Rapids." [Kalliope] (15:3) 93, p. 13.
De CUENCA, Luis Alberto
See CUENCA, Luis Alberto de
1472. De FRATES, Stephen
"Road Kill." [Lactuca] (17) Apr 93, p. 33.
"Shipwrecked." [Lactuca] (17) Apr 93, p. 32.
De IBARBOUROU, Juana
See IBARBOUROU, Juana de
De INSULIS, Alanus
See INSULIS, Alanus de (Alan of Lille)
De IZAGUIRRE, Ester
See IZAGUIRRE, Ester de
1473. De JONG, Daphne
"There's a Hole in the Sky." [Vis] (42) 93, p. 10.
1474. De KOK, Ingrid
"Mending." [BostonR] (18:3/4) Je-Ag 93, p. 32.
"Night Space." [BostonR] (18:3/4) Je-Ag 93, p. 32.
1475. De MARIS, Ron
"The Thing That Waits for You." [LitR] (37:1) Fall 93, p. 38-39.
De MELLO BREYNER ANDRESEN, Sophia
See BREYNER, Sophia de Mello
De MORAES, Vinicius
See MORAES, Vinicius de
De PAGELLA, Angela Blanco Amores
See BLANCO AMORES de PAGELLA, Angela
De PARIS, Marta
See PARIS, Marta de
1476. De RACHEWILTZ, Mary
"Carol called it comfort food." [Interim] (12:1) Spr-Sum 93, p. 39.
"There is something in this house." [Interim] (12:1) Spr-Sum 93, p. 40.
"When the strong ventriloquist crumbles." [Interim] (12:1) Spr-Sum 93, p. 38.
1477. De ROUS, Peter
"Not For." [Bogg] (66) Wint 92-93, p. 10.
De SEGRAIS, Joliveau
See SEGRAIS, Joliveau de
De UNGRIA, Ricardo M.
See UNGRIA, Ricardo M. de

De VEGA, Lope
    See VEGA, Lope de
De VENTADOUR, Bernard
    See VENTADOUR, Bernard de
De VILLENA, Luis Antonio
    See VILLENA, Luis Antonio de
1478. De VITO, E. B.
    "Roles Rewritten." [Comm] (120:13) 16 Jl 93, p. 20.
1479. DEAGON, Andrea Webb
    "First Generation." [LaurelR] (27:1) Wint 93, p. 14.
    "Greek Easter." [Pembroke] (25) 93, p. 57.
    "Here a Different Ocean." [LaurelR] (27:1) Wint 93, p. 15-16.
    "Through the Window." [Journal] (17:2) Fall-Wint 93, p. 29-30.
1480. DEAN, Debra Kang
    "After Long Thought, I Submit My Resignation to the University." [TarRP] (33:1)
        Fall 93, p. 51.
    "Calling from the Gate." [BambooR] (57) Wint 93, p. 156.
    "Catch and Release." [TarRP] (33:1) Fall 93, p. 52.
    "Pineapples" (for Garrett Hongo). [TarRP] (33:1) Fall 93, p. 50-51.
1481. DEANE, Seamus
    "Love Poem." [GrandS] (11:4, #44) 93, p. 29.
    "The Sense of an Ending." [GrandS] (11:4, #44) 93, p. 30-31.
    "The Siege of Derry." [GrandS] (11:4, #44) 93, p. 26-27.
    "The Winter That Succeeded." [GrandS] (11:4, #44) 93, p. 28.
1482. DEANOVICH, Connie
    "Addition to Hitchcock." [NewAW] (11) Sum-Fall 93, p. 80-81.
    "Marie Antoinette Ocean." [NewAW] (11) Sum-Fall 93, p. 82.
DeAVILA, Leonora
    See De AVILA, Leonora
1483. DEBELJAK, Ales
    "Fearful Moments" (tr. by the author and Kelly Hawkins). [NoDaQ] (61:1) Wint 93,
        p. 58.
    "In this moment, in the twilight of a cold room, thunder approaches" (tr. by
        Christopher Merrill, w. the author). [ProseP] (2) 93, p. 28.
    "Indifferently, he watched her through the shadows of furniture" (tr. by Christopher
        Merrill, w. the author). [ProseP] (2) 93, p. 29.
1484. DEBNEY, Jack
    "Alexandria: Coda to Cavafy's 'The City'." [Stand] (34:2) Spr 93, p. 76.
    "The North." [Stand] (34:2) Spr 93, p. 77.
1485. DEBORAH
    "Reflections on My Lesbian Body" (September 26, 1992, New moon). [SinW] (49)
        Spr-Sum 93, p. 15.
1486. DEBOVIAN, Sebastian
    "A Little Extortion on Traction Ave." [ChironR] (12:3, #36) Aut 93, p. 6.
    "The Open Mic Massacre." [ChironR] (12:3, #36) Aut 93, p. 6.
    "To Wordsworth." [ChironR] (12:3, #36) Aut 93, p. 6.
1487. DeCARTERET, Mark
    "Monsters Playing Kissing Games." [Caliban] (12) 93, p. 187.
1488. DECKER, Diana
    "Chase for One Lover Alone" (tr. of Christina Peri Rossi). [QRL] (12:32/33) 93, p.
        275-277.
    "Girls" (tr. of Christina Peri Rossi). [QRL] (12:32/33) 93, p. 274-275.
    "Language" (tr. of Christina Peri Rossi). [QRL] (12:32/33) 93, p. 274.
    "Prayer" (tr. of Christina Peri Rossi). [QRL] (12:32/33) 93, p. 277-278.
    "Prehistory" (tr. of Christina Peri Rossi). [QRL] (12:32/33) 93, p. 274.
    "Reminiscence" (tr. of Christina Peri Rossi). [QRL] (12:32/33) 93, p. 278.
    "A Virus Named AIDS" (tr. of Christina Peri Rossi). [QRL] (12:32/33) 93, p. 278 -
        279.
    "Women's Condition" (tr. of Christina Peri Rossi). [QRL] (12:32/33) 93, p. 273-274.
1489. DECKER, Donna
    "Grandma Gladys." [ApalQ] (38) 92, p. 74-75.
1490. DECKER, Lareina
    "Los Lugares Adonde Voy" (from "Families, Streets and Dreams," a
        poetry/photography event by 3rd grade students, Whittier Elementary, Tulsa).
        [Nimrod] (37:1) Fall-Wint 93, p. 89.

DECKER

"The Places I Go" (from "Families, Streets and Dreams," a poetry/photography
    event by 3rd grade students, Whittier Elementary, Tulsa). [Nimrod] (37:1)
    Fall-Wint 93, p. 89.
1491. DeCOURCY, Lynne Hugo
"From the Manger." [CentR] (37:2) Spr 93, p. 370-371.
"Her Loneliness." [CentR] (37:3) Fall 93, p. 526.
"In the School of Dance." [CentR] (37:3) Fall 93, p. 524-525.
"Versions." [Calyx] (14:3) Sum 93, p. 53-55.
1492. DEFENDI, Adrienne S.
"April Fool's Day, Happy Birthday" (for Billy). [Footwork] (23) 93, p. 82.
"Expulsion" (for JF). [Footwork] (23) 93, p. 83.
"Five Attempts: No Way to Talk Around the Hole." [Footwork] (23) 93, p. 82-83.
"Praying Mantis." [Footwork] (23) 93, p. 82-83.
1493. DeFOE, Mark
"American Dream." [HighP] (8:1) Spr 93, p. 73-74.
"Coming Out of the Discount Store." [HolCrit] (30:3) Je 93, p. 19.
"When Grandfather Tours the Countryside." [Elf] (3:3) Fall 93, p. 26.
DeFRATES, Stephen
    See De FRATES, Stephen
Degli ALBIZZI, Niccolò
    See ALBIZZI, Niccolò degli
1494. DEGUTYTE, Janina
"Holy June" (tr. by Lionginas Pazusis, w. Bradley R. Strahan). [Vis] (43) 93, p. 35.
"To Live" (tr. by Lionginas Pazusis, w. Bradley R. Strahan). [Vis] (43) 93, p. 35.
1495. DEIKE, Marta
"Dreams of Interpretation." [CentralP] (22) Spr 93, p. 107-109.
DeINSULIS, Alanus
    See INSULIS, Alanus de (Alan of Lille)
DeJONG, Daphne
    See De JONG, Daphne
Del CASTILLO, Amelia
    See CASTILLO, Amelia del
Del PINO, José Manuel
    See PINO, José Manuel del
1496. DELANO, Page Dougherty
"Cat Deaths." [SenR] (23:1/2) Wint 93, p. 99-100.
"History." [13thMoon] (11:1/2) 93, p. 24-27.
"I Don't Know Blues." [GettyR] (6:1) Wint 93, p. 36-37.
"V-Girls." [KenR] (NS 15:2) Spr 93, p. 133-136.
1497. DELANTY, Greg
"According to the Horticulturist, It Is Unlikely Our Fuchsia Will Survive the
    Winter." [GreenMR] (NS 6:2) Sum-Fall 93, p. 37.
"At a Low Point." [SouthernR] (29:1) Wint, Ja 93, p. 172.
"On Skellig Michael." [AntR] (51:4) Fall 93, p. 562.
1498. DELEA, Christine
"What I Am Saying." [BellArk] (9:5) S-O 93, p. 10.
1499. DELEY, John Paul
"Beginning Apart." [JamesWR] (10:3) Spr 93, p. 6.
"Chastity Imposes No Conditions." [EvergreenC] (8:2) Sum-Fall 93, p. 56.
"Indifferent Paradise." [FreeL] (11) Wint 93, p. 20.
"Just Wonders." [EvergreenC] (8:2) Sum-Fall 93, p. 55.
1500. DELIGIORGIS, Stavros
"Love Song" (tr. of Paul Celan). [WorldL] (4) 93, p. 23.
1501. DELISLE, Greg
"The Sun" (for C.W.). [CreamCR] (17:2) Fall 93, p. 177.
"Unfinished Ode: to a Lightbulb" (for J.). [RiverS] (38) 93, p. 69-70.
1502. DellaROCCA, L. (Lenny)
"The Man Who Played Bagpipes." [BellArk] (9:6) N-D 93, p. 22.
"Neo." [PoetL] (88:4) Wint 93-94, p. 24.   •
"The Work of Saints" (Selections: 2 poems). [Nimrod] (37:1) Fall-Wint 93, p. 70 -
    76.
1503. Delos SANTOS, P.
"Gwendolyn." [HawaiiR] (17:1, #37) Spr 93, p. 216.
"Waiting." [HawaiiR] (17:1, #37) Spr 93, p. 215.
1504. DeLOTTO, Jeffrey
"Al-Husn, in Northern Jordan." [LitR] (37:1) Fall 93, p. 60-61.

"The First Snow." [CumbPR]] (13:1) Fall 93, p. 60.
1505. DEMCAK, Andrew
"Dime." [ChironR] (12:4/13:1, #37/38) Wint 93-Spr 94, p. 23.
"First Crush." [ChironR] (12:3, #36) Aut 93, p. 7.
"Liars." [ChironR] (12:4/13:1, #37/38) Wint 93-Spr 94, p. 22.
"Reading a Poetry Assignment on Wednesday at 11:09 p.m." [ChironR] (12:4/13:1, #37/38) Wint 93-Spr 94, p. 22.
"A Root Story." [Pearl] (19) Fall-Wint 93, p. 12.
"Seaward." [ChironR] (12:4/13:1, #37/38) Wint 93-Spr 94, p. 22.
"Traffic Was Stopped on P.V. Drive North." [ChironR] (12:4/13:1, #37/38) Wint 93-Spr 94, p. 23.
"Valentine." [ChironR] (12:3, #36) Aut 93, p. 7.
DeMELLO BREYNER ANDRESEN, Sophia
See BREYNER, Sophia de Mello
1506. DEMIENTIEFF, Martha
"Going Away." [Descant] (24:3, #82) Fall 93, p. 115.
"Mental Health Meeting." [Descant] (24:3, #82) Fall 93, p. 113.
"Our Language." [Descant] (24:3, #82) Fall 93, p. 117-118.
1507. DEMING, Alison H.
"Camp Tontozona." [HayF] (12) Spr-Sum 93, p. 80-81.
1508. DEMKO, Robert
"Military Park." [Footwork] (23) 93, p. 60.
1509. DeMOTT, Robert
"Confession: After Earthquake." [CimR] (104) Jl 93, p. 154-155.
1510. DEMPSTER, Barry
"The Dead Are Watching Us." [Arc] (30) Spr 93, p. 39-40.
"Sunday School and the Promised Land." [Arc] (30) Spr 93, p. 35-36.
"Swinging into Space." [Arc] (30) Spr 93, p. 37-38.
1511. DeNICOLA, Deborah
"Like a God." [Journal] (17:1) Spr-Sum 93, p. 41-42.
"Red Shoes." [ApalQ] (38) 92, p. 68-70.
"Where Divinity Begins." [Journal] (17:1) Spr-Sum 93, p. 39-40.
1512. DeNIORD, Chard
"The Dolphin." [Iowa] (23:3) Fall 93, p. 141-142.
"Field." [Iowa] (23:3) Fall 93, p. 140-141.
"Houses." [NewEngR] (15:4) Fall 93, p. 146.
"On the Mountain of Spices." [HarvardR] (3) Wint 93, p. 122-123.
"The Police." [Agni] (37) 93, p. 274-275.
"The Present." [NewEngR] (15:4) Fall 93, p. 145.
"Romance." [NewEngR] (15:4) Fall 93, p. 143-144.
"Shaman." [NoAmR] (278:2) Mr-Ap 93, p. 10.
"Silver Shrine." [NewEngR] (15:4) Fall 93, p. 141-143.
1513. DENNEY, Reuel
"Ars Poetica." [QRL] (12:32/33) 93, p. 114.
"Dragonfly Days." [QRL] (12:32/33) 93, p. 116.
"Remembering the Scholar." [QRL] (12:32/33) 93, p. 116-117.
"To the Finder." [QRL] (12:32/33) 93, p. 115-116.
1514. DENNIS, Carl
"Cedar Point." [PraS] (67:3) Fall 93, p. 58-59.
"The Dead." [DenQ] (27:4) Spr 93, p. 53.
"The Great Day." [ParisR] (35:128) Fall 93, p. 258.
"Integer." [ParisR] (35:128) Fall 93, p. 257.
"Jacob and Esau." [PraS] (67:3) Fall 93, p. 60.
"The Many." [DenQ] (27:4) Spr 93, p. 54-55.
"Night Drive." [AmerPoR] (22:5) S-O 93, p. 56.
"The Oral Tradition." [NewRep] (209:3/4) 19-26 Jl 93, p. 42.
"The Pancake Hour." [Salm] (100) Fall 93, p. 160-161.
"Self and Soul." [DenQ] (27:4) Spr 93, p. 56-57.
"Seven Days." [KenR] (NS 15:1) Wint 93, p. 139.
"Swindle." [PraS] (67:3) Fall 93, p. 57-58.
"To the Soul." [PraS] (67:3) Fall 93, p. 56-57.
"Track Meet." [KenR] (NS 15:1) Wint 93, p. 140.
"Two or Three Wishes." [KenR] (NS 15:1) Wint 93, p. 141.
"Uses of the Past." [Salm] (98/99) Spr-Sum 93, p. 76-77.
1515. DENNIS, Rodney G.
"By the New York Public Library." [HarvardR] (4) Spr 93, p. 112.

1516. DENNIS, William
"Shore." [JlNJPo] (15:2) Aut 93, p. 1-3.
1517. DENNY, Alma
"To Butter a Bagel." [Light] (8) Wint 93, p. 13.
1518. DENNY, David
"The Happy Ones." [SlipS] (13) 93, p. 44.
"Zen and the Art of Marriage." [DogRR] (12:1, #23) Spr-Sum 93, p. 9.
1519. DENT, Peter
"Mare Glaciale." [Os] (37) Wint 93, p. 4.
"River" (Excerpt). [Os] (37) Wint 93, p. 4.
1520. DENT, Tory
"Family Romance." [KenR] (NS 15:3) Sum 93, p. 112-113.
"Listen." [Agni] (37) 93, p. 96-97.
"Many Rivers to Cross." [KenR] (NS 15:3) Sum 93, p. 113-116.
"Poem for a Poem" (for Jade). [Agni] (37) 93, p. 98-99.
"Spared." [KenR] (NS 15:1) Wint 93, p. 41-42.
1521. DEPPE, Theodore
"The Last Summer of America." [GreenMR] (NS 6:2) Sum-Fall 93, p. 25-26.
1522. DEPRÉ, Louise
"Certains Novembres." [WestCL] (27:3, #12) Wint 93-94, p. 59-60.
1523. DEPTA, Victor M.
"Cousin Michael and the Hognose Snake." [CentR] (37:2) Spr 93, p. 373.
"Strange Hope." [CentR] (37:2) Spr 93, p. 372.
1524. DER-HOVANESSIAN, Diana
"At Kirsanov's Burial" (tr. of Andrei Voznesensky, w. David Sloane). [Vis] (42) 93,
p. 34.
"Dialogue Before Death (1983)" (tr. of Nina Berberova, w. Marsbed Hablanian).
[Agni] (38) 93, p. 106.
"Earth" (tr. of Arevshad Avakian). [Vis] (43) 93, p. 6-7.
"Enough to Make Him Howl" (tr. of Vahakn Davtian). [Vis] (43) 93, p. 6.
"Goya." [LitR] (36:2) Wint 93, p. 160.
"Pine Tree." [GrahamHR] (17) Fall 93, p. 64-65.
"Translating" (The Mary Elinore Smith Poetry Prize). [AmerS] (62:3) Sum 93, p.
363-364.
"Your Name" (tr. of Maria Banus, w. the author). [Vis] (42) 93, p. 32-33.
1525. Der WILDE ALEXANDER (13th-century)
"When We Were Children" (tr. by David Ferry). [Raritan] (13:1) Sum 93, p. 30-31.
DeRACHEWILTZ, Mary
See De RACHEWILTZ, Mary
1526. DERGE, William
"Pedal Music." [ArtfulD] (24/25) 93, p. 105.
"Waxing." [ArtfulD] (24/25) 93, p. 104.
1527. DEROUCHIA, Marcia
"Fire Tender." [Blueline] (14) 93, p. 96.
DeROUS, Peter
See De ROUS, Peter
1528. DERRICOTTE, Toi
"My Mouth." [NewL] (59:4) 93, p. 97.
"Squeaky Bed." [PaintedB] (50/51) 93, p. 114.
1529. DERRY, Paul "X"
"The Zipper." [NewYorkQ] (51) 93, p. 82.
1530. DESAUTELS, Denise
"Vues de Près." [WestCL] (27:3, #12) Wint 93-94, p. 56-58.
1531. DESQUIRON OLIVA, Antonio
"Un Bailoteo del Alma." [LindLM] (12:2/4) Ap-D 93, p. 11.
"Mancha de Lluvia." [LindLM] (12:2/4) Ap-D 93, p. 11.
"Miras el Ala." [LindLM] (12:2/4) Ap-D 93, p. 11.
"Oración." [LindLM] (12:2/4) Ap-D 93, p. 11.
"La Ruta 16." [LindLM] (12:2/4) Ap-D 93, p. 11.
1532. DESROCHERS, Kerry
"In my tree." [PraF] (14:3) Aut 93, p. 33.
1533. DeSTEFANO, Darin
"InCityFrozen." [Talisman] (11) Fall 93, p. 202-203.
1534. DESY, Peter
"Alzheimer's." [FourQ] (7:2) Fall 93, p. 26.
"Departures." [SoCoast] (15) Je 93, p. 32-33.

"Down Front." [PoetL] (88:2) Sum 93, p. 10.
"Even Then" (for Dolly). [Poem] (70) N 93, p. 60.
"Family Matters, Sex, and Other Concerns." [Poem] (70) N 93, p. 59.
"Getting It Right." [Poem] (70) N 93, p. 62.
"Grief." [Paint] (19:38) Aut 92, p. 36.
"How to Commit Suicide." [ApalQ] (39) 93, p. 33.
"It Can't Be Spring." [Footwork] (23) 93, p. 93.
"Last Fight." [TampaR] (7) Fall 93, p. 59.
"Not Dancing: Sex in the 40's." [OnTheBus] (6:1, #13) Wint 93-Spr 94, p. 78.
"Ohio Vital Statistics." [RiverC] (14:1) Fall 93, p. 25-26.
"Pepsi Plant, Detroit." [PaintedHR] (9) Spr 93, p. 6.
"Residual." [Poem] (70) N 93, p. 61.
"Sin in the 50's." [OnTheBus] (5:2, #12) Sum-Fall 93, p. 58.
"Sister Mary Lucinda." [SlipS] (13) 93, p. 50.
"Thinking of Getting Remarried in a Time of Shifting Roles." [Footwork] (23) 93, p. 95.
"Uncle Jim." [SlipS] (13) 93, p. 51.
"Visiting the Henry Ford Estate, July, 1991." [WebR] (17) Fall 93, p. 104.
"Why We Bombed Hiroshima" (For Jonathan Holden). [Paint] (19:38) Aut 92, p. 37.
1535. DEUTCH, Richard
"The Drunkard's Prayer." [QRL] (12:32/33) 93, p. 403.
"In Passing." [QRL] (12:32/33) 93, p. 403-404.
"Vincent's Prayer" (after J. Brevert). [Vis] (41) 93, p. 23.
1536. DEUTSCH, Helen
"Four Poems" (2.1, 2.5, 2.14, 4.7. tr. of Propertius). [TriQ] (87) Spr-Sum 93, p. 225 - 232.
1537. DEV SEN, Nabaneeta
"Another Country" (tr. by Sunil B. Ray and Carolyne Wright w. the author). [AmerPoR] (22:4) Jl-Ag 93, p. 25.
"Antara" (4, tr. by Sunil B. Ray, Nandana Dev Sen and Carolyne Wright w. the author). [AmerPoR] (22:4) Jl-Ag 93, p. 24.
"The Child's Saying" (in Bengali and English, tr. by Paramita Banerjee and Carolyne Wright w. the author). [HawaiiR] (17:1, #37) Spr 93, p. 90-91.
"Mosquito Net" (tr. by Paramita Banerjee, Nandana Dev Sen and Carolyne Wright w. the author). [AmerPoR] (22:4) Jl-Ag 93, p. 25.
"Prison Island Exile" (tr. by Sunil B. Ray, Nandana Dev Sen and Carolyne Wright w. the author). [AmerPoR] (22:4) Jl-Ag 93, p. 24.
"The Swaying Lotus" (tr. by Sunil B. Ray, Nandana Dev Sen and Carolyne Wright w. the author). [AmerPoR] (22:4) Jl-Ag 93, p. 24.
"The Temple" (in Bengali and English, tr. by Paramita Banerjee and Carolyne Wright w. the author). [HawaiiR] (17:1, #37) Spr 93, p. 88-89.
"When It Rains" (tr. by Sunil B. Ray, Nandana Dev Sen and Carolyne Wright w. the author). [AmerPoR] (22:4) Jl-Ag 93, p. 24.
1538. DEV SEN, Nandana
"Antara" (4, tr. of Nabaneeta Dev Sen, w. Sunil B. Ray, Carolyne Wright and the author). [AmerPoR] (22:4) Jl-Ag 93, p. 24.
"Mosquito Net" (tr. of Nabaneeta Dev Sen, w. Paramita Banerjee, Carolyne Wright and the author). [AmerPoR] (22:4) Jl-Ag 93, p. 25.
"Prison Island Exile" (tr. of Nabaneeta Dev Sen, w. Sunil B. Ray, Carolyne Wright and the author). [AmerPoR] (22:4) Jl-Ag 93, p. 24.
"The Swaying Lotus" (tr. of Nabaneeta Dev Sen, w. Sunil B. Ray, Carolyne Wright and the author). [AmerPoR] (22:4) Jl-Ag 93, p. 24.
"When It Rains" (tr. of Nabaneeta Dev Sen, w. Sunil B. Ray, Carolyne Wright and the author). [AmerPoR] (22:4) Jl-Ag 93, p. 24.
DeVEGA, Lope
See VEGA, Lope de
1539. DeVEGH, Diana
"Night Visit." [CentralP] (22) Spr 93, p. 47.
1540. DEVENISH, Alan
"Desperate Seeks Same." [PoetryNW] (34:3) Aut 93, p. 12.
"Mon Semblable." [PoetryNW] (34:3) Aut 93, p. 16.
"Praying for Rain." [PoetryNW] (34:3) Aut 93, p. 13-15.
"Read This Now." [PoetryNW] (34:3) Aut 93, p. 15.
1541. DEVICH, Alana
"Sneaking Out." [Sequoia] (34/35) 92-93, p. 34.

DeVITÓ

DeVITO, E. B.
    See De VITO, E. B.
1542. DEVLIN, Denis
    "Palm" (tr. of Paul Valéry). [QRL] (12:32/33) 93, p. 535-537.
1543. DEWDNEY, Christopher
    "A Natural History of Southwestern Ontario" (Excerpts). [GrandS] (12:1, #45) 93, p. 46-48.
1544. DEWEESE, Jeanne
    "No title: In the beginning" (tr. of Tadeusz Rozewicz). [ContextS] (3:1) 93, p. 30.
    "No title: It's high time" (To the memory of Konstanty Puzyna, tr. of Tadeusz Rozewicz). [ContextS] (3:1) 93, p. 32.
    "Still Trying" (tr. of Tadeusz Rozewicz). [ContextS] (3:1) 93, p. 29.
    "'Success' and Requests" (tr. of Tadeusz Rozewicz). [ContextS] (3:1) 93, p. 31-32.
1545. DeWINTER, Corrine
    "The Pearl Diver." [Crucible] (29) Fall 93, p. 13.
    "Sad Numbers." [Plain] (13:3) Spr 93, p. 34.
1546. DeWITT, Jim
    "I Do Hate Lollipops." [PikeF] (11) Fall 93, p. 5.
DeWITT, Susan Kelly
    See KELLY-DeWITT, Susan
1547. DEY, Richard Morris
    "Mailboat." [CaribbeanW] (7) 93, p. 46.
DEYU, Miao
    See MIAO, Deyu
1548. DHARMARAJ, Ramola
    "Full of Rain, the Word." [GreenMR] (NS 6:1) Wint-Spr 93, p. 131-132.
    "In Passing." [Agni] (38) 93, p. 100-102.
    "Listen, the Children." [GreenMR] (NS 6:1) Wint-Spr 93, p. 129-130.
    "The Way Extends" (For Paul). [NowestR] (31:3) 93, p. 51.
1549. DHARWADKER, Vinay
    "Thirty Years Ago, in a Suburb of Bombay." [CumbPR] (12:2) Spr 93, p. 26.
Di . . .
    See also names beginning with "Di" without the following space, filed below in their alphabetic positions, e.g., DiPALMA
DI, Xue
    See XUE, Di
1550. Di IASI, Camilla
    "Eurydice" (tr. by Diane Lunde). [13thMoon] (11:1/2) 93, p. 211.
    "Summer" (tr. by Diane Lunde). [13thMoon] (11:1/2) 93, p. 210.
Di MANNO, Yves
    See MANNO, Yves Di
1551. Di PASQUALE, Emanuel
    "Ezra Pound, Ode." [NewYorkQ] (52) 93, p. 68.
1552. Di PRIMA, Diane
    "Rant." [PoetryUSA] (25/26) 93, p. 44.
1553. Di SALVATORE, Brian
    "Degrees of Gray at Northside" (w. Kenny Briggs and Lora Jansson). [CutB] (40) Spr 93, p. 101-102.
1554. Di SUVERO, Victor
    "Questions." [OnTheBus] (5:2, #12) Sum-Fall 93, p. 59.
1555. DIA!KWAIN
    "Catching a Porcupine" (tr. of ǀXam (Bushman) oral records by Stephen Watson). [BostonR] (18:3/4) Je-Ag 93, p. 30.
    "Prayer to the New Moon" (tr. of ǀXam (Bushman) oral records by Stephen Watson). [BostonR] (18:3/4) Je-Ag 93, p. 30.
1556. DIAL, Bob
    "Summersounds." [Writer] (106:6) Je 93, p. 19-20.
1557. DIAMOND, Olivia
    "Before the Subdivision." [BellArk] (9:2) Mr-Ap 93, p. 8.
DIAN, Li
    See LI, Dian
DIANA JEAN
    See JEAN, Diana
1558. DIAZ GARCIA, Jesús
    "Seguidillas de Santiago, Nacido en Denton." [InterPR] (19:2) Fall 93, p. 28.

" *Seguidillas* to Santiago, Born in Denton" (tr. by Leslie Palmer and Ishmael
Bustinza). [InterPR] (19:2) Fall 93, p. 29.
1559. DICE, Richard B.
"Jigglebustation (n.)" (Amelia One-Liner Award). [Amelia] (7:2, #21) 93, p. 111.
1560. DICKERMAN, Laura
"Dragons." [AnthNEW] (5) 93, p. 11.
1561. DICKEY, James
"The Scratch." [QRL] (12:32/33) 93, p. 404-405.
1562. DICKEY, R. P.
"Arap-Psychology" (The Opposite of Parapsychology). [Light] (6) Sum 93, p. 10.
"Epitaph for J.V. Cunningham (1911-1985)." [Light] (6) Sum 93, p. 9.
"Notion." [Light] (5) Spr 93, p. 20.
1563. DICKEY, William
"Dorothy Later." [SouthernR] (29:2) Spr, Ap 93, p. 300-303.
1564. DICKINSON, Emily
"As Imperceptibly As Grief." [SoCoast] (15) Je 93, p. 62.
"Some Keep the Sabbath Going to Church." [SoCoast] (15) Je 93, p. 63.
1565. DICKINSON, Patricia
"Eye to Eye." [LaurelR] (27:2) Sum 93, p. 74.
1566. DICKINSON, Stephanie
"Carol." [NewYorkQ] (52) 93, p. 49.
1567. DICKSON, John
"The Appraisal of Days." [IllinoisR] (1:1) Fall 93, p. 19.
"As It Was in the Beginning." [Poetry] (162:4) Jl 93, p. 214-215.
"Breakfast at the Harrison Grill." [PikeF] (11) Fall 93, p. 13.
"The Courtship of Whales." [Elf] (3:1) Spr 93, p. 24.
"The Force That Drives the Tulip Drives the Ox." [Elf] (3:1) Spr 93, p. 22-23.
"Natural Selection." [WillowR] (20) Spr 93, p. 14-15.
"Two Sides of the Afternoon." [WillowR] (20) Spr 93, p. 16-17.
1568. DICKSON, Ray Clark
"Barbara by the Sea" (for Barbara at 92, Avila Beach, California). [WormR] (33:1,
#129) 93, p. 36.
"Be Proud You Are an Intellectual." [WormR] (33:1, #129) 93, p. 36-37.
"The Collector." [WormR] (33:1, #129) 93, p. 35-36.
"Diacritic." [WormR] (33:1, #129) 93, p. 36.
"Key Lime Pie." [WormR] (33:1, #129) 93, p. 35.
"On an Island in the Silence of the Stream." [WormR] (33:1, #129) 93, p. 35.
1569. DIETZ, Megan
"He'll Have to Climb." [HiramPoR] (53/54) Fall 92-Sum 93, p. 33-34.
1570. DIETZ, Sheila
"Blue Piping." [DenQ] (27:3) Wint 93, p. 21.
"The Daily Work" (tr. of Ida Gerhardt). [Vis] (41) 93, p. 22.
"Thasos" (tr. of Ida Gerhardt). [Vis] (43) 93, p. 18.
1571. DIFALCO, Sam
"First Poke Your Eyes." [Caliban] (13) 93, p. 115.
"Thinning Train of Summer." [Caliban] (13) 93, p. 114.
1572. DiFALIO, Sam
"One Version of the Struggle." [SlipS] (13) 93, p. 60.
1573. DIGBY, John
"Lines to a Dead Thrush" (from *To Amuse a Shrinking Sun*, 1985). [PoetryUSA]
(25/26) 93, p. 9.
1574. DIGGES, Deborah
"The Afterlife." [Ploughs] (19:4) Wint 93-94, p. 56-57.
"Late Summer." [YaleR] (81:3) Jl 93, p. 58-59.
"The Little Book of Hand Shadows." [Atlantic] (271:6) Je 93, p. 84.
"Nursing the Hamster." [NewYorker] (69:2) 1 Mr 93, p. 78.
1575. DIGIORNO, Geri
"The Red Shoes." [Bogg] (66) 93, Reviews suppl., p. 25.
"So What's the Worst That Could Happen?" [Bogg] (66) Wint 92-93, p. 28.
1576. DIL, Shaheen F.
"In the Jungle." [FourQ] (7:2) Fall 93, p. 62.
1577. DILL, Emil P.
"Greyhound Rock." [ColEng] (55:3) Mr 93, p. 326-327.
1578. DILLAN, Pamela
"Full Fridge on Bank Street." [AntigR] (92) Wint 93, p. 118.
"The Peacefull Province." [AntigR] (93-94) Spr-Sum 93, p. 254.

DILLAN

"Six Burnt Croissants." [AntigR] (93-94) Spr-Sum 93, p. 253.
1579. DILLARD, Annie
"An Acquaintance in the Heavens" (from Martha Evans Martin and Donald Howard
Menzel, *The Friendly Stars*, 1907, 1964). [OntR] (39) Fall-Wint 93-94, p. 9.
"Free Fall" (from David W. McKay and Bruce G. Smith, *Space Science Projects for
Young Scientists*, 1986). [OntR] (39) Fall-Wint 93-94, p. 11.
"I Think Continually of Those Who Went Truly Ape" (from *The Mysterious Senses
of Animals*, Droscher). [OntR] (39) Fall-Wint 93-94, p. 10.
"Index of First Lines" (from *The Penguin Book of Contemporary Irish Poetry* and
Poets from the North of Ireland). [NewRep] (209:18) 1 N 93, p. 40.
"Mornings Like This" (David Grayson, *The Countryman's Year*, 1936). [GeoR]
(47:3) Fall 93, p. 454.
"The Muse and the Poet" (from Francis Buckland, *Buckland's Curiosities of Natural
History*, 1858, 1860, 1865). [OntR] (39) Fall-Wint 93-94, p. 5-6.
"The Naturalist at Large on the Delaware River" (from Charles C. Abbott, M.D.,
Waste-land Wanderings, 1887). [OntR] (39) Fall-Wint 93-94, p. 7-8.
"A Visit to the Mayo Clinic" (From *Nervousness, Indigestion, and Pain* by Walter
C. Alvarez, M.D., Mayo Clinic, 1943). [HarvardR] (5) Fall 93, p. 52-54.
1580. DILLHUNT, C. X.
"How to Read a Poem." [Asylum] (8) 93, p. 12.
1581. DILLING, Angie
"The End." [CoalC] (7) Apr 93, p. 24.
1582. DILLON, Andrew
"Clarifications." [SoDakR] (31:2) Sum 93, p. 136.
"Donation" (for Glenn Platt). [BellArk] (9:5) S-O 93, p. 9.
"For a Dead Cardinal Below the Window." [CapeR] (28:2) Fall 93, p. 7.
"Last Night, After the Party." [CapeR] (28:2) Fall 93, p. 6.
"A Midwestern Vocabulary." [SoDakR] (31:2) Sum 93, p. 135.
"The Route." [BellR] (16:1/2) Spr-Fall 93, p. 30.
"The Woods near Eureka, California." [CumbPR]] (13:1) Fall 93, p. 78.
1583. DILSAVER, Paul
"Charting." [Pearl] (19) Fall-Wint 93, p. 70.
"Rx for Modern Times." [DogRR] (12:1, #23) Spr-Sum 93, p. 19.
DiMANNO, Yves
See MANNO, Yves di
1584. DIMITROVA, Blaga
"In the Mouthcage" (tr. by Ludmilla Popova-Wightman). [Vis] (43) 93, p. 7.
"Interior with Faded Colors" (tr. by Lisa Sapinkopf and Georgi Belev). [Paint]
(19:38) Aut 92, p. 69.
"Labyrinth: The Shadow of the Wind" (in Bulgarian and English, tr. by Ludmilla
Popova-Wightman). [US1] (28/29) 93, p. 11.
"Who Cares for the Blind Stork" (tr. by Lisa Sapinkopf and Georgi Belev). [Paint]
(19:38) Aut 92, p. 68.
1585. DIMOULA, Kiki
"Progress" (tr. by Eleni Fourtouni). [PoetryC] (13:3) 93, p. 21.
"Two Small Poems for a Riddle and a Street" (tr. by Eleni Fourtouni). [PoetryC]
(13:3) 93, p. 21.
"Under the Influence of Autumn" (tr. by Eleni Fourtouni). [PoetryC] (13:3) 93, p.
21.
1586. DINE, Carol
"Swan." [SpoonR] (18:2) Sum-Fall 93, p. 19.
1587. DINGS, Fred
"The Piano Player." [PoetL] (88:1) Spr 93, p. 27.
1588. DINSMORE, Danika
"For Alice Notley." [13thMoon] (12:1/2) 93-94, p. 24.
1589. DIOMEDE, Matthew
"A Winter Past" (tr. of Salvatore Quasimodo). [ApalQ] (35) 90, p. 42.
1590. DION, Marc Munroe
"Advice from a Hard Guy" (To Grandpa Vinnie). [NewL] (60:1) 93, p. 35.
"Cynthia." [NewL] (60:1) 93, p. 36.
"Throwing the Sofa Out the Window." [NewL] (60:1) 93, p. 37.
1591. DiPALMA, Ray
"Agent." [Epoch] (42:3) 93, p. 311.
"Bel Canto Telegram." [Arshile] (2) 93, p. 25.
"Blue Star." [Talisman] (11) Fall 93, p. 243.
"Interrupted Version." [NorthStoneR] (11) 93, p. 104.

"Love at the Base of the Spine." [Epoch] (42:3) 93, p. 312.
"Mercator." [GrandS] (12:2, #46) Sum 93, p. 168.
"October 27th October 27th." [Arshile] (2) 93, p. 24.
"The Peripheral Marathon." [Arshile] (2) 93, p. 26.
"Razor Roxit." [Epoch] (42:3) 93, p. 310.
"Rebus Feast." [NorthStoneR] (11) 93, p. 105.
"Technicians in the Capitol." [Talisman] (11) Fall 93, p. 242.
DiPASQUALE, Emanuel di
　　See Di PASQUALE, Emanuel
DiPRIMA, Diane
　　See Di PRIMA, Diane
DiSALVATORE, Brian
　　See Di SALVATORE, Brian
1592. DISCH, Tom (Thomas M.)
"The Cardinal Detoxes: A Play in One Act." [Hudson] (46:1) Spr 93, p. 57-76.
"Christmas Guilt." [Poetry] (163:3) D 93, p. 148.
"The Garage Sale As a Spiritual Exericse." [Poetry] (163:3) D 93, p. 147.
"Museum Visits." [Light] (7) Aut 93, p. 14.
"A New Covenant." [Chelsea] (55) 93, p. 38-39.
"Song of the belt." [Light] (6) Sum 93, p. 20.
"The Suicide's Picnic." [Light] (8) Wint 93, p. 12.
1593. DISCHELL, Stuart
"The Chamber." [ColR] (20:2) Fall 93, p. 128-129.
"The Genius." [Agni] (37) 93, p. 141-142.
1594. DISSANAYAKE, Wimal
"Mrs. Yoshida." [HawaiiR] (17:1, #37) Spr 93, p. 139.
DiSUVERO, Victor
　　See Di SUVERO, Victor
1595. DITSKY, John
"Japonais." [MalR] (105) Wint 93, p. 79.
"The League of Failed Poets." [CumbPR]] (13:1) Fall 93, p. 35.
"Soap Opera." [MalR] (105) Wint 93, p. 80.
1596. DIVAKARUNI, Chitra
"The Bathers." [13thMoon] (11:1/2) 93, p. 30.
"The Geography Lesson." [Footwork] (23) 93, p. 2.
"Going Home Day." [Footwork] (23) 93, p. 4-5.
"The Grandmothers." [13thMoon] (11:1/2) 93, p. 29.
"Heaven." [13thMoon] (11:1/2) 93, p. 28.
"I Do Not Understand" (tr. of Jaynati Sen). [Prima] (16/17) 93, p. 92-93.
"The Infirmary." [Footwork] (23) 93, p. 2-3.
"Learning to Dance." [Footwork] (23) 93, p. 3-4.
"The Sound of Leaves" (tr. of Begum Razia Husain). [Prima] (16/17) 93, p. 94-95.
"Storm at Point Sur." [Thrpny] (52) Wint 93, p. 11.
"The Walk." [Footwork] (23) 93, p. 1-2.
1597. DIXON, Betty L.
"Taylor's Chapel." [SoCoast] (14) Ja 93, p. 8.
1598. DIXON, John
"Places Left" (3 poems). [Verse] (10:1) Spr 93, p. 56-57.
1599. DIXON, K. Reynolds
"Ceremonial." [SouthernPR] (33:1) Spr 93, p. 26.
1600. DIXON, Linda Silance
"Passing Along Parallels" (inspired by lines from Jorie Graham's "Detail from the
　　Creation of Man" and C. K. Williams' "My Mother's Lips"). [13thMoon]
　　(11:1/2) 93, p. 31.
1601. DIZDAR, Mak
"The Stone Sleeper" (Selections: 2 poems, tr. by Francis R. Jones). [NoDaQ] (61:1)
　　Wint 93, p. 59-62.
1602. DJANIKIAN, Gregory
"My Father Teaches Me a Kind of Driving." [GrahamHR] (17) Fall 93, p. 20-23.
"The Persistence of Zachary" (for my son, age 7). [BelPoJ] (44:1) Fall 93, p. 34-35.
"The Teenager." [CimR] (105) O 93, p. 77-78.
1603. DJORDJEVIC, Milan
"Orange" (tr. by the author). [NoDaQ] (61:1) Wint 93, p. 63.
"Pure Colors" (tr. by the author). [NoDaQ] (61:1) Wint 93, p. 63-64.
1604. DLUGOS, Tim
"Night Life" (for Ed Cox). [PaintedB] (50/51) 93, p. 83.

1605. DOBLES, Julieta
"Amar en Jerusalen" (Selections: 2 poems). [Luz] (3) Ja 93, p. 21-27.
1606. DOBYNS, Stephen
"Cemetery Nights II." [NewEngR] (15:1) Wint 93, p. 114-115.
"The Community." [Ploughs] (19:4) Wint 93-94, p. 23-24.
"Pastel Dresses." [Ploughs] (19:4) Wint 93-94, p. 25-26.
"Red Geraniums." [GettyR] (6:4) Aut 93, p. 631.
"Roughhousing." [GettyR] (6:4) Aut 93, p. 632.
"Santiago: Five Men in the Street." [Border] (2) Spr 93, p. 15-16.
"Santiago: Forestal Park." [Ploughs] (19:4) Wint 93-94, p. 21-22.
"Santiago: Plaza de Armas." [Border] (2) Spr 93, p. 17.
"Somewhere It Still Moves." [Ploughs] (19:4) Wint 93-94, p. 19-20.
"Tenderly." [Ploughs] (19:4) Wint 93-94, p. 27-28.
1607. DOCHERTY, Brian
"Suspended Sentence." [Verse] (10:1) Spr 93, p. 58.
1608. DODD, Wayne
"Asserting, Threatening, Promising, Declaring." [DenQ] (27:4) Spr 93, p. 98-99.
"In Medias Res: A Definition." [WestB] (31/32) 93, p. 65.
"In Medias Res: A Definition" (corrected reprint from 31/32). [WestB] (33) 93, p. 30.
"Let's Face It, You Say, Let's Say Distance." [DenQ] (27:4) Spr 93, p. 95-96.
"Poem About Nothing." [DenQ] (27:4) Spr 93, p. 97-98.
"Variation on a Theme." [DenQ] (27:4) Spr 93, p. 96-97.
1609. DODSON, Keith
"The Optometrist Worries Me About." [Bogg] (66) Wint 92-93, p. 45.
1610. DODSON, Keith A.
"All Too Soon." [Pearl] (19) Fall-Wint 93, p. 51.
"Clothes Make the Man." [Pearl] (17) Spr 93, p. 75.
"My Daughters Look." [Pearl] (19) Fall-Wint 93, p. 51.
1611. DOHEN, Leslie
"California." [Vis] (42) 93, p. 9.
1612. DOLA, Ken
"The Faller." [VirQR] (69:4) Aut 93, p. 653-655.
"Nature Lessons." [VirQR] (69:4) Aut 93, p. 650-653.
1613. DOLAN, Kristen L.
"Blue Baby" (for Eartha Kitt). [BrooklynR] (10) 93, p. 6-7.
1614. DOLIN, Sharon
"If My Mother." [Poetry] (162:6) S 93, p. 315-316.
"The Visit." [Poetry] (162:6) S 93, p. 317.
1615. DOLL, Diane
"Please Send." [Light] (5) Spr 93, p. 37.
1616. DOLOWICH, Madeline
"Elm Street." [Footwork] (23) 93, p. 84.
1617. DOLTON, Alexia Lyn
"Stereotypes." [SlipS] (13) 93, p. 45.
1618. DOMANSKI, Don
"Excathedra" (2 poems). [PoetryC] (13:3) 93, p. 19.
"Lines Written Beneath a Stone." [PoetryC] (13:3) 93, p. 19.
"Morpheus and the Candle-Skin." [PoetryC] (13:3) 93, p. 18.
"Uncle X Dying Alone in a Field." [PoetryC] (13:3) 93, p. 19.
1619. DOMINA, Lynn
"Deathbed, Before." [Vis] (42) 93, p. 38.
1620. DONAGHY, Michael
"Acts of Contrition." [Verse] (10:1) Spr 93, p. 11.
"The Heirloom." [Poetry] (161:4) Ja 93, p. 191.
"Lives of the Artists." [Poetry] (161:4) Ja 93, p. 189-190.
"Lives of the Artists." [Verse] (10:1) Spr 93, p. 11-12.
"True." [Verse] (10:1) Spr 93, p. 12-14.
1621. DONAHUE, Joseph
"Flash Cards" (4 selections). [Talisman] (10) Spr 93, p. 73.
"Lament." [HeavenB] (10) Wint-Spr 93, p. 40-41.
1622. DONALDSON, Jeffery
"The Man Who Drew Days." [AntigR] (95) Aut 93, p. 148-149.
"Visions of Marthe Bonnard." [ParisR] (35:126) Spr 93, p. 250-256.
1623. DONALDSON, Judith
"Midwife." [NewYorkQ] (50) 93, p. 80.

1624. DONG, Jiping
"The Finale" (tr. of Jiaxin Wang, w. Stephen Haven). [AmerPoR] (22:6) N-D 93, p. 37.
"Poetry" (to Haizi, tr. of Jiaxin Wang, w. Stephen Haven). [AmerPoR] (22:6) N-D 93, p. 38.
1625. DONLAN, John
"Artifact." [MalR] (105) Wint 93, p. 27.
"Immune." [MalR] (105) Wint 93, p. 28.
"Plunge Pool." [MalR] (105) Wint 93, p. 26.
1626. DONNELLY, P. N. W.
"My Father's Letters." [Bogg] (66) Wint 92-93, p. 68.
1627. DONNELLY, Susan
"At Baldpate Hospital." [PassN] (14:1) Sum 93, p. 6-7.
"Earrings." [PassN] (14:1) Sum 93, p. 8.
1628. DONOGHUE, John
"Blame." [RiverC] (14:1) Fall 93, p. 45.
"Eel." [WillowS] (32) Sum 93, p. 12.
"Moraine." [RiverC] (14:1) Fall 93, p. 46.
"Positive." [WillowS] (32) Sum 93, p. 13.
1629. DONOVAN, Gerard
"The Cross-Man." [SenR] (23:1/2) Wint 93, p. 89-90.
1630. DONOVAN, Karen
"The Mutual Animosity of Houses." [DenQ] (27:3) Wint 93, p. 22.
1631. DONOVAN, Katie
"Achill." [SenR] (23:1/2) Wint 93, p. 36-37.
"Harvest." [SenR] (23:1/2) Wint 93, p. 34-35.
"In the Hazel Wood." [SenR] (23:1/2) Wint 93, p. 32-33.
"Underneath Our Skirts." [SenR] (23:1/2) Wint 93, p. 30-31.
1632. DONOVAN, Stewart
"Cape Breton's Oral Tradition" (for Leon Dubinsky). [AntigR] (93-94) Spr-Sum 93, p. 262-263.
"First Charlotte Street Show, 1959." [AntigR] (93-94) Spr-Sum 93, p. 257.
"Homemade Stars" (for Frances MacDonald, R.N.). [AntigR] (95) Aut 93, p. 44.
"Liscomb Sanctuary" (In memoriam for the 26 coal miners who died at Plymouth, Nova Scotia." [AntigR] (92) Wint 93, p. 49-50.
"The White Buildings on Shea's Hill" (for Ann MacLellan Donovan). [AntigR] (93 - 94) Spr-Sum 93, p. 258-261.
1633. DOOLEY, Tim
"Resistance." [SouthernR] (29:1) Wint, Ja 93, p. 149.
"Working from Home." [SouthernR] (29:1) Wint, Ja 93, p. 149-151.
DOOLITTLE, Hilda
See H. D.
1634. DOPP, Jamie
"Depression Glass." [AntigR] (93-94) Spr-Sum 93, p. 180.
"Howard." [AntigR] (93-94) Spr-Sum 93, p. 178-179.
1635. DOR, Moshe
"The Art of Waiting" (tr. by Barbara Goldberg, w. the author). [Trans] (28) Spr 93, p. 159.
"December" (tr. by Barbara Goldberg, w. the author). [Trans] (28) Spr 93, p. 159.
"Goliath" (tr. by Barbara Goldberg, w. the author). [Trans] (28) Spr 93, p. 158.
"Orangutan" (tr. by Elaine Magarrell). [PoetL] (88:1) Spr 93, p. 53.
"Shampoo" (tr. by Barbara Goldberg, w. the author). [Trans] (28) Spr 93, p. 157.
"Without Commitments" (tr. by Elaine Magarrell). [PoetL] (88:1) Spr 93, p. 54.
1636. DORESKI, William
"Creation Myth." [PassN] (14:1) Sum 93, p. 15-16.
"Lycidas." [SoCarR] (26:1) Fall 93, p. 113-114.
"Poem with a Familiar Ending." [PassN] (14:1) Sum 93, p. 14.
"Primary Season." [Contact] (11:65/66/67) Spr 93, p. 36.
"Punk Flesh." [SlipS] (13) 93, p. 65.
"To Live and Die in L.A." [NewYorkQ] (51) 93, p. 88.
1637. DORF, Marilyn
"Chokecherries." [Northeast] (5:8) Spr-Sum 93, p. 4.
"He Doesn't Like to Be Liked." [Plain] (13:3) Spr 93, p. 24.
"The Summer the Crows Cried My Name." [Plain] (14:1) Fall 93, p. 31.

1638. DORGAN, Theo
  "The Chinese Notebook" (Selections, tr. of Demosthenes Agrafiotis, w. the author,
    Tony Curtis, Pat Boran, and Kate Newman). [Sulfur] (32) Spr 93, p. 206-212.
1639. DORION, Hélène
  "Poèmes" (3 poems). [Os] (36) Spr 93, p. 7-9.
1640. DORN, Alfred
  "Addicted." [Sparrow] (60) Sum 93, p. 50.
  "Facets of a Name." [Sparrow] (60) Sum 93, p. 50.
1641. DORNER, Nancy L.
  "Lament." [ChrC] (110:5) 17 F 93, p. 164.
D'ORS, Miguel
  See ORS, Miguel d'
1642. DORSETT, Robert
  "Defeat" (tr. of Wen Yi-Duo). [HawaiiR] (17:1, #37) Spr 93, p. 121.
  "Roman Tomb." [InterPR] (19:2) Fall 93, p. 78.
  "Snowfall (on not giving in to government concessions)" (tr. of Wen Yi-Duo).
    [HawaiiR] (17:1, #37) Spr 93, p. 122.
1643. DORSETT, Thomas
  "Concerning Bedrooms and Bestsellers." [Light] (6) Sum 93, p. 16.
  "Sonnet from London" (tr. of Vinicius de Moraes, w. Moyses Purisch). [InterPR]
    (19:2) Fall 93, p. 33.
  "Sonnet to Winter" (tr. of Vinicius de Moraes, w. Moyses Purisch). [InterPR] (19:2)
    Fall 93, p. 31.
1644. DOTY, Catherine
  "For May Is the Month of Our Mother" (For Laurie and Rosemary). [JINJPo] (15:2)
    Aut 93, p. 9.
  "Phone Call from Tempe." [Footwork] (23) 93, p. 91.
  "Why I Don't Drive a New Car." [Footwork] (23) 93, p. 91.
  "A Woman Who Liked Babies." [Footwork] (23) 93, p. 92.
1645. DOTY, Mark
  "Beach Roses." [Art&Und] (2:3) Special Edition 93, p. 11.
  "Brilliance." [PoetryE] (35) Spr 93, p. 156-157.
  "Description." [YaleR] (81:4) O 93, p. 64-66.
  "Difference." [Boulevard] (8:1, #22) Spr 93, p. 166-168.
  "Four Cut Sunflowers, One Upside Down." [GeoR] (47:1) Spr 93, p. 53-54.
  "Surrealism: Essay and Rhapsody." [IndR] (16:1) Spr 93, p. 134-137.
1646. DOUBIAGO, Sharon
  "Body" (from "Rodeo"). [WillowS] (31) Wint 93, p. 66-67.
1647. DOUGALL, Lucy
  "Merry Dancers." [BellArk] (9:1) Ja-F 93, p. 13.
  "Up-Helly-A." [BellArk] (9:1) Ja-F 93, p. 12.
  "Winter Gales in Orkney." [BellArk] (9:1) Ja-F 93, p. 12.
1648. DOUGHERTY, Edward A.
  "Atlantic City." [WestB] (31/32) 93, p. 31.
  "A Single Strand Holds Us All." [Elf] (3:2) Sum 93, p. 38.
  "Why I Think About Hiroshima & Nagasaki." [WestB] (31/32) 93, p. 32-33.
1649. DOUGHERTY, Mary Ellen
  "Mulberry Time." [ChrC] (110:17) 19-26 My 93, p. 558.
1650. DOUGHERTY, Sean Thomas
  "Just Before Curfew (Rattling Chains)." [Contact] (11:65/66/67) Spr 93, p. 60.
  "March." [AnthNEW] (5) 93, p. 23.
  "Ode to a Bottle of Cheap Wine." [Lactuca] (17) Apr 93, p. 38.
  "Poem for Tony." [SlipS] (13) 93, p. 77.
1651. DOUGHERTY, Tommy, III
  "Cita's Sister." [ChironR] (12:4/13:1, #37/38) Wint 93-Spr 94, p. 35.
1652. DOUGLAS, Jim
  "One More Sunrise." [SlipS] (13) 93, p. 98-99.
1653. DOUGLASS, M. Scott
  "American Storm." [SlipS] (13) 93, p. 84-85.
  "Anticipation." [Gypsy] (20) Sum 93, p. 42.
  "Birch River." [SlipS] (13) 93, p. 88.
  "Keeping America Beautiful." [SlipS] (13) 93, p. 87.
  "Memory of Stone." [SlipS] (13) 93, p. 87.
  "This Bloody Thing." [SlipS] (13) 93, p. 84.
  "A View from the Highway." [SlipS] (13) 93, p. 86.

1654. DOUSKEY, Franz
  "The Madhouse." [NewYorkQ] (51) 93, p. 39.
  "Wilding." [NewYorkQ] (50) 93, p. 54.
1655. DOVE, Richard
  "Guided Tour of a Well-Known House" (tr. of Michael Kruger). [NewYorker]
      (69:42) 13 D 93, p. 96.
1656. DOVE, Rita
  "Lost Brilliance: Poems to Persephone and Demeter" (Chapbook: 9 poems).
      [BlackWR] (20:1) Fall-Wint 93, p. 45-56.
  "The Oriental Ballerina" (Georgianna Magdalena Hord, 1896-1979). [NewEngR]
      (15:1) Wint 93, p. 116-117.
1657. DOW, Leslie Smith
  "Dreams of Milk and Honey." [PottPort] (15:1) Spr-Sum 93, p. 66.
  "Hurricane Hazel." [PottPort] (15:1) Spr-Sum 93, p. 65.
1658. DOW, Mark
  "Mississippi Situation." [Pequod] (35) 93, p. 135-136.
  "One Fell Swoop." [Pequod] (35) 93, p. 137.
  "She (In the Cleared Field)." [Crazy] (45) Wint 93, p. 122-130.
1659. DOWD, Juditha
  "At the Edge of Stage Three." [US1] (28/29) 93, p. 19.
  "Conversing with an Orange." [JINJPo] (15:1) Spr 93, p. 38.
  "Fragment under Florescent Light." [Footwork] (23) 93, p. 104.
1660. DOWNE, Lise
  "Abundance of Shores." [Avec] (6:1) 93, p. 50.
  "Vehicle." [Avec] (6:1) 93, p. 49.
1661. DOWNE, Susan
  "Holy Week." [PraF] (14:3) Aut 93, p. 42.
1662. DOWNING, Ben
  "Cartographer's Tombstone." [SouthwR] (78:2) Spr 93, p. 277.
  "Onomathesia" (Vico's term for Adam's naming of the animals). [Poetry] (163:3) D
      93, p. 130.
  "Pieces of Pangaea." [Poetry] (162:5) Ag 93, p. 268.
  "Ranakpur" (Rajasthan, India). [Poetry] (162:5) Ag 93, p. 269.
  "Saudades" (For H.M.C.). [Poetry] (162:5) Ag 93, p. 269.
1663. DOWSE, George
  "Autoexec.Wkn." [Writer] (106:10) O 93, p. 26.
1664. DOYLE, Lynn
  "Rote of Forgetfulness." [EngJ] (82:8) D 93, p. 79.
1665. DOYLE, Owen
  "Before and After a Coup d'Etat." [HarvardR] (3) Wint 93, p. 138.
1666. DOYLE, Sally
  "The Fever Squeezes the House." [CentralP] (22) Spr 93, p. 121.
  "Hoofbeats." [CentralP] (22) Spr 93, p. 122.
  "Shepherding" (Excerpt). [Avec] (6:1) 93, p. 125.
  "Turn on the Lights, for Christssake." [Avec] (6:1) 93, p. 126.
1667. DRABIK, Grazyna
  "The Brief Life of Our Ancestors" (tr. of Wislawa Szymborska, w. Austin Flint).
      [QRL] (12:32/33) 93, p. 340-341.
  "Dealings with the Dead" (tr. of Wislawa Szymborska, w. Austin Flint). [QRL]
      (12:32/33) 93, p. 345.
  "End of the Century" (tr. of Wislawa Szymborska, w. Austin Flint). [QRL]
      (12:32/33) 93, p. 344-345.
  "The First Photograph of Hitler" (tr. of Wislawa Szymborska, w. Austin Flint).
      [QRL] (12:32/33) 93, p. 348.
  "Funeral" (tr. of Wislawa Szymborska, w. Austin Flint). [QRL] (12:32/33) 93, p.
      346.
  "Miracle Fair" (tr. of Wislawa Szymborska, w. Austin Flint). [QRL] (12:32/33) 93,
      p. 347-348.
  "People on a Bridge" (tr. of Wislawa Szymborska, w. Austin Flint). [QRL]
      (12:32/33) 93, p. 342-344.
  "Possibilities" (tr. of Wislawa Szymborska, w. Austin Flint). [QRL] (12:32/33) 93,
      p. 349-350.
  "Stage-Fright" (tr. of Wislawa Szymborska, w. Austin Flint). [QRL] (12:32/33) 93,
      p. 350-351.
  "To the Ark" (tr. of Wislawa Szymborska, w. Austin Flint). [QRL] (12:32/33) 93, p.
      341-342.

1668. DRAGE, John
"A Villanelle." [Bogg] (66) Wint 92-93, p. 34.
1669. DRAGON, Andrea Webb
"Stations of the Cross." [13thMoon] (12:1/2) 93-94, p. 22-23.
1670. DRAKE, Barbara
"Friendly Fire." [RiverS] (37) 93, p. 55.
"Telling About It." [RiverS] (37) 93, p. 56.
1671. DRAKE, Chris
"Fiyeda" (tr. of Fujii Sadakazu). [ChiR] (39:3/4) 93, p. 218-220.
1672. DRAKE, James
"Science and Snacks." [AnotherCM] (25) Spr 93, p. 30-34.
1673. DRAKE, Jeannette
"John Cage Collage in the Marble Hall." [SouthernR] (29:4) Aut, O 93, p. 723-724.
"Sunday Jazz." [SouthernR] (29:4) Aut, O 93, p. 724-725.
1674. DRECHSLER, Mark
"Gravity." [OnTheBus] (5:2, #12) Sum-Fall 93, p. 60.
"With a Whimper." [HampSPR] Wint 93, p. 27.
1675. DRESBACH, D. P.
"Photosynthesis." [Poetry] (161:6) Mr 93, p. 327.
DRESSAY, Anne Le
    See Le DRESSAY, Anne
1676. DREW, George
"The Four-Hundred Player of the Game" (For Lena Spencer). [Salm] (97) Wint 93,
    p. 112-114.
"Nelson Crocket's Pants." [Blueline] (14) 93, p. 78.
"Old Black Suit." [Blueline] (14) 93, p. 79.
1677. DREXEL, John
"She Cunsults Her Maps." [HampSPR] Wint 93, p. 53.
1678. DREXLER, R. D.
"Beruit." [PoetC] (25:1) Fall 93, p. 9.
"Italiam Non Sponde Sequor." [PoetC] (25:1) Fall 93, p. 10.
1679. DRISCOLL, Mary
"The Dowels." [GreenMR] (NS 6:2) Sum-Fall 93, p. 79.
"Widow's Walk" (for Joe). [GreenMR] (NS 6:2) Sum-Fall 93, p. 78.
1680. DRIZHAL, Peter
"Continent of Mental Lapses" (Excerpt). [RagMag] (11:1) 93, p. 18.
"Trash" (from "Continent of Mental Lapses"). [Lactuca] (17) Apr 93, p. 45.
"The Windows That Eyeball the Street." [SlipS] (13) 93, p. 90.
1681. DROP, Mimi
"Bound." [OnTheBus] (6:1, #13) Wint 93-Spr 94, p. 80.
"From a Distance." [OnTheBus] (5:2, #12) Sum-Fall 93, p. 61.
1682. DRUM, David
"The Alchemist" (to Frank O'Hara). [NorthStoneR] (11) 93, p. 178-179.
"Gaslight" (a poem about the past). [NorthStoneR] (11) 93, p. 180-181.
1683. DRURY, John
"Hareton Earnshaw, 1803: 'Hareton Earnshaw, 1500'." [WestHR] (47:3) Fall 93, p.
    292.
"Storm on Fishing Bay." [WestHR] (47:3) Fall 93, p. 291.
Du . . .
    See also names beginning with "Du" without the following space, filed below in
        their alphabetic positions, e.g., DuPLESSIS.
1684. Du BÉARN, Roger
"Clerihews for the Clerisy II." [AmerS] (62:4) Aut 93, p. 528-530.
1685. Du BELLAY, Joachim
"Regrets" (I and II, tr. by Thomas Carper). [Sparrow] (60) Sum 93, p. 53-54.
1686. Du BOUCHET, André
"Ash Shading into Blue" (shortened verson prepared by the author, tr. by David
    Mus). [HarvardR] (4) Spr 93, p. 83-95.
"Dictation" (tr. by David Mus). [DenQ] (27:4) Spr 93, p. 58-60.
1687. DUARTE, Mario
"In New Orleans." [SycamoreR] (5:1) Wint 93, p. 35.
"To the Spider of My Hand." [GreenMR] (NS 6:1) Wint-Spr 93, p. 33.
DuBÉARN, Roger
    See Du BÉARN, Roger
DuBELLAY, Joachim du
    See Du BELLAY, Joachim

1688. DUBIE, Norman
"A Dream of the Three Sisters." [NewEngR] (15:1) Wint 93, p. 118-119.
"Elegy for My Brother." [SouthernR] (29:1) Wint, Ja 93, p. 144-145.
"The Mercy Seat" (for Jack). [ColR] (20:1) Spr 93, p. 62-63.
"The Siege of Leningrad." [ColR] (20:1) Spr 93, p. 64-65.
1689. DuBOIS, Barbara
"Centimentality." [Light] (6) Sum 93, p. 10.
DuBOUCHET, André
See Du BOUCHET, André
1690. DUCHARME, Mark
"Landscape Over Some Film of Godard's." [Talisman] (10) Spr 93, p. 138-140.
1691. DUCKWORTH, Penelope
"Keeping Time" (In memory of James Luguri, 1948-1985, teacher and friend).
[AmerS] (62:4) Aut 93, p. 562-563.
1692. DUCLOS, Jeff
"Like Glass." [OnTheBus] (6:1, #13) Wint 93-Spr 94, p. 81-82.
1693. DUDIS, Ellen Kirvin
"The Man Who Set His Son on Fire." [Border] (2) Spr 93, p. 18.
1694. DUDLEY, Ellen
"The Fortune." [TriQ] (88) Fall 93, p. 78.
"Recidivist." [TriQ] (88) Fall 93, p. 80-81.
"Washington DC, 1990." [TriQ] (88) Fall 93, p. 79.
1695. DUEHR, Gary
"Annihilation." [NoDaQ] (61:4) Fall 93, p. 149.
"Who Fell." [OnTheBus] (5:2, #12) Sum-Fall 93, p. 62.
1696. DUEMER, Joseph
"Dog Before the World." [Manoa] (5:1) Sum 93, p. 139-140.
"Evening Air." [Manoa] (5:1) Sum 93, p. 138.
"Ocean Park (I)" (after Richard Diebenkorn). [DenQ] (28:1) Sum 93, p. 28-29.
"Ocean Park (II)." [DenQ] (28:1) Sum 93, p. 29-30.
"The Thing, 1951." [Manoa] (5:1) Sum 93, p. 140-141.
"What to Listen for in Music" (for David Rakowski). [Manoa] (5:1) Sum 93, p. 141.
1697. DUFAULT, Peter Kane
"Chess Piece." [NewYorker] (69:32) 4 O 93, p. 176.
1698. DUFF, S. K.
"Between Summer and Winter." [Art&Und] (2:4) O-N 93, p. 11.
1699. DUFFIN, Brent
"Revisiting a Mountain Town" (tr. of Sin Kyong-rim, w. Yang Seung-Tai).
[SpoonR] (18:1) Wint-Spr 93, p. 40.
1700. DUFFIN, K. E.
"Deliveries." [SouthwR] (78:2) Spr 93, p. 229.
"Harbor at Old Saybrook." [HarvardR] (5) Fall 93, p. 95.
"In the World." [SouthwR] (78:2) Spr 93, p. 229-230.
1701. DUFFY, John
"Angelus." [Stand] (34:3) Sum 93, p. 11.
"The Narrow Road to the Deep North." [Verse] (10:1) Spr 93, p. 82.
"What I See." [Verse] (10:1) Spr 93, p. 83.
1702. DUFFY, Patty
"In gray morning fog" (Lucille Sandberg Haiku Award, 2nd place). [Amelia] (7:2,
#21) 93, p. 14.
1703. DUHAMEL, Denise
"The Amorous Husband and the Premenstrual Wife." [SilverFR] (24) Wint 93, p.
20.
"Black Barbie History." [Footwork] (23) 93, p. 95.
"The Consequences of Wife-Swapping with a Giant" (From the Inuit tale).
[HarvardR] (5) Fall 93, p. 54.
"The Dark." [ChironR] (12:1, #34) Spr 93, p. 39.
"Four Hours." [WestB] (31/32) 93, p. 149.
"The Future of Vaginas and Penises." [Chelsea] (55) 93, p. 40.
"Making Money" (for Maureen Seaton). [OntR] (39) Fall-Wint 93-94, p. 104-105.
"Native American Barbie." [Footwork] (23) 93, p. 95.
"Oriental Barbie." [Footwork] (23) 93, p. 95.
"Ortho-Novum 777." [ArtfulD] (24/25) 93, p. 58.
"The Rapture." [ArtfulD] (24/25) 93, p. 57.
"Shame." [SilverFR] (24) Wint 93, p. 18-19.
"Three Wishes." [Chelsea] (55) 93, p. 41-42.

"The Tornado-Drawer." [Confr] (51) Sum 93, p. 229.
"The Ugly Step Sister." [OntR] (39) Fall-Wint 93-94, p. 105-106.
"Why, on a Bad Day, I Can Relate to the Manatee." [HarvardR] (4) Spr 93, p. 101.
"You." [ChironR] (12:1, #34) Spr 93, p. 39.
DUK-SOO, Moon
  See MOON, Duk-soo
1704. DUKE, Lee
  "The 522nd Liberates Dachau." [OnTheBus] (6:1, #13) Wint 93-Spr 94, p. 83.
1705. DUKES, Thomas
  "Minerva, Ohio." [Poetry] (162:6) S 93, p. 345.
1706. DUMARS, Denise
  "A Few Moments." [Pearl] (17) Spr 93, p. 47.
  "Green Salsa" (w. Todd Mecklem). [Pearl] (19) Fall-Wint 93, p. 8.
  "Lunch with the Boss." [Pearl] (17) Spr 93, p. 47.
  "Testing the Aubergine." [Amelia] (7:2, #21) 93, p. 31.
1707. DUNCAN, Almeda C.
  "Poems, Poems, Poems." [Eyeball] (2) 93, p. 14.
1708. DUNCAN, Graham
  "Father and Son in 1934 Attend the Sunday Ball Game, Arriving and Leaving
      Separately." [Plain] (14:1) Fall 93, p. 19.
1709. DUNCAN, J. Alexandra
  "The Language of Flowers." [PraF] (14:4) Wint 93-94, p. 76-79.
1710. DUNCAN, Robert
  "The Mabinogion" (Excerpt). [QRL] (12:32/33) 93, p. 405-406.
  "A New Poem" (for Jack Spicer). [QRL] (12:32/33) 93, p. 406-407.
1711. DUNFORD, Mary C.
  "Meridel Le Sueur." [NorthStoneR] (11) 93, p. 173.
1712. DUNGAN, S. L.
  "Hammer Death" (for Joe Orton). [OnTheBus] (5:2, #12) Sum-Fall 93, p. 63.
1713. DUNHAM, Vera Sandomirskaia
  "Almost over the abyss, at the very edge of the branch" (tr. of Galina Gamper). [Elf]
      (3:2) Sum 93, p. 31.
  "Here is the vessel from which I must drown" (tr. of Galina Gamper). [Elf] (3:2)
      Sum 93, p. 32.
1714. DUNHILL, Christina
  "To One of Her Sisters." [TampaR] (7) Fall 93, p. 50.
1715. DUNLOP, Lane
  "Rain" (tr. of Francis Ponge). [QRL] (12:32/33) 93, p. 492.
1716. DUNLOP, Nancy
  "One Day with Honeysuckle." [13thMoon] (12:1/2) 93-94, p. 25-27.
1717. DUNMORE, Helen
  "Rubbing Down the Horse." [Verse] (10:2) Sum 93, p. 3.
  "Three Ways of Recovering a Body." [Verse] (10:2) Sum 93, p. 4.
1718. DUNN, Douglas
  "Disenchantments: Night Thoughts for March 1991." [SouthernR] (29:4) Aut, O 93,
      p. 726-741.
1719. DUNN, Stephen
  "Ars Poetica." [OhioR] (50) 93, p. 94-95.
  "Aubade" (After Philip Dacey). [PaintedB] (50/51) 93, p. 113.
  "Kansas." [NewEngR] (15:1) Wint 93, p. 120.
  "Language." [Poetry] (162:6) S 93, p. 311.
  "Men in the Sky." [AmerPoR] (22:3) My-Je 93, p. 34.
  "Some Things I Wanted to Say to You." [AmerPoR] (22:3) My-Je 93, p. 34.
  "The Woman with Five Hearts." [GeoR] (47:2) Sum 93, p. 329-330.
1720. DUNN, Steven
  "Father, Mother, Robert Henley, Who Hanged Himself in the Ninth Grade, et al."
      [IndR] (16:1) Spr 93, p. 12.
1721. DUNN, Susan E.
  "My Mother's Story." [WillowS] (33) Wint 93, p. 52-53.
1722. DUNN, Terrence E.
  "The Thirsty Heart." [OnTheBus] (6:1, #13) Wint 93-Spr 94, p. 84-85.
1723. DUNNE, Loretta
  "Sex Appeal." [Footwork] (23) 93, p. 74.
1724. DUNWOODY, Michael
  "2. Leda and the Swans." [JamesWR] (10:4) Sum 93, p. 18.
  "3. Sisyphus in the Wartime Housing Projects." [JamesWR] (10:4) Sum 93, p. 18.

"Euridice at THE HAPPY TAP." [JamesWR] (10:4) Sum 93, p. 18.
"Narcissus Goes Down the Third Time." [AntigR] (95) Aut 93, p. 26.
1725. DUO, Duo
"In England" (tr. by Jin Zhong and Stephen Haven). [AmerPoR] (22:6) N-D 93, p. 36.
"It Is" (tr. by Jin Zhong and Stephen Haven). [AmerPoR] (22:6) N-D 93, p. 35.
"Longevity" (tr. by Jin Zhong and Stephen Haven). [AmerPoR] (22:6) N-D 93, p. 35.
"One Story Contains All His Past" (tr. by Jin Zhong and Stephen Haven). [AmerPoR] (22:6) N-D 93, p. 36.
"The Window That Loves to Weep" (tr. by Jin Zhong and Stephen Haven). [AmerPoR] (22:6) N-D 93, p. 36.
1726. DuPLESSIS, Rachel Blau
"Copying" (poem with long prose introduction). [Sulfur] (33) Fall 93, p. 257-272.
"Four Drafts" (15-18). [Sulfur] (32) Spr 93, p. 41-63.
1727. DUPLIJ, Steven
"Duet." [DogRR] (12:2, #24) Fall-Wint 93, p. 25.
"Full Moon." [Interim] (12:1) Spr-Sum 93, p. 45-46.
"The noble riff-raff." [Gypsy] (20) Sum 93, p. 41.
1728. DUPONT, Christopher
"The The." [NewYorkQ] (51) 93, p. 81.
1729. DUPUIS, Howard
"Life Is a Bunch of Moments." [PoetryE] (36) Fall 93, p. 123.
1730. DURBIN, Libby A.
"Metabolism." [CutB] (40) Spr 93, p. 176.
1731. DUTESCU-COLIBAN, Taina
"31 August 1986, 12:28 A.M. (Earthquake Time)" (tr. of Gabriel Chifu, w. Adam Sorkin). [IndR] (16:2) Fall 93, p. 82.
"Drawing Close" (tr. of Gabriel Chifu, w. Adam Sorkin). [IndR] (16:2) Fall 93, p. 84.
"Stubborn" (tr. of Gabriel Chifu, w. Adam Sorkin). [IndR] (16:2) Fall 93, p. 83.
DUYN, Mona van
    See Van DUYN, Mona
1732. DVORACHEK, Dorothy
"Matter of Fact" (Young Writers, age 17). [PikeF] (11) Fall 93, p. 18.
1733. DWORKIN, Joy
"Celibacy." [Epiphany] (4:2) Ap 93, p. 88.
1734. DWYER, Deirdre
"Anchored off Koh Tao." [AntigR] (93-94) Spr-Sum 93, p. 292.
"Coconut Island." [AntigR] (93-94) Spr-Sum 93, p. 291.
"Countries into Words." [AntigR] (93-94) Spr-Sum 93, p. 293.
"Sevilla Cathedral." [TickleAce] (26) Fall-Wint 93, p. 39-40.
"Since I've Come Inland." [AntigR] (93-94) Spr-Sum 93, p. 294.
"Some Aspects of the Real Alcazar, Sevilla." [TickleAce] (26) Fall-Wint 93, p. 38.
1735. DWYER, Neal Michael
"Avenue des Fleurs." [TarRP] (32:2) Spr 93, p. 38.
"Un Commencement." [TarRP] (32:2) Spr 93, p. 36.
"Gypsy Child." [TarRP] (32:2) Spr 93, p. 37.
"St. Paul de Vence." [TarRP] (32:2) Spr 93, p. 37.
1736. DYBEK, Stuart
"Alba." [Light] (5) Spr 93, p. 18.
"The Begonia and I." [PoetryE] (36) Fall 93, p. 29.
"Cranking the Louvers." [TarRP] (32:2) Spr 93, p. 40.
"Descent." [TarRP] (32:2) Spr 93, p. 39-40.
"Golden Shades." [PoetryE] (36) Fall 93, p. 30.
"Revelation." [Boulevard] (8:2/3, #23/24) Fall 93, p. 93-94.
"Symptoms of Drought." [TarRP] (32:2) Spr 93, p. 39.
1737. DYER, Eric
"Explaining the Eastern Wahoo Tree to Girl Scouts." [CumbPR] (12:2) Spr 93, p. 45.
"The Mouth." [CumbPR]] (13:1) Fall 93, p. 74-75.
1738. DYER, Linda
"View." [SmPd] (30:3, #89) Fall 93, p. 28.
1739. DYKERS, Anne
"Vanity." [GreenMR] (NS 6:2) Sum-Fall 93, p. 38.

1740. DYLAN, Bob
"Bob Dylan's Greatest Hits II." [VirQR] (69:1) Wint 93, p. 154.
"Original Basement Tapes." [VirQR] (69:1) Wint 93, p. 153.
1741. DYMOND, Justine
"My Neighbor Asks My Mother." [CimR] (105) O 93, p. 80-81.
1742. EADDY, Felton
"Oh! To Daufuskie (dah first key)." [AfAmRev] (27:1) Spr 93, p. 128-129.
1743. EADY, Cornelius
"Anger." [PraS] (67:3) Fall 93, p. 11.
"The Cab Driver Who Ripped Me Off." [Callaloo] (16:3) Sum 93, p. 678-680.
"The Death of Sam Patch." [PraS] (67:3) Fall 93, p. 12-13.
"Fetchin' Bones." [Pequod] (35) 93, p. 115.
"Hard Times." [Drumvoices] (2:1/2) Fall-Wint 92-93, p. 124.
"I Just Wanna Testify." [Pequod] (35) 93, p. 117.
"I Know (I'm Losing You)." [Pequod] (35) 93, p. 114.
"A Little Bit of Soap." [Pequod] (35) 93, p. 114.
"One Kind Favor." [Pequod] (35) 93, p. 115.
"Papa Was a Rolling Stone." [Drumvoices] (2:1/2) Fall-Wint 92-93, p. 122.
"Photo of Dexter Gordon, About to Solo, 1965." [PraS] (67:3) Fall 93, p. 11-12.
"Photo of Miles Davis at Lennies-on-the-Turnpike, 1968." [KenR] (NS 15:4) Fall
93, p. 147.
"A Rag, a Bone, and a Hank of Hair." [Pequod] (35) 93, p. 116-117.
"Rodney King Blues." [PraS] (67:3) Fall 93, p. 9-10.
"A Small Moment." [KenR] (NS 15:4) Fall 93, p. 146.
"A Small Moment." [PraS] (67:3) Fall 93, p. 9.
"Soothe Me." [Pequod] (35) 93, p. 116.
"Walt Whitman Mall." [PraS] (67:3) Fall 93, p. 8.
"You Don't Miss Your Water." [Pequod] (35) 93, p. 118.
"Youngblood." [Drumvoices] (2:1/2) Fall-Wint 92-93, p. 123.
1744. EAGAN, Matthew
"Mountain." [BellArk] (9:2) Mr-Ap 93, p. 6.
1745. EARL, Martin
"Leipzig." [Iowa] (23:3) Fall 93, p. 165.
"Luanda by Night." [Iowa] (23:3) Fall 93, p. 163-164.
"Mahler's Shed." [Iowa] (23:3) Fall 93, p. 164-165.
1746. EASTER, Charles
"Dry Twigs." [JINJPo] (15:1) Spr 93, p. 23.
1747. EASTMAN, Deborah
"Why I Like to Eat Red Meat." [AnthNEW] (5) 93, p. 18.
1748. EASTWOOD, D. J.
"The Angel." [TickleAce] (26) Fall-Wint 93, p. 69.
"A Doll House" (For Bernard and Dick. Competition Winner, 3rd). [TickleAce] (25)
Spr-Sum 93, p. 127-132.
"A Milkman Goes to Court." [TickleAce] (24) Fall-Wint 92, p. 117-118.
"Your Dream of Moose." [TickleAce] (24) Fall-Wint 92, p. 116.
1749. EATON, Charles Edward
"The Anvil." [Pembroke] (25) 93, p. 109-110.
"The Bath." [Poem] (70) N 93, p. 28.
"Claws." [HolCrit] (30:4) O 93, p. 19.
"Close Quarters." [LaurelR] (27:2) Sum 93, p. 58.
"The Diamond Clip." [Poem] (70) N 93, p. 29.
"Extramadura." [Pembroke] (25) 93, p. 108.
"The House on the Hill." [LullwaterR] (4:2) Spr-Sum 93, p. 41.
"The Lynx." [Paint] (19:38) Aut 92, p. 21.
"The Midget." [QRL] (12:32/33) 93, p. 407.
"The Mountain Gorillas." [Paint] (19:38) Aut 92, p. 24.
"The Queue." [Paint] (19:38) Aut 92, p. 25.
"Screwdriver." [CreamCR] (17:2) Fall 93, p. 110.
"Sleeping Car." [Paint] (19:38) Aut 92, p. 22.
"The Spool." [Paint] (19:38) Aut 92, p. 26.
"Squeeze Play." [SoCarR] (26:1) Fall 93, p. 146.
"The Truss." [CentR] (37:2) Spr 93, p. 382.
"Untitled Picture." [Paint] (19:38) Aut 92, p. 23.
"Wild Oats." [LullwaterR] (4:2) Spr-Sum 93, p. 124.
1750. EAVES, Will
"Evacuees." [Verse] (10:1) Spr 93, p. 101.

1751. EBERHART, Richard
"A Dream." [NewEngR] (15:1) Wint 93, p. 121-122.
"On Seeing an Egyptian Mummy in Berlin, 1932." [QRL] (12:32/33) 93, p. 408.
"Reality." [AnthNEW] (5) 93, p. 7.
1752. ECHELBERGER, M. J.
"The All-Night Hotline and Drop-In Center." [ChironR] (12:1, #34) Spr 93, p. 40.
"Undressing." [ChironR] (12:4/13:1, #37/38) Wint 93-Spr 94, p. 25.
"Words of Comfort." [ChironR] (12:1, #34) Spr 93, p. 40.
1753. ECKLUND, George
"Two Cardinals." [SycamoreR] (5:1) Wint 93, p. 34.
1754. ECONOMOU, George
"De Planctu Naturae" (Selection, tr. of Alanus de (Alan of Lille) Insulis). [Sulfur]
    (33) Fall 93, p. 80-82.
"Piers Plowman (The C-Text)" (tr. of William Langland). [Sulfur] (33) Fall 93, p.
    115-117.
1755. EDDY, Elizabeth
"And That's What the Devil Was Told." [Light] (8) Wint 93, p. 12.
"The Crab in 1932." [Light] (7) Aut 93, p. 9.
1756. EDDY, Gary
"First Lecture on Poetry." [Farm] (10:2) Fall-Wint 93-94, p. 86.
"Second Lecture on Poetry." [Farm] (10:2) Fall-Wint 93-94, p. 87.
"Writing Exercises." [Farm] (10:2) Fall-Wint 93-94, p. 88.
1757. EDELMANN, Carolyn Foote
"American Gothic" (Grant Wood painting of severe New England couple, austere
    house). [Footwork] (23) 93, p. 54.
"Bonnard's Wife" (Cannes 1988 / Princeton 1990). [US1] (28/29) 93, p. 28.
"Impostor." [Footwork] (23) 93, p. 54.
"Ink." [Footwork] (23) 93, p. 54.
"Ogunquit Danse Macabre." [Footwork] (23) 93, p. 54.
1758. EDELSTEIN, Susan
"Sitting Shivah." [WestCL] (27:1, #10) Spr 93, p. 116-117.
1759. EDITH, Patricia
"Morning" (for Corazon Amurao). [Calyx] (15:1) Wint 93-94, p. 38-39.
1760. EDKINS, Anthony
"The Art Center." [SpiritSH] (58) 93, p. 14.
"The End of the Welfare State." [SpiritSH] (58) 93, p. 11.
"Moving Apart." [SpiritSH] (58) 93, p. 14.
"Poeme Trouve." [SpiritSH] (58) 93, p. 13.
"Premonition of Passage." [SpiritSH] (58) 93, p. 12.
"The Right Reader." [SpiritSH] (58) 93, p. 13.
"Spectator Sport." [SpiritSH] (58) 93, p. 13.
"Still Life with Statement." [SpiritSH] (58) 93, p. 14.
1761. EDMOND, Murray
"Snips & Spins" (3 selections). [WestCL] (27:2, #11) Fall 93, p. 58-59.
1762. EDMONDS, Lisa A.
"Double Target." [SinW] (49) Spr-Sum 93, p. 44-45.
"Making Amends." [Pearl] (17) Spr 93, p. 55.
1763. EDMONDSON, Richard
"Conventional Wisdom." [PoetryUSA] (25/26) 93, p. 53.
1764. EDMUNDS, Martin
"The High Road to Taos" (Selections: I-II). [GrandS] (12:2, #46) Sum 93, p. 215 -
    219.
"Weathering" (for Carol Moldaw). [SouthwR] (78:2) Spr 93, p. 244.
1765. EDSON, Russell
"Allegory." [ProseP] (2) 93, p. 32.
"Bread." [ProseP] (1) 92, p. 27.
"Cock-a-Doodle-Doo." [ProseP] (1) 92, p. 28.
"The Decaying Man." [Asylum] (8) 93, p. 127.
"One Man's Story." [ProseP] (1) 92, p. 29.
"Round." [Asylum] (8) 93, p. 127.
"The Traveling Circus." [ProseP] (2) 93, p. 30.
"Windows." [ProseP] (2) 93, p. 31.
1766. EDWARDS, Duane
"Crazy Louie." [Confr] (51) Sum 93, p. 245.
1767. EDWARDS, Elizabeth
"The Chronic Liar Buys a Canary." [SouthernR] (29:3) Sum, Jl 93, p. 575.

EDWARDS

148

"Perspectives." [AntR] (51:3) Sum 93, p. 383.
1768. EDWARDS, Robert
"Bud." [SlipS] (13) 93, p. 35-36.
"Elephant Butte, Utah" (for Leslie). [HawaiiR] (17:3, #39) Fall 93, p. 64-65.
"Green Peaches." [BlackBR] (17) Sum-Fall 93, p. 5.
"Hubbel Trading Post." [DogRR] (12:2, #24) Fall-Wint 93, p. 28-29.
"A Man Looking at Jim Fletcher's Painting, 'The Warrior and His Death
Companion'." [SnailPR] (3:1) Fall-Wint 93, p. 6-7.
"Mars Hill." [SnailPR] (3:1) Fall-Wint 93, p. 8-10.
"Memorial Day." [HawaiiR] (17:3, #39) Fall 93, p. 90.
"The Woman on Summer Street." [Vis] (41) 93, p. 33.
1769. EGER, Ernestina N.
"Aniversario." [BilingR] (18:1) Ja-Ap 93, p. 63.
"Oracion Agnostica: Respuesta a Quevedo" (a la memoria de Lázaro Manuel Costa
Acosta, 2 septiembre 1941-9 Mayo 1989). [BilingR] (18:1) Ja-Ap 93, p. 61-
63.
1770. EGGAN, Ferd
"My Love Is a Kayak Man from Sweden." [YellowS] (42) Wint-Spr 93, p. 20.
1771. EHRET, Terry
"The Truth." [Sun] (212) Ag 93, p. 14.
1772. EHRHART, W. D.
"Flying to the Moon." [PaintedB] (50/51) 93, p. 47.
1773. EHRLICH, Linda C.
"Travelling Over the Mountains" (for Y.). [InterPR] (19:2) Fall 93, p. 73.
1774. EIBEL, Deborah
"A Gold Ring." [PraS] (67:4) Wint 93, p. 75.
"Modern Marriage, Postmodern Marriage." [PraS] (67:4) Wint 93, p. 76.
"The National Anthem." [PraS] (67:4) Wint 93, p. 73.
"Now You Can Study." [PraS] (67:4) Wint 93, p. 77.
"Studying." [PraS] (67:4) Wint 93, p. 73-74.
"Versions." [PraS] (67:4) Wint 93, p. 74.
1775. EICHNER, Maura
"House Painters." [ChrC] (110:17) 19-26 My 93, p. 566.
1776. EIGNER, Janet B.
"Chamber Music Two." [Eyeball] (2) 93, p. 13-14.
"Rite to Life." [Eyeball] (2) 93, p. 14.
"Something to Do with Hunted Animals." [HawaiiR] (17:1, #37) Spr 93, p. 118.
1777. EIGNER, Larry
"Again dawn." [PoetryUSA] (25/26) 93, p. 19.
"Aug 19 90   1 6 9 1." [Talisman] (10) Spr 93, p. 17.
"Fate and the Future." [PoetryUSA] (25/26) 93, p. 19.
"Flat sky going down to leaves." [PoetryUSA] (25/26) 93, p. 26.
"The Hours, Keepers of Heaven." [Sulfur] (33) Fall 93, p. 6-7.
"May 8 -24 90   1 6 8 5" (After the file *Ecstasy (Ekstase)*, 1933, Czech, some of
it). [Talisman] (10) Spr 93, p. 16.
"No Dream?" [PoetryUSA] (25/26) 93, p. 38.
"Sept 26 91   1 6 9 7 .x x x x." [Talisman] (10) Spr 93, p. 18.
"Sunday, Real" (two for Michael McClure). [PoetryUSA] (25/26) 93, p. 38.
1778. EIMERS, Nancy
"Betty and Joe." [PraS] (67:3) Fall 93, p. 148-149.
"The Dark Back Then." [PraS] (67:3) Fall 93, p. 147-148.
"Joy to the World." [ParisR] (35:127) Sum 93, p. 49-51.
"On the Phone with My Parents." [ParisR] (35:127) Sum 93, p. 52-53.
"The Pelican Girl." [NoAmR] (278:4) Jl-Ag 93, p. 44.
1779. EINZIG, Barbara
"Anything Can Happen to a Body Like a Brick" (— George Oppen). [AmerPoR]
(22:2) Mr-Ap 93, p. 3.
"Secrets." [AmerPoR] (22:2) Mr-Ap 93, p. 4-5.
1780. EISDORFER, Sandra
"The Gift." [Art&Und] (2:2) My-Je 93, p. 9.
1781. EISELE, Thomas
"The apparel of anger is often something old." [PoetryE] (36) Fall 93, p. 140.
"Between contemplation & action." [PoetryE] (36) Fall 93, p. 139.
"Buddhism, Hunduism, Shintoism, Calvinism." [PoetryE] (36) Fall 93, p. 142.
"I am sitting by a pond." [PoetryE] (36) Fall 93, p. 141.
"Reincarnation" (for Rosa). [PoetryE] (36) Fall 93, p. 138.

1782. EISEN, Christine
    "Chaconne." [BellArk] (9:4) Jl-Ag 93, p. 9.
    "Matin." [BellArk] (9:3) My-Je 93, p. 13.
    "Morning." [BellArk] (9:3) My-Je 93, p. 13.
    "Ninstint" (Ancient Haida village in the Queen Charlotte Islands). [BellArk] (9:6)
        N-D 93, p. 12.
    "Perceptions." [BellArk] (9:5) S-O 93, p. 8.
1783. EISENHOWER, Cathy
    "Waiting in the Car for My Father at the Youngstown Sheet & Tube." [WillowS]
        (31) Wint 93, p. 52.
1784. EISENLOHR, Kurt
    "Movement." [Asylum] (8) 93, p. 122.
1785. EISIMINGER, Skip
    "Communique from Tithonus." [Light] (5) Spr 93, p. 20.
    "Fran's Revenge." [SoCoast] (15) Je 93, p. 28.
    "Futile Determination." [Light] (6) Sum 93, p. 12.
1786. EISNER, Amy
    "Charles I at Trial." [HarvardA] (128:1) Fall 93, p. 16.
    "A Da Vinci Autopsy." [HarvardA] (128:1) Fall 93, p. 19.
    "Slate Mine, Wales." [HarvardA] (127:2) Wint 93, p. 18.
1787. EKBOIR, Julia
    "Orbitas Transparentes" (from "Orbitas Transparentes"). [Luz] (5) N 93, p. 64.
1788. EL CID (Anonymous)
    "Poem of the Cid" (Selections, tr. by Paul Blackburn). [Sulfur] (33) Fall 93, p. 175 -
        184.
1789. ELBERT, Samuel
    "Careful of the Day" (tr. of Moa Tetua, w. Muriel Rukeyser). [Sulfur] (33) Fall 93,
        p. 256.
    "Rari for O'Otua" (tr. of Moa Tetua, w. Muriel Rukeyser). [Sulfur] (33) Fall 93, p.
        255.
    "Rari for Tahia and Piu" (tr. of Moa Tetua, w. Muriel Rukeyser). [Sulfur] (33) Fall
        93, p. 253-254.
    "A True Confession" (tr. of Moa Tetua, w. Muriel Rukeyser). [Sulfur] (33) Fall 93,
        p. 255-256.
1790. ELDER, Mary
    "Blue." [GreensboroR] (54) Sum 93, p. 3.
1791. ELEFTHERIOU, Stephanie
    "Catching Time." [Interim] (12:1) Spr-Sum 93, p. 8.
    "Seeds." [Interim] (12:1) Spr-Sum 93, p. 9.
1792. ELIAS-BURSAC, Ellen
    "Dear Birch" (to Anamarija Persola, tr. of Enes Kisevic). [NoDaQ] (61:1) Wint 93,
        p. 97.
    "An Exiled Child's Letter" (tr. of Enes Kisevic). [NoDaQ] (61:1) Wint 93, p. 95-96.
    "Forgive Them, O Lord" (tr. of Enes Kisevic). [NoDaQ] (61:1) Wint 93, p. 97.
1793. ELLEDGE, Jim
    "Duckling, Swan." [CimR] (104) Jl 93, p. 146-147.
    "Strangers: An Essay." [ApalQ] (39) 93, p. 46-48.
    "To Them This May Consume." [CimR] (104) Jl 93, p. 143-145.
1794. ELLEFSON, J. C.
    "Denying the Afternoon with Miss Mei Li." [AntigR] (92) Wint 93, p. 123-124.
    "Expatriate Babble." [InterPR] (19:2) Fall 93, p. 81-82.
    "The Expatriate Returns to Dream Street." [WestB] (33) 93, p. 12.
    "Getting Inside the University of the Road." [CentR] (37:3) Fall 93, p. 527.
    "In the Middle of the Tall Night in the Cobble-Stone City, Captain James — the
        Sailor Man — Heads for Home." [LullwaterR] (4:2) Spr-Sum 93, p. 68-69.
    "Sunday in Babylon." [Gypsy] (20) Sum 93, p. 22.
    "We Gypsies." [InterPR] (19:2) Fall 93, p. 83.
1795. ELLINGSEN, Steven
    "Peach Trees." [ChrC] (110:23) 11-18 Ag 93, p. 765.
ELLINGSON, Alice Olds
    See OLDS-ELLINGSON, Alice
ELLIOT, William P. Haynes
    See HAYNES/ELLIOT, William P.
1796. ELLIOTT
    "Bir's Song." [SinW] (51) Wint 93-94, p. 38-39.

150

1797. ELLIOTT, David
   "Haiku" (3 poems). [Northeast] (5:9) Wint 93-94, p. 22.
1798. ELLIS, Denny
   "The way to keep your body thin" (Amelia One-Liner Award). [Amelia] (7:2, #21) 93, p. 52.
1799. ELLIS, Scott
   "When the Moon Drifts Away." [PraF] (14:3) Aut 93, p. 43.
1800. ELLIS, Thomas Sayers
   "A Kiss in the Dark." [Callaloo] (16:3) Sum 93, p. 532.
   "Shooting Back." [Callaloo] (16:3) Sum 93, p. 533.
   "Starchild" (for Garry Shider). [Agni] (38) 93, p. 3.
   "Tambourine" (For the Reverend Ida Ellis). [HarvardR] (5) Fall 93, p. 117.
1801. ELLISON, Carol
   "Wrecks." [Parting] (6:1) Sum 93, p. 1.
1802. ELLISON, Julie
   "Midlife Lullaby." [Witness] (7:1) 93, p. 64-65.
   "Stephanie Gorski Weeps When Her Car Is Towed." [Witness] (7:1) 93, p. 66-67.
1803. ELLMAN, Kitsey
   "A Map of the World." [Witness] (7:1) 93, p. 9.
1804. ELLSWORTH, Anne
   "Solitary Cheating." [ChironR] (12:4/13:1, #37/38) Wint 93-Spr 94, p. 15.
1805. ELMAN, Richard
   "Smoker" (for Louis Asekoff). [Agni] (37) 93, p. 207-208.
1806. ELOVIC, Barbara
   "The Lineup." [OnTheBus] (5:2, #12) Sum-Fall 93, p. 67.
1807. ELSBERG, John
   "The Beach" (In memoriam, David Jaffé, 1911-1990, for whom, and with whom, this poem was written). [Bogg] (66) Wint 92-93, p. 15.
   "A Disquisition on 'Red'." [Wind] (23:72) 93, p. 8.
   "Sprung." [DogRR] (12:1, #23) Spr-Sum 93, p. 49.
1808. ELTON, W. R.
   "Nietzsche's Cat." [DenQ] (27:4) Spr 93, p. 111-112.
1809. ELUARD, Paul
   "First" (Selections: I, VI, XX, XXIX, tr. by Russell Smith). [Quarry] (42:1) 93, p. 121-123.
EMBSE, Jayne von der
   See Von der EMBSE, Jayne
1810. EMERY, Michael J.
   "Playroom a Plus." [JamesWR] (10:3) Spr 93, p. 9.
1811. EMERY, Nona
   "Look Death in the Eye." [OnTheBus] (5:2, #12) Sum-Fall 93, p. 68-69.
1812. EMERY, Thomas
   "Indiana Thunderstorm." [Outbr] (24) 93, p. 57-58.
   "Organic." [Outbr] (24) 93, p. 59-60.
1813. EMMONS, Chalon
   "Grammar and Usage." [IndR] (16:2) Fall 93, p. 153.
1814. EMMONS, Jeanne
   "Advent." [ChrC] (110:36) 15 D 93, p. 1269.
1815. ENDO, Russell Susumu
   "Coconut Don Fu Delight." [Ploughs] (19:1) Spr 93, p. 56-59.
   "Movable Rings." [HawaiiR] (17:1, #37) Spr 93, p. 86.
   "Origin of the Milky Way." [HawaiiR] (17:1, #37) Spr 93, p. 87.
1816. ENGELS, John
   "Autumn Poem." [NewEngR] (15:1) Wint 93, p. 123.
   "Confessions of a Peeping Tom." [QRL] (12:32/33) 93, p. 408-409.
   "Dead Pig." [KenR] (NS 15:1) Wint 93, p. 144-145.
   "Newborn" (for Henry Matthew Amistadi). [KenR] (NS 15:1) Wint 93, p. 146.
   "Turtle Hunter." [SouthernR] (29:1) Wint, Ja 93, p. 177.
1817. ENGELS, Stacy
   "Raven." [AntigR] (92) Wint 93, p. 82.
1818. ENGLE, John D., Jr.
   "Senior Question." [Light] (6) Sum 93, p. 20.
1819. ENGLER, Robert Klein
   "Mary Magdalene Thinks of Cherries." [Border] (2) Spr 93, p. 19.
1820. ENGLISH, Sandra
   "Found some space." [Drumvoices] (1:1/2) Fall-Wint 91-92, p. 13.

"Neighborhood Woman." [Drumvoices] (1:1/2) Fall-Wint 91-92, p. 13.
"Pacific Ocean Time." [Drumvoices] (1:1/2) Fall-Wint 91-92, p. 14.
"You know you've really wound up my heart." [Drumvoices] (1:1/2) Fall-Wint 91 - 92, p. 14.
1821. ENGMAN, John
"After Edvard Munch." [NorthStoneR] (11) 93, p. 182.
"Clear Nights." [Caliban] (13) 93, p. 112.
"Decoys." [NorthStoneR] (11) 93, p. 183.
"An Elephant." [NorthStoneR] (11) 93, p. 184-185.
"Goldfish at Loring Pond." [IndR] (16:2) Fall 93, p. 15.
"Terrible Weather Conditions." [Caliban] (13) 93, p. 113.
1822. ENGONOPOULOS, Nikos
"Maria of the Night" (tr. by Martin McKinsey). [ProseP] (1) 92, p. 30.
"The Shipwrecks' Cabal" (tr. by Martin McKinsey). [ProseP] (1) 92, p. 31.
1823. ENGSTROM-HEG, Bob
"The Formation of Vegetable Mould, Through the Action of Worms, with Observations on Their Habits (God to Darwin)." [ChrC] (110:12) 14 Apr 93, p. 398.
1824. ENRIGHT, Sean
"Boy Meets Globe." [Journal] (17:2) Fall-Wint 93, p. 63-64.
"The Old Story." [Journal] (17:2) Fall-Wint 93, p. 65-66.
"Your Celebrated Summer" (after Horace, Book 4, Ode VII). [GrahamHR] (17) Fall 93, p. 92-93.
1825. ENSING, Riemke
"Molly." [Vis] (41) 93, p. 34-35.
"Poems from the Japanese" (I & II, for Izumi). [Vis] (41) 93, p. 19.
1826. ENSLER, Eve
"All of Us Are Leaving" (Photographs by Ariel Orr Jordan). [Art&Und] (2:2) My-Je 93, p. 30-32.
"A Terrorist Angel" (For Richard). [Art&Und] (2:3) Special Edition 93, p. 9.
1827. ENSLIN, Theodore
"Abendmusik." [Conjunc] (21) 93, p. 96-108.
"Late As Budding Node" (for Judith Fitzgerald). [Talisman] (10) Spr 93, p. 19-22.
"Stalking." [QRL] (12:32/33) 93, p. 409.
"Temptation" (for Diane and Thomas Bouchard). [QRL] (12:32/33) 93, p. 409.
1828. ENZENSBERGER, Hans Magnus
"Gillis van Coninxloo, Landscape" (Wood, 65 by 119 cm, tr. by Reinhold Grimm). [NowestR] (31:1) 93, p. 93.
"In Memory of William Carlos Williams" (tr. by Christopher Levenson). [QRL] (12:32/33) 93, p. 410.
"Old Revolution" (tr. by Reinhold Grimm). [NowestR] (31:1) 93, p. 92.
"The Poison" (tr. by Reinhold Grimm). [NowestR] (31:1) 93, p. 94.
"Sleeping Pill" (tr. by Reinhold Grimm). [NowestR] (31:1) 93, p. 91.
EPHESUS, Hipponax of
See HIPPONAX of Ephesus
1829. EPLING, Kathy
"In These Days Hooked like Railway Cars." [PoetL] (88:3) Fall 93, p. 8.
1830. EQUI, Elaine
"Renga" (w. Martine Bellen and Melanie Neilson). [Conjunc] (21) 93, p. 263-268.
"To Harry Crosby at the Hotel des Artistes." [Chelsea] (55) 93, p. 43.
1831. ERB, Elke
"Rip Van Winkle" (tr. by Rosmarie Waldrop). [ProseP] (2) 93, p. 34.
"The Way We Live" (tr. by Rosmarie Waldrop). [ProseP] (2) 93, p. 33.
1832. ERHARDT, Jean
"2 Corinthians." [Kalliope] (15:3) 93, p. 28.
1833. ERLY, Corinne
"Road Crew." [LitR] (37:1) Fall 93, p. 97.
1834. ERNST, Myron
"Florida Pools." [HiramPoR] (53/54) Fall 92-Sum 93, p. 35.
"For Spring." [PoetryE] (36) Fall 93, p. 110.
"A Game for November." [Poem] (70) N 93, p. 65.
"Poland" (From Gdansk to Wloclawek). [SouthernHR] (27:2) Spr 93, p. 149.
"Safety First." [Poem] (70) N 93, p. 63.
"Winter." [Poem] (70) N 93, p. 64.
1835. ERPENBECK, John
"The Words" (tr. by Gisela Argyle). [PoetryC] (13:2) 93, p. 21.

152

ESAREY

1836. ESAREY, Gary
"What I did as a boy was cowboy, really." [DogRR] (12:2, #24) Fall-Wint 93, p. 23.
1837. ESHLEMAN, Clayton
"Ground." [NoDaQ] (61:2) Spr 93, p. 44.
"The loss of Eternity." [NewAW] (11) Sum-Fall 93, p. 33.
"Marginalia to Baudelaire." [AmerLC] (5) 93, p. 101.
"Still-Life, with Huidobro." [NewAW] (11) Sum-Fall 93, p. 34.
"Under World Arrest" (Selections: 10 poems). [Sulfur] (32) Spr 93, p. 95-112.
1838. ESPADA, Martín
"Mi Vida" (Chelsea, Massachusetts, 1987). [KenR] (NS 15:1) Wint 93, p. 5.
"White Birch." [NoDaQ] (61:2) Spr 93, p. 45-46.
"Who Burns for the Perfection of Paper." [Ploughs] (19:1) Spr 93, p. 80.
1839. ESPAILLAT, Rhina P.
"The Nightingale Has No Objection" (No Le Entristece el Ruiseñor Su Suerte, tr. by
the author). [Sparrow] (60) Sum 93, p. 43.
1840. ESPOSITO, Nancy
"The Carousel Club, 1957." [QRL] (12:32/33) 93, p. 124-125.
"The Light Through the Pig." [QRL] (12:32/33) 93, p. 121-123.
"Mêm' Rain." [QRL] (12:32/33) 93, p. 117-119.
"Snake Charmer." [QRL] (12:32/33) 93, p. 120-121.
"Supposing That Truth Is a Woman — What Then?" [QRL] (12:32/33) 93, p. 123 -
124.
"What There Is." [QRL] (12:32/33) 93, p. 126.
1841. ESPRIU, Salvador
"XVII. Could it be that the long protruding tongue" (tr. by Adela Robles Salz).
[Iowa] (23:2) Spr-Sum 93, p. 3.
1842. ESPY, Willard
"Its the Bottom of the Eighth, and So Far They've Knocked Every Pitcher Out of the
Box" (A Monitory Sonnet Sequence on Saints, Sicknesses, and Baseball
Teams). [Light] (5) Spr 93, p. 22.
1843. ESSENIN
"Three Prayers for the First Forty Days of the Dead" (tr. by W. S. Merwin and Olga
Carlisle). [QRL] (12:32/33) 93, p. 411-413.
1844. ESSINGER, Cathryn
"English 123 Discusses Virginia Woolf." [PoetryNW] (34:1) Spr 93, p. 36-37.
1845. ESTABROOK, Michael
"Bahama Blue Beetle." [WindO] (57) Fall 93, p. 3.
"Cows." [WormR] (33:1, #129) 93, p. 22.
"Dishes & Diapers." [ChironR] (12:4/13:1, #37/38) Wint 93-Spr 94, p. 15.
"Dried Out Plants." [WormR] (33:1, #129) 93, p. 22.
"Gasoline." [WindO] (57) Fall 93, p. 5.
"Harvard." [WindO] (57) Fall 93, p. 32.
"Opinionless." [WormR] (33:1, #129) 93, p. 21.
"Outtakes of Mom When Young" (or fragments of a life). [Pearl] (17) Spr 93, p.
107-109.
"September 21, 1993." [HampSPR] Wint 93, p. 54.
"Surfer's Thighs." [SlipS] (13) 93, p. 94.
"When Things End Sometimes They Go Back to the Beginning." [WormR] (33:1,
#129) 93, p. 21.
"Windowless Rooms." [WindO] (57) Fall 93, p. 6.
1846. ESTABROOK, Susan
"My Life." [OnTheBus] (5:2, #12) Sum-Fall 93, p. 70-71.
1847. ESTEBAN, Cooper
"St. Thomas in Heaven." [HampSPR] Wint 93, p. 17.
"Wicked Stepmother." [HampSPR] Wint 93, p. 17.
1848. ESTELLÉS, Vicent Andrés
"Cry in the Night" (tr. by Adela Robles Salz). [Iowa] (23:2) Spr-Sum 93, p. 4.
"Flèrida" (tr. by Adela Robles Salz). [Iowa] (23:2) Spr-Sum 93, p. 4-5.
"The Lovers" (tr. by Adela Robles Salz). [Iowa] (23:2) Spr-Sum 93, p. 5.
1849. ESTES, Angie
"Poems." [Verse] (10:3) Wint 93, p. 106.
1850. ESTÉS, Clarissa Pinkola
"The Giggly Girls or the Fourth Opening." [ColR] (20:2) Fall 93, p. 35-36.
"La Muerte, Patron Saint of Writers." [ColR] (20:2) Fall 93, p. 37-38.
1851. ESTREICH, George
"Twilight, Poconos." [Ascent] (17:3) Spr 93, p. 25.

ETSUKO, Morimoto
See MORIMOTO, Etsuko
1852. ETTER, Carrie
"Honeymoon." [PoetC] (25:1) Fall 93, p. 18.
"Pears." [WestB] (31/32) 93, p. 123.
"Plunging into the River." [Arshile] (1) Spr 93, p. 64-65.
"Present Tense." [PoetC] (25:1) Fall 93, p. 19.
"Sixteen." [CapeR] (28:2) Fall 93, p. 9.
"The Staged Confession." [WestB] (33) 93, p. 27.
"The Uncelebrated Birthday." [PoetC] (24:2) Wint 93, p. 23.
"Vigil." [Arshile] (1) Spr 93, p. 63.
1853. ETTER, Dave
"For Miles and Miles." [ClockR] (8:1/2) 93, p. 126-127.
"Forklift." [IllinoisR] (1:1) Fall 93, p. 53.
"The Lion Tamer's Daughter." [PoetC] (24:2) Wint 93, p. 31.
1854. ETZWILER, R. Lee
"Minotaurs in Love." [Pearl] (19) Fall-Wint 93, p. 55.
1855. EUBANKS, Georgann
"In Unison." [Vis] (41) 93, p. 7.
1856. EURIPIDES
"Andromache" (Excerpt, tr. by Herbert Golder). [Pequod] (35) 93, p. 41-42.
1857. EVANS, Christine
"Venice Wind-Catchers" (Young Writers, age 14). [PikeF] (11) Fall 93, p. 19.
EVANS, Craig Crist
See CRIST-EVANS, Craig
1858. EVANS, David
"Reincarnation." [BellArk] (9:5) S-O 93, p. 9.
"Umatilla to Spokane." [BellArk] (9:5) S-O 93, p. 7.
1859. EVANS, Jack
"The Cat Food Factory." [ChiR] (39:1) 93, p. 1-2.
"The Nanny." [ProseP] (2) 93, p. 35.
1860. EVANS, Jamie Lee
"I'm No Poet" (for Lisa Horan, my lover, who always introduces me as her poet -
girlfriend). [SinW] (50) Sum-Fall 93, p. 86-88.
1861. EVANS, Kathy
"For Jacques-Henri Lartigue, Who as a Child Mourned the Death of Moments."
[DenQ] (27:3) Wint 93, p. 25.
"Losing It." [DenQ] (27:3) Wint 93, p. 23-24.
1862. EVANS, Lee
"Night Hags Over America" (for Debroah Tobola). [CreamCR] (17:2) Fall 93, p.
190-191.
1863. EVANS, Mari
"How Sudden Dies the Blooming" (For Paula Cooper and All the Other Children on
Death Row). [Drumvoices] (2:1/2) Fall-Wint 92-93, p. 126.
"Johnetta Betch Cole" (Spelman College, November 1988). [Drumvoices] (2:1/2)
Fall-Wint 92-93, p. 127.
"A Man without Food." [Drumvoices] (2:1/2) Fall-Wint 92-93, p. 125.
1864. EVANS, Michael
"Self-Portrait at the Embrace." [IndR] (16:2) Fall 93, p. 190-191.
1865. EVANS, R. Daniel
"Auschwitz." [PaintedB] (50/51) 93, p. 111.
1866. EVANS, Robert W.
"Mary Babnick Brown's Incredible Hair." [CapeR] (28:2) Fall 93, p. 39.
1867. EVARTS, Prescott
"Marks of Spiritual Punctuation." [CimR] (103) Ap 93, p. 96-97.
"Rooftops." [CimR] (103) Ap 93, p. 97.
1868. EVERDING, Kelly
"Unpleasantness." [Caliban] (12) 93, p. 136-137.
1869. EWART, Gavin
"The Horrible Santas." [Light] (8) Wint 93, p. 8.
"Lewis Carroll Advocates Severe Discipline." [Light] (8) Wint 93, p. 10.
"A Romantic Occasion." [Light] (6) Sum 93, p. 16.
1870. EWING, Blair
"Euphony." [CapeR] (28:1) Spr 93, p. 17.
1871. EXNER, Richard
"Born" (tr. by William Cross). [LitR] (36:2) Wint 93, p. 162.

"Boucher in the Grand Palais (Thirteen Fragments About Nakedness)" (tr. by
William Cross). [Chelsea] (54) 93, p. 30-33.
"Fall" (tr. by Martha Collins). [SnailPR] (3:1) Fall-Wint 93, p. 16-17.
"Light, Near Perth" (tr. by William Cross). [Vis] (41) 93, p. 43.
"The Onset of Winter" (tr. by William Cross). [LitR] (36:2) Wint 93, p. 163.
"Question" (tr. by William Cross). [Chelsea] (54) 93, p. 33.
"Trains" (tr. by William Cross). [Chelsea] (54) 93, p. 34.
"Valyermo, St. Andrew's" (winter evening, after Complin. Tr. by Martha Collins).
[GrahamHR] (17) Fall 93, p. 76.
EYCK, Richard Ten
    See TenEYCK, Richard
1872. FABILLI, Mary
    "The Last Cigarettes of Aurora Bligh." [PoetryUSA] (25/26) 93, p. 24.
1873. FACKNITZ, Susan V.
    "The Soul in Its Predicament" (for David Hallman). [LouisL] (10:1) Spr 93, p. 45 -
    46.
1874. FAGAN, Kathy
    " *California*, She Replied." [ParisR] (35:129) Wint 93, p. 228.
    "Her Advice to the Still Life Painter." [ParisR] (35:129) Wint 93, p. 227.
    " *There Are Plenty of Angels,* She Said in the LADIES." [ParisR] (35:129) Wint 93,
    p. 226.
1875. FAGLES, Robert
    "Achilles and Cygus." [QRL] (12:32/33) 93, p. 414.
    "Achilles and Penthesileia." [QRL] (12:32/33) 93, p. 413-414.
    "The Pair-Oared Shell" (after the painting by Thomas Eakins). [SewanR] (101:1) Ja -
    Mr, Wint 93, p. 34.
    "Rain, Steam, and Speed" (after the painting by Turner). [SewanR] (101:1) Ja-Mr,
    Wint 93, p. 33.
1876. FAIN, Sharon
    "Walking in the Oakland Hills After the October Fire." [Calyx] (14:3) Sum 93, p.
    38-39.
1877. FAINLIGHT, Ruth
    "The Bowl." [NewYorker] (69:34) 18 O 93, p. 87.
    "A Mourner." [NewYorker] (68:48) 18 Ja 93, p. 76.
1878. FAIRCHILD, B. H.
    "The Ascension of Ira Campbell." [QRL] (12:32/33) 93, p. 129-130.
    "The Death of a Small Town." [QRL] (12:32/33) 93, p. 130.
    "The *Dumka.*" [QRL] (12:32/33) 93, p. 127-128.
    "Old Men Playing Basketball." [Poetry] (162:4) Jl 93, p. 223.
    "Old Men Playing Basketball." [QRL] (12:32/33) 93, p. 126-127.
    "Song" (Bert Fairchild, 1906-1990). [QRL] (12:32/33) 93, p. 128-129.
1879. FAIRLEY, Lorraine
    "Blasphemy." [Dandel] (20:1) 93, p. 44-45.
1880. FAIZ, Faiz Ahmed (Faiz Ahmad)
    "Heart's Companion." [Agni] (37) 93, p. 146.
    "Visitors" (tr. by Daud Kamal). [Vis] (43) 93, p. 55.
1881. FALCO, Edward
    "In the Green Drawing Room at Hollins College." [HiramPoR] (53/54) Fall 92-Sum
    93, p. 36.
    "Winners." [PennR] (5:2) 93, p. 41.
FALCO, Sam di
    See DIFALCO, Sam
1882. FALCONER, Sandra Evans
    "McGuire, McGoo." [PikeF] (11) Fall 93, p. 35.
FALIO, Sam di
    See DiFALIO, Sam
1883. FALK, Jonathan
    "Aggregation." [HampSPR] Wint 93, p. 58.
    "Second Growth." [HampSPR] Wint 93, p. 58.
1884. FALLEDER, Arnold
    "I Oblige the Dean of Enrollment by Writing a Recommendation for My Daughter."
    [OnTheBus] (5:2, #12) Sum-Fall 93, p. 72.
1885. FALLER, Francis
    "Agnostalgia." [BostonR] (18:3/4) Je-Ag 93, p. 32.
    "Remembering Solomon Mahlangu, Reburied This Week." [BostonR] (18:3/4) Je -
    Ag 93, p. 32.

1886. FALVIUS SPURIUS
   "Flavius Spurius Replies" (tr. by Jack Flavin). [SpoonR] (18:1) Wint-Spr 93, p. 43.
1887. FAMA, Maria
   "Coats." [Footwork] (23) 93, p. 101.
   "Eravamo a Napoli." [Footwork] (23) 93, p. 101-102.
   "The Ghost in My Bed." [Footwork] (23) 93, p. 101.
1888. FAMER, Rod
   "Stolen" (The first two lines, the two "stolen" lines, are a sentence written by T.S.
      Eliot). [DogRR] (12:1, #23) Spr-Sum 93, p. 2.
1889. FAN, Xinmin
   "The Knife" (tr. of Jiaxin Wang, w. Stephen Haven). [AmerPoR] (22:6) N-D 93, p.
      37.
1890. FARALLO, Livio
   "Detente." [SlipS] (13) 93, p. 106-108.
   "Like Any Hall of Famer." [SlipS] (13) 93, p. 104-105.
1891. FAREWELL, Patricia
   "At the Motel Coffee Shop." [NewYorkQ] (52) 93, p. 48.
   "Letting Go." [NewYorkQ] (51) 93, p. 52.
1892. FARGAS, Laura
   "Actively Speciating Even Now." [Poetry] (162:4) Jl 93, p. 194.
   "Grass the Fine Body Hairs of Earth." [Poetry] (162:4) Jl 93, p. 194.
   "Timshel: Thou Mayest." [GeoR] (47:4) Wint 93, p. 664-665.
   "Wave & Particle." [GeoR] (47:1) Spr 93, p. 60.
   "Winter, Leper of the World" (after Rouault). [GeoR] (47:1) Spr 93, p. 60.
1893. FARGNOLI, Patricia
   "Weed in Drought." [MidwQ] (34:2) Wint 93, p. 214.
1894. FARIS, Jordan
   "First Love." [DogRR] (12:2, #24) Fall-Wint 93, p. 26.
1895. FARLEY, Joseph
   "Birds." [PaintedB] (50/51) 93, p. 104.
   "Flashback II." [SlipS] (13) 93, p. 76.
   "Hog." [Pearl] (19) Fall-Wint 93, p. 70.
   "The Mountain." [Bogg] (66) Wint 92-93, p. 50.
1896. FARLEY, Roger
   "Lent." [Sequoia] (34/35) 92-93, p. 55.
1897. FARMER, Rod
   "Details." [Elf] (3:3) Fall 93, p. 33.
   "Island." [Wind] (23:72) 93, p. 8.
   "A Thrown Stone." [WebR] (17) Fall 93, p. 68.
1898. FARMER, Steven
   "Relay." [Avec] (6:1) 93, p. 39-42.
1899. FARNSWORTH, John
   "Holy Water." [ChironR] (12:4/13:1, #37/38) Wint 93-Spr 94, p. 29.
1900. FARNSWORTH, Robert
   "After Dinner." [BelPoJ] (43:3) Spr 93, p. 30-31.
   "An Eagle Finer Than Truth" (In Memoriam A.K.H.). [SouthernR] (29:2) Spr, Ap
      93, p. 306-307.
   "Lot for Sale." [BelPoJ] (43:3) Spr 93, p. 31.
1901. FARQUHAR, Dion
   "Left Us Talking" (For Vivian and Gene). [SinW] (49) Spr-Sum 93, p. 75-76.
1902. FARR, Robert
   "Avalokitesvara" (the buddha of compassion). [Lactuca] (17) Apr 93, p. 9.
   "Chromatography." [Lactuca] (17) Apr 93, p. 9-10.
   "Postcard to My Father." [Lactuca] (17) Apr 93, p. 10-11.
1903. FARR, Sheila
   "The Sari Thief." [NewYorkQ] (50) 93, p. 70.
1904. FARRAH, George
   "Ignore the Wires" (Selections: 3 poems). [WashR] (18:6) Ap-My 93, p. 23.
1905. FARRELL, Kate
   "Albert Pinkham Ryder's 'Dead Bird'." [AntigR] (92) Wint 93, p. 93.
   "Environs of Tangiers 1912." [AntigR] (92) Wint 93, p. 92.
   "Geography." [AntigR] (92) Wint 93, p. 94.
   "In Memory of Patrick Kavanagh (1905-1967)." [AntigR] (92) Wint 93, p. 91.
   "Mushrooms." [AntigR] (92) Wint 93, p. 95.
1906. FARRELL, Pamela B.
   "Mayflower's Yellow Rose." [Footwork] (23) 93, p. 122.

"Pride." [Footwork] (23) 93, p. 121.
1907. FASCIANI, Joseph E.
"Another First Day" (for Arthur Hoehn). [AmerS] (62:2) Spr 93, p. 246.
"November 24, 1969." [OnTheBus] (5:2, #12) Sum-Fall 93, p. 73.
1908. FASEL, Ida
"Gothic." [ChrC] (110:36) 15 D 93, p. 1269.
"Listening to Brahms." [CapeR] (28:1) Spr 93, p. 39.
"With This Ring." [ChrC] (110:8) 10 Mr 93, p. 266.
1909. FAUDREE, Paja
"Awake." [Agni] (37) 93, p. 35-36.
"Lefty." [Agni] (37) 93, p. 37.
1910. FAULKNER, Pete
"English Summer, 1861." [Bogg] (66) Wint 92-93, p. 16.
1911. FAUVELL, Anne
"Riding Cross-Bronx Expressway." [Writer] (106:6) Je 93, p. 20.
1912. FAY, Steve
"The Milkweed Parables." [TriQ] (88) Fall 93, p. 53-66.
"Science." [SnailPR] (3:1) Fall-Wint 93, p. 20.
1913. FEDERMAN, Raymond
"A Little Request" (w. George Chambers). [ProseP] (2) 93, p. 21.
"The Princess and the Frog" (w. George Chambers). [ProseP] (2) 93, p. 20.
1914. FEDERSPIEL, Jürg
"Paracelsus" (Für Margarita, in German and English, tr. by Ellen and Ernest H. von
Nardroff). [LitR] (36:4) Sum 93, p. 548-549.
1915. FEDO, David
"Unknown Poets, Unremembered People." [PoetryE] (36) Fall 93, p. 124-125.
1916. FEENY, Thomas
"Little Man" (tr. of Alfonsina Storni). [SnailPR] (3:1) Fall-Wint 93, p. 22.
1917. FEHLER, Gene
"Modern Medicine: Pro and Con." [Light] (5) Spr 93, p. 21.
"Only Jump Up on the Table." [Light] (7) Aut 93, p. 21.
"Pitcher: A Sestina." [Spitball] (45) Fall 93, p. 15-16.
FEI, Moi
See MOI, Fei
1918. FEIN, Richard J.
"Kafka and Milena in Bed." [GrahamHR] (17) Fall 93, p. 88-89.
1919. FEINFELD, D. A.
"For Howard Nemerov" (1920-1991). [CapeR] (28:1) Spr 93, p. 15.
1920. FEINSTEIN, Robert N.
"Naked Ape." [HolCrit] (30:5) D 93, p. 20.
"Ogden Nash Revisited." [Bogg] (66) Wint 92-93, p. 37.
"The Right of Opinion." [Amelia] (7:2, #21) 93, p. 37.
"Unsung Hero." [Amelia] (7:2, #21) 93, p. 37.
1921. FEINSTEIN, Sascha
"Misterioso." [DenQ] (27:3) Wint 93, p. 26-27.
1922. FEIRSTEIN, Frederick
"Creature of History: A Sequence" (9 poems). [QRL] (12:32/33) 93, p. 131-141.
1923. FELD, Andrew
"Not Included in This Landscape." [ParisR] (35:128) Fall 93, p. 147.
1924. FELDMAN, Irving
"Interrupted Prayers." [ParisR] (35:126) Spr 93, p. 139-144.
"Variations on a Theme by May Swenson" (In memory of May). [ParisR] (35:127)
Sum 93, p. 201-203.
"Warm Enough." [YaleR] (81:1) Ja 93, p. 85-88.
1925. FELDMAN, Laura
"High Mortgages" (from a collaboration with Jean Miller). [Avec] (6:1) 93, p. 61.
"Iatrogenic" (from a collaboration with Jean Miller). [Avec] (6:1) 93, p. 62.
1926. FELDMAN, Marilyn
"Birds." [BrooklynR] (10) 93, p. 77.
1927. FELDMAN, Ruth
"The Hypocrite" (from "Neurosuite," tr. of Margherita Guidacci). [InterPR] (19:2)
Fall 93, p. 51.
"Instant" (from "Hive of Mirrors," tr. of Gina Labriola). [NewRena] (8:3, #26) Spr
93, p. 57.
"Kite" (to F., from "Hive of Mirrors," tr. of Gina Labriola). [NewRena] (8:3, #26)
Spr 93, p. 55.

"Night" (tr. of Lucio Piccolo, w. B. Swann). [QRL] (12:32/33) 93, p. 488-489.
"The Wind Is Hungry" (from "Hive of Mirrors," tr. of Gina Labriola). [NewRena]
   (8:3, #26) Spr 93, p. 53.
1928. FELICIANO, Margarita
   "Be-In" (in Spanish and English, tr. by Margarita Feliciano). [InterPR] (19:1) Spr
      93, p. 4-5.
   "Be-In" (tr. of Margarita Feliciano). [InterPR] (19:1) Spr 93, p. 4-5.
1929. FELSTINER, John
   "Tenebrae" (English tr. of Paul Celan). [TriQ] (87) Spr-Sum 93, p. 196-197.
FEMINA, Gerry La
   See LaFEMINA, Gerry
1930. FENG, Anita N.
   "By the Blue Flame of 2 AM." [PraS] (67:1) Spr 93, p. 123.
   "An Old Recipe." [IllinoisR] (1:1) Fall 93, p. 22.
   "Something About Not Being Safe." [NowestR] (31:2) 93, p. 19.
   "The Street of Chinese Restaurants." [PraS] (67:1) Spr 93, p. 122-123.
   "The Third Visit." [NowestR] (31:2) 93, p. 20.
1931. FENN, Kimball
   "Things Have a Way of Getting Away." [Thrpny] (54) Sum 93, p. 15.
1932. FENSTERMAKER, Vesle
   "The Consumers." [HopewellR] (5) 93, p. 96.
1933. FENTON, James
   "For Andrew Wood." [NewYRB] (40:21) 16 D 93, p. 16.
1934. FERGUSON, Judith
   "Body Language" (with love, to my father). [HangL] (62) 93, p. 23.
1935. FERLINGHETTI, Lawrence
   "A Buddha in the Woodpile." [Tricycle] (3:2) Wint 93, p. 33.
1936. FERMO, Teri
   "You." [Nimrod] (37:1) Fall-Wint 93, p. 77-79.
1937. FERNANDEZ, Amando
   "La Presencia" (con Reinaldo Arenas). [LindLM] (12:1) Mr 93, p. 12.
1938. FERNANDEZ, Mauricio
   "Las Cartas Extranjeras." [LindLM] (12:1) Mr 93, p. 4.
   "Más Números y una Palabra." [LindLM] (12:1) Mr 93, p. 4.
   "País Portátil." [LindLM] (12:1) Mr 93, p. 4.
1939. FERNANDEZ, Raúl
   "3:00 P.M." [Americas] (21:2) Sum 93, p. 70.
   "Mistakes." [Americas] (21:2) Sum 93, p. 70.
   "Poor Us." [Americas] (21:2) Sum 93, p. 69.
1940. FERNAU, Sandra
   "Intersection Blood" (Excerpt). [13thMoon] (12:1/2) 93-94, p. 28-29.
1941. FERNCASE, Anne
   "And Then." [TickleAce] (23) Spr-Sum 92, p. 69-71.
1942. FERRA, Lorraine
   "January." [BellArk] (9:4) Jl-Ag 93, p. 1.
   "This World." [BellArk] (9:4) Jl-Ag 93, p. 8.
1943. FERRARELLI, Rina
   "Linens." [ArtfulD] (24/25) 93, p. 14.
   "Maybe Even This Memory Is Useless" (tr. of Leonardo Sinisgalli). [ArtfulD]
      (24/25) 93, p. 15.
1944. FERRARI, Mary
   "Evening in South Africa." [HangL] (63) 93, p. 11.
   "The Golden Highway to Boipatong." [HangL] (63) 93, p. 8-9.
   "Johannesburg Jacarandas" (for Menzi Ndaba). [HangL] (63) 93, p. 10-11.
1945. FERRATER, Gabriel
   "A Furtive Life" (tr. by Michael Barea). [Vis] (43) 93, p. 9.
   "My Reader" (tr. by Michael Barea). [Vis] (43) 93, p. 9.
1946. FERREIRO, Celso Emilio
   "The Lesson" (tr. by Marian H. Moore). [Vis] (43) 93, p. 22.
   "Sweet Autumn" (tr. by Marian H. Moore). [Vis] (43) 93, p. 21.
1947. FERRO, Jeanpaul
   "Bend Sinister." [DogRR] (12:1, #23) Spr-Sum 93, p. 18.
1948. FERRY, David
   "Tu Ne Quaesieris" (Ode I.11, tr. of Horace). [BostonR] (18:6) D 93-Ja 94, p. 35.
   "When We Were Children" (tr. of a poem by the 13th-century poet known as der
      Wilde Alexander). [Raritan] (13:1) Sum 93, p. 30-31.

1949. FESSLER, Michael
"Silver." [WormR] (33:4, #132) 93, p. 181.
"Stamped Objects." [WormR] (33:4, #132) 93, p. 180-181.
FICK, Marlon Ohnesorge
See OHNESORGE-FICK, Marlon
1950. FICKERT, Kurt
"Going Back to a December Day." [Elf] (3:2) Sum 93, p. 43.
1951. FIELD, Andrew
"Lord Byron in Family Therapy." [WestHR] (47:1) Spr 93, p. 58-59.
1952. FIELD, Edward
"Dying." [PaintedB] (50/51) 93, p. 72-73.
"New Yorkers." [Pearl] (17) Spr 93, p. 42.
"One More for the Quilt" (For Seth Allen). [Art&Und] (2:2) My-Je 93, p. 43.
"The Scream." [Art&Und] (2:2) My-Je 93, p. 42.
"The Veteran." [Art&Und] (2:2) My-Je 93, p. 41.
1953. FIELD, Greg
"The Sky Opens." [LaurelR] (27:2) Sum 93, p. 75.
1954. FIELD, Simon
"Homeward Turn." [Bogg] (66) Wint 92-93, p. 19.
1955. FIELD, Susan
"Beyond 65." [SpoonR] (18:2) Sum-Fall 93, p. 74.
"Learning to Read." [SpoonR] (18:2) Sum-Fall 93, p. 73.
1956. FIELDS, Gregory A.
"This Is Important." [SpoonR] (18:1) Wint-Spr 93, p. 120.
1957. FIELDS, Leslie
"Sea-Cucumber." [CapeR] (28:2) Fall 93, p. 10.
1958. FIFER, Kenneth
"In the Talmud." [AmerPoR] (22:4) Jl-Ag 93, p. 31.
1959. FILES, Meg
"The Love Hunter" (For Larry Stallings, murdered 10/3/92). [Vis] (42) 93, p. 35.
1960. FILKINS, Peter
"Christmas at the Airport." [Hellas] (4:1) Spr 93, p. 25.
"The Film." [HiramPoR] (53/54) Fall 92-Sum 93, p. 101.
"Traveling in America." [Agni] (37) 93, p. 209-211.
1961. FILKOVA, Fedya
"Vulnerability" (tr. by Lisa Sapinkopf and Georgi Belev). [Paint] (19:38) Aut 92, p. 72.
1962. FILLMORE, Adrienne
"Shoot-out at Sun-down." [Writer] (106:6) Je 93, p. 18.
1963. FINALE, Frank
"Looking for Miss Gordon." [NewRena] (8:3, #26) Spr 93, p. 49.
"Lost." [NewRena] (8:3, #26) Spr 93, p. 50.
"Sunday." [NewRena] (8:3, #26) Spr 93, p. 51.
1964. FINCH, Annie
"The Last Mer-Mother." [SoCoast] (14) Ja 93, p. 17-19.
"The Pitcher." [Sparrow] (60) Sum 93, p. 21.
"The Raptor." [Sparrow] (60) Sum 93, p. 48.
1965. FINCH, Roger
"Auto-da-Fé." [HiramPoR] (53/54) Fall 92-Sum 93, p. 37.
"If This Is Belgium." [Poem] (70) N 93, p. 18.
"Snow Angel." [Poem] (70) N 93, p. 19.
1966. FINCKE, Gary
"Coal." [PaintedB] (50/51) 93, p. 77.
"Disrepair." [LaurelR] (27:1) Wint 93, p. 12-13.
"The Egypt Street." [FourQ] (7:1) Spr 93, p. 14.
"Goldilocks." [WebR] (17) Fall 93, p. 105.
"The Great Chain of Being." [MissouriR] (16:2) 93, p. 105-116.
"The Living Fence." [Outbr] (24) 93, p. 95.
"Reversing the Process." [Outbr] (24) 93, p. 93-94.
"The Theories for Ball Lightning." [PennR] (5:2) 93, p. 28.
"The Thoreau Cane." [PoetL] (88:1) Spr 93, p. 41-42.
"What the Lecturer Showed Us." [Outbr] (24) 93, p. 96.
"Why We Care About Quarks." [KenR] (NS 15:4) Fall 93, p. 111.
1967. FINK, Robert A.
"Breakdown." [Border] (2) Spr 93, p. 20.
"Life Imitates Art in Abilene." [Border] (2) Spr 93, p. 21-22.

1968. FINKEL, Donald
"Andante Cantabile" (tr. of Bei Dao, w. Xueliang Chen). [SenR] (23:1/2) Wint 93,
p. 158-159.
"Archaic Figurine from Nayarit." [QRL] (12:32/33) 93, p. 415.
"Bridge" tr. of Bei Dao, w. Xueliang Chen). [DenQ] (28:1) Sum 93, p. 24.
"Commercial" (tr. of Bei Dao, w. Xueliang Chen). [SenR] (23:1/2) Wint 93, p. 157.
"Deserted City" (tr. of Bei Dao, w. Xueliang Chen). [ManhatR] (7:1) Fall 93, p. 51.
"Exile." [DenQ] (27:4) Spr 93, p. 5.
"Guide to Summer" (tr. of Bei Dao, w. Xueliang Chen). [SenR] (23:1/2) Wint 93, p.
160.
"Hurried Night" (tr. of Bei Dao, w. Xueliang Chen). [SenR] (23:1/2) Wint 93, p.
161.
"The Invention of Strangers." [ManhatR] (7:1) Fall 93, p. 62.
"Loyalty" (tr. of Bei Dao, w. Xueliang Chen). [ManhatR] (7:1) Fall 93, p. 49.
"Night Patrol" (tr. of Bei Dao, w. Xueliang Chen). [ManhatR] (7:1) Fall 93, p. 50.
"Notes of an Afternoon" (tr. of Bei Dao, w. Xueliang Chen). [ManhatR] (7:1) Fall
93, p. 52.
"On Eternity" (tr. of Bei Dao, w. Xueliang Chen). [ManhatR] (7:1) Fall 93, p. 55.
"Piano Man." [ManhatR] (7:1) Fall 93, p. 61.
"Portrait" (tr. of Bei Dao, w. Xueliang Chen). [SenR] (23:1/2) Wint 93, p. 162.
"Scenery" (tr. of Bei Dao, w. Xueliang Chen). [ManhatR] (7:1) Fall 93, p. 54.
"Song for Syrinx and Pennywhistle." [QRL] (12:32/33) 93, p. 414.
"Sower" (tr. of Bei Dao, w. Xueliang Chen). [SenR] (23:1/2) Wint 93, p. 163.
"Untitled: At the front, defending the mother tongue" (tr. of Bei Dao, w. Xueliang
Chen). [ManhatR] (7:1) Fall 93, p. 53.
"Variations" (tr. of Bei Dao, w. Xueliang Chen). [ManhatR] (7:1) Fall 93, p. 48.
"Waiting for a Heart." [ParisR] (35:127) Sum 93, p. 131-133.
1969. FINKELSTEIN, Caroline
"Autumn Again." [VirQR] (69:3) Sum 93, p. 501-502.
"Contradiction This Spring." [AntR] (51:2) Spr 93, p. 231.
"The Dwelling." [TriQ] (89) Wint 93-94, p. 185.
"The Lovers." [VirQR] (69:3) Sum 93, p. 500-501.
"See the Pyramids." [VirQR] (69:3) Sum 93, p. 502.
"Thanksgiving." [SenR] (23:1/2) Wint 93, p. 113.
1970. FINKELSTEIN, Miriam
"Unraveling." [Comm] (120:11) 4 Je 93, p. 22.
1971. FINKELSTEIN, Norman
"Imaginary Photographs" (Excerpts). [Talisman] (10) Spr 93, p. 148-149.
"Klamm." [Salm] (100) Fall 93, p. 164-165.
1972. FINLEY, L. D.
"Christmas Remembrance for an Arkanasas House" (803 Champagnolle Road, El
Dorado, AR). [Poem] (69) My 93, p. 30.
"Dawn of the Barn Buring" (Ellis County, OK, 1931). [Poem] (69) My 93, p. 28-29.
"Woman Quilter — Woodard, Oklahoma." [Poem] (69) My 93, p. 26-27.
1973. FINLEY, Michael
"The Newmans of Connecticut." [HiramPoR] (53/54) Fall 92-Sum 93, p. 38.
1974. FINNEGAN, James
"Gone Bad." [Chelsea] (54) 93, p. 99.
"Martyr of These Miles and Hours." [Chelsea] (54) 93, p. 100.
1975. FINNELL, Dennis
"Acmeist." [MassR] (34:4) Wint 93-94, p. 544.
"Ballade, U.S.A." (after one of Villon's "poems in slang"). [LaurelR] (27:2) Sum 93,
p. 88-89.
"The Book of Moonlight." [SouthernPR] (33:2) Fall 93, p. 53.
"Cupola." [PraS] (67:3) Fall 93, p. 122-123.
"Invasions of Privacies." [LaurelR] (27:2) Sum 93, p. 89-90.
"The Irish Wilderness." [DenQ] (27:3) Wint 93, p. 28-29.
"The Last Sky." [SouthernPR] (33:2) Fall 93, p. 52-53.
"Many Happy Returns." [LaurelR] (27:2) Sum 93, p. 90.
"Rapunzel, Rapunzel." [IllinoisR] (1:1) Fall 93, p. 16-17.
1976. FINNEY, Janice
"Our Living Room." [PoetryE] (36) Fall 93, p. 63-64.
1977. FIORINI, Greg
"The Lateen Cross." [Writer] (106:10) O 93, p. 27.
1978. FIORITO, Joe
"Eskimos Carving." [Grain] (21:2) Sum 93, p. 53.

"Last April." [Grain] (21:2) Sum 93, p. 54.
1979. FIRER, Susan
"Building the House of Crazy." [ChiR] (39:1) 93, p. 81-82.
"God Sightings." [CreamCR] (17:2) Fall 93, p. 175.
"I, the Excommunicate." [CreamCR] (17:2) Fall 93, p. 172-173.
"The Mongolian Contortionist with Pigeons." [ChiR] (39:1) 93, p. 79-80.
"Phantom Love." [ChiR] (39:1) 93, p. 83-85.
"Saint Wilgefortis." [CreamCR] (17:2) Fall 93, p. 174.
FIRMAT, Gustavo Pérez
See PÉREZ FIRMAT, Gustavo
1980. FIRNBERG, Virginia
"Arched Neck." [Avec] (6:1) 93, p. 131-132.
1981. FISCHER, Neil
"His Forearm Across My Mouth." [JamesWR] (10:2) Wint 93, p. 17.
1982. FISCHER, Norman
"Success" (Excerpt). [ChiR] (39:3/4) 93, p. 74.
1983. FISCHEROVA, Sylva
"For Greater Precision" (tr. by Vera Orac and Stuart Friebert). [Field] (49) Fall 93,
p. 86.
"Land of Mud" (Warsaw-Leningrad Express, tr. by Vera Orac and Stuart Friebert).
[Field] (49) Fall 93, p. 88.
"A Totally New Time, a Completely New Era" (tr. by Vera Orac and Stuart
Friebert). [Field] (49) Fall 93, p. 87.
1984. FISH, Cheryl
"For Mutual Consent." [NewAW] (11) Sum-Fall 93, p. 103.
"Undulation." [Talisman] (10) Spr 93, p. 159.
1985. FISHER, George William
"Poem with Prologue." [PaintedB] (50/51) 93, p. 92.
1986. FISHER, Joan
"January 25, 1993." [AnotherCM] (26) Fall 93, p. 11-12.
"November 16, 1988." [AnotherCM] (26) Fall 93, p. 13-14.
1987. FISHER, Marilyn
"You, Snake." [Elf] (3:3) Fall 93, p. 36.
1988. FISHEYE, Kaula
"Mele Ko'ihonua no Lili'u" (A genealogical chant for Lili'u, tr. by Lilikala
Kame'eleihiwa). [HawaiiR] (16:3, #36) Wint 93, p. 13.
1989. FISHMAN, Charles
"For My Body." [Boulevard] (8:1, #22) Spr 93, p. 117.
"A Goddess." [Gaia] (1/2) Ap-Jl 93, p. 47.
"A Space Telescope." [Gaia] (1/2) Ap-Jl 93, p. 47.
1990. FISHMAN, Lisa
"Night Skiing." [LouisL] (10:1) Spr 93, p. 3.
"Three-Quarter Moon." [PoetryNW] (34:4) Wint 93-94, p. 44.
"Tracks" (Winner, 1993 Louisiana Literature Prize for Poetry). [LouisL] (10:1) Spr
93, p. 1-2.
1991. FISK, Brent
"Dress." [BellArk] (9:2) Mr-Ap 93, p. 8.
1992. FISK, Molly
"I Recommend Norway." [PassN] (14:2) Wint 93, p. 51.
"On the Disinclination to Scream." [OnTheBus] (5:2, #12) Sum-Fall 93, p. 74-75.
1993. FITCH, John Hawk
"Haiku." [HiramPoR] (53/54) Fall 92-Sum 93, p. 39.
"Sway." [HiramPoR] (53/54) Fall 92-Sum 93, p. 39.
1994. FITTERMAN, Robert
"American History: the Snap Wyatt Poems." [WestCL] (27:2, #11) Fall 93, p. 13-19.
"Here and Then" (to Kim). [GrandS] (12:1, #45) 93, p. 150-151.
1995. FITZPATRICK, Janice
"Last Light on the Keel" (for J. H. Fitzpatrick). [US1] (28/29) 93, p. 28.
1996. FITZPATRICK, Mark
"Sanctuary." [Parting] (6:1) Sum 93, p. 31.
"The Serpent." [Poem] (70) N 93, p. 46.
"The Vision." [Poem] (70) N 93, p. 47.
1997. FITZSIMMONS, Thomas
"Power — Three Lectures." [Nimrod] (37:1) Fall-Wint 93, p. 112.
1998. FIX, Charlene
"Night Diving." [PraF] (14:2) Sum 93, p. 21.

161

1999. FIXEL, Lawrence
"Goodbye Home. Hello Somewhere." [ProseP] (2) 93, p. 36-37.
"Looking Backward" (1969). [Talisman] (11) Fall 93, p. 132-133.
"On the Death of Aldo Moro" (Rome, May 9, 1978). [Talisman] (11) Fall 93, p. 133-134.
"What the Wastebasket Tells" (1940)." [Talisman] (11) Fall 93, p. 130.
"Year of the Bloodhound" (1952). [Talisman] (11) Fall 93, p. 130-131.
"Year of the Bloodhound" (Duncan's Version). [Talisman] (11) Fall 93, p. 131-132.
FLAMME, Michelle la
See La FLAMME, Michelle
2000. FLANDERS, Jane
"Aunt Maude's Pocketbook." [QRL] (12:32/33) 93, p. 147.
"Blue Lobster." [QRL] (12:32/33) 93, p. 143-144.
"The Bow." [QRL] (12:32/33) 93, p. 142-143.
"From a Family Obituary: October 8, 1887" (Goerge Snowberger, age 77 years, death by drowning). [QRL] (12:32/33) 93, p. 147-148.
"Gifts." [QRL] (12:32/33) 93, p. 141-142.
"The Hard Way." [QRL] (12:32/33) 93, p. 144-145.
"The Nest." [QRL] (12:32/33) 93, p. 146-147.
"Sheba." [QRL] (12:32/33) 93, p. 145-146.
2001. FLAVIN, Jack
"Fair Exchange" (tr. of Catullus). [SpoonR] (18:1) Wint-Spr 93, p. 42.
"Flavius Spurius Replies" (tr. of Falvius Spurius). [SpoonR] (18:1) Wint-Spr 93, p. 43.
"Letter to Flavius" (tr. of Catullus). [ApalQ] (35) 90, p. 49.
"Poem After Sappho" (tr. of Catullus). [ApalQ] (35) 90, p. 51.
"A Selection of Epigrams" (tr. of Catullus, Juvenal, and Martial). [SpoonR] (18:1) Wint-Spr 93, p. 41.
"Suffenus" (tr. of Catullus). [ApalQ] (35) 90, p. 50.
2002. FLEISCHMANN, Daniel Ari
"Synonyms." [Pearl] (17) Spr 93, p. 45.
2003. FLEMING, Robert
"Nutty." [Contact] (11:65/66/67) Spr 93, p. 62.
2004. FLESHMAN, Rob
"Seems Like an Ocean Between Us." [SouthernPR] (33:2) Fall 93, p. 27-28.
2005. FLETCHER, Andy
"Archbishops." [Bogg] (66) Wint 92-93, p. 58.
2006. FLETCHER, Luellen
"The World Series." [Spitball] (44) Sum 93, p. 13-14.
2007. FLINT, Austin
"The Brief Life of Our Ancestors" (tr. of Wislawa Szymborska, w. Grazyna Drabik). [QRL] (12:32/33) 93, p. 340-341.
"Dealings with the Dead" (tr. of Wislawa Szymborska, w. Grazyna Drabik). [QRL] (12:32/33) 93, p. 345.
"End of the Century" (tr. of Wislawa Szymborska, w. Grazyna Drabik). [QRL] (12:32/33) 93, p. 344-345.
"The First Photograph of Hitler" (tr. of Wislawa Szymborska, w. Grazyna Drabik). [QRL] (12:32/33) 93, p. 348.
"Funeral" (tr. of Wislawa Szymborska, w. Grazyna Drabik). [QRL] (12:32/33) 93, p. 346.
"Miracle Fair" (tr. of Wislawa Szymborska, w. Grazyna Drabik). [QRL] (12:32/33) 93, p. 347-348.
"People on a Bridge" (tr. of Wislawa Szymborska, w. Grazyna Drabik). [QRL] (12:32/33) 93, p. 342-344.
"Possibilities" (tr. of Wislawa Szymborska, w. Grazyna Drabik). [QRL] (12:32/33) 93, p. 349-350.
"Stage-Fright" (tr. of Wislawa Szymborska, w. Grazyna Drabik). [QRL] (12:32/33) 93, p. 350-351.
"To the Ark" (tr. of Wislawa Szymborska, w. Grazyna Drabik). [QRL] (12:32/33) 93, p. 341-342.
2008. FLINT, Elizabeth
"Cutting Remarks." [PennR] (5:2) 93, p. 23.
"Physical Geology." [PennR] (5:2) 93, p. 24-25.
2009. FLINTOFF, Eddie
"Dark Afternoon" (tr. of Luis Cernuda). [InterPR] (19:2) Fall 93, p. 23.
"The Garden" (tr. of Luis Cernuda). [InterPR] (19:2) Fall 93, p. 19, 21.

2010. FLOCK, Miriam
"Homebody." [SouthwR] (78:2) Spr 93, p. 230.
"If Ontogeny Does Not Recapitulate Phylogeny, Then What Is Metaphor?" [Poetry]
(161:4) Ja 93, p. 203.
2011. FLOYD, Claire
"After the War." [Writer] (106:3) Mr 93, p. 25.
2012. FLYNN, A. Benington
"For All I Know, In a Cleared Patch of Wood a Granite Rock Floats Free of Gravity
Unseen by You or Me, Therefore." [SmPd] (30:2, #88) Spr 93, p. 35.
"Of Saints Sleeping." [SmPd] (30:2, #88) Spr 93, p. 35.
"Reappraisal While Sliding Down a Trough Made Slick by Watery Lies and
Layoffs." [SmPd] (30:2, #88) Spr 93, p. 36.
2013. FLYNN, Nicholas
"Fuckability." [GrahamHR] (17) Fall 93, p. 18-19.
2014. FLYTHE, Starkey
"Man Wearing Neck Collar Entering Lawyer's Office." [LullwaterR] (4:2) Spr-Sum
93, p. 66-67.
FOE, Mark de
See DeFOE, Mark
2015. FOERSTER, Richard
"Late Summer, Chill Nights." [SoCoast] (15) Je 93, p. 47.
"Life Drawing." [Poetry] (162:4) Jl 93, p. 192.
"Sansevieria." [GettyR] (6:3) Sum 93, p. 506-507.
2016. FOGAL, Michele
"Magic Dog Man." [PraF] (14:3) Aut 93, p. 51.
2017. FOGARTY, Mark
"Hawthorne." [Footwork] (23) 93, p. 78.
"Niagara." [JlNJPo] (15:1) Spr 93, p. 40.
2018. FOGEL, Alice B.
"Fishing." [WorldL] (4) 93, p. 21-22.
"See, the Smell of My Son." [WorldL] (4) 93, p. 20.
2019. FOGG, Margaret A.
"Marry Me." [PraF] (14:3) Aut 93, p. 52.
2020. FOLEY, Adelle
"For Judy & Richard Segasture Upon Their Departure for Phoenix (Keep in
Touch)." [PoetryUSA] (25/26) 93, p. 30.
2021. FOLEY, Jack
"Wings." [PoetryUSA] (25/26) 93, p. 26.
2022. FOLEY, Louis
"Punch-Drunk." [Bogg] (66) Wint 92-93, p. 66.
2023. FOLLETT, C. B.
"In the Forest." [HeavenB] (10) Wint-Spr 93, p. 10.
"The Moth." [Calyx] (14:3) Sum 93, p. 43.
"The Picker." [Border] (2) Spr 93, p. 25.
"There Is a Snake Which Has Appeared Here. Come See the God!" (Hapur, India).
[SoCoast] (15) Je 93, p. 50-51.
"Western Hemlock." [DogRR] (12:1, #23) Spr-Sum 93, p. 4.
2024. FOLSOM, Eric
"The Wise." [TickleAce] (23) Spr-Sum 92, p. 35.
2025. FONG, Peter
"I Honestly Don't Remember." [Parting] (6:1) Sum 93, p. 11.
"Noon Sun, East Bay." [Parting] (6:1) Sum 93, p. 7.
2026. FONTENOT, Ken
"Bees" (tr. of Heinz Piontek). [AmerPoR] (22:2) Mr-Ap 93, p. 42.
"Getting Something Done" (tr. of Heinz Piontek). [AmerPoR] (22:2) Mr-Ap 93, p.
42.
"How Music Fought Its Way Through" (tr. of Heinz Piontek). [AmerPoR] (22:2)
Mr-Ap 93, p. 42.
"Return to a Spring Full of Little Boys." [KenR] (NS 15:1) Wint 93, p. 95-96.
2027. FOOTMAN, Jennifer
"Dali's January Moon." [Descant] (24:2, #81) Sum 93, p. 7.
"Distances." [PraS] (67:4) Wint 93, p. 61.
"Father." [PraS] (67:4) Wint 93, p. 60.
"Kensington Place." [PraS] (67:4) Wint 93, p. 59-60.
"Lunar Eclipse 16th Aug 1989." [Descant] (24:2, #81) Sum 93, p. 9.
"Patient." [Arc] (31) Aut 93, p. 72-74.

2028. FORCHÉ, Carolyn
"The Notebook of Uprisings." [AmerPoR] (22:1) Ja-F 93, p. 26-29.
2029. FORD, Cathy
"Also, How I Lost Her." [CanLit] (138/139) Fall-Wint 93, p. 52.
2030. FORD, Michael C.
"The Demented Chauffeur." [OnTheBus] (5:2, #12) Sum-Fall 93, p. 76-77.
"Treason Would Fain Be in One So Fair." [OnTheBus] (6:1, #13) Wint 93-Spr 94, p. 91.
2031. FORD, William
"Desert Romance." [PoetC] (25:1) Fall 93, p. 33.
"Of Ray Young Bear, Des Moines Poetry Festival 1992." [PoetC] (25:1) Fall 93, p. 34.
2032. FORHAN, Chris
"But Look Where Sadly the Poor Wretch Comes Reading." [WillowS] (31) Wint 93, p. 74.
"Panorama Without a View." [WestB] (31/32) 93, p. 33.
"Sanctum Sanctorum." [ArtfulD] (24/25) 93, p. 113.
2033. FORMAN, Ethan
"Metro Station VDNKH." [AntigR] (93-94) Spr-Sum 93, p. 183.
"The Unmaking of Stalin." [AntigR] (93-94) Spr-Sum 93, p. 181-182.
2034. FORNOFF, Frederick
"Geografía Invisible de América" (Selections: 2 poems, tr. of Laureano Albán). [Luz] (4) My 93, p. 9-24.
"Itinerary of Sleep" (from "Autumn's Legacy," tr. of Laureano Albán). [Luz] (5) N 93, p. 49.
2035. FORSSTRÖM, Tua
"I Stopped Too Long" (tr. by David McDuff). [Stand] (34:4) Aut 93, p. 33.
"There Is a Door" (tr. by David McDuff). [Stand] (34:4) Aut 93, p. 33.
2036. FORST, Eric
"Charting Particulars." [HawaiiR] (17:3, #39) Fall 93, p. 42.
2037. FORT, Charles
"For Two Daughters." [AmerPoR] (22:6) N-D 93, p. 56.
2038. FORTIN, Célyne
"Histoire d'Hiver." [Os] (37) Wint 93, p. 12-13.
2039. FORTUNATO-GALT, Margot
"After Dachau." [SpoonR] (18:2) Sum-Fall 93, p. 83-85.
2040. FOSS, Phillip
"There Is Failure to Ignite, As If There Were No Air." [Avec] (6:1) 93, p. 127-128.
2041. FOSTER, Barbara
"Lament for Frida Kahlo." [LindLM] (12:2/4) Ap-D 93, p. 23.
2042. FOSTER, Clarise
"Paper Swans." [PraF] (14:1) Spr 93, p. 122.
2043. FOSTER, Greg
"The Sick Child: Homage to Edvard Munch." [Crazy] (44) Spr 93, p. 66-67.
2044. FOSTER, Jeanne
"The Gate." [QRL] (12:32/33) 93, p. 152-153.
"The Pelican." [QRL] (12:32/33) 93, p. 157-158.
"Summer, 1987." [QRL] (12:32/33) 93, p. 149-150.
"Transplant." [QRL] (12:32/33) 93, p. 154-157.
"The Yellow Stone." [QRL] (12:32/33) 93, p. 150-152.
2045. FOSTER, Karen
"I. To All the Old Apollos." [NewYorkQ] (51) 93, p. 83.
"II. To Artemis, Protector of the Newly Born." [NewYorkQ] (51) 93, p. 83.
2046. FOSTER, Linda Nemec
"The Awkward Young Girl Approaching You" (for Gary Gildner). [IndR] (16:1) Spr 93, p. 163-164.
"Colors from the City of White: Photographs from Bielsko-Biala" (for Agnieszka). [ArtfulD] (24/25) 93, p. 10-11.
"Forgiving the Dead." [ArtfulD] (24/25) 93, p. 8-9.
"Fragments of Athena." [OnTheBus] (6:1, #13) Wint 93-Spr 94, p. 92-93.
"Inevitable Meetings" (tr. of Ewa Parma, w. Beata Kane). [InterPR] (19:2) Fall 93, p. 67.
"Karol's Bridge in Prague, Watercolor" (tr. of Ewa Parma, w. Beata Kane). [ArtfulD] (24/25) 93, p. 12.
"Men as Fathers" (for Tom). [IndR] (16:1) Spr 93, p. 165.

"Ode to My Knee" (or, I Love Reminiscing, tr. of Ewa Parma, w. Beata Kane). [InterPR] (19:2) Fall 93, p. 63.
"On the Second Day of Christmas" (tr. of Ewa Parma, w. the author). [ArtfulD] (24/25) 93, p. 13.
"On the Way" (for prophets, poets, visionaries and Miss Holly Golightly in her journey, tr. of Ewa Parma, w. Beata Kane). [InterPR] (19:2) Fall 93, p. 65.
"The Tao of Junk Mail." [ChironR] (12:4/13:1, #37/38) Wint 93-Spr 94, p. 15.
"The Therapeutist: After Magritte." [PassN] (14:1) Sum 93, p. 37.
"The Town That Voted the Earth Flat." [ArtfulD] (24/25) 93, p. 7.
2047. FOSTER, Michael
"Climacteric" (for Danny). [RagMag] (11:2) 93, p. 95-96.
"The Dancer." [CoalC] (7) Apr 93, p. 17.
"Light Change." [Poem] (70) N 93, p. 14.
"A Light Within the Light." [Poem] (70) N 93, p. 11.
"Matrimonial." [RagMag] (11:2) 93, p. 99.
"Only in America." [RagMag] (11:2) 93, p. 97-98.
"Snow Day." [Poem] (70) N 93, p. 12.
"Western Movie" (the final scene). [Poem] (70) N 93, p. 13.
2048. FOSTER, Robert
"For George" (d. November 24, 1993). [Grain] (21:3) Fall 93, p. 125.
2049. FOSTER, Sesshu
"Postcard to Akemi Miyazawa." [PaintedHR] (9) Spr 93, p. 9.
"Untitled: Little Joe was a vicious drunk." [Parting] (6:1) Sum 93, p. 63.
"Untitled: Peel the roof off Chemo's bakery and empty the glass case of pan dulce." [Caliban] (12) 93, p. 15.
"Untitled: The ringing sound when you lost your sense of humor." [Caliban] (12) 93, p. 14.
"Untitled: There was this big great dane that ran all over the neighborhood biting kids." [Caliban] (12) 93, p. 12.
"Untitled: Xiomara, she treats me well." [Caliban] (12) 93, p. 13.
2050. FOSTER, Tonya M.
"The Rape." [WestHR] (47:2) Sum 93, p. 166-167.
"What Remains." [WestHR] (47:2) Sum 93, p. 168-169.
2051. FOURTOUNI, Eleni
"The Doubt" (tr. of Melissanthi). [PoetryC] (13:3) 93, p. 20.
"The Ewe of the Vapors" (Selections: 1-2, tr. of Athena Papadaki). [PoetryC] (13:3) 93, p. 22.
"Marking Time" (tr. of Melissanthi). [PoetryC] (13:3) 93, p. 20.
"My Little Heart at Night" (tr. of Katerina Anghelaki Rooke). [PoetryC] (13:3) 93, p. 23.
"Progress" (tr. of Kiki Dimoula). [PoetryC] (13:3) 93, p. 21.
"Speaking of Eyes" (tr. of Katerina Anghelaki Rooke). [PoetryC] (13:3) 93, p. 23.
"Two Small Poems for a Riddle and a Street" (tr. of Kiki Dimoula). [PoetryC] (13:3) 93, p. 21.
"Under the Influence of Autumn" (tr. of Kiki Dimoula). [PoetryC] (13:3) 93, p. 21.
2052. FOWLER, Anne Carroll
"Fragments for an Elegy" (For Jotham Pierce, 1915-1990). [LitR] (36:2) Wint 93, p. 174-175.
2053. FOWLER, Ezra
"Where I Pray." [HeavenB] (10) Wint-Spr 93, p. 46.
2054. FOWLER, Sherman L.
"Bearing Witness." [Drumvoices] (1:1/2) Fall-Wint 91-92, p. 17.
"Blowin' in the Breeze" (Poetic dispatch from Ibadan, Nigeria to East St. Louis, IL, 1969). [Drumvoices] (1:1/2) Fall-Wint 91-92, p. 15-16.
"City-Street." [Drumvoices] (1:1/2) Fall-Wint 91-92, p. 18.
"Encounter with an African Princess." [Drumvoices] (1:1/2) Fall-Wint 91-92, p. 18.
"Lesson #121: Weights and Measures." [Drumvoices] (1:1/2) Fall-Wint 91-92, p. 19.
"Lesson #122: Weights and Measures." [Drumvoices] (1:1/2) Fall-Wint 91-92, p. 19.
"Rites de Passion." [Drumvoices] (1:1/2) Fall-Wint 91-92, p. 21.
"Street Cornor Man" [sic]. [Drumvoices] (1:1/2) Fall-Wint 91-92, p. 20-21.
"Three Who Passed: 1987 (Baldwin / Killens / Washington)." [Drumvoices] (1:1/2) Fall-Wint 91-92, p. 17.
2055. FOX, Hugh
"Acolytes of the Chaos-God: Embarcadero Center." [Pembroke] (25) 93, p. 63.

"Broken Plate Mask." [SlipS] (13) 93, p. 66-67.
"Calling The Dead and pushing back time." [Pembroke] (25) 93, p. 62.
"The Light." [Caliban] (13) 93, p. 52-53.
"Making Stands." [Bogg] (66) Wint 92-93, p. 6.
"Merry Christmas, Happy New Year." [ChironR] (12:4/13:1, #37/38) Wint 93-Spr 94, p. 31.
"Mood-Swings." [Lactuca] (17) Apr 93, p. 14.
"Theater." [Pearl] (17) Spr 93, p. 12.
"Theater." [Pembroke] (25) 93, p. 61.
2056. FOX, Joan
"Roots." [Calyx] (15:1) Wint 93-94, p. 12-13.
2057. FOX, Siv Cedering
"A Raccoon." [QRL] (12:32/33) 93, p. 416.
2058. FOX, Skip
"The Computer Drops an *e* Grates." [Talisman] (11) Fall 93, p. 276.
"Where Would You Want the Rail?" [Talisman] (11) Fall 93, p. 276.
2059. FOXCROFT, Bill
"My Father and I." [Grain] (21:1) Spr 93, p. 77.
"When Light Falls." [Event] (22:3) Wint 93-94, p. 68-69.
2060. FOY, John
"Local Superstition." [NewYorker] (69:33) 11 O 93, p. 78.
2061. FRACH, Shannon
"Welcome to America." [ChironR] (12:1, #34) Spr 93, p. 43.
2062. FRAGOS, Emily
"The Skater." [Parting] (6:2) Wint 93, p. 24.
2063. FRAIND, Lori C.
"If We Can Unwind." [Kalliope] (15:3) 93, p. 8-9.
2064. FRAKES, Clint
"Kaliyugen." [Caliban] (12) 93, p. 118-119.
2065. FRAMPTON, Jaime
"Wild." [JINJPo] (15:1) Spr 93, p. 28-29.
2066. FRANC-NOHAIN (Maurice-Etienne Legrand)
"Le Ballon de Football, ou le Moyen de Parvenir." [Hudson] (45:4) Wint 93, p. 681 - 682.
"The Soccer Ball, or How to Succeed in Life" (tr. by Norman R. Shapiro). [Hudson] (45:4) Wint 93, p. 682.
2067. FRANCE, Peter
"Salute — To Singing" (Selections from 36 variations on themes from Chuvash and Tatar folksongs, tr. of Gennady Aygi). [Verse] (10:2) Sum 93, p. 86-87.
2068. FRANCIS, Matthew
"After the Bee." [Stand] (34:4) Aut 93, p. 66-67.
2069. FRANCIS, Robert
"Appraisal." [PoetL] (88:2) Sum 93, p. 47.
"The Great Wind." [PoetL] (88:2) Sum 93, p. 47.
2070. FRANCIS, Scott
"Clown Sees Fox in the Water's Reflection." [HolCrit] (30:2) Ap 93, p. 18.
"Fox Abandons Hope, Almost." [Poem] (70) N 93, p. 33.
"Fox Clownhunts in a Temple's Rock and Sand Garden." [Poem] (70) N 93, p. 32.
"Fox Gains in Courage." [Poem] (70) N 93, p. 30.
"Fox Weeps, Cured of Amnesia." [Poem] (70) N 93, p. 31.
2071. FRANETA, Sonja
"Girlfriend" (tr. of Marina Tsvetaeva). [RiverS] (37) 93, p. 29-31.
2072. FRANK, Bernhard
"Amusement Park Reflections" (tr. of M. Winkler). [InterPR] (19:1) Spr 93, p. 6-7.
"Chassidim Dancing" (tr. of Nelly Sachs). [Vis] (42) 93, p. 14.
"The Evening Slips Off Me" (tr. of M. Winkler). [InterPR] (19:1) Spr 93, p. 12-13.
"I Don't Know When" (tr. of M. Winkler). [InterPR] (19:1) Spr 93, p. 8-9.
"The White Tulips" (tr. of M. Winkler). [InterPR] (19:1) Spr 93, p. 10-11.
2073. FRANK, Edwin
"Portrait." [Agni] (37) 93, p. 15-16.
2074. FRANKLIN, Walt
"Oak." [Gaia] (1/2) Ap-Jl 93, p. 20.
"Sycamore Bridge." [Gaia] (1/2) Ap-Jl 93, p. 20.
2075. FRANSWAY, Rebecca
"On the Way to Human Anatomy." [OnTheBus] (6:1, #13) Wint 93-Spr 94, p. 94.

2076. FRANZEN, Cola
"Cipher" (tr. of Saúl Yurkievich). [GrahamHR] (17) Fall 93, p. 30.
"Farewell Song for the Author" (tr. of Alicia Borinsky). [WorldL] (4) 93, p. 18.
"Insomnia" (tr. of Abu 'Amir ibn Al-Hammarh, 12th c.). [Luz] (5) N 93, p. 15.
"Opening" (tr. of Saúl Yurkievich). [GrahamHR] (17) Fall 93, p. 29.
"The Separation" (tr. of Alicia Borinsky). [WorldL] (4) 93, p. 19.
"Sketch" (tr. of Saúl Yurkievich). [GrahamHR] (17) Fall 93, p. 31-32.
"Summer" (tr. of Alicia Borinsky). [WorldL] (4) 93, p. 18.
2077. FRASER, Kathleen
"The Care of Things" (2 excerpts, tr. of Daniela Attanasio, w. Alberto Rossatti).
    [13thMoon] (11:1/2) 93, p. 206-207.
"Desert Poem" (Excerpts, tr. of Toni Maraini, w. Alberto Rossatti). [13thMoon]
    (11:1/2) 93, p. 212-214.
"Dirge" (tr. of Giovanna Sandri, w. the author). [13thMoon] (11:1/2) 93, p. 219.
"(From One of Zeami's Texts)" (tr. of Giovanna Sandri, w. the author). [13thMoon]
    (11:1/2) 93, p. 221.
"The Girl of Seven Spirits" (tr. of Sara Zanghi, w. Alberto Rossatti). [13thMoon]
    (11:1/2) 93, p. 216.
"Poem: You should remember" (tr. of Sara Zanghi, w. Alberto Rossatti).
    [13thMoon] (11:1/2) 93, p. 217.
"Sleep" (Selection: -20-, tr. of Amelia Rosselli). [13thMoon] (11:1/2) 93, p. 215.
"Springtime" (tr. of Giovanna Sandri, w. the author). [13thMoon] (11:1/2) 93, p.
    222.
"To Re-angle Axes" (tr. of Giovanna Sandri, w. the author). [13thMoon] (11:1/2)
    93, p. 220.
2078. FRASER, Sanford
"Robot Man." [NewYorkQ] (50) 93, p. 61.
FRATES, Stephen de
    See De FRATES, Stephen
FRATRIK, Julie Cooper
    See COOPER-FRATRIK, Julie
2079. FRATTALI, Steven
"My Heart Toward Evening" (tr. of Georg Trakl). [GrahamHR] (17) Fall 93, p. 74.
"To One Who Died Young" (tr. of Georg Trakl). [GrahamHR] (17) Fall 93, p. 75.
"To the Boy Elis" (tr. of Georg Trakl). [GrahamHR] (17) Fall 93, p. 73.
2080. FRATUS, David
"The Girl Dressed in Blue Feathers." [HiramPoR] (53/54) Fall 92-Sum 93, p. 102.
"The Newcomers." [HiramPoR] (53/54) Fall 92-Sum 93, p. 103.
2081. FRAZER, Vernon
"Nice People." [DogRR] (12:1, #23) Spr-Sum 93, p. 42-43.
2082. FRAZIER, Jan
"Mango." [ArtfulD] (24/25) 93, p. 69.
2083. FREEBAIRN, Rachel
"Joe" (Young Writers, age 12). [PikeF] (11) Fall 93, p. 19.
2084. FREEBERG, William
"Boy of the Americas: Raptures of the Seattle Trade Years." [JamesWR] (11:1) Fall
    93, p. 19.
2085. FREEDMAN, Robert
"Our Last Day of Freedom." [WestB] (31/32) 93, p. 167-168.
2086. FREELAND, Charles
"Biography." [Epiphany] (4:3) Jl 93, p. 174.
"Concerning Classified Ads." [Epiphany] (4:3) Jl 93, p. 165.
"Concerning Fractal Geometry." [Epiphany] (4:3) Jl 93, p. 173.
"Concerning Horror Movies." [Epiphany] (4:3) Jl 93, p. 164.
"Concerning Life on the Island." [Epiphany] (4:3) Jl 93, p. 172.
"Concerning the Death of Irony." [Epiphany] (4:3) Jl 93, p. 166-170.
"Direction." [Epiphany] (4:3) Jl 93, p. 171.
"Missing." [CimR] (103) Ap 93, p. 91-92.
"Necessary Racket." [CinPR] (24) Spr 93, p. 27.
2087. FREEMAN, Glenn
"Chaos Physics." [Parting] (6:2) Wint 93, p. 22-23.
"Her Becoming." [Plain] (14:1) Fall 93, p. 14.
2088. FREEMAN, Jan
"Broken." [AmerPoR] (22:6) N-D 93, p. 24.
"Mountain Rhyme." [AmerV] (30) 93, p. 92.

2089. FREEMAN, Jessica
"No Put-Up Job." [CoalC] (7) Apr 93, p. 20.
2090. FREEMAN, Suzanne
"The Bodhisattva Wore a String Tie." [OnTheBus] (6:1, #13) Wint 93-Spr 94, p.
95.
2091. FREISINGER, Randall R.
"The Psychological Present." [CentR] (37:3) Fall 93, p. 540-541.
"Shit Happens." [TarRP] (33:1) Fall 93, p. 43.
"Winter Storm." [CreamCR] (17:2) Fall 93, p. 206-207.
2092. FRETWELL, Kathy
"Language, Cool Down." [PottPort] (15:1) Spr-Sum 93, p. 77-78.
"The Pigskin's Pout." [Bogg] (66) Wint 92-93, p. 57.
"To Dream, to Sleep." [PraF] (14:2) Sum 93, p. 31.
"To My Cousin." [PraF] (14:2) Sum 93, p. 30.
2093. FRIAR, Kimon
"Midnight Stroll" (Scripture of the Blind, 1972, tr. of Yannis Ritsos, w. Kostas
Myrsiades). [HarvardR] (5) Fall 93, p. 132-133.
"Necessary Explanation" (Exercises, 1950-60, tr. of Yannis Ritsos). [HarvardR] (5)
Fall 93, p. 135.
2094. FRID, Marcia C.
"Butterflies." [PraS] (67:4) Wint 93, p. 58.
2095. FRIEBERT, Stuart
"Adam's Needle, Eve's Thread." [SycamoreR] (5:1) Wint 93, p. 28.
"The Arrow" (tr. of Marin Sorescu, w. Adriana Varga). [Field] (48) Spr 93, p. 45.
"As How." [Shen] (43:3) Fall 93, p. 114.
"Autumn Night" (Excerpt, tr. of Judita (Judith) Vaiciunaite, w. Viktoria
Skrupskelis). [AntigR] (93-94) Spr-Sum 93, p. 188.
"Babblers." [Witness] (7:1) 93, p. 87.
"The Bank's Going to Play." [Witness] (7:1) 93, p. 86.
"Behind My Back" (tr. of Karl Krolow). [JamesWR] (10:3) Spr 93, p. 13.
"Big Hole." [Shen] (43:3) Fall 93, p. 115.
"Black Mirror" (tr. of Judita Vaiciunaite, w. Viktoria Skrupskelis). [ParisR] (35:128)
Fall 93, p. 272-273.
"Dark White Paint." [JamesWR] (10:2) Wint 93, p. 17.
"Departure" (tr. of Karl Krolow). [HarvardR] (5) Fall 93, p. 47.
"Dolly Varden." [Gaia] (1/2) Ap-Jl 93, p. 48.
"Dragonflies" (tr. of Judita Vaiciunaite, w. Viktoria Skrupskelis). [LitR] (37:1) Fall
93, p. 86.
"Dry Moon." [CentR] (37:3) Fall 93, p. 531.
"Egg Roast" (for MS). [CentR] (37:3) Fall 93, p. 531.
"Elepaio." [Ascent] (18:1) Fall 93, p. 40.
"Feather Merchant." [OnTheBus] (6:1, #13) Wint 93-Spr 94, p. 96.
"Fence Mouse." [ContextS] (3:1) 93, p. 28.
"Flatfish." [HarvardR] (5) Fall 93, p. 106.
"For Greater Precision" (tr. of Sylva Fischerová, w. Vera Orac). [Field] (49) Fall 93,
p. 86.
"Fresh Salt." [OnTheBus] (5:2, #12) Sum-Fall 93, p. 80.
"Funeral Pie." [HarvardR] (4) Spr 93, p. 80.
"Go-Behind." [WillowS] (31) Wint 93, p. 78.
"Goat's Hair." [Journal] (17:1) Spr-Sum 93, p. 65.
"Goose Egg." [Event] (22:1) Spr 93, p. 49.
"Growing Cheese." [WebR] (17) Fall 93, p. 106.
"The Imagining Eye." [CentR] (37:3) Fall 93, p. 532-533.
"In Memoriam" (tr. of Judita (Judith) Vaiciunaite, w. Viktoria Skrupskelis).
[AntigR] (93-94) Spr-Sum 93, p. 187.
"In My Old Age" (tr. of Karl Krolow). [HarvardR] (5) Fall 93, p. 47.
"In the Hospital" (tr. of Judita Vaiciunaite, w. Viktoria Skrupskelis). [LitR] (37:1)
Fall 93, p. 86.
"Innocence" (tr. of Marin Sorescu, w. Adriana Varga). [Field] (48) Spr 93, p. 47.
"Land of Mud" (Warsaw-Leningrad Express, tr. of Sylva Fischerová, w. Vera Orac).
[Field] (49) Fall 93, p. 88.
"Meeting Ezra Pound" (tr. of Miroslav Holub, w. Dana Hábová). [Field] (49) Fall
93, p. 12.
"Milk Toast." [OnTheBus] (5:2, #12) Sum-Fall 93, p. 80.
"The Next Move." [WritersF] (19) 93, p. 89.
"On Heat and Cold." [NoAmR] (278:1) Ja-F 93, p. 11.

"Samovar." [NewAW] (11) Sum-Fall 93, p. 98.
"September Night" (tr. of Judita Vaiciunaite, w. Viktoria Skrupskelis). [ParisR]
(35:128) Fall 93, p. 271.
"Shifting the Rod." [CinPR] (24) Spr 93, p. 25.
"Sin" (tr. of Marin Sorescu, w. Adriana Varga). [Field] (48) Spr 93, p. 46.
"Sisters" (tr. of Judita Vaiciunaite, w. Viktoria Skrupskelis). [MalR] (102) Spr 93, p.
57.
"Sleeplessness" (tr. of Judita Vaiciunaite, w. Viktoria Skrupskelis). [ParisR]
(35:128) Fall 93, p. 272.
"Spring" (tr. of Judita Vaiciunaite, w. Viktoria Skrupskelis). [ParisR] (35:128) Fall
93, p. 271.
"Stele for Catullus" (tr. of Karl Krolow). [Os] (37) Wint 93, p. 9.
"A Totally New Time, a Completely New Era" (tr. of Sylva Fischerová, w. Vera
Orac). [Field] (49) Fall 93, p. 87.
"Vilnius. Archaeology" (tr. of Judita Vaiciunaite, w. Viktoria Skrupskelis). [ParisR]
(35:128) Fall 93, p. 273.
"While We Watch." [SycamoreR] (5:2) Sum 93, p. 76.
"Young Thoreau." [Ascent] (18:1) Fall 93, p. 41.
2096. FRIED, Michael
"The Limits of Safety." [AntR] (51:2) Spr 93, p. 237.
2097. FRIEDLANDER, Benjamin
"My Brother Fell" (Excerpts). [Avec] (6:1) 93, p. 51-53.
2098. FRIEDMAN, Alan H.
"Summer '90." [DenQ] (27:3) Wint 93, p. 30.
2099. FRIEDMAN, Jeff
"Beyond the Rain" (Editors' Prize Winner). [MissouriR] (16:1) 93, p. 159.
"Desire" (Editors' Prize Winner). [MissouriR] (16:1) 93, p. 160-161.
"Scattering the Ashes" (Editors' Prize Winner). [MissouriR] (16:1) 93, p. 162-163.
"The Talker" (Editors' Prize Winner). [MissouriR] (16:1) 93, p. 158.
2100. FRIEDMAN, Lisa
"Condolence." [BellArk] (9:1) Ja-F 93, p. 5.
"Page Turner for J.R. and Eddie." [BellArk] (9:4) Jl-Ag 93, p. 10.
2101. FRIEDMAN, Stan
"Blame It on the Dress." [BelPoJ] (43:4) Sum 93, p. 20-21.
2102. FRIEL, Raymond
"Bel Air." [Verse] (10:1) Spr 93, p. 63.
2103. FRIEND, Robert
"The Ballad of the Missing Mosquito" (For Jeannie who complained that
mosquitoes invisible to me were biting her). [Light] (8) Wint 93, p. 9.
"Christopher Columbus" (tr. of Simon, Nachmias, w. Michel Konstantyn). [Trans]
(28) Spr 93, p. 105.
"I Don't Understand Russian, and I Translate" (tr. of Simon, Nachmias, w. Michel
Konstantyn). [Trans] (28) Spr 93, p. 106.
"The Odor of Lemon, the Odor of Sweat Reminds Me of Love" (tr. of Simon,
Nachmias, w. Michel Konstantyn). [Trans] (28) Spr 93, p. 104.
2104. FRIES, Kenny
"Dressing the Wound." [JamesWR] (10:4) Sum 93, p. 6.
2105. FRIESEN, Patrick
"Talking 3 A.M." [PraF] (14:4) Wint 93-94, p. 20-22.
2106. FRIGGIERI, Oliver
"Skin Diver" (tr. of Daniel Massa). [Vis] (43) 93, p. 41.
"Twilight" (tr. of Mario Azzopardi). [Vis] (43) 93, p. 40.
"Two Singers" (tr. of Anton Buttigieg). [Vis] (43) 93, p. 41.
2107. FRIMAN, Alice
"Canal and Towpath" (Indianapolis, January 1991). [WindO] (57) Fall 93, p. 16-17.
"Harry's Girl." [Confr] (51) Sum 93, p. 230.
"In Neutral." [Shen] (43:2) Sum 93, p. 106.
"In That Apartment, in That City." [HopewellR] (5) 93, p. 102.
2108. FRISARDI, Andrew
"La Vita Nuova" (Selection: Chapter XXIII: "Donna pietosa," tr. of Dante
Alighieri). [CumbPR]] (13:1) Fall 93, p. 43.
"La Vita Nuova" (Selection: Chapter XXVI: "Tanto gentile e tanto," tr. of Dante
Alighieri). [CumbPR]] (13:1) Fall 93, p. 45.
"La Vita Nuova" (Selection: Chapter XLI: "Oltre la spera," tr. of Dante Alighieri).
[CumbPR]] (13:1) Fall 93, p. 47.

2109. FRÖME, Carol
"Vantage Point in Light." [SycamoreR] (5:1) Wint 93, p. 18-19.
2110. FROST, Carol
"Country." [GettyR] (6:3) Sum 93, p. 407.
"Spinners." [GettyR] (6:3) Sum 93, p. 408-409.
2111. FROST, Celestine
"Birth." [SoCarR] (26:1) Fall 93, p. 145.
"! It invites direct experience." [Talisman] (10) Spr 93, p. 125.
"November." [SoCarR] (26:1) Fall 93, p. 144-145.
2112. FROST, Elisabeth (Elisabeth A.)
"Pines." [DenQ] (28:2) Fall 93, p. 9.
"Prose #2." [MassR] (34:4) Wint 93-94, p. 589.
2113. FROST, Helen
"Between the Church and Its Mountain." [Gaia] (3) O 93, p. 8.
2114. FROST, Richard
"The Book of Games." [GettyR] (6:3) Sum 93, p. 426.
"The Change." [ParisR] (35:128) Fall 93, p. 146.
"The Indian." [ParisR] (35:128) Fall 93, p. 145.
"Neighbor Blood." [ParisR] (35:128) Fall 93, p. 144.
2115. FRUMKIN, Gene
"History, Biography: French Series" (Selections: 14-15, 18). [Caliban] (12) 93, p. 82-84.
2116. FRY, Jane Gilliat
"Attention!" [Light] (7) Aut 93, p. 10.
2117. FRY, Nan
"The Mother-and-Child Riddle." [Gaia] (3) O 93, p. 13-14.
"Riddle" (Eyeglasses). [Kalliope] (15:2) 93, p. 59.
"Riddle" (The Ozone Layer). [Kalliope] (15:2) 93, p. 58.
2118. FU, Liang
"Frenzied Fingers" (tr. by Dian Li). [GreenMR] (NS 6:2) Sum-Fall 93, p. 154.
2119. FUHR, Ellen J.
"Unchaste Virgin." [Bogg] (66) Wint 92-93, p. 22.
2120. FUHRMAN, Joanna
"The Assassin of Light." [HangL] (63) 93, p. 13.
"From the Abstract to the Real." [HangL] (62) 93, p. 24.
"Love Poem." [HangL] (63) 93, p. 14.
"Now I'm New and Improved." [HangL] (63) 93, p. 14.
2121. FUJII, Sadakazu
"Fiyeda" (tr. by Chris Drake). [ChiR] (39:3/4) 93, p. 218-220.
2122. FUJIWARA, no Tameie
"His word means nothing" (tr. by Sam Hamill). [ChiR] (39:3/4) 93, p. 203.
2123. FUJIWARA, no Teika
"Coming slowly home" (tr. by Sam Hamill). [ChiR] (39:3/4) 93, p. 203.
2124. FULKER, Tina
"Daddy." [Bogg] (66) Wint 92-93, p. 42.
"For Jack Kerouac." [Bogg] (66) Wint 92-93, p. 41-42.
"Manchester." [Bogg] (66) Wint 92-93, p. 16.
"Towards the End." [Bogg] (66) Wint 92-93, p. 42.
"West End Girl" (Excerpt, for Candice). [Bogg] (66) Wint 92-93, p. 9.
2125. FULLER, Ann Wood
"A Change of Light." [CumbPR] (12:2) Spr 93, p. 37.
"Thanksgiving." [CumbPR]] (13:1) Fall 93, p. 73.
2126. FULLER, Janice
"Cryptogram." [Crucible] (29) Fall 93, p. 24.
2127. FULLER, Tonda K.
"You Never Compared Me to a Summer's Day." [QW] (37) Sum-Fall 93, p. 206.
2128. FULLER, William
"American Gothic." [CoalC] (7) Apr 93, p. 40.
"The Reading Seas." [Avec] (6:1) 93, p. 34-37.
2129. FULTON, Alice
"About Face." [Chelsea] (55) 93, p. 46.
"Immersion." [Chelsea] (55) 93, p. 44-45.
"Industrial Lace." [NewYorker] (69:22) 19 Jl 93, p. 64.
"The Priming Is a Negligee." [SouthwR] (78:1) Wint 93, p. 52-53.
"Sketch" (for Hank De Leo). [SouthwR] (78:1) Wint 93, p. 51-52.

2130. FULTON, Robin
"Closing Scene." [Verse] (10:3) Wint 93, p. 111.
"The Cuckoo" (tr. of Tomas Tranströmer). [ManhatR] (7:1) Fall 93, p. 10.
"From July 1990" (tr. of Tomas Tranströmer). [ManhatR] (7:1) Fall 93, p. 11.
"Lugubrious Gondola No. 2" (tr. of Tomas Tranströmer). [ManhatR] (7:1) Fall 93,
   p. 7-9.
"A Sketch from 1844" (tr. of Tomas Tranströmer). [Verse] (10:3) Wint 93, p. 102.
"Three Stanzas" (tr. of Tomas Tranströmer). [Verse] (10:3) Wint 93, p. 101.
2131. FUNGE, Robert
"Bourbon" (with apologies to archy). [Light] (5) Spr 93, p. 14.
"The Gospel According to Perse and Others." [LitR] (37:1) Fall 93, p. 41.
"Hungers." [BelPoJ] (43:4) Sum 93, p. 5.
"Moondust." [SoDakR] (31:3) Fall 93, p. 100.
"Snapshots." [LitR] (37:1) Fall 93, p. 40.
"This." [Footwork] (23) 93, p. 125.
2132. FUNK, Allison
"After Dark." [Poetry] (162:4) Jl 93, p. 195-196.
"Blondin." [Poetry] (162:4) Jl 93, p. 198.
"Faultline." [Poetry] (162:4) Jl 93, p. 196-197.
2133. FURBISH, Dean
"Autumn in Mikhailovskoye" (tr. of Viktor Sosnora). [InterPR] (19:1) Spr 93, p. 34 -
   39.
"The ear no longer hears the echo" (tr. of Viktor Sosnora). [InterPR] (19:1) Spr 93,
   p. 26-29.
"September" (tr. of Viktor Sosnora). [InterPR] (19:1) Spr 93, p. 30-33.
"Winter Road" (tr. of Viktor Sosnora). [InterPR] (19:1) Spr 93, p. 40-41.
2134. FURBUSH, Matthew
"Portrait from the Age of Henry the Eighth" (After the Portrait of Robert Cheseman
   by Hans Holbein). [TexasR] (14:1/2) Spr-Sum 93, p. 94-95.
2135. FUSCO, Peter
"Awake." [Light] (8) Wint 93, p. 8.
"Like a Leaf" (tr. of Hyon-Jong Chong, w. Wolhee Choe). [WebR] (17) Fall 93, p.
   25.
"Rise and Fall." [BrooklynR] (10) 93, p. 17.
2136. FUSEK, Serena
"Close the Doors, They're Coming in the Windows." [Lactuca] (17) Apr 93, p. 14.
"Peregrine." [Lactuca] (17) Apr 93, p. 13.
"Raid." [Lactuca] (17) Apr 93, p. 12.
"When the Outside Gets In." [Lactuca] (17) Apr 93, p. 12.
"Wood's Edge." [Lactuca] (17) Apr 93, p. 13.
G., S. M.
   See S. M. G.
2137. GABBARD, G. N.
"The Even Shorter Gavin Ewart." [Light] (8) Wint 93, p. 11.
"Fünf Fantasiestücke in Harry Grahams Manier." [Light] (7) Aut 93, p. 16.
2138. GABIN, Patricia
"Barefoot in the Kitchen." [PraF] (14:1) Spr 93, p. 119.
"Insanity Runs in the Family." [PraF] (14:1) Spr 93, p. 118.
2139. GABIS, Rita
"Leaving." [PassN] (14:2) Wint 93, p. 4.
"Washing Beans." [Colum] (20) Sum 93, p. 25.
"Wishes." [PassN] (14:2) Wint 93, p. 3.
2140. GABRIEL, Margaret
"Late of April." [TickleAce] (26) Fall-Wint 93, p. 109.
"Wood Mentor." [AntigR] (93-94) Spr-Sum 93, p. 189-190.
2141. GADE, Lisa
"Boston Marriage" (In Victorian times, a living arrangement between two women).
   [Kalliope] (15:2) 93, p. 56.
2142. GADJANSKI, Ivan
"Balkan Street" (tr. by Karolina Udovicki). [NoDaQ] (61:1) Wint 93, p. 73-76.
"Summing Up" (tr. by Karolina Udovicki). [NoDaQ] (61:1) Wint 93, p. 77.
2143. GALAS, Diamanda
"Let's Not Chat About Despair." [Art&Und] (2:1) Ja-F 93, back cover.
2144. GALE, E. A.
"Mr. Gianelli Installing Window Screens." [SoCoast] (15) Je 93, p. 30-31.

2145. GALEF, David
"Enthalpy." [Light] (5) Spr 93, p. 10.
2146. GALGUERA, Robin Boody
"Perdida." [NewL] (59:3) 93, p. 83.
2147. GALLAGHER, Kenneth T.
"Children" (Original untitled, tr. of Heinrich Heine). [SpiritSH] (58) 93, p. 28-29.
"Extinguished" (tr. of Heinrich Heine). [SpiritSH] (58) 93, p. 29.
"Friends" (tr. of Heinrich Heine). [SpiritSH] (58) 93, p. 31.
"Her Family" (tr. of Heinrich Heine). [SpiritSH] (58) 93, p. 30.
2148. GALLAGHER, Linda Pergolizzi
"The Truest Sight." [Hellas] (4:1) Spr 93, p. 66.
2149. GALLAGHER, Owen
"Daddy Was Always Mammy." [Verse] (10:1) Spr 93, p. 100.
2150. GALLAGHER, Tess
"As If He Were Free" (for Salman). [PennR] (5:2) 93, p. 1-3.
"Black Pudding." [NewEngR] (15:1) Wint 93, p. 124-125.
"Cameo." [NewL] (59:4) 93, p. 69.
"Close to Me Now." [Pequod] (35) 93, p. 143.
"Ebony." [NewEngR] (15:1) Wint 93, p. 125.
"Invaded by Souls." [NewL] (59:4) 93, p. 66-67.
"Kiss Pressed Like a Flower." [NewL] (59:4) 93, p. 68.
"Knotted Letter." [Pequod] (35) 93, p. 141-142.
2151. GALLAHER, Cynthia
"Northern Spotted Owl." [Gaia] (3) O 93, p. 31.
2152. GALLAHER, Edwin
"Jocasta." [ParisR] (35:128) Fall 93, p. 263.
"Postcard to Cynthia Macdonald in Italy." [ParisR] (35:128) Fall 93, p. 264.
"Upstairs at the Copernican Revolution." [ParisR] (35:128) Fall 93, p. 264.
2153. GALLER, David
"Against Memory." [QRL] (12:32/33) 93, p. 167-168.
"Berryman Reading, 1964." [QRL] (12:32/33) 93, p. 168-170.
"Forbidden Things." [QRL] (12:32/33) 93, p. 160-161.
"From a Train Window at Night." [SouthernR] (29:2) Spr, Ap 93, p. 298-299.
"Ghosts." [QRL] (12:32/33) 93, p. 163-164.
"Helplessness (IV)." [Pequod] (36) 93, p. 80.
"Husk." [QRL] (12:32/33) 93, p. 162.
"Inferno" (for Robert Stock). [QRL] (12:32/33) 93, p. 158-160.
"Justice, 1937." [QRL] (12:32/33) 93, p. 162-163.
"Meditation on a Writer's Notebook." [QRL] (12:32/33) 93, p. 166.
"Mouths." [SouthernR] (29:2) Spr, Ap 93, p. 297-298.
"The New Highway Song." [QRL] (12:32/33) 93, p. 167.
"On Hearing the World Premiere of —'s New York." [QRL] (12:32/33) 93, p. 165 -
166.
"Orpheus Ascending." [QRL] (12:32/33) 93, p. 164.
2154. GALLIK, Daniel
"Athlete: At Seventeen." [WindO] (57) Fall 93, p. 8.
"A Few Words Were All He Needed." [WindO] (57) Fall 93, p. 9.
"What Is In a Canadian Boy's Blood." [WindO] (57) Fall 93, p. 7.
2155. GALLOWAY, Terry
"Monologue" (from the play "Lardo Weeping"). [AmerV] (32) 93, p. 3-7.
GALT, Margot Fortunato
See FORTUNATO-GALT, Margot
2156. GALVIN, Brendan
"Apple Talk." [PraS] (67:1) Spr 93, p. 50-51.
"Norwegians at the Shetland Hotel." [GeoR] (47:3) Fall 93, p. 575.
"October Swallows." [BlackWR] (20:1) Fall-Wint 93, p. 60-61.
"Pococurante." [Shen] (43:4) Wint 93, p. 22.
"The Portuguese Uncle." [Shen] (43:1) Spr 93, p. 82-83.
"Rained Out." [Atlantic] (271:4) Ap 93, p. 99.
"Seeing for Ourselves." [PraS] (67:1) Spr 93, p. 51-52.
"The Soul Is Not Colorless." [BlackWR] (20:1) Fall-Wint 93, p. 62.
"The Stones of Callanish" (Outer Hebrides). [GeoR] (47:3) Fall 93, p. 574-575.
"The Thief of Your Poem." [PoetC] (24:3) Spr 93, p. 44.
"Under My Stornoway Hat." [GettyR] (6:3) Sum 93, p. 390-391.
"Wild Blackberries." [Shen] (43:4) Wint 93, p. 21.

2157. GALVIN, James
"Independence Day, 1956: A Fairy Tale." [NewYorker] (69:20) 5 Jl 93, p. 66.
"Indirective." [ParisR] (35:128) Fall 93, p. 207-209.
"The Sacral Dreams of Ramon Fernandez." [ColR] (20:1) Spr 93, p. 97-102.
"Trespassers." [NewYorker] (69:32) 4 O 93, p. 166.
2158. GALVIN, Martin
"Grieving, for Five Voices." [PoetC] (24:2) Wint 93, p. 11.
"Little Tavern, Georgetown." [PoetL] (88:1) Spr 93, p. 45-46.
GAMA, Steven da
See DaGAMA, Steven
2159. GAMBILL, Gina
"Let Us Eat." [OnTheBus] (5:2, #12) Sum-Fall 93, p. 81.
"Mother, I Have Broken Ribs." [OnTheBus] (6:1, #13) Wint 93-Spr 94, p. 97.
2160. GAMPER, Galina
"Almost over the abyss, at the very edge of the branch" (tr. by Vera Sandomirskaia
Dunham). [Elf] (3:2) Sum 93, p. 31.
"Here is the vessel from which I must drown" (tr. by Vera Sandomirskaia Dunham).
[Elf] (3:2) Sum 93, p. 32.
"I invoke you: our shyness and our courage, return" (tr. by Judy Hogan and Yelena
Sidarova). [Elf] (3:2) Sum 93, p. 31.
2161. GANASSI, Ian
"The Immovable Object." [OnTheBus] (6:1, #13) Wint 93-Spr 94, p. 98.
"A Shattered Glass." [Pequod] (36) 93, p. 81.
2162. GANDER, Forrest
"Desnudo / Aguafuerte" (2 selections, tr. of Monica Mansour). [ProseP] (1) 92, p.
56.
"The second Presence" (for Jack Gilbert and the Manyoshu). [Conjunc] (21) 93, p.
61-63.
2163. GANESH, Chitra
"There Are Two Days I Remember" (Poets of High School Age). [HangL] (62) 93,
p. 93.
2164. GANEV, Nedelcho
"The Soul" (tr. by Lisa Sapinkopf, w. Georgi Belev). [Agni] (37) 93, p. 260.
2165. GANGATIRIYA
"I made a hut" (Songs from the Theragatha: Songs of the Buddhist Monks, circa 450
B.C.E.). [Tricycle] (2:3) Spr 93, p. 39.
2166. GANGEMI, Kenneth
"Twenty Facts." [Caliban] (12) 93, p. 95.
2167. GANICK, Peter
"Code Zero" (Selections: 3 poems). [Avec] (6:1) 93, p. 74-75.
2168. GANNON, Mary
"Ars Poetica." [AntR] (51:3) Sum 93, p. 371.
"Between Sisters." [PassN] (14:1) Sum 93, p. 17.
"General Delivery" (for R.C.). [AntR] (51:3) Sum 93, p. 370.
2169. GARCIA, Albert
"Skunk Talk." [HampSPR] Wint 93, p. 50.
2170. GARCIA, Diana
"La Curandera." [KenR] (NS 15:4) Fall 93, p. 15.
"Other Marías." [KenR] (NS 15:4) Fall 93, p. 14-15.
"Las Rubias." [KenR] (NS 15:4) Fall 93, p. 11-13.
"When Living Was a Labor Camp Called Montgomery." [KenR] (NS 15:4) Fall 93,
p. 10-11.
GARCIA, Jesús Díaz
See DIAZ GARCIA, Jesús
2171. GARCIA, José
"Second Series" (Selections: 36, 53, 88, from *3 x 111 Tristychs*, tr. of Yannis Ritsos,
w. Adamantia García-Baltatzi). [LitR] (36:2) Wint 93, p. 247.
"Third Series" (Selections: 5, 28, 57, 63, 68, 94, from *3 x 111 Tristychs*, tr. of
Yannis Ritsos, w. Adamantia García-Baltatzi). [LitR] (36:2) Wint 93, p. 247-
248.
"With the moonlight a butterfly" (tr. of Yannis Ritsos, w. Adamandia Baltatzi).
[Vis] (41) 93, p. 18.
2172. GARCIA, Michael
"Ideas In and Out." [Americas] (21:2) Sum 93, p. 71.
2173. GARCIA, Richard
"Doing the Tarantella with Lola Montez." [AntR] (51:3) Sum 93, p. 388.

173

"The Experts, the Man in the Street, the Crowd." [ColR] (20:2) Fall 93, p. 44-45.
"No Quarrels Today." [ColR] (20:2) Fall 93, p. 39-41.
"Open Letter to My Friends." [ColR] (20:2) Fall 93, p. 42-43.
"Some Mornings." [ColR] (20:2) Fall 93, p. 183.
"While Trading Clothes in a Rest Stop Bathroom." [GettyR] (6:1) Wint 93, p. 56.
2174. GARCIA-BALTATZI, Adamantia
"Second Series" (Selections: 36, 53, 88, from *3 x 111 Tristychs*, tr. of Yannis Ritsos,
w. José García). [LitR] (36:2) Wint 93, p. 247.
"Third Series" (Selections: 5, 28, 57, 63, 68, 94, from *3 x 111 Tristychs*, tr. of
Yannis Ritsos, w. José García). [LitR] (36:2) Wint 93, p. 247-248.
"With the moonlight a butterfly" (tr. of Yannis Ritsos, w. Jose Garcia). [Vis] (41)
93, p. 18.
2175. GARCIA GOMES, Emilio
"Insomnio" (Spanish tr. of Abu Amir Ben Al-Hammara, 12th c.). [Luz] (5) N 93, p.
15.
2176. GARCIA MONTERO, Luis
"To Federico with Some Violets" (Selection: III, tr. by Cecilia C. Lee and Laura
Higgins). [LitR] (36:3) Spr 93, p. 371-372.
2177. GARDIEN, Kent
"I Saw You There." [WestHR] (47:4) Wint 93, p. 390.
"On the Asphalt Road." [WestHR] (47:4) Wint 93, p. 388-389.
"Peter and Roxanne." [WestHR] (47:4) Wint 93, p. 391.
"Rio Frio" (in Spanish and English). [Border] (2) Spr 93, p. 26-27.
"Wrappings." [QRL] (12:32/33) 93, p. 416-417.
2178. GARDINER, Sheila
"Lunalilo House." [HawaiiR] (17:1, #37) Spr 93, p. 123.
2179. GARDNER, Eric
"Train." [PikeF] (11) Fall 93, p. 13.
"You Wouldn't Listen." [Pearl] (17) Spr 93, p. 64.
2180. GARDNER, Geoffrey
"1939-1945 Poèmes" (Excerpt in English, tr. of Jules Supervielle). [SycamoreR]
(5:2) Sum 93, p. 101.
"Fable du Monde" (Excerpt in English, tr. of Jules Supervielle). [SycamoreR] (5:2)
Sum 93, p. 103.
"The First Days of the World (God Speaks)" (tr. of Jules Supervielle). [SycamoreR]
(5:2) Sum 93, p. 99.
2181. GARDNER, Humphrey
"Subway / Underground." [TickleAce] (23) Spr-Sum 92, p. 61.
"Wanderer Gone West." [TickleAce] (23) Spr-Sum 92, p. 62.
2182. GARDNER, Philip
"Elegy for William Mathias." [TickleAce] (25) Spr-Sum 93, p. 207.
"Fourth of July in North Orange, Mass." (i.m. Arthur Shaw). [TickleAce] (26) Fall -
Wint 93, p. 42.
"Ham Spray." [TickleAce] (23) Spr-Sum 92, p. 88.
"Levelling." [TickleAce] (25) Spr-Sum 93, p. 204.
"New Year's Eve, 1992" (for Tom and Alice). [TickleAce] (25) Spr-Sum 93, p. 205 -
206.
"Oriel Road." [TickleAce] (23) Spr-Sum 92, p. 89.
"Sabang, 1964." [TickleAce] (26) Fall-Wint 93, p. 41.
2183. GARDNER, Stephen
"The Broken Gull." [SoCoast] (15) Je 93, p. 11.
"Guests." [TexasR] (14:1/2) Spr-Sum 93, p. 96.
"Holy." [SnailPR] (3:1) Fall-Wint 93, p. 23.
2184. GARDNER, Thomas
"Strike Rally." [HolCrit] (30:2) Ap 93, p. 13.
2185. GARLAND, Max
"County Night." [Poetry] (163:1) O 93, p. 21.
"The Missiles, 1962." [GettyR] (6:4) Aut 93, p. 596-597.
2186. GARMON, John Frederic
"The Cochise Tax." [PraS] (67:3) Fall 93, p. 135.
"The Land of the Cochise Apaches." [PraS] (67:3) Fall 93, p. 132.
"The Silence of Cochise." [PraS] (67:3) Fall 93, p. 134.
"The Words of the White Eyes." [PraS] (67:3) Fall 93, p. 133.
2187. GARNER, Marguerite
"Hung Gao Liang (Red Sorghum Wine)" (Tien An Men Square). [SoCoast] (14) Ja
93, p. 40.

2188. GARREN, Christine
"Guide." [GreensboroR] (55) Wint 93-94, p. 18.
"Histories." [GreensboroR] (55) Wint 93-94, p. 16.
"Purple Passion." [GreensboroR] (55) Wint 93-94, p. 17.
2189. GARRETT, Dana
"Loblolly Pine." [BlackBR] (17) Sum-Fall 93, p. 21.
"Traffic Report." [BlackBR] (17) Sum-Fall 93, p. 20.
2190. GARRETT, Nancy Fales
"Listening." [HangL] (62) 93, p. 25.
2191. GARRETT, Nola
"The Pastor's Wife Considers African Violets, the Annunciation and the Practice of
Church Suppers." [ChrC] (110:20) 30 Je-7 Jl 93, p. 674.
2192. GARRIGUE, Jean
"Studies for an Actress." [QRL] (12:32/33) 93, p. 417-422.
2193. GARRISON, David
"Mountains on the Moon." [BellArk] (9:5) S-O 93, p. 11.
"Seagull." [Wind] (23:72) 93, p. 9-10.
"Song for Basho." [ArtfulD] (24/25) 93, p. 143-146.
2194. GARRISON, Deborah
"Maybe There's No Going Back." [NewYorker] (69:31) 27 S 93, p. 70.
2195. GARRISON, Jay
"Hospitality." [Plain] (13:2) Wint 93, p. 6.
2196. GARRISON, Peggy
"The Date." [Footwork] (23) 93, p. 126.
"Elegy for Cuz" (1942-1980). [Footwork] (23) 93, p. 127.
"Her Talisman." [Footwork] (23) 93, p. 126.
"Learning to Swim." [Footwork] (23) 93, p. 126-127.
2197. GARTEN, Bill
"Frame 323." [PoetL] (88:3) Fall 93, p. 44.
2198. GARWOOD, Galen
"Floating Parables." [JamesWR] (11:1) Fall 93, p. 11.
2199. GASH, Sondra
"At the Retreat." [US1] (28/29) 93, p. 5.
2200. GASKI, Harald
"The Trek of the Wind" (Selections, tr. of Nils-Aslak Valkeapää, w. Lars Nordström
and Ralph Salisbury). [SilverFR] (24) Wint 93, p. 31-38.
2201. GASKIN, Claire
"Untitled: I sob in a deserted city." [DogRR] (12:2, #24) Fall-Wint 93, p. 20.
"Untitled: I write with clear water   Birds singing." [DogRR] (12:2, #24) Fall-Wint
93, p. 21.
"Untitled: In a cafe   Birds fly round our table." [DogRR] (12:2, #24) Fall-Wint 93,
p. 21.
2202. GASPAR, Frank (Frank X.)
"Absolution." [TampaR] (6) Spr 93, p. j30.
"Beggars and Angels." [SewanR] (101:3) Jl-S, Sum 93, p. 330.
"Desire." [SewanR] (101:3) Jl-S, Sum 93, p. 331-332.
"Eucharist." [Hudson] (46:2) Sum 93, p. 328.
"Lamentation." [Hudson] (46:2) Sum 93, p. 323-325.
"Lover." [PoetL] (88:4) Wint 93-94, p. 17-18.
"Mission." [GettyR] (6:1) Wint 93, p. 101-102.
"Stealing." [TampaR] (6) Spr 93, p. 31-32.
"What Death with Love Must Have to Do." [GettyR] (6:1) Wint 93, p. 99.
"The Wine at Cana." [GettyR] (6:1) Wint 93, p. 100-101.
"Winter Berries." [Hudson] (46:2) Sum 93, p. 326-327.
2203. GASPARINI, Leonard
"Lines Written After a Sleepless Night." [AntigR] (95) Aut 93, p. 144.
2204. GASTIGER, Joseph
"Hivaoa." [AnotherCM] (25) Spr 93, p. 40-41.
2205. GATES, Beatrix
"Triptych" (for Ron King, Lynnsey Carroll and Tracy Sampson). [KenR] (NS 15:2)
Spr 93, p. 146-155.
2206. GAUCHERON, Jacques
"I am woman she says" (from *Entre mon ombre et la lumière*, tr. by Patrick
Williamson). [Verse] (10:1) Spr 93, p. 99.

2207. GAULIS, Louis
"The Rendez-Vous at Cophinou" (tr. by Richard Kopp). [LitR] (36:4) Sum 93, p. 528.
"Le Rendez-Vous de Cophinou." [LitR] (36:4) Sum 93, p. 529.
2208. GAUTHIER, Marcel
"Envy." [GreensboroR] (54) Sum 93, p. 31.
2209. GAVRILOVIC, Manojle
"Building a City" (tr. by Vasa D. Mihailovich). [NoDaQ] (61:1) Wint 93, p. 78.
"The Master of Bees" (tr. by Vasa D. Mihailovich). [NoDaQ] (61:1) Wint 93, p. 78.
2210. GAVRONSKY, Serge
"Fields of Words" (Selections: 3 poems). [WashR] (19:1) Je-Jl 93, p. 6.
"Untitled: I said the forest." [ContextS] (3:1) 93, p. 24.
"Untitled: This movie, see I wanted to take you to." [ContextS] (3:1) 93, p. 24.
2211. GAWON, Jackie
"Fill 'Er Up." [NewYorkQ] (51) 93, p. 64.
2212. GAY, Zan
"Last Two Jars of Pears on a Shelf." [Crucible] (29) Fall 93, p. 14.
2213. GEAREN, Cameron K.
"Sifting." [SpoonR] (18:2) Sum-Fall 93, p. 31.
2214. GEARHART, Michael
"White." [ApalQ] (39) 93, p. 39.
2215. GEAUVREAU, Cherie
"Cantabile." [CapilR] (2:10) Spr 93, p. 39.
"Inversion." [PraF] (14:2) Sum 93, p. 39.
"Locus." [CapilR] (2:10) Spr 93, p. 37.
"The Onion Song." [CapilR] (2:10) Spr 93, p. 33-35.
"A Poem for Two Sisters." [CapilR] (2:10) Spr 93, p. 36.
"The Shadow of the Crow." [CapilR] (2:10) Spr 93, p. 30-32.
"Twentysome." [CapilR] (2:10) Spr 93, p. 38.
2216. GEBLER, Katie
"Winter '65." [Writer] (106:6) Je 93, p. 19.
2217. GEDDES, Gary
"Fusiles y Frijoles." [PoetryC] (13:3) 93, p. 14.
2218. GELETA, Greg
"Train Set." [PaintedB] (50/51) 93, p. 15.
2219. GELINEAU, Christine
"Cast." [BelPoJ] (43:3) Spr 93, p. 8.
"Inheritance." [BelPoJ] (43:3) Spr 93, p. 9.
"Naming the Child." [Footwork] (23) 93, p. 110.
"Reply to Sirens." [Footwork] (23) 93, p. 109-110.
"Survivor." [Footwork] (23) 93, p. 109.
2220. GELMAN, Juan
"Errata" (tr. by Otis Bilodeau). [MassR] (33:4) Wint 92-93, p. 614-615.
"Lament for the Death of Parsifal Hoolig" (tr. by Otis Bilodeau). [MassR] (33:4) Wint 92-93, p. 612-613.
"Lament for the Nape of Tom Steward's Neck" (tr. by Otis Bilodeau). [MassR] (33:4) Wint 92-93, p. 613-614.
"On Poetry" (tr. by Joan Lindgren). [SenR] (23:1/2) Wint 93, p. 129-130.
"Rain" (tr. by Joan Lindgren). [SenR] (23:1/2) Wint 93, p. 131.
"They Say" (tr. by Joan Lindgren). [SenR] (23:1/2) Wint 93, p. 125-126.
"Women" (tr. by Joan Lindgren). [SenR] (23:1/2) Wint 93, p. 127-128.
2221. GELSANLITER, David
"He hated to see his young daughter go." [NewYorkQ] (51) 93, p. 54.
2222. GEMIN, Pamela
"July." [BellArk] (9:6) N-D 93, p. 1.
"Waking Differently." [BellArk] (9:6) N-D 93, p. 12.
2223. GENEGA, Paul
"The Oyster" (from M.F.K. Fisher). [Outbr] (24) 93, p. 31-32.
"Puffins." [Outbr] (24) 93, p. 33.
GENER-MATHISEN, Aina
See GERNER-MATHISEN, Aina
2224. GENN, Gottfried
"September" (tr. by Edgar Lohner and Cid Corman). [QRL] (12:32/33) 93, p. 377 - 378.

176

GENOWAYS

2225. GENOWAYS, Ted
"Defining Life in the Sonora." [Poem] (70) N 93, p. 8.
"Hoop." [Plain] (14:1) Fall 93, p. 12-13.
"Llano Estacado." [Poem] (70) N 93, p. 9.
"Phone Call from Tucson, AZ to Lindon, NE." [Poem] (70) N 93, p. 10.
2226. GENT, Andrew
"Someone Speaks." [ChiR] (39:2) 93, p. 65.
2227. GENTILCORE, Roxanne M.
"Letter to a Friend." [AntigR] (92) Wint 93, p. 96.
2228. GENTRY, Jane
"Epiphany 1992." [HolCrit] (30:2) Ap 93, p. 16.
"In the Darkness." [HolCrit] (30:2) Ap 93, p. 18.
2229. GEORGE, Anthony
"Nervous Breakdown Blues." [Footwork] (23) 93, p. 125.
2230. GEORGE, Beth
"(This Isn't a Smile, It's a Smirk.)" [Bogg] (66) Wint 92-93, p. 61.
2231. GEORGE, Diana Hume
"Lovers, Union Station, Chicago." [SpoonR] (18:1) Wint-Spr 93, p. 36-39.
"Wearing a Human Face" (Carlsbad Caverns, New Mexico). [GeoR] (47:1) Spr 93,
    p. 95-97.
2232. GEORGE, Emery
"Backbird: Poems on the World and Work of Franz Kafka" (Excerpt). [AmerPoR]
    (22:4) Jl-Ag 93, p. 31.
"Forced March" (tr. of Miklós Radnóti). [BelPoJ] (44:1) Fall 93, p. 48.
2233. GEORGE, Faye
"Daphne" (For Robert Graves). [Poetry] (163:2) N 93, p. 88.
"Homestead, Florida" (March 20, 1979). [Interim] (12:2) Fall-Wint 93, p. 7.
"Journal Entry, July 28, 1972." [PoetC] (25:1) Fall 93, p. 7-8.
"Six Times Stronger Than Steel." [Interim] (12:2) Fall-Wint 93, p. 6.
2234. GEORGE, Gerald
"Night" (tr. of Paul jRodenko). [Vis] (41) 93, p. 7.
2235. GEORGE, Stefan
"The Park They Say Is Dead" (tr. by Robert B. Hass). [BlackWR] (20:1) Fall-Wint
    93, p. 119.
2236. GEORGIEV, Marin
"Riverbend" (tr. by Lisa Sapinkopf and Georgi Belev). [Paint] (19:38) Aut 92, p. 57.
"Silence" (tr. by Lisa Sapinkopf and Georgi Belev). [Paint] (19:38) Aut 92, p. 56.
2237. GERGELY, Agnes
"Imago 7: Elegy for the Images of Christopher Okigbo" (tr. by Nathaniel Tarn).
    [GrandS] (12:1, #45) 93, p. 99-100.
"Imago 8: Proportions" (tr. by Nathaniel Tarn). [GrandS] (12:1, #45) 93, p. 96-97.
"Imago 9: The Parchment" (tr. by Nathaniel Tarn). [GrandS] (12:1, #45) 93, p. 97 -
    98.
2238. GERHARDT, Ida
"The Daily Work" (tr. by Sheila Dietz). [Vis] (41) 93, p. 22.
"Thasos" (tr. by Sheila Dietz). [Vis] (43) 93, p. 18.
2239. GERLACH, Lee
"Ghazals III." [GrahamHR] (17) Fall 93, p. 7-12.
"May — There is a flue trapped in the beehive." [Verse] (10:1) Spr 93, p. 34.
GERMAIN, Sheryl St.
    See ST. GERMAIN, Sheryl
2240. GERNER-MATHISEN, Aina
"Black Spruce" (tr. of Astrid Hjertenaes Andersen, w. Suzanne Bachner). [MassR]
    (34:4) Wint 93-94, p. 503.
"Double Image" (tr. of Astrid Hjertenaes Andersen, w. Suzanne Bachner). [Vis] (43)
    93, p. 42.
"Image" (tr. of Astrid Hjertenaes Andersen, w. Suzanne Bachner). [Vis] (43) 93, p.
    42.
"Impressions from the Legends about The Twelve Constellations" (tr. of Astrid
    Hjertenaes Andersen, w. Suzanne Bachner). [NewYorkQ] (52) 93, p. 51-54.
"Winter sine Anno" (tr. of Astrid Hjertenaes Andersen, w. Suzanne Bachner).
    [WillowS] (33) Wint 93, p. 20-21.
2241. GEROV, Alexander
"Mice" (tr. by Lisa Sapinkopf, w. Georgi Belev). [Agni] (37) 93, p. 258.
2242. GERSHATOR, David
"Terra Incognita / Taino Incognito." [CaribbeanW] (7) 93, p. 16-17.

177

2243. GERSTLE, Val
"Mom Told Me to Grow Up and Win the Nobel Prize." [ProseP] (1) 92, p. 32.
2244. GERSTLER, Amy
"Her Account of Herself." [Arshile] (2) 93, p. 22-23.
"An Invalid." [AmerPoR] (22:1) Ja-F 93, p. 30.
"A Love Story." [Arshile] (2) 93, p. 20-21.
"She Senses the Presence of a Dead Suitor in Her Room." [Chelsea] (55) 93, p. 47 -
48.
2245. GERVIN, Charles A.
"For Kevin Ziegler." [JamesWR] (10:4) Sum 93, p. 18.
2246. GERWIRTZMAN, Liz
"Sarah's Laughter." [Sequoia] (34/35) 92-93, p. 84-85.
2247. GERY, John
"Two Mississippis" (for Rebecca & Darryl). [Iowa] (23:2) Spr-Sum 93, p. 129-130.
2248. GESSNER, Kathryn H.
"Winter Break from College after My Father's Plane Crash." [LouisL] (10:1) Spr 93,
p. 52.
2249. GEVIRTZ, Susan
"Anaxsa Fragment: Coming to New Land." [Avec] (6:1) 93, p. 136-145.
"Pathment." [BlackBread] (3) 93, p. 55-67.
2250. GEX-BREAUX, Quo Vadis
"Aging." [AfAmRev] (27:1) Spr 93, p. 130.
"The Long and Short of It." [AfAmRev] (27:1) Spr 93, p. 130.
2251. GFOELLER, Michael
"Al-Bukhari." [BellArk] (9:5) S-O 93, p. 9.
"Al-Ghazali in Jerusalem." [BellArk] (9:5) S-O 93, p. 9.
"Al-Mu'tazilah." [BellArk] (9:5) S-O 93, p. 9.
2252. GHIMOSOULIS, Kostís
"Berlin Poem" (from *To Stóma Kléftis*, Athens, 1886, tr. by Yannis Goumas). [Os]
(36) Spr 93, p. 30.
"Pointed Hour" (from *To Stóma Kléftis*, Athens, 1886, tr. by Yannis Goumas). [Os]
(36) Spr 93, p. 31.
2253. GHIU, Bogdan
"Prologue to the Book" (tr. by Adam Sorkin, w. the author). [Vis] (43) 93, p. 50.
GHOLOSON, Christien
See GHOLSON, Christien
2254. GHOLSON, Christien
"Circle." [BellArk] (9:3) My-Je 93, p. 8.
"The Glass Tower." [ChironR] (12:1, #34) Spr 93, p. 35.
"I Am the Bodhisattva Who Saves the People on This Bus from the Smell of My
Feet." [ChironR] (12:1, #34) Spr 93, p. 35.
"I Swim in the Golden Heat of Jazz's Pure-Land of Anarchy." [BellArk] (9:4) Jl-Ag
93, p. 10.
"I Write to the One I Love Who Lives on in My Boots." [BellArk] (9:2) Mr-Ap 93,
p. 25.
"No Windows." [Lactuca] (17) Apr 93, p. 39-40.
"Part Your Lips." [BellArk] (9:3) My-Je 93, p. 9.
"Untitled: Sketch: Jacquie reading Blofeld's 'Wheel of Life' in Christmas light."
[BellArk] (9:1) Ja-F 93, p. 22.
"What It's Like to Be an Angel." [BellArk] (9:1) Ja-F 93, p. 25.
"When Spring Finally Came, After a Terrible Winter: A Watercolor." [BellArk]
(9:6) N-D 93, p. 13.
2255. GIBB, Robert
"Gnats." [KenR] (NS 15:3) Sum 93, p. 49-50.
"Moths." [KenR] (NS 15:3) Sum 93, p. 47-48.
"Mushrooms." [KenR] (NS 15:3) Sum 93, p. 48-49.
"My Life in Song." [CinPR] (24) Spr 93, p. 68-69.
"Nocturne." [SouthernR] (29:3) Sum, Jl 93, p. 577-578.
"The Orchard." [HampSPR] Wint 93, p. 7-9.
"Revelation." [SouthernR] (29:3) Sum, Jl 93, p. 576-577.
"The Shape of the Goddess in Homestead Park." [SouthernR] (29:3) Sum, Jl 93, p.
578-579.
2256. GIBBONS, Reginald
"Folk Saying." [QRL] (12:32/33) 93, p. 174-175.
"Historic Site." [QRL] (12:32/33) 93, p. 177.
"In a Bar with CNN on TV." [QRL] (12:32/33) 93, p. 170-171.

"Plains Hope." [QRL] (12:32/33) 93, p. 175-176.
"Quiet" (Quartz Mountain, Oklahoma). [QRL] (12:32/33) 93, p. 175.
"Reminiscence of a Distant Exile, Or, Song of Houston." [ChiR] (39:1) 93, p. 60-61.
"Simple Sentence." [QRL] (12:32/33) 93, p. 176-177.
"With Wings / Con Alas, Versos de Invierno para Hugo / Winter Lines for Hugo."
    [QRL] (12:32/33) 93, p. 171-173.
"Worship." [QRL] (12:32/33) 93, p. 173-174.
2257. GIBSON, Grace Loving
"Heron." [Crucible] (29) Fall 93, p. 36.
2258. GIBSON, John
"Spätlese." [CumbPR]] (13:1) Fall 93, p. 34.
2259. GIBSON, L. G.
"If I met him   if he wanted me." [PraF] (14:3) Aut 93, p. 122.
"Love, it left me." [PraF] (14:3) Aut 93, p. 122.
2260. GIBSON, Margaret
"At the Ravine." [GeoR] (47:1) Spr 93, p. 81-82.
"Blessing." [SouthernR] (29:4) Aut, O 93, p. 742-743.
"A Call to Worship" (from "Radiation"). [OhioR] (49) 93, p. 94.
"Prayer Ascending, Prayer Descending." [SouthernR] (29:4) Aut, O 93, p. 743-744.
2261. GIBSON, Max
"Lara and the New World." [Vis] (42) 93, p. 11-12.
2262. GIBSON, Stephen
"The Ax-Murder of Trotsky by Ramon Mercader, Mexico, Agusut 20, 1940."
    [ApalQ] (39) 93, p. 52.
"The Baccae: The Deaths of Benito Mussolini and Claretta Petacci, Milan, April 29,
    1945." [ApalQ] (39) 93, p. 51.
"Moral." [Chelsea] (54) 93, p. 97.
"Squid." [Chelsea] (54) 93, p. 95.
"Tadamori and the Oil Thief" (after Hiroshige, 19th century). [Chelsea] (54) 93, p.
    96.
2263. GIBSON, Stephen Robert
"Hotel Ballrooms." [PoetryNW] (34:2) Sum 93, p. 25.
2264. GIELLA, Al
"Just for Fun." [Footwork] (23) 93, p. 72.
"A Little Nothing." [Footwork] (23) 93, p. 73.
"Paterson, N.J." (a National Monument). [Footwork] (23) 93, p. 73.
"Paterson Re-Visited" (from Los Angeles). [Footwork] (23) 93, p. 72.
"Urban Love." [Footwork] (23) 93, p. 73.
2265. GIESECKE, Lee
"Emergency." [Bogg] (66) Wint 92-93, p. 8.
2266. GIGANTE, Denise
"Advance of the Bone Flutist." [AnotherCM] (26) Fall 93, p. 17.
2267. GILBERT, Alan
"Mixed Signals." [Agni] (38) 93, p. 114-115.
2268. GILBERT, Celia
"A Vision." [HarvardR] (3) Wint 93, p. 81.
2269. GILBERT, Christopher
"A Chance Between Things." [Obs] (8:1) Spr-Sum 93, p. 86-87.
"Getting Over There (Outside Mendocino)." [RiverS] (39) 93, p. 19.
"Metaphor for Something That Plays Us / Remembering Eric Dolphy." [Obs] (8:1)
    Spr-Sum 93, p. 84-86.
2270. GILBERT, David
"Unbound." [Caliban] (12) 93, p. 138-139.
2271. GILBERT, Jack
"Hard Wired." [NewL] (60:1) 93, p. 31.
"Harm and Boon in the Meetings." [NewL] (60:1) 93, p. 29.
"How to Love the Dead." [NewL] (60:1) 93, p. 33.
"I Imagine the Gods." [NewL] (60:1) 93, p. 30.
"Thinking About Ecstasy." [NewL] (60:1) 93, p. 32.
2272. GILBERT, Margaret
"Faulkner at Work." [NewYorkQ] (52) 93, p. 67.
2273. GILDNER, Gary
"Close to Trees." [GeoR] (47:1) Spr 93, p. 42.
"First Poem from Slovakia: A Dream in the Carpathians." [CutB] (39) Wint 93, p.
    37-38.

179

2274. GILFOND, Henry
"Holocaust." [CentR] (37:3) Fall 93, p. 542-543.
2275. GILL, Evalyn Pierpoint
"Photographer." [Crucible] (29) Fall 93, p. 38.
2276. GILL, Gagan
"The Fifth Man" (tr. by Mrinal Pande and Arlene Zide). [Prima] (16/17) 93, p. 87.
2277. GILL, James Vladimir
"Man and His Shadow" (From *La part de l'ombre*, tr. of Jean Tardieu). [ProseP] (2) 93, p. 93.
"Meudon" (After Rodin). [ProseP] (2) 93, p. 38.
"Paper Women" (From *Pièces brèves en quart de ton*, tr. of Jean Pierre Vallotton). [ProseP] (2) 93, p. 95.
"Vertigo" (From *La part de l'ombre*, tr. of Jean Tardieu). [ProseP] (2) 93, p. 92.
2278. GILL-LONERGAN, Janet
"Of Wars and Such." [BellArk] (9:1) Ja-F 93, p. 12.
2279. GILLIHAN, Sean
"Directions to the House" (for Rick). [PaintedHR] (8) Wint 93, p. 5.
2280. GILLILAND, Gail
"Siblings." [Plain] (13:3) Spr 93, p. 18.
2281. GILLILAND, Mary
"Desire at Work." [Bogg] (66) Wint 92-93, p. 48.
"Leveled" (excerpts: four of ten phases. The Nimrod/Hardman Awards: Finalist). [Nimrod] (37:1) Fall-Wint 93, p. 52-55.
2282. GILLIS, Don
"On the 'Son of Man' by Gerry Squires." [TickleAce] (23) Spr-Sum 92, p. 57.
2283. GILLMAN, Richard
"Together Among Monarchs." [SewanR] (101:3) Jl-S, Sum 93, p. 333-334.
2284. GILSDORF, Ethan
"Letter from Japan" (after, and for, Massie Okamoto). [NewYorkQ] (52) 93, p. 46-47.
2285. GILSON, Annette
"Ways to Give Way." [SouthernPR] (33:1) Spr 93, p. 42-43.
2286. GILSON, William
"The Blue Lamp." [Epiphany] (4:3) Jl 93, p. 197.
"Breakfast." [CapeR] (28:1) Spr 93, p. 4.
GINEBRA, Arminda Valdés
See VALDÉS GINEBRA, Arminda
2287. GINSBERG, Allen
"Fighting Society." [Sulfur] (32) Spr 93, p. 113.
"Food for Thought, or Just Deserts" (M.F.A. Workshop w. Marie Hasten, Howard Glyn, Pamela Hughes, M. R. Syneck, Lisbeth Keiley, Mary Greene and David Trinidad, Nov. 21, 1988). [BrooklynR] (10) 93, p. 94-95.
"Hospital Window." [PaintedB] (50/51) 93, p. 88-89.
"Mind Writing Slogans." [Sulfur] (32) Spr 93, p. 125-127.
"Poem in the Form of a Snake That Bites Its Tail." [Sulfur] (32) Spr 93, p. 118-124.
2288. GINSBERG, Aren
"How to Love a Colorblind Artist." [EngJ] (82:3) Mr 93, p. 93.
2289. GIOIA, Dana
"Theseus Describes the King of Hell" (Adapted from Seneca's "Hercules Furens"). [Hellas] (4:2) Fall 93, p. 43.
2290. GIOSEFFI, Daniela
"Flying Home to Jersey from the Top of the Empire State." [Footwork] (23) 93, p. 157-158.
"The Girl with Purple Hair." [Footwork] (23) 93, p. 156.
"The Mother at the Zoo." [Footwork] (23) 93, p. 156-157.
2291. GISCOMBE, C. S.
"Look Ahead — Look South" (Selections: 3 poems). [Obs] (8:1) Spr-Sum 93, p. 88-89.
"This Way" (opening poem of the sequence, "Blue Hole, Flood Waters, Little Miami River"). [CinPR] (24) Spr 93, p. 64-67.
2292. GITZEN, Julian
"Cleaning Day in the Garage." [LouisL] (10:2) Fall 93, p. 55.
"Flossie's Clematis." [LouisL] (10:2) Fall 93, p. 52.
"Late Arrivals." [LouisL] (10:2) Fall 93, p. 54.
"A Witness to the Moment." [LouisL] (10:2) Fall 93, p. 53.

2293. GIUSSANI, Silvio
"Abel and Abel" (tr. by Gayle Ridinger). [Verse] (10:2) Sum 93, p. 21.
"In the Distance" (tr. by Gayle Ridinger). [Verse] (10:2) Sum 93, p. 22.
"Vegetable Calendar" (tr. by Gayle Ridinger). [Verse] (10:2) Sum 93, p. 21.
2294. GIZZI, Peter
"Façades for Theron Ware." [GrandS] (12:2, #46) Sum 93, p. 79-83.
2295. GLADDING, Jody
"Blue Willow." [Agni] (37) 93, p. 8.
"Indian Paint." [Agni] (37) 93, p. 6.
"Silver Queen." [Agni] (37) 93, p. 5.
"Uncle." [Agni] (37) 93, p. 7.
2296. GLADE, Jon Forrest
"Black Bridge." [Pearl] (17) Spr 93, p. 65.
"Burn Victim" (Fitzsimons Army Hospital, 1969). [ChironR] (12:4/13:1, #37/38)
Wint 93-Spr 94, p. 26.
"Going Under." [ChironR] (12:4/13:1, #37/38) Wint 93-Spr 94, p. 26.
"Med-Evac." [ChironR] (12:4/13:1, #37/38) Wint 93-Spr 94, p. 26.
2297. GLANCY, Diane
"Buffalo Jump, Blue Mounds, Minnesota." [Agni] (38) 93, p. 68.
"The Deer Rider." [CreamCR] (17:1) Spr 93, p. 3.
"Light Beneath the Skin (or Pronoun 2)." [GreenMR] (NS 6:1) Wint-Spr 93, p. 86.
"Promoting Neurite Growth in the Mammalian Nervous System" (a seminar notice
in the biology department, Macalester College). [NorthStoneR] (11) 93, p.
138-139.
"A Walk on a Country Road 16 Miles Northeast of Iowa City." [NorthStoneR] (11)
93, p. 139.
2298. GLANCY, Gabrielle
"A Boy, a Woman, a Blackbird." [GlobalCR] (2) Fall 93, p. 40-41.
"The Goat." [AntR] (51:4) Fall 93, p. 566.
"In Visible Light." [Agni] (37) 93, p. 13-14.
"Meditation on the Law of Changes." [AmerPoR] (22:5) S-O 93, p. 44.
"Then We Found the River" (for Margaret). [KenR] (NS 15:4) Fall 93, p. 17.
"Understanding Fog." [AmerPoR] (22:5) S-O 93, p. 45.
"Weed." [GlobalCR] (2) Fall 93, p. 42-43.
"The World from Under." [Ploughs] (19:1) Spr 93, p. 188.
2299. GLASCO, Sue
"Moon and Stars." [EngJ] (82:6) O 93, p. 93.
2300. GLASER, Elton
"Christmas This Side of the Golden Gate." [GettyR] (6:4) Aut 93, p. 671-673.
"Endsheet." [GeoR] (47:4) Wint 93, p. 655-656.
"Family Possessions." [LouisL] (10:1) Spr 93, p. 26-28.
"Genealogy." [CreamCR] (17:1) Spr 93, p. 70.
"Pilgrimage." [LouisL] (10:1) Spr 93, p. 24-25.
"Principles of Conversion." [SouthernHR] (27:2) Spr 93, p. 132.
"Revolver." [CinPR] (24) Spr 93, p. 71.
"Shucking." [Border] (2) Spr 93, p. 29-30.
"Uphill Battle." [HampSPR] Wint 93, p. 10.
"Venice." [LaurelR] (27:2) Sum 93, p. 102-105.
2301. GLASER, Kirk
"The Chain." [Thrpny] (52) Wint 93, p. 20.
2302. GLASER, Michael S.
"Changing Address Books." [Footwork] (23) 93, p. 18.
"Hand" (for Kathy). [Footwork] (23) 93, p. 17.
"The Shapes of Things" (for Joshua). [Footwork] (23) 93, p. 17-18.
"Stay Awake." [Footwork] (23) 93, p. 18.
"Wanting to Be Like God." [Footwork] (23) 93, p. 18.
2303. GLASS, Terrence
"The Shape of a Scream." [HawaiiR] (17:1, #37) Spr 93, p. 208-209.
2304. GLASSER, Jane Ellen
"My Daughter the Thief." [Kalliope] (15:2) 93, p. 61.
"New Tenants." [SouthernPR] (33:1) Spr 93, p. 56-57.
2305. GLATT, Lisa
"Favors." [OnTheBus] (5:2, #12) Sum-Fall 93, p. 82.
"What the Fast Girl Knows" (for Karin Cook, the nieces, and all the daughters).
[Pearl] (17) Spr 93, p. 7.

2306. GLAVE, Thomas
    "The Korean Market." [Callaloo] (16:3) Sum 93, p. 684.
    "Our Lives." [Callaloo] (16:3) Sum 93, p. 685.
2307. GLAZE, Andrew
    "Cristina's Song." [Light] (8) Wint 93, p. 20.
    "An Honorary Habsburg." [LullwaterR] (4:2) Spr-Sum 93, p. 36-37.
    "Light Brigade." [LullwaterR] (4:2) Spr-Sum 93, p. 96.
    "Please Take the Joy of It" (tr. of Osip Mandelstam). [NewYorkQ] (52) 93, p. 47.
2308. GLAZER, Jane
    "Some Trick of Light." [AntR] (51:1) Wint 93, p. 95.
2309. GLAZER, Michele
    "A Convoluted Red Wad of Concentric Circles Stuck on an Attenuated Column and
        Having an Aroma, to My Wife." [ColEng] (55:8) D 93, p. 905-906.
    "Fruit Flies to the Too Ripe Fruit." [ColEng] (55:8) D 93, p. 904.
    "His Thighs Strange. Broken. Knowledgeable." [OnTheBus] (6:1, #13) Wint 93-Spr
        94, p. 99.
    "It Is Hard to Look at What We Came to Think We'd Come to See." [Ploughs]
        (19:1) Spr 93, p. 74-75.
    "My." [OnTheBus] (6:1, #13) Wint 93-Spr 94, p. 99.
    "Summer, & Her Painted Flowers." [Ploughs] (19:1) Spr 93, p. 72-73.
2310. GLEASON, James
    "Available Light." [TarRP] (32:2) Spr 93, p. 31-32.
2311. GLEASON, Marian
    "Auditorium." [ChrC] (110:9) 17 Mr 93, p. 295.
2312. GLEASON, Rebecca Jane
    "This Suit." [HampSPR] Wint 93, p. 40-41.
2313. GLENDAY, John
    "Artillery Horses Under Fire" (from "Whitman's War"). [Event] (22:1) Spr 93, p. 31.
    "Driving Cattle Through Washington" (from "Whitman's War"). [Event] (22:1) Spr
        93, p. 30.
    "Our Wonderful Inventions" (The Patent Office in Washington . . ., from
        "Whitman's War"). [Event] (22:1) Spr 93, p. 33.
    "Whitman Visits the Armory Square Hospital" (from "Whitman's War"). [Event]
        (22:1) Spr 93, p. 32.
2314. GLENN, Laura
    "The Moment." [Ascent] (18:1) Fall 93, p. 65.
    "The Spiral." [MassR] (34:4) Wint 93-94, p. 633-634.
2315. GLICK, G. Wayne
    "Tijuana Haiku." [ChrC] (110:16) 12 My 93, p. 519.
2316. GLICKMAN, Susan
    "For the Young Woman Who Left the Room When I Read a Poem About Chld
        Abuse." [Event] (22:2) Sum 93, p. 29.
    "The Lost Child" (1-2). [PraS] (67:4) Wint 93, p. 78-80.
2317. GLOEGGLER, Tony
    "June, 1987." [Bogg] (66) Wint 92-93, p. 27.
    "Leaning back in his leather lounge chair." [NewYorkQ] (51) 93, p. 55.
    "Uncle Dom." [SlipS] (13) 93, p. 61-62.
2318. GLORIA, Eugene
    "Rizal's Ghost." [MidAR] (14:1) 93, p. 126-127.
    "Thie Promise." [MidAR] (14:1) 93, p. 125.
2319. GLOVER, Jon
    "Glass Goblet." [Stand] (34:4) Aut 93, p. 30.
    "Thirty Miles East of Niagara" (for Dorothy Shaver). [Stand] (34:2) Spr 93, p. 44 -
        47.
2320. GLYN, Howard
    "Food for Thought, or Just Deserts" (M.F.A. Workshop w. Marie Hasten, Pamela
        Hughes, M. R. Syneck, Lisbeth Keiley, Mary Greene, David Trinidad and
        Allen Ginsberg, Nov. 21, 1988). [BrooklynR] (10) 93, p. 94-95.
2321. GNUP-KRUIP, Valentina
    "Reds, Purples, Blues." [HiramPoR] (53/54) Fall 92-Sum 93, p. 40.
2322. GODING, Cecile
    "White Space." [PoetryNW] (34:3) Aut 93, p. 24.
2323. GODOY, Iliana
    "Invicta Carne" (De: *Invicta carne*, México: Ediciones Armella, 1989).
        [Trasimagen] (1:1) Otoño-Invierno 93, p. 1-3.

2324. GOEDICKE, Patricia
"The Adventure." [WillowS] (32) Sum 93, p. 7-10.
"Because We Are Not Separate." [CutB] (40) Spr 93, p. 52-54.
"Danger of Falling." [NoDaQ] (61:3) Sum 93, p. 7-9.
"The Life of Each Seed." [SouthernR] (29:4) Aut, O 93, p. 745-746.
"Look, It's Poetry!" [NewEngR] (15:4) Fall 93, p. 93-97.
"Moments the Body Rises." [TarRP] (32:2) Spr 93, p. 3-6.
"Snow." [DenQ] (27:3) Wint 93, p. 31-32.
"The Three Tortoise Secret-of-the-World Power Plant." [NoDaQ] (61:3) Sum 93, p.
    10-11.
"Wild Card." [WillowS] (32) Sum 93, p. 11.
2325. GOERNER, Leslie
"Grace Notes." [BellArk] (9:6) N-D 93, p. 13.
"Prospect." [BellArk] (9:6) N-D 93, p. 13.
"Sifting Through." [BellArk] (9:6) N-D 93, p. 13.
"Through the Fire." [BellArk] (9:6) N-D 93, p. 13.
2326. GOETSCH, Douglas
"Father's Day, 1993." [HampSPR] Wint 93, p. 59-60.
"Folds." [HampSPR] Wint 93, p. 59.
2327. GOETZ, Melody
"Coffee Shop, 1991 (after Iraq, after Ethiopia, after Bangladesh)." [PraF] (14:2)
    Sum 93, p. 37.
"New World." [PraF] (14:2) Sum 93, p. 38.
"Snapshot: Express to Winnipeg." [PraF] (14:2) Sum 93, p. 38.
2328. GOGOL, John M.
"At E.'s Home in Vresice" (tr. of Reiner Kunze). [QRL] (12:32/33) 93, p. 455-456.
"A Campfire and Ants" (tr. of Alexander Solzhenitsyn). [QRL] (12:32/33) 93, p.
    521-522.
"Hungarian Rhapsody 66" (for Tibor Déry, tr. of Reiner Kunze). [QRL] (12:32/33)
    93, p. 456.
2329. GOLD, Nili
"Lying on the Water" (tr. of Dahlia Ravikovitch). [Trans] (28) Spr 93, p. 167-168.
2330. GOLD, Sid
"There." [ProseP] (1) 92, p. 33.
2331. GOLDBARTH, Albert
"400,000." [Boulevard] (8:1, #22) Spr 93, p. 32-33.
"Acquisitions." [Epoch] (42:1) 93, p. 97-99.
"American Koan." [Light] (6) Sum 93, p. 6.
"The American Photographic Postcard: 1900-1920." [IllinoisR] (1:1) Fall 93, p. 58 -
    60.
"American Tune." [Light] (6) Sum 93, p. 5.
"And Now Let's Check the Map." [PraS] (67:1) Spr 93, p. 47-48.
"The Animals." [SouthwR] (78:1) Wint 93, p. 130-131.
"Arguing Bartusiak." [Poetry] (163:3) D 93, p. 131-132.
"Birds." [PoetC] (25:1) Fall 93, p. 26.
"The Bonds." [Poetry] (162:2) My 93, p. 71-72.
"A Book Left Open in the Bathroom." [Light] (6) Sum 93, p. 6.
"Days with the Family Realist." [OntR] (38) Spr-Sum 93, p. 44.
"Doctor Nitty-Gritty." [Epoch] (42:1) 93, p. 100-102.
"Donald Duck in Danish." [NewEngR] (15:1) Wint 93, p. 126-131.
"Effect Over Distance." [Poetry] (162:2) My 93, p. 73-74.
"The Emergence of Flight from Aristotle's Mud." [OntR] (38) Spr-Sum 93, p. 42-43.
"Engravings in the Books of the 17th Century Scientist/Mystic Athanasius Kircher"
    (with an epigraph from a video catalogue). [Epoch] (42:1) 93, p. 94-96.
"Entire Lives." [NewYorker] (68:49) 25 Ja 93, p. 76-77.
"Etymology: the Com- of 'Compassion'." [DenQ] (27:4) Spr 93, p. 72-74.
"Fang." [Agni] (37) 93, p. 244-247.
"Figurating." [Light] (6) Sum 93, p. 3.
"Flu Song." [Light] (6) Sum 93, p. 5.
"Fraud." [WillowS] (33) Wint 93, p. 8-9.
"The Glimpse of Flabbergassment." [WillowS] (33) Wint 93, p. 7.
"A Haiku." [Light] (6) Sum 93, p. 3.
"Harmonica." [Light] (6) Sum 93, p. 5.
"A Histry F Censrship." [Light] (6) Sum 93, p. 5.
"Humdingers Kneeslappers Sidesplitters & Yuks." [ClockR] (8:1/2) 93, p. 140-141.
"An Invocation." [PoetryNW] (34:1) Spr 93, p. 12-13.

183

"It's Twenty Degrees, and It's Snowing, and I'm in My Livingroom, Idly
    Contemplating a Page of Grimy Erasure." [PoetC] (25:1) Fall 93, p. 24-25.
"'Jeff' of 'Mutt and Jeff' Leans on Air." [PraS] (67:1) Spr 93, p. 45-46.
"Kansas: Stories." [GeoR] (47:4) Wint 93, p. 749-751.
"Little, Big." [PoetryNW] (34:1) Spr 93, p. 11-12.
"Marriage, and Other Science Fiction." [ParisR] (35:126) Spr 93, p. 44-50.
"Minute Mysteries." [IndR] (16:2) Fall 93, p. 115-116.
"Pillows." [IllinoisR] (1:1) Fall 93, p. 21.
"The Professor of Strangeness Out for a Walk." [WillowS] (33) Wint 93, p. 10.
"Public Life." [MichQR] (32:1) Wint 93, p. 39-40.
"Radio Pope." [OhioR] (50) 93, p. 17-53.
"Refinement." [GeoR] (47:4) Wint 93, p. 752-753.
"Repeated Sightings." [PraS] (67:1) Spr 93, p. 46-47.
"Spaces." [Poetry] (163:3) D 93, p. 132-133.
"A Spin Around the Countryside." [Light] (6) Sum 93, p. 3.
"Stephen Hawking, Walking." [CreamCR] (17:2) Fall 93, p. 154-155.
"Tee-Hees / The Call to the Ark." [LaurelR] (27:2) Sum 93, p. 69-70.
"That Shape." [LaurelR] (27:2) Sum 93, p. 66-67.
"Thawed." [Boulevard] (8:1, #22) Spr 93, p. 34-35.
"There." [ClockR] (8:1/2) 93, p. 139.
"Totem." [PraS] (67:1) Spr 93, p. 49.
"Two Readings." [Light] (6) Sum 93, p. 4-5.
"Untitled: The philosopher, who knows nothing is 'real'." [Light] (6) Sum 93, p. 3.
"A Walk in the City." [LaurelR] (27:2) Sum 93, p. 67-69.
"With Lettuce." [OnTheBus] (5:2, #12) Sum-Fall 93, p. 83.
"A Woman Bathing in a Stream, 1654." [Boulevard] (8:2/3, #23/24) Fall 93, p. 28 -
    30.
"The Yoking of the Two Modes." [Poetry] (163:3) D 93, p. 134-135.
"Zen America '89." [Light] (6) Sum 93, p. 6.
2332. GOLDBERG, Barbara
"Alarums and Excursions." [Light] (8) Wint 93, p. 6.
"The Art of Waiting" (tr. of Moshe Dor, w. the author). [Trans] (28) Spr 93, p. 159.
"Crazy Jane's Return." [Light] (8) Wint 93, p. 5.
"December" (tr. of Moshe Dor, w. the author). [Trans] (28) Spr 93, p. 159.
"Goliath" (tr. of Moshe Dor, w. the author). [Trans] (28) Spr 93, p. 158.
"It Needs Brains." [Light] (8) Wint 93, p. 6.
"Marvelous Pursuits." [Light] (8) Wint 93, p. 3-5.
"Shampoo" (tr. of Moshe Dor, w. the author). [Trans] (28) Spr 93, p. 157.
2333. GOLDBERG, Beckian Fritz
"The Betrayer." [NewEngR] (15:4) Fall 93, p. 67.
"Everything Where I Left It." [Field] (48) Spr 93, p. 12-13.
"I Have Set My Heart on the Sparrow." [Field] (48) Spr 93, p. 10-11.
"My Bomb." [GettyR] (6:1) Wint 93, p. 166-167.
"Rebirth." [GettyR] (6:1) Wint 93, p. 162-163.
"Refugees." [GettyR] (6:1) Wint 93, p. 164-165.
"Refugees." [Harp] (286:1715) Ap 93, p. 36.
"The Subject." [NewEngR] (15:4) Fall 93, p. 66.
GOLDBERG, Caryn Mirriam
    See MIRRIAM-GOLDBERG, Caryn
2334. GOLDBERG, Janet
"The Error." [Turnstile] (4:1) 93, p. 18-19.
2335. GOLDBERGER, Iefke
"Encounter in The Hague." [Vis] (41) 93, p. 42.
"Leap Year." [Rosebud] (1:1) Wint 93, p. 90.
2336. GOLDBLATT, Eli
"Army Barbers." [LouisL] (10:2) Fall 93, p. 31-32.
2337. GOLDEMBERG, Isaac
"Body of Love" (tr. by Veronica Miranda). [Luz] (3) Ja 93, p. 18.
"Dreams" (2 poems from "La Vida al Contado," tr. by Veronica Miranda). [Luz] (5)
    N 93, p. 73, 75.
"Hagada." [Trasimagen] (1:1) Otoño-Invierno 93, p. 38.
"Sueños" (2 poems from "La Vida al Contado"). [Luz] (5) N 93, p. 72, 74.
"La Vida al Contado" (Selections: 4 poems). [Luz] (3) Ja 93, p. 17-20.
2338. GOLDEN, Gail
"Warsaw Pediatrics 1939" (for Dr. Adina Szwajger 1918-1993). [Vis] (42) 93, p.
    15-16.

184

2339. GOLDENSOHN, Barry
"Fresh Air." [Salm] (100) Fall 93, p. 163.
"Song to a Porcupine in Mating Season." [Salm] (100) Fall 93, p. 162-163.
"Sweet Town." [Agni] (38) 93, p. 137.
2340. GOLDENSOHN, Lorrie
"Bus Ride South." [Salm] (98/99) Spr-Sum 93, p. 74-75.
"L'Espirt de L'Escalier." [Salm] (98/99) Spr-Sum 93, p. 73.
"Things." [Salm] (98/99) Spr-Sum 93, p. 71-72.
2341. GOLDER, Herbert
"Andromache" (Excerpt, tr. of Euripides). [Pequod] (35) 93, p. 41-42.
2342. GOLDMAN, Judith
"4 in a Cave" (Selections: III-IV, w. Lisa Jarnot). [13thMoon] (12:1/2) 93-94, p. 34 - 35.
2343. GOLDMAN, Judy
"Getting My Children to Rub My Feet." [MidwQ] (34:2) Wint 93, p. 215.
2344. GOLDMAN, Kathleen Zeisler (Kathy)
"Fire Not Water." [OnTheBus] (6:1, #13) Wint 93-Spr 94, p. 101.
"'Is This a Feminist Statement?' She Asked, Dismayed." [OnTheBus] (6:1, #13) Wint 93-Spr 94, p. 100-101.
"The Right Way to Be a Woman." [Pearl] (19) Fall-Wint 93, p. 9.
"Toward Water" (for Tanya). [OnTheBus] (5:2, #12) Sum-Fall 93, p. 84.
"Water Through Rock." [Northeast] (5:9) Wint 93-94, p. 17.
2345. GOLDMAN, Paula
"The Bather" (after "The Morning Bath," by Degas). [ClockR] (8:1/2) 93, p. 75-76.
"Edgar Degas (1834-1917)." [ClockR] (8:1/2) 93, p. 77.
"Eve's Daughters." [Kalliope] (15:3) 93, p. 12.
2346. GOLDSMITH, Bonnie Zucker
"Credo." [SpoonR] (18:2) Sum-Fall 93, p. 100-101.
"Refugees." [SpoonR] (18:2) Sum-Fall 93, p. 97-99.
2347. GOLDSTEIN, Laurence
"The Sports Complex." [Agni] (37) 93, p. 300-301.
2348. GOLDSTEIN-JACKSON, Kevin
"4-Letter Word." [Bogg] (66) Wint 92-93, p. 35.
2349. GOLDSWORTHY, Peter
"A Brief Introduction to Philosophy." [Verse] (10:2) Sum 93, p. 88-91.
"A Statistician to His Love." [BelPoJ] (44:2) Wint 93-94, p. 6.
"Suicide on Christmas Eve." [BelPoJ] (44:2) Wint 93-94, p. 7.
2350. GOLFFING, Francis
"(Antigone, Act II)" (after Sophocles, tr. of Friedrich Hölderlin). [SpiritSH] (58) 93, p. 18.
"Greece" (1st Version, tr. of Friedrich Hölderlin). [SpiritSH] (58) 93, p. 20.
"Oedipus at Colonus" (lines 668-693, after Sophocles, tr. of Friedrich Hölderlin). [SpiritSH] (58) 93, p. 19.
"Three Fragments of Pindar" (tr. of Friedrich Hölderlin). [SpiritSH] (58) 93, p. 17.
"A Vanished House." [QRL] (12:32/33) 93, p. 422-423.
2351. GOLL, Yvan
"The Crucified Swimmer" (tr. by Galway Knnell). [QRL] (12:32/33) 93, p. 423-424.
2352. GOMEZ, Luis Marcelino
"Como un Río." [LindLM] (12:1) Mr 93, p. 15.
"De Noche." [LindLM] (12:1) Mr 93, p. 15.
2353. GOMEZ, María Edna
"La Noche Es un Mar Profundo." [Luz] (5) N 93, p. 22.
2354. GOMEZ, Robert P.
"Hacia Ti." [Americas] (21:1) Spr 93, p. 69-70.
2355. GOMPERT, Chris
"Bunker Watch" (for Les Kay). [PoetC] (24:3) Spr 93, p. 33.
"Still Life." [PoetC] (24:3) Spr 93, p. 34.
2356. GON, Sam, III
"Night at Hakioawa." [BambooR] (57) Wint 93, p. 157.
"Po Hakioawa." [BambooR] (57) Wint 93, p. 157.
2357. GONET, Jill
"And Other Fantasy Lovers." [Agni] (37) 93, p. 87-88.
GONG-CHAE, Chung
   See CHUNG, Gong-chae

2358. GONTAREK, Leonard
"The Pillow Book of Leonard Gontarek" (9 selections). [PaintedB] (50/51) 93, p. 32-33.
2359. GONZALES-PRIETO, D. C.
"Kissing." [Sonora] (24/25) Spr 93, p. 109-110.
2360. GONZALEZ, Angel
"Cemetery in Colliure" (tr. by Steven Ford Brown). [QW] (37) Sum-Fall 93, p. 90 - 91.
"The Day Has Gone" (tr. by Cecilia C. Lee and Laura Higgins). [LitR] (36:3) Spr 93, p. 373-374.
"Erudites on Campus" (tr. by Steven Ford Brown and Gutierrez Revuelta). [HarvardR] (3) Wint 93, p. 142.
"Residential Zone" (tr. by Steven Ford Brown). [QW] (37) Sum-Fall 93, p. 92-93.
2361. GONZALEZ, Marcial
"Oysters." [ColR] (20:2) Fall 93, p. 52-53.
2362. GONZALEZ, Ray
"Four Times the Feast." [ColR] (20:2) Fall 93, p. 54-56.
"The Magnets" (on turning forty). [ColR] (20:2) Fall 93, p. 59-61.
"Song for the Lizard Painted on the Plate." [ColR] (20:2) Fall 93, p. 57-58.
2363. GOOBIE, Beth
"After the Resurrection." [CapilR] (2:11) Sum 93, p. 83-84.
"Black Bethlehem Star." [CapilR] (2:11) Sum 93, p. 81-82.
"Blueprint of Face." [CapilR] (2:11) Sum 93, p. 91-92.
"Cleaning Out the Locker." [CapilR] (2:11) Sum 93, p. 89-90.
"Just After I Knew." [CapilR] (2:11) Sum 93, p. 88.
"Two Brothers." [CapilR] (2:11) Sum 93, p. 85-87.
2364. GOODAN, Kevin
"St. Patrick's Day at the Oxford Bar" (for Mike Craig). [CutB] (39) Wint 93, p. 84.
2365. GOODIN, Thom
"The Slopping Crew." [Journal] (17:1) Spr-Sum 93, p. 45-46.
2366. GOODISON, Lorna
"Mother the Great Stones Got to Move." [Drumvoices] (3:1/2) Fall-Wint 93-94, p. 14-15.
"Nanny." [Drumvoices] (3:1/2) Fall-Wint 93-94, p. 13.
2367. GOODMAN, Brent
"Embalming." [FreeL] (12) Sum 93, p. 24-25.
"The Nutcracker Seat." [FreeL] (12) Sum 93, p. 25.
2368. GOODMAN, Diane
"Near Autumn." [IndR] (16:2) Fall 93, p. 100.
2369. GOODMAN, Henrietta
"Evensong." [PassN] (14:2) Wint 93, p. 6.
2370. GOODMAN, Michael
"Monumentum Aere." [PoetryNW] (34:1) Spr 93, p. 22-23.
2371. GOODMAN, Miriam
"Anxiety of Ten O'Clock." [Poetry] (162:5) Ag 93, p. 271.
"Hospital Visit." [Footwork] (23) 93, p. 49.
"Hungry." [Poetry] (162:5) Ag 93, p. 271.
"Shopping Trip." [ProseP] (1) 92, p. 34.
"Square I." [HarvardR] (3) Wint 93, p. 162.
"Tenants." [Footwork] (23) 93, p. 50.
"Widowed." [Poetry] (162:5) Ag 93, p. 270.
2372. GOODMAN, Ronald
"Dogbone." [AmerPoR] (22:1) Ja-F 93, p. 31.
2373. GORBANEVSKAYA, Natalya
"Untitled: When you begin to stumble on the simplest of words" (tr. by Lara Shapiro). [Asylum] (8) 93, p. 88.
2374. GORDON, C.
"Love Poem." [SouthernPR] (33:2) Fall 93, p. 13.
2375. GORDON, G. Timothy
"Navajo." [Border] (2) Spr 93, p. 31.
2376. GORDON, Jean
"Revealing German." [Pequod] (36) 93, p. 82-83.
2377. GORDON, Pamela K.
"I Grew Two Voices" (w. Monifa Atungaye Love). [Eyeball] (2) 93, p. 24-25.
2378. GORRELL, Nancy
"Grandma Came Down." [Footwork] (23) 93, p. 114.

"The Motor." [Blueline] (14) 93, p. 35.
"The Motor." [Footwork] (23) 93, p. 114-115.
"The River." [Footwork] (23) 93, p. 115.
2379. GORRELL, Robert
"Jet Flight." [Interim] (12:2) Fall-Wint 93, p. 4.
2380. GORRICK, Anne
"Flokati." [CreamCR] (17:1) Spr 93, p. 76.
2381. GOSSE, Peter
"Who Knows Who She Was" (tr. by Gisela Argyle). [PoetryC] (13:2) 93, p. 23.
2382. GOSSETT, Hattie
"In the Window/Monk." [AfAmRev] (27:4) Wint 93, p. 571-572.
2383. GOTERA, Vince
"Heirloom." [RiverS] (37) 93, p. 65-66.
"Mosquito / Manila Haiku." [MidAR] (14:1) 93, p. 39-40.
"Swimmers." [BambooR] (57) Wint 93, p. 159-160.
"Teaching Mary Ann Mah Jong." [BambooR] (57) Wint 93, p. 158.
"Uncle Ray Shoots Craps with Elvis." [RiverS] (37) 93, p. 67-68.
2384. GOTT, George
"Latitudes." [MidwQ] (35:1) Aut 93, p. 38.
GOTT, Lucy Pollard
See POLLARD-GOTT, Lucy
2385. GOULD, Janice
"Outside Language" (In memory of Rod McElroy). [AmerPoR] (22:4) Jl-Ag 93, p. 34.
2386. GOULD, Roberta
"Family Portrait" (Zacualpan, Mexico). [Border] (2) Spr 93, p. 32.
2387. GOUMAS, Yannis (Yannis A.)
"Berlin Poem" (from To Stóma Kléftis, Athens, 1886, tr. of Kostís Ghimosoúlis). [Os] (36) Spr 93, p. 30.
"Daughter" (tr. of Alexandra Plastira). [Vis] (43) 93, p. 25.
"Hangouts" (from Sto Gyrisma Tis Méras, Athens, 1992, tr. of Yánnis Kondós). [Os] (36) Spr 93, p. 33.
"The Mine" (from Idíis Sómasi, Athens, 1886, " (tr. of Thanásis Hadjópoulos). [Os] (36) Spr 93, p. 28.
"Mother and Son." [MalR] (103) Sum 93, p. 83.
"Pointed Hour" (from To Stóma Kléftis, Athens, 1886, tr. of Kostís Ghimosoúlis). [Os] (36) Spr 93, p. 31.
"Rainbow" (from Idíis Sómasi, Athens, 1886, tr. of Thanásis Hadjópoulos). [Os] (36) Spr 93, p. 26.
"The Resurrected" (tr. of Alexandra Plastira). [Vis] (43) 93, p. 25.
"So Much for Traveling" (from Sto Gyrisma Tis Méras, Athens, 1992, tr. of Yánnis Kondós). [Os] (36) Spr 93, p. 32.
"Spas" (from Idíis Sómasi, Athens, 1886, " (tr. of Thanásis Hadjópoulos). [Os] (36) Spr 93, p. 27.
"Winter Afternoons" (tr. of Stratis Paschalis). [Vis] (43) 93, p. 24-25.
2388. GOUSOPOULOS, Zaffi
"Four Greek Men." [Dandel] (20:1) 93, p. 8-9.
2389. GOVE, Jim
"It Was Toward the End of the Revolution That Tatanya Melanovna Became a Sensation in Petersburg." [ChironR] (12:4/13:1, #37/38) Wint 93-Spr 94, p. 5.
"Moonshot." [ChironR] (12:4/13:1, #37/38) Wint 93-Spr 94, p. 5.
"On My Wedding Day." [ChironR] (12:4/13:1, #37/38) Wint 93-Spr 94, p. 5.
"When word came about christ's return." [SmPd] (30:1, #87) Wint 93, p. 18.
2390. GOWER, John
"The Hunter." [Stand] (34:3) Sum 93, p. 64.
2391. GOY, E. D.
"Moonlight on the Sea" (tr. of Dragutin Tadijanovic). [NoDaQ] (61:1) Wint 93, p. 187.
"My Sister Takes the Milk to Town" (tr. of Dragutin Tadijanovic). [NoDaQ] (61:1) Wint 93, p. 186.
2392. GOYETTE, Susan
"Faith" (from the ark to the flood). [TickleAce] (25) Spr-Sum 93, p. 180.
"Sinking." [TickleAce] (25) Spr-Sum 93, p. 179.
2393. GRAB, Sally
"Blue Van." [Sequoia] (34/35) 92-93, p. 12.

2394. GRABOWSKI, Artur
"Expect the Worst" (tr. of Adam Michajlow, w. Chris Hurford). [Verse] (10:2) Sum 93, p. 43.
2395. GRAFF, Christian (Christian T.)
"Savages Sighted Wandering Aimlessly." [Lactuca] (17) Apr 93, p. 22.
"A Walk on the Beach with Hitler." [SmPd] (30:2, #88) Spr 93, p. 8.
2396. GRAHAM, David
"Et in Arcadia Ego." [TampaR] (6) Spr 93, p. 9.
2397. GRAHAM, Desmond
"Acis and Galatea" (i.m. Keith Douglas 1920-1944). [AntigR] (93-94) Spr-Sum 93, p. 41.
"Flowers and Creatures." [AntigR] (93-94) Spr-Sum 93, p. 42.
"Fruit" (for Daniela). [AntigR] (93-94) Spr-Sum 93, p. 43-44.
"Little Nanna." [AntigR] (93-94) Spr-Sum 93, p. 45.
"They Said." [AntigR] (93-94) Spr-Sum 93, p. 39-40.
2398. GRAHAM, Jorie
"Annunciation with a Bullet in It." [NewYorker] (69:36) 1 N 93, p. 109.
"An Artichoke for Montesquieu." [NewEngR] (15:1) Wint 93, p. 132.
"In the Hotel" (3:17 A.M.). [NewYorker] (69:7) 5 Ap 93, p. 80-81.
"March 7th." [NewYorker] (69:1) 22 F 93, p. 112.
"San Sepolcro." [SouthernR] (29:2) Spr, Ap 93, p. 269-270.
"Subjectivity." [ParisR] (35:128) Fall 93, p. 132-138.
2399. GRAHAM, Neile
"The Tree in the World." [Arc] (31) Aut 93, p. 8.
2400. GRAHAM, Shirley
"The Blue Angel" (Chagall). [PoetL] (88:2) Sum 93, p. 44.
"Four Bathers" (Cezanne). [PoetL] (88:2) Sum 93, p. 45.
"The Reclining Poet" (Chagall). [PoetL] (88:2) Sum 93, p. 43.
"Window in the Country, 1915" (Chagall). [PoetL] (88:2) Sum 93, p. 42.
2401. GRAHAM, Taylor
"After the Flood." [CoalC] (7) Apr 93, p. 13.
"Building a Fire in June." [TexasR] (14:3/4) Fall-Wint 93, p. 73.
"For Old Dog, a September Walk." [Outbr] (24) 93, p. 88.
"Just Before Dawn." [Ascent] (17:3) Spr 93, p. 43.
"Little Boy Lost." [PaintedHR] (9) Spr 93, p. 16.
"Picking Ticks" (conversations with an old dog). [Parting] (6:2) Wint 93, p. 29.
"Searching for Grandpa." [PaintedHR] (9) Spr 93, p. 17.
"Why They Split." [CoalC] (7) Apr 93, p. 14.
2402. GRAHAM, W. S.
"Listen. Put on Morning." [QRL] (12:32/33) 93, p. 424-425.
"My Final Bread." [QRL] (12:32/33) 93, p. 425-426.
2403. GRAJEDA, Valerie
"A Gray Matter." [Sequoia] (34/35) 92-93, p. 30-31.
2404. GRANT, Paul
"Baltimore Bouquet." [HampSPR] Wint 93, p. 28.
"The Father's Life, the Mother's Death." [Gaia] (1/2) Ap-Jl 93, p. 51.
"Fire Tower." [Gaia] (3) O 93, p. 38.
"Foxes." [HampSPR] Wint 93, p. 28.
"Housekeeping." [Plain] (14:1) Fall 93, p. 23.
"Quotas." [IndR] (16:1) Spr 93, p. 63.
"Samaras." [IndR] (16:1) Spr 93, p. 64-65.
"Velada" (Night Vigil). [Gaia] (1/2) Ap-Jl 93, p. 52.
2405. GRAPES, Jack
"All the Way Back." [SycamoreR] (5:2) Sum 93, p. 70.
"The Easy Part." [SycamoreR] (5:2) Sum 93, p. 72.
"Nothing Left to Chance." [SycamoreR] (5:2) Sum 93, p. 71.
2406. GRAPES, Lori
"Easter." [PoetryE] (36) Fall 93, p. 21-22.
"The Secret of Life." [PoetryE] (36) Fall 93, p. 19-20.
2407. GRASNICK, Ulrich
"About the Clocks" (tr. by Gisela Argyle). [PoetryC] (13:2) 93, p. 22.
2408. GRASSETTI, Nélida
"Imagenes I." [Luz] (5) N 93, p. 56.
"Imagenes en Dos Tiempos." [Luz] (5) N 93, p. 58.
"Images I" (tr. by Veronica Miranda). [Luz] (5) N 93, p. 57.
"Images in Two Times" (tr. by Veronica Miranda). [Luz] (5) N 93, p. 59.

2409. GRAVES, Michael
"On Kitty Kelly's Book." [HolCrit] (30:2) Ap 93, p. 19.
"When Grad Prof Swears." [HolCrit] (30:4) O 93, p. 18.
2410. GRAY, Dorothy Randall
"Too Soon." [Drumvoices] (3:1/2) Fall-Wint 93-94, p. 98-100.
2411. GRAY, Douglas
"Mermaids Invade Seacoast Town" (Tabloid Headline). [Poem] (69) My 93, p. 64 -
65.
"Returning to Standard Time." [MidwQ] (35:1) Aut 93, p. 39.
"Words on the Moon." [RiverC] (13:1) Fall 92, p. 52-53.
2412. GRAY, Janet
"The Big One." [Caliban] (12) 93, p. 35.
"Conditions of Production." [Caliban] (12) 93, p. 34.
2413. GRAY, Pamela
"3 Out of 4 (or More): a Lament for 3 Out of 4 (or More) Voices." [SinW] (50)
Sum-Fall 93, p. 62-65.
"This Pantoum Was Not On My Schedule." [SinW] (51) Wint 93-94, p. 66-67.
2414. GRAY, Pat
"News, Always the Same" (after Nina Cassian). [PoetryE] (36) Fall 93, p. 132.
2415. GRAY, Robert
"I Do Not Sleep Well in This Place on the Hill" (from *The Weakest Kind of Fruit*).
[JamesWR] (11:1) Fall 93, p. 4.
2416. GRAY, Stephen
"Sex and Drugs in the Caribbean: Ferry to Port Royal (1992)." [CaribbeanW] (7) 93,
p. 44-45.
2417. GREEAR, Mildred
"The Dahlia Man." [ChatR] (13:4) Sum 93, p. 48-49.
"Moving." [ChatR] (13:3) Spr 93, p. 74.
2418. GREEN, Benjamin
"July" ("Day," "Night"). [BellArk] (9:4) Jl-Ag 93, p. 1.
"September: An Act of Renunciation." [DogRR] (12:2, #24) Fall-Wint 93, p. 4.
2419. GREEN, Daniel
"Filial Affection." [RagMag] (11:1) 93, p. 87.
"Fitting in 1913." [Gaia] (3) O 93, p. 8.
2420. GREEN, Jaki Shelton
"Auction Block." [AfAmRev] (27:1) Spr 93, p. 131-132.
"That Boy from Georgia Is Coming Through Here." [AfAmRev] (27:4) Wint 93, p.
629-630.
"Untitled: Where does the slave woman's face." [AfAmRev] (27:1) Spr 93, p. 132.
2421. GREEN, Janet M.
"Goldenrod." [Pembroke] (25) 93, p. 13.
2422. GREEN, Paul
"Horns." [Talisman] (11) Fall 93, p. 257.
"Inner." [Talisman] (11) Fall 93, p. 257.
"A Saucepan for Three Planets" (illustrations by Irving Stettner). [WorldL] (4) 93, p.
44-46.
2423. GREEN, Paula
"Say When." [WestCL] (27:2, #11) Fall 93, p. 50-51.
2424. GREENBAUM, Jessica
"Tolstoy's Snowball." [SouthwR] (78:3) Sum 93, p. 412.
2425. GREENBERG, Alvin
"Bad Weather." [TarRP] (32:2) Spr 93, p. 16.
"The Barges at Night on the Ohio River." [CinPR] (24) Spr 93, p. 56.
"Camptown Races" (from a sequence entitled "An Ordinary Childhood"). [LaurelR]
(27:1) Wint 93, p. 84.
"Coal Chute" (from a sequence entitled "An Ordinary Childhood"). [LaurelR] (27:1)
Wint 93, p. 84-85.
"Elegy in Blue and White." [Agni] (38) 93, p. 185-186.
"Raven Afternoon." [CinPR] (24) Spr 93, p. 54-55.
"Taxonomy" (from a sequence entitled "An Ordinary Childhood"). [LaurelR] (27:1)
Wint 93, p. 85-86.
"Wise Guy." [GeoR] (47:1) Spr 93, p. 100.
2426. GREENBERG, Barbara (Barbara L.)
"The Education." [PoetryNW] (34:1) Spr 93, p. 26.
"Haze." [PraS] (67:1) Spr 93, p. 52-53.
"The Impasse." [PassN] (14:2) Wint 93, p. 12.

"Oral History." [PoetryNW] (34:1) Spr 93, p. 25.
"Strings." [PoetryNW] (34:1) Spr 93, p. 24.
2427. GREENBLATT, Ray
"Guilt." [CoalC] (7) Apr 93, p. 34.
"Night Walk at Shepherd's Landing." [CoalC] (7) Apr 93, p. 34.
2428. GREENE, Jeffrey
"East Shore, New Haven Harbor." [Pequod] (36) 93, p. 84-85.
"Far Sleep." [SouthwR] (78:3) Sum 93, p. 426.
2429. GREENE, Mary
"Food for Thought, or Just Deserts" (M.F.A. Workshop w. Marie Hasten, Howard
Glyn, Pamela Hughes, M. R. Syneck, Lisbeth Keiley, David Trinidad and
Allen Ginsberg, Nov. 21, 1988). [BrooklynR] (10) 93, p. 94-95.
2430. GREENE, Robin
"The Landscape of Desire." [SouthernPR] (33:2) Fall 93, p. 31-32.
2431. GREENHALGH, Chris
"Blue Territory." [Verse] (10:2) Sum 93, p. 19.
"Coffee-Break." [Verse] (10:1) Spr 93, p. 80.
"Introducing 'Love'." [Verse] (10:2) Sum 93, p. 20.
2432. GREENLAW, Lavinia
"Thanksgiving on Ghost Ranch." [NewYorker] (69:39) 22 N 93, p. 96.
2433. GREENWALD, Martha
"The Story of the Day." [Poetry] (163:1) O 93, p. 29.
"Sunday Afternoon Palindrome." [Poetry] (163:1) O 93, p. 30.
"Sunset District: Diminished Seventh." [NewEngR] (15:2) Spr 93, p. 119.
2434. GREENWALD, Roger
"Reunion." [Pequod] (36) 93, p. 86.
"The." [PoetL] (88:1) Spr 93, p. 33-34.
2435. GREENWAY, William
"Anniversary." [Poetry] (161:5) F 93, p. 257.
"Apnea." [SouthernPR] (33:1) Spr 93, p. 28.
"Child of Many Prayers." [SpoonR] (18:1) Wint-Spr 93, p. 13.
"Everything That Rises Must Convene." [Poem] (69) My 93, p. 59.
"For My Friends, Who Complain That I Never Write Anything Happy." [Poetry]
(163:3) D 93, p. 156.
"Forecast." [Poem] (69) My 93, p. 61.
"Foundlings." [Poem] (69) My 93, p. 60.
"Homemade Guilt." [Elf] (3:3) Fall 93, p. 37.
"Missing You at Long John Silver's." [SouthernPR] (33:1) Spr 93, p. 27.
"New House on the Market." [XavierR] (13:1) Spr 93, p. 52.
"Seventh Heaven." [Poetry] (163:3) D 93, p. 155.
"Skin." [XavierR] (13:1) Spr 93, p. 53.
"The Texas Chainsaw Revival." [LaurelR] (27:1) Wint 93, p. 87.
"Traumerei." [SpoonR] (18:1) Wint-Spr 93, p. 12.
2436. GREER, Jeffrey
"Cezanne's 'Preparation for the Funeral'" (For Robbie Bowers, 1966-1979). [QW]
(37) Sum-Fall 93, p. 208.
"The Manager of the Apollo Drive-In Prepares for Winter." [MidAR] (14:1) 93, p.
143-144.
2437. GREGER, Debora
"Easter 1991." [Poetry] (162:1) Ap 93, p. 16-17.
"Eve at the Paradise." [Poetry] (162:1) Ap 93, p. 19-20.
"The Flea Market at the End of History." [GettyR] (6:2) Spr 93, p. 226-227.
"The Frog in the Swimming Pool." [NewRep] (208:7) 15 F 93, p. 38.
"The Further Travels of Marco Polo." [NewRep] (208:26) 28 Je 93, p. 41.
"In the Museum of the Eighteenth Century." [Poetry] (162:1) Ap 93, p. 17-18.
"Keats in Ohio." [Field] (48) Spr 93, p. 28-29.
"Memories of the Atomic Age: Richland, Washington." [GettyR] (6:4) Aut 93, p.
598-600.
"The Mosaic of Creation" (San Marco, Venice). [Poetry] (163:3) D 93, p. 126-128.
"Ovid on the Outer Cape." [NoAmR] (278:3) My-Je 93, p. 29.
"The Patron Saint of Venice." [Nat] (257:10) 4 O 93, p. 362.
"La Petite Danseuse de Quatorze Ans." [YaleR] (81:1) Ja 93, p. 90-91.
"Rilke in the Middle Ages." [PartR] (60:3) Sum 93, p. 422-423.
"Sepia." [Field] (48) Spr 93, p. 30-31.
"Sunday at the Ruins." [Nat] (256:13) 5 Ap 93, p. 460.
"Les Très Riches Heures de Paris." [Poetry] (163:3) D 93, p. 125.

2438. GREGERMAN, Debra
"Frontier." [PraS] (67:1) Spr 93, p. 128-129.
"High Speed." [PraS] (67:1) Spr 93, p. 126.
"Homeland." [PraS] (67:1) Spr 93, p. 127-128.
"Passage." [PraS] (67:1) Spr 93, p. 127.
2439. GREGERSON, Linda
"Bunting." [TriQ] (89) Wint 93-94, p. 210-214.
"For the Taking." [Atlantic] (272:5) N 93, p. 132.
"The Resurrection of the Body" (For Caroline Bynum). [Poetry] (162:1) Ap 93, p. 14-15.
"Salt." [ColR] (20:1) Spr 93, p. 80-83.
2440. GREGG, Andrew P.
"Mixed Doubles." [Parting] (6:2) Wint 93, p. 18.
2441. GREGG, Linda
"After Actium: Loss Filling the Emptiness." [AmerPoR] (22:6) N-D 93, p. 5.
"At Home." [IndR] (16:1) Spr 93, p. 19.
"The Bounty After the Bounty." [AmerPoR] (22:6) N-D 93, p. 5.
"A Bracelet of Bright Hair About the Bone." [NewL] (60:1) 93, p. 101.
"The Clapping." [AmerPoR] (22:6) N-D 93, p. 4.
"Colonus." [NewL] (60:1) 93, p. 103.
"The Delicate Thing." [ColR] (20:1) Spr 93, p. 60-61.
"The Edge of Something." [AmerPoR] (22:6) N-D 93, p. 4.
"The Enormous Engine." [NewL] (60:1) 93, p. 102.
"Fishing in the Keep of Silence." [AmerPoR] (22:6) N-D 93, p. 6.
"The Life of Literature." [Hudson] (45:4) Wint 93, p. 534, 536.
"The Lost Bells of Heaven." [AmerPoR] (22:6) N-D 93, p. 3.
"Official Love Story." [AmerPoR] (22:6) N-D 93, p. 5.
"Past Perfect." [AmerPoR] (22:6) N-D 93, p. 6.
"The Resurrection." [AmerPoR] (22:6) N-D 93, p. 5.
"Sometimes." [AmerPoR] (22:6) N-D 93, p. 5.
"There Is a Sweetness in It." [AmerPoR] (22:6) N-D 93, p. 4.
"The Weight." [AmerPoR] (22:6) N-D 93, p. 3.
"What Is Kept." [AmerPoR] (22:6) N-D 93, p. 6.
2442. GREGOR, Arthur
"One Word." [Nat] (256:21) 31 My 93, p. 750.
"Unencumbered." [QRL] (12:32/33) 93, p. 426.
2443. GREGORY, Horace
"The Muse Behing the Laurel." [QRL] (12:32/33) 93, p. 426-427.
2444. GREGORY, James
"A Dead Man's Shoes." [OnTheBus] (6:1, #13) Wint 93-Spr 94, p. 102.
2445. GREGORY, Robert
"For the Scythian Princess They Found in the Mud." [SilverFR] (24) Wint 93, p. 28.
"Galore" (for Meg O'Brien). [SilverFR] (24) Wint 93, p. 30.
"How I Became the Glorious Mr. Dot." [RiverS] (37) 93, p. 4-5.
"In the Waiting Room." [HeavenB] (10) Wint-Spr 93, p. 54.
"Milk in a Cup Can Be Used for Divination." [SilverFR] (24) Wint 93, p. 29.
"A Pleasant Song about the Time before Items." [RiverS] (37) 93, p. 2-3.
"Yet to Be Reconciled with the Reality of the Dark (Princess Shikishi)." [HeavenB] (10) Wint-Spr 93, p. 24.
2446. GRENNAN, Eamon
"Angel Looking Away." [NewEngR] (15:4) Fall 93, p. 116-117.
"Bridge." [Nat] (257:11) 11 O 93, p. 404.
"Dog." [Poetry] (163:2) N 93, p. 75-76.
"Falling Asleep." [NewEngR] (15:4) Fall 93, p. 117-118.
"Ghosts." [NewYorker] (69:16) 7 Je 93, p. 68.
"Granny." [Nat] (256:25) 28 Je 93, p. 914.
"Headlines." [CreamCR] (17:1) Spr 93, p. 78-79.
"Heirloom." [NewYorker] (69:40) 29 N 93, p. 104.
"Marginal." [NewEngR] (15:4) Fall 93, p. 118-119.
"Monastery, School, Cloud." [Nat] (256:18) 10 My 93, p. 642.
"Neighbour." [SouthwR] (78:4) Aut 93, p. 537.
"Outing." [OntR] (39) Fall-Wint 93-94, p. 97-99.
"Pause." [NewYorker] (68:50) 1 F 93, p. 60.
"Smoke." [CreamCR] (17:1) Spr 93, p. 80-82.
"Sons." [Nat] (256:18) 10 My 93, p. 642.
"Such a State." [OntR] (39) Fall-Wint 93-94, p. 100.

"Two Climbing." [Field] (48) Spr 93, p. 91-94.
"What Doesn't Happen." [NewRep] (209:6) 9 Ag 93, p. 40.
"With Youngest Daughter at Parents' Grave." [SouthwR] (78:4) Aut 93, p. 536.
2447. GREY, John
"The Killers of Everything." [SnailPR] (3:1) Fall-Wint 93, p. 14.
"My Mother's Poets." [ChrC] (110:6) 24 F 93, p. 206.
2448. GREY, Robert
"Narrow Gauge." [CumbPR] (12:2) Spr 93, p. 30-31.
"New Year's Eve." [CumbPR] (12:2) Spr 93, p. 29.
"Opening." [SnailPR] (3:1) Fall-Wint 93, p. 31.
"Self Reliance." [SnailPR] (3:1) Fall-Wint 93, p. 30.
2449. GRIBBLE, John
"Ohioans." [Pearl] (19) Fall-Wint 93, p. 75.
2450. GRICE, Dorsey
"At Age Eleven I Killed a Child." [SouthernPR] (33:1) Spr 93, p. 37.
2451. GRICE, Gordon
"The Ballerina." [SycamoreR] (5:1) Wint 93, p. 41.
"Burned." [CinPR] (24) Spr 93, p. 40-42.
"Faith." [ChironR] (12:1, #34) Spr 93, p. 38.
"Her Husband's Name." [ChironR] (12:1, #34) Spr 93, p. 38.
"Sundown." [Sonora] (24/25) Spr 93, p. 21.
2452. GRIFFIN, Frank James
"Owed to Ogden." [Light] (5) Spr 93, p. 25.
2453. GRIFFIN, Gail
"Pandora." [PassN] (14:2) Wint 93, p. 57.
"The Year of the Horse, 4688" (for a birthday). [PassN] (14:2) Wint 93, p. 55-56.
2454. GRIFFIN, James
"Inside Out." [PoetL] (88:3) Fall 93, p. 21-22.
2455. GRIFFIN, Walter
"Anima." [ChironR] (12:4/13:1, #37/38) Wint 93-Spr 94, p. 30.
"Anima." [KenR] (NS 15:4) Fall 93, p. 16.
"The Bones of Montgomery Clift." [Amelia] (7:2, #21) 93, p. 26.
"The Descent." [ChironR] (12:4/13:1, #37/38) Wint 93-Spr 94, p. 30.
"The Descent." [SouthernR] (29:3) Sum, Jl 93, p. 582-583.
"Night Snow." [SouthernR] (29:3) Sum, Jl 93, p. 583.
"Other Cities." [Amelia] (7:2, #21) 93, p. 25.
"Outlaws." [Amelia] (7:2, #21) 93, p. 24-25.
"The Season of the Falling Face." [ChironR] (12:4/13:1, #37/38) Wint 93-Spr 94, p. 30.
"The Season of the Falling Face." [HawaiiR] (17:3, #39) Fall 93, p. 41.
"The Swimmer." [Amelia] (7:2, #21) 93, p. 26.
"Trigger Housings." [Amelia] (7:2, #21) 93, p. 24.
"Weight." [Amelia] (7:2, #21) 93, p. 26-27.
2456. GRIFFITH, Gail W.
"Buick Electra." [Vis] (41) 93, p. 30-31.
"Miss Bea Cuts the Lights." [Vis] (41) 93, p. 29.
2457. GRIFFITH, Kevin
"Detour." [SoCoast] (15) Je 93, p. 53.
"In the Middle of Nowhere." [PoetL] (88:4) Wint 93-94, p. 16.
"North of Bridgeport, Morel Hunting." [ColEng] (55:4) Ap 93, p. 429.
2458. GRIGG, Phoebe
"Under Control" (for Sambo). [DogRR] (12:2, #24) Fall-Wint 93, p. 19.
2459. GRILIKHES, Alexandra
"Pittsburgh." [PaintedB] (50/51) 93, p. 38-39.
2460. GRILLO, Paul
"Bride 1949." [PaintedB] (50/51) 93, p. 24.
"Oil for the Lamps of China." [PaintedB] (50/51) 93, p. 25.
"A Postcard from Wildwood." [PaintedB] (50/51) 93, p. 25.
"Spider and Squirrel Nightfall Construction." [PaintedB] (50/51) 93, p. 24.
2461. GRIMES, Linda Sue
"Chief Muncie" (for Thomas Thornburg). [Elf] (3:4) Wint 93, p. 34-35.
"Driving." [Elf] (3:4) Wint 93, p. 33.
2462. GRIMES, Susan
"Target Quilt" (for Sallie). [13thMoon] (11:1/2) 93, p. 32.

2463. GRIMM, Reinhold
"Gillis van Coninxloo, Landscape" (Wood, 65 by 119 cm, tr. of Hans Magnus Enzensberger). [NowestR] (31:1) 93, p. 93.
"Old Revolution" (tr. of Hans Magnus Enzensberger). [NowestR] (31:1) 93, p. 92.
"The Poison" (tr. of Hans Magnus Enzensberger). [NowestR] (31:1) 93, p. 94.
"Sleeping Pill" (tr. of Hans Magnus Enzensberger). [NowestR] (31:1) 93, p. 91.
2464. GRINDLEY, Carl
"The Shadow of Hanged Man" (8 selections). [Quarry] (42:2) 93, p. 25-32.
2465. GRISWOLD, Jay
"The Dream." [DogRR] (12:1, #23) Spr-Sum 93, p. 20-21.
"Europe." [WritersF] (19) 93, p. 157.
"Indifference." [NewRena] (8:3, #26) Spr 93, p. 28.
"The Insomnia of the Portrait." [Plain] (13:3) Spr 93, p. 9.
"Meditation at Red Canyon." [ChironR] (12:4/13:1, #37/38) Wint 93-Spr 94, p. 47.
"Over Boulder." [Crucible] (29) Fall 93, p. 18.
"Rumors." [NewRena] (8:3, #26) Spr 93, p. 27.
2466. GRIVICH, Peter
"Elementary Algebra." [TexasR] (14:1/2) Spr-Sum 93, p. 97.
2467. GROLMES, Sam
"Identity." [Talisman] (10) Spr 93, p. 101.
2468. GROSHOLZ, Emily
"Anna." [Hudson] (46:1) Spr 93, p. 178.
"Where the Sky Used to Be." [Hudson] (46:1) Spr 93, p. 177.
2469. GROSS, Luray
"Clayton." [Footwork] (23) 93, p. 52.
"Saturday During the War." [Footwork] (23) 93, p. 52.
"Two Teachers at a Window" (for Peter Wood). [US1] (28/29) 93, p. 13.
2470. GROSS, Pamela
"At the March Equinox." [Comm] (120:5) 12 Mr 93, p. 10.
"Some Notes in the Margin." [Poetry] (163:1) O 93, p. 28.
"The Wing as Lever / Air as Fulcrum." [SouthernR] (29:3) Sum, Jl 93, p. 610-611.
2471. GROSSMAN, Allen
"Great Work Farm Elegy." [ColR] (20:1) Spr 93, p. 6-14.
"Stanzas on the Snowfall" (October 22, 1939). [AmerPoR] (22:1) Ja-F 93, p. 31-33.
2472. GROSSMAN, K. Margaret
"For My Husband Who Wants to Know What's Going to Happen This Anniversary." [CinPR] (24) Spr 93, p. 16-17.
2473. GROSZ, Christiane
"And the Toy Boat Is Ready to Go" (tr. by Gisela Argyle). [PoetryC] (13:2) 93, p. 22.
"Your Three Wishes" (tr. by Gisela Argyle). [PoetryC] (13:2) 93, p. 22.
2474. GROVE, C. L.
"Amoebas." [Light] (5) Spr 93, p. 13.
"Atlantis." [Light] (6) Sum 93, p. 10.
"Lemmings." [Light] (8) Wint 93, p. 9.
"The Pterodactyl." [Light] (7) Aut 93, p. 8.
"Says Pat, on the shore of the Irish Sea." [Light] (7) Aut 93, p. 24.
"Vultures." [Light] (6) Sum 93, p. 12.
2475. GROVE, Jamie
"God of the Desert Night." [Elf] (3:4) Wint 93, p. 29.
2476. GROVER, Dorys Crow
"The Washita." [Border] (2) Spr 93, p. 33.
2477. GROW, Mary
"Random." [Footwork] (23) 93, p. 100.
"Two Pasts and a Present." [Footwork] (23) 93, p. 100.
2478. GRUBB, David H.
"The Rain Children." [Verse] (10:2) Sum 93, p. 66.
"Stanley Spencer Arriving in Heaven" (for Nick and Mary Parry). [Verse] (10:2) Sum 93, p. 66-68.
2479. GRUHN, Hollace
"On the Rosebud" (A Plainsongs Award Poem). [Plain] (13:3) Spr 93, p. 5.
"Sunrise." [Plain] (14:1) Fall 93, p. 9.
2480. GRUMMAN, Bob
"Mathemaku for John Martone." [PoetryUSA] (25/26) 93, p. 11.
"Mathemaku No. 3." [PoetryUSA] (25/26) 93, p. 11.
"Mathemaku No. 10." [PoetryUSA] (25/26) 93, p. 10.

2481. GRUMMER, Greg
"After the Divorce." [LullwaterR] (4:2) Spr-Sum 93, p. 98-99.
"Appledore, On the Island of Shoals." [AmerPoR] (22:2) Mr-Ap 93, p. 43.
"Conception." [IndR] (16:2) Fall 93, p. 39.
"Getting Ready for Bed." [AmerPoR] (22:2) Mr-Ap 93, p. 43.
"Murmurs from the Cult of Marriage Counselors." [LullwaterR] (4:2) Spr-Sum 93,
    p. 35.
2482. GU, Cheng
"Gate of Virtue and Victory (De Sheng Men)" (tr. by Yanbing Chen and John
    Rosenwald). [ChiR] (39:3/4) 93, p. 292.
2483. GU, Zhongxing
"Vineyard" (tr. of Mang Ke, w. Willis Barnstone and Tony Barnstone). [ChiR]
    (39:3/4) 93, p. 289.
2484. GUAN, Yonghe
"Dew Drops" (in Chinese and English, tr. by Li Xi-jian and Gordon Osing). [PikeF]
    (11) Fall 93, p. 15.
2485. GUENTHER, Charles
"The Damaged Crop" (tr. of René Char). [QRL] (12:32/33) 93, p. 392-393.
"Fascinating Four" (tr. of René Char). [QRL] (12:32/33) 93, p. 393.
2486. GUENTHER, Gabriele
"Barlach Sculpture." [Arc] (31) Aut 93, p. 71.
"Delphine, at Twenty-Two." [Quarry] (42:3) 93, p. 83.
2487. GUEST, Barbara
"Riddance." [PoetryUSA] (25/26) 93, p. 38.
"Stripped Tales." [Conjunc] (20) 93, p. 78-81.
2488. GUEVARA, Maurice Kilwein
"Cofradia." [Poetry] (161:5) F 93, p. 264.
"Tombstones." [Poetry] (161:5) F 93, p. 263.
2489. GUIDACCI, Margherita
"The Hypocrite" (from "Neurosuite," tr. by Ruth Feldman). [InterPR] (19:2) Fall 93,
    p. 51.
"L'Ipocrita" (from "Neurosuite"). [InterPR] (19:2) Fall 93, p. 50.
2490. GUIDINETTI, Elda
"Beyond Real Space Time" (tr. by Stephen Sartarelli). [LitR] (36:4) Sum 93, p. 482 -
    489.
2491. GUILD, Wendy
"Satin Mules." [DogRR] (12:1, #23) Spr-Sum 93, p. 38.
2492. GUILLEMOT, Cecile
"It's the Truth." [PraF] (14:3) Aut 93, p. 53.
2493. GUILLÉN, Jorge
"Perfection" (tr. by Carolyne Wright). [HarvardR] (5) Fall 93, p. 28.
"The Sea in the Wind" (tr. by Carolyne Wright). [HarvardR] (5) Fall 93, p. 28.
2494. GUILLEVIC, Eugène
"Fabliette de la Souris." [Hudson] (45:4) Wint 93, p. 678.
"The Mouse" (tr. by Norman R. Shapiro). [Hudson] (45:4) Wint 93, p. 678.
2495. GUILLORY, Dan
"Cajun Doctor." [ClockR] (8:1/2) 93, p. 41-44.
GUIN, Ursula K. le
    See Le GUIN, Ursula K.
2496. GUISTA, Michael
"Angels." [SpoonR] (18:2) Sum-Fall 93, p. 86.
2497. GUNDERSON, Keith
"Baja Journal" (Excerpts). [NorthStoneR] (11) 93, p. 174-177.
GUNDY, Douglas van
    See Van GUNDY, Douglas
2498. GUNDY, Jeff
"An Afternoon in the Country of the Calm Down." [CinPR] (24) Spr 93, p. 8-9.
"And So Heavy with Life the Crust of the World Is Still." [CinPR] (24) Spr 93, p. 7.
"Because I Have No Daughters." [CinPR] (24) Spr 93, p. 10-11.
"The Best Defense, or Recklessness Part One." [CinPR] (24) Spr 93, p. 12.
"Butter." [ArtfulD] (24/25) 93, p. 75.
"Fine New Stances Toward the World." [Paint] (19:38) Aut 92, p. 40-41.
"For the Soft God Paula." [SpoonR] (18:2) Sum-Fall 93, p. 75-76.
"Reckoning." [ArtfulD] (24/25) 93, p. 74.
"Squirrels." [Farm] (10:2) Fall-Wint 93-94, p. 62-63.

2499. GUNN, L. S.
"I Come Home." [TampaR] (6) Spr 93, p. 23.
2500. GUNN, Thom
"Final Song" (for Jeffrey Dahmer). [Salm] (100) Fall 93, p. 145-146.
"Lament" (from *The Man with Night Sweats*, winner of the Lenore Marshall/Nation
Poetry Prize, 1993). [Nat] (257:19) 6 D 93, p. 703.
"Troubadour" (songs for Jeffrey Dahmer). [Thrpny] (55) Fall 93, p. 7.
"Yellow Pitcher Plant." [BostonR] (18:3/4) Je-Ag 93, p. 22.
2501. GUNSTROM, Nickie J.
"A Sport of Nature." [Border] (2) Spr 93, p. 34.
2502. GUO, Wei
"Resurrection" (tr. of Shu Ting, w. Ginny MacKenzie). [MidAR] (14:1) 93, p. 41 -
42.
2503. GUREVICH, Liliya
"Herd of gray horses." [Amelia] (7:2, #21) 93, p. 68.
2504. GURLEY, James
"Bluesong." [Arc] (31) Aut 93, p. 4-5.
"On the Theory of Transformation." [PoetryNW] (34:4) Wint 93-94, p. 32-33.
"Zodiacal Light." [Arc] (31) Aut 93, p. 6-7.
2505. GUSSLER, Phyllis Sanchez
"Riding the Mad Mouse" (1993 Lullwater Prize for Poetry Winner). [LullwaterR]
(4:2) Spr-Sum 93, p. 10-11.
"Running Wire." [SouthernPR] (33:2) Fall 93, p. 22-23.
"Temple de Las." [LullwaterR] (4:2) Spr-Sum 93, p. 73-75.
2506. GUSTAFSON, Jim
"Language and Humility." [HangL] (63) 93, p. 15.
2507. GUSTAFSSON, Lars
"Aristotle and the Crayfish" (tr. by Yvonne L. Sandstroem). [NewYorker] (69:16) 7
Je 93, p. 84-85.
"An Audience with the Muse" (tr. by Yvonne L. Sandstroem). [QRL] (12:32/33) 93,
p. 178-179.
"Border Zone, Minefield, Snow East of Bebra" (tr. by Christopher Middleton).
[QRL] (12:32/33) 93, p. 188.
"Elegy for the Old Mexican Woman and Her Dead Child" (tr. by Yvonne L.
Sandstroem). [QRL] (12:32/33) 93, p. 181-183.
"For All Those Who Wait for Time to Pass" (tr. by Yvonne L. Sandstroem). [QRL]
(12:32/33) 93, p. 181.
"The Geography of the Department of Geography" (A Ghost Ballad, tr. by Yvonne
L. Sandstroem). [QRL] (12:32/33) 93, p. 183-188.
"Itemized Expenses" (August Strindberg 1849-1912, tr. by Yvonne L. Sandstroem).
[QRL] (12:32/33) 93, p. 180.
"The Order of Grace" (tr. by Yvonne L. Sandstroem). [QRL] (12:32/33) 93, p. 179.
"Sonnet of the Beginning and the End" (tr. by Yvonne L. Sandstroem). [QRL]
(12:32/33) 93, p. 179-180.
2508. GUSTAVSON, Jeffrey
"Is Light." [Poetry] (163:2) N 93, p. 94-95.
"Newborn." [NewYorker] (69:31) 27 S 93, p. 86.
GUT, Karen Alkalay
See ALKALAY-GUT, Karen
GUTIERREZ REVUELTA, Pedro
See REVUELTA, Gutierrez
2509. GUTTMAN, Assia
"In the Middle of This Century" (tr. of Yehuda Amichai). [QRL] (12:32/33) 93, p.
367-368.
"Like Our Bodies' Imprint" (tr. of Yehuda Amichai). [QRL] (12:32/33) 93, p. 368.
2510. GUTTMANN, Kaitlyn
"Untitled: She made me sing." [13thMoon] (12:1/2) 93-94, p. 30.
2511. GVOZDZIUS, Vidas
"Instructions on Catching a Salmon." [PaintedHR] (9) Spr 93, p. 33.
2512. GYLYS, Beth
"Painting, Time, and the Music Box." [SoCoast] (14) Ja 93, p. 56-57.
2513. H. D.
"Sheltered Garden" (illustrated by Claire Heimarck). [MassR] (34:2) Sum 93, p.
254-256.
HA, Jin
See JIN, Ha

2514. HAAREN, Michael
"The difference between the wrong word and the right" (Amelia One-Liner Award).
[Amelia] (7:2, #21) 93, p. 34.
"If genius is nine-tenths tenacity" (Amelia One-Liner Award). [Amelia] (7:2, #21)
93, p. 127.
"In the bowling alley of egalitarian ideologies." [Amelia] (7:2, #21) 93, p. 79.
"One rarely finds a bra without a catch" (Amelia One-Liner Award). [Amelia] (7:2,
#21) 93, p. 62.
"The true measure of a man's mind" (Amelia One-Liner Award). [Amelia] (7:2, #21)
93, p. 36.
"Where the doctor may see a brilliant technique" (Amelia One-Liner Award).
[Amelia] (7:2, #21) 93, p. 33.
2515. HABER, Leo
"On Hearing Mendelssohn's Oratotio *Elijah*." [ProseP] (1) 92, p. 35-36.
2516. HABLANIAN, Marsbed
"Dialogue Before Death (1983)" (tr. of Nina Berberova, w. Diana Der -
Hovanessian). [Agni] (38) 93, p. 106.
2517. HABOVA, Dána
"The Autumn Orchard" (tr. of Miroslav Holub, w. David Young). [PartR] (60:3)
Sum 93, p. 419.
"Half a Hedgehog" (tr. of Miroslav Holub, w. David Young). [Field] (49) Fall 93, p.
18-19.
"Hemophilia/Los Angeles" (tr. of Miroslav Holub, w. David Young). [Field] (49)
Fall 93, p. 30-31.
"Meeting Ezra Pound" (tr. of Miroslav Holub, w. Stuart Friebert). [Field] (49) Fall
93, p. 12.
"Seeing" (tr. of Miroslav Holub, w. David Young). [Field] (49) Fall 93, p. 25-26.
2518. HACKER, Marilyn
"An Absent Friend." [Boulevard] (8:1, #22) Spr 93, p. 47.
"For a Fiftieth Anniversay." [ParisR] (35:128) Fall 93, p. 254-255.
"Street Scenes." [TriQ] (89) Wint 93-94, p. 202-205.
"Year's End" (I.M. Audre Lorde and Sonny Wainwright). [ParisR] (35:128) Fall 93,
p. 255-256.
2519. HACKER, Neva
"Aerodynamics." [WebR] (17) Fall 93, p. 108.
"Alison As in Dreams of Dreaming." [WebR] (17) Fall 93, p. 107.
2520. HACKETT, Bob
"Sick Farm." [PoetL] (88:2) Sum 93, p. 18.
2521. HADAS, Rachel
"Absence." [Contact] (11:65/66/67) Spr 93, p. 50.
"Advice to a Friend" (to Phillis Levin). [Salm] (98/99) Spr-Sum 93, p. 84-85.
"Along Edges" (to Mark Rudman). [Contact] (11:65/66/67) Spr 93, p. 48-49.
"The Blessing." [HarvardR] (4) Spr 93, p. 20.
"The Empty Bed." [Thrpny] (53) Spr 93, p. 20.
"Faultlines." [ColEng] (55:7) N 93, p. 782.
"A Glimpse of Simon Verity." [NewRep] (208:11) 15 Mr 93, p. 41.
"Lower Level, Room EE." [WestHR] (47:4) Wint 93, p. 386.
"Orange." [BostonR] (18:3/4) Je-Ag 93, p. 16.
"The Swan" (tr. of Charles Baudelaire). [Pequod] (35) 93, p. 66-67.
"The Theft." [Contact] (11:65/66/67) Spr 93, p. 46-48.
"Upon My Mother's Death." [Pequod] (35) 93, p. 159-160.
"Walking to School" (recipient of The Hellas Award, 1993). [Hellas] (4:2) Fall 93,
p. 49-50.
"The Wall of Remembrance." [Contact] (11:65/66/67) Spr 93, p. 50.
"Winter Night." [WestHR] (47:4) Wint 93, p. 387.
2522. HADDAWAY, J. L.
"If Wishes Were Horses." [HiramPoR] (53/54) Fall 92-Sum 93, p. 41.
"When Fat Girls Dream." [HiramPoR] (53/54) Fall 92-Sum 93, p. 42.
"Woman Abducted from Ohio Home by Aliens." [CinPR] (24) Spr 93, p. 34-35.
2523. HADDOCK, Lillian
"Autorretrato" (Homenaje a Van Gogh). [Trasimagen] (1:1) Otoño-Invierno 93, p.
42.
"Canto a la Luz." [Trasimagen] (1:1) Otoño-Invierno 93, p. 43.
"La Otra Cara." [Trasimagen] (1:1) Otoño-Invierno 93, p. 43.

2524. HADJOPOULOS, Thanásis
   "The Mine" (from *Idíis Sómasi*, Athens, 1886, " (tr. by Yannis Goumas). [Os] (36)
      Spr 93, p. 28.
   "Rainbow" (from *Idíis Sómasi*, Athens, 1886, tr. by Yannis Goumas). [Os] (36) Spr
      93, p. 26.
   "Spas" (from *Idíis Sómasi*, Athens, 1886, " (tr. by Yannis Goumas). [Os] (36) Spr
      93, p. 27.
2525. HAENEL, Paul R.
   "Immigrants in Arlington." [PoetL] (88:3) Fall 93, p. 36.
   "Snake" (after che). [Parting] (6:2) Wint 93, p. 1.
2526. HAGER, Stephanie
   "My Long-Spent Body." [OnTheBus] (5:2, #12) Sum-Fall 93, p. 85.
   "Not." [OnTheBus] (5:2, #12) Sum-Fall 93, p. 85.
   "So That I Might Be Held." [BellR] (16:1/2) Spr-Fall 93, p. 85.
   "The Sweater." [OnTheBus] (6:1, #13) Wint 93-Spr 94, p. 103.
2527. HAGERMAN, Keppel
   "Colors of Port-au-Prince." [CaribbeanW] (7) 93, p. 30.
   "Dock Lady." [CaribbeanW] (7) 93, p. 31.
2528. HAGINS, Jerry
   "Morning Glory." [PaintedB] (50/51) 93, p. 115.
2529. HAGUE, Richard
   "How It Is in Fishing." [ProseP] (1) 92, p. 38.
   "In a New Year and Old Moon." [CinPR] (24) Spr 93, p. 26.
   "Snail." [ProseP] (1) 92, p. 37.
2530. HAHM, Hyeryon
   "Comparative Literature" (tr. by Edward W. Poitras). [ChiR] (39:3/4) 93, p. 244 -
      245.
2531. HAHN, Alex
   "How to Order Chamomile Tea." [Pearl] (19) Fall-Wint 93, p. 68.
   "Moustache." [ChironR] (12:3, #36) Aut 93, p. 31.
2532. HAHN, Elizabeth
   "A Finding." [AnthNEW] (5) 93, p. 10.
2533. HAHN, Kimiko
   "The Iris." [AmerV] (30) 93, p. 44.
2534. HAHN, Oscar
   "Death Sits at the Foot of My Bed" (tr. by William Lawlor). [Vis] (41) 93, p. 22.
   "Visiones de San Narciso." [XavierR] (13:1) Spr 93, p. 62.
   "Visions of Saint Narcissus" (tr. by James Hoggard). [XavierR] (13:1) Spr 93, p. 62.
2535. HAHN, Robert
   "All Clear." [ParisR] (35:127) Sum 93, p. 142-143.
   "Conversation with a Dealer, about a Painting in Private Hands." [ParisR] (35:127)
      Sum 93, p. 141.
   "Mob Rules." [ParisR] (35:127) Sum 93, p. 143-144.
   "Tell the Truth." [ParisR] (35:127) Sum 93, p. 139-140.
2536. HAHN, S. C.
   "Missing Entries from a Polish-English Dictionary." [ProseP] (1) 92, p. 39.
   "Omaha." [ProseP] (2) 93, p. 39-40.
2537. HAHN, Sumi
   "This October Light." [TexasR] (14:3/4) Fall-Wint 93, p. 74.
2538. HAHN, Susan
   "Bone." [VirQR] (69:1) Wint 93, p. 90-91.
   "Half Price." [PraS] (67:3) Fall 93, p. 15.
   "Heart." [Atlantic] (272:6) D 93, p. 71.
   "Incontinence." [Poetry] (162:6) S 93, p. 330.
   "Insomnia." [Poetry] (162:6) S 93, p. 329.
   "Mania." [PraS] (67:3) Fall 93, p. 14.
   "Transplant." [VirQR] (69:1) Wint 93, p. 90.
2539. HAI, Zi
   "Chapter IX: Hometown (September)" (tr. by Dian Li). [GreenMR] (NS 6:2) Sum -
      Fall 93, p. 138-140
2540. HAILE, Mark
   "John." [JamesWR] (10:4) Sum 93, p. 8.
2541. HAINES, Anne
   "Telling Stories, The Evening Star." [PraS] (67:3) Fall 93, p. 16-17.
2542. HAINES, John
   "Age of Bronze." [Hudson] (46:2) Sum 93, p. 289-290.

"Diminishing Credo." [GreenMR] (NS 6:2) Sum-Fall 93, p. 7-8.
"Hotel Laundromat." [Hudson] (46:3) Aut 93, p. 526-527.
"Night." [Hudson] (46:2) Sum 93, p. 292-293.
"Sinister Earth." [GreenMR] (NS 6:2) Sum-Fall 93, p. 5-6.
"Tondo of Hell." [Hudson] (46:2) Sum 93, p. 290-291.
2543. HAINES, John Francis
"The Park Keeper." [Bogg] (66) Wint 92-93, p. 64.
2544. HAINES, Sekyo N.
"Songs from the Riverbank" (tr. of Kim Sowôl). [HarvardR] (4) Spr 93, p. 146.
2545. HAINING, James
"Big Tires for Chris Hagen." [GrandS] (12:3, #47) Fall 93, p. 95.
"The Broad Highway." [GrandS] (12:3, #47) Fall 93, p. 96.
"The Rose Chapel" (for Carrie). [GrandS] (11:4, #44) 93, p. 93, p. 189.
HAIXIN, Xu
See XU, Haixin
HAKEN, Kathleen ten
See Ten HAKEN, Kathleen
2546. HALA
"The Gathasaptasati" (Selections of poems in Maharastri Prakit collected by Hala, tr.
by Martha Ann Selby). [Sulfur] (33) Fall 93, p. 54-57.
2547. HALE, T.
"Scratch." [GreensboroR] (55) Wint 93-94, p. 50.
2548. HALEVI, Yehuda
"Axiom" (tr. by Ammiel Alcalay). [Sulfur] (33) Fall 93, p. 194-195.
"Before Departure" (tr. by Ammiel Alcalay). [Sulfur] (33) Fall 93, p. 194.
"An Exchange Between Levi Ibn Al-Tabban and Yehuda Halevi" (tr. by Ammiel
Alcalay). [Sulfur] (33) Fall 93, p. 198.
"Love Poem" (tr. by Ammiel Alcalay). [Sulfur] (33) Fall 93, p. 195.
"Love Song" (tr. by Ammiel Alcalay). [Sulfur] (33) Fall 93, p. 197.
"Poem in Parts" (tr. by Ammiel Alcalay). [Sulfur] (33) Fall 93, p. 196-197.
2549. HALEY, Heather
"How to Live with a Bitch." [OnTheBus] (6:1, #13) Wint 93-Spr 94, p. 104-105.
2550. HALKO, Gabrielle
"Asylum." [BlackWR] (20:1) Fall-Wint 93, p. 117-118.
2551. HALL, Daniel
"Bartholomew's Cobble." [ParisR] (35:129) Wint 93, p. 92-93.
"Chez Nguyen." [YaleR] (81:3) Jl 93, p. 84-86.
"Mangosteens." [NewRep] (209:23) 6 D 93, p. 48.
"Rising and Falling." [YaleR] (81:3) Jl 93, p. 91-92.
"A Trellis" (for my mother). [YaleR] (81:3) Jl 93, p. 87-90.
2552. HALL, Donald
"Don't Be Afraid." [Pequod] (35) 93, p. 128.
"Flaccus, Drive Up." [PartR] (60:1) Wint 93, p. 95-96.
"H.F." [Nat] (256:16) 26 Ap 93, p. 568.
"Her Face." [GeoR] (47:2) Sum 93, p. 252.
"Horsecollar Is Rarely." [SouthernHR] (27:1) Wint 93, p. 26.
"The Hunters." [NewRep] (209:1) 5 Jl 93, p. 39.
"I Suppose You've Noticed." [SouthernHR] (27:1) Wint 93, p. 27.
"The Island." [GettyR] (6:2) Spr 93, p. 300-301.
"It Was Sigmund" (from *The Museum of Clear Ideas*). [Shen] (43:1) Spr 93, p. 108-
109.
"Let Engine Cowling." [Pequod] (35) 93, p. 125-126.
"The Life of the Party." [Nat] (257:21) 20 D 93, p. 776.
"Nothing, My Aging Flaccus." [Pequod] (35) 93, p. 127.
"O Camilla, Is It." [PartR] (60:1) Wint 93, p. 96.
"Or Say: While Your Old Lovers." [SouthernHR] (27:1) Wint 93, p. 28.
"The Profession." [GettyR] (6:2) Spr 93, p. 302.
"Ric's Progress." [OnTheBus] (6:1, #13) Wint 93-Spr 94, p. 106-115.
"Ship of State, High Tide" (from *The Museum of Clear Ideas*). [Shen] (43:1) Spr 93,
p. 109-110.
"Spring Glen." [Nat] (257:14) 1 N 93, p. 512.
"Venetian Nights." [Thrpny] (54) Sum 93, p. 27.
"When I Was Young." [CreamCR] (17:1) Spr 93, p. 83.
"When the Young Husband." [Atlantic] (271:3) Mr 93, p. 74.
"Young Edgar." [GettyR] (6:2) Spr 93, p. 303.

2553. HALL, Judith
"A Lullaby." [ParisR] (35:129) Wint 93, p. 182.
"Reruns in the Oncologist's Waiting Room." [ParisR] (35:129) Wint 93, p. 178-179.
"Rimbaud's Cancer." [ParisR] (35:129) Wint 93, p. 179-180.
"Stamina." [ParisR] (35:129) Wint 93, p. 181.
2554. HALL, Julie
"Nissiros." [Nat] (257:13) 25 O 93, p. 464.
2555. HALL, Kathryn
"Last Minute Instructions." [CentR] (37:3) Fall 93, p. 513-517.
2556. HALL, Leilani
"Ginseng" (for Oravie). [ArtfulD] (24/25) 93, p. 70.
"Letter to My Postmaster." [PoetL] (88:1) Spr 93, p. 23.
"Tattooed" (for V.S.). [LaurelR] (27:1) Wint 93, p. 41.
"To a Pulaski County Prisoner" (on finding an envelope in Bates Salvageyard).
    [LaurelR] (27:1) Wint 93, p. 40.
2557. HALL, Mary
"Minuet." [AmerS] (62:1) Wint 93, p. 53-54.
2558. HALL, Sidney L., Jr.
"Apollo Loxias." [HampSPR] Wint 93, p. 65.
"The Cold" (after Seferis). [MidwQ] (34:2) Wint 93, p. 216.
"Of Lines Poetic." [HampSPR] Wint 93, p. 65.
"To My Patron and Friend Maecenas" (Horace, Odes I, i). [GrahamHR] (17) Fall 93,
    p. 90-91.
2559. HALLA, R. Chris
"The Paperboy's Father." [Northeast] (5:9) Wint 93-94, p. 7-9.
2560. HALLAWELL, Susan
"Eighth Grade Acrostic." [Agni] (37) 93, p. 31.
"Testimony of the Female Serial Killer." [Agni] (37) 93, p. 32.
2561. HALLERMAN, Victoria
"On the Ferry, Reading the Lives of Astronomers." [NoDaQ] (61:4) Fall 93, p. 65 -
    66.
"Waking to Names of the Dead." [GlobalCR] (1) Spr 93, p. 48-49.
2562. HALLIDAY, Mark
"The Ivory Novel." [DenQ] (27:3) Wint 93, p. 33-35.
"Self There Then." [IndR] (16:1) Spr 93, p. 49-50.
"Taipei Tangle." [IndR] (16:1) Spr 93, p. 51.
"The White Helmet." [Poetry] (162:6) S 93, p. 337.
2563. HALLMUNDSSON, Hallberg
"He Lay There and Was a Great Lover in a Night Without Civilization" (tr. of
    Torgeir Schjerven). [GrandS] (12:3, #47) Fall 93, p. 125.
"Memories in Winter time" (tr. of Steinunn Sigurdardottir). [Vis] (43) 93, p. 27-28.
2564. HALME, Kathleen
"Working Out in the New South." [SouthernPR] (33:1) Spr 93, p. 11-12.
2565. HALPERIN, Joan
"Growing Up." [LaurelR] (27:1) Wint 93, p. 55.
2566. HALPERIN, Mark
"Abe Lincoln, the First Jewish President." [NowestR] (31:1) 93, p. 65-66.
"Bulltrout" (for Jim Spotts). [PraS] (67:1) Spr 93, p. 144-145.
"Calendar Thunderhead." [WillowS] (32) Sum 93, p. 56.
"Cold." [PraS] (67:1) Spr 93, p. 146.
"Splinter." [GreenMR] (NS 6:2) Sum-Fall 93, p. 116-117.
"Waiting." [NowestR] (31:1) 93, p. 67-68.
2567. HALPERN, Daniel
"Homage to N." (after Chekhov). [OntR] (39) Fall-Wint 93-94, p. 40-44.
2568. HALSCHEID, Therése
"Magic Word." [Footwork] (23) 93, p. 51.
2569. HALSTED, Isabella
"Columbia Journal." [HangL] (62) 93, p. 26.
2570. HAMANN, Shannon
"The Babysitter." [HawaiiR] (17:2, #38) Spr 93, p. 39-41.
"The Farm." [Vis] (42) 93, p. 37.
"The Kite." [MassR] (34:1) Spr 93, p. 31-33.
"Man's Fate." [HawaiiR] (17:2, #38) Spr 93, p. 72-73.
"Possess-possess." [Zyzzyva] (9:2) Sum 93, p. 112-113.
"Three." [NewYorkQ] (52) 93, p. 79-81.

2571. HAMBRICK, Jack
   "Dealing with the Dark." [Shen] (43:2) Sum 93, p. 58.
   "Koan for a Friend." [Shen] (43:2) Sum 93, p. 57.
   "Napalm." [Shen] (43:2) Sum 93, p. 56.
2572. HAMBURGER, Michael
   "Alchemical" (tr. of Paul Celan). [QRL] (12:32/33) 93, p. 391-392.
   "Leap-Centuries" (tr. of Paul Celan). [QRL] (12:32/33) 93, p. 390-391.
2573. HAMEL, Madonna
   "Sister Jupiter's Rubber Soul." [CapilR] (2:10) Spr 93, p. 89-97.
2574. HAMER, Forrest
   "Getting Happy." [Zyzzyva] (9:2) Sum 93, p. 32-33.
2575. HAMERSKI, Susan
   "The Heart in Its Wisdom Can Melt Stone" (w. Beverly Voldseth). [RagMag] (11:2)
       93, p. 50.
2576. HAMILL, Sam (See also HAMILL, Samuel E.)
   "After Coltrane's 'I'll Get By'." [ChiR] (39:3/4) 93, p. 119.
   "Already mother's breasts hung low with the years" (tr. of Reizei Tamesuke). [ChiR]
       (39:3/4) 93, p. 203.
   "Coming slowly home" (tr. of Fujiwara no Teika). [ChiR] (39:3/4) 93, p. 203.
   "Dreaming of My Wife" (tr. of Yuan Chen). [Pequod] (36) 93, p. 13.
   "Elegy: O loveliest daughter of Hsieh" (tr. of Yuan Chen). [Pequod] (36) 93, p. 9.
   "Empty House" (tr. of Yuan Chen). [Pequod] (36) 93, p. 14.
   "His word means nothing" (tr. of Fujiwara no Tameie). [ChiR] (39:3/4) 93, p. 203.
   "In the long evening" (tr. of 9th century anonymous Japanese poem). [Pequod] (36)
       93, p. 15.
   "Now I go to live" (tr. of 9th century anonymous Japanese poem). [Pequod] (36) 93,
       p. 16.
   "Return to Wang River" (tr. of Wang Wei). [AmerPoR] (22:2) Mr-Ap 93, p. 46.
   "Three Dreams in Chiang-ling" (tr. of Yuan Chen). [Pequod] (36) 93, p. 10-12.
   "What the Water Knows." [AmerPoR] (22:1) Ja-F 93, p. 34.
2577. HAMILL, Samuel E. (See also HAMILL, Sam)
   "We walked on nights after work." [RagMag] (11:1) 93, p. 39.
2578. HAMILTON, Alfred Starr
   "Highways." [JINJPo] (15:2) Aut 93, p. 24.
   "The Only Pebble on the Beach." [JINJPo] (15:2) Aut 93, p. 23.
   "The Storm." [Footwork] (23) 93, p. 12.
   "War." [Footwork] (23) 93, p. 12.
2579. HAMILTON, Carol
   "An Offering." [CapeR] (28:2) Fall 93, p. 5.
2580. HAMILTON, Fritz
   "1st Bath." [PikeF] (11) Fall 93, p. 5.
   "Bones Equal!" (for Lezli). [DogRR] (12:2, #24) Fall-Wint 93, p. 42.
   "The Flowers Are Screaming." [SmPd] (30:1, #87) Wint 93, p. 36.
   "Human Condition!" [Asylum] (8) 93, p. 128.
   "In Touch at Last." [Asylum] (8) 93, p. 139.
   "Making It Right! (for David)." [PikeF] (11) Fall 93, p. 9.
2581. HAMILTON, M.
   "A Late February Storm." [Light] (5) Spr 93, p. 7.
2582. HAMMER, Mark M.
   "Blaue Nacht." [SouthernPR] (33:1) Spr 93, p. 20-21.
2583. HAMMOND, Catherine
   "Bog Man." [PassN] (14:1) Sum 93, p. 2-4.
   "The Principle of Plenitude." [ChiR] (39:2) 93, p. 106-107.
   "When a Woman's Hair Catches Fire." [ChiR] (39:2) 93, p. 104-105.
2584. HAMMOND, Karla M.
   "Taurus." [Footwork] (23) 93, p. 11.
   "Words for a Friend" (for Peter S. Beagle). [Footwork] (23) 93, p. 11.
2585. HAMOD, Sam
   "And This Forever" (Shari). [Footwork] (23) 93, p. 9.
   "At Fakhani, the Shoe" (For Greg Orfalea, who was there). [Footwork] (23) 93, p. 9 -
       10.
   "The Bedouin Dress." [Footwork] (23) 93, p. 9.
   "Keeping That Cancer Letter to Myself: Flying to Romania" (for my mother).
       [Footwork] (23) 93, p. 8.
2586. HAMPDEN, Holly
   "The Lock-Keeper of Josselin." [Stand] (35:1) Wint 93-94, p. 35.

HAN, Niu
    See NIU, Han
2587. HANAGRID, Samuel Ben Yosef Halevi (Isma'il Ibn Nagrela)
    "The Earthquake (1047)" (tr. by Peter Cole). [Sulfur] (33) Fall 93, p. 191-193.
    "The Miracle at Sea" (tr. by Peter Cole). [Sulfur] (33) Fall 93, p. 186-190.
2588. HANCOCK, Hugh
    "Cheese." [Amelia] (7:2, #21) 93, p. 70.
2589. HANDLER, Joan Cusack
    "Hopeless." [Nimrod] (37:1) Fall-Wint 93, p. 113.
    "In this Big Bed." [JINJPo] (15:1) Spr 93, p. 33.
    "Perhaps It Started." [US1] (28/29) 93, p. 17.
    "A Portrait of a Woman and the Shadow of a Man." [JINJPo] (15:1) Spr 93, p. 32.
    "To Here." [Kalliope] (15:2) 93, p. 30-31.
2590. HANDLIN, Jim
    "The Chesterfields: A Daguerreotype." [Footwork] (23) 93, p. 159-160.
    "Lovers." [Footwork] (23) 93, p. 159.
    "Snowfield with Crows." [Footwork] (23) 93, p. 159.
2591. HANDY, Nixeon Civille
    "Four A.M." [Blueline] (14) 93, p. 60.
2592. HANEY, Michelle
    "A Poem by Michelle" (from "Families, Streets and Dreams," a poetry/photography
        event by 3rd grade students, Whittier Elementary, Tulsa). [Nimrod] (37:1)
        Fall-Wint 93, p. 88.
    "Un Poema por Michelle" (from "Families, Streets and Dreams," a
        poetry/photography event by 3rd grade students, Whittier Elementary, Tulsa).
        [Nimrod] (37:1) Fall-Wint 93, p. 88.
2593. HANIFAN, Jill
    "Dear sister Now I Am Away." [HeavenB] (10) Wint-Spr 93, p. 55.
2594. HANKS, D. Trinidad
    "Color Struck." [AfAmRev] (27:3) Fall 93, p. 473.
    "I Been Fractured." [AfAmRev] (27:3) Fall 93, p. 474.
2595. HANKS, Donna
    "Weeds Happen." [Border] (2) Spr 93, p. 35.
2596. HANLEN, Jim
    "Assignment on the Teacher's Desk." [EngJ] (82:3) Mr 93, p. 92.
2597. HANLEY, Aedan (Aedan Alexander)
    "The City Makes New Grass and Curbs and Brother Booker Blesses the Street."
        [Obs] (8:1) Spr-Sum 93, p. 90-91.
    "How I Learned That Men and Trees Don't Grow in Kansas." [CimR] (102) Ja 93, p.
        83.
    "When Louanne Gave a Haircut." [Bogg] (66) Wint 92-93, p. 63.
2598. HANLEY, Mizzy
    "A Minister Changes Congregations." [PoetL] (88:1) Spr 93, p. 28.
2599. HANNAH, Susan
    "East Thirtieth Street." [Interim] (12:2) Fall-Wint 93, p. 28-29.
    "Woman off Physics, November 1991." [Interim] (12:2) Fall-Wint 93, p. 27-28.
2600. HANNEMANN, Dee
    "Pixilated Geese." [RagMag] (11:1) 93, p. 19.
2601. HANNS, Genine
    "The Ice Princess." [Dandel] (20:1) 93, p. 13.
2602. HANSBURY, Gia
    "Size Queen, a Love Poem for 2 Strippers." [OnTheBus] (6:1, #13) Wint 93-Spr 94,
        p. 116-118.
2603. HANSEN, Daniel
    "Grampa buried the cow." [NewYorkQ] (51) 93, p. 67.
2604. HANSEN, Jeff
    "Bush vs Clinton, 1992." [WashR] (19:2) Ag-S 93, p. 8.
    "Measurements." [WashR] (19:2) Ag-S 93, p. 8.
    "Researchers in the Human Sciences." [WashR] (19:2) Ag-S 93, p. 8.
2605. HANSEN, L.
    "Hand-Picked Rose of a Fading Dream." [ChangingM] (25) Wint-Spr 93, p. 27.
2606. HANSEN, Paul
    "Inscribed at the Temple of Immortal Roaming" (tr. of Wei the Wild). [ChiR]
        (39:3/4) 93, p. 255.
    "White Chrysanthemums" (tr. of Wei the Wild). [ChiR] (39:3/4) 93, p. 255.

2607. HANSEN, Tom
"Cleave a Piece of Wood, I Am There." [LitR] (37:1) Fall 93, p. 35.
"Haystack at Sunset Near Giverny" (Monet, 1891). [LitR] (37:1) Fall 93, p. 34.
"Shadows." [HolCrit] (30:5) D 93, p. 19.
2608. HANSEN, Twyla
"At the Prairie, the Day Before" (for Kathleen Claire). [NoDaQ] (61:2) Spr 93, p. 90-91.
"Gophers." [SoDakR] (31:3) Fall 93, p. 102.
2609. HANSON, Thor
"My Rock at Hidden Valley." [DogRR] (12:2, #24) Fall-Wint 93, p. 5.
2610. HANZLICEK, C. G.
"The Cave." [NoAmR] (278:5) S-O 93, p. 11.
2611. HARAWAY, Fran
"What's in a Locker?" [EngJ] (82:2) F 93, p. 90.
2612. HARDEMAN, Kmur
"For a Friend." [Eyeball] (2) 93, p. 43-44.
2613. HARDENBROOK, Yvonne
"In our identical shirts we hug ourselves hugging each other" (Amelia One-Liner Award). [Amelia] (7:2, #21) 93, p. 63.
2614. HARDER, Dan
"Driving Like Mad." [Border] (2) Spr 93, p. 36.
"Take, for Example / the Pristine Air." [PoetryUSA] (25/26) 93, p. 12.
"You/ with the Hundred Tongues of Fear." [PoetryUSA] (25/26) 93, p. 18.
2615. HARDIN, Jeff
"Fairgrounds." [QW] (37) Sum-Fall 93, p. 94.
"For the Asthmatic." [HayF] (12) Spr-Sum 93, p. 96.
2616. HARDING, Deborah
"She Had Twins and Moved to Paris." [CimR] (105) O 93, p. 95-96.
2617. HARDING, Gunnar
"The Enchanted World of Fairytale" (tr. by Anselm Hollo). [ManhatR] (7:1) Fall 93, p. 16.
"Many Were Here, But They Left Again" (tr. by Anselm Hollo). [ManhatR] (7:1) Fall 93, p. 17-19.
2618. HARDING-RUSSELL, Gillian
"Baby Laurie Arthur's Here." [Grain] (21:3) Fall 93, p. 73-74.
"Joshua and Jesse." [PraF] (14:4) Wint 93-94, p. 44-46.
"Old Bert." [PraF] (14:4) Wint 93-94, p. 46-47.
2619. HARER, Katharine
"March — In the Year of the Heart." [OnTheBus] (5:2, #12) Sum-Fall 93, p. 86-87.
2620. HARGRAVES, Joseph
"Mail." [EvergreenC] (8:1) Spr-Sum 93, p. 51-52.
2621. HARILAOS, Adelia
"Soy una Criatura Marina" (from "Ser de Agua"). [Luz] (5) N 93, p. 44.
2622. HARIS, Leslie
"I'm a Happy Person" (Young Writers, age 13). [PikeF] (11) Fall 93, p. 18.
2623. HARJO, Joy
"The Dawn Appears with Butterflies." [KenR] (NS 15:3) Sum 93, p. 68-69.
"Mourning Song." [KenR] (NS 15:3) Sum 93, p. 70.
"The Place the Musician Became a Bear on the Streets of a City Meant to Kill Him" (for Jim Pepper). [KenR] (NS 15:3) Sum 93, p. 67-68.
2624. HARKINS, Patricia
"In Memory of Audre Lorde, Clifford Lashley and Fritz Henle: Sister of Light" (A Tribute to Audre Lorde — November 1992). [CaribbeanW] (7) 93, p. 7.
2625. HARLEY, Peter
"Conscience." [TickleAce] (25) Spr-Sum 93, p. 187-189.
"Famous Doctor." [TickleAce] (23) Spr-Sum 92, p. 21.
"I Promised My Love I Would Boil Her a Herring." [TickleAce] (23) Spr-Sum 92, p. 22.
"An Isolated Piano Note." [TickleAce] (26) Fall-Wint 93, p. 77.
"She Titupped along the Quai Henri Quatre." [TickleAce] (26) Fall-Wint 93, p. 78.
"Stunned in the Garden of Luxembourg." [TickleAce] (23) Spr-Sum 92, p. 20.
"Two of a Kind." [TickleAce] (24) Fall-Wint 92, p. 91-92.
2626. HARMAN, Padi
"Modern Jesus" (2 poems). [ChironR] (12:3, #36) Aut 93, p. 30.
2627. HARMON, Geoff W.
"In Response to Cole Porter's 'You're the Top'." [ChironR] (12:3, #36) Aut 93, p. 25.

"Transitions, 1979-1992." [ChironR] (12:3, #36) Aut 93, p. 25.
2628. HARMON, William
"Marimba Eroica." [CarolQ] (45:3) Sum 93, p. 30-34.
"The Office of Revels." [CarolQ] (46:1) Fall 93, p. 52-53.
2629. HARMS, James
"Field Trip to My First Time." [PoetryNW] (34:3) Aut 93, p. 44-45.
"The Other World." [ColEng] (55:3) Mr 93, p. 323.
2630. HARNETT, Gerald
"An Indian Legend Says." [Amelia] (7:2, #21) 93, p. 111.
2631. HARP, Jerry
"The Millennium Turning." [Verse] (10:1) Spr 93, p. 37.
"To a High-School Sophomore Who Requested a Love Poem." [Light] (5) Spr 93, p.
15.
2632. HARPER, Cynthia J.
"White Nightmare." [ContextS] (3:1) 93, p. 19.
2633. HARPER, Kate Gale
"Beethoven Reminds Me." [Arshile] (1) Spr 93, p. 30.
2634. HARPER, L. L. (Linda Lee)
"First Ride." [WestB] (33) 93, p. 10-11.
"Horace." [PassN] (14:1) Sum 93, p. 23.
"Teaching Composition." [MassR] (34:4) Wint 93-94, p. 620.
2635. HARPER, Lea
"Commencement of Tai Chi." [AntigR] (93-94) Spr-Sum 93, p. 46.
2636. HARPER, Michael S.
"Dear John, Dear Coltrane." [CarolQ] (45:3) Sum 93, 45th Anniversary section, p.
20-21.
"We Assume" (On the death of our son, Reuben Masai Harper). [QRL] (12:32/33)
93, p. 427-428.
2637. HARPER, Sue
"The Brush Salesman from Leeds." [AntigR] (92) Wint 93, p. 119.
"My Family." [AntigR] (92) Wint 93, p. 120.
2638. HARPOOTIAN, Alysia K.
"I Don't Know How to Sew Buttons." [HawaiiR] (17:1, #37) Spr 93, p. 92.
"Not Calico." [SmPd] (30:1, #87) Wint 93, p. 16.
"Two Minutes After I Told You to Leave." [SmPd] (30:1, #87) Wint 93, p. 16.
2639. HARRINGTON, Anthony
"Kilmeresque." [Light] (6) Sum 93, p. 8.
"Postdiluvian." [Light] (5) Spr 93, p. 13.
2640. HARRINGTON, Ed
"Having Done So." [OnTheBus] (5:2, #12) Sum-Fall 93, p. 88.
"On the Substance of Things." [OnTheBus] (5:2, #12) Sum-Fall 93, p. 88.
2641. HARRIS, Claire
"Framed." [Callaloo] (16:1) Wint 93, p. 30.
"Mysteries." [Callaloo] (16:1) Wint 93, p. 31-32.
"Sister (Y)our Manchild at the Close of the Twentieth Century." [Arc] (30) Spr 93,
p. 45-53.
2642. HARRIS, Craig
"State of Grace" (For Lawrence Washington). [Art&Und] (2:3) Special Edition 93,
p. 8.
2643. HARRIS, Greg
"Fragments of a Progression." [ClockR] (8:1/2) 93, p. 68-70.
2644. HARRIS, James
"Fathers and Sons." [Pequod] (36) 93, p. 87-88.
2645. HARRIS, Jana
"Oh How Can I Keep on Singing?" (Selections: 2 poems, w. photos). [OntR] (39)
Fall-Wint 93-94, p. 67-82.
2646. HARRIS, Joseph
"The Butterfly." [Amelia] (7:2, #21) 93, p. 56.
"Pasquinade." [Light] (5) Spr 93, p. 7.
2647. HARRIS, Judith
"My Father, After Summer Storms." [GreensboroR] (54) Sum 93, p. 58-59.
"The Tea Party." [WebR] (17) Fall 93, p. 122-123.
2648. HARRIS, Lynn Farmer
"Airlink." [LullwaterR] (4:2) Spr-Sum 93, p. 104.
HARRIS, MacDonald
See HEINEY, Donald (MacDonald Harris)

2649. HARRIS, Maureen
"A Blue Grief" (for Lynda). [PraF] (14:2) Sum 93, p. 47.
"Blue Willow." [MalR] (105) Wint 93, p. 14.
"Death of the Marlboro Man" (In Memoriam, F.B., February 1992). [MalR] (105)
Wint 93, p. 15.
"The Lost Son." [PraF] (14:2) Sum 93, p. 48.
2650. HARRIS, Peter
"Sirrah." [PassN] (14:2) Wint 93, p. 46.
HARRIS, Robert Dassanowsky
See DASSANOWSKY-HARRIS, Robert
2651. HARRIS-BOARDMAN, Paul
"Ice-Fishing" (for Paul Harris). [Amelia] (7:2, #21) 93, p. 17-19.
2652. HARRIS-WILLIAMS, Ann
"Persistent Karma." [Obs] (8:2) Fall-Wint 93, p. 96-97.
"Three Women." [Obs] (8:2) Fall-Wint 93, p. 98-99.
"Written in the Margin." [Obs] (8:2) Fall-Wint 93, p. 99-100.
2653. HARRISON, Chris
"Alone, Dark and Sleepless." [OnTheBus] (5:2, #12) Sum-Fall 93, p. 89-90.
"Walking the Alley." [OnTheBus] (5:2, #12) Sum-Fall 93, p. 90.
2654. HARRISON, Guy
"The River's Tale" (The Nimrod/Hardman Awards: Honorable Mention). [Nimrod]
(37:1) Fall-Wint 93, p. 45-51.
2655. HARRISON, Jeffrey
"Entry in a Baby Book: Two Weeks" (After Christopher Smart). [Poetry] (161:6) Mr
93, p. 331-332.
"The Ganges at Benares." [PartR] (60:2) Spr 93, p. 241-243.
"Lord, Deliver Us from This Affliction." [Agni] (37) 93, p. 287.
"Mayflies." [SouthernR] (29:3) Sum, Jl 93, p. 571-572.
"A New Year's Trek." [SouthernR] (29:3) Sum, Jl 93, p. 568-571.
"Physics for Poets." [NewRep] (208:18) 3 My 93, p. 41.
"Political Poem." [Poetry] (161:4) Ja 93, p. 216.
"Shaker Chair." [Poetry] (161:6) Mr 93, p. 333.
2656. HARRISON, Jim
"Coyote No. 1." [CutB] (39) Wint 93, p. 78.
2657. HARRISON, Neil
"Watering the Horses." [WritersF] (19) 93, p. 102.
2658. HARRISON, Pamela
"Poetry." [SouthernPR] (33:1) Spr 93, p. 8.
"Soul in Paraphrase." [GreenMR] (NS 6:2) Sum-Fall 93, p. 40.
2659. HARROD, Lois Marie
"Coming Backstage After a Young Man's Performance." [PassN] (14:1) Sum 93, p.
18.
"Ellsworth Kelly's *White Curve VIII*." [Epiphany] (4:3) Jl 93, p. 199.
"Henry Moore's *Three Motives Against a Wall*." [PassN] (14:1) Sum 93, p. 19.
"Ice Storm." [SouthernPR] (33:1) Spr 93, p. 19-20.
"Lament for Icarus." [SouthernPR] (33:1) Spr 93, p. 18-19.
"My Sister Sends Photos of Her Divorce." [US1] (28/29) 93, p. 17.
"That Same Prayer." [Epiphany] (4:2) Ap 93, p. 105-106.
2660. HARRY, Anna Nelson
"Lament for Eyak." [ChiR] (39:3/4) 93, p. 159-160.
2661. HARSENT, David
"A Child's Bestiary" (Selections: 3 poems). [ChiR] (38:4) 93, p. 127-133.
"Mother and Child." [Verse] (10:1) Spr 93, p. 79.
2662. HART, Anne
"Lazarus the Cat, Nineteen." [TickleAce] (26) Fall-Wint 93, p. 75.
"Strange Newes from the New-found Lande." [TickleAce] (26) Fall-Wint 93, p. 76.
2663. HART, David
"For All Our Presence." [Stand] (35:1) Wint 93-94, p. 64.
2664. HART, Frank
"This Drove Me Nuts." [Spitball] (43) Spr 93, p. 43.
2665. HART, Henry
"Neighbor." [GrahamHR] (17) Fall 93, p. 37-38.
"Pan in Winter." [GrahamHR] (17) Fall 93, p. 36.
2666. HARTER, Penny
"The Llano." [Gaia] (3) O 93, p. 18.
"Moon Over the Sangre de Cristos." [Gaia] (3) O 93, p. 18.

2667. HARTMAN, Geoffrey
"Sanctification" (after Solomon Bar Simson, 12th c.). [WestHR] (47:4) Wint 93, p.
353-355.
2668. HARTMAN, Steven
"The Four Thousand Four Hundred & Two Faces of Dada" (for Ken DiMaggio).
[SlipS] (13) 93, p. 102.
"I Want to Plug My Ears with Cotton." [SlipS] (13) 93, p. 101.
2669. HARTWICH, Jacqueline
"After Heated Words, the Snow." [Gaia] (3) O 93, p. 11.
"Journal from My Night Hotel." [ProseP] (2) 93, p. 41.
"Note to a Silent Member of the Committee." [Prima] (16/17) 93, p. 42-43.
2670. HARVEY, Charles W.
"Eddy." [JamesWR] (10:4) Sum 93, p. 5.
2671. HARVEY, Gayle Elen
"Stephanie's Bees." [LullwaterR] (4:2) Spr-Sum 93, p. 45.
2672. HARVEY, John
"The Battle of Anghiari." [ParisR] (35:128) Fall 93, p. 217.
"Look at This Wound." [WestHR] (47:2) Sum 93, p. 192-193.
"The Persian War after Marathon" (for Lucy Logsdon). [ParisR] (35:128) Fall 93, p.
218.
"Sitting in the Drake." [ParisR] (35:128) Fall 93, p. 219-220.
2673. HARVEY, Matt
"Old Scarecrow Cowley." [Plain] (13:2) Wint 93, p. 19.
2674. HARVOR, Elisabeth
"The Damp Hips of the Women." [AmerV] (31) 93, p. 31-32.
2675. HARWELL, Kimberly
"The First Girl I Kiss." [Pearl] (19) Fall-Wint 93, p. 14.
2676. HARWOOD, Lee
"The Artful Dodger." [HarvardR] (3) Wint 93, p. 127.
"Waunfawr and After / 'The Collar Work Begins'." [Agni] (38) 93, p. 80.
2677. HASHIMOTO, Sharon
"Camano Island: Birthday Poem for My Brother." [PraS] (67:3) Fall 93, p. 130-131.
"Reparations." [PraS] (67:3) Fall 93, p. 131.
"Window Light." [PraS] (67:3) Fall 93, p. 126-130.
2678. HASKINS, Lola
"Angel del Temblor." [Kalliope] (15:3) 93, p. 23-24.
"El Café." [MissouriR] (16:2) 93, p. 32.
"The Carver of Masks." [MissouriR] (16:2) 93, p. 29.
"The Composer Interviews Her Piece." [Kalliope] (15:3) 93, p. 22.
"Cuando Morimos." [MissouriR] (16:2) 93, p. 30.
"Economics." [BelPoJ] (43:3) Spr 93, p. 18.
"Employment." [BelPoJ] (44:2) Wint 93-94, p. 47-48.
"Juan of the Angels." [MissouriR] (16:2) 93, p. 28.
"Kevin Plays the Goldberg Variations." [BelPoJ] (43:3) Spr 93, p. 17.
"Leggiero." [BelPoJ] (43:3) Spr 93, p. 17.
"Lengthening Light." [MissouriR] (16:2) 93, p. 33
"Meteor Shower." [SouthernPR] (33:1) Spr 93, p. 17-18.
"Seeing the thin-sliced moon." [SouthernPR] (33:1) Spr 93, p. 18.
"Three Views from the Latin American Summit" (Guadalajara, Jalisco 1991).
[MissouriR] (16:2) 93, p. 31.
"Uchepas." [Ploughs] (19:4) Wint 93-94, p. 85.
"Waiting for the Bus." [Boulevard] (8:2/3, #23/24) Fall 93, p. 200-201.
2679. HASS, Robert (See also HASS, Robert B.; HASS, Robert Bernard)
"Calm." [NewEngR] (15:1) Wint 93, p. 133.
"The Gardens of Warsaw." [HarvardR] (3) Wint 93, p. 38-39.
"Lithuania, After Fifty-two Years" (tr. of Czeslaw Milosz, w. the author).
[NewYorker] (69:25) 9 Ag 93, p. 70-71.
"A Man-Fly" (tr. of Czeslaw Milosz, w. the author). [NewYorker] (69:6) 29 Mr 93,
p. 60.
"Sarajevo" (tr. of Czeslaw Milosz, w. the author). [NewRep] (209:17) 25 O 93, p.
16.
"Shunga." [NewEngR] (15:1) Wint 93, p. 134.
"Woe!" (tr. of Czeslaw Milosz, w. the author). [NewYorker] (69:14) 24 My 93, p.
74.

205

2680. HASS, Robert B. (*See also* HASS, Robert; HASS, Robert Bernard)
"The Park They Say Is Dead" (tr. of Stefan George). [BlackWR] (20:1) Fall-Wint 93, p. 119.
2681. HASS, Robert Bernard (*See also* HASS, Robert; HASS, Robert B.)
"Monarchs." [SewanR] (101:3) Jl-S, Sum 93, p. 335-336.
2682. HASSELSTROM, Linda
"Pecking Order." [PraS] (67:1) Spr 93, p. 129-130.
2683. HASTEN, Marie
"Food for Thought, or Just Deserts" (M.F.A. Workshop w. Howard Glyn, Pamela Hughes, M. R. Syneck, Lisbeth Keiley, Mary Greene, David Trinidad and Allen Ginsberg, Nov. 21, 1988). [BrooklynR] (10) 93, p. 94-95.
2684. HASTIE, Stella
"Paseo Bolivar." [SouthernPR] (33:1) Spr 93, p. 46-47.
"Portrait." [SouthernPR] (33:1) Spr 93, p. 47-48.
2685. HASTINGS, John R.
"Of Corsets, a Sonnet." [DogRR] (12:1, #23) Spr-Sum 93, p. 7.
2686. HASTINGS, Nancy Peters
"Lilies." [Plain] (13:2) Wint 93, p. 25.
"Lost." [ContextS] (3:1) 93, p. 10.
2687. HASTINGS, Steven
"Apostle." [Verse] (10:2) Sum 93, p. 25.
2688. HATCHETT, Richard
"Thrown." [SouthernHR] (27:2) Spr 93, p. 164.
2689. HATHAWAY, Michael
"Elusive Pisces." [JamesWR] (10:2) Wint 93, p. 17.
2690. HATHAWAY, William
"The Roots of Sweetness." [Epoch] (42:1) 93, p. 103-107.
2691. HATTERSLEY, Michael E.
"Body Knowledge" (To John Ashbery). [Poetry] (163:1) O 93, p. 37-38.
2692. HAUG, James
"Dead Man at the Party." [LitR] (37:1) Fall 93, p. 73.
"Rocks My Pillow Too." [Witness] (7:1) 93, p. 29.
"Trade Wind." [Witness] (7:1) 93, p. 28.
2693. HAUGOVA, Mila
"Autumn Light" (tr. by Ellen Rosenbaum). [OxfordM] (9:1) Spr-Sum 93, p. 32-33.
2694. HAUK, Barbara
"Presence of Death in the Living Room." [OnTheBus] (5:2, #12) Sum-Fall 93, p. 91.
"A Proper Blank Wall." [ChironR] (12:4/13:1, #37/38) Wint 93-Spr 94, p. 29.
2695. HAUPTMAN, Terry
"Bloodstar" (Santa Fe). [13thMoon] (11:1/2) 93, p. 34.
"The Politics of Grief." [Caliban] (13) 93, p. 102-103.
"Shekinah." [Caliban] (13) 93, p. 100-101.
"Stealing Thundaah: Out Dare and Around." [13thMoon] (11:1/2) 93, p. 33.
"The Twenty-First Century." [Caliban] (12) 93, p. 162-163.
2696. HAUSER, Alisa
"Grandpa." [RagMag] (11:2) 93, p. 44-45.
"Paranoia." [RagMag] (11:2) 93, p. 46.
"Phillip Rutland." [RagMag] (11:2) 93, p. 43.
"Sagging Chests" (Young Writers, age 15). [PikeF] (11) Fall 93, p. 20.
2697. HAVEN, Stephen
"Change" (tr. of Jiaxin Wang, w. Jin Zhong). [AmerPoR] (22:6) N-D 93, p. 38.
"Facing a Stone" (tr. of Moi Fei, w. Jin Zhong). [AmerPoR] (22:6) N-D 93, p. 34.
"Falling Snow" (tr. of Moi Fei, w. Jin Zhong). [AmerPoR] (22:6) N-D 93, p. 34.
"The Finale" (tr. of Jiaxin Wang, w. Dong Jiping). [AmerPoR] (22:6) N-D 93, p. 37.
"In England" (tr. of Duo Duo, w. Jin Zhong). [AmerPoR] (22:6) N-D 93, p. 36.
"Instant" (tr. of Moi Fei, w. Jin Zhong). [AmerPoR] (22:6) N-D 93, p. 34.
"Iron" (tr. of Jiaxin Wang, w. Jin Zhong). [AmerPoR] (22:6) N-D 93, p. 38.
"It Is" (tr. of Duo Duo, w. Jin Zhong). [AmerPoR] (22:6) N-D 93, p. 35.
"The Knife" (tr. of Jiaxin Wang, w. Fan Xinmin). [AmerPoR] (22:6) N-D 93, p. 37.
"Longevity" (tr. of Duo Duo, w. Jin Zhong). [AmerPoR] (22:6) N-D 93, p. 35.
"One Story Contains All His Past" (tr. of Duo Duo, w. Jin Zhong). [AmerPoR] (22:6) N-D 93, p. 36.
"Orchard" (tr. of Moi Fei, w. Jin Zhong). [AmerPoR] (22:6) N-D 93, p. 34.
"Poetry" (to Haizi, tr. of Jiaxin Wang, w. Dong Jiping). [AmerPoR] (22:6) N-D 93, p. 38.

"Railway Station" (tr. of Jiaxin Wang, w. Jin Zhong). [AmerPoR] (22:6) N-D 93, p. 37.

"Staircase" (written in my old home at the Gate of Peace, tr. of Jiaxin Wang, w. Jin Zhong). [AmerPoR] (22:6) N-D 93, p. 37.

"That Stone" (tr. of Moi Fei, w. Jin Zhong). [AmerPoR] (22:6) N-D 93, p. 34.

"The Window That Loves to Weep" (tr. of Duo Duo, w. Jin Zhong). [AmerPoR] (22:6) N-D 93, p. 36.

2698. HAVENER, Sandra
"Frackle." [SinW] (51) Wint 93-94, p. 74.

2699. HAWKHEAD, John
"Enter the VIRUS." [Bogg] (66) Wint 92-93, p. 49.

2700. HAWKINS, Hunt
"Ears." [Writer] (106:12) D 93, p. 16.
"Honeymoon." [Writer] (106:12) D 93, p. 18.
"My Wife's Shoes." [Writer] (106:12) D 93, p. 16.
"The Prejohn." [Writer] (106:12) D 93, p. 17.
"Pumpkin Lust." [SouthernR] (29:1) Wint, Ja 93, p. 152.
"Something Not There." [SouthernR] (29:1) Wint, Ja 93, p. 153.

2701. HAWKINS, Kelly
"Fearful Moments" (tr. of Ales Debeljak, w. the author). [NoDaQ] (61:1) Wint 93, p. 58.

2702. HAWKINS, Sharon
"Bodywork." [Arc] (31) Aut 93, p. 75-76.
"A Woman Is Drawing Her Mother." [Arc] (31) Aut 93, p. 77-78.

2703. HAWKS, Tom
"Almanac, 1978." [SenR] (23:1/2) Wint 93, p. 112.

2704. HAWLEY, Mary Kathleen
"Godlines." [Epiphany] (4:3) Jl 93, p. 200.
"La Judicial." [Epiphany] (4:3) Jl 93, p. 201-202.

2705. HAXTON, Brooks
"Crow Call." [TriQ] (88) Fall 93, p. 147.
"Dialogue of Soul & Stone." [Atlantic] (272:4) O 93, p. 72.
"Hypothetical." [YaleR] (81:1) Ja 93, p. 89.
"An Interval of Five Tones Being the Dominant." [ParisR] (35:128) Fall 93, p. 221.
"Scaffold." [TriQ] (88) Fall 93, p. 145-146.

2706. HAYDON, Rich
"Betting Seeds." [BellArk] (9:2) Mr-Ap 93, p. 9.
"Crow Light." [CapeR] (28:2) Fall 93, p. 29.
"The In Between." [BellArk] (9:2) Mr-Ap 93, p. 9.
"The Wood Pile." [BellArk] (9:4) Jl-Ag 93, p. 22.

2707. HAYES, J. Michael
"Godlike Freedoms to Dream up Destiny." [PoetryUSA] (25/26) 93, p. 53.

2708. HAYES, John
"And I'm Still Waiting" (Young Writers, age 12). [PikeF] (11) Fall 93, p. 18.

2709. HAYES, Noreen
"Remodeling." [SpiritSH] (58) 93, p. 10.

2710. HAYFORD, James
"Egress." [HarvardR] (4) Spr 93, p. 155.
"My Window." [HarvardR] (3) Wint 93, p. 108.
"To Robert Forst: A Letter Never Sent." [HarvardR] (3) Wint 93, p. 109.

2711. HAYMAN, Dick
"Air Fairs." [Light] (5) Spr 93, p. 14.
"Eggsaggeration." [Light] (6) Sum 93, p. 12.
"Gilded Rule." [Light] (6) Sum 93, p. 19.
"My Pets." [Light] (8) Wint 93, p. 22.

2712. HAYMON, Ava Leavell
"White Picket Fence" (after a watercolor by Judi Betts). [Vis] (42) 93, p. 22.

2713. HAYNES, Linda Collins
"A Kind of Ascension." [HopewellR] (5) 93, p. 62.

2714. HAYNES, Robert (Robert E.)
"In the Workshop." [PoetryNW] (34:2) Sum 93, p. 17-18.
"Rule for the New Liar." [PoetryNW] (34:2) Sum 93, p. 19-20.
"What I Could Be." [PoetryNW] (34:2) Sum 93, p. 18-19.
"Wherever You Go." [PoetL] (88:2) Sum 93, p. 7.

2715. HAYNES/ELLIOTT, William P.
"Deli Coffee." [Pearl] (17) Spr 93, p. 79.

207

HAYSOM

2716. HAYSOM, Jenny
"Blueberry Gleaner." [Quarry] (42:3) 93, p. 112.
"Dandelion Cross." [Quarry] (42:3) 93, p. 110.
"Fresh from a Shredding." [Quarry] (42:3) 93, p. 113.
"Pictograph." [Quarry] (42:3) 93, p. 111.
"Woman from the Waiting Room." [Quarry] (42:3) 93, p. 109.
2717. HAYWARD, Camille
"Becoming." [BellArk] (9:2) Mr-Ap 93, p. 5.
"Charcoal Drawing." [BellArk] (9:2) Mr-Ap 93, p. 5.
"In the Lifting of Faces." [BellArk] (9:2) Mr-Ap 93, p. 5.
"Let There Be Words." [BellArk] (9:2) Mr-Ap 93, p. 5.
"Naming" (After Margaret Wise Brown's "Goodnight Moon"). [BellArk] (9:2) Mr -
Ap 93, p. 5.
"Pears." [BellArk] (9:2) Mr-Ap 93, p. 5.
2718. HAZEN, James
"One Way Street Game, 1943." [Blueline] (14) 93, p. 77.
2719. HAZEN, Michael
"The Unknown Player." [Spitball] (43) Spr 93, p. 60.
2720. HAZO, Samuel
"The Year of the Horse." [AmerS] (62:2) Spr 93, p. 281-282.
HE, Ou Yang Jiang
See OU YANG, Jiang He
2721. HEAD, Gwen
"Fools the Eye" (after teaching during Artfort week at Ford Worden State Park,
Washington). [NorthStoneR] (11) 93, p. 60.
"The Mask." [NorthStoneR] (11) 93, p. 58-59.
"The Press Poem" (for Scott). [NorthStoneR] (11) 93, p. 57.
2722. HEAD, Robert
"Moment." [Bogg] (66) Wint 92-93, p. 47.
2723. HEADDON, Bill
"Wreckage 1944." [CoalC] (7) Apr 93, p. 18.
2724. HEALEY, Stephen
"The Past." [BlackWR] (19:1) Fall-Wint 92, p. 87-88.
"Pastoral." [HawaiiR] (17:2, #38) Spr 93, p. 3.
"Picture." [HawaiiR] (17:3, #39) Fall 93, p. 58-59.
"The Things That Have Never Happened Before." [IndR] (16:2) Fall 93, p. 178-179.
2725. HEANEY, Seamus
"The Birthplace." [NewEngR] (15:1) Wint 93, p. 136-137.
"Field Work." [NewEngR] (15:1) Wint 93, p. 135.
"The Flight Path" (for Donald Davie). [Thrpny] (52) Wint 93, p. 5.
"Mint." [NewRep] (208:25) 21 Je 93, p. 45.
"The Modern Mistress." [Verse] (10:3) Wint 93, p. 87.
"Poet's Chair" (for Carolyn Mulholland). [Agni] (38) 93, p. 1-2.
"Postscript." [TickleAce] (26) Fall-Wint 93, p. 5.
"The Rainstick" (for Rand and Beth). [NewRep] (208:12) 22 Mr 93, p. 42.
"To a Dutch Potter in Ireland" (for Sonja Landweer). [Thrpny] (53) Spr 93, p. 15.
2726. HEATH-STUBBS, John
"Poem After Solstice." [QRL] (12:32/33) 93, p. 428-429.
2727. HÉBERT, Anne
"The Closed Room" (tr. by A. Poulin). [QRL] (12:32/33) 93, p. 190-191.
"Inventory" (tr. by A. Poulin). [QRL] (12:32/33) 93, p. 189-190.
"More and More Narrow" (tr. by A. Poulin). [QRL] (12:32/33) 93, p. 191.
"Small Dead Girl" (tr. by A. Poulin). [QRL] (12:32/33) 93, p. 191-192.
2728. HECHT, Anthony
"Adam." [QRL] (12:32/33) 93, p. 429-430.
"Going the Rounds: A Sort of Love Poem." [QRL] (12:32/33) 93, p. 430-432.
"A Ruminant." [SouthernR] (29:4) Aut, O 93, p. 747.
2729. HECHT, Roger
"After Kristallnacht." [QRL] (12:32/33) 93, p. 433-434.
2730. HECHT, Susan
"Margaret Mead's Refrigerator." [HawaiiR] (17:2, #38) Spr 93, p. 19.
2731. HECK, April
"The Wife in the Window, the Woman Bending in the Sun." [ArtfulD] (24/25) 93, p.
100-101.
2732. HECKMAN, Julie
"Family." [EvergreenC] (8:1) Spr-Sum 93, p. 66-67.

2733. HEDDEREL, Vance Philip
"Mysteries." [PoetryE] (36) Fall 93, p. 117.
2734. HEDEEN, Paul M.
"Metempsychosis" (for a soldier and townsman, dead, at last, of AIDS). [Confr] (51)
Sum 93, p. 221.
HEDGE COKE, A. A.
See COKE, A. A. Hedge
2735. HEDLEY, Leslie Woolf
"Behold the Men, 1945." [FreeL] (12) Sum 93, p. 4-6.
2736. HEDLUND, Dorothy Swaner
"We row the johnboat" (Lucille Sandberg Haiku Award, 3rd honorable mention).
[Amelia] (7:2, #21) 93, p. 43.
2737. HEFFERNAN, Michael
"A Catch in the Breath." [Shen] (43:1) Spr 93, p. 44-45.
"A Girl Sings to Moravia at the World's End." [Shen] (43:3) Fall 93, p. 26-27.
"The Moving Statue at Melleray." [Shen] (43:1) Spr 93, p. 46.
"Truth." [GettyR] (6:2) Spr 93, p. 322.
"Watering Impatiens." [GettyR] (6:2) Spr 93, p. 323.
HEG, Bob Engstrom
See ENGSTROM-HEG, Bob
2738. HEGLAND, Jean
"The Crone I Will Become." [Calyx] (14:3) Sum 93, p. 16.
2739. HEIGHTON, Steven
"As We Forget Them." [PoetryC] (13:2) 93, p. 4.
"Birthday." [Arc] (30) Spr 93, p. 43.
"Deaf-Mute." [PoetryC] (13:2) 93, p. 4.
"Graveyards in the North Country" (for Jeff). [PoetryC] (13:2) 93, p. 4.
"Hikers." [Arc] (30) Spr 93, p. 42.
"Lightning Bolt in the Black-Out." [LitR] (37:1) Fall 93, p. 17.
"To Our Eyes the Blind Man." [Arc] (30) Spr 93, p. 41.
2740. HEIKKINEN, Jim
"Tongue and Groove." [TampaR] (7) Fall 93, p. 11.
2741. HEIM, Scott
"Chilly." [Arshile] (2) 93, p. 34.
"The Death of Anthony Perkins." [ProseP] (2) 93, p. 42-44.
"Jack." [Farm] (10:2) Fall-Wint 93-94, p. 75-76.
"Loving the Angel." [Pearl] (19) Fall-Wint 93, p. 21.
"Safe." [Arshile] (2) 93, p. 35-36.
2742. HEINE, Heinrich
"Children" (Original untitled, tr. by Kenneth T. Gallagher). [SpiritSH] (58) 93, p.
28-29.
"Extinguished" (tr. by Kenneth T. Gallagher). [SpiritSH] (58) 93, p. 29.
"Friends" (tr. by Kenneth T. Gallagher). [SpiritSH] (58) 93, p. 31.
"Her Family" (tr. by Kenneth T. Gallagher). [SpiritSH] (58) 93, p. 30.
2743. HEINEY, Donald (MacDonald Harris)
"The Old Man." [Pearl] (19) Fall-Wint 93, p. 6.
2744. HEINLEIN, David A.
"New Jersey Diviner." [US1] (28/29) 93, p. 13.
2745. HEINY, Katherine
"Four Endings." [HangL] (63) 93, p. 18.
"Mad Doctor." [HangL] (63) 93, p. 19.
"On the Night My Brother Moved in with His Girlfriend." [HangL] (63) 93, p. 17.
"The Plot to Kill My Grandmother" (for Kitty Lei). [HangL] (63) 93, p. 16.
2746. HEINZ, Suzanne
"A Poem About Breasts." [Dandel] (20:1) 93, p. 14.
2747. HEISE, Thomas
"Posterestante." [Parting] (6:2) Wint 93, p. 16.
2748. HEISLER, Eva
"Margaret Fuller, Pregnant — December 1847" (Discovery-The Nation '93
Prizewinning Poet). [Nat] (256:17) 3 My 93, p. 604.
"The Woman in the Closet." [Nat] (257:3) 19 Jl 93, p. 110.
2749. HEJDA, Zbynek
"A Fable" (tr. by Ellen Rosenbaum). [OxfordM] (9:1) Spr-Sum 93, p. 85-87.
2750. HEJINIAN, Lyn
"Sleeps" (Excerpts). [BlackBread] (3) 93, p. 37-44.

"Sleeps" (Selections: 6, 35, 39, for Lauri Nykopp). [GrandS] (11:4, #44) 93, p. 60 - 65.
2751. HELD, Dennis
"Satan Owns a Boneyard." [CutB] (39) Wint 93, p. 79-80.
2752. HELD, George
"How Sweet the Bye and Bye" (for JBH). [Comm] (120:21) 3 D 93, p. 14.
"Osprey." [Hellas] (4:1) Spr 93, p. 22.
2753. HELLER, Chaia Zblocki
"I Don't Touch My Breasts Anymore." [SinW] (49) Spr-Sum 93, p. 74.
2754. HELLER, Dorothy
"Don't Bank on It!" [Light] (7) Aut 93, p. 11.
2755. HELLER, Liane
"As Always." [AntigR] (95) Aut 93, p. 60-61.
"Point No Point, B.C." [AntigR] (95) Aut 93, p. 62.
"Summer Swelled, Whirred." [AntigR] (95) Aut 93, p. 63.
2756. HELLER, Michael
"About the Capitals." [Talisman] (11) Fall 93, p. 125.
"At Work." [Talisman] (11) Fall 93, p. 122-123.
"Balkan Moon and Sun" (for Rachel). [Talisman] (11) Fall 93, p. 126-127.
"Wednesday." [Talisman] (11) Fall 93, p. 124.
2757. HELLEW, Joyce
"Very Red." [NewYorkQ] (51) 93, p. 66.
2758. HELMINSKI, Kabir Edmund
"And He Is With Us" (tr. of Jelaluddin Rumi). [Sun] (212) Ag 93, p. 39.
"Didn't I Say" (tr. of Jelaluddin Rumi). [Sun] (212) Ag 93, p. 39.
"Search the Darkness" (tr. of Jelaluddin Rumi). [Sun] (212) Ag 93, p. 39.
2759. HELSTERN, Linda Lizut
"The Eye of the Hawk." [SoDakR] (31:1) Spr 93, p. 83.
"For the Deer." [SoDakR] (31:1) Spr 93, p. 80.
"The Living Mountain." [SoDakR] (31:1) Spr 93, p. 84.
"Out of the Darkness." [CapeR] (28:1) Spr 93, p. 38.
"The Path of Darkness." [SoDakR] (31:1) Spr 93, p. 79.
"Without Eyes." [SoDakR] (31:1) Spr 93, p. 81-82.
2760. HELWIG, David
"A Random Gospel" (Selections 6 poems). [MalR] (102) Spr 93, p. 30-35.
2761. HELWIG, Susan L. (Susan Lucinda)
"Exposure." [PraF] (14:3) Aut 93, p. 13.
"Poetry Teacher." [Bogg] (66) Wint 92-93, p. 36.
2762. HEMAN, Bob
"Description." [Caliban] (13) 93, p. 80.
"Enclosure." [Caliban] (13) 93, p. 80.
"Tribe." [Caliban] (13) 93, p. 80.
2763. HEMLEY, Robin
"Strikebreaker" (in "The Big Ear"). [WillowS] (32) Sum 93, p. 45-46.
2764. HEMMINGER, Bill
"To an African Friend, After His Announcing His Intention to Move to the United States." [HopewellR] (5) 93, p. 58-59.
"While walking softely within these walls." [HopewellR] (5) 93, p. 60-61.
2765. HEMPHILL, Caroline
"Do the Dead Dream of Waking?" [BlackWR] (19:2) Spr-Sum 93, p. 20.
"Reunion." [BlackWR] (19:2) Spr-Sum 93, p. 21.
2766. HENDERSHOT, Cynthia
"Twenty Shores." [Asylum] (8) 93, p. 60-64.
2767. HENDERSON, Donna
"Cave Painting." [Gaia] (1/2) Ap-Jl 93, p. 33.
"Dawn." [Gaia] (1/2) Ap-Jl 93, p. 33.
2768. HENDRICKSON, John
"The Electronic Generation." [WeberS] (10:2) Spr-Sum 93, p. 62.
"No Sparrow Falls." [WeberS] (10:2) Spr-Sum 93, p. 62.
HENDRICKSON, S. B. Jones
See JONES-HENDRICKSON, S. B.
2769. HENKE, Mark
"Preview." [OnTheBus] (5:2, #12) Sum-Fall 93, p. 92.
2770. HENLEY, Jim
"A Maxim." [HolCrit] (30:2) Ap 93, p. 14.

2771. HENN, Mary Ann
"Parody on E. Dickinson." [Footwork] (23) 93, p. 121.
2772. HENNEDY, Hugh
"April Music." [HawaiiR] (17:2, #38) Spr 93, p. 52.
2773. HENNEN, Tom
"Finding Horse Skulls on a Day That Smelled Like Flowers." [NorthStoneR] (11)
93, p. 27.
2774. HENNESSEY, Bill
"Nude in the Street." [SlipS] (13) 93, p. 92.
"This Light of Physics." [CapeR] (28:2) Fall 93, p. 8.
2775. HENNESSY, Eileen
"Footnotes to a History of the Flood." [WestHR] (47:4) Wint 93, p. 373.
"Hare and Hounds." [WestHR] (47:4) Wint 93, p. 371.
"Water Babies." [WestHR] (47:4) Wint 93, p. 372.
2776. HENNING, Barbara
"Planks and Boards." [PaintedB] (52) 93, p. 16-17.
2777. HENRIE, Carol
"Affection." [PoetryNW] (34:1) Spr 93, p. 40.
"Cuddyre." [PoetryNW] (34:1) Spr 93, p. 41-42.
"Song Accompanied by Tuneless Whistling." [PoetryNW] (34:1) Spr 93, p. 39-40.
2778. HENRY, Daniel
"Morning Poem." [EngJ] (82:1) Ja 93, p. 87.
2779. HENRY, Gerrit
"And Any Other." [Chelsea] (55) 93, p. 49.
"Petit Grand Mal." [NewAW] (11) Sum-Fall 93, p. 106.
2780. HENRY, Patrick
"12:44 A.M." (tr. of Nina Iskrenko, w. John High). [Talisman] (11) Fall 93, p. 239 -
241.
2781. HENRY, Ron
"Sans Serif: Blue Ridge Parkway, March 1989." [HiramPoR] (53/54) Fall 92-Sum
93, p. 43.
2782. HENSON, David
"Lunch Hour." [Asylum] (8) 93, p. 114.
"A Man Awakens at Dawn, Steps Out of Bed, and Rises to the Ceiling." [Asylum]
(8) 93, p. 114.
"Till Death Do They Part." [Asylum] (8) 93, p. 114.
"Time Machine." [PaintedHR] (9) Spr 93, p. 19.
2783. HENSON, Sandra Meek
"Refugee." [MassR] (34:3) Aut 93, p. 431-432.
2784. HENSON, Stuart
"The Bee Nativity." [CumbPR] (12:2) Spr 93, p. 23.
"The Players." [CumbPR] (12:2) Spr 93, p. 21-22.
"A Postcard to John Greening." [CumbPR] (12:2) Spr 93, p. 24.
2785. HENTZ, Robert R.
"The Forlorn Hope." [DogRR] (12:1, #23) Spr-Sum 93, p. 25.
"The Nagging Question." [CapeR] (28:2) Fall 93, p. 21.
"One That Will Do to Swell a Progress." [DogRR] (12:1, #23) Spr-Sum 93, p. 24.
2786. HERAS SANCHEZ, Antonio
"Uno" (from "Entre Somnolencias, Insomnio y Sueños"). [Luz] (5) N 93, p. 27.
2787. HERBERT, W. N.
"Whispering Through Ice." [Verse] (10:3) Wint 93, p. 108-110.
2788. HERBERT, Zbigniew
"Achilles, Penthesilea" (tr. by Joseph Brodsky). [NewYRB] (40:17) 21 O 93, p. 22.
"The Death of Lev" (tr. by John and Bogdana Carpenter). [NewYorker] (69:4) 15
Mr 93, p. 78.
2789. HERBST, Nikki
"First Poem About My Father." [AntR] (51:4) Fall 93, p. 555.
"Lightning." [DenQ] (27:3) Wint 93, p. 36.
"Set Theory" (A Conversation with My Mother). [GeoR] (47:2) Sum 93, p. 240-241.
"Whirligigs." [BlackWR] (20:1) Fall-Wint 93, p. 25.
2790. HERMAN-SEKULIC, Maja
"Flaubert" (tr. of Milan Milisic). [NoDaQ] (61:1) Wint 93, p. 113.
"Gumbo" (in memoriam Milan Milisic). [NoDaQ] (61:1) Wint 93, p. 79.
"Treacherously, from Behind" (tr. of Milan Milisic). [NoDaQ] (61:1) Wint 93, p.
112.

211

2791. HERMSEN, Terry (Terry A.)
"Pegasus" (for Christopher Merrill). [Journal] (17:2) Fall-Wint 93, p. 39-40.
"Stories on the Mountain." [AntigR] (93-94) Spr-Sum 93, p. 87-88.
2792. HERNANDEZ, David
"3rd World This." [Footwork] (23) 93, p. 15.
"Armitage Street." [Footwork] (23) 93, p. 13.
"Bus-Boy Secrets." [Footwork] (23) 93, p. 16.
"Florencia." [Footwork] (23) 93, p. 14.
"For My Friend and Partner in Poems and Conspiracies: Alfredo Matías."
[Footwork] (23) 93, p. 14.
"Fragments of a Spanish Marriage." [Footwork] (23) 93, p. 16.
"Longings on a Sunday Morning." [Footwork] (23) 93, p. 15.
"My Grammar School Sweetheart Came from a Broken Home." [Footwork] (23) 93,
p. 14.
"Ode to a 60's Militant." [Footwork] (23) 93, p. 16.
"Why I Don't Drive a Car." [Footwork] (23) 93, p. 15.
2793. HERNANDEZ, Francisco
"Autograph" (tr. by John Oliver Simon). [ArtfulD] (24/25) 93, p. 40.
2794. HERNANDEZ, Mario
"To His Wife Who Works Days from Her Husband Who Works Nights." [PraS]
(67:3) Fall 93, p. 116-117.
2795. HERNANDEZ, Orlando Jose
"A Woman Kneeling in the Big City" (Selections: 5 poems, Spanish tr. of Elizabeth
Macklin). [Trasimagen] (1:1) Otoño-Invierno 93, p. 22-25.
2796. HERNANDEZ-SENTER, Juan
"1/14/90." [Americas] (21:2) Sum 93, p. 54.
"7 de Mayo." [Americas] (21:2) Sum 93, p. 52-53.
"Así Es." [Americas] (21:2) Sum 93, p. 58.
"Enero." [Americas] (21:2) Sum 93, p. 55.
"Sin Energía." [Americas] (21:2) Sum 93, p. 50-51.
"El Toño Loco de la Placita de Guadalupe." [Americas] (21:2) Sum 93, p. 57.
"Traducciones." [Americas] (21:2) Sum 93, p. 56.
2797. HERRERA, Juan Felipe
"Iowa Blues Bar Spiritual." [NewEngR] (15:1) Wint 93, p. 138-140.
2798. HERRON, Elizabeth
"Rosa, Maria, Lucia." [SlipS] (13) 93, p. 52-53.
2799. HERSHEY, Laura
"Canyon." [SinW] (49) Spr-Sum 93, p. 114.
"A Mother Tells." [Kaleid] (27) Sum-Fall 93, p. 36.
"Self-Body-Portrait." [SinW] (49) Spr-Sum 93, p. 39.
2800. HERSHON, Robert
"The Cowboy and the Farmer Should be Friends." [HangL] (63) 93, p. 24.
"Cut Flowers." [BrooklynR] (10) 93, p. 42.
"Dupe University." [PoetryNW] (34:3) Aut 93, p. 38-39.
"Fish Name." [HangL] (63) 93, p. 22.
"Floating Hats." [HangL] (63) 93, p. 20.
"Into a Punchline." [HangL] (63) 93, p. 21-22.
"Kid Moves Out." [HangL] (63) 93, p. 23.
"Manager Fired, Managed Named." [PoetryNW] (34:3) Aut 93, p. 38.
"A Primer for Tonight's Audience." [BrooklynR] (10) 93, p. 43.
"Someone from Around Here." [WilliamMR] (31) 93, p. 80-81.
"What We Whistle While We Work." [WilliamMR] (31) 93, p. 18.
"Who's Who in the East." [PoetryNW] (34:3) Aut 93, p. 37-38.
2801. HERZ, Steve
"He Saw the Mounds of Hair Under Glass." [HolCrit] (30:5) D 93, p. 17.
2802. HESKIN, J. D.
"My Heart Does Not Leap." [RagMag] (11:2) 93, p. 35.
2803. HESLOP, Helen
"A Picture of Both My Sons." [Verse] (10:2) Sum 93, p. 98-99.
2804. HESS, Errol
"The Quaker Dreams of Violence." [Lactuca] (17) Apr 93, p. 60.
2805. HESS, Sonya
"A Little Supper Music." [Caliban] (12) 93, p. 81.
"Talk Too Much." [Caliban] (12) 93, p. 80.
2806. HETHERINGTON, John A.
"Hat Face" (from "Yichud"). [PoetryUSA] (25/26) 93, p. 30.

"Mendocino Sea Chair" (from "Yichud"). [PoetryUSA] (25/26) 93, p. 18.
"Winterkill" (from "Yichud"). [PoetryUSA] (25/26) 93, p. 18.
2807. HETTICH, Michael
"Common Birds" (Miami, June 1992). [Gaia] (1/2) Ap-Jl 93, p. 2.
"First Love." [PoetryE] (36) Fall 93, p. 118.
"Trust." [PoetryE] (36) Fall 93, p. 119-120.
2808. HETTLINGER, Graham
"Waiting for the Electric Train to Leningrad." [Field] (48) Spr 93, p. 43.
2809. HEWITT, Christopher
"All I Know to Do." [Art&Und] (2:4) O-N 93, p. 14.
2810. HEWITT, George
"Sestina." [WritersF] (19) 93, p. 86-87.
2811. HEWSON, John
"Requiem for Ray" (For Raymond Boileau, alias Ray Waters). [TickleAce] (24)
        Fall-Wint 92, p. 95.
2812. HEYEN, William
"Among the Stars." [OntR] (39) Fall-Wint 93-94, p. 83.
"Crazy Horse Mnemonic." [AmerPoR] (22:6) N-D 93, p. 21.
"Eidolons." [OntR] (39) Fall-Wint 93-94, p. 83-84.
"The Hunter." [SenR] (23:1/2) Wint 93, p. 88.
"A Long Island Fish Story." [PaintedB] (50/51) 93, p. 42.
"The Meeting." [OntR] (39) Fall-Wint 93-94, p. 85-86.
"November 11, 1918." [OhioR] (50) 93, p. 16.
"The Rope." [AmerPoR] (22:6) N-D 93, p. 22.
"Seneca Country." [SenR] (23:1/2) Wint 93, p. 86-87.
"The Shopper." [OntR] (39) Fall-Wint 93-94, p. 86-87.
"Tongue." [AmerPoR] (22:6) N-D 93, p. 21.
2813. HIBBARD, Kate Lyn
"The Metamorphosis." [Calyx] (14:3) Sum 93, p. 12.
2814. HICKMAN, Amy S.
"Legend." [WestB] (31/32) 93, p. 25.
2815. HICKMAN, David
"51. I laugh not knowing: The wind above." [InterPR] (19:2) Fall 93, p. 84.
"59. Visitations. Shields in the sky." [InterPR] (19:2) Fall 93, p. 85.
"60. The day is where we never arrive." [InterPR] (19:2) Fall 93, p. 86.
"To Silence." [GreensboroR] (54) Sum 93, p. 115.
2816. HICKMAN, Lou Ella
"Needle's Eye" (Mark 10:25). [Comm] (120:11) 4 Je 93, p. 22.
HICKS, Glenda Lindsey
        See LINDSEY-HICKS, Glenda
2817. HICKS, John V.
"The Snake." [Event] (22:2) Sum 93, p. 50.
2818. HICOK, Bob
"As It Is." [PoetryE] (36) Fall 93, p. 50.
"The Dead." [SouthernPR] (33:1) Spr 93, p. 55-56.
"Front Porch, Listening." [PoetryNW] (34:3) Aut 93, p. 33-34.
"Idiot-Savant." [PoetryNW] (34:3) Aut 93, p. 34-36.
"Man of the House." [PoetryE] (36) Fall 93, p. 49.
"A Night at Modern Prototype." [CreamCR] (17:2) Fall 93, p. 204-205.
"Random Events." [CreamCR] (17:2) Fall 93, p. 202-203.
"Two Alarm Fire." [OnTheBus] (5:2, #12) Sum-Fall 93, p. 93.
"Weather." [SouthernR] (29:3) Sum, Jl 93, p. 573-574.
2819. HIER, Grant
"Unarmed Heart." [SlipS] (13) 93, p. 47.
2820. HIESTAND, Emily
"As a Flaneuse" (Memorial Day, 1993). [Verse] (10:3) Wint 93, p. 91.
"In the Hollow of an Intricate City." [GeoR] (47:2) Sum 93, p. 360-361.
"Making Hot Oil." [GeoR] (47:3) Fall 93, p. 509-510.
"Our So Subtle City." [MichQR] (32:2) Spr 93, p. 248.
2821. HIGGINBOTHAM, Patricia
"Calling the Eagle." [Elf] (3:1) Spr 93, p. 40.
"Equilibrium." [Elf] (3:3) Fall 93, p. 24.
2822. HIGGINS, Anne
"In the English Class." [ColEng] (55:5) S 93, p. 538.
2823. HIGGINS, Frank
"Haiku" (3 poems). [NewL] (60:1) 93, p. 81.

213

HIGGINS

2824. HIGGINS, Laura
"Blindman's Bluff" (tr. of María Victoria Atencia, w. Cecilia C. Lee). [LitR] (36:3)
Spr 93, p. 359.
"Call Me" (— Lou Reed. Tr. of Roger Wolfe, w. Cecilia C. Lee). [LitR] (36:3) Spr
93, p. 387.
"The Day Has Gone" (tr. of Angel González, w. Cecilia C. Lee). [LitR] (36:3) Spr
93, p. 373-374.
"Diotima to Her Most Dedicated Student" (tr. of Ana Rossetti, w. Cecilia C. Lee).
[LitR] (36:3) Spr 93, p. 380.
"The Eyes of the Bull" (tr. of Rafael Alberti, w. Cecilia C. Lee). [LitR] (36:3) Spr
93, p. 356.
"The Flight into Egypt" (tr. of Luis Alberto de Cuenca, w. Cecilia C. Lee). [LitR]
(36:3) Spr 93, p. 368.
"Four Roses" (tr. of Luis Antonio de Villena, w. Cecilia C. Lee). [LitR] (36:3) Spr
93, p. 386.
"Julia" (tr. of Luis Alberto de Cuenca, w. Cecilia C. Lee). [LitR] (36:3) Spr 93, p.
368.
"Martha and Mary" (tr. of María Victoria Atencia, w. Cecilia C. Lee). [LitR] (36:3)
Spr 93, p. 360.
"Secret, Ancient Voices of the Night" (Selections: II, IV, tr. of Julia Uceda, w.
Cecilia C. Lee). [LitR] (36:3) Spr 93, p. 383-384.
"Splendor Veritatis" (tr. of Miguel d'Ors, w. Cecilia C. Lee). [LitR] (36:3) Spr 93, p.
370.
"That Sweet Atmosphere of Tango Around Three" (tr. of Luis Antonio de Villena,
w. Cecilia C. Lee). [LitR] (36:3) Spr 93, p. 385-386.
"This Everlasting Evening" (tr. of Rafael Alberti, w. Cecilia C. Lee). [LitR] (36:3)
Spr 93, p. 357.
"To Federico with Some Violets" (Selection: III, tr. of Luis García Montero, w.
Cecilia C. Lee). [LitR] (36:3) Spr 93, p. 371-372.
"With the Table Ready" (tr. of María Victoria Atencia, w. Cecilia C. Lee). [LitR]
(36:3) Spr 93, p. 360.
2825. HIGGINS, Rita Ann
"Always a Bridesmaid." [SenR] (23:1/2) Wint 93, p. 49-51.
"Breech" (for Victor Luftig). [SenR] (23:1/2) Wint 93, p. 52.
"He Is Not Thinking About Last Night." [SenR] (23:1/2) Wint 93, p. 45-48.
2826. HIGGINS, Tiffany M.
"The Angel and I Resolute the Homo." [KenR] (NS 15:4) Fall 93, p. 158-160.
2827. HIGH, John
"12:44 A.M." (tr. of Nina Iskrenko, w. Patrick Henry). [Talisman] (11) Fall 93, p.
239-241.
2828. HIGHFIELD, Arnold
"From Exile." [CaribbeanW] (7) 93, p. 20.
"The Guineaman." [CaribbeanW] (7) 93, p. 18-19.
2829. HIGHTOWER, Scott
"Un Chant d'Amour" (David Wojnarowicz, 1954-1992). [MinnR] (NS 40) Spr-Sum
93, p. 35-36.
"Self-Portrait, Collage" (Gael Pittman, 1953-1990). [MinnR] (NS 40) Spr-Sum 93,
p. 37.
"The Showing of the Instruments" (Upon reading Michel Foucault's *Discipline and
Punish* and observing Fra Angelico's *St. Lawrence Before Valerianus*). [Salm]
(97) Wint 93, p. 100-101.
"With an Instinctive Certainty of the Charms of the Modish, 'for the Fairest'."
[SouthwR] (78:3) Sum 93, p. 357-359.
2830. HIHARA, Masahiko
"Winter Light" (tr. by Akemi Nakamura and Tony Whedon). [GreenMR] (NS 6:2)
Sum-Fall 93, p. 73.
2831. HIKMET, Nazim
"Since I Was Thrown Inside" (tr. by Blasing and Konuk). [SouthernR] (29:2) Spr,
Ap 93, p. 239-241.
2832. HILBERRY, Conrad
"Spoon." [TarRP] (33:1) Fall 93, p. 46.
2833. HILBERT, Donna
"Bad Times Barbie." [Pearl] (19) Fall-Wint 93, p. 15.
"The Body Is." [ChironR] (12:3, #36) Aut 93, p. 16.
"Dad, on the Anniversary of Your Death." [Pearl] (17) Spr 93, p. 103.
"The Doctor Book." [ChironR] (12:3, #36) Aut 93, p. 16.

"Fear II." [Pearl] (17) Spr 93, p. 102.
"Vocabulary Builders." [ChironR] (12:3, #36) Aut 93, p. 16.
2834. HILL, Adam Craig
"The Jeweler." [PoetryNW] (34:2) Sum 93, p. 13-14.
2835. HILL, Crag (See also HILL, Craig)
"Poetic Trace." [Contact] (11:65/66/67) Spr 93, p. 51.
2836. HILL, Craig (See also HILL, Crag)
"There There" (Excerpts). [PoetryUSA] (25/26) 93, p. 29, 30.
2837. HILL, Eric
"A City State." [TickleAce] (24) Fall-Wint 92, p. 93.
"The River Again." [TickleAce] (24) Fall-Wint 92, p. 94.
2838. HILL, Geoffrey
"Cycle" (William Arrowsmith 1924-1992). [Arion] (2:2/3) Spr-Fall 92-93, p. 216 - 217.
2839. HILL, Gerald
"Memory and Rowboat (A Diary)." [MalR] (103) Sum 93, p. 88-91.
2840. HILL, Henry F.
"Building for the Past." [Light] (6) Sum 93, p. 10.
"R.I.P." [Light] (6) Sum 93, p. 19.
2841. HILL, Lindsay
"Socket." [Caliban] (13) 93, p. 56-67.
2842. HILL, Norah
"Present." [Stand] (34:2) Spr 93, p. 24-25.
2843. HILL, Pamela Steed
"The Anniversary of Nothing." [ChiR] (39:2) 93, p. 66-67.
"The Distance." [RagMag] (11:2) 93, p. 78-79.
"Dressing for the Funeral." [Plain] (13:2) Wint 93, p. 22.
"The Feast of the Tangible." [Plain] (13:2) Wint 93, p. 33.
"In Praise of Motels." [AntR] (51:2) Spr 93, p. 248-249.
2844. HILLARD, Jeffrey
"Between Trees" (on a photograph by Jon Christopher Hughes). [Border] (2) Spr 93, p. 37-38.
2845. HILLES, Rick
"Artisans of the Tomb." [CreamCR] (17:2) Fall 93, p. 165.
"A Brief Folklore of Typography." [Colum] (20) Sum 93, p. 115-116.
"Evidence." [MalR] (105) Wint 93, p. 11.
"Insleave for A Hieroglyphic Key to Spiritual Mysteries: Published Posthumously in Stockholm, 1784" (for Swedenborg). [MalR] (105) Wint 93, p. 12-13.
2846. HILLES, Robert
"I Expect the Devil." [PraF] (14:4) Wint 93-94, p. 102-103.
2847. HILLILA, Bernhard
"Flies in Uardere." [HopewellR] (5) 93, p. 84.
2848. HILLMAN, Brenda
"Black Rose." [Pequod] (35) 93, p. 133.
"Cheap Gas." [HarvardR] (3) Wint 93, p. 9-10.
"Male Nipples." [MichQR] (32:4) Fall 93, p. 574-575.
"Possible Companion." [Pequod] (35) 93, p. 129.
"Sorrow of Matter." [DenQ] (27:4) Spr 93, p. 40-41.
"The Spark." [HarvardR] (3) Wint 93, p. 6-8.
"Split Tractate." [Pequod] (35) 93, p. 130-132.
"Torn Shadow." [PartR] (60:2) Spr 93, p. 239-240.
2849. HILLRINGHOUSE, Mark
"Tomato Soup." [HangL] (62) 93, p. 27.
2850. HILTON, David
"Enisled." [PoetryNW] (34:4) Wint 93-94, p. 27-29.
"La Familia Sagrada." [PoetL] (88:1) Spr 93, p. 24-26.
"Tin Whistle." [PoetryNW] (34:4) Wint 93-94, p. 29-30.
2851. HILYARD, J.
"Concrete Shadows." [BlackBR] (17) Sum-Fall 93, p. 34-35.
2852. HIND, Stephen
"Humanities Lecture." [Farm] (10:1) Spr-Sum 93, p. 32.
2853. HINDE, Walter D.
"XIV. A Memory" (taken from a sequence called 'The Tokaido'). [Stand] (34:3) Sum 93, p. 53.
"Wildings, Lavenham." [Stand] (34:3) Sum 93, p. 53.

2854. HINRICHSEN, Dennis
"Detail from *The Garden of Earthly Delights*." [PoetryNW] (34:3) Aut 93, p. 3-8.
"Drawn to Water" (near the wastewater treatment facility). [PoetryNW] (34:3) Aut 93, p. 9-10.
2855. HINSEY, E. C.
"Planisféria, Map of the World, Lisbon, 1554." [SouthernPR] (33:2) Fall 93, p. 57.
2856. HINTON, David
"Cold Creek" (tr. of Meng Chiao). [Sulfur] (33) Fall 93, p. 140-145.
"Laments of the Gorges" (tr. of Meng Chiao). [Sulfur] (33) Fall 93, p. 145-151.
2857. HINTZ, Paul J.
"In the Long Run." [RagMag] (11:1) 93, p. 45-46.
"The Mute." [RagMag] (11:1) 93, p. 43.
"The Pinch Hitter in the Bottom of the Ninth." [RagMag] (11:1) 93, p. 44.
2858. HINZ-PENNER, Raylene
"Domestication." [CinPR] (24) Spr 93, p. 14.
2859. HIPOLITO, Terry
"Casting Off." [SoCoast] (15) Je 93, p. 55.
2860. HIPPONAX of Ephesus
"Complete Poems" (tr. by Anselm Hollo). [Sulfur] (33) Fall 93, p. 103-114.
2861. HIRAIDE, Takashi
"For the Fighting Spirit of the Walnut" (selections, tr. by Robert Leutner). [Stand] (34:2) Spr 93, p. 34-40.
2862. HIRATA, Toshiko
"Flowers" (tr. by Robert Brady and Odagawa Kazuko). [ChiR] (39:3/4) 93, p. 214-215.
HIROAKI, Sato
See SATO, Hiroaki
HIROMI, Ito
See ITO, Hiromi
2863. HIROZAWA, Shurei
"Manoa Before Dawn." [HawaiiR] (17:3, #39) Fall 93, p. 11.
2864. HIRSCH, Edward
"From a Train" (Hofmannsthal in Greece). [Nat] (256:11) 22 Mr 93, p. 391.
"In the Midnight Hour." [DenQ] (27:4) Spr 93, p. 36-38.
"Luminist Paintings at the National Gallery." [PartR] (60:1) Wint 93, p. 96-97.
"My Father's Back." [NewEngR] (15:1) Wint 93, p. 141-142.
"Orpheus Ascending." [Nat] (256:9) 8 Mr 93, p. 312.
"Orpheus: The Descent." [TriQ] (89) Wint 93-94, p. 177.
"The Renunciation of Poetry" (Hofmannsthal in Athens, 1908). [Poetry] (163:1) O 93, p. 31-32.
"Solstice." [SycamoreR] (5:1) Wint 93, p. 40.
"Sortes Vergilianae" (The Fortuneteller's Words to the Poet). [Nat] (256:12) 29 Mr 93, p. 426.
"Unearthly Voices" (Hofmannsthal at the Monastery of St. Luke). [TriQ] (89) Wint 93-94, p. 174-176.
2865. HIRSCH, Steve (*See also* HIRSCH, Steven)
"Dishwasher's Lament." [SlipS] (13) 93, p. 38.
2866. HIRSCH, Steven (*See also* HIRSCH, Steve)
"Archeology." [HeavenB] (10) Wint-Spr 93, p. 61.
"Tyrannical Stream" (The making of a tyrant: A Well-sourced financial product). [HeavenB] (10) Wint-Spr 93, p. 51-53.
2867. HIRSCHFIELD, Ted
"The Cathedral at Ulm." [CapeR] (28:1) Spr 93, p. 26.
"Jesus in Cape Girardeau." [CapeR] (28:1) Spr 93, p. 23.
"Judson Baptist Church." [CapeR] (28:1) Spr 93, p. 25.
"Onward, Christian Soldiers." [CapeR] (28:1) Spr 93, p. 24.
"Orbiting God." [CapeR] (28:2) Fall 93, p. 44.
"Waiting for the New Madrid Earthquake." [CapeR] (28:2) Fall 93, p. 42-43.
2868. HIRSCHMAN, Jack
"Balkan Irony." [ChironR] (12:4/13:1, #37/38) Wint 93-Spr 94, p. 3.
"Black Puddle: April 18" (tr. of Rocco Scotellaro. Translation dedicated to the memory of Bob Kaufman, who was born on April 18). [Arshile] (2) 93, p. 61, 63.
"Black Stone on a White Stone" (tr. of Cesar Valljo). [ChironR] (12:4/13:1, #37/38) Wint 93-Spr 94, p. 3.
"Collected Sunshine" (for Celia). [Arshile] (1) Spr 93, p. 72.

"Enough with This Horible War" (tr. of Ferruccio Brugnaro). [Arshile] (2) 93, p. 59.
"National Pastime." [ChironR] (12:4/13:1, #37/38) Wint 93-Spr 94, p. 3.
"On Censorship." [Arshile] (1) Spr 93, p. 73.
"On Writing Poems Directly on a Typewriter Again After 15 Years." [Talisman]
    (11) Fall 93, p. 166.
"Other Nights" (tr. of Anna Lombardo, w. Antonella Soldaini). [Arshile] (2) 93, p.
    55, 57.
"Steps Were" (tr. of Francesco Moisio). [Arshile] (2) 93, p. 53.
2869. HIRSHFIELD, Jane
"1973." [QRL] (12:32/33) 93, p. 202-203.
"Courtship." [Thrpny] (54) Sum 93, p. 31.
"Each Step." [QRL] (12:32/33) 93, p. 200.
"Empedocles' Physics." [QRL] (12:32/33) 93, p. 197.
"Even the Vanishing Housed." [QRL] (12:32/33) 93, p. 198-199.
"The Fire." [NewL] (59:4) 93, p. 29.
"The Fish." [Ploughs] (19:1) Spr 93, p. 186.
"For a Gelding." [QRL] (12:32/33) 93, p. 198.
"The Heart As Origami." [QRL] (12:32/33) 93, p. 195.
"History As the Painter Bonnard." [QRL] (12:32/33) 93, p. 194-195.
"The House in Winter." [QRL] (12:32/33) 93, p. 199.
"Meeting the Light Completely." [Zyzzyva] (9:3) Fall 93, p. 121.
"Percolation" (Calligraphy by Michele Laporte). [Tricycle] (3:1) Fall 93, p. 58.
"Red Poppies." [Nat] (257:15) 8 N 93, p. 543.
"The Ritual." [NewL] (59:4) 93, p. 31.
"The Shadow." [QRL] (12:32/33) 93, p. 192.
"The Shadow" (Calligraphy by Michele Laporte). [Tricycle] (3:1) Fall 93, p. 59.
"The Stone of Heaven." [QRL] (12:32/33) 93, p. 201.
"A Sweetening All Around Me As It Falls." [QRL] (12:32/33) 93, p. 196-197.
"The Sweetness of Apples, of Figs." [DenQ] (27:4) Spr 93, p. 39.
"The Tea Light of Late September." [Ploughs] (19:1) Spr 93, p. 185.
"This Love." [QRL] (12:32/33) 93, p. 202.
"The Water Diamonds." [NewL] (59:4) 93, p. 30.
"The Wedding." [QRL] (12:32/33) 93, p. 193-194.
"The Weighing." [QRL] (12:32/33) 93, p. 195-196.
"The Window." [Ploughs] (19:1) Spr 93, p. 183-184.
2870. HIX, Blacky
"The Prison Room." [ChironR] (12:1, #34) Spr 93, p. 44.
2871. HIX, H. Edgar
"P. C. Compatible." [SoCoast] (15) Je 93, p. 29.
2872. HIX, H. L.
"Countless Dark Bodies Are to Be Inferred Near the Sun" (— Nietzsche, *Beyond
    Good and Evil*). [GeoR] (47:2) Sum 93, p. 358.
"Objects Contain the Possibility of All Situations" (— Wittgenstein, *Tractatus
    2.014*). [GeoR] (47:2) Sum 93, p. 359.
"On Rising from Bed, Obliterate the Print of Your Body" (—Pythagoras).
    [LaurelR] (27:1) Wint 93, p. 44.
"One Is the Point." [Harp] (287:1719) Ag 93, p. 26.
2873. HLAVSA, Virginia V.
"The Expedition." [Comm] (120:17) 8 O 93, p. 15.
"From the River Merchant: A Letter." [GrahamHR] (17) Fall 93, p. 24.
"Undercover Agent at Work." [Pearl] (17) Spr 93, p. 15.
2874. HO, Chi Minh
"The Prison Poems of Ho Chi Minh" (Selections, Photographs by Larry Towell, tr.
    by Dang The Binh). [Quarry] (42:1) 93, p. 69-84.
2875. HOAGLAND, Tony
"Arrows." [DenQ] (28:1) Sum 93, p. 32-33.
"The Confessional Mode." [NoAmR] (278:2) Mr-Ap 93, p. 35.
"The Invention of Feedback." [HarvardR] (5) Fall 93, p. 18-19.
2876. HOAGLAND, William
"Conservatory" (For Hiram Hoskin, 1911-1988). [SycamoreR] (5:1) Wint 93, p. 56 -
    57.
2877. HOBBS, Blair
"Hell Cat's Best Friend." [LaurelR] (27:1) Wint 93, p. 58.
"Recreation." [LaurelR] (27:1) Wint 93, p. 58-59.
2878. HOBBS, James
"The 'Likes' of Sandhill Cranes." [Plain] (13:2) Wint 93, p. 26.

"Voices of America." [SoDakR] (31:3) Fall 93, p. 58.
2879. HOCHEL, Brano
"XXX. By the number thirty-eight bus down Dostojevsky Lane" (tr. by Stephánia
Allen and James Sutherland-Smith). [OxfordM] (9:1) Spr-Sum 93, p. 48-49.
"I've Seen God Only Twice" (tr. by Stephánia Allen and James Sutherland-Smith).
[OxfordM] (9:1) Spr-Sum 93, p. 47-48.
"Micro-stories" (5 selections, tr. by Stephánia Allen and James Sutherland-Smith).
[OxfordM] (9:1) Spr-Sum 93, p. 49-50.
2880. HOCHMAN, Benjamin
"Evolution and Poetry." [Light] (6) Sum 93, p. 8.
2881. HOCHMAN, Sandra
"Crucifix." [QRL] (12:32/33) 93, p. 434-435.
2882. HOCQUARD, Emmanuel
"Theory of Tables" (Selections: 16-20, tr. by Michael Palmer). [Avec] (6:1) 93, p.
25-29.
"Theory of Tables" (Selections: 40-50, tr. by Michael Palmer). [Sulfur] (32) Spr 93,
p. 156-161.
2883. HODGE, Jan D.
"A Harp Sounds Midnight" (for Gary Frahm). [Elf] (3:1) Spr 93, p. 34.
"Trial." [SoCoast] (15) Je 93, p. 27.
2884. HODGE, Lonnie
"Duck Eye." [Vis] (42) 93, p. 7.
"The Only Photograph of Our Affair." [AlabamaLR] (7:1) 93, p. 15.
2885. HODGE, Margaret
"How Fur Seals Keep Warm" (Selections: 5 poems). [BellArk] (9:6) N-D 93, p. 4.
2886. HODGEN, John
"Old Men in Restrooms." [Sun] (207) Mr 93, p. 29.
"This Life, This Word Unsaid." [Sun] (206) F 93, p. 10-11.
2887. HODGES, Gregg
"Desert Love, or Echo's Revenge." [ParisR] (35:128) Fall 93, p. 222-223.
2888. HODGINS, Philip
"A Half-Remembered Visit." [Nimrod] (36:2) Spr-Sum 93, p. 87-88.
"Swine Dysentery." [Verse] (10:1) Spr 93, p. 7.
2889. HOEFER, David
"Caterwaul." [Talisman] (11) Fall 93, p. 205.
"Riot Trousers." [Talisman] (11) Fall 93, p. 204.
2890. HOEPPNER, Edward Haworth
"Crows." [DogRR] (12:1, #23) Spr-Sum 93, p. 10-11.
"Echolocation." [Journal] (17:2) Fall-Wint 93, p. 23-24.
"Low Pressure." [Journal] (17:2) Fall-Wint 93, p. 25.
"Salvador's Ox." [Farm] (10:2) Fall-Wint 93-94, p. 15-16.
"Summer's End." [RagMag] (11:2) 93, p. 5.
2891. HOERTER, R. C.
"Modi Tchaikovsky Names the Sixth Symphony." [MidAR] (14:1) 93, p. 155-156.
2892. HOEY, Allen
"Angels." [CimR] (102) Ja 93, p. 78.
"February." [TexasR] (14:3/4) Fall-Wint 93, p. 76-77.
"A Stricter Means." [SouthernHR] (27:1) Wint 93, p. 58.
2893. HOFER, Jen
"Birthday Letter" (for J.C.D. in Costa Rica). [13thMoon] (12:1/2) 93-94, p. 31-32.
2894. HOFER, Marianna
"Late Summer Heat Wave." [PikeF] (11) Fall 93, p. 9.
"Tattoo." [PikeF] (11) Fall 93, p. 35.
2895. HOFFMAN, Janice
"Sitting in a Doghouse." [WindO] (57) Fall 93, p. 27.
2896. HOFFMANN, Roald
"Breaking." [Confr] (51) Sum 93, p. 232.
2897. HOGAN, Judy
"I invoke you: our shyness and our courage, return" (tr. of Galina Gamper, w.
Yelena Sidarova). [Elf] (3:2) Sum 93, p. 31.
2898. HOGAN, Linda
"The Alchemists." [AmerPoR] (22:3) My-Je 93, p. 6.
"Bear Fat." [AmerPoR] (22:3) My-Je 93, p. 3.
"Chambered Nautilus." [AmerPoR] (22:3) My-Je 93, p. 7.
"Crossings." [AmerPoR] (22:3) My-Je 93, p. 3.
"The Direction of Light." [AmerPoR] (22:3) My-Je 93, p. 8.

"Harvesters of Night and Water." [AmerPoR] (22:3) My-Je 93, p. 4-5.
"Origins of Corn." [AmerPoR] (22:3) My-Je 93, p. 8.
"Return: Buffalo." [AmerPoR] (22:3) My-Je 93, p. 4.
"Sickness." [AmerPoR] (22:3) My-Je 93, p. 7.
"Skin." [AmerPoR] (22:3) My-Je 93, p. 5.
"Travelers." [AmerPoR] (22:3) My-Je 93, p. 6.
2899. HOGAN, Wayne
"Faith of an Old Man." [DogRR] (12:2, #24) Fall-Wint 93, p. 35.
"My Elvis Sighting." [Light] (8) Wint 93, p. 10.
"What They've Come Up With." [DogRR] (12:2, #24) Fall-Wint 93, p. 34.
2900. HOGGARD, James
"Flyfishing." [Hellas] (4:2) Fall 93, p. 69.
"Visions of Saint Narcissus" (tr. of Oscar Hahn). [XavierR] (13:1) Spr 93, p. 62.
2901. HOGGARD, Lynn
"Angle Markers (Poteaux d'Angle)" (Excerpts, tr. of Henri Michaux). [Chelsea] (54)
93, p. 26-27.
2902. HOGUE, Cynthia
"Falling." [HeavenB] (10) Wint-Spr 93, p. 32-33.
"Modern Times." [HeavenB] (10) Wint-Spr 93, p. 8.
2903. HOH, Barbara
"Ramen." [RagMag] (11:2) 93, p. 6.
2904. HOLAHAN, Susan
"At the Funeral of the Second Mrs. Wilson." [FreeL] (12) Sum 93, p. 9.
"Fengdu Infrastructure." [FreeL] (12) Sum 93, p. 8.
"Sister Betty Reads the Whole You." [BlackWR] (19:2) Spr-Sum 93, p. 22.
2905. HOLBROOK, John
"Manti High on Heaven, Manti Back on Earth." [BellArk] (9:3) My-Je 93, p. 9.
"A Story Worth Repeating" (After Ted Levin in Harrowsmith). [BellArk] (9:3) My -
Je 93, p. 23.
2906. HOLDEN, Jonathan
"Love in the Time of Cholera." [SouthernR] (29:1) Wint, Ja 93, p. 157-158.
2907. HÖLDERLIN, Friedrich
"(Antigone, Act II)" (after Sophocles, tr. by Francis Golffing). [SpiritSH] (58) 93, p.
18.
"Greece" (1st Version, tr. by Francis Golffing). [SpiritSH] (58) 93, p. 20.
"The Half of Life" (tr. by Liz Rosenberg and Denny Schmidt). [GrahamHR] (17)
Fall 93, p. 109.
"Oedipus at Colonus" (lines 668-693, after Sophocles, tr. by Francis Golffing).
[SpiritSH] (58) 93, p. 19.
"On tawny leaves rests the grape, the hope of wine" (tr. by Liz Rosenberg and
Denny Schmidt). [GrahamHR] (17) Fall 93, p. 111.
"Ripe, in fire dipped, broiled" (tr. by Liz Rosenberg and Denny Schmidt).
[GrahamHR] (17) Fall 93, p. 108.
"Three Fragments of Pindar" (tr. by Francis Golffing). [SpiritSH] (58) 93, p. 17.
"To Diotima" (tr. by Liz Rosenberg and Denny Schmidt). [GrahamHR] (17) Fall 93,
p. 110.
HOLENIA, Alexander Lernet
See LERNET-HOLENIA, Alexander
2908. HOLINGER, Richard
"Papyrus." [NewRena] (8:3, #26) Spr 93, p. 29.
2909. HOLLAHAN, Eugene
"Variations on a Variation by Stevens." [LitR] (37:1) Fall 93, p. 98.
"Vetting." [WindO] (57) Fall 93, p. 30.
"The Zoo in the Zodiac." [Verse] (10:1) Spr 93, p. 41-42.
2910. HOLLANDER, Jean
"The Banality of Good." [US1] (28/29) 93, p. 21.
"In Lenk We Read the *Zauberberg* in German." [Footwork] (23) 93, p. 47.
"King Kong Daddy at the Movies." [Footwork] (23) 93, p. 48.
"Light on Oil and Water." [Footwork] (23) 93, p. 47.
"'The Law — She Is an Ass' in Sacramento." [Footwork] (23) 93, p. 48.
2911. HOLLANDER, John
"Bread-and-Butter!" [PartR] (60:1) Wint 93, p. 93-95.
"A Shadow of a Great Rock in a Weary Land" (title of a drawing by Thomas Cole).
[NewRep] (209:22) 29 N 93, p. 44.
"The Tesserae" (Selections: 5 poems). [Raritan] (12:3) Wint 93, p. 16-25.

2912. HOLLANDER, Martha
"Requiem." [PartR] (60:3) Sum 93, p. 427.
"Vertigo: A Letter from San Francisco." [SouthwR] (78:2) Spr 93, p. 192-193.
2913. HOLLANDER, Robert
"After the Gypsies" (for Maria Teresa and Fiorella). [AmerS] (62:4) Aut 93, p. 526 - 527.
2914. HOLLEY, Margaret
"Anchoring Out." [Poem] (70) N 93, p. 22.
"Galileo in the Snow." [Poetry] (161:4) Ja 93, p. 207-208.
"The Gallery of Owls." [Poetry] (161:4) Ja 93, p. 209-210.
"Kore in Bloom." [SouthernR] (29:3) Sum, Jl 93, p. 562-563.
"A Minnow for Morris Graves." [Poem] (70) N 93, p. 23.
"Queen Anne's Lace." [Poem] (70) N 93, p. 24-25.
2915. HOLLO, Anselm
"Blue Ceiling." [HangL] (63) 93, p. 26-30.
"Complete Poems" (tr. of Hipponax of Ephesus). [Sulfur] (33) Fall 93, p. 103-114.
"A Dog's Bark Away, Where the Cigar" (tr. of Ernst Brunner). [ManhatR] (7:1) Fall 93, p. 13.
"The Enchanted World of Fairytale" (tr. of Gunnar Harding). [ManhatR] (7:1) Fall 93, p. 16.
"Many Were Here, But They Left Again" (tr. of Gunnar Harding). [ManhatR] (7:1) Fall 93, p. 17-19.
"Prime the Wall That You Pass" (tr. of Ernst Brunner). [ManhatR] (7:1) Fall 93, p. 12.
2916. HOLLOWAY, Glenna
"Cutting a Finger on Obsidian" (to Georgia O'Keeffe). [HolCrit] (30:3) Je 93, p. 18.
"Glimpses." [ChrC] (110:27) 6 O 93, p. 928.
"A Passing Acquaintance with Death on the Desert" (Literary Contest Winner, 2nd Prize). [Crucible] (29) Fall 93, p. 4-5.
2917. HOLLOWAY, John
"The Dying God." [Hudson] (46:2) Sum 93, p. 354.
"It Takes Time." [Hudson] (46:2) Sum 93, p. 353.
2918. HOLM, Bill
"Black Duck Love Song" (for John and Lorna Rezmerski). [NorthStoneR] (11) 93, p. 186.
2919. HOLMAN, Amy
"And Gently." [HawaiiR] (16:3, #36) Wint 93, p. 58.
2920. HOLMAN, Bob
"We Are the Dinosaur." [Drumvoices] (2:1/2) Fall-Wint 92-93, p. 196-197.
2921. HOLMES, Clyde
"Storm Lantern" (Cwm Hesgin). [Verse] (10:1) Spr 93, p. 82.
2922. HOLMES, Darryl
"Carolina (For Kelly)." [BrooklynR] (10) 93, p. 21.
"Circles" (for Malcolm X on the 66th anniversary of his birth). [Drumvoices] (2:1/2) Fall-Wint 92-93, p. 213-214.
2923. HOLMES, Elizabeth
"The Tale of the Fan." [GettyR] (6:1) Wint 93, p. 87.
2924. HOLMES, Janet
"The Love of the Flesh." [TarRP] (32:2) Spr 93, p. 12-13.
"Neons." [Shen] (43:2) Sum 93, p. 22-24.
2925. HOLSTAD, Scott C.
"But It's a Lot Like Wearing a Raincoat." [ChironR] (12:3, #36) Aut 93, p. 20.
"Gesture." [Pearl] (19) Fall-Wint 93, p. 14.
"Melting Pot." [ChironR] (12:3, #36) Aut 93, p. 20.
"Wear and Tear." [BlackBR] (17) Sum-Fall 93, p. 8-9.
2926. HOLT, Lois
"At Sea Colony — Tattoos and Telltale Signs." [Crucible] (29) Fall 93, p. 8-9.
HOLT, Sophie Jasson
See JASSON-HOLT, Sophie
HOLTEN, Dan von
See Von HOLTEN, Dan
2927. HOLUB, Miroslav
"The Autumn Orchard" (tr. by Dána Habóva and David Young). [PartR] (60:3) Sum 93, p. 419.
"Half a Hedgehog" (tr. by Dana Hábová and David Young). [Field] (49) Fall 93, p. 18-19.

"Hemophilia/Los Angeles" (tr. by Dana Hábová and David Young). [Field] (49) Fall 93, p. 30-31.
"In the Microscope" (tr. by Ian Milner). [Field] (49) Fall 93, p. 9.
"The Journey" (tr. by David Young and the author). [PartR] (60:3) Sum 93, p. 418-419.
"Meeting Ezra Pound" (tr. by Dana Hábová and Stuart Friebert). [Field] (49) Fall 93, p. 12.
"Seeing" (tr. by Dana Hábová and David Young). [Field] (49) Fall 93, p. 25-26.
2928. HOLZER, Madeleine Fuchs
"The Foxtrot." [Pearl] (17) Spr 93, p. 110.
"In the Beginning." [Pearl] (17) Spr 93, p. 110.
"The Work of Men's Hands." [Pearl] (19) Fall-Wint 93, p. 18.
2929. HOMER
"Odysseus at Home" (tr. by David Mason and Yiorgos Chouliaras). [CumbPR]] (13:1) Fall 93, p. 27.
2930. HOMER, Art
"Bucky Takes Time Off." [Journal] (17:1) Spr-Sum 93, p. 47-48.
2931. HONG, Sara
"Pillow" (written in memory of Young Choon Hong). [MassR] (34:3) Aut 93, p. 455-456.
2932. HONGO, Garrett (Garrett Kaoru)
"Looking at Kilauea." [Ploughs] (19:4) Wint 93-94, p. 183-187.
"Village: Kahuku-Mura." [NewEngR] (15:1) Wint 93, p. 143-144.
2933. HOOGESTRAAT, Jane
"Background Music." [Poetry] (163:2) N 93, p. 80-81.
2934. HOOGLAND, Cornelia
"Boulevard of Plums the Morning They Open." [MalR] (105) Wint 93, p. 36.
"Daughter in Spring." [AntigR] (93-94) Spr-Sum 93, p. 90.
"Green Thief." [AntigR] (93-94) Spr-Sum 93, p. 89.
"Here and Now." [MalR] (105) Wint 93, p. 34-35.
"Here's Me at 40." [PraS] (67:4) Wint 93, p. 48-49.
"This Girl." [Grain] (21:2) Sum 93, p. 126.
"Traveling on a Sunday Afternoon." [PraS] (67:4) Wint 93, p. 47-48.
"Your Coat to Somebody Colder." [PraS] (67:4) Wint 93, p. 49-50.
2935. HOOPER, Patricia
"Annunciations." [Poetry] (161:6) Mr 93, p. 320-321.
"At the Storm Door." [WilliamMR] (31) 93, p. 98.
"The Fox." [MidwQ] (34:2) Wint 93, p. 217.
"Intimations." [CinPR] (24) Spr 93, p. 20-21.
"The Plum Tree." [SycamoreR] (5:2) Sum 93, p. 80-81.
"The Shadblow Trees." [RiverS] (38) 93, p. 68.
"Spring Snow." [MidwQ] (34:2) Wint 93, p. 218.
2936. HOOPER, Virginia
"Composure." [NewAW] (11) Sum-Fall 93, p. 70-71.
"This Distance." [NewAW] (11) Sum-Fall 93, p. 68-69.
2937. HOOPER-TODD, Nita
"I'm a Poem." [Pearl] (17) Spr 93, p. 82.
2938. HOOVER, J. B.
"About Inge." [WillowS] (31) Wint 93, p. 50-51.
2939. HOPE, Akua Lezli (Akua Leslie)
"950 Hoe Avenue (the Bronx)." [Obs] (8:2) Fall-Wint 93, p. 101-102.
"CHAZ" (for you). [Obs] (8:2) Fall-Wint 93, p. 103-104.
"Coffee" (a found poem). [Contact] (11:65/66/67) Spr 93, p. 29.
"Imprint" (for Shimmer). [Obs] (8:2) Fall-Wint 93, p. 107.
"My Muse Relentless." [Obs] (8:2) Fall-Wint 93, p. 104-105.
"New David" (for D.G.W.C.). [Contact] (11:65/66/67) Spr 93, p. 28-29.
"Remember the Source." [Obs] (8:2) Fall-Wint 93, p. 107-108.
"Scent." [Obs] (8:2) Fall-Wint 93, p. 105-106.
"So Much to Show, Tell." [Obs] (8:2) Fall-Wint 93, p. 106.
"Water Bears No Scars." [Obs] (8:2) Fall-Wint 93, p. 102-103.
2940. HOPE, Andrew
"Tlingit Market II." [ChiR] (39:3/4) 93, p. 156.
2941. HOPES, David
"Almost Middle Aged, Running Chunns Cove." [Elf] (3:1) Spr 93, p. 36-37.
"Morning Songs." [Elf] (3:1) Spr 93, p. 35.

"Nighthawks, Blasted from Their Customary Air." [HiramPoR] (53/54) Fall 92-Sum 93, p. 104.
2942. HOPKINS, Gerard Manley
    "Spelt from Sibyl's Leaves." [PoetryUSA] (25/26) 93, p. 9.
2943. HOPPEY, Tim
    "The Buzzing in My Balls." [Pearl] (19) Fall-Wint 93, p. 66.
    "The Christmas Castle." [RagMag] (11:2) 93, p. 72-73.
    "Gams." [RagMag] (11:2) 93, p. 76.
    "How Is It?" [RagMag] (11:2) 93, p. 74.
    "Our Mad Nest." [RagMag] (11:2) 93, p. 70.
    "Planting the Lion's Paw" (For Tiffany Keyes). [RagMag] (11:2) 93, p. 71.
    "A Thirst for Work." [RagMag] (11:2) 93, p. 75.
2944. HORACE
    "IV.11" (tr. by Joseph S. Salemi). [CarolQ] (45:2) Wint 93, p. 70-71.
    "Odes I, V" (tr. by Richard O'Connell). [Light] (7) Aut 93, p. 15.
    "Tu ne Quaesieris" (Ode I.11, tr. by David Ferry). [BostonR] (18:6) D 93-Ja 94, p. 35.
2945. HORNER, Karla
    "Moving the Bed." [Parting] (6:1) Sum 93, p. 30.
2946. HORODYSKA, Ewa
    "Letter from the Land of the Red Roofs. To Anna Maria. To Pawka Marcinkiewicz" (tr. of Jacek Podsiadlo, w. Chris Hurford). [Verse] (10:2) Sum 93, p. 42.
    "Mr. and Mrs. Von Kleist" (tr. of Marcin Swietlicki). [Verse] (10:2) Sum 93, p. 36.
    "Sosnowiec Is Like a Woman" (tr. of Marcin Baran). [Stand] (34:3) Sum 93, p. 17.
    "Sosnowiec Is Like a Woman" (tr. of Marcin Baran). [Verse] (10:2) Sum 93, p. 41.
2947. HORSTING, Eric
    "Eventually." [Paint] (19:38) Aut 92, p. 42.
    "Forgiveness: Mother Learns to Talk." [Journal] (17:1) Spr-Sum 93, p. 64.
    "Holland: *Hungerwinter* (The War Years End)." [DenQ] (27:3) Wint 93, p. 37.
2948. HORTON, Barbara (Barbara Savadge)
    "A Candle Burning at the Edge of Time." [WebR] (17) Fall 93, p. 76.
    "First Star." [SouthernPR] (33:1) Spr 93, p. 52.
    "Listen." [PoetryNW] (34:4) Wint 93-94, p. 17-18.
    "A Quality of Wind." [PoetryNW] (34:4) Wint 93-94, p. 18-19.
    "To Heather, Away" (Honorable Mention, Poetry Award). [NewL] (59:2) 93, p. 42.
    "Waving Goodbye." [SouthernPR] (33:1) Spr 93, p. 53-54.
2949. HORTSCH, Dan
    "The Last Time I Saw My Daughter." [WritersF] (19) 93, p. 120-121.
2950. HORVATH, Brooke
    "The *Encyclopaedia Britannica* Uses Down Syndrome to Define 'Monster'." [ProseP] (2) 93, p. 45-46.
    "Tomorrow We Discuss Cottonwoods." [ArtfulD] (24/25) 93, p. 118.
2951. HORVATH, Linda M.
    "Long Shots Sheldom Come In." [ChironR] (12:3, #36) Aut 93, p. 15.
2952. HOSKIN, William D.
    "At East Sandwich Beach in September." [HiramPoR] (53/54) Fall 92-Sum 93, p. 106.
    "Lobster." [HiramPoR] (53/54) Fall 92-Sum 93, p. 105.
2953. HOSKINS, Katherine
    "Spleen." [QRL] (12:32/33) 93, p. 435.
2954. HOSPITAL, Carolina
    "Another Editorial." [ApalQ] (38) 92, p. 46.
2955. HOSTETLER, Ann
    "Improvisations." [CreamCR] (17:2) Fall 93, p. 171.
2956. HOSTETLER, Sheri
    "Probe on Occupation." [13thMoon] (11:1/2) 93, p. 35-36.
2957. HOSTOVSKY, P. (Paul)
    "The Chicken Tree." [JINJPo] (15:1) Spr 93, p. 13.
    "Emergency." [JINJPo] (15:1) Spr 93, p. 12.
    "Little League." [JINJPo] (15:1) Spr 93, p. 11.
    "Little League." [Sparrow] (60) Sum 93, p. 32.
    "The Slide in Kindergarten." [JINJPo] (15:1) Spr 93, p. 14.
    "Trombone Baseball." [JINJPo] (15:1) Spr 93, p. 15.
2958. HOTHAM, Gary
    "Haiku" (2 poems). [Northeast] (5:9) Wint 93-94, p. 19.

2959. HOTINCEANU, Radu
"The Art of Eating." [Footwork] (23) 93, p. 124.
2960. HOUCHIN, Ron
"Little Vessels." [CinPR] (24) Spr 93, p. 61.
"Night Janitor." [CinPR] (24) Spr 93, p. 60.
2961. HOUGHTON, Tim (Timothy)
"Below Two Skies." [DenQ] (27:3) Wint 93, p. 38-39.
"The Leaves of December." [Wind] (23:72) 93, p. 11.
2962. HOUSER, Kathleen
"The White Cup." [NorthStoneR] (11) 93, p. 120.
2963. HOUSSOUBA, Mohomodou
"All the Time Ahead" (Republic of Mali). [PikeF] (11) Fall 93, p. 9.
2964. HOUSTMAN, Dale M.
"There Is Also a City." [Caliban] (12) 93, p. 135.
2965. HOUSTON, Beth
"The Night of Christ's Birth." [LitR] (36:2) Wint 93, p. 161.
"Prose Poem: Clair's semi-yuppie calico kitchen with an assertive twinge." [SoCarR] (26:1) Fall 93, p. 179-180.
"A True Story." [SoCarR] (26:1) Fall 93, p. 178-179.
"When the Lord God Gathered Up the Spirit of Virginia Woolf." [MassR] (34:1) Spr 93, p. 63-64.
2966. HOUSTON, Lisa
"The Blur of Intention." [Avec] (6:1) 93, p. 92.
2967. HOUSTON, Peyton
"Birthdays." [KenR] (NS 15:4) Fall 93, p. 72.
"The Box of the Special Silence." [KenR] (NS 15:4) Fall 93, p. 73.
HOUTEN, Lois van
    See Van HOUTEN, Lois
HOVANESSIAN, Diana Der
    See DER-HOVANESSIAN, Diana
2968. HOWARD, Ben
"Lydia Sails to Byzantium" (from the sequence: 1-2, 5). [LaurelR] (27:1) Wint 93, p. 42-43.
2969. HOWARD, Eugene
"Reading Robert Hayden on a Quiet Morning." [PaintedB] (50/51) 93, p. 79.
2970. HOWARD, Justice
"Plumbers of the Liquid Word, or: How to Be a Good Poet." [ChironR] (12:1, #34) Spr 93, p. 41.
2971. HOWARD, Matthew
"Infidelity." [JamesWR] (10:3) Spr 93, p. 14.
2972. HOWARD, Richard
"Among the Missing." [NewYorker] (69:25) 9 Ag 93, p. 54.
"Correspondences" (Les Fleurs du Mal, tr. of Pierre Charles Baudelaire). [HarvardR] (5) Fall 93, p. 140.
"Further Triangulations" (after an initial three, some years back). [Verse] (10:3) Wint 93, p. 92-93.
"Like Most Revelations" (Reprinted from The Boston Phoenix, after Morris Louis). [DenQ] (28:1) Sum 93, p. 34.
"A Lost Art" (Vienna, 1805). [Poetry] (161:5) F 93, p. 280-283.
"My Last Hustler." [Salm] (100) Fall 93, p. 140-141.
"Pastoral Remains (Hitherto Unpublished) from the Rectory" (Boulge, Suffolk, 1852). [QRL] (12:32/33) 93, p. 435-439.
"Poem for Valéry Larbaud" (tr. of Saint-John Perse). [QRL] (12:32/33) 93, p. 487 - 488.
"The Twain Meeting" (Tokyo, 1992). [Chelsea] (55) 93, p. 50-54.
"Visitations." [MichQR] (32:4) Fall 93, p. 521-528.
2973. HOWE, Fanny
"Democracy: Chapters in Verse." [TriQ] (87) Spr-Sum 93, p. 59-70.
2974. HOWE, Ken
"Notes on Mushrooms." [WestCL] (27:2, #11) Fall 93, p. 33-34.
"Regina." [WestCL] (27:2, #11) Fall 93, p. 30.
"Second Illustrated Advertisement for Jerry's Barber Shop." [WestCL] (27:2, #11) Fall 93, p. 31-32.
2975. HOWE, Marie
"A Certain Light." [NewEngR] (15:4) Fall 93, p. 170-171.
"Death, the Last Visit." [Conscience] (14:4) Wint 93-94, p. 45.

"How Some of It Happened." [NewEngR] (15:4) Fall 93, p. 171-172.
"Just Now." [NewEngR] (15:4) Fall 93, p. 172-173.
"The Promise." [HarvardR] (5) Fall 93, p. 62.
2976. HOWE, Susan (*See also* HOWE, Susan Elizabeth)
    "Melville's Marginalia" (part 2, selections). [AmerPoR] (22:1) Ja-F 93, p. 39-40.
2977. HOWE, Susan Elizabeth (*See also* HOWE, Susan)
    "Canyonlands." [WeberS] (10:3) Fall 93, p. 84.
    "Insomniac." [WeberS] (10:3) Fall 93, p. 85-86.
    "Liberty Enlightening the World: The Statue Has Her Say." [WeberS] (10:3) Fall
        93, p. 81-82.
    "On Losing My Camera Below Dead Horse Point." [WeberS] (10:3) Fall 93, p. 85.
    "The Recreational Parachutist" (for Laird). [WeberS] (10:3) Fall 93, p. 82-83.
2978. HOWELL, Christopher
    "The Puppet's Obsession." [PoetL] (88:3) Fall 93, p. 40.
    "Ships." [CarolQ] (45:2) Wint 93, p. 23.
    "Someone Else." [WillowS] (31) Wint 93, p. 73.
    "Through a Rift in the Natural Fabric." [PoetL] (88:3) Fall 93, p. 39.
    "Window." [GettyR] (6:4) Aut 93, p. 700-701.
2979. HOWELL, David
    "Days in India." [BellR] (16:1/2) Spr-Fall 93, p. 40-50.
2980. HOWELL, Heidi A.
    "An Uncorrected Room" (Selections 4 poems). [WashR] (19:3) O-N 93, p. 8-9.
2981. HOWER, Mary
    "Woman with a Crow." [Thrpny] (55) Fall 93, p. 22.
2982. HOWINGTON, Robert W.
    "A Crazy Guy Put a Gun to Bukowski's Head Once." [WormR] (33:4, #132) 93, p.
        174.
    "Go Out Like a Real Man." [NewYorkQ] (51) 93, p. 65.
    "One of Those Moments in Life Where Nothing Is Going on But the Rent."
        [WormR] (33:4, #132) 93, p. 173.
    "Procrastination Is Rampant at H.U.D." [WormR] (33:4, #132) 93, p. 174.
    "There Was a Young Female Clerk." [WormR] (33:4, #132) 93, p. 175.
2983. HOYRD, André
    "When You Died Willie." [JamesWR] (10:3) Spr 93, p. 6.
2984. HRISTIC, Jovan
    "Barbarians" (tr. by Bernard Johnson). [NoDaQ] (61:1) Wint 93, p. 81.
    "Orators Make Speeches on the Squares" (tr. by Bernard Johnson). [NoDaQ] (61:1)
        Wint 93, p. 82.
    "Socrates on the Battlefield" (tr. by Bernard Johnson). [NoDaQ] (61:1) Wint 93, p.
        80.
    "Who Still Needs Find Stories?" (tr. by Bernard Johnson). [NoDaQ] (61:1) Wint 93,
        p. 80.
2985. HSU, Hsuan
    "Tapdancing." [WebR] (17) Fall 93, p. 63.
2986. HSÜ, Wei
    "A Traveler Seeks to Send This to Chou Chung Yang" (in Chinese and English, tr.
        by James Cryer). [InterPR] (19:1) Spr 93, p. 60-61.
    "What We Made a Long While Back a Certain Acquaintance Wishes Me to Do
        Again" (in Chinese and English, tr. by James Cryer). [InterPR] (19:1) Spr 93,
        p. 58-59.
HSUAN, Hsu
        See HSU, Hsuan
HUA, Bai
        See BAI, Hua
HUA, Li Min
        See LI, Min Hua
2987. HUANG, Leta
    "Victory Towels" (The Michael Jasper Gioia Award Winner for 1992). [Sequoia]
        (34/35) 92-93, p. 67-68.
2988. HUBBLE, Leslie Norman
    "Aquarium." [NewL] (59:4) 93, p. 93.
    "Memorial Days." [NewL] (59:4) 93, p. 90-91.
    "Psychiatric." [NewL] (59:4) 93, p. 92.
2989. HUBBS, Janet
    "Sunbathing." [ColEng] (55:3) Mr 93, p. 322.

2990. HUBINGER, Bert
"Mientras el Hombre la Admira y la Vulnera." [Sequoia] (34/35) 92-93, p. 63-64.
2991. HUCKENPAHLER, James
"Untitled Number Three." [WashR] (18:5) F-Mr 93, p. 22.
"Untitled Number Two." [WashR] (18:5) F-Mr 93, p. 16.
2992. HUDA, Mohammad Nurul
"Happy Marriage" (tr. of Taslima Nasreen, w. Carolyne Wright and the author).
[TriQ] (89) Wint 93-94, p. 183-184.
"Things Cheaply Had" (tr. of Taslima Nasreen, w. Carolyne Wright and the author).
[TriQ] (89) Wint 93-94, p. 182.
2993. HUDGINS, Andrew
"Blemishes." [MichQR] (32:4) Fall 93, p. 621.
"Burial Insurance." [Poetry] (161:5) F 93, p. 261-262.
"Haircut." [Atlantic] (272:1) Jl 93, p. 94.
"Lieutenant Colonel." [Atlantic] (272:4) O 93, p. 84.
2994. HUDSON, Andrew
"My Sweetheart's Voice." [WashR] (18:5) F-Mr 93, p. 17.
2995. HUDSON, Ann
"August Letter from Grandmother." [Plain] (13:3) Spr 93, p. 35.
2996. HUDSON, Brenda J.
"Magdalena." [Plain] (13:3) Spr 93, p. 30-31.
2997. HUDSON, Carolyn
"April." [BellArk] (9:4) Jl-Ag 93, p. 28.
"Go Fly a Kite." [BellArk] (9:4) Jl-Ag 93, p. 28.
"Textiles." [BellArk] (9:4) Jl-Ag 93, p. 8.
2998. HUDSON, Joe
"Killing Youth." [Gypsy] (20) Sum 93, p. 37.
2999. HUDSON, June
"Jack and June Laughing, 1958." [NewL] (59:4) 93, p. 98-99.
3000. HUDSON, Marjorie
"On the Untimely Death of One Beloved." [Pembroke] (25) 93, p. 102.
3001. HUERTA, Efraín
"Funeral of Words" (tr. by Jim Normington). [Talisman] (10) Spr 93, p. 82.
"The Murder of a Poet While Sleeping" (tr. by Jim Normington). [Talisman] (10)
Spr 93, p. 83-84.
3002. HUESGEN, Jan
"Annealing." [PraF] (14:2) Sum 93, p. 61.
"Self Reflections: The Eve of City Clean-Up." [PraF] (14:2) Sum 93, p. 59-60.
3003. HUFF, Michael
"Prairie Rattler." [CimR] (102) Ja 93, p. 82.
3004. HUFFSTICKLER, Albert
"The Challenge." [WormR] (33:4, #132) 93, p. 175-176.
"Champion" (from a dream). [PaintedB] (50/51) 93, p. 68.
"It's Always Getting Later." [ChironR] (12:3, #36) Aut 93, p. 17.
"Notes from the Underground." [WormR] (33:4, #132) 93, p. 176.
"Tornadoes and Other Hassles." [ChironR] (12:3, #36) Aut 93, p. 17.
3005. HUGGINS, Peter
"Sherlock Holmes in America." [ChatR] (14:1) Fall 93, p. 66.
3006. HUGHES, Benedict
"Untitled Work in Progress." [BrooklynR] (10) 93, p. 32-37.
3007. HUGHES, Daniel
"Cosmic Orpheus." [RiverS] (37) 93, p. 63.
"What Stays." [RiverS] (37) 93, p. 64.
3008. HUGHES, Henry J.
"Talking to the Tortoise." [AntR] (51:2) Spr 93, p. 240.
3009. HUGHES, Ingrid
"Two Lives." [Gypsy] (20) Sum 93, p. 36.
3010. HUGHES, Jack
"Traditional Comforts." [CarolQ] (45:3) Sum 93, p. 35.
3011. HUGHES, Myrna Elana
"Core." [13thMoon] (12:1/2) 93-94, p. 33.
"Enclosure." [ChiR] (39:2) 93, p. 93-96.
3012. HUGHES, Pamela
"Food for Thought, or Just Deserts" (M.F.A. Workshop w. Marie Hasten, Howard
Glyn, M. R. Syneck, Lisbeth Keiley, Mary Greene, David Trinidad and Allen
Ginsberg, Nov. 21, 1988). [BrooklynR] (10) 93, p. 94-95.

225

HUGHES

3013. HUGHES, Sheila Hassell
"Dinner Theatre." [LullwaterR] (4:2) Spr-Sum 93, p. 100.
3014. HUGHES, Sophie
"Benedict, the Blessed One" (Baruch Spinoza, 1632-1677). [Poem] (70) N 93, p. 51.
"The Darkening Green." [Confr] (51) Sum 93, p. 247-248.
3015. HUGHES, Ted
"The Battle of Osfrontis." [QRL] (12:32/33) 93, p. 440-441.
"Black Coat." [NewYorker] (68:47) 11 Ja 93, p. 62-63.
"Crow Lore: Crow's First Lesson." [QRL] (12:32/33) 93, p. 439-440.
"Crow's Last Stand." [QRL] (12:32/33) 93, p. 441.
"Totem." [NewYorker] (69:44) 27 D 93-3 Ja 94, p. 150.
3016. HUGHEY, David V.
"Rain Patterns." [HolCrit] (30:2) Ap 93, p. 15.
3017. HUGO, Richard (Richard F.)
"Glen Uig." [CutB] (40) Spr 93, p. 1-2.
"Keen to Leaky Flowers." [QRL] (12:32/33) 93, p. 441-442.
"Piping to You on Skye from Lewis" (for Iain MacLain). [NewEngR] (15:1) Wint 93, p. 145.
"Pishkun" (For Jackie). [QRL] (12:32/33) 93, p. 442.
3018. HULBERT, Kate
"Jalisco Exhibit 1992: To the Smiling, Seated Woman." [Vis] (41) 93, p. 11.
3019. HULL, C. E.
"Dying Dog Mantra." [Stand] (34:3) Sum 93, p. 48-49.
3020. HULL, Lynda
"Amulets." [Iowa] (23:1) Wint 93, p. 126-128.
"Fortunate Traveller." [Iowa] (23:1) Wint 93, p. 123-125.
"Suite for Emily." [KenR] (NS 15:3) Sum 93, p. 1-11.
3021. HUME, Christine
"Empty Rooms." [AntR] (51:3) Sum 93, p. 375.
3022. HUMES, Harry
"61 North." [WestB] (31/32) 93, p. 47.
"Beach Tent." [NewL] (59:3) 93, p. 91.
"Bear Jam." [PoetryNW] (34:1) Spr 93, p. 3-4.
"Cranes." [PoetC] (24:2) Wint 93, p. 19.
"The Dream." [PoetC] (24:2) Wint 93, p. 20.
"Gathering." [PaintedB] (50/51) 93, p. 58-59.
"My Brother in the grand Canyon." [GettyR] (6:3) Sum 93, p. 417-418.
"My Father's Hands." [PoetryNW] (34:1) Spr 93, p. 5-6.
"Onions." [WestB] (33) 93, p. 29.
"Sitting Still at the End of the Year." [WestB] (31/32) 93, p. 48.
"Stealing Coal." [WestB] (33) 93, p. 28.
"Three Young Women on a Coal Bank." [PoetryNW] (34:1) Spr 93, p. 4-5.
"Two Beautiful Young Women." [GettyR] (6:3) Sum 93, p. 419.
"Two Friends Talking." [WestB] (31/32) 93, p. 49.
"We Want One to Fall." [PennR] (5:2) 93, p. 33.
3023. HUMMER, T. R.
"December 1909." [WestHR] (47:1) Spr 93, p. 80-81.
"Walt Whitman in Hell." [KenR] (NS 15:3) Sum 93, p. 20-32.
3024. HUMPHREY, Paul
"Weep." [Light] (5) Spr 93, p. 10.
3025. HUNOLD, Rose Marie
"Ashanti Market." [Obs] (8:2) Fall-Wint 93, p. 109-110.
3026. HUNT, Anthony
"Mona Island" (tr. of Loreina Santos Silva). [Paint] (19:38) Aut 92, p. 75.
"What the Sea Turtle Said" (tr. of Loreina Santos Silva). [Paint] (19:38) Aut 92, p. 74.
3027. HUNT, Leigh
"The Next Set" (Amelia Encore Award). [Amelia] (7:2, #21) 93, p. 64-65.
3028. HUNTER, Donnell
"At the Bottom of Grand Canyon." [Interim] (12:1) Spr-Sum 93, p. 12.
"Irrational Numbers." [Interim] (12:1) Spr-Sum 93, p. 13.
3029. HUNTER, Emmy
"Organized Toward Night." [Talisman] (11) Fall 93, p. 273-274.
3030. HUNTER, Terrell
"Airmail to Jane." [NewYorkQ] (50) 93, p. 79.

3031. HUNTINGTON, Cynthia
"The Animal." [BostonR] (18:1) Ja-F 93, p. 33.
"Invisible Dark." [BostonR] (18:1) Ja-F 93, p. 33.
"Passing Through Hometown." [BostonR] (18:1) Ja-F 93, p. 33.
"The Place of Beautiful Trees." [BostonR] (18:1) Ja-F 93, p. 33.
"Rhapsody." [BostonR] (18:1) Ja-F 93, p. 33.
"Soldiers on East Park." [GrahamHR] (17) Fall 93, p. 47-48.
3032. HUNTINGTON, Mike
"Leaves and Grass and Missy Hayward's Cup of Coffee." [CoalC] (7) Apr 93, p. 33.
3033. HUPTYCH, Miroslav
"The Grey-headed Griffin" (tr. by Ellen Rosenbaum). [OxfordM] (9:1) Spr-Sum 93,
p. 33-35.
3034. HURDLE, Crystal
"A Visition." [CanLit] (138/139) Fall-Wint 93, p. 71-72.
3035. HURFORD, Chris
"Expect the Worst" (tr. of Adam Michajlow, w. Artur Grabowski). [Verse] (10:2)
Sum 93, p. 43.
"Letter from the Land of the Red Roofs. To Anna Maria. To Pawka Marcinkiewicz"
(tr. of Jacek Podsiadlo, w. Ewa Horodyska). [Verse] (10:2) Sum 93, p. 42.
3036. HURSEY, Brett
"The Girl Who Cuts Your Hair." [BlackWR] (20:1) Fall-Wint 93, p. 120-121.
3037. HUSAIN, Begum Razia
"The Sound of Leaves" (tr. by Chitra Divakaruni). [Prima] (16/17) 93, p. 94-95.
3038. HUTCHINGS, Pat
"Before the Thunder Storm." [Northeast] (5:9) Wint 93-94, p. 3.
"Meditation at the Top of the Mountain." [Northeast] (5:9) Wint 93-94, p. 4.
"Pretty Soon" (A Poem to Peter, for his new parents). [Northeast] (5:9) Wint 93-94,
p. 5-6.
"Telling Erin About Iowa on Office Time." [ColEng] (55:6) O 93, p. 644.
3039. HUTCHISON, Joseph
"The Ache." [TarRP] (32:2) Spr 93, p. 21.
"Black River." [Poetry] (162:6) S 93, p. 348.
"Blue Recitation." [TarRP] (32:2) Spr 93, p. 20.
"Summer Storm." [TarRP] (32:2) Spr 93, p. 20.
"What I Know." [Poetry] (161:5) F 93, p. 256.
3040. HUTCHISON, Scott Travis
"Precedent." [HolCrit] (30:2) Ap 93, p. 17.
3041. HUYETT, Pat
"Breaking Water." [WebR] (17) Fall 93, p. 108.
3042. HYDE, Christine
"A Man Wearing Blue Y Fronts, a Happy Lady and the World." [Bogg] (66) Wint
92-93, p. 48.
HYERYON, Hahm
See HAHM, Hyeryon
3043. HYETT, Barbara Helfgott
"Gray Bat" (Myotis grisescens). [Agni] (37) 93, p. 254.
"Roseate Tern" (Sterna dougalli). [Agni] (37) 93, p. 253.
3044. HYMAN, Ramona L.
"This South" (I & II). [AfAmRev] (27:1) Spr 93, p. 133.
3045. HYMANS, Don
"In Both Ears, Out Some Others" (for Lee Upton). [IndR] (16:2) Fall 93, p. 136.
3046. HYMAS, June Hopper
"Dance to a Primeval Air." [Bogg] (66) Wint 92-93, p. 12.
"Not Like the Red Paint Peoples' Burials." [LaurelR] (27:1) Wint 93, p. 72.
"Preface to the Dictionary of the English Language." [RagMag] (11:2) 93, p. 34.
3047. HYNES, Maureen
"Her Broadloom Dream." [PraF] (14:3) Aut 93, p. 63-65.
HYON-JONG, Chong
See CHONG, Hyônjong (Hyon-Jong)
HYONJONG, Chông
See CHONG, Hyônjong (Hyon-Jong)
IASI, Camilla di
See Di IASI, Camilla
3048. IASIELLO, Mimmo
"Apology." [WebR] (17) Fall 93, p. 61-62.

227

3049. IBARBOUROU, Juana de
"Wait!" (tr. by Marijane Osborn). [Vis] (42) 93, p. 25.
Ibn al-TABBAN, Levi
See AL-TABBAN, Levi Ibn
Ibn NAGRELA, Isma'il
See HANAGRID, Samuel Ben Yosef Halevi (Isma'il Ibn Nagrela)
3050. IBSEN, Arni
"Being 4" (tr. by the author and Peter Ridgewell). [Vis] (42) 93, p. 10.
"Bread" (tr. by the author and Peter Ridgewell). [Vis] (41) 93, p. 35-36.
"The Meaningful Sun" (tr. by Peter Ridgewell). [Vis] (43) 93, p. 28.
3051. IBUR, Jane (Jane Ellen)
"Augusta." [WebR] (17) Fall 93, p. 114-115.
"A Hot Dog Kind of Girl." [Spitball] (43) Spr 93, p. 26-27.
"Spinner Sponn." [Spitball] (43) Spr 93, p. 24-25.
3052. IDOL, John
"In the Pines: For Annie." [Pembroke] (25) 93, p. 106.
"Remembering Lynn." [Pembroke] (25) 93, p. 105.
3053. IERONIM, Ioana
"Audio" (tr. by Adam J. Sorkin). [Vis] (41) 93, p. 5.
"Emigration" (tr. by Adam Sorkin, w. the author). [Vis] (43) 93, p. 48.
"Pieta" (tr. of Anna Blandiana, w. Adam Sorkin). [Vis] (41) 93, p. 39.
3054. IGNATOW, David
"Between Us." [HangL] (62) 93, p. 28.
"Dream III." [ProseP] (2) 93, p. 48.
"East Bronx." [PoetryE] (35) Spr 93, p. 175.
"For Lori." [Pequod] (36) 93, p. 90.
"I See a Truck." [PoetryE] (35) Spr 93, p. 175.
"I Was Angry." [QRL] (12:32/33) 93, p. 444.
"Implicated." [ProseP] (1) 92, p. 40.
"In a Dream." [ProseP] (1) 92, p. 42.
"Its Origin." [Pequod] (36) 93, p. 89.
"The Life Dance." [PoetryE] (35) Spr 93, p. 180-181.
"The Nailhead." [QRL] (12:32/33) 93, p. 443-444.
"Nourish the Crops." [PoetryE] (35) Spr 93, p. 174.
"The Past." [HangL] (62) 93, p. 28.
"Proud of Myself." [ProseP] (1) 92, p. 41.
"Rescue the Dead." [PoetryE] (35) Spr 93, p. 170.
"Ruminating." [ProseP] (2) 93, p. 47.
"The Saint." [PaintedB] (50/51) 93, p. 117.
"Secretly." [PoetryE] (35) Spr 93, p. 180.
"Sleepy." [NewEngR] (15:1) Wint 93, p. 146.
"Surface." [PaintedB] (50/51) 93, p. 117.
"Two Voices." [QRL] (12:32/33) 93, p. 443.
"Walking." [QRL] (12:32/33) 93, p. 444.
3055. IINO, Tomoyuki
"At the Tideland" (tr. of Tanikawa Shuntaro, w. Jon Silkin). [Stand] (34:2) Spr 93,
p. 23.
3056. IKAN, Ron
"Writing." [NorthStoneR] (11) 93, p. 145.
3057. IKEDA, Kanoelani
"Yomesan." [BambooR] (57) Wint 93, p. 161.
3058. ILKOV, Ani
"Evaporations" (tr. by Lisa Sapinkopf and Georgi Belev). [Paint] (19:38) Aut 92, p.
65.
"Green and Gold" (tr. by Lisa Sapinkopf and Georgi Belev). [Paint] (19:38) Aut 92,
p. 64.
3059. ILLAS, Jorge
"Te Di el Nombre de Míriam" (a Míriam). [LindLM] (12:1) Mr 93, p. 31.
3060. ILLYÉS, Gyula
"Successful Effort" (tr. by Bruce Berlind, w. Mária Körösy). [ProseP] (1) 92, p. 43.
3061. ILMET, Peep
"In Retreat" (tr. by Krista Kaer). [CimR] (104) Jl 93, p. 59.
"The Oak Screams Out" (tr. by Krista Kaer). [CimR] (104) Jl 93, p. 58.
"The Present Is Like Sailcloth" (tr. by Krista Kaer). [CimR] (104) Jl 93, p. 58.
3062. ILVES, Toomas H.
"Her Quiet Words Let Loose" (tr. of Doris Kareva). [CimR] (104) Jl 93, p. 60.

"The Night Left a Scent" (tr. of Doris Kareva). [CimR] (104) Jl 93, p. 60.
"There Shall Come No Other and Better World" (tr. of Doris Kareva). [CimR] (104)
Jl 93, p. 61.
3063. IMADA, Adria
"Peeking at My Mother." [BambooR] (57) Wint 93, p. 162-164.
3064. IMBRIGLIO, Catherine
"Block Island Ferry." [NewAW] (11) Sum-Fall 93, p. 97.
"Prosthesis." [NewAW] (11) Sum-Fall 93, p. 96.
"Rumor." [NewAW] (11) Sum-Fall 93, p. 95.
3065. INADA, Lawson Fusao
"Shrinking the Pacific." [ChiR] (39:3/4) 93, p. 87-88.
3066. INAGAWA, Masato
"To Hanawa, Terayama, As Far as Nagare" (tr. by Eric Selland). [ChiR] (39:3/4) 93,
p. 216-217.
3067. INCE, Özdemir
"Pomegranates" (tr. by Simon Pettet and Ülker Ince). [Talisman] (10) Spr 93, p. 86.
"Sage" (tr. by Simon Pettet and Ülker Ince). [Talisman] (10) Spr 93, p. 85.
3068. INCE, Ronald
"Romance has reached the low g's when your date moves down a notch" (Amelia
One-Liner Award). [Amelia] (7:2, #21) 93, p. 57.
3069. INCE, Ülker
"Pomegranates" (tr. of Özdemir Ince, w. Simon Pettet). [Talisman] (10) Spr 93, p.
86.
"Sage" (tr. of Özdemir Ince, w. Simon Pettet). [Talisman] (10) Spr 93, p. 85.
3070. INEZ, Colette
"The Dance of Adolph and Eva." [CreamCR] (17:1) Spr 93, p. 85.
"Having Gone to Glory, Nana Speaks to Me." [NewYorkQ] (52) 93, p. 41.
"How Did They Recognize Autumn in the Dark of the City?" [NewYorkQ] (51) 93,
p. 38.
"In the Country of No Remorse." [CreamCR] (17:1) Spr 93, p. 84.
"Michigan August." [Ploughs] (19:1) Spr 93, p. 31.
"The Old Man, Bereaved, Paces Upstairs in a Jumble of Rooms." [Agni] (37) 93, p.
205.
"The Perseid Meteors of August." [NewYorkQ] (50) 93, p. 43.
"The Red Train." [Caliban] (13) 93, p. 97.
"Refrain for My Sires." [DenQ] (27:4) Spr 93, p. 75.
"The Salmon Has Entered Our Winter." [Caliban] (13) 93, p. 96.
3071. INGERSOLL, Glenn
"Winged Man." [CarolQ] (46:1) Fall 93, p. 35.
3072. INGERSON, Martin I.
"The Telephone." [BellArk] (9:5) S-O 93, p. 11.
3073. INGUANZO, Rosa
"A Gustavo." [LindLM] (12:1) Mr 93, p. 18.
"Seattle." [LindLM] (12:1) Mr 93, p. 18.
"Siesta." [LindLM] (12:1) Mr 93, p. 18.
3074. INMAN, Will
"Dark Flowers." [Asylum] (8) 93, p. 137.
"A Spoon of Water." [Pembroke] (25) 93, p. 59.
3075. INSULIS, Alanus de (Alan of Lille)
"De Planctu Naturae" (Selection, tr. by George Economou). [Sulfur] (33) Fall 93, p.
80-82.
3076. IOANNOU, Susan
"After Many Years: Sonnet." [Descant] (24:2, #81) Sum 93, p. 105.
"A Civilized Life." [TickleAce] (23) Spr-Sum 92, p. 74-78.
"In Gratitude" (for Wentworth Walker). [Quarry] (42:1) 93, p. 124.
"In Middle Age." [TickleAce] (23) Spr-Sum 92, p. 72-73.
"Your Warmth, the Night." [Descant] (24:2, #81) Sum 93, p. 106.
3077. IOSIFOVA, Ekaterina
"If the Silence Should Suddenly Return" (tr. by Lisa Sapinkopf and Georgi Belev).
[Paint] (19:38) Aut 92, p. 70-71.
3078. IRIMIA, M. A.
"Almost Domestic" (tr. of Adrian Popescu, w. A. J. Sorkin). [TampaR] (6) Spr 93,
p. 10.
"Elves" (tr. of Adrian Popescu, w. A. J. Sorkin). [TampaR] (6) Spr 93, p. 11.
3079. IRIZARRY, Katrina
"Math." [Americas] (21:2) Sum 93, p. 71.

3080. IRONS, Jim
"No More Fires to Fight." [OnTheBus] (5:2, #12) Sum-Fall 93, p. 98.
3081. IRVINE, Suey
"In the Mountain View Municipal Parking Lot." [BellArk] (9:4) Jl-Ag 93, p. 28.
3082. IRWIN, Mark
"6 August 1945." [Pequod] (36) 93, p. 91-93.
"Almost Never." [Pequod] (36) 93, p. 94-95.
"Brief History of Desire." [Journal] (17:2) Fall-Wint 93, p. 31-34.
"Robert Mapplethorpe's Photograph of Apollo (1988)." [ParisR] (35:128) Fall 93, p. 224.
"Roses" (For B.N. Nasvytis). [BlackWR] (19:1) Fall-Wint 92, p. 137-139.
3083. ISHIGAKI, Rin
"The Pans, the Pots and the Fire in Front of Me" (tr. by Akemi Nakamura and Tony Whedon). [GreenMR] (NS 6:2) Sum-Fall 93, p. 74-75.
3084. ISHIOKA, Chi
"Waiting for a Wind" (tr. by Akemi Nakamura and Tony Whedon). [GreenMR] (NS 6:2) Sum-Fall 93, p. 77.
3085. ISKRENKO, Nina
"12:44 A.M." (tr. by John High, w. Patrick Henry). [Talisman] (11) Fall 93, p. 239-241.
3086. ISLAS, Maya
"Probablemente al Final" (A Ernesto Briel). [LindLM] (12:1) Mr 93, p. 7.
3087. ISMAIL, Jam
"Spanner/Wrench." [ChiR] (39:3/4) 93, p. 148.
3088. ISMAILI, Rashidah
"Grandmother." [Drumvoices] (3:1/2) Fall-Wint 93-94, p. 59.
"Lover." [Drumvoices] (3:1/2) Fall-Wint 93-94, p. 58.
3089. ISON, John M.
"Crossing." [EvergreenC] (8:2) Sum-Fall 93, p. 8.
3090. ISRAEL, Jack
"The Children." [SouthernPR] (33:1) Spr 93, p. 59-60.
"Deep Green." [RiverC] (14:1) Fall 93, p. 58-59.
3091. ISRAELI, Henry
"Stenographer." [AntigR] (92) Wint 93, p. 73.
"The Storm." [Sonora] (26) Fall 93, p. 77-81.
3092. ITO, Hiromi
"Near Kitami Station on the Odakyu Line" (tr. by Leith Morton). [Sulfur] (32) Spr 93, p. 214-216.
"Snow" (tr. by Leith Morton). [Sulfur] (32) Spr 93, p. 213-214.
"Vinegar and Oil" (tr. by Leith Morton). [Sulfur] (32) Spr 93, p. 216-219.
3093. IUPPA, M. J.
"Chrysalis." [Poetry] (162:1) Ap 93, p. 36.
"Crossings." [Footwork] (23) 93, p. 51.
"The Cutting Garden." [TarRP] (32:2) Spr 93, p. 19.
"Inside the Sound." [Footwork] (23) 93, p. 51.
3094. IVERSON, Teresa
"Giant Sequoia." [Agni] (37) 93, p. 257.
"Kaleidoscope" (apologies to Sir Thomas Browne). [Agni] (37) 93, p. 255-256.
"Quaternary" (tr. of Gottfried Benn). [PartR] (60:3) Sum 93, p. 425-426.
3095. IVEY, John Mark
"Alexander Robinson." [Obs] (8:1) Spr-Sum 93, p. 92.
3096. IVRY, Benjamin
"Stained Glass at Père-Lachaise." [NewYorker] (69:19) 28 Je 93, p. 60.
"Wet Autumn Night." [NewYorker] (69:3) 8 Mr 93, p. 92.
3097. IWERSON, Kristine
"Reckoning." [Pearl] (17) Spr 93, p. 14.
3098. IZAGUIRRE, Ester de
"Fantasma" (from "Si Preguntan por Algien con mi Nombre"). [Luz] (5) N 93, p. 78, 80.
"A Lifetime" (from "Si Preguntan por Algien con mi Nombre," tr. by Angela McEwan). [Luz] (5) N 93, p. 91.
"Mi Vida" (from "Si Preguntan por Algien con mi Nombre"). [Luz] (5) N 93, p. 90.
"Phantom" (from "Si Preguntan por Algien con mi Nombre," tr. by Angela McEwan). [Luz] (5) N 93, p. 79, 81.
3099. JABBOUR, Mick
"To an Umpire." [Spitball] (43) Spr 93, p. 23.

3100. JACCOTTET, Philippe
"L'Ignorant." [LitR] (36:4) Sum 93, p. 527.
"The Unknowing" (tr. by Richard Kopp). [LitR] (36:4) Sum 93, p. 526.
3101. JACKMAN, Vernon L.
"Dawnscape." [CaribbeanW] (7) 93, p. 13.
"The Day After Christmas." [Footwork] (23) 93, p. 52.
"Rock and Relic." [CaribbeanW] (7) 93, p. 14-15.
"Woman's Tongue." [CaribbeanW] (7) 93, p. 12.
3102. JACKOWSKA, Nicki
"Reducing the Dose." [Stand] (34:2) Spr 93, p. 72.
3103. JACKSON, Fleda Brown
"Crows." [SycamoreR] (5:2) Sum 93, p. 83.
"Father Andrew Considers Evil." [WestB] (31/32) 93, p. 141.
"Father Andrew's Creed." [WestB] (31/32) 93, p. 140.
"Magi." [SycamoreR] (5:2) Sum 93, p. 82.
3104. JACKSON, Gale
"Sojourner Truth 1797-1883, If the Truth Be Told." [AmerV] (30) 93, p. 47-56.
3105. JACKSON, John
"Cardinals." [Poetry] (163:1) O 93, p. 14.
"The Dead Orchard." [Poetry] (163:1) O 93, p. 13.
"Lambing, Upstate New York." [Poetry] (162:1) Ap 93, p. 1.
3106. JACKSON, Katherine
"Blue Spring" (for Amy Clampitt). [Verse] (10:3) Wint 93, p. 86.
"Walking Trees." [CumbPR]] (13:1) Fall 93, p. 81.
JACKSON, Kevin Goldstein
See GOLDSTEIN-JACKSON, Kevin
3107. JACKSON, Michael L.
"A Definition of Things." [XavierR] (13:1) Spr 93, p. 15-16.
3108. JACKSON, Reuben
"Steps." [Agni] (37) 93, p. 90-91.
3109. JACKSON, Richard
"My Black Madonna." [Crazy] (45) Wint 93, p. 42-45.
"Objects in This Mirror Are Closer Than They Appear." [Crazy] (45) Wint 93, p. 36-41.
"Unauthorized Autobiography." [NewEngR] (15:4) Fall 93, p. 51-54.
"Waiting for Kafka." [BlackWR] (20:1) Fall-Wint 93, p. 7-8.
3110. JACKSON, Spoon
"Purple Fighter." [PoetryUSA] (25/26) 93, p. 54.
3111. JACOB, Bob
"Luck." [US1] (28/29) 93, p. 14.
3112. JACOB, Max
"Approach to a View in Perspective" (tr. by Michael Benedikt). [QRL] (12:32/33) 93, p. 445.
"Hat" (tr. by Michael Benedikt). [QRL] (12:32/33) 93, p. 444-445.
3113. JACOBES, Catherine M.
"Playa de las Rotas." [BrooklynR] (10) 93, p. 20.
3114. JACOBIK, Gray
"Brain Teasers." [SycamoreR] (5:2) Sum 93, p. 37-38.
"Economies." [Farm] (10:2) Fall-Wint 93-94, p. 18.
"The Gift." [SycamoreR] (5:2) Sum 93, p. 36.
"Love Poem for a Familiar." [Farm] (10:2) Fall-Wint 93-94, p. 17.
"Owls." [SycamoreR] (5:2) Sum 93, p. 35.
"Pace." [OntR] (39) Fall-Wint 93-94, p. 88.
"Processes and Relationships." [CentR] (37:3) Fall 93, p. 534.
"The Seven Sourpusses of Okolona, Illinois." [CentR] (37:3) Fall 93, p. 535-537.
"Stones and Soil." [OntR] (39) Fall-Wint 93-94, p. 89.
"Walking to an Eight O'Clock Class." [OntR] (39) Fall-Wint 93-94, p. 90.
"Window with a Dozen Small Square Panes." [PoetL] (88:2) Sum 93, p. 28.
3115. JACOBS, J. L.
"Relics of an Ice Age." [Caliban] (12) 93, p. 148-149.
3116. JACOBS, Josh
"Funeral Spring." [US1] (28/29) 93, p. 11.
3117. JACOBSEN, Josephine
"After Three Days." [KenR] (NS 15:4) Fall 93, p. 18-19.
"The Blue-Eyed Exterminator." [KenR] (NS 15:4) Fall 93, p. 18.
"The Lawn Bowlers." [TriQ] (88) Fall 93, p. 144.

231

"Softly." [KenR] (NS 15:4) Fall 93, p. 19-20.
3118. JACOBSON, Bonnie
"Cleritwos." [Light] (7) Aut 93, p. 10.
"Shopping for Towels." [Light] (5) Spr 93, p. 15.
"Untitled: Why did the oxymoron cross the road?" [Light] (5) Spr 93, p. 9.
3119. JACQMIN, François
"For an inexhaustible instant I sat" (tr. by Dick Schneider). [ManhatR] (7:1) Fall 93,
p. 23.
"It's not the precision" (tr. by Dick Schneider). [ManhatR] (7:1) Fall 93, p. 25.
"Nothing remains of which one would" (tr. by Dick Schneider). [ManhatR] (7:1)
Fall 93, p. 29.
"The rectangular distress of the city" (tr. by Dick Schneider). [ManhatR] (7:1) Fall
93, p. 27.
"Shrewd is the one who hears nothing" (tr. by Dick Schneider). [ManhatR] (7:1) Fall
93, p. 30.
"Since silence links precaution" (tr. by Dick Schneider). [ManhatR] (7:1) Fall 93, p.
31.
"Snow" (tr. by Dick Schneider). [ManhatR] (7:1) Fall 93, p. 21.
"The snow is everywhere" (tr. by Dick Schneider). [ManhatR] (7:1) Fall 93, p. 24.
"The time comes" (tr. by Dick Schneider). [ManhatR] (7:1) Fall 93, p. 28.
"What one hears when the soul" (tr. by Dick Schneider). [ManhatR] (7:1) Fall 93, p.
22.
"When the snow stopped falling" (tr. by Dick Schneider). [ManhatR] (7:1) Fall 93,
p. 26.
3120. JACQUEZ, Henry
"A Dock Poem" (For A.J.). [FreeL] (12) Sum 93, p. 13.
3121. JAECH, Linda
"Butcher Shop, 1957." [PoetryNW] (34:1) Spr 93, p. 15.
3122. JAEGER, Lowell
"How He Cut Himself Shaving." [Poetry] (162:5) Ag 93, p. 262-263.
"Sweet Citrus." [HighP] (8:1) Spr 93, p. 33-34.
"Yard Work." [PaintedHR] (8) Wint 93, p. 6-7.
3123. JAFFE MAGGIE
"At the Unemployement Office" (after Wislawa Szymborska). [ChironR] (12:1,
#34) Spr 93, p. 32.
"Georg Grosz." [ChironR] (12:1, #34) Spr 93, p. 32.
"Murder, Inc." (After Neruda's "United Fruit Co."). [ChironR] (12:1, #34) Spr 93, p.
32.
3124. JAHANNES, Ja A.
"God." [AfAmRev] (27:1) Spr 93, p. 138.
"Last One in Should Bring the Light." [AfAmRev] (27:1) Spr 93, p. 137.
"Totes." [AfAmRev] (27:1) Spr 93, p. 138.
3125. JAJEH, John
"Aquarium." [BlackWR] (19:1) Fall-Wint 92, p. 157-159.
JAM, Ismail
See ISMAIL, Jam
JAME, Adele Ne
See NeJAME, Adele
3126. JAMES, Cynthia
"Drumology." [Drumvoices] (3:1/2) Fall-Wint 93-94, p. 26.
"Motherhood." [Drumvoices] (3:1/2) Fall-Wint 93-94, p. 27.
"Sing Me a Song, sister." [Drumvoices] (3:1/2) Fall-Wint 93-94, p. 26-27.
3127. JAMES, David
"Finally, the Truth about Critics." [NewYorkQ] (52) 93, p. 82.
"For Most of Us." [LitR] (37:1) Fall 93, p. 96.
"Out of Nothing." [PikeF] (11) Fall 93, p. 3.
"A Poem for Poetry Haters." [SoCoast] (15) Je 93, p. 16-17.
3128. JAMES, Joyce
"Conviction." [RiverC] (14:1) Fall 93, p. 27.
3129. JAMES, Sibyl
"Le Nouveau Temps." [ProseP] (1) 92, p. 44.
"October Lambs." [ProseP] (1) 92, p. 45.
"Stigmata Me, Baby." [Vis] (42) 93, p. 28.
3130. JAMIS, Fayad
"For a Lost Scarf" (to Andres Simor, tr. by John Oliver Simon). [ApalQ] (38) 92, p.
57.

3131. JANECZKO, Paul B.
"Opening Day." [Spitball] (45) Fall 93, p. 70-71.
3132. JANES, Percy
"4:19 a.m." [TickleAce] (23) Spr-Sum 92, p. 59.
"Friedrich Nietzsche" (2 poems. From *The Sea of Faith: Portraits and Sketches*, a suite of poems on the history of Christian thought). [TickleAce] (26) Fall-Wint 93, p. 59-60.
"Jimmy Swaggart" (From *The Sea of Faith: Portraits and Sketches*, a suite of poems on the history of Christian thought). [TickleAce] (26) Fall-Wint 93, p. 61.
"Martin Luther" (2 poems. From *The Sea of Faith: Portraits and Sketches*, a suite of poems on the history of Christian thought). [TickleAce] (26) Fall-Wint 93, p. 57-58.
3133. JANKO, Anna
"Any One of Us" (tr. by David Malcolm and Georgia Scott). [Prima] (16/17) 93, p. 32-33.
3134. JANOWITZ, Phyllis
"Come Onna My House (My House)." [RiverS] (37) 93, p. 50.
"The Necessary Angel." [RiverS] (37) 93, p. 49.
3135. JANSEN, Walfried
"It Would Only Be Right." [PraF] (14:3) Aut 93, p. 74.
3136. JANSMA, Esther
"The Full Women" (tr. by Steve Orlen). [AmerPoR] (22:1) Ja-F 93, p. 42.
"In February" (tr. by Steve Orlen). [AmerPoR] (22:1) Ja-F 93, p. 41.
"Paper Mâché" (tr. by Steve Orlen). [AmerPoR] (22:1) Ja-F 93, p. 42.
"Requiem with Nudes" (for Adriaan Morriën, tr. by Steve Orlen). [AmerPoR] (22:1) Ja-F 93, p. 41.
"Royal Entertainment" (tr. by Steve Orlen). [AmerPoR] (22:1) Ja-F 93, p. 42.
"Sweet Sleeper" (for Casper le Fèvre, tr. by Steve Orlen). [AmerPoR] (22:1) Ja-F 93, p. 41.
"Twins" (for Mireille Jansma, tr. by Steve Orlen). [AmerPoR] (22:1) Ja-F 93, p. 41.
"Under the Old Eyes of the Night" (tr. by the author). [NewYorker] (69:6) 29 Mr 93, p. 81.
"Vertigo" (tr. by Steve Orlen). [AmerPoR] (22:1) Ja-F 93, p. 42.
3137. JANSONE, Inguna
"This Eventide Seems Spilt" (tr. of Amanda Aizpuriete). [CimR] (104) Jl 93, p. 31 - 38.
3138. JANSSON, Lora
"Degrees of Gray at Northside" (w. Kenny Briggs and Brian Di Salvatore). [CutB] (40) Spr 93, p. 101-102.
3139. JANZEN, Jean
"The Gardens of the Body." [Poetry] (162:1) Ap 93, p. 9.
"Snake in the Parsonage." [Journal] (17:1) Spr-Sum 93, p. 43.
"Sometimes Hope" (3rd Prize, 7th Annual Contest). [SoCoast] (15) Je 93, p. 36.
"Stained Glass." [ChrC] (110:25) 8-15 S 93, p. 844.
"Toward the End of the Century." [Poetry] (162:1) Ap 93, p. 10.
3140. JANZEN, Rhoda
"The Place to Vacation." [CumbPR] (12:2) Spr 93, p. 25.
3141. JANZEN, Sonya
"Deciduous Desire." [PraF] (14:3) Aut 93, p. 75.
3142. JAQUISH, Karen I.
"Changing History." [HopewellR] (5) 93, p. 115.
"Midwife: After Chernobyl." [HopewellR] (5) 93, p. 114.
3143. JARAMILLO AGUDELO, Darío
"Frusos" (tr. by Don Share). [Agni] (37) 93, p. 272-273.
"The Morgualos" (tr. by Don Share). [Agni] (37) 93, p. 269-271.
3144. JAREMA, Morgan
"The Formative Years — For a Friend —." [NewYorkQ] (51) 93, p. 68.
3145. JARMAN, Mark
"Drought Rain." [SouthwR] (78:2) Spr 93, p. 212-213.
"Forgotten Infancy, Kentucky." [NewEngR] (15:4) Fall 93, p. 75-76.
"Good Voices." [NewEngR] (15:4) Fall 93, p. 76-77.
"Lost in a Dream." [NewEngR] (15:1) Wint 93, p. 147-148.
"Psalm: Let Us Think of God as a Lover." [Ploughs] (19:4) Wint 93-94, p. 121.
"Remembered Weather." [NewEngR] (15:4) Fall 93, p. 77.
"Unholy Sonnet." [Ploughs] (19:4) Wint 93-94, p. 122.

3146. JARNOT, Lisa
"4 in a Cave" (Selections: III-IV, w. Judith Goldman). [13thMoon] (12:1/2) 93-94,
    p. 34-35.
"Dictionary Love Poem." [BlackBread] (3) 93, p. 74.
"Double Triolet" (w. Lee Ann Brown). [BlackBread] (3) 93, p. 72.
"Heaven Sonnet." [BlackBread] (3) 93, p. 71.
"O'Hara Sonnet." [BlackBread] (3) 93, p. 70.
"Rybaudoure" (for RD). [BlackBread] (3) 93, p. 73.
"Yo Moxley." [BlackBread] (3) 93, p. 75.
3147. JARRELL, Randall
"Eighth Air Force." [QRL] (12:32/33) 93, p. 445-446.
"A Ghost Story." [QRL] (12:32/33) 93, p. 446.
3148. JARVIS, Edward
"A Small Observation." [Light] (8) Wint 93, p. 13.
3149. JASNOWSKI, Tony
"Mama Performs Surgery on a Chicken." [CumbPR] (12:2) Spr 93, p. 14-15.
"A Nun Lifts the Veil." [CumbPR] (12:2) Spr 93, p. 16.
3150. JASSON-HOLT, Sophie
"Decade." [Zyzzyva] (9:4) Wint 93, p. 60-61.
3151. JASTERMSKY, Karen
"& for a Moment I Saw Myself in You" (for Greta Garbo). [AlabamaLR] (7:1) 93,
    p. 38-39.
"At John Reed's Grave." [SpoonR] (18:1) Wint-Spr 93, p. 83-84.
"I'm With You, Anna Akhmatova, On the Bridge." [SpoonR] (18:1) Wint-Spr 93, p.
    82.
"White Cotton Bed Sheets." [AnthNEW] (5) 93, p. 26.
3152. JASTRUN, Tomasz
"Alms" (tr. by Daniel Bourne). [Confr] (51) Sum 93, p. 239.
"Intersection" (tr. by Daniel Bourne). [Witness] (7:1) 93, p. 132.
"Monuments" (tr. by Daniel Bourne). [Confr] (51) Sum 93, p. 238.
"Sleeplessness" (tr. by Daniel Bourne). [Confr] (51) Sum 93, p. 237.
"Tending One's Garden" (tr. by Daniel Bourne). [Witness] (7:1) 93, p. 132.
3153. JAUSS, David
"The Blue Coat." [GeoR] (47:4) Wint 93, p. 771-772.
"Croisett, 1853" (from Saint Flaubert). [DenQ] (27:4) Spr 93, p. 76-77.
"Elegy for a Former Neighbor Whose Name I've Forgotten." [CapeR] (28:1) Spr 93,
    p. 22.
"Hymn of Fire" (John Coltrane, Huntington Hospital, Huntington, New York, July
    17, 1967). [InterPR] (19:2) Fall 93, p. 80.
"Saint Flaubert." [Shen] (43:3) Fall 93, p. 41-43.
3154. JAY, Cellan
"On the Road." [Grain] (21:2) Sum 93, p. 25.
"A Poor Story." [Grain] (21:2) Sum 93, p. 24.
JE-CHUN, Park
    See PARK, Je-chun
3155. JEAN, Diana
"Better Than a Snail's Pace." [OnTheBus] (6:1, #13) Wint 93-Spr 94, p. 79.
"Mouse Perspective." [OnTheBus] (5:2, #12) Sum-Fall 93, p. 99.
3156. JEAN, Veronica
"Lightyears" (for John Dickson). [Elf] (3:3) Fall 93, p. 25.
3157. JEFFERS, Trellie L.
"On the Second Birthday of My Grandson Mikki (June 16, 1991)." [AfAmRev]
    (27:1) Spr 93, p. 135.
"Requiem for a Teacher." [AfAmRev] (27:1) Spr 93, p. 136.
3158. JEFFRIES, Alan T.
"For James Wright." [WormR] (33:3, #131), 93, p. 105.
"On Being Asked to Sign an Organ Donor Card." [WormR] (33:3, #131), 93, p. 106.
3159. JELUSIC, Bozica
"Hyperborean Letter" (tr. by Dasha Culic Nisula). [Vis] (43) 93, p. 11.
3160. JENKINS, Don W.
"Cuymaca Ordinary." [AmerPoR] (22:3) My-Je 93, p. 15.
3161. JENKINS, Louis
"Automobile Repair." [HolCrit] (30:5) D 93, p. 4.
"Fishing Below the Dam." [HolCrit] (30:5) D 93, p. 7-8.
"The Ice Fisherman." [HolCrit] (30:5) D 93, p. 2.
"In the Streets." [HolCrit] (30:5) D 93, p. 5.

"Kansas." [HolCrit] (30:5) D 93, p. 3.
"Oklahoma." [HolCrit] (30:5) D 93, p. 1-2.
"Restaurant Overlooking Lake Superior." [HolCrit] (30:5) D 93, p. 8.
3162. JENKINS, Mike
"Dream Meeting." [CharR] (19:1) Spr 93, p. 92.
"Facing Both Ways." [CharR] (19:1) Spr 93, p. 93.
"Intruder." [CharR] (19:1) Spr 93, p. 96.
"The Memory Dance" (i.m. Philip Greagsby). [CharR] (19:1) Spr 93, p. 94.
"The Mouth." [CharR] (19:1) Spr 93, p. 91.
"Openings." [CharR] (19:1) Spr 93, p. 95.
"Searching the Doll." [CharR] (19:1) Spr 93, p. 90.
3163. JENKINSON, John
"Homegrown Homeopathy." [ChironR] (12:4/13:1, #37/38) Wint 93-Spr 94, p. 44.
3164. JENSEN, Dale
"Hollywood Sidewalks." [Talisman] (11) Fall 93, p. 275.
3165. JENSEN, Doreen
"Night Cry." [Plain] (13:2) Wint 93, p. 23.
3166. JENSEN, Judy
"Stationed in Somalia." [ProseP] (2) 93, p. 49-50.
3167. JENSEN, Laura
"Ethnic." [Field] (49) Fall 93, p. 82-84.
"Reunions." [PoetryNW] (34:4) Wint 93-94, p. 36-39.
"Rotary." [Field] (49) Fall 93, p. 85.
"White Christmas." [Field] (49) Fall 93, p. 80-81.
3168. JEROME, Judson
"Night Comfort." [Elf] (3:2) Sum 93, p. 50.
3169. JEROZAL, Gregory
"The Astrologer Sleeps Nights: A Fable." [HampSPR] Wint 93, p. 67.
3170. JESS
"Song of the Pied Parrot." [PoetryUSA] (25/26) 93, p. 28.
"This Is the Box Pandora Shook." [PoetryUSA] (25/26) 93, p. 28.
3171. JEWELL, Terri L.
"Found Cure Nine." [ContextS] (3:1) 93, p. 23.
JIA-XIN, Wang
    See WANG, Jiaxin
JIANG HE, Ou Yang
    See OU YANG, Jiang He
JIANGING, Zheng
    See ZHENG, Jianging
3172. JIANU, Angela
"Anamorphosis" (tr. of Denisa Comanescu, w. Adam J. Sorkin). [Kalliope] (15:2)
    93, p. 18.
"Atlas" (tr. of Denisa Comanescu, w. Adam J. Sorkin). [Kalliope] (15:2) 93, p. 16.
"Impoverished Land" (tr. of Denisa Comanescu, w. Adam J. Sorkin). [Kalliope]
    (15:2) 93, p. 16.
"Leaving Port" (tr. of Denisa Comanescu, w. Adam J. Sorkin). [Kalliope] (15:2) 93,
    p. 16.
"Unforgiving Joy" (tr. of Denisa Comanescu, w. Adam J. Sorkin). [Kalliope] (15:2)
    93, p. 17.
JIAXIN, Wang
    See WANG, Jiaxin
JIE, Wen
    See WEN, Jie
JIM BILL
    See BILL, Jim
3173. JIMÉNEZ, Félix
"Nocturne of the Rose" (for José Gorostiza, tr. of Xavier Villaurrutia). [GrandS]
    (12:1, #45) 93, p. 172-173.
3174. JIMENEZ CORRETJER, Zoé
"Laberintos" (from "Peomanaciones"). [Luz] (5) N 93, p. 60-63.
3175. JIN, Ha
"I Woke Up — Smiling" (to L.Y.). [Agni] (37) 93, p. 150-151.
"My Mother Also Ate" (for Joey Wolenski). [Agni] (38) 93, p. 21.
"On a Pottery Figure of a Storyteller from the Eastern Han Dynasty (A.D. 25-220)."
    [Agni] (38) 93, p. 20.

3176. JIN, Zhong
"Change" (tr. of Jiaxin Wang, w. Stephen Haven). [AmerPoR] (22:6) N-D 93, p. 38.
"Facing a Stone" (tr. of Moi Fei, w. Stephen Haven). [AmerPoR] (22:6) N-D 93, p. 34.
"Falling Snow" (tr. of Moi Fei, w. Stephen Haven). [AmerPoR] (22:6) N-D 93, p. 34.
"In England" (tr. of Duo Duo, w. Stephen Haven). [AmerPoR] (22:6) N-D 93, p. 36.
"Instant" (tr. of Moi Fei, w. Stephen Haven). [AmerPoR] (22:6) N-D 93, p. 34.
"Iron" (tr. of Jiaxin Wang, w. Stephen Haven). [AmerPoR] (22:6) N-D 93, p. 38.
"It Is" (tr. of Duo Duo, w. Stephen Haven). [AmerPoR] (22:6) N-D 93, p. 35.
"Longevity" (tr. of Duo Duo, w. Stephen Haven). [AmerPoR] (22:6) N-D 93, p. 35.
"One Story Contains All His Past" (tr. of Duo Duo, w. Stephen Haven). [AmerPoR] (22:6) N-D 93, p. 36.
"Orchard" (tr. of Moi Fei, w. Stephen Haven). [AmerPoR] (22:6) N-D 93, p. 34.
"Railway Station" (tr. of Jiaxin Wang, w. Stephen Haven). [AmerPoR] (22:6) N-D 93, p. 37.
"Staircase" (written in my old home at the Gate of Peace, tr. of Jiaxin Wang, w. Stephen Haven). [AmerPoR] (22:6) N-D 93, p. 37.
"That Stone" (tr. of Moi Fei, w. Stephen Haven). [AmerPoR] (22:6) N-D 93, p. 34.
"The Window That Loves to Weep" (tr. of Duo Duo, w. Stephen Haven). [AmerPoR] (22:6) N-D 93, p. 36.
JINGRONG, Chen
    See CHEN, Jingrong
JIPING, Dong
    See DONG, Jiping
3177. JOCKO
"Strange Attractors and the Failure of Simple and Complex Systems." [AntigR] (92) Wint 93, p. 33-34.
"Uphill Struggle." [AntigR] (92) Wint 93, p. 32.
3178. JOCSON, Antonio (Antonio L.)
"A Cure for Smell." [Nimrod] (37:1) Fall-Wint 93, p. 115-116.
"Little Boar's Head." [SpoonR] (18:2) Sum-Fall 93, p. 28-30.
"Monday's End." [Nimrod] (37:1) Fall-Wint 93, p. 117.
"Origami." [PoetL] (88:3) Fall 93, p. 37.
"Prelude to a Miracle." [Sonora] (26) Fall 93, p. 74-75.
3179. JOE, Rita
"Apiksiktuaqn" (To forgive, be forgiven). [PraS] (67:4) Wint 93, p. 82.
"In Order of Line." [PraS] (67:4) Wint 93, p. 81.
3180. JOENS, Harley
"Maple Tree Suffering the County Home." [Northeast] (5:9) Wint 93-94, p. 13.
3181. JOHANSEN, Douglas L.
"Rites in the Bay." [DenQ] (28:1) Sum 93, p. 35.
3182. JOHLER, Walt
"Fantasy." [Wind] (23:72) 93, p. 5.
"Moonup." [Wind] (23:72) 93, p. 5.
3183. JOHNSON, Allen, Jr.
"Perfect Summer Dream." [Light] (6) Sum 93, p. 7.
3184. JOHNSON, Amryl
"By Any Other Name." [13thMoon] (12:1/2) 93-94, p. 100.
"Dual Vision." [13thMoon] (12:1/2) 93-94, p. 94-96.
"Island Woman." [13thMoon] (12:1/2) 93-94, p. 97-98.
"Used to Be." [13thMoon] (12:1/2) 93-94, p. 99.
"Wayward Ballerina." [13thMoon] (12:1/2) 93-94, p. 92-93.
3185. JOHNSON, B. R.
"A Woman's Word." [HolCrit] (30:4) O 93, p. 17.
3186. JOHNSON, Bernard
"Again Kosovo" (tr. of Miodrag Pavlovic). [NoDaQ] (61:1) Wint 93, p. 122-123.
"Barbarians" (tr. of Jovan Hristic). [NoDaQ] (61:1) Wint 93, p. 81.
"Orators Make Speeches on the Squares" (tr. of Jovan Hristic). [NoDaQ] (61:1) Wint 93, p. 82.
"Scout" (tr. of Miodrag Pavlovic). [NoDaQ] (61:1) Wint 93, p. 121-122.
"Socrates on the Battlefield" (tr. of Jovan Hristic). [NoDaQ] (61:1) Wint 93, p. 80.
"Who Still Needs Find Stories?" (tr. of Jovan Hristic). [NoDaQ] (61:1) Wint 93, p. 80.
3187. JOHNSON, Brian (Brian C.)
"Night-Blindness." [ProseP] (2) 93, p. 51.

"The School." [ProseP] (1) 92, p. 46.
"Tale." [Caliban] (13) 93, p. 86.
3188. JOHNSON, Cary Alan
"Numbers." [Art&Und] (2:1) Ja-F 93, p. 25.
3189. JOHNSON, Clifford
"Boys in treetops." [BlackBR] (17) Sum-Fall 93, p. 36.
"Outside tent's screen." [BlackBR] (17) Sum-Fall 93, p. 36.
"White duck frozen in the river's edge." [BlackBR] (17) Sum-Fall 93, p. 36.
3190. JOHNSON, Edward
"America's Game" (for Marge Schott). [Spitball] (45) Fall 93, p. 3.
3191. JOHNSON, Greg
"Heat Wave." [MichQR] (32:1) Wint 93, p. 137.
"Künstlerroman." [Shen] (43:3) Fall 93, p. 96-97.
"Last Request." [OntR] (39) Fall-Wint 93-94, p. 66.
"Lines on Turning Forty." [Poetry] (161:5) F 93, p. 255.
"Somewhere in Georgia." [SoCarR] (25:2) Spr 93, p. 124-125.
"Vanity." [MichQR] (32:1) Wint 93, p. 136.
3192. JOHNSON, Halvard
"La Fauvette des Jardins." [Vis] (42) 93, p. 22.
3193. JOHNSON, Helene
"Trees at Night" (illustrated by Lucy D. Rosenfeld). [MassR] (34:2) Sum 93, p. 250 -
251.
3194. JOHNSON, Jacqueline
"BMC Blues." [Drumvoices] (3:1/2) Fall-Wint 93-94, p. 28.
"Sister Sukie II" (For SJ). [Drumvoices] (3:1/2) Fall-Wint 93-94, p. 29.
3195. JOHNSON, Jim
"The Doctor Said He Suffered a Stroke, in Those Days There Were Many Strokes."
[ProseP] (2) 93, p. 52.
"Headwaters." [NorthStoneR] (11) 93, p. 31.
"Spruce Hen." [ProseP] (1) 92, p. 48.
"The Things a Man Keeps." [ProseP] (1) 92, p. 47.
"Two Horses." [ProseP] (2) 93, p. 53.
3196. JOHNSON, Marael
"Bio-Degrading." [ChironR] (12:1, #34) Spr 93, p. 7.
"Fait Accomplis." [ChironR] (12:1, #34) Spr 93, p. 7.
"Material Girl." [ChironR] (12:1, #34) Spr 93, p. 7.
"Memory Jog." [SlipS] (13) 93, p. 30.
"Mirror Kill Drug." [SlipS] (13) 93, p. 31.
"My Good Performance." [ChironR] (12:1, #34) Spr 93, p. 7.
"Pregnant Pos." [ChironR] (12:1, #34) Spr 93, p. 7.
3197. JOHNSON, Mark Allan
"Alone." [BellArk] (9:2) Mr-Ap 93, p. 7.
"Biscuits and Jam." [BellArk] (9:4) Jl-Ag 93, p. 13.
"Bouquet." [BellArk] (9:6) N-D 93, p. 12.
"Canto XLII." [BellArk] (9:1) Ja-F 93, p. 20.
"Fish Story." [BellArk] (9:6) N-D 93, p. 12.
"From the Earth to the Moon." [BellArk] (9:3) My-Je 93, p. 24.
"The Haunting." [BellArk] (9:1) Ja-F 93, p. 20.
"My Dentist Defends Creationism." [BellArk] (9:1) Ja-F 93, p. 20.
"Perfection." [BellArk] (9:2) Mr-Ap 93, p. 7.
"Recovery." [BellArk] (9:5) S-O 93, p. 11.
"Resurrection." [BellArk] (9:2) Mr-Ap 93, p. 7.
"The Road Not Taken." [BellArk] (9:2) Mr-Ap 93, p. 7.
"Sea Change." [BellArk] (9:1) Ja-F 93, p. 20.
"Solstice." [BellArk] (9:2) Mr-Ap 93, p. 7.
"Still Life." [BellArk] (9:1) Ja-F 93, p. 20.
"Sunday Drive." [BellArk] (9:2) Mr-Ap 93, p. 7.
"Sweet Hitchhiker." [BellArk] (9:5) S-O 93, p. 11.
3198. JOHNSON, Michael (Michael L.)
"The City Is Dead" (tr. of Antonio Colinas). [LitR] (36:3) Spr 93, p. 367.
"From a Child of the Provinces Who Wound Up Livng in a Chagall" (Excerpt, tr. of
Blanca Andreu). [LitR] (36:3) Spr 93, p. 358.
"In Toledo" (tr. of Carlos Sahagún). [LitR] (36:3) Spr 93, p. 382.
"Insomnia" (tr. of Carlos Sahagún). [LitR] (36:3) Spr 93, p. 381.
"Leda" (tr. of Rainer Maria Rilke). [SoCoast] (15) Je 93, p. 39.

237

"Night beyond the Night" (Excerpt, tr. of Antonio Colinas). [LitR] (36:3) Spr 93, p. 366.
"On the Reservation." [Hellas] (4:2) Fall 93, p. 68.
"The Path Blocked by Woods" (tr. of Antonio Colinas). [LitR] (36:3) Spr 93, p. 365 - 366.
"Portrait of Bather" (Excerpt, tr. of Julio Llamazares). [LitR] (36:3) Spr 93, p. 376.
"Reinventing Tradition in Malawi." [Bogg] (66) Wint 92-93, p. 61.
"Sands" (tr. of Carlos Sahagún). [LitR] (36:3) Spr 93, p. 382.
"The Slowness of Oxen" (Excerpt, tr. of Julio Llamazares). [LitR] (36:3) Spr 93, p. 375.
"The Triumph of Idleness" (tr. of Francisco Brines). [LitR] (36:3) Spr 93, p. 361.
3199. JOHNSON, Monique
"Sometimes Hope" (3rd Prize, 7th Annual Contest). [SoCoast] (14) Ja 93, p. 24.
3200. JOHNSON, Nancy
"Meat Counter in Winter." [ApalQ] (38) 92, p. 72-73.
3201. JOHNSON, Nicholas
"My Father's Glass Eye." [Journal] (17:2) Fall-Wint 93, p. 67-68.
3202. JOHNSON, Peter
"19th Hole Condom Poem." [WormR] (33:3, #131), 93, p. 107.
"Five Sure Ways Toward Self-Actualization." [WormR] (33:3, #131), 93, p. 108.
"The Scholar." [WormR] (33:3, #131), 93, p. 108-109.
3203. JOHNSON, Pyke, Jr.
"The Paolo Poems" (dedicated to Paolo Santonocito, second grade, Old Greenwich, CT). [Light] (7) Aut 93, p. 21.
3204. JOHNSON, Sheila Golburgh
"Desert Love." [Writer] (106:10) O 93, p. 25.
"Sighting the Sandhill Crane." [Plain] (13:2) Wint 93, p. 26.
3205. JOHNSON, Stacey Land
"Day of the Dead." [GrandS] (12:1, #45) 93, p. 132-133.
"Texas and Eternity." [Ploughs] (19:1) Spr 93, p. 121.
3206. JOHNSON, Susan
"In the Telling." [Pearl] (17) Spr 93, p. 106.
"Voyager." [GreensboroR] (55) Wint 93-94, p. 88.
3207. JOHNSON, Trasi
"Flight of the Blind Bird." [Agni] (37) 93, p. 248-249.
"The Secret." [Callaloo] (16:3) Sum 93, p. 534-535.
3208. JOHNSON, William
"Late Autumn Run." [PoetryNW] (34:3) Aut 93, p. 11-12.
"Long Body of America." [DenQ] (28:1) Sum 93, p. 36.
3209. JOHNSTON, Andrew
"The Lost Town." [Verse] (10:1) Spr 93, p. 16.
"New House." [Verse] (10:1) Spr 93, p. 15.
"Time Slides." [Verse] (10:1) Spr 93, p. 16.
3210. JOHNSTON, Arnie
"Double Sonnet: Sunday Drive." [Outbr] (24) 93, p. 62.
"Moon Goddess." [Outbr] (24) 93, p. 61.
3211. JOHNSTON, Arnold
"The Poet Gives a Reading." [Elf] (3:1) Spr 93, p. 31.
3212. JOHNSTON, Fred
"My Grandfather in the Back Room." [Grain] (21:1) Spr 93, p. 125.
"The Night Café." [Grain] (21:1) Spr 93, p. 124.
"Voices of the Fathers." [CreamCR] (17:1) Spr 93, p. 71.
3213. JOHNSTON, Jerry
"Miss X" (tr. of Jaime Sabines, w. Christopher Merrill). [RiverS] (39) 93, p. 63.
3214. JOHNSTON, Mark
"At the Drive-In: Winter, 1962." [ChironR] (12:3, #36) Aut 93, p. 15.
"Not the Female Body." [CumbPR] (12:2) Spr 93, p. 34.
"Teaching My Son to Ride His Bike." [SoDakR] (31:2) Sum 93, p. 121-122.
3215. JOHNSTON, Sue Ann
"Fleeing from Baghdad." [Event] (22:2) Sum 93, p. 13.
"Grace." [AntigR] (93-94) Spr-Sum 93, p. 64.
3216. JOLLIFF, William
"Able Hall's Belgiums." [CutB] (39) Wint 93, p. 77.
"Covenant." [HawaiiR] (16:3, #36) Wint 93, p. 64.
"Dr. Kenton Prepares to Run Off to the Creek Again, This Time Dead." [CumbPR] (12:2) Spr 93, p. 57.

"The Farmer from the Mill House Door." [HawaiiR] (16:3, #36) Wint 93, p. 67.
"Feed Beetles." [PaintedB] (49) 93, p. 29.
"For My Son in Mariner Valley" (A Martian Reverie). [Poem] (69) My 93, p. 10.
"A History of Stone." [Poem] (69) My 93, p. 11.
"Merle Haggard, Two Farmers, *The End of the World*" (to Charlie Barrett and Kirk
    Schultz, wherever you are). [WritersF] (19) 93, p. 133.
"Reaching for the Latch." [PaintedB] (49) 93, p. 28.
"The Theologian Talks Baseball" (for John Yeatts). [ChrC] (110:11) 7 Apr 93, p.
    374.
"Tuesday Afternoon, the M & M Tavern." [CumbPR] (12:2) Spr 93, p. 58.
3217. JOLLIMORE, Troy
"Tobekobekon." [MalR] (105) Wint 93, p. 81.
3218. JONAS, Stephen
"IX. Get bombed, piss'd in face." [Talisman] (11) Fall 93, p. 17.
"XII. 'She' only wanted to get up in female attire." [Talisman] (11) Fall 93, p. 17.
"XIII. See by my third eye." [Talisman] (11) Fall 93, p. 18.
"XIV. Those who cultivate their manhood." [Talisman] (11) Fall 93, p. 18.
"XVII. The Sun's rays come in lance over lance." [Talisman] (11) Fall 93, p. 18.
"XXIII. You kno, honey, it's great when ya got ya brandnew money." [Talisman]
    (11) Fall 93, p. 18-19.
"XXVIII. When big daddy Chronos." [Talisman] (11) Fall 93, p. 19-20.
"XXXV. Oh no, you have to keep the lights burning." [Talisman] (11) Fall 93, p. 20.
"XXXVI. Say God came back." [Talisman] (11) Fall 93, p. 20-21.
3219. JONES, Alice
"Beyond Hunger." [Sequoia] (34/35) 92-93, p. 35.
"The Foot." [Zyzzyva] (9:1) Spr 93, p. 55.
"The Guts." [Zyzzyva] (9:1) Spr 93, p. 54.
"Inside Out." [KenR] (NS 15:3) Sum 93, p. 156.
"The Larynx." [Zyzzyva] (9:1) Spr 93, p. 53.
"Offering." [KenR] (NS 15:3) Sum 93, p. 157-158.
"The Taboo." [MassR] (34:3) Aut 93, p. 430.
"The Voice." [MassR] (34:3) Aut 93, p. 429.
3220. JONES, Amy
"Period" (w. Jil P. Weaving). [WestCL] (27:1, #10) Spr 93, p. 75-82.
3221. JONES, Bill
"The Perfect American Poem." [Border] (2) Spr 93, p. 39.
3222. JONES, Billy
"50:50" (Selections: 9, 17). [WormR] (33:1, #129) 93, p. 15.
"Conservation Framing Co." [WormR] (33:1, #129) 93, p. 16.
"Drinking with Sparrows." [WormR] (33:1, #129) 93, p. 16.
"Looks Like Rain." [WormR] (33:1, #129) 93, p. 14.
"Love." [WormR] (33:1, #129) 93, p. 14.
"Love Poems." [WormR] (33:1, #129) 93, p. 15.
"Making Up." [WormR] (33:1, #129) 93, p. 16.
"Mary Smokes, 2." [WormR] (33:1, #129) 93, p. 13.
"Poem for Isaac Shams." [WormR] (33:1, #129) 93, p. 14.
3223. JONES, Charlene D.
"Wisewoman." [PraS] (67:4) Wint 93, p. 83.
3224. JONES, Francis R.
"Byzantium" (tr. of Ivan V. Lalic). [NoDaQ] (61:1) Wint 93, p. 101-102.
"Byzantium" (tr. of Ivan V. Lalic). [NoDaQ] (61:1) Wint 93, p. 101-102.
"Last News of the Little Box" (tr. of Vasko Popa). [NoDaQ] (61:1) Wint 93, p. 131.
"The Little Box" (tr. of Vasko Popa). [NoDaQ] (61:1) Wint 93, p. 129.
"The Little Box's Admirers" (tr. of Vasko Popa). [NoDaQ] (61:1) Wint 93, p. 129 -
    130.
"The Little Box's Prisoners" (tr. of Vasko Popa). [NoDaQ] (61:1) Wint 93, p. 130.
"The Stone Sleeper" (Selections: 2 poems, tr. of Mak Dizdar). [NoDaQ] (61:1) Wint
    93, p. 59-62.
"The Voice Singing in the Gardens" (tr. of Ivan V. Lalic). [NoDaQ] (61:1) Wint 93,
    p. 100-101.
3225. JONES, Ginger
"Crossing." [SouthernHR] (27:3) Sum 93, p. 218.
"For the Book Reviewer Who Laughed." [SouthernHR] (27:2) Spr 93, p. 165.
3226. JONES, Ira B.
"Alley Games / the Awakening." [Obs] (8:2) Fall-Wint 93, p. 111.
"Alley Games 13." [Drumvoices] (2:1/2) Fall-Wint 92-93, p. 198.

3227. JONES, Jake-ann
"Ten Years After Michael." [Eyeball] (2) 93, p. 30-32.
3228. JONES, Jill
"At the Window of a Stranger's House." [Nimrod] (36:2) Spr-Sum 93, p. 56.
"Carnival of the New Colonies." [Vis] (42) 93, p. 13.
"The Desert." [Nimrod] (36:2) Spr-Sum 93, p. 57.
"Inside and Outside Houses." [Nimrod] (36:2) Spr-Sum 93, p. 55.
3229. JONES, John
"On the Flyleaf of Cavafy's Complete Poems." [HangL] (62) 93, p. 29.
"Sonnet for David (Horny Neighbor)." [HangL] (62) 93, p. 29.
3230. JONES, Jordan
"After" (tr. of René Daumal). [Asylum] (8) 93, p. 84.
"Coldly" (tr. of René Daumal). [Asylum] (8) 93, p. 81-82.
"Disillusion" (tr. of René Daumal). [Asylum] (8) 93, p. 82.
"No More" (tr. of René Daumal). [Asylum] (8) 93, p. 85-86.
"Prefatory Nymph" (tr. of René Daumal). [Asylum] (8) 93, p. 81.
"To Nothingness" (tr. of René Daumal). [Asylum] (8) 93, p. 83-84.
"Zen Baker." [PaintedHR] (9) Spr 93, p. 32.
3231. JONES, Leslea Mosher
"Wizard." [AnthNEW] (5) 93, p. 24.
3232. JONES, Mavis
"Anatolia." [TickleAce] (25) Spr-Sum 93, p. 198.
"Connie's Story." [Event] (22:2) Sum 93, p. 14-15.
"In Those Days." [Event] (22:2) Sum 93, p. 16-17.
"On the Antalya Road." [TickleAce] (25) Spr-Sum 93, p. 197.
3233. JONES, Patricia Spears
"Officially Lent." [KenR] (NS 15:4) Fall 93, p. 65-66.
"Sly and the Family Stone under the Big Tit, Atlanta, 1973." [KenR] (NS 15:4) Fall
93, p. 66-68.
3234. JONES, Paul
"Better Tomorrow." [Poetry] (162:3) Je 93, p. 127-128.
"Constellations." [SouthernPR] (33:2) Fall 93, p. 51-52.
"Fatherhood in Middle Age." [Hellas] (4:1) Spr 93, p. 19.
3235. JONES, Richard
"The Black Snake." [OnTheBus] (5:2, #12) Sum-Fall 93, p. 101-102.
"The Hermit." [GreenMR] (NS 6:2) Sum-Fall 93, p. 86-87.
"If I Should Die." [OnTheBus] (5:2, #12) Sum-Fall 93, p. 102.
"My Mother's Handkerchief." [AnotherCM] (25) Spr 93, p. 62-67.
"My Sister's Garden." [Pequod] (36) 93, p. 96-97.
"Pirandellos' Shirt." [CreamCR] (17:1) Spr 93, p. 52-53.
"The Remedy." [WillowR] (20) Spr 93, p. 44-47.
"The Test." [AnotherCM] (25) Spr 93, p. 68-70.
"That Evening." [OnTheBus] (5:2, #12) Sum-Fall 93, p. 100-101.
"Today I Am Wearing a Suit." [Agni] (38) 93, p. 134-136.
3236. JONES, Robert
"Diabetes" (for Jessica). [CapeR] (28:2) Fall 93, p. 38.
"Victorian Cemetery." [CapeR] (28:2) Fall 93, p. 37.
3237. JONES, Rodney
"Contempt." [MichQR] (32:2) Spr 93, p. 249-252.
"Counting Potatoes." [GeoR] (47:3) Fall 93, p. 543.
"Diplomacy." [Chelsea] (55) 93, p. 55-56.
"Failed Memory Exercise." [Chelsea] (55) 93, p. 56-58.
"Fantasia of the Bride." [AmerPoR] (22:6) N-D 93, p. 55.
"The First Brith." [NewEngR] (15:1) Wint 93, p. 149-150.
"Hollywood." [DenQ] (28:1) Sum 93, p. 37-38.
"The Privilege." [Chelsea] (55) 93, p. 58-59.
"Shame the Monsters." [GrandS] (11:4, #44) 93, p. 118-119.
"Threads." [Pequod] (36) 93, p. 98-100.
3238. JONES, Roger
"Contrary." [HampSPR] Wint 93, p. 39.
"The Kite." [Border] (2) Spr 93, p. 40.
"Owl." [ColEng] (55:7) N 93, p. 784.
"Pollen." [Border] (2) Spr 93, p. 41.
"Seafood." [HampSPR] Wint 93, p. 39.
3239. JONES, Seaborn
"First Words." [Pearl] (17) Spr 93, p. 121.

JONES

240

"Six of Diamonds." [Pearl] (17) Spr 93, p. 21.
"This Poem Is Not For You." [RiverS] (37) 93, p. 24.
"World War II." [RiverS] (37) 93, p. 22-23.
JONES, Teruko Anderson
    See ANDERSON-JONES, Teruko
3240. JONES-HENDRICKSON, S. B.
    "Screaming in Our Hearts." [CaribbeanW] (7) 93, p. 49-50.
JONG, Daphne de
    See De JONG, Daphne
JOON, Park
    See PARK, Joon
3241. JOPP, Jessica
    "The History of a Voice" (The 1993 Baxter Hathaway Prize in Poetry: A selection
        from the winning book-length manuscript, with a statement by the judge,
        Alice Fulton). [Epoch] (42:3) 93, p. 283-305.
3242. JORDAN, André
    "Powell Street Lines." [PoetL] (88:3) Fall 93, p. 52.
3243. JORDAN, Barbara
    "Menteth Glen" (for D.R.). [HarvardR] (4) Spr 93, p. 55.
3244. JORDAN, June
    "Poem for Haruko" (from "Haruko/Love Poems"). [Nat] (257:1) 5 Jl 93, p. 40.
    "Poem on the Quantum Mechanics of Breakfast with Haruko" (from "Haruko/Love
        Poems"). [Nat] (257:1) 5 Jl 93, p. 40.
    "Why I Became a Pacifist" (from "Haruko/Love Poems"). [Nat] (257:1) 5 Jl 93, p.
        40.
3245. JORDAN, MaryKate
    "Second Sight." [BellArk] (9:2) Mr-Ap 93, p. 9.
    "Time in a Bottle." [BellArk] (9:1) Ja-F 93, p. 21.
3246. JORON, Andrew
    "Boreal." [Caliban] (13) 93, p. 88-89.
    "Fate Map." [Zyzzyva] (9:4) Wint 93, p. 137-138.
    "Focus Throws." [Talisman] (10) Spr 93, p. 100.
    "Le Nombre des Ombres." [Caliban] (13) 93, p. 87.
    "Seven Gnomonic Measurements." [Talisman] (11) Fall 93, p. 206-208.
3247. JOSEPH, Allison
    "Adolescence." [SpoonR] (18:1) Wint-Spr 93, p. 108.
    "Benediction" (for writers). [Pearl] (17) Spr 93, p. 112.
    "Depots." [Plain] (14:1) Fall 93, p. 10-11.
    "For Those Who Have Asked" (A Plainsongs Award Poem). [Plain] (13:3) Spr 93,
        p. 36-37.
    "Good Humor." [Agni] (37) 93, p. 102-103.
    "Home Girl Steps Out." [GreenMR] (NS 6:1) Wint-Spr 93, p. 110-111.
    "Hospitals." [PaintedHR] (9) Spr 93, p. 28-29.
    "The Inner Life." [Agni] (37) 93, p. 100-101.
    "Inquiry." [OnTheBus] (5:2, #12) Sum-Fall 93, p. 103-104.
    "Living in Someone Else's House." [Plain] (13:2) Wint 93, p. 27.
    "Night Song." [Poem] (69) My 93, p. 22-23.
    "Sweet Soul Music." [GreenMR] (NS 6:1) Wint-Spr 93, p. 112-113.
    "Used Books." [CimR] (103) Ap 93, p. 107-108.
    "Voyage." [Poem] (69) My 93, p. 24-25.
3248. JOSEPH, Lawrence
    "Before Our Eyes." [Verse] (10:2) Sum 93, p. 50-51.
    "In a Fit of My Own Vividness." [Pequod] (35) 93, p. 146.
    "Out of the Blue." [Pequod] (35) 93, p. 144.
    "Over Darkening Gold." [Pequod] (35) 93, p. 147-148.
    "Under a Spell." [Pequod] (35) 93, p. 145.
    "Whose Performance Am I Watching?" [Verse] (10:2) Sum 93, p. 51-52.
3249. JOSHUA, John
    "Paragons in Obscurity." [Plain] (13:3) Spr 93, p. 8.
3250. JOSTS, Ingus
    "First Snow" (tr. of Uldis Berzins). [CimR] (104) Jl 93, p. 39.
    "Moralizing Prose" (tr. of Uldis Berzins). [CimR] (104) Jl 93, p. 39.
JOURNOUD, Claude Royet
    See ROYET-JOURNOUD, Claude
3251. JOY, Eileen A.
    "On the Question of Redemption" (for Maria). [Sun] (213) S 93, p. 37.

241

3252. JOYCE, James
"Never Dreaming He'd Have Two Daughters Die Before Him." [GettyR] (6:4) Aut 93, p. 674-675.
3253. JOYCE, William
"School Days." [WorldL] (4) 93, p. 32-33.
"What the Clouds, the Sky, the Sun, and the Sea Taught Me." [WorldL] (4) 93, p. 30-31.
JUA, CHAKULA CHA (McNeal Cayatte)
See CHAKULA CHA JUA (McNeal Cayatte)
3254. JUDSON, John
"Brule River, Fishing at 60" (for Bob Jackson). [ClockR] (8:1/2) 93, p. 138.
3255. JUGAN, Walis
"Hands and Feet" (tr. by Andrea Lingenfelter). [ChiR] (39:3/4) 93, p. 308-309.
3256. JULIS, Emil
"The dark clouds are getting lower" (tr. by Ellen Rosenbaum). [OxfordM] (9:1) Spr - Sum 93, p. 14.
"The Deserted Kingdom" (tr. by Ellen Rosenbaum). [OxfordM] (9:1) Spr-Sum 93, p. 15.
"Things" (tr. by Ellen Rosenbaum). [OxfordM] (9:1) Spr-Sum 93, p. 14.
"We all go with the flow" (tr. by Ellen Rosenbaum). [OxfordM] (9:1) Spr-Sum 93, p. 15.
3257. JUNG, Brian
"Kandinsky Paints the Deep South." [OnTheBus] (6:1, #13) Wint 93-Spr 94, p. 126.
3258. JUNKINS, Donald
" *Jeu de Boules* at Sunset: Bimini." [GreensboroR] (54) Sum 93, p. 47.
"Out of This Long Waiting and Sleeping." [GreensboroR] (54) Sum 93, p. 48-49.
"Overcast." [AntR] (51:4) Fall 93, p. 553.
3259. JUSTICE, Donald
"In the Attic." [NewEngR] (15:1) Wint 93, p. 151.
"Thinking About the Past." [NewEngR] (15:1) Wint 93, p. 152.
3260. JUSTICE, Laura Denise
"In the Beginning" (for Karl Scheibe). [EvergreenC] (8:2) Sum-Fall 93, p. 39-41.
3261. JUVENAL, et al.
"A Selection of Epigrams" (tr. by Jack Flavin). [SpoonR] (18:1) Wint-Spr 93, p. 41.
3262. KACIAN, Jim
"Diptera." [BelPoJ] (44:1) Fall 93, p. 18-19.
"A Sonnet for Philip Glass." [BelPoJ] (44:1) Fall 93, p. 17.
3263. KACZMARSKYJ, Vera
"Blessed Is He Who Divided into Clean and Unclean" (for Vasyl' Fl'orka, tr. of Ihor Rymaruk). [Pequod] (36) 93, p. 117.
"Diva Obyda" (tr. of Ihor Rymaruk). [Pequod] (36) 93, p. 108.
"I don't Know Where You Came From" (tr. of Ihor Rymaruk). [Pequod] (36) 93, p. 109.
"What Do You See There, Brother" (tr. of Ihor Rymaruk). [Pequod] (36) 93, p. 110.
"You Truly Did Not Imagine It" (tr. of Ihor Rymaruk). [Pequod] (36) 93, p. 111 - 116.
3264. KAER, Krista
"In Retreat" (tr. of Peep Ilmet). [CimR] (104) Jl 93, p. 59.
"Normal People" (tr. of Paul-Eerik Rummo). [CimR] (104) Jl 93, p. 57.
"The Oak Screams Out" (tr. of Peep Ilmet). [CimR] (104) Jl 93, p. 58.
"An Ordinary Madman" (tr. of Paul-Eerik Rummo). [CimR] (104) Jl 93, p. 55.
"The Present Is Like Sailcloth" (tr. of Peep Ilmet). [CimR] (104) Jl 93, p. 58.
"A Quiet Madman" (tr. of Paul-Eerik Rummo). [CimR] (104) Jl 93, p. 55-56.
"A Raving Madman" (tr. of Paul-Eerik Rummo). [CimR] (104) Jl 93, p. 56-57.
3265. KAFATOU, Sarah
"Spring." [HarvardR] (4) Spr 93, p. 37.
3266. KAGEYAMA, Claire
"Dying." [AntR] (51:2) Spr 93, p. 239.
3267. KAHELEMAUNA
"Mau Hawai'i ka Lanakila" (Hawai'i is preserved with victory, tr. by Lilikala Kame'eleihiwa). [HawaiiR] (16:3, #36) Wint 93, p. 14-15.
3268. KAHN, Wilma
"In Memoriam" (For Eric, August 26, 1992). [Art&Und] (2:3) Special Edition 93, p. 10.
"She Said, 'You Are Your Own Worst Enemy'." [13thMoon] (12:1/2) 93-94, p. 36 - 37.

3269. KAISER, Mifanwy (Mifanwy Patricia)
"Coming to Know." [OnTheBus] (5:2, #12) Sum-Fall 93, p. 105-107.
"The Last Dance Saved." [OnTheBus] (6:1, #13) Wint 93-Spr 94, p. 129-131.
"Now I'm Forty-five." [OnTheBus] (6:1, #13) Wint 93-Spr 94, p. 127-129.
"Spaces." [OnTheBus] (6:1, #13) Wint 93-Spr 94, p. 131-132.
3270. KAJOKAS, Donaldas
"Gates" (tr. by Jonas Zdanys). [CimR] (104) Jl 93, p. 21.
"The Well" (tr. by Jonas Zdanys). [CimR] (104) Jl 93, p. 21.
3271. KALAMARAS, George
"18 Past 6." [OnTheBus] (5:2, #12) Sum-Fall 93, p. 108.
3272. KALIKOFF, Beth
"Famous Vegetarians" (3 poems). [ColEng] (55:4) Ap 93, p. 434-436.
KALINSKA, Katarzyna Turaj
See TURAJ-KALINSKA, Katarzyna
3273. KALINSKI, Todd
"Is This What Hemingway Meant?" [CoalC] (7) Apr 93, p. 25.
"Stimulating Yr Gone Relationship." [Pearl] (19) Fall-Wint 93, p. 68.
"What a Gas It Was." [ChironR] (12:4/13:1, #37/38) Wint 93-Spr 94, p. 25.
3274. KALLEBERG, Garrett
"The Garden." [GlobalCR] (2) Fall 93, p. 93-94.
"They Obey the Same Signal." [GlobalCR] (2) Fall 93, p. 95-96.
3275. KAMAL, Daud
"Blindfolded Bull" (tr. of Ahmad Nadeem Qasimi). [Vis] (43) 93, p. 55.
"Visitors" (tr. of Faiz Ahmad Faiz). [Vis] (43) 93, p. 55.
3276. KAMAU, H. B.
"Death of a Black Bird." [ChangingM] (26) Sum-Fall 93, p. 39.
"Even Though I Waited." [ChangingM] (26) Sum-Fall 93, p. 20.
3277. KAME'ELEIHIWA, Lilikala
"'A'ole Hopo iho o Hawai'i" (Hawai'i is not fearful, tr. of S. Pinao). [HawaiiR] (16:3, #36) Wint 93, p. 15.
"Ho'ohui'aina Pala ka Mai'a" (Annexation is Rotten Bananas, tr. of S. Pinao). [HawaiiR] (16:3, #36) Wint 93, p. 14.
"Mau Hawai'i ka Lanakila" (Hawai'i is preserved with victory, tr. of Kahelemauna). [HawaiiR] (16:3, #36) Wint 93, p. 14-15.
"Mele Ko'ihonua no Lili'u" (A genealogical chant for Lili'u, tr. of Kaula Fisheye). [HawaiiR] (16:3, #36) Wint 93, p. 13.
3278. KAMINSKY, Marc
"For Kivi." [HangL] (62) 93, p. 30-36.
"Shiva for Kivi." [HangL] (62) 93, p. 37.
3279. KANASTOGA, Wasabi
"El Elvis." [ColR] (20:2) Fall 93, p. 62-63.
3280. KANCHEV, Nikolai
"Seventh Heaven Can Be Seen at First Glance" (tr. by Lisa Sapinkopf, w. Georgi Belev). [Agni] (37) 93, p. 261.
3281. KANDRE, Mare
"Who Knows Where It Comes From?" [Gypsy] (20) Sum 93, p. 17.
3282. KANE, Beata
"Inevitable Meetings" (tr. of Ewa Parma, w. Linda Nemec Foster). [InterPR] (19:2) Fall 93, p. 67.
"Karol's Bridge in Prague, Watercolor" (tr. of Ewa Parma, w. Linda Nemec Foster). [ArtfulD] (24/25) 93, p. 12.
"Ode to My Knee" (or, I Love Reminiscing, tr. of Ewa Parma, w. Linda Nemec Foster). [InterPR] (19:2) Fall 93, p. 63.
"On the Way" (for prophets, poets, visionaries and Miss Holly Golightly in her journey, tr. of Ewa Parma, w. Linda Nemec Foster). [InterPR] (19:2) Fall 93, p. 65.
3283. KANE, Jean
"Alda on the Street." [SoDakR] (31:3) Fall 93, p. 53-54.
"In Ireland, Shabby Boats Move On." [SoDakR] (31:3) Fall 93, p. 50-51.
"In the Night Kitchen on Emerson Street." [SoDakR] (31:3) Fall 93, p. 52.
3284. KANE, Paul
"Disciples Asleep at Gethsemane." [ParisR] (35:127) Sum 93, p. 42-43.
"Mere Islands." [ParisR] (35:127) Sum 93, p. 44-45.
"Time Was." [ParisR] (35:127) Sum 93, p. 43.
3285. KANG, Un-kyo
"Evening Wind" (tr. by Chang Soo Ko). [Vis] (43) 93, p. 31.

3286. KANGAS, J. R.
"Cut!" [PoetC] (24:2) Wint 93, p. 37.
3287. KANTCHEV, Nikolai
"A Dog's Life" (tr. by Theodore Weiss). [QRL] (12:32/33) 93, p. 204.
"Miracle" (tr. by Theodore Weiss). [QRL] (12:32/33) 93, p. 205.
"O" (tr. by Theodore Weiss). [QRL] (12:32/33) 93, p. 205.
"Snowman" (tr. by Theodore Weiss). [QRL] (12:32/33) 93, p. 206.
"A Starling" (tr. by Theodore Weiss). [QRL] (12:32/33) 93, p. 205.
"To Nail the Evening" (tr. by Theodore Weiss). [QRL] (12:32/33) 93, p. 204.
3288. KANYADI, Sándor
"Bell Inscription" (Ars Poetica, tr. by Bruce Berlind, w. Mária Körösy). [WillowS]
(33) Wint 93, p. 23.
"Mane and Skull" (a fragment, tr. by Bruce Berlind, w. Mária Körösy). [WillowS]
(33) Wint 93, p. 22.
3289. KAPLAN, Allan
"The Exiled Poet Nazim Hikmet Writes a Letter to His Country from Varna,
Bulgaria, a Year Before His Death in 1963." [ApalQ] (38) 92, p. 60-62.
3290. KAPLAN, Joy
"When she is born" (Poets of High School Age). [HangL] (62) 93, p. 78-80.
3291. KAPOOR, Suman K.
"Think Without Words." [GrandS] (12:1, #45) 93, p. 134-135.
3292. KARAGEORGE, Yuri Vidov
"Burgas" (tr. of Snezhina Slavova). [CimR] (102) Ja 93, p. 25.
"Fall" (tr. of Elisaveta Bagryana). [CimR] (102) Ja 93, p. 20.
"Fresh Snow" (tr. of Nevena Stefanova). [CimR] (102) Ja 93, p. 21.
"Horizons" (tr. of Elisaveta Bagryana). [CimR] (102) Ja 93, p. 18.
"Paris" (tr. of Elisaveta Bagryana). [CimR] (102) Ja 93, p. 19-20.
"Parting" (tr. of Snezhina Slavova). [CimR] (102) Ja 93, p. 24.
"Plovdiv" (tr. of Snezhina Slavova). [CimR] (102) Ja 93, p. 23-24.
"The Reason of Nature" (tr. of Nevena Stefanova). [CimR] (102) Ja 93, p. 22.
"What Would It Have Been?" (tr. of Nevena Stefanova). [CimR] (102) Ja 93, p. 21.
3293. KARETNICK, Jen
"Venetian Way." [GreensboroR] (54) Sum 93, p. 32-33.
3294. KAREVA, Doris
"Her Quiet Words Let Loose" (tr. by Toomas H. Ilves). [CimR] (104) Jl 93, p. 60.
"The Night Left a Scent" (tr. by Toomas H. Ilves). [CimR] (104) Jl 93, p. 60.
"There Shall Come No Other and Better World" (tr. by Toomas H. Ilves). [CimR]
(104) Jl 93, p. 61.
3295. KARP, Vickie
"Places You'll Never Go" (for Yehuda Mayer Dym). [NewRep] (209:7) 16 Ag 93, p.
40.
"A Taxi to the Flame." [YaleR] (81:4) O 93, p. 62-63.
3296. KARR, Jay
"The Hunter, Now Butcher, Dances." [Epiphany] (4:2) Ap 93, p. 90.
3297. KARR, Mary
"Grace" (for Marie). [HarvardR] (4) Spr 93, p. 132.
3298. KARR, Muriel
"Abbreviated History of Human Consciousness, 1." [BellArk] (9:5) S-O 93, p. 13.
"Elation Translation for Melinda." [BellArk] (9:5) S-O 93, p. 13.
"Fish Story." [BellArk] (9:2) Mr-Ap 93, p. 14.
"The Grace of Grace." [BellArk] (9:2) Mr-Ap 93, p. 14.
"I Give You Life." [BellArk] (9:1) Ja-F 93, p. 1.
"I Think He's Dead." [PoetryNW] (34:3) Aut 93, p. 41.
"I Win." [BellArk] (9:1) Ja-F 93, p. 1.
"It's Said He'll Die." [PoetryNW] (34:3) Aut 93, p. 40.
"Limitation." [BellArk] (9:2) Mr-Ap 93, p. 14.
"Sail Away." [BellArk] (9:2) Mr-Ap 93, p. 14.
"Shape of Pear." [BellArk] (9:3) My-Je 93, p. 1.
"The Talker the Same." [BellArk] (9:2) Mr-Ap 93, p. 14.
"Then You See." [BellArk] (9:5) S-O 93, p. 13.
"Ting-Lotta." [BellArk] (9:3) My-Je 93, p. 5.
"'Today I Felt Like Matisse,' she Said." [BellArk] (9:2) Mr-Ap 93, p. 14.
"We Belong Together." [BellArk] (9:2) Mr-Ap 93, p. 14.
3299. KASDORF, Julia
"Along Ocean Parkway in Brooklyn." [Field] (48) Spr 93, p. 65-66.
"Ghost." [WestB] (31/32) 93, p. 45-46.

"Sinning." [WestB] (31/32) 93, p. 46-47.
"When Our Women Go Crazy." [Field] (48) Spr 93, p. 66-67.
3300. KASISCHKE, Laura
"Babysitter." [HangL] (62) 93, p. 38-39.
"Conspiracies." [Witness] (7:1) 93, p. 47-49.
"Gawkers Block Traffica After Accident." [Witness] (7:1) 93, p. 40-46.
"Grand Rapids Woman Last Seen at Motel 6." [Epoch] (42:3) 93, p. 318.
"Happy Birthday." [Poetry] (162:2) My 93, p. 88.
"Home." [Epoch] (42:3) 93, p. 314-315.
"House Fable." [Ploughs] (19:4) Wint 93-94, p. 17-18.
"Laundry." [MissouriR] (16:3) 93, p. 102-103.
"Local Legend." [MissouriR] (16:3) 93, p. 107-109.
"Married." [OnTheBus] (5:2, #12) Sum-Fall 93, p. 109.
"Moving Parts." [IndR] (16:1) Spr 93, p. 25-26.
"Plenty." [Epoch] (42:3) 93, p. 316-317.
"Ravine." [IndR] (16:1) Spr 93, p. 23-24.
"River." [BelPoJ] (43:4) Sum 93, p. 32.
"Self-Fulfilling Prophecies." [AnotherCM] (25) Spr 93, p. 71-72.
"Theme Park." [MissouriR] (16:3) 93, p. 110-112.
"Thunder, or A Place in the Sun." [MissouriR] (16:3) 93, p. 104-106.
"The Tribe of Women." [AntR] (51:3) Sum 93, p. 380-382.
"Warning." [MissouriR] (16:3) 93, p. 100-101.
"The Way." [Epoch] (42:3) 93, p. 313.
"The Winter of No Money." [GrahamHR] (17) Fall 93, p. 49-50.
3301. KASZUBA, Sophia
"After the War." [PoetryC] (13:4) 93, p. 7.
"Angels at the Corner." [PoetryC] (13:4) 93, p. 7.
"Cone of Light." [PoetryC] (13:4) 93, p. 7.
"The Engineer." [PoetryC] (13:4) 93, p. 7.
"Fragment From the Age." [Arc] (31) Aut 93, p. 15.
"The Machinery." [Arc] (31) Aut 93, p. 13.
"Pearl Earrings." [AntigR] (92) Wint 93, p. 134.
"Power in Toronto." [AntigR] (92) Wint 93, p. 135.
"The Way Between Them." [Arc] (31) Aut 93, p. 14.
3302. KATES, J. (James, Jim)
"No Need for Bullets, the Heart Explodes on Its Own" (tr. of Tatyana Shcherbina).
[LitR] (37:1) Fall 93, p. 84.
"This wood is bordered by dust and rot" (tr. of Mikhail Aizenberg). [HarvardR] (3)
Wint 93, p. 155.
"Untitled: I sleep in your sweater" (tr. of Tatyana Shcherbina). [PaintedB] (52) 93,
p. 11.
"Untitled: Lightbulbs catch fire. The rooms are full" (tr. of Mikhail Aizenberg).
[RiverS] (39) 93, p. 49.
"Untitled: Take this smudged snapshot for a sign" (tr. of Mikhail Aizenberg).
[RiverS] (39) 93, p. 47.
"What's This Love" (tr. of Alexandra Sozonova). [Vis] (42) 93, p. 24.
3303. KATO, Atsuko
"Poem: It's twilight" (tr. by Akemi Nakamura and Tony Whedon). [GreenMR] (NS
6:2) Sum-Fall 93, p. 72.
3304. KATO, Jukio
"At Toba Seashore" (tr. of Tanikawa Shuntaro, w. Jon Silkin). [Stand] (34:3) Sum
93, p. 50.
3305. KATSIMPALIS, Melissa
"In Thai, This Is Called." [SpoonR] (18:2) Sum-Fall 93, p. 8.
"Racing the Dark Language." [SpoonR] (18:2) Sum-Fall 93, p. 9-10.
"Vivisection" (Life Magazine, Photo Essay, 1960s). [SpoonR] (18:2) Sum-Fall 93,
p. 11-12.
KATSUNORI, Yamazato
See YAMAZATO, Katsunori
3306. KATZ, Daniel S.
"The Goddess." [AntigR] (92) Wint 93, p. 109-110.
3307. KATZ, David M.
"After Coleridge." [SouthwR] (78:1) Wint 93, p. 129.
3308. KATZ, Eliot
"A New Style: Or Would There Be Any Buildings Left Standing If You Crossed a
Post-Structuralist with a Neutron Bomb?" [Footwork] (23) 93, p. 63.

"Post-War Culture." [Footwork] (23) 93, p. 63.
3309. KATZ, Jean
"A Different Poem." [OnTheBus] (6:1, #13) Wint 93-Spr 94, p. 133.
3310. KATZ, Jeffrey
"Putting the House in Order." [SoCoast] (14) Ja 93, p. 6-7.
3311. KATZ, Louise
"Certainly Not." [PennR] (5:2) 93, p. 22.
"Death Sheets." [PennR] (5:2) 93, p. 21.
"Places Like This." [PoetL] (88:2) Sum 93, p. 46.
"When You Were Fifteen." [PennR] (5:2) 93, p. 20.
3312. KATZ, Steven B.
"To the Mystic River Bridge, Boston." [Pembroke] (25) 93, p. 42.
3313. KAUCHER, Candace
"This Wawa Is Out of Applications." [PaintedB] (52) 93, p. 8-9.
3314. KAUFFMAN, Elizabeth Doonan
"An Airplane Is the Silver Cloud" (For Rosy and Roberto Arizmendi, tr. of Luis
Rebaza-Soraluz). [Boulevard] (8:1, #22) Spr 93, p. 185-186.
3315. KAUFFMAN, Janet
"Between the Opera and the Mars Game." [NewAW] (11) Sum-Fall 93, p. 51.
"If the Bicycle Is Painted Blue." [NewAW] (11) Sum-Fall 93, p. 53.
"Oh, Angel, You Skipped the Atlantic." [NewAW] (11) Sum-Fall 93, p. 54.
"They're Sleeping in a Row." [NewAW] (11) Sum-Fall 93, p. 52.
3316. KAUFMAN, Andrew
"The Cinnamon Bay Sonnets" (7 poems). [SpoonR] (18:1) Wint-Spr 93, p. 78-81.
"The Cinnamon Bay Sonnets" (Selections: 15-18). [ColEng] (55:6) O 93, p. 646 -
647.
"The Cinnamon Bay Sonnets" (Selections: 9 poems). [MassR] (34:2) Sum 93, p.
270-274.
"Nocturne." [BrooklynR] (10) 93, p. 53.
3317. KAUFMAN, Shirley
"Letter" (1 & 4, tr. of Meir Wieseltier, w. the author). [Trans] (28) Spr 93, p. 109 -
111.
"Letter" (2-3, tr. of Meir Wieseltier). [KenR] (NS 15:4) Fall 93, p. 21-23.
"Output" (tr. of Meir Wieseltier, w. the author). [Trans] (28) Spr 93, p. 112.
"Poem in November." [Field] (49) Fall 93, p. 89-92.
"Subversion." [QRL] (12:32/33) 93, p. 447.
3318. KAURAKA, Kauraka
"Ode to Maori Women / Tateni No Te Vaine Maori" (in Enlish and a language of
the Cook Islands). [Manoa] (5:1) Sum 93, p. 62.
"The Tropic Bird of Maui / Te-Tavake-a-Maui" (in Enlish and a language of the
Cook Islands). [Manoa] (5:1) Sum 93, p. 62-63.
"Weeping Waters / Vai Tangi" (in Enlish and a language of the Cook Islands).
[Manoa] (5:1) Sum 93, p. 61-62.
3319. KAVEN, Bob
"The Rye Field." [MidwQ] (34:2) Wint 93, p. 219.
"Winter Rain Poem." [MidwQ] (34:2) Wint 93, p. 220.
KAWAJI, Ken Armitage
See ARMITAGE-KAWAJI, Ken
3320. KAY, John
"Understanding Glass." [Pearl] (17) Spr 93, p. 10.
3321. KAZANTZIS, Judith
"Night." [Stand] (34:3) Sum 93, p. 62.
KAZUKO, Odagawa
See ODAGAWA, Kazuko
KAZUKO, Shiraishi
See SHIRAISHI, Kazuko
KE, Mang
See MANG, Ke
K'E-HSIANG, Liu
See LIU K'E-HSIANG
3322. KEAHEY, Debbie
"Danse Winnipeg." [PraF] (14:3) Aut 93, p. 86-87.
3323. KEARLEY, Wade
"Birthmark." [TickleAce] (24) Fall-Wint 92, p. 65.
"On an Almost Empty Wednesday." [TickleAce] (24) Fall-Wint 92, p. 66-67.
"The Plot." [TickleAce] (24) Fall-Wint 92, p. 68.

"Shem Grows Impatient Aboard the Ark." [TickleAce] (25) Spr-Sum 93, p. 195 - 196.
3324. KEARNEY, Kevin R.
"Return from Nepal." [NewRena] (8:3, #26) Spr 93, p. 67-68.
"University of Vienna, 1876." [NewRena] (8:3, #26) Spr 93, p. 69.
"What the Widowers Will Say When the Words Turn to Ice." [NewRena] (8:3, #26) Spr 93, p. 68.
3325. KEATING, Timothy J.
"Abode" (tr. of Alvaro Mutis, w. Robert Bensen). [HarvardR] (4) Spr 93, p. 136.
"Three Images" (tr. of Alvaro Mutis, w. Robert Bensen). [HarvardR] (4) Spr 93, p. 137.
3326. KEATS, John
"When I Have Fears." [AmerPoR] (22:5) S-O 93, p. 28.
3327. KEEFER, Janice Kulyk
"Massacre of the Innocents: Pieter Bruegel the Younger." [Event] (22:1) Spr 93, p. 38-40.
"Models and Their Painters" (Selections: 1-2). [Quarry] (42:1) 93, p. 95-98.
"Oranges" (for my mother). [Event] (22:1) Spr 93, p. 34-35.
"A Rare Photograph Taken Somewhere in Eastern Europe, Probably in 1941." [Event] (22:1) Spr 93, p. 36-37.
"Winter Cemetery: Annapolis." [PraS] (67:4) Wint 93, p. 134-135.
3328. KEELAN, Claudia
"Bartok Widow." [HeavenB] (10) Wint-Spr 93, p. 72.
"The Camera's Eye Turned to You and Then the Beginning of Static." [Boulevard] (8:2/3, #23/24) Fall 93, p. 202-203.
"The End Is an Animal." [DenQ] (27:4) Spr 93, p. 78.
"Free Verse." [DenQ] (28:1) Sum 93, p. 39.
"Indian Paint Brush." [IndR] (16:1) Spr 93, p. 96.
"Lines that Rely on Voice for Authenticity." [NewL] (59:4) 93, p. 95-97.
"Mid, Mid-West." [IndR] (16:1) Spr 93, p. 95.
"The Modern Life of the Soul." [RiverS] (37) 93, p. 54.
"One Parable." [Caliban] (12) 93, p. 128.
"To Sleep." [HeavenB] (10) Wint-Spr 93, p. 72.
3329. KEELEY, Edmund
"From Poseidon" (Repetitions, 1963-65, tr. of Yannis Ritsos). [HarvardR] (5) Fall 93, p. 144-145.
"Marking" (Parentheses, 1950-61, tr. of Yannis Ritsos). [HarvardR] (5) Fall 93, p. 131.
"Maybe, Someday" (Parentheses, 1946-47, tr. of Yannis Ritsos). [HarvardR] (5) Fall 93, p. 134.
"The Meaning of Simplicity" (Parentheses, 1946-47, tr. of Yannis Ritsos). [HarvardR] (5) Fall 93, p. 133-134.
"Miniature" (Parentheses, 1946-47, tr. of Yannis Ritsos). [HarvardR] (5) Fall 93, p. 146-147.
"The More Sufficient" (The Distant, 1975, tr. of Yannis Ritsos). [HarvardR] (5) Fall 93, p. 136.
"Nero's Respite" (tr. of C. P. Cavafy, w. Philip Sherrard). [QRL] (12:32/33) 93, p. 390.
"One of Their Gods" (tr. of C. P. Cavafy, w. Philip Sherrard). [QRL] (12:32/33) 93, p. 389.
"Penelope's Despair" (Repetitions, 1968-69, tr. of Yannis Ritsos). [HarvardR] (5) Fall 93, p. 145.
"Point" (Parentheses, 1950-61, tr. of Yannis Ritsos). [HarvardR] (5) Fall 93, p. 144.
"Triplet" (Parentheses, 1950-61, tr. of Yannis Ritsos). [HarvardR] (5) Fall 93, p. 131.
"Tuesday" (tr. of George Seferis). [QRL] (12:32/33) 93, p. 507-508.
"Waiting for the Barbarians" (tr. of C. P. Cavafy, w. Philip Sherrard). [QRL] (12:32/33) 93, p. 388-389.
"Wednesday" (ad vigilias albas, tr. of George Seferis). [QRL] (12:32/33) 93, p. 509.
3330. KEEN, Paul
"The Anchor." [AntigR] (95) Aut 93, p. 110.
3331. KEEN, Suzanne
"A Psalter" (Selection: ps. 4, 7-8). [Agni] (37) 93, p. 51-55.
3332. KEENAN, Gary
"Point of No Return." [SouthernPR] (33:1) Spr 93, p. 7.
"A Region." [BrooklynR] (10) 93, p. 44-45.

"Slow Storm." [GeoR] (47:3) Fall 93, p. 469-470.
3333. KEENER, LuAnn
"A Terre." [PoetL] (88:2) Sum 93, p. 25.
"Bees in Amber" (Winner of the Chelsea Award for Poetry). [Chelsea] (54) 93, p. 117.
"Bracken" (Winner of the Chelsea Award for Poetry). [Chelsea] (54) 93, p. 119.
"Chambered Nautilus" (Winner of the Chelsea Award for Poetry). [Chelsea] (54) 93, p. 112-115.
"Heartwood" (Winner of the Chelsea Award for Poetry). [Chelsea] (54) 93, p. 116.
"Sharks' Teeth" (Winner of the Chelsea Award for Poetry). [Chelsea] (54) 93, p. 118.
3334. KEFALA, Antigone
"The Actual Places." [Manoa] (5:2) Wint 93, p. 31.
"The Ride." [Manoa] (5:2) Wint 93, p. 31.
3335. KEILEY, Lizbeth (Lisbeth)
"The Event of Her Missing Body." [CinPR] (24) Spr 93, p. 32.
"Food for Thought, or Just Deserts" (M.F.A. Workshop w. Marie Hasten, Howard Glyn, Pamela Hughes, M. R. Syneck, Mary Greene, David Trinidad and Allen Ginsberg, Nov. 21, 1988). [BrooklynR] (10) 93, p. 94-95.
"Until the Shore's Dream Reappears I Hear Its Water Barrel Out from Over." [CinPR] (24) Spr 93, p. 33.
3336. KEIN, Sybil
"Bayou Ballad." [AfAmRev] (27:1) Spr 93, p. 142-143.
3337. KEITH, Bill
"Harlequinode." [AfAmRev] (27:4) Wint 93, p. 627.
"Rendezvous in Bilad-as-Sudan." [AfAmRev] (27:4) Wint 93, p. 628.
3338. KEITH, W. J.
"The Parked Car." [AntigR] (93-94) Spr-Sum 93, p. 78.
3339. KEITHLEY, George
"Dusk" (for Carol). [Colum] (20) Sum 93, p. 47.
"Hawks." [Colum] (20) Sum 93, p. 133-134.
"The Sea." [Agni] (37) 93, p. 221.
3340. KEIZER, Arlene
"Awkward Passions: Confessions of a Black Catholic" (for James Baldwin). [TriQ] (87) Spr-Sum 93, p. 150-153.
"Migrants" (for Ida B. Wells). [TriQ] (87) Spr-Sum 93, p. 154.
3341. KELEN, S. K.
"The Gods' Picnic." [Nimrod] (36:2) Spr-Sum 93, p. 69.
"North West." [Nimrod] (36:2) Spr-Sum 93, p. 71.
"Still Life with Elements." [Nimrod] (36:2) Spr-Sum 93, p. 70.
3342. KELIN, Daniel A., II
"Caution Yellow." [HawaiiR] (17:1, #37) Spr 93, p. 164-165.
3343. KELLER, David
"Above the Churchyard, Crockateemore." [QRL] (12:32/33) 93, p. 206-207.
"At the Stone-Age Tombs." [QRL] (12:32/33) 93, p. 208-209.
"Catching On." [QRL] (12:32/33) 93, p. 209-210.
"Childhood Stories." [GettyR] (6:2) Spr 93, p. 250-251.
"In the New Garden." [US1] (28/29) 93, p. 7.
"In the New World." [QRL] (12:32/33) 93, p. 211-212.
"A New Garden." [QRL] (12:32/33) 93, p. 207-208.
"Poem with a One-Word Title." [GettyR] (6:2) Spr 93, p. 252.
"The Solar System." [QRL] (12:32/33) 93, p. 212-213.
"Trouble in History." [IndR] (16:2) Fall 93, p. 120-121.
"Trouble in History." [QRL] (12:32/33) 93, p. 210-211.
3344. KELLER, Tsipi
"Browsing Through the Album" (tr. of Dan Pagis). [QRL] (12:32/33) 93, p. 269 - 270.
"First Interrogation" (tr. of Dan Pagis). [QRL] (12:32/33) 93, p. 269.
"Fractions of a Lament for a Friend" (tr. of Dan Pagis). [QRL] (12:32/33) 93, p. 271-272.
"Instructions to Crossing the Border" (tr. of Dan Pagis). [QRL] (12:32/33) 93, p. 270.
"Moments of Old Age" (tr. of Dan Pagis). [QRL] (12:32/33) 93, p. 272-273.
"The Portrait" (tr. of Dan Pagis). [QRL] (12:32/33) 93, p. 271.
"The Reparations Draft Agreement" (tr. of Dan Pagis). [QRL] (12:32/33) 93, p. 270 - 271.

248

KELLER

"Someone" (tr. of Dan Pagis). [QRL] (12:32/33) 93, p. 268.
"Testimony" (tr. of Dan Pagis). [QRL] (12:32/33) 93, p. 270.
3345. KELLEY, Tina
"Clytie's Rattling on Again." [BelPoJ] (44:2) Wint 93-94, p. 14-15.
"Silence Deep as the Bone at the Bottom of the Skull." [BelPoJ] (44:2) Wint 93-94,
p. 15.
3346. KELLMAN, Steven G.
"Equanimity." [Light] (6) Sum 93, p. 17.
3347. KELLOGG, David
"Dark Matter." [OnTheBus] (5:2, #12) Sum-Fall 93, p. 110.
3348. KELLY, Brigit Pegeen
"All Wild Animals Were Once Called Deer." [MassR] (34:4) Wint 93-94, p. 616 -
619.
"Courting the Famous Figures at the Grotto of Improbable Thought." [NowestR]
(31:1) 93, p. 6-9.
"Guest Place." [CreamCR] (17:2) Fall 93, p. 163.
"Imagining Their Own Hymns." [NewEngR] (15:1) Wint 93, p. 153-154.
"Of Ancient Origins and War." [AmerV] (31) 93, p. 139-140.
"Song." [SouthernR] (29:4) Aut, O 93, p. 748-750.
"Three Cows and the Moon." [NewEngR] (15:4) Fall 93, p. 177-183.
3349. KELLY, Erren Geraud
"Mirrors." [AfAmRev] (27:1) Spr 93, p. 144-146.
3350. KELLY, Robert
"Flags" (for Nathaniel Tarn). [NewAW] (11) Sum-Fall 93, p. 30-32.
"Pasts." [Sulfur] (33) Fall 93, p. 124-127.
"The Physiology of William Blake." [Conjunc] (21) 93, p. 202-212.
3351. KELLY, Susan
"Metaphor." [Verse] (10:1) Spr 93, p. 83.
3352. KELLY, Timothy
"Closed Head Injury." [Field] (48) Spr 93, p. 16.
"Does Enough Happen?" [Field] (48) Spr 93, p. 17.
"Two Special Senses." [Field] (48) Spr 93, p. 14-15.
3353. KELLY-DeWITT, Susan
"Angel with Cabbage Leaf Wings" (after a sculpture by Jorjana Holden). [ClockR]
(8:1/2) 93, p. 73.
"Banyans." [SpoonR] (18:2) Sum-Fall 93, p. 21-22.
"February Heat." [ClockR] (8:1/2) 93, p. 74-75.
"Rock-O-Plane." [SpoonR] (18:2) Sum-Fall 93, p. 23.
"Turning Point." [SpoonR] (18:2) Sum-Fall 93, p. 20.
3354. KEMBLE, Sarah
"Closet Relation." [HawaiiR] (17:3, #39) Fall 93, p. 100.
"Eternity." [HawaiiR] (17:3, #39) Fall 93, p. 107.
3355. KEMENY, Annemarie
"Contortionists of the Free World." [13thMoon] (11:1/2) 93, p. 38.
"Terza Rima for a Girl Stranded in White." [13thMoon] (11:1/2) 93, p. 37.
3356. KEMMETT, Bill
"The Olympian." [Plain] (14:1) Fall 93, p. 33.
3357. KEMP, Arnold J.
"Assumptions in Flight." [Callaloo] (16:2) Spr 93, p. 306-308.
"Like Sabines." [Agni] (37) 93, p. 48-50.
3358. KEMP, Penn
"Dependencies Depend on These." [WestCL] (27:3, #12) Wint 93-94, p. 51.
"Mutative Metaphors." [WestCL] (27:3, #12) Wint 93-94, p. 52.
"Recycling Relationship." [WestCL] (27:3, #12) Wint 93-94, p. 50.
3359. KEMPA, Rick
"Minions" (mignon, French, darling). [Border] (2) Spr 93, p. 42.
"The One Among the Many." [HighP] (8:1) Spr 93, p. 72.
3360. KEMPHER, Ruth Moon
"Gina's Taste." [ChironR] (12:3, #36) Aut 93, p. 27.
"Her Explanation." [ChironR] (12:4/13:1, #37/38) Wint 93-Spr 94, p. 15.
"The Inventory Queen" (written after reading Wallace Stevens, with lines in
quotation marks from Stevens). [JINJPo] (15:1) Spr 93, p. 9-10.
3361. KEMPNER, Bob
"Near a Wabash River levee raunchy clergymen abound" (First Prize, First Annual
River Rhyme Competition). [Light] (5) Spr 93, p. 29.

249

3362. KENDALL, Tim
"The Potter." [Verse] (10:2) Sum 93, p. 92.
3363. KENDIG, Diane
"Ghazals on Lake Erie in March." [CinPR] (24) Spr 93, p. 52.
"Moving into Minimum Security" (for Rick, Shep, Blue, Earl). [CinPR] (24) Spr 93,
p. 53.
3364. KENDRICK, John
"My Father's Ghost Hangs on My Bones." [Blueline] (14) 93, p. 94-95.
"Paris Brothel." [Blueline] (14) 93, p. 92.
"The Widows of Aflenz" (a small village in Austria which lost nearly 90% of its
men in the War). [Blueline] (14) 93, p. 93.
3365. KENNEDY, Chris
"Broadway Lament: San Francisco, 1978." [CreamCR] (17:2) Fall 93, p. 198-199.
3366. KENNEDY, David
"The Baroque Warehouse — Reflections at Castle Howard." [Stand] (34:2) Spr 93,
p. 43.
3367. KENNEDY, John
"Another Life." [CimR] (102) Ja 93, p. 86-87.
"November Birches" (for Lisa). [SouthernHR] (27:4) Fall 93, p. 346.
"A Waking Call." [PoetC] (24:2) Wint 93, p. 9-10.
"Water Striders" (for Johnny). [PoetL] (88:1) Spr 93, p. 40.
3368. KENNEDY, Melinda
"Befana (January 6)." [MassR] (34:4) Wint 93-94, p. 635-636.
"Towards the End of November." [MassR] (34:4) Wint 93-94, p. 635.
3369. KENNEDY, Monique
"Time Port" (tr. of Nina Malinovski, w. Thomas Kennedy). [Vis] (43) 93, p. 16.
3370. KENNEDY, Terry
"Across the Big Screen." [ContextS] (3:1) 93, p. 21-22.
3371. KENNEDY, Thomas
"Time Port" (tr. of Nina Malinovski, w. Monique Kennedy). [Vis] (43) 93, p. 16.
3372. KENNEDY, X. J.
"The Ballad of Fenimore Woolson and Henry James." [Hudson] (46:2) Sum 93, p.
294-299.
"Coming Close to Drowning." [NorthStoneR] (11) 93, p. 41.
"Down by the rancid River Rockaway." [Light] (7) Aut 93, p. 24.
"Five-and-Dime, Late Thirties." [Boulevard] (8:2/3, #23/24) Fall 93, p. 95-96.
"Japanese Beetles." [NorthStoneR] (11) 93, p. 43-44.
"Poets' Hearts." [NorthStoneR] (11) 93, p. 43.
"Raisins." [NorthStoneR] (11) 93, p. 42.
"Sharing the Onus" (for Richard Moore). [Light] (7) Aut 93, p. 14.
"To Writers Forbidden to Write." [NorthStoneR] (11) 93, p. 42.
3373. KENNELL, Galway
"The Man in the Chair." [NewYorker] (69:1) 22 F 93, p. 162.
3374. KENNELLY, Louise
"Winter Grapes." [Pearl] (19) Fall-Wint 93, p. 8.
3375. KENNEY, Richard
"The Evolution of the Flightless Bird." [NewEngR] (15:1) Wint 93, p. 155-156.
3376. KENNING, Janet
"Letter Not Sent: Woods." [PoetL] (88:4) Wint 93-94, p. 25.
3377. KENNY, Maurice
"Stone Throwing." [ClockR] (8:1/2) 93, p. 83-84.
3378. KENT, Jean
"Cockatoos at Dusk." [Nimrod] (36:2) Spr-Sum 93, p. 10.
3379. KENTER, Robert
"Breakdown on Fourth St." [Writ] (25) 93, p. 21.
"Disease." [Writ] (25) 93, p. 20.
"Furious Motion Blurred." [Writ] (25) 93, p. 24.
"Jacob's Ladder." [Writ] (25) 93, p. 23.
"Power." [Writ] (25) 93, p. 25.
"Visiting an Aunt in New York." [Writ] (25) 93, p. 22.
3380. KENVIN, Natalie
"My Daughter." [HawaiiR] (16:3, #36) Wint 93, p. 68.
3381. KENYON, Jane
"Coats." [NewYorker] (69:13) 17 My 93, p. 64.
"Fear of Death Awakens Me." [Pequod] (35) 93, p. 152.
"Insomnia at the Solstice." [GettyR] (6:2) Spr 93, p. 262-263.

"Moving the Frame." [Atlantic] (272:2) Ag 93, p. 80.
"Potato." [GettyR] (6:2) Spr 93, p. 264.
"Sleepers in Jaipur." [PartR] (60:3) Sum 93, p. 420.
"The Stroller." [Pequod] (35) 93, p. 153-156.
3382. KEPLINGER, David
"Boy with a Pacemaker Blues." [PoetL] (88:2) Sum 93, p. 5.
"Moving." [RiverC] (14:1) Fall 93, p. 65-66.
3383. KERLIKOWSKE, Elizabeth
"The Blue Goose." [RiverC] (14:1) Fall 93, p. 61-64.
3384. KERLINSKY, Nathan
"It Was a Dorm Hall." [Sonora] (24/25) Spr 93, p. 175-176.
3385. KERMAN, Judith
"Acts of Faith." [BlackBR] (17) Sum-Fall 93, p. 13.
"Corpus." [BlackBR] (17) Sum-Fall 93, p. 12.
"The Grammar of Simultaneity." [BlackBR] (17) Sum-Fall 93, p. 11.
3386. KERR, Don
"The Environmentally Sound." [PoetryC] (13:4) 93, p. 24.
"The Old Urge." [Arc] (31) Aut 93, p. 9-10.
"That Was Some Saxaphone" (A C Read). [PoetryC] (13:4) 93, p. 24.
"Trumpet / Sax." [PoetryC] (13:4) 93, p. 24.
3387. KERR, Jake
"Intimate Fishing Secrets." [Pearl] (17) Spr 93, p. 77.
3388. KERR, Milton
"Boogie Woogie at 7:50 AM." [SmPd] (30:3, #89) Fall 93, p. 10.
3389. KERRIGAN, T. S.
"Doorish" (For Elizabeth Carnazzo). [SouthernR] (29:3) Sum, Jl 93, p. 585-587.
"Maugherow." [SouthernR] (29:3) Sum, Jl 93, p. 584-585.
"Roué." [SouthernR] (29:3) Sum, Jl 93, p. 584.
"A Sighting on the River." [SouthernR] (29:3) Sum, Jl 93, p. 587-588.
3390. KERRIGAN, William
"Another." [Hellas] (4:1) Spr 93, p. 92.
"On *Hellas*." [Hellas] (4:1) Spr 93, p. 92.
3391. KESLER, Russ
"His Picture." [Paint] (19:38) Aut 92, p. 39.
"Love Letter." [Paint] (19:38) Aut 92, p. 38.
3392. KESSLER, Jascha
"Angelo Poliziano" (tr. of Kirsti Simonsuuri, w. the author). [SenR] (23:1/2) Wint
    93, p. 166.
"Bird" (tr. of Ottó Orbán, w. Mária Körösy). [InterPR] (19:2) Fall 93, p. 39.
"The Boat" (tr. of Ottó Orbán, w. Mária Körösy). [InterPR] (19:2) Fall 93, p. 47.
"Builders" (tr. of Ottó Orbán, w. Mária Körösy). [InterPR] (19:2) Fall 93, p. 41.
"The General" (tr. of Ottó Orbán, w. Mária Körösy). [InterPR] (19:2) Fall 93, p. 45.
"Guitar" (tr. of Ottó Orbán, w. Mária Körösy). [InterPR] (19:2) Fall 93, p. 49.
"Mythos" (tr. of Kirsti Simonsuuri, w. the author). [SenR] (23:1/2) Wint 93, p. 165.
"On the Law School's Steps" (in Bratislava, tr. of Milan Richter). [OxfordM] (9:1)
    Spr-Sum 93, p. 8-9.
"A Rare Book" (tr. of Kirsti Simonsuuri, w. the author). [SenR] (23:1/2) Wint 93, p.
    164.
"Spoiled Poem" (tr. of Milan Richter). [OxfordM] (9:1) Spr-Sum 93, p. 7.
"A Stroll" (tr. of Ottó Orbán, w. Mária Körösy). [InterPR] (19:2) Fall 93, p. 43.
"Yet I Must" (tr. of Milan Richter). [OxfordM] (9:1) Spr-Sum 93, p. 8.
3393. KESSLER, Sydney
"Beginning the Day with Total Recall of Night Air." [Nimrod] (37:1) Fall-Wint 93,
    p. 118.
"Do You Hear Me?" [Nimrod] (37:1) Fall-Wint 93, p. 119.
KEST, Itamar Yaoz
    See YAOZ-KEST, Itamar
3394. KETCHEK, Michael
"For Men Only." [SlipS] (13) 93, p. 39.
3395. KETTNER, M.
"Over-stimulated." [Bogg] (66) Wint 92-93, p. 27.
3396. KEYS, Kerry Shawn
"Fishing with Izaak Walton." [ChironR] (12:4/13:1, #37/38) Wint 93-Spr 94, p. 11.
"The Glass Cage" (in Lencois). [ChironR] (12:4/13:1, #37/38) Wint 93-Spr 94, p.
    11.
"The Kitchen." [ChironR] (12:4/13:1, #37/38) Wint 93-Spr 94, p. 11.

251

3397. KEYWORTH, Suzanne
"Grandfather William." [SycamoreR] (5:2) Sum 93, p. 32.
"Markers." [NoAmR] (278:6) N-D 93, p. 43.
"Poem for the Brother." [SycamoreR] (5:2) Sum 93, p. 30-31.
3398. KHAIYAT, Mahdy Y.
"Just Married." [Hellas] (4:1) Spr 93, p. 66.
3399. KHRISTMUKTI, Sudha
"A Truce." [ContextS] (3:1) 93, p. 13.
3400. KICKNOSWAY, Faye
"Geography." [Manoa] (5:2) Wint 93, p. 139-141.
3401. KIERNAN, Phyllis
"She Has Her Palm Read." [CinPR] (24) Spr 93, p. 72.
3402. KIESNERS, Diana
"Messages." [AntigR] (93-94) Spr-Sum 93, p. 290.
3403. KIHM, Donald
"Monoliths Near Shiprock, New Mexico." [Wind] (23:72) 93, p. 12.
3404. KIJEWSKI, Bruce
"Little Read Reading Habits." [VirQR] (69:2) Spr 93, p. 260-261.
3405. KILDEGAARD, Athena O.
"A Photograph (Taken 1890)." [Vis] (41) 93, p. 9-10.
3406. KILLEEN, Ger
"A Hearty Welcome to the Antichrist." [AmerPoR] (22:6) N-D 93, p. 18-19.
3407. KILLIAN, Sean
"Native-Made." [AmerLC] (5) 93, p. 70-71.
"Targeted by What Attracts." [AmerLC] (5) 93, p. 72-73.
3408. KIM, Aegina
"Flight." [CreamCR] (17:1) Spr 93, p. 58-59.
3409. KIM, Kwang-sup
"My Mind" (tr. by Chang Soo Ko). [Vis] (43) 93, p. 32.
3410. KIM, Kwang-Wook (1580-1656)
"Toda la gente es tonta" (Spanish tr. by William Martínez Jr.). [Luz] (4) My 93, p. 57.
3411. KIM, Myung Mi
"The Bounty" (Excerpts). [Avec] (6:1) 93, p. 133-135.
"Primer." [Conjunc] (21) 93, p. 52-60.
3412. KIM, Namjo
"Love's Cursive" (Selections: 6, 8, tr. by David R. McCann and Hyun-jae Yee Sallee). [ChiR] (39:3/4) 93, p. 242.
3413. KIM, Sang-Yong (1561-1673)
"El amor es falso" (Spanish tr. by William Martínez Jr.). [Luz] (4) My 93, p. 56.
3414. KIM, Sowôl
"Songs from the Riverbank" (tr. by Sekyo N. Haines). [HarvardR] (4) Spr 93, p. 146.
3415. KIM, Yoon Sik
"Here Stands the Aged Hammurabi, All Flesh and Blood." [Vis] (41) 93, p. 26.-27.
"River Colorado." [NewYorkQ] (51) 93, p. 87.
3416. KIMBALL, Michael
"Looking into the Sun." [CapeR] (28:2) Fall 93, p. 36.
3417. KIMBRELL, James
"Leguminous." [PaintedB] (49) 93, p. 26.
3418. KIME, Peter
"Balding." [BellR] (16:1/2) Spr-Fall 93, p. 71.
"Oranges." [BellR] (16:1/2) Spr-Fall 93, p. 72.
"Stroke." [SouthernPR] (33:1) Spr 93, p. 54-55.
"Things to Do." [BellR] (16:1/2) Spr-Fall 93, p. 70.
3419. KIMM, R.
"General Mail Facility Night Shift Dreams." [RagMag] (11:1) 93, p. 21.
"Oh Darkest Mother." [RagMag] (11:1) 93, p. 20.
3420. KIMMEL, Michael
"The Errors of the Mythopoetic Search." [ChangingM] (26) Sum-Fall 93, p. 10.
3421. KINCAID, Joan Payne
"Five Characters in Search of Reality." [Bogg] (66) Wint 92-93, p. 51.
"Goya." [Confr] (51) Sum 93, p. 256.
"Un Oiseau de Passage." [Bogg] (66) Wint 92-93, p. 36.
"Retrograde." [ContextS] (3:1) 93, p. 42-43.
"Sweetie." [SlipS] (13) 93, p. 49.

3422. KINCZYK, Bohdan
"Ingrid & Elsa." [PraF] (14:3) Aut 93, p. 94.
"On Meeting Lesbia." [PraF] (14:3) Aut 93, p. 94.
3423. KING, Janna
"Directions." [BellArk] (9:4) Jl-Ag 93, p. 23.
"Kindness." [ChatR] (13:2) Wint 93, p. 3-4.
"My Prairie Grandmother." [BellArk] (9:1) Ja-F 93, p. 5.
"Taking Easter Morning Back." [BellArk] (9:4) Jl-Ag 93, p. 23.
"What Children Eat." [CumbPR]] (13:1) Fall 93, p. 41.
3424. KING, Linda
"Fucking in the Spirit." [Pearl] (17) Spr 93, p. 62.
3425. KING, Robert S.
"Against the Graveyard's Greater Wall." [Vis] (41) 93, p. 14.
"Cottonmouth Catchers in a Night Swamp." [WritersF] (19) 93, p. 87.
"Darkness Too Is a Mirror." [HampSPR] Wint 93, p. 6.
"The Gravedigger Wiping Sweat." [HampSPR] Wint 93, p. 6.
"Men." [ChatR] (13:2) Wint 93, p. 7.
"The New World Dictionary." [Elf] (3:3) Fall 93, p. 27.
"Prophets Climbing to Machu Picchu." [LullwaterR] (4:2) Spr-Sum 93, p. 126.
"River Pulse." [Elf] (3:3) Fall 93, p. 27.
3426. KING, Willie James
"The Best I Can." [Obs] (8:2) Fall-Wint 93, p. 112-113.
"Mad Marge Speaks." [Obs] (8:1) Spr-Sum 93, p. 93-94.
3427. KINGS, Graham
"The Hostage Deal." [ChrC] (110:11) 7 Apr 93, p. 365.
3428. KINGSBURY, Eric
"Ariel to Prospero" (A postscript to Shakespeare and Auden). [PikeF] (11) Fall 93,
p. 24.
"Prisoners: From a Diary by Julie H." (Friday March 16, 1990). [PikeF] (11) Fall 93,
p. 5.
"The Women of Ravenna" (Selection: II. Cold Mountain — December 1989).
[PikeF] (11) Fall 93, p. 24.
3429. KINGSTON, Katie
"Construction Workers." [WeberS] (10:2) Spr-Sum 93, p. 59.
"Falling." [WeberS] (10:2) Spr-Sum 93, p. 58.
"From the Gulf." [WeberS] (10:2) Spr-Sum 93, p. 61.
"Kindergarten." [WeberS] (10:2) Spr-Sum 93, p. 60.
"Poetry Class." [WeberS] (10:2) Spr-Sum 93, p. 57.
"Storyteller." [HawaiiR] (16:3, #36) Wint 93, p. 69.
3430. KINKEAD, Mary Ellen
"Road shoulder mail boxes." [EngJ] (82:7) N 93, p. 90.
3431. KINNELL, Galway
"Brother of My Heart" (Etheridge Knight). [PaintedB] (50/51) 93, p. 123.
"The Crucified Swimmer" (tr. of Yvan Goll). [QRL] (12:32/33) 93, p. 423-424.
"In the Bamboo Hut." [NewEngR] (15:1) Wint 93, p. 157.
"My Mother's R and R." [AmerPoR] (22:1) Ja-F 93, p. 43.
"The Night." [AmerPoR] (22:1) Ja-F 93, p. 43.
"Poem: Could it be that the foot." [QRL] (12:32/33) 93, p. 447-448.
"Poem: I long for the mantle." [QRL] (12:32/33) 93, p. 448.
"Rapture." [NewYorker] (68:48) 18 Ja 93, p. 92.
"Showing My Father Through Freedom." [AmerPoR] (22:1) Ja-F 93, p. 44.
3432. KINSELLA, John
"Black Suns." [Nimrod] (36:2) Spr-Sum 93, p. 33.
"Blood and Bone" (a p(r)oem). [Grain] (21:3) Fall 93, p. 100.
"Checking the Sheep Two Mornings After the Glad Day." [Nimrod] (36:2) Spr-Sum
93, p. 34.
"Dissertation on a Wasp's Nest." [Iowa] (23:2) Spr-Sum 93, p. 134-136.
"Harvest." [Grain] (21:3) Fall 93, p. 101-104.
"The Mercury Climbs in Happy Valley." [DogRR] (12:2, #24) Fall-Wint 93, p. 33.
"Notes on Divining." [Nimrod] (36:2) Spr-Sum 93, p. 35.
3433. KINSELLA, Thomas
"Remembering Old Wars." [QRL] (12:32/33) 93, p. 449.
"Traveller." [QRL] (12:32/33) 93, p. 449.
3434. KINSEY, C. A.
"She Is Privileged." [ChironR] (12:3, #36) Aut 93, p. 15.

3435. KIPP, Karen
"Containing the Color Blue." [Iowa] (23:2) Spr-Sum 93, p. 100-101.
"Hyena." [WormR] (33:3, #131), 93, p. 129.
"A Man's Wife." [WormR] (33:3, #131), 93, p. 129.
"Works." [Iowa] (23:2) Spr-Sum 93, p. 99-100.
3436. KIRBY, David
"Anacharsis Cloots." [WormR] (33:4, #132) 93, p. 184-185.
"A Phenomenology of Collusion." [WormR] (33:4, #132) 93, p. 182-183.
"The Potato Mash (More Indefinite and More Soluble)." [SouthernR] (29:3) Sum, Jl
93, p. 601-603.
"The Potato Mash (More Indefinite and More Soluble)." [WormR] (33:4, #132) 93,
p. 186-187.
"A Syllabus of Errors." [WormR] (33:4, #132) 93, p. 185-186.
3437. KIRCHDORFER, Ulf
"Santa speaks" (The Competition). [SmPd] (30:3, #89) Fall 93, p. 8.
3438. KIRCHER, Pamela
"A Kind of Goodbye." [SycamoreR] (5:1) Wint 93, p. 52-53.
3439. KIRCHNER, B. Neal
"Lack of Leda." [Poem] (70) N 93, p. 48.
"Ned Bowen Explains the Mystery of Shroyer Hill." [SoDakR] (31:3) Fall 93, p.
140.
"New Love Too Soon." [Poem] (70) N 93, p. 49.
3440. KIRCHWEY, Karl
"An Aside at the Met" (Attic krater, attributed to Lydos). [ParisR] (35:126) Spr 93,
p. 203-205.
"Aubade, Deer Isle." [ParisR] (35:126) Spr 93, p. 201-203.
"The Crocus." [Boulevard] (8:1, #22) Spr 93, p. 92-94.
"Lest He Put Forth His Hand." [NewYorker] (69:9) 19 Ap 93, p. 78-79.
"Rogue Hydrant, August." [NewYorker] (69:28) 6 S 93, p. 78.
"The Spider's Art." [Nat] (256:9) 8 Mr 93, p. 318.
"Trout Tank, Café Le Sporting." [ParisR] (35:126) Spr 93, p. 200-201.
"Tuesday, August 13, 1912" (Ampersand Mountain, Saranac). [Boulevard] (8:1,
#22) Spr 93, p. 91.
3441. KIRKLAND, Leigh
"At a Café in Hermosa Beach." [WeberS] (10:2) Spr-Sum 93, p. 95.
"For Valerie, Seven Days Out of Detox." [WeberS] (10:2) Spr-Sum 93, p. 96.
"Savoring the Season." [WeberS] (10:2) Spr-Sum 93, p. 95.
3442. KIRKPATRICK, Kathryn
"Good Friday in Logroño." [SycamoreR] (5:1) Wint 93, p. 64-65.
"Sycamore." [Poem] (69) My 93, p. 12.
"What I Knew." [SycamoreR] (5:2) Sum 93, p. 33-34.
3443. KIRKUP, James
"On Watching a Friend Trying to Make Her Baby Drink from a Cup for the First
Time." [Light] (5) Spr 93, p. 17.
"Rum Rhymes and Comic Capers." [Light] (7) Aut 93, p. 22.
3444. KIRSCHNER, Elizabeth
"The Call." [WillowS] (32) Sum 93, p. 22-23.
"Haiku." [NoAmR] (278:5) S-O 93, p. 47.
"The Hatbox." [PraS] (67:3) Fall 93, p. 121-122.
"Postal Routes." [PraS] (67:3) Fall 93, p. 118-121.
"Shameless Light." [PraS] (67:3) Fall 93, p. 117-118.
"Shining Through." [NoDaQ] (61:4) Fall 93, p. 34-35.
3445. KIRSTEN-MARTIN, Diane
"Open Mike: Flashback." [OnTheBus] (5:2, #12) Sum-Fall 93, p. 111.
3446. KISEVIC, Enes
"Dear Birch" (to Anamarija Persola, tr. by Ellen Elias-Bursac). [NoDaQ] (61:1)
Wint 93, p. 97.
"An Exiled Child's Letter" (tr. by Ellen Elias-Bursac). [NoDaQ] (61:1) Wint 93, p.
95-96.
"Forgive Them, O Lord" (tr. by Ellen Elias-Bursac). [NoDaQ] (61:1) Wint 93, p. 97.
3447. KISTNER, John
"These Hands Found." [DenQ] (28:1) Sum 93, p. 41.
"Working Overtime on the Surface of the Sun." [DenQ] (28:1) Sum 93, p. 40.
3448. KITCHENS, Romella D.
"African Ways." [Obs] (8:2) Fall-Wint 93, p. 116.
"Beyond Marietta." [Obs] (8:2) Fall-Wint 93, p. 114-115.

3449. KITLINSKI, Tomek
"Bench Ghetto" (tr. of Artur Przystupa, w. Malgorzata Staniewska). [Verse] (10:2)
Sum 93, p. 39-40.
"The Little Mermaid" (tr. of Katarzyna Turaj-Kalinska, w. Malgorzata Staniewska).
[Verse] (10:2) Sum 93, p. 38.
"To Heloise: Yet Another Letter" (tr. of Katarzyna Turaj-Kalinska, w. Malgorzata
Staniewska). [Verse] (10:2) Sum 93, p. 38.
3450. KITSON, Herb
"Introduction to Poetry / Rhyme." [NewYorkQ] (52) 93, p. 71.
"Teacher's Pet." [ChatR] (13:4) Sum 93, p. 41.
3451. KIZER, Carolyn
"In Hell with Virg and Dan" (Canto XVII, tr. of Dante). [13thMoon] (12:1/2) 93-94,
p. 38-41.
"The Voyager" (for Charles Gullans 1955-1964). [QRL] (12:32/33) 93, p. 450-453.
3452. KLAASSEN, Tonja Gunvaldsen
"Eclipse." [MalR] (103) Sum 93, p. 53.
3453. KLANDER, Sharon
"January 7th: Two Views." [WestHR] (47:3) Fall 93, p. 237.
"On Seeing a Collage by K. Johnson Bowles on Ash Wednesday." [WestHR] (47:3)
Fall 93, p. 238.
3454. KLAPPERT, Peter
"Clerihew: When Irene and Vernon Castle." [Light] (7) Aut 93, p. 10.
"Clerihew: Whenever Catherine Anne Porter." [Light] (6) Sum 93, p. 14.
3455. KLAR, Barbara
"Meadowing." [PraF] (14:3) Aut 93, p. 95-96.
3456. KLEE, Frank
"The Ammo Dump at Dong Ha." [ChrC] (110:15) 5 My 93, p. 486.
"My Father'a Food." [ChrC] (110:16) 12 My 93, p. 522.
"Spirit Wall." [ChrC] (110:32) 10 N 93, p. 1130.
3457. KLEIN, Evan
"Emotional Detachment." [NewYorkQ] (51) 93, p. 69.
3458. KLEIN, Michael
"A Scarcity Model for Waves." [GlobalCR] (2) Fall 93, p. 54.
3459. KLEIN, Shirley
"Poem: As I often dread the morning." [ChironR] (12:3, #36) Aut 93, p. 11.
3460. KLEINSCHMIDT, Edward
"Brisance" (for Tamara Verga, 1970-1991). [GreensboroR] (55) Wint 93-94, p. 53.
"Chances and Hazards." [TampaR] (7) Fall 93, p. 10.
"Do-It-Yourself." [MassR] (34:3) Aut 93, p. 332.
"Isthmus Is a Particularly Difficult Word." [AnotherCM] (26) Fall 93, p. 47-48.
"Love's License." [Journal] (17:2) Fall-Wint 93, p. 28.
"Okeydokey." [Epoch] (42:2) 93, p. 214.
"One Thousand Four Hundred Fifty Two." [ApalQ] (35) 90, p. 25.
"Poetry à Go-Go." [Epoch] (42:2) 93, p. 215.
"Preoccupation." [PassN] (14:2) Wint 93, p. 33.
"To Remain." [NewEngR] (15:1) Wint 93, p. 158-160.
"Veronica." [Agni] (37) 93, p. 149.
"Very." [NoDaQ] (61:2) Spr 93, p. 128.
"The World." [Poetry] (162:6) S 93, p. 312.
3461. KLEPSCH, Nancy
"The Daughters of Lions Are Lions Too" (— Swahili proverb). [13thMoon] (12:1/2)
93-94, p. 42-43.
3462. KLIMEK, Ray
"All the Outside." [US1] (28/29) 93, p. 14.
"Cigars." [US1] (28/29) 93, p. 12.
3463. KLIPSCHUTZ
"White Cabs Connect the Dots All Over Town." [PoetC] (24:2) Wint 93, p. 27-28.
3464. KLOEFKORN, William
"Afternoon in October." [NoDaQ] (61:4) Fall 93, p. 9-10.
"Covenant." [NoDaQ] (61:4) Fall 93, p. 7-8.
"For Some Strange Reason." [LaurelR] (27:2) Sum 93, p. 54-55.
"Hannibal." [NorthStoneR] (11) 93, p. 132.
"Job Printing." [NorthStoneR] (11) 93, p. 130-131.
"Learning the Drum." [NoDaQ] (61:4) Fall 93, p. 5-6.
"Not Dreaming" (at a football game, early fall). [PoetC] (24:2) Wint 93, p. 16.
"Prove It." [PaintedB] (50/51) 93, p. 14.

255

KLYZA

KLYZA, Sheila McGrory
    See McGRORY-KLYZA, Sheila
3465. KNAPP, Trevor West
    "Absence." [ChatR] (14:1) Fall 93, p. 68.
    "Day Lilies." [AlabamaLR] (7:2) 93, p. 4-5.
3466. KNAVE, Brian
    "LX. This morning clouds bunch." [Zyzzyva] (9:3) Fall 93, p. 55.
    "XCIII. At the news of your betrothal." [Zyzzyva] (9:3) Fall 93, p. 55.
3467. KNIFFIN, Tom
    "During a Calm, My Brother and I Clear the Driveway." [BellArk] (9:6) N-D 93, p.
    14.
3468. KNIGHT, Arthur Winfield
    "Cole Younger: Coming." [CoalC] (7) Apr 93, p. 43.
    "Dried Prunes." [SlipS] (13) 93, p. 54.
    "Grace Pretty Shields: Caught." [NewYorkQ] (52) 93, p. 45.
    "Jesse James: Jesus Saves." [CoalC] (7) Apr 93, p. 4.
    "Pamela Many Wounds: Fired." [NewYorkQ] (52) 93, p. 45.
    "Taylor Moore: Queer." [ChironR] (12:1, #34) Spr 93, p. 37.
    "Washing the Dead." [SlipS] (13) 93, p. 55.
3469. KNIGHT, Etheridge
    "Circling the Daughter" (for Tandi). [PaintedB] (50/51) 93, p. 99.
3470. KNIGHT, Lynne
    "The Argument against Chaos." [PraS] (67:3) Fall 93, p. 137-138.
    "The Book of Common Betrayals." [PoetryNW] (34:2) Sum 93, p. 24-25.
    "Boundless Kingdom." [BelPoJ] (44:2) Wint 93-94, p. 31.
    "The Child Is Mother of the Longing." [PraS] (67:3) Fall 93, p. 135-137.
    "Dramatis Personae." [PoetC] (24:3) Spr 93, p. 23.
    "Parallel Lines." [NowestR] (31:3) 93, p. 47-48.
    "Slides." [CreamCR] (17:2) Fall 93, p. 180-182.
3471. KNIGHT, William J.
    "Ode to the New California" (from "I Love America," a poem distributed to
    California Republican legislators). [Harp] (287:1722) N 93, p. 21.
3472. KNIGHT-BOWENS, Eunice
    "One Wing" (For Etheridge). [Eyeball] (2) 93, p. 27.
3473. KNIGHTEN, Merrell
    "Authoritarian." [SoCoast] (15) Je 93, p. 25.
3474. KNOBLOCH, Marta
    "Don Quixote's Counsel to Poets." [Amelia] (7:2, #21) 93, p. 19.
3475. KNOEPFLE, John
    "The Potter" (From Song Dynasty Poems, tr. of Mei Yaochen, w. Wang Shouyi).
    [DogRR] (12:1, #23) Spr-Sum 93, p. 54.
3476. KNOTT, Bill
    "Homicidal Domicile II: Night of the No-Par." [ProseP] (2) 93, p. 54.
3477. KNOX, Caroline
    "Herculaneum." [ApalQ] (35) 90, p. 52-57.
3478. KNUTSON, Nancy Roxbury
    "Clearing." [Elf] (3:4) Wint 93, p. 35.
    "Little Lion." [Kalliope] (15:2) 93, p. 54.
3479. KO, Chang Soo
    "Evening Wind" (tr. of Kang Un-kyo). [Vis] (43) 93, p. 31.
    "Festival in Fishing Village No. 5" (tr. of Je-chun Park). [ChiR] (39:3/4) 93, p. 251.
    "Light" (tr. by the author). [Vis] (43) 93, p. 33.
    "Line Sketch" (No. 2, No. 3., tr. of Moon Duk-soo). [Vis] (43) 93, p. 33.
    "My Mind" (tr. of Kim Kwang-sup). [Vis] (43) 93, p. 32.
    "Poetry Is Wine" (tr. of Chung Gong-chae). [Vis] (43) 93, p. 32.
3480. KO, Un
    "Two Zen Poems" ("Beef," "Mountain's a," tr. by David R. McCann). [ChiR]
    (39:3/4) 93, p. 243.
3481. KO, Won
    "A Little While." [ChiR] (39:3/4) 93, p. 17.
3482. KOBYLARZ, Phil
    "Of Icons and Roaches." [ColR] (20:1) Spr 93, p. 66-68.
3483. KOCBEK, Edvard
    "Occurrence" (tr. by Michael Biggins). [GrandS] (11:4, #44) 93, p. 203.
    "A Plea" (tr. by Michael Biggins). [GrandS] (11:4, #44) 93, p. 204-205.

3484. KOCH, Kenneth
"The New York Times, Sunday, October 25, 1953" (w. John Ashbery). [Chelsea] (55) 93, p. 23-31.
"One Train May Hide Another" (sign at a railroad crossing in Kenya). [NewYRB] (40:7) 8 Ap 93, p. 36.
"Poem: Here there are girls with tearing breasts." [QRL] (12:32/33) 93, p. 453-454.
"A Postcard to Popeye" (w. John Ashbery). [Chelsea] (55) 93, p. 21-22.
"Question in Red Ink." [QRL] (12:32/33) 93, p. 453.
3485. KOCHER, Ruth Ellen
"1944." [AntR] (51:4) Fall 93, p. 563.
3486. KOEHLER, Krzysztof
"Germany, Bavaria" (tr. by Tomek Bieron). [Verse] (10:2) Sum 93, p. 40.
3487. KOEHN, David
"The Professor's Wife to the College Boy." [ArtfulD] (24/25) 93, p. 126.
3488. KOENINGER, Kainoa
"Jamestown." [Obs] (8:2) Fall-Wint 93, p. 117.
"Malaika Waits for the Good Times (Re-Mix Version)." [Obs] (8:2) Fall-Wint 93, p. 120.
"Malaika Waits for the Good Times." [Obs] (8:2) Fall-Wint 93, p. 119-120.
"Minority." [Obs] (8:2) Fall-Wint 93, p. 121.
"Oh Lord, Oh Lord, Oh Lord" (for Jackie Robinson). [Obs] (8:2) Fall-Wint 93, p. 119.
"Scripture of the Heart." [Obs] (8:2) Fall-Wint 93, p. 118.
"Shadow of Ebony." [Obs] (8:2) Fall-Wint 93, p. 117-118.
3489. KOERNER, Edgar
"The Sound of My Father." [SouthernR] (29:3) Sum, Jl 93, p. 612.
"Vienna in New Orleans, 1940." [AmerS] (62:2) Spr 93, p. 232-233.
3490. KOERTGE, Ron
"The Art of Poetry." [ApalQ] (36/37) 91, p. 86.
"Books." [BelPoJ] (43:3) Spr 93, p. 7.
"Field Report from Sodom." [YellowS] (42) Wint-Spr 93, p. 20.
"Lava Soap." [BelPoJ] (43:3) Spr 93, p. 6.
"Models of Instruction That Encourage Critical Thinking." [ChironR] (12:1, #34) Spr 93, p. 6.
"The Other Side." [ApalQ] (38) 92, p. 67.
"Road Kill." [ApalQ] (38) 92, p. 66.
"Snow Tires." [ChironR] (12:1, #34) Spr 93, p. 6.
"The War." [ChironR] (12:1, #34) Spr 93, p. 6.
3491. KOESTENBAUM, Wayne
"Piano Life." [ParisR] (35:129) Wint 93, p. 185-190.
"Rhapsody" (Excerpt). [KenR] (NS 15:3) Sum 93, p. 149-155.
"Star Vehicles." [NewYorker] (69:34) 18 O 93, p. 98.
3492. KOETHE, John
"Argument in Isolation." [SouthwR] (78:1) Wint 93, p. 54-56.
"Leather Slippers." [QRL] (12:32/33) 93, p. 455.
"Montana." [QRL] (12:32/33) 93, p. 454-455.
3493. KOHLER, Charles
"The Jilted Maiden" (tr. of Eduard Mörike). [Stand] (34:3) Sum 93, p. 67.
3494. KOHLER, Sandra
"February." [WestB] (31/32) 93, p. 170.
"How We Grow." [WestB] (31/32) 93, p. 169.
"Parma" (for Roseann Waldstein). [WestB] (33) 93, p. 6-7.
"Sugar." [WestB] (33) 93, p. 5-6.
KOK, Ingrid de
   See De KOK, Ingrid
KOKI, Francisco Alvarez
   See ALVAREZ-KOKI, Francisco
3495. KOLENIC, Ivan
"Skin Is Wrapping for Bones" (tr. by Stephánia Allen and James Sutherland-Smith). [OxfordM] (9:1) Spr-Sum 93, p. 116-117.
3496. KOLODNY, Susan
"Paros, View from the Harbor" (from the series, "Epicleros"). [BlackWR] (19:2) Spr-Sum 93, p. 7.
"Silk." [Calyx] (14:3) Sum 93, p. 13.
3497. KOLUMBAN, Nicholas
"When I Come Home." [PoetryE] (36) Fall 93, p. 9.

3498. KOMPATZKI, Anuschka
"The Color of Your Eyes" (Poets of High School Age). [HangL] (62) 93, p. 80.
3499. KOMUNYAKAA, Yusef
"Betrayals." [OnTheBus] (5:2, #12) Sum-Fall 93, p. 112.
"Birds on a Powerline." [Callaloo] (16:2) Spr 93, p. 303.
"Brass." [HopewellR] (5) 93, p. 10-11.
"The Citadel." [Thrpny] (52) Wint 93, p. 6.
"Crack." [Callaloo] (16:2) Spr 93, p. 304-305.
"Diorama." [IllinoisR] (1:1) Fall 93, p. 35.
"Ecstatic." [OnTheBus] (5:2, #12) Sum-Fall 93, p. 112.
"Genealogy." [Field] (49) Fall 93, p. 64.
"Imhotep." [HarvardR] (5) Fall 93, p. 32.
"Lady Xoc." [Caliban] (13) 93, p. 83.
"Montage: MTV." [IllinoisR] (1:1) Fall 93, p. 12.
"My Father's Love Letters." [Field] (48) Spr 93, p. 70-71.
"Necrophilia." [Caliban] (13) 93, p. 82.
"A Night in Tunisia." [HopewellR] (5) 93, p. 8.
"Nightfall." [IllinoisR] (1:1) Fall 93, p. 18.
"No-Good Blues." [Field] (49) Fall 93, p. 67-70.
"Outside the Blue Nile." [BostonR] (18:6) D 93-Ja 94, p. 16.
"Pain Merchant." [HopewellR] (5) 93, p. 9.
"A Reed Boat." [Thrpny] (54) Sum 93, p. 33.
"Slam, Dunk, & Hook." [Field] (48) Spr 93, p. 68-69.
"Slattees." [Field] (49) Fall 93, p. 65-66.
"Starlight Scope Myopia." [NewEngR] (15:1) Wint 93, p. 161-162.
3500. KONCEL, Mary A.
"After the Weather." [ProseP] (2) 93, p. 55.
"Erma Jacowitts Pleads Her Case." [SycamoreR] (5:2) Sum 93, p. 61.
"The Sun Workers." [SycamoreR] (5:2) Sum 93, p. 62.
3501. KONDOS, Yánnis
"Hangouts" (from Sto Gyrisma Tis Méras, Athens, 1992, tr. by Yannis Goumas). [Os] (36) Spr 93, p. 33.
"So Much for Traveling" (from Sto Gyrisma Tis Méras, Athens, 1992, tr. by Yannis Goumas). [Os] (36) Spr 93, p. 32.
3502. KONESKI, Blaze
"Prayer" (tr. by Dragana Marinkovic and Richard Burns). [NoDaQ] (61:1) Wint 93, p. 98.
3503. KONO, Juliet S.
"At the Point." [HawaiiR] (17:2, #38) Spr 93, p. 23-24.
"Coral Chips." [BambooR] (57) Wint 93, p. 169-170.
"The Iceman." [BambooR] (57) Wint 93, p. 167-168.
"Red-Light District." [BambooR] (57) Wint 93, p. 171-172.
"The Smell of the Sea." [BambooR] (57) Wint 93, p. 165-166.
KONOFALSKI, Wendy Rader
See RADER-KONOFALSKI, Wendy
3504. KONRAD, Linda
"Father's Fall." [EngJ] (82:2) F 93, p. 91.
3505. KONSTANTYN, Michel
"Christopher Columbus" (tr. of Simon, Nachmias, w. Robert Friend). [Trans] (28) Spr 93, p. 105.
"I Don't Understand Russian, and I Translate" (tr. of Simon, Nachmias, w. Robert Friend). [Trans] (28) Spr 93, p. 106.
"The Odor of Lemon, the Odor of Sweat Reminds Me of Love" (tr. of Simon, Nachmias, w. Robert Friend). [Trans] (28) Spr 93, p. 104.
3506. KOO, Carolyn
"Ambivalence." [NewAW] (11) Sum-Fall 93, p. 108.
"Silent Film." [NewAW] (11) Sum-Fall 93, p. 107.
3507. KOOMAN, Ko
"Diminuendo" (from the cycle "For My Unborn Son," tr. of Song Lin, from the Dutch version by Maghiel van Crevel). [GreenMR] (NS 6:2) Sum-Fall 93, p. 144.
"Paul Celan in the Seine" (from the cycle "For My Unborn Son," tr. of Song Lin, from the Dutch version by Maghiel van Crevel). [GreenMR] (NS 6:2) Sum-Fall 93, p. 145.
KOON, Woon
See WOON, Koon

3508. KOONTZ, Haven
"A Crown of Letters to Pancho, After the Fact" (Excerpt). [HopewellR] (5) 93, p. 7.
"The Need for Change." [HopewellR] (5) 93, p. 6.
3509. KOONTZ, Tom
"The Gift." [HopewellR] (5) 93, p. 82.
"A Vampire Song" (for Haven). [HopewellR] (5) 93, p. 83.
3510. KOOSER, Ted
"Abandoned Farmhouse." [EngJ] (82:6) O 93, p. 86.
"An Abandoned Stone Schoolhouse in the Nebraska Sandhills." [PraS] (67:3) Fall
93, p. 64.
"After Burning Off the Garden for Spring." [PraS] (67:3) Fall 93, p. 62-63.
"A Blind Woman." [PraS] (67:3) Fall 93, p. 62.
"City Limits." [PoetryNW] (34:1) Spr 93, p. 10-11.
"In Passing." [PraS] (67:3) Fall 93, p. 61.
"Poem before Breakfast." [PraS] (67:3) Fall 93, p. 65.
"A Sound in the Night." [PraS] (67:3) Fall 93, p. 63.
"Surveyors." [KenR] (NS 15:3) Sum 93, p. 51-52.
"Weather Central." [KenR] (NS 15:3) Sum 93, p. 51.
3511. KOPEC, Carol
"On Hiding." [WebR] (17) Fall 93, p. 72.
3512. KOPLOW, Gail M.
"November." [SinW] (51) Wint 93-94, p. 83-84.
3513. KOPP, Karl
"Cana." [ChironR] (12:3, #36) Aut 93, p. 12.
"The Further Demise of Robin Hood." [CharR] (19:1) Spr 93, p. 85-86.
"Hazard Avenue." [CharR] (19:1) Spr 93, p. 81-85.
"Herrenbad." [ChironR] (12:3, #36) Aut 93, p. 12.
"Rude But Nonetheless an Awakening." [ChironR] (12:3, #36) Aut 93, p. 12.
3514. KOPP, Richard
"The Rendez-Vous at Cophinou" (tr. of Louis Gaulis). [LitR] (36:4) Sum 93, p. 528.
"Service for the Dead" (tr. of Maurice Chappaz). [LitR] (36:4) Sum 93, p. 530.
"The Unknowing" (tr. of Philippe Jaccottet). [LitR] (36:4) Sum 93, p. 526.
3515. KOPPLE, K. A.
"#34. I can't drink" (tr. of Mercedes Roffe). [Sonora] (24/25) Spr 93, p. 18-20.
3516. KÖRÖSY, Mária
"Before a Rendezvous" (tr. of Gyorgy Petri, w. Bruce Berlind). [ConnPR] (12:1) 93,
p. 6.
"Bell Inscription" (Ars Poetica, tr. of Sándor Kányádi, w. Bruce Berlind). [WillowS]
(33) Wint 93, p. 23.
"Bird" (tr. of Ottó Orbán, w. Jascha Kessler). [InterPR] (19:2) Fall 93, p. 39.
"The Boat" (tr. of Ottó Orbán, w. Jascha Kessler). [InterPR] (19:2) Fall 93, p. 47.
"Builders" (tr. of Ottó Orbán, w. Jascha Kessler). [InterPR] (19:2) Fall 93, p. 41.
"Canto" (tr. of Ottó Orbán, w. Bruce Berlind). [CharR] (19:2) Fall 93, p. 144-145.
"Crisis" (tr. of Gyorgy Petri, w. Bruce Berlind). [ConnPR] (12:1) 93, p. 5.
"The General" (tr. of Ottó Orbán, w. Jascha Kessler). [InterPR] (19:2) Fall 93, p. 45.
"Guitar" (tr. of Ottó Orbán, w. Jascha Kessler). [InterPR] (19:2) Fall 93, p. 49.
"How Many" (tr. of Imre Oravecz, w. Bruce Berlind). [ProseP] (1) 92, p. 65.
"I Remember Clearly" (tr. of Imre Oravecz, w. Bruce Berlind). [ProseP] (1) 92, p.
66-67.
"Mane and Skull" (a fragment, tr. of Sándor Kányádi, w. Bruce Berlind). [WillowS]
(33) Wint 93, p. 22.
"Minneapolis Intersection" (a topographical poem, to Ken Bales, tr. of Ottó Orbán,
w. Bruce Berlind). [CharR] (19:2) Fall 93, p. 140-141.
"Oklahoma Gold" (tr. of Ottó Orbán, w. Bruce Berlind). [CharR] (19:2) Fall 93, p.
142-143.
"On My Fifty-First Birthday in Minneapolis" (tr. of Ottó Orbán, w. Bruce Berlind).
[CharR] (19:2) Fall 93, p. 147.
"Snow" (Eyewitness News, Channel Five, Minneapolis-St. Paul, tr. of Ottó Orbán,
w. Bruce Berlind). [CharR] (19:2) Fall 93, p. 140.
"Stopgap Arrangement" (tr. of Gyorgy Petri, w. Bruce Berlind). [ConnPR] (12:1)
93, p. 9.
"A Stroll" (tr. of Ottó Orbán, w. Jascha Kessler). [InterPR] (19:2) Fall 93, p. 43.
"Successful Effort" (tr. of Gyula Illyés, w. Bruce Berlind). [ProseP] (1) 92, p. 43.
"Sunday in a Small American Town" (tr. of Ottó Orbán, w. Bruce Berlind). [CharR]
(19:2) Fall 93, p. 146.

"Thus I Registered" (tr. of Gyorgy Petri, w. Bruce Berlind). [ConnPR] (12:1) 93, p. 10.
"To Kornis" (tr. of Gyorgy Petri, w. Bruce Berlind). [ConnPR] (12:1) 93, p. 11.
"University Commencement" ("The National Weather Service has issued a tornado warning," tr. of Ottó Orbán, w. Bruce Berlind). [CharR] (19:2) Fall 93, p. 147.
3517. KORT, Ellen
"Sheep Station." [Nimrod] (37:1) Fall-Wint 93, p. 120.
3518. KORT, S. (Susanne)
"Bride" (after Life of the Aztecs). [AntigR] (95) Aut 93, p. 76.
"Don Antonio, at His Club, Shares a Secret." [AntigR] (95) Aut 93, p. 77.
"For Esther — (Apoc.)." [NowestR] (31:2) 93, p. 14.
"Fugue." [AntigR] (95) Aut 93, p. 78-79.
"Stranger." [CaribbeanW] (7) 93, p. 39.
"Tone Deaf." [SpoonR] (18:2) Sum-Fall 93, p. 52.
"Tourist Season." [Pearl] (19) Fall-Wint 93, p. 11.
3519. KOSER, Jose
"Autorretrato." [Trasimagen] (1:1) Otoño-Invierno 93, p. 14.
"Vanitas." [Trasimagen] (1:1) Otoño-Invierno 93, p. 15.
3520. KOSSMAN, Nina
"Life within a Museum" (To Osip Mandelstam, in Russian and English, tr. by the author). [InterPR] (19:1) Spr 93, p. 46-49.
"The New Leda" (in Russian and English, tr. by the author). [InterPR] (19:1) Spr 93, p. 52-55.
"On Red Steed" (tr. of Marina Tsvetayva). [Epiphany] (4:3) Jl 93, p. 203-208.
"Shape of a Whisper" (in Russian and English, tr. by the author). [InterPR] (19:1) Spr 93, p. 50-51.
"The Wake" (in Russian and English, tr. by the author). [InterPR] (19:1) Spr 93, p. 42-45.
"Wakefulness" (in Russian and English, tr. by the author). [InterPR] (19:1) Spr 93, p. 56-57.
3521. KOSTELANETZ, Richard
"(Complete) Shorter Stories (1992)." [DogRR] (12:1, #23) Spr-Sum 93, p. 23, 35, 44.
"Epiphanies (1993-A)." [Pembroke] (25) 93, p. 44-48.
"Intelligence of Rhyming: Poems & Stories — VI." [RiverS] (39) 93, p. 50-55.
"It Must Be Love." [Asylum] (8) 93, p. 129.
"Lovings Three: A Collection of Stories" (Excerpt). [WorldL] (4) 93, p. 41-43.
"Minimal Fictions." [SoCarR] (26:1) Fall 93, p. 168-170.
"String Two." [HeavenB] (10) Wint-Spr 93, p. 3-4, 8-11, 17-21, 23-24, 28-33, 40-61.
"Twelve-Tone Row 1." [PoetryUSA] (25/26) 93, p. 16.
3522. KOSTENKO, Lina
"In the Morning" (tr. by Marta Sawczuk). [Vis] (43) 93, p. 53.
"The Mail Box" (tr. by Marta Sawczuk). [Vis] (43) 93, p. 54.
3523. KOSTKOWSKA, Justyna
"An Evening with the Author" (tr. of Leszek Szaruga, w. W.D. and K. B. Snodgrass and Peter Lengyel). [Salm] (97) Wint 93, p. 111.
"Watchman" (for Zbigniew Herbert, tr. of Leszek Szaruga, w. W.D. and K. B. Snodgrass and Peter Lengyel). [Salm] (97) Wint 93, p. 110.
3524. KOSTOLEFSKY, Joseph
"The Tombigbee's ugly, the Hudson's a mess." [Light] (6) Sum 93, p. 22.
3525. KOSTOS, Dean Mayos
"Celestial Rust." [JamesWR] (10:2) Wint 93, p. 11.
KOTARO, Takamura
See TAKAMURA, Kotaro
3526. KOTZIN, Miriam N.
"Divinations." [SouthernHR] (27:2) Spr 93, p. 150.
3527. KOUMJIAN, Vaughn
"The Man Upstairs." [Light] (5) Spr 93, p. 21.
"Past This Ignorant Present" (— Macbeth). [Light] (7) Aut 93, p. 12.
3528. KOUROUS, Sharon
"Each Leaf Individual." [Gaia] (1/2) Ap-Jl 93, p. 21.
"Fire Frets Uneasily on Leaf." [Gaia] (1/2) Ap-Jl 93, p. 21.
3529. KOVACS, Edna
"Fish Magic." [BellArk] (9:5) S-O 93, p. 6.
"Freedom." [BellArk] (9:1) Ja-F 93, p. 21.

"The Good Earth." [BellArk] (9:5) S-O 93, p. 6.
"New Year." [BellArk] (9:2) Mr-Ap 93, p. 13.
"Nocturne." [BellArk] (9:3) My-Je 93, p. 9.
"Runaway Dreamer." [BellArk] (9:1) Ja-F 93, p. 21.
"Where I Come From." [BellArk] (9:2) Mr-Ap 93, p. 13.
3530. KOWALSKI, Patricia J.
      "Disclosure." [HopewellR] (5) 93, p. 101.
3531. KOWIT, Steve
      "From the California Beach Town." [OnTheBus] (6:1, #13) Wint 93-Spr 94, p. 134 -
          135.
      "Jacumba." [NewYorker] (69:29) 13 S 93, p. 102.
      "Perognathus Fallax." [HiramPoR] (53/54) Fall 92-Sum 93, p. 44-45.
      "The Prodigal Son's Brother." [Conscience] (14:1/2) Spr-Sum 93, p. 44.
3532. KOZAK, Roberta
      "The Green Room." [PoetryNW] (34:2) Sum 93, p. 42-44.
      "Swimming Pools from the Air." [PoetryNW] (34:2) Sum 93, p. 40-42.
3533. KOZMA, Lynn
      "Great South Bay." [SmPd] (30:3, #89) Fall 93, p. 29.
3534. KRACHUN, Peggy
      "Misfits in a Singles Bar." [TickleAce] (24) Fall-Wint 92, p. 89-90.
3535. KRAFT, Eugene
      "Calling." [Contact] (11:65/66/67) Spr 93, p. 54.
      "The Common One." [HawaiiR] (16:3, #36) Wint 93, p. 56.
      "Natural Sequence." [Nimrod] (37:1) Fall-Wint 93, p. 121.
3536. KRAJECK, Elizabeth
      "The Branches." [HopewellR] (5) 93, p. 116.
      "For All We Know." [HopewellR] (5) 93, p. 117.
3537. KRAMAN, Cynthia
      "Chaucer at Aldgate." [ParisR] (35:127) Sum 93, p. 40.
      "Chaucer at Park House." [ParisR] (35:127) Sum 93, p. 41.
      "In the Reading Room of the 42nd Street Library." [ParisR] (35:127) Sum 93, p. 38.
      "Nothing But Margery Kempe." [ParisR] (35:127) Sum 93, p. 39.
3538. KRAMER, Aaron
      "The Child and the Old Man" (tr. of Rajzel Zychlinska). [Vis] (41) 93, p. 21.
      "Garbage Truck." [PikeF] (11) Fall 93, p. 35.
      "Ghetto Song" (tr. of anonymous Yiddish poem). [Vis] (41) 93, p. 12.
      "Glaucoma." [CumbPR] (12:2) Spr 93, p. 48.
      "The Lawn." [Confr] (51) Sum 93, p. 252.
3539. KRAMER, Brandi
      "A Case for Mediocrity" (Young Writers, age 11). [PikeF] (11) Fall 93, p. 19.
3540. KRAMER, Karen
      "Lloreda, Llorar, Lluvia" (For Alejandro. Poets of High School Age). [HangL] (62)
          93, p. 81.
3541. KRAMER, Larry
      "Ash." [QRL] (12:32/33) 93, p. 217.
      "Baltimore." [QRL] (12:32/33) 93, p. 219.
      "The Guard." [QRL] (12:32/33) 93, p. 214.
      "The Stewardess." [QRL] (12:32/33) 93, p. 214-215.
      "A View of the Water." [QRL] (12:32/33) 93, p. 219-220.
      "Wild Onions" (A Memoir of West Texas and St. Mary's Academy). [QRL]
          (12:32/33) 93, p. 215-216.
      "The Young Woman at the Window." [QRL] (12:32/33) 93, p. 217-218.
3542. KRAMPF, Thomas
      "Brain Disease." [NewYorkQ] (50) 93, p. 68-69.
3543. KRAPF, Norbert
      "The Meditation Room" (The Bavarian National Museum, Nuremberg, January,
          1989). [BelPoJ] (43:4) Sum 93, p. 22-23.
3544. KRAUS, Sharon
      "The Girls' Home." [SouthernPR] (33:1) Spr 93, p. 64-65.
      "Penance." [SouthernPR] (33:1) Spr 93, p. 65-66.
3545. KRAUSHAAR, Mark
      "Chloral Hydrate, 500 mg May Repeat Times One As Needed for Sleeplessness."
          [SpoonR] (18:1) Wint-Spr 93, p. 112.-113.
      "Fast Loans." [PoetryNW] (34:3) Aut 93, p. 22-23.
      "Free Throw." [Shen] (43:1) Spr 93, p. 58-59.

"I Want the Power to Go Out" (Author's twelve-year-old niece). [GettyR] (6:3) Sum
    93, p. 505.
"Roxanne." [SpoonR] (18:1) Wint-Spr 93, p. 114.
"The Waving Lady." [PoetryNW] (34:3) Aut 93, p. 21-22.
3546. KRAVANJA, Sonja
"The Color of Time" (tr. of Tomaz Salamun). [Pequod] (36) 93, p. 119.
"From Night to Night" (tr. of Tomaz Salamun). [Confr] (51) Sum 93, p. 241.
"Gesture" (tr. of Tomaz Salamun). [Confr] (51) Sum 93, p. 242.
"The Heart of Europe Is Elegant and Dead" (tr. of Tomaz Salamun). [Confr] (51)
    Sum 93, p. 240.
"I Am Abandoning Iconoclastic Levels" (tr. of Tomaz Salamun). [Pequod] (36) 93,
    p. 120-121.
"Word" (tr. of Tomaz Salamun). [Pequod] (36) 93, p. 118.
3547. KRCHOVSKY, J. H.
"Above the morning thrushes are to be heard singing" (tr. by Ellen Rosenbaum).
    [OxfordM] (9:1) Spr-Sum 93, p. 104.
"All writing seems to me today idiotic" (tr. by Ellen Rosenbaum). [OxfordM] (9:1)
    Spr-Sum 93, p. 102.
"Alone with myself and even alone within my very self" (tr. by Ellen Rosenbaum).
    [OxfordM] (9:1) Spr-Sum 93, p. 104.
"Does he want to vanish without a trace" (tr. by Ellen Rosenbaum). [OxfordM] (9:1)
    Spr-Sum 93, p. 101.
"I accidentally poured this lousy coffee on myself" (tr. by Ellen Rosenbaum).
    [OxfordM] (9:1) Spr-Sum 93, p. 101-102.
"I always take my own death with me when I go outside" (tr. by Ellen Rosenbaum).
    [OxfordM] (9:1) Spr-Sum 93, p. 104.
"I go out at night into the garden naked" (tr. by Ellen Rosenbaum). [OxfordM] (9:1)
    Spr-Sum 93, p. 105.
"Shod and clothed I am counting the minutes" (tr. by Ellen Rosenbaum). [OxfordM]
    (9:1) Spr-Sum 93, p. 102-103.
"Whitsunday in St. Nicholas' Cathedral" (tr. by Ellen Rosenbaum). [OxfordM] (9:1)
    Spr-Sum 93, p. 103.
3548. KREBS, Michael
"All the Best Witches Have Been Burned." [DogRR] (12:1, #23) Spr-Sum 93, p. 30.
3549. KREMERS, Carolyn
"Backcountry Unit #12" (for Alaska Governor Walter Hickel). [ProseP] (1) 92, p.
    49-50.
3550. KRESS, Leonard
"Anonymous Church Mural, Harrow Gate Martyrdom of Our Lord." [LullwaterR]
    (4:2) Spr-Sum 93, p. 32-33.
"To Spot the Centralia Mine Fire." [PaintedB] (50/51) 93, p. 103.
3551. KRETZ, T. (Thomas)
"Listing." [SoCoast] (14) Ja 93, p. 44-45.
"Missing the Barque." [ChrC] (110:28) 13 O 93, p. 964.
"Sugar for Diabetics." [Pearl] (17) Spr 93, p. 11.
"Sunday Drive." [HolCrit] (30:2) Ap 93, p. 19.
"Thomas More (1478-1535)." [ChrC] (110:3) 27 Ja 93, p. 84.
"What You Do Not Know." [BellR] (16:1/2) Spr-Fall 93, p. 19.
3552. KRIVANEK, Vladimír
"Pigeons" (tr. by Ewald Osers). [OxfordM] (9:1) Spr-Sum 93, p. 84-85.
3553. KROEKER, G. W.
"Memorial." [Parting] (6:2) Wint 93, p. 17-18.
"Mind Train." [Parting] (6:2) Wint 93, p. 20.
3554. KROLL, Ernest
"Azalea." [Light] (7) Aut 93, p. 1.
"Bird Life in the Business District." [SmPd] (30:3, #89) Fall 93, p. 25.
"Day Lily." [Light] (7) Aut 93, p. 1.
"Dreiser Books Passage." [Bogg] (66) Wint 92-93, p. 37.
"Edges." [TexasR] (14:1/2) Spr-Sum 93, p. 98.
"Les Grandes Chaleurs" (August in France). [Light] (7) Aut 93, p. 19.
"High Summer on High Street" (Newburyport). [Light] (6) Sum 93, p. 7.
"Paging Isaac Watts." [Light] (5) Spr 93, p. 14.
"Paradox." [Light] (7) Aut 93, p. 14.
3555. KROLL, Jeri
"Felis Domestica." [Nimrod] (36:2) Spr-Sum 93, p. 11.

3556. KROLL, Judith
"Buying the Dildo." [QRL] (12:32/33) 93, p. 222-223.
"In Another World." [QRL] (12:32/33) 93, p. 222.
"Unwitnessed Nightfall." [QRL] (12:32/33) 93, p. 221.
3557. KROLOW, Karl
"Behind My Back" (tr. by Stuart Friebert). [JamesWR] (10:3) Spr 93, p. 13.
"Departure" (tr. by Stuart Friebert). [HarvardR] (5) Fall 93, p. 47.
"Encounter on the Street." [Crazy] (44) Spr 93, p. 68.
"In My Old Age" (tr. by Stuart Friebert). [HarvardR] (5) Fall 93, p. 47.
"Stele for Catullus" (tr. by Stuart Friebert). [Os] (37) Wint 93, p. 9.
"Stele fúr Catull." [Os] (37) Wint 93, p. 8.
3558. KROMAN, Deborah
"To Shakespeare on the Death of His Son." [SoCoast] (14) Ja 93, p. 48.
3559. KRONEN, Steve
"Your Voice." [RiverS] (38) 93, p. 5.
3560. KRONENFELD, Judy
"At Home." [PikeF] (11) Fall 93, p. 8.
"The Oranges, the Dog, the Wind." [PikeF] (11) Fall 93, p. 3.
3561. KROSBY, Anne
"Dark Victory." [Calyx] (15:1) Wint 93-94, p. 115.
3562. KROUSE, Matthew
"From the Prophet's Mosque." [BostonR] (18:3/4) Je-Ag 93, p. 31.
"Ram'zaan." [BostonR] (18:3/4) Je-Ag 93, p. 31.
3563. KRUEGER, Michele
"Passion Weather." [MidwQ] (35:1) Aut 93, p. 40.
"Womb Regalia." [MidwQ] (35:1) Aut 93, p. 41.
3564. KRÜGER, Michael
"Guided Tour of a Well-Known House" (tr. by Richard Dove). [NewYorker] (69:42)
13 D 93, p. 96.
"Idylls and Illusions" (Excerpt). [GrandS] (11:4, #44) 93, p. 148-150.
KRUIP, Valentina Gnup
See GNUP-KRUIP, Valentina
3565. KRUT, Robert
"Being Here, Awake." [Footwork] (23) 93, p. 136-137.
3566. KRYSL, Marilyn
"Suite for Kokodicholai, Sri Lanka." [KenR] (NS 15:2) Spr 93, p. 141-143.
3567. KRYSS, Tom
"Baghdad Rainbow." [OnTheBus] (6:1, #13) Wint 93-Spr 94, p. 136.
3568. KUAN, Hsiu
"Bad Government" (tr. by J. P. Seaton). [Sulfur] (33) Fall 93, p. 158.
"Ch'i Liang's Good Wife" (tr. by J. P. Seaton). [Sulfur] (33) Fall 93, p. 154.
"On the Border, Three Poems" (tr. by J. P. Seaton). [Sulfur] (33) Fall 93, p. 152-153.
"Song of the Palace of Ch'en" (tr. by J. P. Seaton). [Sulfur] (33) Fall 93, p. 155.
"Song of the Righteous Man" (tr. by J. P. Seaton). [Sulfur] (33) Fall 93, p. 157.
"Song of the Wasteland" (tr. by J. P. Seaton). [Sulfur] (33) Fall 93, p. 156-157.
"Three Verses on Running into the Taoist Master 'In Emptiness'" (tr. by J. P.
Seaton). [Sulfur] (33) Fall 93, p. 155-156.
"Written in the Mountains" (tr. by J. P. Seaton). [Sulfur] (33) Fall 93, p. 153-154.
3569. KUBICEK, J. L.
"In the Land Where Ludwig Came Only in the Evening." [HampSPR] Wint 93, p.
69.
3570. KUBIE, Rachel
"Dirt Bikes." [ChironR] (12:3, #36) Aut 93, p. 8.
"Eight Tattoos." [ChironR] (12:3, #36) Aut 93, p. 8.
"Up." [ChironR] (12:3, #36) Aut 93, p. 8.
3571. KUCHINSKY, Walter
"Growing Up." [Pearl] (19) Fall-Wint 93, p. 58.
"Small Town." [Footwork] (23) 93, p. 88.
3572. KUDERKO, Lynne
"Colors." [PraS] (67:1) Spr 93, p. 120-121.
"Lessons in Cartography." [Ascent] (17:3) Spr 93, p. 58.
"Photograph for My Father: Kansas Settlers, 1897." [PraS] (67:1) Spr 93, p. 119-
120.
3573. KUENZI, David
"The Citizen's Lobby." [CarolQ] (46:1) Fall 93, p. 14.

3574. KUGLE, Scott
"Taking the Bus along Khayaban-e-Iqbal" (for Sameer on a distant subway).
[HawaiiR] (17:3, #39) Fall 93, p. 91-92.
3575. KUMALO, Lerato
"No More Words Now." [Drumvoices] (3:1/2) Fall-Wint 93-94, p. 89-90.
3576. KUMIN, Maxine
"After the Cleansing of Bosnia." [Nat] (257:11) 11 O 93, p. 402.
"Shelling Jacobs Cattle Beans." [NewEngR] (15:1) Wint 93, p. 163-164.
3577. KUMMER, John
"Selling the Farm." [Farm] (10:1) Spr-Sum 93, p. 128.
3578. KUNDID, David
"The Kurds" (Young Writers, age 11). [PikeF] (11) Fall 93, p. 18.
3579. KUNERT, Günter
"Jewish Cemetery in Weissensee" (tr. by Agnes Stein). [Pequod] (35) 93, p. 104.
3580. KUNITZ, Stanley
"My Mother's Pears." [NewYorker] (69:13) 17 My 93, p. 78.
"Proteus." [NewYorker] (69:23) 26 Jl 93, p. 52.
"Route Six." [NewEngR] (15:1) Wint 93, p. 165-166.
3581. KUNTZ, Laurie
"Survivors." [SouthernPR] (33:2) Fall 93, p. 10.
"Yad Vashem." [SouthernPR] (33:2) Fall 93, p. 17-18.
3582. KUNZE, Reiner
"At E.'s Home in Vresice" (tr. by John M. Gogol). [QRL] (12:32/33) 93, p. 455-456.
"Hungarian Rhapsody 66" (for Tibor Déry, tr. by John M. Gogol). [QRL] (12:32/33)
93, p. 456.
3583. KUO, Michael
"Nightwatch." [Lactuca] (17) Apr 93, p. 31.
3584. KUPECZ, Jim
"My Spiritual Advisor." [Ploughs] (19:1) Spr 93, p. 138-139.
"An Ordinary Woman." [Ploughs] (19:1) Spr 93, p. 140.
3585. KUPFERBERG, Tuli
"The New America." [Contact] (11:65/66/67) Spr 93, p. 5.
3586. KURASCH, Dave
"Coffee, the Cross, Change." [Sonora] (24/25) Spr 93, p. 64-65.
"Grace." [Farm] (10:2) Fall-Wint 93-94, p. 38.
"My Brother's Ballet Dancer." [Sonora] (24/25) Spr 93, p. 62-63.
3587. KURTZAHN, Leslie J.
"Yard Sale." [CumbPR] (12:2) Spr 93, p. 49.
3588. KURZ, Egon
"Go Figure." [Light] (6) Sum 93, p. 10.
3589. KUS, Mira
"I peak around the corner, ask" (tr. by Daniel Bourne). [RiverS] (38) 93, p. 66.
"Love" (tr. by Daniel Bourne). [RiverS] (38) 93, p. 67.
3590. KUSHNER, Dale M.
"Detroit Summer." [HayF] (12) Spr-Sum 93, p. 119.
"Her Garden." [Footwork] (23) 93, p. 30.
"Scapegoat." [Footwork] (23) 93, p. 30.
3591. KUTCHINS, Laurie
"Bones." [Calyx] (15:1) Wint 93-94, p. 10-11.
"Mangos." [Calyx] (15:1) Wint 93-94, p. 8-9.
"Spring." [Calyx] (14:3) Sum 93, p. 34-35.
"The Wind." [Calyx] (14:3) Sum 93, p. 36-37.
3592. KUZMA, Greg
"1000 Schuyler." [PoetC] (25:1) Fall 93, p. 11-15.
"First Frost." [Crazy] (45) Wint 93, p. 82-85.
"John Brehm's Latest Poem." [PraS] (67:3) Fall 93, p. 111-114.
"Pallbearing" (in memory of Kay Patterson). [GreenMR] (NS 6:2) Sum-Fall 93, p.
33-34.
"The Rain." [MassR] (34:2) Sum 93, p. 222-224.
"Rhyme." [HarvardR] (5) Fall 93, p. 40-43.
"The Stars." [PraS] (67:3) Fall 93, p. 106-111.
3593. KWA, Lydia
"As She Caught Death." [WestCL] (27:2, #11) Fall 93, p. 118-119.
"Pasar Malam (Night-Market)." [WestCL] (27:2, #11) Fall 93, p. 117.
"Uniforms." [WestCL] (27:2, #11) Fall 93, p. 120-121.
"Who Is She Beyond." [WestCL] (27:2, #11) Fall 93, p. 122-123.

KWANG-SUP, Kim
   See KIM, Kwang-sup
3594. KYLE, Christiane Jacox
   "Poems of the Mothers" (Selections: 6 poems, tr. of Gabriela Mistral). [Iowa] (23:3)
      Fall 93, p. 170-172.
   "Poems of the Saddest Mother" (Selections: 2 poems, tr. of Gabriela Mistral). [Iowa]
      (23:3) Fall 93, p. 172-173.
3595. KYNELL, Teresa
   "There Are Days." [Elf] (3:1) Spr 93, p. 40.
KYOKO, Mori
   See MORI, Kyoko
KYONG-RIM, Sin
   See SIN, Kyong-rim
La . . .
   See also names beginning with "La" without the following space, filed below in
      their alphabetic positions, e.g., LaSALLE.
3596. La FLAMME, Michelle
   "Erasure." [WestCL] (27:1, #10) Spr 93, p. 29.
   "Turning the Words on Surfaces into Faces Without Masks." [WestCL] (27:1, #10)
      Spr 93, p. 27-28.
3597. La RUE, Mark
   "Punto de Vista." [AmerPoR] (22:5) S-O 93, p. 33.
3598. LaBAR, Ann
   "The Dreaming." [AnthNEW] (5) 93, p. 25.
3599. LaBAW, Dominique
   "Offered and Taken." [AmerPoR] (22:5) S-O 93, p. 24.
   "Personal Cult." [AmerPoR] (22:5) S-O 93, p. 24.
3600. LABÉ, Louise
   "Ten Sonnets" (tr. by Karin Lessing). [Sulfur] (33) Fall 93, p. 29-34.
3601. LABINSKI, Marek
   "From Lively Painful Twigs" (tr. of Halina Poswiatowska). [NewRena] (8:3, #26)
      Spr 93, p. 73.
   "The Sliver of My Imagination" (tr. of Halina Poswiatowska). [NewRena] (8:3, #26)
      Spr 93, p. 71.
3602. LaBOMBARD, Joan
   "The Revenants." [TarRP] (33:1) Fall 93, p. 58.
3603. LABRIOLA, Gina
   "Aquilone" (from "Alveare di Specchi"). [NewRena] (8:3, #26) Spr 93, p. 54.
   "Il Vento Ha Fame" (from "Alveare di Specchi"). [NewRena] (8:3, #26) Spr 93, p.
      52.
   "Instant" (from "Hive of Mirrors," tr. by Ruth Feldman). [NewRena] (8:3, #26) Spr
      93, p. 57.
   "Istante" (from "Alveare di Specchi"). [NewRena] (8:3, #26) Spr 93, p. 56.
   "Kite" (to F., from "Hive of Mirrors," tr. by Ruth Feldman). [NewRena] (8:3, #26)
      Spr 93, p. 55.
   "The Wind Is Hungry" (from "Hive of Mirrors," tr. by Ruth Feldman). [NewRena]
      (8:3, #26) Spr 93, p. 53.
LaBRUNO, Carmen Michael
   See LaBRUNO, Michael (Carmen Michael)
3604. LaBRUNO, Michael (Carmen Michael)
   "Citizens Committees." [Footwork] (23) 93, p. 138.
   "Corrections' Officers Certainly Predate Pyramids." [Footwork] (23) 93, p. 137.
   "Each Breath More Precious." [Footwork] (23) 93, p. 137-138.
   "A Promise Renews Its Intimate Minute." [Footwork] (23) 93, p. 139.
3605. LACABA, Emmanuel
   "Open Letters to Filipino Artists." [Bomb] (45) Fall 93, p. 84.
   "Pateros Blues." [Bomb] (45) Fall 93, p. 84.
3606. LACKEY, Joe
   "The Reading." [Bogg] (66) Wint 92-93, p. 35.
3607. LACOUR, Tyrone
   "Finding Myself." [PoetryUSA] (25/26) 93, p. 54.
3608. LaFEMINA, Gerry
   "Giullian's Pool & Billiards." [Outbr] (24) 93, p. 72-73.
   "Heat Lightning above Lake Michigan." [Outbr] (24) 93, p. 74.
   "Recyclables." [CimR] (103) Ap 93, p. 87-88.

LaFLAMME, Michelle
        See La FLAMME, Michelle
3609. LAGASO, Malia
        "The Woman Who Mistook Her Life As Teatime." [HawaiiR] (17:1, #37) Spr 93, p.
            160-161.
3610. LAGIER, Jennifer
        "Italian American Home School." [Footwork] (23) 93, p. 139.
3611. LAGOMARSINO, Nancy
        "Along for the Ride." [ProseP] (2) 93, p. 116-117.
        "Fear in a Public Place." [ProseP] (2) 93, p. 118.
        "My Grandmother and I Say Goodbye" (to Blanche K. Rice, 1893-1978). [ProseP]
            (2) 93, p. 56.
        "The Provinces of Sleep." [ProseP] (2) 93, p. 118.
3612. LAING, Dilys
        "Kwan Yin" (illustrated by Oriole Farb Feshbach). [MassR] (34:2) Sum 93, p. 252 -
            253.
3613. LAINO, E. J. Miller
        "One of the Professors." [MassR] (34:1) Spr 93, p. 78.
3614. LAIRD, Steven
        "Haiti." [Event] (22:2) Sum 93, p. 42-43.
        "Riches." [Event] (22:2) Sum 93, p. 44.
3615. LAKE, Kathleen
        "My Mother Is Still Alive." [Sun] (207) Mr 93, p. 12.
3616. LAKE, Oliver
        "In Memory of David Hines." [RiverS] (37) 93, 5th preliminary page.
3617. LAKE, Paul
        "Dead Poets Society." [Witness] (7:2) 93, p. 161.
3618. LAKE, Whitney
        "Soap Opera Wedding." [US1] (28/29) 93, p. 8.
3619. LALIC, Ivan V.
        "Byzantium" (tr. by Francis R. Jones). [NoDaQ] (61:1) Wint 93, p. 101-102.
        "The Voice Singing in the Gardens" (tr. by Francis R. Jones). [NoDaQ] (61:1) Wint
            93, p. 100-101.
3620. LALLY, Michael
        "Disco Poetry." [Arshile] (1) Spr 93, p. 11-15.
        "It Takes One to Know One." [Arshile] (1) Spr 93, p. 18-19.
        "Who We Are Now." [Arshile] (1) Spr 93, p. 16-17.
3621. LAMB, Elizabeth Searle
        "Search." [Writer] (106:9) S 93, p. 23.
        "This clear morning." [Writer] (106:9) S 93, p. 23.
3622. LAMB, Jessica
        "Unfinished Adoration." [Shen] (43:1) Spr 93, p. 84-85.
3623. LAMBERT, M. A.
        "Descent." [HiramPoR] (53/54) Fall 92-Sum 93, p. 46.
3624. LaMERS, Joyce
        "Becalmed in the Bermuda Triangle." [Light] (8) Wint 93, p. 23.
        "Double Dactyl." [Light] (6) Sum 93, p. 9.
        "Ill Wind." [Light] (8) Wint 93, p. 12.
        "The Monkey." [Light] (8) Wint 93, p. 22.
        "Stopped at Tahoe for inspection" (Honorable Mention, First Annual River Rhyme
            Competition). [Light] (5) Spr 93, p. 30.
        "When Mongols crossed the River Ob." [Light] (6) Sum 93, p. 22.
3625. LAMMON, Martin
        "The Only Other Beautiful Thing." [WestB] (33) 93, p. 79.
        "Stories a Man Keeps to Himself." [Ploughs] (19:4) Wint 93-94, p. 102-103.
        "Three Short Clay Poems" (for Jack Troy). [WestB] (31/32) 93, p. 12-14.
3626. LAMPORT, Felicia
        "Census and Sensibility." [Light] (5) Spr 93, p. 19.
3627. LANCASTER, J. R.
        "I tried to catch the evening." [PoetryUSA] (25/26) 93, p. 19.
3628. LANDALE, Zoë
        "Genealogy of Colours." [CanLit] (137) Sum 93, p. 19-20.
        "Hands Surprised as Starfish" (for J. age 5 1/2). [CanLit] (137) Sum 93, p. 17.
        "Horeb Revisited, or: Five Ways to Walk Right by a Burning Object." [CanLit]
            (137) Sum 93, p. 18.
        "Manifesto." [PraS] (67:4) Wint 93, p. 84-86.

"Onion Enraged." [MalR] (102) Spr 93, p. 13.
"Purity" (1 & 2). [TickleAce] (25) Spr-Sum 93, p. 174-175.
"The Smell of Hot Metal." [TickleAce] (25) Spr-Sum 93, p. 173.
3629. LANDGRAF, Susan
"On This Hallowed Eve's Night." [Calyx] (15:1) Wint 93-94, p. 6-7.
"Remembering the Egg." [Calyx] (14:3) Sum 93, p. 44.
"Under Heaven." [Calyx] (14:3) Sum 93, p. 45.
3630. LANDIS, Maxine
"Hiding." [OnTheBus] (6:1, #13) Wint 93-Spr 94, p. 138-139.
"In There Anyone Out There in that Editor Suit?" [OnTheBus] (5:2, #12) Sum-Fall
93, p. 113-114.
"Putting Myself on the Couch: Or the Poem I Wrote After I Wrote the Poem."
[OnTheBus] (6:1, #13) Wint 93-Spr 94, p. 137-138.
"Sunday Picnic." [OnTheBus] (5:2, #12) Sum-Fall 93, p. 113.
3631. LANDREY, David
"Dinner Table Scenes" (Excerpt). [Talisman] (11) Fall 93, p. 280-281.
"Divorce Poems" (4 excerpts). [Talisman] (11) Fall 93, p. 277-280.
3632. LANE, Joel
"Equity." [Verse] (10:1) Spr 93, p. 80.
3633. LANE, John
"British Jungle Training School, Macal River." [NorthStoneR] (11) 93, p. 122.
"San Antonio, Cayo District, Belize." [NorthStoneR] (11) 93, p. 121.
"The Watch." [NorthStoneR] (11) 93, p. 123.
3634. LANE, M. Travis
"The Ambience." [PottPort] (15:1) Spr-Sum 93, p. 24.
"Codicil ('Including the Cost of a Monument and Inscription')." [PottPort] (15:1)
Spr-Sum 93, p. 26.
"Dark Harbour, N.B." [PottPort] (15:1) Spr-Sum 93, p. 25.
"Keeping Afloat." [MalR] (103) Sum 93, p. 70-72.
"Vigil for the Disappeared (Los Disparecidos)." [PottPort] (15:1) Spr-Sum 93, p. 25.
3635. LANE, Peter
"Horrors." [Bogg] (66) Wint 92-93, p. 60-61.
3636. LANE, Pinkie Gordon
"Mississippi River Poems." [AfAmRev] (27:1) Spr 93, p. 147-149.
3637. LANG, Doug
"Fabric" (w. Mora Larson, Sherene Offutt and Geoff Suchocki). [WashR] (18:5) F -
Mr 93, p. 18.
3638. LANGAN, Steve
"Driving into the Unbeautiful City." [KenR] (NS 15:1) Wint 93, p. 17-19.
"Learning the Language." [SouthernPR] (33:1) Spr 93, p. 44-45.
3639. LANGHORNE, Henry
"Breakout." [Poem] (70) N 93, p. 3.
"Mt. Pisgah" (Mt. Pisgah, N.C., Feb. 1992). [Poem] (70) N 93, p. 4.
"Riding a Hydrofoil to Budapest." [Poem] (70) N 93, p. 2.
"River Bottom." [Poem] (70) N 93, p. 1.
3640. LANGILLE, Carole (Carole Glasser)
"Fear Ghazal." [PraS] (67:4) Wint 93, p. 88.
"Hansel and Gretel." [PraS] (67:4) Wint 93, p. 87-88.
"Soon the Sea." [AntigR] (95) Aut 93, p. 92.
"Through a Slit in the Tent." [MalR] (105) Wint 93, p. 56-58.
3641. LANGLAND, William
"Piers Plowman (The C-Text)" (tr. by George Economou). [Sulfur] (33) Fall 93, p.
115-117.
3642. LANGTON, Daniel J.
"Imagined, Not Recalled." [ChatR] (13:3) Spr 93, p. 59.
"Just Before December." [Confr] (51) Sum 93, p. 244.
3643. LANSDOWN, Andrew
"Wool on a Wire." [Verse] (10:2) Sum 93, p. 25.
3644. LANTHIER, Kateri
"Copper Cliff." [Grain] (21:2) Sum 93, p. 67.
"Lost-lost Sister." [Grain] (21:2) Sum 93, p. 68.
3645. LAO, Linette
"Peterson's Field Guide to the Beefcake Kings." [Caliban] (13) 93, p. 48-49.
3646. LAOR, Yitzhak
"Only the Body Recalls" (tr. by Gabriel Levin). [Trans] (28) Spr 93, p. 148.

3647. LaPALMA, Marina de Bellagente (Marina de Bellagantu?)
"A millionaire." [Footwork] (23) 93, p. 115.
3648. LARA, Martin
"A Maasai in Flagstaff." [Amelia] (7:2, #21) 93, p. 109.
3649. LAREW, Hiram
"Bubbles Under Ice." [BellR] (16:1/2) Spr-Fall 93, p. 33.
3650. LARK, Gary L.
"Eyes." [Blueline] (14) 93, p. 19.
3651. LARKIN, Joan
"Breathing You In." [HangL] (63) 93, p. 32.
"Frost Warning." [BrooklynR] (10) 93, p. 78.
"In the Duchess" (Sheridan Square, 1971). [HangL] (63) 93, p. 33.
"Inventory." [GlobalCR] (1) Spr 93, p. 1-2.
"Night, St. Mark's Place." [HangL] (63) 93, p. 34.
"Progression." [BrooklynR] (10) 93, p. 79-80.
"To Spirit." [AmerV] (31) 93, p. 127-128.
"Want." [HangL] (63) 93, p. 31.
3652. LARKIN, Mary Ann
"Summer of '82" (for Mark and everyone). [PoetL] (88:2) Sum 93, p. 6.
3653. LaROCQUE, Emma
"Bungee Man Third World Man." [Descant] (24:3, #82) Fall 93, p. 84-85.
3654. LARS, Krystyna
"Found Eye" (tr. by David Malcolm and Georgia Scott). [Prima] (16/17) 93, p. 28 -
29.
"(I) She Writes with Fire" (tr. by David Malcolm and Georgia Scott). [Prima]
(16/17) 93, p. 30.
3655. LARSEN, Jeanne
"A Day of Smoke and Mirrors" (for Randall Flory). [GreensboroR] (55) Wint 93-94,
p. 38-39.
3656. LARSEN, Lance
"February 1922: My Father's Conception." [Hudson] (45:4) Wint 93, p. 620.
3657. LARSON, Jacqueline
"Personal Accounts." [WestCL] (27:1, #10) Spr 93, p. 15-16.
3658. LARSON, Kathryn
"Dusk in the Garden." [Lactuca] (17) Apr 93, p. 21.
"Tiny Dramas." [Lactuca] (17) Apr 93, p. 21.
3659. LARSON, Mora
"Fabric" (w. Doug Lang, Sherene Offutt and Geoff Suchocki). [WashR] (18:5) F-Mr
93, p. 18.
"Untitled: Being against this large white cerebrum in my skull." [WashR] (18:5) F -
Mr 93, p. 22.
"Untitled: I remember when I was younger and everybody was all one big mass of
pulsating stuff." [WashR] (18:5) F-Mr 93, p. 16.
3660. LARSSON, Stig
"Pools of Strong Indian Tea and Urine" (tr. by Rika Lesser). [GrandS] (12:3, #47)
Fall 93, p. 57-61.
3661. LaRUE, Dorie
"Pimps Double Back on Sprague Street." [SouthernPR] (33:2) Fall 93, p. 19-20.
LaRUE, Mark La
See La RUE, Mark
3662. LaSALLE, Peter
"Goalies Are Weird." [Interim] (12:1) Spr-Sum 93, p. 44.
"I've Heard a Lot About You." [Interim] (12:1) Spr-Sum 93, p. 43.
"Reading Moby Dick Aloud to My Dead Nephew." [HampSPR] Wint 93, p. 15.
"Real Life." [InterPR] (19:1) Spr 93, p. 83.
"Villefranche." [CumbPR]] (13:1) Fall 93, p. 32-33.
"What It's All About." [InterPR] (19:1) Spr 93, p. 84.
3663. LASDUN, James
"Lines for a Civic Statue." [NewYorker] (68:47) 11 Ja 93, p. 82.
3664. LASKE, Otto
"Eigenheim." [Os] (37) Wint 93, p. 24.
"Zurück." [Os] (37) Wint 93, p. 25.
3665. LASOEN, Patricia
"The Traveller" (1., 2., 4., introduction, 2nd account, intermission, tr. by Scott
Rollins). [Vis] (43) 93, p. 17.

3666. LASSELL, Michael
"Acrobats." [Amelia] (7:2, #21) 93, p. 35.
"After-image." [Amelia] (7:2, #21) 93, p. 36.
"At the Beach." [Amelia] (7:2, #21) 93, p. 36.
"My Mother's Incest." [CentralP] (22) Spr 93, p. 45.
3667. LASSEN, Sandra Lake
"The Girl in 301." [AnthNEW] (5) 93, p. 21.
3668. LaTERRE, David C.
"Exotica / Babysitting / Scherzo #1." [RagMag] (11:1) 93, p. 10-15.
3669. LATIF, Tariq
"David." [Verse] (10:1) Spr 93, p. 79.
3670. LATIMER, Renate
"Chorus of the Trojan Survivors" (from "Helena," tr. of Inge Merkel). [SouthernHR]
(27:4) Fall 93, p. 360-362.
3671. LATTA, John
"A Letter Beginning with O Thirty." [WestHR] (47:3) Fall 93, p. 239.
"A Letter Beginning with The Tulips." [WestHR] (47:3) Fall 93, p. 240.
"A Summer Night with Thunder." [WillowS] (33) Wint 93, p. 49.
3672. LAU, Carolyn Lei-Lani
"Ha'ina 'ia Mai Ana ka Puana (Let the Story Be Told)." [ChiR] (39:3/4) 93, p. 168 -
174.
3673. LAU, Evelyn
"Adult Entertainment." [PoetryC] (13:2) 93, p. 10.
"Christmas Days." [AnotherCM] (26) Fall 93, p. 56-57.
"Christmas Days." [PoetryC] (13:2) 93, p. 10.
"City at Sunset." [Witness] (7:1) 93, p. 139.
"Economics" (for Lindi St. Clair, pominent British postitute). [Witness] (7:1) 93, p.
142-143.
"I Took the Devil Standing." [AnotherCM] (26) Fall 93, p. 54-55.
"In the House of the Slaves." [PoetryC] (13:2) 93, p. 11.
"My Tragic Opera." [MassR] (34:4) Wint 93-94, p. 519-520.
"Nothing Is Happening." [PoetryC] (13:2) 93, p. 11.
"Small Hours." [PoetryC] (13:2) 93, p. 11.
"Three." [Witness] (7:1) 93, p. 140-141.
"A Visitor." [NewL] (60:1) 93, p. 100.
"You Said Love." [Verse] (10:1) Spr 93, p. 39-40.
3674. LAUBER, Peg
"Going Down." [Wind] (23:72) 93, p. 13.
3675. LAUCIK, Ivan
"Contents of a Fever" (tr. by Stephánia Allen and James Sutherland-Smith).
[OxfordM] (9:1) Spr-Sum 93, p. 105.
3676. LAUE, John
"Around the High School." [EngJ] (82:2) F 93, p. 90.
"Updraft." [EngJ] (82:7) N 93, p. 91.
"The Wastebin." [EngJ] (82:3) Mr 93, p. 92.
3677. LAUGHLIN, J. (James)
"At the End." [Iowa] (23:3) Fall 93, p. 65.
"The Biographer." [NewYorkQ] (50) 93, p. 42.
"Blue Booties & Pink Booties." [Light] (8) Wint 93, p. 14.
"A Certain Impermeable Person." [NewYorkQ] (51) 93, p. 37.
"The Change." [Chelsea] (54) 93, p. 88-89.
"Dawn" (from "Byways," after Daphne and Apollo — Ovid). [Iowa] (23:3) Fall 93,
p. 65-67.
"The Departure." [Iowa] (23:3) Fall 93, p. 63.
"The Emigration." [NewAW] (11) Sum-Fall 93, p. 55.
"In the Highstreet of Tralee." [Iowa] (23:3) Fall 93, p. 64.
"The Lost Song." [Poetry] (163:2) N 93, p. 82.
"My Own Name." [NewYorkQ] (52) 93, p. 43.
"The Old Indian" (for Gary Snyder). [Iowa] (23:3) Fall 93, p. 63.
"The Rain on the Roof." [Iowa] (23:3) Fall 93, p. 64-65.
"She Loves Old Men." [Interim] (12:1) Spr-Sum 93, p. 10.
"Some Amatory Epigrams from the Greek Anthology." [Sulfur] (33) Fall 93, p. 50 -
53.
"The Swarming Bees." [QRL] (12:32/33) 93, p. 456-457.
"There's Never a Never." [Interim] (12:1) Spr-Sum 93, p. 10.
"Three Glimpses." [Thrpny] (53) Spr 93, p. 25.

"The Trophy Wives." [Boulevard] (8:2/3, #23/24) Fall 93, p. 130.
"Why?" [Iowa] (23:3) Fall 93, p. 64.
3678. LAUGHLIN, Kristen
"Charlotte." [HawaiiR] (17:2, #38) Spr 93, p. 6.
3679. LAURENCE, Alexander
"The Death of Audrey." [Pearl] (17) Spr 93, p. 10.
"Strangers Meeting the Course in Painted Voice." [Talisman] (11) Fall 93, p. 271 -
272.
3680. LAURENZ, Alejandra
"Escucha" (del libro *Las hijas de Atthis*). [SinW] (49) Spr-Sum 93, p. 17.
"Listen" (from *Atthis's daughters*, tr. by the author). [SinW] (49) Spr-Sum 93, p. 16.
3681. LAUSTERER, Brent
"Immersion." [HawaiiR] (17:1, #37) Spr 93, p. 71-72.
3682. LAUTERBACH, Ann
"Arm's Reach, Harm's Way." [GlobalCR] (2) Fall 93, p. 7-10.
"Constellation Portrait #3: Sill Life with Crows." [AmerPoR] (22:1) Ja-F 93, p. 45.
"Eclipse" (with erratum note: line 15 should read "They [not the] did not say . . ."').
[DenQ] (28:2) Fall 93, p. 10.
"For Example (8): And the Fire Spread." [NewAW] (11) Sum-Fall 93, p. 1-6.
"Phase." [DenQ] (28:1) Sum 93, p. 42.
"The Prior." [AmerPoR] (22:1) Ja-F 93, p. 44-45.
"Rancor of the Empirical." [Conjunc] (20) 93, p. 83-84.
"The Scene Shifts." [Conjunc] (20) 93, p. 82-83.
"The Tacit." [GlobalCR] (2) Fall 93, p. 5-6.
"The Untelling." [Conjunc] (20) 93, p. 84-85.
3683. LAUX, Dorianne
"After Twelve Days of Rain." [Zyzzyva] (9:4) Wint 93, p. 97-99.
"Finding What's Lost." [Zyzzyva] (9:4) Wint 93, p. 101.
"Homecoming." [TarRP] (32:2) Spr 93, p. 10.
"Landrum's Diner, Reno." [TarRP] (32:2) Spr 93, p. 11.
"The Lovers." [AmerPoR] (22:4) Jl-Ag 93, p. 14.
"Romance." [AmerPoR] (22:4) Jl-Ag 93, p. 13.
"Sunday Radio." [AmerPoR] (22:4) Jl-Ag 93, p. 13.
"The Thief." [AmerPoR] (22:4) Jl-Ag 93, p. 14.
"What Could Happen." [AmerPoR] (22:4) Jl-Ag 93, p. 13.
3684. LAVAZZI, Thomas
"Crossing / Borders" (from "Shake hands and come out fighting"). [AmerPoR]
(22:4) Jl-Ag 93, p. 31.
3685. LAVIGNE, Leslie
"Black Letters of Insensitivity" (tr. of W. A. Shaheen, w. Baidar Bakht). [CanLit]
(136) Spr 93, p. 99-100.
"I'm Mad Because of You" (tr. of W. A. Shaheen, w. Baidar Bakht). [CanLit] (136)
Spr 93, p. 100.
"The Sound of Grief" (tr. of W. A. Shaheen, w. Baidar Bakht). [CanLit] (136) Spr
93, p. 99.
3686. LAWLER, Patrick
"(Dreams)" (Excerpt). [AmerLC] (5) 93, p. 1-8.
3687. LAWLOR, William
"Death Sits at the Foot of My Bed" (tr. of Oscar Hahn). [Vis] (41) 93, p. 22.
3688. LAWNER, Lynne
"And So I Requested a Chair." [Chelsea] (54) 93, p. 59.
"Beach Evening." [Confr] (51) Sum 93, p. 223.
"Nightingales." [Chelsea] (54) 93, p. 57.
"School Friend." [Chelsea] (54) 93, p. 58.
"Surrender." [Confr] (51) Sum 93, p. 222.
3689. LAWRENCE, Anthony
"Gathering Seed" (for Coral Hull). [Nimrod] (37:1) Fall-Wint 93, p. 93.
"Home After Two Weeks Away" (for Trina MacAdam). [Nimrod] (37:1) Fall-Wint
93, p. 91-92.
"The Name, the Bird." [MalR] (104) Fall 93, p. 66-67.
"Soundings." [GreenMR] (NS 6:2) Sum-Fall 93, p. 111-112.
3690. LAWRENCE, D. H.
"Butterfly." [GettyR] (6:2) Spr 93, p. 316-317.
3691. LAWRENCE, Joseph
"Lines Imagined Translated into a Foreign Language." [OntR] (38) Spr-Sum 93, p.
57-60.

3692. LAWRY, Mercedes
"Safe Familiars" (Honorable Mention, 1993 Poetry Competition). [Elf] (3:2) Sum
93, p. 25.
3693. LAWS, Kyle
"Under a Belly of Clouds." [ChironR] (12:3, #36) Aut 93, p. 15.
3694. LAWTON, Harry
"Hearing from Corinna" (For Ruhamah Belle Lay). [PoetL] (88:4) Wint 93-94, p.
49-50.
3695. LAYTON, Irving
"Nest Building" (for David Layton). [CanLit] (136) Spr 93, p. 81.
3696. LAZER, Hank
"Negation" (1-2). [PoetryUSA] (25/26) 93, p. 16, 27.
Le . . .
See also names beginning with "Le" without the following space, filed below in
their alphabetic positions, e.g., LeFEVRE.
3697. Le DRESSAY, Anne
"Black Widow." [AntigR] (95) Aut 93, p. 111-112.
"Letter." [Grain] (21:2) Sum 93, p. 89.
"Saying No to a Vampire." [Grain] (21:2) Sum 93, p. 88.
Le FEMINA, Gary
See LaFEMINA, Gary
3698. Le GUIN, Ursula K.
"A Discourse on Method." [NowestR] (31:2) 93, p. 13.
"The Queen of Spain, Grown Old and Mad, Writes to the Daughter She Imagines
She Had by Christopher Columbus." [CreamCR] (17:2) Fall 93, p. 152-153.
"The Woman and the Soul." [13thMoon] (11:1/2) 93, p. 243-244.
3699. Le PERA, George
"The Trodden Wheel of Andrew Wyeth." [ClockR] (8:1/2) 93, p. 71.
3700. LEA, Sydney
"Athlete's Scars." [MichQR] (32:4) Fall 93, p. 572-573.
"Wedding Anniversary" (for MRB). [NewEngR] (15:1) Wint 93, p. 167-169.
3701. LEADER, Mary
"Girl at Sewing Machine" (after a painting by Edward Hopper). [RiverC] (14:1) Fall
93, p. 67-68.
"Her Door." [VirQR] (69:3) Sum 93, p. 498.
3702. LEAHY, Anna
"Voting for Elvis" (for my sister in Minnesota). [PoetC] (24:3) Spr 93, p. 36-37.
3703. LEAKE, Brent T.
"Death of a Blackman in a Holding Cell." [ChironR] (12:3, #36) Aut 93, p. 24.
"Freedom's Poem." [ChironR] (12:3, #36) Aut 93, p. 24.
"Take a Whiff It's Home." [ChironR] (12:3, #36) Aut 93, p. 24.
"Watching Something Like a Documentary on Ed Sullivan." [Pearl] (19) Fall-Wint
93, p. 82.
3704. LEASE, Joseph
"Footloose radish." [GrandS] (12:2, #46) Sum 93, p. 30-31.
"Hammer." [GrandS] (12:2, #46) Sum 93, p. 29.
"Marathon House." [GrandS] (12:3, #47) Fall 93, p. 26-33.
"The Sun Drench" (for Kimberley Gavin). [SouthwR] (78:4) Aut 93, p. 480-482.
3705. LeBLANC, Diane
"First Week." [AnthNEW] (5) 93, p. 22.
3706. LEBOW, Jeanne
"Flicker." [Border] (2) Spr 93, p. 43-44.
3707. LECKIE, Ross
"Now Hear This." [US1] (28/29) 93, p. 2.
"The Runner." [SouthwR] (78:2) Spr 93, p. 228.
3708. LeCOEUR, Jo
" Envidia Does Not Translate." [Border] (2) Spr 93, p. 46-47.
3709. LECUYER, Tess
"Life Without Nipples." [13thMoon] (11:1/2) 93, p. 39.
3710. LEDDY, Michael
"Closer to Laundry" (for Rob Zseleczky). [Talisman] (10) Spr 93, p. 168.
"Tie and Slur." [Talisman] (10) Spr 93, p. 169.
3711. LEDERER, Katherine
"Near Silk Farm Road." [HarvardR] (4) Spr 93, p. 126.
3712. LEDERHENDLER, Lazer (Laser)
"The Inner City Exhibits" (Selections). [CapilR] (2:10) Spr 93, p. 109-119.

"Versons (of You)." [WestCL] (27:3, #12) Wint 93-94, p. 41-45.
LeDRESSAY, Anne
    See Le DRESSAY, Anne
3713. LEDWIDGE, Francis
    "The Blackbirds." [RiverC] (13:2) Spr 93, p. 19.
3714. LEE, Alice
    "A History Poem." [PraS] (67:4) Wint 93, p. 89.
    "I Dreamed of You Again Last Night." [PraS] (67:4) Wint 93, p. 90.
    "Performance." [PraS] (67:4) Wint 93, p. 90-91.
    "Sister Mary Agnes's Prayer." [PraS] (67:4) Wint 93, p. 91-92.
3715. LEE, Cecilia C.
    "Blindman's Bluff" (tr. of María Victoria Atencia, w. Laura Higgins). [LitR] (36:3)
        Spr 93, p. 359.
    "Call Me" (— Lou Reed. Tr. of Roger Wolfe, w. Laura Higgins). [LitR] (36:3) Spr
        93, p. 387.
    "The Day Has Gone" (tr. of Angel González, w. Laura Higgins). [LitR] (36:3) Spr
        93, p. 373-374.
    "Diotima to Her Most Dedicated Student" (tr. of Ana Rossetti, w. Laura Higgins).
        [LitR] (36:3) Spr 93, p. 380.
    "The Eyes of the Bull" (tr. of Rafael Alberti, w. Laura Higgins). [LitR] (36:3) Spr
        93, p. 356.
    "The Flight into Egypt" (tr. of Luis Alberto de Cuenca, w. Laura Higgins). [LitR]
        (36:3) Spr 93, p. 368.
    "Four Roses" (tr. of Luis Antonio de Villena, w. Laura Higgins). [LitR] (36:3) Spr
        93, p. 386.
    "Julia" (tr. of Luis Alberto de Cuenca, w. Laura Higgins). [LitR] (36:3) Spr 93, p.
        368.
    "Martha and Mary" (tr. of María Victoria Atencia, w. Laura Higgins). [LitR] (36:3)
        Spr 93, p. 360.
    "Secret, Ancient Voices of the Night" (Selections: II, IV, tr. of Julia Uceda, w.
        Laura Higgins). [LitR] (36:3) Spr 93, p. 383-384.
    "Splendor Veritatis" (tr. of Miguel d'Ors, w. Laura Higgins). [LitR] (36:3) Spr 93, p.
        370.
    "That Sweet Atmosphere of Tango Around Three" (tr. of Luis Antonio de Villena,
        w. Laura Higgins). [LitR] (36:3) Spr 93, p. 385-386.
    "This Everlasting Evening" (tr. of Rafael Alberti, w. Laura Higgins). [LitR] (36:3)
        Spr 93, p. 357.
    "To Federico with Some Violets" (Selection: III, tr. of Luis García Montero, w.
        Laura Higgins). [LitR] (36:3) Spr 93, p. 371-372.
    "With the Table Ready" (tr. of María Victoria Atencia, w. Laura Higgins). [LitR]
        (36:3) Spr 93, p. 360.
3716. LEE, David
    "Cigarettes." [PoetryE] (36) Fall 93, p. 67-69.
    "First Turtle." [NewYorkQ] (51) 93, p. 71.
    "For Jan, with Love." [HayF] (12) Spr-Sum 93, p. 64-66.
    "Neighbors." [PoetryE] (36) Fall 93, p. 75-80.
    "The Sawmill Road." [CutB] (40) Spr 93, p. 78-85.
    "Whiskey." [PoetryE] (36) Fall 93, p. 70-74.
3717. LEE, John B.
    "Shovelling Snow with My Sons." [MalR] (104) Fall 93, p. 64-65.
3718. LEE, Lance
    "Rising Faire." [Poem] (70) N 93, p. 56.
    "The South Sussex Downs." [Poem] (70) N 93, p. 55.
3719. LEE, Muna
    "Nothing Is Ours" (tr. of Jorge Carrera Andrade). [QRL] (12:32/33) 93, p. 370-371.
3720. LEE, Pete
    "Admiring the Enemy." [DogRR] (12:2, #24) Fall-Wint 93, p. 52.
    "Bonsai." [WindO] (57) Fall 93, p. 15.
    "The Only Security." [DogRR] (12:2, #24) Fall-Wint 93, p. 52.
    "Sugar." [CoalC] (7) Apr 93, p. 6.
3721. LEE, Priscilla
    "Rain." [MidAR] (14:1) 93, p. 102-103.
3722. LEE, Richard E.
    "Love Stamps." [Pearl] (17) Spr 93, p. 86.
3723. LEE, Stellasue
    "Crossing." [OnTheBus] (5:2, #12) Sum-Fall 93, p. 115.

"The Earthquake." [OnTheBus] (6:1, #13) Wint 93-Spr 94, p. 140.
"Passing without Censure." [OnTheBus] (6:1, #13) Wint 93-Spr 94, p. 140.
3724. LEEDAHL, Shelley A.
"Mysteries." [PraF] (14:1) Spr 93, p. 117.
"A Practical Girl." [PraF] (14:1) Spr 93, p. 116.
"Spiders." [PraF] (14:3) Aut 93, p. 97.
3725. LEFCOWITZ, Barbara F.
"Blue Embroidery." [PoetL] (88:4) Wint 93-94, p. 19.
"Sunday Night at the Gyldenlove Hotel, Oslo." [PaintedB] (50/51) 93, p. 45.
3726. LEFEBURE, Stephen
"The Rejected Suitor." [Gypsy] (20) Sum 93, p. 19.
LeFEMINA, Gary
See LaFEMINA, Gary
3727. LEGGO, Carl
"Growing up Perpendicular on the Side of a Hill." [TickleAce] (23) Spr-Sum 92, p. 25-29.
"I Rescue Del Cashin." [AntigR] (93-94) Spr-Sum 93, p. 76-77.
"I Rescue Del Cashin." [Dandel] (20:1) 93, p. 50-51.
"Nan's Soap." [TickleAce] (26) Fall-Wint 93, p. 80-81.
"Nellie Evans." [TickleAce] (26) Fall-Wint 93, p. 79-80.
"Skipper Saves Copper Cooper." [AntigR] (93-94) Spr-Sum 93, p. 74-75.
"Squid." [TickleAce] (23) Spr-Sum 92, p. 23-24.
"True Romance." [AntigR] (93-94) Spr-Sum 93, p. 71-73.
3728. LEGGOTT, Michele
"Seven from Nine." [WestCL] (27:2, #11) Fall 93, p. 67-73.
LEGRAND, Maurice-Etienne
See FRANC-NOHAIN (MAURICE-ETIENNE LEGRAND)
3729. LEGRIS, Sylvia
"Sorting Through Documents." [PraF] (14:4) Wint 93-94, p. 66-69.
LeGUIN, Ursula K.
See Le GUIN, Ursula K.
3730. LEHMAN, David
"The Case of the Spurious Spouse." [Boulevard] (8:1, #22) Spr 93, p. 49-50.
"Derridadaism" (This poem first appeared in the Times Literary Supplement).
[Light] (6) Sum 93, p. 14.
"The Escape Artist" (In memoriam Graham Greene, 1904-1991). [PartR] (60:3) Sum 93, p. 428-429.
"Infidelity." [ParisR] (35:127) Sum 93, p. 205-206.
"The Moment of Truth." [Boulevard] (8:1, #22) Spr 93, p. 53.
"On the Nature of Desire." [MichQR] (32:4) Fall 93, p. 615-618.
"The Pleasure Principle." [AmerLC] (5) 93, p. 37-38.
"Precocity." [ParisR] (35:127) Sum 93, p. 211.
"The Return." [ParisR] (35:127) Sum 93, p. 208-210.
"The Role Model." [Boulevard] (8:1, #22) Spr 93, p. 51-52.
"September Evening." [Nat] (256:24) 21 Je 93, p. 880.
"Sexism." [ParisR] (35:127) Sum 93, p. 207.
"Shock Therapy." [ParisR] (35:127) Sum 93, p. 204.
"There Comes a Time." [AmerLC] (5) 93, p. 38-39.
3731. LEHR, Genevieve
"My Lover's House: Night Journey." [TickleAce] (24) Fall-Wint 92, p. 38.
"The Parts." [TickleAce] (24) Fall-Wint 92, p. 39.
"Post-Impressions" (for Susan). [TickleAce] (24) Fall-Wint 92, p. 40-41.
"St. John's Christmas 1992: Harvey Road Fire." [TickleAce] (25) Spr-Sum 93, p. 183.
"You Will Be Listening" (Competition Winner, 3rd). [TickleAce] (25) Spr-Sum 93, p. 126.
3732. LEIBMAN, Kenneth C.
"A King, a Sheik, and a Sailor Give a Flower and a Bird to a Beast" (as told by Percy Leigh Samuel Robert Bysshe Blake). [Light] (7) Aut 93, p. 15.
"When that I was and a little tiny boy." [Light] (7) Aut 93, p. 30.
3733. LEICHTY, John
"Two Battlefields." [PikeF] (11) Fall 93, p. 28.
3734. LEIPER, Esther M.
"The Wars of Faery" (For C.S. Lewis. Book II, Canto XI. "Wendelemere", Book II, Canto XII. "Hearts Ease"). [Amelia] (7:2, #21) 93, p. 93-103.

3735. LEITHAUSER, Brad
   "Cattails: A Marsh in March." [NewYorker] (69:5) 22 Mr 93, p. 78.
   "Red Leather Jacket." [Atlantic] (272:2) Ag 93, p. 74.
   "Some Ways Along." [Verse] (10:3) Wint 93, p. 90.
3736. LEITNER, Jerrol
   "Learning to Ride." [EngJ] (82:6) O 93, p. 93.
3737. LELAND, Blake
   "Annunciation." [Epoch] (42:1) 93, p. 110.
   "Thief." [Epoch] (42:1) 93, p. 108-109.
3738. LELAND, Kurt
   "Remedies" (after paintings by Remedios Varo). [BelPoJ] (43:4) Sum 93, p. 11-17.
3739. LELAND, Natasha
   "Where I Look." [HarvardA] (128:1) Fall 93, p. 31.
3740. LELOS, Cynthia
   "Apricot Brandy Flowed." [Pearl] (17) Spr 93, p. 101.
   "Vinnie Died Last Night." [Gypsy] (20) Sum 93, p. 16.
3741. LEM, Carol
   "Didn't They Tell You Stories?" [IllinoisR] (1:1) Fall 93, p. 29-30.
3742. LeMASTERS, Larry
   "A Bent Page." [Writer] (106:3) Mr 93, p. 24.
3743. LEMMON, Amy
   "End of the Day." [CinPR] (24) Spr 93, p. 15.
3744. LENGOLD, Jelena
   "A Suburban Hotel" (tr. by Veno Taufer). [NoDaQ] (61:1) Wint 93, p. 103.
3745. LENGYEL, Peter
   "An Evening with the Author" (tr. of Leszek Szaruga, w. W.D. and K. B. Snodgrass
      and Justyna Kostkowska). [Salm] (97) Wint 93, p. 111.
   "Watchman" (for Zbigniew Herbert, tr. of Leszek Szaruga, w. W.D. and K. B.
      Snodgrass and Justyna Kostkowska). [Salm] (97) Wint 93, p. 110.
3746. LENHART, Gary
   "Cinderella." [HangL] (63) 93, p. 35.
   "Granddad." [HangL] (63) 93, p. 37.
   "Just Off the Bus." [HangL] (63) 93, p. 36.
   "Louise." [HangL] (63) 93, p. 37.
   "Peekaboo." [HangL] (63) 93, p. 36.
3747. LENHART, Michael
   "Resilience." [SlipS] (13) 93, p. 89.
3748. LENIHAN, Dan
   "La Brea Blues." [WormR] (33:3, #131), 93, p. 112-113.
   "Greenhouse Blues" (A Wormword Chapbook). [WormR] (33:2, #130) 93, p. 49 -
      104.
   "I Got the Blues." [WormR] (33:3, #131), 93, p. 112.
   "Larry's Back in Town." [WormR] (33:3, #131), 93, p. 111-112.
   "Sometimes Married Guys Get Phone Calls Like This at Night from Their
      Unmarried Friends." [WormR] (33:3, #131), 93, p. 111.
3749. LENNERTZ, William Ritter
   "9 1 2" (for William O. Ritter, September 27, 1911-March 20, 1992." [Pearl] (19)
      Fall-Wint 93, p. 54.
3750. LENT, Jack
   "The Poem When It Comes." [Spitball] (44) Sum 93, p. 25.
3751. LEON, Dave
   "Rm #2." [Pearl] (17) Spr 93, p. 13.
   "The Winners Inn." [Pearl] (17) Spr 93, p. 13.
3752. LEONG, Russell
   "Unfolding Flowers, Matchless Flames." [Tricycle] (2:3) Spr 93, p. 49-51.
3753. LEONHARDT, Kenneth
   "Don't Back a Laureate." [Light] (6) Sum 93, p. 8.
   "Driving to Judgement." [Light] (5) Spr 93, p. 21.
   "Ode Man Out." [Light] (8) Wint 93, p. 7.
   "The One Who Won." [Light] (7) Aut 93, p. 20.
   "Rhyme Gone to Hell." [Light] (8) Wint 93, p. 11.
   "Rye Bread." [Light] (5) Spr 93, p. 13.
   "Substrata Errata." [Light] (5) Spr 93, p. 24.
3754. LEOPOLD, Joseph
   "An Acrostic for Don Benito." [ApalQ] (35) 90, p. 44.

LePERA

74

LePERA, George
    See Le PERA, George
3755. LERNER, Linda
    "Going Down." [NorthStoneR] (11) 93, p. 92.
3756. LERNET-HOLENIA, Alexander
    "Fragments after Robert Browning" (tr. by Robert Dassanowsky-Harris). [WebR]
        (17) Fall 93, p. 27.
    "Mutiny" (tr. by Robert Dassanowsky-Harris). [WebR] (17) Fall 93, p. 26.
LEROY, Félix Morisseau
    See MORISSEAU-LEROY, Félix
3757. LERZUNDI, Patricio
    "La guerra entre los orejas cortas." [LindLM] (12:2/4) Ap-D 93, p. 6.
    "Jan Pakarati." [LindLM] (12:2/4) Ap-D 93, p. 6.
    "Manuia." [LindLM] (12:2/4) Ap-D 93, p. 6.
    "Mi padre." [LindLM] (12:2/4) Ap-D 93, p. 6.
    "No el sol." [LindLM] (12:2/4) Ap-D 93, p. 6.
    "No tengo ojos." [LindLM] (12:2/4) Ap-D 93, p. 6.
    "Los orejas largas quisieron." [LindLM] (12:2/4) Ap-D 93, p. 6.
3758. LesCARBEAU, Mitchell
    "The Comedy of Memory." [Thrpny] (53) Spr 93, p. 7.
3759. LESHINSKY, Anita
    "The Cocoon." [Footwork] (23) 93, p. 56-57.
    "The Size of Things." [Footwork] (23) 93, p. 56.
3760. LESLIE, Naton
    "The Mechanics of Waiting" (for Meg). [WestB] (33) 93, p. 9-10.
    "Notes Toward Creation." [WestB] (33) 93, p. 8-9.
    "The Word and Wondering Violent." [MassR] (33:4) Wint 92-93, p. 493-494.
3761. LESLIE, Peter
    "Shower in A Major." [PraF] (14:3) Aut 93, p. 104.
3762. LESSER, Rika
    "Fagerfjäll, Tjörn, 1986. For Pentti" (tr. of Göran Sonnevi). [Pequod] (35) 93, p. 26 -
        27.
    "From the cliff at the foot of Skull Mountain" (tr. of Göran Sonnevi). [Pequod] (35)
        93, p. 24-25.
    "Life: It Must Suffice Us." [Pequod] (35) 93, p. 97-99.
    "Mourning Cloak" (tr. of Göran Sonnevi). [Pequod] (35) 93, p. 28-31.
    "Pools of Strong Indian Tea and Urine" (tr. of Stig Larsson). [GrandS] (12:3, #47)
        Fall 93, p. 57-61.
3763. LESSING, Karin
    "Ten Sonnets" (tr. of Louise Labé). [Sulfur] (33) Fall 93, p. 29-34.
3764. LESTER, Kathleen
    "The Missing." [IndR] (16:2) Fall 93, p. 101-102.
3765. LESTER-MASSMAN, G. (Gordon) (See also MASSMAN, Gordon)
    "Lake Under the Skull." [Confr] (51) Sum 93, p. 268.
3766. LEUTNER, Robert
    "For the Fighting Spirit of the Walnut" (selections, tr. of Takashi Hiraide). [Stand]
        (34:2) Spr 93, p. 34-40.
LEV, Dina Ben
    See BEN-LEV, Dina
3767. LEV, Donald
    "On the Genuine." [NewYorkQ] (50) 93, p. 57.
    "Yours Is My Nightmare." [NewYorkQ] (52) 93, p. 44.
3768. LEVANT, Jonathan
    "A Personal System of Symbols." [PikeF] (11) Fall 93, p. 29.
3769. LeVASSEUR, Jeanne
    "Something Inside You." [SpoonR] (18:2) Sum-Fall 93, p. 7.
3770. LEVCHEV, Vladimir
    "Beacon" (In memory of Danila Stoyanova, tr. by Lisa Sapinkopf and Georgi
        Belev). [Paint] (19:38) Aut 92, p. 62.
    "Blue Pond at Berkovitsa" (To Tsvetana, tr. by Lisa Sapinkopf and Georgi Belev).
        [Paint] (19:38) Aut 92, p. 63.
3771. LEVENSON, Christopher
    "Giraffe." [PaintedB] (52) 93, p. 6.
    "In Memory of William Carlos Williams" (tr. of Hans Magnus Enzensberger).
        [QRL] (12:32/33) 93, p. 410.

3772. LEVERTOV, Denise
"Anamnesis at the Faultline" (For Barbara Thomas, after experiencing her
installation, "What Is Found, What Is Lost, What Is Remembered", 1992).
[CarolQ] (45:3) Sum 93, p. 7-8.
"A Blessing." [CarolQ] (45:3) Sum 93, p. 9.
"The Earth Worm." [QRL] (12:32/33) 93, p. 458-459.
"Evening Train." [Field] (48) Spr 93, p. 52-53.
"Face to Face." [QRL] (12:32/33) 93, p. 459.
"A Heresy." [AmerPoR] (22:1) Ja-F 93, p. 47.
"Letter to a Friend." [Field] (48) Spr 93, p. 56-58.
"Luxury." [QRL] (12:32/33) 93, p. 458.
"The Lyre-Treee." [AmerPoR] (22:1) Ja-F 93, p. 47.
"The Past III." [AmerPoR] (22:1) Ja-F 93, p. 47.
"Suspended." [Field] (48) Spr 93, p. 63.
"Thirst Song." [QRL] (12:32/33) 93, p. 459-460.
"The Tide." [Field] (48) Spr 93, p. 61-62.
"U.S. Buried Iraqi Soldiers Alive in Gulf War" (News Report, September 1991).
[Field] (48) Spr 93, p. 59.
3773. LEVI, Steven (Steven C.)
"Miasma fills the valley hiding the contours." [CoalC] (7) Apr 93, p. 35.
"O! Bury me not on the lone prairie" (Amelia One-Liner Award). [Amelia] (7:2,
#21) 93, p. 79.
"With a Month to Go." [Pearl] (19) Fall-Wint 93, p. 565.
3774. LEVIN, Amy
"Long Division." [NoDaQ] (61:4) Fall 93, p. 120-121.
3775. LEVIN, Dana
"The Baby on the Table." [Ploughs] (19:4) Wint 93-94, p. 34-35.
3776. LEVIN, Gabriel
"A Closed Place" (tr. of Leah Ayalon). [Trans] (28) Spr 93, p. 83-84.
"Only the Body Recalls" (tr. of Yitzhak Laor). [Trans] (28) Spr 93, p. 148.
"Second Woman and Insecurity" (tr. of Leah Ayalon). [Trans] (28) Spr 93, p. 85.
"Word Processing" (1-4, tr. of Maya Bejerano). [Trans] (28) Spr 93, p. 66-69.
3777. LEVIN, John
"The Price of Admission" (Special Section: 40 poems). [WormR] (33:3, #131), 93,
p. 133-152.
3778. LEVIN, Philip Dane
"Coming Down." [GreenMR] (NS 6:2) Sum-Fall 93, p. 118-119.
3779. LEVIN, Phillis
"The Afterimage." [ParisR] (35:129) Wint 93, p. 94-95.
"Strophe." [ParisR] (35:129) Wint 93, p. 96.
3780. LEVIN, Susan
"Amnesia." [OnTheBus] (5:2, #12) Sum-Fall 93, p. 125.
"Body Beautiful." [OnTheBus] (6:1, #13) Wint 93-Spr 94, p. 144.
"Buried Alive." [OnTheBus] (6:1, #13) Wint 93-Spr 94, p. 142.
"Campaign." [OnTheBus] (5:2, #12) Sum-Fall 93, p. 127.
"Do You Think of Me." [OnTheBus] (6:1, #13) Wint 93-Spr 94, p. 141.
"Fever." [OnTheBus] (6:1, #13) Wint 93-Spr 94, p. 141.
"First Child." [OnTheBus] (5:2, #12) Sum-Fall 93, p. 123-124.
"For Poetry, My Son." [OnTheBus] (6:1, #13) Wint 93-Spr 94, p. 143-144.
"Homecoming Queen." [OnTheBus] (5:2, #12) Sum-Fall 93, p. 126.
"My Girl." [OnTheBus] (6:1, #13) Wint 93-Spr 94, p. 145.
"New England." [OnTheBus] (5:2, #12) Sum-Fall 93, p. 124.
"Pas de Deux." [OnTheBus] (6:1, #13) Wint 93-Spr 94, p. 142.
"Rich Man, Poor Man." [OnTheBus] (5:2, #12) Sum-Fall 93, p. 122.
"While He Leaves." [OnTheBus] (6:1, #13) Wint 93-Spr 94, p. 143.
3781. LEVINE, Elise
"This Is It." [PraS] (67:4) Wint 93, p. 93.
3782. LEVINE, Mark
"Abstract Poem." [NewYorker] (68:50) 1 F 93, p. 70.
"Capitalism." [ColR] (20:1) Spr 93, p. 49-51.
"My Brother Abel, the Wounded." [ColR] (20:1) Spr 93, p. 54-55.
"New Republics." [NewYorker] (69:18) 21 Je 93, p. 66-67.
"Out by Dark." [ColR] (20:1) Spr 93, p. 56-57.
"Seconds." [ColR] (20:1) Spr 93, p. 52-53.
"Seconds." [CutB] (39) Wint 93, p. 45-46.
"Statues." [NewYorker] (69:8) 12 Ap 93, p. 76.

"You." [CutB] (39) Wint 93, p. 43-44.
3783. LEVINE, Philip
  "Above Jazz." [NewEngR] (15:1) Wint 93, p. 173-174.
  "Belief." [NewEngR] (15:1) Wint 93, p. 170-172.
  "Lame Ducks, 1945." [NewYorker] (69:35) 25 O 93, p. 90.
  "Listen Carefully." [Thrpny] (55) Fall 93, p. 31.
  "My Mother with Purse the Summer They Murdered the Spanish Poet."
      [NewYorker] (69:19) 28 Je 93, p. 85.
  "Ode for Mrs. William Settle." [Atlantic] (272:4) O 93, p. 69.
  "Soul." [Thrpny] (54) Sum 93, p. 12.
3784. LEVINSON, James Heller
  "Bad Boy Emotional-." [OnTheBus] (5:2, #12) Sum-Fall 93, p. 129.
  "Untitled: Bad Boy ro mancin his lady." [ChironR] (12:4/13:1, #37/38) Wint 93-Spr
      94, p. 31.
  "Untitled: Bad Boy un practiced in the art of the interview." [ChironR] (12:4/13:1,
      #37/38) Wint 93-Spr 94, p. 31.
  "Untitled: When whole town talk bout Bad Boy." [ChironR] (12:4/13:1, #37/38)
      Wint 93-Spr 94, p. 31.
3785. LEVINSON, Miriam
  "Geology, Summer 1983." [Agni] (37) 93, p. 114-115.
  "Loneliness Begins" (for Natalie Goldberg). [Conscience] (14:3) Aut 93, p. 47.
3786. LEVITIN, Alexis
  "Almost Nothing" (tr. of Eugenio de Andrade). [WebR] (17) Fall 93, p. 17.
  "Body" (tr. of Eugenio de Andrade). [QRL] (12:32/33) 93, p. 22.
  "Cante Jondo" (tr. of Eugenio de Andrade). [Epiphany] (4:2) Ap 93, p. 114.
  "City" (tr. of Eugenio de Andrade). [Nimrod] (37:1) Fall-Wint 93, p. 96.
  "Early in the Morning" (tr. of Eugenio de Andrade). [QRL] (12:32/33) 93, p. 21.
  "Epitaph" (tr. of Eugenio de Andrade). [Epiphany] (4:2) Ap 93, p. 113.
  "Eros Thanatos" (tr. of Eugenio de Andrade). [Epiphany] (4:2) Ap 93, p. 115.
  "Even in Ruins" (tr. of Eugenio de Andrade). [QRL] (12:32/33) 93, p. 21.
  "Heart of Day" (tr. of Eugenio de Andrade). [TampaR] (7) Fall 93, p. 41.
  "Hoarse Song" (tr. of Eugenio de Andrade). [Epiphany] (4:2) Ap 93, p. 112.
  "The House" (tr. of Eugenio de Andrade). [Nimrod] (37:1) Fall-Wint 93, p. 96.
  "Instances" (tr. of Eugenio de Andrade). [SenR] (23:1/2) Wint 93, p. 155.
  "Introduction to the Song" (tr. of Eugenio Andrade). [Os] (36) Spr 93, p. 13.
  "The Little Persian" (tr. of Eugenio de Andrade). [Nimrod] (37:1) Fall-Wint 93, p.
      98.
  "Nocturne for Two Voices" (tr. of Eugenio de Andrade). [HolCrit] (30:3) Je 93, p.
      15.
  "The Patio Light" (tr. of Eugenio de Andrade). [QRL] (12:32/33) 93, p. 22.
  "Peaches" (tr. of Eugenio de Andrade). [QRL] (12:32/33) 93, p. 22.
  "Receding Surf" (tr. of Eugenio de Andrade). [QRL] (12:32/33) 93, p. 22.
  "Sound" (tr. of Eugenio de Andrade). [WebR] (17) Fall 93, p. 17.
  "Tear" (tr. of Eugenio Andrade). [Os] (36) Spr 93, p. 11.
  "To Waken" (tr. of Eugenio Andrade). [Os] (36) Spr 93, p. 15.
  "What Morning Does He Wish for Still" (tr. of Eugenio de Andrade). [SenR]
      (23:1/2) Wint 93, p. 156.
3787. LEVY, Andrew
  "The American Sublime." [Avec] (6:1) 93, p. 38.
3788. LEVY, Howard
  "Mozart" (Rondo from the Violin Concerto #5 in A Major, K. 219, "The Turkish").
      [Poetry] (161:5) F 93, p. 285.
3789. LEVY, Robert J.
  "Ember." [GettyR] (6:1) Wint 93, p. 136-137.
  "Gray Distance." [GettyR] (6:1) Wint 93, p. 138-139.
  "Housebroken." [Thrpny] (52) Wint 93, p. 18.
3790. LEW, Walter
  "1983" (Selections: III-IV). [ChiR] (39:3/4) 93, p. 252-254.
3791. LEWANDOWSKI, Stephen
  "Poplar Cove." [Contact] (11:65/66/67) Spr 93, p. 31.
  "Rivka's Dream." [Contact] (11:65/66/67) Spr 93, p. 31.
3792. LEWIS, Brad
  "The Big Fight." [AfAmRev] (27:1) Spr 93, p. 150-151.
3793. LEWIS, Diane Quintrall
  "The Visitor" (Selections: 2 poems). [Nimrod] (37:1) Fall-Wint 93, p. 80-81.

3794. LEWIS, Georgeanna I.
"Harvest." [CumbPR] (12:2) Spr 93, p. 53-54.
"The Narrator." [CumbPR] (12:2) Spr 93, p. 52.
"Pity." [CumbPR] (12:2) Spr 93, p. 55-56.
3795. LEWIS, Graham
"Swan." [NewYorkQ] (52) 93, p. 57.
3796. LEWIS, J. Patrick
"The Gentleman Bookworm." [Light] (7) Aut 93, p. 20.
"Great Pitches." [Light] (6) Sum 93, p. 7.
"Midnight Blue" (or, The Cockroach's Song). [Light] (8) Wint 93, p. 21.
"Runaway." [ArtfulD] (24/25) 93, p. 115.
"The Unkindest Cut." [Light] (5) Spr 93, p. 21.
3797. LEWIS, Janet
"Girl Help." [Zyzzyva] (9:2) Sum 93, p. 95.
3798. LEWIS, Joel
"Cool Blue Halo." [Talisman] (11) Fall 93, p. 263-264.
"Minus Water." [AmerLC] (5) 93, p. 78.
"Three AM." [HeavenB] (10) Wint-Spr 93, p. 45.
"Tonto's Expanding Headband." [PaintedB] (52) 93, p. 4.
3799. LEWIS, Lisa
"The Heart and the Symbol." [AntR] (51:1) Wint 93, p. 86-87.
"Hemstitching." [Sequoia] (34/35) 92-93, p. 75-76.
"My Students." [Agni] (37) 93, p. 292-293.
"The Office Watch." [IndR] (16:2) Fall 93, p. 122-123.
"Trains." [GrahamHR] (17) Fall 93, p. 94-97.
3800. LEWIS, Mark
"The Crow." [Gypsy] (20) Sum 93, p. 33.
3801. LEWIS, Peggy Hapke
"To the Librarian at the Tesson Ferry Branch." [WebR] (17) Fall 93, p. 123.
3802. LEWIS, Susan
"Ismene." [GlobalCR] (1) Spr 93, p. 89-93.
3803. LEWYN, Gloria
"Behind the Yellow Hibiscus" (In memory of Juleste). [HawaiiR] (17:2, #38) Spr
93, p. 26-27.
"On Hearing That the Waioli Tea Room Has Closed." [HawaiiR] (17:2, #38) Spr 93,
p. 4-5.
"The Second King of Japan." [GreenMR] (NS 6:2) Sum-Fall 93, p. 35-36.
"Seduced Again by Bukowski." [Pearl] (19) Fall-Wint 93, p. 81.
3804. LEXOW, Melissa
"Man-at-Arms" (Young Writers, age 11). [PikeF] (11) Fall 93, p. 20.
3805. LI, Dian
"The Basic Dress Code for a Poet" (tr. of Wan Xia). [GreenMR] (NS 6:2) Sum-Fall
93, p. 151.
"Chapter IX: Hometown (September)" (tr. of Hai Zi). [GreenMR] (NS 6:2) Sum -
Fall 93, p. 138-140
"A Dozen Things" (tr. of Zhang Xiao Bo). [GreenMR] (NS 6:2) Sum-Fall 93, p.
153.
"Echo" (tr. of Xi Chuan). [GreenMR] (NS 6:2) Sum-Fall 93, p. 148.
"The Eighth Month" (tr. of Zhai Yong Ming). [GreenMR] (NS 6:2) Sum-Fall 93, p.
152.
"Frenzied Fingers" (tr. of Fu Liang). [GreenMR] (NS 6:2) Sum-Fall 93, p. 154.
"The Garden in the Air" (tr. of Ou Yang Jiang He). [GreenMR] (NS 6:2) Sum-Fall
93, p. 143.
"A Hymn to X" (tr. of Song Lin). [GreenMR] (NS 6:2) Sum-Fall 93, p. 146.
"My Seventh Winter in Shanghai" (tr. of Song Lin). [GreenMR] (NS 6:2) Sum-Fall
93, p. 147.
"The Orchard in August" (tr. of Xi Chuan). [GreenMR] (NS 6:2) Sum-Fall 93, p.
149.
"Spider" (tr. of Wan Xia). [GreenMR] (NS 6:2) Sum-Fall 93, p. 150.
"We" (tr. of Ou Yang Jiang He). [GreenMR] (NS 6:2) Sum-Fall 93, p. 141-142.
3806. LI, Min Hua (Louie Crew)
"Mace for the Child Molester." [Footwork] (23) 93, p. 79.
3807. LI, Mingxia
"Epic" (tr. of Yan Li, w. Leonard Schwartz). [AmerLC] (5) 93, p. 83-86.

LI

3808. LI, Po
"Calling on a Taoist Priest in Tai-Tien Mountain But Failing to See Him" (tr. by
    Katie Price). [WillowS] (33) Wint 93, p. 68.
3809. LI, Xi-jian
"Dew Drops" (tr. of Guan Yonghe, w. Gordon Osing). [PikeF] (11) Fall 93, p. 15.
"The Diver" (tr. of Ai Qing, w. Gordon Osing). [PikeF] (11) Fall 93, p. 15.
"Looking up at the Moon" (tr. of Shi Xiang, w. Gordon Osing). [PikeF] (11) Fall 93,
    p. 15.
"Natural Beauty" (tr. of Ba Bulinbuhe, w. Gordon Osing). [PikeF] (11) Fall 93, p.
    15.
"The Seagulls" (tr. of Wen Jie, w. Gordon Osing). [PikeF] (11) Fall 93, p. 14.
"Secret Talking" (tr. of Bai Hua, w. Gordon Osing). [PikeF] (11) Fall 93, p. 15.
"Swallows" (tr. of Miao Deyu, w. Gordon Osing). [PikeF] (11) Fall 93, p. 15.
"The Tree at the Edge of the Precipice" (tr. of Zen Zuo, w. Gordon Osing). [PikeF]
    (11) Fall 93, p. 15.
"The Yellow River and the Carp" (tr. of Niu Han, w. Gordon Osing). [PikeF] (11)
    Fall 93, p. 14.
3810. LI, Yan
"Epic" (tr. by Mingxia Li and Leonard Schwartz). [AmerLC] (5) 93, p. 83-86.
LIAN, Yang
    See YANG, Lian
LIANG, Fu
    See FU, Liang
3811. LIBRO, Antoinette
"Borrowed Flight." [JINJPo] (15:1) Spr 93, p. 18.
3812. LICHTIG, Denise P.
"School Days." [AntR] (51:3) Sum 93, p. 376-377.
3813. LIDDY, James
"Bobby the Commie." [CreamCR] (17:2) Fall 93, p. 144-145.
"Larry Josephs, 34, Writer About AIDS, Dies of the Disease." [CreamCR] (17:2)
    Fall 93, p. 143.
3814. LIDDY, John
"To Marcos in the Coming Years." [BellR] (16:1/2) Spr-Fall 93, p. 68.
"Without Words." [BellR] (16:1/2) Spr-Fall 93, p. 69.
3815. LIEBENTHAL, Jean
"Hortatory." [Light] (8) Wint 93, p. 11.
3816. LIEBERMAN, Laurence
"Curse of the Yellow Bird." [IllinoisR] (1:1) Fall 93, p. 32-34.
"Epidermal Hell." [AmerPoR] (22:1) Ja-F 93, p. 48-49.
"Foreplay and Entrapment." [Crazy] (44) Spr 93, p. 27-32.
"House Walk Over the Mountain" (for Michael Madonick). [Nat] (256:23) 14 Je 93,
    p. 847.
"Love, the Barber." [QRL] (12:32/33) 93, p. 460-461.
"Prayer Against the Curse Bomb." [Boulevard] (8:1, #22) Spr 93, p. 196-200.
"Smuggled Pencil Stubs." [AmerPoR] (22:1) Ja-F 93, p. 48-49.
"The St. Kitts Monkey Feuds." [SewanR] (101:4) O-D, Fall 93, p. 487-488.
"Stool Aid's Song" (for Ginger and Charles Lozar). [TarRP] (33:1) Fall 93, p. 65-67.
"White Tiger and the Mosquitos." [Hudson] (46:3) Aut 93, p. 471-476.
3817. LIEBERMAN, Michael
"Ascent." [WebR] (17) Fall 93, p. 74.
"The Condition of Being." [WebR] (17) Fall 93, p. 73.
3818. LIECHTY, John
"Mexico City." [CapeR] (28:1) Spr 93, p. 27.
3819. LIEN, Hoàng
"Relative Sufferings" (tr. by Phon-anh). [Zyzzyva] (9:4) Wint 93, p. 106.
3820. LIES, Betty
"Lot's Wife 1." [Footwork] (23) 93, p. 140.
"Moon." [US1] (28/29) 93, p. 19.
"Your Anger." [Footwork] (23) 93, p. 140.
3821. LIETZ, Robert
"Commission" (For the Jesuits, their housekeeper, her daughter, murdered by the
    death squads). [CharR] (19:1) Spr 93, p. 97-99.
"Households." [PoetL] (88:4) Wint 93-94, p. 37-38.
3822. LIFSHIN, Lyn
"All the Women Poets I Like Didn't Have Their Fathers." [DogRR] (12:2, #24) Fall -
    Wint 93, p. 30-32.

"Ancient Madonna." [WormR] (33:4, #132) 93, p. 188.
"Auschwitz." [NewYorkQ] (50) 93, p. 48.
"Auschwitz Artists." [NewYorkQ] (50) 93, p. 50.
"Auto Mobile Madonna." [WormR] (33:4, #132) 93, p. 188.
"Avalanche Madonna" (1, 2). [WormR] (33:4, #132) 93, p. 188.
"Barbie Feels There Is Someone Else There Inside Her." [SpoonR] (18:1) Wint-Spr
	93, p. 106-107.
"Barbie Hunts Thru Medical Books Looking for What Is Wrong with Her When She
	Sees Her Birth Date in a Book, Knows She Is Over 30." [ClockR] (8:1/2) 93,
	p. 93-94.
"The Barbie Sister." [SpoonR] (18:1) Wint-Spr 93, p. 102-103.
"Barbie Sits in the Too Cute Chocolate Shop." [SpoonR] (18:1) Wint-Spr 93, p.
	104-105.
"Big Green Sea Turtle Madonna." [WormR] (33:1, #129) 93, p. 19.
"Bored and Adored Madonna." [WormR] (33:1, #129) 93, p. 19.
"The Bowls from Bavaria." [WormR] (33:1, #129) 93, p. 20.
"Broken Refrigerator Madonna." [WormR] (33:1, #129) 93, p. 18.
"Burn Out." [Plain] (13:3) Spr 93, p. 19.
"Cars and Men." [WormR] (33:1, #129) 93, p. 20.
"Children with AIDS Learn to Live without Happily Ever After." [NewYorkQ] (51)
	93, p. 41.
"Cow Girl Madonna." [WormR] (33:1, #129) 93, p. 19.
"Cream of Rice." [RagMag] (11:1) 93, p. 16-17.
"Cruise Madonna." [WormR] (33:4, #132) 93, p. 188.
"Crystal Madonna." [WormR] (33:1, #129) 93, p. 18.
"Dances with Sheep Madonna." [WormR] (33:1, #129) 93, p. 19.
"Daughter of Stockbroker, Beatrice von Guggenburg." [NewYorkQ] (51) 93, p. 40.
"Depression." [US1] (28/29) 93, p. 8.
"Depresssed, She." [WormR] (33:1, #129) 93, p. 18.
"Diamond Madonna." [WormR] (33:1, #129) 93, p. 20.
"Driving Back from the Hospital in the Rain." [SlipS] (13) 93, p. 43.
"Eating Disorder Madonna." [WormR] (33:1, #129) 93, p. 19.
"Editing the Anthology." [PaintedB] (49) 93, p. 30.
"Edward R Murrow." [NewYorkQ] (50) 93, p. 51.
"The Forties." [Caliban] (12) 93, p. 171.
"Georgia O'Keeffe." [ColEng] (55:7) N 93, p. 783.
"Hair Grass and Spiders." [NorthStoneR] (11) 93, p. 125.
"Hair Wreathes." [XavierR] (13:2) Fall 93, p. 93.
"Happy Birthday Mama." [Footwork] (23) 93, p. 163.
"He Said I Don't Enunciate Clearly." [WebR] (17) Fall 93, p. 109-110.
"Hollyhocks Madonna, 1." [WormR] (33:4, #132) 93, p. 188.
"Hookers Near Arbor Hill." [SlipS] (13) 93, p. 41.
"Hydroponic Madonna." [WormR] (33:1, #129) 93, p. 20.
"I Remember Haifa Being Lovely But." [CreamCR] (17:1) Spr 93, p. 27.
"The I.V. As Control." [Pearl] (17) Spr 93, p. 111.
"I Was Four in Dotted." [WilliamMR] (31) 93, p. 64.
"In This Version" (1-3). (A Plainsongs Award Poem). [Plain] (14:1) Fall 93, p. 36 -
	38.
"Inside the Church in Lodz." [BellR] (16:1/2) Spr-Fall 93, p. 82-83.
"It Was Like Having." [NewYorkQ] (52) 93, p. 40.
"It's Been So Long." [WormR] (33:1, #129) 93, p. 18.
"Jade, Emerald Ad Chartreeuse [sic] Light in the Branches." [Footwork] (23) 93, p.
	162-163.
"Jeanne Marie Plouffe." [AntigR] (93-94) Spr-Sum 93, p. 210-211.
"Light in January." [PaintedB] (52) 93, p. 20.
"The Mad Girl Is Flip, Uses Words." [Sun] (212) Ag 93, p. 7.
"The Mad Girl's Mother Lives Vicariously Thru Her Daughters." [OnTheBus] (5:2,
	#12) Sum-Fall 93, p. 130-131.
"Madonna Accused by an Ex-Student of Stealing His Poems She Can't Remember."
	[WindO] (57) Fall 93, p. 33.
"Madonna of the Candidate." [WormR] (33:4, #132) 93, p. 188.
"Madonna of the Confidences." [WormR] (33:1, #129) 93, p. 18.
"Madonna of the Over Reactions." [WormR] (33:1, #129) 93, p. 18.
"Madonna of the Provocations." [WormR] (33:1, #129) 93, p. 19.
"Madonna Who Lives in Terror of Taxes and Men." [WormR] (33:1, #129) 93, p.
	20.

"Madonna Who Starts to Write Prose." [WormR] (33:4, #132) 93, p. 188.
"Mama." [Footwork] (23) 93, p. 163-164.
"March 4th Madonna." [WormR] (33:1, #129) 93, p. 19.
"Material Madonna." [WormR] (33:4, #132) 93, p. 188.
"Mist, February." [NorthStoneR] (11) 93, p. 124.
"Mother and Daughter Swim Icy Chesapeake Bay." [LullwaterR] (4:2) Spr-Sum 93,
    p. 64.
"Musky Nights after Rain Rose." [XavierR] (13:2) Fall 93, p. 91.
"My Mother and the Calendar." [PaintedB] (49) 93, p. 31.
"My Mother, on Stronger Pain Killers." [SlipS] (13) 93, p. 41.
"My Mother Sabotages What Could Be to the End." [Pearl] (17) Spr 93, p. 111.
"My Mother Shaving Her Legs." [WebR] (17) Fall 93, p. 110-111.
"My Mother's Third Call on a Day of Sleet and December Falling." [CreamCR]
    (17:1) Spr 93, p. 29.
"Next Door My Neighbor Is Moving." [Sun] (210) Je 93, p. 28.
"November" (3 poems with same title). [SoDakR] (31:3) Fall 93, p. 46-49.
"The Old Woman in Amsterdam." [CreamCR] (17:1) Spr 93, p. 28.
"On the Way to the Gas, One Woman." [NewYorkQ] (50) 93, p. 49.
"Plastic Surgery Madonna." [WormR] (33:1, #129) 93, p. 19.
"A Plus Madonna." [WormR] (33:1, #129) 93, p. 19.
"The Poetry Workshop Dream." [DogRR] (12:1, #23) Spr-Sum 93, p. 39.
"Pointe Shoes." [WormR] (33:1, #129) 93, p. 18.
"Reading the Poem My Sister Wrote That I Hadn't." [BellR] (16:1/2) Spr-Fall 93, p.
    84.
"Reading Tour." [LitR] (36:2) Wint 93, p. 185.
"Sara 10, Never Talks About." [NewYorkQ] (51) 93, p. 42.
"Snake Dance." [DogRR] (12:2, #24) Fall-Wint 93, p. 50.
"Stitched Up Madonna." [NorthStoneR] (11) 93, p. 126.
"Taking My Mother to the Bathroom." [Sun] (216) D 93, p. 33.
"Taking My Mother's Ring." [SlipS] (13) 93, p. 42.
"That Other May." [Footwork] (23) 93, p. i162.
"This April." [XavierR] (13:2) Fall 93, p. 90.
"This May's a Scorcher." [Footwork] (23) 93, p. 163.
"The Thought of It." [ContextS] (3:1) 93, p. 11.
"Treblinka." [PaintedB] (52) 93, p. 18-19.
"Twisted Cord Madonna" (1, 4). [WormR] (33:1, #129) 93, p. 19.
"Up in the Attic Madonna." [NorthStoneR] (11) 93, p. 126.
"Vincent (Edna St Vincent Millay)." [13thMoon] (11:1/2) 93, p. 40.
"The Way Sun Keeps Falling Away from Every Window." [HeavenB] (10) Wint -
    Spr 93, p. 30-31.
"Whale Watch Madonna." [WormR] (33:1, #129) 93, p. 20.
"With Him." [FreeL] (12) Sum 93, p. 19.
"With You." [XavierR] (13:2) Fall 93, p. 92.
3823. LIGHT, Carol
    "Blue Light." [PraS] (67:1) Spr 93, p. 130-131.
3824. LIGHT, Kate
    "After the Season." [WestHR] (47:4) Wint 93, p. 342.
3825. LIGNELL, Kathleen
    "After Living Too Long in an Arid Country." [HayF] (13) Fall-Wint 93, p. 9.
    "Groundwork." [Gaia] (1/2) Ap-Jl 93, p. 30.
    "Measuring the Coastline." [Gaia] (1/2) Ap-Jl 93, p. 30.
    "Theory of Departure" (I-IV). [SouthernPR] (33:2) Fall 93, p. 46-48.
3826. LIKE, Joseph
    "Postmodern: A Definition." [RiverS] (39) 93, p. 1.
3827. LILBURN, Tim
    "Contemplatio." [MalR] (102) Spr 93, p. 12.
LILLE, Alan of
    See INSULIS, Alanus de (Alan of Lille)
3828. LILLY, Jeffrey
    "Que Hora Budu Ya Là?" [PoetryUSA] (25/26) 93, p. 31.
3829. LILLY, Rebecca (Rebecca A.)
    "August by the Willow." [MidwQ] (35:1) Aut 93, p. 42.
    "Hill's Curve." [LullwaterR] (4:2) Spr-Sum 93, p. 78-79.
    "History." [MidwQ] (35:1) Aut 93, p. 43.
    "Last Week in the Cottage." [MidwQ] (35:1) Aut 93, p. 44.
    "The Movie Palace." [Asylum] (8) 93, p. 120.

"The Secret Identity." [Asylum] (8) 93, p. 120.
"The Window in Wind" (after Charles Wright). [SouthernHR] (27:4) Fall 93, p. 379.
3830. LIM-WILSON, Fatima
"From the Bridal Book II." [MassR] (34:1) Spr 93, p. 34.
"Inventing the Filipino." [KenR] (NS 15:3) Sum 93, p. 92-93.
3831. LIMA, Paul
"I Thought It Would Be Cold." [PraF] (14:2) Sum 93, p. 48-49.
LIN, Song
    See SONG, Lin
3832. LIND, Michael
"Coyoacan." [Hellas] (4:1) Spr 93, p. 63.
"Prothalamion: Tableau Vivant" (For Kevin and Diana). [Hellas] (4:1) Spr 93, p. 64 -
    65.
3833. LINDAHL, David
"At the End" (from *Voices Over the River*). [JamesWR] (10:3) Spr 93, p. 10.
"Blue Earth" (for Sunshine Perlmutter, a two-year-old girl who froze to death on
    Christmas Eve, 1983, from *Voices Over the River*). [JamesWR] (10:3) Spr 93,
    p. 11.
"Un-buh-liev-able" (from *Voices Over the River*). [JamesWR] (10:3) Spr 93, p. 10.
"Elixir." [JamesWR] (10:3) Spr 93, p. 11.
"A Laugh, a Bump, Potato Chips." [JamesWR] (10:3) Spr 93, p. 10.
"Love Poem for a Cook" (from *Voices Over the River*). [JamesWR] (10:3) Spr 93, p.
    11.
"Mad Queers at Union Square" (Protest Rally, January 6, 1984, San Francisco, from
    Voices Over the River). [JamesWR] (10:3) Spr 93, p. 11.
"The Pellet Bucket Coming" (from *Voices Over the River*). [JamesWR] (10:3) Spr
    93, p. 11.
"Voices Over the River" (from *Voices Over the River*). [JamesWR] (10:3) Spr 93, p.
    11.
"When I Am at Uncle Buddy's Grave" (from *Voices Over the River*). [JamesWR]
    (10:3) Spr 93, p. 10.
3834. LINDBERG, Peggy
"Divorce After Many Years." [Plain] (13:2) Wint 93, p. 32.
3835. LINDBLAD, Lois
"Jesus As Infant in a Renaissance Painting." [NorthStoneR] (11) 93, p. 167.
"Leaf Mould." [NorthStoneR] (11) 93, p. 166.
"Without a Net." [NorthStoneR] (11) 93, p. 167.
3836. LINDEMAN, Jack
"2 A.M." [Comm] (120:3) 12 F 93, p. 14.
"Christine in America." [BellArk] (9:6) N-D 93, p. 22.
"Rise 'N Shine." [BellArk] (9:4) Jl-Ag 93, p. 23.
"Rock Jetty." [BellArk] (9:4) Jl-Ag 93, p. 22.
3837. LINDEN, Dianne
"Relieving Beethoven." [Grain] (21:1) Spr 93, p. 78.
3838. LINDGREN, Joan
"On Poetry" (tr. of Juan Gelman). [SenR] (23:1/2) Wint 93, p. 129-130.
"Rain" (tr. of Juan Gelman). [SenR] (23:1/2) Wint 93, p. 131.
"They Say" (tr. of Juan Gelman). [SenR] (23:1/2) Wint 93, p. 125-126.
"Women" (tr. of Juan Gelman). [SenR] (23:1/2) Wint 93, p. 127-128.
3839. LINDGREN, John
"Brass Watch." [Stand] (34:2) Spr 93, p. 74.
"The Hands." [LitR] (36:2) Wint 93, p. 164.
"The Place." [Iowa] (23:1) Wint 93, p. 155.
3840. LINDNER, April
"He Interrupts My Regularly Scheduled Dreams." [Gypsy] (20) Sum 93, p. 10.
"The Wake" (for Andre). [PaintedHR] (8) Wint 93, p. 24-25.
3841. LINDNER, Carl
"The Doctor." [SoCarR] (25:2) Spr 93, p. 126.
"Raining Fire." [Iowa] (23:1) Wint 93, p. 153-154.
"Three Horses in a Field." [FloridaR] (19:1) 93, p. 50-51.
3842. LINDO, Stephen
"B" (Poets of High School Age). [HangL] (63) 93, p. 81.
3843. LINDSAY, Maurice
"The Stroke." [Stand] (34:3) Sum 93, p. 13.
3844. LINDSAY, Sarah
"It Blows, Is Blowing." [InterPR] (19:1) Spr 93, p. 85.

3845. LINDSEY-HICKS, Glenda
"Sun." [TexasR] (14:3/4) Fall-Wint 93, p. 75.
3846. LINEBERGER, James
"American Pie." [CentR] (37:2) Spr 93, p. 378-381.
"Communion." [CentR] (37:2) Spr 93, p. 375.
"Contributor's Note" (for Laura Rosenthal). [RagMag] (11:2) 93, p. 36-38.
"The Corps, and the Corps, and the Corps." [RagMag] (11:2) 93, p. 41.
"Hologram" (For Mike Foster). [CentR] (37:2) Spr 93, p. 376-377.
"Lazarus." [NewYorkQ] (52) 93, p. 58.
"May Day '44." [Verse] (10:1) Spr 93, p. 38.
"Palm Reader." [CentR] (37:2) Spr 93, p. 374-375.
"The Rainman Out of Snow." [RagMag] (11:2) 93, p. 39-40.
"The Waiting Game." [Verse] (10:2) Sum 93, p. 56.
"Why We Quit Having These Things in the First Place." [Sonora] (24/25) Spr 93, p.
173-174.
"Wireless." [CoalC] (7) Apr 93, p. 15-16.
3847. LINEHAN, Don
"Late March Night." [AntigR] (93-94) Spr-Sum 93, p. 289.
3848. LINEHAN, Susan
"Grace." [DogRR] (12:1, #23) Spr-Sum 93, p. 44.
"Waiting for the Archduke" (News item, Nov 3, 1992: The last animal at Sarejevo
Zoo died of starvation after snipers kept the keepers from taking food to the
cages). [BelPoJ] (44:2) Wint 93-94, p. 11.
3849. LINETT, Deena
"Wyoming." [Border] (2) Spr 93, p. 48.
LING, Bei
See BEI, Ling
3850. LINGENFELTER, Andrea
"Desire" (tr. of Zhai Yongming). [ChiR] (39:3/4) 93, p. 296.
"Foxtails" (tr. of K'e-hsiang Liu). [ChiR] (39:3/4) 93, p. 306-307.
"Hands and Feet" (tr. of Walis Jugan). [ChiR] (39:3/4) 93, p. 308-309.
3851. LINK, Anna
"The Flowers of Hell." [CentralP] (22) Spr 93, p. 92.
"What's in it For Me." [CentralP] (22) Spr 93, p. 93.
3852. LINKLATER,Tom
"Some Hug" (Honorable Mention, 1993 Poetry Competition). [Elf] (3:2) Sum 93, p.
26.
3853. LIOTTA, P. H.
"After the Ashbery Reading." [ProseP] (2) 93, p. 57.
"Everyone Will Write Poetry" (tr. of Branko Miljkovic). [Vis] (43) 93, p. 51.
"I Wake Her in Vain" (tr. of Branko Miljkovic). [Vis] (42) 93, p. 29.
"In Melville's Room." [ProseP] (2) 93, p. 58.
"A Poem for Ahab." [ProseP] (1) 92, p. 51-52.
"Sun" (tr. of Branko Miljkovic). [Vis] (43) 93, p. 50.
3854. LIPPMAN, Matthew
"January" (for Karen). [Iowa] (23:2) Spr-Sum 93, p. 131.
"Out of the Air." [MassR] (34:3) Aut 93, p. 365-366.
"Twentieth Century Rant." [Sonora] (26) Fall 93, p. 22-23.
3855. LIPSITZ, Lou
"Anthropology." [Pembroke] (25) 93, p. 70-71.
"Dealing with the Fact That My Daughter Has Not Slept at My House in 14 Years."
[Pembroke] (25) 93, p. 66.
"The Forest in the Palm of My Hand Is Burning." [Caliban] (13) 93, p. 105.
"The Garden." [Pembroke] (25) 93, p. 69.
"Poignant Moment, Listening to 'Lakes' Played by the Pat Metheny Group, Summer,
1984." [Pembroke] (25) 93, p. 67-68.
"Sperm." [Sun] (209) My 93, p. 11.
"Throwing Away Several Pages of Poetry." [LitR] (37:1) Fall 93, p. 62.
"The Turn." [Pembroke] (25) 93, p. 72.
"The Wolf" (for Jon who dreamt of him). [Caliban] (13) 93, p. 104.
"Zhivago." [Pembroke] (25) 93, p. 65.
3856. LIPTON, Elizabeth Wittlin
"Retrato Doble" (de Frida Kahlo). [LindLM] (12:2/4) Ap-D 93, p. 23.
3857. LISCHER, Diane
"Black Bear." [AnthNEW] (5) 93, p. 20.

3858. LISHAN, Stuart
"The Summer Storm." [LitR] (37:1) Fall 93, p. 106.
"What I Hear at the Worm's Campfire: The Greybeard's Story." [OnTheBus] (5:2, #12) Sum-Fall 93, p. 132.
3859. LISK, Thomas
"Pillow Fight at Bologna." [ApalQ] (35) 90, p. 34.
3860. LITT, Iris
"Death of a Friend." [OnTheBus] (6:1, #13) Wint 93-Spr 94, p. 146.
3861. LITT, Toby
"At Night" (tr. of Jirí Orten, w. Tomas Mika). [Verse] (10:1) Spr 93, p. 98.
3862. LITTLE, Geraldine C.
"An Afternoon on the River Dee, Llangollen, Wales." [QRL] (12:32/33) 93, p. 225 - 226.
"An Afternoon on the River Dee, Llangollen, Wales." [WestHR] (47:3) Fall 93, p. 282-283.
"At 'The Boathouse,' Laugharne, Wales." [QRL] (12:32/33) 93, p. 223.
"Cricket: An Elegy." [QRL] (12:32/33) 93, p. 226.
"Jean Garrigue: An Appreciation." [QRL] (12:32/33) 93, p. 224-225.
"Opera for Two Voices." [QRL] (12:32/33) 93, p. 227-229.
"A Rainy Night: The Pine Barrens, N.J." [JINJPo] (15:1) Spr 93, p. 21.
"Speaking to Ockanickon: Talking Across Time." [JINJPo] (15:1) Spr 93, p. 19-20.
3863. LITTLE, Jack
"Ars Longa, Vita Brevis." [Light] (5) Spr 93, p. 8.
"Sibling Rivalry." [Light] (5) Spr 93, p. 18.
3864. LIU, K'e-hsiang
"Foxtails" (tr. by Andrea Lingenfelter). [ChiR] (39:3/4) 93, p. 306-307.
3865. LIU, Newton
"Black Gold" (tr. of Tang Yaping, w. Tony Barnstone). [ChiR] (39:3/4) 93, p. 295.
"Love" (tr. of Xi Murong, w. Tony Barnstone). [ChiR] (39:3/4) 93, p. 305.
"New Discovery" (tr. of Zhang Zhen, w. Tony Barnstone). [ChiR] (39:3/4) 93, p. 294.
"Solar Tide" (from the poem cycle "Nuorilang," tr. of Yang Lian, w. Tony Barnstone). [ChiR] (39:3/4) 93, p. 290-291.
3866. LIU, Timothy
"Aperture." [IndR] (16:2) Fall 93, p. 35.
"Echoes." [KenR] (NS 15:3) Sum 93, p. 146-147.
"Forty-Percent Chance of Rain." [Caliban] (13) 93, p. 98.
"Nude Figure Dancing in the Foreground." [Caliban] (13) 93, p. 99.
"Passion" (for Frank & Michael). [Pequod] (35) 93, p. 149-150.
"Poem: If I held back each word, perhaps." [MassR] (34:4) Wint 93-94, p. 577.
"A Room Without Doors." [RiverS] (37) 93, p. 32.
"Separation." [RiverS] (37) 93, p. 33.
"Survivors." [MassR] (34:4) Wint 93-94, p. 578.
"Thoreau." [KenR] (NS 15:3) Sum 93, p. 148.
"The Tree That Knowledge Is." [Pequod] (35) 93, p. 151.
"White Blossoms." [Caliban] (13) 93, p. 98.
3867. LIYONG, Taban lo
"Counterpart Wife Clementine" (From *Wer pa Lawino*, chapter 2, tr. of Okot p'Bitek). [LitR] (36:2) Wint 93, p. 178-184.
3868. LJUNG, Anne-Marie
"The Baker's Daughter." [Poem] (69) My 93, p. 46-47.
"Eva." [Poem] (69) My 93, p. 48.
"The Owls of St. Anne du Beaupré." [Poem] (69) My 93, p. 45.
3869. LLAMAZARES, Julio
"Portrait of Bather" (Excerpt, tr. by Michael L. Johnson). [LitR] (36:3) Spr 93, p. 376.
"The Slowness of Oxen" (Excerpt, tr. by Michael L. Johnson). [LitR] (36:3) Spr 93, p. 375.
LLOSA, Ricardo Pau
See PAU-LLOSA, Ricardo
3870. LLOYD, D. H.
"Air Quality." [Pearl] (19) Fall-Wint 93, p. 73.
"Ticket." [ChironR] (12:4/13:1, #37/38) Wint 93-Spr 94, p. 29.
"Vice Squad." [Pearl] (19) Fall-Wint 93, p. 73.
3871. LLOYD, Margaret
"After You." [Poem] (69) My 93, p. 7.

"Coming Down Rain from Light." [PassN] (14:1) Sum 93, p. 36.
"The Muse." [GreenMR] (NS 6:2) Sum-Fall 93, p. 80.
"Night Out" (for John). [GreenMR] (NS 6:2) Sum-Fall 93, p. 83.
"Preparing for Winter." [GreenMR] (NS 6:2) Sum-Fall 93, p. 82.
"The Same River." [GreenMR] (NS 6:2) Sum-Fall 93, p. 81.
"Stay With Me, Make Me Still." [Journal] (17:2) Fall-Wint 93, p. 100.
"What She Knows." [Poem] (69) My 93, p. 9.
"What We Forgot." [Poem] (69) My 93, p. 8.
3872. LO, Ch'ing
"Found by the Pool" (tr. by Joseph R. Allen). [ChiR] (39:3/4) 93, p. 301.
Lo LIYONG, Taban
See LIYONG, Taban lo
3873. LOCHHEAD, Douglas
"Love in Places I-X." [AntigR] (93-94) Spr-Sum 93, p. 160-164.
3874. LOCKE, Duane
"A Longing for the Impossible." [AmerPoR] (22:2) Mr-Ap 93, p. 52.
3875. LOCKE, Edward
"The Colonist" (for Sir Humphrey Gilbert, drowned at sea on the voyage home).
[ApalQ] (36/37) 91, p. 76.
"The Stamped." [DenQ] (27:3) Wint 93, p. 40.
"To Be Continued." [Ascent] (17:2) Wint 93, p. 18.
3876. LOCKETT, Reginald
"Ex-Ho." [PoetryUSA] (25/26) 93, p. 31.
"Oaktown, CA." [PoetryUSA] (25/26) 93, p. 19.
"Sixteen Haikrazies From Being in Love" (Selections: 12-16). [PoetryUSA] (25/26)
93, p. 17.
3877. LOCKLIN, Gerald
"The Afternoon After." [WormR] (33:4, #132) 93, p. 209.
"Dickens Dickinson Melville Hardy Hugo." [WormR] (33:3, #131), 93, p. 153-154.
"Does Anyone Ever Learn Anything?" [WormR] (33:1, #129) 93, p. 41.
"Free Speech Can Be Expensive." [WormR] (33:4, #132) 93, p. 208.
"Gimme a Break." [WormR] (33:4, #132) 93, p. 209.
"Good Breeding Will Out." [WormR] (33:3, #131), 93, p. 153.
"Her Finest Quarter-Hour." [WormR] (33:3, #131), 93, p. 154-155.
"How Toad Improved Upon Hensel and Gretel." [WormR] (33:3, #131), 93, p. 155.
"I Do Not Hazard Exegesis." [WormR] (33:4, #132) 93, p. 210.
"I Was Born Before Homogenized Milk." [WormR] (33:1, #129) 93, p. 41-42.
"Like Sleeping on a Gymnasium Floor on an Island in a Typhoon." [WormR] (33:1,
#129) 93, p. 42.
"Little Dove, Who Made Thee?" [Pearl] (17) Spr 93, p. 74.
"My Masterpiece Is Four Hours Shorter Than O'Neill's." [Pearl] (19) Fall-Wint 93,
p. 26.
"Picasso: Still Life with Fruit Dish and Mandolin." [BellR] (16:1/2) Spr-Fall 93, p.
15.
"Probably." [WormR] (33:3, #131), 93, p. 155.
"Rufino Tamayo: The Merry Drinker, 1946." [BellR] (16:1/2) Spr-Fall 93, p. 14.
"Second Grade." [SlipS] (13) 93, p. 109.
"There Are More Where That One Came From." [WormR] (33:1, #129) 93, p. 42.
"They Fertilize My Welcome Mat." [Pearl] (19) Fall-Wint 93, p. 25.
"Things Even Out." [Pearl] (19) Fall-Wint 93, p. 26.
"Walt Kuhn's Gourds, 1937." [WormR] (33:1, #129) 93, p. 43.
"What Does She See in Him." [WormR] (33:4, #132) 93, p. 208.
"Where the Wisecracks Grow." [WormR] (33:4, #132) 93, p. 210.
"'Why,' They Asked Sir Edmund Hillary, 'Did You Want to Scale Mons Veneris?'."
[WormR] (33:1, #129) 93, p. 43.
3878. LOCKWOOD, Virginia C.
"Rock Bottom." [US1] (28/29) 93, p. 15.
3879. LODEN, Rachel
"Check-in at Nurnberg." [ProseP] (2) 93, p. 59.
"In Praise of Darkness." [13thMoon] (11:1/2) 93, p. 41.
3880. LOECHL, Candace
"Coming of Age." [NorthStoneR] (11) 93, p. 116.
"Date Night." [NorthStoneR] (11) 93, p. 118.
"The First Time." [NorthStoneR] (11) 93, p. 117.
"Foxfire." [NorthStoneR] (11) 93, p. 114.
"Like Father, Etc." [NorthStoneR] (11) 93, p. 118.

285

"One Way." [NorthStoneR] (11) 93, p. 113.
"Social Security." [NorthStoneR] (11) 93, p. 115.
"The Thirteenth Floor." [NorthStoneR] (11) 93, p. 119.
3881. LOEWEN, Ann
"The Fall." [TickleAce] (23) Spr-Sum 92, p. 60.
3882. LOFTIS, Norman
"Summer Nights in Chicago." [AmerPoR] (22:3) My-Je 93, p. 41-42.
3883. LOGAN, William
"The Late Perpendicular of England." [Nat] (256:8) 1 Mr 93, p. 276.
"Paradise." [Verse] (10:3) Wint 93, p. 88.
"The Porcelain Head." [Boulevard] (8:2/3, #23/24) Fall 93, p. 129.
"The Shock of the New." [YaleR] (81:2) Ap 93, p. 73.
3884. LOGUE, Christopher
"O come all ye faithful." [ParisR] (35:127) Sum 93, p. 264.
3885. LOHANS, Alison
"Michael, on the Seventh Floor." [Writer] (106:3) Mr 93, p. 24.
3886. LOHMANN, Jeanne
"Griefwork." [PoetryNW] (34:4) Wint 93-94, p. 16.
3887. LOHNER, Edgar
"September" (tr. of Gottfried Genn, w. Cid Corman). [QRL] (12:32/33) 93, p. 377 -
378.
3888. LOMAX, Dana
"It Makes Sense That Lawrence Welk Died on a Sunday." [CapeR] (28:1) Spr 93, p.
42-43.
"Sleeping with Dean, 2:54 a.m." [Blueline] (14) 93, p. 22.
3889. LOMBARDO, Anna
"Altra Notte." [Arshile] (2) 93, p. 54, 56.
"Other Nights" (tr. by Antonella Soldaini and Jack Hirschman). [Arshile] (2) 93, p.
55, 57.
3890. LOMBARDO, Gian
"Droughtmonger." [ProseP] (1) 92, p. 54.
"Learning to Dance for Rain." [Talisman] (10) Spr 93, p. 76.
"Light Singing Before the Earth." [ProseP] (1) 92, p. 53.
"A Virgual Incarnation." [Talisman] (10) Spr 93, p. 76.
"What Goes On." [ProseP] (2) 93, p. 60.
3891. LOMBARDO, Marisa
"During These Hours." [SpiritSH] (58) 93, p. 22.
"Your Liquid Eyes." [SpiritSH] (58) 93, p. 21.
3892. LOMBARDY, Anthony
"Hansel and Gretel." [CumbPR]] (13:1) Fall 93, p. 59.
3893. LOMINAC, Gene
"My Other Son." [HawaiiR] (17:1, #37) Spr 93, p. 66-67.
LONERGAN, Janet Gill
See GILL-LONERGAN, Janet
3894. LONG, Bruce
"To Mistranslate Saudade." [PaintedHR] (8) Wint 93, p. 30-31.
3895. LONG, D. S.
"The Spirit Yard" (found in Johnny Frisbie Hebenstreit's Pukapukan story
"Panikiniki" in School Journal, Part 3, Number 2, 1991). [Manoa] (5:1) Sum
93, p. 231.
"Where the Heron Goes." [Manoa] (5:1) Sum 93, p. 230.
3896. LONG, Doc
"Bay-Bay's Kids." [GreenMR] (NS 6:1) Wint-Spr 93, p. 109.
"Marcus Garvey." [GreenMR] (NS 6:1) Wint-Spr 93, p. 108.
"You Can't Get There from Here." [GreenMR] (NS 6:1) Wint-Spr 93, p. 107.
3897. LONG, Priscilla
"House of Anger." [CumbPR] (12:2) Spr 93, p. 27-28.
3898. LONG, Richard
"Death Is Always Just." [HampSPR] Wint 93, p. 18.
"Peace Bridge, in Light." [HampSPR] Wint 93, p. 18.
3899. LONG, Robert Hill
"Casa del Poeta Tragico." [SouthernHR] (27:3) Sum 93, p. 231.
"Homing In." [Iowa] (23:2) Spr-Sum 93, p. 137-138.
"Hurt to See." [ProseP] (2) 93, p. 61.
"Not Quitting the Choir." [CumbPR]] (13:1) Fall 93, p. 39-40.
"The Past Master." [CumbPR]] (13:1) Fall 93, p. 36-37.

"Slaughter of the Innocents." [CumbPR]] (13:1) Fall 93, p. 38.
"Spit." [PoetryE] (36) Fall 93, p. 81-82.
3900. LONG, Virginia Love
"Ain't Living Long Like This." [ChironR] (12:4/13:1, #37/38) Wint 93-Spr 94, p. 4.
"Aunt Annie and Me." [ChironR] (12:2, #35) Sum 93, p. 9.
"For Shawn." [ChironR] (12:2, #35) Sum 93, p. 9.
"Hecate at Fiftysomething." [Crucible] (29) Fall 93, p. 37.
"Untitled: I have also loved." [ChironR] (12:4/13:1, #37/38) Wint 93-Spr 94, p. 4.
"Where Does This Gladness Come From?" [ChironR] (12:4/13:1, #37/38) Wint 93 -
    Spr 94, p. 4.
3901. LONGENBACH, James
"After Horace." [ParisR] (35:128) Fall 93, p. 215-216.
"After Liszt at the Villa D'Este." [WestHR] (47:2) Sum 93, p. 134-135.
"A Brief History of Landscape Painting in France." [ParisR] (35:128) Fall 93, p.
    212-213.
"Stories Told about the Natural World." [ParisR] (35:128) Fall 93, p. 214-215.
"Unpaintable Landscape." [WestHR] (47:2) Sum 93, p. 133.
"We Are Gathered Here." [SouthwR] (78:3) Sum 93, p. 413.
3902. LONGLEY, Judy
"Bones and Blue" (from "Georgia O'Keeffe" series. The Nimrod/Hardman Awards:
    Finalist). [Nimrod] (37:1) Fall-Wint 93, p. 57.
"Flores, Flores por los Muertos" (For John on the third anniversary of his death).
    [Poetry] (162:1) Ap 93, p. 29.
"Garden Wedding." [Poetry] (162:4) Jl 93, p. 199-200.
"Hunting Lodge, Wakullah Springs, Florida." [Poetry] (162:4) Jl 93, p. 201.
"My Last Door" (from "Georgia O'Keeffe" series. The Nimrod/Hardman Awards:
    Finalist). [Nimrod] (37:1) Fall-Wint 93, p. 58.
"Red Poppy" (from "Georgia O'Keeffe" series. The Nimrod/Hardman Awards:
    Finalist). [Nimrod] (37:1) Fall-Wint 93, p. 56.
3903. LONGLEY, Michael
"Cavafy's Desires." [NewYorker] (69:32) 4 O 93, p. 171.
3904. LONGRIE, Denise
"And Fig Leaves for All." [Gypsy] (20) Sum 93, p. 21.
3905. LONGSTAFF, James
"Adding Up a Dead Uncle." [NorthStoneR] (11) 93, p. 165.
"A Rock Mulls Things Over from a Bend in the Wapsipinicon." [NorthStoneR] (11)
    93, p. 164-165.
3906. LONIDIER, Lynn
"Lesbian Heaven" (In memoriam). [PoetryUSA] (25/26) 93, p. 25.
3907. LOO, Jeffrey
"Death Says." [CapeR] (28:1) Spr 93, p. 19.
3908. LOO, Virginia
"Old Boy News (Same Old Story)" (News Brief March 1992). [HawaiiR] (16:3,
    #36) Wint 93, p. 112.
3909. LOOKINGBILL, Colleen
"A Day by Gain." [Talisman] (11) Fall 93, p. 250.
3910. LOOMIS, Jon
"Common Prayer." [Poetry] (162:6) S 93, p. 327.
"Insomnia." [Poetry] (162:6) S 93, p. 328.
"Overnight in the Cardiac Unit." [NoAmR] (278:3) My-Je 93, p. 17.
"Playing Seven-Card Stud with the Men of My Wife's Family." [AntR] (51:4) Fall
    93, p. 559.
3911. LOONEY, George
"Irrefutable Evidence." [SouthernPR] (33:1) Spr 93, p. 23-24.
"What Might Be Called Burning." [SouthernR] (29:3) Sum, Jl 93, p. 604-605.
"With Bread to Fill the Air" (for Mairi). [CimR] (103) Ap 93, p. 79-81.
"A Woman in a Black Coat Who Could Be Memory." [SouthernPR] (33:1) Spr 93,
    p. 24-26.
3912. LOOTS, Barbara
"Abandoned Artillery: Fort Worden." [SoCoast] (15) Je 93, p. 46.
"Abigail." [Sparrow] (60) Sum 93, p. 45.
"Brother Martin." [ChrC] (110:30) 27 O 93, p. 1056.
LOPE de VEGA
    See VEGA, Lope de
3913. LOPES, Damian
"Six o'clock news peak." [WestCL] (27:3, #12) Wint 93-94, p. 90.

LOPEZ, Carolie Parker
    See PARKER-LOPEZ, Carolie
LOPEZ, Hilda Mundo
    See MUNDO LOPEZ, Hilda
3914. LOPEZ, L. Luis
    "Encounter with La Llorna upon His Return from Harvard." [Americas] (21:2) Sum
        93, p. 59-61.
    "Felina." [Americas] (21:3/4) Fall-Wint 93, p. 88-90.
    "Four Old Men." [Americas] (21:2) Sum 93, p. 62.
    "Niño." [Americas] (21:3/4) Fall-Wint 93, p. 97-98.
    "Solomón." [Americas] (21:3/4) Fall-Wint 93, p. 91-96.
3915. LOPEZ-ADORNO, Pedro
    "Sinsora." [Trasimagen] (1:1) Otoño-Invierno 93, p. 37.
3916. LORDE, Audre
    "Afterimages." [CreamCR] (17:2) Fall 93, p. 119-122.
    "My Fifth Trip to Washington Ended in Northeast Delaware." [PaintedB] (50/51)
        93, p. 56.
    "Need: A Chorale for Black Woman Voices" (For Patricia Cowan and Bobbie Jean
        Graham and the hundreds of other mangled Black Women whose nightmares
        inform these words). [CreamCR] (17:2) Fall 93, p. 112-118.
    "Sister, Morning Is a Time for Miracles." [CreamCR] (17:2) Fall 93, p. 123-124.
3917. LORENZEN, Karl
    "The Lemon." [NewYorkQ] (51) 93, p. 72.
    "Razor Blade Woman." [NorthStoneR] (11) 93, p. 61.
3918. LOTT, Rick
    "The Crucifix Fish." [LitR] (37:1) Fall 93, p. 105.
LOTTO, Jeffrey de
    See DeLOTTO, Jeffrey
3919. LOUDIN, Robert
    "Lover's Moon." [PikeF] (11) Fall 93, p. 9.
3920. LOUIS, Adrian C.
    "Akicita Olowan" (In memory of Robert Gay, 1946-1993). [NewL] (60:1) 93, p. 63 -
        64.
    "Ancient Acid Flashing Back." [ChironR] (12:4/13:1, #37/38) Wint 93-Spr 94, p.
        21.
    "At the House of Ghosts." [ChironR] (12:4/13:1, #37/38) Wint 93-Spr 94, p. 21.
    "Blame It on the Dog, He's Dead." [Lactuca] (17) Apr 93, p. 6.
    "Buffalo Spirit Song" (for Robert Gay, 1946-1993). [Ploughs] (19:4) Wint 93-94, p.
        98.
    "Corral of Flame Horses" (for Lyman Pierce). [NewL] (60:1) 93, p. 65-67.
    "Coyote's Citizenship." [NewL] (60:1) 93, p. 68-69.
    "Delmar Flies Away" (In Memory of Delmar "Fudd" Brewer). [Contact]
        (11:65/66/67) Spr 93, p. 35.
    "The Fine Printing on the Label of a Bottle of Non-alcohol Beer." [NoDaQ] (61:2)
        Spr 93, p. 129-130.
    "For My Lakota Woman." [Contact] (11:65/66/67) Spr 93, p. 35.
    "Free China Girl." [ChironR] (12:4/13:1, #37/38) Wint 93-Spr 94, p. 21.
    "Fullblood Girl on a Blue Horse" (for Jimmy Santiago Baca). [AntR] (51:2) Spr 93,
        p. 242-243.
    "I See an Indian Girl I Used to Know Near Larimer Street in Denver." [Lactuca]
        (17) Apr 93, p. 6.
    "Note to a Culture Vulture." [Ploughs] (19:4) Wint 93-94, p. 99.
    "Notes from Indian Country." [ChironR] (12:4/13:1, #37/38) Wint 93-Spr 94, p. 20.
    "Poems & Fables" (3 poems). [NewL] (60:1) 93, p. 63-69.
    "A Postcard from Devils Tower." [Contact] (11:65/66/67) Spr 93, p. 32-34.
    "Postscript: Devils Tower." [Contact] (11:65/66/67) Spr 93, p. 34.
    "Practicing Death Songs." [AntR] (51:2) Spr 93, p. 244.
    "Reclaiming an Old Debt." [CreamCR] (17:1) Spr 93, p. 8.
    "Rhetorical Judea." [Ploughs] (19:4) Wint 93-94, p. 100-101.
    "Two Prayers for the Sioux." [CreamCR] (17:1) Spr 93, p. 9.
    "Verdell's Morning Constitutional." [ChiR] (38:4) 93, p. 137.
3921. LOUIS, Barbara Anna
    "Questions." [Footwork] (23) 93, p. 102.
LOUIS, Barbra
    See LOUIS, Barbara Anna

3922. LOVE, Monifa Atungaye
"I Grew Two Voices" (w. Pamela K. Gordon). [Eyeball] (2) 93, p. 24-25.
"Talking to Wendy at My Mother's Funeral." [AfAmRev] (27:3) Fall 93, p. 477-478.
3923. LOVE, Shirley
"Out of the Fields." [SoDakR] (31:3) Fall 93, p. 141.
3924. LOVE, Tim
"Therapy." [Verse] (10:1) Spr 93, p. 101.
3925. LOVELACE, Skyler
"Anniversary Waltz." [LaurelR] (27:2) Sum 93, p. 21.
3926. LOVELL, Susan
"Inventive Story Telling." [Verse] (10:1) Spr 93, p. 84.
"Like Remedies." [Verse] (10:1) Spr 93, p. 84.
3927. LOVELL, T.
"Thick With Fingers" (for Olga Astafyeva & Vladamir Druk). [Caliban] (12) 93, p. 175.
3928. LOVINS, Terri
"After." [Calyx] (14:3) Sum 93, p. 40-41.
3929. LOVITT, Robert
"Tai Chi." [ChangingM] (26) Sum-Fall 93, p. 5.
"Two Blackbirds." [ChangingM] (26) Sum-Fall 93, p. 39.
3930. LOW, Denise
"State Street." [WestB] (31/32) 93, p. 16.
LOW, Jackson Mac
See Mac LOW, Jackson
3931. LOWE, Janice
"A Boston Mission." [Callaloo] (16:3) Sum 93, p. 537-538.
"Out East, Hamptonites Share Convictions with Faraway Bronx Neighbors, They Never Leave." [Callaloo] (16:3) Sum 93, p. 536.
3932. LOWELL, Robert
"Arsenio" (after Eugenio Montale). [QRL] (12:32/33) 93, p. 461-463.
"Charles the Fifth and the Peasant" (After Valéry). [QRL] (12:32/33) 93, p. 461.
"The Old Flame." [AmerPoR] (22:1) Ja-F 93, p. 8-9.
3933. LOWENSTEIN, Robert
"Logbook." [Hellas] (4:2) Fall 93, p. 54.
"Reverence for Wood." [DogRR] (12:2, #24) Fall-Wint 93, p. 27.
"Revision." [Wind] (23:72) 93, p. 23.
3934. LOWERY, Janet
"How My Sister Loves Me." [PoetryE] (36) Fall 93, p. 134-135.
"The Other Man." [PoetryE] (36) Fall 93, p. 136.
3935. LOWERY, Joanne
"Anomaly." [LitR] (36:2) Wint 93, p. 176.
"Aunts." [ContextS] (3:1) 93, p. 7.
"Trick of Light." [LitR] (36:2) Wint 93, p. 177.
3936. LOWEY, Stephen
"A Thainglish Collection of Poetry." [WestCL] (27:1, #10) Spr 93, p. 130-134.
3937. LOWMAN, Anthony W.
"Right Now (for Michelle)." [ChironR] (12:4/13:1, #37/38) Wint 93-Spr 94, p. 25.
3938. LOY, Mina
"Brancusi's Golden Bird" (illustrated by Oriole Farb Feshbach). [MassR] (34:2) Sum 93, p. 246-247.
"Gertrude Stein" (illustrated by Oriole Farb Feshbach). [MassR] (34:2) Sum 93, p. 244-245.
3939. LOYNAZ, Dulce María
"Carta de Amor al Rey Tut-Ank-Amen." [Areíto] (4:13) Mayo 93, inside front and back covers.
"La Novia de Lázaro" (A mi hermana Flor. De "Poemas naúfragos"). [Areíto] (4:13) Mayo 93, p. 41-45.
3940. LU, Pauline
"Bird Call Valley" (tr. of Wang Wei). [AmerPoR] (22:2) Mr-Ap 93, p. 45.
3941. LUBESKI, Lori
"Sweet Land of (Fabric) Woven" (Excerpts). [BlackBread] (3) 93, p. 29-36.
3942. LUCAS, Tony
"Bedrock." [SoCoast] (14) Ja 93, p. 36.
"The Departure of Ceolfrith." [SoCoast] (14) Ja 93, p. 37-39.
"Sacramental." [SoCoast] (14) Ja 93, p. 34-35.

3943. LUCINA, Mary
"Fish Story." [RiverC] (14:1) Fall 93, p. 28.
3944. LUDOWESE, Egon
"Farm Accident with Heron and Freckles." [NorthStoneR] (11) 93, p. 93.
"I Have a Hunger." [NorthStoneR] (11) 93, p. 93.
3945. LUDVIGSON, Susan
"After Reading Again a Poet I'd Disparaged." [AmerV] (32) 93, p. 92.
"Blackberries." [Ploughs] (19:1) Spr 93, p. 147.
"Containing the Light." [TarRP] (33:1) Fall 93, p. 53-54.
"Dreaming Another Verson." [SouthernHR] (27:3) Sum 93, p. 249.
"How Seem Bedeviled Be: On the Marriage of Elsie and Wallace Stevens."
    [MichQR] (32:2) Spr 93, p. 188-191.
"It Begins with a Presentiment." [GeoR] (47:2) Sum 93, p. 264-265.
"Lasting." [Ploughs] (19:1) Spr 93, p. 148.
"The Maps of Imagined Geography." [Shen] (43:1) Spr 93, p. 62-63.
"Monde Renversé." [TarRP] (33:1) Fall 93, p. 54.
"Zeus Returns." [SouthernHR] (27:4) Fall 93, p. 364.
3946. LUGO, Josie
"Equal Opportunity" (Young Writers, age 11). [PikeF] (11) Fall 93, p. 18.
3947. LUISI, Carmine
"These Reeds." [Footwork] (23) 93, p. 69.
"View from the Dream House." [Footwork] (23) 93, p. 69-70.
3948. LUM, Wing Tek
"At Middle Age." [HawaiiR] (17:1, #37) Spr 93, p. 44-45.
"I Should Have Known." [HawaiiR] (17:1, #37) Spr 93, p. 46.
"Night Blooming Cereus." [HawaiiR] (17:1, #37) Spr 93, p. 47.
3949. LUMMIS, Suzanne
"No One Escapes from Fresno." [OnTheBus] (6:1, #13) Wint 93-Spr 94, p. 147.
"Unfinished Sonnets." [SouthernPR] (33:2) Fall 93, p. 34-35.
3950. LUMSDEN, Roddy
"Candle." [Verse] (10:3) Wint 93, p. 99.
"The Misanthrope's Afternoon Walk." [Verse] (10:3) Wint 93, p. 98-99.
3951. LUNDE, David
"At the Dead Goat Saloon." [Light] (5) Spr 93, p. 18.
3952. LUNDE, Diane
"Eurydice" (tr. of Camilla Di Iasi). [13thMoon] (11:1/2) 93, p. 211.
"Places" (tr. of Anna Cascella). [13thMoon] (11:1/2) 93, p. 208-209.
"Summer" (tr. of Camilla Di Iasi). [13thMoon] (11:1/2) 93, p. 210.
3953. LUNDQUIST, Anne
"I'm Writing This Poem to Keep Us Alive." [Sequoia] (34/35) 92-93, p. 79-80.
"Words and Babies: Issues of Creation." [Sequoia] (34/35) 92-93, p. 77-78.
3954. LUNNY, Karen Lafferty
"Making Brownies." [EngJ] (82:4) Ap 93, p. 96.
3955. LURIA, Emile
"Tornado Weather." [AmerPoR] (22:4) Jl-Ag 93, p. 31.
3956. LUSH, Laura
"38." [AntigR] (92) Wint 93, p. 138.
"Alicia." [PraS] (67:4) Wint 93, p. 104.
"Darkening In." [PraS] (67:4) Wint 93, p. 103-104.
"Fire Swallower." [PraS] (67:4) Wint 93, p. 105.
3957. LUSK, Daniel
"Blood Sister." [PraS] (67:3) Fall 93, p. 124-125.
"Leaning In." [PraS] (67:3) Fall 93, p. 125-126.
"A Sort of Proof." [WebR] (17) Fall 93, p. 77-78.
"Summer." [US1] (28/29) 93, p. 5.
3958. LUTERMAN, Alison
"33-Year-Old Childless Poet Talks to Cherry Tree." [Kalliope] (15:2) 93, p. 52-53.
"The Garbage Truck at 7:30 A.M." [Sun] (215) N 93, p. 38.
"Healer" (for Robert Heyob). [Sun] (210) Je 93, p. 25.
"Insomnia." [Sun] (213) S 93, p. 28.
"The Landscape of the Breast." [Sun] (208) Ap 93, p. 36.
"The Night Crawlers." [Sun] (211) Jl 93, p. 11.
"Swaying Slightly in Geoff's Hammock." [Sun] (207) Mr 93, p. 16.
3959. LUTHER, Susan
"Agenda." [CentR] (37:3) Fall 93, p. 528-530.

3960. LUTZ, Gary
"Postcard to the Poet from a Jilted Bridegroom." [Light] (5) Spr 93, p. 16.
3961. LUX, Thomas
"A Boat in the Forest." [GreensboroR] (54) Sum 93, p. 16.
"Cows." [NewYorker] (69:7) 5 Ap 93, p. 58.
"The Driver Ant." [PassN] (14:2) Wint 93, p. 44.
"Irony." [PassN] (14:2) Wint 93, p. 42.
"Loudmouth Soup." [AmerPoR] (22:2) Mr-Ap 93, p. 7.
"The Neighborhood of Make Believe." [AmerPoR] (22:2) Mr-Ap 93, p. 7.
"The People of the Other Village." [AmerPoR] (22:2) Mr-Ap 93, p. 6.
"Reject What Confuses You." [PassN] (14:2) Wint 93, p. 45.
"Rhadamanthine" (an inflexibly just or severe judge). [PassN] (14:2) Wint 93, p. 43.
"River Blindness (Onchocerciasis)." [AmerPoR] (22:2) Mr-Ap 93, p. 6.
"Snow As the Rain's Father." [GreensboroR] (54) Sum 93, p. 17.
"A Streak of Blood That Once Was a Tiny Red Spider." [HarvardR] (4) Spr 93, p. 111.
3962. LUXORIUS
"#13. Magus" (tr. by Art Beck). [PassN] (14:1) Sum 93, p. 29.
"#13. Tibi cum non sit diai panis." [PassN] (14:1) Sum 93, p. 28.
"#27. Verum, Fama, tibi vultum pictura notavit." [PassN] (14:1) Sum 93, p. 30.
"#27. Well, Fame, the Painting Is" (tr. by Art Beck). [PassN] (14:1) Sum 93, p. 31.
"#90. Hilderic's Palace" (tr. by Art Beck). [PassN] (14:1) Sum 93, p. 31.
"#90. Hildirici regis fulget mirabile factum." [PassN] (14:1) Sum 93, p. 30.
3963. LUZZI, Joyce K.
"Widow, 1." [CapeR] (28:2) Fall 93, p. 16.
3964. LYLES, Peggy Willis
"Beethoven's Ninth." [Northeast] (5:8) Spr-Sum 93, p. 43.
"Broken shell." [Northeast] (5:8) Spr-Sum 93, p. 43.
3965. LYNCH, Alessandra
"Love Poem." [AmerPoR] (22:2) Mr-Ap 93, p. 17.
"A Sound." [AmerPoR] (22:2) Mr-Ap 93, p. 17.
3966. LYNCH, Annette
"On This Earth." [Gaia] (1/2) Ap-Jl 93, p. 22.
3967. LYNCH, Thomas
"Attende Domine." [RiverS] (38) 93, p. 20.
"In Paradisum." [RiverS] (38) 93, p. 21.
"Inviolata." [RiverS] (38) 93, p. 23.
"Panis Angelicus." [RiverS] (38) 93, p. 22.
3968. LYNN, Catherine
"All the Way Home (Instructions to a 10-year-old)." [ChironR] (12:2, #35) Sum 93, p. 3.
"Bald-Headed Girl (Boston Tenement, 1936)." [ChironR] (12:2, #35) Sum 93, p. 2.
"Denial." [ChironR] (12:2, #35) Sum 93, p. 3.
"Rag Doll Mary." [Pearl] (19) Fall-Wint 93, p. 77-78.
"Survival." [ChironR] (12:2, #35) Sum 93, p. 2.
"Talking Barbie." [Gypsy] (20) Sum 93, p. 5.
"With Apologies to Carl Sandburg." [ChironR] (12:2, #35) Sum 93, p. 3.
"You Know You Are Getting Old When." [Pearl] (17) Spr 93, p. 81-82.
3969. LYNSKEY, Edward (Edward C.)
"Anecdote for the Sleepy Poet." [Plain] (13:2) Wint 93, p. 17.
"The Church Mouse's Trap." [SoCoast] (14) Ja 93, p. 15.
"The Crows' Calling." [FreeL] (12) Sum 93, p. 32.
"Fruit Tramps." [Writer] (106:3) Mr 93, p. 23.
"Fugues in the Gutters." [Elf] (3:4) Wint 93, p. 28.
"Hoyt Knuckles Down." [Spitball] (44) Sum 93, p. 9.
"Mrs. Lincoln Winters in Nice." [ApalQ] (35) 90, p. 26.
"The Paccary's Paradise." [HampSPR] Wint 93, p. 62.
"Putting on the Stutz" (based on John O'Hara's travel piece in *Holiday Magazine*, 1948). [NewL] (60:1) 93, p. 72.
"Swamp Roots." [Farm] (10:1) Spr-Sum 93, p. 124.
"What Was Indigo Then Is Kudzu Now." [HampSPR] Wint 93, p. 62-63.
LYNSKEY, Edward S.
See LYNSKEY, Edward (Edward C.)
3970. LYON, Hillary
"Genealogy." [Poem] (70) N 93, p. 42.

3971. LYON, Rick
"Jimmy." [PartR] (60:2) Spr 93, p. 241.
"Joey." [NoDaQ] (61:3) Sum 93, p. 116.
"Major Scott." [NoDaQ] (61:3) Sum 93, p. 117.
3972. LYONS, Bill
"Early Morning Quiet." [EngJ] (82:1) Ja 93, p. 87.
3973. LYONS, Kimberly
"Razor." [13thMoon] (12:1/2) 93-94, p. 44.
3974. LYONS, Richard
"An Address to Marina Tsvetayeva Curling Inward." [GettyR] (6:4) Aut 93, p. 612 -
613.
"Archaic Smile." [ParisR] (35:128) Fall 93, p. 152-153.
"Blackout" (A.L., 1925-1987). [NoAmR] (278:6) N-D 93, p. 51.
"A Half Inch of Blue Sky." [Crazy] (45) Wint 93, p. 53-63.
"Hours of the Cardinal" (in memory of my mother). [IndR] (16:2) Fall 93, p. 9-14.
"In Defense of the Body." [Crazy] (44) Spr 93, p. 35-36.
"Morning, Merrymeeting Lake." [WestHR] (47:1) Spr 93, p. 28-29.
"Stanzas Written at Baba Yaga's" (in memory of L.S.). [ParisR] (35:128) Fall 93, p.
150-152.
"Summer: Silver Flashing." [WestHR] (47:1) Spr 93, p. 25-27.
"Vantage Point." [ParisR] (35:128) Fall 93, p. 148-150.
3975. LYONS, Robert
"A Stranger in Town." [BellArk] (9:3) My-Je 93, p. 11.
3976. LYONS, Stephen
"Continental Divide." [SpoonR] (18:2) Sum-Fall 93, p. 18.
"Night Currents." [SpoonR] (18:2) Sum-Fall 93, p. 17.
"What Hawks Know." [Grain] (21:1) Spr 93, p. 30.
3977. LYTHGOE, Michael H. (Michael Hugh)
"A Clean Page as a Snowscape." [Elf] (3:1) Spr 93, p. 32-33.
"Lines for a Driftwood Table." [CaribbeanW] (7) 93, p. 23-25.
"Lines for Castaways." [CaribbeanW] (7) 93, p. 21-22.
3978. M.F.A. WORKSHOP (Brooklyn College)
"Food for Thought, or Just Deserts" (w. Marie Hasten, Howard Glyn, Pamela
Hughes, M. R. Syneck, Lisbeth Keiley, Mary Greene, David Trinidad and
Allen Ginsberg, Nov. 21, 1988). [BrooklynR] (10) 93, p. 94-95.
3979. MABUZA, Lindiwe
"Open Season." [Drumvoices] (3:1/2) Fall-Wint 93-94, p. 8-12.
Mac . . .
See also names beginning with Mc . . .
3980. MAC, Kathy
"An Old Woman's Property." [AntigR] (93-94) Spr-Sum 93, p. 280.
3981. Mac CORMACK, Karen
"A Cross." [Avec] (6:1) 93, p. 68.
"From Tafia." [CapilR] (2:10) Spr 93, p. 71.
"Lost Exposures." [Avec] (6:1) 93, p. 67.
"Precious Little." [CapilR] (2:10) Spr 93, p. 79.
"Submitted." [CapilR] (2:10) Spr 93, p. 75-76.
"Ten Day Week." [Avec] (6:1) 93, p. 66.
"Through Have Around." [CapilR] (2:10) Spr 93, p. 80.
"Under." [CapilR] (2:10) Spr 93, p. 73-74.
"Unsafe Soundings." [CapilR] (2:10) Spr 93, p. 77-78.
"Untitled: What's circus in a name?" [CapilR] (2:10) Spr 93, p. 72.
3982. Mac LOW, Jackson
"The Presidents of the United States of America, 1853." [Sulfur] (33) Fall 93, p.
244-248.
3983. MacADAMS, Lewis
"In Ron Bernstein's Office at the Gersh Agency." [Arshile] (1) Spr 93, p. 21.
"Poem: I'm the same age Ted & Jack were." [Arshile] (1) Spr 93, p. 26.
"To Joey." [Arshile] (1) Spr 93, p. 20.
"Today." [Arshile] (1) Spr 93, p. 25.
"What Do I Say About Marriages?" (for Michelle and Bart). [Arshile] (1) Spr 93, p.
22-23.
"Yesterday." [Arshile] (1) Spr 93, p. 24.
3984. MACARI, Anne Marie
"Clare and Francis." [Field] (49) Fall 93, p. 75.

3985. MacCARTHY, Catherine Phil
"Barley Sugar." [SenR] (23:1/2) Wint 93, p. 68-69.
"Lady Chatterly." [SenR] (23:1/2) Wint 93, p. 73-74.
"Sanctuary." [SenR] (23:1/2) Wint 93, p. 70-71.
"Sweet Afton." [SenR] (23:1/2) Wint 93, p. 72.
MacCORMACK, Karen
See Mac CORMACK, Karen
3986. MacCORMAIC, Eoghan
"Multitone Monotone" (reprinted from 22:2). [SenR] (23:1/2) Wint 93, p. 189.
"A Reflection Across the Yard" (reprinted from 22:2). [SenR] (23:1/2) Wint 93, p. 188.
3987. MacDIARMID, Laurie
"Late Afternoon." [LouisL] (10:1) Spr 93, p. 17-20.
"Life after Death." [LouisL] (10:1) Spr 93, p. 20-23.
3988. MacDONALD, Alastair
"From the Pinède, Juan les Pins." [TickleAce] (23) Spr-Sum 92, p. 82-83.
"Green Acorn." [TickleAce] (23) Spr-Sum 92, p. 84-85.
3989. MacDONALD, Cynthia
"The Dreamer on the Stone Couch Dreams and Wakes." [ParisR] (35:128) Fall 93, p. 67-68.
3990. MacDONALD, Ranald
"One Way There and One Way Back." [Verse] (10:2) Sum 93, p. 6.
3991. MacDONALD, Reihana
"Waiting for the Palagi." [HawaiiR] (17:1, #37) Spr 93, p. 93.
"Will There Be No Great Thai Restaurants in a Hundred Years Time?" [HawaiiR] (17:1, #37) Spr 93, p. 94-95.
3992. MacDONALD, Tanis
"Freestone." [PraF] (14:3) Aut 93, p. 105.
3993. MACE, Carroll E.
"Love and Something More" (tr. of Marco Tulio del Arca Saravia). [XavierR] (13:1) Spr 93, p. 44.
"White Rest" (tr. of Marco Tulio del Arca Saravia). [XavierR] (13:1) Spr 93, p. 43.
3994. MacFADYEN, David
"New Life" (tr. of Joseph Brodsky, w. the author). [NewYorker] (69:10) 26 Ap 93, p. 86-87.
3995. MACHACEK, Jan
"The Franciscan Baths" (tr. by Ellen Rosenbaum). [OxfordM] (9:1) Spr-Sum 93, p. 82.
"Robinson" (tr. by Ellen Rosenbaum). [OxfordM] (9:1) Spr-Sum 93, p. 83.
3996. MACHADO, Gladys
"La Casa" (from "Cuentas Claras"). [Luz] (5) N 93, p. 34, 36.
"The House" (from "Cuentas Claras," tr. by Veronica Miranda). [Luz] (5) N 93, p. 35, 37.
"I Belong" (from "Cuentas Claras," tr. by Veronica Miranda). [Luz] (5) N 93, p. 89.
"Pertenezco" (from "Cuentas Claras"). [Luz] (5) N 93, p. 88.
MACHAN, Katharyn Howard
See MACHAN, Katharyn Howd
3997. MACHAN, Katharyn Howd
"At the Abortion Clinic" (corrected reprint from issue No. 26/27). [US1] (28/29) 93, p. 29.
"Fit." [Footwork] (23) 93, p. 17.
"The Professor Stares at Salted Popcorn." [IllinoisR] (1:1) Fall 93, p. 54.
3998. MacINNES, Mairi
"The Anarchist." [QRL] (12:32/33) 93, p. 232-233.
"Camping in Winter" (for Antoinette). [QRL] (12:32/33) 93, p. 231-232.
"The History of Henry Simpson." [QRL] (12:32/33) 93, p. 234-235.
"In the Village." [QRL] (12:32/33) 93, p. 233-234.
"In the Woods." [QRL] (12:32/33) 93, p. 233.
"Insight." [QRL] (12:32/33) 93, p. 229-230.
"A Landscape in the North Riding." [QRL] (12:32/33) 93, p. 230-231.
"Nicholas." [QRL] (12:32/33) 93, p. 230.
"North of San Diego." [QRL] (12:32/33) 93, p. 236.
"November Digging." [QRL] (12:32/33) 93, p. 236-237.
"Passion." [NewYorker] (69:43) 20 D 93, p. 98.
"The Remains of Christmas." [QRL] (12:32/33) 93, p. 235-236.

3999. MacINNIS, Judi
"Ghazals: Electric Lawn-Mower Cords." [PraF] (14:3) Aut 93, p. 106.
4000. MacINTOSH, Joan
"Easter with the Ukrainians." [TickleAce] (23) Spr-Sum 92, p. 58.
4001. MACIOCI, R. Nikolas
"The First of October in Tibet." [Ascent] (17:2) Wint 93, p. 12.
"The Gate of Paradise." [OnTheBus] (5:2, #12) Sum-Fall 93, p. 133.
"Memorial Service in Newark." [CapeR] (28:1) Spr 93, p. 48.
"The Quality of Grace." [Ascent] (17:2) Wint 93, p. 12.
"Swing Shift." [Wind] (23:72) 93, p. 14-15.
4002. MacKAY, Carol L.
"White Sale." [AntigR] (95) Aut 93, p. 118.
4003. MacKENZIE, Ginny
"Resurrection" (tr. of Shu Ting, w. Wei Guo). [MidAR] (14:1) 93, p. 41-42.
4004. MACKENZIE, John
"Language Burns" (for Kelly Rhea). [PraF] (14:3) Aut 93, p. 107.
4005. MacKENZIE, Nancy J.
"Arrow." [Dandel] (20:1) 93, p. 56.
4006. MACKEY, Mary
"My Methodist Grandmother Said." [YellowS] (42) Wint-Spr 93, p. 8-9.
4007. MACKEY, Nathaniel
"Song of the Andoumboulou, 17." [NewAW] (11) Sum-Fall 93, p. 36-40.
4008. MACKIE, Richard
"Scared by a Leaf." [PraF] (14:4) Wint 93-94, p. 101.
4009. MACKINNON, Margaret
"Gauguin in Kansas." [GeoR] (47:4) Wint 93, p. 657-658.
4010. MACKLIN, Elizabeth
"Before Spuyten Duyvil." [NewYorker] (69:11) 3 My 93, p. 78.
"Detail From the Large Work." [Nat] (256:25) 28 Je 93, p. 916.
"Foolishly Halved, I See You." [NewYorker] (68:49) 25 Ja 93, p. 60.
"Given the Questions." [NewYorker] (69:3) 8 Mr 93, p. 80.
"Imagine." [NewYorker] (69:25) 9 Ag 93, p. 62.
"A Woman Kneeling in the Big City" (Selections: 5 poems). [Trasimagen] (1:1)
Otoño-Invierno 93, p. 18-21.
"A Woman Kneeling in the Big City" (Selections: 5 poems, Spanish tr. by Orlando
Jose Hernandez). [Trasimagen] (1:1) Otoño-Invierno 93, p. 22-25.
"You've Just Been Told." [NewYorker] (69:17) 14 Je 93, p. 68.
4011. MacLEAN, Kenneth
"The Turning." [NorthStoneR] (11) 93, p. 84-85.
4012. MacLEAN, Ron
"The Oracle of Repeated Danger." [SouthernPR] (33:2) Fall 93, p. 32-33.
4013. MacLEOD, Heather
"Song of Dying." [Grain] (21:1) Spr 93, p. 103.
"The Warrior." [Grain] (21:1) Spr 93, p. 102.
4014. MacLEOD, Kathryn
"Methods of Hygiene." [Avec] (6:1) 93, p. 59-60.
"Self Defense." [WestCL] (27:1, #10) Spr 93, p. 135-139.
4015. MacLEOD, Sue
"As If" (for 'Saturday,' at 14). [PoetryC] (14:1) 93, p. 17.
"As If It Were a Jigsaw Puzzle Nearly Done." [PoetryC] (14:1) 93, p. 17.
"A House Like This." [PoetryC] (14:1) 93, p. 17.
"Old Lovers Can Be Sighted." [TickleAce] (25) Spr-Sum 93, p. 178.
"Thirsty Dreams." [PottPort] (15:1) Spr-Sum 93, p. 48-49.
MacLOW, Jackson
See Mac LOW, Jackson
4016. MADDEN, Ed
"Angels" (for Mary). [RiverC] (13:1) Fall 92, p. 68-69.
"As Is Death." [ColEng] (55:7) N 93, p. 780.
"Finding the Worry Stones." [ColEng] (55:7) N 93, p. 781.
"Our Lady of the Hubcaps." [Farm] (10:2) Fall-Wint 93-94, p. 39-40.
"Platonism." [RiverC] (13:1) Fall 92, p. 66-67.
"Watermelons." [RiverC] (13:1) Fall 92, p. 64-65.
4017. MADDOX, Marjorie
"Relocation: The Building of the Dyke Levee." [Farm] (10:1) Spr-Sum 93, p. 199.
"Susquehanna." [Farm] (10:1) Spr-Sum 93, p. 200.
"When She Moves Beside Me." [Confr] (51) Sum 93, p. 231.

4018. MADDUX, Carolyn
"Grove Street Hyacinths." [BellArk] (9:3) My-Je 93, p. 1.
"Jean's Garden, Before the Rain." [BellArk] (9:3) My-Je 93, p. 24.
"The Midnight Cows of Holcombe." [BellArk] (9:1) Ja-F 93, p. 14.
"Rosemary Ducks." [BellArk] (9:1) Ja-F 93, p. 22.
"Seven from England." [BellArk] (9:6) N-D 93, p. 6-7.
"Voluntary on a Flight of Angels" (for Jane). [BellArk] (9:5) S-O 93, p. 9.
"What Daffodils Don't Need to Hear." [BellArk] (9:2) Mr-Ap 93, p. 1.
4019. MADIGAN, Rick
"Forgetfulness, with Ghost and Snow." [Crazy] (44) Spr 93, p. 33-34.
4020. MADISON, Deborah Kaplan
"Thinking of You." [CentralP] (22) Spr 93, p. 102-104.
"To My Father — Who Raped Me." [CentralP] (22) Spr 93, p. 105.
4021. MADONICK, Michael David
"On Moving to Illinois." [CimR] (103) Ap 93, p. 85-86.
"The Pirate Map" (for Paul Friedman). [CimR] (103) Ap 93, p. 83-85.
"The Professor." [SouthernHR] (27:4) Fall 93, p. 320-322.
4022. MADSON, Arthur
"How to Grow Young Painting Pictures." [PikeF] (11) Fall 93, p. 3.
4023. MADUEÑO, Amalio
"Abiquiu." [Americas] (21:3/4) Fall-Wint 93, p. 80.
"Apache Tear." [Americas] (21:3/4) Fall-Wint 93, p. 85-86.
"Ballad of Friendship Through the Ages" (After C.D. de Andrade). [Americas]
    (21:3/4) Fall-Wint 93, p. 83-84.
"Black Mesa." [Americas] (21:3/4) Fall-Wint 93, p. 79.
"Black Mesa, More or Less." [Americas] (21:3/4) Fall-Wint 93, p. 78.
"Las Cruces." [Poetry] (162:2) My 93, p. 68.
"Home Boy Carvajal." [Americas] (21:3/4) Fall-Wint 93, p. 77.
"The Love of García." [Americas] (21:3/4) Fall-Wint 93, p. 82.
"Piñón." [Americas] (21:3/4) Fall-Wint 93, p. 81.
"Sanctuary of Chimayo." [Americas] (21:3/4) Fall-Wint 93, p. 87.
4024. MAGARRELL, Elaine
"Orangutan" (tr. of Moshe Dor). [PoetL] (88:1) Spr 93, p. 53.
"Without Commitments" (tr. of Moshe Dor). [PoetL] (88:1) Spr 93, p. 54.
4025. MAGEE, Kevin
"For dear life." [Talisman] (11) Fall 93, p. 251.
"Millstone." [Sulfur] (33) Fall 93, p. 118-122.
"Sculpt." [Talisman] (11) Fall 93, p. 252.
"Tedium Drum" (Excerpts from Part III). [Sulfur] (32) Spr 93, p. 148-151.
"We have here no one and you are welcome." [Talisman] (11) Fall 93, p. 251.
4026. MAGER, Don
"A Fly." [CapeR] (28:1) Spr 93, p. 9.
"Holding One's Lover" (from Leaps #42). [EvergreenC] (8:1) Spr-Sum 93, p. 75.
"Nipples." [KenR] (NS 15:1) Wint 93, p. 43-44.
"Plots" (for Bill). [NoDaQ] (61:4) Fall 93, p. 36-37.
"Results: HIV Positive" (from Leaps #58). [JamesWR] (10:3) Spr 93, p. 9.
4027. MAGGI, Maria Theresa
"The Blank World." [BlackWR] (19:1) Fall-Wint 92, p. 56-63.
4028. MAGGIO, Mike
"Friday Morning — Amman." [ApalQ] (38) 92, p. 63-64.
4029. MAGGS, Randall
"Fer de Lance" (Competition Winner, 1st). [TickleAce] (25) Spr-Sum 93, p. 118 -
    119.
4030. MAGIERA, Mark
"As I Drove Past the Old Man Watering His Wife on the Lawn." [Pearl] (19) Fall -
    Wint 93, p. 66.
4031. MAGINNES, Al
"Capitulation." [Shen] (43:4) Wint 93, p. 104-105.
"Dancing Alone." [Shen] (43:4) Wint 93, p. 103.
"Harness." [Poetry] (163:3) D 93, p. 140.
"How We Listen." [TexasR] (14:3/4) Fall-Wint 93, p. 78-79.
"The Slow Hours." [IndR] (16:2) Fall 93, p. 141-142.
4032. MAGNER, James, Jr.
"Creature of God." [HiramPoR] (53/54) Fall 92-Sum 93, p. 47.
4033. MAGORIAN, James
"Feeding Birds." [CreamCR] (17:1) Spr 93, p. 7.

"Uncle Clinton's Decoy." [Thrpny] (52) Wint 93, p. 16.
4034. MAHAKALA
"This lady who cremates the dead" (Songs from the Theragatha: Songs of the Buddhist Monks, circa 450 B.C.E.). [Tricycle] (2:3) Spr 93, p. 39.
4035. MAHAPATRA, Anuradha
"Another Spring, Darkness" (tr. by Paramita Banerjee and Carolyne Wright). [AmerPoR] (22:4) Jl-Ag 93, p. 22.
"Biography" (tr. by Paramita Banerjee and Carolyne Wright). [MidAR] (14:1) 93, p. 99.
"The Boy" (tr. by Jyotirmoy Datta and Carolyne Wright). [MidAR] (14:1) 93, p. 98.
"City Nocturne" (tr. by Paramita Banerjee and Carolyne Wright). [AmerPoR] (22:4) Jl-Ag 93, p. 22.
"Friend" (tr. by Paramita Banerjee and Carolyne Wright). [AmerPoR] (22:4) Jl-Ag 93, p. 23.
"Impatient" (tr. by Paramita Banerjee and Carolyne Wright). [AmerPoR] (22:4) Jl - Ag 93, p. 21.
"The Monster" (tr. by Paramita Banerjee and Carolyne Wright). [AmerPoR] (22:4) Jl-Ag 93, p. 22.
"Night Reader" (tr. by Paramita Banerjee and Carolyne Wright). [AmerPoR] (22:4) Jl-Ag 93, p. 23.
"Pyre Tender" (in Bengali and English, tr. by Paramita Banerjee and Carolyne Wright w. the author). [HawaiiR] (17:1, #37) Spr 93, p. 219-220.
"Tamboura" (tr. by Paramita Banerjee and Carolyne Wright). [MidAR] (14:1) 93, p. 100-101.
"You (II.)" (tr. by Paramita Banerjee and Carolyne Wright). [AmerPoR] (22:4) Jl - Ag 93, p. 22.
4036. MAHAPATRA, Jayanta
"Afterward." [Hudson] (45:4) Wint 93, p. 615.
"Enterprise." [Hudson] (45:4) Wint 93, p. 616.
4037. MAHER, Mary
"Oasis." [Bogg] (66) Wint 92-93, p. 9-10.
4038. MAHLE, Benj
"Advice to My Son." [RagMag] (11:1) 93, p. 55.
"Aliens Can Be Dumb Too." [RagMag] (11:1) 93, p. 58.
"Double Standard." [RagMag] (11:1) 93, p. 56.
"Gathering." [RagMag] (11:1) 93, p. 51.
"Guardian." [RagMag] (11:1) 93, p. 53.
"Guitar Man." [RagMag] (11:1) 93, p. 51.
"If Looking, Like." [RagMag] (11:1) 93, p. 59.
"In Essence." [RagMag] (11:1) 93, p. 57.
"Introduction." [RagMag] (11:1) 93, p. 54.
"Remembrance." [RagMag] (11:1) 93, p. 52.
"Running Water." [RagMag] (11:1) 93, p. 60.
"Vermilion Rain." [RagMag] (11:1) 93, p. 62-63.
"Wedding Photo." [RagMag] (11:1) 93, p. 61.
4039. MAHOLA, Mzikayise
"The Idea." [BostonR] (18:3/4) Je-Ag 93, p. 31.
"Next Time Use a Rope." [BostonR] (18:3/4) Je-Ag 93, p. 31-32.
4040. MAHONE, Michael
"Valentine." [Elf] (3:4) Wint 93, p. 32.
4041. MAHONEY, Lisa
"Cyclist in Winter Air." [Amelia] (7:2, #21) 93, p. 110-111.
"Hospital Room in Yellow and Green." [GreensboroR] (54) Sum 93, p. 78-79.
"Sherwood Estates." [SycamoreR] (5:2) Sum 93, p. 65.
4042. MAHONEY, Maryjo
"Nurse Waking." [KenR] (NS 15:4) Fall 93, p. 90.
4043. MAIER, Carol
"Anonymous (Fifteenth Century)" (from "Angel Dust," tr. of Carlota Caulfield). [Luz] (5) N 93, p. 69.
"Zazen" (from "Angel Dust," tr. of Carlota Caulfield). [Luz] (5) N 93, p. 40.
4044. MAILLARD, Keith
"Late Variant." [MalR] (102) Spr 93, p. 14-19.
4045. MAIO, Samuel
"Black Monday." [Paint] (19:38) Aut 92, p. 27.
"Regrets Only." [Paint] (19:38) Aut 92, p. 28.

MAIPING, Chen
See CHEN, Maiping
4046. MAIR, Catherine
"Moss." [Bogg] (66) Wint 92-93, p. 64.
4047. MAIR, Denis
"Couldn't Get Flatter" (tr. of Ah Wu). [ChiR] (39:3/4) 93, p. 297.
4048. MAJ, Bronislaw
"Untitled: Night, the mountains, a storm. The shelter packed with people" (tr. by Daniel Bourne). [CharR] (19:2) Fall 93, p. 91.
"Untitled: Not at once did you grasp the message" (tr. by Daniel Bourne). [CharR] (19:2) Fall 93, p. 89.
"Untitled: Through the weight of this uneasy summer's air" (tr. by Daniel Bourne). [CharR] (19:2) Fall 93, p. 90.
"Untitled: Weighed down by his bags, gray whiskers on his chin" (tr. by Daniel Bourne). [CharR] (19:2) Fall 93, p. 91.
"Untitled: Whenever he described to me this park, this pathway" (tr. by Daniel Bourne). [CharR] (19:2) Fall 93, p. 90.
"Untitled: Who will bear witness to these times" (tr. by Daniel Bourne). [CharR] (19:2) Fall 93, p. 92.
4049. MAJKA, Christopher
"Real Boreal, Arboreal." [TickleAce] (26) Fall-Wint 93, p. 82-83.
4050. MAJOR, Alice
"Concubine." [Dandel] (20:1) 93, p. 18.
"For All That." [Dandel] (20:1) 93, p. 19.
"Opticks." [AntigR] (95) Aut 93, p. 64.
4051. MAJOR, Clarence
"Words into Words Won't Go." [PaintedB] (50/51) 93, p. 120.
4052. MAJOR, Devorah
"#3. Interracial Series." [OnTheBus] (5:2, #12) Sum-Fall 93, p. 134.
4053. MAJOZO, Estella Conwill
"Gwendolyn Was Here/Is" (for Gwendolyn Brooks). [Drumvoices] (3:1/2) Fall - Wint 93-94, p. 48-49.
"Spider-Woman" (for Toni Morrison). [Drumvoices] (3:1/2) Fall-Wint 93-94, p. 48.
"A Voice" (for June Jordan). [Drumvoices] (3:1/2) Fall-Wint 93-94, p. 49-50.
4054. MAKALANI, Minkah
"A Dancing Memory / or a Love from Prison" (for joy williams). [Obs] (8:2) Fall - Wint 93, p. 122-123.
"The System of Mellon's Hell" (for trina & asia). [Obs] (8:2) Fall-Wint 93, p. 123 - 124.
"The Wind Still Breezes Your Name" (for Oscar Bills, Jr 1969-1991). [Obs] (8:2) Fall-Wint 93, p. 124-127.
4055. MAKELL, Tali
"Fluorescent Sorrow" (tr. of Goran Tomcic, w. Ines Modrcin and the author). [PoetL] (88:1) Spr 93, p. 49.
"Here" (tr. of Goran Tomcic, w. Ines Modrcin and the author). [PoetL] (88:1) Spr 93, p. 50.
4056. MAKKAD, Satwinder
"Let Us Save" (a song). [HawaiiR] (17:3, #39) Fall 93, p. 108.
4057. MAKSIMOVIC, Desanka
"Anticipation" (tr. by Richard Burns and Jasna B. Misic). [NoDaQ] (61:1) Wint 93, p. 105.
"I Have No More Time" (tr. by Richard Burns and Jasna B. Misic). [NoDaQ] (61:1) Wint 93, p. 104.
"Loneliness" (tr. by Biljana D. Obradovic). [PraS] (67:1) Spr 93, p. 80.
"Morana" (tr. by Marie Schulte). [NoDaQ] (61:1) Wint 93, p. 106.
"Morana's Lullaby" (tr. by Marie Schulte). [NoDaQ] (61:1) Wint 93, p. 107.
"Nobody Knows" (tr. by Richard Burns and Jasna B. Misic). [NoDaQ] (61:1) Wint 93, p. 105.
"Poetry Reading" (tr. by Biljana D. Obradovic). [PraS] (67:1) Spr 93, p. 78-79.
"Speak Softly" (tr. by Richard Burns and Jasna B. Misic). [NoDaQ] (61:1) Wint 93, p. 105.
"To Mothers" (tr. by Biljana D. Obradovic). [PraS] (67:1) Spr 93, p. 80-81.
4058. MALANGA, Gerard
"A Last Poem." [PaintedB] (50/51) 93, p. 130-131.
4059. MALCHIODI, Giancarlo
"The Godfather's last Hurrah." [Nimrod] (37:1) Fall-Wint 93, p. 122-123.

4060. MALCOLM, David
"Any One of Us" (tr. of Anna Janko, w. Georgia Scott). [Prima] (16/17) 93, p. 32 - 33.
"Found Eye" (tr. of Krystyna Lars, w. Georgia Scott). [Prima] (16/17) 93, p. 28-29.
"I See the Future" (tr. of Anna Czekanowicz, w. Georgia Scott). [Prima] (16/17) 93, p. 31.
"(I) She Writes with Fire" (tr. of Krystyna Lars, w. Georgia Scott). [Prima] (16/17) 93, p. 30.
4061. MALDEN, Ann-Britt M.
"Cry of the Black Crow — and I'm the Glitter Easy." [WillowS] (31) Wint 93, p. 46 - 47.
4062. MALDONADO, Jesús María (El Flaco).
"Buñuelitos." [Americas] (21:1) Spr 93, p. 73.
"Cuando Yo Crezca." [Americas] (21:1) Spr 93, p. 74.
"Pesadilla No Soñada." [Americas] (21:1) Spr 93, p. 71-72.
"Respeto y Amor Sincero" (Para me ahijado Martín Cervantes de Mabton, Washington). [Americas] (21:1) Spr 93, p. 75-76.
4063. MALIK, Irfan
"Just beside us a flock of days" (tr. by Lisa Sapinkopf and the author). [Sun] (213) S 93, p. 31.
"Last night very late" (tr. by Lisa Sapinkopf and the author). [Sun] (213) S 93, p. 31.
"On the grave of my hunger" (tr. by Lisa Sapinkopf and the author). [Sun] (213) S 93, p. 31.
"The slope of the church roof" (tr. by Lisa Sapinkopf and the author). [Sun] (213) S 93, p. 31.
4064. MALINOVSKI, Nina
"Time Port" (tr. by Monique and Thomas Kennedy). [Vis] (43) 93, p. 16.
4065. MALLARMÉ, Stéphane
"Funereal Toast" (for Théophile Gautier, tr. by Henry Weinfield). [Pequod] (36) 93, p. 30-31.
"Funereal Toast" (for Théophile Gautier, tr. by Henry Weinfield). [Talisman] (10) Spr 93, p. 130-131.
"Prose" (for des Esseintes, tr. by Henry Weinfield). [Pequod] (36) 93, p. 33-34.
"The Tomb of Charles Baudelaire" (tr. by Henry Weinfield). [Talisman] (11) Fall 93, p. 157.
"The Tomb of Edgar Poe" (tr. by Henry Weinfield). [Pequod] (36) 93, p. 32.
4066. MALONE, Jacqueline
"Potatoes." [CumbPR]] (13:1) Fall 93, p. 9.
"Stonehenge." [CumbPR]] (13:1) Fall 93, p. 10-11.
"Waiting" (Robert Penn Warren Poetry Prize Winner, Third Prize). [CumbPR]] (13:1) Fall 93, p. 8.
4067. MALONE, Joe
"Earthward Gliding" (tr. of Bernard de Ventadour). [Hellas] (4:2) Fall 93, p. 60, 62.
4068. MALOUF, Diana
"In a far-away land alone in my thoughts I live." [WorldO] (25:2) Wint 93-94, p. 37.
4069. MALTA, Víctor Guillermo
"Epejos Negros / Los Caminos del Silencio" (Selections: XX, XXII, XXIX). [Luz] (4) My 93, p. 48-50.
"Epejos Negros / Los Caminos del Silencio" (Selections: XXVI). [Luz] (5) N 93, p. 47.
4070. MALTMAN, Kim
"Black Clouds." [PoetryC] (13:3) 93, p. 4.
"A Brightly Lit Ship" (w. Roo Borson and Andy Patton in the collaborative writing group "Pain-not-Bread"). [PoetryC] (13:4) 93, p. 9.
"Chipmunks Enter the World of Don McKay and Jan Zwicky" (w. Roo Borson and Andy Patton in the collaborative writing group "Pain-not-Bread"). [PoetryC] (13:4) 93, p. 9.
"Cook." [PoetryC] (13:3) 93, p. 5.
"Gentleness." [PoetryC] (13:3) 93, p. 4.
"Introduction to the Introduction to Wang Wei" (w. Roo Borson and Andy Patton. Winner of the 1993 Long Poem Prize). [MalR] (103) Sum 93, p. 16-27.
"Pruner Speculates on Oscar Night" (w. Roo Borson and Andy Patton in the collaborative writing group "Pain-not-Bread"). [PoetryC] (13:4) 93, p. 8.
"Small Poem About Peripheral Matters." [PoetryC] (13:3) 93, p. 5.
4071. MALTON, Helena
"Bleeding." [PottPort] (15:1) Spr-Sum 93, p. 79-80.

"Parasite." [PottPort] (15:1) Spr-Sum 93, p. 81.
4072. MALYON, Carol
"In This Place Scented of Lilacs." [PoetryC] (13:4) 93, p. 15.
"Man on Verandah" (for a painting by Alex Colville). [Bogg] (66) Wint 92-93, p. 24.
"Poets East of the Don." [PoetryC] (13:4) 93, p. 15.
"Through the Window in the Subway Station Ceiling, Angels." [PoetryC] (13:4) 93, p. 15.
4073. MAMET, David
"Bad Penny." [Bomb] (45) Fall 93, p. 72.
"Labor Day." [Bomb] (45) Fall 93, p. 72.
"Olympia." [Bomb] (45) Fall 93, p. 72.
"The Pond at Twilight." [Bomb] (45) Fall 93, p. 72.
"Two Colors." [NewYorker] (69:38) 15 N 93, p. 80.
"The Waterworld." [Ploughs] (19:1) Spr 93, p. 187.
4074. MANCUSO, Leni
"10° West of Greenwich." [BelPoJ] (43:4) Sum 93, p. 31.
4075. MANDARINO, Joan
"Children's Mass in Montreal." [AntigR] (93-94) Spr-Sum 93, p. 278.
4076. MANDEL, Charlotte
"Birthday Chorus" (for my daughter Nora. Corrected reprint from issue No. 26/27). [US1] (28/29) 93, p. 29.
"The Fault." [WestB] (33) 93, p. 60-61.
4077. MANDEL, Tom
"An Elegy, After RMR." [NewAW] (11) Sum-Fall 93, p. 22-24.
"On the Black Keys." [NewAW] (11) Sum-Fall 93, p. 17-21.
4078. MANDELL, Arlene L.
"Angry Rooms, Silent Rooms." [Footwork] (23) 93, p. 75.
"Building the Ferris Wheel." [Footwork] (23) 93, p. 76.
"Consciousness Raising Revisited." [Footwork] (23) 93, p. 74.
"How's College?" [Footwork] (23) 93, p. 74-75.
"Route 80." [Footwork] (23) 93, p. 75.
"Seven A.M. on the East Hill." [Footwork] (23) 93, p. 75.
"Turning the Key." [ProseP] (1) 92, p. 55.
4079. MANDELSTAM, Osip
"1920" (tr. by W. S. Merwin and Clarence Brown). [QRL] (12:32/33) 93, p. 463.
"1933" (tr. by W. S. Merwin and Clarence Brown). [QRL] (12:32/33) 93, p. 463.
"Please Take the Joy of It" (tr. by Andrew Glaze). [NewYorkQ] (52) 93, p. 47.
4080. MANEIKIS, Dan
"Motel." [SlipS] (13) 93, p. 99.
"What They Don't Know." [PaintedHR] (8) Wint 93, p. 23.
4081. MANERA, Matthew
"Earthquake." [Dandel] (20:1) 93, p. 5.
4082. MANESIOTIS, Joy
"Not Yet Dead." [VirQR] (69:1) Wint 93, p. 92-93.
"The Reservoir." [VirQR] (69:1) Wint 93, p. 91-92.
4083. MANG, Ke
"Vineyard" (tr. by Tony Barnstone, Willis Barnstone and Gu Zhongxing). [ChiR] (39:3/4) 93, p. 289.
4084. MANGAN, Pat
"The Dog." [NewYorkQ] (52) 93, p. 81.
4085. MANJUL
"Sky" (tr. by Wayne Amtzis). [WebR] (17) Fall 93, p. 16.
4086. MANKIEWICZ, Angela Consolo
"Song of Rabelais." [ChironR] (12:3, #36) Aut 93, p. 31.
4087. MANN, Barbara
"Quartet: Photo Collage." [13thMoon] (11:1/2) 93, p. 42.
4088. MANN, Charles (Charles E., Charles Edward)
"The Boy Who Talked to Birds." [Interim] (12:2) Fall-Wint 93, p. 11.
"Denny's Restaurant, 3:00 PM." [Epiphany] (4:3) Jl 93, p. 196.
"Epernay." [ChatR] (13:2) Wint 93, p. 12-13.
"Seasons" (For Glen Burliegh). [SouthernHR] (27:1) Wint 93, p. 48.
"The Water Tower." [Epiphany] (4:3) Jl 93, p. 195.
4089. MANN, John
"Annunciation." [WestB] (33) 93, p. 59-60.
"La Pie, Monet." [WestB] (33) 93, p. 58-59.

4090. MANNER, Eeva-Liisa
"Deep and Clear" (tr. by Ritva Poom). [Vis] (43) 93, p. 19.
"Hermes" (tr. by Ritva Poom). [Vis] (43) 93, p. 19.
"Last Year in Capricorn" (tr. by Ritva Poom). [Vis] (43) 93, p. 18.
4091. MANNHEIM, Linda
"Dustmice Are the 1950s." [Caliban] (12) 93, p. 168-169.
4092. MANNO, Yves di
"Kambuja: Stelae from the Khmer Empire" (tr. by Nathaniel Tarn). [Sulfur] (33)
Fall 93, p. 206-214.
4093. MANOA, Pio
"A Letter to My Storyteller." [Manoa] (5:1) Sum 93, p. 64-66.
4094. MANOO-RAHMING, Lelawattee
"Trini Tabanca — Carnival 92." [CaribbeanW] (7) 93, p. 47-48.
4095. MANOS, Kenna Creer
"In the Southern Hemisphere." [CanLit] (137) Sum 93, p. 62.
4096. MANSON, Peter
"Superstring Theory." [Verse] (10:2) Sum 93, p. 69.
4097. MANSOUR, Monica
"Desnudo / Aguafuerte" (2 selections, tr. by Forrest Gander). [ProseP] (1) 92, p. 56.
4098. MANTERO, Manuel
"The Art of Going Mad" (tr. by Betty Jean Craige). [LitR] (36:3) Spr 93, p. 378-379.
"This Splendor" (tr. by Betty Jean Craige). [LitR] (36:3) Spr 93, p. 378.
"To Kronos, or Words from a Drunk" (tr. by Betty Jean Craige). [LitR] (36:3) Spr
93, p. 377-378.
4099. MANYARROWS, Victoria Lena
"Have Strength" (Kalliope's Prayer for All Women of the Future). [Kalliope] (15:3)
93, p. 75.
"I Remember the Desert." [Elf] (3:4) Wint 93, p. 36.
"When This Land Was Ours." [SinW] (51) Wint 93-94, p. 17.
4100. MANYÉ i MARTI, Lourdes
"Alone and Silent" (tr. of Miquel Martí i Pol, w. Wayne Cox). [WillowS] (31) Wint
93, p. 80.
"The Aprenticeship of Solitude" (tr. of Miquel Marti i Pol, w. Wayne Cox).
[ClockR] (8:1/2) 93, p. 23.
"Metamorphosis III" (tr. of Miquel Marti i Pol, w. Wayne Cox). [ClockR] (8:1/2)
93, p. 25.
"This Future" (tr. of Miquel Martí i Pol, w. Wayne Cox). [WillowS] (31) Wint 93, p.
80.
"Ultimate Metamorphosis" (tr. of Miquel Marti i Pol, w. Wayne Cox). [ClockR]
(8:1/2) 93, p. 27.
"White on White" (tr. of Miquel Martí i Pol, w. Wayne Cox). [WillowS] (31) Wint
93, p. 79.
4101. MAPANJE, Jack
"To the Unknown Dutch Postcard-Sender (1988)." [KenR] (NS 15:2) Spr 93, p. 131 -
132.
4102. MAPP, Erica
"The Langlois Bridge, March 1888, Arles." [Colum] (20) Sum 93, p. 99.
4103. MARAINI, Toni
"Desert Poem" (Excerpts, tr. by Kathleen Fraser and Alberto Rossatti). [13thMoon]
(11:1/2) 93, p. 212-214.
4104. MARCELLO, Leo Luke
"Fireflies and the Dry-Cleaners." [ContextS] (3:1) 93, p. 17.
"Her Wallpaper." [LouisL] (10:2) Fall 93, p. 56.
"The Infinite Possibilities of Desire." [NorthStoneR] (11) 93, p. 19.
"Local Peaches." [NorthStoneR] (11) 93, p. 19.
4105. MARCH, Andy
"Ah, Star." [PoetryE] (36) Fall 93, p. 88-89.
"Jade Void." [PoetryE] (36) Fall 93, p. 87.
"Song of the Outsized Asteroid." [PoetryE] (36) Fall 93, p. 90-91.
"The Virtue of Poesy." [PoetryE] (36) Fall 93, p. 85-86.
4106. MARCHAND, Blaine
"Released through Stone." [PoetryC] (13:4) 93, p. 10.
"The White Room." [PoetryC] (13:4) 93, p. 10.
4107. MARCHANT, Fred (Frederick J.)
"Fragments on the Last Night." [HarvardR] (4) Spr 93, p. 43-44.
"Herons." [SouthernHR] (27:2) Spr 93, p. 131.

"Starlight Mints." [Journal] (17:2) Fall-Wint 93, p. 69-71.
4108. MARCINKEVICIUS, Justinas
    "Punishment" (tr. by Lionginas Pazusis, w. Bradley R. Strahan). [Vis] (43) 93, p. 36.
4109. MARCUS, Adrianne
    "After the Divorce." [SoDakR] (31:2) Sum 93, p. 103-105.
    "Cinderella." [SoDakR] (31:2) Sum 93, p. 106-107.
    "Fairy Tales." [SoDakR] (31:2) Sum 93, p. 108-109.
4110. MARCUS, Jacqueline
    "Sycamore Bay." [SycamoreR] (5:2) Sum 93, p. 84-85.
4111. MARCUS, Mordecai
    "8:45 P.M." [CapeR] (28:1) Spr 93, p. 6.
    "After the Delivery." [Elf] (3:3) Fall 93, p. 35.
    "Harmless Hours." [PoetC] (25:1) Fall 93, p. 22.
    "Public Needs." [Amelia] (7:2, #21) 93, p. 104-105.
4112. MARCUS, Morton
    "The Big Broadcast." [Caliban] (13) 93, p. 51.
    "The Evil Eye." [Caliban] (13) 93, p. 50.
    "Kisses." [ProseP] (2) 93, p. 62-63.
    "My Aloneness." [Ploughs] (19:1) Spr 93, p. 27-28.
    "Our Star." [Ploughs] (19:1) Spr 93, p. 25-26.
    "The Sorrow of Wood." [ProseP] (2) 93, p. 64.
    "A Universe of Broken Symmetries." [Caliban] (13) 93, p. 51.
4113. MARCUS, Peter
    "Accepting Destruction." [PoetryE] (36) Fall 93, p. 33.
    "The Affair." [Iowa] (23:3) Fall 93, p. 169.
    "Donor." [PoetryE] (36) Fall 93, p. 35.
    "The Insomniac's Pet Shop." [Agni] (37) 93, p. 33.
    "El Mundo del Oro." [WillowS] (33) Wint 93, p. 19.
    "El Mundo del Teror" [sic, i.e. Terror]. [WillowS] (33) Wint 93, p. 18.
    "Not Knowing What Will Heal Him." [WillowS] (33) Wint 93, p. 17.
    "Poem in Honor of the 50th Anniversary of the Navajo Code-Talkers." [Caliban]
        (13) 93, p. 139.
    "Rodin Exhibit on the Rooftop, Metropolitan Museum of Art." [Iowa] (23:3) Fall
        93, p. 168.
    "Song Against Time." [PoetryE] (36) Fall 93, p. 34.
    "To Hear the Chorus Sing." [Agni] (37) 93, p. 34.
    "What Ripens Quickly." [WillowS] (31) Wint 93, p. 75.
4114. MARCUS, Sharon
    "The Night Unloads in Lilacs." [Hellas] (4:2) Fall 93, p. 112-113.
4115. MARENGO, Scott
    "Tabasco on the Table" (for the six who gathered around a table in Louisiana).
        [Confr] (51) Sum 93, p. 257-258.
4116. MARESCA, John
    "Blood Gun." [JamesWR] (10:2) Wint 93, p. 13.
    "Museum." [JamesWR] (10:2) Wint 93, p. 13.
    "Transmission." [JamesWR] (10:2) Wint 93, p. 13.
MARFYNSE, Vanessa
    See MARTYNSE, Vanessa (Marfynse?)
4117. MARGOLIS, Gary
    "Breaker 19." [PennR] (5:2) 93, p. 12.
4118. MARGOSHES, Davie
    "Leave Wife." [PraF] (14:4) Wint 93-94, p. 33-34.
    "Taking Heart." [PraF] (14:4) Wint 93-94, p. 34-35.
4119. MARIC, Dasa
    "Daily Lament" (tr. of Tin Ujevic, w. Richard Burns). [NoDaQ] (61:1) Wint 93, p.
        188-189.
    "Frailty" (tr. of Tin Ujevic, w. Richard Burns). [NoDaQ] (61:1) Wint 93, p. 191.
    "The Necklace" (Selections: XXXII, XXV, XXXI, tr. of Tin Ujevic, w. Richard
        Burns). [NoDaQ] (61:1) Wint 93, p. 190-191.
    "Poems from Hana (1939)" (tr. of Oskar Davico, w. Richard Burns). [NoDaQ]
        (61:1) Wint 93, p. 55-57.
    "Poets" (tr. of A. B. Simic, w. Richard Burns). [NoDaQ] (61:1) Wint 93, p. 174.
    "Star on High" (tr. of Tin Ujevic, w. Richard Burns). [NoDaQ] (61:1) Wint 93, p.
        192.
4120. MARING, Heather
    "My Name Is Campaspe." [WillowS] (31) Wint 93, p. 45.

4121. MARINKOVIC, Dragana
"Prayer" (tr. of Blaze Koneski, w. Richard Burns). [NoDaQ] (61:1) Wint 93, p. 98.
4122. MARINO, Gigi
"Fire." [WillowS] (31) Wint 93, p. 44.
4123. MARINOVICH, Filip
"Sandy" (Poets of High School Age). [HangL] (63) 93, p. 82.
"Toothache and Australia Fantasy" (Poets of High School Age). [HangL] (63) 93, p. 82.
MARIS, Ron de
 See De MARIS, Ron
4124. MARKHAM, E. A.
"Chapter One: Coderington." [CaribbeanW] (7) 93, p. 36-38.
4125. MARKO, Bela
"The Dissected Bird" (tr. by Sylvia Csiffary). [Vis] (41) 93, p. 8.
4126. MARKOVIC, Vito
"Analects" (Selections: 1-2, 24, 27, 31, 33-34, 48, 50, 82, 87, 91, 96, tr. by Richard Burns and Vera Radojevic). [NoDaQ] (61:1) Wint 93, p. 108-109.
4127. MARKS, Gigi
"Additions." [Bomb] (44) Sum 93, p. 66.
"Forgiveness." [Bomb] (44) Sum 93, p. 66.
"Invitation." [RiverC] (14:1) Fall 93, p. 60.
"Lilac." [Bomb] (44) Sum 93, p. 66.
"Martha's Vineyard." [NowestR] (31:3) 93, p. 52-54.
"Open Windows." [Farm] (10:2) Fall-Wint 93-94, p. 61.
"Riverbend." [Bomb] (44) Sum 93, p. 66.
4128. MARKS, Ludek
"I Do No Want to Be" (tr. by Ellen Rosenbaum). [OxfordM] (9:1) Spr-Sum 93, p. 106.
4129. MARKS, Neva E.
"Sound Bites: Early Autumn." [CumbPR]] (13:1) Fall 93, p. 68.
4130. MARKS, Sara
"Consciousness." [HawaiiR] (17:1, #37) Spr 93, p. 70.
4131. MARLATT, David
"Dahlias." [SycamoreR] (5:2) Sum 93, p. 63-64.
"A Hog Slaughtering Woman." [PoetryNW] (34:2) Sum 93, p. 15.
"Mary Agnes." [PassN] (14:2) Wint 93, p. 40.
"The Saint's Cookbook." [PassN] (14:2) Wint 93, p. 41.
"Snapping Beans with the Jehovah's Witness." [PoetryNW] (34:2) Sum 93, p. 16-17.
4132. MARLIS, Stefanie
"Bells." [Manoa] (5:2) Wint 93, p. 30.
"Between Kingdoms." [Manoa] (5:2) Wint 93, p. 29.
"Devolution." [Manoa] (5:2) Wint 93, p. 29-30.
"Possibly." [DenQ] (27:3) Wint 93, p. 41.
"Star Dust." [Poetry] (162:4) Jl 93, p. 220.
4133. MARPLE, Vivian
"About the Carrot." [AntigR] (93-94) Spr-Sum 93, p. 277.
"Of Three Polite Warnings This Is the Second" (From *Shaking the Pumpkin*, Jerome Rothenberg, ed.). [TickleAce] (26) Fall-Wint 93, p. 101-102.
"Wheat." [Grain] (21:1) Spr 93, p. 135.
"When the earthquake hit." [TickleAce] (26) Fall-Wint 93, p. 100.
4134. MARQUART, Debra
"Between Wives." [SouthernPR] (33:2) Fall 93, p. 6-7.
"Somewhere in a House Where You Are Not" (Guy Owen Poetry Prize Winner, Charles Simic, Judge). [SouthernPR] (33:2) Fall 93, p. 5-6.
4135. MARSH, Billie
"All My Friends Advise Me to Start a New Life." [AnthNEW] (5) 93, p. 29.
4136. MARSH, Irene Eberling
"Betty's Dream." [Parting] (6:2) Wint 93, p. 36.
"Fiona's Dream." [Parting] (6:2) Wint 93, p. 24.
4137. MARSH, Sherrie
"San Francisco." [PoetryUSA] (25/26) 93, p. 52.
4138. MARSHALL, B. V.
"Calendar." [Art&Und] (2:1) Ja-F 93, p. 8.
"Hector First Suspects." [Art&Und] (2:1) Ja-F 93, p. 8.
4139. MARSHALL, Gregory
"Messages They Left Behind." [RiverS] (39) 93, p. 65-67.

4140. MARSHALL, Jack
"The Big Brass Handbook: Chapter 2" (Excerpt). [Caliban] (12) 93, p. 158-161.
"Cross-Street." [Ploughs] (19:1) Spr 93, p. 159-160.
"The Home-Front." [Caliban] (12) 93, p. 156-157.
"In Midlife." [Talisman] (11) Fall 93, p. 25-29.
4141. MARSHALL, Tod (Tod T.)
"After Storms." [Farm] (10:2) Fall-Wint 93-94, p. 98.
"Creed." [BellArk] (9:2) Mr-Ap 93, p. 8.
"Fishing." [Farm] (10:1) Spr-Sum 93, p. 98.
"Genesis." [CutB] (39) Wint 93, p. 81-83.
"Lasting Images." [BellArk] (9:3) My-Je 93, p. 8.
"Lasting Images." [BellArk] (9:4) Jl-Ag 93, p. 13.
"Muette Danse" (After W.C.W.). [BellArk] (9:3) My-Je 93, p. 24.
"Muette Danse" (After W.C.W.). [BellArk] (9:4) Jl-Ag 93, p. 10.
"Psalm 118: Taking Out the Trash." [BellArk] (9:4) Jl-Ag 93, p. 7.
"Telescopic." [BellArk] (9:1) Ja-F 93, p. 22.
"Wedding Psalm." [BellArk] (9:2) Mr-Ap 93, p. 8.
4142. MARSOCCI, Raymond
"Resurrection." [ProseP] (1) 92, p. 57.
"Transience." [Journal] (17:2) Fall-Wint 93, p. 17-18.
4143. MARSTELLER, Judith A.
"Penelope's Turn." [EngJ] (82:4) Ap 93, p. 100.
4144. MARTENS, Caroline Rowe
"Haiku: Exhausted." [Amelia] (7:2, #21) 93, p. 83.
4145. MARTENS, Jacinta Taitano
"Dear Mama,/ I Hate Eggs." [ColR] (20:2) Fall 93, p. 31.
"Dear Mama,/ I Love My New Dress." [ColR] (20:2) Fall 93, p. 34.
"Dear Mama,/ I Think I Am Adopted." [ColR] (20:2) Fall 93, p. 33.
"Dear Mama,/ No One Else in the Whole World." [ColR] (20:2) Fall 93, p. 32.
4146. MARTENS, Oscar
"Overhaul." [Arc] (31) Aut 93, p. 11-12.
MARTHA CHRISTINA
    See CHRISTINA, Martha
MARTI, Lourdes Manyé i
    See MANYÉ i MARTI, Lourdes
4147. MARTI, Manuel Luis
"Despertar del Desorden." [Luz] (5) N 93, p. 85.
4148. MARTI i POL, Miquel
"Alone and Silent" (tr. by Wayne Cox and Lourdes Manyé i Martí). [WillowS] (31) Wint 93, p. 80.
"Aprenentatge de la Solitud." [ClockR] (8:1/2) 93, p. 22.
"The Aprenticeship of Solitude" (tr. by Wayne Cox and Lourdes Manyé i Martí). [ClockR] (8:1/2) 93, p. 23.
"Metamorfosi III." [ClockR] (8:1/2) 93, p. 24.
"Metamorfosi Ultima." [ClockR] (8:1/2) 93, p. 26.
"Metamorphosis III" (tr. by Wayne Cox and Lourdes Manyé i Martí). [ClockR] (8:1/2) 93, p. 25.
"This Future" (tr. by Wayne Cox and Lourdes Manyé i Martí). [WillowS] (31) Wint 93, p. 80.
"Ultimate Metamorphosis" (tr. by Wayne Cox and Lourdes Manyé i Martí). [ClockR] (8:1/2) 93, p. 27.
"White on White" (tr. by Wayne Cox and Lourdes Manyé i Martí). [WillowS] (31) Wint 93, p. 79.
4149. MARTIAL
"V.64" (tr. by Joseph S. Salemi). [CarolQ] (45:2) Wint 93, p. 73.
"VI, xii. I've charged the lout next door" (tr. by William Matthews). [IllinoisR] (1:1) Fall 93, p. 41.
"VI.40" (tr. by Joseph S. Salemi). [CarolQ] (45:2) Wint 93, p. 72.
"VI, lxvii. Your Celia keeps company with eunuchs" (tr. by William Matthews). [IllinoisR] (1:1) Fall 93, p. 41.
"VIII, lxxix. Those unlovely friends you drag" (tr. by William Matthews). [IllinoisR] (1:1) Fall 93, p. 41.
"Epigrams" (tr. by D. R. Shackleton Bailey). [GrandS] (12:2, #46) Sum 93, p. 119-124.
"A Selection of Epigrams" (by Martial et al., tr. by Jack Flavin). [SpoonR] (18:1) Wint-Spr 93, p. 41.

4150. MARTIN, Alexander
"Art Therapy." [HawaiiR] (17:1, #37) Spr 93, p. 73.
"Where I Live." [HawaiiR] (17:1, #37) Spr 93, p. 74.
4151. MARTIN, Andrew
"White Sheets." [BrooklynR] (10) 93, p. 89.
4152. MARTIN, Camille
"Untitled: It's winter in the haiku that hardly anyone believed." [Caliban] (12) 93, p. 127.
"Untitled: The inevitable roof with antennae." [Caliban] (12) 93, p. 126.
4153. MARTIN, Carl
"Another Kind of Traffic." [Pembroke] (25) 93, p. 53.
"Just Another Bearish Downsweep." [Pembroke] (25) 93, p. 50.
"On the Allusive Pleasure of Modern Arts." [Pembroke] (25) 93, p. 49.
"Sensibility Shaped by Blood." [Pembroke] (25) 93, p. 51.
"Where It Is and the Colorless Rainbow." [Pembroke] (25) 93, p. 52.
4154. MARTIN, Charles Casey
"Mother's Third Husband." [Agni] (37) 93, p. 202-203.
MARTIN, Diane Kirsten
See KIRSTEN-MARTIN, Diane
4155. MARTIN, Doug
"The Delinquency of Winter." [HawaiiR] (17:3, #39) Fall 93, p. 14-15.
"Stars." [Pearl] (19) Fall-Wint 93, p. 19.
4156. MARTIN, James E.
"The Butcher Shop at Alcara li Fusi, Sicily." [ApalQ] (35) 90, p. 24.
4157. MARTIN, Janette
"Another Portico." [Footwork] (23) 93, p. 57-58.
4158. MARTIN, Mary E.
"Village of the Mermaids" (after a painting by Paul Delvaux). [WestB] (31/32) 93, p. 166-167.
4159. MARTIN, Michael
"Exchange: A Memoir." [Shen] (43:4) Wint 93, p. 49-65.
"On the Sisters." [Shen] (43:2) Sum 93, p. 76-78.
"Return Leter" (to a distant lover). [Shen] (43:2) Sum 93, p. 79-86.
4160. MARTIN, Richard
"Inside." [AnotherCM] (26) Fall 93, p. 77-78.
"Projection." [AnotherCM] (25) Spr 93, p. 79-81.
"Rehearsed in Oblivion." [AnotherCM] (25) Spr 93, p. 82.
4161. MARTINAITIS, Marcelijus
"The Ballads of Kukutis" (Selections: 10 poems, tr. by Laima Sruoginis). [Writ] (25) 93, p. 5-19.
"The Beginning of the Story" (tr. by Laima Sruoginis). [WebR] (17) Fall 93, p. 9.
"An Experiment" (tr. by Laima Sruoginis). [WebR] (17) Fall 93, p. 12-13.
"How Kukutis Regained His Senses" (from "Kukutis's Ballads," tr. by Laima Sruoginyte). [CimR] (104) Jl 93, p. 15-16.
"Kukutis' Appeal to the Alphabet" (tr. by Laima Sruoginis). [WebR] (17) Fall 93, p. 15.
"Kukutis Beats Scholar Pliugzma's Dog" (tr. by Laima Sruoginis). [ArtfulD] (24/25) 93, p. 39.
"Kukutis' Consciousness Becomes Alienated" (tr. by Laima Sruoginis). [Vis] (43) 93, p. 34.
"Kukutis Dreams up Zuveliskes Village in the Cathedral Square" (tr. by Laima Sruoginis). [ArtfulD] (24/25) 93, p. 35-37.
"Kukutis Opens His Eyes" (tr. by Laima Sruoginis). [ArtfulD] (24/25) 93, p. 38.
"Kukutis' Sermon to the Pigs" (from "Kukutis's Ballads," tr. by Laima Sruoginyte). [CimR] (104) Jl 93, p. 16-17.
"Kukutis Wants to See His Homeland" (from "Kukutis's Ballads," tr. by Laima Sruoginyte). [CimR] (104) Jl 93, p. 17-18.
"Kukutis' Words" (tr. by Laima Sruoginis). [WebR] (17) Fall 93, p. 11.
"My Thought-Up Story to Cheer Up Hanged Kukutis" (tr. by Laima Sruoginis). [WebR] (17) Fall 93, p. 14-15.
"Tool's, Word's and People's Confusion" (tr. by Laima Sruoginis). [WebR] (17) Fall 93, p. 10-11.
MARTINAITUS, Marcelijus
See MARTINAITIS, Marcelijus

4164. MARTINEZ, Alejandro
"Seeing" (from "Families, Streets and Dreams," a poetry/photography event by 3rd grade students, Whittier Elementary, Tulsa). [Nimrod] (37:1) Fall-Wint 93, p. 86.
"Viendo" (from "Families, Streets and Dreams," a poetry/photography event by 3rd grade students, Whittier Elementary, Tulsa). [Nimrod] (37:1) Fall-Wint 93, p. 86.
4165. MARTINEZ, Dionisio D.
"Alternating Current." [GreenMR] (NS 6:1) Wint-Spr 93, p. 29.
"Bad Alchemy" (for Gayle Natale, 1944-1990). [MichQR] (32:1) Wint 93, p. 22-24.
"The Doppler Effect." [GreenMR] (NS 6:1) Wint-Spr 93, p. 31.
"Kinescope." [DenQ] (28:1) Sum 93, p. 44.
"Some Bitterness Always." [GreenMR] (NS 6:1) Wint-Spr 93, p. 30.
"Sometimes the Obvious Is a Blessing." [GreenMR] (NS 6:1) Wint-Spr 93, p. 32.
"Syllogism." [DenQ] (28:1) Sum 93, p. 43.
"Talking to Myself at the Once in a Blue Moon Café." [ApalQ] (38) 92, p. 51-52.
"Temporary Losses" (for my sister). [GreenMR] (NS 6:1) Wint-Spr 93, p. 28.
"Veinna, Ohio." [ApalQ] (38) 92, p. 53-56.
"William Pachner: View from a Passing Train." [TampaR] (7) Fall 93, p. 25.
4166. MARTINEZ, Jan
"Apprendiz de Fuego." [CuadP] (7:21) S-D 93, p. 75.
"Cenizas Quedan." [CuadP] (7:21) S-D 93, p. 80-81.
"Claroscuro." [CuadP] (7:21) S-D 93, p. 79.
"La Danza Derretida" (a mi hermano Ernesto in memoriam). [CuadP] (7:21) S-D 93, p. 77.
"La Debil Llama." [CuadP] (7:21) S-D 93, p. 79-80.
"La Lampara." [CuadP] (7:21) S-D 93, p. 78.
"Narciso." [CuadP] (7:21) S-D 93, p. 79.
"Phosphoros." [CuadP] (7:21) S-D 93, p. 76.
"Pirotecnia." [CuadP] (7:21) S-D 93, p. 81.
"La Rosa de Ceniza." [CuadP] (7:21) S-D 93, p. 80.
"La Tarde Encendida." [CuadP] (7:21) S-D 93, p. 78.
"La Vela Olvidada." [CuadP] (7:21) S-D 93, p. 76.
4167. MARTINEZ, Mark L.
"The Kiss" (for August). [EvergreenC] (8:1) Spr-Sum 93, p. 43.
4168. MARTINEZ, Ramon
"The Dancer (June 22, 1987)" (for Fred Astaire). [ColR] (20:2) Fall 93, p. 107.
"Silky Sullivan." [ColR] (20:2) Fall 93, p. 105-106.
"Who Is the Novice in This Poem and What Is She Doing Here?" [ColR] (20:2) Fall 93, p. 108-109.
4169. MARTINEZ, Valerie
"Outside: Winter Solstice." [PraS] (67:3) Fall 93, p. 115.
"Prayer." [PraS] (67:3) Fall 93, p. 114-115.
4170. MARTINEZ, William, Jr.
"El amor es falso" (Spanish tr. of Kim Sang-Yong, 1561-1673). [Luz] (4) My 93, p. 56.
"¿Cuándo se hizo el vino?" (Spanish tr. of anonymous Korean Sijo). [Luz] (4) My 93, p. 56.
"Durante el viento helado de anoche nevó y nevó" (Spanish tr. of Yu Ung-Bu, d. 1456). [Luz] (4) My 93, p. 56.
"En la montaña con agua clara hago casa de hierbas junto a la roca" (Spanish tr. of anonymous Korean Sijo). [Luz] (4) My 93, p. 56.
"El pino solitario junto al río es fuerte y recto" (Spanish tr. of anonymous Korean Sijo). [Luz] (4) My 93, p. 56.
"Toda la gente es tonta" (Spanish tr. of Kim Kwang-Wook, 1580-1656). [Luz] (4) My 93, p. 57.
4171. MARTORY, Pierre
"American Nocturne" (tr. by John Ashbery). [AmerPoR] (22:5) S-O 93, p. 10-11.
"Between Her and Me" (tr. by John Ashbery). [AmerPoR] (22:5) S-O 93, p. 11.
"Coming and Going" (tr. by John Ashbery). [Poetry] (162:3) Je 93, p. 133.
"Dune" (tr. by John Ashbery). [AmerPoR] (22:5) S-O 93, p. 8.
"Elegy: Adieu near those fields that smoke disembowels" (tr. by John Ashbery). [Poetry] (162:3) Je 93, p. 135.
"From Here On" (tr. by John Ashbery). [AmerPoR] (22:5) S-O 93, p. 9.
"The Landscape Is Behind the Door" (tr. by John Ashbery). [AmerPoR] (22:5) S-O 93, p. 10.

"The Landscapist" (tr. by John Ashbery). [AmerPoR] (22:5) S-O 93, p. 9.
"Ma Chandelle Est Morte" (tr. by John Ashbery). [AmerPoR] (22:5) S-O 93, p. 8.
"A Night on the Dead Sea" (tr. by John Ashbery). [AmerPoR] (22:5) S-O 93, p. 11.
"Passing the Frontier" (tr. by John Ashbery). [Poetry] (162:3) Je 93, p. 132.
"Poem: How do you say tomorrow in this country?" (tr. by John Ashbery).
    [AmerPoR] (22:5) S-O 93, p. 8.
"What I Say, Perhaps, Isn't True" (tr. by John Ashbery). [AmerPoR] (22:5) S-O 93,
    p. 11.
"Wine" (tr. by John Ashbery). [Poetry] (162:3) Je 93, p. 134.
4172. MARTYNSE, Vanessa (Marfynse?)
    "Now I Know There Are Bored People Everywhere" (For Dorothy Barresi).
        [Footwork] (23) 93, p. 116.
4173. MARVEL, Catherine
    "Museum of Comparative Zoology." [BlackWR] (19:2) Spr-Sum 93, p. 67.
    "Physical Measurements in Aphasia." [BlackWR] (19:2) Spr-Sum 93, p. 69-70.
    "Pieta." [AntR] (51:2) Spr 93, p. 232.
    "Viral Surgery." [BlackWR] (19:2) Spr-Sum 93, p. 68.
4174. MARVIN, John
    "Where It's At." [HiramPoR] (53/54) Fall 92-Sum 93, p. 48-51.
4175. MARZAN, Julio
    "Disharmonies in Unpredicted Snow." [Americas] (21:3/4) Fall-Wint 93, p. 106 -
        107.
    "Grand Central Station." [Americas] (21:3/4) Fall-Wint 93, p. 104.
    "Summer Cousin." [Americas] (21:3/4) Fall-Wint 93, p. 108.
    "Volkswagen on Calle Cerra." [Americas] (21:3/4) Fall-Wint 93, p. 105.
MASAHIKO, Hihara
    See HIHARA, Masahiko
4176. MASARIK, Al
    "Fantasy Poems." [OnTheBus] (5:2, #12) Sum-Fall 93, p. 135.
    "Free to Walk." [OnTheBus] (5:2, #12) Sum-Fall 93, p. 136.
    "Lure." [PaintedB] (50/51) 93, p. 11.
4177. MASINI, Donna
    "At the Exhibit of Peter Hujar's Photographs, Grey Art Gallery, NYC, 1990."
        [Pequod] (35) 93, p. 100-101.
    "Beauty" (for Steven Festa). [Pequod] (35) 93, p. 102-103.
    "Diorama." [Boulevard] (8:2/3, #23/24) Fall 93, p. 46-47.
    "For My Husband Sleeping Alone" (Honorable Mention, Poetry Award). [NewL]
        (59:2) 93, p. 76-77.
4178. MASON, David
    "At a Cabin in the Pecos." [SewanR] (101:4) O-D, Fall 93, p. 486.
    "The Ball of Yarn" (tr. of Yiorgos Chouliaras, w. the author). [Os] (36) Spr 93, p.
        24.
    "Cold Thoughts." [SewanR] (101:4) O-D, Fall 93, p. 485.
    "The Day Arrives" (tr. of Yiorgos Chouliaras, w. the author). [HangL] (63) 93, p. 7.
    "Demetrius Phalereus" (Historical Poem, tr. of Yiorgos Chouliaras, w. the author).
        [Poetry] (162:3) Je 93, p. 137.
    "Elegy." [Pequod] (36) 93, p. 101.
    "The Grapes" (tr. of Yiorgos Couliaras, w. the author). [HarvardR] (5) Fall 93, p.
        172.
    "The Last Garden." [SewanR] (101:4) O-D, Fall 93, p. 484.
    "Occupied City" (tr. of Yiorgos Chouliaras, w. the author). [Poetry] (162:3) Je 93, p.
        137.
    "Odysseus at Home" (tr. of Homer, w. Yiorgos Chouliaras). [CumbPR]] (13:1) Fall
        93, p. 27.
    "Of the Sea" (3 poems, 1-3, tr. of Yiorgos Chouliaras, w. the author). [HarvardR] (3)
        Wint 93, p. 147.
    "Refugees" (from Fast Food Classics, Athens, 1992, tr. of Yiorgos Chouliaras, w.
        the author). [Os] (36) Spr 93, p. 25.
    "Regarding the Investment of the Ship Owner Mr. Andreas Embeirikos in a Blast
        Furnace (March 1935)" (tr. of Yiorgos Chouliaras, w. the author). [HangL]
        (63) 93, p. 6.
    "The Rhythm of Work." [HarvardR] (4) Spr 93, p. 69.
    "The Saint" (tr. of Yiorgos Chouliaras, w. the author). [HangL] (63) 93, p. 7.
    "The Signals" (tr. of Yiorgos Chouliaras, w. the author). [Poetry] (162:3) Je 93, p.
        136.

"What Obstructs Literature" (tr. of Yiorgos Chouliaras, w. the author). [HangL] (63) 93, p. 7.
4179. MASON, Janet
"In Those Days." [SinW] (51) Wint 93-94, p. 24-25.
"This Fragile Sphere." [Pearl] (19) Fall-Wint 93, p. 65.
"Why I Hate Earth Day." [SinW] (51) Wint 93-94, p. 23.
"You Know I Used to Work in the Sex Industry." [SinW] (49) Spr-Sum 93, p. 36 - 37.
4180. MASON, Keith Antar
"L.A. on the Half Shell." [Eyeball] (2) 93, p. 13.
4181. MASON, L. G.
"Tango of the Dragonflies." [Northeast] (5:8) Spr-Sum 93, p. 6.
4182. MASON, Lucinda
"Ms. Mason, your (ahem) love poetry." [ChangingM] (25) Wint-Spr 93, p. 33.
4183. MASON, Matt
"The Last and Longest Conversation." [ChangingM] (25) Wint-Spr 93, p. 17.
4184. MASSA, Daniel
"Skin Diver" (tr. by Oliver Friggieri). [Vis] (43) 93, p. 41.
4185. MASSEY, Maria Guadalupe
"Mississippi Dogs" (dedicated to musicians I have known). [Eyeball] (2) 93, p. 29.
"Salsa at Midnight." [Eyeball] (2) 93, p. 28.
4186. MASSMAN, Gordon (See also LESTER-MASSMAN, G. (Gordon))
"III. I roll off her — satisfied, fired, heart." [YellowS] (43) Fall 93, p. 29.
MASTERS, Larry Le
See LeMASTERS, Larry
4187. MASTERSON, Dan
"Severn Sketches Keats and Writes to Brown." [SewanR] (101:3) Jl-S, Sum 93, p. 352-353.
4188. MASUDA, Barry
"No Mo' Fish on Maui." [HawaiiR] (17:2, #38) Spr 93, p. 25.
4189. MATA, Josi
"Someday." [SinW] (51) Wint 93-94, p. 34-35.
4190. MATANDA, Wonga
"The Worker." [XavierR] (13:1) Spr 93, p. 17.
4191. MATHIS, Cleopatra
"The Fighter." [KenR] (NS 15:3) Sum 93, p. 143-145.
"The Story." [Ploughs] (19:4) Wint 93-94, p. 58-59.
"Who Knows." [KenR] (NS 15:3) Sum 93, p. 142-143.
MATHISEN, Aina Gerner (Aina Gener)
See GERNER-MATHISEN, Aina
4192. MATHUR, Shakunt
"Chilka Lake" (tr. by Aruna Sitesh and Arlene Zide). [Prima] (16/17) 93, p. 90-91.
4193. MATSON, Clive
"Back Words." [HangL] (63) 93, p. 39-40.
"Light Splinters." [OnTheBus] (6:1, #13) Wint 93-Spr 94, p. 148.
"Slope Breast." [HangL] (63) 93, p. 38-39.
4194. MATSON, Suzanne
"Flagstaff." [HarvardR] (4) Spr 93, p. 37.
"The Wreck of Days." [IndR] (16:1) Spr 93, p. 186-190.
MATSUO, Basho
See BASHO, Matsuo
4195. MATTAWA, Khaled
"Arriving at Pier House Hotel" (Key West, Florida). [GreenMR] (NS 6:1) Wint-Spr 93, p. 42-43.
"The Bloomingfoods Promise." [KenR] (NS 15:1) Wint 93, p. 131-132.
"Cairene Sloth Song." [WillowS] (33) Wint 93, p. 12-13.
"For Etel Adnan." [WillowS] (33) Wint 93, p. 14-16.
"General Italo Balbo" (Tripoli, 1937). [GrahamHR] (17) Fall 93, p. 86-87.
"Herodotus on a Date." [KenR] (NS 15:1) Wint 93, p. 132-133.
"In the Shower Room." [GreenMR] (NS 6:1) Wint-Spr 93, p. 44-45.
"Istanbul, 1923." [Caliban] (12) 93, p. 75-76.
"Love Song." [SycamoreR] (5:2) Sum 93, p. 46.
"Picaresque." [SycamoreR] (5:2) Sum 93, p. 43-45.
"Visiting Jonah." [Caliban] (12) 93, p. 77.
"Watermeldon Tales." [KenR] (NS 15:1) Wint 93, p. 128-130.
"Zai El-Hawa." [Sonora] (26) Fall 93, p. 25-26.

4196. MATTERN, Evelyn
"Before the General Strike." [InterPR] (19:1) Spr 93, p. 79-80.
"Bethlehem." [ChrC] (110:36) 15 D 93, p. 1260.
"Standoff." [ChrC] (110:21) 14-21 Jl 93, p. 718.
"Stones: Holy Land 1988." [InterPR] (19:1) Spr 93, p. 81-82.
MATTHAIS, John
See MATTHIAS, John
4197. MATTHEWS, Mary
"What I Mean by His Bones." [PassN] (14:2) Wint 93, p. 28.
4198. MATTHEWS, Patricia
"Eat That Chicken." [WestB] (31/32) 93, p. 136-137.
"Homemade Mincemeat." [WestB] (31/32) 93, p. 137.
"Little Blue Nude" (after a painting by Renoir). [CreamCR] (17:1) Spr 93, p. 33.
"Shower." [WestB] (31/32) 93, p. 136.
4199. MATTHEWS, William
"VI, xii. I've charged the lout next door" (tr. of Martial). [IllinoisR] (1:1) Fall 93, p. 41.
"VI, lxvii. Your Celia keeps company with eunuchs" (tr. of Martial). [IllinoisR] (1:1) Fall 93, p. 41.
"VIII, lxxix. Those unlovely friends you drag" (tr. of Martial). [IllinoisR] (1:1) Fall 93, p. 41.
"Bmp Bmp." [NewEngR] (15:1) Wint 93, p. 176-177.
"Bob Marley's Hair." [Ploughs] (19:4) Wint 93-94, p. 139.
"Fear of Reconstruction." [QRL] (12:32/33) 93, p. 464.
"Hip Replacement." [TarRP] (33:1) Fall 93, p. 56-57.
"Last Words." [Poetry] (161:4) Ja 93, p. 198.
"New Folsom Prison." [Ploughs] (19:4) Wint 93-94, p. 142.
"Old Folsom Prison." [Ploughs] (19:4) Wint 93-94, p. 141.
"Phone Log." [TarRP] (33:1) Fall 93, p. 56.
"Poem Ending with a Line from Dante." [NewYorker] (69:40) 29 N 93, p. 110.
"President Reagan's visit to New York, October 1984." [Ploughs] (19:4) Wint 93-94, p. 140.
"A Serene Heart at the Movies." [Poetry] (162:3) Je 93, p. 126.
"Social Notes from All Over: Mt. Olympus." [DenQ] (27:4) Spr 93, p. 79.
"A Telegram from the Muse." [Poetry] (161:4) Ja 93, p. 200.
"Time." [Poetry] (162:3) Je 93, p. 126.
"The Time of Our Lives." [Poetry] (162:3) Je 93, p. 125.
"Visiting Hours." [Poetry] (161:4) Ja 93, p. 199.
"Why We Are Truly a Nation." [QRL] (12:32/33) 93, p. 464.
4200. MATTHIAS, John
"From Small Chimes, One voice" (Selections: VI-VII, tr. of Goran Sonnevi). [Vis] (43) 93, p. 52.
"Mozart Variations" (2 & 3, tr. of Goran Sonnevi, w. Goran Printz-Pahlson). [Vis] (42) 93, p. 23.
"An Orphic Legacy" (tr. of Branko Miljkovic, w. Vladeta Vuckovic). [NoDaQ] (61:1) Wint 93, p. 114.
"The Singer of Tales" (for Charles Simic). [NoDaQ] (61:1) Wint 93, p. 110-111.
"To the Earth Right Now" (tr. of Branko Miljkovic, w. Vladeta Vuckovic). [NoDaQ] (61:1) Wint 93, p. 115.
4201. MATTINGLY, Tracy
"Requiem." [Journal] (17:2) Fall-Wint 93, p. 76-78.
4202. MAULSBY, Vernon
"Deception." [Obs] (8:2) Fall-Wint 93, p. 128.
"Shame." [Obs] (8:2) Fall-Wint 93, p. 130.
"To the Black Woman on the Postcard" (Ada Overton Walker 1880-1914). [Obs] (8:2) Fall-Wint 93, p. 129-130.
"Why Chicken Places Give Me Nightmares." [Obs] (8:2) Fall-Wint 93, p. 129.
4203. MAURER, Bonnie
"Human Nature." [HopewellR] (5) 93, p. 118.
4204. MAURER, J. W.
"Yeast." [Light] (5) Spr 93, p. 13.
4205. MAXFIELD, Brad
"Old Cars." [Ascent] (17:2) Wint 93, p. 46.
4206. MAXSON, H. A.
"June 12, 1812: Egg Harbor." [CimR] (104) Jl 93, p. 156.

4207. MAXWELL, Glyn
"But Work." [PartR] (60:1) Wint 93, p. 100.
"The Day After Christmas." [Stand] (34:2) Spr 93, p. 6.
"Flood Before and After." [PartR] (60:1) Wint 93, p. 98-99.
4208. MAXWELL, Mary
"Nausicaa: The Movie." [WestHR] (47:2) Sum 93, p. 106-109.
"Sonnet 52: In every beauty lies some hidden sorrow" (tr. of Walter Benjamin).
[Pequod] (35) 93, p. 70.
4209. MAYBERRY, Stephen
"Eye on the Sparrow." [NewYorkQ] (51) 93, p. 73.
4210. MAYER, Barbara J.
"Birdland" (Literary Contest Winner, Sam Ragan Prize). [Crucible] (29) Fall 93, p.
7.
4211. MAYER, Bernadette
"Ice Cube Epigrams." [GrandS] (11:4, #44) 93, p. 190-193.
4212. MAYERS, Florence Cassen
"Fishing Blues." [Poetry] (162:5) Ag 93, p. 277.
"Hootenanny." [Confr] (51) Sum 93, p. 264-265.
"Letter to Dara, June." [ArtfulD] (24/25) 93, p. 55.
"The Mild Sorrows of Travel." [AmerLC] (5) 93, p. 79-80.
"What City." [ArtfulD] (24/25) 93, p. 54.
"Your Poem: Boat to Saltaire." [Poetry] (162:5) Ag 93, p. 278.
4213. MAYERSON, Charlotte
"In Historic Perspective." [MinnR] (NS 40) Spr-Sum 93, p. 18.
4214. MAYES, Frances
"Spring Equinox." [ColEng] (55:3) Mr 93, p. 324-325.
4215. MAYHOOD, Clifton
"Scenes of Male-Feminine Mystique in P-Town." [JamesWR] (11:1) Fall 93, p. 17.
4216. MAYNE, Robert L.
"Another Seascape." [SpoonR] (18:1) Wint-Spr 93, p. 30.
"Toad." [SpoonR] (18:1) Wint-Spr 93, p. 28-29.
4217. MAYO, Cathy
"Jehovah's Witnesses." [Bogg] (66) Wint 92-93, p. 26.
4218. MAYO, Jeanette
"In Memory of Martha." [RagMag] (11:1) 93, p. 22-23.
"Pilgrimage." [RagMag] (11:1) 93, p. 24-25.
4219. MAZILESCU, Virgil
"A doua poveste pentru stefana." [InterPR] (19:2) Fall 93, p. 56.
"Cîntecul lui guillaume." [InterPR] (19:2) Fall 93, p. 58.
"Dormi dragostea mea." [InterPR] (19:2) Fall 93, p. 60.
"The End of the History Lesson (Professor Guillaume)" (tr. by Thomas C. Carlson
and Dumitru Radu Popa). [WillowS] (32) Sum 93, p. 25.
"Guillaume's Song" (tr. by Thomas C. Carlson and Dumitru Radu Popa). [InterPR]
(19:2) Fall 93, p. 59.
"Not a monument have I raised in your soul" (tr. by Thomas C. Carlson and Dumitru
Radu Popa). [InterPR] (19:2) Fall 93, p. 53.
"Nu un monument am ridicat in sufletul tau." [InterPR] (19:2) Fall 93, p. 52.
"Opinions About Guillaume" (tr. by Thomas C. Carlson and Dumitru Radu Popa).
[WillowS] (32) Sum 93, p. 24.
"Second Fairy Tale for Stefana" (tr. by Thomas C. Carlson and Dumitru Radu
Popa). [InterPR] (19:2) Fall 93, p. 57.
"Sleep My Love" (tr. by Thomas C. Carlson and Dumitru Radu Popa). [InterPR]
(19:2) Fall 93, p. 61.
"Vei auzi din nou: fii inima mea." [InterPR] (19:2) Fall 93, p. 54.
"You Will Hear Once More: Be My Heart" (tr. by Thomas C. Carlson and Dumitru
Radu Popa). [InterPR] (19:2) Fall 93, p. 55.
4220. MAZUR, Gail
"Lilacs on Brattle Street." [PartR] (60:1) Wint 93, p. 102-103.
"Pennies from Heaven." [CreamCR] (17:1) Spr 93, p. 99-100.
4221. MAZZARO, Jerome
"Flights." [SouthwR] (78:2) Spr 93, p. 278.
4222. MAZZOCCO, Robert
"Metamorphosen." [NewYorker] (69:11) 3 My 93, p. 84.
4223. MAZZOTTI, José Antonio
"(......................?)" (tr. by G. J. Racz). [SenR] (23:1/2) Wint 93, p. 145.
"The Anti- *Ars Poetica*" (tr. by G. J. Racz). [SenR] (23:1/2) Wint 93, p. 144.

"Dante and Virgil Descend into Hell" (tr. by G. J. Racz). [SenR] (23:1/2) Wint 93, p.
  140-143.
"I Love Your Freedom" (tr. by G. J. Racz). [SenR] (23:1/2) Wint 93, p. 146.
"On the Late Massacre in Lima: June 19, 1986" (tr. by G. J. Racz). [SenR] (23:1/2)
  Wint 93, p. 151-153.
"Pablo Guevara's Vision" (tr. by G. J. Racz). [SenR] (23:1/2) Wint 93, p. 139.
"The Pond" (tr. by G. J. Racz). [SenR] (23:1/2) Wint 93, p. 147-150.
"Tullumayu" (tr. by G. J. Racz). [SenR] (23:1/2) Wint 93, p. 154.

Mc...
          See also names beginning with Mac...
4224. McADAMS, Janet
  "After the War." [TriQ] (87) Spr-Sum 93, p. 144-146.
  "The Children's Corner." [NoAmR] (278:6) N-D 93, p. 41.
  "Heart." [Asylum] (8) 93, p. 25.
  "Leaving the Old Gods." [TriQ] (87) Spr-Sum 93, p. 148-149.
  "Paradise" (a letter). [IndR] (16:1) Spr 93, p. 132-133.
  "El Salvador del Mundo." [TriQ] (87) Spr-Sum 93, p. 147.
4225. McALPINE, Katherine
  "And the Lord Said, 'Hey, Like Everything's Cool'." [Light] (5) Spr 93, p. 23.
  "Book Contest Bile." [Sparrow] (60) Sum 93, p. 19.
  "Caveat Scriptor." [Light] (8) Wint 93, p. 18.
  "The Coast of Maine" (with apologies to Lord Byron, who'd have understood).
    [Light] (5) Spr 93, p. 18.
  "Nursery Rhyme" (for "the friendly folks at Green Hill Gardens"). [Light] (7) Aut
    93, p. 7.
  "Pièce de Résistance." [Light] (8) Wint 93, p. 12.
  "Rural Development." [Light] (6) Sum 93, p. 19.
  "The Three Marias of East Third Street." [SlipS] (13) 93, p. 68.
  "To a Feminist Collective." [Sparrow] (60) Sum 93, p. 19.
  "Wood Work." [Hellas] (4:2) Fall 93, p. 64.
4226. McANDREW, Donald A.
  "Poemwalls." [EngJ] (82:7) N 93, p. 91.
  "Washing Windows and Writing." [EngJ] (82:3) Mr 93, p. 93.
4227. McARTHUR, Mac
  "We Sat in Open Fields." [JamesWR] (10:2) Wint 93, p. 10.
4228. McAULEY, James J.
  "Career Changes." [CimR] (105) O 93, p. 93-94.
  "A Shift in the Wind" (for Dave and Beth Britt). [CimR] (105) O 93, p. 92-93.
  "Woman at a Window." [CimR] (105) O 93, p. 91-92.
4229. McAULIFFE,, Paul C.
  "Where's My Money." [Pearl] (19) Fall-Wint 93, p. 75.
4230. McBREEN, Joan
  "The Little Street" (after Vermeer, Rijksmuseum, Amsterdam). [SenR] (23:1/2)
    Wint 93, p. 63-64.
  "The Mountain Ash." [SenR] (23:1/2) Wint 93, p. 65.
  "The Nest." [SenR] (23:1/2) Wint 93, p. 62.
4231. McBRIDE, Elizabeth
  "Corozal." [Chelsea] (54) 93, p. 54.
  "Inca Doves." [Chelsea] (54) 93, p. 55-56.
4232. McBRIDE, Mekeel
  "City Sky Line Painted on a Blind eye." [VirQR] (69:3) Sum 93, p. 495-496.
  "Dreaming Space Awake." [VirQR] (69:3) Sum 93, p. 494-495.
  "Some Kisses for Bill." [VirQR] (69:3) Sum 93, p. 492-494.
4233. McBRIDE, Regina
  "Cinderella" (for Sheila). [Caliban] (12) 93, p. 143-144.
  "The Management of Dolls." [MassR] (34:1) Spr 93, p. 127-128.
4234. McBRIDE, Timothy Patrick
  "Snow Fence." [SenR] (23:1/2) Wint 93, p. 91.
  "An Urban Myth." [SenR] (23:1/2) Wint 93, p. 92-93.
4235. McCAFFERY, Steve
  "Instruction Manual." [Avec] (6:1) 93, p. 129-130.
4236. McCAFFREY, Kevin
  "Weehawken Once." [JINJPo] (15:2) Aut 93, p. 32.
4237. McCALLUM, Paddy
  "Slumber Music." [CanLit] (136) Spr 93, p. 39-43.

310

McCANLESS

4238. McCANLESS, Katherine
"Used to This Kind of Heat." [AlabamaLR] (7:2) 93, p. 25-27.
4239. McCANN, David R.
"Autumn Songs" (1 poem, tr. of Sô Chôngju). [QRL] (12:32/33) 93, p. 309.
"Conversation with Parnassus" (tr. of Sô Chôngju). [QRL] (12:32/33) 93, p. 312-313.
"Kilimanjaro's Self-Introduction" (tr. of Sô Chôngju). [QRL] (12:32/33) 93, p. 310-311.
"Love's Cursive" (Selections: 6, 8, tr. of Kim , w. Hyun-jae Yee Sallee). [ChiR] (39:3/4) 93, p. 242.
"Mountain Poem of Korea" (tr. of Sô Chôngju). [QRL] (12:32/33) 93, p. 313-314.
"Poem of Puu Kalena, Hawaiian Mountain Goddess" (tr. of Sô Chôngju). [QRL] (12:32/33) 93, p. 311-312.
"Spring Songs" (3 poems, tr. of Sô Chôngju). [QRL] (12:32/33) 93, p. 307-308.
"Story from the Mountains of North Carolina" (tr. of Sô Chôngju). [QRL] (12:32/33) 93, p. 312.
"Summer Songs" (2 poems, tr. of Sô Chôngju). [QRL] (12:32/33) 93, p. 308-309.
"Two Zen Poems" ("Beef," "Mountain's a," tr. of Un Ko). [ChiR] (39:3/4) 93, p. 243.
"Winter Songs" (2 poems, tr. of Sô Chôngju). [QRL] (12:32/33) 93, p. 309-310.
4240. McCANN, Janet
"And If." [PoetC] (25:1) Fall 93, p. 16.
"Christmas Party at the German Teacher's." [WindO] (57) Fall 93, p. 18.
"Sex Trees." [Prima] (16/17) 93, p. 20-21.
"Spinning Jenny." [13thMoon] (11:1/2) 93, p. 43.
4241. McCARRISTON, Linda
"Second Marriage." [NewEngR] (15:1) Wint 93, p. 175.
4242. McCARTHY, Joanne
"At Last." [BellR] (16:1/2) Spr-Fall 93, p. 18.
"Not a Green Thumb." [BellR] (16:1/2) Spr-Fall 93, p. 17.
"This Bird." [BellR] (16:1/2) Spr-Fall 93, p. 16.
4243. McCARTHY, Lee
"Santa Paula." [Sun] (215) N 93, p. 32.
4244. McCARTHY, Maureen
"Puddles." [Event] (22:1) Spr 93, p. 56.
"A Summer Day." [Event] (22:1) Spr 93, p. 57.
4245. McCARTHY, Thomas
"Cataloguing Twelve Fenian Novels" (2 selections: 364, 327.415, from Seven Winters in Paris). [NorthStoneR] (11) 93, p. 210.
4246. McCARTIN, James T.
"JFK and Martin Luther King." [Footwork] (23) 93, p. 81-82.
4247. McCASLIN, Susan
"The Angelology" (Selections: 12 poems). [BellArk] (9:1) Ja-F 93, p. 8-9.
4248. McCAUGHEY, Kevin
"The Sound of Kennels" (for Biff, who doesn't like people). [ClockR] (8:1/2) 93, p. 125.
4249. McCLANAHAN, Rebecca
"Afterglow" (For my first husband). [Poetry] (163:3) D 93, p. 151-152.
"The Angle of Shadow, the Angle of Light." [SouthernPR] (33:1) Spr 93, p. 8-9.
"Ex-Brother-in-Law." [Poetry] (163:3) D 93, p. 150-151.
"Sidekick." [Poetry] (163:3) D 93, p. 153-154.
4250. McCLATCHY, J. D.
"After Ovid" (for Amy Clampitt. Metamorphoses, XIV, 530-565). [Verse] (10:3) Wint 93, p. 94.
"Found Parable." [NewYorker] (69:38) 15 N 93, p. 72.
4251. McCLAURIN, Irma
"Pearl's Song." [Drumvoices] (3:1/2) Fall-Wint 93-94, p. j38.
"The Power of Names." [Drumvoices] (3:1/2) Fall-Wint 93-94, p. 39.
4252. McCLELLAN, Jane
"Those Who've Survived Open-Heart Surgery." [WebR] (17) Fall 93, p. 62.
4253. McCLELLAN, Michael W.
"Apocalypse: The Early Years." [SmPd] (30:3, #89) Fall 93, p. 11.
"The Fallen Nest." [FreeL] (11) Wint 93, p. 12.
4254. McCLURE, Michael
"The Foam" (from the sequence, Fields). [PoetryUSA] (25/26) 93, p. 14-15.
"Gorgeousness." [NewYorkQ] (51) 93, p. 29.

"Pieces for Robert Creeley." [NewYorkQ] (50) 93, p. 44-45.
4255. McCOMBS, Davis
    "Apprentice." [HarvardA] (128:4, [i.e. 127:4]) Sum 93, p. 13.
    "April Fifth, Nineteen Hundred Eighty-Three" (First Prize). [HarvardA] (127:3) Spr
        93, p. 11.
    "First Reading." [HarvardA] (127:2) Wint 93, p. 31.
4256. McCOMBS, Judith
    "Pictures Not in Our Albums." [PoetryNW] (34:4) Wint 93-94, p. 24.
4257. McCONNELL, Sharon Brown
    "Early Riser." [Wind] (23:72) 93, p. 16.
    "March Quest." [Wind] (23:72) 93, p. 16.
4258. McCORD, Andrew
    "Frames of a Coptic Funeral" (after Sebastião Salgado). [GrandS] (11:4, #44) 93, p.
        80.
    "The Ganges in Flood." [GrandS] (12:3, #47) Fall 93, p. 34-35.
4259. McCORD, Sandy
    "Pressing Needs." [HiramPoR] (53/54) Fall 92-Sum 93, p. 52.
    "Where Is Cinderella When I Need Her?" [CapeR] (28:2) Fall 93, p. 50.
4260. McCORKLE, James
    "The Bat." [Manoa] (5:1) Sum 93, p. 9-11.
    "The Jetty." [Pequod] (35) 93, p. 134.
    "Lake Snow." [Turnstile] (4:1) 93, p. 71-72.
    "Pyromancy." [Manoa] (5:1) Sum 93, p. 11-13.
    "The Shark." [Manoa] (5:1) Sum 93, p. 13-14.
4261. McCORMICK, Brian
    "Inside the Inside of the Moon." [Descant] (24:2, #81) Sum 93, p. 29-30.
4262. McCORMICK, Marilyn
    "Asparagus." [OnTheBus] (6:1, #13) Wint 93-Spr 94, p. 149.
4263. McCOSKER, Karen
    "Vathi" (For Reynolds). [HarvardR] (5) Fall 93, p. 148-149.
4264. McCOWN, Clint
    "The Weather of the Game." [SewanR] (101:1) Ja-Mr, Wint 93, p. 35-36.
4265. McCOY, Mary
    "Mary's World." [AnthNEW] (5) 93, p. 27.
4266. McCOY, Valerie Stevens
    "Red Eye." [Kalliope] (15:2) 93, p. 55.
4267. McCRANIE, Bob
    "Flounder" (for M.A.). [JamesWR] (10:3) Spr 93, p. 4.
    "The Folding Table War." [JamesWR] (10:3) Spr 93, p. 4.
4268. McCRARY, Jim
    "Inspired by a Rumor That Edward Abbey Was Spotted Last Week at a Hardware
        Store in Espanola, New Mexico." [Caliban] (12) 93, p. 183.
    "Untitled 7/23/91." [CoalC] (7) Apr 93, p. 39.
4269. McCRAY, Jane
    "Mantra." [HeavenB] (10) Wint-Spr 93, p. 46.
4270. McCRORIE, Edward
    "After the Ballet." [SpiritSH] (58) 93, p. 4.
    "Deaf at the Beach." [SpiritSH] (58) 93, p. 3.
    "Four Years." [SpiritSH] (58) 93, p. 5.
    "Sappho on the East Side." [SpiritSH] (58) 93, p. 6.
4271. McCULLOUGH, L. E.
    "Buddy Lee Perriman Reflects on the Persian Gulf Crisis, Day 15." [HawaiiR]
        (17:1, #37) Spr 93, p. 158.
    "Club Lido, Kansas City, 1944." [SlipS] (13) 93, p. 80.
    "Club Lido, Kansas City, 1944." [SmPd] (30:3, #89) Fall 93, p. 32.
    "Cumbia." [SmPd] (30:3, #89) Fall 93, p. 31.
    "Hey You Sitting There Looking at This." [HawaiiR] (17:1, #37) Spr 93, p. 159.
    "Romance Type Poem for Miz Martinez." [SmPd] (30:3, #89) Fall 93, p. 30.
4272. McCULLOUGH, Ron
    "Baptism." [Writer] (106:10) O 93, p. 27.
4273. McCURDY, Harold
    "At the Nursing Home." [ChrC] (110:24) 25 Ag-1 S 93, p. 806.
4274. McCURRY, Jim
    "Dogwag Bummerstead." [Farm] (10:2) Fall-Wint 93-94, p. 64.
4275. McDADE, Thomas Michael
    "By Five A.M." [CoalC] (7) Apr 93, p. 3.

"Pirate." [Border] (2) Spr 93, p. 49.
4276. McDANIEL, Wilma Elizabeth
"All I Saw Was Painted Fruit." [HangL] (63) 93, p. 44.
"Breaking the Drought." [HangL] (63) 93, p. 41.
"Day After John Berryman's Suicide January 8, 1972." [WormR] (33:1, #129) 93, p. 10.
"Genetic Pattern." [WormR] (33:1, #129) 93, p. 11.
"Mr. Matson's Super Abundance." [WormR] (33:1, #129) 93, p. 11.
"My Favorite Paperweight." [HangL] (63) 93, p. 45.
"Nitpicker." [WormR] (33:1, #129) 93, p. 11.
"Our Neighbor Neil." [HangL] (63) 93, p. 42.
"Sweat." [HangL] (63) 93, p. 43.
"Two Cousins." [WormR] (33:1, #129) 93, p. 11.
"Widower and Son — 1926." [WormR] (33:1, #129) 93, p. 10.
4277. McDERMOTT, John
"A Path of wet leaves." [US1] (28/29) 93, p. 5.
"Warm living room rug." [US1] (28/29) 93, p. 18.
4278. McDIARMID, Leigh
"Madame Est Servie." [BellR] (16:1/2) Spr-Fall 93, p. 21.
4279. McDONALD, Agnes
"Summer, and the House Finally Crumbles." [Pembroke] (25) 93, p. 104.
4280. McDONALD, David
"Windsong?. Windpoem?. Whatever!!!" [Elf] (3:2) Sum 93, p. 39.
4281. McDONALD, Paul
"First Communion." [CoalC] (7) Apr 93, p. 11.
4282. McDONALD, Walter
"Boys and Their Fathers' Shotguns." [IllinoisR] (1:1) Fall 93, p. 28.
"Bulls in a World They Owned." [PoetL] (88:3) Fall 93, p. 6.
"Crouched at Lake Raven." [HampSPR] Wint 93, p. 49.
"Falling in Love over Dallas." [PoetL] (88:3) Fall 93, p. 7.
"Fields of Buffalo." [SewanR] (101:1) Ja-Mr, Wint 93, p. 37.
"The Graves in Estacado Canyon." [Manoa] (5:2) Wint 93, p. 111-112.
"The Last Saloon in Slaton." [Manoa] (5:2) Wint 93, p. 110-111.
"Mending Fence on Hardscrabble." [SewanR] (101:1) Ja-Mr, Wint 93, p. 38.
"Nights Without Rockets." [GeoR] (47:3) Fall 93, p. 562.
"Rain Two Times a Year." [ArtfulD] (24/25) 93, p. 116.
"Saturday Night Cafés." [GreensboroR] (54) Sum 93, p. 50.
"Seconds of Free Fall and Chaos." [AmerS] (62:2) Spr 93, p. 260.
"The Summer Before the War." [HampSPR] Wint 93, p. 49.
"The Summer before the War." [NoDaQ] (61:3) Sum 93, p. 162.
"Uncle Douglas and the Whirring Blades." [BostonR] (18:3/4) Je-Ag 93, p. 42.
"Under Hardscrabble Skies." [Manoa] (5:2) Wint 93, p. 110.
"West Texas." [Border] (2) Spr 93, p. 50.
4283. McDONOUGH, Tracy Lee
"Improvisations on a Secret Theme." [RagMag] (11:2) 93, p. 22.
"When She Stitched the Flag." [RagMag] (11:2) 93, p. 20-21.
4284. McDOUGALL, Bonnie S.
"Requiem" (for the victims of June Fourth, tr. of Bei Dao, w. Chen Maiping). [ChiR] (39:3/4) 93, p. 288.
4285. McDOUGLE, Tom
"Cedarsmoke." [Poem] (70) N 93, p. 6-7.
4286. McDOWELL, Nick
"Footloose." [OntR] (38) Spr-Sum 93, p. 20-23.
4287. McDOWELL, Robert
"For Lysa, That She May Rise Early." [SycamoreR] (5:1) Wint 93, p. 45.
"A Little Prayer for a Barn, for a Tree." [SycamoreR] (5:1) Wint 93, p. 42.
"The Pact." [Hudson] (46:1) Spr 93, p. 145-155.
"Women in Vats: Indian Summer Vinegar Factory." [SycamoreR] (5:1) Wint 93, p. 43-44.
4288. McDUFF, David
"I Stopped Too Long" (tr. of Tua Forsström). [Stand] (34:4) Aut 93, p. 33.
"There Is a Door" (tr. of Tua Forsström). [Stand] (34:4) Aut 93, p. 33.
4289. McDUFFIE, Carrington
"The Cord." [OnTheBus] (5:2, #12) Sum-Fall 93, p. 137-138.
"The Day Speaks." [OnTheBus] (5:2, #12) Sum-Fall 93, p. 137.
"The Girl That Got Away." [OnTheBus] (6:1, #13) Wint 93-Spr 94, p. 150.

"Mystery Kiss." [OnTheBus] (5:2, #12) Sum-Fall 93, p. 137.
"When the Snow Falls in Summer." [OnTheBus] (6:1, #13) Wint 93-Spr 94, p. 150 - 151.
"Woman in the Pool." [OnTheBus] (5:2, #12) Sum-Fall 93, p. 138.
4290. McELROY, Colleen J.
"Caution: This Woman Brakes for Memories." [Ploughs] (19:1) Spr 93, p. 193-194.
"Paris Subway Tango." [Ploughs] (19:1) Spr 93, p. 191-192.
4291. McEWAN, Angela
"Dreamcats." [Luz] (5) N 93, p. 38.
"The Encircling Memory" (from "Sombra de Luna," tr. of Francisco Alvarez-Koki). [Luz] (5) N 93, p. 29, 31.
"Even at Night" (from "That Ancient Devotion," tr. of Verónica Miranda). [Luz] (5) N 93, p. 25.
"The Garden of Your Delights" (tr. of Ana Rossetti). [Luz] (3) Ja 93, p. 13.
"Gatos Soñados" (tr. by the author). [Luz] (5) N 93, p. 39.
"I Say a Little Prayer" (tr. of Ana Rossetti). [Luz] (3) Ja 93, p. 15.
"A Lifetime" (from "Si Preguntan por Algien con mi Nombre," tr. of Ester de Izaguirre). [Luz] (5) N 93, p. 91.
"Ocean Dream" (from "That Ancient Devotion," tr. of Verónica Miranda). [Luz] (5) N 93, p. 43.
"Phantom" (from "Si Preguntan por Algien con mi Nombre," tr. of Ester de Izaguirre). [Luz] (5) N 93, p. 79, 81.
"Walking with Blackie" (tr. of Luis Zalema). [ApalQ] (38) 92, p. 38-39.
"The Wrangler Kid" (tr. of Ana Rossetti). [Luz] (3) Ja 93, p. 11.
4292. McFADDEN, David
"Blue Angel." [MalR] (105) Wint 93, p. 87-88.
"Much Ado about Nothing." [MalR] (105) Wint 93, p. 85-86.
"Timon of Athens." [MalR] (105) Wint 93, p. 82-84.
4293. McFARLAND, JoAnne
"Daughter." [Obs] (8:1) Spr-Sum 93, p. 95.
"Elisabeth." [Obs] (8:1) Spr-Sum 93, p. 99.
"Intone." [Obs] (8:1) Spr-Sum 93, p. 97-99.
"Nappy." [Obs] (8:1) Spr-Sum 93, p. 96-97.
"Victim." [Obs] (8:1) Spr-Sum 93, p. 96.
4294. McFARLAND, Ron
"Baking Pies." [HiramPoR] (53/54) Fall 92-Sum 93, p. 53.
"Ballgloves." [Spitball] (43) Spr 93, p. 45.
"Dreaming of Baseball." [Spitball] (45) Fall 93, p. 45-46.
"The Nightmare of My Worst Professor." [HampSPR] Wint 93, p. 55.
"O Henry's Go-Go Cafe" (Kennewick, Washington). [Wind] (23:72) 93, p. 17-18.
"Objet d'Art." [HampSPR] Wint 93, p. 55.
"Photo of a Minor League Baseball Team, ca. 1952." [Spitball] (43) Spr 93, p. 44.
"The Poet's Crisis." [SoCoast] (14) Ja 93, p. 46-47.
4295. McFEE, Michael
"The All-Dog Siren Choir." [Poetry] (162:5) Ag 93, p. 252.
"Answering Machine." [Poetry] (161:5) F 93, p. 258-259.
"Clotheslines." [Poetry] (162:5) Ag 93, p. 254.
"Grave Grass." [Poetry] (161:5) F 93, p. 260.
"Pas de Deux." [Poetry] (162:5) Ag 93, p. 253.
4296. McGAHEY, Jeanne
"Inter-Species." [QRL] (12:32/33) 93, p. 238.
"The Old Ones." [QRL] (12:32/33) 93, p. 239-240.
4297. McGARRIE, Ken
"Maxwell." [CoalC] (7) Apr 93, p. 32.
4298. McGEE, Lynn
"Cars" (for my father). [OntR] (38) Spr-Sum 93, p. 81-82.
"Maggie, and How I Hurt Her." [OntR] (38) Spr-Sum 93, p. 84-86.
"Power." [PaintedB] (52) 93, p. 21-25.
"Tooth, Fang, Tusk." [OntR] (38) Spr-Sum 93, p. 82-84.
4299. McGEE, Marc
"My Poodle Can't Swim." [FreeL] (11) Wint 93, p. 7.
"State Fair." [FreeL] (11) Wint 93, p. 11.
4300. McGHEE, Claudia
"Fingertips." [SlipS] (13) 93, p. 57.
"Questions Asked of Women at a NYC Bus Stop." [Asylum] (8) 93, p. 20.

4301. McGINNIS, Eva
"Veteran — WWII." [Border] (2) Spr 93, p. 51.
4302. McGLINN, Ann
"Dyeing Wool." [Poem] (69) My 93, p. 50.
"Maria's Skin." [Poem] (69) My 93, p. 49.
4303. McGONAGALL, William
"The Hen it is a noble beast." [Light] (7) Aut 93, p. 30.
4304. McGONAGLE, Sandra
"Disemboweled." [HawaiiR] (17:1, #37) Spr 93, p. 15.
"I Never Thought About It." [HawaiiR] (17:1, #37) Spr 93, p. 15.
4305. McGOOKEY, Kathleen
"Lilies." [BlackWR] (19:1) Fall-Wint 92, p. 136.
"Lying about Money." [ProseP] (1) 92, p. 58.
"Man Posing As Cheerleader Sentenced." [WestB] (33) 93, p. 74.
"We Think the Heart Can Hold Most Anything." [ProseP] (2) 93, p. 65.
4306. McGOWAN, James D.
"In Maine." [HiramPoR] (53/54) Fall 92-Sum 93, p. 108.
"'Little Venice,' Mykonos." [HiramPoR] (53/54) Fall 92-Sum 93, p. 107.
4307. McGRATH, Campbell
"Angels and the Bars of Manhattan" (for Bruce). [Ploughs] (19:4) Wint 93-94, p.
170-172.
"Blue Tulips and Night Train for Jack Kerouac's Grave." [PoetryE] (36) Fall 93, p.
55-62.
"Rock Falls, Illinois." [PoetryE] (36) Fall 93, p. 51-52.
"Shrimp Boats, Biloxi." [PoetryE] (36) Fall 93, p. 53-54.
"Smokestacks, Chicago." [GettyR] (6:3) Sum 93, p. 490-491.
"Sugar Skulls, Oaxaca" (for Gram Parsons). [GettyR] (6:3) Sum 93, p. 492-493.
"Two Figures with Heat Lightning in the Sangre de Cristo Mountains." [Boulevard]
(8:2/3, #23/24) Fall 93, p. 68-69.
4308. McGRATH, Carmelita
"Annie, Telling Stories." [TickleAce] (25) Spr-Sum 93, p. 172.
"At a Funeral." [TickleAce] (25) Spr-Sum 93, p. 171.
"De Chirico's Girl Doesn't Sleep All Night." [TickleAce] (25) Spr-Sum 93, p. 167 -
168.
"Floating." [TickleAce] (25) Spr-Sum 93, p. 169-170.
4309. McGRATH, Thomas
"Welcome." [PaintedB] (50/51) 93, p. 9.
4310. McGRORY-KLYZA, Sheila
"Craft." [Poem] (69) My 93, p. 31.
4311. McGUCKIAN, Medbh
"The Dream-Language of Fergus." [MichQR] (32:1) Wint 93, p. 122-123.
"Speaking into the Candles." [MichQR] (32:1) Wint 93, p. 130-131.
"Story Between Two Notes." [MichQR] (32:1) Wint 93, p. 128-129.
4312. McGUIRE, Catherine
"Dishes." [Bogg] (66) Wint 92-93, p. 59.
4313. McGUIRT, C. Ra
"Negative Paranoia." [Pearl] (19) Fall-Wint 93, p. 74.
"On the Wings of a Fallen Angel." [Pearl] (19) Fall-Wint 93, p. 74.
"We'll Understand It All By and By." [Pearl] (17) Spr 93, p. 83.
4314. McHUGH, Heather
"Unguent." [HarvardR] (5) Fall 93, p. 23.
"Whose Move." [PaintedB] (50/51) 93, p. 64.
4315. McILVOY, Kevin
"Election Day Barrel Fire." [SpoonR] (18:2) Sum-Fall 93, p. 50-51.
4316. McINNIS, Nadine
"Balance." [Event] (22:3) Wint 93-94, p. 50-51.
"Famous Moments." [MalR] (104) Fall 93, p. 74-79.
"The History of the World." [PoetryC] (13:4) 93, p. 18.
"Line-Men." [Event] (22:3) Wint 93-94, p. 52-55.
"Night Neighbors." [PoetryC] (13:4) 93, p. 19.
4317. McKAY, Don
"Advanced Automotive Science." [TickleAce] (23) Spr-Sum 92, p. 13.
"The Laugh." [MalR] (105) Wint 93, p. 68.
"Matériel." [Quarry] (42:1) 93, p. 107-114.
"Short Fat Flicks." [MalR] (105) Wint 93, p. 69-71.

4318. McKAY, Linda Back
"Winter or Another Land." [Vis] (41) 93, p. 25.
4319. McKAY, Matthew
"The Dice." [CapeR] (28:1) Spr 93, p. 8.
4320. McKEAN, Doug
"Young Maiden." [ChironR] (12:1, #34) Spr 93, p. 44.
4321. McKEE, Glenn
"Another Night Alone." [OnTheBus] (6:1, #13) Wint 93-Spr 94, p. 152.
4322. McKEE, Louis
"Last Call." [PaintedB] (50/51) 93, p. 132.
4323. McKEITHEN, Anne
"Circle of Fire." [SouthernPR] (33:2) Fall 93, p. 21-22.
4324. McKENDRICK, Jamie
"The Master Stroke" (for Xon de Ros). [NewRep] (209:5) 2 Ag 93, p. 42.
4325. McKENTY, Bob
"Auto Erotica" (Confessions of a Wanton Car Phone). [Light] (7) Aut 93, p. 12.
"Déjà Vu" (Second Prize, First Annual River Rhyme Competition). [Light] (5) Spr
93, p. 29.
"The Giant Panda." [Light] (6) Sum 93, p. 12.
"Lamen 'Tater." [Light] (5) Spr 93, p. 12.
"On Cabbages and Kings." [Light] (7) Aut 93, p. 10.
"The Sloth." [Light] (7) Aut 93, p. 8.
"Sufferin' from Succotash." [Light] (8) Wint 93, p. 13.
"La-Z-Boy." [Light] (7) Aut 93, p. 14.
4326. McKENZIE, Joy
"The Lepidopterist." [Vis] (41) 93, p. 28.
4327. McKENZIE, Lee
"Growing Up Backward." [SpoonR] (18:1) Wint-Spr 93, p. 118-119.
"The Poet Reports to the Dean That She, During Recent Sabbatical Leave." [Pearl]
(17) Spr 93, p. 80.
4328. McKERNAN, John
"Blue Sky January 1 63 Outside Nebraska?" [CharR] (19:1) Spr 93, p. 87.
"Cosmology." [FreeL] (12) Sum 93, p. 29.
"I Am Going to Vanish." [Wind] (23:72) 93, p. 19-20.
"I Feel My Left Hand Its Flesh Its Bones Its Muscles." [Parting] (6:2) Wint
93, p. 26.
"Saturday Morning 4/26/80, Huntington Galleries." [SouthernPR] (33:2) Fall 93, p.
55.
"Sunday Afternoon." [VirQR] (69:2) Spr 93, p. 261-262.
"Terminology." [VirQR] (69:2) Spr 93, p. 262-263.
"The Voice of the Miller Cries Out." [Wind] (23:72) 93, p. 19.
4329. McKIERNAN, Ethna
"Alzheimer's Weather." [NorthStoneR] (11) 93, p. 101-102.
"The Children Beckon, Late." [NorthStoneR] (11) 93, p. 102.
"A Woman Remembers Her Ex-Husband." [NorthStoneR] (11) 93, p. 103.
4330. McKIM, Elizabeth
"Onion." [PaintedB] (50/51) 93, p. 102.
4331. McKINNEY, Joshua
"Woman Hit by Lightning." [SouthernPR] (33:1) Spr 93, p. 60-61.
4332. McKINNON, Patrick
"Belize I Miss Your Albert Street." [RagMag] (11:2) 93, p. 26.
"Hal's Dad Cracks Up." [RagMag] (11:2) 93, p. 23-25.
"My Father Was a Carny Man." [ChironR] (12:4/13:1, #37/38) Wint 93-Spr 94, p.
45.
"Poem for My Hate & Rage." [RagMag] (11:2) 93, p. 27-28.
"Thank You Note." [RagMag] (11:2) 93, p. 29.
4333. McKINNON, W. Steve
"Soviet Joke." [Pearl] (17) Spr 93, p. 89.
4334. McKINSEY, Martin
"Evening Walk" (tr. of Yannis Ritsos). [ProseP] (2) 93, p. 80.
"Locomotion and Landscape" (for Yannis Ritsos, 1909-1990). [WebR] (17) Fall 93,
p. 67.
"The Luminosity of Sheets" (Selections: 3-4). [Ploughs] (19:1) Spr 93, p. 116-118.
"Maria of the Night" (tr. of Nikos Engonopoulos). [ProseP] (1) 92, p. 30.
"One Skit, Then Another" (tr. of Yannis Ritsos). [ProseP] (2) 93, p. 79.
"The Shipwrecks' Cabal" (tr. of Nikos Engonopoulos). [ProseP] (1) 92, p. 31.

"Tributaries." [WebR] (17) Fall 93, p. 67.
4335. McLAUGHLIN, Catherine
"All That Fall" (— Samuel Beckett). [SouthernR] (29:3) Sum, Jl 93, p. 561.
"Blue Collars." [CreamCR] (17:1) Spr 93, p. 6.
4336. McLAUGHLIN, Dorothy
"Sunday After Thanksgiving." [Footwork] (23) 93, p. 46.
4337. McLAUGHLIN, Rosemary
"Green." [JINJPo] (15:1) Spr 93, p. 41-43.
4338. McLAUGHLIN, Walt
"Angling." [DogRR] (12:1, #23) Spr-Sum 93, p. 11.
4339. McLAUGHLIN-CARRUTH, Joe-Anne
"Coming Home From the Circus My Son Makes Me Promise Not to Say 'Bear'" (For
Adam). [Poetry] (161:5) F 93, p. 275.
"Ode for Adam." [Poetry] (161:5) F 93, p. 274.
"The Parents They Would Be" (For M. and M.). [Poetry] (161:5) F 93, p. 273.
4340. McLEOD, Donald
"The Middle-Aged Lazy Fox Keeps on Circling." [HampSPR] Wint 93, p. 20.
4341. McLEOD, Margaret
"Ghost Child." [Event] (22:2) Sum 93, p. 25-28.
4342. McLEOD, Milt
"Season of Flies" (Soweto, 1982). [ApalQ] (36/37) 91, p. 71.
4343. McMAHON, Lynne
"A Boy's Life." [NewYorker] (69:10) 26 Ap 93, p. 76.
"December 31st." [NewYorker] (69:44) 27 D 93-3 Ja 94, p. 117.
"Deference." [Atlantic] (271:4) Ap 93, p. 98.
"Polite Nods from the Host." [NewYorker] (69:14) 24 My 93, p. 61.
"Storm Sketch." [YaleR] (81:3) Jl 93, p. 57.
"Toboggan." [Nat] (257:21) 20 D 93, p. 780.
"Work." [ColR] (20:1) Spr 93, p. 84-85.
4344. McMAHON, Michael B.
"Pins and Combs." [HiramPoR] (53/54) Fall 92-Sum 93, p. 54.
4345. McMANUS, James
"23." [AntR] (51:2) Spr 93, p. 235.
"Counting Her Syllables Before They're Hatched." [SpoonR] (18:1) Wint-Spr 93, p.
101.
"Spike Logic." [Salm] (100) Fall 93, p. 142-144.
"Twelfth Night." [Atlantic] (271:4) Ap 93, p. 98.
4346. McMORRIS, Mark
"Au Café Noir." [Chelsea] (54) 93, p. 63.
"Evening." [Chelsea] (54) 93, p. 62.
4347. McMULLEN, Richard E.
"It Came to Him." [Comm] (120:13) 16 Jl 93, p. 18.
4348. McNAIR, Wesley
"The Bird Man." [SouthernR] (29:4) Aut, O 93, p. 751-753.
"Young Man Going Uphill with a Bird." [WillowS] (33) Wint 93, p. 67.
4349. McNALL, Sally Allen
"Conversations: The Battle." [NoDaQ] (61:2) Spr 93, p. 131.
4350. McNAMARA, Robert
"At the Side Door, Holy Epiphany" (for Bob Meyer). [BellR] (16:1/2) Spr-Fall 93,
p. 100.
"Be That Someone." [BellR] (16:1/2) Spr-Fall 93, p. 101.
"In the Wake of the Strafing and Bombing, My Sullen Silence." [BellR] (16:1/2)
Spr-Fall 93, p. 99.
4351. McNEIL, Elizabeth
"In Common Ground." [HayF] (12) Spr-Sum 93, p. 89-90.
4352. McNEIL, Jean
"The Clearance." [AntigR] (93-94) Spr-Sum 93, p. 9-10.
"Tender Is the North." [AntigR] (93-94) Spr-Sum 93, p. 7-8.
4353. McNEILL, Christine
"Human Remains Safely Contained." [Verse] (10:1) Spr 93, p. 85.
"Second Language." [Verse] (10:1) Spr 93, p. 86.
"To See Is Only a Lanugage." [Stand] (35:1) Wint 93-94, p. 11.
4354. McNULTY, Ted
"Coal." [Verse] (10:3) Wint 93, p. 97.
"McGwinn and Son." [SouthernPR] (33:2) Fall 93, p. 18.

4355. McPHERSON, James L.
"Body Language." [Chelsea] (54) 93, p. 98.
4356. McPHERSON, Michael
"The Hearing." [Manoa] (5:1) Sum 93, p. 210-211.
"Maalaea Bay." [Manoa] (5:1) Sum 93, p. 211.
"Toda Drug." [BambooR] (57) Wint 93, p. 173.
4357. McPHERSON, Sandra
"An Acre of Bird's-Foot Trefoil and Morning Glory in a Beach Swale." [Field] (49)
Fall 93, p. 45-46.
"Chain." [WestHR] (47:4) Wint 93, p. 383.
"The Context of a Nectie Quilt, Silk and Satins, 1940s." [NewRep] (208:13) 29 Mr
93, p. 48.
"Desert Night, Las Vegas." [Field] (49) Fall 93, p. 47.
"My Personal Hercules." [ParisR] (35:127) Sum 93, p. 123.
"Ode to Early Work." [ParisR] (35:127) Sum 93, p. 120-121.
"Preface in Invisible Ink to Accompany the Gift of a Blank Book." [WestHR] (47:4)
Wint 93, p. 384-385.
"Signs of Salvation." [Iowa] (23:2) Spr-Sum 93, p. 62.
"Six Movements for Portraits of Erzulie" (Spirit Flags, Sewn in Haiti, 1990). [Iowa]
(23:2) Spr-Sum 93, p. 59-61.
"Trading." [ParisR] (35:127) Sum 93, p. 121-122.
4358. McQUILKIN, Rennie
"Birthday at the Motor Vehicle Dept." [Poetry] (162:6) S 93, p. 335-336.
4359. McRAY, Paul
"Lucy, Refusing to Listen to Bruckner." [WindO] (57) Fall 93, p. 28.
"The Stone." [Footwork] (23) 93, p. 85.
"Under the Desert." [RiverS] (39) 93, p. 77.
4360. McSWEEN, Harold B.
"My First Duchess." [PoetC] (25:1) Fall 93, p. 21.
4361. McVARISH, Emily
"The Waker's Loss." [Zyzzyva] (9:4) Wint 93, between pages 80 and 81.
4362. McVEIGH, Jane
"The Woman in the Supermarket" (for Stephen Dunn). [CreamCR] (17:2) Fall 93, p.
196-197.
4363. McWHIRTER, George
"Diary Without Dates, VIII" (tr. of Homero Aridjis). [Chelsea] (54) 93, p. 22-24.
"Greek Things" (tr. of Homero Aridjis). [PoetryC] (13:4) 93, p. 20.
"Hernan Cortes Sails" (tr. of Homero Aridjis). [Chelsea] (54) 93, p. 25.
"The House of Hernan Cortes, Antigua, Veracruz" (tr. of Homero Aridjis). [Chelsea]
(54) 93, p. 25.
"Lunar Variations" (tr. of Homero Aridjis). [PoetryC] (13:4) 93, p. 20.
"These Are the Sleeping Conditions" (tr. of Homero Aridjis). [MalR] (102) Spr 93,
p. 72-73.
4364. MEACHAM, Mark
"Imago." [SouthernPR] (33:1) Spr 93, p. 41.
4365. MEAD, Jane
"La Guardia, the Story." [AmerPoR] (22:2) Mr-Ap 93, p. 41.
"In the Parking Lot at the Junior College on the Eve of a Presidential Election."
[BelPoJ] (44:1) Fall 93, p. 24-26.
"Problem Performed by Shadows." [BelPoJ] (44:1) Fall 93, p. 22-23.
"To Whatever Remains of Caedmon Wherever It's Remaining." [ColR] (20:1) Spr
93, p. 86-87.
4366. MEAD, Matthew
"Pruzzian Elegy" (tr. of Johannes Bobrowski, w. Ruth Mead). [QRL] (12:32/33) 93,
p. 384-386.
4367. MEAD, Ruth
"Pruzzian Elegy" (tr. of Johannes Bobrowski, w. Matthew Mead). [QRL] (12:32/33)
93, p. 384-386.
4368. MEADE, Gordon
"Animal, Vegetable, or Mineral." [AntigR] (92) Wint 93, p. 7.
"The Barley Poem." [AntigR] (92) Wint 93, p. 8-9.
4369. MEADOWS, Debra F.
"&/He's Got a Music/Magic." [Drumvoices] (2:1/2) Fall-Wint 92-93, p. 199-200.
4370. MEALY, Rosemari
"Death Haunts the Brave." [Drumvoices] (3:1/2) Fall-Wint 93-94, p. 47.

4371. MEAS, M. Minford
"Apples and Such." [Light] (5) Spr 93, p. 12.
"On Her Head." [Light] (5) Spr 93, p. 20.
4372. MECKLEM, Todd
"Green Salsa" (w. Denise Dumars). [Pearl] (19) Fall-Wint 93, p. 8.
4373. MEDENICA, Susan
"Red Tail Sin." [Gaia] (1/2) Ap-Jl 93, p. 2.
4374. MEDINA, Pablo
"Calle de la Amargura." [AmerPoR] (22:3) My-Je 93, p. 16.
"Nocturno de Washington" (for Marta Sánchez Lowery). [AmerPoR] (22:3) My-Je
93, p. 17.
"Nothing Nietzsche." [AmerPoR] (22:3) My-Je 93, p. 16.
"To Celia." [ApalQ] (36/37) 91, p. 77.
4375. MEEHAN, Paula
"City." [SenR] (23:1/2) Wint 93, p. 38-41.
4376. MEEK, Ed
"Hard Times." [NoDaQ] (61:4) Fall 93, p. 130.
4377. MEGAW, Neill
"Docking, Midmorning." [CumbPR]] (13:1) Fall 93, p. 42.
"Driving Up Baja California, Norte." [SoCoast] (14) Ja 93, p. 29.
"Fat Angels." [SoCoast] (14) Ja 93, p. 30.
"Honfleur" (Lithograph by Simon Chaye). [CapeR] (28:1) Spr 93, p. 33.
"The Host." [SoCoast] (14) Ja 93, p. 31.
"Little Jack Horner Lives." [Hellas] (4:1) Spr 93, p. 31.
"Manifest Destiny." [HampSPR] Wint 93, p. 24.
"Multiple Personality." [Hellas] (4:1) Spr 93, p. 32.
"The Muse As Recording Angel." [SoCoast] (15) Je 93, p. 15.
"The Obligations of Furniture." [Light] (7) Aut 93, p. 19.
"Oread." [SoCoast] (14) Ja 93, p. 32.
"Seeing Things." [SoCoast] (14) Ja 93, p. 26-27.
"Silence, Listening to Silence." [CumbPR]] (13:1) Fall 93, p. 63-64.
"Stone in the Shallows." [Hellas] (4:2) Fall 93, p. 67.
"Translations." [CumbPR]] (13:1) Fall 93, p. 61.
"Truce." [SoCoast] (14) Ja 93, p. 28.
"Vows" (A Fragment from a Lost Restoration Comedy). [Light] (5) Spr 93, p. 17.
4378. MEHRHOFF, Charlie
"Banshee" (For John Wright). [FreeL] (11) Wint 93, p. 29.
"Brave in It." [HeavenB] (10) Wint-Spr 93, p. 11.
"Deanna Maria." [ChironR] (12:3, #36) Aut 93, p. 13.
"Fact." [Asylum] (8) 93, p. 102.
"Father I Starve." [WorldL] (4) 93, p. 37.
"In the Half Life." [FreeL] (11) Wint 93, p. 28-29.
"Manhattan." [DogRR] (12:1, #23) Spr-Sum 93, p. 40.
"Passing Through." [ChironR] (12:3, #36) Aut 93, p. 13.
"The President of the United States." [DogRR] (12:1, #23) Spr-Sum 93, p. 40.
"Proem: i call it *the staple job* because misanthropy is paradise." [WorldL] (4) 93, p.
37.
"Temporary Resurrection #408." [SlipS] (13) 93, p. 5.
4379. MEHROTRA, Arvind Krishna
"To an Unborn Daughter." [GettyR] (6:2) Spr 93, p. 238.
4380. MEI, Yaochen
"The Potter" (From Song Dynasty Poems, tr. by John Knoepfle and Wang Shouyi).
[DogRR] (12:1, #23) Spr-Sum 93, p. 54.
4381. MEIKSIN, Judy
"Holiday Season at the White House." [MinnR] (NS 40) Spr-Sum 93, p. 9.
4382. MEINBRESSE, Tim
"Gravity Looms on the Other Side of the Stumbling Block." [Pearl] (19) Fall-Wint
93, p. 22.
"Hell Is Wherever I Am." [SlipS] (13) 93, p. 58.
"Hermaphrodite." [SlipS] (13) 93, p. 59.
4383. MEINHARD, Hermine
"Guatemala." [WillowS] (32) Sum 93, p. 14-15.
"A Piece of Lightning." [ProseP] (1) 92, p. 59.
4384. MEINKE, Peter
"The Attack." [GeoR] (47:4) Wint 93, p. 693-694.
"Caitlin in Fiesole." [ApalQ] (35) 90, p. 29-31.

"Portrait: White on White." [ApalQ] (39) 93, p. 38.
"Rage." [ApalQ] (39) 93, p. 37.
"Spanish Moss" (for Timothy). [TampaR] (6) Spr 93, p. 33.
4385. MEISTER, Peter
"Thomas." [ChrC] (110:30) 27 O 93, p. 1036.
4386. MEJIA, Claudia
"Symbiotic." [WashR] (18:5) F-Mr 93, p. 5.
"Untitled: Insanity creeping up behind me." [WashR] (18:5) F-Mr 93, p. 20.
"Untitled: Of typewritten pages and greased thumbs leafing over painted objects in a room." [WashR] (18:5) F-Mr 93, p. 5.
"Untitled: Plastic nostrils and everything in them." [WashR] (18:5) F-Mr 93, p. 22.
"Untitled: Splinters on my tongue." [WashR] (18:5) F-Mr 93, p. 20.
"What Is Next?" [WashR] (18:5) F-Mr 93, p. 5.
4387. MELCHER, Michael
"Golden." [Talisman] (11) Fall 93, p. 227.
4388. MELEAGER
"Some Amatory Epigrams from the Greek Anthology" (tr. by James Laughlin). [Sulfur] (33) Fall 93, p. 50-51.
4389. MELÉNDEZ, Gabriel
"The Heart Dances with Malinche. El Corazon Baila con la Malinche." [ColR] (20:2) Fall 93, p. 97-98.
4390. MELISSANTHI
"The Doubt" (tr. by Eleni Fourtouni). [PoetryC] (13:3) 93, p. 20.
"Marking Time" (tr. by Eleni Fourtouni). [PoetryC] (13:3) 93, p. 20.
4391. MELLIN, Lilace A.
"A Pond Reflection." [DogRR] (12:2, #24) Fall-Wint 93, p. 24.
4392. MELLINGER, Maria
"I(f)-55." [BellArk] (9:3) My-Je 93, p. 19.
"It Is Believing." [BellArk] (9:4) Jl-Ag 93, p. 7.
"A Very Short Story." [BellArk] (9:3) My-Je 93, p. 23.
"What Am I to Do With." [BellArk] (9:4) Jl-Ag 93, p. 7.
MELLO BREYNER ANDRESEN, Sophia de
See BREYNER, Sophia de Mello
4393. MELNICK, Patrice
"Awa Speaks." [XavierR] (13:1) Spr 93, p. 13-14.
4394. MELNYCZUK, Askold
"After a Snowfall on the Second Day of Spring in 1992" (For Gus and Eiko). [Poetry] (161:6) Mr 93, p. 326.
"The Current Radio." [PartR] (60:2) Spr 93, p. 244-245.
"Late." [AmerPoR] (22:3) My-Je 93, p. 56.
4395. MELO, Michael
"Unlearning English." [Zyzzyva] (9:2) Sum 93, p. 87-91.
4396. MELVIN, John
"Utility Pole." [CinPR] (24) Spr 93, p. 50.
4397. MEMMER, Philip
"Wisdom." [PoetC] (24:3) Spr 93, p. 39.
4398. MEMMOLO, Dan
"When the Vision Comes." [Elf] (3:3) Fall 93, p. 32-33.
4399. MENAMIN, Margaret
"Where Last I Saw You" (reipient of the Editors' Distinguished Entry Award, 1993 Poetry Competition). [Elf] (3:2) Sum 93, p. 24.
4400. MENASHE, Samuel
"Down to Earth." [PartR] (60:2) Spr 93, p. 246.
"Hallelujah." [PartR] (60:2) Spr 93, p. 245.
"Old as the Hills" (for John Thornton). [PartR] (60:2) Spr 93, p. 246.
4401. MENDEL, Stephanie
"She Told Us to Bury Her." [Pearl] (17) Spr 93, p. 103.
4402. MENDEZ, Estrellita
"Almost a Game." [OnTheBus] (6:1, #13) Wint 93-Spr 94, p. 153.
"Arthur Adams Works the Mint." [OnTheBus] (5:2, #12) Sum-Fall 93, p. 139.
4403. MENEBROKER, Ann
"Night Poem." [PaintedB] (50/51) 93, p. 30.
"An Old Wounded Cow Talks to the Mountain" (For Ben). [Pearl] (17) Spr 93, p. 63.
4404. MENG, Chiao
"Cold Creek" (tr. by David Hinton). [Sulfur] (33) Fall 93, p. 140-145.

"Laments of the Gorges" (tr. by David Hinton). [Sulfur] (33) Fall 93, p. 145-151.
MENOZZI, Wallis Wilde
    See WILDE-MENOZZI, Wallis
4405. MERCK, Bryan E.
    "That Day at Arnaud's Mill, Risking Poetry." [HiramPoR] (53/54) Fall 92-Sum 93,
        p. 55-56.
4406. MEREDITH, Connie
    "Wild Woman." [SinW] (49) Spr-Sum 93, p. 89.
4407. MEREDITH, Joseph
    "All-Star" (for AMM in his tenth summer). [PaintedB] (50/51) 93, p. 35.
    "Hunter's Moon" (Jiggs' Field, 1990. For J. H.). [FourQ] (7:1) Spr 93, p. 10-12.
    "Osprey." [FourQ] (7:1) Spr 93, p. 12-13.
4408. MERKEL, Inge
    "Chorus of the Trojan Survivors" (from "Helena," tr. by Renate Latimer).
        [SouthernHR] (27:4) Fall 93, p. 360-362.
4409. MERKEL, Marie
    "Given the Choice." [CarolQ] (45:3) Sum 93, p. 12.
    "Waiting at the Coronet" (in Greenport, L.I.). [CarolQ] (45:3) Sum 93, p. 11.
    "Walking Until You Come Home." [NewRep] (209:24) 13 D 93, p. 45.
4410. MERRILL, Christopher
    "The Fence." [ParisR] (35:127) Sum 93, p. 124-125.
    "Hourly" (tr. of Jaime Sabines). [RiverS] (39) 93, p. 61.
    "In this moment, in the twilight of a cold room, thunder approaches" (tr. of Ales
        Debeljak, w. the author). [ProseP] (2) 93, p. 28.
    "Indifferently, he watched her through the shadows of furniture" (tr. of Ales
        Debeljak, w. the author). [ProseP] (2) 93, p. 29.
    "Interior" (tr. of André Breton). [RiverS] (39) 93, p. 59.
    "Miss X" (tr. of Jaime Sabines, w. Jerry Johnston). [RiverS] (39) 93, p. 63.
    "Should, Should Not" (variation on a theme by Czeslaw Milosz). [ParisR] (35:127)
        Sum 93, p. 125-127.
4411. MERRILL, James
    "Days of 1964." [QRL] (12:32/33) 93, p. 466-467.
    "The Doodler." [QRL] (12:32/33) 93, p. 464-466.
    "Family Week at Oracle Ranch." [NewYorker] (69:1) 22 F 93, p. 166-167.
    "Volcanic Holiday." [ColR] (20:1) Spr 93, p. 106-108.
4412. MERRIMAN, Patience
    "The Night Table." [PaintedB] (50/51) 93, p. 37.
4413. MERRITT, Constance
    "Lullaby." [Callaloo] (16:2) Spr 93, p. 324.
4414. MERRYMAN, Molly
    "Tight Jeans." [Confr] (51) Sum 93, p. 265.
MERS, Joyce la
    See LaMERS, Joyce
4415. MERTON, Andrew
    "Preemie." [Conscience] (14:4) Wint 93-94, p. 43.
    "Valentine." [Conscience] (14:4) Wint 93-94, p. 15.
4416. MERTON, Thomas J.
    "Ariadne." [QRL] (12:32/33) 93, p. 468.
    "The Regret." [QRL] (12:32/33) 93, p. 469.
4417. MERWIN, W. S.
    "1920" (tr. of Osip Mandelstam, w. Clarence Brown). [QRL] (12:32/33) 93, p. 463.
    "1933" (tr. of Osip Mandelstam, w. Clarence Brown). [QRL] (12:32/33) 93, p. 463.
    "Authority." [ColR] (20:1) Spr 93, p. 25.
    "Color Merchants." [Poetry] (163:1) O 93, p. 11.
    "Commemoratives." [PartR] (60:2) Spr 93, p. 238.
    "Dry Ground." [NewYorker] (69:21) 12 Jl 93, p. 68.
    "Entry." [Poetry] (163:1) O 93, p. 10.
    "Forgotten Streams." [PartR] (60:2) Spr 93, p. 237-238.
    "Francois de Maynard, Poet — 1582-1645." [PoetryNW] (34:2) Sum 93, p. 4-5.
    "Garden." [Hudson] (46:3) Aut 93, p. 491.
    "Hölderlin at the River." [ParisR] (35:128) Fall 93, p. 65.
    "Ill Wind." [PoetryNW] (34:2) Sum 93, p. 3.
    "In the Doorway." [Nat] (256:22) 7 Je 93, p. 810.
    "Lackawanna." [QRL] (12:32/33) 93, p. 470-471.
    "Lark." [QRL] (12:32/33) 93, p. 469-470.
    "Night Singing." [ParisR] (35:128) Fall 93, p. 64.

"Oak Time." [Poetry] (163:1) O 93, p. 12.
"Old Question." [Field] (49) Fall 93, p. 49.
"One of the Lives." [NewYRB] (40:8) 22 Ap 93, p. 15.
"One Time." [Field] (49) Fall 93, p. 48.
"Other Time." [Atlantic] (271:5) My 93, p. 82.
"Purgatorio" (Canto V, tr. of Dante). [Poetry] (162:3) Je 93, p. 152-156.
"Purgatorio, Canto II" (Excerpt, tr. of Dante). [OhioR] (50) 93, p. 11-15.
"Quince." [QRL] (12:32/33) 93, p. 471.
"Romanesque." [NewYorker] (69:4) 15 Mr 93, p. 72.
"Season." [NewYorker] (69:29) 13 S 93, p. 62.
"Snake." [NewYorker] (69:36) 1 N 93, p. 98.
"The Stone." [ParisR] (35:128) Fall 93, p. 66.
"Three Prayers for the First Forty Days of the Dead" (tr. of Essenin, w. Olga
    Carlisle). [QRL] (12:32/33) 93, p. 411-413.
"Walkers." [ColR] (20:1) Spr 93, p. 26-27.
"The West Window." [NewYorker] (68:51) 8 F 93, p. 70.
"White Morning." [PartR] (60:2) Spr 93, p. 237.
"Who It Is." [QRL] (12:32/33) 93, p. 471-472.
4418. MERZLAK, Regina
    "Myths." [SpiritSH] (58) 93, p. 26.
    "Night Snow." [SpiritSH] (58) 93, p. 27.
4419. MESMER, Sharon
    "The End" (for Barbara Paley-Israel). [BrooklynR] (10) 93, p. 56.
    "Love Is a Many Splendored Thing, in Brooklyn." [BrooklynR] (10) 93, p. 57-58.
4420. MESSER, Sarah
    "Widow's Hole." [Calyx] (15:1) Wint 93-94, p. 52-53.
4421. MESSO, George
    "Antique" (tr. of Arthur Rimbaud). [Pearl] (19) Fall-Wint 93, p. 12.
4422. MÉSZÖLY, Miklós
    "Christmas, Nineteen-fifties" (tr. by John Bátki). [HarvardR] (3) Wint 93, p. 49.
4423. METODIEV, Ivan
    "These Things from Words" (tr. by Lisa Sapinkopf and Georgi Belev). [Paint]
        (19:38) Aut 92, p. 60.
    "This Crow" (tr. by Lisa Sapinkopf and Georgi Belev). [Paint] (19:38) Aut 92, p. 61.
4424. METZ, Jerred
    "But the Pecculations." [NorthStoneR] (11) 93, p. 128.
    "A Few Words More." [NorthStoneR] (11) 93, p. 127.
    "Locks" (Winner with "An Old Story," Best Pair of Poems). [ContextS] (3:1) 93, p.
        3.
    "No, Not Victimized." [NorthStoneR] (11) 93, p. 127.
    "An Old Story" (Winner with "Locks," Best Pair of Poems). [ContextS] (3:1) 93, p.
        3.
    "So Mr. Rogers Became." [NorthStoneR] (11) 93, p. 128.
4425. METZGER, Danny
    "Where It All Began." [PoetryUSA] (25/26) 93, p. 54.
4426. MEW, Michael S.
    "The Poor House." [SmPd] (30:1, #87) Wint 93, p. 20.
4427. MEYER, David C.
    "Adolescent Magic in my 46th Year." [Elf] (3:3) Fall 93, p. 20.
    "The Blessing Way" (recipient of The Ruth Cable Memorial Prize, 1993 Poetry
        Competition). [Elf] (3:2) Sum 93, p. 22-23.
    "Even If the Snow Should Fall" (for Pat, early December). [Elf] (3:3) Fall 93, p. 22 -
        23.
    "Fire and Ashes" (for Pat). [Elf] (3:2) Sum 93, p. 33.
    "How Might This Corner Come to Be?" (for Pat). [Elf] (3:3) Fall 93, p. 21.
4428. MEYER, Thomas
    "Acts of Compensation." [Conjunc] (21) 93, p. 271.
    "Candlemas." [Conjunc] (21) 93, p. 271-272.
    "The Ceration." [Conjunc] (21) 93, p. 269-271.
    "Drought in the Alps." [Conjunc] (21) 93, p. 272.
    "Egyptian Cotton." [Conjunc] (21) 93, p. 273.
    "Endive." [Conjunc] (21) 93, p. 274-275.
    "The Flood." [Conjunc] (21) 93, p. 271.
    "The Great Wall." [Conjunc] (21) 93, p. 272.
    "The Midnight Sun." [Conjunc] (21) 93, p. 272-273.
    "Ordinary Questions." [Conjunc] (21) 93, p. 275.

"The Principle." [Conjunc] (21) 93, p. 276.
"A Summer Place." [Conjunc] (21) 93, p. 276.
4429. MEYERS, Brad
"Jump." [BellArk] (9:4) Jl-Ag 93, p. 10.
"Traveler." [BellArk] (9:6) N-D 93, p. 12.
4430. MEYERS, Linda Curtis
"After the Dish Ran Away with the Spoon." [HawaiiR] (17:2, #38) Spr 93, p. 84.
4431. MEYERS, Susan
"My Mother, Her Mornings." [GreensboroR] (55) Wint 93-94, p. 36-37.
4432. MEZEY, Naomi
"Absence" (tr. of Jorge Luis Borges, w. Robert Mezey). [SenR] (23:1/2) Wint 93, p. 120.
4433. MEZEY, Robert
"1891" (tr. of Jorge Luis Borges). [ArtfulD] (24/25) 93, p. 45.
"Absence" (tr. of Jorge Luis Borges, w. Naomi Mezey). [SenR] (23:1/2) Wint 93, p. 120.
"Allusion to the Death of Colonel Francisco Borges (1833-74)" (tr. of Jorge Luis Borges, w. R. G. Barnes). [NowestR] (31:3) 93, p. 59.
"Buenos Aires" (tr. of Jorge Luis Borges). [MissouriR] (16:3) 93, p. 32.
"A Compass" (tr. of Jorge Luis Borges). [Poetry] (162:3) Je 93, p. 158.
"James Joyce" (tr. of Jorge Luis Borges, w. Dick Barnes). [ArtfulD] (24/25) 93, p. 41.
"Limits" (tr. of Jorge Luis Borges, w. R. G. Barnes). [Poetry] (162:3) Je 93, p. 157 - 158.
"The Night They Held a Wake on the Southside" (To Letizia Alvarez de Toledo, tr. of Jorge Luis Borges). [MissouriR] (16:3) 93, p. 26-27.
"Of Which Nothing Is Known" (tr. of Jorge Luis Borges). [SenR] (23:1/2) Wint 93, p. 124.
"On Forgetting a Dream" (To Viviana Aguilar, tr. of Jorge Luis Borges, w. R. G. Barnes). [NowestR] (31:3) 93, p. 60.
"The Other Tiger" (tr. of Jorge Luis Borges). [MissouriR] (16:3) 93, p. 28-29.
"Poem about Quantity" (tr. of Jorge Luis Borges). [NewYRB] (40:12) 24 Je 93, p. 35.
"Religio Medici, 1643" (tr. of Jorge Luis Borges). [SenR] (23:1/2) Wint 93, p. 119.
"A Rose and Milton." [NowestR] (31:3) 93, p. 61.
"Sleep" (tr. of Jorge Luis Borges). [Poetry] (162:3) Je 93, p. 159.
"The Tango" (tr. of Jorge Luis Borges). [SenR] (23:1/2) Wint 93, p. 121-123.
"Texas (2)" (tr. of Jorge Luis Borges). [ArtfulD] (24/25) 93, p. 42.
"To the One Reading Me" (tr. of Jorge Luis Borges). [MissouriR] (16:3) 93, p. 25.
"Truco" (tr. of Jorge Luis Borges, w. Dick Barnes). [ArtfulD] (24/25) 93, p. 44.
4434. MIAO, Deyu
"Swallows" (in Chinese and English, tr. by Li Xi-jian and Gordon Osing). [PikeF] (11) Fall 93, p. 15.
4435. MICHAEL, Marilyn
"Woman at the Door." [Sequoia] (34/35) 92-93, p. 14.
4436. MICHAELS, Anne
"The Passionate World." [Event] (22:2) Sum 93, p. 7-8.
"The Second Search." [Event] (22:2) Sum 93, p. 9-12.
"Skin Divers." [Arc] (30) Spr 93, p. 55-57.
"Wild Horses." [Arc] (30) Spr 93, p. 58.
4437. MICHAELS, Judith
"On the Loss of Lemon." [JINJPo] (15:1) Spr 93, p. 8.
4438. MICHAJLOW, Adam
"Expect the Worst" (tr. by Artur Grabowski and Chris Hurford). [Verse] (10:2) Sum 93, p. 43.
4439. MICHAUD, Michael Gregg
"10-22-89." [Amelia] (7:2, #21) 93, p. 74.
"11-26-89." [Amelia] (7:2, #21) 93, p. 77-78.
"December 22, 1989." [Amelia] (7:2, #21) 93, p. 76.
"January 27, 1990: P.M." [Amelia] (7:2, #21) 93, p. 77.
"November 5, 1989." [Amelia] (7:2, #21) 93, p. 74-75.
"November 6, 1989: Morning." [Amelia] (7:2, #21) 93, p. 76.
"Ruega por Nosotros." [JamesWR] (10:3) Spr 93, p. 13.
4440. MICHAUX, Henri
"Angle Markers (Poteaux d'Angle)" (Excerpts, tr. by Lynn Hoggard). [Chelsea] (54) 93, p. 26-27.

"Demain N'Est Pas Encore." [WashR] (19:2) Ag-S 93, p. 15.
"Not Again" (tr. by Dennis Barone). [WashR] (19:2) Ag-S 93, p. 15.
4441. MICHELSON, Peter
"Colombo Airport." [AnotherCM] (25) Spr 93, p. 89-90.
"Nature or Nurture." [AnotherCM] (25) Spr 93, p. 91.
4442. MICUS, Edward
"612 A." [Chelsea] (54) 93, p. 94.
"Sylvia." [Chelsea] (54) 93, p. 93.
4443. MIDDLEBROOKS, Phyllis
"Portrait." [PaintedB] (50/51) 93, p. 50-51.
4444. MIDDLETON, Christopher
"Border Zone, Minefield, Snow East of Bebra" (tr. of Lars Gustafsson). [QRL]
(12:32/33) 93, p. 188.
"Naked Truth." [Thrpny] (52) Wint 93, p. 18.
"The Parrot House on Bruton Street, 1830" (Edward Lear). [NewYorker] (69:7) 5
Ap 93, p. 70.
"A Picture Which Magritte Deferred." [Thrpny] (55) Fall 93, p. 25.
"Poem Written After Contemplating the Adverb 'Primarily'." [QRL] (12:32/33) 93,
p. 472-473.
"Reflections" (tr. of Ljubo Wiesner). [NewYorker] (69:41) 6 D 93, p. 52.
4445. MIDDLETON, David
"Oak Alley" (For L.P.S.). [SewanR] (101:2) Ap-Je, Spr 93, p. 145-148.
4446. MIDDLETON, Peter
"Paternalisms" (Selections: 2-3, 5). [Avec] (6:1) 93, p. 54-58.
4447. MIDGE, Tiffany
"Iron Eyes Cody." [CutB] (40) Spr 93, p. 170.
4448. MIHAILOVICH, Vasa D.
"Building a City" (tr. of Manojle Gavrilovic). [NoDaQ] (61:1) Wint 93, p. 78.
"The Master of Bees" (tr. of Manojle Gavrilovic). [NoDaQ] (61:1) Wint 93, p. 78.
4449. MIKA, Tomas
"At Night" (tr. of Jirí Orten, w. Toby Litt). [Verse] (10:1) Spr 93, p. 98.
4450. MIKES, Petr
"Canto" (tr. by the author, w. Wanda Boeke). [OxfordM] (9:1) Spr-Sum 93, p. 115.
"I'm tortured" (tr. by the author, w. Wanda Boeke). [OxfordM] (9:1) Spr-Sum 93, p.
113.
"A Lost Street" (tr. by the author, w. Wanda Boeke). [OxfordM] (9:1) Spr-Sum 93,
p. 114.
"The Memory of the Wound III" (tr. by the author, w. Wanda Boeke). [OxfordM]
(9:1) Spr-Sum 93, p. 114.
"Parable" (tr. by the author, w. Wanda Boeke). [OxfordM] (9:1) Spr-Sum 93, p. 113.
"The space of my sleep" (tr. by the author, w. Wanda Boeke). [OxfordM] (9:1) Spr-
Sum 93, p. 114.
"To Ross and His Children" (tr. by the author, w. Wanda Boeke). [OxfordM] (9:1)
Spr-Sum 93, p. 113-114.
"To William Blake" (tr. by the author, w. Wanda Boeke). [OxfordM] (9:1) Spr-Sum
93, p. 115.
MIKIO, Yonaha
See YONAHA, Mikio
4451. MIKITA, Nancy
"The Facts Speak." [HampSPR] Wint 93, p. 23.
"Song." [DogRR] (12:1, #23) Spr-Sum 93, p. 5.
"Wisdom." [HampSPR] Wint 93, p. 23.
4452. MIKKELSEN, Robert S.
"Boneyard." [WeberS] (10:3) Fall 93, p. 126-127.
"September Song." [WeberS] (10:3) Fall 93, p. 125-126.
4453. MIKULEC, Patrick B.
"The Advantage of Spiders." [Interim] (12:1) Spr-Sum 93, p. 4.
"Among Tea Roses." [Interim] (12:1) Spr-Sum 93, p. 7.
"The Ballet." [Interim] (12:1) Spr-Sum 93, p. 5.
"Man Crying on the Sidewalk." [Interim] (12:1) Spr-Sum 93, p. 6.
MILANÉS, Cecilia Rodriguez
See RODRIGUEZ MILANÉS, Cecilia
4454. MILBURN, Suzan
"Family Tradition." [PraF] (14:2) Sum 93, p. 72.
"Nana Knew Men Were Different." [PraF] (14:2) Sum 93, p. 73.
"Sandwiched." [Dandel] (20:1) 93, p. 59-60.

4455. MILES, Josephine
"Botany." [QRL] (12:32/33) 93, p. 473-474.
"Skin." [QRL] (12:32/33) 93, p. 473.
4456. MILES, Ron
"Banff Centred." [AntigR] (93-94) Spr-Sum 93, p. 279.
4457. MILES, Steve
"After Lovemaking." [Plain] (14:1) Fall 93, p. 8-9.
4458. MILISIC, Milan
"Flaubert" (tr. by Maja Herman-Sekulic). [NoDaQ] (61:1) Wint 93, p. 113.
"Treacherously, from Behind" (tr. by Maja Herman-Sekulic). [NoDaQ] (61:1) Wint
93, p. 112.
4459. MILITANO, Carmelo
"Winter Afternoon." [PraF] (14:3) Aut 93, p. 52.
4460. MILJKOVIC, Branko
"Everyone Will Write Poetry" (tr. by P. H. Liotta). [Vis] (43) 93, p. 51.
"I Wake Her in Vain" (tr. by P. H. Liotta). [Vis] (42) 93, p. 29.
"An Orphic Legacy" (tr. by John Matthias and Vladeta Vuckovic). [NoDaQ] (61:1)
Wint 93, p. 114.
"Sun" (tr. by P. H. Liotta). [Vis] (43) 93, p. 50.
"To the Earth Right Now" (tr. by John Matthias and Vladeta Vuckovic). [NoDaQ]
(61:1) Wint 93, p. 115.
4461. MILLAY, Edna St. Vincent
"Love Is Not All" (with music by Alva Henderson, March 1991). [Sparrow] (60)
Sum 93, p. 9-15.
4462. MILLER, A. McA.
"A Moving Man Goes On." [QW] (37) Sum-Fall 93, p. 95.
4463. MILLER, Alexander L.
"Standing in the World's Most Renowned Concert Hall." [HawaiiR] (16:3, #36)
Wint 93, p. 97.
4464. MILLER, Ann
"Cathedral." [HampSPR] Wint 93, p. 11-12.
"Vipunen's Gift." [HampSPR] Wint 93, p. 12-13.
4465. MILLER, Carolyn
"After Cocteau: Beauty's Father in the Castle of the Beast" (for Lee Hildreth).
[PaintedHR] (9) Spr 93, p. 10-11.
4466. MILLER, D. Patrick
"Lullaby." [Sun] (206) F 93, p. 38.
4467. MILLER, David
"Drunk Talking to No One." [Callaloo] (16:3) Sum 93, p. 492-493.
"In My Dream." [Callaloo] (16:3) Sum 93, p. 491.
"Sundays." [Callaloo] (16:3) Sum 93, p. 490.
4468. MILLER, Deborah (Deborah M.)
"Almost Lost in Translation" (for Betty Fukuyama). [BellArk] (9:3) My-Je 93, p.
23.
"Growth." [PraF] (14:4) Wint 93-94, p. 22.
"I am Judas Too." [PraF] (14:4) Wint 93-94, p. 23.
"Sisters in Rain." [BellR] (16:1/2) Spr-Fall 93, p. 34.
"Three Months Without Electricity." [BellArk] (9:1) Ja-F 93, p. 5.
4469. MILLER, Derek
"A Year." [HangL] (63) 93, p. 47.
4470. MILLER, E. Ethelbert
"A Death in the Family." [Footwork] (23) 93, p. 141.
"Malcolm X, 1964." [Footwork] (23) 93, p. 140.
"Malcolm X, August 1952." [Footwork] (23) 93, p. 140.
"Malcolm X, February 1965." [Footwork] (23) 93, p. 140.
"W.E.B. DuBois." [Footwork] (23) 93, p. 141.
4471. MILLER, E. S.
"Go South, Old Man." [Light] (8) Wint 93, p. 8.
"Napoli è Vecchia." [Light] (8) Wint 93, p. 18.
4472. MILLER, Errol
"The American Artist." [Gaia] (3) O 93, p. 33.
"At Control Point 0." [Footwork] (23) 93, p. 38.
"Beyond Blue Bayou." [Caliban] (13) 93, p. 148.
"Crossing into Urbana." [RagMag] (11:1) 93, p. 81.
"Delta Blues." [Footwork] (23) 93, p. 38-39.
"Ebb-Tide." [CentR] (37:3) Fall 93, p. 546-547.

"The Eclipse." [Caliban] (13) 93, p. 146-147.
"Eternity." [FourQ] (7:2) Fall 93, p. 44-45.
"Far-Off Atlantic Nights." [Plain] (13:2) Wint 93, p. 10.
"For Farris." [Parting] (6:2) Wint 93, p. 35.
"For Northern Papa." [Plain] (13:3) Spr 93, p. 32.
"For the Cutover Woods of Dixie." [CentR] (37:3) Fall 93, p. 544-545.
"Going." [HiramPoR] (53/54) Fall 92-Sum 93, p. 57-58.
"Gulf Stream Mediation." [Interim] (12:2) Fall-Wint 93, p. 14.
"The Ice Age in Dixie." [XavierR] (13:2) Fall 93, p. 44-45.
"Joe Boxer." [Parting] (6:2) Wint 93, p. 34.
"Just Off Highway 82 East." [Bogg] (66) Wint 92-93, p. 43.
"Lord Set My Feet on Higher Ground." [CentR] (37:3) Fall 93, p. 547.
"Mystic." [Pearl] (17) Spr 93, p. 54.
"The New South." [Northeast] (5:9) Wint 93-94, p. 10-11.
"Old Dominion Prose." [Verse] (10:1) Spr 93, p. 32-33.
"On Past Georgia." [CimR] (105) O 93, p. 89-90.
"On the Necessity of Surrealism." [Caliban] (12) 93, p. 129.
"Our Town." [Footwork] (23) 93, p. 37-38.
"Poetic Wisdom." [PaintedHR] (9) Spr 93, p. 31.
"The Reward of Harvest, Then" (for Atlantis in the autumn). [SmPd] (30:1, #87) Wint 93, p. 22.
"Room of Rooms." [BlackBR] (17) Sum-Fall 93, p. 23-24.
"The Service Charge." [RagMag] (11:1) 93, p. 80.
"South of Boston." [Crucible] (29) Fall 93, p. 15-16.
"The Southern Collection." [LouisL] (10:1) Spr 93, p. 55-56.
"The Spider's Net." [PoetL] (88:4) Wint 93-94, p. 45.
"Steel City Blues." [AlabamaLR] (7:1) 93, p. 21-23.
"This Place Looking Out Upon." [Parting] (6:2) Wint 93, p. 3.
"To Bend the Sun." [Paint] (19:38) Aut 92, p. 43.
"Where the Delta Ends." [ContextS] (3:1) 93, p. 12.
MILLER, Erroll
    See MILLER, Errol
4473. MILLER, Heather Ross
    "Heal-All." [Turnstile] (4:1) 93, p. 73.
4474. MILLER, Jane
    "Countryside." [KenR] (NS 15:1) Wint 93, p. 136-137.
    "The Impossible." [AmerPoR] (22:1) Ja-F 93, p. 50-51.
    "More or Less a Sorrow." [KenR] (NS 15:1) Wint 93, p. 138.
    "The Poet." [ColR] (20:1) Spr 93, p. 47-48.
    "Turning Over the Earth." [CreamCR] (17:2) Fall 93, p. 201.
4475. MILLER, Jennifer
    "Lullaby for a Showgirl." [Footwork] (23) 93, p. 71.
4476. MILLER, Joel B.
    "Gilding the Lily." [SnailPR] (3:1) Fall-Wint 93, p. 24.
    "One for Alzheimer." [SnailPR] (3:1) Fall-Wint 93, p. 25.
4477. MILLER, John N.
    "Almost to Hau'ula." [HawaiiR] (16:3, #36) Wint 93, p. 57.
    "Dakota Abstract." [Interim] (12:1) Spr-Sum 93, p. 17.
    "Museum Pieces." [Interim] (12:1) Spr-Sum 93, p. 15-16.
    "With Walt Whitman in Freiburg." [Interim] (12:1) Spr-Sum 93, p. 14-15.
4478. MILLER, Kate Berne
    "Women with Knives" (for Gloria). [SinW] (49) Spr-Sum 93, p. 38.
4479. MILLER, Kevin
    "Reunion on the Northfork." [CutB] (40) Spr 93, p. 171.
4480. MILLER, L. K.
    "Sonnet to Sustenance, or, How Do I Love Thee, Food" (with apologies to Elizabeth Barrett Browning). [EngJ] (82:1) Ja 93, p. 86.
4481. MILLER, Leslie Adrienne
    "Gacela of Departed Love" (after Lorca). [Nimrod] (37:1) Fall-Wint 93, p. 41.
    "Pandare." [Nimrod] (37:1) Fall-Wint 93, p. 40.
    "Sleeping Out" (The Nimrod/Hardman Awards: First Honorable Mention). [Nimrod] (37:1) Fall-Wint 93, p. 38-39.
4482. MILLER, Melissa
    "Flowa." [HawaiiR] (17:1, #37) Spr 93, p. 16-17.
4483. MILLER, Philip
    "Angel." [Confr] (51) Sum 93, p. 250.

"Baby Dolls." [ColEng] (55:5) S 93, p. 535-536.
"Death Camp Documentary in Gray and White" (At the time of liberation). [Poetry]
    (162:3) Je 93, p. 141.
"Falling Off." [NewL] (60:1) 93, p. 75.
"Fathers." [Poetry] (162:6) S 93, p. 321.
"Full Moon Madness." [PoetL] (88:3) Fall 93, p. 34.
"Hard Eyes." [Confr] (51) Sum 93, p. 249-250.
"Magician" (for Keith Denniston). [ColEng] (55:5) S 93, p. 534-535.
"The Man Who Wears a Hat." [FreeL] (11) Wint 93, p. 13.
"The Man Who Wears No Hat." [CoalC] (7) Apr 93, p. 19.
"Maturity." [CapeR] (28:2) Fall 93, p. 13.
"Mean." [CoalC] (7) Apr 93, p. 7-8.
"Our Dogs." [PoetC] (25:1) Fall 93, p. 27-28.
"What It Comes Down To." [Poetry] (162:6) S 93, p. 322.
"Winning." [Poetry] (162:6) S 93, p. 319-320.
4484. MILLER, Stephen Paul
    "All Visual Materials Emit Countless Cartoon Bubbles." [Talisman] (11) Fall 93, p.
        138-141.
4485. MILLER, Tyrus
    "Hydrogen: Lightness." [AmerLC] (5) 93, p. 60.
4486. MILLER, William
    "Delta Winter." [ChatR] (13:3) Spr 93, p. 60-61.
    "Eldridge Cleaver Addresses the East Lake Baptist Church." [Confr] (51) Sum 93, p.
        254-255.
    "Frederick Douglass: the Last Day of Slavery." [Poem] (69) My 93, p. 53.
    "The Wolf's Reply." [Poem] (69) My 93, p. 54.
MILLER LAINO, E. J.
    See LAINO, E. J. Miller
4487. MILLET, T. Lane
    "Naked Charm." [CanLit] (136) Spr 93, p. 4.
4488. MILLETT, John
    "Concorde." [Vis] (42) 93, p. 4.
    "The Foxes." [Bogg] (66) Wint 92-93, p. 40.
    "Nareen Singing." [Bogg] (66) Wint 92-93, p. 40.
    "The Tennis Club." [Bogg] (66) Wint 92-93, p. 40-41.
4489. MILLIGAN, Marjorie
    "Crescent Park." [ProseP] (2) 93, p. 66.
    "Voodoo Summer Job." [ProseP] (2) 93, p. 67.
4490. MILLIGAN, Paula
    "Lake Union, Early Spring." [BellArk] (9:3) My-Je 93, p. 1.
    "Revalations [Revelations?] Under Oak and Stars." [BellArk] (9:2) Mr-Ap 93, p. 9.
4491. MILLIS, Christopher
    "The Alzheimer's Monkeys" (for J.B.). [Agni] (37) 93, p. 56.
    "On Hearing About the Disappearance of Frogs." [Agni] (37) 93, p. 57.
4492. MILLS, David
    "The Lourdes Prayer" (in memory of Audre Lorde). [Eyeball] (2) 93, p. 19.
4493. MILLS, J.
    "After a Month." [SoCoast] (15) Je 93, p. 37.
4494. MILLS, Jess
    "Rio del Mar." [BellArk] (9:4) Jl-Ag 93, p. 23.
    "Starting Over." [CapeR] (28:2) Fall 93, p. 25.
4495. MILLS, Ralph J., Jr.
    "Blue / Flowers" (variation on Jaccottet). [NorthStoneR] (11) 93, p. 135.
    "Bluish / Chimney Smoke." [TarRP] (32:2) Spr 93, p. 32.
    "Day Of." [NorthStoneR] (11) 93, p. 136.
    "Deft / Wind." [NorthStoneR] (11) 93, p. 134.
    "Empty / Day." [TarRP] (32:2) Spr 93, p. 33.
    "Evening Song." [IllinoisR] (1:1) Fall 93, p. 65.
    "Fruits So / Bunched." [NorthStoneR] (11) 93, p. 137.
    "Song." [NorthStoneR] (11) 93, p. 133.
4496. MILLS, Wilmer Hastings
    "Confessions of a Steeplejack." [TarRP] (32:2) Spr 93, p. 14-15.
    "The Welder." [CimR] (105) O 93, p. 79.
4497. MILLSTONE, John
    "The Education of Hawa." [BelPoJ] (44:2) Wint 93-94, p. 8-9.
    "The Turtle." [BelPoJ] (44:2) Wint 93-94, p. 10.

4498. MILNER, Ian
"In the Microscope" (tr. of Miroslav Holub). [Field] (49) Fall 93, p. 9.
4499. MILNER, Mark
"Lit. Crit." [Dandel] (20:1) 93, p. 58.
4500. MILOSZ, Czeslaw
"Lithuania, After Fifty-two Years" (tr. by the author and Robert Hass). [NewYorker]
(69:25) 9 Ag 93, p. 70-71.
"A Man-Fly" (tr. by the author and Robert Hass). [NewYorker] (69:6) 29 Mr 93, p.
60.
"Sarajevo" (tr. by the author and Robert Hass). [NewRep] (209:17) 25 O 93, p. 16.
"To Allen Ginsberg" (tr. by the author). [HarvardR] (3) Wint 93, p. 50-51.
"Woe!" (tr. by the author and Robert Hass). [NewYorker] (69:14) 24 My 93, p. 74.
4501. MILTNER, Robert
"Hypothermia." [ProseP] (1) 92, p. 61.
"Orphanesque." [Gaia] (1/2) Ap-Jl 93, p. 45.
"A Shoebox." [ProseP] (1) 92, p. 60.
4502. MILTON, John
"When I Consider How My Light Is Spent." [AmerPoR] (22:5) S-O 93, p. 28.
4503. MIMNERMOS of Kolophon
"Mimnermos: the Brainsex Paintings" (A Translation of the Fragments by Anne
Carson). [QRL] (12:32/33) 93, p. 94-96.
4504. MIMS, Kevin
"Born on the Moon." [Thrpny] (53) Spr 93, p. 22.
"My Life as a Comic Strip." [IndR] (16:2) Fall 93, p. 149-150.
"Power Surge on Hummingbird Lane." [FreeL] (12) Sum 93, p. 26.
"Spell-Check." [FreeL] (12) Sum 93, p. 27.
"Umpteen." [IndR] (16:2) Fall 93, p. 148.
MINAMIKO, Nagashima
See NAGASHIMA, Minamiko
4505. MINCZESKI, John
"Breaking It Off." [SpoonR] (18:2) Sum-Fall 93, p. 78-79.
"Initiation." [SpoonR] (18:2) Sum-Fall 93, p. 81-82.
"Mud Daubers." [SpoonR] (18:2) Sum-Fall 93, p. 80.
4506. MINEHAN, Mike
"In March We're Going to Egypt." [Bogg] (66) Wint 92-93, p. 7.
4507. MINET, Lawrence
"Eve Reflecting on Her Fall from Innocence." [Poem] (69) My 93, p. 1.
MING, Zhai Yong
See ZHAI, Yong Ming
MINGXIA, Li
See LI, Mingxia
4508. MINICH, Jan C.
"Peavine Canyon." [WeberS] (10:1) Wint 93, p. 64-65.
"Riverbottom." [WeberS] (10:1) Wint 93, p. 66.
"Somewhere within Reach, for Sarah." [WeberS] (10:1) Wint 93, p. 65.
4509. MINNIS, Chelsey (Merrit Chelsey)
"Cryogenics." [OnTheBus] (5:2, #12) Sum-Fall 93, p. 140.
"Driving." [OnTheBus] (6:1, #13) Wint 93-Spr 94, p. 154.
"Lizzie Design." [SilverFR] (24) Wint 93, p. 13-17.
"Normally." [Caliban] (12) 93, p. 52.
"Snakes." [Caliban] (12) 93, p. 51.
"Spring." [Caliban] (12) 93, p. 50.
"Summer Ends Tonight." [Bogg] (66) Wint 92-93, p. 20.
"Tattoos." [OnTheBus] (5:2, #12) Sum-Fall 93, p. 140.
MINORU, Yoshioka
See YOSHIOKA, Minoru
4510. MINTZER, Elaine
"Alarm." [Pearl] (17) Spr 93, p. 56.
"In the Dark." [OnTheBus] (5:2, #12) Sum-Fall 93, p. 141.
"Mother Day." [OnTheBus] (6:1, #13) Wint 93-Spr 94, p. 155.
"No Complaints." [OnTheBus] (6:1, #13) Wint 93-Spr 94, p. 155.
4511. MIODUCHOWSKA, Anna
"May Frolic." [PraF] (14:3) Aut 93, p. 87.
4512. MIRANDA, Verónica
"Aun Que Noche" (from "Esa Antigua Constancia"). [Luz] (5) N 93, p. 24.
"Body of Love" (tr. of Isaac Goldemberg). [Luz] (3) Ja 93, p. 18.

"The Dream Remains" (from "Soñadores, soñad," tr. of Alejandro Roemmers). [Luz] (5) N 93, p. 87.
"Dreams" (2 poems from "La Vida al Contado," tr. of Isaac Goldemberg). [Luz] (5) N 93, p. 73, 75.
"El — Mentido Adios." [Luz] (3) Ja 93, p. 31.
"El — Presencia." [Luz] (3) Ja 93, p. 33.
"Ella — No Es Fácil." [Luz] (3) Ja 93, p. 32.
"Even at Night" (from "That Ancient Devotion," tr. by Angela McEwan). [Luz] (5) N 93, p. 25.
"The House" (from "Cuentas Claras," tr. of Gladys Machado). [Luz] (5) N 93, p. 35, 37.
"I Belong" (from "Cuentas Claras," tr. of Gladys Machado). [Luz] (5) N 93, p. 89.
"Images I" (tr. of Nélida Grassetti). [Luz] (5) N 93, p. 57.
"Images in Two Times" (tr. of Nélida Grassetti). [Luz] (5) N 93, p. 59.
"Insomnia" (from "Soñadores, soñad," tr. of Alejandro Roemmers). [Luz] (5) N 93, p. 17.
"Mar en Sueño" (from "Esa Antigua Constancia"). [Luz] (5) N 93, p. 42.
"Ocean Dream" (from "That Ancient Devotion," tr. by Angela McEwan). [Luz] (5) N 93, p. 43.
"Rio Soy." [Luz] (3) Ja 93, p. 30.
4513. MIRIKITANI, Janice
"Desert Flowers." [Drumvoices] (2:1/2) Fall-Wint 92-93, p. 129-131.
"For My Father." [Drumvoices] (2:1/2) Fall-Wint 92-93, p. 128-129.
"Salad." [Drumvoices] (2:1/2) Fall-Wint 92-93, p. 131.
"We, the Dangerous." [Drumvoices] (2:1/2) Fall-Wint 92-93, p. 132-133.
4514. MIRRIAM-GOLDBERG, Caryn
"Hurricane Sestina." [ChironR] (12:4/13:1, #37/38) Wint 93-Spr 94, p. 27.
4515. MISANCHUK, Melanie
"James." [PraF] (14:3) Aut 93, p. 107.
4516. MISHKIN, Julia
"Agua Alta." [QRL] (12:32/33) 93, p. 240-241.
"Letters from a Dry Island 1: Greenwich Mean Time." [QRL] (12:32/33) 93, p. 246 - 247.
"Letters from a Dry Island 7: The Young Men." [QRL] (12:32/33) 93, p. 249.
"Maurice Ravel at the Piano." [QRL] (12:32/33) 93, p. 247-248.
"Schumann: Answer to Joachim." [QRL] (12:32/33) 93, p. 244-246.
"Self-Portrait with Dying Empire." [QRL] (12:32/33) 93, p. 241-244.
4517. MISIC, Jasna B.
"Anticipation" (tr. of Desanka Maksimovic, w. Richard Burns). [NoDaQ] (61:1) Wint 93, p. 105.
"I Have No More Time" (tr. of Desanka Maksimovic, w. Richard Burns). [NoDaQ] (61:1) Wint 93, p. 104.
"Nobody Knows" (tr. of Desanka Maksimovic, w. Richard Burns). [NoDaQ] (61:1) Wint 93, p. 105.
"Speak Softly" (tr. of Desanka Maksimovic, w. Richard Burns). [NoDaQ] (61:1) Wint 93, p. 105.
4518. MISTRAL, Gabriela
"Poems of the Mothers" (Selections: 6 poems, tr. by Christiane Jacox Kyle). [Iowa] (23:3) Fall 93, p. 170-172.
"Poems of the Saddest Mother" (Selections: 2 poems, tr. by Christiane Jacox Kyle). [Iowa] (23:3) Fall 93, p. 172-173.
4519. MITCHAM, Judson
"Click." [RiverS] (38) 93, p. 29.
"The Mystery." [SouthernR] (29:3) Sum, Jl 93, p. 609.
"The Widow's Desire." [RiverS] (38) 93, p. 26-28.
"A World Beneath." [SouthernR] (29:3) Sum, Jl 93, p. 606-608.
4520. MITCHELL, Elaine
"Urban Chivalry." [Light] (6) Sum 93, p. 17.
4521. MITCHELL, Felicia
"Lost in Austin." [Border] (2) Spr 93, p. 52.
4522. MITCHELL, Gwendolyn
"Book Learning." [AmerV] (32) 93, p. 23.
4523. MITCHELL, Hayley R.
"Another child Outgrows Her Hobbyhorse." [Pearl] (17) Spr 93, p. 58.
"Broken." [ChironR] (12:4/13:1, #37/38) Wint 93-Spr 94, p. 10.
"Garden Party." [ChironR] (12:4/13:1, #37/38) Wint 93-Spr 94, p. 10.

"My Father Was Electrocuted." [ChironR] (12:4/13:1, #37/38) Wint 93-Spr 94, p.
    10.
4524. MITCHELL, Homer
    "Bone and Blowdown." [Blueline] (14) 93, p. 1.
    "St. Lawrence Winter." [Blueline] (14) 93, p. 2.
    "Touched by Frost." [Blueline] (14) 93, p. 3.
4525. MITCHELL, John
    "54 in Butiaba." [NorthStoneR] (11) 93, p. 159.
    "The Armageddon Rose." [NorthStoneR] (11) 93, p. 156-157.
    "The Diversity University Controversy." [NorthStoneR] (11) 93, p. 157.
    "My Father's Pliers." [NorthStoneR] (11) 93, p. 158.
    "Riddle." [NorthStoneR] (11) 93, p. 158.
    "Seven Crows." [NorthStoneR] (11) 93, p. 158.
4526. MITCHELL, Karen
    "Honeysuckles." [Callaloo] (16:3) Sum 93, p. 485-486.
    "Music." [Callaloo] (16:3) Sum 93, p. 487.
    "Separations." [Callaloo] (16:3) Sum 93, p. 488-489.
4527. MITCHELL, Rick
    "Yesterday's Barn." [ChironR] (12:1, #34) Spr 93, p. 37.
4528. MITCHELL, Roger
    "Accident Report." [HopewellR] (5) 93, p. 14-15.
    "Cloudy Feather." [SpoonR] (18:2) Sum-Fall 93, p. 13.
    "Driving, Some Used Cars." [HopewellR] (5) 93, p. 16-17.
    "For Instance." [PoetryNW] (34:1) Spr 93, p. 17-19.
    "Old Road" (for C.). [OhioR] (50) 93, p. 102-103.
    "Rendered World." [SpoonR] (18:2) Sum-Fall 93, p. 14-15.
    "Segments of Spine." [HopewellR] (5) 93, p. 12-13.
    "These Days." [TarRP] (32:2) Spr 93, p. 21.
    "What Happens Next." [OhioR] (50) 93, p. 100-101.
4529. MITCHNER, Gary
    "He Is Dead." [WestHR] (47:4) Wint 93, p. 367-369.
    "Turning In on Itself." [WestHR] (47:4) Wint 93, p. 366.
4530. MITRA-BANERJEE, Swapna
    "The Diamond of Character" (tr. of Kabita Sinha, w. Carolyne Wright). [AmerPoR]
        (22:4) Jl-Ag 93, p. 26.
    "I Left a Long Time Back" (tr. of Kabita Sinha, w. Carolyne Wright). [HarvardR]
        (3) Wint 93, p. 97.
    "The Last Door's Name Is Sorrow" (tr. of Kabita Sinha, w. Carolyne Wright).
        [AmerPoR] (22:4) Jl-Ag 93, p. 27.
4531. MIYOSHI, Tatsuji
    "Baby Carriages" (tr. by Akemi Nakamura and Tony Whedon). [GreenMR] (NS
        6:2) Sum-Fall 93, p. 69.
    "Double Scenery" (tr. by Akemi Nakamura and Tony Whedon). [GreenMR] (NS
        6:2) Sum-Fall 93, p. 70.
    "Maruki Bridge" (tr. by Akemi Nakamura and Tony Whedon). [GreenMR] (NS 6:2)
        Sum-Fall 93, p. 68.
4532. MIZER, Ray
    "Carnality." [Elf] (3:2) Sum 93, p. 40-41.
    "Confessional Type of Poem." [BellArk] (9:5) S-O 93, p. 12.
    "End Notes." [BellArk] (9:5) S-O 93, p. 24.
    "Horns That Blow at Midnight." [RagMag] (11:2) 93, p. 42.
    "Hunger Strike." [WebR] (17) Fall 93, p. 75.
    "Late for the Sky" (incited by the thoughts of David Lavery in his book *The
        Mentality of the Space Age*). [BellArk] (9:2) Mr-Ap 93, p. 3.
    "Mixmaster." [Gypsy] (20) Sum 93, p. 40.
    "Seafarer." [BellArk] (9:1) Ja-F 93, p. 22.
    "Terms of Collection." [Plain] (13:2) Wint 93, p. 17.
    "Thurbers." [BellArk] (9:6) N-D 93, p. 11.
MO, Fei
        See ALSO MOI, Fei
4533. MOAN, Tamara
    "Tracks and Ties" (for my brother). [BambooR] (57) Wint 93, p. 174-175.
4534. MOBILIO, Albert
    "The Causes Tighten." [Talisman] (10) Spr 93, p. 117-118.
    "Talus Slope." [GrandS] (11:4, #44) 93, p. 78-79.

MOCK

330

4535. MOCK, Jeff
"Another Angel." [Crazy] (44) Spr 93, p. 54-56.
"First Year in Gettysburg." [Ascent] (17:3) Spr 93, p. 24.
"Glass." [HarvardR] (3) Wint 93, p. 76-77.
"Lazarus Envisions His Next Accident." [LaurelR] (27:2) Sum 93, p. 16-17.
"Lazarus Steals a Compact Car." [LaurelR] (27:2) Sum 93, p. 13-16.
"Lazarus Under the New Moon Dreaming." [LaurelR] (27:2) Sum 93, p. 12.
"The Presence of Absence." [BlackWR] (20:1) Fall-Wint 93, p. 85.
"Without You" (Danny Maitland, 1977-1993). [BlackWR] (20:1) Fall-Wint 93, p. 86-87.
4536. MODRCIN, Ines
"Fluorescent Sorrow" (tr. of Goran Tomcic, w. Tali Makell and the author). [PoetL] (88:1) Spr 93, p. 49.
"Here" (tr. of Goran Tomcic, w. Tali Makell and the author). [PoetL] (88:1) Spr 93, p. 50.
4537. MOE, Frederick
"Anthroposcopy." [Elf] (3:1) Spr 93, p. 38.
"For Dennis" (1951-1992). [ChangingM] (26) Sum-Fall 93, p. 13.
"In October." [Elf] (3:1) Spr 93, p. 39.
4538. MOE, Rita
"Homecoming." [NorthStoneR] (11) 93, p. 79.
"Malice." [NorthStoneR] (11) 93, p. 78.
4539. MOFFEIT, Tony
"Dreaming of Crazy Horse." [ChironR] (12:3, #36) Aut 93, p. 27.
"Indian Summer." [Amelia] (7:2, #21) 93, p. 106.
4540. MOFFET, Penelope
"Desert Woman." [Colum] (20) Sum 93, p. 97-98.
"Poem on Progress." [OnTheBus] (5:2, #12) Sum-Fall 93, p. 142.
4541. MOHAMMED, Rukia
"Images." [Eyeball] (2) 93, p. 15.
"Nduta." [Eyeball] (2) 93, p. 15.
4542. MOHR, Bill
"Asparagus." [OnTheBus] (5:2, #12) Sum-Fall 93, p. 143.
"Barely Holding Distant Things Apart." [Asylum] (8) 93, p. 18-40.
"Cro-Magnon." [AntR] (51:4) Fall 93, p. 560-561.
"It Is Difficult to Remember a Name in a Lanugage You Don't Speak" (— David Antin). [Pearl] (17) Spr 93, p. 97.
"Powdered Sugar." [Pearl] (17) Spr 93, p. 98.
"Waiting for the Paint to Dry." [Pearl] (19) Fall-Wint 93, p. 24.
4543. MOHRING, Ron
"The Culvert" (after Sharon Olds). [JamesWR] (10:3) Spr 93, p. 14.
4544. MOHYLYNY, Attila
"Night Melodies: A Cycle" (tr. by Michael Naydan). [Agni] (38) 93, p. 110-113.
4545. MOI, Fei
"Facing a Stone" (tr. by Jin Zhong and Stephen Haven). [AmerPoR] (22:6) N-D 93, p. 34.
"Falling Snow" (tr. by Jin Zhong and Stephen Haven). [AmerPoR] (22:6) N-D 93, p. 34.
"Instant" (tr. by Jin Zhong and Stephen Haven). [AmerPoR] (22:6) N-D 93, p. 34.
"Orchard" (tr. by Jin Zhong and Stephen Haven). [AmerPoR] (22:6) N-D 93, p. 34.
"That Stone" (tr. by Jin Zhong and Stephen Haven). [AmerPoR] (22:6) N-D 93, p. 34.
4546. MOISIO, Francesco
"Erano Passi." [Arshile] (2) 93, p. 52.
"Steps Were" (tr. by Jack Hirschman). [Arshile] (2) 93, p. 53.
4547. MOLDAW, Carol
"Chalkmarks on Stone." [NewRep] (209:11) 13 S 93, p. 40.
"From Assisi" (for J. O.). [NewRep] (208:6) 8 F 93, p. 38.
"In Memoriam: Franklin Walker III 1954-1988." [BostonR] (18:2) Mr-Ap 93, p. 23.
MOLEN, Robert vander
See VanderMOLEN, Robert
4548. MOLIERE
"Sganarelle, or The Imaginary Cuckold" (Comedy in 24 Scenes, 1660, tr. by Richard Wilbur). [GettyR] (6:2) Spr 93, p. 193-225.
4549. MÖLLER, Susann
"Marionette." [AmerPoR] (22:6) N-D 93, p. 32.

4550. MOLTON, Warren Lane
"If God Is a Diviner." [ChrC] (110:17) 19-26 My 93, p. 556.
4551. MOMOI, Beverly Acuff
"In the Tenth Mounth, There Are Flowers." [RiverS] (38) 93, p. 72-77.
4552. MONAGAN, George C.
"Uncle Jack." [Wind] (23:72) 93, p. 21.
4553. MONAHAN, Jean
"Gretel, Lost" (for John). [GrahamHR] (17) Fall 93, p. 39.
4554. MONROE, Melissa
"Odex — Scenarios for a Functionoid" (described in Asimov and Frenkel, *Robots*).
    [KenR] (NS 15:4) Fall 93, p. 87-88.
"Pandora" (described in *Into the Heart of the Mind* by Frank Rose). [KenR] (NS
    15:4) Fall 93, p. 88.
"R.M.I. 3" (The *New York Times*, March 18, 1987). [KenR] (NS 15:4) Fall 93, p. 89.
4555. MONTAGUE, John
"Foreign Field." [NewEngR] (15:1) Wint 93, p. 178-179.
4556. MONTALE, Eugenio
"The Arno at Rovezzano" (tr. by William Arrowsmith). [Pequod] (36) 93, p. 22.
"Götterdämmerung" (tr. by William Arrowsmith). [Pequod] (36) 93, p. 17.
"In Smoke" (tr. by William Arrowsmith). [Pequod] (36) 93, p. 18.
"Late at Night" (tr. by William Arrowsmith). [Pequod] (36) 93, p. 21.
"Men Who Turn Back" (tr. by William Arrowsmith). [Pequod] (36) 93, p. 23.
"Nothing Serious" (tr. by William Arrowsmith). [Pequod] (36) 93, p. 19.
"Time and Times" (tr. by William Arrowsmith). [Pequod] (36) 93, p. 20.
"Xenia" (1964-1966 — in memory of the poet's wife, tr. by Helen Barolini). [QRL]
    (12:32/33) 93, p. 474-475.
MONTERO, Luis García
    See GARCIA MONTERO, Luis
4557. MONTEZ, Susan
"Aubade in Modified Second Asclepiadean." [SoCoast] (15) Je 93, p. 26.
"The Catacombs." [ChatR] (13:4) Sum 93, p. 40.
"Illinois Fantasy." [NewYorkQ] (51) 93, p. 70.
"Last Poem of the Season." [CreamCR] (17:1) Spr 93, p. 31.
"Three Dreams: South Bronx." [HangL] (63) 93, p. 48.
"The Travel Industry." [13thMoon] (11:1/2) 93, p. 44.
4558. MONTGOMERY, M. S.
"The Golden Age of Gay Literature." [Art&Und] (2:3) Special Edition 93, p. 10.
4559. MONTGOMERY, Missy Marie
"Race Point." [PassN] (14:2) Wint 93, p. 29.
4560. MONTGOMERY, Nan
"Akhmatova." [RagMag] (11:2) 93, p. 61.
"Boabab Trees." [RagMag] (11:2) 93, p. 63.
"Sin." [RagMag] (11:2) 93, p. 62.
4561. MONTLLOR, Ovidi
"A Letter Home" (tr. by Adela Robles Salz). [Iowa] (23:2) Spr-Sum 93, p. 6-7.
4562. MOODY, Carla
"Fortunate." [Drumvoices] (2:1/2) Fall-Wint 92-93, p. 201-202.
"A Short Poem." [Drumvoices] (2:1/2) Fall-Wint 92-93, p. 202.
4563. MOODY, Shirley
"Milton's Daughters." [Crucible] (29) Fall 93, p. 27-28.
4564. MOOERS, Vernon
"Fenway Park." [TickleAce] (23) Spr-Sum 92, p. 90-91.
"Night Sounds of Cave Creatures." [AntigR] (93-94) Spr-Sum 93, p. 194-197.
4565. MOOLTEN, David
"The Airman's Father." [TampaR] (6) Spr 93, p. 44.
"Bio 7." [SouthernR] (29:1) Wint, Ja 93, p. 165-167.
"The Brother I Never Had." [SouthernR] (29:1) Wint, Ja 93, p. 167-168.
"'Cuda." [KenR] (NS 15:4) Fall 93, p. 69-71.
"The Enlightenment." [Boulevard] (8:1, #22) Spr 93, p. 194-195.
"Having Come This Way." [IndR] (16:1) Spr 93, p. 130.
"Losing It." [Shen] (43:2) Sum 93, p. 60-61.
"Omission." [SouthernR] (29:1) Wint, Ja 93, p. 164-165.
"Precision Bomb Run, Tkyo, 1945." [Shen] (43:2) Sum 93, p. 62-63.
"Rescue." [TampaR] (6) Spr 93, p. 42-43.
4566. MOON, Duk-soo
"Line Sketch" (No. 2, No. 3., tr. by Chang Soo Ko). [Vis] (43) 93, p. 33.

4567. MOON, Janell
"Going Fishing." [Art&Und] (2:4) O-N 93, p. 14.
4568. MOORE, Barbara
"Too Much." [HiramPoR] (53/54) Fall 92-Sum 93, p. 59-60.
4569. MOORE, Cynthia
"The Clearing" (for Tom). [PoetL] (88:4) Wint 93-94, p. 35-36.
4570. MOORE, Dalian
"Colombian Priestess" (Winner Marguerette Cummins Broadside Award). [Amelia] (7:2, #21) 93, broadside supplment.
4571. MOORE, George B.
"New Year." [InterPR] (19:1) Spr 93, p. 75-76.
"Totem." [InterPR] (19:1) Spr 93, p. 77-78.
4572. MOORE, Honor
"Bucharest, 1989." [ParisR] (35:128) Fall 93, p. 142-143.
4573. MOORE, Lenard D.
"Collards." [Agni] (37) 93, p. 113.
"Land Changes." [AfAmRev] (27:1) Spr 93, p. 152.
"Message to Etheridge Knight." [PaintedB] (50/51) 93, p. 23.
"Root Song" (for Eugene B. Redmond). [Eyeball] (2) 93, p. 47.
4574. MOORE, Marian H.
"The Lesson" (tr. of Celso Emilio Ferreiro). [Vis] (43) 93, p. 22.
"Sweet Autumn" (tr. of Celso Emilio Ferreiro). [Vis] (43) 93, p. 21.
4575. MOORE, Marianne
"By Disposition of Angels." [QRL] (12:32/33) 93, p. 475-476.
"Voracities and Verities Sometimes Are Interacting." [QRL] (12:32/33) 93, p. 476.
"What Are Years?" (illustrated by Claire Heimarck). [MassR] (34:2) Sum 93, p. 248-249.
4576. MOORE, Mary (Mary Barbara)
"Dean, Keeping Bees in Kentucky." [PraS] (67:3) Fall 93, p. 159-160.
"Fontanel." [Poetry] (163:3) D 93, p. 136.
"Like a Great Wind" (Honorable Mention, Poetry Award). [NewL] (59:2) 93, p. 41.
"Parachute" (Honorable Mention, Poetry Award). [NewL] (59:2) 93, p. 39-40.
"Sebastopol." [PraS] (67:3) Fall 93, p. 159.
4577. MOORE, Miles David
"Fatslug and the Bumperstickers." [Bogg] (66) Wint 92-93, p. 8.
"William McGonagall Meets Ogden Nash in Heaven." [Light] (5) Spr 93, p. 27-28.
4578. MOORE, Richard
"April Is the Cruelest Month." [Sparrow] (60) Sum 93, p. 43.
"Christmas Day." [SewanR] (101:2) Ap-Je, Spr 93, p. 150.
"The Cinder." [Agni] (37) 93, p. 302-303.
"Cosi Fan Tutte." [Light] (8) Wint 93, p. 18.
"The Devaluation." [Light] (5) Spr 93, p. 3.
"Elocution Lesson." [Light] (5) Spr 93, p. 3.
"Enfin" (After "Troilus and Criseyde," Book III, lines 1-49). [Hellas] (4:2) Fall 93, p. 44-45.
"For a Feminist." [Light] (5) Spr 93, p. 3.
"The Helicopter." [Light] (5) Spr 93, p. 5.
"Lassitude" (tr. of Paul Verlaine). [SewanR] (101:4) O-D, Fall 93, p. 562.
"Marital Nirvana." [Light] (5) Spr 93, p. 6.
"The Mirror." [SewanR] (101:2) Ap-Je, Spr 93, p. 149.
"The Mouse Whole: An Epic" (Selection: "The Mouse's Wedding"). [Light] (5) Spr 93, p. 4.
"On Cooking a Gourmet Dinner." [Light] (7) Aut 93, p. 8.
"On Receiving a Contract to Translate *The Iliad*." [Light] (5) Spr 93, p. 6.
"On Saving Art, Beauty, Spirit, Etc." (A Voice from the Curia). [Light] (5) Spr 93, p. 6.
"Out of It." [Light] (5) Spr 93, p. 6.
"Overheard at a Feminist Conference." [Light] (5) Spr 93, p. 6.
"Personal Ad." [Light] (5) Spr 93, p. 6.
"The Poet Finds Himself." [Light] (5) Spr 93, p. 5.
"Talk." [Light] (5) Spr 93, p. 3.
"Technology Transcendent." [Light] (8) Wint 93, p. 8.
"The Universality of Experience." [Light] (5) Spr 93, p. 6.
"The Vulgar Materialist." [Light] (8) Wint 93, p. 17.
"When the Muse Is Absent." [Light] (5) Spr 93, p. 6.
"Words of Experience." [Light] (5) Spr 93, p. 6.

4579. MOORE, Roger
"Daffodils" (For my mother). [PottPort] (15:1) Spr-Sum 93, p. 27.
"Portrait of My Father the Last Day I Saw Him Alive in the Nursing Home."
[PottPort] (15:1) Spr-Sum 93, p. 28.
4580. MOORE, Rosalie
"Moving, by Roads Moved." [QRL] (12:32/33) 93, p. 476-477.
"Parade with Piccolos." [QRL] (12:32/33) 93, p. 477.
4581. MOORE, Todd
"6 Year Old." [ChironR] (12:1, #34) Spr 93, p. 3.
"Besides the Money." [ChironR] (12:1, #34) Spr 93, p. 3.
"Blood & Dreams" (Selections). [SpoonR] (18:1) Wint-Spr 93, p. 59-65.
"The First Thing." [Pearl] (19) Fall-Wint 93, p. 57.
"The First Time." [ChironR] (12:1, #34) Spr 93, p. 3.
"Harry Was." [SlipS] (13) 93, p. 62.
"I Bought the." [Pearl] (17) Spr 93, p. 70.
"I Didn't Know." [Pearl] (19) Fall-Wint 93, p. 57.
"I Took a." [SlipS] (13) 93, p. 63.
"I've Never Told." [ChironR] (12:1, #34) Spr 93, p. 3.
"Macklin Was." [Pearl] (17) Spr 93, p. 70.
"Miller & I Were." [ChironR] (12:4/13:1, #37/38) Wint 93-Spr 94, p. 46.
"Mud, Sky, Stars, Wind" (based loosely on the Mormon journal of William Marks).
[SpoonR] (18:1) Wint-Spr 93, p. 66-73.
"Sometimes." [ChironR] (12:1, #34) Spr 93, p. 3.
"Those Times I." [OnTheBus] (5:2, #12) Sum-Fall 93, p. 144.
"The Whole Idea." [ChironR] (12:1, #34) Spr 93, p. 3.
4582. MOORE, Val
"Grass Roots." [SoCoast] (15) Je 93, p. 43.
4583. MOORHEAD, Andrea
"Below Orford." [Os] (36) Spr 93, p. 19.
"Body without Light." [Os] (36) Spr 93, p. 21.
"The Flowers in Sinsheim." [Os] (37) Wint 93, p. 29-33.
"Night Brings Its Own Sadness." [Os] (36) Spr 93, p. 18.
"Only Aachen." [Os] (36) Spr 93, p. 16.
4584. MORA, Pat
" Cuentista: Story Teller." [Footwork] (23) 93, p. 1.
"Sueño de Miel." [ColR] (20:2) Fall 93, p. 77-78.
"Woman and Tree." [Footwork] (23) 93, p. 1.
4585. MORAES, Vinicius de
"Soneto ao Inverno." [InterPR] (19:2) Fall 93, p. 30.
"Soneto de Londres." [InterPR] (19:2) Fall 93, p. 32.
"Sonnet from London" (tr. by Thomas Dorsett and Moyses Purisch). [InterPR]
(19:2) Fall 93, p. 33.
"Sonnet to Winter" (tr. by Thomas Dorsett and Moyses Purisch). [InterPR] (19:2)
Fall 93, p. 31.
4586. MORAMARCO, Fred
"The Picture I Didn't Take" (for Stephen). [Pearl] (17) Spr 93, p. 99.
4587. MORAN, Ronald
"Double Imaging." [ChironR] (12:1, #34) Spr 93, p. 23.
"Homecomings." [SnailPR] (3:1) Fall-Wint 93, p. 11.
"Set Apart from the World." [Northeast] (5:9) Wint 93-94, p. 23.
4588. MORAN, Sandra
"Lady Dorrance." [NewYorkQ] (52) 93, p. 83.
4589. MORCHELES, Barbara Wind
"The Room at Gedney Farm." [Footwork] (23) 93, p. 58.
4590. MOREA, J. M.
"The Unfolding Eye." [EvergreenC] (8:2) Sum-Fall 93, p. 71-72.
4591. MOREHEAD, Jamie O.
"Introduction: How to Get Your Wings." [HiramPoR] (53/54) Fall 92-Sum 93, p.
109.
4592. MOREJON, Nancy
"Elegia a Maurice Bishop." [Drumvoices] (3:1/2) Fall-Wint 93-94, p. 77-79.
"Elegy for Maurice Bishop" (tr. by Lisa Davis). [Drumvoices] (3:1/2) Fall-Wint 93 -
94, p. 79-81.
"The Nightingale and Death" (tr. by Lisa Davis). [Drumvoices] (3:1/2) Fall-Wint
93-94, p. 76-77.
"El Ruiseñor y la Muerte." [Drumvoices] (3:1/2) Fall-Wint 93-94, p. 76.

MOREJON

334

"A Simple Truth" (from a construction worker, my friend, tr. by Lisa Davis).
    [Drumvoices] (3:1/2) Fall-Wint 93-94, p. 82.
"Simple Verdad" (de un constructor amigo). [Drumvoices] (3:1/2) Fall-Wint 93-94,
    p. 82.
4593. MORELAND, Jane
    "Into the Night." [BelPoJ] (44:2) Wint 93-94, p. 30.
4594. MORELLI, Jenny
    "Abingdon Square." [GrandS] (12:3, #47) Fall 93, p. 126-127.
4595. MORENO, Cristina
    "I lived in a time of revolution at 18" (Poets of High School Age). [HangL] (62) 93,
        p. 84.
    "Take me down to the MEXICAN moon" (Poets of High School Age). [HangL] (62)
        93, p. 82-83.
4596. MORENO, Gean
    "Gonzalo Arango." [Americas] (21:1) Spr 93, p. 66-67.
    "Hole Digger." [TampaR] (7) Fall 93, p. 12-13.
    "Hunting Horn." [GreenMR] (NS 6:1) Wint-Spr 93, p. 26-27.
    "The Painter Pedro Moreno." [Americas] (21:1) Spr 93, p. 68.
    "Reinaldo Arenas." [Americas] (21:1) Spr 93, p. 62-63.
    "Second-Hand." [GreenMR] (NS 6:1) Wint-Spr 93, p. 24.
    "A Visit." [GreenMR] (NS 6:1) Wint-Spr 93, p. 25.
    "Years of Apocalypse" (after the paintings of Humberto Calzada). [Americas] (21:1)
        Spr 93, p. 64-65.
4597. MORGAN, Bill
    "As Eyesight in Darkness." [PikeF] (11) Fall 93, p. 35.
4598. MORGAN, Elizabeth Seydel
    "Moon Arrangement." [PassN] (14:2) Wint 93, p. 17.
    "Unarmed." [SouthernR] (29:4) Aut, O 93, p. 755.
    "Valdosta." [SouthernR] (29:4) Aut, O 93, p. 754.
4599. MORGAN, Frederick
    "Breathing Space." [SewanR] (101:3) Jl-S, Sum 93, p. 337-338.
    "The Sign." [AmerS] (62:2) Spr 93, p. 210-212.
4600. MORGAN, John
    "The Wedge." [QRL] (12:32/33) 93, p. 250-257.
4601. MORGAN, Robert
    "Husk and Germ." [VirQR] (69:2) Spr 93, p. 253.
    "Music of the Spheres." [Poetry] (163:1) O 93, p. 16.
    "P." [Poetry] (161:4) Ja 93, p. 204.
    "Scarifying." [Atlantic] (271:6) Je 93, p. 61.
    "Sour Acres." [Shen] (43:3) Fall 93, p. 98.
    "The Strange Attractor." [Shen] (43:3) Fall 93, p. 99.
    "Wild Peavines." [Atlantic] (272:2) Ag 93, p. 81.
4602. MORI, Kyoko
    "For My Youngest Aunt." [PassN] (14:2) Wint 93, p. 35-36.
    "Four Scenes with the Sea: Love and Solitude." [PassN] (14:2) Wint 93, p. 37-39.
    "Landscape: January 1991." [Footwork] (23) 93, p. 13.
4603. MORIARTY, Michael
    "Chamber Music." [NewYorkQ] (51) 93, p. 43-44.
    "Chamber Music." [NewYorkQ] (52) 93, p. 38-39.
    "While Waiting to Audition for the Role of Ben Stone in Law and Order."
        [NewYorkQ] (50) 93, p. 40.
4604. MÖRIKE, Eduard
    "The Jilted Maiden" (tr. by Charles Kohler). [Stand] (34:3) Sum 93, p. 67.
4605. MORIMOTO, Etsuko
    "Her cherry red lips" (Lucille Sandberg Haiku Award, 1st place). [Amelia] (7:2,
        #21) 93, p. 10.
4606. MORIN, SkyBlue
    "Big Medicine Sacred White Buffalo." [PraS] (67:4) Wint 93, p. 107-108.
    "White Buffalo Calf Woman's Spirit." [PraS] (67:4) Wint 93, p. 106-107.
4607. MORISSEAU-LEROY, Felix
    "The Cross" (from "Diacoute," tr. by Suze Baron). [NewYorkQ] (51) 93, p. 76-77.
    "Diacoute" (Excerpt). [NewYorkQ] (51) 93, p. 75.
4608. MORITZ, A. F.
    "Catalpa in Flower." [SouthwR] (78:2) Spr 93, p. 214.
    "Founders." [PartR] (60:3) Sum 93, p. 431-432.
    "In the Desert." [Hudson] (45:4) Wint 93, p. 619.

"Untreated Condition." [Comm] (120:4) 26 F 93, p. 12.
4609. MORITZ, Dennis
    "We honor our love in the breach." [PaintedB] (50/51) 93, p. 96.
4610. MORLEY, David
    "Mosquito." [Stand] (35:1) Wint 93-94, p. 30-34.
    "What You Do and What You Say." [Verse] (10:1) Spr 93, p. 54-55.
4611. MORLEY, Marjorie (Marjorie Se Dora)
    "Beyond the Casinos" (for the RAM). [BellArk] (9:1) Ja-F 93, p. 23.
    "Grandmother: An Interior Dialogue." [BellArk] (9:3) My-Je 93, p. 8.
    "An Hour with Longfellow." [BellArk] (9:1) Ja-F 93, p. 23.
4612. MORPHEW, Melissa
    "In the Moonlight." [Poem] (69) My 93, p. 17.
    "Sitting Up with Thomas (Aged 2)." [Poem] (69) My 93, p. 18.
4613. MORRILL, Ann
    "Each Sound a Bird." [RagMag] (11:2) 93, p. 94.
    "Shadow Dancing" (Dominican Republic, 1988). [RagMag] (11:2) 93, p. 93.
4614. MORRILL, Donald
    "Blue Star Home." [SouthernR] (29:4) Aut, O 93, p. 756.
    "The Travertines." [ApalQ] (38) 92, p. 59.
4615. MORRIS, Bernard E.
    "57. It isn't war you fear so much as peace." [Plain] (13:3) Spr 93, p. 13.
    "Deciduous." [CinPR] (24) Spr 93, p. 46-47.
    "I Turn to You Unfaithful." [Plain] (13:2) Wint 93, p. 12.
4616. MORRIS, Cecil (Cecil W.)
    "Adult Swimming at Johnson Pool." [HampSPR] Wint 93, p. 30.
    "Down to the Creek." [HiramPoR] (53/54) Fall 92-Sum 93, p. 61-62.
    "Longing for Summer." [EngJ] (82:4) Ap 93, p. 97.
    "Loving Like the Water." [Poem] (69) My 93, p. 16.
    "Signs." [HampSPR] Wint 93, p. 31-32.
    "Teaching Dreams." [EngJ] (82:5) S 93, p. 104.
    "To Tell the Truth." [Poem] (69) My 93, p. 15.
    "The Treasure in Books." [HampSPR] Wint 93, p. 31.
4617. MORRIS, Daniel
    "Poem Written in the Logic of Late Capitalism." [Agni] (37) 93, p. 286.
4618. MORRIS, David
    "Willie and I Discuss Myths of Sacrifice." [ApalQ] (36/37) 91, p. 75.
4619. MORRIS, Herbert
    "The Neighbor's Son." [QRL] (12:32/33) 93, p. 478-479.
    "Now the Fitzgerald Brothers Growing Older" (for Lynn Sharon Schwartz). [Salm]
        (100) Fall 93, p. 150-159.
    "One Hundred Versions of the Peaceable Kingdom" (Edward Hicks painted the
        Peaceable Kingdom over one hundred times). [Salm] (97) Wint 93, p. 104-
        109.
    "Painting Elena Passacantando's Door." [Crazy] (45) Wint 93, p. 73-81.
    "Truffaut." [Crazy] (45) Wint 93, p. 64-72.
4620. MORRIS, Paul
    "The Magic Flute." [Sonora] (26) Fall 93, p. 63-64.
4621. MORRIS, Peter
    "The Fatherland." [ChironR] (12:1, #34) Spr 93, p. 24.
    "Flaws of the Flawless" (Special Section: 21 poems). [WormR] (33:1, #129) 93, p.
        25-34.
    "I Was Gullible." [ChironR] (12:1, #34) Spr 93, p. 24.
    "Stingers." [ChironR] (12:1, #34) Spr 93, p. 24.
4622. MORRISON, Danny
    "Reflections." [SenR] (23:1/2) Wint 93, p. 172-173.
4623. MORRISON, Kathi
    "Playing with Tar." [NewYorkQ] (52) 93, p. 84.
4624. MORRISON, R. H.
    "Basic Operations" (tr. of Joaquin Antonio Peñalosa). [AntigR] (95) Aut 93, p. 91.
    "Blind from Birth" (tr. of Joaquin Antonio Peñalosa). [AntigR] (95) Aut 93, p. 81.
    "The Cathedral" (tr. of Joaquin Antonio Peñalosa). [AntigR] (95) Aut 93, p. 89.
    "Farewell to the Sea." [SouthernR] (29:1) Wint, Ja 93, p. 178.
    "The Housing Problem" (tr. of Joaquin Antonio Peñalosa). [AntigR] (95) Aut 93, p.
        83.
    "The Mirror." [Hellas] (4:2) Fall 93, p. 13.

"Problems of Botany" (tr. of Joaquin Antonio Peñalosa). [AntigR] (95) Aut 93, p. 85.
"Sagesse" (Selections: 4 poems, tr. of Paul Verlaine). [AntigR] (93-94) Spr-Sum 93, p. 120-129.
"The Tattooed Cities" (tr. of Joaquin Antonio Peñalosa). [AntigR] (95) Aut 93, p. 87.
4625. MORRISON, Richard
"The Accident." [Vis] (42) 93, p. 27.
4626. MORRO, Henry J.
"Cousin." [ChironR] (12:1, #34) Spr 93, p. 31.
"Growing Up Short." [ChironR] (12:1, #34) Spr 93, p. 31.
"Nudist Camps & Queers, 1964." [ChironR] (12:1, #34) Spr 93, p. 31.
4627. MORSE, Michael
"Ave Maria." [Iowa] (23:2) Spr-Sum 93, p. 105-106.
"Kinglet Banding." [AntR] (51:4) Fall 93, p. 558.
"Untitled: That a body might sag with many weights." [Iowa] (23:2) Spr-Sum 93, p. 104.
4628. MORTAL, Anna
"Rite of Passage." [13thMoon] (12:1/2) 93-94, p. 45.
4629. MORTIMER, Henry L., Jr.
"Patchwork." [WestB] (33) 93, p. 44-45.
"Poem for Wendell." [WestB] (33) 93, p. 45.
4630. MORTIMER, Peter
"Dying to Shout." [Stand] (34:2) Spr 93, p. 10-11.
4631. MORTON, Colin
"At a Nameless Bend in the River." [MalR] (105) Wint 93, p. 24-25.
4632. MORTON, Colleen
"Approximate." [YellowS] (42) Wint-Spr 93, p. 29.
"Belief." [SycamoreR] (5:1) Wint 93, p. 66-67.
"Her Ecstasy." [YellowS] (42) Wint-Spr 93, p. 29.
"Poem for the Dead Mother." [YellowS] (42) Wint-Spr 93, p. 29.
4633. MORTON, Leith
"Near Kitami Station on the Odakyu Line" (tr. of Hiromi Ito). [Sulfur] (32) Spr 93, p. 214-216.
"Snow" (tr. of Hiromi Ito). [Sulfur] (32) Spr 93, p. 213-214.
"The Touched, Loonies, Full Moon" (tr. of Shiraishi Kazuko). [ChiR] (39:3/4) 93, p. 206-210.
"Vinegar and Oil" (tr. of Hiromi Ito). [Sulfur] (32) Spr 93, p. 216-219.
4634. MOSES, Daniel David
"Ballad About Light in Winter." [PoetryC] (14:1) 93, p. 4.
"Blues Around a Barn." [Arc] (30) Spr 93, p. 25.
"Last Blues" (23 October 1990). [Arc] (30) Spr 93, p. 26-27.
"May Blues." [Arc] (30) Spr 93, p. 28.
"Shine." [Arc] (30) Spr 93, p. 29.
"The Solstice Blues." [PoetryC] (14:1) 93, p. 4.
"A Song Among Beds." [PoetryC] (14:1) 93, p. 4.
4635. MOSS, Donald Jordan
"Marvel® Wonder." [EvergreenC] (8:1) Spr-Sum 93, p. 9.
4636. MOSS, Howard
"Gulls." [QRL] (12:32/33) 93, p. 479-480.
4637. MOSS, Jacqueline
"Bitter Cup." [Pearl] (17) Spr 93, p. 61.
4638. MOSS, Melissa Iris
"New Moon." [Kalliope] (15:3) 93, p. 32-33.
4639. MOSS, Stanley
"Masque for Paul Celan." [Pequod] (35) 93, p. 105-106.
"On Hearing Celan's Son Is an Aerialist Not a Juggler." [Pequod] (35) 93, p. 108.
"On Hearing Paul Celan's Son Is a Juggler." [Pequod] (35) 93, p. 107.
"Widow." [Pequod] (35) 93, p. 109.
4640. MOSS, Thylias
"Beanstalk Dreams." [RiverS] (38) 93, p. 62-63.
"First Storm Warning of the Season." [Nat] (257:5) 9-16 Ag 93, p. 187.
"Games." [ColR] (20:1) Spr 93, p. 74-76.
"Heads." [MichQR] (32:3) Sum 93, p. 406-407.
"Holding." [Callaloo] (16:1) Wint 93, p. 18-19.
"In the Pit of Crinoline Ruffles." [Nat] (257:17) 22 N 93, p. 630.

337

MOSS

"The Lighter Side of Shadows of Monsters." [Nat] (257:17) 22 N 93, p. 630.
"Mission" (for Jill). [MichQR] (32:3) Sum 93, p. 404-405.
"One Year Sonny Stabs Himself." [Callaloo] (16:1) Wint 93, p. 22.
"Remembering Kitchens." [Callaloo] (16:1) Wint 93, p. 20-21.
"Renegade Angels." [ColR] (20:2) Fall 93, p. 130-131.
4641. MOSSMAN, James K.
"South Shore Summer." [AntigR] (92) Wint 93, p. 136-137.
4642. MOTT, Michael
"Autumn, Odysseus." [TarRP] (33:1) Fall 93, p. 59.
"Byron at Missolonghi." [SewanR] (101:3) Jl-S, Sum 93, p. 339.
"Hamlet." [SewanR] (101:4) O-D, Fall 93, p. 520.
"Taino." [Stand] (34:4) Aut 93, p. 34-36.
MOTT, Robert de
See DeMOTT, Robert
4643. MOURÉ, Erin
"Corrections to the Saints: Transubstantial." [Arc] (31) Aut 93, p. 56.
"A Glass Look Over a High Hill." [Arc] (31) Aut 93, p. 27-28.
"Halls." [Arc] (31) Aut 93, p. 18-26.
"The Purposes of Skin." [Arc] (31) Aut 93, p. 29-33.
4644. MOUSA, Munif
"Beirut" (in Arabic and English, tr. by Elias G. Abu-Saba). [InterPR] (19:1) Spr 93, p. 20-21.
"Lamentation" (in Arabic and English, tr. by Elias G. Abu-Saba). [InterPR] (19:1) Spr 93, p. 22-25.
4645. MOXLEY, Jennifer
"Untitled: You drew me under yards of bad luck." [13thMoon] (12:1/2) 93-94, p. 46.
4646. MOYLAN, Chris
"The Blessed." [ProseP] (2) 93, p. 68.
4647. MOYLES, Lois
"Exams." [NewYorker] (69:31) 27 S 93, p. 58.
MU, Tu
See TU, Mu
MU, Yang
See YANG, Mu
4648. MUELLER, Jenny
"Allegory." [ColR] (20:1) Spr 93, p. 32-33.
"The Plaintiffs." [ColR] (20:1) Spr 93, p. 30-31.
4649. MUELLER, John
"The Gate" (Tell Notiz, Part I: Excerpts). [PoetryUSA] (25/26) 93, p. 17, 18.
4650. MUELLER, Lavonne
"Colette's Cat." [ApalQ] (39) 93, p. 34-35.
4651. MUELLER, Lisel
"Happy and Unhappy Families" (I-II). [PoetryNW] (34:4) Wint 93-94, p. 40-41.
"Heartland." [Poetry] (163:2) N 93, p. 79.
4652. MUKS, Roberts
"1,980th Christmas" (tr. by Guna Kupcs Chaberek). [GrahamHR] (17) Fall 93, p. 42.
"Bakchum." [Lactuca] (17) Apr 93, p. 34.
"A Brief Meeting" (tr. by Guna Kupcs Chaberek). [Lactuca] (17) Apr 93, p. 36.
"Issavienojums." [Lactuca] (17) Apr 93, p. 36.
"Ka Parlekt Savai Enai." [Lactuca] (17) Apr 93, p. 37.
"Leaping Over My Shadow" (tr. by Guna Kupcs Chaberek). [Lactuca] (17) Apr 93, p. 37.
"More About Crocodiles" (tr. by Guna Kupcs Chaberek). [Lactuca] (17) Apr 93, p. 35.
"Reflecting" (tr. by Guna Kupcs Chaberek and Ed Chaberek). [GrahamHR] (17) Fall 93, p. 43.
"To Bakchus" (tr. by Guna Kupcs Chaberek). [Lactuca] (17) Apr 93, p. 34.
"Vel par Krokodiliem." [Lactuca] (17) Apr 93, p. 35.
4653. MULDER, Tiny
"Conversation" (tr. by Henry Baron). [Vis] (43) 93, p. 20.
"Words" (tr. by Henry Baron). [Vis] (43) 93, p. 20.
4654. MULDOON, Paul
"Cows" (for Dermot Seymour). [Ploughs] (19:4) Wint 93-94, p. 159-161.
4655. MULHERN, Maureen
"Lava." [Poetry] (162:2) My 93, p. 90.

"Sleep as Travel." [PraS] (67:3) Fall 93, p. 139.
"The Visitor." [PraS] (67:3) Fall 93, p. 138-139.
4656. MULKERN, Terence
"Naturalist's Notes." [PoetryNW] (34:1) Spr 93, p. 37-39.
4657. MULKEY, Richard
"*Mijikayo" (*A Japanese term for the short nights of late spring and early
    summer). [HolCrit] (30:5) D 93, p. 16.
4658. MULLEN, Harryette
"Muse & Drudge" (Selections: 1-6). [Agni] (37) 93, p. 58-63.
4659. MULLEN, Jack
"The American Name." [WestHR] (47:2) Sum 93, p. 138-139.
"The Beard." [WestHR] (47:2) Sum 93, p. 140-141.
"Couple Touring Black Places." [WestHR] (47:2) Sum 93, p. 136-137.
4660. MULLEN, Laura
"The Castle." [Agni] (37) 93, p. 17-18.
"The French Lesson." [ColR] (20:1) Spr 93, p. 28-29.
"House." [Agni] (37) 93, p. 19-26.
"House." [AmerLC] (5) 93, p. 18.
"House-Hunting." [SycamoreR] (5:2) Sum 93, p. 52-53.
"Memorial." [SycamoreR] (5:2) Sum 93, p. 56.
"A Retelling." [AmerLC] (5) 93, p. 19-21.
"A Series of Failures So That I'm Sick of the Word." [SycamoreR] (5:2) Sum 93, p.
    54-55.
"Structures." [AmerLC] (5) 93, p. 21-24.
"Two Novels." [SycamoreR] (5:2) Sum 93, p. 50-51.
"The Visible World." [BlackWR] (19:2) Spr-Sum 93, p. 107-108.
4661. MULLIGAN, J. B.
"The Universe Next Door." [Parting] (6:2) Wint 93, p. 23.
4662. MULLINS, Brighde
"At the Lakehouse." [ColR] (20:1) Spr 93, p. 77-79.
"Idle Aria in Battery Park." [Chelsea] (55) 93, p. 61.
"Sand Lake." [Chelsea] (55) 93, p. 60.
4663. MULLINS, Terence Y.
"First Person Singular." [ChrC] (110:15) 5 My 93, p. 488.
4664. MULRANE, Scott
"The Grand Entrance." [Sequoia] (34/35) 92-93, p. 23.
4665. MUNDO LOPEZ, Hilda
"Poemas: a Alba Díaz." [Trasimagen] (1:1) Otoño-Invierno 93, p. 32-33.
4666. MUNK, Robert L.
"Charlie's One-eyed Loiter." [Eyeball] (2) 93, p. 39.
4667. MUÑOZ, Charles
"Fifth Symphony." [CreamCR] (17:1) Spr 93, p. 16.
"For Edward Abbey." [CreamCR] (17:1) Spr 93, p. 18-19.
"Journey." [CreamCR] (17:2) Fall 93, p. 126-129.
"A Photograph of Buchenwald." [CreamCR] (17:1) Spr 93, p. 17.
"Wet Basement: an Elegy." [LitR] (36:2) Wint 93, p. 173.
4668. MUNRO, Jane (Jane Southwell)
"Dream Tiger." [CapilR] (2:11) Sum 93, p. 61-63.
"Fishing Sonnet." [CapilR] (2:11) Sum 93, p. 59-60.
"Grief Notes & Animal Dreams." [Event] (22:2) Sum 93, p. 45-47.
"Helicopter by the Lake." [CapilR] (2:11) Sum 93, p. 55-56.
"It's in the Kitchen." [CapilR] (2:11) Sum 93, p. 57-58.
"Romance." [CapilR] (2:11) Sum 93, p. 54.
"Salt Woman." [CanLit] (137) Sum 93, p. 61.
"The Wake After Maxie's Funeral." [Quarry] (42:3) 93, p. 82.
"Wanting." [Event] (22:2) Sum 93, p. 48-49.
"Washday." [CanLit] (137) Sum 93, p. 62.
4669. MUNRO, Peter
"Divorce." [SouthernPR] (33:1) Spr 93, p. 30-31.
4670. MURA, David
"Gardens We Have Left." [GreenMR] (NS 6:1) Wint-Spr 93, p. 145-153.
"Issei Strawberry." [RiverS] (39) 93, p. 45.
4671. MURANAKA, Daryl
"The Japanese: a Prose Poem." [HawaiiR] (17:1, #37) Spr 93, p. 14.
4672. MURAWSKI, Elisabeth (Elisabeth A.)
"Alex Walking." [HolCrit] (30:3) Je 93, p. 14.

"The Arrival of Grace" (Robert Penn Warren Poetry Prize Winner, Third Prize).
    [CumbPR]] (13:1) Fall 93, p. 6-7.
"A Declaration." [PoetryNW] (34:4) Wint 93-94, p. 26.
"Driving on Empty." [PoetryNW] (34:1) Spr 93, p. 33-35.
"Por Nada." [ChrC] (110:35) 8 D 93, p. 1231.
MURONG, Xi
    See XI, Murong
4673. MURPHY, Carol Darnell
    "For Milton's Granddaughters." [PraS] (67:1) Spr 93, p. 82.
4674. MURPHY, Erin
    "All's Hollow." [Field] (49) Fall 93, p. 71.
    "Descartes's Lover." [Field] (49) Fall 93, p. 72-74.
4675. MURPHY, J. K.
    "The Flag." [Verse] (10:1) Spr 93, p. 4.
    "Full Cycle." [Verse] (10:1) Spr 93, p. 4.
4676. MURPHY, Kay
    "Snapshots from the Border." [WillowR] (20) Spr 93, p. 28-31.
    "The Trucker's Head Music." [LouisL] (10:1) Spr 93, p. 15-16.
4677. MURPHY, Maureen
    "Still Life with Muscovy Ducks." [WebR] (17) Fall 93, p. 124.
4678. MURPHY, Patricia
    "The Tumor." [Iowa] (23:3) Fall 93, p. 137.
4679. MURPHY, Peter E.
    "The Formality." [BelPoJ] (44:2) Wint 93-94, p. 12-13.
    "Leaving Atlantic City." [JINJPo] (15:2) Aut 93, p. 35.
4680. MURPHY, Rich
    "Clocksville." [InterPR] (19:2) Fall 93, p. 75.
    "The Office Supply." [InterPR] (19:2) Fall 93, p. 76.
4681. MURPHY, S. Michelle
    "Girl in a Fish Bowl." [ProseP] (2) 93, p. 70.
    "Knowing the Place." [ProseP] (2) 93, p. 69.
4682. MURPHY, Sheila E.
    "Accrue a manifest St. Jude thing." [Avec] (6:1) 93, p. 45.
    "And the creased mechanics of detritus." [Talisman] (11) Fall 93, p. 230.
    "Between Mountains." [Talisman] (11) Fall 93, p. 229.
    "Blueprint." [HeavenB] (10) Wint-Spr 93, p. 69.
    "Every Future Climb." [WindO] (57) Fall 93, p. 34.
    "First Impression." [HeavenB] (10) Wint-Spr 93, p. 69.
    "Heal Protocol." [Talisman] (10) Spr 93, p. 90.
    "Heavens uploaded seem to chaperone the monsters." [Avec] (6:1) 93, p. 43.
    "I rinse you in what's mine." [Talisman] (11) Fall 93, p. 230.
    "I Walk." [Talisman] (10) Spr 93, p. 90.
    "Innocent Bystanders." [13thMoon] (11:1/2) 93, p. 45.
    "Red Poppy — O'Keeffe, 1927." [Talisman] (11) Fall 93, p. 230.
    "Self Portrait." [13thMoon] (11:1/2) 93, p. 45.
    "Squaw Peak in Sepia." [HeavenB] (10) Wint-Spr 93, p. 69.
    "Thank you for pinstripe (cozy place to sit and wield my pen." [Avec] (6:1) 93, p.
        44.
    "Things to Read." [ChironR] (12:4/13:1, #37/38) Wint 93-Spr 94, p. 46.
    "Uncompass." [Talisman] (10) Spr 93, p. 90.
4683. MURPHY, Susan
    "Elegy for Laverne." [Prima] (16/17) 93, p. 65.
4684. MURRAY, G. E.
    "Art of a Cold Sun." [SewanR] (101:2) Ap-Je, Spr 93, p. 151.
    "Hide & Seek" (Adventures in the Art Trade). [Ascent] (18:1) Fall 93, p. 42-43.
    "Nudes & Interiors" (I-II). [IllinoisR] (1:1) Fall 93, p. 52.
    "True Stories about Color." [SewanR] (101:2) Ap-Je, Spr 93, p. 152.
4685. MURRAY, Joan
    "Epithalamium." [PraS] (67:1) Spr 93, p. 75-78.
4686. MURRAY, Les
    "Dead Trees in the Dam." [Verse] (10:1) Spr 93, p. 3.
    "Kimberley Brief." [PartR] (60:1) Wint 93, p. 103-107.
    "Late Summer Fires." [Verse] (10:1) Spr 93, p. 3.
    "Mollusc." [Nimrod] (36:2) Spr-Sum 93, p. 142.
    "The Say-But-the-Word Centurion Attempts a Summary." [Comm] (120:6) 26 Mr
        93, p. 12.

4687. MURRAY, Lloyd
"Sound Burier." [Light] (7) Aut 93, p. 10.
"What Profits." [Light] (5) Spr 93, p. 23.
4688. MUS, David
"Ash Shading into Blue" (shortened verson prepared by the author, tr. of André du
Bouchet). [HarvardR] (4) Spr 93, p. 83-95.
"Dictation" (tr. of André Du Bouchet). [DenQ] (27:4) Spr 93, p. 58-60.
"January 23 — I go out / Le 23 janvier — Je sors." [Conjunc] (20) 93, p. 70-71.
"Nothing here which won't remember me / Rien, ici, qui ne se souvienne de moi."
[Conjunc] (20) 93, p. 66-67.
"The One Alternative / L'un Alternatif" (Excerpt). [Conjunc] (20) 93, p. 64-65.
"Overflow / Trop-Plein" (Excerpt). [Conjunc] (20) 93, p. 72-73.
"You can only feel the wind here in spurts / Ici le vent ne se fait sentir que par
bouffées." [Conjunc] (20) 93, p. 68-69.
4689. MUSCHG, Adolf
"Als ein Stern Fiel." [LitR] (36:4) Sum 93, p. 553.
"Just as a Star" (tr. by Ellen and Ernest H. von Nardroff). [LitR] (36:4) Sum 93, p.
552.
4690. MUSGRAVE, John
"I knelt before my friend, unable." [CoalC] (7) Apr 93, p. 28.
"On Snipers, Laughter and Death: Vietnam Poems" (To Wilda Bartlett Musgrave,
July 29, 1924-June 9, 1987. Special chapbook issue). [CoalC] (6) Mr 93, 36 p.
4691. MUSGRAVE, Susan
"Forcing the Narcissus." [PraS] (67:4) Wint 93, p. 108-109.
"The Gift." [PraS] (67:4) Wint 93, p. 109-110.
4692. MUSIAL, Grzegorz
"Death of an Actress, Berlin 1937" (tr. by Lia Purpura). [Vis] (43) 93, p. 44.
"In This House" (tr. by Lia Purpura). [Vis] (43) 93, p. 43.
4693. MUSKE, Carol
"Barra de Navidad: Postscript" (for my sister). [ColR] (20:1) Spr 93, p. 71-73.
"Kenya." [Poetry] (161:6) Mr 93, p. 334-336.
4694. MUSKIE-DUKE, Carol
"Unsent Letter 2." [RiverS] (39) 93, p. 33-34.
4695. MUTIS, Alvaro
"Abode" (tr. by Robert Bensen and Timothy J. Keating). [HarvardR] (4) Spr 93, p.
136.
"Three Images" (tr. by Robert Bensen and Timothy J. Keating). [HarvardR] (4) Spr
93, p. 137.
4696. MUTTON, Paul
"An Abandoned Car." [Quarry] (42:1) 93, p. 58.
"Knives for the Mushroom." [Quarry] (42:3) 93, p. 77.
"Poem for the All-Canadian Bookstore." [Quarry] (42:3) 93, p. 78.
"Shadow." [Quarry] (42:3) 93, p. 79.
4697. MYATT, Stacy
"Buttercup Park." [ClockR] (8:1/2) 93, p. 104.
"The Musicians." [ClockR] (8:1/2) 93, p. 103.
"Racine Street." [ClockR] (8:1/2) 93, p. 105.
4698. MYCUE, Edward
"Dispute." [BellR] (16:1/2) Spr-Fall 93, p. 22.
"The Door to a Wall." [JamesWR] (10:4) Sum 93, p. 8.
"Evening — 'So This Is My Life Now'." [JamesWR] (10:4) Sum 93, p. 8.
"None on the daffodil dish." [Talisman] (11) Fall 93, p. 265.
"Telephone Poles." [JamesWR] (10:4) Sum 93, p. 8.
4699. MYERS, Jack
"Bread, Meat, Greens, and Soap." [Poetry] (162:2) My 93, p. 78-79.
"The Stripper." [Poetry] (162:2) My 93, p. 80-81.
4700. MYERS, Neil
"Berkshire Morning, for My Mother." [OhioR] (50) 93, p. 108.
"Homage, Basho." [CharR] (19:2) Fall 93, p. 122.
"Seasonal." [CharR] (19:2) Fall 93, p. 121.
4701. MYLES, Eileen
"Meow Mix." [Arshile] (1) Spr 93, p. 46-47.
"Taxing." [BrooklynR] (10) 93, p. 18-19.
4702. MYRSIADES, Kostas
"Midnight Stroll" (Scripture of the Blind, 1972, tr. of Yannis Ritsos, w. Kimon
Friar). [HarvardR] (5) Fall 93, p. 132-133.

341

4703. MYRVAAGNES, Naomi
"Crossword." [OnTheBus] (6:1, #13) Wint 93-Spr 94, p. 156-157.
4704. MYSKO, Madeleine
"Couplets for the Novelist." [Sparrow] (60) Sum 93, p. 34.
"Letter." [Sparrow] (60) Sum 93, p. 35.
"On My Forty-fifth Birthday." [Sparrow] (60) Sum 93, p. 33.
"Thursday." [Hellas] (4:2) Fall 93, p. 58.
"A Wash." [Sparrow] (60) Sum 93, p. 33.
MYUNG, Mi Kim
    See KIM, Myung Mi
4705. NACCA, Judy
"The Ritual Quiet." [Elf] (3:4) Wint 93, p. 37.
4706. NACHMIAS, Simon,
"Christopher Columbus" (tr. by Robert Friend and Michel Konstantyn). [Trans] (28)
    Spr 93, p. 105.
"I Don't Understand Russian, and I Translate" (tr. by Robert Friend and Michel
    Konstantyn). [Trans] (28) Spr 93, p. 106.
"Tne Odor of Lemon, the Odor of Sweat Reminds Me of Love" (tr. by Robert Friend
    and Michel Konstantyn). [Trans] (28) Spr 93, p. 104.
4707. NADAL, Bobbie Su
"Jazz Me, Baby." [HarvardR] (5) Fall 93, p. 129-130.
4708. NADEL, Arl Spencer
"6/29/92." [SinW] (49) Spr-Sum 93, p. 71-72.
"The Bus." [SinW] (49) Spr-Sum 93, p. 60-61.
4709. NADELMAN, Cynthia
"The Poet and the Journalist." [GettyR] (6:3) Sum 93, p. 527-528.
"Soir Bleu." [GettyR] (6:3) Sum 93, p. 525-526.
4710. NAGAMURA, Kit Pancoast
"Blue Skiff." [HawaiiR] (17:3, #39) Fall 93, p. 62-63.
4711. NAGANAWA, Arlene
"How White the Lilies." [MidAR] (14:1) 93, p. 123.
"Not Wishes" (for Mike Namiki, 1949-81). [MidAR] (14:1) 93, p. 124.
4712. NAGASHIMA, Minamiko
"May" (tr. by Akemi Nakamura and Tony Whedon). [GreenMR] (NS 6:2) Sum-Fall
    93, p. 71.
4713. NAGLE, Alice Connelly
"In the Cemetery." [OnTheBus] (5:2, #12) Sum-Fall 93, p. 146.
"Not Only That Shattered Day." [OnTheBus] (5:2, #12) Sum-Fall 93, p. 145.
4714. NAGLE, Christian
"Nostalgia and Complaint of the America Buffalo." [LullwaterR] (4:2) Spr-Sum 93,
    p. 101.
4715. NAGLER, Robert
"Beginning, Middle, End." [SlipS] (13) 93, p. 72.
"The City of Richmond." [XavierR] (13:2) Fall 93, p. 76.
"Hagiographies." [SlipS] (13) 93, p. 71.
"Leng-Tch'e (An Execution by Dismemberment, 1905)" (Cf. *Pekin qui s'en va*, Ed.
    A. Maloine, Paris, 1913). [WormR] (33:1, #129) 93, p. 1-2.
"M.I.A." [Bogg] (66) Wint 92-93, p. 67.
"On an Etching, 'Antiope,' by Dunoyer de Segozac." [AnotherCM] (25) Spr 93, p.
    117.
"Photograph of a Woman Falling" (After an untitled photograph by Lejaren A.
    Hiller, 1938). [SlipS] (13) 93, p. 70.
"Pier." [WormR] (33:1, #129) 93, p. 2.
"Shadow." [WormR] (33:1, #129) 93, p. 3.
"She Turns the Ceramic Dogs in, toward the Living Room, Meaning: My Husband
    Is Here." [NewYorkQ] (52) 93, p. 85.
NAGRELA, Isma'il Ibn
    See HANAGRID, Samuel Ben Yosef Halevi (Isma'il Ibn Nagrela)
4716. NAGY, Agnes Nemes
"Comparison" (tr. by Bruce Berlind). [AmerPoR] (22:1) Ja-F 93, p. 7.
"The Geyser" (tr. by Bruce Berlind). [AmerPoR] (22:1) Ja-F 93, p. 5-6.
"The Sleeping Horsemen" (tr. by Bruce Berlind). [AmerPoR] (22:1) Ja-F 93, p. 6.
"Statues" (tr. by Bruce Berlind). [AmerPoR] (22:1) Ja-F 93, p. 5.
"Trees" (tr. by Bruce Berlind). [AmerPoR] (22:1) Ja-F 93, p. 6-7.
4717. NAIDEN, James
"Crabs" (w. Jeff Beddow). [NorthStoneR] (11) 93, p. 168-169.

"Poem in Jeff Beddow's Absence" (w. Michael Tjepkes). [NorthStoneR] (11) 93, p. 170.

4718. NAIM, C. M.
"After You Come" (tr. of Azra Abbas). [Prima] (16/17) 93, p. 83.
"Bitch" (tr. of Azra Abbas). [Prima] (16/17) 93, p. 84-85.
"It Has Been Written" (tr. of Parween Shakir). [Prima] (16/17) 93, p. 86.

4719. NAKAMOTO, Renée K.
"Quintet." [HawaiiR] (17:1, #37) Spr 93, p. 136.

4720. NAKAMURA, Akemi
"Baby Carriages" (tr. of Tatsuji Miyoshi, w. Tony Whedon). [GreenMR] (NS 6:2) Sum-Fall 93, p. 69.
"Double Scenery" (tr. of Tatsuji Miyoshi, w. Tony Whedon). [GreenMR] (NS 6:2) Sum-Fall 93, p. 70.
"Maruki Bridge" (tr. of Tatsuji Miyoshi, w. Tony Whedon). [GreenMR] (NS 6:2) Sum-Fall 93, p. 68.
"May" (tr. of Minamiko Nagashima, w. Tony Whedon). [GreenMR] (NS 6:2) Sum - Fall 93, p. 71.
"Osteon / the Atelier of Bones, Invention in Two Voices, D Minor" (tr. of Atsusuke Tanaka, w. Tony Whedon). [GreenMR] (NS 6:2) Sum-Fall 93, p. 76.
"The Pans, the Pots and the Fire in Front of Me" (tr. of Rin Ishigaki, w. Tony Whedon). [GreenMR] (NS 6:2) Sum-Fall 93, p. 74-75.
"Poem: It's twilight" (tr. of Atsuko Kato, w. Tony Whedon). [GreenMR] (NS 6:2) Sum-Fall 93, p. 72.
"Waiting for a Wind" (tr. of Chi Ishioka, w. Tony Whedon). [GreenMR] (NS 6:2) Sum-Fall 93, p. 77.
"Winter Light" (tr. of Masahiko Hihara, w. Tony Whedon). [GreenMR] (NS 6:2) Sum-Fall 93, p. 73.

4721. NALLEY, Richard
"Salt Tears." [GrandS] (12:3, #47) Fall 93, p. 158-159.

NAMJO, Kim
See KIM, Namjo

NANAO, Sakaki
See SAKAKI, Nanao

4722. NARAYANAN, Vivek
"An Austrian Visa Office in Budapest." [GrahamHR] (17) Fall 93, p. 71-72.
"Learning to Drown." [GrahamHR] (17) Fall 93, p. 66-68.
"Two Hymns." [GrahamHR] (17) Fall 93, p. 69-70.

NARDROFF, Ellen von
See Von NARDROFF, Ellen

NARDROFF, Ernest H. von
See Von NARDROFF, Ernest H.

4723. NARES, James
"The Curve" (w. David Rattray). [Conjunc] (20) 93, p. 9-14.

4724. NASH, Florence
"Last Hunt." [GreensboroR] (55) Wint 93-94, p. 35.

4725. NASH, Midred
"Sisyphus's Sibling." [Light] (7) Aut 93, p. 7.

4726. NASH, Roger
"Heritage." [CanLit] (137) Sum 93, p. 7.
"Preparations for a Journey." [MalR] (102) Spr 93, p. 100-101.
"The Presence of Absences." [MalR] (102) Spr 93, p. 99.

4727. NASH, Susan Smith
"Letters from Marilyn." [Talisman] (10) Spr 93, p. 163-167.

4728. NASON, Jim
"Bathing Malcolm." [EvergreenC] (8:2) Sum-Fall 93, p. 80-81.

4729. NASREEN, Taslima
"Happy Marriage" (tr. by Mohammad Nurul Huda and Carolyne Wright, w. the author). [TriQ] (89) Wint 93-94, p. 183-184.
"Things Cheaply Had" (tr. by Mohammad Nurul Huda and Carolyne Wright, w. the author). [TriQ] (89) Wint 93-94, p. 182.

NATALE, Nanci Roth
See ROTH-NATALE, Nanci

4730. NATHAN, Leonard (Leonard E.)
"Ark." [Atlantic] (271:2) F 93, p. 84.
"The Art of Crickets." [PoetL] (88:4) Wint 93-94, p. 46.
"Circlings." [NewYorker] (69:39) 22 N 93, p. 68.

343

NATHAN

"In the Retirement Home." [SouthwR] (78:4) Aut 93, p. 538.
"Mamie Sharp." [Witness] (7:1) 93, p. 96-97.
"The Matchmaker in Flight." [QRL] (12:32/33) 93, p. 480.
"Outside the Window." [PraS] (67:3) Fall 93, p. 140-141.
"The Presences." [PraS] (67:3) Fall 93, p. 140.
"Vision in the Ice Cream Parlor." [Witness] (7:1) 93, p. 95.
4731. NATHAN, Norman
"Bleak Thought." [SpiritSH] (58) 93, p. 40.
"Flourishing Gnarled." [Poem] (69) My 93, p. 68.
"The Universal Waste Basket." [SpiritSH] (58) 93, p. 40.
4732. NATHANIEL, Isabel
"The Jewels of Windsor" (Sotheby exhibit and sale, Geneva). [Field] (48) Spr 93, p. 37.
"Lost in the Forest Near Nacogdoches." [Nat] (256:21) 31 My 93, p. 748.
"Miss Blue." [Field] (48) Spr 93, p. 40-41.
"The Weepers." [Field] (48) Spr 93, p. 38-39.
4733. NATT, Gregory
"Judgment Day." [ProseP] (1) 92, p. 62.
4734. NAVE, Frank
"Bowled Over." [Drumvoices] (1:1/2) Fall-Wint 91-92, p. 38-40.
"East Boogie Rap" (from the play "East Boogie," Act 1, Scene 1). [Drumvoices] (1:1/2) Fall-Wint 91-92, p. 30-32.
4735. NAYDAN, Michael (Michael M.)
"An Ironic Nocturne" (tr. of Oksana Zabuzhko). [Agni] (37) 93, p. 276.
"Letter from a Summer Home" (tr. of Oksana Zabuzhko). [Agni] (37) 93, p. 277-278.
"Night Melodies: A Cycle" (tr. of Attila Mohylyny). [Agni] (38) 93, p. 110-113.
4736. NAYLOR, Paul
"First-Order Enthymeme." [Talisman] (11) Fall 93, p. 258.
"Second-Order Enthymeme." [Talisman] (11) Fall 93, p. 258.
"Third-Order Enthymeme." [Talisman] (11) Fall 93, p. 258.
4737. NDLOVU, Lorraine Nomadlozi
"Dear Father." [Drumvoices] (3:1/2) Fall-Wint 93-94, p. 57.
"Tell Me, Mama." [Drumvoices] (3:1/2) Fall-Wint 93-94, p. 56.
Ne JAME, Adele
    See NeJAME, Adele
4738. NEALON, Mary Jane
"Short Journey: Four Months After Diagnosis." [MinnR] (NS 40) Spr-Sum 93, p. 38.
4739. NECAKOV, Lillain
"Caucasians." [PoetryC] (13:2) 93, p. 5.
"Starch Bosom." [PoetryC] (13:2) 93, p. 5.
"Tattooed Fish." [PoetryC] (13:2) 93, p. 5.
"Warm Wood." [PoetryC] (13:2) 93, p. 5.
4740. NECKER, Robert
"First ideas of pale and dusty death." [SmPd] (30:3, #89) Fall 93, p. 9.
"Sunday." [SmPd] (30:3, #89) Fall 93, p. 9.
4741. NEEDELL, Claire
"Excavations." [Talisman] (10) Spr 93, p. 23-25.
4742. NEELD, Judith
"A Flock of Golden-Eyes." [Pembroke] (25) 93, p. 94.
"From the Artist, Letter to Arthur Stieglitz" (On John Martin's *Maine Islands*). [TexasR] (14:1/2) Spr-Sum 93, p. 99.
4743. NEELY, Kim
"Glass." [SlipS] (13) 93, p. 16.
4744. NEILSON, Melanie
"Renga" (w. Martine Bellen and Elaine Equi). [Conjunc] (21) 93, p. 263-268.
4745. NeJAME, Adele
"A Bedouin's Dream." [Manoa] (5:2) Wint 93, p. 108-109.
4746. NEJAR, Carlos
"The Age of the Dawn" (Excerpts, tr. by Madeleine Picciotto). [QRL] (12:32/33) 93, p. 257-262.
NEJAT, Murat Nemet
    See NEMET-NEJAT, Murat
4747. NEKOLA, Charlotte
"For My Father." [Footwork] (23) 93, p. 99.

"Nuclear Age." [Footwork] (23) 93, p. 98-99.
"The Wrong Town." [Footwork] (23) 93, p. 99.
4748. NELMS, Sheryl L.
"Country Cream." [ChironR] (12:4/13:1, #37/38) Wint 93-Spr 94, p. 46.
"Do Da Day" (from *Audio Visual Poetry Foundation*, Issue #4, Marianna, Florida).
[Kaleid] (26) Wint-Spr 93, p. 30.
"Outhouse Blues." [Border] (2) Spr 93, p. 53.
"Sonoran Variegation." [Bogg] (66) Wint 92-93, p. 19.
"The Writing Life: As It Should Be." [DogRR] (12:1, #23) Spr-Sum 93, p. 6-7.
4749. NELSON, Eric
"Art of the Middle Ages." [SouthernR] (29:3) Sum, Jl 93, p. 581.
"The Rose Bus." [SouthernR] (29:3) Sum, Jl 93, p. 580.
4750. NELSON, Gale
"Ode" (for Alison). [Agni] (37) 93, p. 79-83.
4751. NELSON, George
"A Suite of Objects." [AnotherCM] (26) Fall 93, p. 90.
4752. NELSON, Howard
"Deer on the Ballfield." [TarRP] (33:1) Fall 93, p. 32.
4753. NELSON, J.
"Urinals." [PraF] (14:3) Aut 93, p. 110.
4754. NELSON, Jo
"Road Warrior." [Plain] (13:3) Spr 93, p. 12.
4755. NELSON, Joyce
"Dear Miss Angela D." [MalR] (104) Fall 93, p. 69.
"Standing Watch." [MalR] (104) Fall 93, p. 68.
"The Tooth." [MalR] (104) Fall 93, p. 70.
4756. NELSON, Kay
"A Night in the Emergency Room." [Crucible] (29) Fall 93, p. 30.
"Silent Scream." [Pembroke] (25) 93, p. 64.
4757. NELSON, Kurt
"At Six with Grandpa" (Young Writers, age 12). [PikeF] (11) Fall 93, p. 19.
4758. NELSON, Ryan
"The Merry-Go-Round at Hieronymus Park." [Plain] (14:1) Fall 93, p. 22-23.
4759. NELSON, Sandra
"Contrapasta Boy." [WritersF] (19) 93, p. 121.
"Distemper." [LouisL] (10:1) Spr 93, p. 50-51.
"Stoves." [Iowa] (23:3) Fall 93, p. 76.
"What a Comet Is." [Iowa] (23:3) Fall 93, p. 77-79.
"When She Used to Be Pretty." [Iowa] (23:3) Fall 93, p. 76-77.
4760. NELSON, Sara
"Outside the Medical Supply Shop." [13thMoon] (11:1/2) 93, p. 48.
"Reading Critical Theory to My Mother Over the Phone." [13thMoon] (11:1/2) 93,
p. 47.
4761. NELSON, Sharon H.
"Mother in the Kitchen" (for Ronnie R. Brown). [Arc] (31) Aut 93, p. 68-69.
4762. NELSON-TAKIGUCHI, Mimi
"Boston, 1971." [OnTheBus] (5:2, #12) Sum-Fall 93, p. 150.
4763. NEMEROV, Howard
"Brainstorm." [QRL] (12:32/33) 93, p. 480-481.
4764. NEMET-NEJAT, Murat
"Vocabularies of Space" (Excerpt). [Talisman] (11) Fall 93, p. 162.
4765. NEPO, Mark
"Polo." [MassR] (33:4) Wint 92-93, p. 616-617.
4766. NESANOVICH, Stella
"Dark Turns" (For a Friend Diagnosed with Multiple Sclerosis). [XavierR] (13:1)
Spr 93, p. 63.
4767. NESSUNO, Santo
"Like Spikes." [Hellas] (4:1) Spr 93, p. 90-91.
4768. NESTER, Daniel M.
"The Aesthetics of the Pennsauken Mart." [Eyeball] (2) 93, p. 27.
"Freddie's Elegy" (Freddie Mercury, 1946-1991). [MinnR] (NS 40) Spr-Sum 93, p.
22-23.
"To a Young Poet." [Eyeball] (2) 93, p. 28.
4769. NESTER, Richard
"Baptism at Bluegill Pond." [GrahamHR] (17) Fall 93, p. 103-104.
"Cleaning the Ground." [Callaloo] (16:3) Sum 93, p. 686.

"Earth and Sky." [Callaloo] (16:3) Sum 93, p. 687.
"Long Jump, Berlin, 1936." [DogRR] (12:2, #24) Fall-Wint 93, p. 18-19.
"My Morning Walk, a Lament for Eyes." [CapeR] (28:1) Spr 93, p. 47.
"Pennsylvania Turnpike, West" (for Albert Einstein). [SycamoreR] (5:2) Sum 93, p. 47-48.
"Three Views of Narrative." [SenR] (23:1/2) Wint 93, p. 94-96.
4770. NEUER, Linda
"Hide and Seek." [PoetC] (24:2) Wint 93, p. 33.
4771. NEUMAN, Claudia
"For You." [OnTheBus] (5:2, #12) Sum-Fall 93, p. 152.
"Mark Does Pipes." [OnTheBus] (5:2, #12) Sum-Fall 93, p. 151-152.
"One More Sunday." [OnTheBus] (6:1, #13) Wint 93-Spr 94, p. 158.
4772. NEVA, Judith
"The Clockmaker." [Vis] (41) 93, p. 16.
4773. NEVERSILOVA, Olga
"Without Words" (tr. by Bronislava Volkova). [Vis] (43) 93, p. 12.
4774. NEVILL, Sue
"Dressed to Die." [AntigR] (92) Wint 93, p. 62.
"Ducks on Thin Ice." [Dandel] (20:1) 93, p. 6.
"Pacific Composition." [MalR] (103) Sum 93, p. 41.
4775. NEWCOMB, P. F.
"Fisherman Blues." [CapeR] (28:2) Fall 93, p. 34.
4776. NEWELL, Jeff
"The End of an Era." [WillowS] (33) Wint 93, p. 46-47.
4777. NEWELL, Michael L.
"For James Edmundson as Willy Loman" (at the Oregon Shakespeare Festival, 1981). [ColEng] (55:5) S 93, p. 540.
"School Metaphors." [BellArk] (9:6) N-D 93, p. 9.
4778. NEWLAND, Emily
"On the Other Side of the Oasis." [Light] (6) Sum 93, p. 16.
4779. NEWMAN, Amy
"La Pensée" (for Camille Claudel. 15th Anniversary Contest Winner, 2nd Place — Poetry). [IndR] (16:1) Spr 93, p. 66.
4780. NEWMAN, David
"The Dildo." [ChironR] (12:4/13:1, #37/38) Wint 93-Spr 94, p. 18.
4781. NEWMAN, Kate
"The Chinese Notebook" (Selections, tr. of Demosthenes Agrafiotis, w. the author, Theo Dorgan, Tony Curtis, and Pat Boran). [Sulfur] (32) Spr 93, p. 206-212.
4782. NEWMAN, P. B.
"A Certain Slant of Light" (The Nimrod/Hardman Awards: Finalist). [Nimrod] (37:1) Fall-Wint 93, p. 59.
"Virginia Murray" (My Mother's Reflections). [Crucible] (29) Fall 93, p. 10.
NEWMAN, R. Pastorio
See PASTORIO-NEWMAN, R.
4783. NEWTON, Peter
"There's something about a grown man fishing for change" (Amelia One-Liner Award). [Amelia] (7:2, #21) 93, p. 119.
4784. NGAI, Sianne
"Position." [Caliban] (13) 93, p. 108-109.
4785. NGUYEN, Emily
"The Open Sleeve of Love." [US1] (28/29) 93, p. 19.
"Persimmon Tree." [US1] (28/29) 93, p. 6.
4786. NIATUM, Duane
"Conch Oracles on the Elders' Path." [ChiR] (39:3/4) 93, p. 107-109.
"Late Summer Evening Near the Hoko River." [GreenMR] (NS 6:1) Wint-Spr 93, p. 85.
4787. NICHOL, Allison J.
"Lessons" (for Gay). [EvergreenC] (8:2) Sum-Fall 93, p. 7.
4788. NICHOLAS, Douglas
"V. Footsoldier's Slow Drag and Breakdown." [Sonora] (26) Fall 93, p. 67-68.
4789. NICHOLLS, Sandra
"Ear Training." [AntigR] (93-94) Spr-Sum 93, p. 106.
"The Long Distance." [AntigR] (93-94) Spr-Sum 93, p. 107.
"My Father's Binoculars." [PoetryC] (14:1) 93, p. 5.
"Real Estate." [PoetryC] (14:1) 93, p. 5.

346

NICHOLS

4790. NICHOLS, Krista
"Afternoon." [AmerV] (30) 93, p. 72.
4791. NICHOLS-ORIANS, Judith
"Counting." [HayF] (12) Spr-Sum 93, p. 118.
4792. NICHOLSON, Kelly Robin
"The Winter of Our Summer." [PraF] (14:3) Aut 93, p. 111.
4793. NICKEL, Barbara
"Two Loves." [AntigR] (95) Aut 93, p. 131-132.
"Uncle John Got Married." [Grain] (21:3) Fall 93, p. 124.
4794. NICKSON, Richard
"The Decoyed Mistress." [Light] (8) Wint 93, p. 15.
NICOLA, Deborah de
See De NICOLA, Deborah
4795. NIDITCH, B. Z.
"Budapest." [Caliban] (12) 93, p. 176.
"Creativity Returns." [Colum] (20) Sum 93, p. 58.
"Diego Rivera." [BlackBR] (17) Sum-Fall 93, p. 29.
"Franz Kline." [BlackBR] (17) Sum-Fall 93, p. 28.
"Howard Nemerov" (In Memoriam). [HolCrit] (30:2) Ap 93, p. 17.
"In Adolescence." [Light] (5) Spr 93, p. 9.
"Kid's Day." [SpiritSH] (58) 93, p. 37.
"Latin Lover." [Contact] (11:65/66/67) Spr 93, p. 27.
"Lenin." [LitR] (36:2) Wint 93, p. 186.
"Los Angeles, 1990." [Caliban] (12) 93, p. 177.
"Max Ernst." [BlackBR] (17) Sum-Fall 93, p. 28.
"Murphy's Law." [SpiritSH] (58) 93, p. 38.
"Orozco." [BlackBR] (17) Sum-Fall 93, p. 25.
"Sequeiros." [BlackBR] (17) Sum-Fall 93, p. 26.
"Somnambulist Poet." [DogRR] (12:2, #24) Fall-Wint 93, p. 49.
"To Be Continued." [SpiritSH] (58) 93, p. 36.
"Two in July." [HayF] (13) Fall-Wint 93, p. 97.
"Writer's Block." [SpiritSH] (58) 93, p. 39.
NIDITICH, B. Z.
See NIDITCH, B. Z.
4796. NIELSEN, Dan
"Bad Start." [ChironR] (12:4/13:1, #37/38) Wint 93-Spr 94, p. 46.
"The Dells." [Pearl] (17) Spr 93, p. 93.
"Loyal to Our Species." [Bogg] (66) Wint 92-93, p. 5.
"Man Are So Shallow." [WormR] (33:3, #131), 93, p. 130.
"A Perfect Moment." [WormR] (33:3, #131), 93, p. 130.
"Poet & Critic: the Danger." [ChironR] (12:1, #34) Spr 93, p. 41.
"A Serious Feminist." [ChironR] (12:4/13:1, #37/38) Wint 93-Spr 94, p. 35.
"So I'm Not Handy." [WormR] (33:3, #131), 93, p. 130.
"What Gave Me Away?" [SlipS] (13) 93, p. 92.
4797. NIELSEN, Kristy
"Arms That Hold Me Back." [SpoonR] (18:2) Sum-Fall 93, p. 57-60.
"The Girl Calls Herself Gentle Names." [IllinoisR] (1:1) Fall 93, p. 66-68.
"A Girl Needs Something of Her Own." [IllinoisR] (1:1) Fall 93, p. 7-10.
"Magic Learned on Men." [PoetC] (25:1) Fall 93, p. 23.
"A Measure of the Sin." [SpoonR] (18:2) Sum-Fall 93, p. 61-65.
"The Song of Regrets." [SpoonR] (18:2) Sum-Fall 93, p. 66-72.
4798. NIEMEYER, Carl
"Laser Opera, July 3, 1991." [DenQ] (27:4) Spr 93, p. 25-26.
NIETO, Catherine Rodriguez
See RODRIGUEZ-NIETO, Catherine
4799. NIGHTINGALE, Eric
"Reunion." [RagMag] (11:2) 93, p. 51.
4800. NIMNICHT, Nona
"Interior with Two Women at a Linen Chest" (after Pieter de Hooch). [PoetryNW]
(34:4) Wint 93-94, p. 33.
4801. NIMS, John Frederick
"Almsgiving." [Light] (5) Spr 93, p. 23.
"Dictionary." [Light] (6) Sum 93, p. 8.
"Dover Sole" (by Joe E. Skilmer). [Sparrow] (60) Sum 93, p. 55.
"Grammarian." [Light] (6) Sum 93, p. 10.
"Mondrian." [Light] (5) Spr 93, p. 9.

"Political Correctitude." [Light] (7) Aut 93, p. 11.
"Renoir." [Light] (5) Spr 93, p. 9.
"Sonnet Right Off the Bat" (tr. of Lope de Vega). [Sparrow] (60) Sum 93, p. 18.
"Three Epigrams." [GeoR] (47:2) Sum 93, p. 266.
NIORD, Chard de
    See DeNIORD, Chard
4802. NISSAN, Gilla
    "Batman Is Depressed." [OnTheBus] (6:1, #13) Wint 93-Spr 94, p. 159.
    "Non-Biodegradable." [OnTheBus] (5:2, #12) Sum-Fall 93, p. 153.
4803. NISULA, Dasha Culic
    "Hyperborean Letter" (tr. of Bozica Jelusic). [Vis] (43) 93, p. 11.
    "Late Summer" (tr. of Irena Vrkljan). [Vis] (43) 93, p. 10.
4804. NITYCHORUK, Margaret
    "Rescue Tips" (for the snow white prince). [PraF] (14:3) Aut 93, p. 112.
4805. NIU, Han
    "The Yellow River and the Carp" (in Chinese and English, tr. by Li Xi-jian and
        Gordon Osing). [PikeF] (11) Fall 93, p. 14.
4806. NIVEN, Julie
    "By Memory." [BellArk] (9:5) S-O 93, p. 10.
    "Spring Planting." [BellArk] (9:5) S-O 93, p. 24.
4807. NIXON, David Michael
    "Blue Dust." [Gypsy] (20) Sum 93, p. 32.
    "Sister, Lend Me." [SoCoast] (15) Je 93, p. 35.
4808. NIXON, John, Jr.
    "Club from a Deck of Concrete Cards." [QW] (37) Sum-Fall 93, p. 85.
    "Coat of Arms." [Light] (5) Spr 93, p. 26.
    "Haut Goût." [ChrC] (110:19) 16-23 Je 93, p. 621.
    "Making Love." [ChrC] (110:10) 24-31 Mr 93, p. 327.
4809. NIXON, Sallie
    "Portrait of Hunger" (From an Associated Press Photograph, *The Charlotte
        Observer*, 1-12-92). [Crucible] (29) Fall 93, p. 35.
4810. NOBLES, Edward
    "Loss" (Selections: 1-7). [Pequod] (35) 93, p. 163-168.
    "Near Incident." [Witness] (7:2) 93, p. 93.
    "Sunday in the Park." [Witness] (7:2) 93, p. 92.
4811. NOETHE, Sheryl
    "Losing Eurydice, Neutrinos & Quarks." [CutB] (40) Spr 93, p. 55-56.
4812. NOGUERE, Suzanne
    "My Sister's Window." [Sparrow] (60) Sum 93, p. 49.
    "We Who In." [Sparrow] (60) Sum 93, p. 49.
4813. NOHRNBERG, Peter
    "National." [HarvardA] (128:4, [i.e. 127:4]) Sum 93, p. 20.
4814. NOLAN, Eamon
    "Socrates." [SenR] (23:1/2) Wint 93, p. 180-181.
    "Soldier." [SenR] (23:1/2) Wint 93, p. 182.
4815. NOLAN, Pat
    "In the Driver's Seat" (for Andrei Codrescu). [HangL] (62) 93, p. 40-42.
4816. NOLDE, Carol J.
    "Tattooed." [Outbr] (24) 93, p. 24.
    "Windfalls." [Outbr] (24) 93, p. 25.
4817. NOLLET, Tara
    "Transparencies." [PraF] (14:3) Aut 93, p. 132.
NOONAN, Mary-Beth O'Shea
    See O'SHEA-NOONAN, Mary-Beth
NOORD, Barbara van
    See Van NOORD, Barbara
4818. NORDBRANDT, Henrik
    "The Cemetery" (tr. by Alex Taylor). [Vis] (41) 93, p. 14.
    "Chora" (tr. by Alex Taylor). [Vis] (43) 93, p. 16.
    "Gobi" (tr. by Alex Taylor). [Vis] (41) 93, p. 13.
    "I Talk About You" (tr. by Anne Born). [Verse] (10:1) Spr 93, p. 97.
    "Street" (tr. by Alex Taylor). [Vis] (42) 93, p. 23.
4819. NORDFORS, Douglas
    "Tess of the D'Urbervilles." [QW] (37) Sum-Fall 93, p. 96.
4820. NORDHAUS, Jean
    "Arroyo Seco: A House at the Crossroads." [QRL] (12:32/33) 93, p. 264-265.

348

NORDHAUS

"From a Window in Jerusalem." [Poetry] (163:1) O 93, p. 33.
"The Infant King." [QRL] (12:32/33) 93, p. 265-266.
"Santa Fe: A Jewish Wife, 1895." [QRL] (12:32/33) 93, p. 266-267.
"Silk." [Poetry] (163:1) O 93, p. 34.
"Small Worries." [QRL] (12:32/33) 93, p. 267-268.
"The Stammer." [Poetry] (163:1) O 93, p. 36.
"Thread Box." [QRL] (12:32/33) 93, p. 268.
"Trouble with Consonants." [QRL] (12:32/33) 93, p. 265.
"The Weekly Loaf." [Poetry] (163:1) O 93, p. 35.
"The White Meal." [QRL] (12:32/33) 93, p. 263-264.
4821. NORDSTRÖM, Lars
"The Trek of the Wind" (Selections, tr. of Nils-Aslak Valkeapää, w. Ralph Salisbury
and Harald Gaski). [SilverFR] (24) Wint 93, p. 31-38.
4822. NORINE, William
"In Memoriam, Virgil Fish, 1925-1977)." [WilliamMR] (31) 93, p. 39.
4823. NORMAN, Anita
"Heartwell." [Plain] (13:3) Spr 93, p. 13.
4824. NORMINGTON, Jim
"Funeral of Words" (tr. of Efraín Huerta). [Talisman] (10) Spr 93, p. 82.
"The Murder of a Poet While Sleeping" (tr. of Efraín Huerta). [Talisman] (10) Spr
93, p. 83-84.
4825. NORMOYLE, Michele
"A Woman of Parts." [WestCL] (27:3, #12) Wint 93-94, p. 46-49.
4826. NORRIS, Leslie
"The Beautiful Young Devon Shorthorn Bull Sexton Hyades XXXIII." [TarRP]
(33:1) Fall 93, p. 19.
"Calling Him Home." [Atlantic] (271:3) Mr 93, p. 100.
"I.M. Reverend Lawrence Scanlan, D.D., 1843-1915, First Bishop of Salt Lake."
[TarRP] (33:1) Fall 93, p. 25-28.
"Water." [TarRP] (33:1) Fall 93, p. 1-2.
4827. NORSE, Harold
"Seismic Events" (separate chapbook bound in issue). [Contact] (11:65/66/67) Spr
93, 15 p.
"Walt Whitman Called Today" (for jack foley). [PoetryUSA] (25/26) 93, p. 27.
4828. NORTH, Charles
"Aug.-Dec. for Jimmy Schuyler." [Talisman] (11) Fall 93, p. 30-34.
"Shooting for Line" (for Bob Hershon). [HangL] (62) 93, p. 43-46.
4829. NORTH, William
"Those Stains." [ChrC] (110:11) 7 Apr 93, p. 365.
4830. NORTHCUTT, Derek
"He's Making a Movie." [ChironR] (12:1, #34) Spr 93, p. 34.
"Tough as a Bone." [ChironR] (12:1, #34) Spr 93, p. 34.
4831. NORTHROP, Kate
"When My Father Goes Down." [PaintedHR] (9) Spr 93, p. 30-31.
4832. NORTHUP, Harry E.
"A Shaman Purpose a Minute." [OnTheBus] (5:2, #12) Sum-Fall 93, p. 154-155.
4833. NOTEBOOM, Erin
"The Last Child in Hamlin." [Plain] (13:2) Wint 93, p. 18.
4834. NOTLEY, Alice
"Désamère" (Excerpt). [Talisman] (11) Fall 93, p. 4-10.
"Faces Imagined Rise Up." [RiverS] (37) 93, p. 16-21.
"In April." [Arshile] (1) Spr 93, p. 59-60.
"Your Angels." [OnTheBus] (6:1, #13) Wint 93-Spr 94, p. 160-165.
4835. NOTO, John
"Cyclonic thoughts encase the rain-engines of imagination." [Caliban] (13) 93, p.
155.
"Folds." [Caliban] (12) 93, p. 94.
"March Storm— Contusion." [Talisman] (11) Fall 93, p. 193.
"The Moonraker (Rocky Pt., Pacifica)." [Talisman] (11) Fall 93, p. 192.
"Motor-Balancing the Untimed Snow: Ella Waking." [Caliban] (13) 93, p. 94.
4836. NOVACK, Barbara
"Elsewhere." [CapeR] (28:2) Fall 93, p. 40-41.
"The Painters." [CapeR] (28:1) Spr 93, p. 21.
"Pas de Deux." [SoCoast] (14) Ja 93, p. 16.

4837. NOVAK, Boris
"Heavenly Flower" (tr. of Josip Osti, w. Ruzha Cleaveland). [WebR] (17) Fall 93, p. 29.
"Rose Garden" (tr. of Josip Osti, w. Ruzha Cleaveland). [WebR] (17) Fall 93, p. 29.
"The Stake Stabbing the Tongue Has Sprouted Leaves" (tr. of Josip Osti, w. Ruzha Cleaveland). [WebR] (17) Fall 93, p. 29.
"Suddenly Everyone Beheld an Empty Sky" (tr. of Josip Osti, w. Ruzha Cleaveland). [WebR] (17) Fall 93, p. 28.
"Vanilla's Fragrance, Peppermint's Scent" (tr. of Josip Osti, w. Ruzha Cleaveland). [WebR] (17) Fall 93, p. 28.

4838. NOVAK, Emily R.
"For L." [13thMoon] (12:1/2) 93-94, p. 47.
"Untitled: Woman in a sailor suit." [13thMoon] (12:1/2) 93-94, p. 48.

4839. NOVAK, Katherine Bush
"It's This I Ask." [SpoonR] (18:1) Wint-Spr 93, p. 26.
"Wherein Wife Urges Sale of Gun." [SpoonR] (18:1) Wint-Spr 93, p. 27.

4840. NOWAK, Mark
"How shall I praise you, polis, as the center or the snare at the center." [NowestR] (31:1) 93, p. 64.
"Off-shore, even if there was a shore, some distance from it." [Talisman] (11) Fall 93, p. 226.
"The porch the things around them, the trees." [NowestR] (31:1) 93, p. 63.

4841. NUÑEZ, Fernando
"En la Siesta" (a Pierre Loti). [LindLM] (12:1) Mr 93, p. 18.
"Mi Casa." [LindLM] (12:1) Mr 93, p. 18.
"Sin Título: Estoy amenazado de muerte, cada día." [LindLM] (12:1) Mr 93, p. 18.

4842. NURKSE, D.
"The Bed of Coals." [ManhatR] (7:1) Fall 93, p. 57.
"Customs." [WestB] (31/32) 93, p. 28.
"Dawn Kitchen." [ManhatR] (7:1) Fall 93, p. 56.
"Evening Practice." [ManhatR] (7:1) Fall 93, p. 58.
"The Last Night of Exile." [ManhatR] (7:1) Fall 93, p. 60.
"Lying In." [ManhatR] (7:1) Fall 93, p. 59.
"Pause at Delta Assembly." [WestB] (33) 93, p. 47.

4843. NUTTER, Geoffrey
"Parallel Sky-Lines." [ColR] (20:1) Spr 93, p. 42-46.

4844. NUTTER, Jude
"Back View." [IndR] (16:2) Fall 93, p. 38.
"The Graves of Animals." [IndR] (16:2) Fall 93, p. 36-37.

4845. NYE, Naomi Shihab
"Arabic" (Jordan, 1992). [GreenMR] (NS 6:1) Wint-Spr 93, p. 46.
"Arabic Coffee." [PaintedB] (50/51) 93, p. 94.
"Estate Sale: The Scrabble Game of a Dead Woman." [HayF] (12) Spr-Sum 93, p. 36-37.
"His Secret." [HayF] (12) Spr-Sum 93, p. 35.
"How Long Peace Takes." [ArtfulD] (24/25) 93, p. 99.
"Lullaby for Regret." [ArtfulD] (24/25) 93, p. 98.
"Morning Glory." [TarRP] (33:1) Fall 93, p. 62-63.
"Passing the Refugee Camp" (Occupied Territories / Palestine, 1993). [TarRP] (33:1) Fall 93, p. 60-62.
"Telling Less." [HayF] (12) Spr-Sum 93, p. 38.

4846. NYHART, Al
"Driving with the Dead." [PaintedB] (49) 93, p. 33.
"Near Danant." [PaintedB] (49) 93, p. 32.

4847. NYHART, Nina
"At the Grave." [ProseP] (1) 92, p. 64.
"Ghost Triptych." [ProseP] (2) 93, p. 71.
"Worm." [ProseP] (1) 92, p. 63.

4848. NYSTROM, Debra
"Mary Before the Pageant." [VirQR] (69:3) Sum 93, p. 496-497.
"What Are We?" [IndR] (16:2) Fall 93, p. 105-106.

4849. NYSTROM, Karen
"Crossed Histories." [IndR] (16:2) Fall 93, p. 137-138.
"Mythic Sorbet." [AnotherCM] (25) Spr 93, p. 118-120.

4850. OAKES, Jennifer Callin (J. Cailin, J. Caillin)
"In a Moment." [BlackWR] (20:1) Fall-Wint 93, p. 122-124.

"Potential: Two Times." [NoDaQ] (61:4) Fall 93, p. 98-99.
4851. OAKES, Randy W.
"Newlywed." [PoetryE] (36) Fall 93, p. 121.
4852. OAKS, Jeff
"Hunger." [PennR] (5:2) 93, p. 34-35.
4853. OATES, Joyce Carol
"The Black Glove: A Rapture." [WestHR] (47:2) Sum 93, p. 164-165.
4854. OBERC
"I Want to Walk." [Pearl] (17) Spr 93, p. 70.
"What Pisses Me Off." [Pearl] (17) Spr 93, p. 70.
4855. OBRADOVIC, Biljana D.
"Loneliness" (tr. of Desanka Maksimovic). [PraS] (67:1) Spr 93, p. 80.
"Poetry Reading" (tr. of Desanka Maksimovic). [PraS] (67:1) Spr 93, p. 78-79.
"To Mothers" (tr. of Desanka Maksimovic). [PraS] (67:1) Spr 93, p. 80-81.
4856. O'BRIAN, Catherine
"Silent Playgrounds." [CharR] (19:2) Fall 93, p. 115-116.
4857. O'BRIEN, Geoffrey
"Intercept." [Talisman] (11) Fall 93, p. 284-287.
4858. O'BRIEN, Laurie
"34 Kreuzer" (Second Place, annual Paintbrush Award, 1993). [PaintedHR] (10)
    Fall 93, p. 9.
"L'Art de Toucher le Clavecin" (Bach, after Couperin). [Poetry] (162:1) Ap 93, p. 6.
"Ballroom Dancing." [RiverC] (13:1) Fall 92, p. 61.
"Cages for the Dead." [RiverC] (13:1) Fall 92, p. 59.
"Casey Dying." [RiverC] (13:1) Fall 92, p. 60.
"My Mother, Memphis, 1931." [RiverC] (13:1) Fall 92, p. 62-63.
"Playing Bach." [CapeR] (28:2) Fall 93, p. 4.
"Rogues' Codes." [Poetry] (162:1) Ap 93, p. 7-8.
"Solving for N." [HeavenB] (10) Wint-Spr 93, p. 43.
"Suppose Heaven." [ApalQ] (39) 93, p. 40.
4859. O'BRIEN, Pamela S.
"Fire." [Blueline] (14) 93, p. 75.
O'BRIEN, Susan Roney
    See RONEY-O'BRIEN, Susan
4860. OCHESTER, Ed
"Ohio." [Ploughs] (19:4) Wint 93-94, p. 143.
4861. O'CONGHALAIGH, Tarlac
"Gulags." [SenR] (23:1/2) Wint 93, p. 174.
"Letter to a Bishop." [SenR] (23:1/2) Wint 93, p. 175-178.
"Love and Beauty Saves the World." [SenR] (23:1/2) Wint 93, p. 179.
4862. O'CONNELL, Richard
"Odes I, V" (tr. of Horace). [Light] (7) Aut 93, p. 15.
"Raimondo de Soncino, Agent of the Duke of Milan, to the Duke, 18 December
    1497." [ApalQ] (35) 90, p. 21-23.
4863. O'CONNOR, Christine
"The House on the Boulevard." [Footwork] (23) 93, p. 94.
4864. O'CONNOR, Deirdre
"At the Edge of the Amish Orchard" (for my mother). [HayF] (13) Fall-Wint 93, p.
    95.
"Braid." [PaintedB] (49) 93, p. 35.
"Broken Arm." [LaurelR] (27:1) Wint 93, p. 17.
"Commencement." [RiverC] (14:1) Fall 93, p. 89.
"Everything in Relation to the Sky." [RiverC] (14:1) Fall 93, p. 90.
"The Hiss of the Spirit as It Leaves a Woman's Body." [HayF] (13) Fall-Wint 93, p.
    92.
"Name." [RiverC] (14:1) Fall 93, p. 91-92.
"Playing Boggle in the Psych Ward." [PaintedB] (49) 93, p. 34.
"Something Meaner." [LaurelR] (27:1) Wint 93, p. 17.
"These Many Tricks." [HayF] (13) Fall-Wint 93, p. 93-94.
"Traveling at Night in Fukushima." [RiverC] (14:1) Fall 93, p. 93-94.
4865. O'CONNOR, John
"Ah Ha." [Bogg] (66) Wint 92-93, p. 47.
4866. O'CONNOR, Mark
"Arnhem Land." [Nimrod] (36:2) Spr-Sum 93, p. 92.
"Fig." [Nimrod] (36:2) Spr-Sum 93, p. 90.
"The Grasshopper Man." [Nimrod] (36:2) Spr-Sum 93, p. 91.

"Nourlangie Cave at Night" (July 17, 1992). [Nimrod] (36:2) Spr-Sum 93, p. 89.
"Portrait by the Artist" (Nourlangie Caves, Kakadu). [Nimrod] (36:2) Spr-Sum 93,
    p. 93.
4867. O'CONNOR, Mike
    "Elegy for a Log-Truck Driver." [ChiR] (39:3/4) 93, p. 102-106.
    "Mad Woman" (tr. of anonymous poem from Tiananmen Square, Spring 1989).
        [ChiR] (39:3/4) 93, p. 284-286.
    "Tonight Martial Law Was Imposed" (tr. of anonymous poem from Tiananmen
        Square, Spring 1989). [ChiR] (39:3/4) 93, p. 286-287.
    "Words for Xn" (tr. of anonymous poem from Tiananmen Square, Spring 1989).
        [ChiR] (39:3/4) 93, p. 287.
4868. ODAGAWA, Kazuko
    "Flowers" (tr. of Toshiko Hirata, w. Robert Brady). [ChiR] (39:3/4) 93, p. 214-215.
4869. ODAM, Joyce
    "The Death Album." [Parting] (6:1) Sum 93, p. 24.
    "Displacement." [Parting] (6:2) Wint 93, p. 35.
    "Gail in New York." [Parting] (6:1) Sum 93, p. 46.
    "Years Later." [Parting] (6:2) Wint 93, p. 36.
4870. ODLIN, Reno
    "St.-Trophime 1956-Rosedale 1958." [AntigR] (95) Aut 93, p. 124.
4871. O'DONNELL, Isobel
    "Trays." [PaintedB] (49) 93, p. 27.
4872. O'DONNELL, Louise
    "I'm Not Alice." [AntigR] (93-94) Spr-Sum 93, p. 255.
4873. O'DONNELL, Mary
    "Farming in Doohat." [SenR] (23:1/2) Wint 93, p. 81-82.
    "Kate O'Brien Weekender Meets La Leche Leaguers." [SenR] (23:1/2) Wint 93, p.
        84-85.
    "Song Before Birth." [SenR] (23:1/2) Wint 93, p. 83.
4874. O'DOWD, Paddy
    "Historically Speaking." [SenR] (23:1/2) Wint 93, p. 185.
4875. O'DWYER, Tess
    "And Now" (tr. of Giannina Braschi). [LitR] (36:2) Wint 93, p. 148.
    "Eggs are months and days too" (tr. of Giannina Braschi). [Trasimagen] (1:1)
        Otoño-Invierno 93, p. 35.
    "Empire of Dreams" (Excerpt, tr. of Giannina Braschi). [Agni] (37) 93, p. 250.
    "I Am the Shepherd of Water" (tr. of Giannina Braschi). [LitR] (36:2) Wint 93, p.
        149.
    "It wasn't fire" (from "El Imperiod de los sueños," tr. of Giannina Braschi). [Luz] (5)
        N 93, p. 21.
    "On the Top Floor of the Empire State" (tr. of Giannina Braschi). [LitR] (36:2) Wint
        93, p. 148.
    "This is different" (tr. of Giannina Braschi). [Trasimagen] (1:1) Otoño-Invierno 93,
        p. 35.
    "The world is a billiard ball" (tr. of Giannina Braschi). [Trasimagen] (1:1) Otoño -
        Invierno 93, p. 35.
    "The world is a doll house" (tr. of Giannina Braschi). [Trasimagen] (1:1) Otoño -
        Invierno 93, p. 35.
    "The world is blank" (tr. of Giannina Braschi). [Trasimagen] (1:1) Otoño-Invierno
        93, p. 35.
4876. OEHRING, Connie
    "Driving North" (for Shaune). [HighP] (8:3) Wint 93, p. 89-90.
4877. OFFUTT, Sherene
    "Compulsive Gambling." [WashR] (18:5) F-Mr 93, p. 22.
    "Fabric" (w. Doug Lang, Mora Larson and Geoff Suchocki). [WashR] (18:5) F-Mr
        93, p. 18.
    "Genes." [WashR] (18:5) F-Mr 93, p. 20.
    "September 30, 10:00 p.m." [WashR] (18:5) F-Mr 93, p. 8.
    "Tables." [WashR] (18:5) F-Mr 93, p. 22.
    "The Weather." [WashR] (18:5) F-Mr 93, p. 22.
4878. OGDEN, Hugh
    "Devotions." [PoetL] (88:3) Fall 93, p. 47-48.
    "Survivor." [Blueline] (14) 93, p. 100-101.
    "Yale Medical Center, the Evoked Response" (for Annette). [PoetL] (88:3) Fall 93,
        p. 45-46.

4879. O'GRADY, Jennifer
"Illuminated Page." [Poetry] (161:6) Mr 93, p. 322.
"One Explanation." [GeoR] (47:2) Sum 93, p. 251.
"The Surrealist Learns to Fly." [Poetry] (161:6) Mr 93, p. 323.
4880. O'HAGAN, Felim
"A History of Prisoners." [SenR] (23:1/2) Wint 93, p. 186-187.
4881. O'HAGAN, Rory
"Father." [PraF] (14:3) Aut 93, p. 113.
4882. O'HARA, Mark
"The Composer's Dream." [WilliamMR] (31) 93, p. 17.
"Planting" (after a story by the sister of James M. Floyd). [JINJPo] (15:1) Spr 93, p. 22.
4883. O'HAY, Charles
"Forecasting." [Pearl] (17) Spr 93, p. 15.
4884. O'HEHIR, Diana
"Good Man Blues." [Shen] (43:3) Fall 93, p. 113.
"Summoning a Boat." [Shen] (43:3) Fall 93, p. 112.
4885. O'HERN, James
"Bones." [OnTheBus] (5:2, #12) Sum-Fall 93, p. 157.
"Drugstore Cowboy." [OnTheBus] (5:2, #12) Sum-Fall 93, p. 156.
"Grendel's Song." [OnTheBus] (6:1, #13) Wint 93-Spr 94, p. 166-167.
"Portents." [OnTheBus] (5:2, #12) Sum-Fall 93, p. 158.
4886. OHNESORGE-FICK, Marlon
"Anniversary." [DenQ] (27:3) Wint 93, p. 42-43.
"Carp Lake." [AntR] (51:1) Wint 93, p. 89.
"To My Wife." [AntR] (51:1) Wint 93, p. 88.
4887. OJAIDE, Tanure
"Ivwri: Invoking the Warrior Spirit." [Paint] (20:39/40) Spr-Aut 93, p. 239-248.
OKOT p'BITEK
See p'BITEK, Okot
4888. OKTENBERG, Adrian
"Ch'iu Chin, Beheaded, 1907." [AmerV] (31) 93, p. 131.
4889. OLDER, Julia
"I Will Die of Cancer of the Spine" (tr. of Boris Vian). [ApalQ] (39) 93, p. 29-30.
"The Spiders" (tr. of Boris Vian). [Vis] (42) 93, p. 14-15.
"Sunday in San Miguel." [Border] (2) Spr 93, p. 54.
4890. OLDKNOW, Antony
"Eyes." [Asylum] (8) 93, p. 9.
"Horse Swimming." [NoDaQ] (61:2) Spr 93, p. 132.
"Inside the Eyelids." [CreamCR] (17:1) Spr 93, p. 11.
4891. OLDS, Jennifer
"Conversationally." [PoetL] (88:1) Spr 93, p. 20.
"Country and Western Torch Song." [SlipS] (13) 93, p. 81-83.
"The Girl, the Parrot, the Ghost." [PoetL] (88:1) Spr 93, p. 21.
4892. OLDS, Sharon
"1954" (for Stephanie Bryan). [Ploughs] (19:4) Wint 93-94, p. 43-44.
"After My Mother Was Done With Me." [AmerPoR] (22:3) My-Je 93, p. 22.
"The Borders." [Ploughs] (19:4) Wint 93-94, p. 42.
"Boulder Creek." [AmerPoR] (22:1) Ja-F 93, p. 56.
"The Couple Waking Up in the Hotel Mirror." [AmerPoR] (22:3) My-Je 93, p. 21.
"Emily Dickinson's Writing Table in Her Bedroom at the Homestead, Amherst, Mass." [GrandS] (11:4, #44) 93, p. 246-247.
"First Weeks." [AmerPoR] (22:3) My-Je 93, p. 21.
"The Knowing." [AmerPoR] (22:1) Ja-F 93, p. 55.
"The Necklace." [GrandS] (11:4, #44) 93, p. 248.
"Parts of the Body" (Berlin airport, 1932). [NewEngR] (15:1) Wint 93, p. 180.
"Poem to the Reader." [AmerPoR] (22:3) My-Je 93, p. 20.
"The Shore." [AmerPoR] (22:1) Ja-F 93, p. 56.
"These Days." [AmerPoR] (22:1) Ja-F 93, p. 56.
"To My Husband." [AmerPoR] (22:1) Ja-F 93, p. 55.
4893. OLDS-ELLINGSON, Alice
"About-the-City Poems." [PikeF] (11) Fall 93, p. 28.
"Letter to Orpheus." [PikeF] (11) Fall 93, p. 9.
4894. OLEAF, Jerry
"The Good Day." [Footwork] (23) 93, p. 141.
"Inscription in Stone." [Footwork] (23) 93, p. 141.

"A Shadow." [Footwork] (23) 93, p. 141.
"The Sylphe." [Footwork] (23) 93, p. 142.
4895. OLESON, Anne Britting
"The Glove." [Spitball] (44) Sum 93, p. 3.
4896. OLINKA, Sharon
"The Legacy." [ApalQ] (35) 90, p. 45-46.
4897. OLIPHANT, Andries Walter
"Childhood in Heidelberg." [BostonR] (18:3/4) Je-Ag 93, p. 31.
"Rivers." [BostonR] (18:3/4) Je-Ag 93, p. 31.
OLIVA, Antonio Desquirón
See DESQUIRON OLIVA, Antonio
4898. OLIVAS, Henry Claro, Jr.
"The Unreal." [OnTheBus] (5:2, #12) Sum-Fall 93, p. 159.
4899. OLIVE, Harry
"Green Spring in the Morning." [Elf] (3:4) Wint 93, p. 23.
"Here." [Elf] (3:4) Wint 93, p. 24.
"Lost in the Iodine of Green Kelp Seas." [Plain] (13:3) Spr 93, p. 14.
"Reaching Out Past Pale Illuminations." [Elf] (3:4) Wint 93, p. 21.
"Sometimes, I Think We Are All Sunblasted Birds." [Elf] (3:2) Sum 93, p. 35.
"There Is a Joyous Sound." [Elf] (3:2) Sum 93, p. 34.
"To Win Deliverance." [Elf] (3:4) Wint 93, p. 22.
4900. OLIVER, Mary
"August." [Poetry] (162:5) Ag 93, p. 249.
"Beside the Waterfall." [Poetry] (162:5) Ag 93, p. 250-251.
"In Pobiddy, Georgia." [SouthernR] (29:1) Wint, Ja 93, p. 154-155.
"Little Owl Who Lives in the Orchard." [PoetryE] (35) Spr 93, p. 15-16.
"Owl in the Winter Trees." [Colum] (20) Sum 93, p. 7-8.
"A Poem for the Blue Heron." [NewEngR] (15:1) Wint 93, p. 181-182.
"The Sea Mouse." [Atlantic] (271:1) Ja 93, p. 100.
"Spiders." [AmerV] (30) 93, p. 39.
"Warblers." [SouthernR] (29:1) Wint, Ja 93, p. 155-156.
"When Death Comes." [PoetryE] (35) Spr 93, p. 18-19.
"White Owl Flies Into and Out of the Field." [PoetryE] (35) Spr 93, p. 13-14.
"Work." [Colum] (20) Sum 93, p. 9.
4901. OLIVER, Raymond
"Diminishment." [Thrpny] (53) Spr 93, p. 29.
"Length of Life." [Thrpny] (53) Spr 93, p. 29.
"Old Man." [Thrpny] (53) Spr 93, p. 29.
4902. OLSEN, Lance
"Arrival." [ColEng] (55:1) Ja 93, p. 76.
"Giving Birth." [BellR] (16:1/2) Spr-Fall 93, p. 51.
"Pelt." [BellR] (16:1/2) Spr-Fall 93, p. 52.
4903. OLSEN, William
"Death of the Blues." [ChiR] (38:4) 93, p. 138.
"Hereafter." [ParisR] (35:126) Spr 93, p. 213.
"The Mysteries of the End." [Crazy] (45) Wint 93, p. 46-52.
"Old World Light." [ParisR] (35:126) Spr 93, p. 212-123.
"Slow Train North" (after I.B. Singer). [MichQR] (32:1) Wint 93, p. 20-21.
4904. OLSON, David
"An Oklahoma Birth." [WestB] (33) 93, p. 64.
4905. OLSON, Jennifer DeAnn
"The Blizzard Rope, Armistice Day, 1940" (for Clara and Ralph Hanson).
[RagMag] (11:2) 93, p. 30-31.
"The Open Door." [RagMag] (11:2) 93, p. 32-33.
4906. OLSON, John
"Amphibious Muse." [NewAW] (11) Sum-Fall 93, p. 89-90.
"Andalusian Fog." [NewAW] (11) Sum-Fall 93, p. 91-92.
"Armoire." [Caliban] (12) 93, p. 30-31.
"Gothic Mud." [NewAW] (11) Sum-Fall 93, p. 87-88.
"Perturbed Guitar with Boom and Bow." [NewAW] (11) Sum-Fall 93, p. 93-94.
"Sudden from Heaven." [Caliban] (12) 93, p. 28-29.
4907. OLSON, Toby
"A Note." [PaintedB] (50/51) 93, p. 107.
4908. OLSSON, Kurt S.
"Only Son" (Greensboro Review Literary Award Poem: Honorable Mention).
[GreensboroR] (55) Wint 93-94, p. 106.

4909. OLSZEWSKI, Greg
   "I Bought a Yesteryear Major-league Replica Cap." [Spitball] (45) Fall 93, p. 13.
4910. O'MALLEY, Mary
   "Forgive Me That I Am Coping Badly" (After Akhmatova). [SenR] (23:1/2) Wint 93, p. 26.
   "Scars." [SenR] (23:1/2) Wint 93, p. 25.
   "The Shape of Saying." [SenR] (23:1/2) Wint 93, p. 20.
   "The Storm." [SenR] (23:1/2) Wint 93, p. 23-24.
   "Tracing" (For my Father and Richard Murphy). [SenR] (23:1/2) Wint 93, p. 21-22.
4911. O'NAN, Stewart
   "Body Count." [ChatR] (13:4) Sum 93, p. 44-45.
   "The Last Corn of Summer." [ChatR] (13:4) Sum 93, p. 46-47.
4912. O'NEILL, Brendan
   "Socrates." [AlabamaLR] (7:1) 93, p. 16-17.
4913. O'NEILL, Brian
   "Blizzard." [SoCarR] (25:2) Spr 93, p. 127-128.
   "Winter Run" (for Rory Holscher). [HopewellR] (5) 93, p. 75-80.
4914. O'NEILL, Elizabeth Stone
   "Metronome." [NewRena] (8:3, #26) Spr 93, p. 113-114.
4915. O'NEILL, John
   "Bear." [CanLit] (137) Sum 93, p. 74.
   "Grand Canyon." [PoetryC] (13:4) 93, p. 14.
   "Monument Valley." [PoetryC] (13:4) 93, p. 14.
   "On the Big Rez." [PoetryC] (13:4) 93, p. 14.
   "Patti Catches a Ride, Mojave." [PoetryC] (13:4) 93, p. 14.
4916. ONESS, Chad
   "August 1990." [BlackWR] (20:1) Fall-Wint 93, p. 59.
   "Not Grace Exactly" (for Boyd White). [SoCoast] (15) Je 93, p. 52.
4917. OPPEDAHL, Rachel
   "Far Away from the House and the Voices, the Crying, the Slam of the Back Screen Door." [SoCoast] (15) Je 93, p. 34.
4918. OPPEN, George
   "Nation." [Thrpny] (52) Wint 93, p. 16.
   "Street." [AmerPoR] (22:5) S-O 93, p. 31.
4919. ORAC, Vera
   "For Greater Precision" (tr. of Sylva Fischerová, w. Stuart Friebert). [Field] (49) Fall 93, p. 86.
   "Land of Mud" (Warsaw-Leningrad Express, tr. of Sylva Fischerová, w. Stuart Friebert). [Field] (49) Fall 93, p. 88.
   "A Totally New Time, a Completely New Era" (tr. of Sylva Fischerová, w. Stuart Friebert). [Field] (49) Fall 93, p. 87.
4920. ORAVECZ, Imre
   "How Many" (tr. by Bruce Berlind, w. Mária Körösy). [ProseP] (1) 92, p. 65.
   "I Remember Clearly" (tr. by Bruce Berlind, w. Mária Körösy). [ProseP] (1) 92, p. 66-67.
   "It Happened in the Afternoon" (tr. by Bruce Berlind). [ProseP] (2) 93, p. 72-73.
   "Now Then" (tr. by Bruce Berlind). [ProseP] (2) 93, p. 74-75.
   "September, 1972" (2 selections, tr. by Bruce Berlind). [Talisman] (11) Fall 93, p. 266-267.
   "September, 1972" (3 selections, tr. by Bruce Berlind). [Talisman] (10) Spr 93, p. 79-81.
   "Today, Accidentally" (tr. by Bruce Berlind). [BostonR] (18:1) Ja-F 93, p. 25.
4921. ORBAN, Ottó
   "Bird" (tr. by Jascha Kessler, w. Mária Körösy). [InterPR] (19:2) Fall 93, p. 39.
   "The Boat" (tr. by Jascha Kessler, w. Mária Körösy). [InterPR] (19:2) Fall 93, p. 47.
   "Builders" (tr. by Jascha Kessler, w. Mária Körösy). [InterPR] (19:2) Fall 93, p. 41.
   "Canto" (tr. by Bruce Berlind and Mária Körösy). [CharR] (19:2) Fall 93, p. 144 - 145.
   "Csónak." [InterPR] (19:2) Fall 93, p. 46.
   "Építök." [InterPR] (19:2) Fall 93, p. 40.
   "The General" (tr. by Jascha Kessler, w. Mária Körösy). [InterPR] (19:2) Fall 93, p. 45.
   "Gitár." [InterPR] (19:2) Fall 93, p. 48.
   "Guitar" (tr. by Jascha Kessler, w. Mária Körösy). [InterPR] (19:2) Fall 93, p. 49.
   "Madár." [InterPR] (19:2) Fall 93, p. 38.

"Minneapolis Intersection" (a topographical poem, to Ken Bales, tr. by Bruce
   Berlind and Mária Körösy). [CharR] (19:2) Fall 93, p. 140-141.
"Oklahoma Gold" (tr. by Bruce Berlind and Mária Körösy). [CharR] (19:2) Fall 93,
   p. 142-143.
"On My Fifty-First Birthday in Minneapolis" (tr. by Bruce Berlind and Mária
   Körösy). [CharR] (19:2) Fall 93, p. 147.
"Séta." [InterPR] (19:2) Fall 93, p. 42.
"Snow" (Eyewitness News, Channel Five, Minneapolis-St. Paul, tr. by Bruce
   Berlind and Mária Körösy). [CharR] (19:2) Fall 93, p. 140.
"A Stroll" (tr. by Jascha Kessler, w. Mária Körösy). [InterPR] (19:2) Fall 93, p. 43.
"Sunday in a Small American Town" (tr. by Bruce Berlind and Mária Körösy).
   [CharR] (19:2) Fall 93, p. 146.
"Tábonok." [InterPR] (19:2) Fall 93, p. 44.
"University Commencement" ("The National Weather Service has issued a tornado
   warning," tr. by Bruce Berlind and Mária Körösy). [CharR] (19:2) Fall 93, p.
   147.
4922. ORELLI, Giorgio
   "Blu di Metilene." [LitR] (36:4) Sum 93, p. 495.
   "Methylene Blue" (tr. by Stephen Sartarelli). [LitR] (36:4) Sum 93, p. 494.
4923. OREM, Laura L.
   "The Diplomats." [Nimrod] (37:1) Fall-Wint 93, p. 82.
   "In Water." [Nimrod] (37:1) Fall-Wint 93, p. 83.
ORIANS, Judith Nichols
   See NICHOLS-ORIANS, Judith
4924. ORLANDERSMITH, Dael
   "Evangeline." [Bomb] (45) Fall 93, p. 75.
   "The Poet" (for Patricia Smith). [Bomb] (45) Fall 93, p. 75.
   "What the British Bluez Boyz Dream." [Bomb] (45) Fall 93, p. 75.
4925. ORLEN, Steve
   "The Full Women" (tr. of Esther Jansma). [AmerPoR] (22:1) Ja-F 93, p. 42.
   "In February" (tr. of Esther Jansma). [AmerPoR] (22:1) Ja-F 93, p. 41.
   "Paper Mâché" (tr. of Esther Jansma). [AmerPoR] (22:1) Ja-F 93, p. 42.
   "Requiem with Nudes" (for Adriaan Morriën, tr. of Esther Jansma). [AmerPoR]
      (22:1) Ja-F 93, p. 41.
   "Royal Entertainment" (tr. of Esther Jansma). [AmerPoR] (22:1) Ja-F 93, p. 42.
   "Sweet Sleeper" (for Casper le Fèvre, tr. of Esther Jansma). [AmerPoR] (22:1) Ja-F
      93, p. 41.
   "Twins" (for Mireille Jansma, tr. of Esther Jansma). [AmerPoR] (22:1) Ja-F 93, p.
      41.
   "Vertigo" (tr. of Esther Jansma). [AmerPoR] (22:1) Ja-F 93, p. 42.
4926. ORLOVITZ, Gil
   "Art of the Sonnet: LXIX." [QRL] (12:32/33) 93, p. 482.
4927. ORLOWSKY, Dzvinia
   "The Joke." [Agni] (38) 93, p. 105.
4928. ORMSBY, Eric
   "Antlion." [NewYorker] (69:36) 1 N 93, p. 84.
   "Childhood House." [NewYorker] (68:49) 25 Ja 93, p. 80.
   "The Crossing." [PoetryC] (14:1) 93, p. 10.
   "Florida Bay." [SouthernR] (29:2) Spr, Ap 93, p. 308-311.
   "For a Modest God." [NewYorker] (69:30) 20 S 93, p. 104.
   "Fragrances." [NewRep] (208:14) 5 Ap 93, p. 45.
   "Getting Ready for the Night." [NewYorker] (69:3) 8 Mr 93, p. 60.
   "Grasses in November." [Blueline] (14) 93, p. 104.
   "Origins." [NewRep] (208:16) 19 Ap 93, p. 42.
   "Railway Stanzas." [Blueline] (14) 93, p. 102-103.
4929. OROZCO, Olga
   "Personal Stamp" (tr. by Mary Crow). [SenR] (23:1/2) Wint 93, p. 132-133.
   "Somber Cantata" (tr. by Mary Crow). [SenR] (23:1/2) Wint 93, p. 136-138.
   "To Make a Talisman" (tr. by Mary Crow). [SenR] (23:1/2) Wint 93, p. 134-135.
4930. ORR, Gregory
   "Glukupikron" (To Sappho). [Poetry] (163:2) N 93, p. 85.
   "I Found a Bird." [OhioR] (50) 93, p. 60-62.
   "Orpheus and Eurydice." [Poetry] (163:2) N 93, p. 86.
4931. ORR, Thomas Alan
   "White Flower of Wild Blackberry." [HopewellR] (5) 93, p. 61.

4932. ORS, Miguel d'
"Splendor Veritatis" (tr. by Cecilia C. Lee and Laura Higgins). [LitR] (36:3) Spr 93, p. 370.
4933. ORTEN, Jiří
"At Night" (tr. by Toby Litt and Tomas Mika). [Verse] (10:1) Spr 93, p. 98.
4934. ORTIZ, Chris
"Life in a Mirror." [WindO] (57) Fall 93, p. 36.
4935. ORTIZ, Hector
"I Remember." [Footwork] (23) 93, p. 37.
4936. ORTIZ, Simon J.
"History's Midst." [WritersF] (19) 93, p. 19.
"No Weather Map But Poetry." [WritersF] (19) 93, p. 20.
"The Unfolding Mystery." [PaintedB] (50/51) 93, p. 80.
"Waiting for a Friend." [WritersF] (19) 93, p. 18.
ORTIZ COFER, Judith
See COFER, Judith Ortiz
4937. ORTIZ RAMIREZ, Gloria
"Pesadilla" (from "La Soledad Es un Espejo"). [Luz] (5) N 93, p. 55.
4938. OSBORN, Bud
"Hounded to the Coast." [Event] (22:3) Wint 93-94, p. 39-49.
4939. OSBORN, Jan
"Women in My Life." [OnTheBus] (6:1, #13) Wint 93-Spr 94, p. 168.
4940. OSBORN, Karen
"All the Long Way." [PoetL] (88:3) Fall 93, p. 41.
4941. OSBORN, Marijane
"Wait!" (tr. of Juana de Ibarbourou). [Vis] (42) 93, p. 25.
4942. OSERS, Ewald
"Abingdon" (tr. of Zdenek Vanicek). [OxfordM] (9:1) Spr-Sum 93, p. 109.
"Everyday Occurrence" (tr. of Ivana Bozdechová). [OxfordM] (9:1) Spr-Sum 93, p. 83-84.
"In the Little Church of St. Mary's" (tr. of Zdenek Vanicek). [OxfordM] (9:1) Spr - Sum 93, p. 107-109.
"Pigeons" (tr. of Vladimír Krivánek). [OxfordM] (9:1) Spr-Sum 93, p. 84-85.
"Sewers (Is This How Love Dies — ?)" (tr. of Josef Simon). [OxfordM] (9:1) Spr - Sum 93, p. 106-107.
4943. O'SHEA-NOONAN, Mary-Beth
"Water Images." [CimR] (105) O 93, p. 87-88.
4944. OSHEROW, Jacqueline
"Eight Months Pregnant in July, High Noon, Segesta." [ParisR] (35:129) Wint 93, p. 84-90.
"Mural from the Temple of Longing Thither" (after Paul Klee). [ParisR] (35:129) Wint 93, p. 91.
4945. OSING, Gordon (Gordon T.)
"Dew Drops" (tr. of Guan Yonghe, w. Li Xi-jian). [PikeF] (11) Fall 93, p. 15.
"The Diver" (tr. of Ai Qing, w. Li Xi-jian). [PikeF] (11) Fall 93, p. 15.
"Looking up at the Moon" (tr. of Shi Xiang, w. Li Xi-jian). [PikeF] (11) Fall 93, p. 15.
"My Chinese Ring" (after Escher's *The Hand Drawing Itself*). [SouthernHR] (27:3) Sum 93, p. 268.
"Natural Beauty" (tr. of Ba Bulinbuhe, w. Li Xi-jian). [PikeF] (11) Fall 93, p. 15.
"The Seagulls" (tr. of Wen Jie, w. Li Xi-jian). [PikeF] (11) Fall 93, p. 14.
"Secret Talking" (tr. of Bai Hua, w. Li Xi-jian). [PikeF] (11) Fall 93, p. 15.
"Swallows" (tr. of Miao Deyu, w. Li Xi-jian). [PikeF] (11) Fall 93, p. 15.
"The Tree at the Edge of the Precipice" (tr. of Zen Zuo, w. Li Xi-jian). [PikeF] (11) Fall 93, p. 15.
"The Yellow River and the Carp" (tr. of Niu Han, w. Li Xi-jian). [PikeF] (11) Fall 93, p. 14.
4946. OSMAN, Jena
"Stray Plenum" (Selection: "Expedition (VII)"). [13thMoon] (12:1/2) 93-94, p. 49 - 52.
4947. OSMOND, R. K.
"Snowshoe Thoughts." [TickleAce] (23) Spr-Sum 92, p. 87.
4948. OSPINA, Doris
"Juego de Imágenes en Azul en Palabras." [Luz] (3) Ja 93, p. 38-39.

4949. OSTI, Josip
"Heavenly Flower" (tr. by Ruzha Cleaveland and Boris Novak). [WebR] (17) Fall 93, p. 29.
"Rose Garden" (tr. by Ruzha Cleaveland and Boris Novak). [WebR] (17) Fall 93, p. 29.
"The Stake Stabbing the Tongue Has Sprouted Leaves" (tr. by Ruzha Cleaveland and Boris Novak). [WebR] (17) Fall 93, p. 29.
"Suddenly Everyone Beheld an Empty Sky" (tr. by Ruzha Cleaveland and Boris Novak). [WebR] (17) Fall 93, p. 28.
"Vanilla's Fragrance, Peppermint's Scent" (tr. by Ruzha Cleaveland and Boris Novak). [WebR] (17) Fall 93, p. 28.
4950. OSTRIKER, Alicia
"Aaron." [13thMoon] (11:1/2) 93, p. 54-55.
"At the Van Gogh Museum" (for Rebecca and Eve. *Vincent's House in Arles*, Riksmuseum Vincent Van Gogh, Amsterdam). [TriQ] (89) Wint 93-94, p. 199.
"Disco." [TriQ] (89) Wint 93-94, p. 198.
"Disco." [US1] (28/29) 93, p. 3.
"The Exchange." [RiverC] (13:2) Spr 93, p. 157-158.
"Exodus." [Iowa] (23:2) Spr-Sum 93, p. 55-58.
"Letter of Inquiry" (for Diana Hume George). [PraS] (67:3) Fall 93, p. 20-21.
"Mark Rothko: Three Paintings." [OntR] (39) Fall-Wint 93-94, p. 45.
"Mastectomy" (for Alison Estabrook). [AmerPoR] (22:3) My-Je 93, p. 32.
"Metaphor" (For Frederick Tibbetts). [Poetry] (162:4) Jl 93, p. 189-190.
"The Nature of Beauty." [PraS] (67:3) Fall 93, p. 18-19.
"The Orange Cat" (For Vikram Seth). [Poetry] (162:4) Jl 93, p. 191.
"Rebecca's Way." [13thMoon] (11:1/2) 93, p. 49-50.
"Recovery Notebook." [PraS] (67:3) Fall 93, p. 22-25.
"Saturday Night." [TriQ] (89) Wint 93-94, p. 195-197.
"The Sisters." [13thMoon] (11:1/2) 93, p. 51.
"The Songs of Miriam." [13thMoon] (11:1/2) 93, p. 52-53.
"Spoon." [PraS] (67:3) Fall 93, p. 26-27.
"The Supreme Theme." [PraS] (67:3) Fall 93, p. 19-20.
"What Was Lost." [AmerPoR] (22:3) My-Je 93, p. 32-33.
"Wintering." [AmerPoR] (22:3) My-Je 93, p. 33.
"Woodland Spring." [OntR] (39) Fall-Wint 93-94, p. 46.
4951. O'TOOLE, John M.
"Darkness Familiar." [Ascent] (17:3) Spr 93, p. 44.
"November Evenings." [Ascent] (17:3) Spr 93, p. 45.
4952. O'TOOLE, Kathleen
"County Antrim Archeology." [Poetry] (162:1) Ap 93, p. 28.
4953. OTT, Gil
"Act of love learned over and over" (for Julia, 5/85). [PaintedB] (50/51) 93, p. 52.
4954. OTT, Martin
"Omer's Gallery." [BlackBR] (17) Sum-Fall 93, p. 6-7.
4955. OTT, Rita
"Pigtailing the Wiring." [BellArk] (9:4) Jl-Ag 93, p. 8.
4956. OTTEN, Charlotte F.
"Sunday Morning in Foster City." [Interim] (12:2) Fall-Wint 93, p. 9.
4957. OTTERY, Jim
"Earthlight." [DenQ] (27:3) Wint 93, p. 44-45.
4958. OU YANG, Jiang He
"The Garden in the Air" (tr. by Dian Li). [GreenMR] (NS 6:2) Sum-Fall 93, p. 143.
"We" (tr. by Dian Li). [GreenMR] (NS 6:2) Sum-Fall 93, p. 141-142.
4959. OVERMAN, Linda Rader
"Walls of Discovery" (dedicated to Mark Tansey). [OnTheBus] (6:1, #13) Wint 93 - Spr 94, p. 169.
4960. OVERSTREET, Roy
"Windows facing north get no sun." [Border] (2) Spr 93, p. 55-56.
4961. OVID
"The Book of Changes I" (Excerpt, from "The Matamorphoses, tr. by David R. Slavitt). [Boulevard] (8:1, #22) Spr 93, p. 110-113.
"The Metamorphoses of Ovid" (Selection: Boox IX, tr. by David R. Slavitt). [TexasR] (14:1/2) Spr-Sum 93, p. 107-108.
"The Tale of Myrrha" (tr. by David R. Slavitt). [GrandS] (12:3, #47) Fall 93, p. 137-143.

"Tiresias and Narcissus" (from "Metamorphoses," Book III, tr. by David R. Slavitt).
[MichQR] (32:4) Fall 93, p. 631-637.
4962. OWECHKO, Hala
"No Thank You." [ChironR] (12:1, #34) Spr 93, p. 44.
4963. OWEN, Deborah L.
"It's Basic" (tr. of Luisa Castro). [LitR] (36:3) Spr 93, p. 362-364.
4964. OWEN, Jan
"It." [Verse] (10:1) Spr 93, p. 6.
"Parabola." [Verse] (10:1) Spr 93, p. 5-6.
"The Treacherous Hour" (The Pyrenees Highway). [Nimrod] (36:2) Spr-Sum 93, p.
86.
4965. OWEN, Sue
"These Fireflies." [Poetry] (162:5) Ag 93, p. 281.
"Three Peas in a Pod." [Iowa] (23:3) Fall 93, p. 75.
4966. OWENBEY, Brian
"What My Mother Left." [ChironR] (12:1, #34) Spr 93, p. 45.
4967. OWENS, June
"Crow Moon." [Amelia] (7:2, #21) 93, p. 110.
4968. OWENS, Rochelle
"Luca: Discourse on Life and Death" (Selection: "Lines/Dust"). [AnotherCM] (25)
Spr 93, p. 135-142.
4969. OWENS, Scott
"February's Air of Waiting." [Crucible] (29) Fall 93, p. 11-12.
"The Inside of Cut Strawberries Is Sharp, Sexual, Pink as Bone." [HayF] (13) Fall -
Wint 93, p. 45.
"Saint Sebastian's Widow." [CreamCR] (17:2) Fall 93, p. 160-162.
"To See If I've Really Done Anything at All." [WebR] (17) Fall 93, p. 101.
"Why I Sometimes Sing the Songs I Hated As a Child." [WebR] (17) Fall 93, p.
102.
"You in the Tomb of My Eyes." [GreensboroR] (54) Sum 93, p. 94-96.
4970. OWENS, Susan
"Off Off Off Off Broadway." [SpoonR] (18:2) Sum-Fall 93, p. 38-40.
4971. OWENS, Suzanne
"Baptism." [CumbPR]] (13:1) Fall 93, p. 88-90.
4972. OWNBEY, Brian
"Detour." [Pembroke] (25) 93, p. 111.
4973. OWSLEY, Charlie
"Picture Show." [Border] (2) Spr 93, p. 57.
4974. OXENBURGH, Peter
"An Abusers' Thesaurus, 1st Edition." [CentralP] (22) Spr 93, p. 20-40.
4975. OXLEY, William
"McGee, Doing for Himself." [Sparrow] (60) Sum 93, p. 47.
"A Sort of City Sonnet." [Sparrow] (60) Sum 93, p. 47.
"The Unignorable Thing." [Sparrow] (60) Sum 93, p. 48.
4976. OZIER, Dan
"Memorabilia." [RagMag] (11:1) 93, p. 78-79.
4977. Π. O.
"Anna." [Manoa] (5:2) Wint 93, p. 143-147.
"Two Men in a Corner." [Manoa] (5:2) Wint 93, p. [Manoa] (5:2) Wint 93, p. 142 -
143.
4978. PACE, Rosalind
"Buying a Dozen Lemons on the Way to Heaven." [AmerPoR] (22:4) Jl-Ag 93, p.
30.
4979. PACERNIK, Gary
"Vision." [HiramPoR] (53/54) Fall 92-Sum 93, p. 63.
PACHÉCO, Robert Vázquez
See VAZQUEZ-PACHÉCO, Robert
4980. PACK, James R.
"The Farmboy, Before He'd Seen Paris" (First Place, Annual Poetry Contest).
[PaintedB] (49) 93, p. 40.
4981. PACKA, Sheila J.
"Migrations" (Duluth, Minnesota). [Ploughs] (19:1) Spr 93, p. 119-120.
"St. Luke's Hospital, Duluth" (to Joanne). [RagMag] (11:1) 93, p. 70-71.
"A Woman Playing Ball." [SinW] (49) Spr-Sum 93, p. 34-35.

4982. PACKARD, William
"Odyssey." [NewYorkQ] (51) 93, p. 45-47.
"Strange." [NewYorkQ] (50) 93, p. 63.
"Virgil to Dante." [NewYorkQ] (52) 93, p. 61.
4983. PACOSZ, Christina
"An Ending." [Outbr] (24) 93, p. 3-4.
"Meditation on a Beaver Pelt." [Outbr] (24) 93, p. 5-7.
4984. PADDOCK, Joe
"Black Smoke." [NorthStoneR] (11) 93, p. 28-29.
"His Horses." [NorthStoneR] (11) 93, p. 30.
4985. PADEL, Ruth
"Archie." [Verse] (10:2) Sum 93, p. 5.
"Trance." [Verse] (10:2) Sum 93, p. 5.
4986. PADGETT, Ron
"5 Poems." [Arshile] (2) 93, p. 19.
"Bedtime Story" (for Katherine Koch). [NewAW] (11) Sum-Fall 93, p. 48.
"The Benefit of Doubt." [NewAW] (11) Sum-Fall 93, p. 47.
"Oil." [Arshile] (2) 93, p. 18.
"Twilight Slide." [Arshile] (2) 93, p. 17.
"A Visit from Hurricane Bob." [NewAW] (11) Sum-Fall 93, p. 49.
"Wickerware." [NewAW] (11) Sum-Fall 93, p. 50.
4987. PADHI, Bibhu
"Father's Voices." [HawaiiR] (17:1, #37) Spr 93, p. 68.
"A Glass of Clear Water" (For Marvin Bell). [Poetry] (161:4) Ja 93, p. 194.
4988. PADILLA, Heberto
"Allan Marquand Espera a Su Compañero de Tenis en el Campo Sur." [LindLM]
    (12:2/4) Ap-D 93, p. 3.
"El Cementerio de Princeton." [LindLM] (12:2/4) Ap-D 93, p. 3.
"Noche de Invierno." [LindLM] (12:2/4) Ap-D 93, p. 3.
"Para Que Te Liberes de un Viejo Pensamiento." [LindLM] (12:2/4) Ap-D 93, p. 3.
4989. PADILLA, Mario René
"My Father's Lullaby." [NewL] (59:3) 93, p. 78-79.
"Paris in the Winter." [AntR] (51:3) Sum 93, p. 373.
"El Pobrecito." [NewL] (59:3) 93, p. 80-81.
4990. PADILLA, Martha
"Alias." [LindLM] (12:1) Mr 93, p. 9.
"Los Duendes." [LindLM] (12:1) Mr 93, p. 9.
"Parodia de la Especie." [LindLM] (12:1) Mr 93, p. 9.
"Ración del Don." [LindLM] (12:1) Mr 93, p. 9.
4991. PADUA, Jose
"The Autobiography of a Tiny Buffalo." [Bomb] (43) Spr 93, p. 82.
"On These Days Driving." [Bomb] (43) Spr 93, p. 82.
4992. PAGE, Carolyn
"Belladonna." [BellR] (16:1/2) Spr-Fall 93, p. 67.
"While Emily." [BellR] (16:1/2) Spr-Fall 93, p. 66.
4993. PAGE, P. K.
"Autumn." [PraS] (67:4) Wint 93, p. 25-26.
"The Gold Sun." [PraS] (67:4) Wint 93, p. 21-22.
"In Memoriuam." [PraS] (67:4) Wint 93, p. 22-23.
"Love's Pavilion." [MalR] (104) Fall 93, p. 16-17.
"Planet Earth." [MalR] (104) Fall 93, p. 20-21.
"The Presences." [MalR] (104) Fall 93, p. 18-19.
"The Sandpiper." [PraS] (67:4) Wint 93, p. 24-25.
PAGELLA, Angela Blanco Amores de
    See BLANCO AMORES de PAGELLA, Angela
4994. PAGH, Nancy
"Anchoring." [PoetryNW] (34:1) Spr 93, p. 20-21.
4995. PAGIS, Dan
"Browsing Through the Album" (tr. by Tsipi Keller). [QRL] (12:32/33) 93, p. 269 -
    270.
"First Interrogation" (tr. by Tsipi Keller). [QRL] (12:32/33) 93, p. 269.
"Fractions of a Lament for a Friend" (tr. by Tsipi Keller). [QRL] (12:32/33) 93, p.
    271-272.
"Instructions to Crossing the Border" (tr. by Tsipi Keller). [QRL] (12:32/33) 93, p.
    270.
"Moments of Old Age" (tr. by Tsipi Keller). [QRL] (12:32/33) 93, p. 272-273.

"The Portrait" (tr. by Tsipi Keller). [QRL] (12:32/33) 93, p. 271.
"The Reparations Draft Agreement" (tr. by Tsipi Keller). [QRL] (12:32/33) 93, p. 270-271.
"Someone" (tr. by Tsipi Keller). [QRL] (12:32/33) 93, p. 268.
"Testimony" (tr. by Tsipi Keller). [QRL] (12:32/33) 93, p. 270.
PAHLITZSCH, Lori Storie
     See STORIE-PAHLITZSCH, Lori
PÅHLSON, Göran Printz
     See PRINTZ-PÅHLSON, Göran
4996. PAHMEIER, Gailmarie
     "Emma Remembers Somethinig of the World Series" (Game 7, October 12, 1967, St. Louis, 7, Boston, 2). [NorthStoneR] (11) 93, p. 160.
     "Emma's Kiss, Redeemed." [NorthStoneR] (11) 93, p. 161.
     "Lines Too Long for a Postcard: Love, Emma." [NorthStoneR] (11) 93, p. 161.
4997. PAIN-NOT-BREAD
     "A Brightly Lit Ship" (by Roo Borson, Kim Maltman and Andy Patton in the collaborative writing group "Pain-not-Bread"). [PoetryC] (13:4) 93, p. 9.
     "Chipmunks Enter the World of Don McKay and Jan Zwicky" (by Roo Borson, Kim Maltman and Andy Patton in the collaborative writing group "Pain-not-Bread"). [PoetryC] (13:4) 93, p. 9.
     "Pruner Speculates on Oscar Night" (by Roo Borson, Kim Maltman and Andy Patton in the collaborative writing group "Pain-not-Bread"). [PoetryC] (13:4) 93, p. 8.
4998. PAINE, Lori
     "One night." [PraF] (14:3) Aut 93, p. 120.
4999. PAINO, Frankie
     "The Battersea Shield" (for Paula Rankin). [GreenMR] (NS 6:2) Sum-Fall 93, p. 124-126.
     "Halfway" (for my father). [GreenMR] (NS 6:2) Sum-Fall 93, p. 127.
     "NDE." [PraS] (67:3) Fall 93, p. 104-105.
     "Once, Love, I Wanted Faith." [PraS] (67:3) Fall 93, p. 101-103.
     "Pietà." [PraS] (67:3) Fall 93, p. 103-104.
5000. PAINO, Gerrie
     "Nightfishing" (for Papa). [SpoonR] (18:1) Wint-Spr 93, p. 96-97.
     "Twins But Not Sisters" (for Paula Rankin). [SpoonR] (18:1) Wint-Spr 93, p. 94-95.
5001. PAKOLA, Richard
     "I Dreamt That Hugo Wolf Got Out of the Asylum." [Lactuca] (17) Apr 93, p. 20.
     "Madness." [Lactuca] (17) Apr 93, p. 19-20.
5002. PALACIO, Donna Wolf
     "Listening to Mozart." [Poetry] (163:1) O 93, p. 23.
5003. PALADINO, Thomas
     "Reverie Over and Above the Essences." [InterPR] (19:1) Spr 93, p. 86-87.
5004. PALEN, John
     "The Groundhog." [WebR] (17) Fall 93, p. 70.
     "Moose." [WebR] (17) Fall 93, p. 69.
     "On Zeno's Bus." [PassN] (14:2) Wint 93, p. 16.
     "Preludes." [WebR] (17) Fall 93, p. 70.
5005. PALEOLOGO, M. P.
     "Caparina." [Footwork] (23) 93, p. 142.
5006. PALMA, Lisa
     "Fisherman." [NewYorkQ] (50) 93, p. 77.
     "School." [NewYorkQ] (51) 93, p. 56.
PALMA, Marina de Bellagente La
     See LaPALMA, Marina de Bellagente
PALMA, Ray di
     See DiPALMA, Ray
5007. PALMER, Joanne
     "5 O'Clock." [BellArk] (9:6) N-D 93, p. 22.
     "Paris Postcard." [BellArk] (9:6) N-D 93, p. 22.
5008. PALMER, John
     "Reserve" (The Outer Banks, N.C.). [AntR] (51:3) Sum 93, p. 369.
5009. PALMER, Leigh
     "A Scratch." [NewEngR] (15:4) Fall 93, p. 104-107.
5010. PALMER, Leslie
     " *Seguidillas* to Santiago, Born in Denton" (tr. of Jesús Díaz García, w. Ishmael Bustinza). [InterPR] (19:2) Fall 93, p. 29.

"Take a Girl Flaubert Doesn't Know." [BellR] (16:1/2) Spr-Fall 93, p. 103.
"Watching Peter Arnett Report from Baghdad." [BellR] (16:1/2) Spr-Fall 93, p. 102.
5011. PALMER, Michael
"Construction of the Museum" (to E.H., 11 apr 91). [AmerPoR] (22:2) Mr-Ap 93, p. 38.
"Flight 1" (tr. of Aleksei Parshchikov). [Avec] (6:1) 93, p. 102.
"H: We sat on the cliff-head." [AmerPoR] (22:2) Mr-Ap 93, p. 37.
"H: Yet the after is still a storm." [AmerPoR] (22:2) Mr-Ap 93, p. 37.
"The Leonardo Improvisations." [Sulfur] (32) Spr 93, p. 152-155.
"Or Anything Resembling It." [AmerPoR] (22:2) Mr-Ap 93, p. 36.
"Theory of Tables" (Selections: 16-20, tr. of Emmanuel Hocquard). [Avec] (6:1) 93, p. 25-29.
"Theory of Tables" (Selections: 40-50, tr. of Emmanuel" Hocquard). [Sulfur] (32) Spr 93, p. 156-161.
"Twenty-four Logics in Memory of Lee Hickman." [AmerPoR] (22:2) Mr-Ap 93, p. 36.
"Untitled (April '91)." [AmerPoR] (22:2) Mr-Ap 93, p. 38.
"Untitled (Far Away Near)" (for the dancers). [ColR] (20:1) Spr 93, p. 38-39.
"Untitled (February '92)." [GrandS] (12:2, #46) Sum 93, p. 136.
"Untitled (kN)." [NewAW] (11) Sum-Fall 93, p. 14.
"Untitled (March '93)." [NewAW] (11) Sum-Fall 93, p. 13.
"Untitled: O you in that little bark" (for D.S.). [Avec] (6:1) 93, p. 1.
"Untitled (September '92)." [GrandS] (12:2, #46) Sum 93, p. 137-139.
"Wheel." [AmerPoR] (22:2) Mr-Ap 93, p. 36.
"Writer's Dream (The Wagon)." [NewAW] (11) Sum-Fall 93, p. 15.
"Writer's Dream (Untitled)." [NewAW] (11) Sum-Fall 93, p. 16.
5012. PALUMBO, Maria
"1941." [NewYorkQ] (50) 93, p. 78.
"Two german officers and their driver." [NewYorkQ] (52) 93, p. 59.
5013. PANDE, Mrinal
"The Fifth Man" (tr. of Gagan Gill, w. Arlene Zide). [Prima] (16/17) 93, p. 87.
5014. PANIKER, Ayyappa
"The Window" (tr. of Savitri Rajeevan, w. Arlene Zide). [Prima] (16/17) 93, p. 88 - 89.
5015. PANKEY, Eric
"Accordance." [TampaR] (6) Spr 93, p. 25.
"Apocryphal Fragments: Excerpts from a Notebook." [RiverS] (39) 93, p. 14-18.
"A Breviary." [RiverC] (13:1) Fall 92, p. 48-51.
"Don Giovanni in Hell." [KenR] (NS 15:3) Sum 93, p. 171-175.
"The Pear as One Example." [GrandS] (12:3, #47) Fall 93, p. 170-171.
"The Resurrection of the Body." [Poetry] (162:1) Ap 93, p. 26.
"Study." [GettyR] (6:1) Wint 93, p. 46.
"Trick Candle." [RiverS] (39) 93, p. 13.
5016. PAOLA, Suzanne
"Flowering Judas." [SouthernHR] (27:3) Sum 93, p. 232-233.
"Glass." [WillowS] (33) Wint 93, p. 24-28.
"Return." [SouthernHR] (27:3) Sum 93, p. 250.
5017. PAPADAKI, Athena
"The Ewe of the Vapors" (Selections: 1-2, tr. by Eleni Fourtouni). [PoetryC] (13:3) 93, p. 22.
5018. PAPE, Greg
"The Ani." [CutB] (40) Spr 93, p. 172.
"Remember the Moose." [CutB] (40) Spr 93, p. 173-175.
5019. PAPE, Ronald
"The Poet as Commuter and Cockroach." [OnTheBus] (5:2, #12) Sum-Fall 93, p. 162.
PAPPAS, Rita Signorelli
See SIGNORELLI-PAPPAS, Rita
5020. PAPPAS, Theresa
"The Church of Perivleptos." [WebR] (17) Fall 93, p. 83.
"His Skin the Color of This Coffee." [BlackWR] (19:2) Spr-Sum 93, p. 9.
"The Night, These Men." [FloridaR] (19:1) 93, p. 26-27.
"Not Watching the Men." [BlackWR] (19:2) Spr-Sum 93, p. 8.
"Playing War." [WebR] (17) Fall 93, p. 82-83.
"The Voice" (a painting by Edvard Munch). [CreamCR] (17:2) Fall 93, p. 151.

5021. PARADIS, Philip
"Bean Soup: or, A Legume Miscellany." [AmerS] (62:1) Wint 93, p. 130-131.
"Dear Neighbor." [CimR] (103) Ap 93, p. 105-106.
"Elegy for Orchardist and Orchard." [CimR] (103) Ap 93, p. 104-105.
"Goldfinch." [CimR] (103) Ap 93, p. 106.
"Tornado Alley." [AmerS] (62:3) Sum 93, p. 419-420.
5022. PARHAM, Robert
"Agamemnon on the Jukebox." [CharR] (19:1) Spr 93, p. 89.
"Beyond the Milking Barn." [CapeR] (28:2) Fall 93, p. 45.
"The Cosmic Significance or Rock and Roll." [HampSPR] Wint 93, p. 68.
"Don't It Make Your Blue Eyes Cry." [SycamoreR] (5:2) Sum 93, p. 66-67.
"Grove Workers at Frost Time." [SouthernHR] (27:4) Fall 93, p. 345.
"In the High Fierce West." [NewRena] (8:3, #26) Spr 93, p. 30.
"Thunderstorm at Night." [Elf] (3:3) Fall 93, p. 31.
5023. PARINI, Jay
"Stars Falling." [NewYorker] (69:24) 2 Ag 93, p. 65.
5024. PARIS, Marta de
"Era Una Vez America" (Selections: 4 poems). [Luz] (4) My 93, p. 26-30.
"El Sueño Que Parece Mío." [Luz] (5) N 93, p. 50-51.
5025. PARK, Anthony
"I've Been Everywhere and Nowhere." [Sonora] (24/25) Spr 93, p. 138-139.
"The Toss of Bones." [ClockR] (8:1/2) 93, p. 45.
"You and I and Sir John Franklin." [WritersF] (19) 93, p. 103.
5026. PARK, Clara Claiborne
"Writing Sonnets." [Sparrow] (60) Sum 93, p. 18.
5027. PARK, Je-chun
"Festival in Fishing Village No. 5" (tr. by Chang Soo Ko). [ChiR] (39:3/4) 93, p.
    251.
5028. PARK, Joon
"The Bookshelf Continuum." [DenQ] (27:3) Wint 93, p. 46.
"Flight of Gravity's Attention." [BlackWR] (20:1) Fall-Wint 93, p. 125.
5029. PARK, William
"Christina." [Stand] (34:3) Sum 93, p. 18-20.
5030. PARKE, Nancy
"Shoe Shop, Urbino." [Comm] (120:14) 13 Ag 93, p. 22.
5031. PARKER, Alan Michael
"The Back Porch." [AntR] (51:1) Wint 93, p. 93.
"Magpie." [TriQ] (89) Wint 93-94, p. 180-181.
5032. PARKER, Jacqueline Dee
"The Architect" (for Gene Lewis, 1934-1985). [PoetC] (24:3) Spr 93, p. 25.
5033. PARKER, Mary Elizabeth
"Boy Playing War." [Vis] (42) 93, p. 36.
"Breath." [SouthernPR] (33:1) Spr 93, p. 29-30.
5034. PARKER, Robert
"City Park." [Dandel] (20:1) 93, p. 41-42.
5035. PARKER-LOPEZ, Carolie
"Going Back to Teaching ESL." [RiverS] (39) 93, p. 57.
5036. PARKS, Ian
"Crossing the Bridge." [ChironR] (12:1, #34) Spr 93, p. 43.
5037. PARMA, Ewa
"Inevitable Meetings" (tr. by Linda Nemec Foster and Beata Kane). [InterPR] (19:2)
    Fall 93, p. 67.
"Karol's Bridge in Prague, Watercolor" (tr. by Linda Nemec Foster and Beata Kane).
    [ArtfulD] (24/25) 93, p. 12.
"Nieuniknione Spotkania." [InterPR] (19:2) Fall 93, p. 66.
"Oda do Wlasnego Kolana" (Czyli Kocham powroty!)." [InterPR] (19:2) Fall 93, p.
    62.
"Ode to My Knee" (or, I Love Reminiscing, tr. by Linda Nemec Foster and Beata
    Kane). [InterPR] (19:2) Fall 93, p. 63.
"On the Second Day of Christmas" (tr. by Linda Nemec Foster and the author).
    [ArtfulD] (24/25) 93, p. 13.
"On the Way" (for prophets, poets, visionaries and Miss Holly Golightly in her
    journey, tr. by Linda Nemec Foster and Beata Kane). [InterPR] (19:2) Fall 93,
    p. 65.
"W Drodze" (prorokom, poetom, wizjonerom i pannie Holly Golightly w podrózy).
    [InterPR] (19:2) Fall 93, p. 64.

363

PARMAN

5038. PARMAN, Susan
"Forces of Nature." [HiramPoR] (53/54) Fall 92-Sum 93, p. 64.
"Sweets for the Dead." [HiramPoR] (53/54) Fall 92-Sum 93, p. 65-66.
5039. PARMENTER, Grace
"Roomful of moonlight" (Lucille Sandberg Haiku Award, 3rd place). [Amelia] (7:2, #21) 93, p. 23.
5040. PARO, Maude
"Poetry is no excuse." [Light] (5) Spr 93, p. 37.
5041. PARSHCHIKOV, Aleksei
"Flight 1" (tr. by Michael Palmer). [Avec] (6:1) 93, p. 102.
5042. PARSONS, Jeff
"Children." [WormR] (33:1, #129) 93, p. 12-13.
"Humility." [WormR] (33:1, #129) 93, p. 12.
"Rites of Wrong." [WormR] (33:1, #129) 93, p. 13.
"Waiters and Geopolitics." [WormR] (33:1, #129) 93, p. 12.
5043. PARTRIDGE, Dixie
"Subsistence." [SouthernPR] (33:1) Spr 93, p. 13-14.
"Unnatural Laws" (Arriving Late with My Father, 77: the Northwest Coastline). [Comm] (120:10) 21 My 93, p. 12.
"Venetian Blinds." [Ploughs] (19:1) Spr 93, p. 76-78.
5044. PASCHALIS, Stratis
"Winter Afternoons" (tr. by Yannis A. Goumas). [Vis] (43) 93, p. 24-25.
5045. PASCHEN, Elise
"I Will Leave You in Possession of the Field" (From Dangerous Liaisons). [Poetry] (162:2) My 93, p. 86.
"Litany." [Poetry] (162:2) My 93, p. 87.
"Voir Dire." [Poetry] (162:2) My 93, p. 85.
5046. PASMAN, Jo Ellen
"Salvation Man." [OnTheBus] (5:2, #12) Sum-Fall 93, p. 163-164.
PASQUALE, Emanuel di
See Di PASQUALE, Emanuel
5047. PASS, John
"And Risen, Celibate." [PoetryC] (13:3) 93, p. 7.
"Lived in Nectar, Absorbed." [PoetryC] (13:3) 93, p. 7.
"A Shadow Play, Romance." [PoetryC] (13:3) 93, p. 7.
5048. PASSARELLA, Lee
"The Monkey's Paw" (for Mrs. Townsley). [LullwaterR] (4:2) Spr-Sum 93, p. 59.
"The Night You Saved the World." [Sun] (208) Ap 93, p. 31.
5049. PASSERA, William E.
"7:30 Sharp." [Light] (7) Aut 93, p. 7.
"The Teacher." [Footwork] (23) 93, p. 64.
"The Teacher." [Pearl] (17) Spr 93, p. 93.
5050. PASTAN, Linda
"The Apple Shrine." [Poetry] (162:2) My 93, p. 63-64.
"At the Jewish Museum" (The Lower East Side: Portal to American Life, 1887 - 1924). [QRL] (12:32/33) 93, p. 482-483.
"Between Generations." [QRL] (12:32/33) 93, p. 483.
"An Early Afterlife." [GeoR] (47:2) Sum 93, p. 284.
"The Floozie Clause." [PaintedB] (50/51) 93, p. 87.
"Gladiola." [Poetry] (162:2) My 93, p. 65.
"Hardwood." [VirQR] (69:1) Wint 93, p. 99.
"In a Northern Country." [Poetry] (163:1) O 93, p. 20.
"May 27." [AmerS] (62:2) Spr 93, p. 245.
"Narcissus at 60." [NewRep] (209:10) 6 S 93, p. 42.
"Snow Showers, a Prothalamion" (For Rachel and David). [Poetry] (163:1) O 93, p. 19.
"Sometimes." [Atlantic] (272:2) Ag 93, p. 81.
"What We Fear Most" (for R after the accident). [VirQR] (69:1) Wint 93, p. 99.
"Wisteria Floribunda." [Poetry] (162:2) My 93, p. 64.
5051. PASTOR, Ned
"If You're Bored, Why Not Nosh on a Bit of Nash?" (A different version of this poem appeared in the Fall, 1986 issue of Amelia). [Light] (5) Spr 93, p. 25.
"Ode to a Fallen Idol." [Light] (6) Sum 93, p. 19.
"Rafting down the Mississippi." [Light] (6) Sum 93, p. 22.
5052. PASTORIO-NEWMAN, R.
"Our Lady of Last Night." [Footwork] (23) 93, p. 143.

364

PASTORIO-NEWMAN

"These Are Acts of Devotion." [Footwork] (23) 93, p. 143.
5053. PATCHEN, Kenneth
"Two for History." [QRL] (12:32/33) 93, p. 483-484.
5054. PATE, Alexs
"Into the Heart." [NorthStoneR] (11) 93, p. 162.
5055. PATERSON, Don
"Beltane." [Verse] (10:2) Sum 93, p. 35.
5056. PATERSON, Stuart A.
"Chowdown." [Verse] (10:1) Spr 93, p. 62.
"The Leaving of Scotland." [Verse] (10:1) Spr 93, p. 59-61.
"Peace Offerings." [Verse] (10:1) Spr 93, p. 59.
"Pollok Park." [Verse] (10:1) Spr 93, p. 61.
"Still." [Verse] (10:1) Spr 93, p. 61.
PATRICIA EDITH
    See EDITH, Patricia
5057. PATTEN, Karl
"Assisi in July." [CinPR] (24) Spr 93, p. 57.
5058. PATTERSON, Raymond R.
"Ars Poetica." [PaintedB] (50/51) 93, p. 10.
"Bent Blues (Captain Lomax Wants to Know)." [Drumvoices] (2:1/2) Fall-Wint 92 -
    93, p. 73.
"Last Mile blues." [Drumvoices] (2:1/2) Fall-Wint 92-93, p. 74.
"No Jive." [Drumvoices] (1:1/2) Fall-Wint 91-92, p. 129.
5059. PATTERSON, Tori
"To a Watery Page." [AntR] (51:4) Fall 93, p. 554.
5060. PATTON, Andy
"A Brightly Lit Ship" (w. Roo Borson and Kim Maltman in the collaborative writing
    group "Pain-not-Bread"). [PoetryC] (13:4) 93, p. 9.
"Chipmunks Enter the World of Don McKay and Jan Zwicky" (w. Roo Borson and
    Kim Maltman in the collaborative writing group "Pain-not-Bread"). [PoetryC]
    (13:4) 93, p. 9.
"Introduction to the Introduction to Wang Wei" (w. Roo Borson and Kim Maltman.
    Winner of the 1993 Long Poem Prize). [MalR] (103) Sum 93, p. 16-27.
"Pruner Speculates on Oscar Night" (w. Roo Borson and Kim Maltman in the
    collaborative writing group "Pain-not-Bread"). [PoetryC] (13:4) 93, p. 8.
5061. PATTON, Christopher
"Cycling on Mayne Island." [PoetryC] (13:4) 93, p. 17.
"Dried Flowers in a Milk Bottle." [PoetryC] (13:4) 93, p. 17.
"Ice Storm." [PoetryC] (13:4) 93, p. 17.
"Tomintoul." [AntigR] (93-94) Spr-Sum 93, p. 212-213.
5062. PATTON, Sarah
"All Day." [Conscience] (14:4) Wint 93-94, p. 6.
"Blues." [Conscience] (14:4) Wint 93-94, p. 41.
"Lost Red Parrots Come Home to the Loquat Tree." [Conscience] (14:3) Aut 93, p.
    25.
"Preparing the Body." [Conscience] (14:1/2) Spr-Sum 93, p. 31.
5063. PAU-LLOSA, Ricardo
"Assimilation." [Verse] (10:1) Spr 93, p. 35.
"Carlos Enriquez." [Footwork] (23) 93, p. 45.
"Fall" (after the sculpture "Icarus" by Gay García). [NoAmR] (278:3) My-Je 93, p.
    15.
"Finally Learning to Hate." [RiverS] (37) 93, p. 12.
"Gracias, Fidel." [GrahamHR] (17) Fall 93, p. 83-85.
"Train to Chicago." [ApalQ] (38) 92, p. 44-45.
"Vigilancia" (after the sculptures of Ronald González). [RiverS] (37) 93, p. 10-11.
5064. PAUL, David John
"Single Beds." [AntigR] (92) Wint 93, p. 43.
"Weaknesses." [AntigR] (92) Wint 93, p. 42.
5065. PAUL, Jay
"The Place Came Over You." [Shen] (43:2) Sum 93, p. 59.
5066. PAUL, Laura
"Sinfonia for Strings." [HiramPoR] (53/54) Fall 92-Sum 93, p. 67.
5067. PAULENICH, Craig
"Hunting Deer." [SpoonR] (18:1) Wint-Spr 93, p. 50-51.
5068. PAVESE, Cesare
"Old Discipline" (tr. by Scott Davison). [CimR] (104) Jl 93, p. 139.

"Other Times" (tr. by Scott Davison). [CimR] (104) Jl 93, p. 141-142.
"Poetica." [ChiR] (38:4) 93, p. 149-150.
"Poetical" (tr. by Scott Davison). [ChiR] (38:4) 93, p. 151-152.
"Sad Wine" (tr. by Scott Davison). [CimR] (104) Jl 93, p. 140-141.
5069. PAVLICH, Walter
"The Ankle of Andromeda." [Manoa] (5:2) Wint 93, p. 94.
"Farmer's Market." [Iowa] (23:1) Wint 93, p. 151.
"Highway 200." [PoetL] (88:1) Spr 93, p. 47.
"Judy Garland Laughing." [LaurelR] (27:1) Wint 93, p. 74.
"Mouthflowers." [Iowa] (23:1) Wint 93, p. 150.
"Newness." [CutB] (39) Wint 93, p. 35-36.
"Notes Toward a Garden Undoing Itself." [LaurelR] (27:1) Wint 93, p. 73.
"Pistachios." [PoetL] (88:2) Sum 93, p. 37-38.
"Ruby Moon" (in memoriam: Ruby Johnson). [PoetL] (88:4) Wint 93-94, p. 15.
"Sarajevo Bear." [Atlantic] (271:3) Mr 93, p. 55.
"Throwing China into the Sea." [YaleR] (81:2) Ap 93, p. 71-72.
"Waiting for the Telephone Repairman to Show." [LaurelR] (27:2) Sum 93, p. 101.
"Walter." [PoetL] (88:4) Wint 93-94, p. 13-15.
"What Should I Write about Today?" [Manoa] (5:2) Wint 93, p. 93-94.
5070. PAVLOV, Konstantin
"The Curious" (tr. by Ludmilla Popova-Wightman). [Vis] (43) 93, p. 8-9.
5071. PAVLOVIC, Miodrag
"Again Kosovo" (tr. by Bernard Johnson). [NoDaQ] (61:1) Wint 93, p. 122-123.
"Scout" (tr. by Bernard Johnson). [NoDaQ] (61:1) Wint 93, p. 121-122.
5072. PAWLAK, Mark
"Similar But Different." [HangL] (62) 93, p. 47-49.
5073. PAYNE, Gerrye
"Two Generations After the Lynching." [Vis] (42) 93, p. 17.
5074. PAYNE, Mark
"Alba." [Talisman] (10) Spr 93, p. 119.
"Belerion." [Talisman] (10) Spr 93, p. 119.
"Poem for a Desert City." [Talisman] (10) Spr 93, p. 119.
5075. PAZUSIS, Lionginas
"Holy June" (tr. of Janina Degutyte, w. Bradley R. Strahan). [Vis] (43) 93, p. 35.
"Punishment" (tr. of Justinas Marcinkevicius, w. Bradley R. Strahan). [Vis] (43) 93,
p. 36.
"Sweet Apples" (tr. of Albinas Zukauskas, w. Bradley R. Strahan). [Vis] (43) 93, p.
37-38.
"To Live" (tr. of Janina Degutyte, w. Bradley R. Strahan). [Vis] (43) 93, p. 35.
5076. p'BITEK, Okot
"Counterpart Wife Clementine" (From *Wer pa Lawino*, chapter 2, tr. by Taban lo
Liyong). [LitR] (36:2) Wint 93, p. 178-184.
5077. PEABODY, Richard
"Bedroom City: A Found Poem" (Paperback Titles). [Bogg] (66) Wint 92-93, inside
back cover.
5078. PEACOCK, Molly
"Greeting Card Verse." [Boulevard] (8:2/3, #23/24) Fall 93, p. 27.
"The Site." [Boulevard] (8:2/3, #23/24) Fall 93, p. 26.
5079. PEACOCK, Thomas Love
"Seamen Three." [Light] (6) Sum 93, p. 22.
5080. PEARCE, Brian Louis
"Smoke Smiler." [SoCoast] (14) Ja 93, p. 54-55.
5081. PEARCE, Robert
"Atavist 2: an Expedition." [TickleAce] (24) Fall-Wint 92, p. 74.
"A Cat in Love." [TickleAce] (24) Fall-Wint 92, p. 75.
5082. PEARL, Dan
"Eastlake Avenue Bar" (for M). [BellArk] (9:3) My-Je 93, p. 24.
"Friends on the Next Street" (After Thomas Hardy). [BellArk] (9:3) My-Je 93, p. 11.
"September Memory: My Father When He Stood." [BellArk] (9:4) Jl-Ag 93, p. 19.
5083. PEARLBERG, Gerry Gomez
"The Circle Being Described." [Art&Und] (2:1) Ja-F 93, p. 7.
5084. PEARN, Victor
"Fifteenth Child." [MidwQ] (34:2) Wint 93, p. 221.
"Origami Meatballs." [PikeF] (11) Fall 93, p. 25.
5085. PEASE, Deborah
"Loss of Soul." [Agni] (38) 93, p. 76.

"Traveler." [CharR] (19:2) Fall 93, p. 117.
5086. PEASE, Robert F.
"Margueritte." [Amelia] (7:2, #21) 93, p. 108.
5087. PECK, Carol F.
"Coyote Lunacy" (Eclipse). [SoCoast] (15) Je 93, p. 13.
5088. PECK, Gail J.
"Guilt Like Salt." [SouthernR] (29:4) Aut, O 93, p. 757-758.
"Landscape." [CimR] (104) Jl 93, p. 148.
"Little Man's Gonna Getcha." [CimR] (104) Jl 93, p. 149.
"Volunteer." [SouthernR] (29:4) Aut, O 93, p. 758-759.
5089. PECK, John
"Dark on Dark." [QRL] (12:32/33) 93, p. 484-485.
"For the Engraver." [QRL] (12:32/33) 93, p. 485.
"In the Twinkling of an Eye." [QRL] (12:32/33) 93, p. 486.
"The Turn." [QRL] (12:32/33) 93, p. 486.
"Weather over the Lake." [PartR] (60:3) Sum 93, p. 420.
5090. PECK, Steven D.
"Accidentals." [Pembroke] (25) 93, p. 41.
5091. PECOR, Amanda
"Cosmology." [WestHR] (47:3) Fall 93, p. 219.
"Invitation." [WestHR] (47:3) Fall 93, p. 223.
"Riddles Wisely Expounded as Beauty Speaks from Sleep." [WestHR] (47:3) Fall 93, p. 224-225.
"Romance." [WestHR] (47:3) Fall 93, p. 220-221.
"Suppose It Were Petrarch." [WestHR] (47:3) Fall 93, p. 222.
5092. PEDERSON, Miriam
"The West of Ireland" (a series: 5 selections). [PassN] (14:2) Wint 93, p. 48-50.
5093. PEDEVILLANO, A. J.
"Breakfast." [Footwork] (23) 93, p. 55.
5094. PEEK, Patricia Randall
"Down to Sleep." [TexasR] (14:3/4) Fall-Wint 93, p. 80.
5095. PEELER, Tim
"Black." [BlackBR] (17) Sum-Fall 93, p. 19.
"I Go After the Clock." [BlackBR] (17) Sum-Fall 93, p. 18.
"Mr. October Came to Catawba County." [Spitball] (45) Fall 93, p. 47.
"So I've Got the Class." [Spitball] (45) Fall 93, p. 30.
PEENEN, H. J. van
See Van PEENEN, H. J.
5096. PEER, Andri
"Ils on Vantüraivels" (Selections: 3 poems in German and English, tr. by Ellen and Ernest H. von Nardroff). [LitR] (36:4) Sum 93, p. 462-467.
5097. PEET, Bridget
"The Flood" (tr. of Franci Zagoricnik, w. Tone Percic). [NoDaQ] (61:1) Wint 93, p. 219-220.
"Mordana" (tr. of Franci Zagoricnik, w. Tone Percic). [NoDaQ] (61:1) Wint 93, p. 214.
"Starting Up" (tr. of Franci Zagoricnik, w. Tone Percic). [NoDaQ] (61:1) Wint 93, p. 212-213.
"Striptease" (tr. of Franci Zagoricnik, w. Tone Percic). [NoDaQ] (61:1) Wint 93, p. 217-218.
"Under Four" (tr. of Franci Zagoricnik, w. Tone Percic). [NoDaQ] (61:1) Wint 93, p. 216-217.
"Under Three" (tr. of Franci Zagoricnik, w. Tone Percic). [NoDaQ] (61:1) Wint 93, p. 215.
5098. PEGRAM, Amelia Blossom
"Prayer." [Drumvoices] (3:1/2) Fall-Wint 93-94, p. 104.
"Spaces to Fill." [Drumvoices] (3:1/2) Fall-Wint 93-94, p. 103.
5099. PEIRCE, Kathleen
"Distance." [Boulevard] (8:2/3, #23/24) Fall 93, p. 67.
"Divided Touch, Divided Color" (— Georges Seurat). [ColR] (20:1) Spr 93, p. 24.
5100. PELENSKY, Olga Anastasia
"Anna Anna" (in the Carpathian Mountains). [Agni] (37) 93, p. 206.
5101. PELLEGRINO, Katherine
"Grandma." [Footwork] (23) 93, p. 144.
5102. PELLETIERE, Marcia
"In Weeds" (for D.L.M.). [PaintedB] (52) 93, p. 5.

5103. PEMBER, John
"Stubs." [Footwork] (23) 93, p. 145.
"'The Thing From Another World' Frozen Fast and Loose." [Footwork] (23) 93, p. 144-145.
"With 28 Flavors, One Must Be Crow." [Footwork] (23) 93, p. 145.
5104. PEÑALOSA, Joaquin Antonio
"Basic Operations" (tr. by R. H. Morrison). [AntigR] (95) Aut 93, p. 91.
"Blind from Birth" (tr. by R. H. Morrison). [AntigR] (95) Aut 93, p. 81.
"La Catedral." [AntigR] (95) Aut 93, p. 88.
"The Cathedral" (tr. by R. H. Morrison). [AntigR] (95) Aut 93, p. 89.
"Ciego de Nacimiento." [AntigR] (95) Aut 93, p. 80.
"Las Ciudades Tatuadas." [AntigR] (95) Aut 93, p. 86.
"The Housing Problem" (tr. by R. H. Morrison). [AntigR] (95) Aut 93, p. 83.
"Operaciones Fundamentales." [AntigR] (95) Aut 93, p. 90.
"El Problema de la Vivienda." [AntigR] (95) Aut 93, p. 82.
"Problemas de Botánica." [AntigR] (95) Aut 93, p. 84.
"Problems of Botany" (tr. by R. H. Morrison). [AntigR] (95) Aut 93, p. 85.
"The Tattooed Cities" (tr. by R. H. Morrison). [AntigR] (95) Aut 93, p. 87.
5105. PENDLETON, Denise
"Moving Closer." [NowestR] (31:1) 93, p. 62.
"String." [TarRP] (32:2) Spr 93, p. 7.
5106. PENN, Peggy
"Phantoms." [BelPoJ] (43:4) Sum 93, p. 36-37.
"Polity." [BelPoJ] (43:4) Sum 93, p. 38.
"Zona Viva: Mexico City Market." [BelPoJ] (43:4) Sum 93, p. 34-35.
5107. PENNANT, Edmund
"Armadillo." [ChironR] (12:4/13:1, #37/38) Wint 93-Spr 94, p. 32.
"Breakup." [LullwaterR] (4:2) Spr-Sum 93, p. 72.
"The Commuter." [ChironR] (12:4/13:1, #37/38) Wint 93-Spr 94, p. 32.
"The Homecoming." [LitR] (36:2) Wint 93, p. 187.
"Reprieve." [LullwaterR] (4:2) Spr-Sum 93, p. 16.
"The Tourist." [ChironR] (12:4/13:1, #37/38) Wint 93-Spr 94, p. 32.
5108. PENNER, Cheryl
"Passage." [Conscience] (14:1/2) Spr-Sum 93, p. 46.
PENNER, Raylene Hinz
See HINZ-PENNER, Raylene
5109. PENNEY, Darby
"The Theory of Bureaucratic Digestion." [13thMoon] (11:1/2) 93, p. 57.
"The Theory of Bureaucratic Elimination." [13thMoon] (11:1/2) 93, p. 56.
"The Theory of Bureaucratic Locomotion." [13thMoon] (11:1/2) 93, p. 58.
5110. PENNISI, Linda
"Resurrection." [MidwQ] (35:1) Aut 93, p. 45.
"War Song." [MidwQ] (35:1) Aut 93, p. 46-47.
5111. PEPPER, Patric
"Evening News." [HiramPoR] (53/54) Fall 92-Sum 93, p. 68-69.
PERA, George le
See Le PERA, George
5112. PERCHAN, Robert (Robert J.)
"Hunger of the Lost Children" (to Mi-ah). [ChironR] (12:1, #34) Spr 93, p. 15.
"Propinquity." [ProseP] (2) 93, p. 77.
"Time." [ProseP] (2) 93, p. 76.
5113. PERCHIK, Simon
"390. Pulling the mirror closer." [SouthernPR] (33:1) Spr 93, p. 30.
"401. Before you even saw a lake." [Poem] (69) My 93, p. 19.
"409. This rain slowly in the dark." [ColEng] (55:8) D 93, p. 906.
"458. You still don't trust seabirds." [Parting] (6:2) Wint 93, p. 32.
"460. What you hear is one winter." [HayF] (13) Fall-Wint 93, p. 23.
"460. What you hear is one winter." [Parting] (6:2) Wint 93, p. 33.
"After all, it was the rain, a day." [CharR] (19:2) Fall 93, p. 107.
"All our clothes, cleansed and nakedness." [PaintedHR] (8) Wint 93, p. 28.
"And the headwind still visible." [Os] (37) Wint 93, p. 35.
"And you, licking this reef." [NowestR] (31:2) 93, p. 15.
"Each night my mouth, my cough, my sweat." [CharR] (19:2) Fall 93, p. 108.
"The Emptiness Between My Hands: Poems to Prove the Photographs in *The Family of Man* Published by the Museum of Modern Art" (chapbook). [DustyD] 93, 24 p.

"I come to this park to train." [SmPd] (30:1, #87) Wint 93, p. 18.
"I open your letter and mouth to mouth." [Sequoia] (34/35) 92-93, p. 7.
"I Tell You." [Vis] (41) 93, p. 18.
"It takes more flickering, wires." [Os] (36) Spr 93, p. 4.
"Just off the ground and the mower." [MassR] (33:4) Wint 92-93, p. 560.
"My Arm and the Night." [CreamCR] (17:1) Spr 93, p. 26.
"Poems from Photographs" (4 poems, with photographs by John Milton). [SoDakR] (31:1) Spr 93, p. 152-162.
"The spider on this curb." [CharR] (19:2) Fall 93, p. 106.
"Spoonfed Step by Step — All Those Years." [LitR] (37:1) Fall 93, p. 57.
"These leaves getting fat." [ColEng] (55:2) F 93, p. 209.
"This Time the splinter, wedged." [Os] (37) Wint 93, p. 34.
"This watchband kept alive." [MassR] (33:4) Wint 92-93, p. 559.
"To start the limp you lace." [Os] (37) Wint 93, p. 36.
"Untitled: My camera kept strapped, frantic." [Caliban] (13) 93, p. 144.
"Untitled: That covers half the Earth with goodbye." [Caliban] (13) 93, p. 145.
"What you hear could be a mountain." [Os] (36) Spr 93, p. 5.
"Without my voice." [PaintedHR] (8) Wint 93, p. 29.
"You can still make out the waterfall." [WilliamMR] (31) 93, p. 75.
"You expect the noon-alarm at City Hall." [PoetL] (88:3) Fall 93, p. 33.

5114. PERCIC, Tone
"The Flood" (tr. of Franci Zagoricnik, w. Bridget Peet). [NoDaQ] (61:1) Wint 93, p. 219-220.
"Mordana" (tr. of Franci Zagoricnik, w. Bridget Peet). [NoDaQ] (61:1) Wint 93, p. 214.
"Starting Up" (tr. of Franci Zagoricnik, w. Bridget Peet). [NoDaQ] (61:1) Wint 93, p. 212-213.
"Striptease" (tr. of Franci Zagoricnik, w. Bridget Peet). [NoDaQ] (61:1) Wint 93, p. 217-218.
"Under Four" (tr. of Franci Zagoricnik, w. Bridget Peet). [NoDaQ] (61:1) Wint 93, p. 216-217.
"Under Three" (tr. of Franci Zagoricnik, w. Bridget Peet). [NoDaQ] (61:1) Wint 93, p. 215.

5115. PEREIRA, Peter
"Peaches." [NoDaQ] (61:3) Sum 93, p. 92-93.
"Visiting My Father's Grave." [NoDaQ] (61:3) Sum 93, p. 91.

5116. PEREIRA, Sam
"The Stereotypical Bear." [AmerPoR] (22:5) S-O 93, p. 24.

5117. PERETZ, Maya
"It's because of flowers" (tr. of Halina Poswiatowska). [SnailPR] (3:1) Fall-Wint 93, p. 3.
"Mirror" (tr. of Halina Poswiatowska). [SnailPR] (3:1) Fall-Wint 93, p. 2.

5118. PÉREZ, Anthony
"Café Havana, Budapest." [ApalQ] (38) 92, p. 40-41.
"Elegy for a Mariachi." [SenR] (23:1/2) Wint 93, p. 101-103.

5119. PÉREZ, Melissa
"The Kindergarten Way." [Americas] (21:2) Sum 93, p. 74.
"Today for Homework." [Americas] (21:2) Sum 93, p. 73.

5120. PEREZ, Michele
"Poetry in Public Places." [NewYorkQ] (52) 93, p. 88.

5121. PEREZ, Nola
"Courtyard Canary." [Outbr] (24) 93, p. 107.

5122. PÉREZ FIRMAT, Gustavo
"Dude Descending a Staircase." [LindLM] (12:1) Mr 93, p. 8.
"Leave-Taking Trio." [LindLM] (12:1) Mr 93, p. 8.

5123. PERI ROSSI, Christina
"Chase for One Lover Alone" (tr. by Diana Decker). [QRL] (12:32/33) 93, p. 275 - 277.
"Girls" (tr. by Diana Decker). [QRL] (12:32/33) 93, p. 274-275.
"Language" (tr. by Diana Decker). [QRL] (12:32/33) 93, p. 274.
"Prayer" (tr. by Diana Decker). [QRL] (12:32/33) 93, p. 277-278.
"Prehistory" (tr. by Diana Decker). [QRL] (12:32/33) 93, p. 274.
"Reminiscence" (tr. by Diana Decker). [QRL] (12:32/33) 93, p. 278.
"A Virus Named AIDS" (tr. by Diana Decker). [QRL] (12:32/33) 93, p. 278-279.
"Women's Condition" (tr. by Diana Decker). [QRL] (12:32/33) 93, p. 273-274.

5124. PERILLO, Lucia Maria
"Boot Camp." [WillowS] (31) Wint 93, p. 81.
"For My Washer and Dryer." [Journal] (17:2) Fall-Wint 93, p. 12-14.
"Pit." [Journal] (17:2) Fall-Wint 93, p. 15-16.
5125. PERKINS, James Ashbrook
"Star Sapphires." [US1] (28/29) 93, p. 21.
5126. PERKINS, Leslie D.
"Aboard a junk along the Wu." [Light] (8) Wint 93, p. 23.
"As I was paddling down the Po" (Honorable Mention, First Annual River Rhyme
Competition). [Light] (5) Spr 93, p. 29.
"The Cinnamon Bear." [Light] (8) Wint 93, p. 21.
"Laundry Day Soliloquy." [SoCoast] (15) Je 93, p. 19.
"While crossing the Styx I could tell." [Light] (6) Sum 93, p. 22.
5127. PERLBERG, Mark
"Geode." [PoetryE] (36) Fall 93, p. 15.
"Self-Portrait: Camille Pissarro." [IllinoisR] (1:1) Fall 93, p. 57.
5128. PERLMAN, John
"In the Shawangunks." [Talisman] (10) Spr 93, p. 94.
"The Natural History of Trees" (Excerpt). [Talisman] (11) Fall 93, p. 228.
5129. PERLOFF, Marjorie
"In the Storm of Roses" (tr. of Ingeborg Bachmann). [Sulfur] (32) Spr 93, p. 165.
"Shadow Roses Shadow" (tr. of Ingeborg Bachmann). [Sulfur] (32) Spr 93, p. 167.
5130. PERREAULT, George
"Tongues." [Shen] (43:3) Fall 93, p. 93.
5131. PERRILLO, Lucia
"On the Sunken Fish Processor, Tenyo Maru." [KenR] (NS 15:3) Sum 93, p. 118 -
119.
"Retablo with Multiple Sclerosis and Saint" (for Vivian Kendall). [KenR] (NS 15:3)
Sum 93, p. 120-123.
"Women Who Sleep on Stones." [KenR] (NS 15:3) Sum 93, p. 117.
5132. PERRINE, Laurence
"Caution to Old Age." [Light] (6) Sum 93, p. 20.
"Does the Lethe." [Light] (8) Wint 93, p. 23.
"An erudite scholar of Michelangelo." [Light] (8) Wint 93, p. 28.
"For each human act there's a place meant." [Light] (8) Wint 93, p. 27.
"Genesis Reconsidered." [Poetry] (163:3) D 93, p. 129.
"'I did what I did,' declared Id." [Light] (8) Wint 93, p. 28.
"If the race wasn't lost from the start." [Light] (8) Wint 93, p. 27.
"If we let the Greeks in, they'll betray us." [Light] (8) Wint 93, p. 27.
"The illusions of youth nearly dead." [Light] (8) Wint 93, p. 28.
"In the spring I am always afraid." [Light] (8) Wint 93, p. 27.
"Limerick: Marianne, an inveterate flirt." [Light] (5) Spr 93, p. 16.
"Limerick: We know about bimbos and hunks." [Light] (6) Sum 93, p. 15.
"O Britain! what glories are thine!" [Light] (8) Wint 93, p. 28.
"Old Faithful." [Light] (6) Sum 93, p. 22.
"On the Atlantic." [Light] (7) Aut 93, p. 24.
"Our God, some contend, is immutable." [Light] (8) Wint 93, p. 28.
"The pretty twins, Lottie and Lou." [Light] (8) Wint 93, p. 28.
"A Purtian looked at his yard." [Light] (8) Wint 93, p. 27.
"The Testments." [Poetry] (163:3) D 93, p. 129.
"There once was a miser who hoarded." [Light] (8) Wint 93, p. 28.
"A Thrice Happy Romance." [Light] (8) Wint 93, p. 15.
"Wariant Villanelle for Two Voices." [Light] (5) Spr 93, p. 9.
5133. PERRY, Aaren Yeatts
"Poem for Lizzy." [PaintedB] (50/51) 93, p. 124-125.
5134. PERRY, Georgette
"Descant." [RagMag] (11:1) 93, p. 67.
5135. PERRY, Kirk Hamlin
"Love (2)." [Caliban] (13) 93, p. 123.
"Self-Portrait." [Caliban] (13) 93, p. 122.
5136. PERRY, Stephen
"Night at the Texas Lone Star Bar." [YellowS] (42) Wint-Spr 93, p. 24-25.
5137. PERSAUD, Sasenarine
"Images of Father in the Cremating Heat." [CaribbeanW] (7) 93, p. 42-43.

5138. PERSE, Saint-John
"Poem for Valéry Larbaud" (tr. by Richard Howard). [QRL] (12:32/33) 93, p. 487 -
488.
5139. PERSONIUS, Gordon
"Dream Time." [Writer] (106:10) O 93, p. 25.
"Game Called." [BellArk] (9:5) S-O 93, p. 28.
5140. PESEROFF, Joyce
"The Camera As Infernal Machine." [13thMoon] (11:1/2) 93, p. 59-60.
"Woman on the Roof." [13thMoon] (11:1/2) 93, p. 61-62.
5141. PETERNEL, Joan
"Doubts of a Poet-Scholar." [LindLM] (12:2/4) Ap-D 93, p. 10.
"The Interpreter on the Santa Maria: Luis de Torres." [LindLM] (12:2/4) Ap-D 93,
p. 10.
"Synecdoche." [LindLM] (12:2/4) Ap-D 93, p. 10.
5142. PETERS, Robert
"Bishop Benson's Wife." [Asylum] (8) 93, p. 8.
"Homage to Derrida." [Pearl] (19) Fall-Wint 93, p. 79.
"Skake Board Man." [Pearl] (19) Fall-Wint 93, p. 78.
5143. PETERSEN, Keith S.
"Visit to the New York Museum of Modern Art." [GreensboroR] (54) Sum 93, p.
80-81.
5144. PETERSON, Allan
"Complexity and Sunburn." [SouthernPR] (33:1) Spr 93, p. 49-51.
"December." [Outbr] (24) 93, p. 27.
"I Better." [Footwork] (23) 93, p. 55.
"Identifiable Wings." [ContextS] (3:1) 93, p. 40-41.
"Power Sources." [Sonora] (26) Fall 93, p. 82.
"Tails You Lose." [BellR] (16:1/2) Spr-Fall 93, p. 98.
"Weather or Bruise." [Outbr] (24) 93, p. 26.
5145. PETERSON, Jim
"The Council." [GeoR] (47:1) Spr 93, p. 83-84.
"Empty Hands." [CreamCR] (17:1) Spr 93, p. 22-23.
"King Queen Jack." [TexasR] (14:3/4) Fall-Wint 93, p. 81-83.
"Work." [PassN] (14:2) Wint 93, p. 31-32.
5146. PETERSON, Lesley
"Triolet: Procrustes Is Diverted." [PraF] (14:3) Aut 93, p. 121.
"Vilanelle: Procrustes Explains." [PraF] (14:3) Aut 93, p. 121-122.
5147. PETERSON, Phyllis K.
"Transcending a Prison." [WorldO] (25:2) Wint 93-94, p. 39.
5148. PETREMAN, David A.
"Ignis Fatuus." [TampaR] (7) Fall 93, p. 51.
5149. PETRI, Gyorgy
"Before a Rendezvous" (tr. by Bruce Berlind, w. Mária Korösy). [ConnPR] (12:1)
93, p. 6.
"Crisis" (tr. by Bruce Berlind, w. Mária Korösy). [ConnPR] (12:1) 93, p. 5.
"Stopgap Arrangement" (tr. by Bruce Berlind, w. Mária Korösy). [ConnPR] (12:1)
93, p. 9.
"Thus I Registered" (tr. by Bruce Berlind, w. Mária Korösy). [ConnPR] (12:1) 93, p.
10.
"To Kornis" (tr. by Bruce Berlind, w. Mária Korösy). [ConnPR] (12:1) 93, p. 11.
5150. PETRIE, Marc
"Elegy to an Adobe Wall" (for Ross Smith, my stepfather). [OnTheBus] (5:2, #12)
Sum-Fall 93, p. 165.
"Green Light." [OnTheBus] (5:2, #12) Sum-Fall 93, p. 165.
"Whirlybird Ride." [OnTheBus] (6:1, #13) Wint 93-Spr 94, p. 170.
5151. PETRIE, Paul
"Ghost Song." [Hellas] (4:1) Spr 93, p. 21.
"Opinions." [ChrC] (110:19) 16-23 Je 93, p. 623.
5152. PETROSKY, Anthony
"Goodbye on the Wind." [GeoR] (47:3) Fall 93, p. 576-577.
5153. PETROV, Aleksandar
"Dinner by Candlelight" (tr. by Richard Burns). [NoDaQ] (61:1) Wint 93, p. 125 -
126.
"Heavenly Firebird" (tr. by Richard Burns). [NoDaQ] (61:1) Wint 93, p. 126-128.
"Poetry Visits an Old Lady" (tr. by Richard Burns). [NoDaQ] (61:1) Wint 93, p.
124-125.

5154. PETRUZELLI, David
"The Meeting." [NewYorker] (69:24) 2 Ag 93, p. 50.
5155. PETTET, Simon
"Echo." [Talisman] (10) Spr 93, p. 157.
"Pomegranates" (tr. of Özdemir Ince, w. Ülker Ince). [Talisman] (10) Spr 93, p. 86.
"Sage" (tr. of Özdemir Ince, w. Ülker Ince). [Talisman] (10) Spr 93, p. 85.
5156. PETTRUCCI, Mario
"George and the Dragon." [CoalC] (7) Apr 93, p. 26.
5157. PEZZULLO, Ralph
"Coca-Cola Man." [Vis] (41) 93, p. 32.
5158. PFEFFERLE, W. T.
"Meetings." [OhioR] (50) 93, p. 99.
5159. PFINGSTON, Roger
"Septicus Interruptus." [HopewellR] (5) 93, p. 28.
5160. PHILIP, M. Nourbese
"Black, Armed and Dangerous." [Drumvoices] (3:1/2) Fall-Wint 93-94, p. 43-46.
5161. PHILIPS, Elizabeth
"The Lake in Winter." [Event] (22:1) Spr 93, p. 42-43.
"Letter." [PraF] (14:4) Wint 93-94, p. 69.
"Nativity." [Event] (22:1) Spr 93, p. 41.
5162. PHILLIPS, Carl
"Any Moment." [PoetL] (88:2) Sum 93, p. 23-24.
"Becoming Miss Holiday." [Agni] (37) 93, p. 30.
"The Captain Hurls the Ship's Log Out to Sea." [Journal] (17:2) Fall-Wint 93, p. 57 -
58.
"Domestic." [IndR] (16:1) Spr 93, p. 27-28.
"For Erin, for Others." [AntR] (51:3) Sum 93, p. 384-385.
"For Joe, Who Is Not at All a Coin." [Journal] (17:1) Spr-Sum 93, p. 35-36.
"From the Devotions." [Journal] (17:1) Spr-Sum 93, p. 38.
"Home Movie." [HangL] (63) 93, p. 49.
"King of Hearts." [IndR] (16:1) Spr 93, p. 29-30.
"A Mathematics of Breathing." [Agni] (37) 93, p. 27-29.
"Passing." [Sequoia] (34/35) 92-93, p. 96-97.
"The Photographer." [IndR] (16:1) Spr 93, p. 31-32.
"Processional." [Journal] (17:1) Spr-Sum 93, p. 37.
"The Reach." [Callaloo] (16:3) Sum 93, p. 530-531.
"Scuttlebutt." [Journal] (17:2) Fall-Wint 93, p. 60-61.
"Sunday." [Callaloo] (16:3) Sum 93, p. 527.
"A Touring Man Loses His Way." [BostonR] (18:3/4) Je-Ag 93, p. 36.
"What Myth Is." [Ploughs] (19:1) Spr 93, p. 29-30.
"What the Cook Said." [Journal] (17:2) Fall-Wint 93, p. 59.
"You Are Here." [Callaloo] (16:3) Sum 93, p. 528-529.
5163. PHILLIPS, Frank Lamont
"Tunnel Rats." [AfAmRev] (27:1) Spr 93, p. 153-154.
5164. PHILLIPS, Louis
"1938: The Brown Bomber Defeats Max Schmeling and Retains His Heavyweight
Championship of the World." [ApalQ] (39) 93, p. 49-50.
"The Birdwatcher." [SycamoreR] (5:1) Wint 93, p. 46.
"The Flood." [CapeR] (28:2) Fall 93, p. 14.
"The Krazy Kat Rag" (Selections: 12-13). [Light] (5) Spr 93, p. 28-29.
"The Krazy Kat Rag" (Selections: 14-16). [Light] (6) Sum 93, p. 20-21.
"The Krazy Kat Rag" (Selections: 17-19). [Light] (7) Aut 93, p. 23.
"The Krazy Kat Rag" (Selections: 20-21). [Light] (8) Wint 93, p. 22-23.
"Night News: August 1986." [ApalQ] (35) 90, p. 38.
"On Reading *The Man in the Gray Flannel Suit* Some 35 Years After Publication."
[NowestR] (31:2) 93, p. 107.
"Out of Time to the Music." [DogRR] (12:1, #23) Spr-Sum 93, p. 23.
"Query." [Light] (8) Wint 93, p. 17.
"What Can Be More Useless Than Happiness?" [Footwork] (23) 93, p. 46.
"Words over the Entranceway to Hell." [TexasR] (14:1/2) Spr-Sum 93, p. 100.
5165. PHILLIPS, Robert
"Carving." [SouthernR] (29:4) Aut, O 93, p. 760-761.
"Face to Face." [Boulevard] (8:2/3, #23/24) Fall 93, p. 131-132.
"On Finding a Former Lover Cut All Dedications to Me from Her *Selected Poems*."
[WestHR] (47:1) Spr 93, p. 24.

5166. PHILLIPS, Sharon
"Starting a Star." [OnTheBus] (6:1, #13) Wint 93-Spr 94, p. 171.
5167. PHILLIPS, Walt
"American Express Accepted." [ChironR] (12:4/13:1, #37/38) Wint 93-Spr 94, p. 44.
"Generally." [BlackBR] (17) Sum-Fall 93, p. 14.
5168. PHILODEMUS
"Some Amatory Epigrams from the Greek Anthology" (tr. by James Laughlin). [Sulfur] (33) Fall 93, p. 53.
5169. PHILP, Geoffrey
"Dance Hall." [CaribbeanW] (7) 93, p. 27-28.
"Hurricane." [CaribbeanW] (7) 93, p. 29.
"John Crow Batty." [CaribbeanW] (7) 93, p. 26.
5170. PHILPOT, Tracy
"A Group Diary." [NewAW] (11) Sum-Fall 93, p. 102.
"How the Crazy Love." [IndR] (16:2) Fall 93, p. 103-104.
"The Serious Blues." [ProseP] (2) 93, p. 78.
5171. PHIPPS, Wanda
"The pendulum is tired" (tr. of Volodymyr Svidzinsky, w. Virlana Tkaz). [Vis] (41) 93, p. 15.
"Tired, Leaning on the Hills" (tr. of Volodymyr Svidzinsky, w. Virlana Tkacz). [Vis] (43) 93, p. 53.
"To Think About Eternity" (tr. of Mykola Riabchuk, w. Virlana Tkaz). [Vis] (41) 93, p. 15.
"Your Last Illusion, or Break Up Sonnets" (inspired by Ted Berrigan's Sonnets). [HangL] (63) 93, p. 50-56.
5172. PHON-ANH
"Relative Sufferings" (tr. of Hoàng Liên). [Zyzzyva] (9:4) Wint 93, p. 106.
PI. O.
See Π. O. (Greek letter at beginning of the 'P' section)
5173. PICARD, Meredith
"The Little Chair." [HampSPR] Wint 93, p. 33.
5174. PICCIOTTO, Madeleine
"The Age of the Dawn" (Excerpts, tr. of Carlos Nejar). [QRL] (12:32/33) 93, p. 257 - 262.
5175. PICCOLO, Lucio
"Night" (tr. by B. Swann and Ruth Feldman). [QRL] (12:32/33) 93, p. 488-489.
5176. PIECHOWICZ, Krzysztof
"Conservation" (tr. by Lia Purpura and the author). [ArtfulD] (24/25) 93, p. 16.
5177. PIERCE, Pamela
"Rendering." [RagMag] (11:1) 93, p. 34.
5178. PIERCY, Marge
"Between Two Hamlets." [CreamCR] (17:2) Fall 93, p. 184-185.
"Councils" (for two voices, female and male). [EngJ] (82:7) N 93, p. 87.
"Too Soon to Be True." [CreamCR] (17:2) Fall 93, p. 186-187.
"What She Tells Herself Before Dialing the Number She Never Has to Look Up." [PaintedB] (50/51) 93, p. 81.
5179. PIERMAN, Carol J.
"Farm Stories." [Contact] (11:65/66/67) Spr 93, p. 55-56.
"For the Organic Farmers" (for Jean Mills and Carol Eichelberger). [Contact] (11:65/66/67) Spr 93, p. 56-57.
"Returning Light." [RiverS] (38) 93, p. 24-25.
5180. PIES, Ronald
"Consultation Request" (*Journal of the American Medical Association*, volume 267, p. 708). [Kaleid] (26) Wint-Spr 93, p. 50.
"Creeping Thyme" (*Riding Down Dark*, 1992). [Kaleid] (26) Wint-Spr 93, p. 50.
"Memento" (*Riding Down Dark*, 1992). [Kaleid] (26) Wint-Spr 93, p. 58.
"To Dr. Paul Mendelsohn, My Former Student, Killed While Jogging" (*Journal of the American Medical Association*, volume 264, p. 568). [Kaleid] (26) Wint-Spr 93, p. 58.
5181. PIGGFORD, George
"Separate Piles." [EvergreenC] (8:2) Sum-Fall 93, p. 16.
5182. PIIRTO, Jane
"La Difunta Correa" (Postcard from San Juan Province, Argentina). [Vis] (41) 93, p. 40-41.

5183. PIKE, Lawrence
"Some Days." [RiverS] (39) 93, p. 56.
5184. PILCHER, Barry Edgar
"Lines of Thought." [Bogg] (66) Wint 92-93, p. 38.
5185. PILKINGTON, Kevin
"Breakfast." [BostonR] (18:6) D 93-Ja 94, p. 22.
"Fleetwood." [BostonR] (18:6) D 93-Ja 94, p. 22.
"From the Roof." [BostonR] (18:6) D 93-Ja 94, p. 22.
"Magis" (Watch Hill, R.I. — for my father). [BostonR] (18:6) D 93-Ja 94, p. 22.
5186. PILLER, John
"Bird Calls." [Amelia] (7:2, #21) 93, p. 53.
"Window Shopping." [PoetryE] (36) Fall 93, p. 113.
"You're Right." [GettyR] (6:4) Aut 93, p. 670.
5187. PILLING, Marilyn
"Father." [Quarry] (42:1) 93, p. 119.
"Henhouse Longing." [Quarry] (42:1) 93, p. 120.
5188. PINAO, S.
"'A'ole Hopo iho o Hawai'i" (Hawai'i is not fearful, tr. by Lilikala Kame'eleihiwa).
[HawaiiR] (16:3, #36) Wint 93, p. 15.
"Ho'ohui'aina Pala ka Mai'a" (Annexation is Rotten Bananas, tr. by Lilikala
Kame'eleihiwa). [HawaiiR] (16:3, #36) Wint 93, p. 14.
5189. PINE, Ana
"Flophouse." [ChironR] (12:1, #34) Spr 93, p. 25.
"Tattooing My Tit / and Other Things in Yuppiedom on Tuesday Morning."
[ChironR] (12:1, #34) Spr 93, p. 25.
5190. PINEGAR, Pat
"Marathon." [TarRP] (33:1) Fall 93, p. 64.
5191. PINES, Paul
"Untitled: Two fingers" (tr. of Maria Rewakowicz). [Agni] (37) 93, p. 281.
PING, Chou
See CHOU, Ping
5192. PING, Wang
"Dream at the Center of a Seed" (Translation Chapbook Series No. 21, 8 poems, tr.
of Xue Di, w. Keith Waldrop). [MidAR] (14:1) 93, p. 63-85.
5193. PINK, D. J.
"The Postmodern Mariner." [WestHR] (47:3) Fall 93, p. 280-281.
5194. PINKWATER, Susan
"Hunger." [NewYorkQ] (52) 93, p. 60.
5195. PINO, José Manuel del
"Doré II. La Pesadilla. The Nightmare" (tr. by G. J. Racz). [AnotherCM] (26) Fall
93, p. 10.
"Sexual Ode I" (tr. by G. J. Racz). [AnotherCM] (26) Fall 93, p. 9.
5196. PINSKY, Robert
"Canto XV" (tr. of Dante Alighieri). [Thrpny] (54) Sum 93, p. 19.
"Flowers." [NewEngR] (15:1) Wint 93, p. 183-184.
"In the First Circle" (A Translation of Dante's Inferno, Canto IV). [NewEngR]
(15:4) Fall 93, p. 55-61.
"Inferno" (Canto VII, tr. of Dante). [Salm] (98/99) Spr-Sum 93, p. 37-41.
"Inferno" (Canto XVI-XVII, tr. of Dante). [Poetry] (162:3) Je 93, p. 143-151.
"Inferno: Canto V (Paolo and Francesca)" (tr. of Dante Alighieri). [AmerPoR]
(22:1) Ja-F 93, p. 57-59.
"Inferno, Canto XIII: The Wood of the Suicides" (tr. of Dante). [BostonR] (18:1) Ja -
F 93, p. 19-21.
"Inferno, Canto XXII: Among the Malebranche" (tr. of Dante). [TriQ] (89) Wint 93 -
94, p. 221-230.
"Soot." [NewYorker] (69:16) 7 Je 93, p. 96.
5197. PIONTEK, Heinz
"Bees" (tr. by Ken Fontenot). [AmerPoR] (22:2) Mr-Ap 93, p. 42.
"Getting Something Done" (tr. by Ken Fontenot). [AmerPoR] (22:2) Mr-Ap 93, p.
42.
"How Music Fought Its Way Through" (tr. by Ken Fontenot). [AmerPoR] (22:2)
Mr-Ap 93, p. 42.
5198. PIPER, Janet
"Behind This Mortal Bone." [Iowa] (23:3) Fall 93, p. 139.
"Cowardice." [Iowa] (23:3) Fall 93, p. 138.
"East Texas Wild Life." [Iowa] (23:3) Fall 93, p. 138.

5199. PIPER, Paul S.
"Measures." [Manoa] (5:2) Wint 93, p. 137-138.
"The Painting." [Manoa] (5:2) Wint 93, p. 136-137.
"The Whales." [BambooR] (57) Wint 93, p. 176.
"Where the Raspberries Grow." [Manoa] (5:2) Wint 93, p. 135-136.
5200. PISTOLAS, Androula Savvas
"For My Mother." [ChironR] (12:1, #34) Spr 93, p. 37.
"The Untold." [ChironR] (12:1, #34) Spr 93, p. 47.
5201. PITTMAN, Al
"Ashes, Ashes! All Fall Down!" (for Gerry Squires). [TickleAce] (25) Spr-Sum 93,
    p. 39-40.
"Kelly at Graveside" (for Rufus Gruinchard). [TickleAce] (25) Spr-Sum 93, p. 34 -
    35.
"Limbo Dancer." [TickleAce] (25) Spr-Sum 93, p. 36-38.
"Lyrinda's Visit." [TickleAce] (25) Spr-Sum 93, p. 31.
"Maiden Voyage" (for Clyde Rose). [TickleAce] (25) Spr-Sum 93, p. 32-33.
5202. PITTMAN, Kyran
"Spider Man." [TickleAce] (23) Spr-Sum 92, p. 36.
5203. PIZER, Nicole
"Macy's Dressing Room." [Asylum] (8) 93, p. 30.
5204. PLANK, Shane P.
"Gods." [Plain] (13:3) Spr 93, p. 19.
5205. PLASTIRA, Alexandra
"Daughter" (tr. by Yannis A. Goumas). [Vis] (43) 93, p. 25.
"The Resurrected" (tr. by Yannis A. Goumas). [Vis] (43) 93, p. 25.
5206. PLATH, Sylvia
"Death & Co." [NewYorker] (69:27) 23-30 Ag 93, p. 151.
"Edge." [NewYorker] (69:27) 23-30 Ag 93, p. 154.
"Letter in November." [NewYorker] (69:27) 23-30 Ag 93, p. 133.
"Medusa." [NewYorker] (69:27) 23-30 Ag 93, p. 93.
"The Rabbit Catcher." [NewYorker] (69:27) 23-30 Ag 93, p. 148.
"Three Women" (a radio play: excerpt). [QRL] (12:32/33) 93, p. 489-491.
"Tulips." [NewYorker] (69:27) 23-30 Ag 93, p. 136-137.
5207. PLATT, Donald
"Childhood." [TriQ] (87) Spr-Sum 93, p. 182.
"First Child." [TriQ] (87) Spr-Sum 93, p. 185.
"My Father's Crucifix." [TriQ] (87) Spr-Sum 93, p. 186.
"The Nakedness of Fathers." [TriQ] (87) Spr-Sum 93, p. 183-184.
"Psalm for the Summer Solstice." [VirQR] (69:4) Aut 93, p. 661-665.
"Welcome Hardings' Clocks & Music Boxes." [VirQR] (69:4) Aut 93, p. 657-661.
5208. PLEIMANN, John F.
"Sending Anna Home." [CapeR] (28:2) Fall 93, p. 46.
PLESSIS, Rachel Blau du
    See DuPLESSIS, Rachel Blau
5209. PLETCHER, Robert
"Iraqi Eviction." [AntigR] (93-94) Spr-Sum 93, p. 230.
"Kuwait Interlude." [AntigR] (93-94) Spr-Sum 93, p. 229.
5210. PLINER, Susan
"Just You at the Last." [KenR] (NS 15:3) Sum 93, p. 178-181.
5211. PLIURA, Vytautas
"Father." [EvergreenC] (8:2) Sum-Fall 93, p. 36.
"I Dreamt of Blowing Up the Dick Clark Show." [JamesWR] (11:1) Fall 93, p. 18.
"When I Cracked His Teeth Out with a Frilly Victorian Lamp by the Bedside He
    Suddenly Remembered Where His Wallet Was." [EvergreenC] (8:2) Sum-Fall
    93, p. 37-38.
5212. PLOTNICK, Harvey
"The Skiptracer." [Rosebud] (1:1) Wint 93, p. 67-68.
5213. PLUMB, Hudson
"Hershey's Cocoa." [Kaleid] (26) Wint-Spr 93, p. 6.
5214. PLUMLY, Stanley
"Armistice Poppies." [Field] (49) Fall 93, p. 93-94.
"The Art of Poetry." [KenR] (NS 15:4) Fall 93, p. 150-153.
"Conan Doyle's Copper Beeches." [KenR] (NS 15:4) Fall 93, p. 148-149.
"Snipers." [Ploughs] (19:4) Wint 93-94, p. 96-97.
"Some Canvases That Will Retain Their Calm Even in the Catastrophe." [QRL]
    (12:32/33) 93, p. 491.

375

"Waders and Swimmers" (Merriman's Cove, Maine). [NewEngR] (15:1) Wint 93, p. 185-186.
"White Oaks Ascending." [KenR] (NS 15:4) Fall 93, p. 149-150.
5215. PLUMPP, Sterling
"Orange Free State" (for Lionel Beukes). [TriQ] (88) Fall 93, p. 156-157.
"Thaba Nchu." [TriQ] (88) Fall 93, p. 153-155.
"Thabong." [TriQ] (88) Fall 93, p. 158-159.
PO, Chu-i
See BAI, Juyi
PO, Li
See LI, Po
5216. POBO, Kenneth
"Over Dust." [AntigR] (93-94) Spr-Sum 93, p. 202.
5217. PODRACKA, Dana
"Without Regard to Autumn" (tr. by Ellen Rosenbaum). [OxfordM] (9:1) Spr-Sum 93, p. 13.
5218. PODSIADLO, Jacek
"Letter from the Land of the Red Roofs. To Anna Maria. To Pawka Marcinkiewicz" (tr. by Ewa Horodyska and Chris Hurford). [Verse] (10:2) Sum 93, p. 42.
5219. PODULKA, Fran
"The Vigil." [SpoonR] (18:2) Sum-Fall 93, p. 16.
5220. POITRAS, Edward W.
"Comparative Literature" (tr. of Hahm Hyeryon). [ChiR] (39:3/4) 93, p. 244-245.
"Punishment" (A Series of Four Poems, tr. of Shin Taechol). [ChiR] (39:3/4) 93, p. 248-250.
"Things That Float in the Air" (tr. of Chông Hyônjong). [ChiR] (39:3/4) 93, p. 246-247.
POL, Miquel Marti i
See MARTI i POL, Miquel
5221. POLAK, Maralyn Lois
"You Wouldn't Know." [PaintedB] (50/51) 93, p. 28-29.
5222. POLANSKY, Mary
"I kneel, and in the center of the rose, amid thorns." [Footwork] (23) 93, p. 129.
"Untitled: It was a spring of cool flowers." [Footwork] (23) 93, p. 129.
"Untitled: It was all there under my grandfather's apple tree." [Footwork] (23) 93, p. 129.
5223. POLITE, Frank
"Bartalk." [OnTheBus] (5:2, #12) Sum-Fall 93, p. 166-167.
5224. POLITO, Robert
"Not the Right Way." [Chelsea] (55) 93, p. 62.
5225. POLK, Geoffrey
"The Last Good Restaurant in New York." [ContextS] (3:1) 93, p. 15-16.
5226. POLKINHORN, Christa
"The Mirror." [CapeR] (28:1) Spr 93, p. 34.
5227. POLLACK, Arlene Joffe
"Willin'." [Bogg] (66) Wint 92-93, p. 45.
5228. POLLARD, Velma
"For the Gentleman of the Waterfront (Feby. 13, 1993)." [CaribbeanW] (7) 93, p. 8-9.
5229. POLLARD-GOTT, Lucy
"What You Don't Need." [PoetryE] (36) Fall 93, p. 107.
5230. POMUS, Doc
"Angel of the evening." [Antaeus] (71/72) Aut 93, p. 166.
"Every night I dream." [Antaeus] (71/72) Aut 93, p. 158.
"Fragments." [Antaeus] (71/72) Aut 93, p. 179.
"Hello Stranger." [Antaeus] (71/72) Aut 93, p. 176-177.
"I knowing I'm getting older every day." [Antaeus] (71/72) Aut 93, p. 162.
"I may be bruised." [Antaeus] (71/72) Aut 93, p. 175-176.
"I want to be somebody's hero sometime." [Antaeus] (71/72) Aut 93, p. 182-183.
"'I'm Temporarily Insane' and Permanently Blue." [Antaeus] (71/72) Aut 93, p. 164.
"Loneliness has chased me into strange corners." [Antaeus] (71/72) Aut 93, p. 162-163.
"Lonely Avenue." [Antaeus] (71/72) Aut 93, p. 160-161.
"Obscene Silly Doggeral. The Ballad of Doc and Lulu." [Antaeus] (71/72) Aut 93, p. 180.
"Prince Valium and King Toot." [Antaeus] (71/72) Aut 93, p. 169-170.

"Protégé." [Antaeus] (71/72) Aut 93, p. 172-173.
"The Real Me." [Antaeus] (71/72) Aut 93, p. 168-169.
"Red wine and blues." [Antaeus] (71/72) Aut 93, p. 171.
"Save the Last Dance for Me." [Antaeus] (71/72) Aut 93, p. 184.
"She's a *midnight lady* in a five o'clock town." [Antaeus] (71/72) Aut 93, p. 163.
"Take your losses and move on." [Antaeus] (71/72) Aut 93, p. 183.
"There's a thin little man." [Antaeus] (71/72) Aut 93, p. 162.
"They Call Me the Barber, or, the Barber's Blues." [Antaeus] (71/72) Aut 93, p. 178 -
    179.
"The Victim." [Antaeus] (71/72) Aut 93, p. 180-181.
"A World I Never Made." [Antaeus] (71/72) Aut 93, p. 182.
"You're Going With Me." [Antaeus] (71/72) Aut 93, p. 166-167.
5231. POND, Judith
"Waves." [Grain] (21:2) Sum 93, p. 141.
5232. PONGE, Francis
"Law and Order" (tr. by Dennis Barone). [WashR] (19:2) Ag-S 93, p. 14.
"Rain" (tr. by Lane Dunlop). [QRL] (12:32/33) 93, p. 492.
"Règle." [WashR] (19:2) Ag-S 93, p. 14.
5233. POOLE, Francis
"Night of the Hunger Moon." [Pearl] (17) Spr 93, p. 12.
5234. POOLE, Joan Lauri
"Queen Anne's Lace." [NewYorkQ] (52) 93, p. 90.
5235. POOM, Ritva
"Deep and Clear" (tr. of Eeva-Liisa Manner). [Vis] (43) 93, p. 19.
"Hermes" (tr. of Eeva-Liisa Manner). [Vis] (43) 93, p. 19.
"Last Year in Capricorn" (tr. of Eeva-Liisa Manner). [Vis] (43) 93, p. 18.
5236. POPA, Dumitru Radu
"The End of the History Lesson (Professor Guillaume)" (tr. of Virgil Mazilescu, w.
    Thomas C. Carlson). [WillowS] (32) Sum 93, p. 25.
"Guillaume's Song" (tr. of Vigil Mazilescu, w. Thomas C. Carlson). [InterPR] (19:2)
    Fall 93, p. 59.
"Not a monument have I raised in your soul" (tr. of Vigil Mazilescu, w. Thomas C.
    Carlson). [InterPR] (19:2) Fall 93, p. 53.
"Opinions About Guillaume" (tr. of Virgil Mazilescu, w. Thomas C. Carlson).
    [WillowS] (32) Sum 93, p. 24.
"Second Fairy Tale for Stefana" (tr. of Vigil Mazilescu, w. Thomas C. Carlson).
    [InterPR] (19:2) Fall 93, p. 57.
"Sleep My Love" (tr. of Vigil Mazilescu, w. Thomas C. Carlson). [InterPR] (19:2)
    Fall 93, p. 61.
"You Will Hear Once More: Be My Heart" (tr. of Vigil Mazilescu, w. Thomas C.
    Carlson). [InterPR] (19:2) Fall 93, p. 55.
5237. POPA, Vasko
"Last News of the Little Box" (tr. by Francis R. Jones). [NoDaQ] (61:1) Wint 93, p.
    131.
"The Little Box" (tr. by Francis R. Jones). [NoDaQ] (61:1) Wint 93, p. 129.
"The Little Box's Admirers" (tr. by Francis R. Jones). [NoDaQ] (61:1) Wint 93, p.
    129-130.
"The Little Box's Prisoners" (tr. by Francis R. Jones). [NoDaQ] (61:1) Wint 93, p.
    130.
5238. POPE, Alexander
"Rondeau" (A paraphrase of Voiture's 'Ou vous tromper bien finement'). [SoCoast]
    (15) Je 93, p. 64.
5239. POPE, Deborah
"Departure, Nice." [PoetC] (24:3) Spr 93, p. 26.
"Forecast." [Poetry] (163:1) O 93, p. 24.
"Hotel, River View." [Poetry] (163:1) O 93, p. 25-26.
"Intermezzo." [PoetryNW] (34:2) Sum 93, p. 12-13.
"Morning After." [PoetC] (24:3) Spr 93, p. 27.
"Picture on the River Cherwell." [Poetry] (162:4) Jl 93, p. 187-188.
"Scientists Search Burial Vault for Seventeenth Century Air." [PoetryNW] (34:2)
    Sum 93, p. 11-12.
"What Is Left to Tell." [PoetL] (88:3) Fall 93, p. 54.
5240. POPE, Deidre
"Palette." [Prima] (16/17) 93, p. 44.

5241. POPESCU, Adrian
"Almost Domestic" (tr. by A. J. Sorkin and M. A. Irimia). [TampaR] (6) Spr 93, p. 10.
"Elves" (tr. by A. J. Sorkin and M. A. Irimia). [TampaR] (6) Spr 93, p. 11.

5242. POPLE, Ian
"The Quiet Limits." [Verse] (10:1) Spr 93, p. 81.

5243. POPOVA-WIGHTMAN, Ludmilla
"The Curious" (tr. of Konstantin Pavlov). [Vis] (43) 93, p. 8-9.
"In the Mouthcage" (tr. of Blaga Dimitrova). [Vis] (43) 93, p. 7.
"Labyrinth: The Shadow of the Wind" (in Bulgarian and English, tr. of Blaga Dimitrova). [US1] (28/29) 93, p. 11.
"Memory of a Dream" (Selections: 2 poems, tr. of Danila Stoianova). [LitR] (37:1) Fall 93, p. 85.

5244. PORTER, Anne
"A Forest Pilgrimage." [Comm] (120:22) 17 D 93, p. 10.

5245. PORTER, Browning
"Three from the Tang Dynasty." [HawaiiR] (17:2, #38) Spr 93, p. 16-18.

5246. PORTER, Caryl
"Posting the Banns." [ChrC] (110:29) 20 O 93, p. 1018.

5247. PORTER, Helen Fogwill
"Sunday Best." [TickleAce] (23) Spr-Sum 92, p. 54-56.

5248. PORTER, Pamela Rice
"The Battering of the Rose." [13thMoon] (12:1/2) 93-94, p. 53-54.

5249. PORTS, Kim
"Before Moving." [Plain] (13:3) Spr 93, p. 15.

5250. PORTUGAL, Anne
"The Comforts of a Bench" (Excerpts, tr. by Norma Cole). [Avec] (6:1) 93, p. 103 - 106.

5251. PORTWOOD, Pamela
"Disaster." [Border] (2) Spr 93, p. 58.
" 'Lavabo' by James McGarrell." [ApalQ] (39) 93, p. 36.

5252. POSMENTIER, Sonya
"Amends with Steady Soil" (Poets of High School Age). [HangL] (63) 93, p. 83.

5253. POSTON, Jane
"The Fish Becomes a Flower." [Writer] (106:6) Je 93, p. 20-21.

5254. POSWIATOWSKA, Halina
"Drzazga Mojej Wyobrazni." [NewRena] (8:3, #26) Spr 93, p. 70.
"From Lively Painful Twigs" (tr. by Marek Labinski). [NewRena] (8:3, #26) Spr 93, p. 73.
"It's because of flowers" (tr. by Maya Peretz). [SnailPR] (3:1) Fall-Wint 93, p. 3.
"Mirror" (tr. by Maya Peretz). [SnailPR] (3:1) Fall-Wint 93, p. 2.
"The Sliver of My Imagination" (tr. by Marek Labinski). [NewRena] (8:3, #26) Spr 93, p. 71.
"Z Zywych Bolesnych Galezi." [NewRena] (8:3, #26) Spr 93, p. 72.

5255. POTOS, Andrea
"Mother's Nerves." [PoetryE] (36) Fall 93, p. 115.
"Papouli" (the word for "Grandfather" in Greek). [PoetryE] (36) Fall 93, p. 116.
"Twenty Years Later, to a Friend." [Calyx] (14:3) Sum 93, p. 42.

5256. POTTER, Carol
"Cairns." [Field] (48) Spr 93, p. 9.
"Upside Down in the Rafters." [Field] (48) Spr 93, p. 8.

5257. POTTER, G. W.
"Sonnet: Thanksgiving Day in England." [NewL] (59:3) 93, p. 88.

5258. POTTER, Sally
"Coming" (Orlando's song). [Bomb] (44) Sum 93, p. 34.

5259. POTTS, Lee W.
"Dark Wood." [PaintedB] (50/51) 93, p. 17.

5260. POTTS, Randall
"A Semblance of Place." [ColR] (20:2) Fall 93, p. 132-134.

5261. POULIN, A.
"The Closed Room" (tr. of Anne Hébert). [QRL] (12:32/33) 93, p. 190-191.
"Inventory" (tr. of Anne Hébert). [QRL] (12:32/33) 93, p. 189-190.
"More and More Narrow" (tr. of Anne Hébert). [QRL] (12:32/33) 93, p. 191.
"Small Dead Girl" (tr. of Anne Hébert). [QRL] (12:32/33) 93, p. 191-192.

5262. POUND, Ezra
"Canto 72" (tr. by the author). [ParisR] (35:128) Fall 93, p. 307-317.

"Canto LXXXIV." [QRL] (12:32/33) 93, p. 493-496.
"Chi e Questa" (after Guido Cavalcanti). [QRL] (12:32/33) 93, p. 496.
5263. POUNTHIOUN, Diallo
    "La Païenne des Vallons" (Extraits). [Os] (36) Spr 93, p. 34-37.
5264. POW, Tom
    "Alberta Morning" (Or How Newness Enters My World)." [PoetryC] (13:4) 93, p. 21.
    "Animal." [Event] (22:1) Spr 93, p. 52-53.
    "New World Dreams." [Stand] (34:3) Sum 93, p. 51.
    "Night-Night." [Event] (22:1) Spr 93, p. 50-51.
    "Swimmers" (Banff November 92). [PoetryC] (13:4) 93, p. 21.
5265. POWELL, Craig
    "Death Poems for My Father" (Frederick Powell 1912-1991). [QRL] (12:32/33) 93, p. 287-288.
    "Ferns." [QRL] (12:32/33) 93, p. 286-287.
    "Flight." [QRL] (12:32/33) 93, p. 281.
    "For Zoe Stephens." [QRL] (12:32/33) 93, p. 283-284.
    "Ghosts." [QRL] (12:32/33) 93, p. 285.
    "The International." [QRL] (12:32/33) 93, p. 282-283.
    "Katie at Twenty-One." [QRL] (12:32/33) 93, p. 281-282.
    "Mulberries." [QRL] (12:32/33) 93, p. 282.
    "Mythologies of Music." [QRL] (12:32/33) 93, p. 285.
    "The Snapshot Never Taken" (October 1940). [QRL] (12:32/33) 93, p. 284.
    "Some Words on a Stranger." [QRL] (12:32/33) 93, p. 286.
    "Vintages" (for David and Nikki). [QRL] (12:32/33) 93, p. 279.
    "Visiting Edwin" (June 20 1967-July 15 1967). [QRL] (12:32/33) 93, p. 279-280.
    "Visitors." [QRL] (12:32/33) 93, p. 280-281.
5266. POWELL, Dannye Romine
    "Almost Fifty." [Crazy] (44) Spr 93, p. 38.
    "The Day You Died I Thought It Would Be As Hard As Having to Haul All My Furniture into the Back Yard Then Sweep Up in Less Than an Hour." [Crazy] (44) Spr 93, p. 37.
5267. POWELL, Joseph
    "Bathing My Son." [QRL] (12:32/33) 93, p. 289-292.
    "The Great Horned Owl." [QRL] (12:32/33) 93, p. 294-295.
    "Leveling Grain." [QRL] (12:32/33) 93, p. 292-294.
5268. POWELL, Lynn
    "Nativity." [ParisR] (35:127) Sum 93, p. 47-48.
    "Revelation." [ParisR] (35:127) Sum 93, p. 46-47.
5269. POWELL, R. J.
    "Corpses in Copses at the Base of Mountain." [AntigR] (93-94) Spr-Sum 93, p. 184.
    "Man Disappears." [AntigR] (93-94) Spr-Sum 93, p. 186.
    "Sisters Die by Drowning." [AntigR] (93-94) Spr-Sum 93, p. 185.
5270. POWER, Marjorie
    "All These Winters." [SouthernPR] (33:1) Spr 93, p. 62.
    "Study in Gray" (for Sylvia Nicholas). [BellR] (16:1/2) Spr-Fall 93, p. 38.
    "Study in Green." [BellR] (16:1/2) Spr-Fall 93, p. 37.
    "Study in Orange." [BellR] (16:1/2) Spr-Fall 93, p. 36.
5271. POWERS, Dan
    "Technical Love #47: Inspection." [WormR] (33:3, #131), 93, p. 113.
5272. POWERS, Michael
    "Strawberries of Wrath." [Pearl] (17) Spr 93, p. 21.
5273. POWERS, Richard L.
    "Things I Can Do Listening to Music." [SouthernPR] (33:1) Spr 93, p. 22-23.
5274. POZZI, Antonio
    "The Nun's Antechamber" (tr. by Deborah Woodard). [ApalQ] (35) 90, p. 28.
    "Venice" (tr. by Deborah Woodard). [ApalQ] (35) 90, p. 27.
5275. PRADO, Adélio
    "Before Names" (tr. by Ellen Watson). [MassR] (34:2) Sum 93, inside front cover.
5276. PRAFKE, Jean
    "Men at Home from the Factory." [ColEng] (55:7) N 93, p. 779.
5277. PRAISNER, Wanda S.
    "Knotted Webbing" (Bambarra Beach, Middle Caicos). [US1] (28/29) 93, p. 15.
5278. PRANGE, Marnie
    "With What Is Left." [CutB] (40) Spr 93, p. 217-218.

5279. PRATT, Charles W.
"The Artichoke" (A Mediation on Marriage). [Light] (8) Wint 93, p. 19.
"Beating the Dead Horse." [Light] (5) Spr 93, p. 14.
"Beatnik Days" (tr. of Arthur Rimbaud). [Light] (7) Aut 93, p. 17.
"The Caterpillow." [Light] (7) Aut 93, p. 21.
"Orchard Story." [ChrC] (110:15) 5 My 93, p. 478.
"The Pleasure of Summer Light." [Light] (6) Sum 93, p. 7.
"A Song from Yeats Country in Praise of the Great Queen." [Light] (8) Wint 93, p. 16.
"Whatever It Was." [SouthernPR] (33:1) Spr 93, p. 39-40.

5280. PREFONTAINE, Jay R.
"After Death." [WritersF] (19) 93, p. 122.

5281. PRELUTSKY, Jack
"I Stared in the Mirror." [Light] (8) Wint 93, p. 16.

5282. PRESS, Karen
"Incarnate Eternity" (Excerpt). [BostonR] (18:3/4) Je-Ag 93, p. 32.

5283. PRESTON, Elaine
"DWF, 36, Sensitive, Stunning, Petite, Sexy . . . ." [NewYorkQ] (52) 93, p. 86-87.

5284. PRESTON, Scott
"Beautiful Ride" (for Simon Ortiz). [ChironR] (12:1, #34) Spr 93, p. 37.
"Learning How to Cry." [ChironR] (12:4/13:1, #37/38) Wint 93-Spr 94, p. 18.

5285. PRICE, Katie
"Actual and Ideal Forms." [Sonora] (24/25) Spr 93, p. 137.
"Atom." [Nimrod] (37:1) Fall-Wint 93, p. 125.
"Calling on a Taoist Priest in Tai-Tien Mountain But Failing to See Him" (tr. of Li Po). [WillowS] (33) Wint 93, p. 68.
"Fragments of Rose." [Nimrod] (37:1) Fall-Wint 93, p. 124.

5286. PRICE, Laurie
"Balance." [Arshile] (2) 93, p. 38.
"Boat." [BlackBread] (3) 93, p. 51.
"Early Sonnet." [Arshile] (2) 93, p. 39.
"The Easy Way." [BlackBread] (3) 93, p. 53.
"Junk." [BlackBread] (3) 93, p. 50.
"Proviso." [Arshile] (2) 93, p. 37.
"Rain." [BlackBread] (3) 93, p. 52.
"Tango." [Arshile] (2) 93, p. 40.

5287. PRICE, Ron
"Sitting on an Eastern Bluff along the Mississippi River." [PaintedB] (50/51) 93, p. 100.

PRIETO, D. C. Gonzales
See GONZALES-PRIETO, D. C.

PRIMA, Diane di
See Di PRIMA, Diane

5288. PRIME, Patricia
"Turn." [Bogg] (66) Wint 92-93, p. 44.

5289. PRINCE, Heather Browne
"Swallowtail Light, Grand Manan Island." [AntigR] (95) Aut 93, p. 37.

5290. PRINTZ-PÅHLSON, Göran
"Acrobats on the Radio: Letter to Newcomb" (For Newcomb Greenleaf, Naropa Institute, Easter 1980). [AnotherCM] (26) Fall 93, p. 111-113.
"Mozart Variations" (2 & 3, tr. of Goran Sonnevi, w. John Matthais). [Vis] (42) 93, p. 23.
"To John at the Summer Solstice, Before His Return" (For John Matthias, Midsummer 1979). [AnotherCM] (26) Fall 93, p. 114-117.

5291. PRINZMETAL, Donna
"The Chant." [ProseP] (1) 92, p. 68-70.

5292. PRITAM, Amrita
"A Meeting" (tr. by Arlene Zide and the author). [Vis] (43) 93, p. 46.

5293. PRITCHARD, Selwyn
"Joining the Imperial Bourgeoisie." [AntigR] (92) Wint 93, p. 24.
"New Stone Age." [Nimrod] (36:2) Spr-Sum 93, p. 41.

5294. PRITCHARD, Sheila Jon
"Childhood." [Writer] (106:3) Mr 93, p. 25.

5295. PRIVETT, Katharine
"The Drunkard's Last Words." [Bogg] (66) Wint 92-93, p. 54.
"Turtle." [FourQ] (7:1) Spr 93, p. 46.

380

5296. PROFFITT, Pamela (Pamela Ann)
"Church Is for Girls." [QW] (37) Sum-Fall 93, p. 204-205.
"The Gardener." [BlackWR] (20:1) Fall-Wint 93, p. 24.
"In a Letter Explaining Everything." [Sonora] (26) Fall 93, p. 71-72.
5297. PROPER, Stan
"Bad Breath Bod." [Pearl] (17) Spr 93, p. 90.
"Professor Ed." [Pearl] (17) Spr 93, p. 90.
5298. PROPERTIUS
"Four Poems" (2.1, 2.5, 2.14, 4.7. tr. by Helen Deutsch). [TriQ] (87) Spr-Sum 93, p. 225-232.
5299. PROSPERE, Susan
"Farm Life." [Field] (48) Spr 93, p. 79-80.
5300. PROVENCHER, Richard (Richard L.)
"Springhill Pen, NS." [PottPort] (15:1) Spr-Sum 93, p. 64.
"St. Peter's Harbour, PEI." [Bogg] (66) Wint 92-93, p. 13.
5301. PRUCHA, Cristine Berg
"Fall Turns Us Too." [Northeast] (5:8) Spr-Sum 93, p. 11.
"Putting the Books Back" (after Philip Levine's "Fear and Fame"). [Northeast] (5:8) Spr-Sum 93, p. 10.
5302. PRUFER, Kevin
"The Lukens Cache, Excavated 1981-1988." [TexasR] (14:1/2) Spr-Sum 93, p. 101 - 102.
5303. PRUNTY, Wyatt
"Blood." [SewanR] (101:1) Ja-Mr, Wint 93, p. 39.
"A Box of Leaves." [Verse] (10:1) Spr 93, p. 34.
"Flying at Night." [SewanR] (101:1) Ja-Mr, Wint 93, p. 40.
"The Inventor." [Shen] (43:1) Spr 93, p. 57.
"A Note of Thanks." [AmerS] (62:1) Wint 93, p. 96-97.
5304. PRZYSTUPA, Artur
"Bench Ghetto" (tr. by Tomek Kitlinski and Malgorzata Staniewska). [Verse] (10:2) Sum 93, p. 39-40.
5305. PULTZ, Constance
"Forgotten Frontier." [TexasR] (14:1/2) Spr-Sum 93, p. 103-104.
"Setting the Stage." [CreamCR] (17:2) Fall 93, p. 170.
5306. PURDY, Richard
"La Risurrettione de Giesu Cristo, 1708." [Descant] (24:2, #81) Sum 93, p. 10-11.
5307. PURISCH, Moyses
"Sonnet from London" (tr. of Vinicius de Moraes, w. Thomas Dorsett). [InterPR] (19:2) Fall 93, p. 33.
"Sonnet to Winter" (tr. of Vinicius de Moraes, w. Thomas Dorsett). [InterPR] (19:2) Fall 93, p. 31.
5308. PURPURA, Lia
"Conservation" (tr. of Krzysztof Piechowicz, w. the author). [ArtfulD] (24/25) 93, p. 16.
"Death of an Actress, Berlin 1937" (tr. of Grzegorz Musial). [Vis] (43) 93, p. 44.
"In This House" (tr. of Grzegorz Musial). [Vis] (43) 93, p. 43.
"Kitchen Study." [HangL] (63) 93, p. 57.
"Late Winter." [IndR] (16:2) Fall 93, p. 77-78.
"A Little Singing." [SenR] (23:1/2) Wint 93, p. 111.
"Tracking X." [IndR] (16:2) Fall 93, p. 79-81.
"Wall Cycle." [IndR] (16:2) Fall 93, p. 75-76.
"With the Cloud Formations." [HayF] (13) Fall-Wint 93, p. 22.
5309. PURSIFULL, Carmen M.
"To You on Wave #10." [HeavenB] (10) Wint-Spr 93, p. 58-59.
5310. PUSTERLA, Fabio
"Concession to Winter" (tr. by Stephen Sartarelli). [LitR] (36:4) Sum 93, p. 490.
"Concessione all'Inverno." [LitR] (36:4) Sum 93, p. 491.
5311. PYBUS, Rodney
"The Presbyterian Reads the Song of Solomon." [Stand] (34:4) Aut 93, p. 65.
"Walls Mating." [Stand] (34:2) Spr 93, p. 42.
5312. PYLE, Wayne
"Sometimes the Coat Closet." [NewYorkQ] (52) 93, p. 89.
5313. QASIMI, Ahmad Nadeem
"Blindfolded Bull" (tr. by Daud Kamal). [Vis] (43) 93, p. 55.
QING, Ai
        See AI, Qing

5314. QUAGLIANO, Tony
"The Leper Eye." [ArtfulD] (24/25) 93, p. 110.
"Letter from Hawai'i to David Ray." [HawaiiR] (17:1, #37) Spr 93, p. 54-55.
"Linkages" (for Barry Peckham). [HawaiiR] (17:1, #37) Spr 93, p. 56.
"The Phoenix Myth." [HawaiiR] (17:2, #38) Spr 93, p. 14.
5315. QUALLS, Suzanne
"Death of a Scholar." [BostonR] (18:5) O-N 93, p. 18.
"Katie Can't Go Out Today." [BostonR] (18:5) O-N 93, p. 18.
"Lament for a Young Son Who Fell from a Roof." [BostonR] (18:5) O-N 93, p. 18.
"Letter to David." [BostonR] (18:5) O-N 93, p. 18.
5316. QUAN, Andy
"The Last Visit." [Grain] (21:2) Sum 93, p. 127-128.
5317. QUARTERMAIN, Meredith
"Animal You." [WestCL] (27:1, #10) Spr 93, p. 114.
"Bark Burn." [WestCL] (27:1, #10) Spr 93, p. 110-112.
"Christ." [WestCL] (27:1, #10) Spr 93, p. 115.
"The Marbled Murrelet." [WestCL] (27:1, #10) Spr 93, p. 113.
5318. QUASIMODO, Salvatore
"A Negro Church in Harlem" (tr. by Will Wells). [ApalQ] (35) 90, p. 43.
"A Winter Past" (tr. by Matthew Diomede). [ApalQ] (35) 90, p. 42.
5319. QUENNEVILLE, Freda
"Having Begonias." [BlackWR] (19:2) Spr-Sum 93, p. 129-130.
5320. QUESADA, Hiram
"The Learning Dungeon." [Americas] (21:2) Sum 93, p. 63-64.
"School — AAAA!!" [Americas] (21:2) Sum 93, p. 64.
"Yo, Man!" [Americas] (21:2) Sum 93, p. 64.
5321. QUESENBERRY, Mattie F.
"Tokens of Living" (for Doug). [HolCrit] (30:2) Ap 93, p. 16.
5322. QUETCHENBACH, Bernard
"Ghost." [FreeL] (11) Wint 93, p. 27.
"Twilight." [FreeL] (11) Wint 93, p. 27.
5323. QUINN, Bernetta
"First Visit to San Michele." [AntigR] (93-94) Spr-Sum 93, p. 24.
"Garden by the Adriatic" (1974). [AntigR] (93-94) Spr-Sum 93, p. 25.
"Honesty Is Hard to Find" (A Celebration for Flannery O'Connor). [AntigR] (93-94)
Spr-Sum 93, p. 26.
"Landscape with the Fall of Icarus." [AntigR] (93-94) Spr-Sum 93, p. 29.
"Mary." [AntigR] (93-94) Spr-Sum 93, p. 28.
"Spring Comes to East Lansing." [AntigR] (93-94) Spr-Sum 93, p. 27.
5324. QUINN, John
"Bonsai." [Hellas] (4:2) Fall 93, p. 108.
"Things As They Are" (for Cana). [HolCrit] (30:5) D 93, p. 15.
"Turned Ermine." [Confr] (51) Sum 93, p. 243.
5325. QUINN, John Robert
"Home-Town Vignette." [Wind] (23:72) 93, p. 22-23.
"Tent Meeting." [Wind] (23:72) 93, p. 22.
5326. QUINONES, Migdalia
"Amor Bilingue." [13thMoon] (12:1/2) 93-94, p. 114.
"April 25th." [13thMoon] (12:1/2) 93-94, p. 112.
"Brown Angel." [13thMoon] (12:1/2) 93-94, p. 116.
"Discussions." [13thMoon] (12:1/2) 93-94, p. 117.
"I Am Here for You." [13thMoon] (12:1/2) 93-94, p. 113.
"A Satire." [13thMoon] (12:1/2) 93-94, p. 115.
5327. QUIÑONEZ, Naomi
"Aye Que Maria Feliz (or Maria Was No Virgin)." [ColR] (20:2) Fall 93, p. 72-73.
"Dali's Watch." [ColR] (20:2) Fall 93, p. 68-69.
"Ultima II True Blood Eye Shadows of the Past." [ColR] (20:2) Fall 93, p. 70-71.
5328. QUINTANA, Leroy
"Dr. Fulton." [ColR] (20:2) Fall 93, p. 65-66.
"Granizo." [ColR] (20:2) Fall 93, p. 64.
"Penney's, Closed Now." [ColR] (20:2) Fall 93, p. 67.
5329. QUINTERO, Henry
"Making Tortillas" (For Allena and my mother). [AntR] (51:3) Sum 93, p. 386-387.
RA, C
See McGUIRT, C. Ra

5330. RAAB, Lawrence
"The House on the Borderland." [NewYorker] (69:1) 22 F 93, p. 120.
"The Revised Versions." [NewYorker] (69:41) 6 D 93, p. 66.
5331. RABASSA, Clementine
"Canticle for a Memory" (tr. of Franciso Arriví). [Luz] (4) My 93, p. 33.
"City Without Me" (tr. of Franciso Arriví). [Luz] (4) My 93, p. 35.
"Upon Cobblestones" (tr. of Franciso Arriví). [Luz] (4) My 93, p. 37.
5332. RABBITT, Thomas
"Another Comedy for Paolo and Francesca." [Ploughs] (19:4) Wint 93-94, p. 134 - 135.
"In Mudville, In a Time of Plague." [Ploughs] (19:4) Wint 93-94, p. 132-133.
"Over All." [Ploughs] (19:4) Wint 93-94, p. 131.
5333. RABIKOVICH, Dahlia
"Gravitation" (tr. by Daniel Weissbort and Orna Raz). [Stand] (34:3) Sum 93, p. 10.
5334. RABINOWITZ, Anna
"Hymn." [BlackWR] (19:1) Fall-Wint 92, p. 9-10.
"Mixed Media" (for my father, 1902-1986). [BlackWR] (19:1) Fall-Wint 92, p. 7-8.
"Through Many Waters, Leaf-Light, the Tree" (for Marilyn Bergner, 1933-1992). [ParisR] (35:129) Wint 93, p. 233.
5335. RABINOWITZ, Sima
"Between the Lines." [SinW] (51) Wint 93-94, p. 26-27.
5336. RABY, Elizabeth
"Bargain." [Lactuca] (17) Apr 93, p. 11.
5337. RACHEL, Naomi
"Hidden Marriage." [HampSPR] Wint 93, p. 16.
"Natural History" (Selections: 3 poems. The Nimrod/Hardman Awards: First Honorable Mention). [Nimrod] (37:1) Fall-Wint 93, p. 42-44.
RACHEWILTZ, Mary de
See De RACHEWILTZ, Mary
5338. RACZ, G. J.
"(......................?)" (tr. of José Antonio Mazzotti). [SenR] (23:1/2) Wint 93, p. 145.
"The Anti- Ars Poetica" (tr. of José Antonio Mazzotti). [SenR] (23:1/2) Wint 93, p. 144.
"Dante and Virgil Descend into Hell" (tr. of José Antonio Mazzotti). [SenR] (23:1/2) Wint 93, p. 140-143.
"Doré II. La Pesadilla. The Nightmare" (tr. of José Manuel del Pino). [AnotherCM] (26) Fall 93, p. 10.
"I Love Your Freedom" (tr. of José Antonio Mazzotti). [SenR] (23:1/2) Wint 93, p. 146.
"On the Late Massacre in Lima: June 19, 1986" (tr. of José Antonio Mazzotti). [SenR] (23:1/2) Wint 93, p. 151-153.
"Pablo Guevara's Vision" (tr. of José Antonio Mazzotti). [SenR] (23:1/2) Wint 93, p. 139.
"The Pond" (tr. of José Antonio Mazzotti). [SenR] (23:1/2) Wint 93, p. 147-150.
"Sexual Ode I" (tr. of José Manuel del Pino). [AnotherCM] (26) Fall 93, p. 9.
"Tullumayu" (tr. of José Antonio Mazzotti). [SenR] (23:1/2) Wint 93, p. 154.
5339. RADAVICH, David
"Crossbred Driver." [PikeF] (11) Fall 93, p. 3.
5340. RADER-KONOFALSKI, Wendy
"The Noise." [BellR] (16:1/2) Spr-Fall 93, p. 90-91.
5341. RADIN, Doris
"After the Shiva." [Footwork] (23) 93, p. 86.
5342. RADNOTI, Miklós
"Forced March" (tr. by Emery George). [BelPoJ] (44:1) Fall 93, p. 48.
5343. RADOJEVIC, Vera
"Analects" (Selections: 1-2, 24, 27, 31, 33-34, 48, 50, 82, 87, 91, 96, tr. of Vito Markovic, w. Richard Burns). [NoDaQ] (61:1) Wint 93, p. 108-109.
"Between Bed and Table" (tr. of Duska Vrhovac, w. Richard Burns). [NoDaQ] (61:1) Wint 93, p. 208.
"Dugout" (I-III, tr. of Duska Vrhovac, w. Richard Burns). [NoDaQ] (61:1) Wint 93, p. 206-207.
"It Doesn't Matter Why" (tr. of Duska Vrhovac, w. Richard Burns). [NoDaQ] (61:1) Wint 93, p. 208.
"Ring-a-by" (tr. of Duska Vrhovac, w. Richard Burns). [NoDaQ] (61:1) Wint 93, p. 207.

"Visitation" (tr. of Duska Vrhovac, w. Richard Burns). [NoDaQ] (61:1) Wint 93, p. 205.

5344. RAFFEL, Burton
"Credo." [ParisR] (35:127) Sum 93, p. 285.
"Folk Talk." [ParisR] (35:127) Sum 93, p. 284.
"I Send Letters." [ParisR] (35:127) Sum 93, p. 283.
"Lovers Losing Lovers." [ParisR] (35:127) Sum 93, p. 282-283.
"The Man with a Hole in His Heart." [ParisR] (35:127) Sum 93, p. 282.
"New Growth / New Time / No Growth / No Time." [WestHR] (47:2) Sum 93, p. 132.
"Rosamund." [ParisR] (35:127) Sum 93, p. 284.

5345. RAFFERTY, Charles
"The Batsto River at Night" (After B. J. Ward). [HiramPoR] (53/54) Fall 92-Sum 93, p. 70.
"Great Egg Harbor Creek." [HiramPoR] (53/54) Fall 92-Sum 93, p. 71-72.
"Snow." [Hellas] (4:2) Fall 93, p. 55-56.
"White-Tailed Deer." [Hellas] (4:2) Fall 93, p. 56.

5346. RAGAN, James
"On Mowing a Lawn." [HampSPR] Wint 93, p. 4-5.
"Remembering Dryden on the People's Road." [HampSPR] Wint 93, p. 5.

5347. RAGSDALE, Leslie Rankin
"3-3-92." [ChironR] (12:4/13:1, #37/38) Wint 93-Spr 94, p. 17.
"Links." [ChironR] (12:4/13:1, #37/38) Wint 93-Spr 94, p. 17.
"Puzzle." [ChironR] (12:4/13:1, #37/38) Wint 93-Spr 94, p. 17.
"Strange Food." [ChironR] (12:4/13:1, #37/38) Wint 93-Spr 94, p. 17.

5348. RAHIM, Jennifer
"Confessions II: A Killing Story." [GrahamHR] (17) Fall 93, p. 40-41.

RAHMING, Lelawattee Manoo
See MANOO-RAHMING, Lelawattee

5349. RAIMUND, Hans
"Allabendlich" (from *Kaputte Mythen*, Salzburg, 1992). [Os] (37) Wint 93, p. 10-11.
"Retzer Sphinx" (from *Kaputte Mythen*, Salzburg, 1992). [Os] (36) Spr 93, p. 22.
"Souvenir" (from *Kaputte Mythen*, Salzburg, 1992). [Os] (36) Spr 93, p. 23.

5350. RAINEY, Joel
"When in Public" (Honorable Mention). [HarvardA] (127:3) Spr 93, p. 13.

5351. RAJEEVAN, Savitri
"The Window" (tr. by Ayyappa Paniker and Arlene Zide). [Prima] (16/17) 93, p. 88 - 89.

5352. RAKOSI, Carl
"Discoveries, Trade Names, Genitals, and Ancienty Instruments." [QRL] (12:32/33) 93, p. 497.
"The Old Man's Hornpipe." [QRL] (12:32/33) 93, p. 496-497.
"Song." [AmerPoR] (22:3) My-Je 93, p. 46.

5353. RALIN, Radoi
"Seduced and Abandoned" (tr. by Lisa Sapinkopf, w. Georgi Belev). [Agni] (37) 93, p. 262-263.

5354. RALPH, Brett
"Tree Limbs Letting Go of Snow." [WillowS] (31) Wint 93, p. 82.

5355. RALSTON, Connie
"Pipe Organ." [ChironR] (12:4/13:1, #37/38) Wint 93-Spr 94, p. 18.

RAMIREZ, Gloria Ortiz
See ORTIZ RAMIREZ, Gloria

5356. RAMKE, Bin
"Humiliation of the Aphorism." [OhioR] (50) 93, p. 84-85.
"The Man Without a Body" (for D.S.). [ChatR] (13:3) Spr 93, p. 58.
"A Tree Full of Fish (Nine Dreams of a Girl)." [AmerV] (32) 93, p. 130-135.

5357. RAMMELKAMP, Charles
"Man's Best Friend." [Pearl] (17) Spr 93, p. 78.
"Unfulfilled Desires Make Lifelong Ideals." [Pearl] (19) Fall-Wint 93, p. 67.

5358. RAMNATH, S.
"Blue Nude." [ChironR] (12:4/13:1, #37/38) Wint 93-Spr 94, p. 46.
"Los Angeles, April 1992." [Gaia] (3) O 93, p. 18.
"Weltschmerz." [ChironR] (12:1, #34) Spr 93, p. 30.

5359. RAMPOLOKENG, Lesego
"For the Oral." [BostonR] (18:3/4) Je-Ag 93, p. 32.

5360. RAMSAY, John
"Catholic Courtship, 1965." [GrahamHR] (17) Fall 93, p. 33-34.
5361. RAMSEY, Jarold
"The Glances." [QRL] (12:32/33) 93, p. 295-296.
"Indian Heaven" (for Charlie Jackson, elder). [QRL] (12:32/33) 93, p. 297-298.
"'October': The Brothers Limbourg." [QRL] (12:32/33) 93, p. 298-299.
"A Presence." [QRL] (12:32/33) 93, p. 300.
"Romanticism, a Sequel." [QRL] (12:32/33) 93, p. 295.
"To Save the Innocent, Anything Possible" (for Sophia). [QRL] (12:32/33) 93, p. 299.
"Working Out" (in memory of Jim Spenko). [QRL] (12:32/33) 93, p. 296-297.
5362. RAMSEY, Paul
"Scenes for a Dying." [PoetL] (88:4) Wint 93-94, p. 51-54.
"Witnessing the Sea." [FourQ] (7:1) Spr 93, p. 9.
5363. RAMSEY, William M.
"Ch'in Concubine by Her Pond." [CumbPR]] (13:1) Fall 93, p. 67.
"The Ch'in Envoy" (Third letter to the Emperor). [CumbPR]] (13:1) Fall 93, p. 65.
"The General." [CumbPR]] (13:1) Fall 93, p. 66.
"Students in Line." [TarRP] (33:1) Fall 93, p. 29.
5364. RANAN, Wendy
"Color Code." [GrahamHR] (17) Fall 93, p. 27.
"Continuity." [GrahamHR] (17) Fall 93, p. 28.
"The Six O'Clock News." [GrahamHR] (17) Fall 93, p. 25.
"Vespers." [GrahamHR] (17) Fall 93, p. 26.
5365. RANCOURT, Jacques
"Looks Like the Day Will Take Its Time" (tr. by Michele Brondy). [Vis] (42) 93, p. 9.
5366. RANDALL, D'Arcy
"Moreton Island." [Nimrod] (36:2) Spr-Sum 93, p. 12.
5367. RANDALL, Margaret
"As the Mountain Comes." [13thMoon] (11:1/2) 93, p. 63.
"Fierce." [13thMoon] (11:1/2) 93, p. 66.
"Free Enterprise, Again." [GreenMR] (NS 6:1) Wint-Spr 93, p. 94-95.
"Polar Bears and Rabbit Watching the Northern Lights" (after a painting by Melissa Miller). [13thMoon] (11:1/2) 93, p. 64-65.
5368. RANDALL-MILLS, Elizabeth
"In the Night." [SpiritSH] (58) 93, p. 41.
5369. RANDOLPH, Sarah
"Water." [Sonora] (26) Fall 93, p. 70.
5370. RANEY, Jennifer
"Untitled: Would proof lie none sweet." [13thMoon] (12:1/2) 93-94, p. 55.
5371. RANGEL-CARLSEN, Ivana
"The Conch" (tr. of Miguel Torga). [Vis] (43) 93, p. 45.
"Emptiness" (tr. of Miguel Torga). [Vis] (43) 93, p. 45.
5372. RANKIN, Rush
"After Death." [HangL] (62) 93, p. 51.
"Gothic Fears." [HangL] (62) 93, p. 50.
5373. RANKINE, Claudia
"Eden." [RiverS] (38) 93, p. 30-31.
"In Transit." [KenR] (NS 15:3) Sum 93, p. 107-111.
"The Man. His Bowl. His Raspberries." [SouthernR] (29:1) Wint, Ja 93, p. 146.
"Man and Woman in Landscape." [SouthernR] (29:1) Wint, Ja 93, p. 147-148.
"Plain Talk." [Agni] (37) 93, p. 77-78.
5374. RANZONI, Patricia
"Progress." [Kalliope] (15:3) 93, p. 14.
"She Can Count on Two Hands the Times She's Gone to a Beauty Parlor Most Times Sorry She Did." [SnailPR] (3:1) Fall-Wint 93, p. 21.
5375. RAPHAEL, Dan
"To Look Between Night." [Caliban] (13) 93, p. 92-93.
5376. RAPOLA, Zachariah
"Virsil for an Urchin." [BostonR] (18:3/4) Je-Ag 93, p. 29-30.
5377. RAPPLEYE, Greg
"I Did Not Request Your Song in My Dreams." [DogRR] (12:1, #23) Spr-Sum 93, p. 41.
"Jefferson Davis, Blackhawk and the Emergence of the Acceptance Principle in Mid-19th Century America." [PassN] (14:1) Sum 93, p. 20-21.

5378. RAPTOSH, Diane
"California Quail." [MalR] (102) Spr 93, p. 93-95.
"Concetta's Essay on Poetry." [MalR] (102) Spr 93, p. 96-98.
5379. RASH, Ron
"Eureka." [SouthernR] (29:1) Wint, Ja 93, p. 181.
"Hellbender." [ColEng] (55:2) F 93, p. 210.
"Yearbook Photograph of the Crest High Future Farmers of America. Dated
January, 1971." [PoetL] (88:3) Fall 93, p. 18.
5380. RASULA, Jed
"Blushing in the Garden of the Animal." [Sulfur] (32) Spr 93, p. 204-205.
5381. RATCLIFFE, Stephen
"—T." [NewAW] (11) Sum-Fall 93, p. 76.
"Scale." [NewAW] (11) Sum-Fall 93, p. 74.
"Smoke." [NewAW] (11) Sum-Fall 93, p. 75.
"Sound/ (system)" (Excerpt). [Talisman] (10) Spr 93, p. 91-93.
"Spaces in the Light Said to Be Where One/ Comes From" (Selections: 74, 76, 80 -
81). [Avec] (6:1) 93, p. 98-101.
"T." [NewAW] (11) Sum-Fall 93, p. 77.
5382. RATHENOW, Lutz
"Jenaer Elegien" (Excerpt). [Os] (36) Spr 93, p. 6.
5383. RATNER, Rochelle
"Photographs." [IllinoisR] (1:1) Fall 93, p. 61-62.
5384. RATTRAY, David
"The Curve" (w. James Nares). [Conjunc] (20) 93, p. 9-14.
"The White Butterfly." [Bomb] (44) Sum 93, p. 82.
5385. RATZLAFF, Keith
"The Amish Visit Pella, Iowa." [Sequoia] (34/35) 92-93, p. 92.
"The Artist Reclining" (after Chagall). [PoetryNW] (34:4) Wint 93-94, p. 15-16.
"Bob and Jack with Chainsaws." [PoetryNW] (34:4) Wint 93-94, p. 14-15.
"In March." [PikeF] (11) Fall 93, p. 13.
"Rough-Cut Head" (after Paul Klee). [Thrpny] (55) Fall 93, p. 27.
5386. RAU, Aurel
"Seven Lean Cows" (tr. by Adam J. Sorkin and Liviu Bleoca). [LullwaterR] (4:2)
Spr-Sum 93, p. 12.
"Sign" (tr. by Adam J. Sorkin and Liviu Bleoca). [LullwaterR] (4:2) Spr-Sum 93, p.
123.
"Writing with a Feather" (tr. by Adam Sorkin, w. the author). [Vis] (43) 93, p. 49.
5387. RAVEN, Tashunka
"Pony Time: Metaphysical Blues on a Lakota Reservation." [FreeL] (12) Sum 93, p.
11.
5388. RAVIKOVITCH, Dahlia
"Lying on the Water" (tr. by Nili Gold). [Trans] (28) Spr 93, p. 167-168.
5389. RAWLES, Richard
"The Naturalist's Emergency." [Outbr] (24) 93, p. 89.
5390. RAWLINGS, Jane B.
"1,000,000,000,000,000,000,000,000" (corrected reprint from issue No. 26/27). [US1]
(28/29) 93, p. 29.
"Here." [US1] (28/29) 93, p. 17.
5391. RAWLS, Joseph M.
"The Two Churches of Chimayó." [ChrC] (110:5) 17 F 93, p. 165.
5392. RAWSON, Eric
"Dear Pound, I Am Leaving England." [IndR] (16:2) Fall 93, p. 8.
"Interval." [IndR] (16:2) Fall 93, p. 7.
"Seclusion in Mexico City." [WebR] (17) Fall 93, p. 65-66.
5393. RAWSON, JoAnna
"After the Verdict." [PassN] (14:1) Sum 93, p. 42-43.
"Django's Guitar." [BlackWR] (19:1) Fall-Wint 92, p. 85.
"Phantom Pain." [PassN] (14:1) Sum 93, p. 41.
5394. RAWSON, Josie
"Diplomatic Imperative." [DenQ] (27:3) Wint 93, p. 47-48.
"Echo of a Scream." [AmerPoR] (22:6) N-D 93, p. 8.
5395. RAY, David
"The Awkwardness Among Men." [Nat] (256:16) 26 Ap 93, p. 571.
"Beggar." [PoetC] (24:3) Spr 93, p. 18.
"A Callgirl in India." [PoetC] (24:3) Spr 93, p. 19-20.
"Elegy for Rajiv." [Contact] (11:65/66/67) Spr 93, p. 30.

"For Rudolf Hoess, Commandant of Auschwitz." [PraS] (67:3) Fall 93, p. 74-77.
"The Guilt Trip." [Footwork] (23) 93, p. 7-8.
"A Hilltop (for Sam)." [FreeL] (12) Sum 93, p. 23.
"Homo Delphinus." [Footwork] (23) 93, p. 7.
"Jack." [NewYorkQ] (52) 93, p. 92.
"Lines for Eudora." [GeoR] (47:4) Wint 93, p. 691-692.
"Milan." [ApalQ] (35) 90, p. 35-36.
"Montreal." [CharR] (19:2) Fall 93, p. 101-102.
"Pantophobic." [CharR] (19:2) Fall 93, p. 98-100.
"Ronda." [ApalQ] (38) 92, p. 65.
"Serial." [CharR] (19:2) Fall 93, p. 96-97.
"Two Mentors." [WestB] (31/32) 93, p. 10-11.
5396. RAY, Janisse
"The Last Canoe Trip" (for Ra, how he lives). [ApalQ] (39) 93, p. 44-45.
5397. RAY, Judy
"Darkroom Variations" (for Lauri, and for her brother Steve). [CharR] (19:2) Fall
93, p. 93.
"For Salman Rushdie, 14 February, 1992" (P.E.N. reading, Dunedin Public Library,
New Zealand). [CharR] (19:2) Fall 93, p. 94.
"Frida Kahlo." [CharR] (19:2) Fall 93, p. 95.
5398. RAY, Leland
"Cemetery, Chapel of the Cross, Flora, Mississippi." [ProseP] (1) 92, p. 71.
5399. RAY, Sunil B.
"Another Country" (tr. of Nabaneeta Dev Sen, w. Carolyne Wright w. the author).
[AmerPoR] (22:4) Jl-Ag 93, p. 25.
"Antara" (4, tr. of Nabaneeta Dev Sen, w. Nandana Dev Sen, Carolyne Wright and
the author). [AmerPoR] (22:4) Jl-Ag 93, p. 24.
"Prison Island Exile" (tr. of Nabaneeta Dev Sen, w. Nandana Dev Sen, Carolyne
Wright and the author). [AmerPoR] (22:4) Jl-Ag 93, p. 24.
"The Swaying Lotus" (tr. of Nabaneeta Dev Sen, w. Nandana Dev Sen, Carolyne
Wright and the author). [AmerPoR] (22:4) Jl-Ag 93, p. 24.
"When It Rains" (tr. of Nabaneeta Dev Sen, w. Nandana Dev Sen, Carolyne Wright
and the author). [AmerPoR] (22:4) Jl-Ag 93, p. 24.
5400. RAY, Yvonne
"Before Sunday School." [WillowR] (20) Spr 93, p. 26.
5401. RAYMOND, Monica
"A Limerick Sequence." [Light] (6) Sum 93, p. 10.
"Toxic Sonnets." [Light] (5) Spr 93, p. 19.
5402. RAZ, Orna
"Gravitation" (tr. of Dahlia Rabikovich, w. Daniel Weissbort). [Stand] (34:3) Sum
93, p. 10.
"Night Temptation" (tr. of Itamar Yaoz-Kest, w. Daniel Weissbort). [Stand] (34:3)
Sum 93, p. 9.
5403. RAZAVI, Rebecca Hopkins
"July 4, 1974-1984" (for Teddy, who wrote in my yearbook, "I'll always remember
you as the girl down the street"). [Epiphany] (4:2) Ap 93, p. 89.
"That Sun Is Gold Blood." [Vis] (42) 93, p. 30-31.
5404. RAZOR BLADE
"X Rated." [CentralP] (22) Spr 93, p. 154-155.
5405. REA, Susan
"Entomology." [Gypsy] (20) Sum 93, p. 9.
"First Snow." [Footwork] (23) 93, p. 65.
"Music Box." [Footwork] (23) 93, p. 65.
"Silence." [Comm] (120:4) 26 F 93, p. 18.
"Twilight." [HolCrit] (30:5) D 93, p. 18.
5406. READER, Willie
"After the Funeral." [Kalliope] (15:2) 93, p. 32.
"The Blacksmith and the Perpetual Mother Machine." [CreamCR] (17:1) Spr 93, p.
87.
"Lunar Eclipse." [Kalliope] (15:2) 93, p. 32.
5407. REAGLER, Robin
"My X." [13thMoon] (12:1/2) 93-94, p. 56.
5408. REARDON, Alissa
"Beginning Art, in Two Parts." [SycamoreR] (5:2) Sum 93, p. 75.
"Early Morning: Ludvika, Sweden." [Poem] (69) My 93, p. 42-43.
"Lapse." [Poem] (69) My 93, p. 41.

"To a Poet, from a Gardner." [Poem] (69) My 93, p. 44.
5409. REBAZA-SORALUZ, Luis
   "An Airplane Is the Silver Cloud" (For Rosy and Roberto Arizmendi, tr. by
       Elizabeth Doonan Kauffman). [Boulevard] (8:1, #22) Spr 93, p. 185-186.
5410. RECHNER, Mary E.
   "Where I Found It First." [Parting] (6:1) Sum 93, p. 42.
5411. RECHNITZ, Emily
   "Compensation." [CimR] (105) O 93, p. 85.
   "Night Session." [CimR] (105) O 93, p. 84.
5412. RECIPUTI, Natalie
   "The Catalpa Tree." [BellArk] (9:2) Mr-Ap 93, p. 4.
   "Just Say." [BellArk] (9:2) Mr-Ap 93, p. 25.
   "Light Observations." [BellArk] (9:2) Mr-Ap 93, p. 4.
   "The Pottery Sailboats." [BellArk] (9:2) Mr-Ap 93, p. 4.
   "Puget Sound." [BellArk] (9:2) Mr-Ap 93, p. 4.
   "Song for a Small Boat Leaving Biloxi on a Night in June, 1979." [BellArk] (9:2)
       Mr-Ap 93, p. 4.
5413. RECTOR, Liam
   "Tonight We Bow." [VirQR] (69:3) Sum 93, p. 497.
RED, Rockin'
   See ROCKIN' RED
5414. REDDAWAY, Richard
   "In the Forest of Signs and Dreams." [WestCL] (27:2, #11) Fall 93, p. 52-53.
5415. REDEN, Lisa
   "Indian Lake." [Blueline] (14) 93, p. 58-59.
5416. REDGROVE, Peter
   "Ab-Teenagers." [ManhatR] (7:1) Fall 93, p. 69-70.
   "Ancient Well." [ManhatR] (7:1) Fall 93, p. 63.
   "Argus." [Verse] (10:1) Spr 93, p. 16-17.
   "As She Left Us." [PoetryUSA] (25/26) 93, p. 47.
   "The Bathsheba Poems." [PoetryUSA] (25/26) 93, p. 48.
   "Dazzle." [PoetryUSA] (25/26) 93, p. 49.
   "The Desert House." [PoetryUSA] (25/26) 93, p. 45.
   "Eight Parents." [ManhatR] (7:1) Fall 93, p. 66.
   "Einstein's Colour." [PoetryUSA] (25/26) 93, p. 45.
   "The Feast Under the Clitoris-Tree." [Verse] (10:1) Spr 93, p. 18.
   "Kind Hands and Soft Voices." [PoetryUSA] (25/26) 93, p. 49.
   "Landscape and Headache." [PoetryUSA] (25/26) 93, p. 48.
   "Llangattock Escarpment in the Black Mirror." [Verse] (10:1) Spr 93, p. 17.
   "Loose Faces." [ManhatR] (7:1) Fall 93, p. 67-68.
   "Mirror." [PoetryUSA] (25/26) 93, p. 49.
   "The Poor Man Naps in the Dunes." [ManhatR] (7:1) Fall 93, p. 64-65.
   "They Come." [ManhatR] (7:1) Fall 93, p. 71.
   "Transform or Perish." [PoetryUSA] (25/26) 93, p. 46.
5417. REDHEAD, Kay
   "Nouvelle Hantise." [PraF] (14:4) Wint 93-94, p. 105.
   "The Song of the Artichoke Lover." [PraF] (14:4) Wint 93-94, p. 104.
5418. REDHILL, Michael
   "Lake Nora" (5 selections). [Quarry] (42:1) 93, p. 48-54.
5419. REDMOND, Eugene B.
   "Aerolingual Poet of Prey" (For Alvin Aubert who surveys Life from the quiet's
       deep see). [Drumvoices] (1:1/2) Fall-Wint 91-92, p. 45-46.
   "Carryover" (Thinking about Jimmy Dixson, Clarence Nelson and Darnell Sullivan).
       [Drumvoices] (1:1/2) Fall-Wint 91-92, p. 49-50.
   "Gwensways" (For Gwendolyn Brooks, 1987). [Drumvoices] (1:1/2) Fall-Wint 91 -
       92, p. 42.
   "His Eminence Plays the Soular System" ([sic]. Following recording session:
       Hammett Bluiett et al., NYC 7/7/87). [Drumvoices] (1:1/2) Fall-Wint 91-92,
       p. 51-52.
   "Milestone: The Birth of an Ancestor" (For Miles Dewey Davis, III, 1926-1991. In
       Memoriam, In Futuriam). [Drumvoices] (1:1/2) Fall-Wint 91-92, p. 41.
   "Models and Mentors" (Written January, 1987 for the SIUE/East St. Louis Pre -
       School Staff). [Drumvoices] (1:1/2) Fall-Wint 91-92, p. 44.
   "The Tigerettes Are Our Monuments" (For the East St. Louis Lincoln Senior High
       School Girls Track Team, 1985-89). [Drumvoices] (1:1/2) Fall-Wint 91-92, p.
       47-49.

5420. REECE, Spencer
"Apollo Mourns Hyacinthus." [RagMag] (11:1) 93, p. 38.
"Chiaroscuro." [RagMag] (11:1) 93, p. 36.
"The Frog." [Dandel] (20:1) 93, p. 7.
"The Past." [RagMag] (11:1) 93, p. 37.
"Two Young Men 23 to 24." [JamesWR] (10:3) Spr 93, p. 14.
5421. REED, Helen
"The Burning Tree" (For M. P.). [WillowR] (20) Spr 93, p. 20.
"Ghosts in Flight." [WillowR] (20) Spr 93, p. 19.
"Going Softly" (For H. K. G.). [WillowR] (20) Spr 93, p. 18.
5422. REED, Ishmael
"Ohun Pataki." [Drumvoices] (2:1/2) Fall-Wint 92-93, p. 75.
5423. REED, John R.
"Bible Studies." [OntR] (39) Fall-Wint 93-94, p. 101-102.
"By Huron." [OntR] (39) Fall-Wint 93-94, p. 103.
5424. REED, Kjersti A.
"During Celibacy the Mind Tends to Wander." [NewEngR] (15:2) Spr 93, p. 133 -
135.
5425. REED, Lori Ann
"Abused Child." [Drumvoices] (1:1/2) Fall-Wint 91-92, p. 60.
"Becoming." [Drumvoices] (1:1/2) Fall-Wint 91-92, p. 59.
"Other Folk's Mirrors." [Drumvoices] (1:1/2) Fall-Wint 91-92, p. 59.
"Rainy Day Nap." [Drumvoices] (1:1/2) Fall-Wint 91-92, p. 60.
"Rodney King Beating: Round Three, or, A Pebble Dropped." [Drumvoices] (1:1/2)
Fall-Wint 91-92, p. 58.
5426. REED, Marthe
"Story" (for Leslie Silko). [WritersF] (19) 93, p. 158.
5427. REED, Tennessee
"Hair." [PoetryUSA] (25/26) 93, p. 50.
"I Don't Stop When I Play Bebop." [PoetryUSA] (25/26) 93, p. 51.
"My Room Rules." [PoetryUSA] (25/26) 93, p. 51.
"The Old Parents Blues." [PoetryUSA] (25/26) 93, p. 51.
"School Spirit." [PoetryUSA] (25/26) 93, p. 51.
5428. REES, Elizabeth
"Castaway." [Confr] (51) Sum 93, p. 267.
"Colleagues." [HiramPoR] (53/54) Fall 92-Sum 93, p. 73.
"Photographed." [FourQ] (7:2) Fall 93, p. 45.
"Something Borrowed, Something Blue." [HiramPoR] (53/54) Fall 92-Sum 93, p.
74.
"Sounding Fields." [Agni] (37) 93, p. 283-284.
5429. REES, Roberta
"Sliding Home." [MalR] (105) Wint 93, p. 64-67.
5430. REESE, Steven
"A Child's Oval Office." [PoetryNW] (34:2) Sum 93, p. 30-31.
"Proposing to the Widow Dewine." [PoetryNW] (34:2) Sum 93, p. 28-30.
"Sunday Bells." [PoetryNW] (34:4) Wint 93-94, p. 21-22.
5431. REEVE, Davd
"Disabled Veteran." [WormR] (33:4, #132) 93, p. 166.
"Paper Boy Stress." [WormR] (33:4, #132) 93, p. 167.
"Roger, the Tattoo Artist." [ChironR] (12:4/13:1, #37/38) Wint 93-Spr 94, p. 44.
"Why I Seldom Read Newspapers." [WormR] (33:4, #132) 93, p. 167.
5432. REEVE, F. D.
"Full Moon in May." [Poetry] (162:2) My 93, p. 91.
"Harbor Island." [SewanR] (101:2) Ap-Je, Spr 93, p. 153.
"The Last Argument." [PoetC] (25:1) Fall 93, p. 36.
"Ragged Island." [Poetry] (162:5) Ag 93, p. 264.
"Rainy Morning." [SewanR] (101:2) Ap-Je, Spr 93, p. 153-154.
"Roller-Coaster." [PoetC] (25:1) Fall 93, p. 35.
"Twilight." [Poetry] (162:2) My 93, p. 92.
5433. REEVES, Sonya
"For My Granma Souter Who Was Wrong About." [Verse] (10:3) Wint 93, p. 104.
5434. REEVES, Trish
"Don't." [NewL] (59:4) 93, p. 26.
"Entrance to the View." [NewL] (59:4) 93, p. 27.
"January." [NewL] (59:4) 93, p. 28.
"Something Infinite." [13thMoon] (11:1/2) 93, p. 67.

5435. REEVES, Troy
"Star of Bethlehem." [ChrC] (110:36) 15 D 93, p. 1269.
5436. REGAN, M.
"Castle." [13thMoon] (12:1/2) 93-94, p. 57.
5437. REGIER, Gail
"Staying Out Late." [MassR] (34:1) Spr 93, p. 42-44.
5438. REHDER, Robert
"On the Nature of Physical Law." [Stand] (35:1) Wint 93-94, p. 12-13.
"Vérollay." [Stand] (35:1) Wint 93-94, p. 12.
5439. REIBETANZ, John
"Ampersand." [MalR] (104) Fall 93, p. 42-43.
"Bough Cottage." [AntigR] (93-94) Spr-Sum 93, p. 111-112.
"Icon." [AntigR] (93-94) Spr-Sum 93, p. 108.
"Landed Immigrants." [AntigR] (93-94) Spr-Sum 93, p. 110.
"Windward." [AntigR] (93-94) Spr-Sum 93, p. 109.
5440. REICHARD, William
"Invert." [BlackWR] (19:1) Fall-Wint 92, p. 179-181.
"It Takes Me." [JamesWR] (11:1) Fall 93, p. 13.
"Poet Whore in the 9th Circle of Hell." [JamesWR] (11:1) Fall 93, p. 16.
"Roland Barthes." [EvergreenC] (8:1) Spr-Sum 93, p. 49-50.
"There Be Monsters Here." [EvergreenC] (8:1) Spr-Sum 93, p. 47-48.
"Without Translation." [JamesWR] (11:1) Fall 93, p. 16.
5441. REID, Alastair
"Things That Might Have Been" (tr. of Jorge Luis Borges). [NewEngR] (15:1) Wint 93, p. 101.
5442. REID, Bethany
"At the Family Cemetery." [Calyx] (14:3) Sum 93, p. 48-49.
"Spell." [Calyx] (14:3) Sum 93, p. 46-47.
"To Carry On" (Arada Taylor Lusk, 1895-1983). [Calyx] (14:3) Sum 93, p. 50-51.
5443. REID, Monty
"Crabapples." [PoetryC] (13:2) 93, p. 18-19.
"The Shale Disparities" (for Jon Whyte). [MalR] (105) Wint 93, p. 19-23.
5444. REIDEL, James
"Grandfather" (for W.H.R.). [Verse] (10:2) Sum 93, p. 53.
"In the Windbreak." [Verse] (10:2) Sum 93, p. 53.
5445. REIMONENQ, Alden
"The Box." [JamesWR] (10:4) Sum 93, p. 6.
5446. REINHARD, John
"Perhaps Our Parents Made Love After All." [PassN] (14:2) Wint 93, p. 52-53.
5447. REINHOLD, Amy
"Forever Bent." [PennR] (5:2) 93, p. 31.
5448. REINKE, Mari
"In Absence." [CapeR] (28:1) Spr 93, p. 20.
5449. REIS, Donna
"Docteur Gachet." [NewYorkQ] (51) 93, p. 74.
REIS, Siri von
See Von REIS, Siri
5450. REISNER, Barbara
"More Than Watchmen for the Morning." [GrahamHR] (17) Fall 93, p. 80-81.
"The Shadow That Trails the Body." [GrahamHR] (17) Fall 93, p. 78-79.
5451. REISS, James
"Crabbing." [WestHR] (47:4) Wint 93, p. 358-359.
"Crickets." [HawaiiR] (17:1, #37) Spr 93, p. 162.
"Dark Conceit." [ParisR] (35:128) Fall 93, p. 266-267.
"Dorland." [ParisR] (35:128) Fall 93, p. 265-266.
"Him." [WestHR] (47:4) Wint 93, p. 357.
5452. REISZ, Martina
"French Kissing." [BellR] (16:1/2) Spr-Fall 93, p. 86.
"Reprise." [BellR] (16:1/2) Spr-Fall 93, p. 87.
"Side Streets." [CapeR] (28:1) Spr 93, p. 1.
5453. REITER, David P.
"Mutton Birds" (Lord Howe Island). [CanLit] (138/139) Fall-Wint 93, p. 34.
5454. REITER, Thomas
"A Farm in Kansas." [Ascent] (18:1) Fall 93, p. 29.
"Fine China." [PoetC] (25:1) Fall 93, p. 3.
"A Prairie Garden." [PoetC] (25:1) Fall 93, p. 4.

"Yellow Man." [CaribbeanW] (7) 93, p. 40-41.
5455. REIZEI, Tamesuke
"Already mother's breasts hung low with the years" (tr. by Sam Hamill). [ChiR] (39:3/4) 93, p. 203.
5456. REMBOLD, Kristen Staby
"Town Line Road, by Bicycle Twenty Years Later." [SoDakR] (31:3) Fall 93, p. 103.
5457. REMMERDE, Jon
"Look for Spring in Life." [BellArk] (9:6) N-D 93, p. 14.
5458. REMOTO, Danton
"Corpus Delicti" (After the Sandiganbayan decision on the Aquino assassination). [Bomb] (45) Fall 93, p. 80.
"To Carlos Orchida." [Bomb] (45) Fall 93, p. 80.
5459. REMSKI, Matthew
"First Sorrowful Mystery: The Agony in the Garden (Repentance)" (Winner of the 1993 Long Poem Prize). [MalR] (103) Sum 93, p. 42-52.
"Peddling Another Go at It." [MalR] (102) Spr 93, p. 78.
"The Refrain Man." [MalR] (102) Spr 93, p. 77.
5460. RENAUD, Jorge A.
"I Glance at Windows." [Americas] (21:3/4) Fall-Wint 93, p. 103.
"Soy Jorge" (for Beth). [Americas] (21:3/4) Fall-Wint 93, p. 99.
"A View, in Lieu of Valentines" (for Aimée). [Americas] (21:3/4) Fall-Wint 93, p. 100.
"Ya Basta / Stream of Consciousness." [Americas] (21:3/4) Fall-Wint 93, p. 101 - 102.
5461. RENDLEMAN, Danny
"Maples." [AntigR] (95) Aut 93, p. 97-98.
5462. RENJILIAN, Jerry
"Vocabulary Lesson." [EngJ] (82:3) Mr 93, p. 92.
5463. RENKL, Margaret
"At Shiloh, For Example." [SouthernHR] (27:3) Sum 93, p. 216-217.
"Elegy in March." [SouthernHR] (27:3) Sum 93, p. 265.
5464. REPETTO, Vittoria
"3 Doctors Discussing Raynard's Syndrome in the Ladies Lounge." [Footwork] (23) 93, p. 116.
"Bus Stop Poem #2." [Footwork] (23) 93, p. 116.
"Lovers and Other Dead Animals." [Footwork] (23) 93, p. 116.
"My Father and I Are Alone Together." [Footwork] (23) 93, p. 116.
5465. REPP, John
"The American English Sentence, the Supple, Unforgiving." [Northeast] (5:8) Spr - Sum 93, p. 44.
"Everywhere We Go." [ColEng] (55:4) Ap 93, p. 431.
"What Left." [Journal] (17:1) Spr-Sum 93, p. 61-62.
5466. RESS, Lisa
"Eve Out of Season." [IllinoisR] (1:1) Fall 93, p. 63.
"Persephone." [IllinoisR] (1:1) Fall 93, p. 15.
5467. RETALLACK, Joan
"Errata 5uite" (Excerpts). [Avec] (6:1) 93, p. 85-88.
5468. REVARD, Carter
"When Earth Brings" (For Joy & Daisy, grandmothers — for Simon, grandfather — for Rainy Dawn & Chris, parents — for Krista Rae, child — and for all our relatives). [Caliban] (12) 93, p. 49.
5469. REVELL, Donald
"City More Than I Suspected" (Excerpt). [DenQ] (28:1) Sum 93, p. 22.
"Cloistered." [AmerPoR] (22:1) Ja-F 93, p. 59.
"Death to Santa Foy." [Agni] (37) 93, p. 147-148.
"An Instrument Also." [SycamoreR] (5:2) Sum 93, p. 21-22.
"The Pillars." [Pequod] (36) 93, p. 60-61.
"The Traveller's Garment." [ColR] (20:1) Spr 93, p. 69-70.
"Voracity." [AmerPoR] (22:1) Ja-F 93, p. 59.
5470. REVUELTA, Gutierrez
"Erudites on Campus" (tr. of Angel González, w. Steven Ford Brown). [HarvardR] (3) Wint 93, p. 142.
REVUELTA, Pedro Gutierrez
See REVUELTA, Gutierrez

5471. REWAK, William J.
"At 4 in the Morning." [WritersF] (19) 93, p. 66.
5472. REWAKOWICZ, Maria
"Untitled: Two fingers" (tr. by Paul Pines). [Agni] (37) 93, p. 281.
5473. REXROTH, Kenneth
"February 1944." [QRL] (12:32/33) 93, p. 499.
"A fervor parches you sometimes." [QRL] (12:32/33) 93, p. 497-498.
"I like to think of you naked." [QRL] (12:32/33) 93, p. 498.
5474. REYES, Carlos
"Sacramento" (for "Ethel" and "Go, Dog, Go!"). [BellR] (16:1/2) Spr-Fall 93, p. 26 -
27.
5475. REYES, Lina Sagaral
"Ichthys." [Bomb] (45) Fall 93, p. 83.
"'Storya" (for Grace and Onang). [Bomb] (45) Fall 93, p. 83.
5476. REYNOLDS, Kurt
"Loss, Grief, and Time." [Art&Und] (2:4) O-N 93, p. 23.
5477. REYNOLDS, Mark
"I Got a New Bed Today." [NewYorkQ] (50) 93, p. 75.
5478. REYNOLDS, Rebecca
"Mattress Cowboys." [US1] (28/29) 93, p. 12.
"Peridot." [US1] (28/29) 93, p. 18.
5479. REZNIKOFF, Charles
"Rivers and Seas, Harbors and Parts" (from "Testimony," 1934). [Sulfur] (33) Fall
93, p. 249-252.
5480. RHINE, David
"A Lament." [ChironR] (12:3, #36) Aut 93, p. 29.
"Separate But United." [ChironR] (12:3, #36) Aut 93, p. 29.
"Terry." [ChironR] (12:3, #36) Aut 93, p. 29.
"While Working." [ChironR] (12:3, #36) Aut 93, p. 29.
5481. RHOADES, Susan M.
"Saplings." [CaribbeanW] (7) 93, p. 35.
5482. RHODENBAUGH, Suzanne
"Litany for the Screened Women." [RiverS] (38) 93, p. 46.
"Our Songs Beginning with If." [CimR] (103) Ap 93, p. 89-90.
"The Trek" (for Stan). [PoetryE] (36) Fall 93, p. 114.
5483. RHODES, Martha
"Elegy." [Agni] (37) 93, p. 282.
"Infestation." [QW] (37) Sum-Fall 93, p. 97.
5484. RIABCHUK, Mykola
"To Think About Eternity" (tr. by Virlana Tkaz and Wanda Phipps). [Vis] (41) 93,
p. 15.
5485. RICCI, L. A.
"My Mother's Voice." [Footwork] (23) 93, p. 89.
5486. RICCIO, Carla
"The Roses." [WilliamMR] (31) 93, p. 78.
5487. RICE, Oliver
"Who Malingers, Who Mimes." [Ascent] (17:2) Wint 93, p. 37.
"The Will of Things in Appalachia." [Ascent] (17:2) Wint 93, p. 37.
5488. RICE, Paul
"Making. Rain." [GeoR] (47:1) Spr 93, p. 120-121.
5489. RICE, William
"Nature Lover." [HarvardR] (4) Spr 93, p. 126.
5490. RICH, Adrienne
"Continuum." [QRL] (12:32/33) 93, p. 501.
"Gabriel." [QRL] (12:32/33) 93, p. 500-501.
"In the Evening." [QRL] (12:32/33) 93, p. 502.
"What Kinds of Times Are These" (corrected reprint from "Not Somewhere Else,
But Here," 77:2/3, Spr-Sum 92). [SouthwR] (78:1) Wint 93, p. 141.
5491. RICH, Mark
"Ears, Not Knees." [Poem] (70) N 93, p. 68.
"That Same, in Winter." [Poem] (70) N 93, p. 69.
"To a Sports-Car-Owning Friend on His Fortieth Birthday" (For Roc Ordman).
[Light] (5) Spr 93, p. 20.
"White Lips." [Poem] (70) N 93, p. 70.
5492. RICH, Susan
"The Beggars" (Zinder, Niger). [SoCoast] (15) Je 93, p. 42.

"The Lost." [HampSPR] Wint 93, p. 14.
"Love in the Time of AIDS." [MassR] (34:1) Spr 93, p. 76-77.
"Men at Work." [BellR] (16:1/2) Spr-Fall 93, p. 20.
5493. RICHARD, Brad
"Aubade." [NoAmR] (278:1) Ja-F 93, p. 37.
"The Domicle." [RiverS] (39) 93, p. 20.
"Hermetic." [RiverS] (39) 93, p. 21.
"Pleasures of a Spring Night." [HayF] (13) Fall-Wint 93, p. 42.
5494. RICHARDS, Marilee
"Captives." [Journal] (17:2) Fall-Wint 93, p. 26-27.
"Events." [SouthernPR] (33:1) Spr 93, p. 68-69.
"The Ladies." [SpoonR] (18:2) Sum-Fall 93, p. 25.
"Munchausen's (By Proxy)." [SpoonR] (18:2) Sum-Fall 93, p. 26-27.
"The Old Men." [SpoonR] (18:2) Sum-Fall 93, p. 24.
5495. RICHARDS, Melanie
"Pandora: The White Gift." [Farm] (10:1) Spr-Sum 93, p. 99.
5496. RICHARDSON, Eve
"Televangelism." [Light] (5) Spr 93, p. 23.
5497. RICHARDSON, Fred
"Give Us This Day." [Pearl] (17) Spr 93, p. 22.
5498. RICHARDSON, James
"In Deer Country." [ParisR] (35:126) Spr 93, p. 206.
5499. RICHERT, Mary
"Uncles." [DenQ] (27:3) Wint 93, p. 49-52.
5500. RICHHARIYA, Sanjeev
"Radio Babylon Goes Off the Air." [Verse] (10:1) Spr 93, p. 57.
5501. RICHMAN, Elliot
"The Blue Cart." [BlackBR] (17) Sum-Fall 93, p. 39.
"Chance Meeting." [Asylum] (8) 93, p. 32.
"Flowering Almond Blossoms." [BlackBR] (17) Sum-Fall 93, p. 30.
"The Fly." [Asylum] (8) 93, p. 32.
"Love American Style: The Holocaust on Washington St. at the Triangle Shirtwaist
Factory Saturday, March 25, 1911, . . . 5:04 PM." [SlipS] (13) 93, p. 100.
"The Man Who Became a Horse." [CoalC] (7) Apr 93, p. 41-42.
"A Midsummer Night's Dream." [Bogg] (66) Wint 92-93, p. 21.
"An October Evening." [Asylum] (8) 93, p. 31.
5502. RICHMAN, Jan
"Ajijic." [Ploughs] (19:4) Wint 93-94, p. 16.
"The Grape." [Nimrod] (37:1) Fall-Wint 93, p. 126.
"Origami for Adults." [Ploughs] (19:4) Wint 93-94, p. 15.
"The Physics of Dating" (Discovery-The Nation '93 Prizewinning Poet). [Nat]
(256:17) 3 My 93, p. 603.
5503. RICHMAN, Robert
"1:00 A.M." [AntR] (51:4) Fall 93, p. 564.
5504. RICHMOND, Steve
"Desenex Every Night" (Special Section: ca. 30 poems). [WormR] (33:4, #132) 93,
p. 189-206.
"Gagaku." [Bogg] (66) Wint 92-93, p. 59.
"Gagaku." [ChironR] (12:1, #34) Spr 93, p. 23.
5505. RICHSTONE, May
"The Clock Is Cuckoo." [Light] (7) Aut 93, p. 7.
"Good Morning." [Light] (8) Wint 93, p. 12.
"It Seemed Like Forever." [Light] (6) Sum 93, p. 17.
"Media." [Light] (7) Aut 93, p. 12.
"We Entitled." [Light] (8) Wint 93, p. 7.
"When Your Teenager Lacks Ambition." [Light] (5) Spr 93, p. 18.
5506. RICHTER, Harvena
"Swamp Light." [SoDakR] (31:2) Sum 93, p. 28-29.
5507. RICHTER, Michael
"From a Distance." [OnTheBus] (5:2, #12) Sum-Fall 93, p. 171.
5508. RICHTER, Milan
"In Frosty March" (tr. by the author). [OxfordM] (9:1) Spr-Sum 93, p. 9.
"On the Law School's Steps" (in Bratislava, tr. by Jascha Kessler). [OxfordM] (9:1)
Spr-Sum 93, p. 8-9.
"Spoiled Poem" (tr. by Jascha Kessler). [OxfordM] (9:1) Spr-Sum 93, p. 7.
"Yet I Must" (tr. by Jascha Kessler). [OxfordM] (9:1) Spr-Sum 93, p. 8.

5509. RICHTER, Stacey
"Carbonation" (1993 Sonora Review Poetry Award Winner). [Sonora] (26) Fall 93,
p. 42.
"Ring Poem." [Sonora] (26) Fall 93, p. 43.
5510. RICKEL, Boyer
"How Say." [NoDaQ] (61:2) Spr 93, p. 133-136.
5511. RICKETTS, Collin
"Morning Gathering." [AnthNEW] (5) 93, p. 12.
5512. RICKS, David
"Ethnic Cleansing." [Poetry] (162:3) Je 93, p. 139.
"Genius Loci." [Poetry] (162:1) Ap 93, p. 5.
5513. RIDDELL, Amy (Amy C.)
"Criminal Intent." [BlackWR] (19:2) Spr-Sum 93, p. 49.
"Lullaby for My Other Mother." [BlackWR] (19:2) Spr-Sum 93, p. 50.
"What I Have Been." [CentralP] (22) Spr 93, p. 152.
5514. RIDGEWELL, Peter
"Being 4" (tr. of Arni Ibsen, w. the author). [Vis] (42) 93, p. 10.
"Bread" (tr. of Arni Ibsen, w. the author). [Vis] (41) 93, p. 35-36.
"The Meaningful Sun" (tr. of Arni Ibsen). [Vis] (43) 93, p. 28.
5515. RIDINGER, Gayle
"Abel and Abel" (tr. of Silvio Giussani). [Verse] (10:2) Sum 93, p. 21.
"In the Distance" (tr. of Silvio Giussani). [Verse] (10:2) Sum 93, p. 22.
"Vegetable Calendar" (tr. of Silvio Giussani). [Verse] (10:2) Sum 93, p. 21.
5516. RIDL, Jack
"If You're Waiting, You May as Well." [Caliban] (12) 93, p. 166-167.
"In the Last Seconds." [Ploughs] (19:1) Spr 93, p. 109.
"Night Gym." [Ploughs] (19:1) Spr 93, p. 110.
"The Second Coming." [PoetryE] (36) Fall 93, p. 28.
5517. RIDLAND, John
"Dust on the Water" (for F. R. Bresgal). [SoCarR] (26:1) Fall 93, p. 6.
"Retitled 'Silent Noon'." [Sparrow] (60) Sum 93, p. 17.
"Sonnet: The National Game." [Sparrow] (60) Sum 93, p. 17.
"Vivid." [SoCarR] (26:1) Fall 93, p. 6.
5518. RIEGEL, Katherine
"January in Indianapolis." [HopewellR] (5) 93, p. 98-99.
"White Tigers." [Plain] (13:2) Wint 93, p. 34.
5519. RIELLY, Edward J.
"Chinese Illusions." [Vis] (41) 93, p. 27.
"Putting a Dog to Sleep." [WebR] (17) Fall 93, p. 68.
5520. RIGG, Sharon
"A Man on the Road." [HiramPoR] (53/54) Fall 92-Sum 93, p. 76-78.
"Sun on the Bottom." [HiramPoR] (53/54) Fall 92-Sum 93, p. 75.
5521. RIGGAN, Nancy
"Diminished Decrepitude." [Bogg] (66) Wint 92-93, p. 25.
5522. RIGSBEE, David
"Hosanna." [AmerPoR] (22:6) N-D 93, p. 33.
"The Mountaintop." [Amelia] (7:2, #21) 93, p. 21.
"Nuages." [Journal] (17:1) Spr-Sum 93, p. 44.
"Only Heaven." [WillowS] (32) Sum 93, p. 26.
"Spaghetti." [SouthernR] (29:3) Sum, Jl 93, p. 593-595.
"The White Rainbow." [TexasR] (14:1/2) Spr-Sum 93, p. 105-106.
5523. RIIS, Sharon
"Poem for Leonard Cohen." [Grain] (21:3) Fall 93, p. 57.
5524. RIKER, William H.
"General Sir Harry Flashman, K.C.B." [Light] (7) Aut 93, p. 10.
5525. RILE, Karen
"The Fear of Being Noticed." [PaintedB] (50/51) 93, p. 57.
5526. RILEY, Joanne Mokosh
"In Tongues" (for my grandmother, Veronika O. Mokos). [Footwork] (23) 93, p. 28 -
29.
"Infant of Prague" (for Veronika). [Footwork] (23) 93, p. 28.
"The Madonna and the Hoe" (for Veronika). [Footwork] (23) 93, p. 29.
5527. RILEY, Michael D.
"Horizons." [Parting] (6:2) Wint 93, p. 4.
"Regret." [Poetry] (162:4) Jl 93, p. 218.

5528. RILKE, Rainer Maria
"Leda" (in German and English, tr. by Michael L. Johnson). [SoCoast] (15) Je 93, p. 38-39.
"Marionettes" (tr. by Michael J. Bugeja). [SoCoast] (15) Je 93, p. 40-41.
5529. RIMBAUD, Arthur
"Antique" (tr. by George Messo). [Pearl] (19) Fall-Wint 93, p. 12.
"Beatnik Days" (tr. by Charles W. Pratt). [Light] (7) Aut 93, p. 17.
"Ma Bohème" (fantaisie). [Light] (7) Aut 93, p. 17.
RIN, Ishigaki
See ISHIGAKI, Rin
5530. RINALDI, Nicholas
"Grammar Lesson." [LitR] (37:1) Fall 93, p. 15.
"Handkerchief." [LitR] (36:2) Wint 93, p. 188.
5531. RIND, Sherry
"The Return to Spain, 1992." [SouthernPR] (33:1) Spr 93, p. 10-11.
5532. RINGER, Darby
"Hide and Seek." [BellArk] (9:1) Ja-F 93, p. 24-25.
5533. RIO, Nela
"Aquella Luz, la Que Estremece" (Selection: II). [Luz] (5) N 93, p. 84.
5534. RIOS, Alberto Alvaro
"Kid Hielero." [ColR] (20:2) Fall 93, p. 84-87.
5535. RIPLEY, Anthony
"Chicago Green" (Honorable Mention, 7th Annual Contest). [SoCoast] (15) Je 93, p. 4-5.
5536. RISTAU, Harland
"The Brief Meeting." [Pearl] (17) Spr 93, p. 24.
5537. RITCHIE, Elisavietta
"Associations en Route to a Bone Scan." [Arc] (31) Aut 93, p. 70.
"Cautionary Tale for a Daughter." [PoetL] (88:3) Fall 93, p. 9-10.
"Note from the Stratosphere." [Kalliope] (15:3) 93, p. 18.
"Pastoral Letter." [NewYorkQ] (51) 93, p. 58.
"Recipe: One Artichoke" (Earlier versions of this poem appeared in *New York Quarterly* and *Raking the Snow*). [Light] (8) Wint 93, p. 13.
"Wild Garlic" (Five Poems from a Sequence). [Confr] (51) Sum 93, p. 233-236.
"Yo-Yo." [Kalliope] (15:3) 93, p. 17.
5538. RITCHINGS, Joan Drew
"Jack-in-the-Box." [Light] (5) Spr 93, p. 17.
5539. RITSOS, Yannis
"Approximately" (*Testimonies B*, 1966, tr. by Nikos Stangos). [HarvardR] (5) Fall 93, p. 133.
"Association" (*Testimonies A*, 1963, tr. by Nikos Stangos). [HarvardR] (5) Fall 93, p. 146.
"The Day of the Sick Man" (*Testimonies B*, 1966, tr. by Nikos Stangos). [HarvardR] (5) Fall 93, p. 132.
"Evening Walk" (tr. by Martin McKinsey). [ProseP] (2) 93, p. 80.
"From Poseidon" (*Repetitions*, 1963-65, tr. by Edmund Keeley). [HarvardR] (5) Fall 93, p. 144-145.
"Marking" (*Parentheses*, 1950-61, tr. by Edmund Keeley). [HarvardR] (5) Fall 93, p. 131.
"Maybe, Someday" (*Parentheses*, 1946-47, tr. by Edmund Keeley). [HarvardR] (5) Fall 93, p. 134.
"The Meaning of Simplicity" (*Parentheses*, 1946-47, tr. by Edmund Keeley). [HarvardR] (5) Fall 93, p. 133-134.
"Midnight Stroll" (*Scripture of the Blind*, 1972, tr. by Kimon Friar and Kostas Myrsiades). [HarvardR] (5) Fall 93, p. 132-133.
"Miniature" (*Parentheses*, 1946-47, tr. by Edmund Keeley). [HarvardR] (5) Fall 93, p. 146-147.
"The More Sufficient" (*The Distant*, 1975, tr. by Edmund Keeley). [HarvardR] (5) Fall 93, p. 136.
"Motionless Swaying" (*Gestures B*, 1969-70, tr. by Nikos Stangos). [HarvardR] (5) Fall 93, p. 136-137.
"Necessary Explanation" (*Exercises*, 1950-60, tr. by Kimon Friar). [HarvardR] (5) Fall 93, p. 135.
"One Skit, Then Another" (tr. by Martin McKinsey). [ProseP] (2) 93, p. 79.
"Penelope's Despair" (*Repetitions*, 1968-69, tr. by Edmund Keeley). [HarvardR] (5) Fall 93, p. 145.

"Point" (*Parentheses*, 1950-61, tr. by Edmund Keeley). [HarvardR] (5) Fall 93, p. 144.
"Second Series" (Selections: 36, 53, 88, from *3 x 111 Tristychs*, tr. by José García and Adamantia García-Baltatzi). [LitR] (36:2) Wint 93, p. 247.
"Third Series" (Selections: 5, 28, 57, 63, 68, 94, from *3 x 111 Tristychs*, tr. by José García and Adamantia García-Baltatzi). [LitR] (36:2) Wint 93, p. 247-248.
"Triplet" (*Parentheses*, 1950-61, tr. by Edmund Keeley). [HarvardR] (5) Fall 93, p. 131.
"With the moonlight a butterfly" (tr. by Jose Garcia and Adamandia Baltatzi). [Vis] (41) 93, p. 18.
5540. RIVARD, David
"Hush & Taunt." [HarvardR] (3) Wint 93, p. 14-15.
5541. RIVERA, Anthony
"School." [Americas] (21:2) Sum 93, p. 66.
"School Days." [Americas] (21:2) Sum 93, p. 67.
5542. RIVERO, Mario
"Motivations of the Day" (tr. by Elizabeth B. Clark). [ApalQ] (36/37) 91, p. 58-60.
"Psalm" (tr. by Elizabeth B. Clark). [ApalQ] (36/37) 91, p. 61.
5543. RIVERS, J. W.
"The Girl Who Dances in Snow." [SoCarR] (25:2) Spr 93, p. 64-71.
5544. RIVKIN, Sophia
"Talk Between Women Is Stitchery." [FreeL] (12) Sum 93, p. 31.
ROBB, Maria Elena Caballero
See CABALLERO-ROBB, Maria Elena
5545. ROBBINS, Anthony
"Hung (17° N 88° W)." [AnotherCM] (26) Fall 93, p. 134-135.
5546. ROBBINS, Doren
"The Dostoyevsky Face and the Other One." [OnTheBus] (5:2, #12) Sum-Fall 93, p. 174.
"Life Before and Life After Tampico" (for Raphael Escamilla). [Caliban] (12) 93, p. 8-11.
"The Rav of Berditchev." [OnTheBus] (5:2, #12) Sum-Fall 93, p. 172-174.
5547. ROBBINS, Martin
"Versions of Shakespeare." [SewanR] (101:4) O-D, Fall 93, p. 508-516.
5548. ROBBINS, Michael
"In Memoriam: Prayers for William Stafford, 1914-1993." [Plain] (14:1) Fall 93, p. 39.
"Poem: It is intelligence" (A Plainsongs Award Poem). [Plain] (14:1) Fall 93, p. 5.
"The Unknowable." [Plain] (13:3) Spr 93, p. 20.
5549. ROBBINS, Richard
"Crack Baby on TV." [PoetryNW] (34:1) Spr 93, p. 14.
"Georgic after an Argument." [IndR] (16:1) Spr 93, p. 138.
"Recovery." [Sonora] (26) Fall 93, p. 69.
5550. ROBERTS, Andy
"Happy." [WindO] (57) Fall 93, p. 31.
"The Sea Chest." [BellArk] (9:5) S-O 93, p. 12.
"Waiting for a Double Espresso in the King Street Coffeehouse." [SlipS] (13) 93, p. 12.
5551. ROBERTS, Beth K.
"Blue Tick." [GettyR] (6:2) Spr 93, p. 356-357.
"Cartoon." [GettyR] (6:2) Spr 93, p. 358.
"Keep House." [GettyR] (6:2) Spr 93, p. 355.
5552. ROBERTS, Betty
"The Window." [Bogg] (66) Wint 92-93, p. 39.
5553. ROBERTS, Gildas
"Doing Good" (Johannesburg, 1939). [TickleAce] (23) Spr-Sum 92, p. 51-52.
5554. ROBERTS, Kim
"Menstrual Cramps." [PoetL] (88:1) Spr 93, p. 36.
"The Nameless." [ChatR] (13:4) Sum 93, p. 42-43.
"Patriotism." [Confr] (51) Sum 93, p. 266.
5555. ROBERTS, Len
"Antique Store, Pecs Hungary." [PoetryNW] (34:1) Spr 93, p. 27-28.
"Counting the Black Angels." [Hudson] (46:2) Sum 93, p. 348-350.
"Courtyard at Home, Before Autumn" (tr. of Sandor Csóori). [Chelsea] (54) 93, p. 28-29.
"Easy to Say, Easy to Say." [Agni] (37) 93, p. 200-201.

"Holding Out the Hands." [NoDaQ] (61:2) Spr 93, p. 137-138.
"It Will Wait." [PaintedB] (50/51) 93, p. 40.
"Joey McGraw's Desk, 1960." [Boulevard] (8:2/3, #23/24) Fall 93, p. 133-135.
"Learning Natural Instincts." [PoetryNW] (34:1) Spr 93, p. 31-32.
"Learning Natural Instincts." [VirQR] (69:4) Aut 93, p. 656-657.
"Learning the Stars." [PoetryNW] (34:1) Spr 93, p. 30-31.
"Near the Paulite Church." [WestB] (31/32) 93, p. 67.
"On Hearing That We Were All Boundless, Unimaginable Energy." [Hudson] (46:2)
    Sum 93, p. 346-347.
"Second-Grade Angel." [Hudson] (46:2) Sum 93, p. 345-346.
"Shrinking As They Rise, The." [WestB] (31/32) 93, p. 66.
"Talking with God." [GettyR] (6:4) Aut 93, p. 686-687.
"Thinning the Walnuts." [NewEngR] (15:4) Fall 93, p. 69-70.
"Trying to Tell My Mother about Her Guardian Angel." [OhioR] (50) 93, p. 72-73.
"The Way I Always Like It." [PoetryNW] (34:1) Spr 93, p. 29.
"What Sins, Now." [NewEngR] (15:4) Fall 93, p. 68-69.
"When the Angel Finally Came Down." [Shen] (43:2) Sum 93, p. 101.
5556. ROBERTS, Mark
    "Giacometti on Parade: Almost Home." [Wind] (23:72) 93, p. 18.
5557. ROBERTS, Stephen R.
    "The Calls." [Farm] (10:2) Fall-Wint 93-94, p. 41.
    "Dreaming the Days." [Pembroke] (25) 93, p. 89.
    "In the Doghouse Stag Cafe." [Gypsy] (20) Sum 93, p. 33.
    "Kindling the Family Orchard." [Pembroke] (25) 93, p. 88.
5558. ROBERTS, Teresa Noelle
    "The Gravedigger." [BellArk] (9:2) Mr-Ap 93, p. 3.
    "Icarus in the Garden." [BellArk] (9:2) Mr-Ap 93, p. 3.
    "Roadside." [BellArk] (9:2) Mr-Ap 93, p. 3.
    "Serenity of Bone." [BellArk] (9:2) Mr-Ap 93, p. 3.
5559. ROBERTS, Tony
    "The Doll's-Eye Maker" (in conversation with Henry Mayhew, 1850). [SoCoast]
        (15) Je 93, p. 20-21.
5560. ROBERTSON, Hugh
    "Reverie." [AntR] (51:1) Wint 93, p. 96.
5561. ROBERTSON, Ken
    "The Normal Man Responds" (Caption in Illinois newspaper: Normal Man Marries
        Oblong Woman). [Light] (5) Spr 93, p. 16.
    "You Have to Go Through Bowlegs." [Light] (6) Sum 93, p. 17.
5562. ROBERTSON, Lisa
    "Eclogue One: Honour" (from "XEclogue"). [CapilR] (2:11) Sum 93, p. 99-106.
5563. ROBERTSON, Louise
    "After the Collapse of a Building." [LullwaterR] (4:2) Spr-Sum 93, p. 109.
5564. ROBERTSON, Wade
    "Dad." [Pearl] (17) Spr 93, p. 98.
5565. ROBERTSON, William
    "Another Lesson in Economics." [CanLit] (138/139) Fall-Wint 93, p. 4.
    "Misplaced." [PraF] (14:4) Wint 93-94, p. 55.
5566. ROBERTUS, Polly M.
    "Hill Country Cedar." [Border] (2) Spr 93, p. 59.
5567. ROBIN, Mark
    "When Dexter Ran Away." [ContextS] (3:1) 93, p. 18.
5568. ROBINSON, Bruce
    "Chicane." [WeberS] (10:2) Spr-Sum 93, p. 82.
    "Cold Storage." [WeberS] (10:2) Spr-Sum 93, p. 84.
    "Only We Can Speak of a Beauty." [WeberS] (10:2) Spr-Sum 93, p. 83.
    "Village Women." [OnTheBus] (6:1, #13) Wint 93-Spr 94, p. 172.
    "Where Books Come In." [XavierR] (13:2) Fall 93, p. 109.
5569. ROBINSON, Curtis W.
    "The Words   5-12-1993." [PoetryUSA] (25/26) 93, p. 55.
5570. ROBINSON, Daniel
    "Fire Scenes" (#1-#6). [Outbr] (24) 93, p. 75-78.
5571. ROBINSON, Edwin Arlington
    "The Clerks." [SoCoast] (15) Je 93, p. 66.
5572. ROBINSON, Elizabeth
    "August." [Sulfur] (32) Spr 93, p. 144-145.
    "Circle." [Talisman] (10) Spr 93, p. 123-124.

"March." [Sulfur] (32) Spr 93, p. 147.
"Nightworks." [Sulfur] (32) Spr 93, p. 145.
"Pendant." [Sulfur] (32) Spr 93, p. 146.
"When That." [Sulfur] (32) Spr 93, p. 146-147.
5573. ROBINSON, G. W.
"Birds Calling in the Valley" (tr. of Wang Wei). [AmerPoR] (22:2) Mr-Ap 93, p. 45.
5574. ROBINSON, Harold McNeil
"Love at a Distance." [Art&Und] (2:1) Ja-F 93, p. 24-25.
5575. ROBINSON, Kit
"Balance Sheet" (Excerpt). [Avec] (6:1) 93, p. 63-65.
5576. ROBINSON, M. Christian
"Thank You America." [PennR] (5:2) 93, p. 29-30.
5577. ROBINSON, Mansel
"Public Relations." [Grain] (21:1) Spr 93, p. 123.
5578. ROBINSON, Mike
"The Magician's Wife." [PoetryNW] (34:4) Wint 93-94, p. 23.
5579. ROBINSON, Peter
"Before an Operation." [Stand] (35:1) Wint 93-94, p. 65.
"A Classical Landscape." [Stand] (35:1) Wint 93-94, p. 65-66.
"Deep North." [Stand] (35:1) Wint 93-94, p. 66.
5580. ROBISON, Margaret
"Apraxia." [Kaleid] (26) Wint-Spr 93, p. 27.
"Before the Moon Was the Moon" (Kindergarten Group Poem written with
    Margaret Robison). [Gaia] (3) O 93, p. 40.
"Red Creek" (Excerpt). [Gaia] (3) O 93, p. 40.
"Sunday Outing." [Gaia] (3) O 93, p. 40.
"We Buried the Salamander." [HayF] (13) Fall-Wint 93, p. 99.
5581. ROBLES SALZ, Adela
"Blisters Sleethe" (tr. of Xavier Rosselló). [Iowa] (23:2) Spr-Sum 93, p. 12.
"Cry in the Night" (tr. of Vicent Andrés Estellés). [Iowa] (23:2) Spr-Sum 93, p. 4.
"Flèrida" (tr. of Vicent Andrés Estellés). [Iowa] (23:2) Spr-Sum 93, p. 4-5.
"How Odd This Landscape" (tr. of Vicent Salvador). [Iowa] (23:2) Spr-Sum 93, p.
    10.
"I Picture the Rain" (tr. of Xavier Rosselló). [Iowa] (23:2) Spr-Sum 93, p. 12-13.
"A Letter Home" (tr. of Ovidi Montllor). [Iowa] (23:2) Spr-Sum 93, p. 6-7.
"The Lovers" (tr. of Vicent Andrés Estellés). [Iowa] (23:2) Spr-Sum 93, p. 5.
"March Wind" (tr. of Vicent Salvador). [Iowa] (23:2) Spr-Sum 93, p. 9.
"Mediterrània" (tr. of Teresa Arenys). [Iowa] (23:2) Spr-Sum 93, p. 8.
"Nobody's Answering Machine" (tr. of Vicent Salvador). [Iowa] (23:2) Spr-Sum 93,
    p. 9-10.
"Now That I Am Forty" (tr. of Vicent Salvador). [Iowa] (23:2) Spr-Sum 93, p. 11.
"Will of a Rich Man" (tr. of Vicent Salvador). [Iowa] (23:2) Spr-Sum 93, p. 9.
"XVII. Could it be that the long protruding tongue" (tr. of Salvador Espriu). [Iowa]
    (23:2) Spr-Sum 93, p. 3.
5582. ROBOTHAM, John
"Clerihews." [DogRR] (12:1, #23) Spr-Sum 93, p. 5, 24, 38-39, 41.
ROCCA, L. Della
    See DellaROCCA, L.
5583. ROCKIN' RED
"Housewarming." [Light] (5) Spr 93, p. 25.
5584. ROCKSON, Annella Moore
"Fishing Guides." [Pembroke] (25) 93, p. 107.
5585. ROCKWELL, Tom
"Country Matters." [NewYorkQ] (50) 93, p. 76.
"I am living among people whose concerns are not mine." [NewYorkQ] (52) 93, p.
    64.
"What am I going to do with all the years." [NewYorkQ] (51) 93, p. 57.
ROCQUE, Emma la
    See LaROCQUE, Emma
5586. RODEMAN, Juliet
"The Idea of Rooks." [DenQ] (27:3) Wint 93, p. 53.
5587. RODENKO, Paul
"Night" (tr. by Gerald George). [Vis] (41) 93, p. 7.
5588. RODIA, Becky
"Summer Jobs." [WillowS] (33) Wint 93, p. 48.

398

RODITI

5589. RODITI, Edouard
"An Atheist's Creed" (10 selections, tr. of Alain Bosquet). [WorldL] (4) 93, p. 6-10.
"Autopsychoanalysis" (For Stanley Moss). [WorldL] (4) 93, p. 27.
"For Federico García Lorca" (tr. of Miguel Torga). [WorldL] (4) 93, p. 3-4.
"No Pasaran!" (tr. of Miguel Torga). [WorldL] (4) 93, p. 5.
"The Warning" (For Norman Manea). [WorldL] (4) 93, p. 26.
5590. RODRIGUEZ, Bill
"Genghis Khan." [WormR] (33:3, #131), 93, p. 118-119.
"Snowball." [WormR] (33:3, #131), 93, p. 118.
5591. RODRIGUEZ, Lola
"To Willie Loman: Life as a Package Deal." [EngJ] (82:4) Ap 93, p. 98.
5592. RODRIGUEZ, Luis J.
"A Fence of Lights." [ColR] (20:2) Fall 93, p. 76.
"Hungry." [GreenMR] (NS 6:1) Wint-Spr 93, p. 34-35.
"The Quiet Women." [ColR] (20:2) Fall 93, p. 74.
"Reflection on El Train Glass." [ColR] (20:2) Fall 93, p. 75.
5593. RODRIGUEZ, Pilar
"Geometria Emocional." [BilingR] (18:1) Ja-Ap 93, p. 57.
"La Mala del Cuento." [BilingR] (18:1) Ja-Ap 93, p. 56.
5594. RODRIGUEZ, W. R.
"The Fountain of Youth." [ProseP] (2) 93, p. 81.
5595. RODRIGUEZ MILANÉS, Cecilia
"Abuelita Poem." [13thMoon] (12:1/2) 93-94, p. 124.
"Donde Esta Tu Abuela?" [13thMoon] (12:1/2) 93-94, p. 121.
"RR in Spanish =." [13thMoon] (12:1/2) 93-94, p. 122.
"Untitled: Our breasts reveal." [13thMoon] (12:1/2) 93-94, p. 123.
5596. RODRIGUEZ-NIETO, Catherine
"On Being Alone: Berkeley 1969" (tr. of Lucha Corpi). [ColR] (20:2) Fall 93, p. 49-51.
5597. ROE, Margie McCreless
"Dealing with Disorder." [ChrC] (110:1) 6-13 Ja 93, p. 21.
5598. ROEMMERS, Alejandro
"The Dream Remains" (from "Soñadores, soñad," tr. by Veronica Miranda). [Luz] (5) N 93, p. 87.
"Insomnia" (from "Soñadores, soñad," tr. by Veronica Miranda). [Luz] (5) N 93, p. 17.
"Insomnio" (from "Soñadores, soñad"). [Luz] (5) N 93, p. 16.
"Queda el Sueño" (from "Soñadores, soñad"). [Luz] (5) N 93, p. 86.
5599. ROEPE, Rebecca A.
"In a College Town." [CumbPR]] (13:1) Fall 93, p. 85-87.
"Upper Westside Commerce." [CumbPR]] (13:1) Fall 93, p. 84.
5600. ROESKE, Paulette
"Tournament of Destruction" (Santa Fe Speedway). [VirQR] (69:1) Wint 93, p. 96-97.
5601. ROFFE, Mercedes
"#34. I can't drink" (tr. by K. A. Kopple). [Sonora] (24/25) Spr 93, p. 18-20.
5602. ROGAL, Stan
"Buzz Buzz." [PraF] (14:4) Wint 93-94, p. 100.
"Personations" (3 poems: 5, 6, 10). [PoetryC] (13:4) 93, p. 25.
"Signals." [PraF] (14:4) Wint 93-94, p. 98.
"Tempus Fugit." [PraF] (14:4) Wint 93-94, p. 99.
"Waterlines." [PraF] (14:4) Wint 93-94, p. 100.
5603. ROGERS, Bertha
"In February, Thinking of the Gulf War." [SmPd] (30:2, #88) Spr 93, p. 7.
5604. ROGERS, Bobby Caudle
"While the River Is Wide." [SouthernR] (29:2) Spr, Ap 93, p. 314-315.
5605. ROGERS, Daryl
"The First Time." [NewYorkQ] (52) 93, p. 91.
5606. ROGERS, Pattiann
"The All-Encompassing" (*Philosopher in Meditation*, Rembrandt). [Hudson] (45:4) Wint 93, p. 609-610.
"Berry Renaissance." [GettyR] (6:3) Sum 93, p. 476-477.
"Considering All the Moving Light, All the Stationary Darkness." [KenR] (NS 15:4) Fall 93, p. 130-131.
"Creating Transfiguration." [GettyR] (6:3) Sum 93, p. 475.
"Death Vision." [KenR] (NS 15:4) Fall 93, p. 129-130.

"Eating Death." [AmerPoR] (22:4) Jl-Ag 93, p. 36.
"Emissaries." [GeoR] (47:1) Spr 93, p. 127-128.
"For Any Known Fact: Nude Walking Alone on a Beach in Moonlight." [GettyR] (6:3) Sum 93, p. 478-479.
"God Alone." [ParisR] (35:128) Fall 93, p. 75-76.
"The Image in a World of Flux." [Iowa] (23:1) Wint 93, p. 18-19.
"Language and Experience." [WestHR] (47:1) Spr 93, p. 21.
"Life and Death: All the Lost Accordions and Concertinas." [Hudson] (45:4) Wint 93, p. 611-612.
"Life in an Expanding Universe." [ParisR] (35:128) Fall 93, p. 76-77.
"The Need to Adore." [CutB] (39) Wint 93, p. 1-2.
"A New Notice of Motion: The Lover Waiting." [KenR] (NS 15:4) Fall 93, p. 128-129.
"The One True God." [CutB] (39) Wint 93, p. 3-4.
"This Kind of Grace." [CutB] (39) Wint 93, p. 5-6.
"Till My Teeth Rattle." [GeoR] (47:1) Spr 93, p. 129.
"Trial and Error." [Iowa] (23:1) Wint 93, p. 19-20.
"Truth As We Know It." [MichQR] (32:3) Sum 93, p. 352-353.
"Whiteout: The Disappearance of Impossibilities." [WestHR] (47:1) Spr 93, p. 22-23.
5607. ROGOFF, Jay
"Extra Innings." [SewanR] (101:2) Ap-Je, Spr 93, p. 210-211.
"Sacrifice." [SewanR] (101:2) Ap-Je, Spr 93, p. 211-212.
"Venera" (Selections: 3 poems). [KenR] (NS 15:3) Sum 93, p. 176-177.
5608. ROGOW, Zack
"Poem in Leopardese" (Bilingual Text fragment, tr. of Virgil Teodorescu, w. Sasha Vlad). [Talisman] (10) Spr 93, p. 155-156.
5609. ROHRER, Matt
"To a Croatian Poet." [CreamCR] (17:2) Fall 93, p. 132.
5610. ROHRER, Michael
"The Grinder's Monkey." [CumbPR] (12:2) Spr 93, p. 39.
"Invitation to a Voyage." [CumbPR] (12:2) Spr 93, p. 42.
"Sinbad." [CumbPR] (12:2) Spr 93, p. 38.
"Traces." [CumbPR] (12:2) Spr 93, p. 40-41.
5611. ROHWER, Lee Orcutt
"Mary's Discontent." [RagMag] (11:2) 93, p. 107.
5612. ROITMAN, Judith
"At the Corner of 9th and Avalon." [RiverC] (13:1) Fall 92, p. 58.
"The Diamond Notebooks II" (Excerpt). [Caliban] (13) 93, p. 140-143.
"Mother Stanzas." [RiverC] (13:1) Fall 92, p. 56-57.
"Third Pantoum for My Parents." [RiverC] (13:1) Fall 92, p. 54-55.
5613. ROLFE, Edwin
"Are You Now or Have You Ever Been." [TriQ] (88) Fall 93, p. 149-150.
"A Letter to the Denouncers." [TriQ] (88) Fall 93, p. 151.
"Not Hatred." [TriQ] (88) Fall 93, p. 148.
"Pastoral — 1954." [TriQ] (88) Fall 93, p. 152.
5614. ROLFE, Rob
"Metamorphosis." [Grain] (21:1) Spr 93, p. 52.
"Myth." [Grain] (21:1) Spr 93, p. 49.
"St Boniface." [Grain] (21:1) Spr 93, p. 50-51.
5615. ROLLINGS, Alane
"Continuity." [DenQ] (28:2) Fall 93, p. 11-12.
"Fighting the Elements." [GettyR] (6:2) Spr 93, p. 304-305.
"Never Stop." [Sonora] (26) Fall 93, p. 3-4.
"Tomorrow Is a Difficult Idea." [TampaR] (6) Spr 93, p. 12-13.
"The Uncrippling." [Sonora] (26) Fall 93, p. 1-2.
5616. ROLLINS, Scott
"The Traveller" (1., 2., 4., introduction, 2nd account, intermission, tr. of Patricia Lasoen). [Vis] (43) 93, p. 17.
5617. ROMANO, Rose
"Dead." [Footwork] (23) 93, p. 41.
"Just a Suggestion." [Footwork] (23) 93, p. 41.
"Looking for Italian Names." [SlipS] (13) 93, p. 96-97.
"Think of Palermo." [Footwork] (23) 93, p. 42.
"This." [Footwork] (23) 93, p. 42.
"Woman in an Attic." [Footwork] (23) 93, p. 39-41.

5618. ROMANY, Celina
"A la Cama, Niños." [Americas] (21:1) Spr 93, p. 45.
"Ábrete Sésamo." [Americas] (21:1) Spr 93, p. 46.
"En Nueva York." [Americas] (21:1) Spr 93, p. 44.
"Oda a la muerte." [Americas] (21:1) Spr 93, p. 47-48.
"Personales." [Americas] (21:1) Spr 93, p. 41.
"Plegaria en Bahía." [Americas] (21:1) Spr 93, p. 42-43.
5619. ROMER, Stephen
"Hibernation." [NewRep] (209:15) 11 O 93, p. 50.
5620. ROMOND, Edwin
"At Night the Characters on My Classroom Shelves Come Out to Party." [EngJ]
(82:4) Ap 93, p. 97.
"Sunday Before Thanksgiving" (from *Home Fire*, Belle Mead Press). [Sun] (205) Ja
93, p. 15.
5621. ROMTVEDT, David
"Another Saigon Intersection." [Sun] (213) S 93, p. 23.
"Deep Blue Flower." [Sun] (214) O 93, p. 19.
"Iris." [PoetryE] (36) Fall 93, p. 26.
"My Daughter's Room." [Sun] (213) S 93, p. 23.
"My Father's Death." [Event] (22:2) Sum 93, p. 18.
"My Flame." [MissouriR] (16:2) 93, p. 171.
"My Job." [Sun] (205) Ja 93, p. 22.
"My Porch." [MissouriR] (16:2) 93, p. 175.
"My Village." [Sun] (205) Ja 93, p. 23.
"My Wife." [MissouriR] (16:2) 93, p. 172.
"Painting the Fence." [MissouriR] (16:2) 93, p. 169.
"The Radio." [MissouriR] (16:2) 93, p. 174.
"Spring Cleaning." [WillowS] (33) Wint 93, p. 65.
"Traffic." [Sun] (205) Ja 93, p. 23.
"Ultimate Nightingale." [AmerPoR] (22:2) Mr-Ap 93, p. 41.
"Welcome." [MissouriR] (16:2) 93, p. 170.
"Windows." [MissouriR] (16:2) 93, p. 173.
"Wyoming I Do Not Own." [AmerPoR] (22:2) Mr-Ap 93, p. 40.
5622. RONAN, John
"Crows Along Paradise Road" (for C. & K. L.). [SoCoast] (15) Je 93, p. 14.
5623. RONEY-O'BRIEN, Susan
"At Noon Hill" (for Caitlin). [PraS] (67:3) Fall 93, p. 28-29.
"Stereognosis." [PraS] (67:3) Fall 93, p. 29.
5624. RONK, Martha
"Arroyo Seco." [Talisman] (10) Spr 93, p. 115.
"The Bitterness of Rousseau." [AntR] (51:2) Spr 93, p. 238.
"The Bus." [Talisman] (10) Spr 93, p. 116.
"Dying." [SouthernR] (29:2) Spr, Ap 93, p. 292.
"Hunger, a Cookbook." [DenQ] (27:4) Spr 93, p. 80-81.
"The Moon." [SouthernR] (29:2) Spr, Ap 93, p. 291-292.
"Neutra's Window." [Talisman] (10) Spr 93, p. 116.
"Paraphrase." [Talisman] (10) Spr 93, p. 116.
"The San Gabriels." [Talisman] (10) Spr 93, p. 115.
"The Sierras." [Talisman] (10) Spr 93, p. 115.
"The Sketch." [SouthernR] (29:2) Spr, Ap 93, p. 291.
5625. ROOKE, Katerina Anghelaki
"My Little Heart at Night" (tr. by Eleni Fourtouni). [PoetryC] (13:3) 93, p. 23.
"Speaking of Eyes" (tr. by Eleni Fourtouni). [PoetryC] (13:3) 93, p. 23.
5626. ROOT, Judith
"In a Flat Between Pianos." [TarRP] (32:2) Spr 93, p. 26.
5627. ROPPEL, Katherine
"Time Piece." [AnthNEW] (5) 93, p. 8.
5628. ROQUEPLAN, Fernand
"Sunrise on Tisang River." [InterPR] (19:2) Fall 93, p. 77.
5629. ROSCHER, Marina (Marina L.)
"The Conch." [Gaia] (3) O 93, p. 5.
"Seven Days in October." [Gaia] (3) O 93, p. 5-6.
"Subsequent Meeting." [ApalQ] (35) 90, p. 41.
5630. ROSE, Anthony
"A New Metropolis." [OnTheBus] (5:2, #12) Sum-Fall 93, p. 175.

5631. ROSE, Jennifer
"First Frost in the Suburbs." [BostonR] (18:2) Mr-Ap 93, p. 15.
"Route One Postcard" (California). [DenQ] (27:3) Wint 93, p. 54.
5632. ROSE, Josh
"Puget Sound." [OnTheBus] (5:2, #12) Sum-Fall 93, p. 176.
"When Girls See Me for the First Time." [OnTheBus] (6:1, #13) Wint 93-Spr 94, p. 173.
5633. ROSE, Wilga
"Tai Chi." [Bogg] (66) Wint 92-93, p. 13.
5634. ROSEN, Deborah Nodler
"Before Boarding." [WillowR] (20) Spr 93, p. 36-37.
5635. ROSEN, Kenneth
"In Defense of the Fallen Clergy." [Ploughs] (19:4) Wint 93-94, p. 123-124.
"Poetry Reading in Pisgah." [Ploughs] (19:4) Wint 93-94, p. 125-126.
5636. ROSEN, Michael J.
"Another View of Penn." [ParisR] (35:126) Spr 93, p. 208-210.
"Expressions in Cement." [ParisR] (35:126) Spr 93, p. 210-211.
"Pilgrim Signs." [SouthwR] (78:1) Wint 93, p. 26-31.
"The Shelving Unit." [TampaR] (6) Spr 93, p. 58-59.
"Watercolors." [ParisR] (35:126) Spr 93, p. 207-208.
5637. ROSEN, Sally
"Definitions of a Kiss." [PoetL] (88:2) Sum 93, p. 15-16.
"Pills, or Why We Got Up This Morning." [PoetL] (88:2) Sum 93, p. 17.
5638. ROSENBAUM, Ellen
"Above the morning thrushes are to be heard singing" (tr. of J. H. Krchovsky).
    [OxfordM] (9:1) Spr-Sum 93, p. 104.
"The Ace" (tr. of Svatava Antosová). [OxfordM] (9:1) Spr-Sum 93, p. 44-46.
"All writing seems to me today idiotic" (tr. of J. H. Krchovsky). [OxfordM] (9:1)
    Spr-Sum 93, p. 102.
"Alone with myself and even alone within my very self" (tr. of J. H. Krchovsky).
    [OxfordM] (9:1) Spr-Sum 93, p. 104.
"Autumn Light" (tr. of Mila Haugová). [OxfordM] (9:1) Spr-Sum 93, p. 32-33.
"The Beast" (tr. of Jáchym Topol). [OxfordM] (9:1) Spr-Sum 93, p. 43-44.
"The dark clouds are getting lower" (tr. of Emil Julis). [OxfordM] (9:1) Spr-Sum 93,
    p. 14.
"The Deserted Kingdom" (tr. of Emil Julis). [OxfordM] (9:1) Spr-Sum 93, p. 15.
"Does he want to vanish without a trace" (tr. of J. H. Krchovsky). [OxfordM] (9:1)
    Spr-Sum 93, p. 101.
"A Dream of Death" (tr. of Ivan Wernisch). [OxfordM] (9:1) Spr-Sum 93, p. 89.
"Eerie Dreams" (tr. of Jáchym Topol). [OxfordM] (9:1) Spr-Sum 93, p. 41-43.
"The End of the World" (tr. of Jáchym Topol). [OxfordM] (9:1) Spr-Sum 93, p. 40 -
    41.
"An Examination of the Body" (tr. of Jan Skácel). [OxfordM] (9:1) Spr-Sum 93, p.
    16-17.
"A Fable" (tr. of Zbynek Hejda). [OxfordM] (9:1) Spr-Sum 93, p. 85-87.
"Farewell Letter" (tr. of Svatava Antosová). [OxfordM] (9:1) Spr-Sum 93, p. 46-47.
"The Franciscan Baths" (tr. of Jan Machácek). [OxfordM] (9:1) Spr-Sum 93, p. 82.
"The Grey-headed Griffin" (tr. of Miroslav Huptych). [OxfordM] (9:1) Spr-Sum 93,
    p. 33-35.
"He was drunk, this time a little less so than other times" (tr. of Ivan Wernisch).
    [OxfordM] (9:1) Spr-Sum 93, p. 89.
"How a Heart Breaks" (tr. of Karel Siktanc). [OxfordM] (9:1) Spr-Sum 93, p. 117 -
    122.
"I accidentally poured this lousy coffee on myself" (tr. of J. H. Krchovsky).
    [OxfordM] (9:1) Spr-Sum 93, p. 101-102.
"I always take my own death with me when I go outside" (tr. of J. H. Krchovsky).
    [OxfordM] (9:1) Spr-Sum 93, p. 104.
"I Do No Want to Be" (tr. of Ludek Marks). [OxfordM] (9:1) Spr-Sum 93, p. 106.
"I go out at night into the garden naked" (tr. of J. H. Krchovsky). [OxfordM] (9:1)
    Spr-Sum 93, p. 105.
"If I am living it is a sign that here nothing is in order" (tr. of Karel Sebek).
    [OxfordM] (9:1) Spr-Sum 93, p. 31-32.
"Invariably I can't rid myself of the feeling" (tr. of Ivan Wernisch). [OxfordM] (9:1)
    Spr-Sum 93, p. 91.
"The king of the fools ordered" (tr. of Ivan Wernisch). [OxfordM] (9:1) Spr-Sum 93,
    p. 88.

"Love Episode" (tr. of Jáchym Topol). [OxfordM] (9:1) Spr-Sum 93, p. 39-40.
"Lubok" (tr. of Ivan Wernisch). [OxfordM] (9:1) Spr-Sum 93, p. 90.
"The Match" (tr. of Lenka Chytilová). [OxfordM] (9:1) Spr-Sum 93, p. 28.
"Morning Song" (to the memory of Osip Mandelstam, tr. of Jiri Rulf). [OxfordM] (9:1) Spr-Sum 93, p. 11-12.
"The nearness of day like the fangs of a wolf" (tr. of Karel Sebek). [OxfordM] (9:1) Spr-Sum 93, p. 32.
"A Night out of Goethe" (tr. of Lenka Chytilová). [OxfordM] (9:1) Spr-Sum 93, p. 28.
"Old-fashioned Language" (tr. of Jirina Salaquardova). [OxfordM] (9:1) Spr-Sum 93, p. 10-11.
"Once there was a fellow" (tr. of Ivan Wernisch). [OxfordM] (9:1) Spr-Sum 93, p. 91.
"A poem comes to me like night dressed in pyjamas" (tr. of Karel Sebek). [OxfordM] (9:1) Spr-Sum 93, p. 28-29.
"Proposal for an Observation" (tr. of Jiri Rulf). [OxfordM] (9:1) Spr-Sum 93, p. 12 - 13.
"Robinson" (tr. of Jan Machácek). [OxfordM] (9:1) Spr-Sum 93, p. 83.
"Shod and clothed I am counting the minutes" (tr. of J. H. Krchovsky). [OxfordM] (9:1) Spr-Sum 93, p. 102-103.
"Sonnet About Those Who Strangled Her" (tr. of Jan Skácel). [OxfordM] (9:1) Spr - Sum 93, p. 17.
"Sonnet on a July Night in the Highlands" (tr. of Jan Skácel). [OxfordM] (9:1) Spr - Sum 93, p. 16.
"A spike in the head during the holidays" (tr. of Karel Sebek). [OxfordM] (9:1) Spr - Sum 93, p. 29-30.
"The Tale of the Angel's Return" (tr. of Jirina Salaquardova). [OxfordM] (9:1) Spr - Sum 93, p. 10.
"There arrives a beast the spring" (tr. of Karel Sebek). [OxfordM] (9:1) Spr-Sum 93, p. 30-31.
"Things" (tr. of Emil Julis). [OxfordM] (9:1) Spr-Sum 93, p. 14.
"Time" (tr. of Jan Skácel). [OxfordM] (9:1) Spr-Sum 93, p. 16.
"We all go with the flow" (tr. of Emil Julis). [OxfordM] (9:1) Spr-Sum 93, p. 15.
"Whitsunday in St. Nicholas' Cathedral" (tr. of J. H. Krchovsky). [OxfordM] (9:1) Spr-Sum 93, p. 103.
"Who could, paid" (tr. of Ivan Wernisch). [OxfordM] (9:1) Spr-Sum 93, p. 88.
"Without Regard to Autumn" (tr. of Dana Podracká). [OxfordM] (9:1) Spr-Sum 93, p. 13.
"Yes yes" (tr. of Ivan Wernisch). [OxfordM] (9:1) Spr-Sum 93, p. 90.
5639. ROSENBERG, Heidi D.
"Una Mujer." [Pearl] (17) Spr 93, p. 11.
5640. ROSENBERG, Liz
"The Half of Life" (tr. of Friedrich Hölderlin, w. Denny Schmidt). [GrahamHR] (17) Fall 93, p. 109.
"Lebanon." [Boulevard] (8:2/3, #23/24) Fall 93, p. 204.
"On tawny leaves rests the grape, the hope of wine" (tr. of Friedrich Hölderlin, w. Denny Schmidt). [GrahamHR] (17) Fall 93, p. 111.
"Ripe, in fire dipped, broiled" (tr. of Friedrich Hölderlin, w. Denny Schmidt). [GrahamHR] (17) Fall 93, p. 108.
"To Diotima" (tr. of Friedrich Hölderlin, w. Denny Schmidt). [GrahamHR] (17) Fall 93, p. 110.
5641. ROSENFELD, Natania
"Poem for My Friend, Nearly a Year After Her Death." [SenR] (23:1/2) Wint 93, p. 108.
"The Safe House." [SenR] (23:1/2) Wint 93, p. 109-110.
5642. ROSENFIELD, Kim
"For Her Only." [BlackBread] (3) 93, p. 17.
"What's a Shook Slicker Bridge?" [BlackBread] (3) 93, p. 16.
5643. ROSENTHAL, David
"To Return." [DenQ] (27:3) Wint 93, p. 55.
5644. ROSENTHAL, Irv
"Fast." [RagMag] (11:1) 93, p. 103.
"Psyche, 6." [RagMag] (11:1) 93, p. 102.
5645. ROSENTHAL, M. L.
"1991-1992" (in memoriam D. H. R.). [SouthernR] (29:3) Sum, Jl 93, p. 558-560.

403

ROSENTHAL

"Three Conversations" (1 For E. R., 2 For E. C., 3 for V. H. R.). [QRL] (12:32/33)
  93, p. 502-503.
5646. ROSENWALD, John
    "Gate of Virtue and Victory (De Sheng Men)" (tr. of Gu Cheng, w. Yanbing Chen).
    [ChiR] (39:3/4) 93, p. 292.
5647. ROSENWASSER, Rena
    "India's Increments." [Talisman] (10) Spr 93, p. 126-129.
5648. ROSENZWEIG, Geri
    "Orpah's Song." [LullwaterR] (4:2) Spr-Sum 93, p. 38.
5649. ROSKOS, David
    "Storm's Opal." [Lactuca] (17) Apr 93, p. 42-44.
5650. ROSS, David
    "How Abstract, the Idea of Mulberries." [BellArk] (9:5) S-O 93, p. 1.
    "Huge Umber." [Northeast] (5:9) Wint 93-94, p. 18.
    "Invocation of the Second Chance." [BellArk] (9:5) S-O 93, p. 1.
    "Notes Concerning the Ontogeny of Flight." [BellArk] (9:5) S-O 93, p. 1.
5651. ROSS, Joyce Elaine
    "A Father's Pain." [OnTheBus] (6:1, #13) Wint 93-Spr 94, p. 174.
5652. ROSS, Linwood M.
    "And I Wanted to Say." [Lactuca] (17) Apr 93, p. 27-30.
    "Causalities." [Lactuca] (17) Apr 93, p. 25-27.
    "The Lyrics of Despair" (For Billie). [AfAmRev] (27:4) Wint 93, p. 631-632.
    "Motherwish." [FreeL] (11) Wint 93, p. 23-24.
    "Poem for the Fat Lady Singing." [Gypsy] (20) Sum 93, p. 52.
    "Reunion: August '89." [AfAmRev] (27:4) Wint 93, p. 632-634.
    "Whore." [ChangingM] (25) Wint-Spr 93, p. 67.
ROSS, Nathan Viste
    See VISTE-ROSS, Nathan
5653. ROSS, Stacey
    "Mama" (tr. of Manlio Argueta, w. Dan Bellm). [KenR] (NS 15:3) Sum 93, p. 94 -
      95.
5654. ROSSATTI, Alberto
    "The Care of Things" (2 excerpts, tr. of Daniela Attanasio, w. Kathleen Fraser).
      [13thMoon] (11:1/2) 93, p. 206-207.
    "Desert Poem" (Excerpts, tr. of Toni Maraini, w. Kathleen Fraser). [13thMoon]
      (11:1/2) 93, p. 212-214.
    "The Girl of Seven Spirits" (tr. of Sara Zanghi, w. Kathleen Fraser). [13thMoon]
      (11:1/2) 93, p. 216.
    "Poem: You should remember" (tr. of Sara Zanghi, w. Kathleen Fraser). [13thMoon]
      (11:1/2) 93, p. 217.
5655. ROSSELLI, Amelia
    "Sleep" (Selection: -20-, tr. by Kathleen Fraser). [13thMoon] (11:1/2) 93, p. 215.
5656. ROSSELLO, Xavier
    "Blisters Sleethe" (tr. by Adela Robles Salz). [Iowa] (23:2) Spr-Sum 93, p. 12.
    "I Picture the Rain" (tr. by Adela Robles Salz). [Iowa] (23:2) Spr-Sum 93, p. 12-13.
5657. ROSSETTI, Ana
    "Chico Wrangler." [Luz] (3) Ja 93, p. 10.
    "Diotima to Her Most Dedicated Student" (tr. by Cecilia C. Lee and Laura Higgins).
      [LitR] (36:3) Spr 93, p. 380.
    "Festividad del Dulcisimo Nombre." [Luz] (3) Ja 93, p. 9-10.
    "The Garden of Your Delights" (tr. by Angela McEwan). [Luz] (3) Ja 93, p. 13.
    "I Say a Little Prayer" (in Spanish and English, tr. by Angela McEwan). [Luz] (3) Ja
      93, p. 14-15.
    "El Jardin de Tus Delicias." [Luz] (3) Ja 93, p. 12.
    "The Wrangler Kid" (tr. by Angela McEwan). [Luz] (3) Ja 93, p. 11.
5658. ROSSETTI, Christina
    "Up-Hill." [Light] (7) Aut 93, p. 24.
5659. ROSSETTI, Dante Gabriel
    "Prolonged Sonnet: Whent he Troops Were Returning from Milan" (tr. of Niccolò
      degli Albizzi). [SoCoast] (15) Je 93, p. 61.
5660. ROSSI, Antonio
    "Compaia sul Monte Sighignola la Prima Neve o Non Compaia." [LitR] (36:4) Sum
      93, p. 493.
    "Whether or Not the First Snow Appears on Mount Sighignola" (tr. by Stephen
      Sartarelli). [LitR] (36:4) Sum 93, p. 492.

ROSSI, Cristina Peri
    See PERI ROSSI, Cristina
5661. ROSSI, Daniel
    "It Comes As No Surprise." [JamesWR] (11:1) Fall 93, p. 7.
5662. ROSSI, Joe
    "Portrait." [HawaiiR] (17:1, #37) Spr 93, p. 217-218.
5663. ROSSI, Lee
    "The Head of a Girl." [ChironR] (12:1, #34) Spr 93, p. 33.
    "Metempsychosis." [OnTheBus] (6:1, #13) Wint 93-Spr 94, p. 175-176.
    "Pleasant Lake — Waiting for My Sister to Deliver." [PoetryE] (36) Fall 93, p. 111 -
        112.
    "Spotting the Goddess." [ChironR] (12:1, #34) Spr 93, p. 33.
    "Venn Logic." [ChironR] (12:1, #34) Spr 93, p. 33.
5664. ROSSINI, Clare
    "The Good Fortune of Others." [AntR] (51:1) Wint 93, p. 94.
    "Still Life With Pear." [SycamoreR] (5:2) Sum 93, p. 41-42.
5665. ROSSINI, Frank
    "George Washington Dies." [ChironR] (12:1, #34) Spr 93, p. 45.
    "Six Chinese Painters." [SilverFR] (24) Wint 93, p. 39-45.
5666. ROSU, Dona
    "The Convicted" (tr. of Marin Sorescu, w. W.D. Snodgrass & Luciana Costea).
        [Salm] (98/99) Spr-Sum 93, p. 81.
    "Fortress" (tr. of Marin Sorescu, w. W.D. Snodgrass & Luciana Costea). [Salm]
        (98/99) Spr-Sum 93, p. 82.
    "Frames" (tr. of Marin Sorescu, w. W.D. Snodgrass & Luciana Costea). [Salm]
        (98/99) Spr-Sum 93, p. 83.
5667. ROTELLA, Alexis
    "Champagne." [Footwork] (23) 93, p. 68.
    "Cheese." [Footwork] (23) 93, p. 68.
    "The Day a Woman Hit a Doe." [Footwork] (23) 93, p. 69.
    "Flame Dance." [Footwork] (23) 93, p. 68.
    "A Good Cry." [ChironR] (12:3, #36) Aut 93, p. 31.
    "Just the Two of Us." [Footwork] (23) 93, p. 68.
    "Private Joy." [Footwork] (23) 93, p. 69.
    "You Can't Win." [Footwork] (23) 93, p. 68.
5668. ROTH, Ron
    "The Red Parrot." [SoDakR] (31:3) Fall 93, p. 137-138.
5669. ROTH-NATALE, Nanci
    "Junk Week." [BellArk] (9:1) Ja-F 93, p. 21.
5670. ROTHENBERG, Jerome
    "Candle Fat" (tr. of Kurt Schwitters). [PoetryUSA] (25/26) 93, p. 15.
    "The Lorca Variation" (Selection: "Second New York Poem"). [Sulfur] (32) Spr 93,
        p. 220-226.
    "An Oracle for Delfi" (for Demosthenes Agrafiotis). [Sulfur] (33) Fall 93, p. 215 -
        223.
    "Subway Poem" (tr. of Kurt Schwitters). [PoetryUSA] (25/26) 93, p. 23.
5671. ROTHENBERG, Susan
    "Parts" (w. Robert Creeley). [Conjunc] (20) 93, p. 87-103.
5672. ROTUNNO, Laura
    "At a Jazz Bar." [Plain] (13:2) Wint 93, p. 16.
    "My Dear Old Uncle Bobby." [Plain] (13:3) Spr 93, p. 28.
5673. ROUBAUD, Jacques
    "Air" (tr. by Rosmarie Waldrop). [Pequod] (36) 93, p. 50.
    "Air, Water, Places, II" (tr. by Rosmarie Waldrop). [Pequod] (36) 93, p. 48.
    "Alive, absent from all life" (tr. by Rosmarie Waldrop). [ManhatR] (7:1) Fall 93, p.
        41.
    "Any, Any Whatever" (tr. by Rosmarie Waldrop). [ManhatR] (7:1) Fall 93, p. 34.
    "Bright World" (tr. by Rosmarie Waldrop). [ManhatR] (7:1) Fall 93, p. 39.
    "Division of Worlds" (tr. by Rosmarie Waldrop). [ManhatR] (7:1) Fall 93, p. 42.
    "Even into the Night" (tr. by Rosmarie Waldrop). [Talisman] (11) Fall 93, p. 11-13.
    "The Idea of Form" (tr. by Rosmarie Waldrop). [NewAW] (11) Sum-Fall 93, p. 56 -
        62.
    "Identity" (tr. by Rosmarie Waldrop). [ManhatR] (7:1) Fall 93, p. 47.
    "In the Ersatz-World" (tr. by Rosmarie Waldrop). [ManhatR] (7:1) Fall 93, p. 33.
    "In these worlds, in every one" (tr. by Rosmarie Waldrop). [ManhatR] (7:1) Fall 93,
        p. 40.

"Lyrical" (tr. by Rosmarie Waldrop). [ManhatR] (7:1) Fall 93, p. 44.
"Plenitude" (tr. by Rosmarie Waldrop). [ManhatR] (7:1) Fall 93, p. 46.
"Preparatory Poem" (tr. by Rosmarie Waldrop). [Pequod] (36) 93, p. 51.
"The Sickness of the Soul, V" (tr. by Rosmarie Waldrop). [Pequod] (36) 93, p. 49.
"That the World Was There" (tr. by Rosmarie Waldrop). [ManhatR] (7:1) Fall 93, p. 45.
"The Way of Examples, II" (tr. by Rosmarie Waldrop). [ManhatR] (7:1) Fall 93, p. 43.
"The Way of Stories" (tr. by Rosmarie Waldrop). [ManhatR] (7:1) Fall 93, p. 36.
"The Way of the Impossible" (tr. by Rosmarie Waldrop). [ManhatR] (7:1) Fall 93, p. 37.
"What to Do with a World" (tr. by Rosmarie Waldrop). [ManhatR] (7:1) Fall 93, p. 38.
"Where time imitates a solid line" (tr. by Rosmarie Waldrop). [ManhatR] (7:1) Fall 93, p. 35.
5674. ROUNER, Rita Rainsford
   "A Work of Spinning" (for T. N. R.). [AmerS] (62:3) Sum 93, p. 452-454.
ROUS, Peter de
   See De ROUS, Peter
5675. ROUSE, Frances
   "Toowoomba in the Fog" (For Chris Mansell in memory of Amelia Earhart and Amy Johnson). [Nimrod] (36:2) Spr-Sum 93, p. 80-81.
5676. ROUSSEAU, Ann
   "Before Dawn." [EngJ] (82:7) N 93, p. 90.
5677. ROXMAN, Susanna
   "The Peat-Bog." [Vis] (41) 93, p. 13.
5678. ROY, Darlene
   "Black Bridge Blues." [Drumvoices] (1:1/2) Fall-Wint 91-92, p. 72-73.
   "Consciousness Rising / Love Rising." [Drumvoices] (1:1/2) Fall-Wint 91-92, p. 76.
   "Dunham's Dance." [Drumvoices] (1:1/2) Fall-Wint 91-92, p. 74.
   "Evolution." [Drumvoices] (1:1/2) Fall-Wint 91-92, p. 68-69.
   "Haiku" (2 poems). [Drumvoices] (1:1/2) Fall-Wint 91-92, p. 69.
   "Malcolmorphosis." [Drumvoices] (1:1/2) Fall-Wint 91-92, p. 70-71.
   "Moving On." [Drumvoices] (1:1/2) Fall-Wint 91-92, p. 67.
5679. ROY, Lucinda
   "Origami." [Shen] (43:1) Spr 93, p. 106-107.
5680. ROY, Margaret
   "On Leaving the Visitor's Interpretative Center: Rain." [Contact] (11:65/66/67) Spr 93, p. 9.
5681. ROYET-JOURNOUD, Claude
   "I.E." (Selections: 9-13, tr. by Keith Waldrop). [Avec] (6:1) 93, p. 93-97.
5682. ROZEWICZ, Tadeusz
   "No title: In the beginning" (tr. by Jeanne Deweese). [ContextS] (3:1) 93, p. 30.
   "No title: It's high time" (To the memory of Konstanty Puzyna, tr. by Jeanne Deweese). [ContextS] (3:1) 93, p. 32.
   "Still Trying" (tr. by Jeanne Deweese). [ContextS] (3:1) 93, p. 29.
   "'Success' and Requests" (tr. by Jeanne Deweese). [ContextS] (3:1) 93, p. 31-32.
5683. RUARK, Gibbons
   "Hybrid Magnolias in Late April." [NewRep] (209:14) 4 O 93, p. 42.
   "This Table." [Shen] (43:3) Fall 93, p. 59.
5684. RUBAVICIUS, Vytautas
   "Accident Not Yet Understood" (tr. by Almantas Samalavicius). [CimR] (104) Jl 93, p. 20.
   "Winter Ideology, 1986" (tr. by Almantas Samalavicius). [CimR] (104) Jl 93, p. 19.
5685. RUBIA, Geraldine
   "Dictionary Sam." [TickleAce] (24) Fall-Wint 92, p. 111-112.
   "Fine Lines." [TickleAce] (23) Spr-Sum 92, p. 32.
   "Flying Sideways." [TickleAce] (23) Spr-Sum 92, p. 31.
   "Kevin." [TickleAce] (23) Spr-Sum 92, p. 33.
   "Should You See Me Naked." [TickleAce] (23) Spr-Sum 92, p. 34.
5686. RUBIN, Mark
   "Introduction to the Asylum." [LaurelR] (27:2) Sum 93, p. 18.
   "The Use of Wrens." [LaurelR] (27:2) Sum 93, p. 19-20.
5687. RUBIN, Stan Sanvel
   "Emily Was Right." [RiverC] (13:1) Fall 92, p. 82.
   "Wreckage." [RiverC] (13:1) Fall 92, p. 83.

5688. RUBINSTEIN, Raphael
    "Requested Rhetoric." [Talisman] (11) Fall 93, p. 161.
5689. RUBIO, Alberto
    "Asleep by the River" (tr. by Steven White). [InterPR] (19:2) Fall 93, p. 35.
    "Durmiendo Junto al Río." [InterPR] (19:2) Fall 93, p. 34.
5690. RUBY, Carmela
    "Suite." [ContextS] (3:1) 93, p. 5.
5691. RUCKER, Trish
    "Emily's Dreams." [SouthernPR] (33:2) Fall 93, p. 49-50.
    "In Your Garden." [PoetryE] (36) Fall 93, p. 18.
5692. RUCKERT, Jan
    "Favorite." [OnTheBus] (5:2, #12) Sum-Fall 93, p. 177.
    "A Simple Design." [OnTheBus] (6:1, #13) Wint 93-Spr 94, p. 177.
5693. RUCKS, Carol
    "All Day Children." [RagMag] (11:1) 93, p. 98.
    "The Beginning of Memory." [RagMag] (11:1) 93, p. 99.
5694. RUDMAN, Mark
    "The Art of Dying" (To the suicides of '50 and '54 — Cesare Pavese, Robert Leeds).
        [Raritan] (13:2) Fall 93, p. 7-8.
    "Pennsylvania Road Trip." [DenQ] (28:1) Sum 93, p. 105.
    "Rider" (Excerpts). [Crazy] (45) Wint 93, p. 131-147.
    "Rider" (Excerpts). [DenQ] (28:2) Fall 93, p. 13-19.
    "The Train." [DenQ] (28:1) Sum 93, p. 45.
5695. RUDNIK, Raphael
    "Thought by Rembrandt's Wife and Model During the Painting of 'Flora'." [QRL]
        (12:32/33) 93, p. 503.
5696. RUDOLF, Anthony
    "Long-term Misunderstanding" (tr. of Ifigenija Zagoricnik-Simonovic, w. the
        author). [NoDaQ] (61:1) Wint 93, p. 222.
    "Love Poem" (tr. of Ifigenija Zagoricnik-Simonovic, w. the author). [NoDaQ] (61:1)
        Wint 93, p. 223.
    "Under the Same Roof" (tr. of Ifigenija Zagoricnik-Simonovic, w. the author).
        [NoDaQ] (61:1) Wint 93, p. 221.
RUE, Dorie La
    See LaRUE, Dorie
RUE, Mark La
    See La RUE, Mark
5697. RUEBOTTOM, Ann
    "Precambrian Strata." [Bogg] (66) Wint 92-93, p. 25.
5698. RUESCHER, Scott
    "First Impression." [Agni] (38) 93, p. 61-63.
5699. RUFF, John
    "A Common Name." [XavierR] (13:2) Fall 93, p. 111.
    "A Poem in Three Parts About My Father." [RiverC] (13:1) Fall 92, p. 78-81.
5700. RUFFLE, Mary
    "Timberland." [KenR] (NS 15:1) Wint 93, p. 97-98.
5701. RUFINUS
    "Some Amatory Epigrams from the Greek Anthology" (tr. by James Laughlin).
        [Sulfur] (33) Fall 93, p. 52-53.
5702. RUKEYSER, Muriel
    "Careful of the Day" (tr. of Moa Tetua, w. Samuel Elbert). [Sulfur] (33) Fall 93, p.
        256.
    "Rari for O'Otua" (tr. of Moa Tetua, w. Samuel Elbert). [Sulfur] (33) Fall 93, p. 255.
    "Rari for Tahia and Piu" (tr. of Moa Tetua, w. Samuel Elbert). [Sulfur] (33) Fall 93,
        p. 253-254.
    "This Place in the Ways" (illustrated by Lucy D. Rosenfeld). [MassR] (34:2) Sum
        93, p. 240-241.
    "A True Confession" (tr. of Moa Tetua, w. Samuel Elbert). [Sulfur] (33) Fall 93, p.
        255-256.
5703. RULF, Jiri
    "Morning Song" (to the memory of Osip Mandelstam, tr. by Ellen Rosenbaum).
        [OxfordM] (9:1) Spr-Sum 93, p. 11-12.
    "Proposal for an Observation" (tr. by Ellen Rosenbaum). [OxfordM] (9:1) Spr-Sum
        93, p. 12-13.
5704. RUMI, Jelaluddin
    "And He Is With Us" (tr. by Kabir Edmund Helminski). [Sun] (212) Ag 93, p. 39.

407

RUMI

"Didn't I Say" (tr. by Kabir Edmund Helminski). [Sun] (212) Ag 93, p. 39.
"Search the Darkness" (tr. by Kabir Edmund Helminski). [Sun] (212) Ag 93, p. 39.
5705. RUMMO, Paul-Eerik
    "Normal People" (tr. by Krista Kaer). [CimR] (104) Jl 93, p. 57.
    "An Ordinary Madman" (tr. by Krista Kaer). [CimR] (104) Jl 93, p. 55.
    "A Quiet Madman" (tr. by Krista Kaer). [CimR] (104) Jl 93, p. 55-56.
    "A Raving Madman" (tr. by Krista Kaer). [CimR] (104) Jl 93, p. 56-57.
5706. RUNCIMAN, Lex
    "Fans." [SouthernR] (29:4) Aut, O 93, p. 762-763.
5707. RUNKLE, Stephen
    "Jouissance." [IndR] (16:2) Fall 93, p. 181.
    "The Loners." [IndR] (16:2) Fall 93, p. 180.
5708. RUNNER, Jennifer
    "A Father" (Luke 5:11). [Poem] (69) My 93, p. 40.
    "Leah" (Genesis 29:1-23). [Poem] (69) My 93, p. 38-39.
5709. RUNYAN, Tana Williams
    "Blank Pages." [PoetryC] (13:3) 93, p. 17.
    "Father Falling." [PoetryC] (13:3) 93, p. 17.
    "Inland Waterways." [PoetryC] (13:3) 93, p. 17.
    "Lines of Descent." [PoetryC] (13:3) 93, p. 17.
5710. RUPCHEV, Georgi
    "Still Life" (tr. by Lisa Sapinkopf, w. Georgi Belev). [Agni] (37) 93, p. 264.
5711. RUSS, Biff
    "Gravity for Beginners" (for my niece). [ApalQ] (36/37) 91, p. 81-82.
5712. RUSS, Don
    "Gothic." [PoetryNW] (34:2) Sum 93, p. 26.
    "Here." [PoetryNW] (34:2) Sum 93, p. 27.
5713. RUSSAKOFF, Molly
    "The Japanese Desire." [PaintedB] (50/51) 93, p. 98.
5714. RUSSELL, CarolAnn
    "Third Eye for Etheridge." [PaintedB] (49) 93, p. 8.
    "This Is No Fairmont in Deadwood." [SpoonR] (18:2) Sum-Fall 93, p. 34-35.
5715. RUSSELL, Frank
    "Before the Beat." [Ploughs] (19:1) Spr 93, p. 107.
    "Flotation Device." [Ploughs] (19:1) Spr 93, p. 108.
RUSSELL, Gillian Harding
    See HARDING-RUSSELL, Gillian
5716. RUSSELL, Hilary
    "The Skyblue Tarp." [CarolQ] (46:1) Fall 93, p. 54.
    "Willis' Fall." [CarolQ] (46:1) Fall 93, p. 55.
5717. RUSSELL, Peter
    "The Death of a Swift." [NoDaQ] (61:1) Wint 93, p. 155-156.
    "False Tracks" (tr. of Matija Beckovic). [NoDaQ] (61:1) Wint 93, p. 31.
    "A Lament for Myself" (A Fragment, tr. of Matija Beckovic). [NoDaQ] (61:1) Wint
        93, p. 33.
    "Matija Beckovic" (tr. of Matija Beckovic). [NoDaQ] (61:1) Wint 93, p. 32.
    "Sarajevo." [NoDaQ] (61:1) Wint 93, p. 156.
5718. RUSSELL, Timothy
    "In Annus Mirabilis." [WestB] (31/32) 93, p. 26.
    "In Disiecta Membra." [Poetry] (163:3) D 93, p. 137.
    "In Dubio." [AnthNEW] (5) 93, p. 9.
    "In Individuo." [WestB] (33) 93, p. 24-25.
    "In Lacrimae." [WestB] (31/32) 93, p. 27.
    "In Opere Citato." [WestB] (33) 93, p. 23-24.
    "In Ultima Thule." [Poetry] (163:3) D 93, p. 138.
    "In Urbe." [ArtfulD] (24/25) 93, p. 128.
    "The Ugliest Flower in the World." [HiramPoR] (53/54) Fall 92-Sum 93, p. 79.
5719. RUSSO, Gianna
    "Directions for Driving the Tamiami Trail." [Gaia] (1/2) Ap-Jl 93, p. 19.
    "Night School: A Dream." [HeavenB] (10) Wint-Spr 93, p. 60.
5720. RUSSO, Linda V.
    "Why I Scrawled on the Back of This Photo the Words 'Late Autumn Sunfall 1979'
        —." [SpoonR] (18:1) Wint-Spr 93, p. 31-32.
5721. RUTH, Barbara
    "The Writer in the Mirror." [SinW] (49) Spr-Sum 93, p. 95-97.

5722. RUTH, Deborah Dashow
"Grounds." [Zyzzyva] (9:4) Wint 93, p. 15.
5723. RUTHCHILD, Geraldine Quietlake
"The Rigors of Death." [PoetL] (88:1) Spr 93, p. 35.
5724. RUTSALA, Vern
"Departures, Arrivals." [DenQ] (27:3) Wint 93, p. 56-57.
"The End of Waiting." [RiverS] (37) 93, p. 79.
"Office Hours Ancestors and Drought." [SouthernPR] (33:2) Fall 93, p. 66-68.
"Reunion on the Weekend of the Fourth." [SouthernPR] (33:2) Fall 93, p. 63-66.
"You Said I Should Look." [RiverS] (37) 93, p. 78.
5725. RUTTER, Mark
"Tory Wig." [HawaiiR] (16:3, #36) Wint 93, p. 124.
5726. RUZESKY, Jay
"Battle of the Monster Trucks." [Grain] (21:1) Spr 93, p. 100.
"Roller Coaster." [Grain] (21:1) Spr 93, p. 101-102.
"Seeing Eye Dog." [Grain] (21:1) Spr 93, p. 99.
"Sneaking into the Stephen Hawking Lecture Then Sneaking Back Out Again."
[PoetryNW] (34:2) Sum 93, p. 9-11.
"The Waitress at the Day and Night." [Caliban] (12) 93, p. 153.
"Woman at the Schwarzenegger Film." [CanLit] (137) Sum 93, p. 40.
5727. RYALS, Mary Jane
"Everglades Canal." [PoetL] (88:2) Sum 93, p. 13-14.
"A Word to Sylvia Plath after Seeing Heptonstall Cemetery." [ApalQ] (36/37) 91, p.
72-73.
5728. RYAN, Florence Holmes
"Wrinkled Night Magic." [Plain] (13:3) Spr 93, p. 16.
5729. RYAN, Gig
"Trade." [Verse] (10:3) Wint 93, p. 105.
5730. RYAN, Gregory A.
"The Abandoned Town." [WilliamMR] (31) 93, p. 100.
"Dead Pet Poem" (for Charles Baudelaire). [Agni] (37) 93, p. 251-252.
"Portage" (for Michael Kaminski). [HawaiiR] (17:3, #39) Fall 93, p. 25-26.
5731. RYAN, Kay
"A Certain Kind of Eden." [TriQ] (89) Wint 93-94, p. 186.
"Emptiness." [Atlantic] (272:2) Ag 93, p. 81.
"Glass Slippers." [TriQ] (89) Wint 93-94, p. 187.
"This Life." [Atlantic] (271:4) Ap 93, p. 99.
5732. RYBICKI, John
"Brother Ben." [PassN] (14:1) Sum 93, p. 9.
"A Tear in Directions." [PassN] (14:1) Sum 93, p. 10.
"Untitled: This ring of fire about my wrists." [PassN] (14:1) Sum 93, p. 9.
5733. RYDBERG, Amy Shea
"Cheap Sneakers." [CapeR] (28:1) Spr 93, p. 14.
"Subway Goddess." [AnthNEW] (5) 93, p. 15.
5734. RYDER, Salmon
"Beth Tatarsky 1948-1992." [US1] (28/29) 93, p. 6.
"The Canon, A Dialogue." [US1] (28/29) 93, p. 27.
5735. RYERSON, Alice
"The Monet Show." [PraS] (67:1) Spr 93, p. 121-122.
5736. RYMARUK, Ihor
"Blessed Is He Who Divided into Clean and Unclean" (for Vasyl' Fl'orka, tr. by
Vera Kaczmarskyj). [Pequod] (36) 93, p. 117.
"Diva Obyda" (tr. by Vera Kaczmarskyj). [Pequod] (36) 93, p. 108.
"I don't Know Where You Came From" (tr. by Vera Kaczmarskyj). [Pequod] (36)
93, p. 109.
"What Do You See There, Brother" (tr. by Vera Kaczmarskyj). [Pequod] (36) 93, p.
110.
"You Truly Did Not Imagine It" (tr. by Vera Kaczmarskyj). [Pequod] (36) 93, p.
111-116.
5737. S. M. G.
"Tattoos." [Writer] (106:10) O 93, p. 27.
SABA, Elias G. Abu-
See ABU-SABA, Elias G.
5738. SABINES, Jaime
"Horal." [RiverS] (39) 93, p. 60.
"Hourly" (tr. by Christopher Merrill). [RiverS] (39) 93, p. 61.

"Miss X" (in Spanish and English, tr. by Christopher Merrill, w. Jerry Johnston).
[RiverS] (39) 93, p. 62-63.
5739. SABINI, Meredith
"As Parts Go." [Pearl] (19) Fall-Wint 93, p. 53.
5740. SACHS, Nelly
"Chassidim Dancing" (tr. by Bernhard Frank). [Vis] (42) 93, p. 14.
5741. SACKS, Peter
"For Leyvick Halpern." [BostonR] (18:3/4) Je-Ag 93, p. 31.
"Pushkin." [BostonR] (18:3/4) Je-Ag 93, p. 31.
SADAKAZU, Fujii
See FUJII, Sadakazu
5742. SADDIK, Orly
"Fog." [EngJ] (82:7) N 93, p. 90.
5743. SADOFF, Ira
"Bud Powell at the Club Montmarte." [CreamCR] (17:1) Spr 93, p. 89.
5744. SAENZ, Benjamin A. (Benjamin Alire)
"Contemplating Roads." [Sequoia] (34/35) 92-93, p. 24-25.
"Coyote." [PraS] (67:3) Fall 93, p. 78-79.
"Uncles (Who Lie Still and Perfect)." [ColR] (20:2) Fall 93, p. 91-96.
"Ventura's Visits." [PraS] (67:3) Fall 93, p. 80-81.
5745. SAFARIK, Allan
"Black Swans." [Spitball] (43) Spr 93, p. 13.
"The Patient." [Event] (22:2) Sum 93, p. 34-35.
"The Veranda." [Event] (22:2) Sum 93, p. 32-33.
5746. SAFFORD, Charles
"Aunt Virginia's Cancer." [SpoonR] (18:1) Wint-Spr 93, p. 86.
"Cancer Child." [SlipS] (13) 93, p. 13.
"A Letter to Marie." [SpoonR] (18:1) Wint-Spr 93, p. 85.
"Living with Cannibals." [SlipS] (13) 93, p. 14.
"Moving." [ClockR] (8:1/2) 93, p. 135.
"Prophecy." [SpoonR] (18:1) Wint-Spr 93, p. 86.
"Vigil." [SlipS] (13) 93, p. 13-14.
5747. SAGAN, Miriam
"Isabel." [Bogg] (66) Wint 92-93, p. 12.
"The Matisse Network." [FreeL] (11) Wint 93, p. 26.
5748. SAGOFF, Maurice
"A Clutter of Clerihews." [Light] (5) Spr 93, p. 8.
5749. SAHAGUN, Carlos
"In Toledo" (tr. by Michael L. Johnson). [LitR] (36:3) Spr 93, p. 382.
"Insomnia" (tr. by Michael L. Johnson). [LitR] (36:3) Spr 93, p. 381.
"Sands" (tr. by Michael L. Johnson). [LitR] (36:3) Spr 93, p. 382.
5750. SAIJO, Albert
"Eyat." [BambooR] (57) Wint 93, p. 182.
"A Kona." [BambooR] (57) Wint 93, p. 177-180.
"Trees." [BambooR] (57) Wint 93, p. 181.
SAINT
See also ST. (filed as spelled)
5751. SAINT, Assotto
"Vital Signs" (for david frechette). [JamesWR] (11:1) Fall 93, p. 10.
5752. SAISER, Marjorie
"I Find a Rock for You." [PraS] (67:3) Fall 93, p. 87.
"Seeing the Scar." [PraS] (67:3) Fall 93, p. 85-86.
"She Is a Woman like Glass." [PraS] (67:3) Fall 93, p. 88.
"Storm at Night." [PraS] (67:3) Fall 93, p. 82-84.
"Washing My Hair in the Platte." [PraS] (67:3) Fall 93, p. 84-85.
"The Wind Picks Up." [Crazy] (44) Spr 93, p. 7-9.
5753. SAJE, Natasha
"Eating Crabs with Bob and Jim." [Shen] (43:2) Sum 93, p. 103.
"Game." [Shen] (43:2) Sum 93, p. 102.
"A Male in the Women's Locker Room." [Ploughs] (19:4) Wint 93-94, p. 76-77.
"A Short History of the Sybarites." [Poetry] (162:2) My 93, p. 66-67.
"Tongues." [PraS] (67:3) Fall 93, p. 67-68.
"What Difference Does It Make?" [Ploughs] (19:1) Spr 93, p. 156-158.
5754. SAKAKI, Nanao
"Altitude 10,700m." [ChiR] (39:3/4) 93, p. 211-213.

5755. SALAAM, Jamil
"The Real Blues." [PoetryUSA] (25/26) 93, p. 52.
5756. SALAMUN, Tomaz
"The Color of Time" (tr. by Sonja Kravanja). [Pequod] (36) 93, p. 119.
"From Night to Night" (tr. by Sonja Kravanja). [Confr] (51) Sum 93, p. 241.
"Gesture" (tr. by Sonja Kravanja). [Confr] (51) Sum 93, p. 242.
"The Heart of Europe Is Elegant and Dead" (tr. by Sonja Kravanja). [Confr] (51)
    Sum 93, p. 240.
"I Am Abandoning Iconoclastic Levels" (tr. by Sonja Kravanja). [Pequod] (36) 93,
    p. 120-121.
"Word" (tr. by Sonja Kravanja). [Pequod] (36) 93, p. 118.
5757. SALAQUARDOVA, Jirina
"Old-fashioned Language" (tr. by Ellen Rosenbaum). [OxfordM] (9:1) Spr-Sum 93,
    p. 10-11.
"The Tale of the Angel's Return" (tr. by Ellen Rosenbaum). [OxfordM] (9:1) Spr -
    Sum 93, p. 10.
5758. SALASIN, Sal
"And drop shortly into some manner of reverie." [AnotherCM] (26) Fall 93, p. 136 -
    138.
5759. SALAZAR, Dixie
"Conversations." [PaintedHR] (9) Spr 93, p. 18-19.
"Three Generations (A Photo)." [QW] (37) Sum-Fall 93, p. 98-99.
5760. SALEH, Dennis
"Summer." [HangL] (63) 93, p. 58.
5761. SALEMI, Joseph S.
"IV.11" (tr. of Horace). [CarolQ] (45:2) Wint 93, p. 70-71.
"V.64" (tr. of Martial). [CarolQ] (45:2) Wint 93, p. 73.
"VI.40" (tr. of Martial). [CarolQ] (45:2) Wint 93, p. 72.
5762. SALERNO, Joe
"The Last Goat in Bergen County." [US1] (28/29) 93, p. 3.
"Waking Up in New Jersey." [MidwQ] (34:2) Wint 93, p. 222.
5763. SALERNO, Mark
"Entertainment Tonight" (for Robert Gill). [Arshile] (2) 93, p. 48.
"Etiquette." [Arshile] (1) Spr 93, p. 39-41.
"February" (for Mark Sanchez). [Arshile] (1) Spr 93, p. 37.
"Futile." [Arshile] (2) 93, p. 47.
"The Good-Bye Sonnet." [Arshile] (1) Spr 93, p. 38.
"Like Them." [Arshile] (2) 93, p. 50.
"Old." [Arshile] (2) 93, p. 46.
"A Politics." [Arshile] (1) Spr 93, p. 42.
"She Wants to Hear the Man I Love." [Arshile] (2) 93, p. 49.
5764. SALINAS, Luis Omar
"I Am America." [NoDaQ] (61:2) Spr 93, p. 188-189.
5765. SALISBURY, Ralph
"The Trek of the Wind" (Selections, tr. of Nils-Aslak Valkeapää, w. Lars Nordström
    and Harald Gaski). [SilverFR] (24) Wint 93, p. 31-38.
5766. SALKEY, Andrew
"After the War on the Land" (In Memory of Victor Jara). [BostonR] (18:5) O-N 93,
    p. 31.
SALLE, Peter la
    See LaSALLE, Peter
5767. SALLEE, Hyun-jae Yee
"Love's Cursive" (Selections: 6, 8, tr. of Kim Namjo, w. David R. McCann). [ChiR]
    (39:3/4) 93, p. 242.
5768. SALLIS, James
"Absence." [ApalQ] (38) 92, p. 71.
"Preparing for the Hurricane." [CharR] (19:2) Fall 93, p. 133.
5769. SALOY, Mona Lisa
"Word Works." [AfAmRev] (27:1) Spr 93, p. 155-156.
5770. SALTER, Mary Jo
"The Hand of Thomas Jefferson" (Philadelphia, 1776). [NewRep] (208:5) 1 F 93, p.
    58.
"Moving." [NewYorker] (69:38) 15 N 93, p. 84.
"What Do Women Want?" [NewYorker] (68:47) 11 Ja 93, p. 74.
"Young Girl Peeling Apples" (Nicholas Maes). [Verse] (10:3) Wint 93, p. 89.

5771. SALTMAN, Bethany
"Amherst Poem." [BrooklynR] (10) 93, p. 68.
"Home in October." [BrooklynR] (10) 93, p. 69.
5772. SALVADOR, Vicent
"How Odd This Landscape" (tr. by Adela Robles Salz). [Iowa] (23:2) Spr-Sum 93,
p. 10.
"March Wind" (tr. by Adela Robles Salz). [Iowa] (23:2) Spr-Sum 93, p. 9.
"Nobody's Answering Machine" (tr. by Adela Robles Salz). [Iowa] (23:2) Spr-Sum
93, p. 9-10.
"Now That I Am Forty" (tr. by Adela Robles Salz). [Iowa] (23:2) Spr-Sum 93, p. 11.
"Will of a Rich Man" (tr. by Adela Robles Salz). [Iowa] (23:2) Spr-Sum 93, p. 9.
SALVATORE, Brian di
See Di SALVATORE, Brian
5773. SALVERDA, Nynke
"My Father Mounted Me." [AnthNEW] (5) 93, p. 30.
SALZ, Adela Robles
See ROBLES SALZ, Adela
5774. SALZMAN, Eva
"Natural Habitats." [NewYorker] (69:20) 5 Jl 93, p. 82.
5775. SALZMANN, Jerome
"Logic kisses." [Bogg] (66) Wint 92-93, p. 17.
"The State." [Bogg] (66) Wint 92-93, p. 17.
5776. SAMALAVICIUS, Almantas
"Accident Not Yet Understood" (tr. of Vytautas Rubavicius). [CimR] (104) Jl 93, p.
20.
"Winter Ideology, 1986" (tr. of Vytautas Rubavicius). [CimR] (104) Jl 93, p. 19.
5777. SAMARAS, Nicholas
"All the Angels Are Dying." [SouthernR] (29:3) Sum, Jl 93, p. 613.
"Jordanville." [HarvardR] (4) Spr 93, p. 31.
"The Mansion of Forgetting." [Poetry] (162:6) S 93, p. 323-324.
5778. SAMPSON, Bob
"Echoes." [Bogg] (66) Wint 92-93, p. 39.
5779. SAMPSON, Dennis
"Working." [AmerS] (62:2) Spr 93, p. 213-215.
5780. SAMYN, Mary Ann
"Light Under the Door." [ContextS] (3:1) 93, p. 6.
"Tides." [DogRR] (12:1, #23) Spr-Sum 93, p. 22.
5781. SANBORNE, Jon
"Dancing Static." [PaintedB] (49) 93, p. 22-23.
"Maryland." [PaintedB] (52) 93, p. 42-43.
"Mr. Crunchy" (after Cornelius Eady). [PaintedB] (49) 93, p. 24-25.
SANCHEZ, Antonio Heras
See HERAS SANCHEZ, Antonio
5782. SANCHEZ, Erika
"Working." [Americas] (21:2) Sum 93, p. 68.
5783. SANDBURG, Carl
"Arms" (For Wallace Stevens). [AmerPoR] (22:6) N-D 93, p. 29.
"I Should Like to Be Hanged on a Summer Afternoon." [AmerPoR] (22:6) N-D 93,
p. 31.
"In Blue Gown and in Black Satin Gown." [AmerPoR] (22:6) N-D 93, p. 29.
"An Interwoven Man and Woman Talked." [AmerPoR] (22:6) N-D 93, p. 29.
"Monday, One P.M." [AmerPoR] (22:6) N-D 93, p. 28.
"Painted Fishes." [AmerPoR] (22:6) N-D 93, p. 28.
"Planked Whitefish." [AmerPoR] (22:6) N-D 93, p. 27.
"Shadows of April and Blue Hills." [AmerPoR] (22:6) N-D 93, p. 29.
"Sherwood Anderson." [AmerPoR] (22:6) N-D 93, p. 31.
"These Valleys Seem Old" (Dedicated to Mrs. Florence Ayscough . . ., whose
translations from inscriptions on Chinese paintings furnished the basis for
these renditions). [AmerPoR] (22:6) N-D 93, p. 28.
"Troth Tryst." [AmerPoR] (22:6) N-D 93, p. 29.
"Vaudeville, 1916." [AmerPoR] (22:6) N-D 93, p. 27.
"Virginia Woolf." [AmerPoR] (22:6) N-D 93, p. 30.
5784. SANDERS, Bonny Barry
"Song for the Scarlet Tanager." [HayF] (13) Fall-Wint 93, p. 96.
5785. SANDERS, David
"Bread-Baking" (tr. of Emile Verhaeren). [Sparrow] (60) Sum 93, p. 51.

"The Falls." [NewL] (59:3) 93, p. 90.
"Here, Now." [Sparrow] (60) Sum 93, p. 51.
5786. SANDERS, Mark
"The Last Night." [CharR] (19:2) Fall 93, p. 118.
"Reunion." [Plain] (13:2) Wint 93, p. 7.
5787. SANDERS, Tony
"April Gold." [WestHR] (47:1) Spr 93, p. 43.
"Art of Silence." [GettyR] (6:4) Aut 93, p. 716.
"The Epigone." [OhioR] (50) 93, p. 86-87.
"Flight Pattern." [WestHR] (47:1) Spr 93, p. 42.
"Frontier Thesis." [WestHR] (47:1) Spr 93, p. 41.
"The Middle Voice." [GettyR] (6:4) Aut 93, p. 718.
"Nocturne." [GettyR] (6:4) Aut 93, p. 717.
"Reverdie." [WestHR] (47:1) Spr 93, p. 44.
"Sunday Evening." [HarvardR] (4) Spr 93, p. 140-141.
"Verisimilitudes" (after a painting by Jane Freilicher). [WestHR] (47:1) Spr 93, p.
45.
"The Warning Track." [ParisR] (35:126) Spr 93, p. 214-224.
5788. SANDOVAL, José-Luis
"Before Eye Could Tell Time." [Americas] (21:1) Spr 93, p. 60.
"Mexicans and Others." [Americas] (21:1) Spr 93, p. 55-56.
"Street Gangs." [Americas] (21:1) Spr 93, p. 61.
"When Eye Was a Child." [Americas] (21:1) Spr 93, p. 57-59.
5789. SANDRI, Giovanna
"A Lucio." [13thMoon] (11:1/2) 93, p. 219.
"(Da un Testo di Zeami)." [13thMoon] (11:1/2) 93, p. 221.
"Dall'invisibile centro / from the invisible centre." [13thMoon] (11:1/2) 93, p. 229.
"Dirge" (tr. by the author and Kathleen Fraser). [13thMoon] (11:1/2) 93, p. 219.
"The Forest King." [13thMoon] (11:1/2) 93, p. 227.
"(From One of Zeami's Texts)" (tr. by the author and Kathleen Fraser). [13thMoon]
(11:1/2) 93, p. 221.
"Hermes" (1-3). [13thMoon] (11:1/2) 93, p. 223-225.
"Primavera." [13thMoon] (11:1/2) 93, p. 222.
"The Queen on the Tower." [13thMoon] (11:1/2) 93, p. 226.
"Riangolare gli Assi." [13thMoon] (11:1/2) 93, p. 220.
"Springtime" (tr. by the author and Kathleen Fraser). [13thMoon] (11:1/2) 93, p.
222.
"To Re-angle Axes" (tr. by the author and Kathleen Fraser). [13thMoon] (11:1/2)
93, p. 220.
"Totem." [13thMoon] (11:1/2) 93, p. 228.
5790. SANDSTROEM, Yvonne L.
"Aristotle and the Crayfish" (tr. of Lars Gustafsson). [NewYorker] (69:16) 7 Je 93,
p. 84-85.
"An Audience with the Muse" (tr. of Lars Gustafsson). [QRL] (12:32/33) 93, p. 178 -
179.
"Elegy for the Old Mexican Woman and Her Dead Child" (tr. of Lars Gustafsson).
[QRL] (12:32/33) 93, p. 181-183.
"For All Those Who Wait for Time to Pass" (tr. of Lars Gustafsson). [QRL]
(12:32/33) 93, p. 181.
"The Geography of the Department of Geography" (A Ghost Ballad, tr. of Lars
Gustafsson). [QRL] (12:32/33) 93, p. 183-188.
"Itemized Expenses" (August Strindberg 1849-1912, tr. of Lars Gustafsson). [QRL]
(12:32/33) 93, p. 180.
"The Order of Grace" (tr. of Lars Gustafsson). [QRL] (12:32/33) 93, p. 179.
"Sonnet of the Beginning and the End" (tr. of Lars Gustafsson). [QRL] (12:32/33)
93, p. 179-180.
5791. SANDY, Stephen
"Downstairs My Son." [GreenMR] (NS 6:2) Sum-Fall 93, p. 39.
5792. SANER, Reg
"Astrophysics." [Ploughs] (19:4) Wint 93-94, p. 181-182.
"Dandelion." [QRL] (12:32/33) 93, p. 305.
"Desert Space." [QRL] (12:32/33) 93, p. 300-301.
"Evening." [QRL] (12:32/33) 93, p. 306.
"Keen Edges." [QRL] (12:32/33) 93, p. 306.
"Landscape with Coyote and Special Effects." [Ploughs] (19:4) Wint 93-94, p. 179 -
180.

"Meanwhile." [QRL] (12:32/33) 93, p. 305-306.
"Postcards from Italy." [QRL] (12:32/33) 93, p. 302-303.
"Rain Near Heart Lake." [QRL] (12:32/33) 93, p. 303-304.
"Spring Song." [QRL] (12:32/33) 93, p. 307.
"Tonto Plateau, Grand Canyon." [QRL] (12:32/33) 93, p. 301.
"Villa That Made Us Clairvoyant." [CharR] (19:2) Fall 93, p. 119-120.
"What Wilderness Tells You." [QRL] (12:32/33) 93, p. 304-305.
5793. SANFORD, Carol
"The Nurturer." [Parting] (6:2) Wint 93, p. 7.
5794. SANFORD, Christy Sheffield
"Italian Smoking Piece" (with Simultaneous Translation). [ApalQ] (39) 93, p. 1-17.
SANG-YONG, Kim
See KIM, Sang-Yong (1561-1673)
5795. SANGER, Judy Firth
"Reverberations of the Day Pheasants Flew Up." [AntR] (51:4) Fall 93, p. 556-557.
5796. SANGER, Richard
"The Tourist at Cadiz." [SouthwR] (78:3) Sum 93, p. 381.
"A Walk in the Fall" (Toronto, Fall 1990). [Quarry] (42:1) 93, p. 41-44.
5797. SANTA CRUZ, Nicomedes
"Black Rhythms of Peru" (tr. by Keith Cartwright). [XavierR] (13:2) Fall 93, p. 27 -
28.
"Ritmos Negros del Perú." [XavierR] (13:2) Fall 93, p. 27-28.
5798. SANTAMARIA, Soledad
"The Call" (tr. by Laura Chesak). [InterPR] (19:2) Fall 93, p. 27.
"La Llamada." [InterPR] (19:2) Fall 93, p. 26.
5799. SANTELLO, Rob
"Tea-stained Lust." [Gypsy] (20) Sum 93, p. 58.
SANTIAGO, José Luis Colon
See COLON SANTIAGO, José Luis
5800. SANTONOCITO, Paula
"Sound All Around." [WestB] (31/32) 93, p. 29.
SANTOS, P. Delos
See Delos SANTOS, P.
5801. SANTOS, Sherod
"Dalai Lama." [Poetry] (161:4) Ja 93, p. 214.
"Empire" (Luxembourg Gardens, 1986). [Iowa] (23:1) Wint 93, p. 101-102.
"Fire." [SouthernR] (29:2) Spr, Ap 93, p. 280-281.
"Married Love." [SouthernR] (29:2) Spr, Ap 93, p. 279.
5802. SANTOS SILVA, Loreina
"Mona Island" (tr. by Anthony Hunt). [Paint] (19:38) Aut 92, p. 75.
"What the Sea Turtle Said" (tr. by Anthony Hunt). [Paint] (19:38) Aut 92, p. 74.
5803. SAPIA, Yvonne
"Washing Your Body." [Kalliope] (15:2) 93, p. 46.
5804. SAPINKOPF, Lisa
"The Apples" (From "Début et fin de la neige," tr. of Yves Bonnefoy). [GreenMR]
(NS 6:1) Wint-Spr 93, p. 156.
"Beacon" (In memory of Danila Stoyanova, tr. of Vladimir Levchev, w. Georgi
Belev). [Paint] (19:38) Aut 92, p. 62.
"Birth" (tr. of Georgi Belev, w. the author). [Stand] (34:3) Sum 93, p. 63.
"Blue Pond at Berkovitsa" (To Tsvetana, tr. of Vladimir Levchev, w. Georgi Belev).
[Paint] (19:38) Aut 92, p. 63.
"Business Trip" (tr. of Georgi Belev, w. the author). [SouthernHR] (27:3) Sum 93,
p. 247.
"Clytemnestra" (tr. of Oksana Zabuzhko, w. the author). [Agni] (38) 93, p. 108-109.
"Dedham, Seen from Langham" (Title of several paintings by Constable. Tr. of
Yves Bonnefoy). [QRL] (12:32/33) 93, p. 58-61.
"Delphic" (Pt. IV, tr. of Sophia de Mello Breyner Andresen). [HarvardR] (4) Spr 93,
p. 149.
"The Dream's Restlessness" (tr. of Yves Bonnefoy). [QRL] (12:32/33) 93, p. 56-58.
"Evaporations" (tr. of Ani Ilkov, w. Georgi Belev). [Paint] (19:38) Aut 92, p. 65.
"The Farewell" (tr. of Yves Bonnefoy). [QRL] (12:32/33) 93, p. 62-63.
"The fast train? The express?" (tr. of Miriana Basheva, w. Georgi Belev). [Agni]
(37) 93, p. 259.
"Fleeting Snow on scarf" (From "Début et fin de la neige," tr. of Yves Bonnefoy).
[GreenMR] (NS 6:1) Wint-Spr 93, p. 155.

"Garden with Stone Wall and Quince Trees" (tr. of Georgi Belev). [Vis] (41) 93, p. 6.
"Gates" (tr. of Georgi Borisov, w. Georgi Belev). [Paint] (19:38) Aut 92, p. 58.
"Give the snow a good interrogation!" (tr. of Georgi Belev). [GreenMR] (NS 6:1) Wint-Spr 93, p. 157.
"Green and Gold" (tr. of Ani Ilkov, w. Georgi Belev). [Paint] (19:38) Aut 92, p. 64.
"The Horse" (tr. of Georgi Borisov, w. Georgi Belev). [Paint] (19:38) Aut 92, p. 59.
"If the Silence Should Suddenly Return" (tr. of Ekaterina Iosifova, w. Georgi Belev). [Paint] (19:38) Aut 92, p. 70-71.
"If there were a sun to see you" (tr. of Georgi Belev, w. the author). [SouthernHR] (27:3) Sum 93, p. 248.
"I'm Listening" (tr. of Sophia de Mello Breyner). [Sun] (209) My 93, p. 15.
"Interior with Faded Colors" (tr. of Blaga Dimitrova, w. Georgi Belev). [Paint] (19:38) Aut 92, p. 69.
"It Was War" (tr. of Miriana Basheva, w. Georgi Belev). [Paint] (19:38) Aut 92, p. 73.
"It's time — farewell to irony!" (tr. of Georgi Belev, w. the author). [HarvardR] (3) Wint 93, p. 170.
"Just beside us a flock of days" (tr. of Irfan Malik, w. the author). [Sun] (213) S 93, p. 31.
"Last night very late" (tr. of Irfan Malik, w. the author). [Sun] (213) S 93, p. 31.
"The Little Square" (tr. of Sophia de Mello Breyner). [Sun] (207) Mr 93, p. 19.
"Mice" (tr. of Alexander Gerov, w. Georgi Belev). [Agni] (37) 93, p. 258.
"Moth" (tr. of Georgi Belev, w. the author). [PennR] (5:2) 93, p. 38.
"On the grave of my hunger" (tr. of Irfan Malik, w. the author). [Sun] (213) S 93, p. 31.
"Part VI From Gypsy Christ" (tr. of Sophia de Mello Breyner). [Sun] (209) My 93, p. 15.
"People who read" (tr. of Oksana Zabuzhko, w. the author). [HarvardR] (4) Spr 93, p. 145.
"Riverbend" (tr. of Marin Georgiev, w. Georgi Belev). [Paint] (19:38) Aut 92, p. 57.
"Seduced and Abandoned" (tr. of Radoi Ralin, w. Georgi Belev). [Agni] (37) 93, p. 262-263.
"Seventh Heaven Can Be Seen at First Glance" (tr. of Nikolai Kanchev, w. Georgi Belev). [Agni] (37) 93, p. 261.
"Silence" (tr. of Marin Georgiev, w. Georgi Belev). [Paint] (19:38) Aut 92, p. 56.
"The slope of the church roof" (tr. of Irfan Malik, w. the author). [Sun] (213) S 93, p. 31.
"Snowflakes" (From "Début et fin de la neige," tr. of Yves Bonnefoy). [GreenMR] (NS 6:1) Wint-Spr 93, p. 154.
"The Soul" (tr. of Nedelcho Ganev, w. Georgi Belev). [Agni] (37) 93, p. 260.
"Still Life" (tr. of Georgi Rupchev, w. Georgi Belev). [Agni] (37) 93, p. 264.
"A Summer's Night" (tr. of Yves Bonnefoy). [QRL] (12:32/33) 93, p. 54-55.
"The Swiftness of the Clouds" (tr. of Yves Bonnefoy). [QRL] (12:32/33) 93, p. 61 - 62.
"These Things from Words" (tr. of Ivan Metodiev, w. Georgi Belev). [Paint] (19:38) Aut 92, p. 60.
"This Crow" (tr. of Ivan Metodiev, w. Georgi Belev). [Paint] (19:38) Aut 92, p. 61.
"Three mares" (tr. of Danila Stoyanova, w. Georgi Belev). [Vis] (41) 93, p. 6.
"The Tree" (tr. of Georgi Belev, w. the author). [PennR] (5:2) 93, p. 37.
"Vision" (tr. of Georgi Belev, w. the author). [Paint] (19:38) Aut 92, p. 66.
"Vulnerability" (tr. of Fedya Filkova, w. Georgi Belev). [Paint] (19:38) Aut 92, p. 72.
"Wedding Song" (tr. of Georgi Belev, w. the author). [PennR] (5:2) 93, p. 39.
"Who Cares for the Blind Stork" (tr. of Blaga Dimitrova, w. Georgi Belev). [Paint] (19:38) Aut 92, p. 68.
"Zoo" (tr. of Georgi Belev, w. the author). [Paint] (19:38) Aut 92, p. 67.
5805. SAPPHIRE
"In My Father's House." [CentralP] (22) Spr 93, p. 133-136.
"In My Father's House." [Drumvoices] (3:1/2) Fall-Wint 93-94, p. 85-88.
"In My Father's House." [Eyeball] (2) 93, p. 4-5.
"Mickey Mouse Was a Scorpio." [CentralP] (22) Spr 93, p. 138-139.
"Rabbit Man." [CentralP] (22) Spr 93, p. 129-131.
"Rabbit Man." [Eyeball] (2) 93, p. 6-7.
"Wild Thing." [Eyeball] (2) 93, p. 7-8.

5806. SARAGO, Dan
"The Bath." [Footwork] (23) 93, p. 146.
"Return to Ellis Island." [Footwork] (23) 93, p. 146-147.
5807. SARAVIA, Marco Tulio del Arca
"Amor y Algo Más." [XavierR] (13:1) Spr 93, p. 44.
"Blanco Descanso." [XavierR] (13:1) Spr 93, p. 43.
"Love and Something More" (tr. by Carroll E. Mace). [XavierR] (13:1) Spr 93, p. 44.
"White Rest" (tr. by Carroll E. Mace). [XavierR] (13:1) Spr 93, p. 43.
5808. SARGENT, Robert
"The Echo." [Pembroke] (25) 93, p. 30.
"Hannah" (1st Samuel 1:1-28). [SoDakR] (31:2) Sum 93, p. 56.
"The Redemptive Figures." [SoDakR] (31:2) Sum 93, p. 55.
5809. SAROYAN, Aram
"Film Noir." [Arshile] (1) Spr 93, p. 27-29.
5810. SARTARELLI, Stephen
"Beyond Real Space Time" (tr. of Elda Guidinetti). [LitR] (36:4) Sum 93, p. 482 - 489.
"Concession to Winter" (tr. of Fabio Pusterla). [LitR] (36:4) Sum 93, p. 490.
"Methylene Blue" (tr. of Giorgio Orelli). [LitR] (36:4) Sum 93, p. 494.
"Whether or Not the First Snow Appears on Mount Sighignola" (tr. of Antonio Rossi). [LitR] (36:4) Sum 93, p. 492.
5811. SARTON, May
"Celebrations 1943" (from the winter 1942 issue of *The University Review*, the predecessor magazine of *New Letters*). [NewL] (60:1) 93, p. 8-9.
5812. SARUBBI, Joanne M.
"The Bell." [Footwork] (23) 93, p. 104.
5813. SASANOV, Catherine
"Demolitions IV." [RiverS] (37) 93, p. 13.
"Excitement, The Need for." [Agni] (37) 93, p. 285.
"Illegals." [Caliban] (13) 93, p. 29.
"Receiving the Violently Killed." [Caliban] (13) 93, p. 30.
"Skeleton Tableau." [RiverS] (37) 93, p. 14.
"Vellum (Ireland)." [Caliban] (13) 93, p. 32.
"Vertical City." [Caliban] (13) 93, p. 31.
5814. SATO, Hiroaki
"A 100-Poem Sequence" (tr. of Princess Shikishi). [Sulfur] (33) Fall 93, p. 58-66.
"The Blowing Whale" (tr. of Kotaro Takamura). [Pembroke] (25) 93, p. 22.
"Book of Geology" (tr. of Kotaro Takamura). [Pembroke] (25) 93, p. 23-24.
"Denying Man" (tr. of Kotaro Takamura). [Pembroke] (25) 93, p. 28-29.
"Dinner at Yonekyu" (tr. of Kotaro Takamura). [Pembroke] (25) 93, p. 17-19.
"Late Night During a Rainy Season" (tr. of Kotaro Takamura). [Pembroke] (25) 93, p. 24-26.
"Lost Mona Lisa" (tr. of Kotaro Takamura). [Pembroke] (25) 93, p. 14-15.
"My Poetry" (tr. of Kotaro Takamura). [Pembroke] (25) 93, p. 27.
"Ogiwara Morie" (tr. of Kotaro Takamura). [Pembroke] (25) 93, p. 21.
"Ready to Be Beheaded" (tr. of Kotaro Takamura). [Pembroke] (25) 93, p. 20.
"Voices" (tr. of Kotaro Takamura). [Pembroke] (25) 93, p. 16-17.
"The Wailing of the Hundred Million" (tr. of Kotaro Takamura). [Pembroke] (25) 93, p. 26-27.
5815. SATTERFIELD, Jane
"The Crossing." [HayF] (13) Fall-Wint 93, p. 81.
5816. SAUL, Scott
"The Stationary Writer" (The Michael Jasper Gioia Award Winner for 1991). [Sequoia] (34/35) 92-93, p. 65-66.
5817. SAUNDERS, Bobbie
"Grief." [13thMoon] (11:1/2) 93, p. 68.
5818. SAVAGE, Hugh
"Borzoi." [Poetry] (163:2) N 93, p. 74.
"Moving House." [Poetry] (162:1) Ap 93, p. 27.
5819. SAVARD, Jeannine
"The Devil's Rope: Confession of an Abductee." [DenQ] (27:3) Wint 93, p. 58-59.
5820. SAVARD, Michel
"Rue Montmartre" (Paris, June 1992). [TickleAce] (25) Spr-Sum 93, p. 199.
5821. SAVITT, Lynne
"Ignition." [NewYorkQ] (50) 93, p. 60.

"Six Things to Know If You Love a Convict." [PaintedB] (50/51) 93, p. 71.
"Sleeping Retrospect of Desire." [NewYorkQ] (51) 93, p. 62.
5822. SAVITT, Wade
"Walking, thumb-sucking within fluid, the self is set against blankness." [US1]
(28/29) 93, p. 12.
5823. SAVOIE, Terry (T. Maurice)
"Impedimenta." [FreeL] (11) Wint 93, p. 14.
"Still Life" (to an abandoned farmhouse). [SpoonR] (18:2) Sum-Fall 93, p. 49.
"Stolen Kisses." [FreeL] (11) Wint 93, p. 15.
5824. SAVVAS, Minas
"A Daughter from the Grave" (tr. of anonymous lament from rural Greece).
[HawaiiR] (17:1, #37) Spr 93, p. 117.
5825. SAWCZUK, Marta
"In the Morning" (tr. of Lina Kostenko). [Vis] (43) 93, p. 53.
"The Mail Box" (tr. of Lina Kostenko). [Vis] (43) 93, p. 54.
5826. SAWYER, Joy
"Los Angeles, April 30, 1992." [NewYorkQ] (52) 93, p. 62-63.
5827. SAWYER, Paul
"On Jenny." [Light] (6) Sum 93, p. 16.
5828. SCAFIDI, Steve
"The Devil in the House." [PoetryNW] (34:3) Aut 93, p. 31.
5829. SCALAPINO, Leslie
"Defoe" (Excerpt). [AmerPoR] (22:1) Ja-F 93, p. 65-66.
"Defoe" (Excerpts). [Conjunc] (20) 93, p. 296-304.
"Waking Life" (Excerpt). [RiverS] (38) 93, p. 58-61.
5830. SCALF, Sue
"After a Long Absence." [AlabamaLR] (7:1) 93, p. 35.
"February '63." [HampSPR] Wint 93, p. 56.
"On Buying a Sprig of Quince." [TarRP] (32:2) Spr 93, p. 17.
5831. SCANTLEBURY, Darren
"Detention." [Americas] (21:2) Sum 93, p. 69.
5832. SCARBROUGH, George
"The Night He Came." [SpiritSH] (58) 93, p. 1-2.
5833. SCATES, Maxine
"She Wrote." [PennR] (5:2) 93, p. 49-54.
5834. SCATTERGOOD, Amy
"A Song for the Daughter I Do Not Have." [Sequoia] (34/35) 92-93, p. 91.
5835. SCHAACK, F. J.
"The Vainglorious Present." [Hellas] (4:1) Spr 93, p. 20.
5836. SCHAEDLER, Brad
"Indian Summer." [Plain] (14:1) Fall 93, p. 32.
"Snow in June" (Laramie, Wyoming). [AlabamaLR] (7:2) 93, p. 17.
"Wyoming Winter Sunset, Ten Miles From Nowhere." [Plain] (13:3) Spr 93, p. 17.
5837. SCHAEFFER, Susan Fromberg
"Gifts." [BrooklynR] (10) 93, p. 86-88.
"The Old Fan." [NorthStoneR] (11) 93, p. 140.
5838. SCHAFFER, Amanda
"The Robin Moor, 1893." [HarvardA] (128:1) Fall 93, p. 9.
"Slides of the Jazz Age" (Second Prize). [HarvardA] (127:3) Spr 93, p. 17.
5839. SCHAFFNER, M. A.
"Mount Vernon." [HampSPR] Wint 93, p. 47-48.
"Niccolo's Ghost." [Sparrow] (60) Sum 93, p. 32.
"On the Death of Park Squirrels." [HampSPR] Wint 93, p. 48.
"Soft Shoulders." [HampSPR] Wint 93, p. 47.
5840. SCHAPIRO, Jane
"Reentry." [Northeast] (5:8) Spr-Sum 93, p. 5.
5841. SCHAPIRO, Lisa
"Tearing Papers." [13thMoon] (12:1/2) 93-94, p. 58.
5842. SCHEELE, Roy
"Certificate." [SouthernR] (29:1) Wint, Ja 93, p. 182-183.
"Nebraska Wine." [Poetry] (161:6) Mr 93, p. 328.
5843. SCHEER, Linda
"Adieu, Chimères, Idéals, Erreurs" (— Rimbaud. Tr. of Rafael Alberti, w. Brian
Swann). [QRL] (12:32/33) 93, p. 11-13.
"Prado Museum" (tr. of Rafael Alberti, w. Brian Swann). [QRL] (12:32/33) 93, p. 8 -
11.

5844. SCHELLING, Andrew
"Greeting the Return of the Wolf to Colorado." [DenQ] (27:4) Spr 93, p. 82.
"Notes and Scraps: 18:XI:92." [Talisman] (11) Fall 93, p. 22-24.
5845. SCHEMM, Ripley
"Flying Home in December" (for Dick). [CutB] (40) Spr 93, p. 19-20.
"Retelling the Story." [CutB] (40) Spr 93, p. 21-22.
5846. SCHENKER, Donald
"Technological Night." [Contact] (11:65/66/67) Spr 93, p. 37.
5847. SCHEWEL, Adam
"Light over Television Hill." [BellR] (16:1/2) Spr-Fall 93, p. 88-89.
5848. SCHIELE, Evelyn
"Daddy's Home." [WillowR] (20) Spr 93, p. 32.
"What You Don't See." [WillowR] (20) Spr 93, p. 33.
5849. SCHILLER, Laura
"The Afterlife Messenger Service." [Turnstile] (4:2) 93, p. 35-36.
5850. SCHJELDAHL, Peter
"Harm." [DenQ] (28:1) Sum 93, p. 50-52.
5851. SCHJERVEN, Torgeir
"He Lay There and Was a Great Lover in a Night Without Civilization" (tr. by
Hallberg Hallmundsson). [GrandS] (12:3, #47) Fall 93, p. 125.
5852. SCHLANGER, Eugene
"Alcibiades" (by Timandra, the courtesan). [AmerS] (62:3) Sum 93, p. 350.
5853. SCHLIPP, Margot
"Anachronisms." [RiverS] (37) 93, p. 1.
5854. SCHLOSS, David
"The Cloak." [Poetry] (162:1) Ap 93, p. 2.
"In a Blue Light." [Poetry] (162:4) Jl 93, p. 210-212.
"The Mind/Body Problem." [Poetry] (162:4) Jl 93, p. 213.
"Tourists Under Glass" (Topkapi). [ParisR] (35:128) Fall 93, p. 229.
"Words Instead of a Thousand Pictures" (The British Museum). [ParisR] (35:128)
Fall 93, p. 228.
5855. SCHMIDT, Denny
"The Half of Life" (tr. of Friedrich Hölderlin, w. Liz Rosenberg). [GrahamHR] (17)
Fall 93, p. 109.
"On tawny leaves rests the grape, the hope of wine" (tr. of Friedrich Hölderlin, w.
Liz Rosenberg). [GrahamHR] (17) Fall 93, p. 111.
"Ripe, in fire dipped, broiled" (tr. of Friedrich Hölderlin, w. Liz Rosenberg).
[GrahamHR] (17) Fall 93, p. 108.
"To Diotima" (tr. of Friedrich Hölderlin, w. Liz Rosenberg). [GrahamHR] (17) Fall
93, p. 110.
5856. SCHMIDT, Jan
"A Woman Without Children." [CreamCR] (17:1) Spr 93, p. 36-39.
5857. SCHMIDT, Katharine A.
"Tabletop." [OnTheBus] (5:2, #12) Sum-Fall 93, p. 178.
5858. SCHMIDT, Paulette
"Westwego" (1917-1922, for M.L., tr. of Philippe Soupault). [ArtfulD] (24/25) 93,
p. 47-53.
5859. SCHMITT, Peter
"Breakfast of Runnersup." [Poetry] (162:4) Jl 93, p. 216-217.
"Shoeshine." [Ploughs] (19:1) Spr 93, p. 102-103.
5860. SCHNEIDER, Annerose D.
"For Suzanne." [Pearl] (17) Spr 93, p. 43.
"Marlene's Grave." [Pearl] (19) Fall-Wint 93, p. 82.
5861. SCHNEIDER, Dick
"For an inexhaustible instant I sat" (tr. of François Jacqmin). [ManhatR] (7:1) Fall
93, p. 23.
"It's not the precision" (tr. of François Jacqmin). [ManhatR] (7:1) Fall 93, p. 25.
"Nothing remains of which one would" (tr. of François Jacqmin). [ManhatR] (7:1)
Fall 93, p. 29.
"The rectangular distress of the city" (tr. of François Jacqmin). [ManhatR] (7:1) Fall
93, p. 27.
"Shrewd is the one who hears nothing" (tr. of François Jacqmin). [ManhatR] (7:1)
Fall 93, p. 30.
"Since silence links precaution" (tr. of François Jacqmin). [ManhatR] (7:1) Fall 93,
p. 31.
"Snow" (tr. of François Jacqmin). [ManhatR] (7:1) Fall 93, p. 21.

"The snow is everywhere" (tr. of François Jacqmin). [ManhatR] (7:1) Fall 93, p. 24.
"The time comes" (tr. of François Jacqmin). [ManhatR] (7:1) Fall 93, p. 28.
"What one hears when the soul" (tr. of François Jacqmin). [ManhatR] (7:1) Fall 93, p. 22.
"When the snow stopped falling" (tr. of François Jacqmin). [ManhatR] (7:1) Fall 93, p. 26.
5862. SCHNEIDERS, Jay
"Making Cider." [Sonora] (26) Fall 93, p. 76.
5863. SCHNEIDRE, P.
"The Second Kind." [OnTheBus] (5:2, #12) Sum-Fall 93, p. 179.
5864. SCHOENBERGER, Nancy
"Girl's Bed." [Boulevard] (8:1, #22) Spr 93, p. 191.
"Nathaniel Hawthorne in Hell." [SouthernHR] (27:3) Sum 93, p. 234.
5865. SCHOFIELD, Don
"I Don't Know the Local." [SouthernPR] (33:2) Fall 93, p. 60-61.
5866. SCHONBRUN, Adam
"My First Day Teaching in a Nursing School." [Footwork] (23) 93, p. 158.
"Poem of Apology." [Footwork] (23) 93, p. 158-159.
5867. SCHÖNMAIER, Eleonore
"Airport Bomb." [PraF] (14:2) Sum 93, p. 87.
"Eszter's Swim." [Dandel] (20:1) 93, p. 10.
"Opa." [PottPort] (15:1) Spr-Sum 93, p. 29.
5868. SCHORB, E. M.
"Art." [TexasR] (14:3/4) Fall-Wint 93, p. 84-85.
"At the Gate." [LitR] (37:1) Fall 93, p. 76.
"Destruction." [AmerS] (62:2) Spr 93, p. 234.
"Like the Titanic." [Pembroke] (25) 93, p. 60.
"The Nun." [HolCrit] (30:3) Je 93, p. 16-17.
"A Tumble for Skelton." [JINJPo] (15:2) Aut 93, p. 21-22.
5869. SCHORB, Michael
"Demise of the Sun Parrot." [Outbr] (24) 93, p. 105.
"Einstein's Violin." [Outbr] (24) 93, p. 106.
5870. SCHORN, Brian
"The Scissors of Max Ernst" (Excerpt). [Caliban] (13) 93, p. 149-150.
5871. SCHOTT, Barbara
"Mango flesh." [PraF] (14:3) Aut 93, p. 65.
5872. SCHOTT, Penelope Scambly
"Desertion" (Honorable Mention, Poetry Award). [NewL] (59:2) 93, p. 75.
"Devotions of May." [AmerV] (32) 93, p. 61-62.
"Women Holding Up the Sky." [US1] (28/29) 93, p. 8.
5873. SCHRAF, Mark
"Hector at the Plate." [Spitball] (44) Sum 93, p. 72-73.
"I Saw Rod Scurry." [Spitball] (43) Spr 93, p. 46-47.
5874. SCHREINER, Steven
"Untitled: Much of marriage is mastery." [RiverS] (37) 93, p. 53.
"Untrue." [RiverS] (37) 93, p. 51-52.
5875. SCHUBERT, David
"Getting a Mosquito." [QRL] (12:32/33) 93, p. 505.
"It Is Sticky in the Subway." [QRL] (12:32/33) 93, p. 504-505.
"No Finis." [QRL] (12:32/33) 93, p. 506.
"Reflections on Violence." [QRL] (12:32/33) 93, p. 506.
"The Skeleton in the Closet." [QRL] (12:32/33) 93, p. 506-507.
5876. SCHUG, Lawrence
"My Wife and the Snake." [RagMag] (11:1) 93, p. 105.
"One Hundred Hawks." [RagMag] (11:1) 93, p. 104.
5877. SCHULER, Christine L.
"Nine Hours at the Benji Cafe in Plains, Montana." [BellArk] (9:5) S-O 93, p. 7.
5878. SCHULER, Robert
"Art Nouveau: Under the Studio Window." [NorthStoneR] (11) 93, p. 155.
"The Ides of April, North." [CoalC] (7) Apr 93, p. 12.
"Late Summer: Harmonie du Jour." [CoalC] (7) Apr 93, p. 12.
"Poem for Jody B." [NorthStoneR] (11) 93, p. 155.
5879. SCHULTE, Jane
"Poplars." [WillowR] (20) Spr 93, p. 39.
5880. SCHULTE, Marie
"Morana" (tr. of Desanka Maksimovic). [NoDaQ] (61:1) Wint 93, p. 106.

"Morana's Lullaby" (tr. of Desanka Maksimovic). [NoDaQ] (61:1) Wint 93, p. 107.
5881. SCHULTZ, Susan M.
"The Lost Country." [Talisman] (11) Fall 93, p. 288.
"The Philosopher's Child." [Verse] (10:2) Sum 93, p. 95-96.
5882. SCHUMAKER, Peggy
"Passing Through, Passing On" (Waipo'o Falls, Kuaui). [PoetC] (24:3) Spr 93, p. 5.
"Ways of Seeing." [PoetC] (24:3) Spr 93, p. 3-4.
5883. SCHWARTZ, Betsy Robin
"Chess Is a Game Where Partners in Play Are Called Opponents." [13thMoon]
(11:1/2) 93, p. 70.
"Dining Out." [13thMoon] (11:1/2) 93, p. 69.
"I Wish." [13thMoon] (11:1/2) 93, p. 69.
"Shana Yardena." [Footwork] (23) 93, p. 127.
"When You Read This Poem Out Loud, Someone Will Call You an Ugly Bitter
Bitch" (for Robin Pastorio Newman). [Footwork] (23) 93, p. 128.
5884. SCHWARTZ, Hillel
"Child. Eight. Autistic." [ColEng] (55:1) Ja 93, p. 80-81.
"Ground Zero." [BelPoJ] (44:2) Wint 93-94, p. 26-27.
"NOR." [CentR] (37:3) Fall 93, p. 551.
"Walking with Donna Near Del Mar." [CentR] (37:3) Fall 93, p. 550.
5885. SCHWARTZ, Leonard
"Difficult Passage." [Talisman] (10) Spr 93, p. 150.
"Epic" (tr. of Yan Li, w. Mingxia Li). [AmerLC] (5) 93, p. 83-86.
5886. SCHWARTZ, Lloyd
"Pornography." [ParisR] (35:127) Sum 93, p. 276-281.
"Three Dreams." [Agni] (38) 93, p. 139-143.
5887. SCHWARTZ, Rick
"Perseus and Andromeda, As If by Emily Dickinson." [Confr] (51) Sum 93, p. 246.
5888. SCHWARTZ, Ruth L.
"Letter from Anywhere." [ArtfulD] (24/25) 93, p. 71.
"Scene with Pelicans." [ArtfulD] (24/25) 93, p. 72.
5889. SCHWARTZHOFF, Kim
"Announcing Your Arrival." [CreamCR] (17:2) Fall 93, p. 139.
"White Fog." [CreamCR] (17:2) Fall 93, p. 138.
5890. SCHWARTZMAN, Adam
"Retief's Kloof." [Verse] (10:3) Wint 93, p. 100.
"Return Journey." [Verse] (10:3) Wint 93, p. 100.
"Umkupozi." [Verse] (10:3) Wint 93, p. 101.
5891. SCHWARZ, Ghita
"Exile." [ProseP] (2) 93, p. 82.
"Refuge." [Caliban] (13) 93, p. 47.
5892. SCHWEIK, Joanne L.
"Shelling Peas" (Honorable Mention, 1993 Poetry Competition). [Elf] (3:2) Sum 93,
p. 27.
5893. SCHWERER, Eric
"Poems of the Bicameral Mind" (Selection: 2. Like Something Too Familiar).
[Sonora] (24/25) Spr 93, p. 22.
5894. SCHWERNER, Armand
"The Air of Performance-a at Liancourt" (for Elise). [AmerPoR] (22:1) Ja-F 93, p.
67.
"Going Places." [AmerPoR] (22:1) Ja-F 93, p. 67.
5895. SCHWITTERS, Kurt
"Candle Fat" (tr. by Jerome Rothenberg). [PoetryUSA] (25/26) 93, p. 15.
"Subway Poem" (tr. by Jerome Rothenberg). [PoetryUSA] (25/26) 93, p. 23.
5896. SCOFIELD, James
"For Sale." [WillowR] (20) Spr 93, p. 38.
"The Holding Shed" (For Ida Gray). [SmPd] (30:1, #87) Wint 93, p. 15.
"The Housekeeper." [Ploughs] (19:1) Spr 93, p. 141-142.
5897. SCOFIELD, Robin
"Occasion of an Unopened Bloom." [WestHR] (47:4) Wint 93, p. 417.
"White Knight, Knave of Hearts." [WestHR] (47:4) Wint 93, p. 416.
5898. SCOPINO, Adriana
"The 10 p.m. Local from DC to NYC." [Lactuca] (17) Apr 93, p. 8.
"At 6:10 I Am Certain You Are." [Lactuca] (17) Apr 93, p. 8.
"Walking." [Lactuca] (17) Apr 93, p. 8.

5899. SCOTELLARO, Rocco
"Black Puddle: April 18" (tr. by Jack Hirschman. Translation dedicated to the
memory of Bob Kaufman, who was born on April 18). [Arshile] (2) 93, p. 61,
63.
"Pozzanghera Nera il Diciotto Aprile." [Arshile] (2) 93, p. 60, 62.
5900. SCOTT, David G. W.
"Last Baskets Before Night" (Greensboro Review Literary Award Poem: Honorable
Mention). [GreensboroR] (55) Wint 93-94, p. 89-90.
"Wile E. Love." [GreensboroR] (55) Wint 93-94, p. 91.
5901. SCOTT, Georgia
"Any One of Us" (tr. of Anna Janko, w. David Malcolm). [Prima] (16/17) 93, p. 32 -
33.
"Found Eye" (tr. of Krystyna Lars, w. David Malcolm). [Prima] (16/17) 93, p. 28 -
29.
"I See the Future" (tr. of Anna Czekanowicz, w. David Malcolm). [Prima] (16/17)
93, p. 31.
"(I) She Writes with Fire" (tr. of Krystyna Lars, w. David Malcolm). [Prima] (16/17)
93, p. 30.
5902. SCOTT, Jo H.
"I Dwell Too Often." [OnTheBus] (6:1, #13) Wint 93-Spr 94, p. 178.
5903. SCOTT, Mary
"Cats." [Gaia] (3) O 93, p. 7.
"For Julie at Tom Thumb." [Gaia] (3) O 93, p. 7.
"The Migrant Lovers." [Gaia] (3) O 93, p. 8.
5904. SCOTT, Peter Dale
"Letter to Paul Alpers." [HarvardR] (4) Spr 93, p. 6-12.
5905. SCOTT, Virginia
"The Breaker-Limbs." [Confr] (51) Sum 93, p. 269.
5906. SCRIMGEOUR, J. D.
"Guitar." [Border] (2) Spr 93, p. 60.
"National Review." [RiverS] (39) 93, p. 27-28.
"Ribbon." [RiverS] (39) 93, p. 29.
"Their Favorite Author." [GreenMR] (NS 6:2) Sum-Fall 93, p. 88-89.
"Valentine's Day, 1991" (for E.F.). [HayF] (13) Fall-Wint 93, p. 21.
5907. SCRIMGEOUR, James R.
"The French Expressionist Idea." [GreenMR] (NS 6:2) Sum-Fall 93, p. 90-91.
5908. SCRUGGS, Patricia L.
"The Desert at Night." [OnTheBus] (6:1, #13) Wint 93-Spr 94, p. 179.
"Letter to Dylan Thomas." [OnTheBus] (5:2, #12) Sum-Fall 93, p. 184.
5909. SCRUTON, James
"In the Age of the Radio Telescope." [Poetry] (163:1) O 93, p. 18.
5910. SEAMAN, Barbara
"Antiphon." [Kaleid] (27) Sum-Fall 93, p. 59.
"Filling in the Blanks." [Kaleid] (27) Sum-Fall 93, p. 60.
"Snowfall at Children's Mercy Hospital." [Kaleid] (27) Sum-Fall 93, p. 56.
"Trading Post." [Plain] (14:1) Fall 93, p. 6-7.
"Wintergrace." [ChrC] (110:36) 15 D 93, p. 1269.
5911. SEARCY, Darlene
"Dream on Daddy." [PraF] (14:3) Aut 93, p. 123.
5912. SEARS, Peter
"The Clearing." [NowestR] (31:1) 93, p. 60.
"What Scared Me As a Boy Was Not My Sex." [NowestR] (31:1) 93, p. 61.
5913. SEATON, J. P.
"Bad Government" (tr. of Kuan Hsiu). [Sulfur] (33) Fall 93, p. 158.
"Ch'i Liang's Good Wife" (tr. of Kuan Hsiu). [Sulfur] (33) Fall 93, p. 154.
"On the Border, Three Poems" (tr. of Kuan Hsiu). [Sulfur] (33) Fall 93, p. 152-153.
"Song of the Palace of Ch'en" (tr. of Kuan Hsiu). [Sulfur] (33) Fall 93, p. 155.
"Song of the Righteous Man" (tr. of Kuan Hsiu). [Sulfur] (33) Fall 93, p. 157.
"Song of the Wasteland" (tr. of Kuan Hsiu). [Sulfur] (33) Fall 93, p. 156-157.
"Three Verses on Running into the Taoist Master 'In Emptiness'" (tr. of Kuan Hsiu).
[Sulfur] (33) Fall 93, p. 155-156.
"Written in the Mountains" (tr. of Kuan Hsiu). [Sulfur] (33) Fall 93, p. 153-154.
5914. SEATON, Maureen
"Astronomy." [IndR] (16:1) Spr 93, p. 117.
"Romancing Debussy." [Poetry] (162:1) Ap 93, p. 3-4.
"Saved." [IndR] (16:1) Spr 93, p. 114-115.

"Self-Portrait with Disasters." [PaintedB] (49) 93, p. 15.
"Torque." [IndR] (16:1) Spr 93, p. 116.
5915. SEAY, Anita
"Passion Vs. Perception." [JINJPo] (15:1) Spr 93, p. 39.
5916. SEBASTIAN, Robert M.
"Billy Graham." [Light] (5) Spr 93, p. 21.
"Bio Bite." [Light] (8) Wint 93, p. 11.
"Chinatown Entree." [Light] (5) Spr 93, p. 13.
"Dear Old Father Marzipano." [Light] (5) Spr 93, p. 26.
"Epitaph for Our Cook." [Light] (7) Aut 93, p. 8.
5917. SEBEK, Karel
"If I am living it is a sign that here nothing is in order" (tr. by Ellen Rosenbaum).
[OxfordM] (9:1) Spr-Sum 93, p. 31-32.
"The nearness of day like the fangs of a wolf" (tr. by Ellen Rosenbaum). [OxfordM]
(9:1) Spr-Sum 93, p. 32.
"A poem comes to me like night dressed in pyjamas" (tr. by Ellen Rosenbaum).
[OxfordM] (9:1) Spr-Sum 93, p. 28-29.
"A spike in the head during the holidays" (tr. by Ellen Rosenbaum). [OxfordM]
(9:1) Spr-Sum 93, p. 29-30.
"There arrives a beast the spring" (tr. by Ellen Rosenbaum). [OxfordM] (9:1) Spr -
Sum 93, p. 30-31.
5918. SECOR, Nanette
"Articles of Faith." [13thMoon] (11:1/2) 93, p. 72.
"A Cure for Back Pain." [Stand] (34:2) Spr 93, p. 63.
5919. SEDWICK, Timothy
"Generation Epitaph." [RagMag] (11:1) 93, p. 82.
5920. SEEHUUS, Tonya R.
"Local Haole." [HawaiiR] (17:1, #37) Spr 93, p. 65.
5921. SEFERIS, George
"Tuesday" (tr. by Edmund Keeley). [QRL] (12:32/33) 93, p. 507-508.
"Wednesday" (ad vigilias albas, tr. by Edmund Keeley). [QRL] (12:32/33) 93, p.
509.
5922. SEGRAIS, Joliveau de
"L'Aigle et le Ver." [Hudson] (45:4) Wint 93, p. 681.
"The Eagle and the Worm" (tr. by Norman R. Shapiro). [Hudson] (45:4) Wint 93, p.
681.
5923. SEIBEL, Mary-Alice
"After the Storm." [Writ] (25) 93, p. 32.
"Alcohol." [Writ] (25) 93, p. 38.
"The Cell." [Writ] (25) 93, p. 34.
"The Crocus." [Writ] (25) 93, p. 36.
"The Hummingbirds." [Writ] (25) 93, p. 35.
"The Moths." [Writ] (25) 93, p. 33.
"The Sea Otters." [Writ] (25) 93, p. 31.
"Victorian Women." [Writ] (25) 93, p. 37.
5924. SEIBLES, Tim
"Cancion" (for Lina del Roble). [GreenMR] (NS 6:1) Wint-Spr 93, p. 103.
"Hardie." [Ploughs] (19:4) Wint 93-94, p. 36-38.
"Outtakes from an Interview with Malcolm X after Mecca" (January 1965).
[Callaloo] (16:3) Sum 93, p. 501-505.
"Shade" (for Joy Nolan). [GreenMR] (NS 6:1) Wint-Spr 93, p. 104-106.
5925. SEID, Christopher
"On a Farm in Nebraska." [Farm] (10:1) Spr-Sum 93, p. 125.
5926. SEIDEL, Frederick
"Autumn." [Raritan] (12:4) Spr 93, p. 28.
"Chartres." [Raritan] (12:4) Spr 93, p. 28.
"Glory." [AmerPoR] (22:1) Ja-F 93, p. 68.
"The Hour." [AmerPoR] (22:1) Ja-F 93, p. 69.
"The Lighting of the Candles." [Raritan] (12:4) Spr 93, p. 29.
"Lorraine Motel, Memphis." [Raritan] (12:4) Spr 93, p. 29.
"The New Woman." [AmerPoR] (22:1) Ja-F 93, p. 69.
"Pol Pot." [AmerPoR] (22:1) Ja-F 93, p. 68.
"Recessional." [Raritan] (12:4) Spr 93, p. 30.
"The Second Coming." [Raritan] (12:4) Spr 93, p. 28.
"Sonnet." [AmerPoR] (22:1) Ja-F 93, p. 68.

"Untitled: Brought to the surface form the floor of the ocean." [Raritan] (12:4) Spr 93, p. 26-27.
5927. SEIDMAN, Hugh
"Eye : Void : Matter." [Talisman] (11) Fall 93, p. 105-109.
5928. SEIFERLE, Rebecca
"Divided Continent." [Calyx] (15:1) Wint 93-94, p. 14-16.
5929. SEIFERT, Jaroslav
"Dedication (A.M.P.)" (tr. by Vera Borkovec). [Vis] (43) 93, p. 15.
"Halley's Comet" (tr. by Vera Borkovec). [Vis] (43) 93, p. 13.
"The Weight of the Earth" (tr. by Vera Borkovec). [Vis] (43) 93, p. 14.
5930. SEILER, Barry
"A Friend of the Family." [Footwork] (23) 93, p. 153.
"Self-Portrait as John Garfield." [Talisman] (11) Fall 93, p. 268-269.
SEKULIC, Maja Herman
See HERMAN-SEKULIC, Maja
5931. SELAWSKY, John (John T.)
"After August." [Poem] (69) My 93, p. 62.
"Resurrection." [Poem] (69) My 93, p. 63.
"Sunday Ride to Brooklyn." [CapeR] (28:2) Fall 93, p. 35.
"Wasp's Sting." [SoDakR] (31:3) Fall 93, p. 101.
5932. SELBY, Martha Ann
"The Gathasaptasati" (Selections, tr. of poems in Maharastri Prakit collected by Hala). [Sulfur] (33) Fall 93, p. 54-57.
5933. SELBY, Spencer
"Dangerous." [Caliban] (12) 93, p. 130.
"Mutation Stops" (For C.L.). [Talisman] (11) Fall 93, p. 235-238.
"Strand." [Caliban] (12) 93, p. 131.
"Treatment." [NewAW] (11) Sum-Fall 93, p. 78-79.
5934. SELFRIDGE, Barbara
"The Napper." [Witness] (7:2) 93, p. 128-129.
5935. SELLAND, Eric
"Elegy" (for Nishiwaki Junzaburo, tr. of Yoshioka Minoru). [ChiR] (39:3/4) 93, p. 204-205.
"To Hanawa, Terayama, As Far as Nagare" (tr. of Inagawa Masato). [ChiR] (39:3/4) 93, p. 216-217.
5936. SELLERS, Heather (Heather Laurie)
"Dolphin City, Neptune Beach." [ApalQ] (36/37) 91, p. 83-84.
"Father Above." [ApalQ] (36/37) 91, p. 85.
"Your Whole Life." [SouthernPR] (33:2) Fall 93, p. 62-63.
5937. SELMAN, Robyn
"21 East 10th, 2BR, WBF, EIK." [AmerPoR] (22:6) N-D 93, p. 23.
"After Amy." [WestHR] (47:3) Fall 93, p. 258-259.
"Exodus." [ParisR] (35:128) Fall 93, p. 324-338.
"Talk Radio." [WestHR] (47:3) Fall 93, p. 256-257.
"They Last." [WestHR] (47:3) Fall 93, p. 260-262.
5938. SELPH, Carl
"Una Nobildonna" (for Dorothy and Charles Hasty). [BellArk] (9:6) N-D 93, p. 23 - 24.
5939. SELTZER, Joanne
"Women of the Future." [Kalliope] (15:3) 93, p. 15.
5940. SELTZER, Michael
"Encomium" (for Nicholas, on his birth day). [AntigR] (93-94) Spr-Sum 93, p. 214 - 215.
5941. SELVING, Jan
"Isabel." [Ploughs] (19:4) Wint 93-94, p. 129-130.
"Offerings." [Ploughs] (19:4) Wint 93-94, p. 127-128.
5942. SEMANSKY, Chris
"Hide & Seek." [AmerLC] (5) 93, p. 25.
"What the Window Cleaner Thought." [WestHR] (47:4) Wint 93, p. 360-363.
5943. SEMENOVICH, Joseph
"Draft-Dodger." [SlipS] (13) 93, p. 67.
"I want these fingers to say." [Footwork] (23) 93, p. 60.
"Rain." [WebR] (17) Fall 93, p. 71-72.
5944. SEMONES, Charles
"In Locust Weather, Speaking of Angels" (for T.J.). [Wind] (23:72) 93, p. 26-27.
"What I've Done with Your 'Nocturne'." [Wind] (23:72) 93, p. 24-25.

423

SEN

5945. SEN, Jayanti
"I Do Not Understand" (tr. by Chitra Divakaruni). [Prima] (16/17) 93, p. 92-93.
SEN, Nabaneeta Dev
See DEV SEN, Nabaneeta
SEN, Nandana Dev
See DEV SEN, Nandana
5946. SENECA
"Trojan Women" (Excerpt, tr. by David R. Slavitt). [Pequod] (35) 93, p. 43-46.
5947. SENS, Jean-Marc
"Long Way Home." [ContextS] (3:1) 93, p. 14.
"A Long Way Home." [Crucible] (29) Fall 93, p. 19.
SENTER, Juan Hernández
See HERNANDEZ-SENTER, Juan
5948. SEQUEIRA, Jose
"Evenings with Grandmother." [ChangingM] (25) Wint-Spr 93, p. 72.
5949. SERAFINO, Alan
"The March Kite." [TickleAce] (25) Spr-Sum 93, p. 201.
5950. SERRANO, Juan
"Public School." [Americas] (21:2) Sum 93, p. 72.
5951. SERRAO, Achille
"There Was a Time" (tr. by Luigi Bonaffini). [Vis] (43) 93, p. 29.
"You see him come, always" (tr. by Luigi Bonaffini). [Vis] (43) 93, p. 30.
5952. SESHADRI, Vijay
"Prothalamion." [Boulevard] (8:2/3, #23/24) Fall 93, p. 183-184.
5953. SETTLE, Judith (Judith H., Judith Holmes)
"Purple Power: A Summer Dream, 1992." [Crucible] (29) Fall 93, p. 20.
"The Winter Closet." [Pembroke] (25) 93, p. 95.
5954. SEUFERT, Christopher K.
"Fishing in Bed." [Verse] (10:1) Spr 93, p. 36.
SEUNG-TAI, Yang
See YANG, Seung-Tai
5955. SEUSS-BRAKEMAN, Diane
"Frog Prince." [PassN] (14:1) Sum 93, p. 38.
"Hope." [PassN] (14:2) Wint 93, p. 13.
"An Inordinate Fondness for Beetles." [PassN] (14:1) Sum 93, p. 39.
"What My Son's Haricut Taught Me About Flying." [PassN] (14:1) Sum 93, p. 40.
5956. SEWELL, Lisa
"The Annoucement." [PassN] (14:2) Wint 93, p. 25.
"The Empty Dish." [PassN] (14:2) Wint 93, p. 21.
"Health." [PassN] (14:2) Wint 93, p. 22.
"One of the Foolish Women." [PassN] (14:2) Wint 93, p. 26.
"Surrender." [PassN] (14:2) Wint 93, p. 23.
"Then I Read About Eve in Paradise Lost." [SouthernPR] (33:2) Fall 93, p. 14-15.
"Then I Read about Eve in *Paradise Lost*." [PassN] (14:2) Wint 93, p. 24.
"Two Lessons in the Sacred." [PassN] (14:2) Wint 93, p. 27.
5957. SEXTON, Anne
"In Celebration of My Uterus." [QRL] (12:32/33) 93, p. 510-511.
5958. SEXTON, Megan
"The Meaning of Bones." [Calyx] (14:3) Sum 93, p. 33.
"Sigmund Freud Writes a Postcard from Coney Island, 1909." [HawaiiR] (17:2, #38) Spr 93, p. 69.
5959. SEYBURN, Patty
"The New Country." [Pearl] (17) Spr 93, p. 105.
"This Is the Middle." [NewYorkQ] (52) 93, p. 93.
5960. SHADOIAN, Jack
"Phasing Out." [PikeF] (11) Fall 93, p. 13.
5961. SHAFFER, Eric Paul
"The Love of Red Soil" (Selections, tr. of Yonaha Mikio, w. Katsunori Yamazato). [ChiR] (39:3/4) 93, p. 223-226.
5962. SHAHEEN, W. A.
"Black Letters of Insensitivity" (tr. by Baidar Bakht and Leslie Lavigne). [CanLit] (136) Spr 93, p. 99-100.
"I'm Mad Because of You" (tr. by Baidar Bakht and Leslie Lavigne). [CanLit] (136) Spr 93, p. 100.
"The Sound of Grief" (tr. by Baidar Bakht and Leslie Lavigne). [CanLit] (136) Spr 93, p. 99.

5963. SHAIDLE, Kathy
"Kahlo." [PoetryC] (13:3) 93, p. 15.
5964. SHAKESPEARE, William
"Shall I Compare Thee to a Summer's Day?" (Sonnet 18, with music by Claudia Lee
Gary Annis). [Sparrow] (60) Sum 93, p. 36-42.
5965. SHAKIR, Parween
"It Has Been Written" (tr. by C. M. Naim). [Prima] (16/17) 93, p. 86.
5966. SHANNON, Lisa
"Blue-Bellied Lizard at Divide Meadow." [PoetL] (88:2) Sum 93, p. 39-41.
5967. SHAPIRO, Alan
"The Letter." [Thrpny] (55) Fall 93, p. 4.
"Sisters" (For Sheila). [Poetry] (161:5) F 93, p. 265.
"Soul." [Poetry] (161:5) F 93, p. 266.
5968. SHAPIRO, David
"After." [AmerPoR] (22:1) Ja-F 93, p. 69.
"A Part for the Part." [AmerPoR] (22:1) Ja-F 93, p. 69.
"Sentences." [PaintedB] (50/51) 93, p. 34.
"Untitled Dreams." [AmerPoR] (22:1) Ja-F 93, p. 69.
5969. SHAPIRO, Gegg
"Apples." [Footwork] (23) 93, p. 96.
5970. SHAPIRO, Harvey
"After the Fall." [Boulevard] (8:2/3, #23/24) Fall 93, p. 186.
"The Collectors." [QRL] (12:32/33) 93, p. 512.
"The Defense." [Talisman] (11) Fall 93, p. 128.
"For Job at Forty." [QRL] (12:32/33) 93, p. 511.
"National Cold Storage Company." [QRL] (12:32/33) 93, p. 512.
"The Old Nostalgia." [QRL] (12:32/33) 93, p. 512-513.
"These Are the Streets." [Boulevard] (8:2/3, #23/24) Fall 93, p. 185.
5971. SHAPIRO, Karl
"Anti-Valentine." [Sparrow] (60) Sum 93, p. 20.
"Creative Writing." [NewYorkQ] (51) 93, p. 4.
"Karl Shapiro" (to Saul Bellow). [NewYorkQ] (50) 93, p. 32.
"M O M A." [Sparrow] (60) Sum 93, p. 21.
"The Sacred Blue." [NewYorkQ] (52) 93, p. 32.
"Ur-Valentine?" (tr. of anonymous 12-13th century poem, based on the literal tr.
from the Middle-High German by Sopie Wilkins). [Sparrow] (60) Sum 93, p.
20.
5972. SHAPIRO, Lara
"Untitled: When you begin to stumble on the simplest of words" (tr. of Natalya
Gorbanevskaya). [Asylum] (8) 93, p. 88.
5973. SHAPIRO, Michael
"Abbey's Land." [SmPd] (30:2, #88) Spr 93, p. 10-11.
"Order *Ephemeroptera*." [SmPd] (30:2, #88) Spr 93, p. 9-10.
"Territory." [SmPd] (30:2, #88) Spr 93, p. 12-13.
5974. SHAPIRO, Norman R.
"The Crayfish and Her Daughter" (tr. of Edme Boursault). [Hudson] (45:4) Wint 93,
p. 680.
"The Eagle and the Worm" (tr. of Joliveau de Segrais). [Hudson] (45:4) Wint 93, p.
681.
"The Mouse" (tr. of Eugène Guillevic). [Hudson] (45:4) Wint 93, p. 678.
"The Soccer Ball, or How to Succeed in Life" (tr. of Franc-Nohain (Maurice -
Etienne Legrand)). [Hudson] (45:4) Wint 93, p. 682.
5975. SHAPIRO, Samantha
"Love Doesn't Come with an Order of Fries" (Poets of High School Age). [HangL]
(62) 93, p. 86.
"Low Ratings" (Poets of High School Age). [HangL] (62) 93, p. 85.
5976. SHAPIRO, Susan
"Sunscreen." [PoetryE] (36) Fall 93, p. 122.
SHARAT CHANDRA, G. S.
See CHANDRA, G. S. Sharat
5977. SHARE, Don
"Frusos" (tr. of Darío Jaramillo Agudelo). [Agni] (37) 93, p. 272-273.
"The Morgualos" (tr. of Darío Jaramillo Agudelo). [Agni] (37) 93, p. 269-271.
5978. SHARER, Donna
"Summertime." [AnotherCM] (25) Spr 93, p. 167-169.

5979. SHARKEY, Lee
"The Dream of Gold." [CreamCR] (17:2) Fall 93, p. 200.
"Fat Woman Talking." [CreamCR] (17:1) Spr 93, p. 12-14.
5980. SHARP, Virginia
"Friday Night." [NewYorkQ] (52) 93, p. 55.
5981. SHAVIT, Dean
"Bar Mitzvah at the Wailing Wall." [TriQ] (89) Wint 93-94, p. 193-194.
"In Her Kitchen." [TriQ] (89) Wint 93-94, p. 192.
"A Marriage." [TriQ] (89) Wint 93-94, p. 190-191.
"Resolution" (for Omar Dohär). [AnotherCM] (26) Fall 93, p. 139-146.
5982. SHAW, Angela
"April." [Chelsea] (55) 93, p. 64.
"Courtesan." [Chelsea] (55) 93, p. 63.
"Heart: A Taunt." [SouthernPR] (33:2) Fall 93, p. 11-12.
"Oyster." [Chelsea] (55) 93, p. 64.
5983. SHAW, Catherine
"The Heaven Bound." [ChrC] (110:27) 6 O 93, p. 938.
5984. SHAW, Craig
"Down to Dream." [Plain] (14:1) Fall 93, p. 34.
5985. SHAW, Deirdre
"The Firefighter." [ChironR] (12:4/13:1, #37/38) Wint 93-Spr 94, p. 44.
"Swallowing" (for KC, who knew). [Pearl] (17) Spr 93, p. 44.
5986. SHAW, Luci
"Edges of Wales." [SoCoast] (14) Ja 93, p. 4.
"St. Frideswide's Chapel, Christ Church, Oxford." [SoCoast] (14) Ja 93, p. 5.
"The Today Show." [SoCoast] (14) Ja 93, p. 3.
5987. SHAW, Robert B.
"Florilegium." [Poetry] (161:4) Ja 93, p. 212-213.
"Halfway." [Poetry] (162:6) S 93, p. 346.
"Ice Time." [NewRep] (209:26) 27 D 93, p. 36.
"Low Tide." [Shen] (43:4) Wint 93, p. 92.
"A Mica Mine." [Shen] (43:4) Wint 93, p. 90-91.
"Night Lights." [Shen] (43:4) Wint 93, p. 93.
"A Pair of Bookends." [Poetry] (161:4) Ja 93, p. 211.
5988. SHAW, Stephen I.
"Sonoluminescence." [Northeast] (5:9) Wint 93-94, p. 14.
5989. SHAWH, Jacquelyn
"Letter from K on a Drunken Raft" (Honorable Mention, 7th Annual Contest).
[SoCoast] (15) Je 93, p. 6-7.
"Sideshow." [CapeR] (28:2) Fall 93, p. 15.
5990. SHCHERBINA, Tatyana
"No Need for Bullets, the Heart Explodes on Its Own" (tr. by J. Kates). [LitR] (37:1)
Fall 93, p. 84.
"Untitled: I sleep in your sweater" (in Russian and English, tr. by J. Kates).
[PaintedB] (52) 93, p. 10-11.
5991. SHEA, Glenn (Glen)
"Epithalamion" (for Tierney and Andy). [SmPd] (30:1, #87) Wint 93, p. 13.
"For Joyce Rankin." [SmPd] (30:1, #87) Wint 93, p. 13.
"It's Then You Begin to Burn Things." [Pearl] (19) Fall-Wint 93, p. 58.
"The Privacies of Light." [SmPd] (30:1, #87) Wint 93, p. 14.
"The World Is Grief" (Saint Kevin at Glendalough). [SmPd] (30:1, #87) Wint 93, p.
14.
5992. SHEA, John
"A Theologian at Prayer." [Comm] (120:2) 29 Ja 93, p. 14.
5993. SHEARD, Norma Voorhees
"Honeysuckle." [CapeR] (28:2) Fall 93, p. 48.
"Returning" (for Jim). [US1] (28/29) 93, p. 3.
5994. SHEARIN, Faith
"Luck." [ChiR] (39:2) 93, p. 31-32.
"Lust." [ChiR] (39:2) 93, p. 30.
"Rescue." [LullwaterR] (4:2) Spr-Sum 93, p. 105.
5995. SHECK, Laurie
"Blue Fragment." [RiverS] (37) 93, p. 36-37.
"Headlights." [RiverS] (37) 93, p. 34-35.
"The Inn." [NewYorker] (68:50) 1 F 93, p. 76.
"Rain." [Ploughs] (19:4) Wint 93-94, p. 54-55.

"Under the Desert." [RiverS] (37) 93, p. 38.
5996. SHECTMAN, Robin
"Arrowheads." [SenR] (23:1/2) Wint 93, p. 116.
5997. SHEEHAN, Marc J.
"For Cesar Vallejo." [ApalQ] (39) 93, p. 54.
"The Living." [SycamoreR] (5:1) Wint 93, p. 51.
"Reading Nietzsche in the Factory Canteen." [ApalQ] (39) 93, p. 55.
5998. SHEELER, Jackie
"Fantasies of Coma" (for Gail Joseph). [Parting] (6:2) Wint 93, p. 30.
"Inheritance." [Gaia] (1/2) Ap-Jl 93, p. 46.
5999. SHELDON, Anne
"497 Mss., or, Processing the Entries." [Bogg] (66) Wint 92-93, p. 34.
"My First Season as an Orioles' Fan Without Orsulak, Billy, and Milligan."
[Spitball] (45) Fall 93, p. 14.
6000. SHELDON, Bill
"Driving." [Bogg] (66) Wint 92-93, p. 24.
6001. SHELDON, Glenn
"One Man's Biography, One Man's Autobiography." [PikeF] (11) Fall 93, p. 29.
"Sister Montego." [Lactuca] (17) Apr 93, p. 46.
6002. SHELLEY, Percy Bysshe
"Ozymandias" (first draft). [Sulfur] (33) Fall 93, p. 282.
6003. SHELLY, Nadine
"Horus." [CapilR] (2:10) Spr 93, p. 123-124.
"Internal Damnation: the Furnace of Angels." [CapilR] (2:10) Spr 93, p. 130-131.
"Ode to a Node (Deja Vu)." [CapilR] (2:10) Spr 93, p. 126-129.
"Vernal Vernacular." [CapilR] (2:10) Spr 93, p. 125.
6004. SHELNUTT, Eve
"Collaborators." [ApalQ] (35) 90, p. 37.
"History." [ArtfulD] (24/25) 93, p. 106.
"Journey." [LullwaterR] (4:2) Spr-Sum 93, p. 125.
"Portrait." [CreamCR] (17:1) Spr 93, p. 86.
"Warning." [LullwaterR] (4:2) Spr-Sum 93, p. 8.
6005. SHELTON, Richard
"Family Memoirs." [ProseP] (2) 93, p. 83.
6006. SHEPARD, Miriam
"On a Morning When the Season Is Most like Itself." [Poem] (69) My 93, p. 36-37.
"The Palimpsest Soul." [Poem] (69) My 93, p. 34.
"Revisiting Eden." [Poem] (69) My 93, p. 35.
6007. SHEPARD, Neil
"Tropical Moment." [DenQ] (27:3) Wint 93, p. 60-62.
"Wuyi Mountain Cave." [WestHR] (47:4) Wint 93, p. 338-339.
6008. SHEPARD, Roy
"Eye Cannot Edit." [ChrC] (110:18) 2-9 Je 93, p. 591.
"Going Back" (Selections: 6 poems. The Pablo Neruda Prize for Poetry: Second
Prize). [Nimrod] (37:1) Fall-Wint 93, p. 31-37.
6009. SHEPHERD, Gail
"Anatomy Lesson." [Boulevard] (8:1, #22) Spr 93, p. 114.
6010. SHEPHERD, J. Barrie
"Anointings." [ChrC] (110:17) 19-26 My 93, p. 552.
"Church Picnic." [ChrC] (110:34) 1 D 93, p. 1206.
"Jurassic Church." [ChrC] (110:28) 13 O 93, p. 978.
"Lent Is." [ChrC] (110:10) 24-31 Mr 93, p. 322.
"Orienting-Lent." [ChrC] (110:6) 24 F 93, p. 197.
"Two Porpoises Passed By." [ChrC] (110:12) 14 Apr 93, p. 390.
"Wednesday's Truth." [ChrC] (110:4) 3-10 F 93, p. 116.
6011. SHEPHERD, Melissa
"De Casibus." [SouthernPR] (33:1) Spr 93, p. 15-17.
6012. SHEPHERD, Reginald
"About the Body, Beauty." [Verse] (10:1) Spr 93, p. 43.
"Ariadne's Dancing Floor." [SouthwR] (78:4) Aut 93, p. 485.
"The Difficult Music." [Nat] (257:13) 25 O 93, p. 476.
"Grass." [HawaiiR] (17:3, #39) Fall 93, p. 61.
"The Lucky One." [GreenMR] (NS 6:1) Wint-Spr 93, p. 102.
"A Man of Reason." [IndR] (16:2) Fall 93, p. 118.
"Narcissus on Echo Beach" (For Jim Bourgeois). [Journal] (17:2) Fall-Wint 93, p.
56.

427

SHEPHERD

"Nijinsky's Winter Afternoon, with Faun." [Agni] (37) 93, p. 104.
"Nuages." [IndR] (16:2) Fall 93, p. 117.
"Perfect." [Nat] (256:24) 21 Je 93, p. 874.
"Sam Cooke Would Be Sixty-One This Year." [GreenMR] (NS 6:1) Wint-Spr 93, p.
    101.
"Sunday." [IndR] (16:2) Fall 93, p. 119.
"Tantalus in May" (Discovery-The Nation '93 Prizewinning Poet). [Nat] (256:17) 3
    My 93, p. 604.
"Two Boys Glimpsed in Late Night." [GreenMR] (NS 6:1) Wint-Spr 93, p. 100.
"Until December." [SouthernPR] (33:2) Fall 93, p. 50-51.
"Until She Returns." [MassR] (34:1) Spr 93, p. 129-130.
"Where When Was." [AntR] (51:1) Wint 93, p. 77.
6013. SHEPPARD, Susan
    "Dream 22: Sitting on a Nest of Swans." [OhioR] (50) 93, p. 96-98.
6014. SHEPPERSON, Janet
    "The Aphrodite Stone." [SenR] (23:1/2) Wint 93, p. 77-78.
    "Madonna of the Spaces." [SenR] (23:1/2) Wint 93, p. 79-80.
    "Private Viewing." [SenR] (23:1/2) Wint 93, p. 75-76.
6015. SHERMAN, Alana
    "He Makes the Figs Our Mouths to Meet." [Elf] (3:1) Spr 93, p. 33.
6016. SHERMAN, Nan
    "Hospital Corridors." [OnTheBus] (6:1, #13) Wint 93-Spr 94, p. 183.
6017. SHERRARD, Philip
    "Nero's Respite" (tr. of C. P. Cavafy, w. Edmund Keeley). [QRL] (12:32/33) 93, p.
        390.
    "One of Their Gods" (tr. of C. P. Cavafy, w. Edmund Keeley). [QRL] (12:32/33) 93,
        p. 389.
    "Waiting for the Barbarians" (tr. of C. P. Cavafy, w. Edmund Keeley). [QRL]
        (12:32/33) 93, p. 388-389.
6018. SHERRILL, Steven
    "Fiddle Player Dreams of Skinks." [HayF] (13) Fall-Wint 93, p. 7.
6019. SHETTERLY, Susan Hand
    "The Owl." [BelPoJ] (43:4) Sum 93, p. 39-41.
6020. SHEVIN, David
    "Dead Horse Breeder Raises a Ruckus with a Beneficiary" (front page headline,
        Wall Street Journal). [Light] (5) Spr 93, p. 14.
    "The New Poetry." [Vis] (42) 93, p. 6.
    "Skink." [Vis] (42) 93, p. 5-6.
6021. SHI, Xiang
    "Looking up at the Moon" (in Chinese and English, tr. by Li Xi-jian and Gordon
        Osing). [PikeF] (11) Fall 93, p. 15.
6022. SHICK, Nicole Alison
    "I Geneviève Bergeron." [PraF] (14:2) Sum 93, p. 71.
    "She Said Poems." [PraF] (14:3) Aut 93, p. 130-132.
    "Your milkyeyed glance." [PraF] (14:2) Sum 93, p. 72.
6023. SHIELDS, Bill
    "A Ghost Poem." [Pearl] (17) Spr 93, p. 69.
    "Ghost Poem for Blacky Hix." [Pearl] (17) Spr 93, p. 69.
    "I Had to Pull the Car Over & Swallow Smoke." [NewYorkQ] (51) 93, p. 60.
    "King Maggot." [ChironR] (12:3, #36) Aut 93, p. 31.
    "Please." [NewYorkQ] (50) 93, p. 74.
    "PTSD." [ChironR] (12:1, #34) Spr 93, p. 13.
6024. SHIKISHI, Princess
    "A 100-Poem Sequence" (tr. by Hiroaki Sato). [Sulfur] (33) Fall 93, p. 58-66.
6025. SHIN, Taechol
    "Punishment" (A Series of Four Poems, tr. by Edward W. Poitras). [ChiR] (39:3/4)
        93, p. 248-250.
6026. SHINDER, Jason
    "Dark Palace" (Gables Theater, Merrick, New York). [Agni] (38) 93, p. 72-74.
    "Love Like a Wolf." [GrahamHR] (17) Fall 93, p. 106.
6027. SHIPPY, Peter Jay
    "Her Planet." [Epoch] (42:2) 93, p. 204-205.
    "Pills for Split Seconds." [DenQ] (27:3) Wint 93, p. 63.
6028. SHIRAISHI, Kazuko
    "The Touched, Loonies, Full Moon" (tr. by Leith Morton). [ChiR] (39:3/4) 93, p.
        206-210.

6029. SHOAF, Diann Blakely
"Corpuscles." [CimR] (102) Ja 93, p. 77.
"Medusa." [Verse] (10:2) Sum 93, p. 54.
6030. SHOLL, Betsy
"Babysitting to Thelonious Monk." [BelPoJ] (44:2) Wint 93-94, p. 20-21.
"Different Porches." [BelPoJ] (44:2) Wint 93-94, p. 22-23.
"Festival in the Park." [MissouriR] (16:3) 93, p. 172-173.
"A Kind of Darkness." [MissouriR] (16:3) 93, p. 174-175.
"Neon Jesus." [MissouriR] (16:3) 93, p. 171.
"The Rim" (for J). [MissouriR] (16:3) 93, p. 178-179.
"With You in the Darkness" (G.W., 1945-1977). [MissouriR] (16:3) 93, p. 176-177.
6031. SHOMER, Enid
"Elegy and Rant for My Father." [Poetry] (162:1) Ap 93, p. 30-31.
"First Day of the Season." [TampaR] (6) Spr 93, p. 56-57.
"Global Aphasia." [Atlantic] (272:6) D 93, p. 94.
"In the Viennese Style." [Poetry] (161:5) F 93, p. 284.
6032. SHOPSIS, Mari
"Drought" (Poets of High School Age). [HangL] (63) 93, p. 84.
"Isabel" (In the spirit of Isabel Allende. Poets of High School Age). [HangL] (63)
93, p. 85-86.
"My Thoughts" (Poets of High School Age). [HangL] (63) 93, p. 86.
6033. SHORE, Jane
"Last Breath." [NewRep] (208:8) 22 F 93, p. 40.
6034. SHORE, Paul
"At the Roger Maris Museum, West Acres Mall, Fargo, North Dakota."
[HopewellR] (5) 93, p. 48.
"Reliquary: Trnava." [HopewellR] (5) 93, p. 48.
6035. SHORT, Gary
"Junk Cars: Mina, Nevada." [OnTheBus] (5:2, #12) Sum-Fall 93, p. 188.
"A New Kind of Delicate." [LaurelR] (27:2) Sum 93, p. 64-65.
"Salt" (First Place, annual Paintbrush Award, 1993). [PaintedHR] (10) Fall 93, p. 5 -
6.
"Third Grade: Later in November 1963" (First Place, annual Paintbrush Award,
1993). [PaintedHR] (10) Fall 93, p. 7.
6036. SHORTEN, Richard
"A Season for Berries." [Poem] (70) N 93, p. 15.
SHOUYI, Wang
See WANG, Shouyi
6037. SHREVE, Sandy
"Walking Back to Sackville." [PottPort] (15:1) Spr-Sum 93, p. 62-63.
6038. SHU, Ting
"Missing You" (tr. by Chou Ping). [ChiR] (39:3/4) 93, p. 293.
"Resurrection" (tr. by Ginny MacKenzie and Wei Guo). [MidAR] (14:1) 93, p. 41 -
42.
6039. SHULTICE, Robert N.
"Rolling Thinking." [OnTheBus] (5:2, #12) Sum-Fall 93, p. 191.
6040. SHULTIS, Michael
"Untitled: We may not have always been masters of ourselves." [Footwork] (23) 93,
p. 122.
6041. SHULTZ, George E.
"Would I?" [Pearl] (19) Fall-Wint 93, p. 20.
6042. SHUMAKER, Peggy
"Censored." [Ploughs] (19:1) Spr 93, p. 34.
"The Day the Leaves Came." [Ploughs] (19:1) Spr 93, p. 33.
"Dust Devil." [AmerPoR] (22:5) S-O 93, p. 34.
"How They Are with Each Other, the Woman, the Man." [AmerPoR] (22:5) S-O 93,
p. 35.
"The Run of Silvers." [AmerPoR] (22:5) S-O 93, p. 35.
"Wide Icy River." [AmerPoR] (22:5) S-O 93, p. 34.
6043. SHUMATE, Kathleen
"False Dawn." [SouthernPR] (33:2) Fall 93, p. 39-42.
SHUNTARO, Tanikawa
See TANIKAWA, Shuntaro
6044. SHURIN, Aaron
"A Door." [Sulfur] (32) Spr 93, p. 135-143.
"The Self." [Conjunc] (20) 93, p. 22-24.

6045. SHUTTLE, Penelope
"Broken Bed." [Verse] (10:2) Sum 93, p. 26.
"Changing." [PoetryUSA] (25/26) 93, p. 47.
"The Demonstration." [ManhatR] (7:1) Fall 93, p. 72.
"If You Were Us, What Would You Do?" [ManhatR] (7:1) Fall 93, p. 73.
"Saying Goodbye to Sweetapple." [Verse] (10:2) Sum 93, p. 27.
"Summer Lilies." [PoetryUSA] (25/26) 93, p. 47.
"A Town I Know" (Padstow). [ManhatR] (7:1) Fall 93, p. 74.
"Travel." [Verse] (10:2) Sum 93, p. 26.
6046. SICOLI, Dan
"Spy." [SlipS] (13) 93, p. 103.
6047. SIDAROVA, Yelena
"I invoke you: our shyness and our courage, return" (tr. of Galina Gamper, w. Judy Hogan). [Elf] (3:2) Sum 93, p. 31.
6048. SIDDONS, Rebecca
"Dinner Party for One." [ApalQ] (39) 93, p. 64.
6049. SIDJAK, Dave
"Her Shapeless Ukraine." [Event] (22:2) Sum 93, p. 21-24.
"Strange Magus." [Event] (22:2) Sum 93, p. 20.
"Sunday, Thinking of What's Been Lost." [Event] (22:2) Sum 93, p. 19.
6050. SIEGEL, Joan I.
"Circulating." [LitR] (36:2) Wint 93, p. 189.
"Seascape with Beach Umbrellas." [CumbPR]] (13:1) Fall 93, p. 28.
6051. SIEGENTHALER, Peter
"Jiaohe." [Os] (37) Wint 93, p. 2.
6052. SIERRA, Sherry
"The Call." [Writer] (106:3) Mr 93, p. 26.
6053. SIEVERS, Kelly
"Cinderella, 1959." [PoetC] (24:3) Spr 93, p. 24.
6054. SIFAKIS, Michael
"Dreams II." [HarvardR] (4) Spr 93, p. 122.
6055. SIGNORELLI-PAPPAS, Rita
"The Artist's Studio." [SnailPR] (3:1) Fall-Wint 93, p. 29.
"Club Desire." [PoetL] (88:4) Wint 93-94, p. 32.
"Desdemona's Mother." [WillowR] (20) Spr 93, p. 27.
"Ghost Story." [SycamoreR] (5:1) Wint 93, p. 62.
"Lament." [SnailPR] (3:1) Fall-Wint 93, p. 28.
"Letter to Marcia." [SycamoreR] (5:1) Wint 93, p. 63.
"Palmerina." [WebR] (17) Fall 93, p. 81.
"Le Train Bleu." [PoetL] (88:4) Wint 93-94, p. 33-34.
"Venice." [SouthernHR] (27:2) Spr 93, p. 148.
"The Village of the Mermaids" (after Paul Delvaux). [CreamCR] (17:1) Spr 93, p. 88.
6056. SIGURDARDOTTIR, Steinunn
"Memories in Winter time" (tr. by Hallberg Hallmundsson). [Vis] (43) 93, p. 27-28.
6057. SIKÉLIANOS, Eléni
"A Thousand Petals Dry Under Sex's Flexed Biceps" (this whole Western scene blown out to sea). [13thMoon] (12:1/2) 93-94, p. 59-62.
6058. SIKTANC, Karel
"How a Heart Breaks" (tr. by Ellen Rosenbaum). [OxfordM] (9:1) Spr-Sum 93, p. 117-122.
6059. SILANO, Martha
"In That Other Universe." [PoetryNW] (34:1) Spr 93, p. 44.
"The Moon." [PoetryNW] (34:1) Spr 93, p. 43.
"Response to a Letter from My Ex." [PoetryNW] (34:1) Spr 93, p. 45.
6060. SILBERG, Richard
"The Crows." [AmerPoR] (22:5) S-O 93, p. 36.
"The Fields." [AmerPoR] (22:5) S-O 93, p. 36.
"For Poetry." [AmerPoR] (22:5) S-O 93, p. 36.
"Poetizing at the Med." [DenQ] (27:3) Wint 93, p. 64.
6061. SILÉN, Iván
"Maestro de Maestros" (A Luis Cernuda). [LindLM] (12:1) Mr 93, p. 10.
"Trilogía de la Maldad" (A los poetas del mundo). [LindLM] (12:1) Mr 93, p. 10.
6062. SILENTIARIUS, Paulus
"Some Amatory Epigrams from the Greek Anthology" (tr. by James Laughlin). [Sulfur] (33) Fall 93, p. 50.

SILESKY

6063. SILESKY, Barry
"Doorbell." [Boulevard] (8:1, #22) Spr 93, p. 192-193.
"Grace Street." [IllinoisR] (1:1) Fall 93, p. 40.
"Place to Hide." [IllinoisR] (1:1) Fall 93, p. 40.
"Their Stories." [OnTheBus] (5:2, #12) Sum-Fall 93, p. 192.
"Tom (d. 1990)." [PoetryE] (36) Fall 93, p. 65-66.
"Voodoo Sonata." [HeavenB] (10) Wint-Spr 93, p. 17-20.
6064. SILEX, Edgar
"Border Patrol." [SlipS] (13) 93, p. 17.
"Laughter." [SlipS] (13) 93, p. 18.
6065. SILKIN, Jon
"At the Tideland" (tr. of Tanikawa Shuntaro, w. Tomoyuki Iino). [Stand] (34:2) Spr
93, p. 23.
"At Toba Seashore" (tr. of Tanikawa Shuntaro, w. Jukio Kato). [Stand] (34:3) Sum
93, p. 50.
"For They Are Beautiful, in Many Languages." [Stand] (34:2) Spr 93, p. 22.
"The Hand's Black Hymns." [Bogg] (66) Wint 92-93, p. 11.
"The Jews in England" (for Emanuel Litvinoff). [NewL] (60:1) 93, p. 71.
"The Jews of England" (for Emanuel Litvinoff). [NewL] (60:1) 93, p. 70.
6066. SILLIMAN, Ron
"(R)" (for Lyn Hejinian — poem's title consists of an upper-case R in a circle).
[Conjunc] (21) 93, p. 166-180.
6067. SILVA, Eddie
"The Elke Sommer Story." [LullwaterR] (4:2) Spr-Sum 93, p. 106-107.
SILVA, Loreina Santos
See SANTOS SILVA, Loreina
6068. SILVA, Lynda S.
"Leaves of an Autumn Past." [Plain] (14:1) Fall 93, p. 18.
6069. SILVA, Sam
"Hog Heaven and Bum Hell." [DogRR] (12:1, #23) Spr-Sum 93, p. 8.
6070. SILVERMAN, David
"Dental." [CreamCR] (17:2) Fall 93, p. 134.
6071. SILVERMAN, Hersch
"Messiah." [Footwork] (23) 93, p. 147-148.
6072. SILVERTHORNE, Marty L.
"October Dogwood." [Pembroke] (25) 93, p. 111.
6073. SIMCOX, Helen Earle
"Watcher at the Cross." [ChrC] (110:7) 3 Mr 93, p. 228.
6074. SIMIC, A. B.
"Poets" (tr. by Richard Burns and Dasa Maric). [NoDaQ] (61:1) Wint 93, p. 174.
6075. SIMIC, Amela
"Sarajevo Sorrow" (Five Poems, tr. of Goran Simic). [Salm] (100) Fall 93, p. 98 -
101.
6076. SIMIC, Charles
"Afternoon Peace." [ArtfulD] (24/25) 93, p. 30.
"The Beggar on Houston Street." [Field] (49) Fall 93, p. 79.
"The Clocks of the Dead." [HarvardR] (4) Spr 93, p. 25.
"The Dead in Photographs." [Field] (49) Fall 93, p. 76.
"Divine Collaborator." [NewAW] (11) Sum-Fall 93, p. 12.
"Dream Avenue." [ArtfulD] (24/25) 93, p. 29.
"Evening Visitor." [ArtfulD] (24/25) 93, p. 31.
"Explaining a Few Things." [NewAW] (11) Sum-Fall 93, p. 8.
"Feast Day." [SouthernR] (29:1) Wint, Ja 93, p. 170-171.
"The Fly." [NewAW] (11) Sum-Fall 93, p. 11.
"Fresh Notions & Co." [Field] (49) Fall 93, p. 78.
"Happiness." [NewAW] (11) Sum-Fall 93, p. 10.
"Heroic Moment." [ProseP] (2) 93, p. 84.
"Hoarder of Tragedy." [Nat] (256:7) 22 F 93, p. 247.
"Late Arrival." [Poetry] (163:1) O 93, p. 9.
"Leaves." [GrandS] (12:1, #45) 93, p. 45.
"Leaves." [Harp] (287:1721) O 93, p. 31.
"The Lovers." [ProseP] (2) 93, p. 87.
"Mad Business." [YaleR] (81:3) Jl 93, p. 53.
"Madame Thebes." [NewYorker] (69:12) 10 My 93, p. 78.
"Make Yourself Invisible." [ProseP] (2) 93, p. 86.
"The Massacre of the Innocents." [Field] (49) Fall 93, p. 77.

"Men Deified Because of Their Cruelty." [SouthernR] (29:1) Wint, Ja 93, p. 171.
"Navigator." [NewEngR] (15:1) Wint 93, p. 187.
"November First." [Nat] (256:7) 22 F 93, p. 247.
"Paper Dolls Cut Out of a Newspaper." [ColR] (20:1) Spr 93, p. 58.
"Pascal's Idea." [YaleR] (81:3) Jl 93, p. 55.
"The Pleasures of Reading." [NewYorker] (69:19) 28 Je 93, p. 74.
"Psalm." [AnotherCM] (26) Fall 93, p. 147.
"A Puppet Play." [ColR] (20:1) Spr 93, p. 59.
"Read Your Fate." [NewYorker] (69:2) 1 Mr 93, p. 70.
"Reading History." [NewYorker] (69:33) 11 O 93, p. 98.
"Romantic Landscape." [Poetry] (163:1) O 93, p. 7.
"Sinister Company." [YaleR] (81:3) Jl 93, p. 56.
"Street." [NewAW] (11) Sum-Fall 93, p. 9.
"The Supreme Moment." [YaleR] (81:3) Jl 93, p. 54.
"Tattooed City." [Poetry] (163:1) O 93, p. 8.
"That Slant of Light." [NewAW] (11) Sum-Fall 93, p. 7.
"The Tower." [Agni] (38) 93, p. 17.
"Via del Tritone." [SouthernR] (29:1) Wint, Ja 93, p. 169.
"Voice from the Cage." [ProseP] (2) 93, p. 85.
"With Charles and Holly at Giubbe Rosse in Florence." [SouthernR] (29:1) Wint, Ja
    93, p. 170.
"The World." [Nat] (256:7) 22 F 93, p. 247.
6077. SIMIC, Goran
    "Sarajevo Sorrow" (Five Poems, tr. by Amela Simic). [Salm] (100) Fall 93, p. 98 -
        101.
6078. SIMMERMAN, Jim
    "Hide Away." [LaurelR] (27:2) Sum 93, p. 38-42.
    "Wheel." [LaurelR] (27:2) Sum 93, p. 38.
6079. SIMMONS, James
    "Marriage Counselling" (Herakles and Daysair). [Grain] (21:2) Sum 93, p. 85-87.
    "Years After." [US1] (28/29) 93, p. 13.
6080. SIMMONS, Jes
    "Hands." [ChangingM] (25) Wint-Spr 93, p. 27.
6081. SIMMS, Kristina
    "Brick Hunters." [Poem] (70) N 93, p. 39.
    "Convoy." [Poem] (70) N 93, p. 38.
6082. SIMON, Anne
    "Great Falls of Paterson." [BellArk] (9:2) Mr-Ap 93, p. 6.
    "Re-Creation." [BellArk] (9:2) Mr-Ap 93, p. 8.
6083. SIMON, Beth
    "She's Done It This Time." [BellR] (16:1/2) Spr-Fall 93, p. 28.
6084. SIMON, Denise K.
    "Swelter." [PoetL] (88:2) Sum 93, p. 29-30.
6085. SIMON, Jacqueline
    "Propagation." [Border] (2) Spr 93, p. 62.
6086. SIMON, John
    "A Tombstone Carved from Speech." [QRL] (12:32/33) 93, p. 513-514.
6087. SIMON, John Oliver
    "Autograph" (tr. of Francisco Hernandez). [ArtfulD] (24/25) 93, p. 40.
    "For a Lost Scarf" (to Andres Simor, tr. of Fayad Jamis). [ApalQ] (38) 92, p. 57.
    "Subjunctive." [ApalQ] (38) 92, p. 58.
    "Why So Many Forms" (tr. of Alberto Blanco). [Agni] (38) 93, p. 4.
6088. SIMON, Josef
    "Sewers (Is This How Love Dies — ?)" (tr. by Ewald Osers). [OxfordM] (9:1) Spr -
        Sum 93, p. 106-107.
6089. SIMON, Maurya
    "Banded Krait." [GeoR] (47:3) Fall 93, p. 561.
    "Last Words." [Poetry] (161:6) Mr 93, p. 338.
    "Revival." [CreamCR] (17:2) Fall 93, p. 194-195.
    "The Sea Sprite, Hermosa Beach." [Journal] (17:2) Fall-Wint 93, p. 62.
    "Shiva's Prowess." [GeoR] (47:3) Fall 93, p. 559-560.
6090. SIMON, Tracey L.
    "The Eternal City." [ApalQ] (35) 90, p. 47-48.
6091. SIMONE, Roberta
    "Clerihew Couple." [Light] (8) Wint 93, p. 15.
    "Clerihew: Jacques Derrida." [Light] (6) Sum 93, p. 14.

432

SIMONOVIC, Ifigenija Zagoricnik
   See ZAGORICNIK-SIMONOVIC, Ifigenija
6092. SIMONS, Edison
   "Mosaico II." [Os] (37) Wint 93, p. 37-38.
6093. SIMONS, Louise
   "Taking in Your Bookstore." [PaintedB] (50/51) 93, p. 54.
   "A Walk in the Woods." [PaintedB] (50/51) 93, p. 55.
6094. SIMONSUURI, Kirsti
   "Angelo Poliziano" (tr. by Jascha Kessler and the author). [SenR] (23:1/2) Wint 93,
      p. 166.
   "Mythos" (tr. by Jascha Kessler and the author). [SenR] (23:1/2) Wint 93, p. 165.
   "A Rare Book" (tr. by Jascha Kessler and the author). [SenR] (23:1/2) Wint 93, p.
      164.
6095. SIMPSON, Anne
   "Floating on a Kitchen Chair." [Grain] (21:3) Fall 93, p. 27-28.
   "Uncle Ted." [Grain] (21:3) Fall 93, p. 29.
6096. SIMPSON, Grace
   "Kansas As Metaphor." [CinPR] (24) Spr 93, p. 48-49.
6097. SIMPSON, Jamie
   "Indian Summer." [Farm] (10:1) Spr-Sum 93, p. 142.
6098. SIMPSON, Louis
   "After a Light Snowfall." [SycamoreR] (5:1) Wint 93, p. 23.
   "Moving the Walls." [QRL] (12:32/33) 93, p. 514-517.
6099. SIMPSON, Matt
   "Write Off." [Verse] (10:2) Sum 93, p. 58.
6100. SIMPSON, Richard
   "Avon Road, 7 AM." [TarRP] (33:1) Fall 93, p. 47.
   "Miles Davis." [TarRP] (33:1) Fall 93, p. 47.
6101. SIMSON, Cari
   "Who Needs Men When You've Got a Fast Car." [AnthNEW] (5) 93, p. 16.
6102. SIN, Kyong-rim
   "Revisiting a Mountain Town" (tr. by Brent Duffin, w. Yang Seung-Tai). [SpoonR]
      (18:1) Wint-Spr 93, p. 40.
6103. SINAVAIANA, Caroline
   "Ianeta's Dance." [Manoa] (5:1) Sum 93, p. 227.
   "Sa Nafanua" (for my sisters). [Manoa] (5:1) Sum 93, p. 227-228.
6104. SINE, Georgia
   "Death of a Biology Teacher." [WillowS] (31) Wint 93, p. 48-49.
6105. SINHA, Kabita
   "Curse" (tr. by Enaksi Chatterjee and Carolyne Wright). [AmerPoR] (22:4) Jl-Ag
      93, p. 27.
   "Departure" (tr. by Enaksi Chatterjee and Carolyne Wright). [AmerPoR] (22:4) Jl -
      Ag 93, p. 26.
   "The Diamond of Character" (tr. by Swapna Mitra-Banerjee and Carolyne Wright).
      [AmerPoR] (22:4) Jl-Ag 93, p. 26.
   "Eve Speaks to God" (tr. by Carolyne Wright, w. the author). [AmerV] (32) 93, p.
      45-47.
   "I Left a Long Time Back" (tr. by Carolyne Wright and Swapna Mitra-Banerjee).
      [HarvardR] (3) Wint 93, p. 97.
   "The Last Door's Name Is Sorrow" (tr. by Swapna Mitra-Banerjee and Carolyne
      Wright). [AmerPoR] (22:4) Jl-Ag 93, p. 27.
   "Last Meeting" (tr. by Enaksi Chatterjee and Carolyne Wright). [AmerPoR] (22:4)
      Jl-Ag 93, p. 26.
   "Party" (tr. by Enaksi Chatterjee and Carolyne Wright). [AmerPoR] (22:4) Jl-Ag 93,
      p. 27.
   "Waterfall" (tr. by Enaksi Chatterjee and Carolyne Wright). [AmerPoR] (22:4) Jl -
      Ag 93, p. 26.
6106. SINISGALLI, Leonardo
   "Maybe Even This Memory Is Useless" (tr. by Rina Ferrarelli). [ArtfulD] (24/25)
      93, p. 15.
6107. SINK, Susan
   "Mercy" (Silver Lake, Michigan). [ChiR] (39:2) 93, p. 20-21.
   "The Way of All the Earth." [ChiR] (39:2) 93, p. 22-23.
6108. SINNETT, Mark
   "Condensations." [AntigR] (93-94) Spr-Sum 93, p. 264.

6109. SINOPOULOS, Takis
"Origin" (tr. by James Stone). [DenQ] (28:1) Sum 93, p. 53.
6110. SIRENS, Patti
"My Grandmother Did the Polka." [PaintedHR] (8) Wint 93, p. 13-15.
6111. SIROWITZ, Hal
"The Double." [Footwork] (23) 93, p. 59.
"Let Me Die First." [HangL] (63) 93, p. 60.
"Mother Talks to the Dead." [Chelsea] (55) 93, p. 65.
"News of My Death." [HangL] (63) 93, p. 59.
"Protect Yourself." [Footwork] (23) 93, p. 59.
"Still Life." [Footwork] (23) 93, p. 59.
"Working for the Future." [Footwork] (23) 93, p. 59.
6112. SISSON, C. H.
"Eppur Si Muove." [PartR] (60:3) Sum 93, p. 421-422.
"Figure." [GrandS] (12:1, #45) 93, p. 66.
"Portrait of the Artist." [GrandS] (12:1, #45) 93, p. 67.
6113. SIT, Joanna
"The Day Old Mermaid Traded Her Fins for Feet." [Pearl] (17) Spr 93, p. 66-67.
"Treasure Island." [ContextS] (3:1) 93, p. 8-9.
6114. SITESH, Aruna
"Chilka Lake" (tr. of Shakunt Mathur, w. Arlene Zide). [Prima] (16/17) 93, p. 90-91.
"Man" (tr. of Archana Varma, w. Arlene Zide). [MalR] (102) Spr 93, p. 50-51.
6115. SITWELL, Edith
"Dirge for the New Sunrise" (Fifteen minutes past eight o'clock, on the morning of
Monday, the 6th of August, 1945). [QRL] (12:32/33) 93, p. 517-518.
6116. SKACEL, Jan
"An Examination of the Body" (tr. by Ellen Rosenbaum). [OxfordM] (9:1) Spr-Sum
93, p. 16-17.
"Sonnet About Those Who Strangled Her" (tr. by Ellen Rosenbaum). [OxfordM]
(9:1) Spr-Sum 93, p. 17.
"Sonnet on a July Night in the Highlands" (tr. by Ellen Rosenbaum). [OxfordM]
(9:1) Spr-Sum 93, p. 16.
"Time" (tr. by Ellen Rosenbaum). [OxfordM] (9:1) Spr-Sum 93, p. 16.
6117. SKARSTEDT, Sonja
"A Demolition Symphony." [PoetryC] (13:3) 93, p. 24.
"Night Ferry Intimations" (en route to Salt Spring Island, B.C.). [PoetryC] (13:3) 93,
p. 24-25.
"The Pen As Spade" (for Seamus Heaney). [PoetryC] (13:3) 93, p. 25.
6118. SKEEN, Tim
"Gameday Saturday Afternoon." [MidAR] (14:1) 93, p. 148-149.
6119. SKELTON, John
"Phyllyp Sparrowe" (Excerpt). [PoetryUSA] (25/26) 93, p. 8.
6120. SKENE, K. V.
"Anthropic Principle Revisited." [CanLit] (138/139) Fall-Wint 93, p. 90.
"Final Anthropic Principle." [CanLit] (138/139) Fall-Wint 93, p. 89-90.
"Gaia." [Quarry] (42:3) 93, p. 81.
"Honeycomb." [AntigR] (93-94) Spr-Sum 93, p. 200.
"Opium" (Parfum). [Quarry] (42:3) 93, p. 80.
"Participatory Anthropic Principle." [CanLit] (138/139) Fall-Wint 93, p. 89.
"Strong Anthropic Principle." [CanLit] (138/139) Fall-Wint 93, p. 88.
"Trellis." [AntigR] (93-94) Spr-Sum 93, p. 199.
"Trinity or Blackberry Stitch" (From "The Arran Designs"). [AntigR] (93-94) Spr -
Sum 93, p. 198.
"Weak Anthropic Principle." [CanLit] (138/139) Fall-Wint 93, p. 88.
"Zig Zag." [AntigR] (93-94) Spr-Sum 93, p. 201.
6121. SKILLMAN, Judith
"The Animals of Complicity." [CreamCR] (17:2) Fall 93, p. 164.
"Complicity." [NowestR] (31:2) 93, p. 16-17.
"Hamilton Street." [PoetC] (25:1) Fall 93, p. 5-6.
"In a Mild Autumn." [WillowS] (32) Sum 93, p. 21.
"The Strads." [SouthernPR] (33:2) Fall 93, p. 24-27.
"The Violin Mark." [NowestR] (31:2) 93, p. 18.
SKILMER, Joe E.
See NIMS, John Frederick
6122. SKINNER, Knute
"It." [NewYorkQ] (50) 93, p. 41.

6123. SKLOOT, Floyd
"Behind Gershwin's Eyes." [Iowa] (23:3) Fall 93, p. 72-74.
"Cannon Beach." [Crazy] (44) Spr 93, p. 65.
"Cape Lookout." [HarvardR] (3) Wint 93, p. 19.
"The Crossing." [PoetC] (24:3) Spr 93, p. 30-31.
"December Dawn." [VirQR] (69:2) Spr 93, p. 253-254.
"Delius & Fenby." [VirQR] (69:2) Spr 93, p. 254-256.
"The End of the Pier." [PoetC] (24:3) Spr 93, p. 28-29.
"Fires." [Iowa] (23:3) Fall 93, p. 71-72.
"Mendelssohn at Thirty-Eight." [AmerS] (62:4) Aut 93, p. 564.
"Ring of Fire." [SilverFR] (24) Wint 93, p. 3-12.
"Rue." [HarvardR] (5) Fall 93, p. 55.
"Sage." [NowestR] (31:1) 93, p. 56.
"The View." [Crazy] (44) Spr 93, p. 64.
"When We Pass." [SoDakR] (31:3) Fall 93, p. 104.
6124. SKOBLE, Martin
"Survival, It's a Gift." [HangL] (63) 93, p. 62.
6125. SKOBLOW, Jeffrey
"Mosquitos & Poison Ivy." [Drumvoices] (2:1/2) Fall-Wint 92-93, p. 134.
"Screen." [Drumvoices] (2:1/2) Fall-Wint 92-93, p. 134.
"Thelonious Dedalus." [Drumvoices] (2:1/2) Fall-Wint 92-93, p. 135.
"Threshold" (tr. by the author). [Verse] (10:3) Wint 93, p. 107.
6126. SKOYLES, John
"After Surgery." [TriQ] (88) Fall 93, p. 76-77.
6127. SKRUPSKELIS, Viktoria
"Autumn Night" (Excerpt, tr. of Judita (Judith) Vaiciunaite, w. Stuart Friebert).
[AntigR] (93-94) Spr-Sum 93, p. 188.
"Black Mirror" (tr. of Judita Vaiciunaite, w. Stuart Friebert). [ParisR] (35:128) Fall
93, p. 272-273.
"Dragonflies" (tr. of Judita Vaiciunaite, w. Stuart Friebert). [LitR] (37:1) Fall 93, p.
86.
"In Memoriam" (tr. of Judita (Judith) Vaiciunaite, w. Stuart Friebert). [AntigR] (93 -
94) Spr-Sum 93, p. 187.
"In the Hospital" (tr. of Judita Vaiciunaite, w. Stuart Friebert). [LitR] (37:1) Fall 93,
p. 86.
"September Night" (tr. of Judita Vaiciunaite, w. Stuart Friebert). [ParisR] (35:128)
Fall 93, p. 271.
"Sisters" (tr. of Judita Vaiciunaite, w. Stuart Friebert). [MalR] (102) Spr 93, p. 57.
"Sleeplessness" (tr. of Judita Vaiciunaite, w. Stuart Friebert). [ParisR] (35:128) Fall
93, p. 272.
"Spring" (tr. of Judita Vaiciunaite, w. Stuart Friebert). [ParisR] (35:128) Fall 93, p.
271.
"Vilnius. Archaeology" (tr. of Judita Vaiciunaite, w. Stuart Friebert). [ParisR]
(35:128) Fall 93, p. 273.
6128. SLACK, Ellen
"The Funeral of My Cousin Phil Maddux: Tinicum, Bucks County, in the Spring."
[PaintedB] (50/51) 93, p. 65.
6129. SLAPIKAS, Carolyn
"An Even Number." [NewYorkQ] (52) 93, p. 65.
6130. SLATER, Barbara
"The Elderly Ladies." [TickleAce] (25) Spr-Sum 93, p. 176-177.
6131. SLATER, Dashka
"What Fish Signify." [Outbr] (24) 93, p. 90.
6132. SLATER, Jeffrey
"Your Name on the AIDS Memorial Quilt." [PoetryNW] (34:3) Aut 93, p. 26-27.
6133. SLAUGHTER, William
"China Lesson." [ProseP] (2) 93, p. 88.
6134. SLAVIN, Corey
"The Real Me." [OnTheBus] (6:1, #13) Wint 93-Spr 94, p. 184-185.
6135. SLAVITT, David (David R.)
"The Book of Changes I" (Excerpt, from "The Matamorphoses, tr. of Ovid).
[Boulevard] (8:1, #22) Spr 93, p. 110-113.
"Bucolic Lines Composed en Route to Lyon's U-Pik-'em Strawberry Fields,
Creedmore, N.C." [Light] (6) Sum 93, p. 17.
"Cézanne Drawing." [PraS] (67:1) Spr 93, p. 41.
"The Emperor's Rejoinder." [Shen] (43:3) Fall 93, p. 75.

"The Greedy Man and the Envious Man" (tr. of Avianus). [GrandS] (12:1, #45) 93, p. 216.
"The Hunter and the Tiger" (tr. of Avianus). [GrandS] (12:1, #45) 93, p. 215.
"Ismene." [Shen] (43:3) Fall 93, p. 76-77.
"Lullaby." [Pequod] (35) 93, p. 157-158.
"The Metamorphoses of Ovid" (Selection: Boox IX, tr. of Ovid). [TexasR] (14:1/2) Spr-Sum 93, p. 107-108.
"Nevelson." [PaintedB] (50/51) 93, p. 46.
"The Penitent Peters" (for Paul Weiss). [SewanR] (101:1) Ja-Mr, Wint 93, p. 41-42.
"Raptures." [PraS] (67:1) Spr 93, p. 39.
"The Storm and the Jar." [Shen] (43:3) Fall 93, p. 78.
"The Tale of Myrrha" (tr. of Ovid). [GrandS] (12:3, #47) Fall 93, p. 137-143.
"Tatiana, Older." [PraS] (67:1) Spr 93, p. 40-41.
"Tiresias and Narcissus" (from "Metamorphoses," Book III, tr. of Ovid). [MichQR] (32:4) Fall 93, p. 631-637.
"Trojan Women" (Excerpt, tr. of Seneca). [Pequod] (35) 93, p. 43-46.
"The Wolf and the Kid" (tr. of Avianus). [GrandS] (12:1, #45) 93, p. 217.
6136. SLAVOVA, Snezhina
"Burgas" (tr. by Yuri Vidov Karageorge). [CimR] (102) Ja 93, p. 25.
"Parting" (tr. by Yuri Vidov Karageorge). [CimR] (102) Ja 93, p. 24.
"Plovdiv" (tr. by Yuri Vidov Karageorge). [CimR] (102) Ja 93, p. 23-24.
6137. SLOANE, David
"At Kirsanov's Burial" (tr. of Andrei Voznesensky, w. Diana Der-Hovanessian). [Vis] (42) 93, p. 34.
6138. SLOMKOWSKA, Lusia
"Cellar Dweller." [PraS] (67:3) Fall 93, p. 69-70.
"Dulcza Wielka" (a village in southern Poland that was destroyed during WWII). [PraS] (67:3) Fall 93, p. 72-73.
"For Andrzej, for Marek, for Szczepan." [PraS] (67:3) Fall 93, p. 71-72.
"Smazyna." [SpoonR] (18:1) Wint-Spr 93, p. 98-99.
"Sto Lat" (A birthday song wishing the celebrant a hundred years of life). [SpoonR] (18:1) Wint-Spr 93, p. 100.
6139. SLOSBERG, Daniel
"Beach Glass." [SoCoast] (15) Je 93, p. 12.
6140. SLOSS, Henry
"The Parthenon." [Poetry] (161:4) Ja 93, p. 217.
6141. SLOWINSKI, S.
"Penthesilea." [Sequoia] (34/35) 92-93, p. 13.
SLUYS, Sharon M. van
See Van SLUYS, Sharon M.
6142. SMAILS, William
"Seal Beach" (Selections: 4 poems). [BellArk] (9:4) Jl-Ag 93, p. 3-7.
6143. SMALLFIELD, Edward
"Firenze" (for Kathleen. Third Place, annual Paintbrush Award, 1993). [PaintedHR] (10) Fall 93, p. 11.
"Island." [Caliban] (13) 93, p. 138.
"Sleepless Nights" (for Eve). [Caliban] (13) 93, p. 136-137.
6144. SMART, Christine
"Plucked." [Grain] (21:1) Spr 93, p. 31.
"Silent Voices." [Grain] (21:1) Spr 93, p. 31.
6145. SMART, Harry
"Oisin and the Angels." [Stand] (34:2) Spr 93, p. 41.
6146. ŚMELCER, John E.
"Gambell, St. Lawrence Island." [ArtfulD] (24/25) 93, p. 73.
6147. SMIDDY, Nina
"The Chair" (for Alex). [Nimrod] (37:1) Fall-Wint 93, p. 129.
"The Christ in My Body." [AmerPoR] (22:1) Ja-F 93, p. 70.
"In Pryor, Oklahoma." [AmerPoR] (22:1) Ja-F 93, p. 71.
"The Lake." [Nimrod] (37:1) Fall-Wint 93, p. 128.
"Naked in the City Where I Honeymooned." [AmerPoR] (22:1) Ja-F 93, p. 71.
"The Pebble." [Nimrod] (37:1) Fall-Wint 93, p. 127.
"Places I've Been, Places I'm Going." [AmerPoR] (22:1) Ja-F 93, p. 71.
"Selah." [AmerPoR] (22:1) Ja-F 93, p. 70.
"Song While Bathing by the Open Window in the Country." [AmerPoR] (22:1) Ja-F 93, p. 71.

"The Weather in My Heart, the Articulate Region Where I live, the Map of the
    Rain." [AmerPoR] (22:1) Ja-F 93, p. 70.
"White" (December, 1986). [AmerPoR] (22:1) Ja-F 93, p. 70.
"The White Ship of My Heart." [AmerPoR] (22:1) Ja-F 93, p. 71.
"YMCA." [AmerPoR] (22:1) Ja-F 93, p. 71.
6148. SMITH, Alan E.
"El cuarto de vidrio." [InterPR] (19:2) Fall 93, p. 24.
"The glass room" (tr. by Mark Smith-Soto). [InterPR] (19:2) Fall 93, p. 25.
6149. SMITH, Arthur
"The River at Land's End." [NoAmR] (278:1) Ja-F 93, p. 20-21.
6150. SMITH, Barbara F.
"No Leap." [Bogg] (66) Wint 92-93, p. 66.
6151. SMITH, Beatrice
"The Five Senses of the Witness." [US1] (28/29) 93, p. 6.
6152. SMITH, Bruce
"Hostile Witness." [Agni] (37) 93, p. 145.
"Mercy." [Agni] (37) 93, p. 143.
"Scenes from a Puppet Play." [Agni] (37) 93, p. 144.
"Summer in the Crumbling State." [HarvardR] (4) Spr 93, p. 100.
6153. SMITH, Caroline
"The Magician of Cracow" (Excerpt). [Stand] (34:2) Spr 93, p. 20-21.
6154. SMITH, Charlie
"At the Hour of Our Birth." [AmerPoR] (22:3) My-Je 93, p. 23.
"The Bad Daughter." [AmerPoR] (22:3) My-Je 93, p. 23.
"Belief." [Field] (49) Fall 93, p. 50.
"The Business." [NewEngR] (15:4) Fall 93, p. 73.
"By-Laws." [NewEngR] (15:4) Fall 93, p. 72.
"The Children's House." [WillowS] (31) Wint 93, p. 71-72.
"The Chinese New Year." [ParisR] (35:126) Spr 93, p. 258-259.
"Defiance." [NewYorker] (69:5) 22 Mr 93, p. 70.
"The Distance." [Field] (49) Fall 93, p. 51.
"The Family Plot." [NewYorker] (69:43) 20 D 93, p. 124.
"Kiss of the Moon." [WillowS] (31) Wint 93, p. 69.
"The Missing." [ChatR] (14:1) Fall 93, p. 58.
"Natural History." [Pequod] (35) 93, p. 119-124.
"Off Season Repairs." [WillowS] (31) Wint 93, p. 70.
"The Sentinel." [NewYorker] (68:51) 8 F 93, p. 94.
"To Lautréamont." [ParisR] (35:126) Spr 93, p. 257-258.
"The Voice." [NewEngR] (15:4) Fall 93, p. 71.
"The White City." [Nat] (256:8) 1 Mr 93, p. 282.
"Wisdom." [NewEngR] (15:4) Fall 93, p. 73-74.
6155. SMITH, Christopher
"The Man Writes, the Woman Listens." [BellArk] (9:5) S-O 93, p. 10.
"To an Old Woman Walking." [BellArk] (9:5) S-O 93, p. 11.
6156. SMITH, Dave
"Crab." [NewEngR] (15:1) Wint 93, p. 188-191.
6157. SMITH, David-Glen
"A Different Landscape." [SpoonR] (18:2) Sum-Fall 93, p. 87-89.
"The Myth of Memory." [ChatR] (14:1) Fall 93, p. 60-61.
"You, in Darkness." [JamesWR] (10:3) Spr 93, p. 14.
6158. SMITH, Douglas Burnet
"Duck-Hooks and Slices: Hazards, Handicaps, Poetry." [Event] (22:1) Spr 93, p. 17 -
    19.
6159. SMITH, Ed
"For the David Murray Octet." [Talisman] (10) Spr 93, p. 158.
"There's Nothing Left in Your File." [Footwork] (23) 93, p. 107.
"The Wind." [Talisman] (10) Spr 93, p. 158.
6160. SMITH, Ellen
"A Parisian Dinner." [ProseP] (1) 92, p. 72.
"Truce." [Pearl] (19) Fall-Wint 93, p. 10.
6161. SMITH, Francis J.
"The Cardinal." [Light] (5) Spr 93, p. 7.
6162. SMITH, Gary
"Fifth Avenue Uptown: James Baldwin, 1924-1987." [AfAmRev] (27:4) Wint 93, p.
    635-638.

437

SMITH

6163. SMITH, Iain Crichton
"Conversion." [Stand] (34:2) Spr 93, p. 54-62.
SMITH, James Sutherland
See SUTHERLAND-SMITH, James
6164. SMITH, Joan Jobe
"Heartthrobs." [ChironR] (12:1, #34) Spr 93, p. 41.
"Purple Hearts." [ChironR] (12:3, #36) Aut 93, p. 11.
6165. SMITH, John
"Cicada." [Footwork] (23) 93, p. 85.
"Judas." [NewYorkQ] (52) 93, p. 95-96.
"The Loved Ones" (a lithograph by Eng Tay). [US1] (28/29) 93, p. 24.
"The Original Tree." [LitR] (37:1) Fall 93, p. 107.
"Ticks." [JlNJPo] (15:2) Aut 93, p. 10.
6166. SMITH, Jonathan
"Notes on a Disremembered Past." [RiverS] (38) 93, p. 87.
6167. SMITH, Jules
"Carnivore Currency." [Pearl] (17) Spr 93, p. 92.
"The History of Shaving." [Pearl] (17) Spr 93, p. 92.
6168. SMITH, Ken
"Johannes from Dresden." [Stand] (34:2) Spr 93, p. 6.
6169. SMITH, Kevin J.
"War Is Hell." [ChironR] (12:1, #34) Spr 93, p. 15.
6170. SMITH, Kirsten
"The Architect's Daughter" (for Kelli Thomas). [HayF] (13) Fall-Wint 93, p. 8.
"The Couple Inside of You." [PoetL] (88:4) Wint 93-94, p. 23.
6171. SMITH, Lawrence R.
"Bivouac" (tr. of Yang Mu, w. Michelle Yeh). [Caliban] (13) 93, p. 118.
"Footsteps" (tr. of Yang Mu, w. Michelle Yeh). [Caliban] (13) 93, p. 117.
"News" (tr. of Yang Mu, w. Michelle Yeh). [Caliban] (13) 93, p. 118.
"The Woman in Black" (tr. of Yang Mu, w. Michelle Yeh). [Caliban] (13) 93, p. 119.
6172. SMITH, Michael S.
"Civil Obedience." [Plain] (14:1) Fall 93, p. 17.
"Feline Mediator." [Hellas] (4:1) Spr 93, p. 26.
"Fourth of July Heritage Festival." [Border] (2) Spr 93, p. 63.
"Halloween." [Plain] (13:2) Wint 93, p. 13.
"Last Will." [SpoonR] (18:2) Sum-Fall 93, p. 37.
"Love's Mileposts." [Footwork] (23) 93, p. 97.
"Nothing to Crow About." [Hellas] (4:1) Spr 93, p. 27.
"The Old Ball Game." [Footwork] (23) 93, p. 97.
"Sententious Blather in the Boneyard." [SpoonR] (18:2) Sum-Fall 93, p. 36.
"Spectator Sport." [BellR] (16:1/2) Spr-Fall 93, p. 58.
"What'll You Give Me For It?" [Sequoia] (34/35) 92-93, p. 98.
6173. SMITH, Noel
"Hiking." [Blueline] (14) 93, p. 31.
6174. SMITH, R. T.
"Black Shawl." [GettyR] (6:4) Aut 93, p. 579.
"Crockett in the Mountains." [Pembroke] (25) 93, p. 100-101.
"Early Daffodils" (For Debora). [Elf] (3:1) Spr 93, p. 26-27.
"The Evidence Suggests She Was Never a Slave." [Crucible] (29) Fall 93, p. 3.
"Fire Blight." [SycamoreR] (5:1) Wint 93, p. 20-22.
"Kilcoolie Fern." [FreeL] (12) Sum 93, p. 20-22.
"Lithograph" (Literary Contest Winner, 1st Prize). [Crucible] (29) Fall 93, p. 1-2.
"Lucia." [GettyR] (6:4) Aut 93, p. 580-582.
"Mist Net." [CimR] (103) Ap 93, p. 100-101.
"Optics." [LullwaterR] (4:2) Spr-Sum 93, p. 62-63.
"Rape Honey." [FreeL] (12) Sum 93, p. 22.
"Rescue." [Elf] (3:1) Spr 93, p. 28-29.
"Strolling Down St. Dominic Hill." [ApalQ] (35) 90, p. 32-33.
"Walter Anderson in Mississippi." [LullwaterR] (4:2) Spr-Sum 93, p. 13-15.
6175. SMITH, Robert L.
"Final Exam." [WormR] (33:4, #132) 93, p. 162-163.
"Nineteen Urn-Thoughts." [WormR] (33:4, #132) 93, p. 161-162.
6176. SMITH, Russell
"First" (Selections: I, VI, XX, XXIX, tr. of Paul Eluard). [Quarry] (42:1) 93, p. 121-123.

6177. SMITH, S. Random
"The Preacher Prays Silently at the Potluck Social." [PoetC] (24:2) Wint 93, p. 32.
6178. SMITH, Shannon
"For the Woman in the Bookstore." [NewYorkQ] (52) 93, p. 94.
"From Rodin's Nightmare of Camille 1917." [InterPR] (19:2) Fall 93, p. 71-72.
6179. SMITH, Susannah
"After the Funeral." [Dandel] (20:1) 93, p. 11-12.
6180. SMITH, Thomas R.
"Grass Growing from a White Pine Stump." [ProseP] (2) 93, p. 90.
"March Wind." [NorthStoneR] (11) 93, p. 18.
"Michael Kincaid's Kitchen." [NorthStoneR] (11) 93, p. 18.
"The Muskie." [CreamCR] (17:2) Fall 93, p. 176.
"Windy Day at Kabekona." [ProseP] (2) 93, p. 89.
6181. SMITH, Todd
"Crossing." [Verse] (10:1) Spr 93, p. 41.
"Love in the Time of Menopause." [Verse] (10:1) Spr 93, p. 40.
6182. SMITH, Tom
"Jack's Beans: A Five-Year Diary" (Selections: 4 poems). [BelPoJ] (44:1) Fall 93, p.
27-33.
"Shelters" (A page of *Jack's Beans: A Five-Year Diary* — August 5). [JamesWR]
(10:4) Sum 93, p. 15.
"Spring Rain" (*Jack's Beans: A Five-Year Diary* — stanzas from April 1952).
[JamesWR] (10:4) Sum 93, p. 15.
"A Winking Eye" (From *Jack's Beans: A Five-Year Diary* — July 14-19, 1953).
[JamesWR] (10:4) Sum 93, p. 15.
6183. SMITH, William D.
"The Broken Vacation." [Footwork] (23) 93, p. 100.
6184. SMITH-SOTO, Mark
"The glass room" (tr. of Alan E. Smith). [InterPR] (19:2) Fall 93, p. 25.
6185. SMITS, Ronald (Ronald F.)
"Agent." [ColEng] (55:5) S 93, p. 533.
"Genu." [PoetryE] (36) Fall 93, p. 14.
"Vision." [Elf] (3:2) Sum 93, p. 42.
6186. SMOCK, Frederick
"I am in matters of love." [PoetryE] (36) Fall 93, p. 105.
"Tender death." [PoetryE] (36) Fall 93, p. 105.
"The thief eschews the dark." [PoetryE] (36) Fall 93, p. 106.
"Under moonlight, & birdbath." [PoetryE] (36) Fall 93, p. 106.
6187. SMUKLER, Linda
"I Came." [13thMoon] (12:1/2) 93-94, p. 63.
"Radio." [ProseP] (2) 93, p. 91.
6188. SMYTH, Jacqui
"Night Mirror." [AntigR] (92) Wint 93, p. 44.
6189. SNEEDEN, Ralph
"The Overgrown Cranberry Bog." [HayF] (13) Fall-Wint 93, p. 20.
6190. SNEYD, Steve
"De Bello Civile." [Bogg] (66) Wint 92-93, p. 26.
6191. SNIDER, Clifton
"The Necessary Sting." [Pearl] (19) Fall-Wint 93, p. 9.
"Negative." [Pearl] (17) Spr 93, p. 9.
"Survivor." [Pearl] (17) Spr 93, p. 8.
6192. SNIDER, Kat
"How to Get a Man." [SlipS] (13) 93, p. 7-8.
6193. SNIVELY, Susan
"Another Life." [Ploughs] (19:4) Wint 93-94, p. 82.
"The Speed of the Drift" (Selections: 2 poems). [Shen] (43:3) Fall 93, p. 44-45.
6194. SNODGRASS, Ann
"Seasonal." [Ploughs] (19:1) Spr 93, p. 32.
6195. SNODGRASS, K. B.
"An Evening with the Author" (tr. of Leszek Szaruga, w. W.D. Snodgrass, Justyna
Kostkowska and Peter Lengyel). [Salm] (97) Wint 93, p. 111.
"Watchman" (for Zbigniew Herbert, tr. of Leszek Szaruga, w. W.D. Snodgrass,
Justyna Kostkowska and Peter Lengyel). [Salm] (97) Wint 93, p. 110.
6196. SNODGRASS, W. D.
"The Ballad of Jesse Helms" (Expletives Deleted and Self-CENSORED).
[HarvardR] (3) Wint 93, p. 117-119.

439

"The Convicted" (tr. of Marin Sorescu, w. Dona Rosu & Luciana Costea). [Salm] (98/99] Spr-Sum 93, p. 81.
"An Evening with the Author" (tr. of Leszek Szaruga, w. K.B. Snodgrass, Justyna Kostkowska and Peter Lengyel). [Salm] (97) Wint 93, p. 111.
"A Flat One." [QRL] (12:32/33) 93, p. 518-521.
"Fortress" (tr. of Marin Sorescu, w. Dona Rosu & Luciana Costea). [Salm] (98/99] Spr-Sum 93, p. 82.
"Frames" (tr. of Marin Sorescu, w. Dona Rosu & Luciana Costea). [Salm] (98/99] Spr-Sum 93, p. 83.
"In Flower" (2 poems: iv. Dandelions, v. Narcissus). [SouthernR] (29:1) Wint, Ja 93, p. 159-160.
"Watchman" (for Zbigniew Herbert, tr. of Leszek Szaruga, w. K.B. Snodgrass, Justyna Kostkowska and Peter Lengyel). [Salm] (97) Wint 93, p. 110.
6197. SNOW, Carol
"Mask Series." [DenQ] (28:2) Fall 93, p. 20-22.
6198. SNOW, Sandra
"The Voyeur." [Plain] (13:2) Wint 93, p. 15.
6199. SNYDER, Gary
"Afloat." [GrandS] (12:1, #45) 93, p. 147-149.
"Steak." [Tricycle] (2:3) Spr 93, p. 30-31.
"Uluru Wild Fig Song." [Zyzzyva] (9:3) Fall 93, p. 122.
"Under the Hills Near the Morava River." [Sulfur] (33) Fall 93, p. 79.
6200. SNYDER, Jennifer
"Train." [AmerPoR] (22:4) Jl-Ag 93, p. 48.
SNYDER, Kaye Bache
See BACHE-SNYDER, Kaye
6201. SÔ, Chôngju
"Autumn Songs" (1 poem, tr. by David R. McCann). [QRL] (12:32/33) 93, p. 309.
"Conversation with Parnassus" (tr. by David R. McCann). [QRL] (12:32/33) 93, p. 312-313.
"Kilimanjaro's Self-Introduction" (tr. by David R. McCann). [QRL] (12:32/33) 93, p. 310-311.
"Mountain Poem of Korea" (tr. by David R. McCann). [QRL] (12:32/33) 93, p. 313-314.
"Poem of Puu Kalena, Hawaiian Mountain Goddess" (tr. by David R. McCann). [QRL] (12:32/33) 93, p. 311-312.
"Spring Songs" (3 poems, tr. by David R. McCann). [QRL] (12:32/33) 93, p. 307-308.
"Story from the Mountains of North Carolina" (tr. by David R. McCann). [QRL] (12:32/33) 93, p. 312.
"Summer Songs" (2 poems, tr. by David R. McCann). [QRL] (12:32/33) 93, p. 308-309.
"Winter Songs" (2 poems, tr. by David R. McCann). [QRL] (12:32/33) 93, p. 309-310.
6202. SOBELMAN, 'Annah
"I Am the No and the Yes." [AntR] (51:1) Wint 93, p. 84.
"Jesus Considers the Night." [ApalQ] (39) 93, p. 56-58.
"The Physics of Desire, As a Milky Thing, Categories." [DenQ] (28:1) Sum 93, p. 54.
6203. SOBIN, Anthony
"Beast." [WillowS] (31) Wint 93, p. 84.
"Problems in Painting: Spring Landscape with Melting Snow." [LitR] (36:2) Wint 93, p. 190.
6204. SOBIN, Gustaf
"Anguish & Metaphor." [Talisman] (10) Spr 93, p. 47.
"Article of Faith." [Talisman] (10) Spr 93, p. 45.
"The Death of Flash-Back." [Talisman] (10) Spr 93, p. 48-49.
"Idiom." [Talisman] (10) Spr 93, p. 46.
"On the Nature of the Iconic." [Talisman] (10) Spr 93, p. 50-51.
"Orpheus Semantic." [DenQ] (28:1) Sum 93, p. 55-57.
6205. SOBSEY, Cynthia
"This Is Our Address." [DogRR] (12:2, #24) Fall-Wint 93, p. 6.
SOCAS, Olga Torres
See TORRES SOCAS, Olga
6206. SOCOLOW, Elizabeth Anne
"Another Conversation with the Beloved." [MichQR] (32:1) Wint 93, p. 109.

440

SOCOLOW

"On Leaving the Big A." [US1] (28/29) 93, p. 4.
6207. SODEN, Christopher S. (Christopher Stephen)
"Rock a Bye." [JamesWR] (11:1) Fall 93, p. 13.
"Shiva." [JamesWR] (10:2) Wint 93, p. 16.
6208. SOFER, Andrew
"The Anatomy of Whales." [PoetL] (88:2) Sum 93, p. 34.
"Baxter State Park, 1975." [PoetL] (88:2) Sum 93, p. 31-32.
"Boarding School Sestina." [PoetL] (88:2) Sum 93, p. 35-36.
"Out of Earshot." [PoetL] (88:2) Sum 93, p. 33.
6209. SOFRANKO, Michael
"My Father's Poker Game." [GreensboroR] (55) Wint 93-94, p. 32-33.
"The Swamp Song." [GreensboroR] (55) Wint 93-94, p. 34.
6210. SOIFER, Mark
"Miracle" (from *The City of Wires*). [Parting] (6:2) Wint 93, p. 9.
6211. SOL, Adam
"45 Assertions." [Caliban] (13) 93, p. 110-111.
"Honey and Plaster." [PikeF] (11) Fall 93, p. 35.
6212. SOLDAINI, Antonella
"Other Nights" (tr. of Anna Lombardo, w. Jack Hirschman). [Arshile] (2) 93, p. 55,
57.
6213. SOLDOFSKY, Alan
"Inventory." [CreamCR] (17:1) Spr 93, p. 32.
6214. SOLE, Kelwyn
"Pillow." [BostonR] (18:3/4) Je-Ag 93, p. 33.
6215. SOLHEIM, James
"Beowulf in Utopia." [LaurelR] (27:1) Wint 93, p. 62-63.
"A Jar of Teeth." [LaurelR] (27:1) Wint 93, p. 64.
"Just Grass: a Prairie Walk." [LaurelR] (27:1) Wint 93, p. 60-62.
"Wrassler Céleste." [LaurelR] (27:1) Wint 93, p. 63.
"Yak" (Selections: Books 4-6). [AnotherCM] (25) Spr 93, p. 170-177.
6216. SOLJAK, Katie
"Sex Fo' Sale." [Pearl] (19) Fall-Wint 93, p. 71-72.
6217. SOLLORS, David Morgan
"Epithalamion" (Wedding Song — For my father). [HangL] (62) 93, p. 88-90.
"The Son of the Muse Plays a Maccaferri" (Poets of High School Age). [HangL]
(62) 93, p. 87.
6218. SOLOMON, Marvin
"AIDS." [Poetry] (162:1) Ap 93, p. 23.
"Aunt Mad." [SmPd] (30:3, #89) Fall 93, p. 26.
"Bloomsburyday." [WormR] (33:4, #132) 93, p. 173.
"Bruises." [PoetL] (88:3) Fall 93, p. 23-24.
"Deep Night." [SouthernPR] (33:1) Spr 93, p. 21-22.
"The Divine Sarah." [Poetry] (162:1) Ap 93, p. 21.
"The Existentialist." [WormR] (33:4, #132) 93, p. 173.
"Fellini y Yo." [PoetL] (88:3) Fall 93, p. 25-26.
"The Mag." [Interim] (12:2) Fall-Wint 93, p. 8-9.
"Nijinsky's Solo." [Poetry] (162:1) Ap 93, p. 22.
"Some Things My Father Liked." [Poetry] (161:5) F 93, p. 271-272.
"South and North." [Wind] (23:72) 93, p. 28.
"Timeclock." [Wind] (23:72) 93, p. 28-29.
"Variation and Centrifuge on 'No Love, No Nothin" (or, Cole Porter, Ethel
Merman, Where Are You?)." [SmPd] (30:1, #87) Wint 93, p. 21.
6219. SOLOMON, Sandy
"Return." [NewYorker] (68:52) 15 F 93, p. 81.
"Tidal Basin, Washington, D.C." [SouthernR] (29:2) Spr, Ap 93, p. 316-317.
6220. SOLOMON, Suzanne A.
"Indicia of Madness." [NewYorkQ] (51) 93, p. 59.
6221. SOLONCHE, J. R.
"At the Reflecting Pool." [AmerLC] (5) 93, p. 102.
6222. SOLWAY, David
"The Ruins of Phylakopi." [CanLit] (136) Spr 93, p. 79.
"Windsurfing." [CanLit] (136) Spr 93, p. 112-113.
6223. SOLZHENITSYN, Alexander
"A Campfire and Ants" (tr. by John M. Gogol). [QRL] (12:32/33) 93, p. 521-522.
6224. SOMMERSTEIN, Carly
"East Side Friday Evening." [13thMoon] (11:1/2) 93, p. 74.

6225. SONDE, Susan
"Ghostbusters." [AnotherCM] (26) Fall 93, p. 148-149.
"Up Periscope." [OnTheBus] (5:2, #12) Sum-Fall 93, p. 197.
6226. SONG, Cathy
"Old Story." [CreamCR] (17:1) Spr 93, p. 74-75.
"Sunworshippers." [Poetry] (162:6) S 93, p. 331-332.
"Vasectomy." [MichQR] (32:4) Fall 93, p. 619-620.
6227. SONG, Lin
"Diminuendo" (from the cycle "For My Unborn Son," tr. by Ko Kooman, from the
    Dutch version by Maghiel van Crevel). [GreenMR] (NS 6:2) Sum-Fall 93, p.
    144.
"A Hymn to X" (tr. by Dian Li). [GreenMR] (NS 6:2) Sum-Fall 93, p. 146.
"My Seventh Winter in Shanghai" (tr. by Dian Li). [GreenMR] (NS 6:2) Sum-Fall
    93, p. 147.
"Paul Celan in the Seine" (from the cycle "For My Unborn Son," tr. by Ko Kooman,
    from the Dutch version by Maghiel van Crevel). [GreenMR] (NS 6:2) Sum-
    Fall 93, p. 145.
6228. SONIAT, Katherine
"Cloister." [QW] (37) Sum-Fall 93, p. 103.
"A Country Grandson, 1920." [QW] (37) Sum-Fall 93, p. 104-105.
"Eddying." [PraS] (67:3) Fall 93, p. 153.
"Forecast: New Orleans." [Shen] (43:1) Spr 93, p. 86.
"Graffiti." [HampSPR] Wint 93, p. 25.
"Harboring." [SouthernR] (29:4) Aut, O 93, p. 764-765.
"Hydra." [PraS] (67:3) Fall 93, p. 154.
"Land Lights: New Orleans." [ChiR] (39:1) 93, p. 77-78.
"Marks of Light." [Iowa] (23:1) Wint 93, p. 22-24.
"Patience." [Thrpny] (55) Fall 93, p. 19.
"Peter." [PraS] (67:3) Fall 93, p. 151-152.
"Selvage." [PraS] (67:3) Fall 93, p. 150-151.
"The Spring House." [Iowa] (23:1) Wint 93, p. 21.
"Wanting It." [HampSPR] Wint 93, p. 25.
6229. SONIK, Madeline
"The Crush." [AntigR] (95) Aut 93, p. 143.
6230. SONNEVI, Göran
"Fagerfjäll, Tjörn, 1986. For Pentti" (tr. by Rika Lesser). [Pequod] (35) 93, p. 26-27.
"From Small Chimes, One voice" (Selections: VI-VII, tr. by John Matthais). [Vis]
    (43) 93, p. 52.
"From the cliff at the foot of Skull Mountain" (tr. by Rika Lesser). [Pequod] (35) 93,
    p. 24-25.
"Mourning Cloak" (tr. by Rika Lesser). [Pequod] (35) 93, p. 28-31.
"Mozart Variations" (2 & 3, tr. by John Matthais and Goran Printz-Pahlson). [Vis]
    (42) 93, p. 23.
SORALUZ, Luis Rebaza
    See REBAZA-SORALUZ, Luis
6231. SORBY, Angela
"Doing Theory." [13thMoon] (11:1/2) 93, p. 76.
"Gossip." [PoetC] (24:3) Spr 93, p. 10.
"That May There Were Alligators in Green Lake." [13thMoon] (11:1/2) 93, p. 75.
6232. SORCIC, Jim
"Ten Reasons Why I Never Made Love to Your Mouth." [YellowS] (43) Fall 93, p.
    9.
"Up All Night." [YellowS] (43) Fall 93, p. 8.
"Walking In, Watching You." [YellowS] (43) Fall 93, p. 8.
6233. SORENSEN, Sally Jo
"The Blend." [Poem] (70) N 93, p. 21.
"A House, and the Fields Beyond." [Poem] (70) N 93, p. 20.
"Incoming." [PoetL] (88:4) Wint 93-94, p. 10.
"Middle Lake." [PaintedB] (50/51) 93, p. 60.
"Mistletoe Tea." [PoetL] (88:4) Wint 93-94, p. 9.
"Somewhere on the Edge of a Field and the Woods." [PoetL] (88:4) Wint 93-94, p.
    11.
6234. SORESCU, Marin
"The Arrow" (tr. by Adriana Varga and Stuart Friebert). [Field] (48) Spr 93, p. 45.
"The Convicted" (tr. by W.D. Snodgrass, w. Dona Rosu & Luciana Costea). [Salm]
    (98/99) Spr-Sum 93, p. 81.

442

SORESCU

"Fortress" (tr. by W.D. Snodgrass, w. Dona Rosu & Luciana Costea). [Salm] (98/99] Spr-Sum 93, p. 82.
"Frames" (tr. by W.D. Snodgrass, w. Dona Rosu & Luciana Costea). [Salm] (98/99] Spr-Sum 93, p. 83.
"Innocence" (tr. by Adriana Varga and Stuart Friebert). [Field] (48) Spr 93, p. 47.
"Sin" (tr. by Adriana Varga and Stuart Friebert). [Field] (48) Spr 93, p. 46.
6235. SORKIN, Adam (Adam J.)
"31 August 1986, 12:28 A.M. (Earthquake Time)" (tr. of Gabriel Chifu, w. Taina Dutescu-Coliban). [IndR] (16:2) Fall 93, p. 82.
"Almost Domestic" (tr. of Adrian Popescu, w. M. A. Irimia). [TampaR] (6) Spr 93, p. 10.
"Anamorphosis" (tr. of Denisa Comanescu, w. Angela Jianu). [Kalliope] (15:2) 93, p. 18.
"Atlas" (tr. of Denisa Comanescu, w. Angela Jianu). [Kalliope] (15:2) 93, p. 16.
"Audio" (tr. of Ioana Ieronim). [Vis] (41) 93, p. 5.
"Circles" (tr. of Lucian Vasiliu, w. the author). [Vis] (43) 93, p. 46.
"Contre Jour" (tr. of Liliana Ursu, w. the author). [Vis] (43) 93, p. 47.
"Drawing Close" (tr. of Gabriel Chifu, w. Taina Dutescu-Coliban). [IndR] (16:2) Fall 93, p. 84.
"Efficiency, Ecstasy" (tr. of Daniela Crasnaru). [AntigR] (93-94) Spr-Sum 93, p. 227.
"Elves" (tr. of Adrian Popescu, w. M. A. Irimia). [TampaR] (6) Spr 93, p. 11.
"Emigration" (tr. of Ioana Ieronim, w. the author). [Vis] (43) 93, p. 48.
"An Immense Hand" (tr. of Magda Carneci, w. the author). [Vis] (43) 93, p. 49.
"Impoverished Land" (tr. of Denisa Comanescu, w. Angela Jianu). [Kalliope] (15:2) 93, p. 16.
"Leaving Port" (tr. of Denisa Comanescu, w. Angela Jianu). [Kalliope] (15:2) 93, p. 16.
"Pieta" (tr. of Anna Blandiana, w. Ioana Ieronim). [Vis] (41) 93, p. 39.
"Prologue to the Book" (tr. of Bogdan Ghiu, w. the author). [Vis] (43) 93, p. 50.
"Seven Lean Cows" (tr. of Aurel Rau, w. Liviu Bleoca). [LullwaterR] (4:2) Spr-Sum 93, p. 12.
"Sign" (tr. of Aurel Rau, w. Liviu Bleoca). [LullwaterR] (4:2) Spr-Sum 93, p. 123.
"Stubborn" (tr. of Gabriel Chifu, w. Taina Dutescu-Coliban). [IndR] (16:2) Fall 93, p. 83.
"Writing with a Feather" (tr. of Aurel Rau, w. the author). [Vis] (43) 93, p. 49.
"Under the Lens" (tr. of Daniela Crasnaru). [AntigR] (93-94) Spr-Sum 93, p. 228.
"Unforgiving Joy" (tr. of Denisa Comanescu, w. Angela Jianu). [Kalliope] (15:2) 93, p. 17.
"Your Thing" (tr. of Lucian Vasiliu, w. the author). [Vis] (43) 93, p. 46.
6236. SORNBERGER, Judith
"Artemisia's Women" (from the paintings of Artemisia Gentileschi, 1593-1652). [AmerV] (31) 93, p. 105-107.
"Dividing the Dolls." [Calyx] (14:3) Sum 93, p. 6-8.
"Fire and Ice." [Calyx] (15:1) Wint 93-94, p. 54-55.
"Mother-in-Law." [Calyx] (15:1) Wint 93-94, p. 56-57.
"The Olson Women and their Hair." [Calyx] (14:3) Sum 93, p. 9-11.
"Woman Alone Under the Lunar Eclipse." [Calyx] (14:3) Sum 93, p. 5.
6237. SORNBERGER, Lisa
"Chest X-Ray." [NewYorkQ] (52) 93, p. 97.
6238. SORRENTINO, Gilbert
"Bliss." [Arshile] (2) 93, p. 33.
"By Degrees Weary." [Arshile] (2) 93, p. 30.
"Depression Canzone." [Arshile] (1) Spr 93, p. 35-36.
"Habituation." [Arshile] (2) 93, p. 31.
"Performance of Music." [Arshile] (2) 93, p. 32.
6239. SOSNORA, Viktor
"Autumn in Mikhailovskoye" (in Russian and English, tr. by Dean Furbish). [InterPR] (19:1) Spr 93, p. 34-39.
"The ear no longer hears the echo" (in Russian and English, tr. by Dean Furbish). [InterPR] (19:1) Spr 93, p. 26-29.
"September" (in Russian and English, tr. by Dean Furbish). [InterPR] (19:1) Spr 93, p. 30-33.
"Winter Road" (in Russian and English, tr. by Dean Furbish). [InterPR] (19:1) Spr 93, p. 40-41.

6240. SOSNOWSKI, David
"Openers." [Confr] (51) Sum 93, p. 255.
6241. SOTERES, Peter
"The Immigrant Voyeur." [LitR] (37:1) Fall 93, p. 42.
6242. SOTO, Gary
"A Better View." [ColR] (20:2) Fall 93, p. 99-100.
"Dare." [RiverS] (38) 93, p. 1.
"Dizzy Girls from the '60s." [OntR] (38) Spr-Sum 93, p. 102-103.
"Industry." [IllinoisR] (1:1) Fall 93, p. 31.
"Planet News." [ColR] (20:2) Fall 93, p. 101-102.
"Probability." [BlackWR] (20:1) Fall-Wint 93, p. 20.
"Prof with Both Hands on the Rail." [ColR] (20:2) Fall 93, p. 103-104.
"Que Pretty In Tejas" (para Sandra). [Nat] (256:18) 10 My 93, p. 644.
"Saturday in Chinatown." [OntR] (38) Spr-Sum 93, p. 101-102.
"Sizing Up a Marriage." [Poetry] (162:4) Jl 93, p. 204-205.
"Some Coins." [Nat] (257:18) 29 N 93, p. 672.
"Summer Marriage" (For Jon Veinberg). [Poetry] (162:4) Jl 93, p. 203.
"Travelling with Tomas." [RiverS] (38) 93, p. 2.
"Water and Light." [Nat] (256:19) 17 My 93, p. 678.
6243. SOTO, Genaro
"The Zoo" (from "Families, Streets and Dreams," a poetry/photography event by 3rd
grade students, Whittier Elementary, Tulsa). [Nimrod] (37:1) Fall-Wint 93, p.
88.
"El Zoologico" (from "Families, Streets and Dreams," a poetry/photography event
by 3rd grade students, Whittier Elementary, Tulsa). [Nimrod] (37:1) Fall-
Wint 93, p. 88.
SOTO, Mark Smith
See SMITH-SOTO, Mark
6244. SOUAID, Carolyn Marie
"Daddy." [AntigR] (93-94) Spr-Sum 93, p. 236.
"Politics." [AntigR] (93-94) Spr-Sum 93, p. 237.
"Thursday." [AntigR] (93-94) Spr-Sum 93, p. 234.
"The Way It Is." [AntigR] (93-94) Spr-Sum 93, p. 235.
6245. SOUPAULT, Philippe
"Westwego" (1917-1922, for M.L., tr. by Paulette Schmidt). [ArtfulD] (24/25) 93, p.
47-53.
6246. SOUSA, Dian
"Jane Is Doing Phone Sex Again." [ChironR] (12:1, #34) Spr 93, p. 43.
6247. SOUTHWICK, Marcia
"Agatha's Butterfly" (based on Agatha Christie's autobiography). [PraS] (67:1) Spr
93, p. 71-73.
"The Bone-Cupboard" (based on Beatrix Potter's journals and letters). [PraS] (67:1)
Spr 93, p. 73-74.
"Dream Factory: The Autobiography of Lana Turner." [SouthernR] (29:2) Spr, Ap
93, p. 276-278.
"I Won't Get Up." [PraS] (67:1) Spr 93, p. 68-69.
"The Kiss." [PraS] (67:1) Spr 93, p. 65-66.
"Picayune." [PraS] (67:1) Spr 93, p. 69-70.
"Take My Wings." [PraS] (67:3) Fall 93, p. 30-31.
"What Should I Do?" [PraS] (67:3) Fall 93, p. 31-33.
"What the Stars Owe Me." [PraS] (67:1) Spr 93, p. 64-65.
"Where Was I?" [PraS] (67:1) Spr 93, p. 67-68.
SOWOL, Kim
See KIM, Sowol
6248. SOWTON, Ian
"That Thin Man" (for Eli Mandel 1922-1992). [CanLit] (136) Spr 93, p. 194.
6249. SOZONOVA, Alexandra
"What's This Love" (tr. by James Kates). [Vis] (42) 93, p. 24.
6250. SPACKS, Barry
"Remembering I.B. Singer." [PaintedHR] (9) Spr 93, p. 20-21.
"Weeper" (for Simms Ingerton). [PaintedHR] (9) Spr 93, p. 21.
"Zen Pace" (For Mark Saunders). [Poetry] (162:6) S 93, p. 349.
6251. SPADY, Susan
"Bruised." [PoetryNW] (34:2) Sum 93, p. 23.
"The Prom Dress." [NowestR] (31:3) 93, p. 49-50.
"The Push-Pull of This Love." [Calyx] (15:1) Wint 93-94, p. 5.

6252. SPAHR, Juliana
"In a clock's small space." [BlackBread] (3) 93, p. 46.
"Introduction" (Excerpts). [WashR] (19:4) D 93-Ja 94, p. 25.
"This a divergence words yellow." [BlackBread] (3) 93, p. 48.
"To yearling place this border." [BlackBread] (3) 93, p. 47.
"Untitled: Held in by the ribs of the garment." [13thMoon] (12:1/2) 93-94, p. 64.
6253. SPALDING, Esta (Esta Alice)
"Belonging to You (A Daughter's Poem)" (for Philip Spalding). [MalR] (104) Fall
93, p. 47-48.
"But Only the Captains of This Earth" (— Melville). [Grain] (21:3) Fall 93, p. 98.
"The Cow." [Grain] (21:3) Fall 93, p. 99.
"Wings & Bones, or, La Rigidité Cadavérique de l'Écriture — Derrida." [MalR]
(104) Fall 93, p. 44-46.
6254. SPANGLE, Doug
"Fairy Tale." [DogRR] (12:1, #23) Spr-Sum 93, p. 33.
"A Thing About Bridges" (for Ivo Andric). [DogRR] (12:1, #23) Spr-Sum 93, p. 32.
6255. SPARA, Walter
"Franz Died." [CoalC] (7) Apr 93, p. 2.
6256. SPARENBERG, David
"Keys" (tr. of Jan Zych, w. Aleksandra Szostalo). [SnailPR] (3:1) Fall-Wint 93, p. 1.
6257. SPARK, Muriel
"That Lonely Shoe Lying on the Road." [NewYorker] (69:30) 20 S 93, p. 82.
6258. SPARLING, George
"Photos of Louise Brooks." [ChironR] (12:4/13:1, #37/38) Wint 93-Spr 94, p. 43.
6259. SPARROW
"The Revolution." [Sun] (214) O 93, p. 11.
"A Testimonial." [Sun] (212) Ag 93, p. 33.
"Umbrella." [Sun] (215) N 93, p. 12.
6260. SPARSHOTT, Francis
"Creativity." [CanLit] (136) Spr 93, p. 114.
"Hero." [CanLit] (136) Spr 93, p. 128.
"Homage to Walt Whitman." [CanLit] (136) Spr 93, p. 81.
"Reluctant Shipwright." [Quarry] (42:3) 93, p. 114-115.
6261. SPASSER, Constance Corzilius
"The New World" (for I. Y. L.). [WillowR] (20) Spr 93, p. 21.
6262. SPAULDING, John
"The Roué at the Breakfast Table, or Breakfast in Bloom." [Light] (6) Sum 93, p.
16.
"Violet." [Light] (7) Aut 93, p. 19.
6263. SPEARS, Heather
"Mammography Survey, Bispebjerg Hospital." [Event] (22:1) Spr 93, p. 28-29.
"Perugia." [Event] (22:1) Spr 93, p. 25.
"The Search for Scarlett." [Event] (22:1) Spr 93, p. 26-27.
6264. SPECTOR, Al
"Uncle Hank." [Wind] (23:72) 93, p. 4.
6265. SPECTOR, Donna
"At the Post Office." [JINJPo] (15:2) Aut 93, p. 25.
"Beauty Is a Burden." [PoetL] (88:2) Sum 93, p. 11.
"My Father's Breakfast." [SycamoreR] (5:2) Sum 93, p. 68-69.
"The Play Is Love." [Footwork] (23) 93, p. 96.
6266. SPEER, Laurel
"Andy & Holly Meet Scott on the Steps of the Parthenon" (Emily Dickinson, Too).
[Footwork] (23) 93, p. 161.
"Discovering Eve." [Footwork] (23) 93, p. 162.
"The Lady in Idaho." [13thMoon] (11:1/2) 93, p. 77.
"Meeting with Dante in a A Narrow Street." [PaintedB] (50/51) 93, p. 106.
"My Hippo." [Footwork] (23) 93, p. 161.
"The Poet Falls Down under Wordsworth in the Afternoon." [Pearl] (17) Spr 93, p.
42.
"Second Chidren." [Footwork] (23) 93, p. 161-162.
6267. SPELIUS, Carol
"Mary, How Does Your Garden Grow." [WindO] (57) Fall 93, p. 24-25.
6268. SPENCE, Michael
"Commonplaces." [PoetryNW] (34:1) Spr 93, p. 32-33.
6269. SPENCER, Linda Moore
"Pine Rest." [Kalliope] (15:2) 93, p. 60.

6270. SPERA, Gabriel
"Antonio in Tijuca." [ChiR] (39:1) 93, p. 94-96.
"Balkan." [Poetry] (162:3) Je 93, p. 138.
"Beach Bum." [ChiR] (39:1) 93, p. 97.
"Corcovado." [ChiR] (38:4) 93, p. 5-7.
"Without a Sequel." [ChiR] (39:1) 93, p. 98.
6271. SPERANZA, Anthony
"The Three Lambs." [Plain] (14:1) Fall 93, p. 7.
6272. SPHERES, Duane
"All Our Seasons" (for Denise). [BellArk] (9:2) Mr-Ap 93, p. 9.
"Willow." [BellArk] (9:1) Ja-F 93, p. 14.
6273. SPICER, Bob
"Prestidigitation." [Bogg] (66) Wint 92-93, p. 22.
6274. SPICER, David
"Heaven." [ChironR] (12:4/13:1, #37/38) Wint 93-Spr 94, p. 46.
6275. SPIER, Margaret
"What's Required Is." [PennR] (5:2) 93, p. 36.
6276. SPIESS, Richard
"What Follows the Death of Your Body." [CreamCR] (17:1) Spr 93, p. 60.
6277. SPINELLI, Eileen
"Dream in the Abstract." [Footwork] (23) 93, p. 26.
"To My Cousin on Star Mountain" (A goodbye). [Footwork] (23) 93, p. 26.
6278. SPIRENG, Matthew J.
"Arrhythmia." [ColEng] (55:7) N 93, p. 783.
"The Bat" (for R.J. Kelly). [HampSPR] Wint 93, p. 57.
"Cutting the Maple." [SpoonR] (18:1) Wint-Spr 93, p. 48-49.
"Four-Leaf Clover." [Blueline] (14) 93, p. 38.
"Illusion." [ChatR] (13:2) Wint 93, p. 5.
"Janet on Thin Ice." [WestB] (31/32) 93, p. 9.
"Standing at an Open Window." [Plain] (14:1) Fall 93, p. 34.
"There Is a Place." [CapeR] (28:1) Spr 93, p. 31.
"They Buried All Their Dead." [BellR] (16:1/2) Spr-Fall 93, p. 31.
"The Throw." [Pembroke] (25) 93, p. 43.
6279. SPIRES, Elizabeth
"The Bodies." [Iowa] (23:1) Wint 93, p. 120-121.
"Celia Dreaming." [NewRep] (208:21) 24 My 93, p. 36.
"The Robed Heart." [Iowa] (23:1) Wint 93, p. 121.
"Sake." [Iowa] (23:1) Wint 93, p. 122.
"The Shadow." [AmerPoR] (22:3) My-Je 93, p. 18.
"Truro." [NewYorker] (69:23) 26 Jl 93, p. 56.
6280. SPIRO, Peter
"An April Morning." [Footwork] (23) 93, p. 33.
"The Avenue X Gang." [Footwork] (23) 93, p. 35.
"A Boy Who's Bright But Awfully Quiet." [Footwork] (23) 93, p. 34.
"Cause and Effect." [Footwork] (23) 93, p. 36.
"My Nextdoor Neighbor, Mrs. Fischetti." [Footwork] (23) 93, p. 35.
"On a Greyhound Back to Base." [Footwork] (23) 93, p. 36.
"On Our Way Toward Literacy." [Footwork] (23) 93, p. 33.
"On the First Day of Class, I Ask My Students Two Questions." [Footwork] (23) 93,
p. 34.
"Some of Them." [Footwork] (23) 93, p. 34.
6281. SPIVACK, Susan Fantl
"Goddess Prayers for the Twenty-first Century" (Selection: "In Your Names
Goddess"). [Kalliope] (15:3) 93, p. 16.
6282. SPLAKE, T. Kilgore
"A Doomsday Library." [Gaia] (3) O 93, p. 32-33.
"John Berryman's Lost Son." [OnTheBus] (5:2, #12) Sum-Fall 93, p. 198-199.
6283. SPRAGUE, Karen
"Ecclesiastical History." [SouthernR] (29:4) Aut, O 93, p. 766.
6284. SPRING, Michael
"After Kicking Off Her Shoes." [BellArk] (9:1) Ja-F 93, p. 22.
"After Your Death." [BellArk] (9:3) My-Je 93, p. 8.
"Building a Soul." [ChironR] (12:3, #36) Aut 93, p. 27.
"Windows." [BellArk] (9:1) Ja-F 93, p. 23.
6285. SPRINGER, Christina
"Dame's Rocket." [Drumvoices] (2:1/2) Fall-Wint 92-93, p. 140.

446
SPRINGER

"In My Garden." [Drumvoices] (2:1/2) Fall-Wint 92-93, p. 139-140.
6286. SPUNGIN, Jennifer
"The Removers." [13thMoon] (11:1/2) 93, p. 78.
SPURIUS, Falvius
See FALVIUS SPURIUS
6287. SPYDELL, Cat
"Indian Head Tavern." [ChironR] (12:4/13:1, #37/38) Wint 93-Spr 94, p. 12.
"Just When I Thought I'd Seen It All." [ChironR] (12:4/13:1, #37/38) Wint 93-Spr 94, p. 12.
"Nature Lovers." [Pearl] (17) Spr 93, p. 59.
6288. SPYKER, James
"I Like Ike." [AntigR] (93-94) Spr-Sum 93, p. 240-241.
"Johnny and the Post-Nuclear Family." [TickleAce] (26) Fall-Wint 93, p. 85-86.
"Speed Reading" (or 160 miles in 90 minutes). [AntigR] (93-94) Spr-Sum 93, p. 238-239.
"A True Artist #1." [AntigR] (93-94) Spr-Sum 93, p. 242.
6289. SRUOGINIS, Laima (*See also* SRUOGINYTE, Laima)
"The Ballads of Kukutis" (Selections: 10 poems, tr. of Marcelijus Martinaitis). [Writ] (25) 93, p. 5-19.
"The Beginning of the Story" (tr. of Marcelijus Martinaitis). [WebR] (17) Fall 93, p. 9.
"An Experiment" (tr. of Marcelijus Martinaitis). [WebR] (17) Fall 93, p. 12-13.
"Kukutis' Appeal to the Alphabet" (tr. of Marcelijus Martinaitis). [WebR] (17) Fall 93, p. 15.
"Kukutis Beats Scholar Pliugzma's Dog" (tr. of Marcelijus Martinaitis). [ArtfulD] (24/25) 93, p. 39.
"Kukutis' Consciousness Becomes Alienated" (tr. of Marcelijus Martinaitus). [Vis] (43) 93, p. 34.
"Kukutis Dreams up Zuveliskes Village in the Cathedral Square" (tr. of Marcelijus Martinaitis). [ArtfulD] (24/25) 93, p. 35-37.
"Kukutis Opens His Eyes" (tr. of Marcelijus Martinaitis). [ArtfulD] (24/25) 93, p. 38.
"Kukutis' Words" (tr. of Marcelijus Martinaitis). [WebR] (17) Fall 93, p. 11.
"My Thought-Up Story to Cheer Up Hanged Kukutis" (tr. of Marcelijus Martinaitis). [WebR] (17) Fall 93, p. 14-15.
"Tool's, Word's and People's Confusion" (tr. of Marcelijus Martinaitis). [WebR] (17) Fall 93, p. 10-11.
6290. SRUOGINYTE, Laima (*See also* SRUOGINIS, Laima)
"How Kukutis Regained His Senses" (from "Kukutis's Ballads," tr. of Marcelijus Martinaitis). [CimR] (104) Jl 93, p. 15-16.
"Kukutis' Sermon to the Pigs" (from "Kukutis's Ballads," tr. of Marcelijus Martinaitis). [CimR] (104) Jl 93, p. 16-17.
"Kukutis Wants to See His Homeland" (from "Kukutis's Ballads," tr. of Marcelijus Martinaitis). [CimR] (104) Jl 93, p. 17-18.
6291. ST. ANDREWS, B. A.
"Blonde Rebellion." [BellR] (16:1/2) Spr-Fall 93, p. 59.
"For Anne Frank." [Comm] (120:1) 15 Ja 93, p. 16.
"Happy Accidents." [SpoonR] (18:1) Wint-Spr 93, p. 14.
"Learning to Float." [Footwork] (23) 93, p. 78.
6292. ST. CLAIR, Philip
"Drought." [GreensboroR] (54) Sum 93, p. 60-61.
"House." [CinPR] (24) Spr 93, p. 28-30.
6293. ST. GERMAIN, Sheryl
"My Body in Summer." [CreamCR] (17:1) Spr 93, p. 90-91.
"Pain Killers." [MassR] (34:1) Spr 93, p. 142-143.
"Rent." [LouisL] (10:1) Spr 93, p. 47-49.
6294. ST. JACQUES, Elizabeth
"A sweatband finds the fieldhand's thirst" (Amelia One-Liner Award). [Amelia] (7:2, #21) 93, p. 87.
6295. ST. JOAN, Jacqueline
"Dead Baby." [DenQ] (28:1) Sum 93, p. 46-49.
6296. ST. THOMASINO, Gregory Vincent
"Go Twenty-Nine." [PoetryUSA] (25/26) 93, p. 27.
"Go Twenty-Six." [PoetryUSA] (25/26) 93, p. 13.
"Igne Fifteen." [PoetryUSA] (25/26) 93, p. 11.
"Igne Nineteen." [PoetryUSA] (25/26) 93, p. 11.

"Igne Thirteen." [PoetryUSA] (25/26) 93, p. 13.
6297. STAFANILE, Selma
"Lorrie." [Sparrow] (60) Sum 93, p. 5.
6298. STAFFORD, Darrell (1914-1993)
"Communion at Coldwater Baptist Church." [AmerPoR] (22:3) My-Je 93, p. 15.
6299. STAFFORD, William (1914-1993)
"After Life's Fever." [OhioR] (50) 93, p. 65.
"Any Morning." [OhioR] (50) 93, p. 63.
"Apologia pro Vita Sua." [FourQ] (7:1) Spr 93, p. 23.
"Assurance." [NowestR] (31:3) 93, first preliminary page.
"An Author's House." [Light] (7) Aut 93, p. 4.
"Bio: Fitting into My Years." [TarRP] (33:1) Fall 93, p. 31.
"Both of You." [FourQ] (7:2) Fall 93, p. 13.
"By the Black Ships." [QRL] (12:32/33) 93, p. 523.
"By the Chapel." [PaintedB] (50/51) 93, p. 84.
"Easter Morning." [CreamCR] (17:1) Spr 93, p. 50.
"Entering History." [Nat] (256:15) 19 Ap 93, p. 534.
"Epiphanies of an Old-Model Hoover." [CreamCR] (17:1) Spr 93, p. 51.
"Evidence." [TarRP] (33:1) Fall 93, p. 30.
"Farrier Talk." [Nat] (256:15) 19 Ap 93, p. 534.
"For Someone Gone." [FourQ] (7:1) Spr 93, p. 23.
"From Tombstones Back Home." [Light] (7) Aut 93, p. 4.
"Getting Going." [Light] (7) Aut 93, p. 3.
"Grandmother." [Elf] (3:3) Fall 93, p. 19.
"Leaving the Island." [HarvardR] (5) Fall 93, p. 36.
"Living Statues." [VirQR] (69:2) Spr 93, p. 251-252.
"Meeting an Old Friend in the Supermarket." [VirQR] (69:2) Spr 93, p. 251.
"Mein Kampf." [GeoR] (47:3) Fall 93, p. 433.
"My Parents Were Simple Folk." [QRL] (12:32/33) 93, p. 522.
"Old Friends." [Interim] (12:1) Spr-Sum 93, p. 3.
"Oldtimers." [Light] (7) Aut 93, p. 5.
"On Standby." [Light] (7) Aut 93, p. 3.
"One Little Witness." [Light] (7) Aut 93, p. 3.
"Opening Scene." [FourQ] (7:1) Spr 93, p. 24.
"Over Montana." [Nat] (256:6) 15 F 93, p. 211.
"Philosophical Investigations." [Light] (7) Aut 93, p. 4.
"Put These in Your Pipe." [Light] (7) Aut 93, p. 5.
"Report from the Heartland." [Plain] (13:3) Spr 93, p. 21.
"A Rock Presented by a Friend from Alaska." [ChiR] (39:3/4) 93, p. 91.
"The Sky." [VirQR] (69:2) Spr 93, p. 252-253.
"Slow News from Our Place." [TarRP] (33:1) Fall 93, p. 31-32.
"Some Notes on the Violin." [Light] (7) Aut 93, p. 6.
"Some People Know." [TarRP] (33:1) Fall 93, p. 30-31.
"Spanish Guitar." [QRL] (12:32/33) 93, p. 522-523.
"Speaking in Tongues." [OhioR] (50) 93, p. 64.
"A Story I Have to Tell You." [Nat] (256:15) 19 Ap 93, p. 534.
"Sympathy." [Light] (7) Aut 93, p. 6.
"The Way I Do It." [Light] (7) Aut 93, p. 5.
"What You Need." [Light] (7) Aut 93, p. 3.
"Worldly Considerations." [Light] (7) Aut 93, p. 4.
6300. STAHLECKER, Beth
"Asking You." [GettyR] (6:2) Spr 93, p. 336.
"The Berkshires: May." [VirQR] (69:1) Wint 93, p. 87.
"Black and White." [GettyR] (6:2) Spr 93, p. 337.
"Cape May Point." [GettyR] (6:2) Spr 93, p. 338.
"Meeting Mr. Doroshenko." [GettyR] (6:2) Spr 93, p. 339.
"News." [SycamoreR] (5:2) Sum 93, p. 88.
"Out Back." [SycamoreR] (5:2) Sum 93, p. 89.
"Practice." [AntR] (51:1) Wint 93, p. 92.
"Rushing Back." [SycamoreR] (5:2) Sum 93, p. 90-92.
"Seems to Me." [SycamoreR] (5:2) Sum 93, p. 93.
"Summertime." [VirQR] (69:1) Wint 93, p. 89.
"Time Off." [VirQR] (69:1) Wint 93, p. 88-89.
"View." [SycamoreR] (5:2) Sum 93, p. 94.
"Waiting." [GettyR] (6:2) Spr 93, p. 340.
"With My Looks." [GettyR] (6:2) Spr 93, p. 341.

448

"World Gone White." [VirQR] (69:1) Wint 93, p. 87-88.
6301. STAINSBY, Martha
"Notes from a Cold Place." [HampSPR] Wint 93, p. 64.
6302. STALLINGS, A. E.
"Eurydice Reveals Her Strength." [BelPoJ] (43:4) Sum 93, p. 10.
"For the Losers of Things." [BelPoJ] (43:4) Sum 93, p. 8.
"Hades Welcomes His Bride." [BelPoJ] (43:4) Sum 93, p. 9.
"The Wife of the Man of Many Wiles." [BelPoJ] (44:2) Wint 93-94, p. 24.
6303. STALLWORTHY, Jon
"The Naming" (for Daphna Erdinast-Vulcan). [NewRep] (208:19) 10 My 93, p. 52.
6304. STAMBLER, Peter
"The Shespak Letters" (Selections: V-VI, XI). [QRL] (12:32/33) 93, p. 314-323.
6305. STAMP, Stephen B.
"Above the Snow Line in Big Sky Country." [AntigR] (95) Aut 93, p. 100.
"Little Big Horn." [AntigR] (95) Aut 93, p. 99.
"Pilgrim's Progress." [AntigR] (95) Aut 93, p. 101.
6306. STANARD, Christopher
"Headline News." [Drumvoices] (2:1/2) Fall-Wint 92-93, p. 204.
"KRS-1." [Drumvoices] (2:1/2) Fall-Wint 92-93, p. 203.
"Mindin' Your Business." [Drumvoices] (2:1/2) Fall-Wint 92-93, p. 203.
"Raindrops." [Drumvoices] (2:1/2) Fall-Wint 92-93, p. 204.
6307. STANDING, Sue
"At the Gedi Ruins." [SouthwR] (78:3) Sum 93, p. 360-361.
"Event Horizon." [HarvardR] (4) Spr 93, p. 54.
6308. STANDLEY, Gerald
"Coquette." [Amelia] (7:2, #21) 93, p. 65.
6309. STANFORD, Ann
"The Gift" (from [The Descent)." [PoetryE] (35) Spr 93, p. 130.
"In the Black Forest" (Selection: 1, from [The Descent)." [PoetryE] (35) Spr 93, p. 129-130.
"The Organization of Space" (Selections: 3-4, from [The Descent)." [PoetryE] (35) Spr 93, p. 128-129.
"Pandora" (from [The Weathercock)." [PoetryE] (35) Spr 93, p. 126-127.
"The Walnuts" (from [The Weathercock)." [PoetryE] (35) Spr 93, p. 127-128.
"The White Horse" (from [The Weathercock)." [PoetryE] (35) Spr 93, p. 124-125.
6310. STANFORD, Frank
"Curse." [ChatR] (13:4) Sum 93, p. 38-39.
"Night of the Following Day." [ChatR] (13:4) Sum 93, p. 37.
6311. STANGOS, Nikos
"Approximately" (Testimonies B, 1966, tr. of Yannis Ritsos). [HarvardR] (5) Fall 93, p. 133.
"Association" (Testimonies A, 1963, tr. of Yannis Ritsos). [HarvardR] (5) Fall 93, p. 146.
"The Day of the Sick Man" (Testimonies B, 1966, tr. of Yannis Ritsos). [HarvardR] (5) Fall 93, p. 132.
"Motionless Swaying" (Gestures B, 1969-70, tr. of Yannis Ritsos). [HarvardR] (5) Fall 93, p. 136-137.
6312. STANHOPE, Patrick
"Rimbaud Takes the Stand." [WebR] (17) Fall 93, p. 41-47.
6313. STANIEWSKA, Malgorzata
"Bench Ghetto" (tr. of Artur Przystupa, w. Tomek Kitlinski). [Verse] (10:2) Sum 93, p. 39-40.
"The Little Mermaid" (tr. of Katarzyna Turaj-Kalinska, w. Tomek Kitlinski). [Verse] (10:2) Sum 93, p. 38.
"To Heloise: Yet Another Letter" (tr. of Katarzyna Turaj-Kalinska, w. Tomek Kitlinski). [Verse] (10:2) Sum 93, p. 38.
6314. STANLEY, Jean (Jean W.)
"From the Louvre to Jeu de Paume." [InterPR] (19:1) Spr 93, p. 88.
"Rustle." [CapeR] (28:1) Spr 93, p. 41.
6315. STANNARD, Julian
"The Corpse." [Verse] (10:3) Wint 93, p. 107.
6316. STANSBERGER, Richard
"Baldy Bateman." [CinPR] (24) Spr 93, p. 74-75.
"Oldest Known." [CinPR] (24) Spr 93, p. 73.
6317. STANTON, Joseph
"Geckos." [BambooR] (57) Wint 93, p. 183-184.

6318. STANTON, Kay
"Inch-Long Baby." [SoCoast] (15) Je 93, p. 24.
6319. STANTON, Maura
"Chairman." [RiverS] (39) 93, p. 10-11.
"The City of the Dead." [SouthernR] (29:2) Spr, Ap 93, p. 286-287.
"Drug Store Trolls." [HopewellR] (5) 93, p. 35.
"Learning to Drive." [SouthernR] (29:2) Spr, Ap 93, p. 284-286.
"October Petunia." [SouthernR] (29:2) Spr, Ap 93, p. 283-284.
"Ode to a Grain of Salt." [HopewellR] (5) 93, p. 36-37.
"Pig." [SouthernR] (29:2) Spr, Ap 93, p. 282-283.
"Sunday Nights in the Fifties." [SycamoreR] (5:2) Sum 93, p. 24-25.
6320. STARCHER, Kirsten
"Bell Island Retrospective." [TickleAce] (26) Fall-Wint 93, p. 106-107.
6321. STARKEY, David
"Advice to My Poetry Students on the Last Day of Class." [HampSPR] Wint 93, p.
75.
"Emerson: Concord, 1882." [ChatR] (13:2) Wint 93, p. 9-10.
"I Am Waiting for a Boat." [CharR] (19:2) Fall 93, p. 129.
"My Wife Is Contemplating Adultery." [WebR] (17) Fall 93, p. 121.
"This Poem Is Not About Charleston, South Carolina." [PoetL] (88:3) Fall 93, p. 51.
"Unfinished: On the Anniversary of Loose Ends." [PoetL] (88:3) Fall 93, p. 49-50.
"What If Lot Says, 'All Right." [WestB] (33) 93, p. 75.
6322. STARRETT, Virginia
"Naked Truth." [Light] (6) Sum 93, p. 12.
"Pig Tales." [Light] (5) Spr 93, p. 13.
6323. STARZ, Maria Elena
"No Se Permite" (In Spanish and English). [Border] (2) Spr 93, p. 64.
6324. STARZEC, Larry
"Genesis." [Farm] (10:1) Spr-Sum 93, p. 31.
6325. STATHIS, Andrew
"Flo." [Lactuca] (17) Apr 93, p. 30-31.
6326. STAUDACHER, Carol
"Telling the Lanugage" (Robert Penn Warren Poetry Prize Winner, Second Prize).
[CumbPR]] (13:1) Fall 93, p. 4-5.
6327. STAUDT, David
"Billboard." [Blueline] (14) 93, p. 32.
"Coop." [Blueline] (14) 93, p. 34.
"Preacher's Camp." [Blueline] (14) 93, p. 33.
6328. STEEL, Ross P.
"Eggplant." [Light] (7) Aut 93, p. 8.
6329. STEELE, Lenora Jean
"A Gentile's Response." [AntigR] (95) Aut 93, p. 115.
"The Sins of Charity." [AntigR] (95) Aut 93, p. 116-117.
"Variations on the Trapped Theme." [AntigR] (95) Aut 93, p. 113-114.
6330. STEELE, Marian
"The Very Old Woman with Total Recall." [SoDakR] (31:2) Sum 93, p. 27.
6331. STEELE, Rebecca
"Mortality" (Young Writers, age 11). [PikeF] (11) Fall 93, p. 20.
6332. STEELE, Timothy
"California Sea Lion." [Thrpny] (52) Wint 93, p. 11.
"Her Memory of the Picnic." [Shen] (43:3) Fall 93, p. 94-95.
"Takeoff." [NewRep] (208:23) 7 Je 93, p. 40.
6333. STEFANILE, Felix
"The Bocce Court on Lewis Avenue" (New York Times photograph, December 2,
1970, by Barton Silverman). [Footwork] (23) 93, p. 149-152.
"Feast of San Gennaro." [Footwork] (23) 93, p. 149.
"Grandfather's Story." [Footwork] (23) 93, p. 148.
"Honorable Army Discharge." [Footwork] (23) 93, p. 148.
"Malespina" (For Lucy). [Footwork] (23) 93, p. 149.
"Marty" (Remembering the great TV play, "Marty," by Paddy Chayevsky).
[Sparrow] (60) Sum 93, p. 46.
"To Father Don Angelo Grillo" (tr. of Torquato Tasso). [Sparrow] (60) Sum 93, p.
55.
STEFANO, Darin de
See DeSTEFANO, Darin

6334. STEFANOVA, Nevena
"Fresh Snow" (tr. by Yuri Vidov Karageorge). [CimR] (102) Ja 93, p. 21.
"The Reason of Nature" (tr. by Yuri Vidov Karageorge). [CimR] (102) Ja 93, p. 22.
"What Would It Have Been?" (tr. by Yuri Vidov Karageorge). [CimR] (102) Ja 93, p. 21.
6335. STEFFLER, John
"Broken Sleep." [TickleAce] (25) Spr-Sum 93, p. 47.
"Corner Brook to Athens by Way of London." [TickleAce] (25) Spr-Sum 93, p. 45.
"Edge of a Field." [TickleAce] (23) Spr-Sum 92, p. 1.
"Hammering." [TickleAce] (25) Spr-Sum 93, p. 49.
"New Desert." [TickleAce] (23) Spr-Sum 92, p. 3.
"Noon." [TickleAce] (24) Fall-Wint 92, p. 72.
"Over Northern Ontario." [TickleAce] (23) Spr-Sum 92, p. 2.
"Primitive Renaissance." [TickleAce] (23) Spr-Sum 92, p. 4-5.
"Repairs." [TickleAce] (25) Spr-Sum 93, p. 48.
"Stepping into the Night." [TickleAce] (24) Fall-Wint 92, p. 69.
"Street-Lights, Leaves." [TickleAce] (24) Fall-Wint 92, p. 70-71.
"There Is Nothing Waiting to Emerge." [TickleAce] (25) Spr-Sum 93, p. 50.
"Thorns and Abrasion." [TickleAce] (25) Spr-Sum 93, p. 46-47.
6336. STEIN, Agnes
"At the End of the Day." [NorthStoneR] (11) 93, p. 39.
"Figures Among the Fauves" (Derain: The Thames, Westminster Bridge). [NorthStoneR] (11) 93, p. 40.
"Jewish Cemetery in Weissensee" (tr. of Günter Kunert). [Pequod] (35) 93, p. 104.
"Tortoise." [NorthStoneR] (11) 93, p. 40.
6337. STEIN, Deborah
"You'd Never now." [US1] (28/29) 93, p. 18.
6338. STEIN, Hannah
"Garter Snake." [PaintedHR] (8) Wint 93, p. 26-27.
"The Road to Giverny." [BelPoJ] (44:2) Wint 93-94, p. 28-29.
"Twin." [AmerV] (32) 93, p. 77-79.
6339. STEIN, Jill
"Changes Brought About by a Baby." [Footwork] (23) 93, p. 53.
"Letter to My Husband in Colorado." [US1] (28/29) 93, p. 24.
"My Friend and I Watch Our Daughters Play on the Lawn Beside the Quaker Meeting House." [Footwork] (23) 93, p. 53.
6340. STEIN, Joyce
"The Concert." [OnTheBus] (6:1, #13) Wint 93-Spr 94, p. 189.
"Goddess." [OnTheBus] (5:2, #12) Sum-Fall 93, p. 200.
6341. STEIN, Julia
"This Year of Floods, Riots and Earthquake" (12 poems). [Pearl] (17) Spr 93, p. 25 - 37.
6342. STEIN, Kevin
"Authorial Distance." [Poetry] (163:2) N 93, p. 77-78.
"First Performance of the Rock 'n' Roll Band *Puce Exit*." [PoetryNW] (34:2) Sum 93, p. 37-39.
"World Without End." [PoetryNW] (34:2) Sum 93, p. 35-37.
6343. STEIN, Michael
"Between Patients." [Agni] (37) 93, p. 288.
"The Way We Love." [Agni] (37) 93, p. 289.
"With a Baby in the Men's Locker Room." [CimR] (103) Ap 93, p. 102-103.
6344. STEINBERG, Alan
"Melville of the North Country." [Contact] (11:65/66/67) Spr 93, p. 10.
6345. STEINBERG, Hugh
"Collage: Murder Mystery" (Source: Weekly World News, April 23, 1991). [GrandS] (12:1, #45) 93, p. 174-175.
"World's Fair" (April 17, 1990, while listening to Ray Bradbury). [GrandS] (12:1, #45) 93, p. 176.
6346. STEINBERG, Llori
"Bio." [OnTheBus] (6:1, #13) Wint 93-Spr 94, p. 190-191.
"Cause & Effect." [OnTheBus] (6:1, #13) Wint 93-Spr 94, p. 191.
6347. STEINBORN, Tamara
"Flowing." [PraF] (14:3) Aut 93, p. 123.
6348. STEINER, Donna
"Acknowledgement III." [PassN] (14:1) Sum 93, p. 11.

451

STEINGESSER

6349. STEINGESSER, Martin
"Those Pelicans." [Border] (2) Spr 93, p. 65.
6350. STEINKE, René
"Emmet Street" (for Joanne Tangorra). [TriQ] (87) Spr-Sum 93, p. 166-167.
"The Psychology of the Sentence: Case Histories." [TriQ] (87) Spr-Sum 93, p. 164-165.
6351. STEINMAN, Lisa M.
"Carslaw's Sequences." [PoetryE] (36) Fall 93, p. 83-84.
"Testimonials from the Boarding House." [MichQR] (32:3) Sum 93, p. 354-356.
6352. STENZEL, Annie
"Some Effects of the Weather." [SpoonR] (18:1) Wint-Spr 93, p. 18.
"Sonnet for Constituents Not Permitted." [SnailPR] (3:1) Fall-Wint 93, p. 18.
6353. STEPANCHEV, Stephen
"Crossed." [NewYorker] (69:18) 21 Je 93, p. 56.
"A Minor Resurrection." [Comm] (120:8) 23 Ap 93, p. 18.
"An Occurrence on Kissena Boulevard." [NewYorkQ] (50) 93, p. 56.
"Shot While Playing in the Street." [NewYorkQ] (51) 93, p. 61.
"Wrecking Ball." [NewYorkQ] (52) 93, p. 42.
6354. STEPHENS, Christine
"Grandfather's Garden." [SycamoreR] (5:2) Sum 93, p. 79.
"Tundra Month." [TarRP] (32:2) Spr 93, p. 35.
6355. STEPHENS, Genevieve
"Sound Bites: Jets." [CumbPR]] (13:1) Fall 93, p. 68.
6356. STEPHENS, Michael
"The Ducks." [PoetL] (88:1) Spr 93, p. 38.
"Magpie." [PoetL] (88:1) Spr 93, p. 37.
"Red Maple." [PoetL] (88:1) Spr 93, p. 39.
6357. STEPHENS, Mora
"Lunch with My Grandparents" (Poets of High School Age). [HangL] (63) 93, p. 88.
"Meeting at the Hotel" (Poets of High School Age). [HangL] (63) 93, p. 89.
"Party Flashback" (Poets of High School Age). [HangL] (63) 93, p. 89.
"Sunflowers Hidden Away" (Poets of High School Age). [HangL] (63) 93, p. 90.
"A Vision of Two Lovers" (Poets of High School Age). [HangL] (63) 93, p. 87.
6358. STEPHENSON, David
"To a Garbage Truck." [Hellas] (4:2) Fall 93, p. 66.
6359. STEPTOE, Lamont B.
"For Jesse Owens." [PaintedB] (50/51) 93, p. 69.
6360. STERLING, Gary
"Sui Generis." [NorthStoneR] (11) 93, p. 163.
6361. STERN, Bert
"Nobody Loves the Dead Enough." [IndR] (16:2) Fall 93, p. 139-140.
6362. STERN, Gerald
"All I Have Are the Tracks." [NewEngR] (15:1) Wint 93, p. 192.
"Birthday." [AmerPoR] (22:1) Ja-F 93, p. 72.
"Hinglish." [AmerPoR] (22:1) Ja-F 93, p. 73.
"My First Kinglet." [NewEngR] (15:1) Wint 93, p. 193-194.
"Odd Mercy." [ColR] (20:1) Spr 93, p. 15-17.
6363. STERN, Joan
"The Bones of Your Name." [CumbPR] (12:2) Spr 93, p. 44.
"New Math." [CumbPR] (12:2) Spr 93, p. 43.
6364. STERN, Robert
"Ruth." [AntigR] (93-94) Spr-Sum 93, p. 216.
6365. STERNLIEB, Barry
"Fractions." [PoetC] (24:3) Spr 93, p. 38.
"Genetics." [PoetryNW] (34:2) Sum 93, p. 8.
"Justifying the Margins." [PoetryNW] (34:2) Sum 93, p. 7-8.
"Pine Judgment" (16th Century Japan). [Poetry] (163:2) N 93, p. 96.
6366. STEUER, Lee
"Bubbling." [Kaleid] (27) Sum-Fall 93, p. 44.
"Occupational Therapy." [Kaleid] (27) Sum-Fall 93, p. 49.
"Psychiatric Dreams." [Kaleid] (27) Sum-Fall 93, p. 47.
"Starting Somewhere." [Kaleid] (27) Sum-Fall 93, p. 49.
6367. STEVENS, A. Wilber
"Counting My Books." [HampSPR] Wint 93, p. 66.
6368. STEVENS, Arethusa
"Severance & Cages." [13thMoon] (12:1/2) 93-94, p. 65.

6369. STEVENS, Geoff
   "Washing Your Hair." [CoalC] (7) Apr 93, p. 23.
6370. STEVENS, Jim
   "Crossing." [Northeast] (5:8) Spr-Sum 93, p. 9.
   "Handicapped." [Light] (5) Spr 93, p. 19.
6371. STEVENS, Lisa
   "Post-Point (1993)." [ChironR] (12:3, #36) Aut 93, p. 13.
6372. STEVENS, Tina
   "It Takes Seventeen Cups of Coffee to Fuel Us from Nebraska to Kentucky and
      Back." [QW] (37) Sum-Fall 93, p. 201-203.
   "Omaha." [PraS] (67:3) Fall 93, p. 157-158.
   "Rosebud." [PraS] (67:3) Fall 93, p. 156-157.
6373. STEVENS, Wallace
   "Attempt to Discover Life." [QRL] (12:32/33) 93, p. 529-530.
   "Burghers of Petty Death." [QRL] (12:32/33) 93, p. 527.
   "The Creations of Sound." [SouthwR] (78:3) Sum 93, p. 313-314.
   "Extraordinary References." [QRL] (12:32/33) 93, p. 529.
   "Human Arrangement." [QRL] (12:32/33) 93, p. 527-528.
   "The Pediment of Appearance." [QRL] (12:32/33) 93, p. 526-527.
   "The Prejudice Against the Past." [QRL] (12:32/33) 93, p. 528.
   "Repetitions of a Young Captain." [QRL] (12:32/33) 93, p. 523-526.
6374. STEVENSON, Anne
   "After You Left." [NewRep] (209:21) 22 N 93, p. 38.
   "Late." [NewRep] (209:16) 18 O 93, p. 46.
   "May Bluebells, Coed Aber Artro" (for Radcliffe Squires). [MichQR] (32:3) Sum
      93, p. 357.
   "A Tricksy June." [NewYorker] (69:18) 21 Je 93, p. 76.
6375. STEVENSON, Diane
   "Get the Picture" (for David Shapiro). [Boulevard] (8:2/3, #23/24) Fall 93, p. 171 -
      172.
6376. STEVENSON, Terry B.
   "Frank." [OnTheBus] (6:1, #13) Wint 93-Spr 94, p. 192.
6377. STEVER, Edward (Edward W., Edward William)
   "The Complete Italian Feast." [Pearl] (19) Fall-Wint 93, p. 69.
   "Eat Your Heat Out." [Pearl] (17) Spr 93, p. 76.
   "Feminine Metaphysics." [Pearl] (19) Fall-Wint 93, p. 69.
   "Gravity, Ya Know." [Pearl] (17) Spr 93, p. 75.
   "Lighter Than Air." [ChironR] (12:1, #34) Spr 93, p. 42.
   "Lipstick." [Pearl] (19) Fall-Wint 93, p. 69.
   "A Matter of Timing" (for Diane Gough). [ChironR] (12:1, #34) Spr 93, p. 42.
   "Tale of Two Heroes." [ChironR] (12:1, #34) Spr 93, p. 42.
   "There Is No Sky." [HeavenB] (10) Wint-Spr 93, p. 31.
   "What They Really Meant." [ChironR] (12:1, #34) Spr 93, p. 42.
   "Wise Choice." [Pearl] (17) Spr 93, p. 75.
6378. STEWARD, D. E.
   "Août." [Caliban] (12) 93, p. 85-90.
   "Chromad." [NewAW] (11) Sum-Fall 93, p. 72-73.
   "Fog." [CharR] (19:2) Fall 93, p. 136-139.
   "Washington — 6288 Ft." [JlNJPo] (15:2) Aut 93, p. 11.
6379. STEWART, Dolores
   "July: Moon of Bird-listening." [Gaia] (3) O 93, p. 38.
   "A Song of the Colony." [HiramPoR] (53/54) Fall 92-Sum 93, p. 80.
   "Testament Not Found in the Dead Sea Scrolls." [Calyx] (14:3) Sum 93, p. 52.
6380. STEWART, Jack
   "I.V." [SouthernHR] (27:2) Spr 93, p. 120.
6381. STEWART, Pamela
   "Flight." [BlackWR] (20:1) Fall-Wint 93, p. 21.
   "Neighbors." [WestB] (31/32) 93, p. 30.
   "Not Just Shadow." [Field] (48) Spr 93, p. 44.
6382. STEWART, Shannon
   "The Canadian Girl 1937." [PoetryC] (13:2) 93, p. 16.
   "December Aquarium." [PoetryC] (13:2) 93, p. 17.
   "Dream." [PraF] (14:1) Spr 93, p. 120-121.
   "Moon & Snail." [PoetryC] (13:2) 93, p. 17.
   "Shiksa." [PraF] (14:1) Spr 93, p. 121-122.
   "The Watercress Gatherer." [Grain] (21:3) Fall 93, p. 54.

6383. STEWART, W. Gregory
"On Matters Equestrian." [Amelia] (7:2, #21) 93, p. 9.
6384. STILES, Guy
"St. Croix 11." [CaribbeanW] (7) 93, p. 32.
6385. STILLMAN, Peter R.
"Coming Down the Kuskokwim." [ColEng] (55:2) F 93, p. 208-209.
6386. STILLWELL, Marie
"Buttercup." [WebR] (17) Fall 93, p. 52.
"The Dream." [WebR] (17) Fall 93, p. 55.
"The First Tutu." [WebR] (17) Fall 93, p. 51.
"Homestead, News from - ." [WebR] (17) Fall 93, p. 53.
"A Lack of Sound." [WebR] (17) Fall 93, p. 52.
"Stone Mountain Man." [WebR] (17) Fall 93, p. 54.
6387. STINUS, Erik
"Chile During the Fifteenth Winter." [Drumvoices] (2:1/2) Fall-Wint 92-93, p. 136.
"An Old Play Re-enacted." [Drumvoices] (2:1/2) Fall-Wint 92-93, p. 136-137.
"Stocktaking." [Drumvoices] (2:1/2) Fall-Wint 92-93, p. 138.
6388. STOCK, Norman
"Do You Want a Chicken Sandwich." [NewYorkQ] (50) 93, p. 58.
6389. STOIANOVA, Danila
"Memory of a Dream" (Selections: 2 poems, tr. by Ludmilla Popova-Wightman).
[LitR] (37:1) Fall 93, p. 85.
6390. STOKES, Denis
"How Rain Arrives." [Quarry] (42:1) 93, p. 36.
6391. STOKESBURY, Leon
"Autumn Rhythm." [NewEngR] (15:4) Fall 93, p. 150-151.
"Unsent Message to My Brother in His Pain." [NewEngR] (15:1) Wint 93, p. 195.
6392. STOLLER, Francy
"Mischa / Mischa Langdon / The Late Sixties / New York Town." [Drumvoices]
(2:1/2) Fall-Wint 92-93, p. 76-77.
6393. STOLOFF, Carolyn
"As Long As I Live." [Talisman] (10) Spr 93, p. 151-152.
"Changing Focus." [Contact] (11:65/66/67) Spr 93, p. 52.
"Defender of the Faith." [Pearl] (17) Spr 93, p. 22.
"For Your Information." [Chelsea] (54) 93, p. 60-61.
"The Headlight Through Us." [SouthernPR] (33:1) Spr 93, p. 51-52.
"Keyholes II." [Pearl] (17) Spr 93, p. 23.
"Last Night News of an Uncle's Death Reached Me." [Pembroke] (25) 93, p. 58.
"Leaving a Head Behind." [Asylum] (8) 93, p. 138.
"Night's Drownings and Resuscitations." [Caliban] (12) 93, p. 32-33.
"Nonetheless." [Contact] (11:65/66/67) Spr 93, p. 53.
"Slides." [Caliban] (13) 93, p. 81.
6394. STONE, Alison
"Her Loving Net." [NewYorkQ] (52) 93, p. 56.
"Holding On." [IllinoisR] (1:1) Fall 93, p. 14.
6395. STONE, Anderson
"Daughter of a Friend." [OnTheBus] (6:1, #13) Wint 93-Spr 94, p. 193.
6396. STONE, Arlene
"Pit Fall." [Vis] (41) 93, p. 43.
6397. STONE, James
"Of Painting" (tr. of C. P. Cavafy). [DenQ] (28:1) Sum 93, p. 25.
"Origin" (tr. of Takis Sinopoulos). [DenQ] (28:1) Sum 93, p. 53.
"Walls" (tr. of C. P. Cavafy). [DenQ] (28:1) Sum 93, p. 25.
6398. STONE, Jennifer
"Love Everlasting." [PoetryUSA] (25/26) 93, p. 25.
6399. STONE, Magi
"Murray Valley" (Australia). [Bogg] (66) Wint 92-93, p. 23.
6400. STONE, Myrna J.
"Michael Mourning." [HawaiiR] (17:1, #37) Spr 93, p. 119.
"War Story." [HawaiiR] (17:1, #37) Spr 93, p. 120.
6401. STONEHAM, Marilyn
"City Sights." [PoetryUSA] (25/26) 93, p. 53.
6402. STONER, Kay
"Burnouts, Both." [EvergreenC] (8:2) Sum-Fall 93, p. 54.
6403. STOOK, B. E.
"Village at Dusk." [Footwork] (23) 93, p. 124.

6404. STORIE-PAHLITZSCH, Lori
"The Dreams of Early Mammals." [PoetL] (88:4) Wint 93-94, p. 7-8.
6405. STORNI, Alfonsina
"Little Man" (tr. by Thomas Feeny). [SnailPR] (3:1) Fall-Wint 93, p. 22.
6406. STORY, Gerturde
"Hot Pillow Poems, Remembered." [PraS] (67:4) Wint 93, p. 152-154.
6407. STOTT, Libby
"Tying One On at the University." [Hellas] (4:1) Spr 93, p. 23.
6408. STOUT, Barbara F.
"Sand Crabs at Lookout Point." [Amelia] (7:2, #21) 93, p. 7.
6409. STOUT, Robert Joe
"The Gate." [RagMag] (11:1) 93, p. 94-97.
"Listening to Spring." [RagMag] (11:1) 93, p. 92-93.
"Lives I Remember Come Back As I Clean the Garage." [Footwork] (23) 93, p. 92.
"Repression." [CapeR] (28:1) Spr 93, p. 37.
6410. STOYANOVA, Danila
"Three mares" (tr. by Lisa Sapinkopf, w. Georgi Belev). [Vis] (41) 93, p. 6.
6411. STRAHAN, B. R. (Bradley R.)
"Baltimore" (for James Taylor — The Baltimore poet, not the singer). [OnTheBus]
(6:1, #13) Wint 93-Spr 94, p. 194.
"Deceitful Landscapes" (tr. of Vlada Urosevic, w. the author). [Vis] (43) 93, p. 39.
"The Garden God" (tr. of Alis Balbierius, w. Jolanta Vitkuaskaite). [Vis] (43) 93, p.
38.
"Holy June" (tr. of Janina Degutyte, w. Lionginas Pazusis). [Vis] (43) 93, p. 35.
"Punishment" (tr. of Justinas Marcinkevicius, w. Lionginas Pazusis). [Vis] (43) 93,
p. 36.
"Regions of Restlessness" (tr. of Vlada Urosevic, w. the author). [Vis] (43) 93, p.
39.
"Regions of Silence" (tr. of Vlada Urosevic, w. the author). [Vis] (43) 93, p. 39.
"Sweet Apples" (tr. of Albinas Zukauskas, w. Lionginas Pazusis). [Vis] (43) 93, p.
37-38.
"To Live" (tr. of Janina Degutyte, w. Lionginas Pazusis). [Vis] (43) 93, p. 35.
6412. STRAND, Mark
"Dark Harbor" (Selections: I-III). [PartR] (60:1) Wint 93, p. 91-93.
"Farewell." [NewYorker] (68:48) 18 Ja 93, p. 58-59.
"In Memoriam." [QRL] (12:32/33) 93, p. 530.
"The Mysterious Maps." [NewYorker] (68:52) 15 F 93, p. 64-65.
"A Poet's Alphabet of Influences" (Selections: A, D, G-I, L-N, S, V-Y). [ColR]
(20:1) Spr 93, p. 90-96.
6413. STRANDQUIST, Bob
"Memory and Flight." [Event] (22:3) Wint 93-94, p. 75-82.
6414. STRANGE, Sharan
"Childhood." [Callaloo] (16:1) Wint 93, p. 15.
"How to Teach Them." [Agni] (37) 93, p. 84-85.
"Looking." [Callaloo] (16:3) Sum 93, p. 539.
"Metaphysical." [Callaloo] (16:3) Sum 93, p. 540.
"Offering." [Callaloo] (16:1) Wint 93, p. 16.
"Snow." [Agni] (37) 93, p. 86.
"Streetcorner Church II: For James Baldwin." [Callaloo] (16:1) Wint 93, p. 17.
6415. STRASSER, Ján
"Between Us" (tr. by Stephánia Allen and James Sutherland-Smith). [OxfordM]
(9:1) Spr-Sum 93, p. 27.
"By the Way" (tr. by Stephánia Allen and James Sutherland-Smith). [OxfordM]
(9:1) Spr-Sum 93, p. 27.
"The Hour of Misrepresentation" (tr. by Stephánia Allen and James Sutherland -
Smith). [OxfordM] (9:1) Spr-Sum 93, p. 26.
6416. STRASSER, Judith
"Chanukah." [PraS] (67:1) Spr 93, p. 141.
"Digging Out." [PraS] (67:1) Spr 93, p. 138-140.
"Natural Buoyancy." [PraS] (67:1) Spr 93, p. 140-141.
6417. STRAUS, Marc (Marc J.)
"Carotid Aneurym." [LullwaterR] (4:2) Spr-Sum 93, p. 95.
"The Collector." [GreensboroR] (54) Sum 93, p. 114.
"Hannibal in the Alps on a Sunday." [PassN] (14:1) Sum 93, p. 27.
"Infomred Consent." [PassN] (14:1) Sum 93, p. 26.

455

"Lecture to Third-Year Medical Students" (for Peter Russo). [KenR] (NS 15:4) Fall
    93, p. 91-92.
"Marlene Dietrich's Dead." [PassN] (14:1) Sum 93, p. 24.
"My Inner Ear." [LullwaterR] (4:2) Spr-Sum 93, p. 44.
"A Pause." [PassN] (14:1) Sum 93, p. 25.
"The Size of the Lesion." [SnailPR] (3:1) Fall-Wint 93, p. 27.
"Uncle Aaron Has Alzheimer's Disease." [SnailPR] (3:1) Fall-Wint 93, p. 26.
6418. STRELOW, Michael
    "Dust." [BellR] (16:1/2) Spr-Fall 93, p. 73.
6419. STREVER, Jan
    "Grace." [BellArk] (9:5) S-O 93, p. 11.
    "Savanna." [BellArk] (9:2) Mr-Ap 93, p. 8.
6420. STRICKLAND, Stephanie
    "Preservation of Order." [AmerLC] (5) 93, p. 44-45.
    "True North" (1-5). [KenR] (NS 15:4) Fall 93, p. 123-127.
6421. STRINGER, A. E.
    "Confessional." [HawaiiR] (17:1, #37) Spr 93, p. 163.
6422. STRINGHAM, Mike
    "Liberation Theology." [CapeR] (28:2) Fall 93, p. 22.
    "Postcard from the West." [CapeR] (28:2) Fall 93, p. 23.
6423. STROFFOLINO, Chris
    "Still Life with Dogma." [Talisman] (10) Spr 93, p. 173.
    "With Vacations Like This, Who Needs a Job." [PaintedB] (49) 93, p. 38.
    "With Vacations Like This, Who Needs a Job." [PaintedB] (50/51) 93, p. 121.
6424. STRONG, Beret E.
    "On the AIDS/Hospice Ward." [MinnR] (NS 40) Spr-Sum 93, p. 10.
6425. STRONG, Tim
    "Beating." [Blueline] (14) 93, p. 52.
6426. STROUD, Diane
    "Lucille." [EngJ] (82:2) F 93, p. 91.
    "The Piano Lesson." [EngJ] (82:6) O 93, p. 93.
6427. STROWBRIDGE, Nellie P.
    "Charles." [TickleAce] (26) Fall-Wint 93, p. 88-89.
    "The Poet's Licence." [TickleAce] (26) Fall-Wint 93, p. 87-88.
6428. STRPKA, Ivan
    "While Unity Lasts" (tr. by Stephánia Allen and James Sutherland-Smith).
        [OxfordM] (9:1) Spr-Sum 93, p. 107.
6429. STRUTHERS, Ann
    "Cherry Trees." [PoetC] (24:3) Spr 93, p. 12.
    "How I Developed a White Marigold." [PoetC] (24:3) Spr 93, p. 11.
    "Spirit Lake and Shang-lin Park" (after a poem by Ssu-ma Hsian-Ju). [Gaia] (1/2)
        Ap-Jl 93, p. 14-15.
    "Three Questions." [SpoonR] (18:1) Wint-Spr 93, p. 109.
    "Waking at Night." [Gaia] (1/2) Ap-Jl 93, p. 15.
6430. STRYK, Dan
    "The Spirit of Old Matresses in Junk Heaps." [SouthernPR] (33:2) Fall 93, p. 23-24.
6431. STRYK, Lucien
    "Voyage." [AmerPoR] (22:1) Ja-F 93, p. 74.
6432. STUART, Dabney
    "The Amber Window." [PassN] (14:2) Wint 93, p. 15.
    "A Few Good Women." [GettyR] (6:4) Aut 93, p. 697-698.
    "Figure on the Edge" (Gillespie Beach, NZ: The Tasman Sea). [WillowS] (31) Wint
        93, p. 68.
    "His Granddaughter Arrives." [VirQR] (69:2) Spr 93, p. 265-266.
    "Mighty Tall and Handsome." [Turnstile] (4:2) 93, p. 103-104.
    "Now and Again." [PoetC] (24:2) Wint 93, p. 6.
    "Panic." [PassN] (14:2) Wint 93, p. 14.
    "Plain Talk" (For Bill and Sue Hoffman). [Turnstile] (4:2) 93, p. 99-100.
    "Standoff." [Light] (6) Sum 93, p. 15.
    "They Fill the Air." [PoetC] (24:2) Wint 93, p. 5.
    "Watermusic." [FourQ] (7:1) Spr 93, p. 32.
    "Will." [Turnstile] (4:2) 93, p. 101-102.
    "Will the Circle Be Unbroken." [PoetC] (24:2) Wint 93, p. 3-4.
    "The Woman on the Fire Escape." [GettyR] (6:4) Aut 93, p. 699.
6433. STUART, Jeremy
    "I'm Sorry for All the Dads." [OnTheBus] (6:1, #13) Wint 93-Spr 94, p. 195.

"The Touch of Velvet." [OnTheBus] (5:2, #12) Sum-Fall 93, p. 201-202.
6434. STUBBS, Andrew
"Country and Western." [PraF] (14:2) Sum 93, p. 81.
"Daedalus." [MalR] (104) Fall 93, p. 24-28.
"Games." [MalR] (104) Fall 93, p. 22-23.
"A Paraplegic's Flying Dreams." [MalR] (104) Fall 93, p. 29-30.
"War." [PraF] (14:2) Sum 93, p. 80.
STUBBS, John Heath
See HEATH-STUBBS, John
6435. STULL, Charlene
"To Be a Folder of the Creek." [GeoR] (47:1) Spr 93, p. 22.
6436. STULL, Richard
"The Song Dropped from Opus 15." [Chelsea] (55) 93, p. 66.
"The War Against Irony." [Chelsea] (55) 93, p. 68.
"When He Was Dead." [Chelsea] (55) 93, p. 67.
6437. STURGEON, Shawn
"The Prince and the Poplars." [ParisR] (35:127) Sum 93, p. 137-138.
"The Witch *Is* Dead." [ParisR] (35:127) Sum 93, p. 138.
6438. STURMANIS, Dona
"You Can Take the Boy Out of the Country." [Grain] (21:2) Sum 93, p. 108-109.
6439. SU, Adrienne
"Alice Descending the Rabbit-Hole." [PraS] (67:3) Fall 93, p. 34-35.
"The Bride." [PraS] (67:3) Fall 93, p. 36-37.
"The Doll's Talk in Translation." [Interim] (12:1) Spr-Sum 93, p. 37.
"The Oracle, After a Long Silence." [NoDaQ] (61:2) Spr 93, p. 159.
"So Help Us." [MidAR] (14:1) 93, p. 13-14.
"Thisbe Changing Her Mind." [MidAR] (14:1) 93, p. 11-12.
"Translation." [Interim] (12:1) Spr-Sum 93, p. 36.
"The Visitors." [MidAR] (14:1) 93, p. 9-10.
6440. SUAREZ, Julia
"Bones." [Salm] (98/99) Spr-Sum 93, p. 78-79.
"Walking with Jeanne." [Salm] (98/99) Spr-Sum 93, p. 80.
6441. SUAREZ, Virgil
"Izquierdo." [ColR] (20:2) Fall 93, p. 88-90.
6442. SUBRAMAN, Belinda
"Clutching the Known." [ChironR] (12:4/13:1, #37/38) Wint 93-Spr 94, p. 18.
"My TV Doesn't Love Me Anymore." [SlipS] (13) 93, p. 64.
6443. SUCHOCKI, Geoff
"American Terrorism." [WashR] (18:5) F-Mr 93, p. 13.
"Fabric" (w. Doug Lang, Mora Larson and Sherene Offutt). [WashR] (18:5) F-Mr
93, p. 18.
6444. SUCOFF, Marjorie
"Cafe." [NorthStoneR] (11) 93, p. 171.
"We Left Our Work." [NorthStoneR] (11) 93, p. 172.
6445. SUERMONDT, Tim
"The Dangerous Women with Their Cellos" (for Donald Revell). [PoetC] (24:3) Spr
93, p. 16.
"Goodbye Margo." [IndR] (16:1) Spr 93, p. 161.
"Hearing Aid for the Younger." [IndR] (16:1) Spr 93, p. 162.
"Pilgrimage in Question." [PoetC] (24:3) Spr 93, p. 15.
6446. SUGIOKA, Kimi
"A Modest Harvest of Stars." [13thMoon] (12:1/2) 93-94, p. 66.
6447. SUK, Julie
"Facing the Truth." [RiverS] (38) 93, p. 64-65.
"Lamentation." [Poetry] (162:5) Ag 93, p. 276.
"Leaving the World We've Loved Speechless." [Poetry] (162:5) Ag 93, p. 275.
"Listening to Rodrigo's Concerto for Guitar." [CreamCR] (17:2) Fall 93, p. 192.
6448. SULKIN, Sidney
"No More to Prophesy" (Excerpts). [QRL] (12:32/33) 93, p. 323-331.
6449. SULLIVAN, Gary
"Watchtower." [Talisman] (10) Spr 93, p. 77-78.
6450. SULLIVAN, Gerald
"Ossipee Lake." [HarvardR] (3) Wint 93, p. 166.
6451. SULLIVAN, James
"The Jetty." [SpiritSH] (58) 93, p. 24-25.
"The Sickening Smile of Jesus." [SpiritSH] (58) 93, p. 23.

6452. SULLIVAN, John
"The Dynamite Confession of Eraser Grunt." [BlackBR] (17) Sum-Fall 93, p. 37-42.
6453. SULLIVAN, Mark
"Instant." [ArtfulD] (24/25) 93, p. 78.
6454. SULLIVAN, Mary Jane
"I Come to This World As Romance Dies." [Contact] (11:65/66/67) Spr 93, p. 58.
"In the Valley of the Moon." [Contact] (11:65/66/67) Spr 93, p. 59.
6455. SUMMERS, Ellen
"My father flew." [HiramPoR] (53/54) Fall 92-Sum 93, p. 110.
6456. SUMNER, David
"The Ultimate Drape." [Bogg] (66) Wint 92-93, p. 49.
6457. SUNDAHL, Daniel James
"Fragment from a Mennonite Journal" (c. 1911). [WebR] (17) Fall 93, p. 64.
"Interjections V-VIII: A Poem for Lyman Larson." [InterPR] (19:1) Spr 93, p. 89 -
90.
"Monet's Breakfast" (for Ellen Frances). [WilliamMR] (31) 93, p. 113.
"Mutatis Mutandis." [Blueline] (14) 93, p. 4.
"Summer Work, 1968." [WillowS] (33) Wint 93, p. 66.
"Vigil Strange" (for John Munchoff). [BambooR] (57) Wint 93, p. 185-186.
6458. SUNDVALL, Herbert
"Black Fruits of August." [BellArk] (9:5) S-O 93, p. 24.
"End of Run." [BellArk] (9:1) Ja-F 93, p. 13.
"Sound Garden" (Magnuson Park, Seattle). [BellArk] (9:5) S-O 93, p. 28.
"Talk Endless as a River" (Based on a passage from Chuang Tzu). [BellArk] (9:5)
S-O 93, p. 12.
6459. SUPERVIELLE, Jules
"1939-1945 Poèmes" (Excerpt in English, tr. by Geoffrey Gardner). [SycamoreR]
(5:2) Sum 93, p. 101.
"1939-1945 Poèmes" (Excerpt). [SycamoreR] (5:2) Sum 93, p. 100.
"Fable du Monde" (Excerpt). [SycamoreR] (5:2) Sum 93, p. 102.
"Fable du Monde" (Excerpt in English, tr. by Geoffrey Gardner). [SycamoreR] (5:2)
Sum 93, p. 103.
"The First Days of the World (God Speaks)" (tr. by Geoffrey Gardner).
[SycamoreR] (5:2) Sum 93, p. 99.
"Premiers Jours du Monde" (Dieu Parle)." [SycamoreR] (5:2) Sum 93, p. 98.
6460. SURANO, Adriana
"Sunlight Through the Window." [Footwork] (23) 93, p. 152.
6461. SURRATT, Jerl
"After You." [MinnR] (NS 40) Spr-Sum 93, p. 34.
6462. SURVANT, Joe
"The World's Largest Flower Is a Parasite." [CinPR] (24) Spr 93, p. 36-37.
6463. SUTHERILL, Colin
"Shorty Rogers at the Scattering of Stan Getz's Ashes." [Verse] (10:2) Sum 93, p.
57.
"Wipers on Full." [Verse] (10:2) Sum 93, p. 57-58.
6464. SUTHERLAND, Kate
"Lucia." [PraF] (14:1) Spr 93, p. 123.
6465. SUTHERLAND-SMITH, James
"XXX. By the number thirty-eight bus down Dostojevsky Lane" (tr. of Brano
Hochel, w. Stephánia Allen). [OxfordM] (9:1) Spr-Sum 93, p. 48-49.
"Bequest (to Other Thieves)" (tr. of Karol Chmel, w. Stephánia Allen). [OxfordM]
(9:1) Spr-Sum 93, p. 116.
"Between Us" (tr. of Ján Strasser, w. Stephánia Allen). [OxfordM] (9:1) Spr-Sum
93, p. 27.
"By the Way" (tr. of Ján Strasser, w. Stephánia Allen). [OxfordM] (9:1) Spr-Sum
93, p. 27.
"Contents of a Fever" (tr. of Ivan Laucík, w. Stephánia Allen). [OxfordM] (9:1) Spr -
Sum 93, p. 105.
"The Hour of Misrepresentation" (tr. of Ján Strasser, w. Stephánia Allen).
[OxfordM] (9:1) Spr-Sum 93, p. 26.
"I've Seen God Only Twice" (tr. of Brano Hochel, w. Stephánia Allen). [OxfordM]
(9:1) Spr-Sum 93, p. 47-48.
"Micro-stories" (5 selections, tr. of Brano Hochel, w. Stephánia Allen). [OxfordM]
(9:1) Spr-Sum 93, p. 49-50.
"Mist" (tr. of Ján Buzássy, w. Stephánia Allen). [OxfordM] (9:1) Spr-Sum 93, p. 26.
"Red Poet" (for Jan Ondrus). [Stand] (34:2) Spr 93, p. 4-5.

"Skepticism" (tr. of Karol Chmel, w. Stephánia Allen). [OxfordM] (9:1) Spr-Sum 93, p. 116.
"Skin Is Wrapping for Bones" (tr. of Ivan Kolenic, w. Stephánia Allen). [OxfordM] (9:1) Spr-Sum 93, p. 116-117.
"Verses" (tr. of Karol Chmel, w. Stephánia Allen). [OxfordM] (9:1) Spr-Sum 93, p. 115-116.
"While Unity Lasts" (tr. of Ivan Strpka, w. Stephánia Allen). [OxfordM] (9:1) Spr - Sum 93, p. 107.
6466. SUTPHEN, Joyce
"The Beginnings of Philosophy." [SpoonR] (18:1) Wint-Spr 93, p. 91.
"Dreaming You Out of Honduras" (for Miguel). [SpoonR] (18:1) Wint-Spr 93, p. 89-90.
6467. SUTTON, Dorothy
"Highway to Nowhere." [SouthernR] (29:2) Spr, Ap 93, p. 320.
6468. SUTTON, Pamela
"Evolution." [PraS] (67:3) Fall 93, p. 146.
"Ornithology of Icarus" (for Joe Hill McClatchey, in memoriam). [DenQ] (27:3) Wint 93, p. 65-66.
SUVERO, Victor Di
    See Di SUVERO, Victor
6469. SUZANNE
"Fire in the Woods, Flood in Town" (for Andrea, 1963-1982). [SinW] (51) Wint 93 - 94, p. 28-29.
6470. SVENVOLD, Mark
"Scarecrows." [LullwaterR] (4:2) Spr-Sum 93, p. 60.
"West Oakland Somniloquy." [LullwaterR] (4:2) Spr-Sum 93, p. 9.
6471. SVIDZINSKY, Volodymyr
"The pendulum is tired" (tr. by Virlana Tkaz and Wanda Phipps). [Vis] (41) 93, p. 15.
"Tired, Leaning on the Hills" (tr. by Virlana Tkacz and Wanda Phipps). [Vis] (43) 93, p. 53.
6472. SVOBODA, Terese
"The Goddess Corn Finds Her Dress in Disarray" (with apologies to Herrick). [Shen] (43:1) Spr 93, p. 60-61.
"Like a Dog, He Hunts in Dream" (— Tennyson). [Agni] (38) 93, p. 69.
"Obscenity." [Ploughs] (19:1) Spr 93, p. 51-52.
"The Pale California Moon." [PraS] (67:3) Fall 93, p. 144-145.
"Public Works." [Ploughs] (19:1) Spr 93, p. 53-54.
"The Quick Cave." [KenR] (NS 15:1) Wint 93, p. 102-104.
"Rogue Transmissions." [PraS] (67:3) Fall 93, p. 143-144.
"Sex." [PraS] (67:3) Fall 93, p. 143.
6473. SWAN, Alison
"If I Could Keep Her, I Would, He Says." [WillowS] (33) Wint 93, p. 11.
6474. SWAN, Marc
"Bottles" (for Tom Kent). [ChironR] (12:3, #36) Aut 93, p. 31.
"Infatuation." [RagMag] (11:2) 93, p. 7-8.
"One More Time." [Pearl] (17) Spr 93, p. 56.
"Pigeon Fucking." [ChironR] (12:4/13:1, #37/38) Wint 93-Spr 94, p. 9.
"The Silk in the Sow's Ear." [RagMag] (11:2) 93, p. 8.
"Sky Above, Water Below." [Pearl] (17) Spr 93, p. 56.
6475. SWANBERG, Ingrid
"The Horses." [Os] (36) Spr 93, p. 38.
6476. SWANDER, Mary
"Mud Road." [PraS] (67:3) Fall 93, p. 155-156.
6477. SWANGER, David
"In This World." [PoetC] (24:3) Spr 93, p. 21.
"Practice: Father and Son." [PoetC] (24:3) Spr 93, p. 22.
"Style" (for Elissa). [GeoR] (47:3) Fall 93, p. 434.
6478. SWANK, R. T.
"Preceding the Sudden Death of Eva Rueda, Newly Famous Spanish Gymnast, on Bouevard St. Germain, No. 133." [SlipS] (13) 93, p. 78.
6479. SWANLUND, Matthew
"My Penis." [ChironR] (12:4/13:1, #37/38) Wint 93-Spr 94, p. 13.
"Right After Breakfast." [ChironR] (12:4/13:1, #37/38) Wint 93-Spr 94, p. 13.
"The Slow Boat to China." [ChironR] (12:4/13:1, #37/38) Wint 93-Spr 94, p. 13.

6480. SWANN, B. (*See also* SWANN, Brian)
"Night" (tr. of Lucio Piccolo, w. Ruth Feldman). [QRL] (12:32/33) 93, p. 488-489.
6481. SWANN, Brian (*See also* SWANN, B.)
"Adieu, Chimères, Idéals, Erreurs" (— Rimbaud. Tr. of Rafael Alberti, w. Linda
  Scheer). [QRL] (12:32/33) 93, p. 11-13.
"The Attic." [Asylum] (8) 93, p. 134.
"Counterpoint." [QRL] (12:32/33) 93, p. 336-337.
"The Director." [ProseP] (1) 92, p. 74.
"The Director." [QRL] (12:32/33) 93, p. 337-338.
"A Dream of Newness." [NewAW] (11) Sum-Fall 93, p. 99-100.
"In the Beginning." [QRL] (12:32/33) 93, p. 333-334.
"Insider Trading." [QRL] (12:32/33) 93, p. 332-333.
"The Meteor and the Deer." [Iowa] (23:1) Wint 93, p. 152.
"Misericordia." [Asylum] (8) 93, p. 134.
"My Wife the Actress." [QRL] (12:32/33) 93, p. 338-339.
"Paysage Moralisé." [QRL] (12:32/33) 93, p. 339.
"Prado Museum" (tr. of Rafael Alberti, w. Linda Scheer). [QRL] (12:32/33) 93, p. 8 -
  11.
"Restoration of a Copy of an Imaginary Painting." [QRL] (12:32/33) 93, p. 331-332.
"Simplification." [ProseP] (1) 92, p. 73.
"The Skull on Its Occiput." [Asylum] (8) 93, p. 134.
"Taking the Sun in a Carpark Beside the East River." [QRL] (12:32/33) 93, p. 339 -
  340.
"The Theme of Power." [QRL] (12:32/33) 93, p. 334-335.
"Translation." [QRL] (12:32/33) 93, p. 333.
"Two Self-Portraits." [Agni] (38) 93, p. 70-71.
"Variations on the First Elegy." [QRL] (12:32/33) 93, p. 335-336.
6482. SWANNELL, Anne
"From a Cafeteria Window." [MalR] (105) Wint 93, p. 77-78.
"Poem to a Daughter." [Grain] (21:1) Spr 93, p. 47-48.
6483. SWANSON, Catherine
"Nativity." [ArtfulD] (24/25) 93, p. 59.
6484. SWARTS, Helene
"O, the Names" (on seeing photographs of Bosnia half a century after the
  Holocaust). [ChrC] (110:9) 17 Mr 93, p. 284.
"Peaks Island, Maine." [AnthNEW] (5) 93, p. 17.
6485. SWARTWOUT, Susan
"Faggot." [IllinoisR] (1:1) Fall 93, p. 64.
6486. SWEENEY, Bill
"The Reels for TR and CJ." [CapeR] (28:1) Spr 93, p. 16.
6487. SWEENEY, Gael
"Storm Front: February 1991." [HiramPoR] (53/54) Fall 92-Sum 93, p. 111.
6488. SWEENEY, Patrick
"Mood." [EngJ] (82:6) O 93, p. 92.
6489. SWEET, John
"Silent Rust." [SlipS] (13) 93, p. 73.
6490. SWEETMAN, Greg
"The News from Grunwaldstrasse." [Verse] (10:1) Spr 93, p. 78.
6491. SWENSEN, Cole
"Animism." [Conjunc] (21) 93, p. 93-94.
"Ghazal of the Empty Thing." [Conjunc] (21) 93, p. 94-95.
"To Carry On." [Conjunc] (21) 93, p. 95.
"To Circumferate." [Conjunc] (21) 93, p. 93.
"To Fall." [Conjunc] (21) 93, p. 95.
"To Irrevoke." [Conjunc] (21) 93, p. 94.
"To Word." [Conjunc] (21) 93, p. 92.
6492. SWENSON, Karen
"Impressions" (for my son). [QRL] (12:32/33) 93, p. 530-531.
"Medias Res." [SouthernPR] (33:2) Fall 93, p. 56.
"We." [GeoR] (47:3) Fall 93, p. 546.
6493. SWENSON, May
"Beginning Ended." [Poetry] (163:2) N 93, p. 67-68.
"Daffodildo." [ParisR] (35:127) Sum 93, p. 272-275.
"Glancing through your letter again I see your phraise" ([sic], from a letter to
  Elizabeth Bishop). [Light] (5) Spr 93, p. 16.
"Guilty." [Nat] (256:3) 25 Ja 93, p. 98.

"Horse." [Nat] (256:3) 25 Ja 93, p. 102.
"In Progress." [Poetry] (163:2) N 93, p. 65-66.
"Logs in the Grate." [YaleR] (81:1) Ja 93, p. 39.
"The Most Important." [Poetry] (163:2) N 93, p. 63-64.
"My Poems." [Nat] (256:3) 25 Ja 93, p. 96.
"Overview." [Poetry] (163:2) N 93, p. 68-69.
"The Sea." [Poetry] (163:2) N 93, p. 69-70.
"Sleeping with Boa." [YaleR] (81:1) Ja 93, p. 37-38.
"[Statement]" (In March 1984, on reading, at an editor's request, a manuscript
      chosen for print, I'm supposed to make a "statement"). [Poetry] (163:2) N 93,
      p. 64-65.
"Under the Best of Circumstances." [Poetry] (163:2) N 93, p. 66-67.
"Weather." [Nat] (256:3) 25 Ja 93, p. 100.
"What I Did on a Rainy Day." [Atlantic] (272:5) N 93, p. 124.
6494. SWIETLICKI, Marcin
"Mr. and Mrs. Von Kleist" (tr. by Ewa Horodyska). [Verse] (10:2) Sum 93, p. 36.
6495. SWIFT, Doug
"Bareback." [AmerPoR] (22:2) Mr-Ap 93, p. 29.
"Beneficence." [AmerPoR] (22:2) Mr-Ap 93, p. 31.
"Deafened." [AmerPoR] (22:2) Mr-Ap 93, p. 30.
"The Fulfillment of Wishes." [AmerPoR] (22:2) Mr-Ap 93, p. 31.
"The Inhuman." [AmerPoR] (22:2) Mr-Ap 93, p. 30.
"Lovers." [AmerPoR] (22:2) Mr-Ap 93, p. 30.
"Memory and Hope." [AmerPoR] (22:2) Mr-Ap 93, p. 29.
"Sister, Aunt, Mother of Poetry Comes for a Visit, Brings Stars" (for Colette Inez).
      [AmerPoR] (22:2) Mr-Ap 93, p. 29.
"The Wait." [AmerPoR] (22:2) Mr-Ap 93, p. 31.
6496. SWILKY, Jody
"Carnations." [GreensboroR] (55) Wint 93-94, p. 51.
6497. SWINTON, John
"Jackie and Campy." [Spitball] (45) Fall 93, p. 8-9.
6498. SWIST, Wally
"The Red Fox." [Outbr] (24) 93, p. 34.
"Returning Back to My Body." [Os] (36) Spr 93, p. 2.
6499. SWOFFORD, Michael
"Raiding Party." [OnTheBus] (5:2, #12) Sum-Fall 93, p. 203.
6500. SYLVAIN, Patrick
"Creativity and Fire." [Ploughs] (19:1) Spr 93, p. 81-82.
"Doo-Bop." [Ploughs] (19:1) Spr 93, p. 83-84.
"Horizon of Gun Butts." [Ploughs] (19:1) Spr 93, p. 85.
6501. SYLVESTER, Janet
"By Now We Were Freezing." [WeberS] (10:1) Wint 93, p. 47-48.
"Goatsbeard." [WeberS] (10:1) Wint 93, p. 48-49.
"In the Descartes Mountains." [WeberS] (10:1) Wint 93, p. 45-46.
"Modern Times." [Boulevard] (8:1, #22) Spr 93, p. 87-90.
6502. SYMONS, M. E.
"Crone." [PraS] (67:4) Wint 93, p. 136-137.
"Gravetalk." [PraS] (67:4) Wint 93, p. 136.
"Link." [PraS] (67:4) Wint 93, p. 137-138.
6503. SYNECK, M. R.
"Food for Thought, or Just Deserts" (M.F.A. Workshop w. Marie Hasten, Howard
      Glyn, Pamela Hughes, Lisbeth Keiley, Mary Greene, David Trinidad and
      Allen Ginsberg, Nov. 21, 1988). [BrooklynR] (10) 93, p. 94-95.
6504. SYNENKO, Anna
"Swan Song (Poem for Nijinsky)." [AntigR] (95) Aut 93, p. 123.
6505. SZANTO, Vera
"Eve's Lament." [DogRR] (12:1, #23) Spr-Sum 93, p. 3.
6506. SZARUGA, Leszek
"An Evening with the Author" (tr. by W.D. and K.B. Snodgrass, w. Justyna
      Kostkowska and Peter Lengyel). [Salm] (97) Wint 93, p. 111.
"Watchman" (for Zbigniew Herbert, tr. by W.D. and K.B. Snodgrass, w. Justyna
      Kostkowska and Peter Lengyel). [Salm] (97) Wint 93, p. 110.
6507. SZCZEPANSKI, Marian
"Daily Offerings." [BellArk] (9:6) N-D 93, p. 7.
"Demonry (1939)" (From a sequence of poems "Paul Klee in the Kunstmuseum,
      Bern"). [Vis] (42) 93, p. 31.

461

"New Poet Sleeps Beside the River." [BellArk] (9:6) N-D 93, p. 9.
"On Stengel Beach." [BellArk] (9:4) Jl-Ag 93, p. 22.
"Packing Nana's Kitchen." [BellArk] (9:4) Jl-Ag 93, p. 8.
"Shine." [BellArk] (9:6) N-D 93, p. 9.
6508. SZE, Arthur
"From the Rooftop." [Contact] (11:65/66/67) Spr 93, p. 51.
"Oolong." [KenR] (NS 15:4) Fall 93, p. 153-157.
6509. SZEMAN, Sherri
"When Bitterness Is All We Have." [HawaiiR] (17:1, #37) Spr 93, p. 210-211.
6510. SZOKE, Donna
"Crisp." [PraF] (14:3) Aut 93, p. 133.
6511. SZOSTALO, Aleksandra
"Keys" (tr. of Jan Zych, w. David Sparenberg). [SnailPR] (3:1) Fall-Wint 93, p. 1.
6512. SZPORLUK, Larissa
"B-b-bluebells." [IndR] (16:1) Spr 93, p. 93-94.
"Devolution." [CinPR] (24) Spr 93, p. 24.
"Field Study: A Sestina." [CinPR] (24) Spr 93, p. 22-23.
"Good-bye." [Agni] (37) 93, p. 279.
"Ideogram." [Agni] (37) 93, p. 280.
"Krell." [IndR] (16:1) Spr 93, p. 88.
"Round Face in a Little Town." [IndR] (16:1) Spr 93, p. 89-90.
"Women of Fable." [IndR] (16:1) Spr 93, p. 91-92.
6513. SZUMOWSKI, Margaret C.
"The Beautiful Nurse." [RiverC] (13:1) Fall 92, p. 74-75.
"Nightcrossing: The Wigella of Christmas." [RiverC] (13:1) Fall 92, p. 77.
"Ruthless as a Tibetan Monk." [MassR] (34:3) Aut 93, p. 346.
"Violinists in the Snow" (after Chagall, for Anna). [RiverC] (13:1) Fall 92, p. 76.
6514. SZYMBORSKA, Wislawa
"The Brief Life of Our Ancestors" (tr. by Grazyna Drabik and Austin Flint). [QRL]
(12:32/33) 93, p. 340-341.
"Brueghel's Two Monkeys" (tr. by Stanislaw Baranczak and Clare Cavanagh).
[NewYorker] (69:5) 22 Mr 93, p. 61.
"Cat in an Empty Apartment" (tr. by Stanislaw Baranczak and Clare Cavanagh).
[NewYRB] (40:17) 21 O 93, p. 42.
"Conversation with a Stone" (tr. by Stanislaw Baranczak and Clare Cavanagh).
[ManhatR] (7:1) Fall 93, p. 79-80.
"Dealings with the Dead" (tr. by Grazyna Drabik and Austin Flint). [QRL]
(12:32/33) 93, p. 345.
"The End and the Beginning" (tr. by Stanislaw Baranczak and Clare Cavanagh).
[NewRep] (208:3) 18 Ja 93, p. 40.
"End of the Century" (tr. by Grazyna Drabik and Austin Flint). [QRL] (12:32/33)
93, p. 344-345.
"The First Photograph of Hitler" (tr. by Grazyna Drabik and Austin Flint). [QRL]
(12:32/33) 93, p. 348.
"Funeral" (tr. by Grazyna Drabik and Austin Flint). [QRL] (12:32/33) 93, p. 346.
"In Heraclitus's River" (tr. by Stanislaw Baranczak and Clare Cavanagh). [Agni]
(38) 93, p. 107.
"Miracle Fair" (tr. by Grazyna Drabik and Austin Flint). [QRL] (12:32/33) 93, p.
347-348.
"No Title Required" (tr. by Stanislaw Baranczak and Clare Cavanagh). [ManhatR]
(7:1) Fall 93, p. 81-82.
"A Paleolithic Fertility Fetish" (tr. by Stanislaw Baranczak and Clare Cavanagh).
[ManhatR] (7:1) Fall 93, p. 78.
"Parting with a View" (tr. by Stanislaw Baranczak and Clare Cavanagh). [TriQ] (89)
Wint 93-94, p. 178-179.
"People on a Bridge" (tr. by Grazyna Drabik and Austin Flint). [QRL] (12:32/33)
93, p. 342-344.
"Possibilities" (tr. by Grazyna Drabik and Austin Flint). [QRL] (12:32/33) 93, p.
349-350.
"Reality Demands" (tr. by Stanislaw Baranczak and Clare Cavanagh). [NewYorker]
(69:2) 1 Mr 93, p. 86-87.
"Stage-Fright" (tr. by Grazyna Drabik and Austin Flint). [QRL] (12:32/33) 93, p.
350-351.
"To the Ark" (tr. by Grazyna Drabik and Austin Flint). [QRL] (12:32/33) 93, p. 341 -
342.

TABBAN, Levi Ibn al-
    See AL-TABBAN, Levi Ibn
6515. TACIUCH, Dean
    "How to Lose What You Never Had." [ContextS] (3:1) 93, p. 43.
    "South." [ContextS] (3:1) 93, p. 20.
6516. TADIJANOVIC, Dragutin
    "Moonlight on the Sea" (tr. by E. D. Goy). [NoDaQ] (61:1) Wint 93, p. 187.
    "My Sister Takes the Milk to Town" (tr. by E. D. Goy). [NoDaQ] (61:1) Wint 93, p. 186.
TAECHOL, Shin
    See SHIN, Taechol
6517. TAGG, John
    "A Blind Mother in the Park." [Hellas] (4:2) Fall 93, p. 46.
    "Sunset." [Sequoia] (34/35) 92-93, p. 54.
6518. TAGGART, John
    "Concetto Spaziale." [NewAW] (11) Sum-Fall 93, p. 35.
    "Greek Lyric Meter." [Talisman] (10) Spr 93, p. 120.
    "Into the Hill Country." [Conjunc] (20) 93, p. 60-63.
6519. TAGGART, Linda
    "Sestina in Photographs." [WillowS] (33) Wint 93, p. 50-51.
6520. TAGLIABUE, John
    "The Planet as the Temple's Inner Shrine." [SouthernPR] (33:2) Fall 93, p. 57-58.
    "Practical Concerns Continue." [Elf] (3:4) Wint 93, p. 26.
    "Predestined Instructive Brother." [Elf] (3:2) Sum 93, p. 36.
    "The Robes of Feathers." [Elf] (3:4) Wint 93, p. 25.
    "A Subject of My Affections, Plus Muse and Person Loved." [Elf] (3:2) Sum 93, p. 37.
6521. TAKAMURA, Kotaro
    "The Blowing Whale" (tr. by Hiroaki Sato). [Pembroke] (25) 93, p. 22.
    "Book of Geology" (tr. by Hiroaki Sato). [Pembroke] (25) 93, p. 23-24.
    "Denying Man" (tr. by Hiroaki Sato). [Pembroke] (25) 93, p. 28-29.
    "Dinner at Yonekyu" (tr. by Hiroaki Sato). [Pembroke] (25) 93, p. 17-19.
    "Late Night During a Rainy Season" (tr. by Hiroaki Sato). [Pembroke] (25) 93, p. 24-26.
    "Lost Mona Lisa" (tr. by Hiroaki Sato). [Pembroke] (25) 93, p. 14-15.
    "My Poetry" (tr. by Hiroaki Sato). [Pembroke] (25) 93, p. 27.
    "Ogiwara Morie" (tr. by Hiroaki Sato). [Pembroke] (25) 93, p. 21.
    "Ready to Be Beheaded" (tr. by Hiroaki Sato). [Pembroke] (25) 93, p. 20.
    "Voices" (tr. by Hiroaki Sato). [Pembroke] (25) 93, p. 16-17.
    "The Wailing of the Hundred Million" (tr. by Hiroaki Sato). [Pembroke] (25) 93, p. 26-27.
TAKASHI, Hiraide
    See HIRAIDE, Takashi
TAKIGUCHI, Mimi Nelson
    See NELSON-TAKIGUCHI, Mimi
6522. TAKSA, Mark
    "A Branch Is Home Plate." [XavierR] (13:1) Spr 93, p. 74.
    "Bright Dancing." [Contact] (11:65/66/67) Spr 93, p. 51.
6523. TALAL, Marilynn
    "The Blue Road." [Poetry] (163:3) D 93, p. 157.
6524. TALL, Deborah
    "A Blue Silk Shirt." [GettyR] (6:1) Wint 93, p. 177.
    "Dead Numbers" (for Ray Carver). [GettyR] (6:1) Wint 93, p. 178.
    "Grounded." [Poetry] (162:2) My 93, p. 75.
6525. TALLEY, Doug
    "A House for the Son." [Hellas] (4:1) Spr 93, p. 28.
6526. TALLMOUNTAIN, Mary
    "Good Grease." [ChiR] (39:3/4) 93, p. 157-158.
6527. TAM, Reuben
    "The Band of the Sea." [BambooR] (57) Wint 93, p. 139.
    "The Fields of January." [BambooR] (57) Wint 93, p. 140.
    "Groundwater." [BambooR] (57) Wint 93, p. 143.
    "Hawaiian Archipelago." [BambooR] (57) Wint 93, p. 144.
    "The Quiet Side of the Island." [BambooR] (57) Wint 93, p. 145.
    "The Rainbow Shower." [BambooR] (57) Wint 93, p. 141-142.
    "A Stone Souvenir." [BambooR] (57) Wint 93, p. 147.

"Waking to Makaleha." [BambooR] (57) Wint 93, p. 146.
6528. TAMMARO, Thom
"Leaves Under Snow." [Sun] (215) N 93, p. 23.
"Reading Stafford Late at Night" (William Stafford, 1914-1993). [NoDaQ] (61:2)
Spr 93, p. 160.
"Walking to My Office on Easter Sunday Morning." [Sun] (208) Ap 93, p. 19.
6529. TANA, Patti
"The Night I Decided." [HiramPoR] (53/54) Fall 92-Sum 93, p. 112.
6530. TANAKA, Atsusuke
"Osteon / the Atelier of Bones, Invention in Two Voices, D Minor" (tr. by Akemi
Nakamura and Tony Whedon). [GreenMR] (NS 6:2) Sum-Fall 93, p. 76.
6531. TANG, Yaping
"Black Gold" (tr. by Tony Barnstone and Newton Liu). [ChiR] (39:3/4) 93, p. 295.
6532. TANGORRA, Joanne
"Velazquez' Venus Makes Her Position Clear" (National Gallery, London).
[13thMoon] (12:1/2) 93-94, p. 67-68.
6533. TANIGAWA, Donna
"Advertisement for Cut-her Lot: Repossessed Body Parts." [HawaiiR] (17:3, #39)
Fall 93, p. 71-73.
6534. TANIKAWA, Shuntaro
"At the Tideland" (tr. by Tomoyuki Iino and Jon Silkin). [Stand] (34:2) Spr 93, p.
23.
"At Toba Seashore" (tr. by Jukio Kato and Jon Silkin). [Stand] (34:3) Sum 93, p. 50.
6535. TANNY, Marlaina B.
"Late One Night on a Car Trip to N.Y." [WorldO] (25:2) Wint 93-94, p. 15.
6536. TAPP, Pamela
"The Fate of Women." [OnTheBus] (6:1, #13) Wint 93-Spr 94, p. 196-197.
6537. TARDIEU, Jean
"Cicada of Space" (tr. by Robert Brown). [PoetL] (88:1) Spr 93, p. 51.
"Lord Vulture Lady Pelican" (tr. by Robert Brown). [PoetL] (88:1) Spr 93, p. 52.
"Man and His Shadow" (From *La part de l'ombre*, tr. by James Vladimir Gill).
[ProseP] (2) 93, p. 93.
"Vertigo" (From *La part de l'ombre*, tr. by James Vladimir Gill). [ProseP] (2) 93, p.
92.
6538. TARLOW, Steven
"Davenning in the Old Age Home." [CumbPR] (12:2) Spr 93, p. 50-51.
"The Jewish Cemetery in Prague — Tisha B'av." [NowestR] (31:3) 93, p. 55-56.
6539. TARN, Nathaniel
"Aspens This Fall" (for Eliot Weinberger & Nina Subin). [GrandS] (12:2, #46) Sum
93, p. 46-48.
"Imago 7: Elegy for the Images of Christopher Okigbo" (tr. of Agnes Gergely).
[GrandS] (12:1, #45) 93, p. 99-100.
"Imago 8: Proportions" (tr. of Agnes Gergely). [GrandS] (12:1, #45) 93, p. 96-97.
"Imago 9: The Parchment" (tr. of Agnes Gergely). [GrandS] (12:1, #45) 93, p. 97 -
98.
"Kambuja: Stelae from the Khmer Empire" (tr. of Yves di Manno). [Sulfur] (33)
Fall 93, p. 206-214.
"Provincial Morning" (for M.). [PaintedB] (50/51) 93, p. 66.
"Red Banner's Whereabouts" (for Robert Kelly). [Conjunc] (20) 93, p. 140-143.
6540. TARPLEY, Natasha
"Debt" (Honorable Mention). [HarvardA] (127:3) Spr 93, p. 35.
6541. TARVER, John
"These Photographers Recede." [DenQ] (27:3) Wint 93, p. 67.
6542. TASSI, Katherine
"Destinations." [NowestR] (31:2) 93, p. 108.
6543. TASSO, Torquato
"To Father Don Angelo Grillo" (tr. by Felix Stefanile). [Sparrow] (60) Sum 93, p.
55.
6544. TATE, James
"The Answering Service." [QRL] (12:32/33) 93, p. 532.
"Color in the Garden." [AmerPoR] (22:1) Ja-F 93, p. 75.
"The Early Years." [NewYorker] (69:9) 19 Ap 93, p. 68.
"A Fox." [NewYorker] (69:17) 14 Je 93, p. 54.
"From an Island." [PaintedB] (49) 93, p. 5.
"A Glowworm, a Lemur, and Some Women." [HarvardR] (5) Fall 93, p. 105-106.
"Head of a White Woman Winking." [AmerPoR] (22:1) Ja-F 93, p. 75.

"Inspiration." [AmerPoR] (22:4) Jl-Ag 93, p. 29.
"Jim Left the Pet Cemetery with a Feeling of Disgust." [NewEngR] (15:4) Fall 93,
    p. 148-149.
"Letting Him Go." [QRL] (12:32/33) 93, p. 531.
"The Life of Poetry." [Hudson] (45:4) Wint 93, p. 536.
"Like a Scarf." [ColR] (20:1) Spr 93, p. 21-23.
"The New Chinese Fiction." [AmerPoR] (22:1) Ja-F 93, p. 76.
"Rainy Day." [PaintedB] (49) 93, p. 4.
"Spring Forward, Fall Back." [AmerPoR] (22:4) Jl-Ag 93, p. 29.
"Tell Them   Was Here" (Constant Defender, 17). [OhioR] (49) 93, p. 111.
"Tortoise Relocation." [AmerPoR] (22:4) Jl-Ag 93, p. 29.
"What the City Was Like." [ColR] (20:1) Spr 93, p. 18-20.
"The Wrong Way Home." [NewEngR] (15:4) Fall 93, p. 149.
6545. TATMAN, Lucy A.
"Like a woman I labored to change." [SinW] (50) Sum-Fall 93, p. 38-39.
TATSUJI, Miyoshi
    See MIYOSHI, Tatsuji
6546. TAUFER, Veno
"A Suburban Hotel" (tr. of Jelena Lengold). [NoDaQ] (61:1) Wint 93, p. 103.
6547. TAUS, Roger
"Bird, Poem @ 06/11/90." [OnTheBus] (5:2, #12) Sum-Fall 93, p. 204.
6548. TAYLOR, Alex
"The Cemetery" (tr. of Henrik Nordbrandt). [Vis] (41) 93, p. 14.
"Chora" (tr. of Henri Nordbrandt). [Vis] (43) 93, p. 16.
"Gobi" (tr. of Henrik Nordbrandt). [Vis] (41) 93, p. 13.
"Street" (tr. of Henrik Nordbrandt). [Vis] (42) 93, p. 23.
6549. TAYLOR, Bruce
"Frank." [Journal] (17:2) Fall-Wint 93, p. 35-36.
"Middle-aged Men, Learning" (four movements). [Journal] (17:2) Fall-Wint 93, p.
    37-38.
"Mine." [MidwQ] (35:1) Aut 93, p. 48.
"Poetry Sex Love Music Booze & Death" (a "lite" sestina). [Epiphany] (4:2) Ap 93,
    p. 107-108.
6550. TAYLOR, Cathy
"Untitled: I was already not too happy that tuesday morning." [Eyeball] (2) 93, p.
    19.
6551. TAYLOR, Craig
"The Politics of Three Horrors." [OnTheBus] (6:1, #13) Wint 93-Spr 94, p. 198.
"Wanting to Enter." [WillowR] (20) Spr 93, p. 34.
6552. TAYLOR, Dannyka
"The Mother Explains the Father to the Son." [Ploughs] (19:4) Wint 93-94, p. 81.
6553. TAYLOR, Joan Imig
"A Desert Change." [WorldO] (25:2) Wint 93-94, p. 36.
6554. TAYLOR, Jon
"Armageddon." [Pearl] (17) Spr 93, p. 24.
"So Granpa Wouldn't Know." [Pearl] (17) Spr 93, p. 65.
6555. TAYLOR, Judith
"Velvet Dips." [OnTheBus] (6:1, #13) Wint 93-Spr 94, p.   199.
6556. TAYLOR, Keith
"Cashier's Dream, the Hunt." [MichQR] (32:1) Wint 93, p. 73.
"Resurrection." [MichQR] (32:1) Wint 93, p. 74-75.
6557. TAYLOR, Marcella
"Steps into Spring." [RagMag] (11:1) 93, p. 7.
6558. TAYLOR, Marilyn
"Clown." [CreamCR] (17:2) Fall 93, p. 125.
"Golden Warriors End Year with Big Loss." [Poetry] (162:4) Jl 93, p. 222.
"What They Don't Know." [PoetL] (88:3) Fall 93, p. 14.
6559. TAYLOR, Ross
"The Room." [VirQR] (69:3) Sum 93, p. 503.
"Toy." [VirQR] (69:3) Sum 93, p. 504.
6560. TAYLOR, Thomas Lowe
"After." [Talisman] (11) Fall 93, p. 260-261.
6561. TAYSON, Richard
"In Sickness and in Health." [MichQR] (32:3) Sum 93, p. 408-409.
"Prophylactic II." [MinnR] (NS 40) Spr-Sum 93, p. 24.

6562. TEAPE, Roland
"Faery Ring." [Dandel] (20:1) 93, p. 57.
6563. TEDESCO, Cynthia
"Prophets." [Caliban] (12) 93, p. 181.
6564. TEJADA, Roberto
"Mirrors for Gold" (for J. W.). [GlobalCR] (1) Spr 93, p. 74-79.
6565. TELLER, Janne
"Playing." [Contact] (11:65/66/67) Spr 93, p. 42.
6566. TEMPLETON, Ardis Possanza
"Self-Portrait: October, 1991." [Footwork] (23) 93, p. 50.

Ten . . .
See also names beginning with "Ten" without the following space, filed below in
their alphabetical positions, e.g., TenEYCK
6567. Ten HAKEN, Kathleen
"Letters from Tucson." [Lactuca] (17) Apr 93, p. 15-18.
6568. TENENBAUM, Molly
"To the Ski Instructor, Regarding the Paradox of Grip and Glide." [ColEng] (55:1)
Ja 93, p. 79-80.
6569. TenEYCK, Richard
"The Night Is Deep." [PoetL] (88:4) Wint 93-94, p. 12.
6570. TEODORESCU, Virgil
"Poem in Leopardese" (Bilingual Text fragment, tr. by Sasha Vlad and Zack
Rogow). [Talisman] (10) Spr 93, p. 155-156.
6571. TEPEXCUINTLE, Alice
"Down the black dirt highways." [CapilR] (2:10) Spr 93, p. 64-68.
"Twenty-Nine Rules About Horses." [CapilR] (2:10) Spr 93, p. 62-63.
"Up River on a Hot Summernite." [CapilR] (2:10) Spr 93, p. 59-61.
6572. TERADA, Rei
"Piero di Cosimo" (after Panofsky). [PartR] (60:3) Sum 93, p. 424-425.
6573. TERMAN, Philip
"Eloquence." [Poetry] (161:5) F 93, p. 268-269.
"For Etheridge Knight." [PoetC] (24:2) Wint 93, p. 12-15.
"G-d." [Poetry] (161:5) F 93, p. 267-268.
"My Father's Mother." [Poetry] (161:5) F 93, p. 269-270.
6574. TERPSTRA, John
"(Blues)." [PoetryC] (13:3) 93, p. 6.
"(Blues, Removed)." [PoetryC] (13:3) 93, p. 6.
"(Rhythm)." [PoetryC] (13:3) 93, p. 6.
6575. TERRANOVA, Elaine
"Melrose Park." [PaintedB] (50/51) 93, p. 70.
"Story in the Style of Henry James." [CreamCR] (17:1) Spr 93, p. 64-65.
TERRE, David C. la
See LaTERRE, David C.
6576. TERRIS, Susan
"False Pregnancy." [PoetL] (88:3) Fall 93, p. 35.
"Flossie." [SpoonR] (18:1) Wint-Spr 93, p. 24-25.
"Future Tense." [Kalliope] (15:3) 93, p. 25.
6577. TERRIS, Virginia
"Fo(u)nd Memories." [13thMoon] (11:1/2) 93, p. 80.
"Just Next Door." [HangL] (63) 93, p. 63.
"Patients." [HangL] (63) 93, p. 63.
"Revelations." [Confr] (51) Sum 93, p. 251.
6578. TETI, Zona
"Tale from Balzac: Bette." [Iowa] (23:2) Spr-Sum 93, p. 65.
"Tess Learns to Be Professional." [Iowa] (23:2) Spr-Sum 93, p. 66.
6579. TETTE, Sharan Flynn
"Down into Mill Valley." [Plain] (13:3) Spr 93, p. 7.
6580. TETUA, Moa
"Careful of the Day" (tr. by Muriel Rukeyser and Samuel Elbert). [Sulfur] (33) Fall
93, p. 256.
"Rari for O'Otua" (tr. by Muriel Rukeyser and Samuel Elbert). [Sulfur] (33) Fall 93,
p. 255.
"Rari for Tahia and Piu" (tr. by Muriel Rukeyser and Samuel Elbert). [Sulfur] (33)
Fall 93, p. 253-254.
"A True Confession" (tr. by Muriel Rukeyser and Samuel Elbert). [Sulfur] (33) Fall
93, p. 255-256.

6581. THALMAN, Mark
"The Only Plaster Casting of *The Thinker* Rodin Made." [CharR] (19:2) Fall 93, p. 103-104.
"The Wheelchair." [Pearl] (19) Fall-Wint 93, p. 53.
6582. THAMAN, Konai
"Your Words." [Manoa] (5:1) Sum 93, p. 232.
6583. THATCHER, Philip
"Three Voices in Stone — Plus Wood." [Event] (22:1) Spr 93, p. 44-48.
6584. THEGE, Michel de Donkoly
"Pylos." [PennR] (5:2) 93, p. 26-27.
6585. THELIN, John R.
"Parole del Politico" (for Cesare Pavese). [Border] (2) Spr 93, p. 66-67.
6586. THEROUX, Alexander
"Consolation of Philosophy." [Conjunc] (20) 93, p. 128.
"Jesus and the Cat." [Conjunc] (20) 93, p. 127.
"Jonah Considers His Right Hand from His Left Hand." [Conjunc] (20) 93, p. 127.
"Lucifer Is Haunted by the Echo of His Last Goodbye." [Conjunc] (20) 93, p. 128 - 129.
"What Mr. Ambidextrine Was Told at Confession at the 31st St. Shrine." [Conjunc] (20) 93, p. 128.
"Willow Tree" (for Peggy Lee). [Conjunc] (20) 93, p. 129.
6587. THESEN, Sharon
"Biography of a Woman." [PoetryC] (14:1) 93, p. 18.
"Eating Smarties in the Truck." [PoetryC] (14:1) 93, p. 18.
"The Lesson Is." [PoetryC] (14:1) 93, p. 19.
"Over & Out." [PoetryC] (14:1) 93, p. 18.
"Sputnik Measures." [PoetryC] (14:1) 93, p. 19.
"Valentine." [PoetryC] (14:1) 93, p. 19.
6588. THIELMAN, James
"Not Far." [Comm] (120:12) 18 Je 93, p. 14.
6589. THILLEMAN, Tod
"I set off from home to define life's way." [Talisman] (10) Spr 93, p. 171.
"I've lifted above to hear below." [Talisman] (10) Spr 93, p. 171.
"Today I walk, a sandwiched event like history." [Talisman] (10) Spr 93, p. 171.
6590. THISTLETHWAITE, Kathy
"The Dragons' Soirée." [SoCoast] (14) Ja 93, p. 14.
6591. THOMAS, Christopher
"Faces II" (after an Urdu Ghazal). [JamesWR] (11:1) Fall 93, p. 7.
6592. THOMAS, Elizabeth
"Crabapple." [SouthernR] (29:1) Wint, Ja 93, p. 161-163.
6593. THOMAS, G. Murray
"The Tattoo." [ChironR] (12:4/13:1, #37/38) Wint 93-Spr 94, p. 45.
6594. THOMAS, Julia
"On Becoming Lovers." [Pearl] (17) Spr 93, p. 14.
6595. THOMAS, Larry D.
"Late Sonata." [ChatR] (13:2) Wint 93, p. 11.
"The red Raging Waters." [TexasR] (14:3/4) Fall-Wint 93, p. 86.
6596. THOMAS, Laurence W.
"Tranquility." [AmerPoR] (22:4) Jl-Ag 93, p. 31.
6597. THOMAS, Randolph
"River." [SpoonR] (18:2) Sum-Fall 93, p. 77.
6598. THOMAS, Sally
"The Farmer's Mistress." [NewRep] (208:1/2) 4-11 Ja 93, p. 34.
"Grandmother Rising." [WillowS] (31) Wint 93, p. 76.
"The Hands." [RiverC] (13:1) Fall 92, p. 70-71.
"An Order for Eucharist." [RiverC] (13:1) Fall 92, p. 72-73.
"Reunion." [NewYorker] (69:24) 2 Ag 93, p. 38.
6599. THOMAS, Stanley J.
"Extended Metaphor." [Bogg] (66) Wint 92-93, p. 7.
6600. THOMAS, Terry
"Looking into Lomans." [Plain] (13:2) Wint 93, p. 35.
"Marginalia." [HampSPR] Wint 93, p. 26.
"Pasta Potion." [Plain] (14:1) Fall 93, p. 28.
6601. THOMAS, Vonnie
"An Ancient Idyll Lives Today." [AnthNEW] (5) 93, p. 28.

6602. THOMIN, Jeanette Barnes
"Bronze Age" (Literary Contest Winner, 2nd Prize). [Crucible] (29) Fall 93, p. 6.
6603. THOMPSON, Clive
"Season's Tickets." [Quarry] (42:2) 93, p. 124.
6604. THOMPSON, Craig
"The Flat." [Border] (2) Spr 93, p. 68.
6605. THOMPSON, Julius E.
"The Make-Believe." [Obs] (8:1) Spr-Sum 93, p. 100.
6606. THOMPSON, Kit
"For Jean MacDonald, b. 1910." [Comm] (120:15) 10 S 93, p. 14.
"When Borges Dreamed." [Comm] (120:9) 7 My 93, p. 21.
6607. THOMPSON, Phyllis Hoge
"1976." [QRL] (12:32/33) 93, p. 357-358.
"Beauty" (for Linda Daniels). [QRL] (12:32/33) 93, p. 352-353.
"Diamond" (The Death of Christian Pons). [QRL] (12:32/33) 93, p. 351-352.
"Faith." [QRL] (12:32/33) 93, p. 354-355.
"The Light on the Door." [QRL] (12:32/33) 93, p. 355-356.
"There's Justice." [QRL] (12:32/33) 93, p. 356-357.
"Tom Singer's Bracelet." [QRL] (12:32/33) 93, p. 353-354.
6608. THOMPSON, Rebecca
"Afternoon of a Yawn." [MidwQ] (34:2) Wint 93, p. 223.
6609. THOMPSON, Tom
"Gently, the Orange." [Stand] (34:2) Spr 93, p. 73.
6610. THOMPSON, W. B.
"Starez Silouan." [Sequoia] (34/35) 92-93, p. 99.
6611. THOMSON, Diana
"St. Peter Healing the Sick with His Shadow" (Masaccio). [ChrC] (110:22) 28 Jl-4
Ag 93, p. 747.
6612. THOMSON, Jeffrey J.
"Listening Again to 'Take the A Train'." [Plain] (14:1) Fall 93, p. 15.
"Phototropism and Sardines" (For Al Salsich). [Plain] (13:3) Spr 93, p. 29.
6613. THOMSON, Taunja
"Dreaming During a Lecture on How to Publish Poetry." [CinPR] (24) Spr 93, p. 62.
6614. THORBURN, Alexander
"The Canal." [Iowa] (23:1) Wint 93, p. 156-157.
"The Library." [Iowa] (23:1) Wint 93, p. 159-160.
"The Soda Fountain." [Iowa] (23:1) Wint 93, p. 158-159.
"The Street Plan." [PoetryNW] (34:4) Wint 93-94, p. 10-11.
"The Timetable." [PoetryNW] (34:4) Wint 93-94, p. 9-10.
6615. THORBURN, Russell
"Apollinaire's Landscapes." [Northeast] (5:8) Spr-Sum 93, p. 12.
6616. THORENSEN, Rik
"For Kim." [Caliban] (12) 93, p. 164.
"Love Poem" (In the rain). [Caliban] (12) 93, p. 165.
"Port of Call." [Asylum] (8) 93, p. 126.
6617. THORN, Arline R.
"Exploring the Poles." [SouthernHR] (27:1) Wint 93, p. 47.
6618. THORNLYRE, Padma J.
"The Moon's Robe." [DogRR] (12:2, #24) Fall-Wint 93, p. 43.
6619. THORNTON, Russell
"The Body of the Whispering." [PoetryC] (13:4) 93, p. 11.
"The Eyes of Travel." [PoetryC] (13:4) 93, p. 11.
6620. THORNTON, Thomas E.
"Birches, Down a 1/4." [EngJ] (82:1) Ja 93, p. 86.
6621. THORPE, Michael
"Trapped Light" (for Lucy, Edmond and Jacob). [AntigR] (92) Wint 93, p. 57-61.
6622. THORPE, Ronald
"Moon Bath." [Footwork] (23) 93, p. 47.
6623. TIBALDO-BONGIORNO, Marylou
"Aunt Mary." [Footwork] (23) 93, p. 103.
"Margarita." [Footwork] (23) 93, p. 103.
6624. TIBBETTS, Elizabeth
"Ida Goes to the Hens." [BelPoJ] (43:3) Spr 93, p. 24-25.
"Institution." [BelPoJ] (44:2) Wint 93-94, p. 18-19.
6625. TIBBETTS, Frederick
"Essays." [NewRep] (208:9) 1 Mr 93, p. 38.

"Motions of the Soul." [YaleR] (81:1) Ja 93, p. 40.
"Remarks on Our City." [ParisR] (35:126) Spr 93, p. 124-126.
"Three Figures." [ParisR] (35:128) Fall 93, p. 73-74.
"A View of the Firmament." [Verse] (10:2) Sum 93, p. 55.
"Winds Becoming North." [US1] (28/29) 93, p. 6.
6626. TICE, Arden (Arden A.)
"I Lie Mauve in the Courtyard." [DogRR] (12:1, #23) Spr-Sum 93, p. 9.
"The Wall." [Gypsy] (20) Sum 93, p. 50.
6627. TIERNEY, Erin C.
"Untitled: becky rosner was the only jewish girl I knew." [Caliban] (12) 93, p. 170.
6628. TIERNEY, Karl
"June 21, 1989." [AmerPoR] (22:2) Mr-Ap 93, p. 18.
"Summer Solstice." [AmerPoR] (22:2) Mr-Ap 93, p. 18.
6629. TIGER, Madeline
"Storms." [Footwork] (23) 93, p. 66.
"Waking Up." [Footwork] (23) 93, p. 66.
"Wet Cellar." [Footwork] (23) 93, p. 66.
"Where I Come From." [US1] (28/29) 93, p. 12.
6630. TILLINGHAST, Richard
"Abbey Hill." [SouthernR] (29:2) Spr, Ap 93, p. 288-289.
"First" (from the Turkish of Sezai Karakoc). [MichQR] (32:2) Spr 93, p. 204-205.
"On a Gothic Ivory" (for James Boyd White). [HarvardR] (3) Wint 93, p. 90-91.
"Sketches." [SouthwR] (78:2) Spr 93, p. 190-191.
"Twos." [Ploughs] (19:1) Spr 93, p. 79.
"The Winter Funerals." [Hudson] (45:4) Wint 93, p. 613-614.
"Wireless." [SouthernR] (29:2) Spr, Ap 93, p. 290.
6631. TIMM, Steve
"The Drift." [RagMag] (11:2) 93, p. 55.
"Gus Is Gone." [RagMag] (11:2) 93, p. 56.
"Tell Them I Sent You." [RagMag] (11:2) 93, p. 60.
"The Walking After the Riding After the Shouting" (Want, Part Thirteen).
[RagMag] (11:2) 93, p. 57-58.
"Want, Part Six." [RagMag] (11:2) 93, p. 59.
6632. TIMS, Jane
"Coltsfoot" (Tussilago Farfara L.). [AntigR] (92) Wint 93, p. 76-77.
"Parting the Collection." [AntigR] (95) Aut 93, p. 133-134.
"Pearly Everlasting" (Anaphalis margaritacea L.). [AntigR] (92) Wint 93, p. 74-75.
"Queen Anne's Lace" (Daucus carota L.). [AntigR] (92) Wint 93, p. 80-81.
"Star-flower" (Trientalis borealis Raf.). [AntigR] (92) Wint 93, p. 78-79.
TING, Shu
   See SHU, Ting
6633. TIRADO, Eduardo
"Macho-Macho-Macho-Man." [Trasimagen] (1:1) Otoño-Invierno 93, p. 64.
6634. TISDEL, Phillip H.
"Lesson in Law." [Amelia] (7:2, #21) 93, p. 55.
"Role Play." [Amelia] (7:2, #21) 93, p. 55-56.
"Seductions." [Amelia] (7:2, #21) 93, p. 54-55.
6635. TIUS, Mary M.
"Riddle: Get the horses! Call the chief!" [Light] (7) Aut 93, p. 13.
6636. TJEPKES, Michael
"Poem in Jeff Beddow's Absence" (w. James Naiden). [NorthStoneR] (11) 93, p.
170.
6637. TKACZ, Virlana
"The pendulum is tired" (tr. of Volodymyr Svidzinsky, w. Wanda Phipps). [Vis]
(41) 93, p. 15.
"Tired, Leaning on the Hills" (tr. of Volodymyr Svidzinsky, w. Wanda Phipps).
[Vis] (43) 93, p. 53.
"To Think About Eternity" (tr. of Mykola Riabchuk, w. Wanda Phipps). [Vis] (41)
93, p. 15.
TKAZ, Virlana
   See TKACZ, Virlana
6638. TOBIN, Daniel
"René Rilke." [SouthernHR] (27:4) Fall 93, p. 380.
6639. TOBIN, Philip
"When Blackbirds and Shadows Traverse the Night." [PoetL] (88:3) Fall 93, p. 28.

6640. TODD, J. C.
"Falls." [VirQR] (69:2) Spr 93, p. 257-259.
6641. TODD, Mike
"My View." [PoetryUSA] (25/26) 93, p. 55.
TODD, Nita Hooper
See HOOPER-TODD, Nita
6642. TODD, Rebecca
"The Reptile Tent." [CinPR] (24) Spr 93, p. 70.
6643. TOFER, Merle
"Just Another Faggot Poet" (for Ana & Dave Christy). [ChironR] (12:1, #34) Spr
93, p. 22.
"New Year." [JamesWR] (10:3) Spr 93, p. 4.
6644. TOKUNO, Ken
"Mortality." [BellArk] (9:5) S-O 93, p. 12.
6645. TOLAN, James
"Should You Die." [LouisL] (10:2) Fall 93, p. 58.
"Without a Sound." [LouisL] (10:2) Fall 93, p. 57.
6646. TOM, Karen
"Untitled: God went down on me in a graveyard." [ChironR] (12:1, #34) Spr 93, p.
45.
6647. TOMASOVICH, Brian
"Labor." [BrooklynR] (10) 93, p. 46-47.
6648. TOMCIC, Goran
"Fluorescent Sorrow" (tr. by Ines Modrcin, the author and Tali Makell). [PoetL]
(88:1) Spr 93, p. 49.
"Here" (tr. by Ines Modrcin, the author and Tali Makell). [PoetL] (88:1) Spr 93, p.
50.
6649. TOMLINSON, Charles
"April for B—" (tr. of Attilio Bertolucci). [TriQ] (88) Fall 93, p. 25.
"Cosmology." [TriQ] (88) Fall 93, p. 22.
"Fires in November" (tr. of Attilio Bertolucci). [TriQ] (88) Fall 93, p. 24.
"Hovingham." [TriQ] (88) Fall 93, p. 21.
"Mad Song." [QRL] (12:32/33) 93, p. 532-533.
"Obsession." [QRL] (12:32/33) 93, p. 533-534.
"October" (tr. of Attilio Bertolucci). [TriQ] (88) Fall 93, p. 26.
"To a Photographer." [TriQ] (88) Fall 93, p. 23.
"To Giuseppe in October" (tr. of Attilio Bertolucci). [TriQ] (88) Fall 93, p. 28.
"To His Mother Whose Name Was Maria" (tr. of Attilio Bertolucci). [TriQ] (88)
Fall 93, p. 27.
6650. TOMLINSON, Rawdon
"Cunningham Burns, Electrician." [Northeast] (5:9) Wint 93-94, p. 12.
"Father's Disaster Tale." [SoCarR] (26:1) Fall 93, p. 112-113.
"First Birthday Sonnet" (for my son, Rawdon Stephen Scott Tomlinson 10/21/91 to
12/12/91). [WritersF] (19) 93, p. 45.
"Job's Comforters" (For Monsignor C.B. Woodrich). [WritersF] (19) 93, p. 44.
"Moonman." [ChatR] (13:2) Wint 93, p. 2.
"Sangre de Cristo, July 4." [Confr] (51) Sum 93, p. 259-260.
TOMOYUKI, Iino
See IINO, Tomoyuki
6651. TOPOL, Jáchym
"The Beast" (tr. by Ellen Rosenbaum). [OxfordM] (9:1) Spr-Sum 93, p. 43-44.
"Eerie Dreams" (tr. by Ellen Rosenbaum). [OxfordM] (9:1) Spr-Sum 93, p. 41-43.
"The End of the World" (tr. by Ellen Rosenbaum). [OxfordM] (9:1) Spr-Sum 93, p.
40-41.
"Love Episode" (tr. by Ellen Rosenbaum). [OxfordM] (9:1) Spr-Sum 93, p. 39-40.
6652. TOPP, Mike
"Country Life." [HangL] (62) 93, p. 60.
"The Godfather." [HangL] (62) 93, p. 60.
"Handy Hint." [Talisman] (11) Fall 93, p. 296.
"Miles to Go." [Talisman] (11) Fall 93, p. 296.
"World Poetry Projections." [Talisman] (11) Fall 93, p. 296.
6653. TORGA, Miguel
"The Conch" (tr. by Ivana Rangel-Carlsen). [Vis] (43) 93, p. 45.
"Emptiness" (tr. by Ivana Rangel-Carlsen). [Vis] (43) 93, p. 45.
"For Federico García Lorca" (tr. by Edouard Roditi). [WorldL] (4) 93, p. 3-4.
"No Pasaran!" (tr. by Edouard Roditi). [WorldL] (4) 93, p. 5.

6654. TORGERSEN, Eric
"The Lone Ranger Rides Off." [PassN] (14:1) Sum 93, p. 12-13.
6655. TORNES, Elizabeth
"Bathing My Grandmother." [Boulevard] (8:2/3, #23/24) Fall 93, p. 187.
6656. TORRA, Joseph
"Livingstone Metalwork." [Talisman] (11) Fall 93, p. 231-232.
6657. TORRES SOCAS, Olga
"45 Horas." [Americas] (21:2) Sum 93, p. 48.
"Retorno a la Realidad." [Americas] (21:2) Sum 93, p. 47.
"Trasplantada." [Americas] (21:2) Sum 93, p. 49.
6658. TORRESON, Rodney
"A Farmwife and Son." [Northeast] (5:9) Wint 93-94, p. 30.
"Purity, a Failure in White Robes, Goes Dreaming in the Far Pasture." [Northeast]
(5:8) Spr-Sum 93, p. 7.
"Thurman Munson." [Spitball] (45) Fall 93, p. 56-57.
"Ties." [Northeast] (5:8) Spr-Sum 93, p. 8.
TOSHIKO, Hirata
See HIRATA, Toshiko
6659. TOTH, Tawni
"Home." [HayF] (13) Fall-Wint 93, p. 80.
6660. TOTTEN, B. R.
"For the Child Stirring." [BellArk] (9:6) N-D 93, p. 8-9.
6661. TOTTEN, Kathryn
"Ebenezer." [WestB] (33) 93, p. 7.
6662. TOVA
"Community Circles." [SinW] (50) Sum-Fall 93, p. 18-27.
6663. TOWLE, Parker
"Cutting Ice." [Blueline] (14) 93, p. 98-99.
6664. TOWNSEND, Ann
"Foolish." [NewL] (59:3) 93, p. 76-77.
"The Rabbit Queen" (Black Hand Gorge Festival, September). [WestHR] (47:2)
Sum 93, p. 190-191.
"Salt for Me." [WestHR] (47:2) Sum 93, p. 188-189.
6665. TOWNSEND, Cheryl (Cheryl A.)
"Escaping." [Amelia] (7:2, #21) 93, p. 45.
"Foreplay." [ChironR] (12:4/13:1, #37/38) Wint 93-Spr 94, p. 45.
"Glazed." [Bogg] (66) Wint 92-93, p. 6.
"I Polished My Nails for This." [Pearl] (17) Spr 93, p. 15.
"I Poured Into." [Pearl] (17) Spr 93, p. 15.
"It's an Art of Balance." [SlipS] (13) 93, p. 33.
"Standards." [ChironR] (12:4/13:1, #37/38) Wint 93-Spr 94, p. 45.
"Unemployment." [ChironR] (12:4/13:1, #37/38) Wint 93-Spr 94, p. 45.
6666. TOY, Lyda
"Reflections by a Window." [Kalliope] (15:2) 93, p. 29.
6667. TRACHTENBERG, Paul
"Life's Sporadic Turnabout." [Pearl] (19) Fall-Wint 93, p. 65.
6668. TRAIL, B. D.
"Lecture." [NewYorkQ] (50) 93, p. 62.
6669. TRAKL, Georg (George)
"An Autumn Evening" (for Karl Rock, tr. by Ned Balbo). [Verse] (10:2) Sum 93, p.
65.
"Dream of Evil" (tr. by Ned Balbo). [Verse] (10:2) Sum 93, p. 65.
"In the Wasteland" (tr. by William Virgil Davis). [Paint] (19:38) Aut 92, p. 54.
"My Heart Toward Evening" (tr. by Steven Frattali). [GrahamHR] (17) Fall 93, p.
74.
"To One Who Died Young" (tr. by Steven Frattali). [GrahamHR] (17) Fall 93, p. 75.
"To the Boy Elis" (tr. by Steven Frattali). [GrahamHR] (17) Fall 93, p. 73.
"Transfigured Fall" (tr. by David Carrara). [Talisman] (11) Fall 93, p. 212.
"A Winter Evening" (tr. by William Virgil Davis). [Paint] (19:38) Aut 92, p. 55.
6670. TRAMMELL, Michael
"Mardi Gras in the Dead of Summer." [PoetL] (88:4) Wint 93-94, p. 21-22.
6671. TRAN, Barbara
"Love and Rice." [AntR] (51:1) Wint 93, p. 91.
6672. TRAN, Truong
"Scars." [NoDaQ] (61:3) Sum 93, p. 148.
"Second Religion." [OnTheBus] (6:1, #13) Wint 93-Spr 94, p. 200.

471

6673. TRANBARGER, Ossie E.
"Time of sugaring" (Lucille Sandberg Haiku Award, 1st honorable mention).
[Amelia] (7:2, #21) 93, p. 32.
6674. TRANSTRÖMER, Tomas
"The Cuckoo" (tr. by Robin Fulton). [ManhatR] (7:1) Fall 93, p. 10.
"From July 1990" (tr. by Robin Fulton). [ManhatR] (7:1) Fall 93, p. 11.
"Lugubrious Gondola No. 2" (tr. by Robin Fulton). [ManhatR] (7:1) Fall 93, p. 7-9.
"A Sketch from 1844" (tr. by Robin Fulton). [Verse] (10:3) Wint 93, p. 102.
"Three Stanzas" (tr. by Robin Fulton). [Verse] (10:3) Wint 93, p. 101.
6675. TRANTER, John
"Anyone Home?" [Nimrod] (36:2) Spr-Sum 93, p. 38-40.
"Australia Day." [Nimrod] (36:2) Spr-Sum 93, p. 36.
"North Woods." [Verse] (10:1) Spr 93, p. 8-10.
"Southlanders." [Nimrod] (36:2) Spr-Sum 93, p. 37.
"Two Views of Lake Placid." [Boulevard] (8:1, #22) Spr 93, p. 132.
6676. TRASK, Haunani-Kay
"Every Island a God." [ChiR] (39:3/4) 93, p. 179.
"Kaulana Na Pua." [HawaiiR] (16:3, #36) Wint 93, p. 40-41.
6677. TRAUNSTEIN, Russ
"Poet's Séance: Stopping by Woods" (News Item: Poets talk to Robert Frost).
[Light] (8) Wint 93, p. 11.
6678. TRAXLER, Patricia
"Death of a Distant In-law." [Agni] (37) 93, p. 198.
"First Prairie Winter." [Agni] (37) 93, p. 199.
6679. TREAT, Jessica
"Letter to My Sister." [Asylum] (8) 93, p. 22.
"Soldier." [Asylum] (8) 93, p. 22.
6680. TREBOR
"My Perfect Androgyne." [ChironR] (12:3, #36) Aut 93, p. 28.
"Our Lady of the Fine Torso (A Vision of Marky Mark in Cavin Kleins)." [ChironR]
(12:3, #36) Aut 93, p. 28.
6681. TREFETHEN, Tracy
"Two Seasons." [AntR] (51:3) Sum 93, p. 379.
6682. TREGEBOV, Rhea
"At or Above the Earth's Surface." [MalR] (105) Wint 93, p. 40-41.
"The Extravagant." [PraS] (67:4) Wint 93, p. 122.
"Filling Out the Form." [PraS] (67:4) Wint 93, p. 119-120.
"For Keith Spicer" (who wanted the nation's poets to solve the unity crisis). [Quarry]
(42:1) 93, p. 45-47.
"Problems." [PraS] (67:4) Wint 93, p. 117-119.
"What Is to Be Done?" (for Ann Ganley, activist, b. 1904, Vitebsk, Russia, d. 1991,
Plainfield, NJ). [PraS] (67:4) Wint 93, p. 120-121.
"Without Asking." [MalR] (105) Wint 93, p. 38-39.
6683. TREITEL, Renata
"Gypsophila" (to L. Anceschi, tr. of Rosita Copioli). [SnailPR] (3:1) Fall-Wint 93,
p. 4.
"The weather is fair, but to not quiver is an unravelling of all yesses" (tr. of Rosita
Copioli). [SnailPR] (3:1) Fall-Wint 93, p. 5.
6684. TREMBLAY, Gail
"An Onondaga Trades with a Woman Who Sings with a Mayan Tongue." [Calyx]
(15:1) Wint 93-94, p. 47.
"Surviving." [Calyx] (15:1) Wint 93-94, p. 46.
6685. TREMBLAY, Mildred
"Regina Vagina." [Dandel] (20:1) 93, p. 15-17.
6686. TREMMEL, Robert
"I Read Two Articles in the Paper This Morning." [PoetryNW] (34:4) Wint 93-94,
p. 13.
"Prajna Paramita." [MidwQ] (34:2) Wint 93, p. 224-225.
"Renting Videos." [PoetryNW] (34:4) Wint 93-94, p. 12-13.
6687. TRETHEWEY, Eric
"Wait." [Poetry] (162:4) Jl 93, p. 208-209.
6688. TRETHEWEY, Natasha
"Drapery Factory, Gulfport, Mississippi 1956." [Agni] (37) 93, p. 65.
"Flounder." [Callaloo] (16:1) Wint 93, p. 33.
"Naola Beauty Academy, New Orleans, Louisiana 1943." [Agni] (37) 93, p. 64.

TRETHEWEY

472

"Three Photographs" (from the "American Highways and Byways" series by Clifton
  Johnson, 1902). [Callaloo] (16:3) Sum 93, p. 521-523.
6689. TRICARICO, Danny
  "Roses" (for Colleen). [Pearl] (17) Spr 93, p. 55.
6690. TRILLIN, Calvin
  "Adieu, George Bush." [Nat] (256:3) 25 Ja 93, p. 77.
  "Adieu, Whizzer." [Nat] (256:14) 12 Ap 93, p. 473.
  "The Ballad of Zoë Baird." [Nat] (256:6) 15 F 93, p. 185.
  "Baseball's Back." [Nat] (256:17) 3 My 93, p. 581.
  "Blues, by Wanderin' Willie Clinton." [Nat] (256:25) 28 Je 93, p. 893.
  "Busy, Busy, Busy." [Nat] (256:15) 19 Ap 93, p. 509.
  "Change in Travel Plans." [Nat] (256:23) 14 Je 93, p. 821.
  "A Cheer, of Sorts, for Arafat." [Nat] (257:10) 4 O 93, p. 341.
  "Clinton Presides Over the Signing." [Nat] (257:11) 11 O 93, p. 378.
  "Clinton Redux." [Nat] (257:20) 13 D 93, p. 717.
  "Curse." [Nat] (256:4) 1 F 93, p. 112.
  "Customer Persistence." [Nat] (256:12) 29 Mr 93, p. 401.
  "Dole." [Nat] (256:22) 7 Je 93, p. 761.
  "Don't Leave Us, Di." [Nat] (257:22) 27 D 93, p. 789.
  "Ed Rollins Speaks." [Nat] (257:19) 6 D 93, p. 681.
  "The Final Shocker." [Nat] (256:8) 1 Mr 93, p. 257.
  "The Forest Summit Issue." [Nat] (256:16) 26 Ap 93, p. 545.
  "Gergen, Gergen." [Nat] (257:5) 9-16 Ag 93, p. 161.
  "Gore Redux." [Nat] (257:13) 25 O 93, p. 449.
  "A Health Care Plan Is Sent to Congress." [Nat] (257:17) 22 N 93, p. 609.
  "Hollywood Goes Too Far." [Nat] (257:7) 6-13 S 93, p. 233.
  "Japanese Slump." [Nat] (257:21) 20 D 93, p. 753.
  "Just Cool It." [Nat] (257:8) 20 S 93, p. 270.
  "A Life in the Senate." [Nat] (257:18) 29 N 93, p. 645.
  "Lingering Reflections on a Populist Inaugural." [Nat] (256:7) 22 F 93, p. 221.
  "Mission to Mars." [Nat] (257:9) 27 S 93, p. 305.
  "Observations at a Clinton Press Conference." [Nat] (256:1) 4-11 Ja 93, p. 5.
  "Obsession." [Nat] (256:11) 22 Mr 93, p. 365.
  "On a Four-President Press Conference." [Nat] (257:12) 18 O 93, p. 413.
  "On Attempting to Comment on the First One Hundred Days." [Nat] (256:20) 24
    My 93, p. 689.
  "On Military Intervention." [Nat] (257:14) 1 N 93, p. 485.
  "On the Accusation That Former Italian Premier Giulio Andreotti Kissed the Mafia's
    Boss of Bosses." [Nat] (256:19) 17 My 93, p. 653.
  "On the Appointment of David Gergen as White House Communications Director."
    [Nat] (256:24) 21 Je 93, p. 857.
  "On the Nomination of Ruth Bader Ginsburg." [Nat] (257:2) 12 Jl 93, p. 53.
  "The Phillies vs. Toronto." [Nat] (257:16) 15 N 93, p. 558.
  "Poet at a Loss." [Nat] (256:21) 31 My 93, p. 725.
  "Rostenkowski Accused." [Nat] (257:6) 23-30 Ag 93, p. 198.
  "Saddam Hussein, Saddam Hussein." [Nat] (257:3) 19 Jl 93, p. 89.
  "Saved From Lani Guinier." [Nat] (257:1) 5 Jl 93, p. 5.
  "The Senate Confirms Janet Reno, 98-0." [Nat] (256:13) 5 Ap 93, p. 437.
  "A Short History of Lloyd Bentsen's Dealing with Special Interests." [Nat] (256:2)
    18 Ja 93, p. 41.
  "Thoughts on Filibustering." [Nat] (256:18) 10 My 93, p. 617.
  "Thoughts on the Senator from Georgia Who Might Have Been President." [Nat]
    (256:9) 8 Mr 93, p. 293.
  "Welcome, President Clinton." [Nat] (256:5) 8 F 93, p. 149.
  "Whatever Happened to Cyprus?" [Nat] (257:4) 26 Jl-2 Ag 93, p. 125.
  "Who?" [Nat] (257:15) 8 N 93, p. 521. Corrected reprint [Nat] (257:16) 15 N 93, p.
    600.
6691. TRINIDAD, David
  "3 a.m." [IllinoisR] (1:1) Fall 93, p. 20.
  "Family Portrait, 1963." [IllinoisR] (1:1) Fall 93, p. 24-27.
  "Food for Thought, or Just Deserts" (M.F.A. Workshop w. Marie Hasten, Howard
    Glyn, Pamela Hughes, M. R. Syneck, Lisbeth Keiley, Mary Greene and Allen
    Ginsberg, Nov. 21, 1988). [BrooklynR] (10) 93, p. 94-95.
  "Something's Got to Give." [Chelsea] (55) 93, p. 69-71.
  "The Ten Best Episodes of *The Patty Duke Show*." [IllinoisR] (1:1) Fall 93, p. 11.

6692. TRIPLETT, Pimone
"Persephone and Hades." [ParisR] (35:128) Fall 93, p. 225-227.
6693. TRITICA, John
"Brooklyn and Back" (for David Abel and Kathy Kuehn). [Talisman] (11) Fall 93,
p. 282-283.
6694. TRIVELPIÈCE, Laurel
"Preparation." [PoetL] (88:3) Fall 93, p. 11.
6695. TRIVERS, Mildred Raynolds
"The House on Bitterstrasse." [HopewellR] (5) 93, p. 97.
6696. TROUPE, Quincy
"Perennial Ritual" (For all the dictators of Haiti & anywhere else). [Drumvoices]
(1:1/2) Fall-Wint 91-92, p. 136.
6697. TROWBRIDGE, William
"Help Wanted." [TarRP] (32:2) Spr 93, p. 35.
"Interstate" (I-35 North, Iowa). [GeoR] (47:3) Fall 93, p. 521.
"Kong Views an Experimental Art Film at the City Library." [PoetC] (24:2) Wint
93, p. 42.
"Miss Snider." [TarRP] (32:2) Spr 93, p. 34.
6698. TROY, Jack
"In Kenyon's Fields." [WestB] (31/32) 93, p. 14-15.
TRUONG, Tran
See TRAN, Truong
6699. TRUSSELL, Robert
"The Feet of Pilgrims." [NewL] (60:1) 93, p. 74-75.
6700. TSALOUMAS, Dimitris
"Song of the Just." [CentR] (37:2) Spr 93, p. 369.
6701. TSVETAEVA, Marina
"Girlfriend" (tr. by Sonja Franeta). [RiverS] (37) 93, p. 29-31.
"On Red Steed" (tr. by Nina Kossman). [Epiphany] (4:3) Jl 93, p. 203-208.
TSVETAYEVA, Marina
See TSVETAEVA, Marina
6702. TU, Mu
"Coming Home" (tr. by David Young). [Field] (48) Spr 93, p. 21.
"Late Summer Evening" (tr. by David Young). [Field] (48) Spr 93, p. 23.
"Morning on the River" (tr. by David Young). [Field] (48) Spr 93, p. 20.
"Pien River Freezing Over" (tr. by David Young). [Field] (48) Spr 93, p. 18.
"Saying Goodbye" (tr. by David Young). [Field] (48) Spr 93, p. 24.
"Spring in the South" (tr. by David Young). [Field] (48) Spr 93, p. 22.
"Unable to Cross at Yunzhi" (tr. by David Young). [Field] (48) Spr 93, p. 19.
6703. TUCKER, David
"The Men Decide." [Boulevard] (8:2/3, #23/24) Fall 93, p. 170.
6704. TUCKER, Martin
"An Artist's Life" (for Alfred Van Loen, 1924-1993). [Confr] (51) Sum 93, p. 228.
6705. TUDOR, Amy Liann
"Highway 51, New Mexico." [NewYorkQ] (52) 93, p. 98.
6706. TUDOR, Leo
"Giacumbert Nau" (Selections, tr. by Ellen and Ernest H. von Nardroff). [LitR]
(36:4) Sum 93, p. 454-457.
6707. TUFTS, Carol
"Extended Care Facility." [Poem] (69) My 93, p. 33.
"Too Little Care." [Poem] (69) My 93, p. 32.
6708. TUGEND, Alina
"On the Bus." [SoCoast] (14) Ja 93, p. 33.
6709. TULLIS, Rod (See also TULLOSS, Rod)
"Dementia." [SpoonR] (18:2) Sum-Fall 93, p. 117.
"Filling Station Poems." [SpoonR] (18:2) Sum-Fall 93, p. 111-114.
"In the Act of Becoming Timeless." [SpoonR] (18:1) Wint-Spr 93, p. 74-75.
"The Light of This March Day." [SpoonR] (18:1) Wint-Spr 93, p. 76-77.
"The Perche Creek Trestle." [SpoonR] (18:2) Sum-Fall 93, p. 115-116.
"A View from the Truckstop." [CinPR] (24) Spr 93, p. 59.
6710. TULLOSS, Rod (See also TULLIS, Rod)
"Degrees of Unsolvability" (for Charles Entrekin). [US1] (28/29) 93, p. 28.
"Feeding My Angel" (for Gerald Jorge Lee). [US1] (28/29) 93, p. 17.
6711. TUMBALÉ, Elkion
"On Ya 'Gin." [Bogg] (66) Wint 92-93, p. 58.

6712. TURAJ-KALINSKA, Katarzyna
    "The Little Mermaid" (tr. by Tomek Kitlinski and Malgorzata Staniewska). [Verse]
        (10:2) Sum 93, p. 38.
    "To Heloise: Yet Another Letter" (tr. by Tomek Kitlinski and Malgorzata
        Staniewska). [Verse] (10:2) Sum 93, p. 38.
6713. TURCO, Lewis
    "Arachnophobia." [SouthernHR] (27:4) Fall 93, p. 378.
    "Letter to W. D. S." [HolCrit] (30:3) Je 93, p. 3.
    "Monophobia: The Fear of Loneliness." [NewYorkQ] (51) 93, p. 63.
    "Papyrophobia: The Fear of Paper." [NewYorkQ] (50) 93, p. 55.
6714. TURCOTTE, James
    "The Death Show." [MinnR] (NS 40) Spr-Sum 93, p. 11.
6715. TURK, Penelope Bryant
    "Mending Test" (Apologies to Robert Frost). [EngJ] (82:1) Ja 93, p. 86.
6716. TURNER, Alberta
    "Birthday Poem." [Journal] (17:1) Spr-Sum 93, p. 31.
    "The Everlasting Yes." [Journal] (17:1) Spr-Sum 93, p. 34.
    "A Kind of Loving." [13thMoon] (11:1/2) 93, p. 81.
    "Lions' Mouths." [Journal] (17:1) Spr-Sum 93, p. 33.
    "The Match." [Journal] (17:2) Fall-Wint 93, p. 11.
    "Rope." [Journal] (17:2) Fall-Wint 93, p. 8-9.
    "Saved." [Journal] (17:2) Fall-Wint 93, p. 10.
    "Trepidations." [Journal] (17:1) Spr-Sum 93, p. 32.
6717. TURNER, Bill
    "Relax, Petrarch!" [Sparrow] (60) Sum 93, p. 16.
6718. TURNER, Frederick
    "Death Mass." [Crazy] (45) Wint 93, p. 14-35.
    "In a Season of Political Faction." [Sparrow] (60) Sum 93, p. 29.
    "On Glenn Gould's Goldberg Variations, Sainte-Colombe, Marais, Radnoti and
        Petrarch." [Sparrow] (60) Sum 93, p. 29.
6719. TURNER, Jack
    "Re-Creation." [Poetry] (161:4) Ja 93, p. 215.
6720. TURNER, Ken
    "Downstairs." [Footwork] (23) 93, p. 119.
    "Standing Room." [Footwork] (23) 93, p. 120.
    "Starlings." [Footwork] (23) 93, p. 119.
    "Touchdown." [Footwork] (23) 93, p. 119.
6721. TURNER, Seneca
    "For Etheridge." [Drumvoices] (2:1/2) Fall-Wint 92-93, p. 224-225.
6722. TUTWILER, Mary
    "Hanging Tree." [LouisL] (10:1) Spr 93, p. 60-61.
6723. TWICHELL, Chase
    "Animal Graves." [NewEngR] (15:4) Fall 93, p. 122-123.
    "Bear on Scale." [NewEngR] (15:4) Fall 93, p. 125-126.
    "The Devil I Don't Know." [NewEngR] (15:4) Fall 93, p. 120-121.
    "Girl with Sad Face." [OntR] (38) Spr-Sum 93, p. 63.
    "The Ruiner of Lives." [OntR] (38) Spr-Sum 93, p. 61-62.
    "The Rule of the North Star." [NewEngR] (15:4) Fall 93, p. 124-125.
    "Snow in Condoland." [Nat] (256:11) 22 Mr 93, p. 388.
    "Stripped Car." [NewEngR] (15:4) Fall 93, p. 126-128.
    "Touch-Me-Not." [GeoR] (47:1) Spr 93, p. 39-41.
6724. TWITTY, Anne
    "Hermana" (Fragment, tr. of Magali Alabau). [Luz] (4) My 93, p. 40-47.
    "To Be a Deserter" (tr. of Magali Alabau). [AmerV] (31) 93, p. 120.
6725. TYSH, Chris
    "Car Men, a Play in D" (Excerpt). [Talisman] (10) Spr 93, p. 95-96.
6726. TZAGOLOFF, Helen
    "Important Telephone Numbers." [NewYorkQ] (52) 93, p. 70.
6727. UCEDA, Julia
    "Secret, Ancient Voices of the Night" (Selections: II, IV, tr. by Cecilia C. LeeLaura
        Higgins). [LitR] (36:3) Spr 93, p. 383-384.
6728. UDOVICKI, Karolina
    "Balkan Street" (tr. of Ivan Gadjanski). [NoDaQ] (61:1) Wint 93, p. 73-76.
    "Summing Up" (tr. of Ivan Gadjanski). [NoDaQ] (61:1) Wint 93, p. 77.
6729. UIAGALELEI, Matthew
    "Cedilla." [HawaiiR] (17:3, #39) Fall 93, p. 132.

"Circumflex." [HawaiiR] (17:3, #39) Fall 93, p. 133.
"Green Dodge." [HawaiiR] (17:3, #39) Fall 93, p. 27-28.
"Water." [HawaiiR] (17:3, #39) Fall 93, p. 69.
6730. UJEVIC, Tin
"Daily Lament" (tr. by Richard Burns and Dasa Maric). [NoDaQ] (61:1) Wint 93, p. 188-189.
"Frailty" (tr. by Richard Burns and Dasa Maric). [NoDaQ] (61:1) Wint 93, p. 191.
"The Necklace" (Selections: XXXII, XXV, XXXI, tr. by Richard Burns and Dasa Maric). [NoDaQ] (61:1) Wint 93, p. 190-191.
"Star on High" (tr. by Richard Burns and Dasa Maric). [NoDaQ] (61:1) Wint 93, p. 192.
6731. ULKU, A. K.
"Willow." [BlackWR] (19:2) Spr-Sum 93, p. 131.
6732. ULLMAN, Leslie
"The Mountain Outside My Window." [Poetry] (163:1) O 93, p. 17.
6733. ULMER, James
"Fallingwater." [Crazy] (44) Spr 93, p. 48-49.
"Portraits in Green." [Crazy] (44) Spr 93, p. 50-51.
"A Season." [Border] (2) Spr 93, p. 69-70.
"Six Thin Ladders" (2 selections. First Runner Up, Poetry Award). [NewL] (59:2) 93, p. 115-117.
"Summoning." [Crazy] (44) Spr 93, p. 43-47.
UN, Ko
    See KO, Un
UN-KYO, Kang
    See KANG, Un-kyo
6734. UNDERWOOD, Pat
"Dusting Doll Dishes." [PoetC] (25:1) Fall 93, p. 17.
6735. UNDERWOOD, Robert
"At the Gym." [Pearl] (17) Spr 93, p. 76.
"Quake Fever." [WormR] (33:4, #132) 93, p. 172.
"Sequel." [WormR] (33:4, #132) 93, p. 172.
"Shortchanged." [WormR] (33:4, #132) 93, p. 172.
"Why Little Red Riding Hood Couldn't Happen Today." [Pearl] (17) Spr 93, p. 76.
UNG-BU, Yu
    See YU, Ung-Bu (d. 1456)
6736. UNGER, David
"Gringo Ghost." [WritersF] (19) 93, p. 90.
6737. UNGRIA, Ricardo M. de
"Avatar at the Gas Station, Lower East Side." [Bomb] (45) Fall 93, p. 82.
"Bienvenido." [Bomb] (45) Fall 93, p. 82.
6738. UNGRICH, Rick
"Havasu Falls." [Kaleid] (26) Wint-Spr 93, p. 40.
6739. UNSINO, Stephen
"Snow Wine" (tr. of Alexander Blok). [TampaR] (6) Spr 93, p. 41.
6740. UPDIKE, John
"Academy." [OntR] (38) Spr-Sum 93, p. 46.
"At the End of the Rainbow." [OntR] (38) Spr-Sum 93, p. 45.
"Brazil." [Boulevard] (8:1, #22) Spr 93, p. 30.
"Fall." [Pequod] (35) 93, p. 78.
"The House Growing." [Pequod] (35) 93, p. 77-78.
"Montes Veneris." [NewYorker] (69:15) 31 My 93, p. 46.
"São Paulo." [Boulevard] (8:1, #22) Spr 93, p. 29.
"Upon Looking into Sylvia Plath's Letters Home." [Boulevard] (8:1, #22) Spr 93, p. 31.
6741. UPTON, Elaine Maria
"Overcoming Anthropology." [Drumvoices] (3:1/2) Fall-Wint 93-94, p. 101.
"Story." [Drumvoices] (3:1/2) Fall-Wint 93-94, p. 102.
6742. UPTON, Lee
"Brave Spirit." [SycamoreR] (5:1) Wint 93, p. 36-37.
"Contemporary Fragment (I)." [Epoch] (42:2) 93, p. 201.
"The Crossing of Orchids." [Field] (48) Spr 93, p. 50-51.
"The Fish House." [BlackWR] (19:1) Fall-Wint 92, p. 86.
"Ocean Cave." [AmerPoR] (22:5) S-O 93, p. 25.
"Psychic's Holiday." [AmerPoR] (22:5) S-O 93, p. 25.
"To See You Again." [Field] (48) Spr 93, p. 48-49.

"A Tour." [SycamoreR] (5:1) Wint 93, p. 38-39.
"Walled Garden." [AmerLC] (5) 93, p. 26.
"Woman in an Interior" (— Edouard Vuillard). [Epoch] (42:2) 93, p. 202-203.
6743. URDANG, Constance
"Goodbye, 1992" (for A.M.F.). [OntR] (39) Fall-Wint 93-94, p. 108.
"Her Studio." [CharR] (19:2) Fall 93, p. 128.
"In Rivera's Studio." [Border] (2) Spr 93, p. 71.
"In the Weather." [CharR] (19:2) Fall 93, p. 125.
"Into the Trees." [YaleR] (81:2) Ap 93, p. 28-29.
"Jaap's House." [CharR] (19:2) Fall 93, p. 126.
"Landmarks." [CharR] (19:2) Fall 93, p. 127.
"Lines for My Grandmother's Grave." [QRL] (12:32/33) 93, p. 534-535.
"Mexico." [CharR] (19:2) Fall 93, p. 124.
"Night Voices." [Border] (2) Spr 93, p. 72.
"Reincarnation." [OntR] (39) Fall-Wint 93-94, p. 107.
6744. UROSEVIC, Vlada
"Deceitful Landscapes" (tr. by Bradley R. Strahan and the author). [Vis] (43) 93, p. 39.
"Regions of Restlessness" (tr. by Bradley R. Strahan and the author). [Vis] (43) 93, p. 39.
"Regions of Silence" (tr. by Bradley R. Strahan and the author). [Vis] (43) 93, p. 39.
6745. URSU, Liliana
"Contre Jour" (tr. by Adam Sorkin, w. the author). [Vis] (43) 93, p. 47.
6746. USCHUK, Pamela
"Accord." [HighP] (8:3) Wint 93, p. 97-98.
"The Fifth World Nation Attends Sunset on Wolf Creek Pass" (for Frank Bergon).
[HighP] (8:3) Wint 93, p. 99-100.
6747. VAICIUNAITĖ, Judita (Judith)
"Autumn Night" (Excerpt, tr. by Viktoria Skrupskelis and Stuart Friebert). [AntigR] (93-94) Spr-Sum 93, p. 188.
"Black Mirror" (tr. by Viktoria Skrupskelis and Stuart Friebert). [ParisR] (35:128) Fall 93, p. 272-273.
"Dragonflies" (tr. by Viktoria Skrupskelis and Stuart Friebert). [LitR] (37:1) Fall 93, p. 86.
"In Memoriam" (tr. by Viktoria Skrupskelis and Stuart Friebert). [AntigR] (93-94) Spr-Sum 93, p. 187.
"In the Hospital" (tr. by Viktoria Skrupskelis and Stuart Friebert). [LitR] (37:1) Fall 93, p. 86.
"September Night" (tr. by Viktoria Skrupskelis and Stuart Friebert). [ParisR] (35:128) Fall 93, p. 271.
"Sisters" (tr. by Viktoria Skrupskelis and Stuart Friebert). [MalR] (102) Spr 93, p. 57.
"Sleeplessness" (tr. by Viktoria Skrupskelis and Stuart Friebert). [ParisR] (35:128) Fall 93, p. 272.
"Spring" (tr. by Viktoria Skrupskelis and Stuart Friebert). [ParisR] (35:128) Fall 93, p. 271.
"Vilnius. Archaeology" (tr. by Viktoria Skrupskelis and Stuart Friebert). [ParisR] (35:128) Fall 93, p. 273.
6748. VAIL, Desire
"Coyaba" (From: *See How Wet the Street Sounds*, 1992). [Kaleid] (27) Sum-Fall 93, p. 29.
"Moving In." [Blueline] (14) 93, p. 18.
"See" (From: *See How Wet the Street Sounds*, 1992). [Kaleid] (27) Sum-Fall 93, p. 56.
6749. VALAORITIS, Nanos
"Moving Targets." [Asylum] (8) 93, p. 124.
"Rule Number Three." [Asylum] (8) 93, p. 124.
6750. VALDÉS, Gina
"Changing the World." [Americas] (21:1) Spr 93, p. 53-54.
"English con Salsa." [Americas] (21:1) Spr 93, p. 49-50.
"Los Angeles." [Americas] (21:1) Spr 93, p. 51-52.
6751. VALDÉS GINEBRA, Arminda
"Sombras Imaginarias" (Selection: X). [Luz] (5) N 93, p. 83.
6752. VALENTINE, Jean
"After a Mastectomy." [AmerV] (32) 93, p. 12.
"The Childhood House." [NewYorker] (69:41) 6 D 93, p. 137.

"The Inside Angel." [GlobalCR] (2) Fall 93, p. 1.
"The Suicides." [NewYorker] (69:12) 10 My 93, p. 87.
"To the Black Madonna of Chartres." [Atlantic] (271:4) Ap 93, p. 90.
"World Light." [NewYorker] (69:35) 25 O 93, p. 98.
6753. VALÉRY, Paul
    "Palm" (tr. by Denis Devlin). [QRL] (12:32/33) 93, p. 535-537.
6754. VALESIO, Paolo
    "Il Figlio dell'Uomo Fa l'Aeroplano." [Footwork] (23) 93, p. 113-114.
    "A Prayer for the Buddha." [Footwork] (23) 93, p. 112.
    "Preghiera al Buddha." [Footwork] (23) 93, p. 112-113.
    "The Son of Man Plays Airplane." [Footwork] (23) 93, p. 113.
    "Spendere il Cielo." [Footwork] (23) 93, p. 112.
    "Spending Heaven." [Footwork] (23) 93, p. 112.
6755. VALINOTTI, Nick
    "Coastal Advisory" (for my father). [BrooklynR] (10) 93, p. 54.
6756. VALIS, Noël
    "Belfast Elegy." [ProseP] (2) 93, p. 94.
    "When I Really Dream." [13thMoon] (11:1/2) 93, p. 82.
6757. VALKEAPÄÄ, Nils-Aslak
    "The Trek of the Wind" (Selections, tr. by Lars Nordström, Ralph Salisbury and
        Harald Gaski). [SilverFR] (24) Wint 93, p. 31-38.
6758. VALLE, Carmen
    "Civil Register" (tr. by the author). [Trasimagen] (1:1) Otoño-Invierno 93, p. 40.
    "Genealogia." [Trasimagen] (1:1) Otoño-Invierno 93, p. 39.
    "Registro Civil." [Trasimagen] (1:1) Otoño-Invierno 93, p. 40.
6759. VALLE, Francisco
    "Estella Inscrita." [InterPR] (19:2) Fall 93, p. 36.
    "Inscribed Stele" (tr. by Steven White). [InterPR] (19:2) Fall 93, p. 37.
6760. VALLEJO, César
    "Black Stone on a White Stone" (tr. by Jack Hirschman). [ChironR] (12:4/13:1,
        #37/38) Wint 93-Spr 94, p. 3.
    "Trilce" (Selection: I, in Spanish). [MassR] (34:2) Sum 93, p. 1 84.
    "Trilce" (Selections: I-III, IX-XI, XIII, XV, tr. by Magda Bogin). [MassR] (34:2)
        Sum 93, p. 185-192.
6761. VALLONE, Antonio
    "Sex Education." [NowestR] (31:3) 93, p. 45.
    "Sperm Bank: A Post-Modern Love Story." [NowestR] (31:3) 93, p. 46.
6762. VALLOTTON, Jean Pierre
    "Paper Women" (From Pièces brèves en quart de ton, tr. by James Vladimir Gill).
        [ProseP] (2) 93, p. 95.
VALVERDE, Alfonso Barrera
    See BARRERA VALVERDE, Alfonso
6763. VALVIS, James
    "About Your Iguana." [ChironR] (12:4/13:1, #37/38) Wint 93-Spr 94, p. 16.
    "The Tree." [Pearl] (19) Fall-Wint 93, p. 56.
    "Upon Receiving a Fan Letter Asking Me to Explain One of My Poems." [ChironR]
        (12:4/13:1, #37/38) Wint 93-Spr 94, p. 16.
    "What Exactly Is a Valvis?" [ChironR] (12:4/13:1, #37/38) Wint 93-Spr 94, p. 16.
Van . . .
    See also names beginning with "Van" without the following space, filed below in
        their alphabetic positions.
Van CREVEL, Maghiel
    See CREVEL, Maghiel van
6764. Van DUYN, Mona
    "Into Mexico." [QRL] (12:32/33) 93, p. 538-539.
6765. Van GUNDY, Douglas
    "Ankle Deep in the Madison River." [BellArk] (9:1) Ja-F 93, p. 13.
    "Sketch." [BellArk] (9:1) Ja-F 93, p. 5.
6766. Van HOUTEN, Lois
    "Butterflies Save Me from the Cold." [Footwork] (23) 93, p. 76.
    "The Lilacs." [Footwork] (23) 93, p. 76-77.
    "Miss Edda Mc Clanahan." [Footwork] (23) 93, p. 77.
6767. Van NOORD, Barbara
    "Between Seasons." [Comm] (120:7) 9 Ap 93, p. 22.
    "In the frozen Bracken" (for Pat, on the death of her mother). [Poem] (70) N 93, p.
        66.

"Ralph Steiner's Photograph: 'Hanging Sheets'." [Poem] (70) N 93, p. 67.
6768. Van PEENEN, H. J.
    "At Lovegene's Gallery." [BellArk] (9:2) Mr-Ap 93, p. 13.
    "Death of the Woodcutter" (tr. of Alfonso Barrera Valverde). [InterPR] (19:2) Fall
        93, p. 15, 17.
    "If, Then" (Agouti, Corcovado Rain Forest). [BellArk] (9:2) Mr-Ap 93, p. 13.
    "An Introduction" (tr. of Alfonso Barrera Valverde). [InterPR] (19:2) Fall 93, p. 13.
    "Meditation on the Unknown" (tr. of Alfonso Barrera Valverde). [InterPR] (19:2)
        Fall 93, p. 5, 7.
    "Much to Be Said" (Sloth, Tortuguero Rain Forest). [BellArk] (9:2) Mr-Ap 93, p. 8.
    "A Song of Simple Love" (tr. of Alfonso Barrera Valverde). [InterPR] (19:2) Fall
        93, p. 9, 11.
6769. Van SLUYS, Sharon M.
    "Garden without Flowers." [PoetC] (24:2) Wint 93, p. 40-41.
6770. Van WALLEGHEN, Michael
    "Crawlspace." [SouthernR] (29:3) Sum, Jl 93, p. 591-592.
6771. Van WERT, William (William F.)
    "Grief Stages." [PaintedB] (50/51) 93, p. 62.
6772. Van WINCKEL, Nance
    "Ghost Pig." [GrandS] (11:4, #44) 93, p. 173.
    "Girl with Wood." [IndR] (16:1) Spr 93, p. 180.
    "Hurry, Get Up, There's Work to Do." [PoetryNW] (34:4) Wint 93-94, p. 35-36.
    "Insemination Tango." [Ploughs] (19:1) Spr 93, p. 190.
    "John the Baptist. Two Hungers." [NowestR] (31:3) 93, p. 57.
    "Local Anesthetic: A Woman's Womb Is Opened" (Los Angeles, Oct. 1991).
        [AmerV] (32) 93, p. 117-119.
    "Nicholas by the River." [Ploughs] (19:1) Spr 93, p. 189.
    "Old Man Watching the Storm." [ChiR] (39:1) 93, p. 46-47.
    "Our House Was Full without Us." [ChiR] (39:1) 93, p. 44-45.
    "Par Nothing." [PoetryNW] (34:4) Wint 93-94, p. 34.
6773. Van ZANT, Frank
    "Coping with Touch" (for Patricia). [ChangingM] (25) Wint-Spr 93, p. 33.
6774. VANCE, Bob
    "A Christmas Story." [ChangingM] (26) Sum-Fall 93, p. 72.
6775. VANDENBERG, Katrina
    "The Problem with the Pills." [MidAR] (14:1) 93, p. 152-154.
6776. VANDERLIP, Brian
    "Benares." [Event] (22:2) Sum 93, p. 37-41.
6777. VanderMOLEN, Robert
    "The North Starts Here." [ArtfulD] (24/25) 93, p. 111.
VanDUYN, Mona
    See Van DUYN, Mona
VanGUNDY, Douglas
    See Van GUNDY, Douglas
6778. VANICEK, Zdenek
    "Abingdon" (tr. by Ewald Osers). [OxfordM] (9:1) Spr-Sum 93, p. 109.
    "In the Little Church of St. Mary's" (tr. by Ewald Osers). [OxfordM] (9:1) Spr-Sum
        93, p. 107-109.
VanNOORD, Barbara
    See Van NOORD, Barbara
VanPEENEN, H. J.
    See Van PEENEN, H. J.
VanSLUYS, Sharon M.
    See Van SLUYS, Sharon M.
6779. VANSPANCKEREN, Kathryn
    "The Servant's Happiness." [13thMoon] (12:1/2) 93-94, p. 69-70.
6780. VANTOMME, Dianne
    "Mordant Greenery." [OnTheBus] (5:2, #12) Sum-Fall 93, p. 205.
VanWALLEGHEN, Michael
    See Van WALLEGHEN, Michael
VanWINCKEL, Nance
    See Van WINCKEL, Nance
6781. VARGA, Adriana
    "The Arrow" (tr. of Marin Sorescu, w. Stuart Friebert). [Field] (48) Spr 93, p. 45.
    "Innocence" (tr. of Marin Sorescu, w. Stuart Friebert). [Field] (48) Spr 93, p. 47.
    "Sin" (tr. of Marin Sorescu, w. Stuart Friebert). [Field] (48) Spr 93, p. 46.

6782. VARGAS, Michelle
   "About My Country" (Poets of High School Age). [HangL] (62) 93, p. 91.
   "Wine Glass" (Poets of High School Age). [HangL] (62) 93, p. 91.
6783. VARMA, Archana
   "Man" (tr. by Aruna Sitesh and Arlene Zide). [MalR] (102) Spr 93, p. 50-51.
6784. VARNER, William
   "Flowers." [PoetL] (88:3) Fall 93, p. 13.
   "Swimming at Night." [PoetL] (88:3) Fall 93, p. 12.
6785. VARNES, Kathrine
   "Connecting the Dots." [AmerV] (31) 93, p. 24-25.
6786. VARNEY, Vic
   "Untitled: You can tell a lot about a country by its Madonna." [Sonora] (26) Fall 93,
      p. 19-20.
6787. VARON, Susan
   "Zen Water." [Outbr] (24) 93, p. 8-9.
6788. VASCONCELLOS, Cherry Jean
   "Every Night." [Pearl] (19) Fall-Wint 93, p. 48.
   "The Week the Dog Went Blind." [Pearl] (19) Fall-Wint 93, p. 48.
6789. VASILIU, Lucian
   "Circles" (tr. by Adam Sorkin, w. the author). [Vis] (43) 93, p. 46.
   "Your Thing" (tr. by Adam Sorkin, w. the author). [Vis] (43) 93, p. 46.
VASSEUR, Jeanne le
   See LeVASSEUR, Jeanne
6790. VAUGHN, Michael J.
   "Cadenza." [Elf] (3:4) Wint 93, p. 30.
   "Globe Street." [Elf] (3:4) Wint 93, p. 31.
6791. VAULTONBURG, Thomas L.
   "The Empty Angel." [SlipS] (13) 93, p. 74.
   "Play Directions for an Impromptu Creation of the Ideal Universe." [Pearl] (17) Spr
      93, p. 83.
   "Silence." [SlipS] (13) 93, p. 75.
6792. VAZIRANI, Reetika
   "Aunt Juni in Her Japanese Garden." [CumbPR]] (13:1) Fall 93, p. 70-71.
   "Aunt Juni's Carousel Horse." [CumbPR]] (13:1) Fall 93, p. 72.
   "Calcutta, for Jai." [Callaloo] (16:3) Sum 93, p. 509-510.
   "Mrs. Biswas Banishes a Female Relative." [Callaloo] (16:3) Sum 93, p. 508.
   "Mrs. Biswas Giving Advice to a Granddaughter." [Callaloo] (16:3) Sum 93, p. 506 -
      507.
   "Thinking about Citizenship While the Workmen Are Here" (for R.M.H., 1904 -
      1990). [KenR] (NS 15:1) Wint 93, p. 1-4.
6793. VAZQUEZ-PACHÉCO, Robert
   "New Ceremonies." [JamesWR] (10:4) Sum 93, p. 5.
6794. VEASEY, Jack
   "Wounded Animals." [PaintedB] (50/51) 93, p. 109.
6795. VEAZEY, Mary
   "Advanced St. Ives Riddle." [Light] (8) Wint 93, p. 11.
   "Petty Cash." [Light] (7) Aut 93, p. 13.
6796. VEGA, Janine Pommy
   "Epiphany." [Bogg] (66) Wint 92-93, p. 3-5.
   "Sick Room." [HangL] (63) 93, p. 70-71.
   "Word Up" (for the women in the Bayview Workshop, Bayview Correctional
      Facility for Women, New York City, June 1990). [HangL] (63) 93, p. 71.
6797. VEGA, Lope de
   "Sonnet Right Off the Bat" (tr. by John Frederick Nims). [Sparrow] (60) Sum 93, p.
      18.
VEGH, Diana de
   See DeVEGH, Diana
6798. VEINBERG, Jon
   "The Rain's Burden" (in memory of Ernesto Trejo). [QW] (37) Sum-Fall 93, p. 100 -
      102.
6799. VENTADOUR, Bernard de
   "Earthward Gliding" (in Provençal and English, tr. by Joe Malone). [Hellas] (4:2)
      Fall 93, p. 60-63.
6800. VENTOLA, John L.
   "On Strike." [Elf] (3:4) Wint 93, p. 32.

6801. VERA, A.
"It was at your funeral." [ChangingM] (25) Wint-Spr 93, p. 32.
6802. VERDICCHIO, Pasquale
"Terra Mara" (Selections, work in progress: 5 poems). [Footwork] (23) 93, p. 153 -
154.
6803. VERHAEREN, Emile
"Bread-Baking" (tr. by David Sanders). [Sparrow] (60) Sum 93, p. 51.
6804. VERILLA, Joseph
"Another Love Affair." [Footwork] (23) 93, p. 31-32.
6805. VERLAINE, Paul
"Langueur." [SewanR] (101:4) O-D, Fall 93, p. 561-562.
"Lassitude" (tr. by Richard Moore). [SewanR] (101:4) O-D, Fall 93, p. 562.
"Sagesse" (Selections: 4 poems, in French and English, tr. by R. H. Morrison).
[AntigR] (93-94) Spr-Sum 93, p. 120-129.
6806. VERLAINE, Tim
"Beauty Trip." [Bomb] (43) Spr 93, p. 42.
"Mars." [Bomb] (43) Spr 93, p. 42.
"Rhyme." [Bomb] (43) Spr 93, p. 43.
"This Tune." [Bomb] (43) Spr 93, p. 43.
6807. VERNY, Thomas R.
"Season's Greetings." [Footwork] (23) 93, p. 154.
VERONICA JEAN
See JEAN, Veronica
6808. VERTREACE, Martha (Martha M.)
"An Acceptable Sacrifice." [Gaia] (1/2) Ap-Jl 93, p. 46.
"Black Cameo." [Prima] (16/17) 93, p. 98-99.
"A Document in Madness." [SouthernHR] (27:3) Sum 93, p. 266-267.
"Pathfinder." [WebR] (17) Fall 93, p. 99-100.
6809. VIAN, Boris
"I Will Die of Cancer of the Spine" (tr. by Julia Older). [ApalQ] (39) 93, p. 29-30.
"The Spiders" (tr. by Julia Older). [Vis] (42) 93, p. 14-15.
6810. VIERECK, Peter
"Time Enough." [Agni] (38) 93, p. 138.
6811. VIETTI, Vicki
"Diary Entry, 1862." [WillowR] (20) Spr 93, p. 23-25.
6812. VILLANUEVA, Alma
"Trust." [Footwork] (23) 93, p. 12.
6813. VILLANUEVA-COLLADO, Alfredo
"Prosas para Arturo R." [Trasimagen] (1:1) Otoño-Invierno 93, p. 16-17.
6814. VILLAURRUTIA, Xavier
"Nocturne of the Rose" (for José Gorostiza, tr. by Félix Jiménez). [GrandS] (12:1,
#45) 93, p. 172-173.
6815. VILLENA, Luis Antonio de
"Four Roses" (tr. by Cecilia C. Lee and Laura Higgins). [LitR] (36:3) Spr 93, p. 386.
"That Sweet Atmosphere of Tango Around Three" (tr. by Cecilia C. Lee and Laura
Higgins). [LitR] (36:3) Spr 93, p. 385-386.
6816. VINCENT, John
"Young Man and Sailor" (after a drawing by Lorca). [JamesWR] (11:1) Fall 93, p.
6.
6817. VINOGRAD, Julia
"Scarecrow." [OnTheBus] (6:1, #13) Wint 93-Spr 94, p. 202.
6818. VINZ, Mark
"Family Still Life." [NoDaQ] (61:3) Sum 93, p. 61.
"A Mighty Fortress." [NoDaQ] (61:2) Spr 93, p. 205.
"Rhubarb." [NoDaQ] (61:3) Sum 93, p. 62.
6819. VIOLI, Paul
"The Laws of Casuality" (Excerpt). [FreeL] (12) Sum 93, p. 14-15.
"Scatter." [PaintedB] (52) 93, p. 44-45.
6820. VIRTUE, Linda
"To Jon." [Footwork] (23) 93, p. 70-71.
6821. VISTE-ROSS, Nathan
"Sonata" (to Louise). [NorthStoneR] (11) 93, p. 20-21.
6822. VITKUASKAITE, Jolanta
"The Garden God" (tr. of Alis Balbierius, w. Bradley R. Strahan). [Vis] (43) 93, p.
38.

481

VITO, E. B. de
    See De VITO, E. B.
6823. VIVANTE, Arturo
    "At the White Horse Tavern" (to Dylan Thomas). [Footwork] (23) 93, p. 5.
6824. VIVAR, Alicia Galaz
    "El Orden y los Dias." [InterPR] (19:1) Spr 93, p. 14.
    "The Order and the Days" (tr. by Oliver Welden). [InterPR] (19:1) Spr 93, p. 13.
6825. VIZENOR, Gerald
    Haiku (several poems in his article "The Envoy to Haiku"). [ChiR] (39:3/4) 93, p. 55-62.
6826. VLAD, Sasha
    "Poem in Leopardese" (Bilingual Text fragment, tr. of Virgil Teodorescu, w. Zack Rogow). [Talisman] (10) Spr 93, p. 155-156.
6827. VLASOPOLOS, Anca
    "Birding Once More." [Interim] (12:1) Spr-Sum 93, p. 20.
    "Common Knowledge." [Interim] (12:1) Spr-Sum 93, p. 19.
    "Even Song." [Interim] (12:1) Spr-Sum 93, p. 18.
    "First the Uterus." [Interim] (12:1) Spr-Sum 93, p. 21.
    "Midwest, Summer Storm." [CreamCR] (17:1) Spr 93, p. 30.
6828. VNUCAK, Ann
    "Anthropology." [BlackWR] (19:2) Spr-Sum 93, p. 109.
6829. VOGEL, Angela
    "The Dani." [FreeL] (11) Wint 93, p. 15.
6830. VOGEL, Frank
    "Margaret As Windfall" (For Her Birthday). [Light] (8) Wint 93, p. 20.
6831. VOISINE, Connie
    "Home From School." [MidAR] (14:1) 93, p. 141-142.
    "The Hunchback Sits Up at His Funeral." [NewYorkQ] (51) 93, p. 84.
6832. VOLD, Jan Erik
    "Elk" (tr. by the author). [ManhatR] (7:1) Fall 93, p. 14-15.
6833. VOLDSETH, Beverly
    "The Heart in Its Wisdom Can Melt Stone" (w. Susan Thurston Hamerski). [RagMag] (11:2) 93, p. 50.
    "A New Era." [RagMag] (11:1) 93, p. 72.
6834. VOLKMAN, Karen
    "Casanova in Love." [Poetry] (162:4) Jl 93, p. 221.
    "Equations." [ParisR] (35:128) Fall 93, p. 81.
    "Looking Back." [ParisR] (35:128) Fall 93, p. 79-80.
    "Persephone at Home." [ParisR] (35:128) Fall 93, p. 78-79.
6835. VOLKMER, Jon
    "The Line of Aridity." [SoDakR] (31:1) Spr 93, p. 98-99.
    "The Penates." [Hellas] (4:1) Spr 93, p. 58-60.
6836. VOLKOVA, Bronislava
    "A Certain Poem Comes As Fear" (tr. by the author). [Vis] (43) 93, p. 12.
    "Without Words" (tr. of Olga Neversilova). [Vis] (43) 93, p. 12.
6837. Von der EMBSE, Jayne
    "Anne's Blue Glass Gets Broken in the Earthquake." [Sequoia] (34/35) 92-93, p. 57-58.
6838. Von HOLTON, Dan
    "Foreclosure." [PikeF] (11) Fall 93, p. 29.
6839. Von NARDROFF, Ellen
    "Giacumbert Nau" (Selections, tr. of Leo Tudor, w. Ernest H. von Nardroff). [LitR] (36:4) Sum 93, p. 454-457.
    "Ils on Vantüraivels" (Selections: 3 poems, tr. of Andri Peer, w. Ernest H. von Nardroff). [LitR] (36:4) Sum 93, p. 462-467.
    "Just as a Star" (tr. of Adolf Muschg, w. Ernest H. von Nardroff). [LitR] (36:4) Sum 93, p. 552.
    "Paracelsus" (For Margarita, tr. of Jürg Federspiel, w. Ernest H. von Nardroff). [LitR] (36:4) Sum 93, p. 548-549.
    "Participation" (tr. of Erika Burkart, w. Ernest H. von Nardroff). [LitR] (36:4) Sum 93, p. 550.
6840. Von NARDROFF, Ernest H.
    "Giacumbert Nau" (Selections, tr. of Leo Tudor, w. Ellen von Nardroff). [LitR] (36:4) Sum 93, p. 454-457.
    "Ils on Vantüraivels" (Selections: 3 poems, tr. of Andri Peer, w. Ellen von Nardroff). [LitR] (36:4) Sum 93, p. 462-467.

"Just as a Star" (tr. of Adolf Muschg, w. Ellen von Nardroff). [LitR] (36:4) Sum 93,
    p. 552.
"Paracelsus" (For Margarita, tr. of Jürg Federspiel, w. Ellen von Nardroff). [LitR]
    (36:4) Sum 93, p. 548-549.
"Participation" (tr. of Erika Burkart, w. Ellen von Nardroff). [LitR] (36:4) Sum 93,
    p. 550.
6841. Von REIS, Siri
    "A Diet of Glass." [ParisR] (35:126) Spr 93, p. 129-130.
    "Glittering Ghost." [ParisR] (35:126) Spr 93, p. 132-133.
    "In Amber." [ParisR] (35:126) Spr 93, p. 130-131.
    "Luminist, National Gallery." [ParisR] (35:126) Spr 93, p. 131-132.
    "Quasi-stellar Object." [ParisR] (35:126) Spr 93, p. 128.
    "Vast Problem Still Obscure." [ParisR] (35:126) Spr 93, p. 128-129.
    "The Very Large Telescope." [ParisR] (35:126) Spr 93, p. 127.
Von WYSOCKI, Gisela
    See WYSOCKI, Gisela von
6842. VOSS, Fred
    "1982." [ChironR] (12:2, #35) Sum 93, p. 6.
    "Arrangement." [ChironR] (12:2, #35) Sum 93, p. 6.
    "Better." [ChironR] (12:2, #35) Sum 93, p. 5.
    "Blessed." [ChironR] (12:2, #35) Sum 93, p. 4.
    "The Devil." [ChironR] (12:2, #35) Sum 93, p. 6.
    "Double Standard." [ChironR] (12:2, #35) Sum 93, p. 5.
    "Feelers." [Pearl] (19) Fall-Wint 93, p. 17.
    "Full Speed Ahead." [ChironR] (12:2, #35) Sum 93, p. 6.
    "The Game Tried to Go On." [ChironR] (12:2, #35) Sum 93, p. 7.
    "Getting It Together." [ChironR] (12:2, #35) Sum 93, p. 8.
    "Goodguys." [ChironR] (12:2, #35) Sum 93, p. 7.
    "Hope." [ChironR] (12:2, #35) Sum 93, p. 8.
    "I Had a Lot to Learn." [Pearl] (19) Fall-Wint 93, p. 17.
    "Intrepid." [ChironR] (12:2, #35) Sum 93, p. 7.
    "The Laboratory." [ChironR] (12:2, #35) Sum 93, p. 6.
    "Man About Town." [ChironR] (12:2, #35) Sum 93, p. 8.
    "Night Shift." [ChironR] (12:2, #35) Sum 93, p. 7.
    "Not Long for This World." [SlipS] (13) 93, p. 32.
    "Out on a Limb." [Pearl] (17) Spr 93, p. 87.
    "Paradise." [ChironR] (12:2, #35) Sum 93, p. 4.
    "Partypooper." [ChironR] (12:2, #35) Sum 93, p. 8.
    "The Perfect Host." [ChironR] (12:2, #35) Sum 93, p. 4.
    "Protection." [ChironR] (12:2, #35) Sum 93, p. 4.
    "A Reason to Live." [ChironR] (12:2, #35) Sum 93, p. 5.
    "Seesaw." [ChironR] (12:2, #35) Sum 93, p. 5.
    "A Serious Smoker." [ChironR] (12:2, #35) Sum 93, p. 8.
    "Surprise." [ChironR] (12:2, #35) Sum 93, p. 5.
    "Tough Audience." [ChironR] (12:2, #35) Sum 93, p. 7.
    "Worse Than I Thought." [Pearl] (17) Spr 93, p. 87.
6843. VOZNESENSKY, Andrei
    "At Kirsanov's Burial" (tr. by Diana Der-Hovanessian and David Sloane). [Vis] (42)
        93, p. 34.
6844. VRHOVAC, Duska
    "Between Bed and Table" (tr. by Richard Burns and Vera Radojevic). [NoDaQ]
        (61:1) Wint 93, p. 208.
    "Dugout" (I-III, tr. by Richard Burns and Vera Radojevic). [NoDaQ] (61:1) Wint
        93, p. 206-207.
    "It Doesn't Matter Why" (tr. by Richard Burns and Vera Radojevic). [NoDaQ]
        (61:1) Wint 93, p. 208.
    "Ring-a-by" (tr. by Richard Burns and Vera Radojevic). [NoDaQ] (61:1) Wint 93, p.
        207.
    "Visitation" (tr. by Richard Burns and Vera Radojevic). [NoDaQ] (61:1) Wint 93, p.
        205.
6845. VRKLJAN, Irena
    "Late Summer" (tr. by Dasha Culic Nisula). [Vis] (43) 93, p. 10.
6846. VUCKOVIC, Vladeta
    "An Orphic Legacy" (tr. of Branko Miljkovic, w. John Matthias). [NoDaQ] (61:1)
        Wint 93, p. 114.

"To the Earth Right Now" (tr. of Branko Miljkovic, w. John Matthias). [NoDaQ] (61:1) Wint 93, p. 115.
6847. WADE, Cory
"The Dog Without Fleas." [Sequoia] (34/35) 92-93, p. 15-17.
6848. WADSWORTH, William
"Bloom's Photograph." [ParisR] (35:126) Spr 93, p. 54-55.
"Saturn." [ParisR] (35:126) Spr 93, p. 53-54.
"The Snake in the Garden Considers Daphne." [ParisR] (35:126) Spr 93, p. 51.
"The Spider." [ParisR] (35:126) Spr 93, p. 52.
6849. WAGNER, Anneliese
"A Direction in Life." [LullwaterR] (4:2) Spr-Sum 93, p. 102-103.
6850. WAGNER, Robert
"What He Said When His Wife Asked Him to Mow the Lawn." [Bogg] (66) Wint 92-93, p. 50.
6851. WAGNER, Shari
"Second Language (Somalia, 1973)." [HopewellR] (5) 93, p. 100.
6852. WAGNER, Shelly
"A Happy Poem." [HampSPR] Wint 93, p. 37-38.
"Ruth Stone Reading My Poem." [OnTheBus] (5:2, #12) Sum-Fall 93, p. 206.
"Thomas's Birthday." [TriQ] (88) Fall 93, p. 85-86.
"Treasure." [TriQ] (88) Fall 93, p. 84.
"Wet." [HampSPR] Wint 93, p. 36.
"What If?" [TriQ] (88) Fall 93, p. 87.
6853. WAGONER, David
"In a Field of Wild Flowers." [Poetry] (163:1) O 93, p. 4-5.
"Old Men Going to Bed." [NewRep] (209:19) 8 N 93, p. 42.
"On a Mountainside." [Poetry] (163:1) O 93, p. 1-3.
"On the Forest Floor." [Poetry] (163:1) O 93, p. 6.
"On the Plains." [Poetry] (163:1) O 93, p. 3-4.
WAI-LIM, Yip
See YIP, Wai-lim
6854. WAISMAN, Sergio Gabriel
"Six-four." [HangL] (63) 93, p. 72.
6855. WAITE, Genez
"Tattoos." [OnTheBus] (6:1, #13) Wint 93-Spr 94, p. 203.
6856. WAITE, Wendy
"Sounding." [BelPoJ] (44:2) Wint 93-94, p. 5.
6857. WAITTS, Fileman
"Colcothar." [CarolQ] (46:1) Fall 93, p. 36-37.
6858. WAKOSKI, Diane
"The Bluejay at the Nearly Empty Feeder" (for Jason Appelman). [AnotherCM] (26) Fall 93, p. 169-170.
"The Emerald Tattooed on My Arm." [CreamCR] (17:2) Fall 93, p. 178-179.
"Hummingbirds, Dazzling in from the Calif Desert" (for Craig Cotter and WCW). [13thMoon] (12:1/2) 93-94, p. 71.
"Point Dume." [AnotherCM] (26) Fall 93, p. 171-172.
"Portrait of a Lady." [AnotherCM] (26) Fall 93, p. 178.
"Salt Free Talk" (for Norman Hindley). [AnotherCM] (26) Fall 93, p. 173-175.
"Salt Marsh" (a tribute to Bob Peters). [AnotherCM] (26) Fall 93, p. 179-180.
"The Silky Islands." [13thMoon] (12:1/2) 93-94, p. 73-74.
"Silver Arrows." [Contact] (11:65/66/67) Spr 93, p. 26.
"Sudden Mendenhall Glacier." [13thMoon] (12:1/2) 93-94, p. 72.
"The Summer Nuthatch." [Contact] (11:65/66/67) Spr 93, p. 25.
"Unlike Stars." [Contact] (11:65/66/67) Spr 93, p. 24.
"White Cardamom" (for Norman Hindley). [AnotherCM] (26) Fall 93, p. 176-177.
6859. WALCOTT, Derek
"A Far Cry from Africa" (from "In a Green Night," 1962). [Drumvoices] (2:1/2) Fall-Wint 92-93, p. 14.
"For Adrian, April 14, 1986" (To Grace, Ben, Judy, Junior, Norline, Katryn, Gem, Stanley, and Diana). [Drumvoices] (2:1/2) Fall-Wint 92-93, p. 18-19.
"Frederiksted, Dusk" (from "Sea Grapes"). [CaribbeanW] (7) 93, p. 62.
"Gros-Ilet." [Drumvoices] (2:1/2) Fall-Wint 92-93, p. 17.
"In the Virgins" (For Bill and Pat Strachan. From "The Star-Apple Kingdom"). [CaribbeanW] (7) 93, p. 63-64.
"Menelaus." [Drumvoices] (2:1/2) Fall-Wint 92-93, p. 22.

484

WALCOTT

"New World" (From "Sea Grapes," 1976). [Drumvoices] (2:1/2) Fall-Wint 92-93, p. 15.
"Omeros" (2 excerpts). [Drumvoices] (2:1/2) Fall-Wint 92-93, p. 23-25.
"Origins" (for Veronica Jenkin). [Drumvoices] (2:1/2) Fall-Wint 92-93, p. 10-13.
"Saint Lucia's First Communion." [Drumvoices] (2:1/2) Fall-Wint 92-93, p. 16.
"The Young Wife" (For Nigel). [Drumvoices] (2:1/2) Fall-Wint 92-93, p. 20-21.
6860. WALD, Diane
"Positive Negative." [ProseP] (1) 92, p. 75.
6861. WALDEN, T.
"The Homely Soldier." [Asylum] (8) 93, p. 126.
6862. WALDEN, William
"Caveat." [Light] (6) Sum 93, p. 17.
6863. WALDERS, Davi
"Oil Men at a Jewish Cemetery." [Border] (2) Spr 93, p. 73-74.
"To the Whiteness of Bone." [Vis] (41) 93, p. 37-38.
6864. WALDMAN, Anne
"Before You Drop Off Read This." [PaintedB] (50/51) 93, p. 129.
"Early." [13thMoon] (12:1/2) 93-94, p. 75-76.
"Exteriority." [RiverS] (37) 93, p. 57-59.
"Night Wing" (for the painter Yvonne Jacquette). [AmerPoR] (22:1) Ja-F 93, p. 76.
"Okay the Dream." [Talisman] (11) Fall 93, p. 135.
"West Point." [AmerPoR] (22:6) N-D 93, p. 40.
6865. WALDMAN, John
"Akin to Ashes." [CreamCR] (17:2) Fall 93, p. 188-189.
6866. WALDMAN, Ken
"Atop Mt. Baker." [Lactuca] (17) Apr 93, p. 41-42.
"Dear Dad." [WritersF] (19) 93, p. 121.
"Nome Industry." [SoDakR] (31:3) Fall 93, p. 134.
"The Shooting Lesson." [Lactuca] (17) Apr 93, p. 41.
"Small Planes Near Nome." [SoDakR] (31:3) Fall 93, p. 135.
"Third Street, Nome." [SoDakR] (31:3) Fall 93, p. 136.
6867. WALDNER, Liz
"On the Way." [NewAW] (11) Sum-Fall 93, p. 105.
"Rampant." [Talisman] (11) Fall 93, p. 259.
"Request for a Little Water Music from the Night." [13thMoon] (12:1/2) 93-94, p. 77-78.
"Whim." [NewAW] (11) Sum-Fall 93, p. 104.
"With the Tongues of Angels." [MassR] (34:4) Wint 93-94, p. 504.
6868. WALDRON, Peggy L.
"Second-Mortgage Lovers." [HolCrit] (30:2) Ap 93, p. 14.
6869. WALDROP, Jason
"History." [Sequoia] (34/35) 92-93, p. 95.
6870. WALDROP, Keith
"Dream at the Center of a Seed" (Translation Chapbook Series No. 21, 8 poems, tr. of Xue Di, w. Wang Ping). [MidAR] (14:1) 93, p. 63-85.
"I.E." (Selections: 9-13, tr. of Claude Royet-Journoud). [Avec] (6:1) 93, p. 93-97.
6871. WALDROP, Rosmarie
"Air" (tr. of Jacques Roubaud). [Pequod] (36) 93, p. 50.
"Air, Water, Places, II" (tr. of Jacques Roubaud). [Pequod] (36) 93, p. 48.
"Alive, absent from all life" (tr. of Jacques Roubaud). [ManhatR] (7:1) Fall 93, p. 41.
"Any, Any Whatever" (tr. of Jacques Roubaud). [ManhatR] (7:1) Fall 93, p. 34.
"Bright World" (tr. of Jacques Roubaud). [ManhatR] (7:1) Fall 93, p. 39.
"Division of Worlds" (tr. of Jacques Roubaud). [ManhatR] (7:1) Fall 93, p. 42.
"Even into the Night" (tr. of Jacques Roubaud). [Talisman] (11) Fall 93, p. 11-13.
"Grandmother" (tr. of Gisela von Wysocki). [WorldL] (4) 93, p. 24-25.
"The Idea of Form" (tr. of Jacques Roubaud). [NewAW] (11) Sum-Fall 93, p. 56-62.
"Identity" (tr. of Jacques Roubaud). [ManhatR] (7:1) Fall 93, p. 47.
"In the Ersatz-World" (tr. of Jacques Roubaud). [ManhatR] (7:1) Fall 93, p. 33.
"In these worlds, in every one" (tr. of Jacques Roubaud). [ManhatR] (7:1) Fall 93, p. 40.
"A Key into the Language of America" (2 selections). [Talisman] (11) Fall 93, p. 233-234.
"A Key into the Language of America" (Selections). [Sulfur] (33) Fall 93, p. 230-235.
"Localization." [Conjunc] (20) 93, p. 146.

"Lyrical" (tr. of Jacques Roubaud). [ManhatR] (7:1) Fall 93, p. 44.
"Outermost." [Conjunc] (20) 93, p. 147.
"Pleasure Principle." [Conjunc] (20) 93, p. 145.
"Plenitude" (tr. of Jacques Roubaud). [ManhatR] (7:1) Fall 93, p. 46.
"Preparatory Poem" (tr. of Jacques Roubaud). [Pequod] (36) 93, p. 51.
"Reading Freud." [GrandS] (12:2, #46) Sum 93, p. 39-41.
"Rip Van Winkle" (tr. of Elke Erb). [ProseP] (2) 93, p. 34.
"The Sickness of the Soul, V" (tr. of Jacques Roubaud). [Pequod] (36) 93, p. 49.
"Split Infinites." [Caliban] (12) 93, p. 38-39.
"That the World Was There" (tr. of Jacques Roubaud). [ManhatR] (7:1) Fall 93, p. 45.
"To Wit a Very Small Gland." [Conjunc] (20) 93, p. 148.
"The Vital Knot." [Conjunc] (20) 93, p. 144.
"The Way of Examples, II" (tr. of Jacques Roubaud). [ManhatR] (7:1) Fall 93, p. 43.
"The Way of Stories" (tr. of Jacques Roubaud). [ManhatR] (7:1) Fall 93, p. 36.
"The Way of the Impossible" (tr. of Jacques Roubaud). [ManhatR] (7:1) Fall 93, p. 37.
"The Way We Live" (tr. of Elke Erb). [ProseP] (2) 93, p. 33.
"What to Do with a World" (tr. of Jacques Roubaud). [ManhatR] (7:1) Fall 93, p. 38.
"Where time imitates a solid line" (tr. of Jacques Roubaud). [ManhatR] (7:1) Fall 93, p. 35.
6872. WALEY, Arthur
"Lao-Tzu" (tr. of Po Chu-i). [NewYorkQ] (51) 93, p. 98.
"Taoist Song" (tr. of Chi K'ang). [NewYorkQ] (51) 93, p. 98.
6873. WALKER, Alice
"New Face." [Agni] (38) 93, p. 171.
6874. WALKER, Beth
"Arrowheads" (near the Obion River, Nov. 1990). [CreamCR] (17:1) Spr 93, p. 43.
"Becoming Woman." [CreamCR] (17:1) Spr 93, p. 44-45.
6875. WALKER, Henry M.
"Snail-Shell" (tr. of Ruben Darío). [Asylum] (8) 93, p. 136.
6876. WALKER, Jeanne Murray
"I. Frederick: The Decision." [PaintedB] (52) 93, p. 46.
"II. Marta: The First Year in Minnesota." [PaintedB] (52) 93, p. 47-48.
"III. Henrietta: Farming." [PaintedB] (52) 93, p. 49.
"IV. Frederick: The Drought." [PaintedB] (52) 93, p. 50.
"V. Marta: Inventing Herself." [PaintedB] (52) 93, p. 51.
"After Image." [WestB] (31/32) 93, p. 125.
"Aunt Joe Plays with the Children." [PraS] (67:1) Spr 93, p. 143.
"The Aunt Joe Poems" (10 poems). [MidwQ] (34:3) Spr 93, p. 311-321.
"Bjorn Larsen and Aunt Joe at the Dump." [PraS] (67:1) Spr 93, p. 143-144.
"A Caution to Us." [WestB] (31/32) 93, p. 126.
"Christina Johnson: The Mother." [QRL] (12:32/33) 93, p. 359.
"David Johnson: The Thief." [QRL] (12:32/33) 93, p. 363-364.
"Harold Lindgrin: The Judge." [QRL] (12:32/33) 93, p. 362-363.
"Josephine Johnson: The Sister." [QRL] (12:32/33) 93, p. 360-361.
"Keeping the Plane Up." [Poetry] (162:2) My 93, p. 70.
"Learning to Swim in Lake Adley" (for Elaine Terranova). [PraS] (67:1) Spr 93, p. 142.
"Letter Home, 1860." [WestB] (31/32) 93, p. 124.
"The National Enquirer Headline Writer Calls Etheridge Knight to Interview Him about Gravity." [PaintedB] (50/51) 93, p. 76.
"Ollie Olsen: The Accomplice." [QRL] (12:32/33) 93, p. 360.
"Roy Uhde: The Sheriff." [QRL] (12:32/33) 93, p. 362.
6877. WALKER, Larry
"And That's What I Felt When I Heard Them." [SpoonR] (18:1) Wint-Spr 93, p. 88.
"Designs of Skin, Religion, and Trade." [SpoonR] (18:1) Wint-Spr 93, p. 87.
6878. WALKER, Lolalee
"A Woman's Place." [NewYorkQ] (52) 93, p. 73-74.
6879. WALL, Kathleen
"Ariadne." [AntigR] (95) Aut 93, p. 102-104.
"Untitled: I confess I love the ambiguity of distance." [CanLit] (137) Sum 93, p. 39.
6880. WALLACE, Bruce
"Sunday." [Plain] (13:2) Wint 93, p. 11.

6881. WALLACE, D. M.
"Sieves." [SilverFR] (24) Wint 93, p. 23.
6882. WALLACE, Helen Pruitt
"Studying Your Hands." [TampaR] (7) Fall 93, p. 42.
6883. WALLACE, Jan
"Horse Heart." [PoetryNW] (34:2) Sum 93, p. 21-22.
"Plenty." [PoetryNW] (34:2) Sum 93, p. 20-21.
6884. WALLACE, Mark
"Black Longing Allows Calm Keys." [WashR] (19:2) Ag-S 93, p. 17.
"Emblems Merge Blood, Lick Empires, Map Song." [WashR] (19:2) Ag-S 93, p. 17.
"Melville, Even, Lives Various Illusions, Leaves Learned Evidence." [WashR]
    (19:2) Ag-S 93, p. 17.
"They're Closing It Down But It's Still going On." [Talisman] (10) Spr 93, p. 172.
6885. WALLACE, N. (Naomi)
"Meat Strike." [AmerV] (32) 93, p. 56.
"Meat Strike." [Stand] (35:1) Wint 93-94, p. 7.
"Preparing for War" (In Memory of Paul Barrat). [Nat] (256:6) 15 F 93, p. 204.
"Preparing for War" (in memory of Paul Barret). [Verse] (10:1) Spr 93, p. 28.
"Prophet Having Seen Jesus Perform a Miracle." [Verse] (10:1) Spr 93, p. 29.
"Sonnet Framing the Thoughts of a Forefather Before the Pequot Battle." [Iowa]
    (23:2) Spr-Sum 93, p. 63.
"Sonnet Framing the Thoughts of a Forefather Before the Pequot Battle." [Stand]
    (35:1) Wint 93-94, p. 6.
"St. Francis and the Hawk." [Iowa] (23:2) Spr-Sum 93, p. 64.
"Touching in the Sweatshop." [Stand] (35:1) Wint 93-94, p. 8.
"Unrepentant Witch Burned for Adultery in 1503." [Iowa] (23:2) Spr-Sum 93, p. 64.
6886. WALLACE, Robert
"Noon." [LaurelR] (27:1) Wint 93, p. 75.
"The Pool Clock." [LaurelR] (27:1) Wint 93, p. 75.
"Window in March." [LaurelR] (27:1) Wint 93, p. 76.
6887. WALLACE, Ronald
"Ballade of David Parsons" (for my father, 1925-1980). [Nat] (256:1) 4-11 Ja 93, p.
    31.
"Canzone: Siesta Key." [ApalQ] (36/37) 91, p. 78-80.
"A Cry in the Night." [PraS] (67:1) Spr 93, p. 133-134.
"February 29." [PoetL] (88:2) Sum 93, p. 9.
"Fishing." [Poem] (70) N 93, p. 45.
"Grandfather, His Book." [Poetry] (161:4) Ja 93, p. 197.
"The Heron." [ArtfulD] (24/25) 93, p. 107.
"Honky-Tonk." [PoetryNW] (34:3) Aut 93, p. 30-31.
"Oriole's Nest." [ArtfulD] (24/25) 93, p. 109.
"Poison Ivy." [Boulevard] (8:2/3, #23/24) Fall 93, p. 199.
"Running." [PraS] (67:1) Spr 93, p. 132-133.
"Stone Crab Claws." [ArtfulD] (24/25) 93, p. 108.
"Therapy." [PoetL] (88:2) Sum 93, p. 8.
6888. WALLACE, T. H. S.
"A Guide to Ancient Places." [ChironR] (12:1, #34) Spr 93, p. 15.
6889. WALLACE, Terry Smith
"Ars Poetica." [PaintedB] (50/51) 93, p. 90.
6890. WALLACE-CRABBE, Chris
"In the Buda Hills." [Nimrod] (36:2) Spr-Sum 93, p. 77.
"The Invitation." [Nimrod] (36:2) Spr-Sum 93, p. 76.
"Love Talk." [Nimrod] (36:2) Spr-Sum 93, p. 75.
"Ode to Morpheus." [HarvardR] (4) Spr 93, p. 68.
"Song As Song." [Verse] (10:2) Sum 93, p. 24.
"Summer's Breath." [Verse] (10:2) Sum 93, p. 23.
6891. WALLACH, Martin
"Living in Hope." [Poem] (70) N 93, p. 53.
"Seeing Things." [Poem] (70) N 93, p. 54.
"The Silver Streak." [Poem] (70) N 93, p. 52.
6892. WALLACK, Susan
"Diogenes in Athens." [Calyx] (15:1) Wint 93-94, p. 33.
WALLEGHEN, Michael van
    See Van WALLEGHEN, Michael
6893. WALLER, Margaret
"The Cloth." [TickleAce] (24) Fall-Wint 92, p. 113.

487

WALLING

6894. WALLING, Mark
    "A Concrete Eternity." [WeberS] (10:1) Wint 93, p. 99.
6895. WALLS, Michael
    "Incan Forests." [Poem] (70) N 93, p. 5.
6896. WALPOLE, Peter
    "All the Things We Know Better Than." [CumbPR] (12:2) Spr 93, p. 11.
    "Not Myself Today, I Hope." [CumbPR] (12:2) Spr 93, p. 10.
6897. WALSH, Des
    "Glynmill Inn Bar, Corner Brook, December 2, 1992." [TickleAce] (25) Spr-Sum
        93, p. 69.
    "New World Island, Notre Dame Bay." [TickleAce] (25) Spr-Sum 93, p. 70.
6898. WALSH, Marty
    "American Crow." [Bogg] (66) Wint 92-93, p. 62.
    "Like an Odysseus Doomed" (A Plainsongs Award Poem). [Plain] (13:2) Wint 93,
        p. 36-37.
    "Worms." [BelPoJ] (43:3) Spr 93, p. 5.
6899. WALSH, Sydney
    "Long Lunch." [Arshile] (2) 93, p. 28-29.
6900. WALSTORM, Anthony
    "Chinese Cantos." [Gypsy] (20) Sum 93, p. 41.
6901. WALSWORTH, Sarah
    "My Love Is Caught Descending." [13thMoon] (12:1/2) 93-94, p. 79-80.
6902. WALTERS, Wendy S.
    "I Bite the Onion." [Obs] (8:1) Spr-Sum 93, p. 101-102.
    "Stone Love." [Obs] (8:1) Spr-Sum 93, p. 102-103.
6903. WALTON, Anthony
    "A Lament for the State of Ohio as a Lament for Ohio State." [PraS] (67:1) Spr 93,
        p. 136-138.
    "Third Shift." [PraS] (67:1) Spr 93, p. 134-136.
6904. WALZER, Kevin
    "The Courage of My Fiction" (Cincinnati). [WestB] (31/32) 93, p. 8-9.
    "Nude on a Cincinnati Porch." [CinPR] (24) Spr 93, p. 18.
6905. WAN, Xia
    "The Basic Dress Code for a Poet" (tr. by Dian Li). [GreenMR] (NS 6:2) Sum-Fall
        93, p. 151.
    "Spider" (tr. by Dian Li). [GreenMR] (NS 6:2) Sum-Fall 93, p. 150.
6906. WANEK, Connie
    "January." [GreenMR] (NS 6:2) Sum-Fall 93, p. 109-110.
    "Wild Apples." [VirQR] (69:3) Sum 93, p. 498-500.
WANG, Jia-Xin
    See WANG, Jiaxin
6907. WANG, Jiaxin
    "Change" (tr. by Jin Zhong and Stephen Haven). [AmerPoR] (22:6) N-D 93, p. 38.
    "The Finale" (tr. by Dong Jiping and Stephen Haven). [AmerPoR] (22:6) N-D 93, p.
        37.
    "Iron" (tr. by Jin Zhong and Stephen Haven). [AmerPoR] (22:6) N-D 93, p. 38.
    "The Knife" (tr. by Fan Xinmin and Stephen Haven). [AmerPoR] (22:6) N-D 93, p.
        37.
    "Poetry" (to Haizi, tr. by Dong Jiping and Stephen Haven). [AmerPoR] (22:6) N-D
        93, p. 38.
    "Railway Station" (tr. by Jin Zhong and Stephen Haven). [AmerPoR] (22:6) N-D 93,
        p. 37.
    "Staircase" (written in my old home at the Gate of Peace, tr. by Jin Zhong and
        Stephen Haven). [AmerPoR] (22:6) N-D 93, p. 37.
6908. WANG, Lenore Baeli
    "Dispute." [Footwork] (23) 93, p. 61.
    "The Lotus Leaver." [Kalliope] (15:3) 93, p. 26-27.
WANG, Ping
    See PING, Wang
6909. WANG, Shouyi
    "The Potter" (From Song Dynasty Poems, tr. of Mei Yaochen, w. John Knoepfle).
        [DogRR] (12:1, #23) Spr-Sum 93, p. 54.
6910. WANG, Wei
    "Bird Call Valley" (tr. by Pauline Lu). [AmerPoR] (22:2) Mr-Ap 93, p. 45.
    "Bird-Singing Stream" (tr. by Wai-lim Yip). [AmerPoR] (22:2) Mr-Ap 93, p. 45.

"Birds Calling in the Valley" (tr. by G. W. Robinson). [AmerPoR] (22:2) Mr-Ap 93, p. 45.
"Birds Sing in the Ravine" (tr. by Tony Barnstone, Willis Barnstone and Xu Haixin). [AmerPoR] (22:2) Mr-Ap 93, p. 45.
"Deer Park" (tr. by Tony Barnstone, Willis Barnstone and Xu Haixin). [AmerPoR] (22:2) Mr-Ap 93, p. 46.
"Return to Wang River" (tr. by Sam Hamill). [AmerPoR] (22:2) Mr-Ap 93, p. 46.
"Return to Wang River" (tr. by Tony Barnstone, Willis Barnstone and Xu Haixin). [AmerPoR] (22:2) Mr-Ap 93, p. 46.
"You Asked About My Life. I Send You, Pei Di, These Lines" (tr. by Tony Barnstone, Willis Barnstone and Xu Haixin). [AmerPoR] (22:2) Mr-Ap 93, p. 46.

6911. WANG, Yun
"April White Blossoms." [PennR] (5:2) 93, p. 18-19.
"Beneath the Painted Shrine." [GreenMR] (NS 6:1) Wint-Spr 93, p. 53.
"The Buffalo Man." [GreenMR] (NS 6:1) Wint-Spr 93, p. 50-51.
"Jealousy." [GreenMR] (NS 6:1) Wint-Spr 93, p. 52.
"Without Fear." [PennR] (5:2) 93, p. 17.

6912. WANLESS, Norma
"Ancestralidades" (w. Pro'logo de Iliana Godoy y Introducción de Guillermo Rousset Banda). [Trasimagen] (1:1) Otoño-Invierno 93, p. 4-8.
"Ancestralities" (tr. by the author, w. Pro'logo de Iliana Godoy y Introducción de Guillermo Rousset Banda). [Trasimagen] (1:1) Otoño-Invierno 93, p. 9-13.

6913. WARAT, Ruth
"Characters Around a Soriano Painting. Art in Miami." [SenR] (23:1/2) Wint 93, p. 104-105.

6914. WARD, Adam
"Talk to Me." [BrooklynR] (10) 93, p. 4-5.

6915. WARD, Dave
"Street Girl." [Bogg] (66) Wint 92-93, p. 17.

6916. WARD, David C.
"Internal Differences." [Wind] (23:72) 93, p. 20.

6917. WARD, Jerry W., Jr.
"The Faculty Club: A Table of Truth." [XavierR] (13:2) Fall 93, p. 62.
"Losing Memory." [XavierR] (13:2) Fall 93, p. 61.
"Mississippi: Bell Zone 1." [XavierR] (13:2) Fall 93, p. 63.
"Walls." [XavierR] (13:2) Fall 93, p. 64-65.

6918. WARD, Robert R.
"Forever Is Not as Long as You Might Think." [Gaia] (3) O 93, p. 22.
"In the Garden." [Gaia] (3) O 93, p. 22.
"Piano Passage." [PaintedHR] (9) Spr 93, p. 7.

6919. WARDEN, Marine Robert
"Armageddon." [Pearl] (19) Fall-Wint 93, p. 7.
"Drowned Sailor 1946." [Pearl] (19) Fall-Wint 93, p. 7.

6920. WARLAND, Betsey
"The Body the Archive." [WestCL] (27:1, #10) Spr 93, p. 55-58.

6921. WARNER, Gale
"Green Heron." [WestB] (31/32) 93, p. 107.
"If." [Gaia] (1/2) Ap-Jl 93, p. 1.
"Myxomatosis" (an infectious and fatal disease of rabbits, artificially introduced into Great Britain . . . to keep down the rabbit population). [Gaia] (1/2) Ap-Jl 93, p. 1.
"Reading Plato." [Agni] (37) 93, p. 290-291.

6922. WARNER, James
"The Bird-Temple." [Event] (22:3) Wint 93-94, p. 70.
"The Ring." [Event] (22:3) Wint 93-94, p. 71.

6923. WARNER, Marilyn
"Heron." [BellArk] (9:5) S-O 93, p. 6.

6924. WARNER, Patrick
"Turf." [TickleAce] (24) Fall-Wint 92, p. 42.

6925. WARREN, Gerald
"Sound Bites: Taste of Morning Breakfast." [CumbPR]] (13:1) Fall 93, p. 68-69.

6926. WARREN, Rebecca
"Fu Hao." [InterPR] (19:1) Spr 93, p. 67-68.

489

6927. WARREN, Robert Penn
"Snowshoeing Back to Camp in Gloaming." [NewEngR] (15:1) Wint 93, p. 197 -
198.
"Timeless, Twinned." [NewEngR] (15:1) Wint 93, p. 199.
"Weather Report." [NewEngR] (15:1) Wint 93, p. 196.
"Will Work for Food." [Atlantic] (271:2) F 93, p. 94.
6928. WARREN, Rosanna
"Antietam Creek" (22,000 dead September 17, 1862). [NewEngR] (15:1) Wint 93,
p. 200.
6929. WARREN, Shirley
"Fishing, Winter 1989" (In memory of Norman and Ivy Lake). [GeoR] (47:3) Fall
93, p. 544-545.
"Watering Place." [CreamCR] (17:2) Fall 93, p. 107.
"We Lay Down Worlds." [Poem] (69) My 93, p. 66-67.
6930. WARROCK, Anna M.
"Heart, Hurt." [HarvardR] (4) Spr 93, p. 121.
6931. WARSAW, Irene
"The Greeks Had a Word for Me." [Light] (6) Sum 93, p. 13.
6932. WARSH, Lewis
"Actual Size." [AmerPoR] (22:5) S-O 93, p. 4.
"Black Bread with Russian Dressing." [AmerPoR] (22:5) S-O 93, p. 6.
"Blue Turban." [AmerPoR] (22:5) S-O 93, p. 5.
"Different Trains." [Talisman] (11) Fall 93, p. 37-47.
"Elegy." [AmerPoR] (22:5) S-O 93, p. 6.
"Evidence." [AmerPoR] (22:5) S-O 93, p. 5.
"Grace Notes." [AmerPoR] (22:5) S-O 93, p. 5.
"A Man Escaped." [AmerPoR] (22:5) S-O 93, p. 3.
"Mirror's Edge." [AmerPoR] (22:5) S-O 93, p. 3.
"Mistaken Identity." [AmerPoR] (22:5) S-O 93, p. 3.
"Overture." [AmerPoR] (22:5) S-O 93, p. 4.
"Pictures." [AmerPoR] (22:5) S-O 93, p. 6.
"The Possessed." [AmerPoR] (22:5) S-O 93, p. 3.
"Thwarted Suitor." [AmerPoR] (22:5) S-O 93, p. 5.
"To the Household Goddess." [AmerPoR] (22:5) S-O 93, p. 5.
6933. WARSHAWSKI, Morrie
"The Inventory of Rage." [ApalQ] (36/37) 91, p. 64.
6934. WARWICK, Betsey
"Invasion." [OnTheBus] (6:1, #13) Wint 93-Spr 94, p. 205.
"Mission." [OnTheBus] (6:1, #13) Wint 93-Spr 94, p. 205.
"Rosa." [OnTheBus] (6:1, #13) Wint 93-Spr 94, p. 204.
"Valentine's Day After Watching Too Much Television the Night Before."
[OnTheBus] (6:1, #13) Wint 93-Spr 94, p. 205.
6935. WARWICK, Ioanna-Veronika
"Civilization." [PoetL] (88:1) Spr 93, p. 43.
"Coleus." [SycamoreR] (5:2) Sum 93, p. 26-27.
"The Heirloom." [SycamoreR] (5:2) Sum 93, p. 28-29.
"I Want to Know How Rilke Did It." [HayF] (12) Spr-Sum 93, p. 108.
"In the Mirror." [PoetL] (88:4) Wint 93-94, p. 29.
"Knowing the Way." [MassR] (33:4) Wint 92-93, p. 491-492.
"Letter From a Schoolfriend." [OnTheBus] (5:2, #12) Sum-Fall 93, p. 207-209.
"San Diego in Late October." [CimR] (102) Ja 93, p. 84-85.
"Saying Goodbye." [LaurelR] (27:2) Sum 93, p. 45-46.
"Scars." [Plain] (14:1) Fall 93, p. 26.
"Warsaw at Night." [HayF] (12) Spr-Sum 93, p. 107.
"Warsaw at Night." [LaurelR] (27:2) Sum 93, p. 44-45.
6936. WASHBUSH, Judy
"To a Statue I Would Like to Know." [Pearl] (17) Spr 93, p. 54.
6937. WASSERBURG, Charles
"Video." [TriQ] (89) Wint 93-94, p. 188-189.
6938. WASSERMAN, Rosanne
"Putting in a Word." [Boulevard] (8:1, #22) Spr 93, p. 187-189.
6939. WATERHOUSE, Philip A.
"Home Planet." [RagMag] (11:2) 93, p. 86.
"Horizons." [Gypsy] (20) Sum 93, p. 51.
"Horseboy." [RagMag] (11:2) 93, p. 85.
"Mail Call." [RagMag] (11:2) 93, p. 87.

WATERHOUSE

490

"Phone Sex." [RagMag] (11:2) 93, p. 84.
6940. WATERS, Chris
"Homecoming." [HampSPR] Wint 93, p. 43.
"Title-at-End-Poem." [Pearl] (19) Fall-Wint 93, p. 80.
6941. WATERS, Jacqueline
"#77 Revisited" (Poets of High School Age). [HangL] (62) 93, p. 92-93.
6942. WATERS, Mary Ann
"The Corrector Speaks" (At the Plantin-Moretus Printing Office, Antwerpen,
Flanders, 1675). [GettyR] (6:1) Wint 93, p. 160-161.
"One." [FreeL] (11) Wint 93, p. 3.
"Poetry Workshop: The Extra-Large Muse." [Witness] (7:2) 93, p. 46-47.
6943. WATERS, Michael
"The '66 Mets." [MissouriR] (16:1) 93, p. 174.
"Christ at the Apollo, 1962" (for Andrew Hudgins). [MissouriR] (16:1) 93, p. 175.
"First Lesson: Winter Trees." [MissouriR] (16:1) 93, p. 176.
"First Mile." [MissouriR] (16:1) 93, p. 177.
"God at Forty." [OhioR] (50) 93, p. 7-8.
"Green Ash, Red Maple, Black Gum." [GettyR] (6:1) Wint 93, p. 24.
"On the Afternoon of the Prom." [PaintedB] (50/51) 93, p. 48.
"Stoning the Birds." [MissouriR] (16:1) 93, p. 172-173.
"Two Baths" (Ios). [AmerPoR] (22:2) Mr-Ap 93, p. 51.
6944. WATKINS, Klyd
"Origin of the Constellation Called Froggey's New Year's Eve." [SouthernPR]
(33:1) Spr 93, p. 31-33.
"What a Hooting Glory, the Geese Alanding." [Plain] (14:1) Fall 93, p. 16.
6945. WATKINS, Steve
"Car Plunges Off Ridge Road into Creek, Couple Survives." [HampSPR] Wint 93,
p. 51-52.
6946. WATKINS, Vernon
"The Cave-Drawing." [QRL] (12:32/33) 93, p. 539-541.
6947. WATKINS, William John
"Anniversary Poem to an Ex-Wife." [JINJPo] (15:2) Aut 93, p. 33.
"The Dead of Al-Julaydah, Jan. 14." [Gypsy] (20) Sum 93, p. 51.
"Existential Moments." [Hellas] (4:2) Fall 93, p. 115.
"No Heavy Lifting." [WritersF] (19) 93, p. 88.
"Now Is the Time to Love Quirks." [HiramPoR] (53/54) Fall 92-Sum 93, p. 82-83.
"Reason Is a Zoning Commissioner." [JINJPo] (15:2) Aut 93, p. 34.
"Secret Sale." [Hellas] (4:2) Fall 93, p. 114.
"Sisyphus Rolls His Ball Up Mobius Hill." [HiramPoR] (53/54) Fall 92-Sum 93, p.
81.
6948. WATSON, Craig
"The Arc of the Jumper" (Excerpts). [Avec] (6:1) 93, p. 22-24.
"The Arc of the Jumper" (Selctions: three sections). [Talisman] (10) Spr 93, p. 146 -
147.
6949. WATSON, Ellen
"Before Names" (tr. of Adélio Prado). [MassR] (34:2) Sum 93, inside front cover.
6950. WATSON, Lawrence
"Patience." [PoetC] (24:2) Wint 93, p. 38.
"Poem for My Father." [Paint] (19:38) Aut 92, p. 35.
6951. WATSON, Randall
"The Art of Mapplethorpe's Work." [Chelsea] (54) 93, p. 91-92.
"The Nail Star." [Chelsea] (54) 93, p. 90-91.
"Skull the Apostate (On Physics)." [NoAmR] (278:4) Jl-Ag 93, p. 25.
6952. WATSON, Stephen
"Catching a Porcupine" (tr. of Dia!kwain from !Xam (Bushman) oral records).
[BostonR] (18:3/4) Je-Ag 93, p. 30.
"Prayer to the New Moon" (tr. of Dia!kwain from !Xam (Bushman) oral records).
[BostonR] (18:3/4) Je-Ag 93, p. 30.
6953. WATTERSON, William Collins
"Rex Jacobus Ludi." [SewanR] (101:4) O-D, Fall 93, p. 517-519.
6954. WATTISON, Meredith
"Edvard Munch's Magnetic Shoes." [Vis] (41) 93, p. 17.
"'Extinct Moon' No. 15." [Vis] (41) 93, p. 17.
6955. WATTS, Charles
"Bread and Wine (after Hölderlin)." [ChiR] (39:3/4) 93, p. 133-137.

491

6956. WATTS, David
"Getting Ready to Take Off from Cleveland Hopkins Airport in What Feels Like a Hurricane." [SpoonR] (18:1) Wint-Spr 93, p. 110-111.
6957. WATTS, Enos
"Speer at Spandau, Remembering." [TickleAce] (24) Fall-Wint 92, p. 96-97.
6958. WAUGH, Robert H.
"Deer-Gutting." [LaurelR] (27:2) Sum 93, p. 43.
6959. WAYBRANT, Linda
"It's True He Met Her at Druxy's & His Coffee Was Cold Before She Offered Him a Seat." [AntigR] (93-94) Spr-Sum 93, p. 256.
6960. WAYMAN, Tom
"Country Incomplete." [Hudson] (45:4) Wint 93, p. 603-605.
"The Hallows." [Event] (22:3) Wint 93-94, p. 63.
"Mountain Elegy" (Dave Bostock). [OntR] (38) Spr-Sum 93, p. 106-109.
"Pasture." [Event] (22:3) Wint 93-94, p. 64-65.
"Praise." [PoetryC] (14:1) 93, p. 13.
"The Quarrel." [OntR] (38) Spr-Sum 93, p. 104-105.
"Reverend Billy." [Quarry] (42:1) 93, p. 57.
"Snow." [Quarry] (42:1) 93, p. 35-36.
"The Tree." [PoetryC] (14:1) 93, p. 13.
"Waley, Waley." [Hudson] (45:4) Wint 93, p. 605-608.
6961. WAYNE, Val
"For Joe, 20 December 1991" (In memory of Joseph Chadwick, June 5, 1954-April 9, 1992). [HawaiiR] (17:1, #37) Spr 93, p. iv.
6962. WEARNE, Alan
"Barb at Dot's Wedding" (Excerpt). [Manoa] (5:2) Wint 93, p. 65-68.
6963. WEATHERFORD, Carole Boston
"Charleston Baskets." [Calyx] (15:1) Wint 93-94, p. 48-51.
"Juchitec Market Women." [Border] (2) Spr 93, p. 75.
"Parade at Elmina Castle." [Obs] (8:1) Spr-Sum 93, p. 104-105.
"Sciatica." [AfAmRev] (27:3) Fall 93, p. 475-476.
"Sciatica." [Footwork] (23) 93, p. 123.
"White Water." [Pearl] (17) Spr 93, p. 93.
6964. WEATHERS, Winston
"Aubade, 1954." [CharR] (19:2) Fall 93, p. 109.
"On Entering the Hospice." [Poetry] (162:1) Ap 93, p. 24.
"A Sacrament." [Poetry] (162:1) Ap 93, p. 25.
6965. WEAVER, Margaret
"The Cove at Evening." [PoetL] (88:4) Wint 93-94, p. 42.
6966. WEAVER, Michael S.
"The Blue Ford, 1958." [JlNJPo] (15:1) Spr 93, p. 4-5.
"Bootleg Whiskey for Twenty-Five Cents." [Footwork] (23) 93, p. 7.
"Easy Living" (for Dorothy West). [KenR] (NS 15:3) Sum 93, p. 160-161.
"An Elegy for Lorraine Hansberry." [Pequod] (35) 93, p. 161-162.
"Elsie's Pearl Necklace." [JlNJPo] (15:1) Spr 93, p. 6-7.
"The Forgotten Park." [Footwork] (23) 93, p. 6.
"Jukebox 1946." [Footwork] (23) 93, p. 6.
"The Lawn." [JlNJPo] (15:1) Spr 93, p. 1-2.
"A Life in a Steel Mill." [PaintedB] (50/51) 93, p. 67.
"Liu Huifang." [CreamCR] (17:1) Spr 93, p. 48-49.
"A Morning with Abby Shahn." [CreamCR] (17:1) Spr 93, p. 46-47.
"Otis' Leather Jacket." [JlNJPo] (15:1) Spr 93, p. 3.
"Party." [Footwork] (23) 93, p. 6.
"Science." [KenR] (NS 15:3) Sum 93, p. 159.
6967. WEAVER, Robert
"And Are We So Divided?" [DogRR] (12:1, #23) Spr-Sum 93, p. 25.
6968. WEAVER, Roger
"At the Source." [CharR] (19:1) Spr 93, p. 102.
"She's Gone." [PaintedHR] (8) Wint 93, p. 16.
6969. WEAVING, Jil P.
"Period" (w. Amy Jones). [WestCL] (27:1, #10) Spr 93, p. 75-82.
6970. WEBB, Charles
"After Not Winning the Yale Poetry Prize." [MichQR] (32:1) Wint 93, p. 71-72.
"At Summer's End." [TampaR] (7) Fall 93, p. 66-67.
"Back Flip." [AntR] (51:2) Spr 93, p. 234.
"Born to Whine." [WormR] (33:3, #131), 93, p. 110-111.

WEBB

"Braille." [BlackWR] (20:1) Fall-Wint 93, p. 83.
"Existentialists." [PoetL] (88:4) Wint 93-94, p. 41.
"Fall in L.A." [CinPR] (24) Spr 93, p. 58.
"Fog." [HiramPoR] (53/54) Fall 92-Sum 93, p. 85-86.
"Forest Service Cabin #114." [SoCoast] (14) Ja 93, p. 20-21.
"If We Become Famous Lovers." [TampaR] (7) Fall 93, p. 65.
"Judgment Call." [WormR] (33:3, #131), 93, p. 109-110.
"A Philosophical Question." [Pearl] (17) Spr 93, p. 46.
"Picking Her Up at the Airport." [Asylum] (8) 93, p. 21.
"Premiere." [PoetL] (88:4) Wint 93-94, p. 39-40.
"To Beat the Shit Out of Someone." [ChironR] (12:3, #36) Aut 93, p. 9.
"Unravelling." [HiramPoR] (53/54) Fall 92-Sum 93, p. 84.
"Watch for Deer" (1st Prize, 7th Annual Contest). [SoCoast] (14) Ja 93, p. 22-23.
6971. WEBB, Martha
"Kulaiwi: Source of Bone." [BambooR] (57) Wint 93, p. 187.
6972. WEBB, Robert (Robert T.)
"Midtown Gym, 1991" (To David Simanoff). [Amelia] (7:2, #21) 93, p. 108.
"Postcard: 'Distant View of the Forbidden City'." [AntigR] (93-94) Spr-Sum 93, p. 130.
"Smiler" (for Erin). [Amelia] (7:2, #21) 93, p. 107.
6973. WEBB, Sarah
"In la Cabaña." [ApalQ] (39) 93, p. 53.
6974. WEBER, Lori
"In a Tribal Society." [TickleAce] (26) Fall-Wint 93, p. 108.
6975. WEBER, Mark
"The Bones of an Ancient Thesaurus" (24 poems). [Pearl] (19) Fall-Wint 93, p. 27 - 47.
"A Bunch of Nuts." [ChironR] (12:3, #36) Aut 93, p. 2.
"Care for a Spot of Scotch Ol' Boy?" [Pearl] (17) Spr 93, p. 20.
"The Homeless." [ChironR] (12:1, #34) Spr 93, p. 47.
"It's Good But It Ain't Heroin." [ChironR] (12:3, #36) Aut 93, p. 3.
"L.A. Cops." [ChironR] (12:3, #36) Aut 93, p. 3.
"Love and Booze." [ChironR] (12:3, #36) Aut 93, p. 3.
"My 2¢ Worth." [Gypsy] (20) Sum 93, p. 34.
"Rock Garden & Decaffeinated Tea." [Gypsy] (20) Sum 93, p. 34.
"Same Sidewalk." [ChironR] (12:3, #36) Aut 93, p. 2.
"Sunday Drivers." [ChironR] (12:3, #36) Aut 93, p. 3.
"Typically Left-Handed & Oblivious." [ChironR] (12:3, #36) Aut 93, p. 2.
6976. WEBSTER, Catherine
"Drylot." [BellArk] (9:3) My-Je 93, p. 3-5.
"Hey, Rube." [BellArk] (9:2) Mr-Ap 93, p. 22-24.
"Wheelbarrow." [BellArk] (9:1) Ja-F 93, p. 6-7.
6977. WEBSTER, Diane
"After the snow melt." [DogRR] (12:2, #24) Fall-Wint 93, p. 32.
"Home alone." [DogRR] (12:2, #24) Fall-Wint 93, p. 32.
"Sprigs of grass greening." [DogRR] (12:2, #24) Fall-Wint 93, p. 32.
6978. WEDDE, Ian
"The Insomniac's Lexicon." [WestCL] (27:2, #11) Fall 93, p. 48-49.
"Six False Starts. No Stops. Getting Homesick." [WestCL] (27:2, #11) Fall 93, p. 47.
6979. WEDDLE, Jeff
"Above All This Grinning Confusion." [ChironR] (12:4/13:1, #37/38) Wint 93-Spr 94, p. 9.
"Cruise." [HawaiiR] (17:1, #37) Spr 93, p. 137.
"Homeless Nixon." [SlipS] (13) 93, p. 95.
6980. WEE, Karen Herseth
"Creatureliness" (24 March). [RagMag] (11:1) 93, p. 49.
"In Used Light." [RagMag] (11:1) 93, p. 47.
6981. WEEKS, Evelyne
"Appalachia I." [HolCrit] (30:5) D 93, p. 15.
6982. WEEKS, Robert Lewis
"And Only Then." [HampSPR] Wint 93, p. 73.
"Another Lesson." [CumbPR]] (13:1) Fall 93, p. 14-18.
"Confessions of One or the Other." [CumbPR]] (13:1) Fall 93, p. 12-13.
"A Little Speech Called Silence." [HampSPR] Wint 93, p. 73.
"These Minutes." [HiramPoR] (53/54) Fall 92-Sum 93, p. 87-88.

493

6983. WEHRSPANN, Jodie
"A Dream." [EvergreenC] (8:1) Spr-Sum 93, p. 65.
WEI, Guo
See GUO, Wei
WEI, Hsü
See HSÜ, Wei
6984. WEI, the Wild
"Inscribed at the Temple of Immortal Roaming" (tr. by Paul Hansen). [ChiR]
(39:3/4) 93, p. 255.
"White Chrysanthemums" (tr. by Paul Hansen). [ChiR] (39:3/4) 93, p. 255.
6985. WEIDMAN, Phil
"Ever So Close." [WormR] (33:4, #132) 93, p. 207.
"Friends." [WormR] (33:4, #132) 93, p. 207.
"Suburbanites." [Bogg] (66) Wint 92-93, p. 44.
"Trade-Off." [WormR] (33:4, #132) 93, p. 207.
"Tricked." [WormR] (33:4, #132) 93, p. 207.
6986. WEIGEL, John A.
"An Alternative." [Light] (8) Wint 93, p. 8.
6987. WEIGHTMAN, Sharon
"A Command of Language." [BelPoJ] (43:4) Sum 93, p. 6-7.
6988. WEIGL, Bruce
"Bear Meadow." [Ploughs] (19:4) Wint 93-94, p. 40-41.
"Care." [AmerPoR] (22:1) Ja-F 93, p. 78.
"Cleaning Out the Shaker Gears, Elyria Foundry, Elyria, Ohio 1971." [AmerPoR]
(22:1) Ja-F 93, p. 77.
"Elegy for Peter." [AmerPoR] (22:1) Ja-F 93, p. 79.
"Meditation at Melville Ave." [WillowS] (32) Sum 93, p. 18-19.
"On the Ambiguity of Injury and Pain." [Ploughs] (19:4) Wint 93-94, p. 39.
"The One." [AmerPoR] (22:1) Ja-F 93, p. 78.
"Rib." [WillowS] (32) Sum 93, p. 20.
"Sitting with Buddhist Monks, Hue 1967." [AmerPoR] (22:1) Ja-F 93, p. 77.
6989. WEIL, James L.
"Like Them" (for Bill). [Northeast] (5:8) Spr-Sum 93, p. 3.
6990. WEIN, Terren Ilana
"Cuttings." [BellArk] (9:2) Mr-Ap 93, p. 9.
"The Swing." [BellArk] (9:2) Mr-Ap 93, p. 13.
6991. WEINBERGER, Florence
"The End of Black and White." [OnTheBus] (5:2, #12) Sum-Fall 93, p. 210.
6992. WEINER, Joshua
"Who They Were." [Thrpny] (53) Spr 93, p. 19.
6993. WEINFIELD, Henry
"Funereal Toast" (for Théophile Gautier, tr. of Stéphane Mallarmé). [Pequod] (36)
93, p. 30-31.
"Funereal Toast" (for Théophile Gautier, tr. of Stéphane Mallarmé). [Talisman] (10)
Spr 93, p. 130-131.
"Prose" (for des Esseintes, tr. of Stéphane Mallarmé). [Pequod] (36) 93, p. 33-34.
"The Tomb of Charles Baudelaire" (tr. of Stéphane Mallarmé). [Talisman] (11) Fall
93, p. 157.
"The Tomb of Edgar Poe" (tr. of Stéphane Mallarmé). [Pequod] (36) 93, p. 32.
6994. WEINGARTEN, Roger
"Crawling Between Earth and Heaven." [NoAmR] (278:6) N-D 93, p. 19.
"E.S.P." [ParisR] (35:126) Spr 93, p. 64-65.
"Geography IV." [ParisR] (35:126) Spr 93, p. 66.
"P.S." [ParisR] (35:126) Spr 93, p. 62-63.
6995. WEINMAN, Paul
"Build Your Very Own Homeless Apartment." [Pearl] (19) Fall-Wint 93, p. 76.
6996. WEINRAUB, Richard
"Subtitles." [ChangingM] (25) Wint-Spr 93, p. 67.
6997. WEINSTEIN, Debra
"Onanism." [GlobalCR] (1) Spr 93, p. 21-22.
6998. WEINTRAUB, Rachel
"Rites" (For Diane Foug). [Boulevard] (8:1, #22) Spr 93, p. 190.
6999. WEIS, Lyle
"Burning Slocan." [TickleAce] (25) Spr-Sum 93, p. 184.
7000. WEISBERG, Barbara
"Borderline." [BrooklynR] (10) 93, p. 8.

"Schedule." [Border] (2) Spr 93, p. 77.
7001. WEISS, David
"Wind." [Atlantic] (272:2) Ag 93, p. 80.
7002. WEISS, Elisabeth
"Alan Davis." [Crazy] (44) Spr 93, p. 71.
7003. WEISS, Theodore
"A Dog's Life" (tr. of Nikolai Kantchev). [QRL] (12:32/33) 93, p. 204.
"A Midsummer Nightmare." [QRL] (12:32/33) 93, p. 541-543.
"Miracle" (tr. of Nikolai Kantchev). [QRL] (12:32/33) 93, p. 205.
"O" (tr. of Nikolai Kantchev). [QRL] (12:32/33) 93, p. 205.
"Snowman" (tr. of Nikolai Kantchev). [QRL] (12:32/33) 93, p. 206.
"A Starling" (tr. of Nikolai Kantchev). [QRL] (12:32/33) 93, p. 205.
"To Nail the Evening" (tr. of Nikolai Kantchev). [QRL] (12:32/33) 93, p. 204.
7004. WEISSBORT, Daniel
"Gravitation" (tr. of Dahlia Rabikovich, w. Orna Raz). [Stand] (34:3) Sum 93, p. 10.
"Night Temptation" (tr. of Itamar Yaoz-Kest, w. Orna Raz). [Stand] (34:3) Sum 93,
p. 9.
7005. WEISSLITZ, E. F.
"Fugitive." [Event] (22:2) Sum 93, p. 36.
7006. WEISSMANN, Gordon
"Mommy." [CentralP] (22) Spr 93, p. 14-18.
7007. WEITZ, William
"Split." [WormR] (33:3, #131), 93, p. 131-132.
"They Dance." [WormR] (33:3, #131), 93, p. 132.
7008. WELBOURN, Cynthia
"A Snow Day." [Pearl] (17) Spr 93, p. 57.
"Washing Out Lingerie." [Pearl] (17) Spr 93, p. 58.
7009. WELCH, Don
"Last Scene in *The Prince of Toads*." [LaurelR] (27:2) Sum 93, p. 91.
"There Is No Wind in Heaven." [GeoR] (47:2) Sum 93, p. 242.
7010. WELCH, John
"Recess." [BellArk] (9:5) S-O 93, p. 24.
7011. WELCH, Liliane
"Common Ground" (for M. Travis Lane). [PraS] (67:4) Wint 93, p. 148-149.
"Ravaged." [PraS] (67:4) Wint 93, p. 149.
"This Is My Language" (Ginette Knaff's Monotype 1992). [PraS] (67:4) Wint 93, p.
151.
"Winter Morning." [PraS] (67:4) Wint 93, p. 150.
7012. WELDEN, Oliver
"The Order and the Days" (tr. of Alicia Galaz Vivar). [InterPR] (19:1) Spr 93, p. 13.
7013. WELISH, Marjorie
"As Though Through a Tunnel." [Talisman] (10) Spr 93, p. 97.
"Bodiless, Bodiless in Translation" (I-III). [Sulfur] (32) Spr 93, p. 252-254.
"Crude Misunderstandings." [NewAW] (11) Sum-Fall 93, p. 26.
"Drastic Measures." [Sulfur] (32) Spr 93, p. 273-274.
"Grace's Tree, II." [Talisman] (10) Spr 93, p. 98.
"Guitars and Tigers." [Sulfur] (32) Spr 93, p. 275.
"Henry Cowell Plays the Standards." [Sulfur] (32) Spr 93, p. 276-278.
"Michelangelesque." [DenQ] (27:4) Spr 93, p. 18-19.
"Nowhere More Vivid." [DenQ] (27:4) Spr 93, p. 18.
"Of a Display." [DenQ] (27:4) Spr 93, p. 22-24.
"Opera." [NewAW] (11) Sum-Fall 93, p. 28-29.
"Pre-Echo." [Sulfur] (32) Spr 93, p. 270-272.
"Suppressed Misfortunes." [DenQ] (27:4) Spr 93, p. 20-21.
"Vocabularies." [NewAW] (11) Sum-Fall 93, p. 27.
"The World Map." [NewAW] (11) Sum-Fall 93, p. 25.
7014. WELKER, Holly
"Bad Habits." [CumbPR] (12:2) Spr 93, p. 17-18.
"Because I Used to Be a Good Girl." [TriQ] (87) Spr-Sum 93, p. 155-156.
"Dynamics." [TriQ] (87) Spr-Sum 93, p. 157.
"If I Had a Lover." [CumbPR] (12:2) Spr 93, p. 19-20.
"The Word Thistle." [HayF] (12) Spr-Sum 93, p. 117.
7015. WELLINGTON, Jan
"Mystery Lives Even in New Jersey." [ProseP] (1) 92, p. 76-78.
7016. WELLS, Will
"A Negro Church in Harlem" (tr. of Salvatore Quasimodo). [ApalQ] (35) 90, p. 43.

"Past Midnight, I Soak My Feet, Ravenna, 1317." [ApalQ] (38) 92, p. 80-81.
7017. WELNA, Judy
"To My Daughter." [AnthNEW] (5) 93, p. 19.
7018. WELTER, Matt
"Heading Home to You." [ChangingM] (26) Sum-Fall 93, p. 5.
7019. WEN, Jie
"The Seagulls" (in Chinese and English, tr. by Li Xi-jian and Gordon Osing).
[PikeF] (11) Fall 93, p. 14.
7020. WEN, Yi-Duo
"Defeat" (tr. by Robert Dorsett). [HawaiiR] (17:1, #37) Spr 93, p. 121.
"Snowfall (on not giving in to government concessions)" (tr. by Robert Dorsett).
[HawaiiR] (17:1, #37) Spr 93, p. 122.
7021. WENBORN, Neil
"The Holidaymakers." [NewRena] (8:3, #26) Spr 93, p. 99-100.
"Landscape with Houses." [NewRena] (8:3, #26) Spr 93, p. 101.
7022. WENDELL, Julia
"In the Pasture of Dead Horses." [Journal] (17:2) Fall-Wint 93, p. 72-73.
7023. WENTHE, William
"The Blue Ridge: Heraclitus." [SouthernR] (29:3) Sum, Jl 93, p. 564-566.
"December Walk in Low Country." [SouthernHR] (27:4) Fall 93, p. 363.
"Enniscorthy, Virginia." [CimR] (102) Ja 93, p. 79-80.
"First Walk." [CimR] (102) Ja 93, p. 81.
"Flood." [RiverC] (14:1) Fall 93, p. 47-48.
"The Garden." [HampSPR] Wint 93, p. 21-22.
"Invitation to a Wedding." [SouthernR] (29:3) Sum, Jl 93, p. 566-567.
"Trout Fly." [TarRP] (32:2) Spr 93, p. 22-23.
7024. WENTZ, Stephen W.
"Picking Chokeberries." [SmPd] (30:1, #87) Wint 93, p. 17.
7025. WERNER, Judith
"Alice at the Hearth." [SoDakR] (31:2) Sum 93, p. 156.
"For My Son." [Sequoia] (34/35) 92-93, p. 26-27.
"Hubby, Pass the Beer" (with apologies to Edna St. Vincent Millay). [FourQ] (7:1)
Spr 93, p. 59.
"Photographer's Sestina." [Elf] (3:3) Fall 93, p. 34.
"The Sacrifice." [Vis] (41) 93, p. 24-25.
7026. WERNISCH, Ivan
"A Dream of Death" (tr. by Ellen Rosenbaum). [OxfordM] (9:1) Spr-Sum 93, p. 89.
"He was drunk, this time a little less so than other times" (tr. by Ellen Rosenbaum).
[OxfordM] (9:1) Spr-Sum 93, p. 89.
"Invariably I can't rid myself of the feeling" (tr. by Ellen Rosenbaum). [OxfordM]
(9:1) Spr-Sum 93, p. 91.
"The king of the fools ordered" (tr. by Ellen Rosenbaum). [OxfordM] (9:1) Spr-Sum
93, p. 88.
"Lubok" (tr. by Ellen Rosenbaum). [OxfordM] (9:1) Spr-Sum 93, p. 90.
"Once there was a fellow" (tr. by Ellen Rosenbaum). [OxfordM] (9:1) Spr-Sum 93,
p. 91.
"Who could, paid" (tr. by Ellen Rosenbaum). [OxfordM] (9:1) Spr-Sum 93, p. 88.
"Yes yes" (tr. by Ellen Rosenbaum). [OxfordM] (9:1) Spr-Sum 93, p. 90.
WERT, William (William F.) van
See VAN WERT, William (William F.)
7027. WESLOWSKI, Dieter.
"After November Rains." [Os] (36) Spr 93, p. 3.
"And Rain." [Os] (37) Wint 93, p. 3.
"Experiments." [PaintedHR] (8) Wint 93, p. 11.
"I Count the Beery-Lanterns." [Nimrod] (37:1) Fall-Wint 93, p. 130.
"I Haven't Given Up." [PoetryE] (36) Fall 93, p. 16.
"I Used to Think Salt." [Caliban] (12) 93, p. 69.
"Night." [HawaiiR] (17:2, #38) 93, p. 42.
"Now, When I Pass the Chabad House." [Os] (37) Wint 93, p. 3.
"Poem Beginning with a Line from Canto LXXXVI of Pound." [Caliban] (13) 93, p.
90-91.
"Radiance of the Hundred Door Cast." [Caliban] (12) 93, p. 67.
"Rheumatic." [Sequoia] (34/35) 92-93, p. 14.
"She Cuts Stars." [PoetryE] (36) Fall 93, p. 17.
"Snow." [Nimrod] (37:1) Fall-Wint 93, p. 130.
"There Will Be Another Time." [GrahamHR] (17) Fall 93, p. 105.

"You Are Not For My Eyes." [Caliban] (12) 93, p. 68.
7028. WEST, Kathleene
"Because She Is Allowing Herself Some Choice in This Life." [PraS] (67:3) Fall 93, p. 100-101.
"The Body Politic." [13thMoon] (11:1/2) 93, p. 83-84.
"Chichicastenango Sestina" (after a line by Marilyn Hacker). [PraS] (67:3) Fall 93, p. 98-99.
"For My Widowed Sister." [CreamCR] (17:2) Fall 93, p. 148-149.
"The Peony Background." [CreamCR] (17:2) Fall 93, p. 146-147.
"Romance Language." [PraS] (67:3) Fall 93, p. 99-100.
"Shopping for the Revolution." [13thMoon] (11:1/2) 93, p. 85-86.
7029. WEST, Rex
"An Image Comes." [Gaia] (1/2) Ap-Jl 93, p. 13.
7030. WEST, Richard M.
"The Yellow Cat." [WormR] (33:3, #131), 93, p. 121-122.
7031. WESTERFIELD, Nancy (Nancy G.)
"Barbie's Exciting Life." [CreamCR] (17:2) Fall 93, p. 193.
"Biblical Olympics." [ChrC] (110:17) 19-26 My 93, p. 563.
"The Department Head." [Plain] (13:2) Wint 93, p. 9.
"Infantry Reunion." [PoetL] (88:3) Fall 93, p. 30.
"The Man at the Doorway" (Hiram Hisanori Kano, priest, 1889-1988, arrested Sunday Dec. 7, 1941, interned until war's end). [ChrC] (110:34) 1 D 93, p. 1210.
"Where the Train Carries You." [Comm] (120:1) 15 Ja 93, p. 12.
7032. WESTWOOD, Norma
"Family Gathering." [Parting] (6:2) Wint 93, p. 25.
7033. WETZSTEON, Rachel
"Dissolving Views." [ParisR] (35:128) Fall 93, p. 269-270.
"Drinks in the Town Square." [ParisR] (35:128) Fall 93, p. 268.
"In Memory of W. H. Auden." [WestHR] (47:4) Wint 93, p. 412-415.
"Metamorphosis." [CumbPR] (12:2) Spr 93, p. 46.
"Speech after a Spectacle." [CumbPR] (12:2) Spr 93, p. 47.
7034. WEUVE, Denise R.
"Siren." [Pearl] (19) Fall-Wint 93, p. 16.
7035. WEVILL, Sharon
"Poet in a Tattered Yellow Dress." [Border] (2) Spr 93, p. 78.
7036. WEXLER, Evelyn
"The Tutor (Budapest, 1936)." [ApalQ] (38) 92, p. 42-43.
7037. WEXLER, Philip
"Conversation in Produce." [Gypsy] (20) Sum 93, p. 35.
7038. WHALE, John
"1790s Diary." [Stand] (35:1) Wint 93-94, p. 9.
7039. WHALEN, Benji
"Maps." [BellR] (16:1/2) Spr-Fall 93, p. 92.
7040. WHALEN, Tom
"The Bridge." [ProseP] (2) 93, p. 96.
"It's So Nice." [ProseP] (1) 92, p. 80.
"The Next Morning." [ProseP] (1) 92, p. 81.
"Rooftops." [ProseP] (1) 92, p. 79.
7041. WHEATCROFT, John
"Family Outing: Yorkshire." [PaintedB] (49) 93, p. 36-37.
"Hannah." [FourQ] (7:2) Fall 93, p. 14.
"Hooked Ram." [SoDakR] (31:3) Fall 93, p. 44-45.
"The Portland Vase." [GrahamHR] (17) Fall 93, p. 60-63.
"Sign in the London Underground." [SoDakR] (31:3) Fall 93, p. 43.
"Spice Island" (For Josephine and Eric Jacobsen). [GrahamHR] (17) Fall 93, p. 53 - 59.
7042. WHEATLEY, Patience
"Cave Drawing." [PottPort] (15:1) Spr-Sum 93, p. 82-86.
"Gynechologist." [PraS] (67:4) Wint 93, p. 139.
7043. WHEATWIND, Marie-Elise
"Los Perdidos: 'Angel'." [OnTheBus] (5:2, #12) Sum-Fall 93, p. 211.
7044. WHEDON, Tony
"Baby Carriages" (tr. of Tatsuji Miyoshi, w. Akemi Nakamura). [GreenMR] (NS 6:2) Sum-Fall 93, p. 69.
"Before Bodhidarma, Emptiness." [CharR] (19:1) Spr 93, p. 105.

"Double Scenery" (tr. of Tatsuji Miyoshi, w. Akemi Nakamura). [GreenMR] (NS
    6:2) Sum-Fall 93, p. 70.
"Leg Trap." [SpoonR] (18:2) Sum-Fall 93, p. 43.
"Maruki Bridge" (tr. of Tatsuji Miyoshi, w. Akemi Nakamura). [GreenMR] (NS 6:2)
    Sum-Fall 93, p. 68.
"May" (tr. of Minamiko Nagashima, w. Akemi Nakamura). [GreenMR] (NS 6:2)
    Sum-Fall 93, p. 71.
"Osteon / the Atelier of Bones, Invention in Two Voices, D Minor" (tr. of Atsusuke
    Tanaka, w. Akemi Nakamura). [GreenMR] (NS 6:2) Sum-Fall 93, p. 76.
"The Pans, the Pots and the Fire in Front of Me" (tr. of Rin Ishigaki, w. Akemi
    Nakamura). [GreenMR] (NS 6:2) Sum-Fall 93, p. 74-75.
"Poem: It's twilight" (tr. of Atsuko Kato, w. Akemi Nakamura). [GreenMR] (NS
    6:2) Sum-Fall 93, p. 72.
"Seeing Your Face." [SpoonR] (18:2) Sum-Fall 93, p. 44.
"Still Life." [PassN] (14:1) Sum 93, p. 22.
"Waiting for a Wind" (tr. of Chi Ishioka, w. Akemi Nakamura). [GreenMR] (NS
    6:2) Sum-Fall 93, p. 77.
"Winter Light" (tr. of Masahiko Hihara, w. Akemi Nakamura). [GreenMR] (NS 6:2)
    Sum-Fall 93, p. 73.
7045. WHEELER, Charles B.
    "The Creative Writing Class Goes on Safari." [CumbPR]] (13:1) Fall 93, p. 76-77.
    "Le Déjeuner sur l'Herbe." [SouthernPR] (33:1) Spr 93, p. 49.
    "Gay Chimp Falls in Love with Circus Dwarf." [Ascent] (17:2) Wint 93, p. 38-39.
    "Paradise Permanently Lost." [Light] (7) Aut 93, p. 18.
7046. WHEELER, Sue
    "Exotic." [PraS] (67:4) Wint 93, p. 147.
    "The Laws of Gravity." [PoetryC] (13:3) 93, p. 16.
    "Lineage." [PoetryC] (13:3) 93, p. 16.
    "Look at Us." [Event] (22:3) Wint 93-94, p. 56.
    "Minus 0.3." [Event] (22:1) Spr 93, p. 58.
    "Scaffolds Everywhere." [PoetryC] (13:3) 93, p. 16.
    "Thai Restaurant, Edmonton." [MalR] (105) Wint 93, p. 37.
7047. WHEELER, Susan
    "Forgetting the Liberty." [13thMoon] (12:1/2) 93-94, p. 81.
    "Framingham." [Witness] (7:2) 93, p. 27.
    "The Hair on Your Chest." [Chelsea] (55) 93, p. 74.
    "Instructions." [Chelsea] (55) 93, p. 75.
    "No Mo Faith in the Stepsa Salvation." [Sequoia] (34/35) 92-93, p. 83.
    "Ordination." [Sequoia] (34/35) 92-93, p. 82.
    "Peanut Agglutinin." [Witness] (7:2) 93, p. 26.
    "You Should Know" (Prose Poems After Catullus). [Chelsea] (55) 93, p. 72-73.
7048. WHITAKER, Caleb
    "Two Poems of Awakening." [ChatR] (13:4) Sum 93, p. 50-52.
7049. WHITE, A. Bethany
    "Promised to a Dead Man." [RiverS] (37) 93, p. 27.
    "Uncle Means Stop." [RiverS] (37) 93, p. 28.
7050. WHITE, Boyd
    "Cooking with Bradley" (for Bradley P. Ross). [PraS] (67:3) Fall 93, p. 44-45.
    "Flowers Become a Job You Can Never Finish" (for Carolyn Jacobson). [PraS]
        (67:3) Fall 93, p. 46.
    "Thallium Poisoning." [PraS] (67:3) Fall 93, p. 43-44.
7051. WHITE, Calvin
    "Seen from a Balcony on Carral Street." [TickleAce] (23) Spr-Sum 92, p. 37.
    "Wing Chou." [TickleAce] (23) Spr-Sum 92, p. 38-39.
7052. WHITE, Claire Nicolas
    "Lost Daughter." [PartR] (60:3) Sum 93, p. 429-430.
7053. WHITE, Francia
    "June." [GlobalCR] (1) Spr 93, p. 29-30.
7054. WHITE, Gail
    "Anima." [Hellas] (4:1) Spr 93, p. 30.
    "Boating on the Mississippi." [Light] (8) Wint 93, p. 23.
    "Ghost Talk." [CapeR] (28:2) Fall 93, p. 20.
    "Gravity, Grace." [Hellas] (4:1) Spr 93, p. 29.
    "Letter to My Friend in the Convent." [CreamCR] (17:2) Fall 93, p. 111.
    "On Reading John Donne's Sermons." [HampSPR] Wint 93, p. 61.
    "Pilgrims in Assisi." [ChrC] (110:26) 22-29 S 93, p. 898.

"Preposterous Pets." [Light] (7) Aut 93, p. 20.
"The Secret Faith." [HampSPR] Wint 93, p. 61.
"Slug Song." [Light] (8) Wint 93, p. 21.
"We punted on the Hellespont." [Light] (7) Aut 93, p. 24.
"Wetbacks cross the Rio Grande" (Honorable Mention, First Annual River Rhyme
    Competition). [Light] (5) Spr 93, p. 30.
7055. WHITE, J. P.
"Cane." [Crazy] (44) Spr 93, p. 85-86.
"Christmas Eve at the Plantation." [HighP] (8:1) Spr 93, p. 30-32.
"Cleaning the Book Shelf." [Crazy] (44) Spr 93, p. 82-84.
"The Dancing Girls at the Diplomat" (Hollywood, Florida). [Crazy] (44) Spr 93, p.
    87-89.
"The Tree." [MassR] (34:4) Wint 93-94, p. 533-534.
7056. WHITE, John
"For Miles." [CapeR] (28:2) Fall 93, p. 2-3.
7057. WHITE, Julianne
"Divorce." [EngJ] (82:6) O 93, p. 92.
7058. WHITE, Julie Herrick
"The Green Grocer's Daughters." [Pearl] (17) Spr 93, p. 104.
7059. WHITE, Lucia Stanton
"The Woman With a Perfect Garden." [AmerV] (30) 93, p. 25-26.
7060. WHITE, Michael
"Camille Monet sur Son Lit de Mort" (for Jackie). [NewRep] (208:15) 12 Ap 93, p.
    41.
"Her Mother's House." [Journal] (17:2) Fall-Wint 93, p. 75.
7061. WHITE, Mimi
"Old Hat." [Vis] (42) 93, p. 19.
"Over Lunch with My Father." [Vis] (42) 93, p. 18-19.
"A Simple Love Story." [Poetry] (162:2) My 93, p. 89.
7062. WHITE, Patrick
"What I Wanted to Be to You." [Arc] (30) Spr 93, p. 61.
7063. WHITE, Philip
"Night Traffic Over North Street." [SouthernPR] (33:1) Spr 93, p. 43-44.
"The View from Home" (for Cherry Douch). [CreamCR] (17:2) Fall 93, p. 158-159.
7064. WHITE, Sharon
"Fall." [Northeast] (5:9) Wint 93-94, p. 24.
7065. WHITE, Steven
"Asleep by the River" (tr. of Alberto Rubio). [InterPR] (19:2) Fall 93, p. 35.
"Inscribed Stele" (tr. of Francisco Valle). [InterPR] (19:2) Fall 93, p. 37.
7066. WHITE, Tinker
"Red Bank, N.J. (1941-45)." [JINJPo] (15:1) Spr 93, p. 24-27.
7067. WHITEHEAD, Thomas
"Lost on the Quad." [Light] (6) Sum 93, p. 12.
"Old Anew." [Poem] (70) N 93, p. 50.
7068. WHITFIELD, Toni
"Perfect Legs." [CapeR] (28:1) Spr 93, p. 35.
7069. WHITLEDGE, Jane
"Telling Our Lives: Susan's Turn." [Kalliope] (15:2) 93, p. 57.
7070. WHITMAN, Walt
"America to the Old World Bards." [QRL] (12:32/33) 93, p. 544.
"I Stand and Look." [QRL] (12:32/33) 93, p. 544.
"Sunrise." [QRL] (12:32/33) 93, p. 544.
"To What You Said." [QRL] (12:32/33) 93, p. 543-544.
7071. WHITMORE, S.
"Body Boby Air." [PoetL] (88:2) Sum 93, p. 19-20.
"Keeps on Turning." [PoetL] (88:2) Sum 93, p. 21-22.
7072. WHITNEY, J. D.
"Grandmother: tries lending dogs to people." [Northeast] (5:9) Wint 93-94, p. 31.
"Grandmother: warns the children NOT to play with their bellybuttons." [Northeast]
    (5:9) Wint 93-94, p. 32.
7073. WHITNEY, Ross R.
"In the Stable." [PoetryNW] (34:1) Spr 93, p. 46-47.
"Snow." [FreeL] (11) Wint 93, p. 25.
"The Swansong of J. Richard Bachman." [Light] (7) Aut 93, p. 16.
"That He Will Wake." [PoetryNW] (34:3) Aut 93, p. 25.
"The Water Breather" (for Norman Fruman). [BelPoJ] (43:3) Spr 93, p. 10-13.

499

WHITT

7074. WHITT, Laurie Anne
"The Absinthe-Drinker" (After the painting "L'absynthe" by Edgar Degas).
[CreamCR] (17:2) Fall 93, p. 140-142.
7075. WHITTEMORE, Christine
"The Season of Persimmons" (for you, after thirteen years). [Hellas] (4:1) Spr 93, p.
56-57.
7076. WHITTEMORE, Marie
"Towards a Ridge of Blue Sky." [AntR] (51:4) Fall 93, p. 552.
7077. WHITTER, Gail D.
"Adorning her with jewels." [Bogg] (66) 93, Reviews suppl., p. 4.
"Bathing she spots." [Bogg] (66) 93, Reviews suppl., p. 4.
"Busted." [Bogg] (66) 93, Reviews suppl., p. 4.
"Cricket crawling." [Bogg] (66) 93, Reviews suppl., p. 4.
"Slap the shore." [Bogg] (66) 93, Reviews suppl., p. 4.
7078. WICKS, Susan
"Changeling." [Verse] (10:3) Wint 93, p. 103.
"Many." [Verse] (10:3) Wint 93, p. 102.
"Spider Naevus." [Verse] (10:3) Wint 93, p. 103.
7079. WIDERKEHR, Richard
"Night Fields." [WritersF] (19) 93, p. 135.
7080. WIDUP, David
"The Picture Show." [OnTheBus] (6:1, #13) Wint 93-Spr 94, p. 206.
"A Stolen Moment." [OnTheBus] (5:2, #12) Sum-Fall 93, p. 212-213.
7081. WIEDER, Laurance
"Deafened." [Boulevard] (8:2/3, #23/24) Fall 93, p. 169.
"Shake." [Boulevard] (8:2/3, #23/24) Fall 93, p. 168.
7082. WIEGEL, Nancy J.
"Parade." [Kalliope] (15:2) 93, p. 45.
7083. WIENS, Paul
"Metabolism" (Hieronymous Bosch. Tr. by Gisela Argyle). [PoetryC] (13:2) 93, p.
23.
7084. WIESE, Brooke
"Confession of Julio Gonzalez" (as taken by Police Sgt. Michael Geary, 48th
Precinct). [BrooklynR] (10) 93, p. 22-23.
"Three Tanka Because John" (for Sebastian). [HawaiiR] (17:1, #37) Spr 93, p. 75.
7085. WIESELTIER, Meir
"Letter" (1 & 4, tr. by Shirley Kaufman, w. the author). [Trans] (28) Spr 93, p. 109 -
111.
"Letter" (2-3, tr. by Shirley Kaufman). [KenR] (NS 15:4) Fall 93, p. 21-23.
"Output" (tr. by Shirley Kaufman, w. the author). [Trans] (28) Spr 93, p. 112.
7086. WIESNER, Ljubo
"Reflections" (tr. by Christopher Middleton). [NewYorker] (69:41) 6 D 93, p. 52.
7087. WIGGS, Terry
"Don't Tell Me You Don't Like Bukowski." [ChironR] (12:1, #34) Spr 93, p. 45.
"A Lion Turns Seventy." [ChironR] (12:4/13:1, #37/38) Wint 93-Spr 94, p. 44.
7088. WIGHT, Ernest A., Jr.
"Mooz." [Interim] (12:2) Fall-Wint 93, p. 5.
WIGHTMAN, Ludmilla Popova
See POPOVA-WIGHTMAN, Ludmilla
7089. WILBORN, William
"News" (after Breughel). [Hellas] (4:2) Fall 93, p. 107.
"Of Arms." [Poetry] (161:5) F 93, p. 276-277.
7090. WILBUR, Richard
"The Agent." [QRL] (12:32/33) 93, p. 546-547.
"A Digression." [NewYorker] (69:26) 16 Ag 93, p. 68.
"Flumen Tenebrarum." [QRL] (12:32/33) 93, p. 545.
"Sganarelle, or The Imaginary Cuckold" (Comedy in 24 Scenes, 1660, tr. of
Molière). [GettyR] (6:2) Spr 93, p. 193-225.
7091. WILCOX, Lois White
"The Peevement of Achievement." [Light] (5) Spr 93, p. 24.
7092. WILCOX, Luman E.
"Springtime for Some: Expounding on a Theme of Ezra." [Light] (5) Spr 93, p. 7.
7093. WILCZYK, Wojciech
"Manoeuvres" (tr. by Tomek Bieron). [Verse] (10:2) Sum 93, p. 37.
"Translation from the Chinese" (tr. by Tomek Bieron). [Verse] (10:2) Sum 93, p. 37.

7094. **WILD, Gerald**
"Cello at Barnes Lake." [Elf] (3:4) Wint 93, p. 27.

7095. **WILD, Peter**
"Adam Names the Animals." [Elf] (3:3) Fall 93, p. 30.
"Calligraphy." [HiramPoR] (53/54) Fall 92-Sum 93, p. 89.
"Chinese Restaurants." [NoDaQ] (61:4) Fall 93, p. 150-151.
"Columbus, New Mexico." [AnotherCM] (26) Fall 93, p. 181.
"The Concert." [ApalQ] (35) 90, p. 39-40.
"Cowboys." [FreeL] (11) Wint 93, p. 6.
"Doctor." [OnTheBus] (6:1, #13) Wint 93-Spr 94, p. 207.
"The Evolution of the Piano." [PoetL] (88:4) Wint 93-94, p. 48.
"The Happy Camper." [ChatR] (13:3) Spr 93, p. 57.
"Lost Dogs." [FreeL] (11) Wint 93, p. 4.
"A Novel about Dentists." [BellR] (16:1/2) Spr-Fall 93, p. 35.
"Pets." [FreeL] (11) Wint 93, p. 5.
"Pussy Willows." [GreenMR] (NS 6:2) Sum-Fall 93, p. 95.
"Slaves." [LaurelR] (27:1) Wint 93, p. 35.
"The Truth about AIDS." [PoetL] (88:4) Wint 93-94, p. 47.
"The View from My Lawyer's Office." [ArtfulD] (24/25) 93, p. 117.
"Watches." [OnTheBus] (5:2, #12) Sum-Fall 93, p. 214.

WILD, Wei the
See WEI, the Wild

7096. **WILDE-MENOZZI, Wallis**
"At Three or Four." [KenR] (NS 15:1) Wint 93, p. 143.
"California Immortality" (for L. L. Cavalli-Sforza). [MalR] (103) Sum 93, p. 87.
"Late Spring." [SouthwR] (78:4) Aut 93, p. 483-484.
"Sewing: Nineteenth-Century Sampler." [AmerV] (31) 93, p. 94-100.
"Wash, Early Monday." [KenR] (NS 15:1) Wint 93, p. 142-143.
"With Both Hands." [MalR] (103) Sum 93, p. 86.

7097. **WILDER, Rex**
"Balcony" (Port-la-Galère). [YellowS] (42) Wint-Spr 93, p. 19.
"A Cote d'Azur Dessert for Two" (for Kellianne). [YellowS] (42) Wint-Spr 93, p. 19.
"Recessional." [Ploughs] (19:1) Spr 93, p. 55.
"Séverine Between Marriages." [YellowS] (42) Wint-Spr 93, p. 18.

7098. **WILDMAN, Ed**
"I Chose the Law." [AntigR] (93-94) Spr-Sum 93, p. 59-60.
"So You Won't Have to Ask Why I Don't Do Criminal Law Anymore." [AntigR] (93-94) Spr-Sum 93, p. 56-58.

7099. **WILDONGER, Jill**
"At the Edge of the Pool" (Poets of High School Age). [HangL] (63) 93, p. 91.
"Let Me Go" (Poets of High School Age). [HangL] (63) 93, p. 92.
"My Friend" (Poets of High School Age). [HangL] (63) 93, p. 91.

7100. **WILEY, Peter J.**
"Gophers." [GrahamHR] (17) Fall 93, p. 107.

7101. **WILK, Melvin**
"Mornings on the Air at Ten." [Poetry] (162:4) Jl 93, p. 206-207.

7102. **WILKES, Kennette H.**
"Absolution." [ChangingM] (25) Wint-Spr 93, p. 72.

7103. **WILKIE, Rodger I.**
"Ronald." [TickleAce] (26) Fall-Wint 93, p. 62-65.

7104. **WILKINS, Sopie**
"Ur-Valentine?" (tr. of anonymous 12-13th century Middle-High German poem, re - translated by Karl Shapiro). [Sparrow] (60) Sum 93, p. 20.

7105. **WILKINSON, Claude**
"Blackberry Fools." [Poem] (70) N 93, p. 57.
"Epoch." [Poem] (70) N 93, p. 58.

7106. **WILLARD, Nancy**
"The Alligator Wrestler." [NewYorker] (69:10) 26 Ap 93, p. 70.
"Angels Among the Servants." [NewYorker] (69:33) 11 O 93, p. 91.
"The Bell Ringers of Kalamazoo." [PassN] (14:2) Wint 93, p. 34.
"The Burning at Neilson's Farm." [NewL] (59:3) 93, p. 54-55.
"Harpo and the Angel." [LaurelR] (27:2) Sum 93, p. 86-87.
"The Patience of Bathtubs." [NewEngR] (15:4) Fall 93, p. 147.
"Still Life with Drive-In." [LaurelR] (27:2) Sum 93, p. 87.
"The Totems." [NewL] (59:3) 93, p. 53.

7107. WILLEY, Rosemary
"All the Needs." [Poetry] (161:4) Ja 93, p. 221-222.
"The Fitting Room." [IndR] (16:1) Spr 93, p. 191.
7108. WILLHOFT, David
"You Can't Say." [Plain] (14:1) Fall 93, p. 11.
WILLIAMS, Ann Harris
See HARRIS-WILLIAMS, Ann
7109. WILLIAMS, C. K.
"Artemis." [NewEngR] (15:1) Wint 93, p. 201.
"Dashed Off" (tr. of Adam Zagajewski, w. the author). [OhioR] (50) 93, p. 9-10.
"The Dirty Talker, Boston." [NewEngR] (15:1) Wint 93, p. 202.
"Shame." [NewEngR] (15:1) Wint 93, p. 202-203.
7110. WILLIAMS, David L.
"In Quest." [ChrC] (110:14) 28 Apr 93, p. 454.
7111. WILLIAMS, Diane
"The Goal." [DenQ] (28:1) Sum 93, p. 59.
"My Reaction to Life." [DenQ] (28:1) Sum 93, p. 58.
"Speech." [DenQ] (28:1) Sum 93, p. 60.
7112. WILLIAMS, Eran
"Ptolemy and Me." [OnTheBus] (5:2, #12) Sum-Fall 93, p. 215.
7113. WILLIAMS, Joe
"Wisdom." [SlipS] (13) 93, p. 69.
7114. WILLIAMS, Jonathan
"New Metafours." [JamesWR] (11:1) Fall 93, p. 4.
7115. WILLIAMS, Linda Paglierani
"Sundays Were Religious Days." [AmerPoR] (22:6) N-D 93, p. 32.
7116. WILLIAMS, Lisa
"Out of These Days." [LouisL] (10:2) Fall 93, p. 61-62.
"The Rattlesnake" (for my father). [Crazy] (44) Spr 93, p. 39-40.
7117. WILLIAMS, Mo
"Only Saints May Wash Their Hands in Memory." [Kalliope] (15:3) 93, p. 29.
7118. WILLIAMS, Roger
"Poor Bird." [VirQR] (69:3) Sum 93, p. 504-505.
7119. WILLIAMS, Rynn
"Da Vinci's Man" (for my father). [Footwork] (23) 93, p. 90.
"Small Visits." [Footwork] (23) 93, p. 89-90.
"Water Witch." [Footwork] (23) 93, p. 89.
7120. WILLIAMS, Tyrone
"Earthbound." [Drumvoices] (2:1/2) Fall-Wint 92-93, p. 79.
"Sleeping Sickness" (for Lee and Steven). [Drumvoices] (2:1/2) Fall-Wint 92-93, p. 79.
7121. WILLIAMS, William Carlos
"The Bitter World of Spring." [QRL] (12:32/33) 93, p. 548.
"The Clouds III (Scherzo)." [QRL] (12:32/33) 93, p. 551.
"Dactyls — From Theocritus: Idyl I." [QRL] (12:32/33) 93, p. 551-556.
"The Dish of Fruit." [QRL] (12:32/33) 93, p. 550.
"The Goat." [QRL] (12:32/33) 93, p. 550.
"Lament." [QRL] (12:32/33) 93, p. 548-549.
"Sunflowers." [QRL] (12:32/33) 93, p. 550-551.
"To a Lovely Old Bitch." [QRL] (12:32/33) 93, p. 549.
7122. WILLIAMSON, Alan
"Fire and Flood." [SouthwR] (78:3) Sum 93, p. 382.
"For My Daughter, Leaving." [Zyzzyva] (9:2) Sum 93, p. 68-69.
7123. WILLIAMSON, Greg
"Boy with a Baseball Bat." [Hellas] (4:1) Spr 93, p. 62.
"Chant Royal." [YaleR] (81:4) O 93, p. 67-69.
"The River-Merchant's Wife: A Letter." [PoetC] (24:3) Spr 93, p. 17.
"Walter Parmer." [CumbPR]] (13:1) Fall 93, p. 19-23.
7124. WILLIAMSON, Patrick
"I am woman she says" (tr. of Jacques Gaucheron from *Entre mon ombre et la lumière*). [Verse] (10:1) Spr 93, p. 99.
7125. WILLIAMSON, Rosemarie
"Cookie Crisis." [Writer] (106:7) Jl 93, p. 21.
"Disturbing Thought." [Writer] (106:7) Jl 93, p. 21.
"Dog Days." [Writer] (106:7) Jl 93, p. 21.
"A Dress Unknown." [Writer] (106:7) Jl 93, p. 20.

"A Fiery Courtship." [Writer] (106:7) Jl 93, p. 20.
"Holloween Costume Contest." [Writer] (106:7) Jl 93, p. 21.
"Ill Wind." [Writer] (106:7) Jl 93, p. 19.
"Live and Learn." [Writer] (106:7) Jl 93, p. 21.
"Once Over Lightly." [Writer] (106:7) Jl 93, p. 20.
"Pa for the Course." [Writer] (106:7) Jl 93, p. 20.
"Quandary." [Writer] (106:7) Jl 93, p. 46.
"Saturday's Child." [Writer] (106:7) Jl 93, p. 20.
"A Seedy Story." [Writer] (106:7) Jl 93, p. 19.
"Sun-Room Scenario." [Writer] (106:7) Jl 93, p. 21.
7126. WILLIS, Dawn (Dawn Diez)
"The Door Closing." [TarRP] (33:1) Fall 93, p. 57.
"Lazarus." [SouthernPR] (33:2) Fall 93, p. 48-49.
"Trapeze in Autumn." [BelPoJ] (43:3) Spr 93, p. 32.
"Tsubuka" (for Professor Hitoshi Igarashi). [BelPoJ] (43:3) Spr 93, p. 33.
7127. WILLIS, Elizabeth
"Songs for A." (Excerpts). [13thMoon] (12:1/2) 93-94, p. 82-84.
7128. WILLIS, Irene
"Becoming Hard of Hearing." [US1] (28/29) 93, p. 4.
"Dancing Feet." [Crazy] (44) Spr 93, p. 41.
"When the Beat Comes Back." [Crazy] (44) Spr 93, p. 42.
"The Yellow Shirt." [LaurelR] (27:1) Wint 93, p. 77-79.
7129. WILLIS, Paul
"Easter in the Campground." [ChrC] (110:11) 7 Apr 93, p. 365.
7130. WILLIS, William
"The Pirate Ship." [WashR] (18:5) F-Mr 93, p. 22.
7131. WILLOUGHBY, Jennifer
"Critical History." [Nimrod] (37:1) Fall-Wint 93, p. 61.
"For Herr Neumann, Retiring to Las Vegas" (The Nimrod/Hardman Awards:
Finalist). [Nimrod] (37:1) Fall-Wint 93, p. 60.
7132. WILLOUGHBY, N. C. Dylan
"Language Barrier." [Blueline] (14) 93, p. 60.
7133. WILLS, Matthew
"Postman Says." [Bogg] (66) Wint 92-93, p. 51.
"Shorter." [Light] (6) Sum 93, p. 17.
7134. WILLSON, John
"The Persistence of Memory" (To Salvador Dali, 1904-1989). [SycamoreR] (5:1)
Wint 93, p. 29-33.
7135. WILMARTH, Richard
"When I Socially Interact with All of My Sick Friends." [BlackBR] (17) Sum-Fall
93, p. 10.
7136. WILMER, Mary
"The Gannet (A Sestina)." [Crucible] (29) Fall 93, p. 26.
7137. WILNER, Eleanor
"Admonition." [BostonR] (18:6) D 93-Ja 94, p. 28.
"Ambition." [HawaiiR] (17:3, #39) Fall 93, p. 128-131.
"Amelia." [PraS] (67:1) Spr 93, p. 32-34.
"American Painting, with Rain." [PraS] (67:1) Spr 93, p. 26-29.
"Demolition." [PraS] (67:1) Spr 93, p. 35-36.
"Desertsong" (Meditation on a Dance by Jeff Duncan, In Memoriam). [PaintedB]
(50/51) 93, p. 126-127.
"How to Get in the Best Magazines." [PraS] (67:3) Fall 93, p. 4-6.
"The Mulch" (for Sujata and Michael and Jenny Mira). [PraS] (67:1) Spr 93, p. 37 -
38.
"Operations: Desert Shield, Desert Storm." [Calyx] (15:1) Wint 93-94, p. 34-37.
"Recurrence in Another Tongue: Homage to Tristia and Osip Mandelstam." [PraS]
(67:1) Spr 93, p. 30-32.
"The Walls" (for Melanie). [PraS] (67:1) Spr 93, p. 22-26.
"Women Talking." [PraS] (67:3) Fall 93, p. 6-7.
7138. WILOCH, Thomas
"My Crime." [HawaiiR] (17:1, #37) Spr 93, p. 221.
"My Promise." [HawaiiR] (17:1, #37) Spr 93, p. 221.
"The Regret." [HawaiiR] (17:1, #37) Spr 93, p. 221.
7139. WILSON, Armin
"O" (On reading some comments on "OM" in Justus George Lawler's "Celestial
Pantomine," 11 March, 1993). [Gypsy] (20) Sum 93, p. 27.

7140. WILSON, Barbara Hurd
"Canning Beets." [Footwork] (23) 93, p. 155.
"Caving without the Shaman." [Outbr] (24) 93, p. 112-113.
"New Age Bear." [Outbr] (24) 93, p. 114.
"On the Morning of Our 20th Anniversary." [Footwork] (23) 93, p. 154.
"Teacher." [Footwork] (23) 93, p. 155-156.
7141. WILSON, Betty
"Dryland Farmer." [Grain] (21:2) Sum 93, p. 116.
7142. WILSON, David
"Vice." [Bogg] (66) Wint 92-93, p. 65.
WILSON, Fatima Lim
   See LIM-WILSON, Fatima
7143. WILSON, Ian Randall
"Fall." [Bogg] (66) Wint 92-93, p. 47.
7144. WILSON, Jack Lowther
"Fabrics." [TickleAce] (23) Spr-Sum 92, p. 80.
"Herons." [TickleAce] (23) Spr-Sum 92, p. 81.
7145. WILSON, Joyce
"Woman in the Dunes." [HarvardR] (3) Wint 93, p. 158.
7146. WILSON, Marilyn
"Lady in Mink." [Crucible] (29) Fall 93, p. 25.
7147. WILSON, Miles
"Into It." [NoAmR] (278:3) My-Je 93, p. 20.
"Stripper." [Poetry] (162:2) My 93, p. 82.
7148. WILSON, Patrice M.
"The End, the Beginning." [HawaiiR] (17:1, #37) Spr 93, p. 48-49.
"Portia." [HawaiiR] (17:2, #38) Spr 93, p. 2.
"Whether the Thing in Nature Speaks to You or Not." [HawaiiR] (17:1, #37) Spr 93, p. 50-51.
7149. WILSON, Paul
"Dreaming My Father's Body" (Excerpt). [Dandel] (20:1) 93, p. 47.
"Father's Gloves." [Dandel] (20:1) 93, p. 46.
"Not a Love Story." [PraF] (14:2) Sum 93, p. 88.
"Pounding." [PraF] (14:2) Sum 93, p. 89.
7150. WILSON, Randy
"On the Last Morning." [SlipS] (13) 93, p. 39.
7151. WILSON, Steve
"The Past: A Letter." [ProseP] (2) 93, p. 97.
"Solicitude." [ProseP] (1) 92, p. 82.
7152. WIMAN, Christian
"Storm Cellar." [PassN] (14:2) Wint 93, p. 47.
7153. WIMP, Jet
"Invocation." [PaintedB] (50/51) 93, p. 13.
7154. WINANS, A. D.
"Ode to Clint Eastwood." [Pearl] (17) Spr 93, p. 19.
7155. WINCH, Terence
"The Art of Percussion." [AmerPoR] (22:4) Jl-Ag 93, p. 32.
"In the Big Blue Buildings." [AmerPoR] (22:4) Jl-Ag 93, p. 32.
"Instant Systems." [AmerPoR] (22:4) Jl-Ag 93, p. 32.
WINCKEL, Nance van
   See Van WINCKEL, Nance
7156. WINDAHL, Gibb
"Speaking in Tongues." [GeoR] (47:4) Wint 93, p. 758-759.
7157. WINDHAM, Stephen
"Near Death Experience." [PoetryE] (36) Fall 93, p. 7.
7158. WINFIELD, William
"The Language of Crows." [PoetL] (88:4) Wint 93-94, p. 28.
WING, Tek Lum
   See LUM, Wing Tek
7159. WINGATE, Steve
"What Flashes Before You." [Pearl] (19) Fall-Wint 93, p. 50.
7160. WINK, Jodeen
"I Have This Poem. It Has No Name." [RagMag] (11:2) 93, p. 68.
"In August." [RagMag] (11:1) 93, p. 69.
"Keeping Company." [RagMag] (11:1) 93, p. 69.
"(Old News) Dear Cynthia." [RagMag] (11:2) 93, p. 69.

"The Reason I Refused My X Husband's Last Name." [RagMag] (11:1) 93, p. 68.
"Skeletons." [RagMag] (11:2) 93, p. 67.
7161. WINKLER, M.
"Amusement Park Reflections" (in Hebrew and English, tr. by Bernhard Frank).
[InterPR] (19:1) Spr 93, p. 6-7.
"The Evening Slips Off Me" (in Hebrew and English, tr. by Bernhard Frank).
[InterPR] (19:1) Spr 93, p. 12-13.
"I Don't Know When" (in Hebrew and English, tr. by Bernhard Frank). [InterPR]
(19:1) Spr 93, p. 8-9.
"The White Tulips" (in Hebrew and English, tr. by Bernhard Frank). [InterPR]
(19:1) Spr 93, p. 10-11.
WINTER, Corrine de
   See DeWINTER, Corrine
7162. WINTER, Jonah
"The Black Hole." [ChiR] (38:4) 93, p. 54-56.
"Missing Panels from an Altarpiece." [Field] (48) Spr 93, p. 42.
"Mojo." [ChiR] (38:4) 93, p. 57.
"Postcards from Paradise." [ChiR] (38:4) 93, p. 50-53.
"Sestina: My Women." [NewYorkQ] (51) 93, p. 86.
"Unrequited Love: A Slide Presentation." [ChiR] (39:2) 93, p. 81-85.
7163. WINTER, Kathleen
"My Heart Is Not As Strong As Birds'" (with music by Eric West). [TickleAce] (25)
Spr-Sum 93, p. 202-203.
7164. WINTERER, Heather
   "Moranbah." [Nimrod] (36:2) Spr-Sum 93, p. 85.
"Precaution." [Nimrod] (36:2) Spr-Sum 93, p. 83-84.
"Precaution." [Nimrod] (37:1) Fall-Wint 93, p. 94-95.
7165. WINTERS, Anne
"Sonnet: Now the god of rainy August hangs his mask." [NewYorker] (69:28) 6 S
93, p. 87.
7166. WINTERS, Mary
"The Big Livingroom." [JINJPo] (15:2) Aut 93, p. 12.
"Childhood." [Plain] (14:1) Fall 93, p. 20.
"Only One Promise" (A Plainsongs Award Poem). [Plain] (13:3) Spr 93, p. 22.
"Red Overcoming." [Gaia] (3) O 93, p. 12.
"Some Moments on Earth." [PaintedHR] (9) Spr 93, p. 8-9.
"Taunted." [Gaia] (1/2) Ap-Jl 93, p. 22.
"Tests." [JINJPo] (15:2) Aut 93, p. 13.
"Trophy." [XavierR] (13:2) Fall 93, p. 110.
"Vision." [Gaia] (3) O 93, p. 12.
7167. WINTHROP, Jeanette I.
"The First Time." [HampSPR] Wint 93, p. 45.
"In My Mother's Kitchen, 1943." [HampSPR] Wint 93, p. 44.
"Watching the Moon with My Husband." [AntigR] (93-94) Spr-Sum 93, p. 30.
7168. WINTROUB, Bob
"Lana Turner." [OnTheBus] (6:1, #13) Wint 93-Spr 94, p. 208.
"Reflections." [OnTheBus] (6:1, #13) Wint 93-Spr 94, p. 208.
"Sarajevo." [OnTheBus] (6:1, #13) Wint 93-Spr 94, p. 208.
7169. WIRAM, Frieda K.
"As If It Were." [HiramPoR] (53/54) Fall 92-Sum 93, p. 90.
7170. WISCHNER, Claudia M.
"For Persephone." [Sequoia] (34/35) 92-93, p. 18.
"Rubyglass." [Sequoia] (34/35) 92-93, p. 19.
7171. WISE, Marie Gray
"Memorial Day, 1985" (For John Crawford, Jr.). [Footwork] (23) 93, p. 26.
7172. WISEMAN, Jonathan
"Zundel." [Grain] (21:3) Fall 93, p. 38.
7173. WITEK, Terri
"A Good Life." [SouthernR] (29:2) Spr, Ap 93, p. 318-319.
"Ouija Boards." [NewYorkQ] (52) 93, p. 72.
"Rewind." [Shen] (43:1) Spr 93, p. 104-105.
7174. WITHERSPOON, Richard
"Sorrel and Tamarind Teas." [JamesWR] (10:3) Spr 93, p. 5.
7175. WITT, Harold
"American Lit: A Psalm of Life." [WritersF] (19) 93, p. 69.
"Bane" (from "American Lit"). [BellArk] (9:2) Mr-Ap 93, p. 21.

"Behind It All." [WindO] (57) Fall 93, p. 12.
"Carmen in Verona." [WindO] (57) Fall 93, p. 13.
"An Early Sequence" (from "American Lit"). [BellArk] (9:2) Mr-Ap 93, p. 21.
"Fahrenheit 451." [CharR] (19:2) Fall 93, p. 130.
"Fallen Leaf." [Elf] (3:1) Spr 93, p. 41.
"Gail White." [CharR] (19:2) Fall 93, p. 132.
"Jean Stafford." [CharR] (19:2) Fall 93, p. 131.
"Jethro Martin, Elvis Impersonator." [WormR] (33:1, #129) 93, p. 23.
"The Last Day at Safeway." [WindO] (57) Fall 93, p. 14.
"Loma Prieta." [BellArk] (9:5) S-O 93, p. 7.
"Nights in San Jose." [CharR] (19:2) Fall 93, p. 130.
"The Odd Couple." [WormR] (33:1, #129) 93, p. 24.
"Old Hat in a New Wave" (a play in one act). [BellArk] (9:5) S-O 93, p. 21-24.
"One Flew Over the Cuckoo's Nest" (American Lit). [NewYorkQ] (50) 93, p. 59.
"Paging Through the Tavern Post and Reading Steve Yamamoto's Haikus Again."
    [CharR] (19:2) Fall 93, p. 132.
"Pooh." [Interim] (12:1) Spr-Sum 93, p. 11.
"So Many Poets." [PoetC] (24:3) Spr 93, p. 45.
"Someone Though" (from "American Lit"). [BellArk] (9:2) Mr-Ap 93, p. 21.
"Spingarn." [CharR] (19:2) Fall 93, p. 131.
"A Summer Visit." [LitR] (37:1) Fall 93, p. 18-19.
"This Swallowtail." [BellArk] (9:5) S-O 93, p. 6.
"Trash." [WritersF] (19) 93, p. 68.
"Trying the New Volvo." [BellArk] (9:2) Mr-Ap 93, p. 8.
"Why John Sanderson Won't Go Back To Where He Came From or Anywhere
    Else." [WormR] (33:1, #129) 93, p. 23-24.
"Yes, Bill." [Sparrow] (60) Sum 93, p. 16.
WITT, Jim de
    See DeWITT, Jim
7176. WITTE, Francine
    "Alien Story." [PoetC] (24:2) Wint 93, p. 25-26.
    "When the Last Beatle Dies." [GreensboroR] (54) Sum 93, p. 93.
    "Yin/Yang." [CreamCR] (17:1) Spr 93, p. 34.
7177. WITTE, George
    "The Secret Fire." [PoetC] (24:3) Spr 93, p. 13-14.
    "To Be Opened in the Event." [SouthwR] (78:3) Sum 93, p. 383-384.
    "Voiceover." [NewYorkQ] (51) 93, p. 85.
7178. WITTE, John
    "Chopper." [OntR] (38) Spr-Sum 93, p. 19.
    "Why." [OntR] (38) Spr-Sum 93, p. 17-18.
7179. WITTE, Phyllis
    "The Wonderwheel at Coney Island." [BrooklynR] (10) 93, p. 55.
7180. WITTWER, Rodney
    "Border Reports." [HayF] (12) Spr-Sum 93, p. 121.
    "Children's Games" (after Bruegel). [CreamCR] (17:2) Fall 93, p. 183.
    "Drawing the Storm." [HayF] (12) Spr-Sum 93, p. 122-123.
    "Gone & Gone." [Ploughs] (19:1) Spr 93, p. 161-162.
7181. WOHLFELD, Valerie
    "Sea." [Pequod] (35) 93, p. 138-140.
7182. WOJAHN, David
    "Elegy for Empire." [ChiR] (39:2) 93, p. 1-3.
    "Human Form" (Loyola Park). [TriQ] (89) Wint 93-94, p. 215-216.
    "New Orleans, Unearthing." [Boulevard] (8:2/3, #23/24) Fall 93, p. 25.
    "Postmodern." [Boulevard] (8:2/3, #23/24) Fall 93, p. 23-24.
    "Tomis." [TriQ] (89) Wint 93-94, p. 217-219.
7183. WOLBRINK, Paul
    "Killer Teach." [EngJ] (82:5) S 93, p. 104.
7184. WOLF, David
    "Elsewhere and Otherwise." [CapeR] (28:1) Spr 93, p. 32.
    "Maneuvers." [PoetC] (24:2) Wint 93, p. 21.
7185. WOLF, Michele
    "The Blind Spot." [SouthernPR] (33:1) Spr 93, p. 33-35.
    "Flamingo Sunset." [AntR] (51:4) Fall 93, p. 565.
    "Man with Picture Frame" (90th and Third, NYC). [Poetry] (163:3) D 93, p. 149.
7186. WOLFE, John
    "Having Gotten Your Phone Number." [AnotherCM] (26) Fall 93, p. 182.

7187. WOLFE, Roger
"Call Me" (— Lou Reed. Tr. by Cecilia C. Lee and Laura Higgins). [LitR] (36:3)
Spr 93, p. 387.

WOLHEE, Choe
See CHOE, Wolhee

7188. WOLMAN, Kenneth
"Ezra Pound: Binghampton, New York, 11/2/72." [NewYorkQ] (52) 93, p. 69.

7189. WOMACK, R. T.
"Mill Ball." [Spitball] (45) Fall 93, p. 25.

WON, Ko
See KO, Won

7190. WONG, Doris
"Angels & Artichokes." [CreamCR] (17:1) Spr 93, p. 62-63.
"A Suicide Note." [CreamCR] (17:1) Spr 93, p. 61.

7191. WOO, Daniel Schroyer
"Graphology." [HawaiiR] (17:1, #37) Spr 93, p. 52.
"The Theory of Flight." [HawaiiR] (17:1, #37) Spr 93, p. 53.

7192. WOOD, Eve (Eve E. M.)
"Advice Before Marrying." [PoetC] (24:2) Wint 93, p. 24.
"Hope." [AntR] (51:4) Fall 93, p. 551.

7193. WOOD, James
"The Borrowed Wife." [ColR] (20:1) Spr 93, p. 40-41.
"From Thes Hye Hilles, As When a Spryng Doth Fall" (— Sir Thomas Wyatt).
[MassR] (34:2) Sum 93, p. 296.
"A Town Lit by the Sea." [MassR] (34:2) Sum 93, p. 295.

7194. WOOD, Jean
"A* Wonderland Party" (*Alzheimer's). [HiramPoR] (53/54) Fall 92-Sum 93, p. 91 -
92.

7195. WOOD, Susan
"Geography." [ParisR] (35:128) Fall 93, p. 69-70.
"Swamp." [ParisR] (35:128) Fall 93, p. 71-72.

7196. WOODARD, Deborah
"The Nun's Antechamber" (tr. of Antonio Pozzi). [ApalQ] (35) 90, p. 28.
"Venice" (tr. of Antonio Pozzi). [ApalQ] (35) 90, p. 27.

7197. WOODBURY, Elizabeth
"After the Fall." [Blueline] (14) 93, p. 97.
"Ballet Lesson." [Blueline] (14) 93, p. 97.

7198. WOODCOCK, Bruce
"Totem and Taboo." [Pearl] (17) Spr 93, p. 101.

7199. WOODCOCK, George
"The Six Toms" (a suite of poems with dedicatory afterword). [Quarry] (42:3) 93, p.
116-122.

7200. WOODMAN, Jay
"Bloubergstrand." [BellArk] (9:4) Jl-Ag 93, p. 23.
"Elephants." [BellArk] (9:3) My-Je 93, p. 24.

7201. WOODRUFF, Paul
"Li Ch'ing-Chau." [Vis] (41) 93, p. 20.
"Museums of Antiquity." [Vis] (41) 93, p. 12.

7202. WOODS, John
"Beset." [PoetryNW] (34:2) Sum 93, p. 46.
"Henry Wiggins' Reading Matter." [PoetryNW] (34:2) Sum 93, p. 44-45.
"Lessons of the War, 1945." [PoetryNW] (34:2) Sum 93, p. 47.
"The Pathologist's Report." [PoetryNW] (34:2) Sum 93, p. 46.
"Return to the Love Canal." [PoetryNW] (34:2) Sum 93, p. 45.
"W.A.S.P., White Anglo-Saxon Protestant." [Northeast] (5:9) Wint 93-94, p. 29.

7203. WOODS, Peggy
"Defining." [13thMoon] (12:1/2) 93-94, p. 85.

7204. WOODSUM, Douglas
"Carving Your Future." [NoDaQ] (61:4) Fall 93, p. 49-51.
"An Impartial Answer." [CutB] (39) Wint 93, p. 39-40.
"Love Ravages the Tree of Life" (to the memory of Allen Barnett). [PraS] (67:3)
Fall 93, p. 141-142.

7205. WOODWARD, Gerard
"Night Bus." [Stand] (34:2) Spr 93, p. 51.

7206. WOODWORTH, Marc
"Letter from Paris." [Salm] (97) Wint 93, p. 102-103.

507

"Lovis Corinth at Walchensee." [ParisR] (35:126) Spr 93, p. 60-61.
"Sophia Tolstoy at Yasnaya Polyana." [Salm] (100) Fall 93, p. 147-149.
7207. WOODY, Elizabeth
"Translation of Blood Quantum." [ChiR] (39:3/4) 93, p. 89-90.
7208. WOOLLATT, Richard
"Walking Estero." [Dandel] (20:1) 93, p. 29-30.
7209. WOON, Koon
"It Isn't Because the Years Like Water Leak from My Hands." [Contact]
(11:65/66/67) Spr 93, p. 43.
7210. WOOSTER, Jack
"AC Transit." [OnTheBus] (5:2, #12) Sum-Fall 93, p. 223-224.
7211. WORLEY, James
"Messiah." [ChrC] (110:8) 10 Mr 93, p. 270.
"Newton." [ChrC] (110:24) 25 Ag-1 S 93, p. 809.
"Saints." [ChrC] (110:1) 6-13 Ja 93, p. 18.
7212. WORLEY, Jeff
"The Bookkeeper's Other Life." [CinPR] (24) Spr 93, p. 31.
"December 24, 1959." [PoetryNW] (34:4) Wint 93-94, p. 25.
"How They Come Back to Us." [PoetC] (24:2) Wint 93, p. 17.
"IBM Memo: Mouse Balls Available as Field Replacement Unit (FRU)" (a found
poem). [SouthernPR] (33:1) Spr 93, p. 70.
"Lance and Andi: Friends Gone West." [SoDakR] (31:1) Spr 93, p. 53-62.
"Late Night Caller." [HarvardR] (5) Fall 93, p. 19.
"Legacy." [PoetC] (24:2) Wint 93, p. 18.
"Luck." [ColEng] (55:4) Ap 93, p. 430.
"Nature." [Boulevard] (8:2/3, #23/24) Fall 93, p. 49-51.
"Newspaper Columnist Dies While Snorkeling" (Darrell Sifford, 60, . . . died
yesterday while snorkeling off the coast of Belize). [Boulevard] (8:2/3,
#23/24) Fall 93, p. 52.
"Our Softball Tournament Rained Out, I Settle in with Some Bourbon and Watch
the Leaves." [ChiR] (39:1) 93, p. 58-59.
"Seminal Statement." [FloridaR] (19:1) 93, p. 72-73.
"Sin." [BlackWR] (19:2) Spr-Sum 93, p. 132.
"Sitting on the Back Porch the Night Before Our First Family Reunion in 15 Years."
[LitR] (37:1) Fall 93, p. 20.
"The Weather." [LitR] (36:2) Wint 93, p. 157.
7213. WORMSER, Baron
"August 22, 1990 (Iraq and Kuwait)." [ManhatR] (7:1) Fall 93, p. 75-76.
"Cow Symphony" (for Janet). [BelPoJ] (43:3) Spr 93, p. 15.
"For D.R., Dead of AIDS at age 25." [DenQ] (27:4) Spr 93, p. 34.
"Haircut (1956)." [BelPoJ] (43:3) Spr 93, p. 16.
"The Poverty of Theory." [Poetry] (162:4) Jl 93, p. 202.
"A Quiet Life." [ManhatR] (7:1) Fall 93, p. 77.
"Simon Turetzky Who Died at Dachau." [DenQ] (27:4) Spr 93, p. 35.
"Tricia LeClair." [BelPoJ] (43:3) Spr 93, p. 14.
"Young Ahab." [DenQ] (27:4) Spr 93, p. 33.
7214. WOROZBYT, Theodore, Jr.
"Accident." [NowestR] (31:2) 93, p. 109-111.
"Bone China." [SouthernPR] (33:1) Spr 93, p. 48.
"Napoleon's Snuffbox." [PoetL] (88:4) Wint 93-94, p. 5-6.
7215. WORTSMAN, Peter
"Cunning Convertibles" (from Observations on Urban Fauna). [ProseP] (2) 93, p.
99.
"Lonesome Ceilings" (from Observations on Urban Fauna). [ProseP] (2) 93, p. 98.
"A Postcard from Cairo." [ProseP] (1) 92, p. 84.
"Racing to Istanbul." [ProseP] (1) 92, p. 85.
"The Riddle of the Sphinx." [ProseP] (1) 92, p. 83.
"So Many Things Still Aching to Be Described" (from Observations on Urban
Fauna). [ProseP] (2) 93, p. 102.
"The Twilight's Last Gleaming" (from Observations on Urban Fauna). [ProseP] (2)
93, p. 101.
"Where Names Come From" (for Russell Edson, from Observations on Urban
Fauna). [ProseP] (2) 93, p. 100.
7216. WREGGITT, Andrew
"Jardin du Luxembourg." [PoetryC] (14:1) 93, p. 6.
"John Smith." [PoetryC] (14:1) 93, p. 6.

"Zhivago's Fire." [PoetryC] (14:1) 93, p. 7.
7217. WREN, Andrea M.
"125th Street." [Drumvoices] (1:1/2) Fall-Wint 91-92, p. 96.
"The Block" (re: romare bearden). [Obs] (8:1) Spr-Sum 93, p. 106-107.
"Caterfly" (thoughts of Suz). [Drumvoices] (1:1/2) Fall-Wint 91-92, p. 94.
"Down the Road" (for me and Askhari). [Drumvoices] (1:1/2) Fall-Wint 91-92, p. 95.
"Effie's Excursion." [Obs] (8:1) Spr-Sum 93, p. 109-110.
"Girthia." [Obs] (8:1) Spr-Sum 93, p. 108.
"Gray-Eyed Effie" (at 94). [Obs] (8:1) Spr-Sum 93, p. 108-109.
"Haiku: I shade myself in." [Drumvoices] (1:1/2) Fall-Wint 91-92, p. 96.
"Homecoming." [AfAmRev] (27:1) Spr 93, p. 157.
"A Martyr's Lament." [Drumvoices] (1:1/2) Fall-Wint 91-92, p. 97.
"Mother Girthia." [Obs] (8:1) Spr-Sum 93, p. 107-108.
"Reunion." [Drumvoices] (1:1/2) Fall-Wint 91-92, p. 97.
"Talking Back." [Drumvoices] (1:1/2) Fall-Wint 91-92, p. 93.
"Youth." [Drumvoices] (1:1/2) Fall-Wint 91-92, p. 93.
7218. WRENN, Elizabeth
"The Number Five and Blue." [13thMoon] (12:1/2) 93-94, p. 86-88.
7219. WRIGHT, Bil
"Wedding Dress." [JamesWR] (10:4) Sum 93, p. 8.
7220. WRIGHT, C. D.
"Approximately Forever." [Epoch] (42:2) 93, p. 199.
"Crescent." [Epoch] (42:2) 93, p. 198.
"Everything Good between Men and Women." [Epoch] (42:2) 93, p. 195.
"Key Episodes from an Earthly Life." [AmerLC] (5) 93, p. 61-62.
"Ponds, in Love." [Epoch] (42:2) 93, p. 200.
"Song of the Gourd." [ProseP] (1) 92, p. 86.
"Sonic Relations." [Epoch] (42:2) 93, p. 196-197.
"Tours." [PaintedB] (50/51) 93, p. 93.
"With Grass As Their Witness." [AmerLC] (5) 93, p. 63.
7221. WRIGHT, Carolyne
"Another Country" (tr. of Nabaneeta Dev Sen, w. Sunil B. Ray w. the author). [AmerPoR] (22:4) Jl-Ag 93, p. 25.
"Another Spring, Darkness" (tr. of Anuradha Mahapatra, w. Paramita Banerjee). [AmerPoR] (22:4) Jl-Ag 93, p. 22.
"Antara" (4, tr. of Nabaneeta Dev Sen, w. Sunil B. Ray, Nandana Dev Sen and the author). [AmerPoR] (22:4) Jl-Ag 93, p. 24.
"Biography" (tr. of Anuradha Mahapatra, w. Paramita Banerjee). [MidAR] (14:1) 93, p. 99.
"The Boy" (tr. of Anuradha Mahapatra, w. Jyotirmoy Datta). [MidAR] (14:1) 93, p. 98.
"The Child's Saying" (tr. of Nabaneeta Dev Sen, w. Paramita Banerjee and the author). [HawaiiR] (17:1, #37) Spr 93, p. 91.
"City Nocturne" (tr. of Anuradha Mahapatra, w. Paramita Banerjee). [AmerPoR] (22:4) Jl-Ag 93, p. 22.
"Curse" (tr. of Kabita Sinha, w. Enaksi Chatterjee). [AmerPoR] (22:4) Jl-Ag 93, p. 27.
"Departure" (tr. of Kabita Sinha, w. Enaksi Chatterjee). [AmerPoR] (22:4) Jl-Ag 93, p. 26.
"The Diamond of Character" (tr. of Kabita Sinha, w. Swapna Mitra-Banerjee). [AmerPoR] (22:4) Jl-Ag 93, p. 26.
"Eve Speaks to God" (tr. of Kabita Sinha, w. the author). [AmerV] (32) 93, p. 45-47.
"Flowers in Winter" (1992 John Williams Andrews Prize Winner). [PoetL] (88:1) Spr 93, p. 8-19.
"Friend" (tr. of Anuradha Mahapatra, w. Paramita Banerjee). [AmerPoR] (22:4) Jl-Ag 93, p. 23.
"Happy Marriage" (tr. of Taslima Nasreen, w. Mohammad Nurul Huda and the author). [TriQ] (89) Wint 93-94, p. 183-184.
"I Left a Long Time Back" (tr. of Kabita Sinha, w. Swapna Mitra-Banerjee). [HarvardR] (3) Wint 93, p. 97.
"Impatient" (tr. of Anuradha Mahapatra, w. Paramita Banerjee). [AmerPoR] (22:4) Jl-Ag 93, p. 21.
"The Last Door's Name Is Sorrow" (tr. of Kabita Sinha, w. Swapna Mitra-Banerjee). [AmerPoR] (22:4) Jl-Ag 93, p. 27.

"Last Meeting" (tr. of Kabita Sinha, w. Enaksi Chatterjee). [AmerPoR] (22:4) Jl-Ag 93, p. 26.
"The Monster" (tr. of Anuradha Mahapatra, w. Paramita Banerjee). [AmerPoR] (22:4) Jl-Ag 93, p. 22.
"Mosquito Net" (tr. of Nabaneeta Dev Sen, w. Paramita Banerjee, Nandana Dev Sen and the author). [AmerPoR] (22:4) Jl-Ag 93, p. 25.
"Night Reader" (tr. of Anuradha Mahapatra, w. Paramita Banerjee). [AmerPoR] (22:4) Jl-Ag 93, p. 23.
"Night Walk Around Green Lakes." [CreamCR] (17:2) Fall 93, p. 135.
"Party" (tr. of Kabita Sinha, w. Enaksi Chatterjee). [AmerPoR] (22:4) Jl-Ag 93, p. 27.
"Perfection" (tr. of Jorge Guillén). [HarvardR] (5) Fall 93, p. 28.
"Prison Island Exile" (tr. of Nabaneeta Dev Sen, w. Sunil B. Ray, Nandana Dev Sen and the author). [AmerPoR] (22:4) Jl-Ag 93, p. 24.
"Pyre Tender" (tr. of Anuradha Mahapatra, w. Paramita Banerjee and the author). [HawaiiR] (17:1, #37) Spr 93, p. 220.
"Return to Sender?" [CreamCR] (17:2) Fall 93, p. 136-137.
"The Sea in the Wind" (tr. of Jorge Guillén). [HarvardR] (5) Fall 93, p. 28.
"The Swaying Lotus" (tr. of Nabaneeta Dev Sen, w. Sunil B. Ray, Nandana Dev Sen and the author). [AmerPoR] (22:4) Jl-Ag 93, p. 24.
"Tamboura" (tr. of Anuradha Mahapatra, w. Paramita Banerjee). [MidAR] (14:1) 93, p. 100-101.
"The Temple" (tr. of Nabaneeta Dev Sen, w. Paramita Banerjee and the author). [HawaiiR] (17:1, #37) Spr 93, p. 89.
"Things Cheaply Had" (tr. of Taslima Nasreen, w. Mohammad Nurul Huda and the author). [TriQ] (89) Wint 93-94, p. 182.
"This Night Train" (tr. of Gita Chattopadhyay, w. Paramita Banerjee). [Prima] (16/17) 93, p. 82.
"Thou Art Durga" (tr. of Gita Chattopadhyay, w. Paramita Banerjee). [Prima] (16/17) 93, p. 81.
"Waterfall" (tr. of Kabita Sinha, w. Enaksi Chatterjee). [AmerPoR] (22:4) Jl-Ag 93, p. 26.
"When It Rains" (tr. of Nabaneeta Dev Sen, w. Sunil B. Ray, Nandana Dev Sen and the author). [AmerPoR] (22:4) Jl-Ag 93, p. 24.
"You (II.)" (tr. of Anuradha Mahapatra, w. Paramita Banerjee). [AmerPoR] (22:4) Jl-Ag 93, p. 22.
7222. WRIGHT, Charles
"Morandi II." [YaleR] (81:2) Ap 93, p. 26.
"Paesaggio Notturno." [NewYorker] (69:22) 19 Jl 93, p. 52.
"Self-Portrait." [NewEngR] (15:1) Wint 93, p. 204.
"Waiting for Tu Fu." [GettyR] (6:1) Wint 93, p. 85-86.
"Watching the Equinox Arrive in Charlottesville, September 1992." [ColR] (20:1) Spr 93, p. 103-105.
7223. WRIGHT, Dave
"The Prototype Bimbo, Grotesquely Preserved." [Bogg] (66) Wint 92-93, p. 67.
7224. WRIGHT, Franz
"Abridged Dictionary of Synonyms and Phrases for Chronic Alcohol Abuse." [Field] (49) Fall 93, p. 56-59.
"Van Gogh's 'Undergrowth with Two Figures'." [Field] (49) Fall 93, p. 55.
7225. WRIGHT, G. T.
"Cricket." [NorthStoneR] (11) 93, p. 86.
"Delphi." [NorthStoneR] (11) 93, p. 88-91.
"Disengagement." [NorthStoneR] (11) 93, p. 87.
"Program." [NorthStoneR] (11) 93, p. 87.
7226. WRIGHT, Howard
"Dog." [Verse] (10:2) Sum 93, p. 98.
"A Landing Place." [Bogg] (66) Wint 92-93, p. 65.
7227. WRIGHT, James
"Butterfly Fish." [GettyR] (6:2) Spr 93, p. 317.
"The Continental Can Company at Six O'Clock." [AmerPoR] (22:6) N-D 93, p. 51.
"The Doors." [QRL] (12:32/33) 93, p. 557.
"Poem on a Trip to Ohio." [QRL] (12:32/33) 93, p. 556-557.
"Some Places in America Are Anonymous." [QRL] (12:32/33) 93, p. 556.
"To Harvey, Who Traced the Circulation." [QRL] (12:32/33) 93, p. 557-558.
7228. WRIGHT, Justin
"Small Talk" (for Kelly Grey). [BlackWR] (20:1) Fall-Wint 93, p. 22-23.

7229. WRIGHT, Kirby
"Kung Yee Fat Choy." [ProseP] (2) 93, p. 103.
"Life Extension." [ArtfulD] (24/25) 93, p. 125.
"Pool." [CapeR] (28:2) Fall 93, p. 28.
7230. WRIGHT, Leilani
"Native Fever." [HawaiiR] (17:2, #38) Spr 93, p. 63-68.
"Red Oasis." [HayF] (13) Fall-Wint 93, p. 46.
"Solitary" (tr. of Margarita Carrera). [InterPR] (19:1) Spr 93, p. 17, 19.
"Spore." [Vis] (42) 93, p. 8.
7231. WRIGHT, Tim
"Dawn, Blocker's Landing." [ColEng] (55:8) D 93, p. 907.
7232. WRIGLEY, Robert
"A Cappella" (for Marnie Bullock). [CutB] (40) Spr 93, p. 15-18.
"Benton's Persephone." [PoetryNW] (34:2) Sum 93, p. 31-32.
"The Bramble." [GeoR] (47:1) Spr 93, p. 117-119.
"Homage." [Poetry] (162:5) Ag 93, p. 255-256.
"Little Deaths." [Poetry] (162:1) Ap 93, p. 33-34.
"The Speed of Light." [PoetryNW] (34:2) Sum 93, p. 33-34.
"Treating the Spring Box." [PoetryNW] (34:2) Sum 93, p. 32-33.
7233. WROBLEWSKI, Michele
"Honeymoon." [Gaia] (3) O 93, p. 35.
WU, Ah
See AH, Wu
7234. WURSTER, Michael
"The Cemetery." [Bogg] (66) Wint 92-93, p. 63.
"The Difference Between Prose and Free Verse." [PennR] (5:2) 93, p. 32.
"Generation." [CapeR] (28:2) Fall 93, p. 24.
"No censorship." [PennR] (5:2) 93, p. 56.
7235. WYATT, Charles
"Afternoon of a Faun." [BelPoJ] (43:3) Spr 93, p. 26-29.
"The Land of Bears." [Ascent] (17:3) Spr 93, p. 57.
"Loutre Creek." [Sequoia] (34/35) 92-93, p. 6.
"Over the Undertaker." [Sequoia] (34/35) 92-93, p. 5.
"Portrait." [SoCoast] (15) Je 93, p. 56-57.
"Rembrandt Drawings" (3 poems). [TriQ] (87) Spr-Sum 93, p. 190-192.
"Saskia Looking Out of a Window, c. 1633-34." [AnotherCM] (25) Spr 93, p. 178.
"Vision." [CumbPR] (12:2) Spr 93, p. 36.
7236. WYATT, Thomas (Sir, ca. 1536)
"In Mourning Wise." [Pequod] (35) 93, p. 10-11.
7237. WYDE, Stephen
"Out of Nowhere" (from *On the Bum*). [PoetryUSA] (25/26) 93, p. 52.
"Singing for a Little Change" (from *On the Bum*). [PoetryUSA] (25/26) 93, p. 52.
7238. WYE, Pamela
"Brain Rain" (Nine 2-pagers of Images & Text). [Sulfur] (32) Spr 93, p. 279-297.
7239. WYLAM, John
"Estrangement." [LaurelR] (27:2) Sum 93, p. 62.
"Green Shade." [LaurelR] (27:2) Sum 93, p. 63.
"So Many Selves." [Nimrod] (37:1) Fall-Wint 93, p. 131.
7240. WYLER, Susan Logothetis
"Stuck." [OnTheBus] (6:1, #13) Wint 93-Spr 94, p. 209-212.
"This Great Weight." [OnTheBus] (6:1, #13) Wint 93-Spr 94, p. 212-214.
7241. WYLEY, Enda
"Eating Baby Jesus." [SenR] (23:1/2) Wint 93, p. 55-56.
"Graveyard Picnic." [SenR] (23:1/2) Wint 93, p. 54.
"Indian Death Song." [SenR] (23:1/2) Wint 93, p. 60-61.
"Storm." [SenR] (23:1/2) Wint 93, p. 53.
"You Checked Beneath Your Bed." [SenR] (23:1/2) Wint 93, p. 57-59.
7242. WYLIE, Susan
"Venus After Dark." [PassN] (14:1) Sum 93, p. 5.
"The Waves Roll In" (Ensenada, Mexico). [PassN] (14:1) Sum 93, p. 5.
7243. WYREBEK, M.
"Recovery." [VirQR] (69:1) Wint 93, p. 95-96.
"Red Tee Shirt." [VirQR] (69:1) Wint 93, p. 94-95.
"A Reminder." [VirQR] (69:1) Wint 93, p. 93-94.
"Still Awake." [VirQR] (69:1) Wint 93, p. 94.

511

7244. WYSHYNSKI, James
"The Day in Question." [RiverS] (39) 93, p. 32.
7245. WYSOCKI, Gisela von
"Grandmother" (tr. by Rosmarie Waldrop). [WorldL] (4) 93, p. 24-25.
7246. WYTTENBERG, Victoria
"Blue Moon." [PoetryNW] (34:1) Spr 93, p. 7-9.
"For My Oldest Child." [MalR] (102) Spr 93, p. 39-40.
"Miranda." [PoetryNW] (34:1) Spr 93, p. 6-7.
"This Is Not My Life, But the Life I Would Like." [MalR] (102) Spr 93, p. 37-38.
"Tulips" (for John). [MalR] (102) Spr 93, p. 36.
7247. XI, Chuan
"Echo" (tr. by Dian Li). [GreenMR] (NS 6:2) Sum-Fall 93, p. 148.
"The Orchard in August" (tr. by Dian Li). [GreenMR] (NS 6:2) Sum-Fall 93, p. 149.
"To Robinson Jeffers" (tr. of Bei Ling, w. Tony Barnstone). [ChiR] (39:3/4) 93, p. 298.
7248. XI, Murong
"Love" (tr. by Tony Barnstone and Newton Liu). [ChiR] (39:3/4) 93, p. 305.
"The Rainy Night" (tr. by Jianging Zheng and Angela Ball). [MidAR] (14:1) 93, p. 46.
XI-JIAN, Li
    See LI, Xi-jian
XIA, Wan
    See WAN, Xia
7249. XIA, Yu
"Simple Future Tense" (tr. by Michelle Yeh). [ChiR] (39:3/4) 93, p. 303-304.
XIANG, Shi
    See SHI, Xiang
XINMIN, Fan
    See FAN, Xinmin
7250. XU, Haixin
"Birds Sing in the Ravine" (tr. of Wang Wei, w. Tony Barnstone and Willis Barnstone). [AmerPoR] (22:2) Mr-Ap 93, p. 45.
"Deer Park" (tr. of Wang Wei, w. Tony Barnstone and Willis Barnstone). [AmerPoR] (22:2) Mr-Ap 93, p. 46.
"Return to Wang River" (tr. of Wang Wei, w. Tony Barnstone and Willis Barnstone). [AmerPoR] (22:2) Mr-Ap 93, p. 46.
"You Asked About My Life. I Send You, Pei Di, These Lines" (tr. of Wang Wei, w. Tony Barnstone and Willis Barnstone). [AmerPoR] (22:2) Mr-Ap 93, p. 46.
7251. XUE, Di
"Dream at the Center of a Seed" (Translation Chapbook Series No. 21, 8 poems, tr. by Wang Ping and Keith Waldrop). [MidAR] (14:1) 93, p. 63-85.
XUELIANG, Chen
    See CHEN, Xueliang
7252. YAKE, William
"Among Lakes." [BellArk] (9:3) My-Je 93, p. 10-11.
"Lines and Photographs." [BellArk] (9:4) Jl-Ag 93, p. 22.
7253. YAMADA, Leona
"Poi Bowl." [HawaiiR] (17:1, #37) Spr 93, p. 69.
"September for Joe" (Joseph K. Chadwick: June 5, 1954-April 9, 1992, and, for Clifford). [HawaiiR] (17:1, #37) Spr 93, p. v.
7254. YAMANAKA, Lois-Ann
"Chicken Pox." [HawaiiR] (17:1, #37) Spr 93, p. 18-19.
"Dead Dogs R I P." [HangL] (63) 93, p. 74-75.
"Kala — Seventh Grade, Me — Sixth Grade Sitting on Our Bikes by the Catholic Church." [HangL] (63) 93, p. 76.
"Saturday Night at the Pahala Theater" (poems: special double issue). [BambooR] (58/59) 93, 143 p.
"Yarn Wig." [MichQR] (32:1) Wint 93, p. 36-38.
7255. YAMASHITA, Jolyn Marie
"An Eighth Grader's Prayer." [HawaiiR] (17:1, #37) Spr 93, p. 212-213.
"Waimanalo." [HawaiiR] (17:1, #37) Spr 93, p. 214.
7256. YAMAZATO, Katsunori
"The Love of Red Soil" (Selections, tr. of Yonaha Mikio, w. Eric Paul Shaffer). [ChiR] (39:3/4) 93, p. 223-226.
7257. YAMRUS, John
"One Tough Mother." [Bogg] (66) Wint 92-93, p. 31-32.

YAN, Li
    See LI, Yan
YANBING, Chen
    See CHEN, Yanbing
7258. YANG, Lian
    "Solar Tide" (from the poem cycle "Nuorilang," tr. by Tony Barnstone and Newton
        Liu). [ChiR] (39:3/4) 93, p. 290-291.
7259. YANG, Mu
    "An Autumnal Prayer to Tu Fu" (tr. by Joseph R. Allen). [ChiR] (39:3/4) 93, p. 302.
    "Bivouac" (tr. by Michelle Yeh and Lawrence R. Smith). [Caliban] (13) 93, p. 118.
    "Footsteps" (tr. by Michelle Yeh and Lawrence R. Smith). [Caliban] (13) 93, p. 117.
    "News" (tr. by Michelle Yeh and Lawrence R. Smith). [Caliban] (13) 93, p. 118.
    "The Woman in Black" (tr. by Michelle Yeh and Lawrence R. Smith). [Caliban]
        (13) 93, p. 119.
7260. YANG, Seung-Tai
    "Revisiting a Mountain Town" (tr. of Sin Kyong-rim, w. Brent Duffin). [SpoonR]
        (18:1) Wint-Spr 93, p. 40.
YAOCHEN, Mei
    See MEI, Yaochen
7261. YAOZ-KEST, Itamar
    "Night Temptation" (tr. by Daniel Weissbort and Orna Raz). [Stand] (34:3) Sum 93,
        p. 9.
YAPING, Tang
    See TANG, Yaping
7262. YASUTOME, Kay
    "Nam Cuts." [PennR] (5:2) 93, p. 13-16.
7263. YATCHISIN, George
    "Leavings." [HeavenB] (10) Wint-Spr 93, p. 43.
    "Near to Prayer." [HeavenB] (10) Wint-Spr 93, p. 3.
    "Thought Patterns Hazy." [LaurelR] (27:2) Sum 93, p. 60-61.
    "Upon Finding in a Volume of William Blake a Card Pledging Love Forever from
        an Ex-Lover." [PaintedB] (49) 93, p. 9.
7264. YATES, J. Michael
    "Sign." [CanLit] (137) Sum 93, p. 48.
7265. YATES, Steve
    "Afterlife." [Epiphany] (4:2) Ap 93, p. 117.
    "From His Porch in Galloway." [Epiphany] (4:2) Ap 93, p. 119-120.
    "From His Porch in Galloway." [SoDakR] (31:3) Fall 93, p. 98-99.
    "From His Porch in Galloway." [TexasR] (14:3/4) Fall-Wint 93, p. 87-88.
    "A Love We Have at the Start" (Oaklawn Park). [Epiphany] (4:2) Ap 93, p. 116.
    "Remember Home Art" (Old woman looking at sun swathe on her carpet).
        [Epiphany] (4:2) Ap 93, p. 118.
    "Sawhorse with a Wife Sitting Against It." [Epiphany] (4:2) Ap 93, p. 121-122.
7266. YAU, Emily
    "Doves" (November 18, 1947, Shanghai, tr. of Chen Jingrong). [ConnPR] (12:1) 93,
        p. 13.
    "Flowers, Trees, Clouds" (Fall 1981, Beijing, tr. of Chen Jingrong). [ConnPR]
        (12:1) 93, p. 12.
    "The Poetry Dream Dance" (For my readers). [ConnPR] (12:1) 93, p. 14-15.
7267. YAU, John
    "Mr Dead and Mrs Free." [Talisman] (11) Fall 93, p. 14-15.
    "Second Diptych." [PaintedB] (50/51) 93, p. 31.
    "Second Diptych." [Talisman] (11) Fall 93, p. 15-16.
    "Self Portrait with Max Beckmann." [Epoch] (42:1) 93, p. 111-112.
7268. YBARRA, Ricardo Means
    "Smokey." [KenR] (NS 15:2) Spr 93, p. 137-140.
7269. YEATS, William Butler
    "The Man and the Echo." [HarvardR] (4) Spr 93, p. 97-98.
YEE SALLEE, Hyun-jae
    See SALLEE, Hyun-jae Yee
7270. YEH, Jane
    "Palliative." [HarvardA] (128:4, [i.e. 127:4]) Sum 93, p. 30.
    "Untitled: I've gotten nothing for weeks." [HarvardA] (128:4, [i.e. 127:4]) Sum 93,
        p. 8.
    "Vesuvius" (in the priests' quarters. Third Prize). [HarvardA] (127:3) Spr 93, p. 25.

7271. YEH, Michelle
"Bivouac" (tr. of Yang Mu, w. Lawrence R. Smith). [Caliban] (13) 93, p. 118.
"Footsteps" (tr. of Yang Mu, w. Lawrence R. Smith). [Caliban] (13) 93, p. 117.
"News" (tr. of Yang Mu, w. Lawrence R. Smith). [Caliban] (13) 93, p. 118.
"Simple Future Tense" (tr. of Xia Yu). [ChiR] (39:3/4) 93, p. 303-304.
"The Woman in Black" (tr. of Yang Mu, w. Lawrence R. Smith). [Caliban] (13) 93,
   p. 119.
7272. YELLE, Gerald
"No Apology, No Clarity the Waves Speak in Tongues." [Sonora] (26) Fall 93, p.
   39-41.
7273. YENSER, Stephen
"Art History." [ParisR] (35:126) Spr 93, p. 262.
"Blue Guide." [ParisR] (35:129) Wint 93, p. 37-44.
"Carnal Knowledge." [ParisR] (35:126) Spr 93, p. 260-261.
"Sentence." [SouthwR] (78:2) Spr 93, p. 276.
"Voices." [ParisR] (35:126) Spr 93, p. 263.
7274. YEO, Marg
"Working on It." [AmerV] (32) 93, p. 18-19.
YI-DUO, Wen
   See WEN, Yi-Duo
7275. YIP, Wai-lim
"Bird-Singing Stream" (tr. of Wang Wei). [AmerPoR] (22:2) Mr-Ap 93, p. 45.
7276. YODER, Sherida
"Moving Days (A Poem in Two Parts)." [Footwork] (23) 93, p. 108.
"Patched Quilt (For Aunt Grace)." [Footwork] (23) 93, p. 108.
7277. YONAHA, Mikio
"The Love of Red Soil" (Selections, tr. by Katsunori Yamazato and Eric Paul
   Shaffer). [ChiR] (39:3/4) 93, p. 223-226.
YONGHE, Guan
   See GUAN, Yonghe
YONGMING, Zhai
   See ZHAI, Yongming
YOON, Sik Kim
   See KIM, Yoon Sik
7278. YORK, John T.
"A Stout One." [InterPR] (19:2) Fall 93, p. 79.
7279. YOSHIOKA, Minoru
"Elegy" (for Nishiwaki Junzaburo, tr. by Eric Selland). [ChiR] (39:3/4) 93, p. 204 -
   205.
7280. YOUNG, Brian
"Town." [Sonora] (26) Fall 93, p. 24.
7281. YOUNG, Clifford
"A Poem for Joe" (In memory of Joseph Chadwick, June 5, 1954-April 9, 1992).
   [HawaiiR] (17:1, #37) Spr 93, p. iv.
7282. YOUNG, David
"The Autumn Orchard" (tr. of Miroslav Holub, w. Dána Habóva). [PartR] (60:3)
   Sum 93, p. 419.
"Chopping Garlic." [NewEngR] (15:4) Fall 93, p. 168.
"Coming Home" (tr. of Tu Mu). [Field] (48) Spr 93, p. 21.
"Half a Hedgehog" (tr. of Miroslav Holub, w. Dana Hábová). [Field] (49) Fall 93, p.
   18-19.
"Hemophilia/Los Angeles" (tr. of Miroslav Holub, w. Dana Hábová). [Field] (49)
   Fall 93, p. 30-31.
"The Journey" (tr. of Miroslav Holub, w. the author). [PartR] (60:3) Sum 93, p. 418 -
   419.
"Late Summer Evening" (tr. of Tu Mu). [Field] (48) Spr 93, p. 23.
"Morning on the River" (tr. of Tu Mu). [Field] (48) Spr 93, p. 20.
"Pien River Freezing Over" (tr. of Tu Mu). [Field] (48) Spr 93, p. 18.
"Poem for Adlai Stevenson and Yellow Jackets." [NewEngR] (15:4) Fall 93, p. 169.
"Saying Goodbye" (tr. of Tu Mu). [Field] (48) Spr 93, p. 24.
"Seeing" (tr. of Miroslav Holub, w. Dana Hábová). [Field] (49) Fall 93, p. 25-26.
"Spring in the South" (tr. of Tu Mu). [Field] (48) Spr 93, p. 22.
"Unable to Cross at Yunzhi" (tr. of Tu Mu). [Field] (48) Spr 93, p. 19.
7283. YOUNG, Dean
"Another of the Body's Stories." [AnotherCM] (26) Fall 93, p. 185-186.
"Centrifuge" (for Mark Halliday). [NewAW] (11) Sum-Fall 93, p. 83-84.

"Guidebook." [PoetryNW] (34:4) Wint 93-94, p. 46-47.
"I Love How One Season Ends in the Middle of Another." [DenQ] (28:1) Sum 93,
p. 61-62.
"Immortality." [Crazy] (44) Spr 93, p. 75-76.
"Knight in Error." [Crazy] (44) Spr 93, p. 77-78.
"My Own Recognizance." [Crazy] (44) Spr 93, p. 72-74.
"Paradise" (for David Wojahn). [Crazy] (44) Spr 93, p. 79-81.
"Ready-Made Bouquet." [Ploughs] (19:4) Wint 93-94, p. 78-80.
"Upon Hearing of My Friend's Marriage Breaking Up." [Thrpny] (54) Sum 93, p. 5.
"What I Thought I Loved." [AnotherCM] (26) Fall 93, p. 183-184.
"White Crane." [PoetryNW] (34:4) Wint 93-94, p. 45.
7284. YOUNG, Gary
"Because a world may be called into being." [Sonora] (24/25) Spr 93, p. 66.
"Four Days." [BlackWR] (20:1) Fall-Wint 93, p. 84.
"My son wakes screaming." [Journal] (17:1) Spr-Sum 93, p. 60.
7285. YOUNG, George
"The Miracle." [Northeast] (5:9) Wint 93-94, p. 20-21.
7286. YOUNG, Gretel
"Two Sisters Were Walking by the River." [Asylum] (8) 93, p. 28.
7287. YOUNG, James
"Two Sided Tape for One Track Minds." [WashR] (18:5) F-Mr 93, p. 9.
7288. YOUNG, Jill
"Hap." [Pearl] (17) Spr 93, p. 94.
7289. YOUNG, Jim
"Cataclysms." [Elf] (3:2) Sum 93, p. 41.
7290. YOUNG, Kevin
"Casting." [Callaloo] (16:3) Sum 93, p. 542-543.
"Central Standard Time." [KenR] (NS 15:1) Wint 93, p. 99.
"Clyde Peeling's Reptiland in Allenwood, Pennsylvania." [Agni] (37) 93, p. 9-11.
"Driving Independence Day." [KenR] (NS 15:1) Wint 93, p. 100.
"The Escape Artist." [Callaloo] (16:3) Sum 93, p. 546-547.
"Everywhere Is Out of Town" (for Maceo Parker & the JB Horns). [Agni] (37) 93,
p. 12.
"Field Trip." [Callaloo] (16:3) Sum 93, p. 544-545.
"The Living." [Poetry] (162:6) S 93, p. 343-344.
"No Offense." [KenR] (NS 15:1) Wint 93, p. 101.
"The Preserving." [Ploughs] (19:1) Spr 93, p. 145-146.
"The Slaughter." [Ploughs] (19:1) Spr 93, p. 143-144.
7291. YOUNG, Michael T.
"The Curious Little Girl" (A painting by Camille Corot. Corrected reprint from
#51/52). [HiramPoR] (53/54) Fall 92-Sum 93, p. 93.
7292. YOUNG, Patricia
"Miss Harkins." [CanLit] (136) Spr 93, p. 44.
"Party Talk." [PoetryC] (14:1) 93, p. 12.
"Tree Fort." [PoetryC] (14:1) 93, p. 12.
"When the Body Speaks to the Heart It Says." [CanLit] (136) Spr 93, p. 114.
7293. YOUNG, Roselyn
"Barbara at Forty-five." [EngJ] (82:8) D 93, p. 82.
7294. YOUNG, Tony
"Empty Hallways" (Special thanks to Faye Kicknosway). [HawaiiR] (17:1, #37) Spr
93, p. 138.
7295. YOUNG BEAR, Ray (Ray A.)
"Father Scarmark — World War I Hero — and Democracy." [Ploughs] (19:1) Spr
93, p. 86-89.
"Summer Tripe Dream and Concrete Leaves." [Ploughs] (19:1) Spr 93, p. 90-91.
7296. YSKAMP, Amanda
"Kiss Chase." [Thrpny] (54) Sum 93, p. 33.
"Soundings: Doppler's Doppleganger." [Outbr] (24) 93, p. 108-109.
7297. YU, Ung-Bu (d. 1456)
"Durante el viento helado de anoche nevó y nevó" (Spanish tr. by William Martínez
Jr.). [Luz] (4) My 93, p. 56.
YU, Xia
See XIA, Yu
7298. YUAN, Chen
"Dreaming of My Wife" (tr. by Sam Hamill). [Pequod] (36) 93, p. 13.
"Elegy: O loveliest daughter of Hsieh" (tr. by Sam Hamill). [Pequod] (36) 93, p. 9.

515

YUAN

"Empty House" (tr. by Sam Hamill). [Pequod] (36) 93, p. 14.
"Three Dreams in Chiang-ling" (tr. by Sam Hamill). [Pequod] (36) 93, p. 10-12.
7299. YUAN, Ch'iung-ch'iung
"The Understanding" (tr. by Steve Bradbury). [MidAR] (14:1) 93, p. 15.
7300. YUE, An
"Being a Hero Once." [Interim] (12:2) Fall-Wint 93, p. 31.
"A Visit to Qin Dynasty Terracottas." [Interim] (12:2) Fall-Wint 93, p. 30.
YUE, Zhi-Qiang
See YUE, An
YUN, Wang
See WANG, Yun
7301. YUNGKANS, Jonathan
"Playing with Dolls." [Pearl] (17) Spr 93, p. 95.
7302. YUP, Paula
"Grandfather." [MidAR] (14:1) 93, p. 45.
"This Is the Body" (for Eric Turkington). [MidAR] (14:1) 93, p. 43-44.
7303. YURKIEVICH, Saúl
"Cipher" (tr. by Cola Franzen). [GrahamHR] (17) Fall 93, p. 30.
"Opening" (tr. by Cola Franzen). [GrahamHR] (17) Fall 93, p. 29.
"Sketch" (tr. by Cola Franzen). [GrahamHR] (17) Fall 93, p. 31-32.
7304. YUSON, Alfred A.
"The Homebody Goes on Tour." [Bomb] (45) Fall 93, p. 81.
"Kibitzer." [Bomb] (45) Fall 93, p. 81.
7305. YVONNE
"Wife of the Bath." [Contact] (11:65/66/67) Spr 93, p. 59.
7306. ZABLE, Jeffrey
"Chickenology." [NewYorkQ] (52) 93, p. 76.
7307. ZABOROWSKI, Karen Copeland
"Watching Them Ride the Rides." [US1] (28/29) 93, p. 5.
7308. ZABRANSKY, Richard
"The Missed Conception That Might Have Been Christ." [SlipS] (13) 93, p. 48-49.
"Nights at Londeon With Tess." [PoetryE] (36) Fall 93, p. 8.
"Zeroes." [CapeR] (28:2) Fall 93, p. 32-33.
7309. ZABUZHKO, Oksana
"Clytemnestra" (tr. by Lisa Sapinkopf, w. the author). [Agni] (38) 93, p. 108-109.
"An Ironic Nocturne" (tr. by Michael M. Naydan). [Agni] (37) 93, p. 276.
"Letter from a Summer Home" (tr. by Michael M. Naydan). [Agni] (37) 93, p. 277 -
278.
"People who read" (tr. by Lisa Sapinkopf and the author). [HarvardR] (4) Spr 93, p.
145.
7310. ZACHARY
"Of Weeds." [QW] (37) Sum-Fall 93, p. 106-107.
7311. ZAGAJEWSKI, Adam
"Dashed Off" (tr. by the author and C. K. Williams). [OhioR] (50) 93, p. 9-10.
7312. ZAGORICNIK, Franci
"The Flood" (tr. by Tone Percic and Bridget Peet). [NoDaQ] (61:1) Wint 93, p. 219 -
220.
"Mordana" (tr. by Tone Percic and Bridget Peet). [NoDaQ] (61:1) Wint 93, p. 214.
"Starting Up" (tr. by Tone Percic and Bridget Peet). [NoDaQ] (61:1) Wint 93, p.
212-213.
"Striptease" (tr. by Tone Percic and Bridget Peet). [NoDaQ] (61:1) Wint 93, p. 217 -
218.
"Under Four" (tr. by Tone Percic and Bridget Peet). [NoDaQ] (61:1) Wint 93, p.
216-217.
"Under Three" (tr. by Tone Percic and Bridget Peet). [NoDaQ] (61:1) Wint 93, p.
215.
7313. ZAGORICNIK-SIMONOVIC, Ifigenija
"Long-term Misunderstanding" (tr. by Anthony Rudolf and the author). [NoDaQ]
(61:1) Wint 93, p. 222.
"Love Poem" (tr. by Anthony Rudolf and the author). [NoDaQ] (61:1) Wint 93, p.
223.
"Under the Same Roof" (tr. by Anthony Rudolf and the author). [NoDaQ] (61:1)
Wint 93, p. 221.
7314. ZALEMA, Luis
"Walking with Blackie" (tr. by Angela McEwan). [ApalQ] (38) 92, p. 38-39.

7315. ZALLER, Robert
"Clytemnestras" (tr. of Lili Bita). [AmerPoR] (22:3) My-Je 93, p. 43.
"The Death of Polycrates." [AmerPoR] (22:3) My-Je 93, p. 45.
"The Debut" (tr. of Lili Bita). [AmerPoR] (22:3) My-Je 93, p. 43.
"Herbert's Pebble." [AmerPoR] (22:3) My-Je 93, p. 44.
"Poem on a Line by Parra." [AmerPoR] (22:3) My-Je 93, p. 44.
"Today" (tr. of Lili Bita). [AmerPoR] (22:3) My-Je 93, p. 43.
"Treml." [AmerPoR] (22:3) My-Je 93, p. 44.
7316. ZAMORA, Bernice
"Endurance." [ColR] (20:2) Fall 93, p. 111.
"Recounting the Day" (2 poems: "June 17, 1984," "June 1, 1984"). [ColR] (20:2)
Fall 93, p. 112-113.
"Stearn Wharf." [ColR] (20:2) Fall 93, p. 110.
7317. ZANDER, William
"Voices." [JINJPo] (15:2) Aut 93, p. 16-17.
"Winter Trees." [WritersF] (19) 93, p. 67.
7318. ZANDVAKILI, Katayoon
"Hansel and Gretel." [HawaiiR] (16:3, #36) Wint 93, p. 104.
7319. ZANGHI, Sara
"The Girl of Seven Spirits" (tr. by Kathleen Fraser and Alberto Rossatti).
[13thMoon] (11:1/2) 93, p. 216.
"Poem: You should remember" (tr. by Kathleen Fraser and Alberto Rossatti).
[13thMoon] (11:1/2) 93, p. 217.
7320. ZAREMBA, Donald
"Momentum." [CoalC] (7) Apr 93, p. 22.
"On the Interstate." [PoetL] (88:3) Fall 93, p. 38.
7321. ZARIN, Cynthia
"Song." [NewRep] (208:24) 14 Je 93, p. 48.
"The Venetian Optician." [ParisR] (35:126) Spr 93, p. 264-267.
7322. ZARRIN, Ali
"Songs of Fire" (tr. of Manuchehr Atashi). [Vis] (43) 93, p. 43.
7323. ZARUCCHI, Roy
"Meeting in Hawaii." [OnTheBus] (5:2, #12) Sum-Fall 93, p. 225.
7324. ZARZYSKI, Paul
"The Day the Black Man Came like an Angel." [PraS] (67:3) Fall 93, p. 163-164.
"The Day the War Began." [PraS] (67:3) Fall 93, p. 162-163.
"Just War." [PraS] (67:3) Fall 93, p. 161-162.
"Linguistics." [PraS] (67:3) Fall 93, p. 165-166.
"Playing Favorites." [PraS] (67:3) Fall 93, p. 160-161.
"Words Growing Wild in the Woods." [CutB] (40) Spr 93, p. 117-118.
"Zarzyski Curses the Burning of His Bro, Zozobra, Old Man Gloom." [CutB] (40)
Spr 93, p. 119-120.
7325. ZAUHAR, David
"Your Parents Get the News You Are Dead." [ChironR] (12:3, #36) Aut 93, p. 11.
7326. ZAWINSKI, Andrena
"Reading Early Morning (or I Could Commit Justifiable Homicide)." [PaintedHR]
(8) Wint 93, p. 12.
7327. ZDANYS, Jonas
"Gates" (tr. of Donaldas Kajokas). [CimR] (104) Jl 93, p. 21.
"The Well" (tr. of Donaldas Kajokas). [CimR] (104) Jl 93, p. 21.
7328. ZEALAND, Karen
"As a child, I Couldn't Float." [SouthernPR] (33:2) Fall 93, p. 15-16.
"Hope Is the Thing with Feathers." [Outbr] (24) 93, p. 80.
"To a Former Lover." [Outbr] (24) 93, p. 79.
7329. ZEIDNER, Lisa
"The Mesopotamian Tool Room." [PaintedB] (50/51) 93, p. 20-21.
7330. ZEIGER, Gene
"Above the Harbor." [CarolQ] (45:2) Wint 93, p. 24.
"The Dog's Life." [ProseP] (2) 93, p. 104.
"Heaven: A Definition." [ProseP] (1) 92, p. 87.
"The Hole." [ProseP] (2) 93, p. 105.
7331. ZEIGER, Lila
"Jacob." [FreeL] (11) Wint 93, p. 21-22.
7332. ZELEZNIK, Mari E.
"Last Row, Last Seat." [HawaiiR] (16:3, #36) Wint 93, p. 65-66.

7333. ZELLER, Muriel
"The Bathtub Planter." [BellArk] (9:1) Ja-F 93, p. 13.
7334. ZELVIN, Elizabeth
"The Baby in Group." [Art&Und] (2:2) My-Je 93, p. 9.
7335. ZEN, Zuo
"The Tree at the Edge of the Precipice" (in Chinese and English, tr. by Li Xi-jian
and Gordon Osing). [PikeF] (11) Fall 93, p. 15.
7336. ZEPPA, Mary
"Why Men Won't Ask for Directions" (for Bob Zeppa, 1942-1986). [NewYorkQ]
(52) 93, p. 75.
7337. ZERDEN, Deborah
"Coney Island Beach." [Chelsea] (54) 93, p. 64-65.
7338. ZHAI, Yongming (Yong Ming)
"Desire" (tr. by Andrea Lingenfelter). [ChiR] (39:3/4) 93, p. 296.
"The Eighth Month" (tr. by Dian Li). [GreenMR] (NS 6:2) Sum-Fall 93, p. 152.
7339. ZHANG, Xiao Bo
"A Dozen Things" (tr. by Dian Li). [GreenMR] (NS 6:2) Sum-Fall 93, p. 153.
7340. ZHANG, Zhen
"New Discovery" (tr. by Tony Barnstone and Newton Liu). [ChiR] (39:3/4) 93, p.
294.
ZHEN, Zhang
  See ZHANG, Zhen
7341. ZHENG, Jianging
"The Rainy Night" (tr. of Xi Murong, w. Angela Ball). [MidAR] (14:1) 93, p. 46.
ZHONG, Jin
  See JIN, Zhong
ZHONGXING, Gu
  See GU, Zhongxing
ZI, Hai
  See HAI, Zi
7342. ZIDE, Arlene
"Chilka Lake" (tr. of Shakunt Mathur, w. Aruna Sitesh). [Prima] (16/17) 93, p. 90 -
91.
"The Fifth Man" (tr. of Gagan Gill, w. Mrinal Pande). [Prima] (16/17) 93, p. 87.
"Man" (tr. of Archana Varma, w. Aruna Sitesh). [MalR] (102) Spr 93, p. 50-51.
"A Meeting" (tr. of Amrita Pritam, w. the author). [Vis] (43) 93, p. 46.
"Welcoming All Comers" (tr. of Kirti Chaudhury). [Vis] (43) 93, p. 26.
"The Window" (tr. of Savitri Rajeevan, w. Ayyappa Paniker). [Prima] (16/17) 93, p.
88-89.
"The Windows" (tr. of Vijaya Dabbe). [Vis] (43) 93, p. 31.
7343. ZIEROTH, Dale
"Building Consensus." [MalR] (105) Wint 93, p. 42-43.
"Time Over Earth." [CanLit] (138/139) Fall-Wint 93, p. 21-22.
"When We First Felt Our Minds." [MalR] (105) Wint 93, p. 44-45.
7344. ZIKA, B. Lynne
"My First Best Friend." [OnTheBus] (6:1, #13) Wint 93-Spr 94, p. 215.
7345. ZIMLER, Richard
"Hermitage" (tr. of Al Berto). [JamesWR] (11:1) Fall 93, p. 18.
"A Return to Simple Stories" (tr. of Al Berto). [JamesWR] (11:1) Fall 93, p. 20.
7346. ZIMMER, Paul
"Big Blue Train." [Iowa] (23:2) Spr-Sum 93, p. 132-133.
"The Longing Season." [NewEngR] (15:4) Fall 93, p. 174.
"The Map." [NewEngR] (15:4) Fall 93, p. 176.
"A Rant Against Losses" (for Tom Lloyd). [NewEngR] (15:4) Fall 93, p. 175.
7347. ZIMMERMAN, Edwin
"Dido Was Smitten." [PartR] (60:2) Spr 93, p. 243.
7348. ZIMMERMAN, Irene
"And It Was Night" (John 13:20). [ChrC] (110:11) 7 Apr 93, p. 365.
7349. ZIMMERMAN, Lisa Horton
"Sewing Batman's Cape After the Funeral of a Friend's Son." [Sun] (212) Ag 93, p.
27.
7350. ZIMROTH, Evan
"On Hearing That Childbirth Is Like Orgasm" (in ad for the author's book *Dead,
Dinner, or Naked*). [TriQ] (87) Spr-Sum 93, p. 5.
7351. ZINFON, Gerald J.
"Castle Moats of New Hampshire." [BellArk] (9:2) Mr-Ap 93, p. 12.

518

ZINFON

"Fruit and Produce — by U.P." [BellArk] (9:1) Ja-F 93, p. 11.
"Harvest Snow." [BellArk] (9:6) N-D 93, p. 14.
"Sand Dance." [BellArk] (9:3) My-Je 93, p. 19.
"Summer Ice." [BellArk] (9:4) Jl-Ag 93, p. 14.
7352. ZINNES, Harriet
"Bowl of Fruit." [AmerPoR] (22:4) Jl-Ag 93, p. 35.
"Correspondences." [LullwaterR] (4:2) Spr-Sum 93, p. 7.
"Fugitive." [LullwaterR] (4:2) Spr-Sum 93, p. 77.
"Two Birds." [AmerPoR] (22:4) Jl-Ag 93, p. 35.
7353. ZISQUIT, Linda
"The Ant." [BostonR] (18:1) Ja-F 93, p. 17.
"Apprehension of Beauty." [BostonR] (18:1) Ja-F 93, p. 17.
"Ethics of the Fathers." [BostonR] (18:1) Ja-F 93, p. 17.
"Eve." [BostonR] (18:1) Ja-F 93, p. 17.
"Istehar Returning." [BostonR] (18:1) Ja-F 93, p. 17.
"A Modern Midrash." [BostonR] (18:1) Ja-F 93, p. 17.
"A Simple Man." [BostonR] (18:1) Ja-F 93, p. 17.
"Summer at War." [BostonR] (18:1) Ja-F 93, p. 17.
"Vertical." [HarvardR] (5) Fall 93, p. 95.
7354. ZIVANCEVIC, Nina
"The Elegance of a Withered Flower." [Talisman] (11) Fall 93, p. 262.
"If You Just Imagine" (tr. by the author). [NoDaQ] (61:1) Wint 93, p. 224.
"Love" (tr. by the author). [NoDaQ] (61:1) Wint 93, p. 226.
"On Death." [Talisman] (11) Fall 93, p. 262.
"Transparency" (tr. by the author). [NoDaQ] (61:1) Wint 93, p. 225.
7355. ZIZIK, Joel
"Army Basic Training." [JamesWR] (10:2) Wint 93, p. 20.
"A Private Urge to Travel." [JamesWR] (10:2) Wint 93, p. 20.
7356. ZMIRAK, John
"Lee in New Orleans" (For Donald Davidson). [SoCarR] (26:1) Fall 93, p. 110-111.
7357. ZOLF, Rachel
"Chrysalis." [PraF] (14:1) Spr 93, p. 125.
"How curious" (with thanks to Lady Wishfort, "as I'm a person"). [PraF] (14:1) Spr 93, p. 124.
"I remember you" (with thanks to Joy Kogawa and ee commings). [PraF] (14:1) Spr 93, p. 126.
"Warm fuzzy phrases" (written under *The Passion*-ate influence of Jeannette Winterson). [PraF] (14:1) Spr 93, p. 127.
7358. ZONAILO, Carolyn
"The Attic Room." [PraS] (67:4) Wint 93, p. 123-125.
"Distance." [PoetryC] (13:2) 93, p. 12.
"A Summer Swim." [PoetryC] (13:2) 93, p. 12.
"Walls." [PoetryC] (13:2) 93, p. 13.
7359. ZORDANI, Bob
"Elegy: No God can make my words ring free or clang." [Poem] (69) My 93, p. 58.
"Epileptic's Song." [WillowR] (20) Spr 93, p. 35.
"Letter to an Old Flame." [Shen] (43:1) Spr 93, p. 28.
"A Picnic in June." [Shen] (43:1) Spr 93, p. 29.
"Vagina Dentata." [ChangingM] (25) Wint-Spr 93, p. 66.
"Washerwoman's Song." [Poem] (69) My 93, p. 55.
"Your Life Without Me." [Poem] (69) My 93, p. 56-57.
7360. ZUBER, Isabel
"Knell." [GreensboroR] (54) Sum 93, p. 131.
"Surcease." [Prima] (16/17) 93, p. 106.
7361. ZUBICK, Kelleen
"Mercy." [MassR] (34:3) Aut 93, p. 344-345.
7362. ZUCKERMAN, Lonnie
"The Golden Ring." [Americas] (21:2) Sum 93, p. 63.
7363. ZUKAUSKAS, Albinas
"Sweet Apples" (tr. by Lionginas Pazusis, w. Bradley R. Strahan). [Vis] (43) 93, p. 37-38.
7364. ZUKOFSKY, Louis
"All of December Toward New Year's." [QRL] (12:32/33) 93, p. 558-559.
"Reading and Talking." [QRL] (12:32/33) 93, p. 559-561.
7365. ZULAUF, Sander
"Always Less." [Blueline] (14) 93, p. 74.

"In Memoriam: Howard Nemerov." [SewanR] (101:2) Ap-Je, Spr 93, p. 155.
ZUO, Zen
    See ZEN, Zuo
7366. ZVERINA, Robert
    "The Night Before Christmas." [SoCoast] (15) Je 93, p. 54.
7367. ZWEIG, Martha
    "Not Mowing." [CarolQ] (45:2) Wint 93, p. 27.
    "On Stannard Mountain." [Poetry] (163:2) N 93, p. 71.
    "Over Again." [Epoch] (42:3) 93, p. 320.
    "The Particulars." [Epoch] (42:3) 93, p. 319.
    "Powers" (A Chapbook). [Manoa] (5:1) Sum 93, p. 91-97.
7368. ZWICKY, Fay
    "Akibat." [Nimrod] (36:2) Spr-Sum 93, p. 73.
    "Perdjodohan." [Nimrod] (36:2) Spr-Sum 93, p. 74.
7369. ZWICKY, Jan
    "Adagio, K. 219." [MalR] (105) Wint 93, p. 8.
    "Bartók's Roumanian Dances." [MalR] (105) Wint 93, p. 5.
    "Brahms' Clarinet Quintet in B Minor, Op. 115." [MalR] (105) Wint 93, p. 9.
    "Musicians." [MalR] (105) Wint 93, p. 10.
    "Open Strings." [MalR] (105) Wint 93, p. 6-7.
7370. ZYCH, Jan
    "Keys" (tr. by Aleksandra Szostalo and David Sparenberg). [SnailPR] (3:1) Fall -
        Wint 93, p. 1.
7371. ZYCHLINSKA, Rajzel
    "The Child and the Old Man" (tr. by Aaron Kramer). [Vis] (41) 93, p. 21.
7372. ZYDEK, Fredrick (Frederick)
    "Advice for Tending the Ego." [HiramPoR] (53/54) Fall 92-Sum 93, p. 94.
    "Indian Statue: Pioneer Park." [Confr] (51) Sum 93, p. 253.
    "Looking for God at the Supermarket" (for Tom). [ChrC] (110:22) 28 Jl-4 Ag 93, p.
        744.
    "Twenty Fourth Meditation: Man to Man." [CharR] (19:2) Fall 93, p. 110-113.
    "Vision Through a White Stone." [ChrC] (110:21) 14-21 Jl 93, p. 714.
    "Year End Monologue with Inner Space" (for John Ciardi). [Amelia] (7:2, #21) 93,
        p. 57.

Title Index

Titles are arranged alphanumerically, with numerals filed in numerical order before letters. Each title is followed by one or more author entry numbers, which refer to the numbered entries in the first part of the volume. Entry numbers are preceded by a space colon space (:). Any numeral which preceeds the space colon space (:) is part of the title, not an entry number. Poems with "Untitled" in the title position are entered under "Untitled" followed by the first line of the poem and also directly under the first line. Numbered titles are entered under the number and also under the part following the number.

(......................?) : 4223, 5338.
1:00 A.M. : 5503.
1/14/90 : 2796.
I. Frederick: The Decision : 6876.
1. quick i the death of thing : 1353.
(I) She Writes with Fire : 3654, 4060, 5901.
I. To All the Old Apollos : 2045.
1st Bath : 2580.
2 A.M. : 360, 3836.
2 Corinthians : 1832.
2. Leda and the Swans : 1724.
II. Marta: The First Year in Minnesota : 6876.
II. To Artemis, Protector of the Newly Born : 2045.
3:00 P.M. : 1939.
3-3-92 : 5347.
3 a.m. : 6691.
3 Doctors Discussing Raynard's Syndrome in the Ladies Lounge : 5464.
III. Henrietta: Farming : 6876.
III. I roll off her — satisfied, fired, heart : 4186.
#3. Interracial Series : 4052.
3 Out of 4 (or More): a Lament for 3 Out of 4 (or More) Voices : 2413.
3. Sisyphus in the Wartime Housing Projects : 1724.
3rd World This : 2792.
IV.11 : 2944, 5761.
4:19 a.m. : 3132.
IV. Frederick: The Drought : 6876.
4 in a Cave : 2342, 3146.
4-Letter Word : 2348.
4. where's Jack Was : 1353.
5° : 1112.
V.64 : 4149, 5761.
V. Footsoldier's Slow Drag and Breakdown : 4788.
V. Marta: Inventing Herself : 6876.
5 O'Clock : 5007.
5 Poems : 4986.

VI, xii. I've charged the lout next door : 4149, 4199.
6/29/92 : 4708.
VI.40 : 4149, 5761.
VI, lxvii. Your Celia keeps company with eunuchs : 4149, 4199.
6 August 1945 : 3082.
6 Year Old : 4581.
7/23/91 : 4268.
7:30 Sharp : 5049.
7 de Mayo : 2796.
8:45 P.M. : 4111.
VIII, lxxix. Those unlovely friends you drag : 4149, 4199.
9 1 2 : 3749.
IX. Get bombed, piss'd in face : 3218.
10-22-89 : 4439.
The 10 p.m. Local from DC to NYC : 5898.
10° West of Greenwich : 4074.
11-26-89 : 4439.
12:44 A.M. : 2780, 2827, 3085.
XII. 'She' only wanted to get up in female attire : 3218.
#13. Magus : 423, 3962.
XIII. See by my third eye : 3218.
#13. Tibi cum non sit diai panis : 3962.
XIV. A Memory : 2853.
XIV. Those who cultivate their manhood : 3218.
XVII. Could it be that the long protruding tongue : 1841, 5581.
XVII. The Sun's rays come in lance over lance : 3218.
18 Past 6 : 3271.
19th Hole Condom Poem : 3202.
21 East 10th, 2BR, WBF, EIK : 5937.
21st of February : 897, 1033.
23 : 4345.
XXIII. You kno, honey, it's great when ya got ya brandnew money : 3218.
#27. Verum, Fama, tibi vultum pictura notavit : 3962.

#27. Well, Fame, the Painting Is : 423, 3962.
XXVIII. When big daddy Chronos : 3218.
XXX. By the number thirty-eight bus down
    Dostojevsky Lane : 100, 2879, 6465.
XXX: How lonely the spirit of Erich Fromm
    : 302.
30 Windsor : 434.
31 August 1986, 12:28 A.M. (Earthquake
    Time) : 1087, 1731, 6235.
33 3/4 : 1006.
33-Year-Old Childless Poet Talks to Cherry
    Tree : 3958.
#34. I can't drink : 3515, 5601.
34 Kreuzer : 4858.
XXXV. Oh no, you have to keep the lights
    burning : 3218.
XXXVI. Say God came back : 3218.
38 : 3956.
45 Assertions : 6211.
45 Horas : 6657.
50:50 : 3222.
51. I laugh not knowing: The wind above :
    2815.
54 in Butiaba : 4525.
57. It isn't war you fear so much as peace :
    4615.
59. Visitations. Shields in the sky : 2815.
60. The day is where we never arrive : 2815.
LX. This morning clouds bunch : 3466.
61 North : 3022.
The '66 Mets : 6943.
#77 Revisited : 6941.
#90. Hilderic's Palace : 423, 3962.
#90. Hildirici regis fulget mirabile factum :
    3962.
XCIII. At the news of your betrothal : 3466.
A 100-Poem Sequence : 5814, 6024.
105 Degrees : 526.
125th Street : 7217.
390. Pulling the mirror closer : 5113.
401. Before you even saw a lake : 5113.
409. This rain slowly in the dark : 5113.
458. You still don't trust seabirds : 5113.
460. What you hear is one winter : 5113.
497 Mss., or, Processing the Entries : 5999.
The 522nd Liberates Dachau : 1704.
612 A : 4442.
636 11th : 1140.
950 Hoe Avenue (the Bronx) : 2939.
1000 Schuyler : 3592.
1790s Diary : 7038.
1891 : 643, 4433.
1920 : 782, 4079, 4417.
1933 : 782, 4079, 4417.
1938: The Brown Bomber Defeats Max
    Schmeling and Retains His
    Heavyweight Championship of the
    World : 5164.
1939-1945 Poèmes : 2180, 6459, 6459.
1941 : 5012.
1944 : 3485.
1953 : 947.
1954 : 4892.
1966: The Stone Mason's Funeral : 445.
1968 : 383.
1973 : 2869.

1976 : 6607.
1,980th Christmas : 1035, 4652.
1982 : 6842.
1983 : 3790.
1991-1992 : 5645.
400,000 : 2331.
1,000,000,000,000,000,000,000 : 5390.
A Alba Díaz : 4665.
A Bride Abattue : 880.
A Cappella : 7232.
A-driftin' down the Allagash : 1192.
A Gustavo : 3073.
A la Cama, Niños : 5618.
A Lucio : 5789.
A Quien Escribo Yo : 330.
A Terre : 3333.
A* Wonderland Party : 7194.
Aaron : 4950.
Ab-Teenagers : 5416.
Abandoned Artillery: Fort Worden : 3912.
An Abandoned Car : 4696.
Abandoned Farmhouse : 3510.
An Abandoned Stone Schoolhouse in the
    Nebraska Sandhills : 3510.
The Abandoned Town : 5730.
Abandoning his house : 440.
The Abandonment of the Body : 836.
Abbey Hill : 6630.
Abbey's Land : 5973.
Abbreviated History of Human
    Consciousness, 1 : 3298.
Abe Lincoln, the First Jewish President :
    2566.
Abel and Abel : 2293, 5515.
Abendmusik : 1827.
Abiding : 790.
Abigail : 3912.
Abingdon : 4942, 6778.
Abingdon Square : 4594.
Abiquiu : 4023.
Able Hall's Belgiums : 3216.
Aboard a junk along the Wu : 5126.
Abode : 471, 3325, 4695.
About Face : 2129.
About Inge : 2938.
About My Country : 6782.
About the Body, Beauty : 6012.
About the Capitals : 2756.
About the Carrot : 4133.
About-the-City Poems : 4893.
About the Clocks : 188, 2407.
About to Move : 214.
About Your Iguana : 6763.
Above All This Grinning Confusion : 6979.
Above Jazz : 3783.
Above the Churchyard, Crockateemore :
    3343.
Above the Harbor : 7330.
Above the morning thrushes are to be heard
    singing : 3547, 5638.
Above the Mountains : 670.
Above the Snow Line in Big Sky Country :
    6305.
Above the White Sheet : 425.
Abraham : 711.
Abrete Sésamo : 5618.

Abridged Dictionary of Synonyms and
    Phrases for Chronic Alcohol Abuse :
    7224.
Absence : 643, 2521, 3465, 4432, 4433,
    5768.
The Absent : 1045.
The Absent Father : 460.
An Absent Friend : 2518.
The Absinthe-Drinker : 7074.
Absolution : 2202, 7102.
Abstract Poem : 3782.
Abuelita Poem : 5595.
Abundance of Shores : 1660.
Abused Child : 5425.
An Abusers' Thesaurus, 1st Edition : 4974.
AC Transit : 7210.
Academy : 6740.
The Academy : 692.
An Acceptable Sacrifice : 6808.
Accepting Destruction : 4113.
Accident : 7214.
The Accident : 702, 742, 4625.
Accident Not Yet Understood : 5684, 5776.
Accident Report : 4528.
Accidentals : 5090.
An Accompaniment to the Rain : 757.
Accord : 6746.
Accordance : 5015.
According to Legend : 546.
According to the Horticulturist, It Is Unlikely
    Our Fuchsia Will Survive the Winter :
    1497.
Accrue a manifest St. Jude thing : 4682.
The Ace : 173, 5638.
The Ache : 3039.
Achill : 1631.
Achilles and Cygus : 1875.
Achilles and Penthesileia : 1875.
Achilles, Penthesilea : 756, 2788.
The Acid Rumor : 996.
Acis and Galatea : 2397.
Acknowledgement III : 6348.
Acmeist : 1975.
Acolytes of the Chaos-God: Embarcadero
    Center : 2055.
An Acquaintance in the Heavens : 1579.
Acquisitions : 2331.
An Acre of Bird's-Foot Trefoil and Morning
    Glory in a Beach Swale : 4357.
Acrobats : 3666.
Acrobats on the Radio: Letter to Newcomb :
    5290.
Across the Big Screen : 3370.
An Acrostic for Don Benito : 3754.
Act of love learned over and over : 4953.
Actively Speciating Even Now : 1892.
Acts of Compensation : 4428.
Acts of Contrition : 1620.
Acts of Faith : 3385.
Actual and Ideal Forms : 5285.
The Actual Places : 3334.
Actual Size : 6932.
Ad Libitum : 778.
Adagio, K. 219 : 7369.
Adam : 2728.
Adam Names the Animals : 7095.

Adam's Needle, Eve's Thread : 2095.
Addicted : 1640.
Adding Up a Dead Uncle : 3905.
Adding Water to Your Specimen May Cause
    You to Test Positive : 282.
Addition to Hitchcock : 1482.
Additions : 4127.
An Address to Marina Tsvetayeva Curling
    Inward : 3974.
Adeline Stephen : 652.
Adieu : 399.
Adieu, Chimères, Idéals, Erreurs : 62, 5843,
    6481.
Adieu, George Bush : 6690.
Adieu, Whizzer : 6690.
Admiring the Enemy : 3720.
Admonition : 7137.
Adolescence : 3247.
Adolescent Magic in my 46th Year : 4427.
The Adopted : 1224.
Adorning her with jewels : 7077.
Adult Education : 1025.
Adult Entertainment : 3673.
Adult Swimming at Johnson Pool : 4616.
Adultery : 1232, 1378.
Advance of the Bone Flutist : 2266.
Advanced Automotive Science : 4317.
Advanced St. Ives Riddle : 6795.
The Advantage of Spiders : 4453.
Advent : 904, 1814.
Advent: Snow Incantation : 417.
The Adventure : 2324.
Advertisement for Cut-her Lot: Repossessed
    Body Parts : 6533.
Advice Before Marrying : 7192.
Advice for Tending the Ego : 7372.
Advice from a Hard Guy : 1590.
Advice to a Friend : 2521.
Advice to My Poetry Students on the Last
    Day of Class : 6321.
Advice to My Son : 4038.
Aerodynamics : 2519.
Aerolingual Poet of Prey : 5419.
The Aesthetics of the Pennsauken Mart :
    4768.
The Affair : 4113.
Affection : 2777.
Afloat : 6199.
African Sleeping Sickness : 1196.
African Ways : 3448.
After : 1425, 3230, 3928, 5968, 6560.
After a Late Latin Dinner at the Centro
    Español : 1226.
After a Light Snowfall : 6098.
After a Long Absence : 5830.
After a Mastectomy : 6752.
After a Month : 4493.
After a Snowfall on the Second Day of
    Spring in 1992 : 4394.
After Actium: Loss Filling the Emptiness :
    2441.
After After : 1392.
After all, it was the rain, a day : 5113.
After Amy : 5937.
After Another War : 824.
After August : 5931.

After Burning Off the Garden for Spring :
    3510.
After Cocteau: Beauty's Father in the Castle
    of the Beast : 4465.
After Coleridge : 3307.
After Coltrane's 'I'll Get By' : 2576.
After Dachau : 2039.
After Dark : 2132.
After Death : 5280, 5372.
After Dinner : 264, 1900.
After Edvard Munch : 1821.
After Heated Words, the Snow : 2669.
After Horace : 3901.
After-image : 3666.
After Image : 6876.
After Kicking Off Her Shoes : 6284.
After Kristallnacht : 2729.
After Life's Fever : 6299.
After Liszt at the Villa D'Este : 3901.
After Living Too Long in an Arid Country :
    3825.
After Long Thought, I Submit My
    Resignation to the University : 1480.
After Lovemaking : 4457.
After Many Years: Sonnet : 3076.
After Marriage : 850.
After Mourning : 225.
After My Mother Was Done With Me : 4892.
After Not Winning the Yale Poetry Prize :
    6970.
After November Rains : 7027.
After Observing American Bureaucracy
    10.91 : 511.
After One Year in Exeter, New Hampshire :
    168.
After Ovid : 4250.
After Oz : 836.
After Reading Again a Poet I'd Disparaged :
    3945.
After Reading Charles Dickens' Biography
    by Peter Ackroyd in Southern Florida :
    1226.
After School : 466.
After Storms : 4141.
After Surgery : 6126.
After That : 1380.
After the Ashbery Reading : 3853.
After the Ballet : 4270.
After the Bee : 2068.
After the Big Earth- : 344.
After the Cicadas : 1233.
After The Circus at Santa Maria del Mar :
    1133.
After the Cleansing of Bosnia : 3576.
After the Collapse of a Building : 5563.
After the Delivery : 4111.
After the Dish Ran Away with the Spoon :
    4430.
After the Divorce : 2481, 4109.
After the Fall : 5970, 7197.
After the Flood : 2401.
After the Funeral : 5406, 6179.
After the Gypsies : 2913.
After the King's Cross Fire : 1446.
After the Quarrel : 1397.
After the Resurrection : 2363.

After the Season : 3824.
After the Shiva : 5341.
After the snow melt : 6977.
After the Storm : 1435, 5923.
After the Survivors Are Gone : 298.
After the Verdict : 5393.
After the War : 2011, 3301, 4224.
After the War on the Land : 5766.
After the Weather : 3500.
After Three Days : 3117.
After Twelve Days of Rain : 3683.
After You : 3871, 6461.
After You Come : 2, 4718.
After You Died : 1382.
After You Left : 6374.
After Your Death : 6284.
Afterglow : 4249.
The Afterimage : 3779.
Afterimages : 3916.
Afterlife : 926, 7265.
The Afterlife : 1574.
The Afterlife Messenger Service : 5849.
Aftermath : 1238.
Afternoon : 4790.
The Afternoon After : 3877.
Afternoon in October : 3464.
An Afternoon in the Country of the Calm
    Down : 2498.
Afternoon Meeting with an Angel : 405.
Afternoon of a Faun : 7235.
Afternoon of a Yawn : 6608.
An Afternoon on the River Dee, Llangollen,
    Wales : 3862.
Afternoon Peace : 6076.
Afterward : 4036.
Again dawn : 1777.
Again Kosovo : 3186, 5071.
Against Memory : 2153.
Against the Black Wind : 1369.
Against the Graveyard's Greater Wall : 3425.
Agamemnon on the Jukebox : 5022.
Agatha's Butterfly : 6247.
Age 5 Born with AIDS : 923.
Age of Bronze : 2542.
The Age of Nostalgia : 91.
The Age of the Dawn : 4746, 5174.
An Age with Sunspots : 998.
Agenda : 3959.
Agent : 1591, 6185.
The Agent : 7090.
Aggregation : 1883.
Aging : 2250.
The Aging Saboteur Remembers the Majestic
    : 894.
Agnostalgia : 1885.
The Agnostic Returns to Town : 315.
Agua Alta : 4516.
Ah Ha : 4865.
Ah, Look! : 838.
Ah, Star : 4105.
AIDS : 6218.
L'Aigle et le Ver : 5922.
Ain't Living Long Like This : 3900.
Air : 530, 5673, 6871.
Air Fairs : 2711.

The Air of Performance- α at Liancourt : 5894.
Air Quality : 3870.
Air, Water, Places, II : 5673, 6871.
Airborne : 844.
Airfield : 231.
Airlink : 2648.
Airmail to Jane : 3030.
The Airman's Father : 4565.
An Airplane Is the Silver Cloud : 3314, 5409.
Airport Bomb : 5867.
Ajijic : 5502.
Akhmatova : 4560.
Akibat : 7368.
Akicita Olowan : 3920.
Akin to Ashes : 6865.
Al-Bukhari : 2251.
Al-Ghazali in Jerusalem : 2251.
Al-Husn, in Northern Jordan : 1504.
Al-Mu'tazilah : 2251.
Los Alamos, 1945 : 91.
Alan Davis : 7002.
Alarm : 4510.
Alarums and Excursions : 2332.
Alba : 1736, 5074.
Albania & the Death of Enver Hoxha : 79.
Albert Einstein Explains Relativity Once and For All : 1238.
Albert Pinkham Ryder's 'Dead Bird' : 1905.
Alberta Morning : 5264.
Albino : 855.
Alchemical : 1026, 2572.
The Alchemist : 1682.
The Alchemists : 2898.
Alcibiades : 5852.
Alcohol : 989, 5923.
Alda on the Street : 3283.
Alex Walking : 4672.
Alexander Robinson : 3095.
Alexandria: Coda to Cavafy's 'The City' : 1484.
Alias : 4990.
Alice at the Hearth : 7025.
Alice Descending the Rabbit-Hole : 6439.
Alice, Waiting : 625.
Alice's Right Foot, Esq : 625.
Alicia : 3956.
Alien Story : 7176.
Aliens Can Be Dumb Too : 4038.
Alison As in Dreams of Dreaming : 2519.
Alita : 41.
Alive, absent from all life : 5673, 6871.
All Blues : 213.
All Clear : 2535.
All Day : 1241, 5062.
All Day Children : 5693.
The All-Dog Siren Choir : 4295.
The All-Encompassing : 5606.
All for once I melt to like it : 150.
All I Have Are the Tracks : 6362.
All I Know to Do : 2809.
All I Saw Was Painted Fruit : 4276.
All My Friends : 838.
All My Friends Advise Me to Start a New Life : 4135.

The All-Night Hotline and Drop-In Center : 1752.
All-Night Radio : 639.
All of December Toward New Year's : 7364.
All of Us Are Leaving : 1826.
All our clothes, cleansed and nakedness : 5113.
All Our Seasons : 6272.
All Souls' Day : 909.
All-Star : 4407.
All That Fall : 4335.
All the Angels Are Dying : 5777.
All the Best Witches Have Been Burned : 3548.
All the Long Way : 4940.
All the Needs : 7107.
All the Noise of the World : 446.
All the Outside : 3462.
All the Things We Know Better Than : 6896.
All the Time Ahead : 2963.
All the Way Back : 2405.
All the Way Home (Instructions to a 10-year - old) : 3968.
All the Women Poets I Like Didn't Have Their Fathers : 3822.
All These Winters : 5270.
All Too Soon : 1610.
All Visual Materials Emit Countless Cartoon Bubbles : 4484.
All Wild Animals Were Once Called Deer : 3348.
All writing seems to me today idiotic : 3547, 5638.
All Your Jabber of All Those People — Big : 1324.
Allabendlich : 5349.
Allan Marquand Espera a Su Compañero de Tenis en el Campo Sur : 4988.
Allegory : 923, 1765, 4648.
Allen Ginsberg on the Citadel: Halifax, 1986 : 1105.
Alley Games 13 : 3226.
Alley Games / the Awakening : 3226.
Alligator Holes Down Along About Old Dock : 121.
The Alligator Wrestler : 7106.
All's Hollow : 4674.
Allusion to the Death of Colonel Francisco Borges (1833-74) : 354, 643, 4433.
Almanac, 1978 : 2703.
Almost a Game : 4402.
Almost Domestic : 3078, 5241, 6235.
Almost Fifty : 5266.
Almost Lost in Translation : 4468.
Almost Middle Aged, Running Chunns Cove : 2941.
Almost Never : 3082.
Almost Nothing : 143, 3786.
Almost over the abyss, at the very edge of the branch : 1713, 2160.
Almost Spring : 537.
Almost There : 503.
Almost to Hau'ula : 4477.
Alms : 665, 3152.
Almsgiving : 4801.
Alone : 838, 3197.

Alone and Silent : 1305, 4100, 4148.
Alone, Dark and Sleepless : 2653.
Alone with myself and even alone within my
    very self : 3547, 5638.
Along Edges : 2521.
Along for the Ride : 3611.
Along Ocean Parkway in Brooklyn : 3299.
Already mother's breasts hung low with the
    years : 2576, 5455.
Als ein Stern Fiel : 4689.
Also, How I Lost Her : 2029.
Also Lawyers : 837.
Alteration : 979.
Alternating Current : 4165.
An Alternative : 6986.
Altitude 10,700m : 5754.
Altra Notte : 3889.
Always a Bridesmaid : 2825.
Always Less : 7365.
Alzheimer's : 1534.
The Alzheimer's Monkeys : 4491.
Alzheimer's Weather : 4329.
Amar en Jerusalen : 1605.
Amaryllis : 876.
The Amateur Matador : 206.
Amazing Journey : 1429.
The Amber Window : 6432.
The Ambience : 3634.
Ambition : 7137.
Ambivalence : 3506.
Amelia : 7137.
Amends with Steady Soil : 5252.
America : 837.
America to the Old World Bards : 7070.
The American Artist : 4472.
American Crow : 6898.
American Dream : 1493.
The American English Sentence, the Supple,
    Unforgiving : 5465.
American Express Accepted : 5167.
American Gothic : 1757, 2128.
American History: the Snap Wyatt Poems :
    1994.
American Koan : 2331.
American Lit: A Psalm of Life : 7175.
The American Name : 4659.
American Nocturne : 214, 4171.
American Painting, with Rain : 7137.
American Parnassas : 1025.
The American Photographic Postcard: 1900 -
    1920 : 2331.
American Pie : 3846.
An American Primitive: *Before the Fall* :
    278.
American Sky : 1283.
American Storm : 1653.
The American Sublime : 3787.
American Terrorism : 6443.
American Tune : 2331.
America's Game : 3190.
Amherst Poem : 5771.
The Amish Visit Pella, Iowa : 5385.
The Ammo Dump at Dong Ha : 3456.
Amnesia : 3780.
Amoebas : 2474.
Among Lakes : 7252.

Among Tea Roses : 4453.
Among the Divided Lilies : 897.
Among the Missing : 2972.
Among the Stars : 2812.
Amor Bilingue : 5326.
El amor es falso : 3413, 4170.
Amor y Algo Más : 5807.
The Amorous Husband and the Premenstrual
    Wife : 1703.
El Amparo : 1226.
Ampersand : 5439.
Amphibious Muse : 4906.
Amulets : 3020.
Amusement Park Reflections : 2072, 7161.
Anacharsis Cloots : 3436.
Anachronisms : 5853.
Analects : 862, 4126, 5343.
Anamnesis at the Faultline : 3772.
Anamorphosis : 1215, 3172, 6235.
The Anarchist : 3998.
Anatolia : 3232.
Anatomy Lesson : 113, 923, 6009.
The Anatomy of Nostalgia : 908.
The Anatomy of Whales : 6208.
The Anatomy Theater at Padua : 620.
Anaxsa Fragment: Coming to New Land :
    2249.
Ancestralidades : 6912.
Ancestralities : 6912.
The Anchor : 3330.
Anchored off Koh Tao : 1734.
Anchoring : 4994.
Anchoring Out : 2914.
Ancient Acid Flashing Back : 3920.
An Ancient Idyll Lives Today : 6601.
Ancient Madonna : 3822.
Ancient Well : 5416.
And Also from the Son : 904.
And Any Other : 2779.
And Are We So Divided? : 6967.
And drop shortly into some manner of reverie
    : 5758.
And Fig Leaves for All : 3904.
& for a Moment I Saw Myself in You : 3151.
And Gently : 2919.
And He Is With Us : 2758, 5704.
&/He's Got a Music/Magic : 4369.
And I Wanted to Say : 5652.
And If : 4240.
And I'm Still Waiting : 2708.
And It Was Night : 7348.
And Now : 715, 4875.
And Now Let's Check the Map : 2331.
And Only Then : 6982.
And Other Fantasy Lovers : 2357.
And Rain : 7027.
And Risen, Celibate : 5047.
And So Heavy with Life the Crust of the
    World Is Still : 2498.
And So I Requested a Chair : 3688.
And That's What I Felt When I Heard Them :
    6877.
And That's What the Devil Was Told : 1755.
And the creased mechanics of detritus : 4682.

And the Fish with the Yellow Eyes and the
    Green Tail Fins Leaped into the
    Volcano : 838.
And the headwind still visible : 5113.
And the Lord Said, 'Hey, Like Everything's
    Cool' : 4225.
And the Stars Were Shining : 214.
And the Toy Boat Is Ready to Go : 188,
    2473.
And Their Voices a River : 1383.
And Then : 1941.
And This Forever : 2585.
And Wylde for to Hold : 752.
And you, licking this reef : 5113.
Andalusian Fog : 4906.
Andante Cantabile : 436, 1076, 1968.
Andriaen Adriaensz : 1298.
Andromache : 1856, 2341.
Andy & Holly Meet Scott on the Steps of the
    Parthenon : 6266.
Anecdote for the Sleepy Poet : 3969.
An Anecdote of the Double Ninth Festival :
    1047.
Angel : 4483.
The Angel : 1748.
The Angel and I Resolute the Homo : 2826.
Angel del Temblor : 2678.
Angel Looking Away : 2446.
Angel of the evening : 5230.
Angel Sighted from Airliner! : 1025.
Angel with Cabbage Leaf Wings : 3353.
Angelo Poliziano : 3392, 6094.
The Angelology : 4247.
Angels : 2496, 2892, 4016.
Angels Among the Servants : 7106.
Angels Among Us : 865.
Angels & Artichokes : 7190.
Angels and the Bars of Manhattan : 4307.
Angels at the Corner : 3301.
An Angel's Time : 429.
Angelus : 1701.
Anger : 1743.
Angle Markers (Poteaux d'Angle) : 2901,
    4440.
The Angle of Shadow, the Angle of Light :
    4249.
Angling : 4338.
Angry Rooms, Silent Rooms : 4078.
Anguish & Metaphor : 6204.
The Ani : 5018.
Anima : 2455, 7054.
Animal : 5264.
The Animal : 3031.
Animal Graves : 6723.
Animal, Vegetable, or Mineral : 4368.
Animal You : 5317.
The Animals : 2331.
The Animals of Complicity : 6121.
Animism : 6491.
Aniversario : 1062, 1769.
Ankle Deep in the Madison River : 6765.
The Ankle of Andromeda : 5069.
Anna : 2468, 4977.
Anna Anna : 5100.
Annealing : 3002.

Anne's Blue Glass Gets Broken in the
    Earthquake : 6837.
Annie, Telling Stories : 4308.
Annihilation : 1695.
Anniversary : 1294, 1392, 2435, 4886.
The Anniversary : 1313.
Anniversary of a Drowning : 1045.
The Anniversary of Nothing : 2843.
Anniversary Poem to an Ex-Wife : 6947.
Anniversary Waltz : 77, 3925.
The Annoucement : 5956.
Announcing Your Arrival : 5889.
Annunciation : 3737, 4089.
Annunciation with a Bullet in It : 2398.
Annunciations : 2935.
Anointings : 6010.
Anomaly : 3935.
Anonimo (Siglo XV) : 1018.
Anonymous : 881.
Anonymous Church Mural, Harrow Gate
    Martyrdom of Our Lord : 3550.
Anonymous (Fifteenth Century) : 1018,
    4043.
Another : 979, 3390.
Another Angel : 4535.
Another Cat with Too Many Lives : 1238.
Another child Outgrows Her Hobbyhorse :
    4523.
Another Comedy for Paolo and Francesca :
    5332.
Another Conversation with the Beloved :
    6206.
Another Country : 1537, 5399, 7221.
Another Day in Valhalla : 836.
Another Dream of Paleography : 908.
Another Editorial : 2954.
Another First Day : 1907.
Another Kind of Traffic : 4153.
Another Lesson : 6982.
Another Lesson in Economics : 5565.
Another Life : 3367, 6193.
Another Love Affair : 6804.
Another Night Alone : 4321.
Another of the Body's Stories : 7283.
Another Portico : 4157.
Another Saigon Intersection : 5621.
Another Seascape : 4216.
Another Spring, Darkness : 318, 4035, 7221.
Another View of Penn : 5636.
Answering Machine : 4295.
The Answering Service : 6544.
The Ant : 7353.
Antara : 1537, 1538, 5399, 7221.
Antecedents : 207.
Anthropic Principle Revisited : 6120.
Anthropology : 3855, 6828.
Anthroposcopy : 4537.
Anti-Valentine : 5971.
The Anti- *Ars Poetica* : 4223, 5338.
Anticipation : 862, 1653, 4057, 4517.
Antietam Creek : 6928.
(Antigone, Act II) : 2350, 2907.
Antiphon : 5910.
Antique : 1468, 4421, 5529.
Antique Store, Pecs Hungary : 5555.
Antlion : 4928.

Antonio in Tijuca : 6270.
The Anvil : 1749.
Anxiety of Ten O'Clock : 2371.
An Anxious Dream : 1034.
Any, Any Whatever : 5673, 6871.
Any Moment : 5162.
Any Morning : 6299.
Any One of Us : 3133, 4060, 5901.
Anyone Home? : 6675.
Anything Can Happen to a Body Like a
    Brick : 1779.
Anything You Decide Changes Your Life :
    875.
'A'ole Hopo iho o Hawai'i : 3277, 5188.
Août : 6378.
Apache Tear : 4023.
Aperture : 3866.
The Aphrodite Stone : 6014.
Apiksiktuaqn : 3179.
Apnea : 2435.
Apocalypse: The Early Years : 4253.
Apocryphal Fragments: Excerpts from a
    Notebook : 5015.
Apollinaire's Landscapes : 6615.
Apollo Loxias : 2558.
Apollo Mourns Hyacinthus : 5420.
Apologia pro Vita Sua : 6299.
Apologies : 80.
Apologizing to the Bees : 1204.
Apology : 278, 3048.
The Apostates Stop for a Phosphate : 853.
Apostle : 2687.
Appalachia I : 6981.
Appalling : 1174.
The apparel of anger is often something old :
    1781.
The Apple Shrine : 5050.
Apple Talk : 2156.
Appledore, On the Island of Shoals : 2481.
Apples : 5969.
The Apples : 636, 5804.
Apples and Such : 4371.
Applied Science : 678.
Appraisal : 2069.
The Appraisal of Days : 1567.
Apprehension of Beauty : 7353.
Aprendiz de Fuego : 4166.
Apprentice : 4255.
Approach to a View in Perspective : 458,
    3112.
Approximate : 4632.
Approximately : 5539, 6311.
Approximately Forever : 7220.
Apraxia : 5580.
Aprenentatge de la Solitud : 4148.
The Aprenticeship of Solitude : 1305, 4100,
    4148.
Apricot Brandy Flowed : 3740.
April : 2997, 5982.
April 25th : 5326.
(April '91) : 5011.
April Fifth, Nineteen Hundred Eighty-Three :
    4255.
April Fool's Day, Happy Birthday : 1492.
April for B— : 522, 6649.
April Gold : 5787.

April Is the Cruelest Month : 4578.
An April Morning : 6280.
April Music : 2772.
April Snow : 890.
April White Blossoms : 6911.
Aquarium : 2988, 3125.
Aquella Luz, la Que Estremece : 5533.
Aquilone : 3603.
Arabic : 4845.
Arabic Coffee : 4845.
Arabic Music : 6.
Arachnophobia : 6713.
Arap-Psychology : 1562.
The Arc of the Jumper : 6948.
The Arcades : 1432.
Arcana Mundi : 417.
Archaeology : 943.
Archaic Figurine from Nayarit : 1968.
Archaic Smile : 3974.
Archbishops : 2005.
Arched Neck : 1980.
Archeology : 2866.
Archie : 4985.
The Archipelago : 214.
The Architect : 5032.
The Architect's Daughter : 6170.
Arctic Tern : 931.
Are Sin Disease and Death Real? : 916.
Are You Now or Have You Ever Been :
    5613.
Arethusa, Deep : 217.
Arguing Bartusiak : 2331.
The Argument against Chaos : 3470.
Argument in Isolation : 3492.
An Argument with Wordsworth : 1263.
Argus : 5416.
Ariadne : 4416, 6879.
Ariadne's Dancing Floor : 6012.
Ariel to Prospero : 3428.
Aristotle and the Crayfish : 2507, 5790.
Ark : 4730.
Armadillo : 5107.
Armageddon : 6554, 6919.
The Armageddon Rose : 4525.
Armistice Poppies : 5214.
Armitage Street : 2792.
Armoire : 4906.
Arms : 5783.
Arm's Reach, Harm's Way : 3682.
Arms That Hold Me Back : 4797.
Army Barbers : 2336.
Army Basic Training : 7355.
Arnhem Land : 4866.
The Arno at Rovezzano : 204, 4556.
Around at Our Place : 296.
Around the High School : 3676.
Arrangement : 6842.
Arrhythmia : 6278.
Arrival : 4902.
The Arrival of Grace : 4672.
Arriving at Pier House Hotel : 4195.
Arrow : 4005.
The Arrow : 2095, 6234, 6781.
Arrowheads : 5996, 6874.
Arrows : 2875.
Arroyo Seco : 5624.

Arroyo Seco: A House at the Crossroads :
    4820.
Ars Longa, Vita Brevis : 3863.
Ars Poetica : 151, 1513, 1719, 2168, 5058,
    6889.
Arsenio : 3932.
Art : 5868.
The Art Center : 1760.
L'Art de Toucher le Clavecin : 4858.
Art History : 7273.
Art Nouveau: Under the Studio Window :
    5878.
Art of a Cold Sun : 4684.
The Art of Crickets : 4730.
The Art of Dying : 5694.
The Art of Eating : 2959.
The Art of Going Mad : 1310, 4098.
The Art of Gratitude : 764.
The Art of Improvisation : 1371.
The Art of Mapplethorpe's Work : 6951.
The Art of Percussion : 7155.
The Art of Poetry : 3490, 5214.
Art of Silence : 5787.
The Art of Speeding : 214.
Art of the Middle Ages : 4749.
Art of the Sonnet: LXIX : 4926.
The Art of Waiting : 1635, 2332.
Art Therapy : 4150.
Arte Poetica (One More) : 461, 976.
Arte Poetica, Otra : 461.
Artemesia Gentileschi Speaks : 5.
Artemis : 7109.
Artemisia's Women : 6236.
The Artful Dodger : 2676.
Arthur Adams Works the Mint : 4402.
The Artichoke : 5279.
An Artichoke for Montesquieu : 2398.
Article of Faith : 6204.
Articles of Faith : 5918.
Artifact : 1625.
Artillery Horses Under Fire : 2313.
Artisans of the Tomb : 2845.
An Artist in Winter : 973.
The Artist Reclining : 5385.
An Artist's Life : 6704.
The Artist's Studio : 6055.
As a child, I Couldn't Float : 7328.
As a Flaneuse : 2820.
As Always : 2755.
As Eyesight in Darkness : 4597.
As How : 2095.
As I Drove Past the Old Man Watering His
    Wife on the Lawn : 4030.
As I often dread the morning : 3459.
As I was paddling down the Po : 5126.
As If : 4015.
As If He Were Free : 2150.
As If It Were : 7169.
As If It Were a Jigsaw Puzzle Nearly Done :
    4015.
As Imperceptibly As Grief : 1564.
As in a Pourtract : 124.
As Is Death : 4016.
As It Is : 2818.
As It Was in the Beginning : 1567.
As Long As I Live : 6393.

As Parts Go : 5739.
As She Caught Death : 3593.
As She Left Us : 5416.
As the Mountain Comes : 5367.
As Though Through a Tunnel : 7013.
As We Forget Them : 2739.
As we were sailing off Bizerte : 1192.
The Ascension of Ira Campbell : 1878.
Ascent : 3817.
Aschenbach in Venice : 1197.
Ash : 3541.
Ash Shading into Blue : 1686, 4688.
Ash Wednesday : 654.
Ashanti Market : 3025.
The Ashes : 341.
Ashes, Ashes! All Fall Down! : 5201.
Así Es : 2796.
An Aside at the Met : 3440.
Asking You : 6300.
Asleep by the River : 5689, 7065.
Asparagus : 4262, 4542.
Aspens This Fall : 6539.
Aspirin : 73.
The Assassin of Light : 2120.
Asserting, Threatening, Promising, Declaring
    : 1608.
Assignment on the Teacher's Desk : 2596.
Assimilation : 5063.
Assisi in July : 5057.
Assistant : 1095.
Association : 5539, 6311.
Associations en Route to a Bone Scan : 5537.
Assumptions in Flight : 3357.
Assurance : 6299.
The Astrologer Sleeps Nights: A Fable :
    3169.
Astronomy : 5914.
Astrophysics : 5792.
Asylum : 2550.
At 4 in the Morning : 5471.
At 6:10 I Am Certain You Are : 5898.
At 7 AM the River : 1226.
At 78, Marge Goes River Rafting : 1203.
At a Cabin in the Pecos : 4178.
At a Café in Hermosa Beach : 3441.
At a Farm in Dutch County : 1141.
At a Funeral : 4308.
At a Jazz Bar : 5672.
At a Low Point : 1497.
At a Nameless Bend in the River : 4631.
At Age Eleven I Killed a Child : 2450.
At Baldpate Hospital : 1627.
At Burt Lake : 151.
At Control Point 0 : 4472.
At East Sandwich Beach in September :
    2952.
At E.'s Home in Vresice : 2328, 3582.
At Fakhani, the Shoe : 2585.
At first, I couldn't open the door : 1138.
At Home : 2441, 3560.
At Home Within : 865.
At John Reed's Grave : 3151.
At Kirsanov's Burial : 1524, 6137, 6843.
At Last : 4242.
At Lovegene's Gallery : 6768.
At Middle Age : 3948.

At Night : 3861, 4449, 4933.
At Night in Late Fall : 749.
At Night the Characters on My Classroom Shelves Come Out to Party : 5620.
At Noon Hill : 5623.
At or Above the Earth's Surface : 6682.
At Quarry Hill Cemetery, an Angel : 551.
At School : 654.
At Sea Colony — Tattoos and Telltale Signs : 2926.
At Seven Months : 1082.
At Seventeen : 73.
At Shiloh, For Example : 5463.
At Six with Grandpa : 4757.
At Summer's End : 6970.
At the Abortion Clinic : 3997.
At the Babe Ruth Museum : 1259.
At the Beach : 3666.
At 'The Boathouse,' Laugharne, Wales : 3862.
At the Bottom of Grand Canyon : 3028.
At the Cafe Barbar : 992.
At the Corner of 9th and Avalon : 5612.
At the Crossroads : 299, 843.
At the Dead Goat Saloon : 3951.
At the Drive-In: Winter, 1962 : 3214.
At the Edge of Stage Three : 1659.
At the Edge of the Amish Orchard : 4864.
At the Edge of the Pool : 7099.
At the End : 3677, 3833.
At the End of the Day : 6336.
At the End of the Rainbow : 6740.
At the Exhibit of Peter Hujar's Photographs, Grey Art Gallery, NYC, 1990 : 4177.
At the Family Cemetery : 5442.
At the front, defending the mother tongue : 436, 1076, 1968.
At the Funeral of the Second Mrs. Wilson : 2904.
At the Gate : 5868.
At the Gedi Ruins : 6307.
At the Grave : 4847.
At the Gym : 6735.
At the Hour of Our Birth : 6154.
At the House of Ghosts : 3920.
At the Jewish Museum : 5050.
At the Lakehouse : 4662.
At the March Equinox : 2470.
At the Motel Coffee Shop : 1891.
At the news of your betrothal : 3466.
At the Nursing Home : 4273.
At the Point : 3503.
At the Post Office : 6265.
At the Prairie, the Day Before : 2608.
At the Ravine : 2260.
At the Reflecting Pool : 6221.
At the Retreat : 2199.
At the Roger Maris Museum, West Acres Mall, Fargo, North Dakota : 6034.
At the Side Door, Holy Epiphany : 4350.
At the Source : 6968.
At the Special Olympics : 1247.
At the Stillborn Grave : 620.
At the Stone-Age Tombs : 3343.
At the Storm Door : 2935.
At the Synchrotron Lab : 400.

At the Tideland : 3055, 6065, 6534.
At the Unemployement Office : 3123.
At the Van Gogh Museum : 4950.
At the White Horse Tavern : 6823.
At the Window : 666.
At the Window of a Stranger's House : 3228.
At the Y : 654.
At Three or Four : 7096.
At Toba Seashore : 3304, 6065, 6534.
At Work : 2756.
Atalanta in Cleveland : 858.
Atavist 2: an Expedition : 5081.
An Atheist's Creed : 657, 5589.
Athlete: At Seventeen : 2154.
Athlete's Scars : 3700.
Atiq : 207.
Atlantic City : 1648.
Atlantis : 2474.
Atlas : 1215, 3172, 6235.
Atom : 5285.
Atop Mt. Baker : 6866.
Atrocities : 1343.
The Attack : 4384.
Attempt to Discover Life : 6373.
Attende Domine : 3967.
Attention! : 2116.
The Attic : 6481.
The Attic Room : 7358.
Au Café Noir : 4346.
Aubade : 1719, 5493.
Aubade, 1954 : 6964.
Aubade, Deer Isle : 3440.
Aubade in Modified Second Asclepiadean : 4557.
Auction Block : 2420.
An Audience with the Muse : 2507, 5790.
Audio : 3053, 6235.
Auditorium : 2311.
Aug 19 90   1 6 9 1 : 1777.
Aug.-Dec. for Jimmy Schuyler : 4828.
August : 4900, 5572.
August 5 : 1369.
August 6, 1989 : 1257.
August 22, 1990 (Iraq and Kuwait) : 7213.
August 1990 : 4916.
August by the Willow : 3829.
August Letter from Grandmother : 2995.
Augusta : 3051.
Aun Que Noche : 4512.
Aunt Annie and Me : 3900.
Aunt Joe Plays with the Children : 6876.
The Aunt Joe Poems : 6876.
Aunt Juni in Her Japanese Garden : 6792.
Aunt Juni's Carousel Horse : 6792.
Aunt Mad : 6218.
Aunt Mary : 6623.
Aunt Maude's Pocketbook : 2000.
Aunt Virginia's Cancer : 5746.
Aunts : 3935.
Aurora Leigh : 799.
Auschwitz : 1865, 3822.
Auschwitz Artists : 3822.
Australia Day : 6675.
An Austrian Visa Office in Budapest : 4722.
Authorial Distance : 6342.
Authoritarian : 3473.

Authority : 4417.
Authorized Version : 466.
An Author's House : 6299.
Auto-da-Fé : 1965.
Auto Erotica : 4325.
Auto Mobile Madonna : 3822.
Autobiographical Notes : 309.
The Autobiography of a Tiny Buffalo : 4991.
Autoexec.Wkn : 1663.
Autograph : 2793, 6087.
Automobile Repair : 3161.
Autopsychoanalysis : 5589.
Autorretrato : 2523, 3519.
Autumn : 4993, 5926.
Autumn Again : 1969.
An Autumn Evening : 303, 6669.
Autumn Fires : 299, 843.
Autumn in Mikhailovskoye : 2133, 6239.
Autumn Light : 2693, 5638.
Autumn Night : 2095, 6127, 6747.
Autumn, Odysseus : 4642.
The Autumn Orchard : 2517, 2927, 7282.
Autumn Poem : 1816.
Autumn Rain in Tel Aviv : 117, 591.
Autumn Rhythm : 6391.
Autumn Songs : 4239, 6201.
An Autumnal Prayer to Tu Fu : 96, 7259.
Autumnal Primer : 333.
Available Light : 2310.
Avalanche Madonna : 3822.
Avalokitesvara : 1902.
Avatar at the Gas Station, Lower East Side : 6737.
Ave Maria : 4627.
Avenue des Fleurs : 1735.
The Avenue X Gang : 6280.
The Aviator's Restaurant : 363.
Una Avispa Cruzo el Himen de la Ventana : 461.
Avon Road, 7 AM : 6100.
Awa Speaks : 4393.
Awake : 1909, 2135.
Awakening : 231.
Awful Coffee : 723.
Awkward Passions: Confessions of a Black Catholic : 3340.
The Awkward Young Girl Approaching You : 2046.
The Awkwardness Among Men : 5395.
The Ax-Murder of Trotsky by Ramon Mercader, Mexico, Agusut 20, 1940 : 2262.
Axiom : 67, 2548.
Aye Que Maria Feliz (or Maria Was No Virgin) : 5327.
Azalea : 3554.
An Azure Shadowed Room : 1146.
B : 3842.
B-b-bluebells : 6512.
Babblers : 2095.
The baby always gets heavier : 671.
Baby Carriages : 4531, 4720, 7044.
Baby Dolls : 4483.
The Baby in Group : 7334.
Baby Laurie Arthur's Here : 2618.
The Baby on the Table : 3775.

Baby Poems : 485.
Babysitter : 3300.
The Babysitter : 2570.
The Babysitter's Loss : 881.
Babysitting to Thelonious Monk : 6030.
The Bacchae on the Docks at Tenth Street : 101.
The Baccae: The Deaths of Benito Mussolini and Claretta Petacci, Milan, April 29, 1945 : 2262.
Bachelor Brothers : 1383.
Bachelor Party : 837.
Back Flip : 6970.
The Back Porch : 5031.
Back Road, Amherst Virginia : 670.
Back View : 4844.
Back Words : 4193.
Backbird: Poems on the World and Work of Franz Kafka : 2232.
Backcountry Unit #12 : 3549.
Background Music : 2933.
Backward Dancer : 603.
Backwater : 1024.
Bad Alchemy : 4165.
Bad Boy Emotional- : 3784.
Bad Boy ro mancin his lady : 3784.
Bad Boy un practiced in the art of the interview : 3784.
Bad Breath Bod : 5297.
The Bad Daughter : 6154.
A Bad Day for Possums : 1311.
Bad Government : 3568, 5913.
Bad Habits : 7014.
Bad Penny : 4073.
Bad Start : 4796.
Bad Times Barbie : 2833.
Bad Weather : 2425.
Baghdad Rainbow : 3567.
Bagpipe Dream : 618.
Bahama Blue Beetle : 1845.
Un Bailoteo del Alma : 1531.
The Bait : 1448.
Baja Journal : 2497.
Bakchum : 4652.
The Baker's Daughter : 3868.
Baking Pies : 4294.
Balance : 4316, 5286.
Balance Sheet : 5575.
Balanchine's *Western Symphony* : 1275.
Le Balcon : 754.
Balcony : 7097.
Balcony Poem #7 : 1343.
Bald-Headed Girl (Boston Tenement, 1936) : 3968.
Balding : 3418.
The Balding Animal Lover : 1058.
Baldy Bateman : 6316.
Balkan : 6270.
Balkan Irony : 2868.
Balkan Moon and Sun : 2756.
Balkan Street : 2142, 6728.
Ball : 510.
The Ball of Yarn : 1104, 4178.
Ballad About Light in Winter : 4634.
The Ballad of Fenimore Woolson and Henry James : 3372.

Ballad of Friendship Through the Ages : 4023.
The Ballad of Jesse Helms : 6196.
The Ballad of the Missing Mosquito : 2103.
The Ballad of Zoë Baird : 6690.
Ballade of David Parsons : 6887.
The Ballade of Dead Ladies : 1169.
Ballade, U.S.A : 1975.
The Ballads of Kukutis : 4161, 6289.
The Ballerina : 2451.
The Ballet : 4453.
Ballet Lesson : 7197.
Ballgloves : 4294.
Le Ballon de Football, ou le Moyen de Parvenir : 2066.
Ballroom Dancing : 4858.
Balsamroot, Paintbrush and Lomatium on a Slope : 625.
Baltimore : 3541, 6411.
Baltimore Bouquet : 2404.
Bamboo Shoots in Asia : 1340.
The Banality of Good : 2910.
The Band of the Sea : 6527.
Banded Krait : 6089.
Bane : 7175.
Banff Centred : 4456.
The Bank's Going to Play : 2095.
Banshee : 4378.
Banyans : 3353.
Baptism : 4272, 4971.
Baptism at Bluegill Pond : 4769.
A Bar in the Islands : 965.
Bar Mitzvah at the Wailing Wall : 5981.
Barb at Dot's Wedding : 6962.
Barbara at Forty-five : 7293.
Barbara by the Sea : 1568.
Barbarians : 2984, 3186.
Barbie Feels There Is Someone Else There Inside Her : 3822.
Barbie Hunts Thru Medical Books Looking for What Is Wrong with Her When She Sees Her Birth Date in a Book, Knows She Is Over 30 : 3822.
The Barbie Sister : 3822.
Barbie Sits in the Too Cute Chocolate Shop : 3822.
Barbie's Exciting Life : 7031.
Bareback : 6495.
Barefoot in the Kitchen : 2138.
Barely Holding Distant Things Apart : 4542.
Barfight : 231.
Bargain : 5336.
The Barges at Night on the Ohio River : 2425.
Bark Burn : 5317.
Barlach Sculpture : 2486.
The Barley Poem : 4368.
Barley Sugar : 3985.
Barn : 527.
The Barn's Blue Light : 345.
The Baroque Warehouse — Reflections at Castle Howard : 3366.
Barra de Navidad: Postscript : 4693.
Barrens : 994.
Bartalk : 5223.
Barter : 17.

Bartholomew's Cobble : 2551.
Bartok Widow : 3328.
Bartók's Roumanian Dances : 7369.
Baseball's Back : 6690.
Basement Barber : 1095.
The Basic Dress Code for a Poet : 3805, 6905.
Basic Operations : 4624, 5104.
Basta con Questa Atroce Guerra : 806.
Bastille Day : 561.
The Bat : 4260, 6278.
Bath : 780.
The Bath : 1749, 5806.
The Bather : 2345.
The Bathers : 1596.
Bathing Lenin : 1122.
Bathing Malcolm : 4728.
Bathing My Father : 1150.
Bathing My Grandmother : 6655.
Bathing My Son : 5267.
Bathing she spots : 7077.
The Bathsheba Poems : 5416.
The Bathtub Planter : 7333.
Batman Is Depressed : 4802.
Bats : 344.
The Batsto River at Night : 5345.
The Battering of the Rose : 5248.
The Battersea Shield : 4999.
The Battle of Anghiari : 2672.
The Battle of Osfrontis : 3015.
Battle of the Monster Trucks : 5726.
Baxter State Park, 1975 : 6208.
Bay-Bay's Kids : 3896.
Bayou Ballad : 3336.
Be-In : 1928.
Be Proud You Are an Intellectual : 1568.
Be That Someone : 4350.
The Beach : 1807.
Beach Bum : 6270.
Beach Evening : 3688.
Beach Glass : 6139.
Beach Post Office : 512.
Beach Roses : 1645.
Beach Sight : 573.
Beach Tent : 3022.
Beachcombing : 468.
Beacon : 442, 3770, 5804.
Beaded Tongue and Groove : 1167.
Bean Soup: or, A Legume Miscellany : 5021.
Beanstalk Dreams : 4640.
Bear : 4915.
The Bear : 1397.
Bear Fat : 2898.
Bear Jam : 3022.
Bear Meadow : 6988.
Bear on Scale : 6723.
The Beard : 4659.
Bearing Witness : 2054.
Beast : 6203.
The Beast : 5638, 6651.
Beating : 6425.
Beating the Dead Horse : 5279.
Beatnik Days : 5279, 5529.
The Beautiful Nurse : 6513.
Beautiful Ride : 5284.

The Beautiful Young Devon Shorthorn Bull
    Sexton Hyades XXXIII : 4826.
Beauty : 4177, 6607.
Beauty Is a Burden : 6265.
The Beauty of Illness: A Family Vacation up
    in Michigan : 726.
Beauty Trip : 6806.
Becalmed in the Bermuda Triangle : 3624.
Because a world may be called into being :
    7284.
Because I Have No Daughters : 2498.
Because I Used to Be a Good Girl : 7014.
Because Now : 897.
Because She Is Allowing Herself Some
    Choice in This Life : 7028.
Because We Are Not Separate : 2324.
becky rosner was the only jewish girl I knew
    : 6627.
Becoming : 2717, 5425.
Becoming Hard of Hearing : 7128.
Becoming Miss Holiday : 5162.
Becoming Woman : 6874.
The Bed of Coals : 4842.
The Bedouin Dress : 2585.
A Bedouin's Dream : 4745.
Bedrock : 3942.
Bedroom City: A Found Poem : 5077.
Bedside : 897, 1033.
Bedtime Story : 838, 4986.
Bee : 296.
Bee-Keeping : 686.
The Bee Man : 602.
The Bee Nativity : 2784.
Beechey Island : 181.
Bees : 1112, 2026, 5197.
Bees in Amber : 3333.
Beethoven Reminds Me : 2633.
Beethoven's Ninth : 3964.
Befana (January 6) : 3368.
Before a Rendezvous : 498, 3516, 5149.
Before an Operation : 5579.
Before and After a Coup d'Etat : 1665.
Before Boarding : 5634.
Before Bodhidarma, Emptiness : 7044.
Before Dawn : 5676.
Before Departure : 67, 2548.
Before Eye Could Tell Time : 5788.
Before Moving : 5249.
Before Names : 5275, 6949.
Before Our Eyes : 3248.
Before Persephone : 1240.
Before Spuyten Duyvil : 4010.
Before Sunday School : 5400.
Before the Beat : 5715.
Before the General Strike : 4196.
Before the Moon Was the Moon : 5580.
Before the Subdivision : 1557.
Before the Thunder Storm : 3038.
Before You Drop Off Read This : 6864.
Before you even saw a lake : 5113.
Beggar : 5395.
The Beggar on Houston Street : 6076.
The Beggars : 5492.
Beggars and Angels : 2202.
Beginning Apart : 1499.
Beginning Art, in Two Parts : 5408.

Beginning Ended : 6493.
Beginning, Middle, End : 4715.
The Beginning of Memory : 5693.
The Beginning of the Story : 4161, 6289.
Beginning the Day with Total Recall of Night
    Air : 3393.
The Beginnings of Philosophy : 6466.
Beginnings of the Ice Age : 879.
The Begonia and I : 1736.
Behind Gershwin's Eyes : 6123.
Behind His Eyes : 342.
Behind It All : 7175.
Behind My Back : 2095, 3557.
Behind the Yellow Hibiscus : 3803.
Behind This Mortal Bone : 5198.
Behold the Men, 1945 : 2735.
Being 4 : 3050, 5514.
Being a Hero Once : 7300.
Being against this large white cerebrum in
    my skull : 3659.
Being Here, Awake : 3565.
Beirut : 11, 4644.
Bel Air : 2102.
Bel Canto Telegram : 1591.
Belerion : 5074.
Belfast Elegy : 6756.
Belief : 3783, 4632, 6154.
Belize I Miss Your Albert Street : 4332.
The Bell : 5812.
Bell Inscription : 498, 3288, 3516.
Bell Island Retrospective : 6320.
The Bell Ringers of Kalamazoo : 7106.
Belladonna : 4992.
Bellies : 1272.
Bells : 4132.
Belonging to You (A Daughter's Poem) :
    6253.
Below Orford : 4583.
Below Two Skies : 2961.
Beltane : 5055.
Benares : 6776.
Bench Ghetto : 3449, 5304, 6313.
Bend Sinister : 1947.
Bending with the Wind : 253.
Beneath the Painted Shrine : 6911.
Benedict, the Blessed One : 3014.
Benediction : 3247.
Beneficence : 6495.
The Benefit of Doubt : 4986.
Benny : 491.
Bent Blues (Captain Lomax Wants to Know)
    : 5058.
A Bent Page : 3742.
Benton's Persephone : 7232.
Beowulf in Utopia : 6215.
Bequest (to Other Thieves) : 100, 1096,
    6465.
Berkshire Morning, for My Mother : 4700.
The Berkshires: May : 6300.
Berlin Poem : 2252, 2387.
Berry Renaissance : 5606.
Berryman Reading, 1964 : 2153.
Beruit : 1678.
Beset : 7202.
Beside the Road : 665.
Beside the Waterfall : 4900.

Besides the Money : 4581.
The Best Defense, or Recklessness Part One : 2498.
The Best I Can : 3426.
Beth Tatarsky 1948-1992 : 5734.
Bethlehem : 4196.
Betrayals : 3499.
The Betrayer : 2333.
Better : 6842.
Better Than a Snail's Pace : 3155.
Better Tomorrow : 3234.
A Better View : 6242.
Betting Seeds : 2706.
Betty and Joe : 1778.
Betty's Birthday : 510.
Betty's Dream : 4136.
Between 3 and 4 A.M. : 10.
Between a Pig and a Baby : 149.
Between Bed and Table : 862, 5343, 6844.
Between contemplation & action : 1781.
Between Generations : 5050.
Between Grief and Nothing : 368.
Between Her and Me : 214, 4171.
Between Kingdoms : 4132.
Between Mountains : 4682.
Between Patients : 6343.
Between Seasons : 6767.
Between Sisters : 2168.
Between Stations : 1410.
Between Summer and Winter : 1698.
Between the Church and Its Mountain : 2113.
Between the House and the Sky : 370.
Between the Lines : 5335.
Between the Opera and the Mars Game : 3315.
Between Trees : 2844.
Between Two Hamlets : 5178.
Between Us : 100, 3054, 6415, 6465.
Between Wives : 4134.
Beyond 65 : 1955.
Beyond Blue Bayou : 4472.
Beyond Hunger : 3219.
Beyond Las Nieves : 1226.
Beyond Marietta : 3448.
Beyond Real Space Time : 2490, 5810.
Beyond the Casinos : 4611.
Beyond the Milking Barn : 5022.
Beyond the Rain : 2099.
Bible Studies : 5423.
Biblical Olympics : 7031.
Bicycle Days : 424.
Bienvenido : 6737.
Big Blue Train : 7346.
The Big Brass Handbook: Chapter 2 : 4140.
The Big Broadcast : 4112.
Big Dick : 408.
The Big Fight : 3792.
Big Green Sea Turtle Madonna : 3822.
Big Hole : 2095.
The Big Livingroom : 7166.
Big Medicine Sacred White Buffalo : 4606.
The Big One : 2412.
Big Tires for Chris Hagen : 2545.
Billboard : 6327.
Billboards : 1321.
Billy Graham : 5916.

Bio : 6346.
Bio 7 : 4565.
Bio Bite : 5916.
Bio-Degrading : 3196.
Bio: Fitting into My Years : 6299.
The Biographer : 3677.
Biography : 318, 2086, 4035, 7221.
Biography of a Woman : 6587.
Birch River : 1653.
Birches, Down a 1/4 : 6620.
Bird : 3392, 3516, 4921.
Bird Call Valley : 3940, 6910.
Bird Calls : 5186.
Bird Life in the Business District : 3554.
The Bird Man : 4348.
Bird, Poem @ 06/11/90 : 6547.
Bird-Singing Stream : 6910, 7275.
The Bird-Temple : 6922.
Birding Once More : 6827.
Birdland : 4210.
Birds : 1895, 1926, 2331.
Birds Calling in the Valley : 5573, 6910.
Birds on a Powerline : 3499.
Birds Sing in the Ravine : 362, 363, 6910, 7250.
The Birdwatcher : 5164.
Bir's Song : 1796.
Birth : 442, 2111, 5804.
Birthday : 2739, 6362.
Birthday at the Motor Vehicle Dept : 4358.
Birthday Chorus : 4076.
Birthday Letter : 2893.
Birthday Poem : 6716.
Birthday Presence : 625.
Birthdays : 2967.
Birthmark : 3323.
The Birthplace : 2725.
Birthright : 287.
Biscuits and Jam : 3197.
Bishop Benson's Wife : 5142.
Bitch : 2, 4718.
Bitter Cup : 4637.
The Bitter World of Spring : 7121.
The Bitterness of Rousseau : 5624.
Bivouac : 6171, 7259, 7271.
Bjorn Larsen and Aunt Joe at the Dump : 6876.
Black : 5095.
Black and Blind : 344.
Black and White : 6300.
Black and White Hell : 838.
Black, Armed and Dangerous : 5160.
Black Barbie History : 1703.
Black Bear : 3857.
Black Bethlehem Star : 2363.
Black Bread with Russian Dressing : 6932.
Black Bridge : 2296.
Black Bridge Blues : 5678.
Black Cameo : 6808.
Black Clouds : 4070.
Black Coat : 3015.
Black Duck Love Song : 2918.
Black Fruits of August : 6458.
The Black Glove: A Rapture : 4853.
Black Gold : 362, 3865, 6531.
The Black Hole : 7162.

Black Ibises : 1226.
Black Letters of Insensitivity : 294, 3685, 5962.
Black Lid : 1380.
Black Longing Allows Calm Keys : 6884.
Black Mesa : 4023.
Black Mesa, More or Less : 4023.
Black Mirror : 2095, 6127, 6747.
Black Monday : 4045.
Black Mulberry : 620.
Black Pudding : 2150.
Black Puddle: April 18 : 2868, 5899.
Black Rhythms of Peru : 988, 5797.
Black River : 3039.
Black Rose : 2848.
Black Shawl : 6174.
Black Smoke : 4984.
The Black Snake : 3235.
Black Spring : 211.
Black Spruce : 127, 274, 2240.
Black Stone on a White Stone : 2868, 6760.
Black Suns : 3432.
Black Swans : 5745.
Black Widow : 899, 3697.
Blackberries : 3945.
Blackberry Fools : 7105.
The Blackbirds : 3713.
Blackout : 3974.
The Blacksmith and the Perpetual Mother Machine : 5406.
Blame : 1628.
Blame It on Jack : 344.
Blame It on the Dog, He's Dead : 3920.
Blame It on the Dress : 2101.
Blanch Wilcox Brown : 783.
Blanco Descanso : 5807.
Blank Pages : 5709.
The Blank World : 4027.
Blanket Weather : 90.
Blasphemy : 1879.
Blaue Nacht : 2582.
Bleak Thought : 4731.
Bleeding : 4071.
Bleeding Heart : 807.
Blemishes : 2993.
The Blend : 6233.
Blessed : 6842.
The Blessed : 4646.
Blessed Is He Who Divided into Clean and Unclean : 3263, 5736.
Blessing : 2260.
A Blessing : 3772.
The Blessing : 2521.
The Blessing Way : 4427.
Blessings on the Stomach, the Body's Inner Furnace : 604.
Blind from Birth : 4624, 5104.
A Blind Mother in the Park : 6517.
The Blind Spot : 7185.
A Blind Woman : 3510.
Blindfolded Bull : 3275, 5313.
Blindman's Bluff : 224, 2824, 3715.
The Blindness Desired : 1304.
Bliss : 225, 6238.
Blisters Sleethe : 5581, 5656.
Blizzard : 4913.

The Blizzard Rope, Armistice Day, 1940 : 4905.
The Block : 7217.
Block Island Ferry : 3064.
Blocked Writer : 1168.
Blonde Rebellion : 6291.
Blondin : 2132.
Blood : 5303.
Blood and Bone : 3432.
Blood & Dreams : 4581.
Blood Gun : 4116.
Blood Rain : 900.
Blood Sister : 3957.
Bloodstar : 2695.
Bloody Men : 1263.
The Bloomingfoods Promise : 4195.
Bloom's Photograph : 6848.
Bloomsbury Remembered : 1358.
Bloomsburyday : 6218.
Bloubergstrand : 7200.
Blow as Deep as You Want to Blow : 172.
Blowin' in the Breeze : 2054.
The Blowing Whale : 5814, 6521.
Blowjob Bonnet vs. War Bonnet : 172.
Blowjob Mantra : 172.
Blu di Metilene : 4922.
Blue : 1790.
Blue Angel : 4292.
The Blue Angel : 2400.
Blue Baby : 1613.
Blue-Bellied Lizard at Divide Meadow : 5966.
Blue Blood : 999.
Blue Booties & Pink Booties : 3677.
The Blue Cart : 5501.
Blue Ceiling : 2915.
The Blue Coat : 3153.
Blue Collars : 4335.
Blue Donuts : 1399.
Blue Dust : 4807.
Blue Earth : 3833.
Blue Embroidery : 3725.
The Blue-Eyed Exterminator : 3117.
Blue Flower : 211.
Blue / Flowers : 4495.
The Blue Ford, 1958 : 6966.
Blue Fragment : 5995.
The Blue God : 306.
Blue Gone to Black : 742.
The Blue Goose : 3383.
A Blue Grief : 2649.
Blue Guide : 7273.
Blue Hill Fair : 168.
The Blue Lamp : 2286.
Blue Light : 3823.
Blue Lobster : 2000.
Blue Moon : 7246.
Blue Mountain Autumn : 488.
Blue Nude : 5358.
Blue Piping : 1570.
Blue Pond at Berkovitsa : 442, 3770, 5804.
Blue Recitation : 3039.
The Blue Ridge: Heraclitus : 7023.
The Blue Road : 6523.
Blue Room, Blue Horse : 361.
Blue Screen : 129.

A Blue Silk Shirt : 6524.
Blue Skiff : 4710.
Blue Sky January 1 63 Outside
    Nebraska? : 4328.
Blue Spring : 3106.
Blue Star : 1591.
Blue Star Home : 4614.
Blue Territory : 2431.
Blue Tick : 5551.
Blue Train Rant : 483.
Blue Tulips and Night Train for Jack
    Kerouac's Grave : 4307.
Blue Turban : 6932.
Blue Van : 2393.
Blue Willow : 2295, 2649.
Blue Window : 1440.
Blueberry Gleaner : 2716.
Bluebird : 1091.
Bluegrass : 241.
The Bluejay at the Nearly Empty Feeder :
    6858.
Blueprint : 4682.
Blueprint of Face : 2363.
Blues : 1448, 5062.
(Blues) : 6574.
Blues Around a Barn : 4634.
Blues, by Wanderin' Willie Clinton : 6690.
[Blues for Ron Dellums] : 186.
Blues in the Night : 1366.
Blues in the Valley : 121.
(Blues, Removed) : 6574.
Bluesong : 2504.
Bluish / Chimney Smoke : 4495.
Blur of Atoms : 170.
The Blur of Intention : 2966.
Blushing in the Garden of the Animal : 5380.
BMC Blues : 3194.
Bmp Bmp : 4199.
Boabab Trees : 4560.
Boarding School Sestina : 6208.
Boat : 5286.
The Boat : 3392, 3516, 4921.
A Boat in the Forest : 3961.
Boating on the Mississippi : 7054.
Bob and Jack with Chainsaws : 5385.
Bob Dylan's Greatest Hits II : 1740.
Bob Marley's Hair : 4199.
Bobby the Commie : 3813.
The Bocce Court on Lewis Avenue : 6333.
The Bodhisattva Wore a String Tie : 2090.
The Bodies : 6279.
Bodiless, Bodiless in Translation : 7013.
Body : 143, 1646, 3786.
Body Beautiful : 3780.
Body Boby Air : 7071.
Body Count : 4911.
Body Fascists : 777.
The Body Holographic : 521.
The Body Is : 2833.
Body Knowledge : 2691.
Body Language : 1934, 4355.
Body of Love : 2337, 4512.
Body of Night : 1247.
The Body of the Whispering : 6619.
The Body Politic : 7028.
The Body the Archive : 6920.

Body without Light : 4583.
Bodywork : 2702.
The Bog : 654.
Bog Life, Lake and Outlet : 865.
Bog Man : 2583.
Bogged in Ogden : 585.
The Bonds : 2331.
Bone : 2538.
Bone and Blowdown : 4524.
The Bone Carriage Answers : 266.
Bone China : 7214.
The Bone-Cupboard : 6247.
The Bone Room : 181.
Bones : 3591, 4885, 6440.
Bones and Blue : 3902.
Bones Equal! : 2580.
The Bones of an Ancient Thesaurus : 6975.
The Bones of Montgomery Clift : 2455.
The Bones of Your Name : 6363.
Boneyard : 4452.
Bonnard's Wife : 1757.
Bonsai : 3720, 5324.
Boogie Woogie at 7:50 AM : 3388.
The Book : 1371.
Book Contest Bile : 4225.
Book Learning : 4522.
A Book Left Open in the Bathroom : 2331.
The Book of Changes I : 4961, 6135.
The Book of Common Betrayals : 3470.
The Book of Games : 2114.
Book of Geology : 5814, 6521.
The Book of Kells : 1383.
The Book of Moonlight : 1975.
The Book of the Dead Man : 448.
The Book of the Dead Man (#23) : 448.
The Book of the Dead Man (#27) : 448.
The Book of the Dead Man (#28) : 448.
The Book of the Dead Man (#33) : 448.
The Bookkeeper's Other Life : 7212.
Books : 3490.
Books Fall from Love : 848.
The Bookshelf Continuum : 5028.
Boot Camp : 5124.
Bootleg Whiskey for Twenty-Five Cents :
    6966.
Border Patrol : 6064.
Border Reports : 7180.
Border Zone, Minefield, Snow East of Bebra
    : 2507, 4444.
Borderline : 7000.
The Borders : 4892.
Boreal : 3246.
Bored and Adored Madonna : 3822.
Born : 1336, 1871.
Born Free : 1164.
Born of Water and the Spirit : 855.
Born on the Moon : 4504.
Born to Whine : 6970.
Borrowed Flight : 3811.
The Borrowed Wife : 7193.
Borzoi : 5818.
Bosnia's Christian Soldiers : 1273.
Boston, 1971 : 4762.
Boston Marriage : 2141.
A Boston Mission : 3931.
Botany : 4455.

Botany and Memory : 356.
Both of You : 6299.
Bottles : 6474.
Boucher in the Grand Palais (Thirteen Fragments About Nakedness) : 1336, 1871.
Bough Cottage : 5439.
Boulder Creek : 4892.
Boulevard of Plums the Morning They Open : 2934.
Bound : 1681.
Boundless Kingdom : 3470.
The Bounty : 3411.
The Bounty After the Bounty : 2441.
Bouquet : 3197.
Bourbon : 2131.
The Bow : 2000.
Bowen Island : 1159.
The Bowl : 1877.
Bowl of Fruit : 7352.
Bowl of Progresso Minestrone : 1269.
Bowled Over : 4734.
The Bowls from Bavaria : 3822.
The Box : 870, 5445.
A Box of Leaves : 5303.
The Box of the Special Silence : 2967.
The Boy : 1422, 4035, 7221.
A Boy, a Woman, a Blackbird : 2298.
Boy Meets Globe : 1824.
Boy of the Americas: Raptures of the Seattle Trade Years : 2084.
Boy Playing War : 5033.
The Boy Who Lives in the Backyard : 1119.
The Boy Who Talked to Birds : 4088.
A Boy Who's Bright But Awfully Quiet : 6280.
Boy with a Baseball Bat : 7123.
Boy with a Pacemaker Blues : 3382.
Boys and Their Fathers' Shotguns : 4282.
Boys in treetops : 3189.
A Boy's Life : 4343.
Bracelet : 326.
A Bracelet of Bright Hair About the Bone : 2441.
Bracken : 3333.
Brahms' Clarinet Quintet in B Minor, Op. 115 : 7369.
Braid : 4864.
Braille : 6970.
Brain Damage : 35.
Brain Disease : 3542.
Brain Rain : 7238.
Brain Teasers : 3114.
Brainstorm : 4763.
The Bramble : 7232.
A Branch Is Home Plate : 6522.
The Branches : 3536.
Brancusi's Golden Bird : 3938.
Brass : 3499.
Brass Watch : 3839.
Brave in It : 4378.
The Brave Siesta : 486.
Brave Spirit : 6742.
Brazil : 6740.
La Brea Blues : 3748.
Bread : 1122, 1765, 3050, 5514.

Bread-and-Butter! : 2911.
Bread and Wine (after Hölderlin) : 6955.
Bread-Baking : 5785, 6803.
Bread, Meat, Greens, and Soap : 4699.
Bread Route : 1202.
Breakdown : 1967.
Breakdown on Fourth St : 3379.
Breaker 19 : 4117.
The Breaker-Limbs : 5905.
Breakfast : 2286, 5093, 5185.
Breakfast at the Harrison Grill : 1567.
Breakfast in the Orchard : 1362.
Breakfast of Runnersup : 5859.
Breakfast with Seymour : 80.
Breaking : 2896.
Breaking It Off : 4505.
Breaking the Drought : 4276.
Breaking Water : 3041.
Breakout : 3639.
Breakup : 5107.
Breath : 50, 5033.
Breath Becomes Life : 1099.
The Breathers, St. Mark's Lighthouse : 917.
Breathing : 1294.
Breathing Space : 4599.
Breathing You In : 3651.
Breech : 2825.
A Breviary : 5015.
Briar Rose Defunct : 784.
Brick Hunters : 6081.
Bride : 3518.
The Bride : 6439.
Bride 1949 : 2460.
Bridge : 436, 1076, 1968, 2446.
The Bridge : 848, 7040.
A Brief Folklore of Typography : 2845.
A Brief History of Asylum : 752.
Brief History of Desire : 3082.
A Brief History of Landscape Painting in France : 3901.
A Brief Introduction to Philosophy : 2349.
The Brief Life of Our Ancestors : 1667, 2007, 6514.
A Brief Meeting : 1035, 4652.
The Brief Meeting : 5536.
Bright Dancing : 6522.
Bright World : 5673, 6871.
A Brightly Lit Ship : 653, 4070, 4997, 5060.
Brilliance : 1645.
Bringing in the Horses : 142.
Brisance : 3460.
British Jungle Training School, Macal River : 3633.
The Broad Highway : 2545.
Broadway Lament: San Francisco, 1978 : 3365.
Broken : 2088, 4523.
Broken Arm : 4864.
Broken Bed : 6045.
Broken Circle : 632.
Broken Glass : 802.
The Broken Gull : 2183.
Broken Plate Mask : 2055.
Broken Refrigerator Madonna : 3822.
Broken shell : 3964.
Broken Shells : 764.

Broken Sleep : 6335.
The Broken Vacation : 6183.
Bronze Age : 6602.
The Bronze Slave : 473.
Brooklyn and Back : 6693.
Brother Ben : 5732.
The Brother I Never Had : 4565.
Brother Martin : 3912.
Brother of My Heart : 3431.
Brothers : 361, 834.
Brought to the surface form the floor of the ocean : 5926.
Brown Angel : 5326.
Browsing Through the Album : 3344, 4995.
Brueghel's Two Monkeys : 327, 1022, 6514.
A bruise, from purple to yellow : 1138.
Bruised : 6251.
Bruises : 6218.
Brule River, Fishing at 60 : 3254.
Brunanburh, 937 A.D. : 355, 643.
The Brush Salesman from Leeds : 2637.
Bubbles Under Ice : 3649.
Bubbling : 6366.
Bucharest, 1989 : 4572.
Bucky Takes Time Off : 2930.
Bucolic Lines Composed en Route to Lyon's U-Pik-'em Strawberry Fields, Creedmore, N.C. : 6135.
Bud : 1768.
Bud Powell at the Club Montmarte : 5743.
Budapest : 1204, 4795.
A Buddha in the Woodpile : 1935.
Buddhism, Hunduism, Shintoism, Calvinism : 1781.
Buddy Lee Perriman Reflects on the Persian Gulf Crisis, Day 15 : 4271.
Buenos Aires : 643, 4433.
Buffalo Jump, Blue Mounds, Minnesota : 2297.
The Buffalo Man : 6911.
Buffalo Spirit Song : 3920.
Buick Electra : 2456.
Build Your Very Own Homeless Apartment : 6995.
Builders : 3392, 3516, 4921.
Building a City : 2209, 4448.
Building a Fire in June : 2401.
Building a Soul : 6284.
Building Consensus : 7343.
Building for the Past : 2840.
Building the Ferris Wheel : 4078.
Building the House of Crazy : 1979.
Built to Commemorate an Indian Burial Ground : 554.
Bulbs : 1433.
Bull Shot : 1274.
The Bulldozer's Syntax : 177.
Bulls in a World They Owned : 4282.
Bulltrout : 2566.
The Bully : 838.
The Bumble Bee : 559.
A Bunch of Nuts : 6975.
Bunched in My Fist Like September : 1291.
Bundle of Strawberries : 831.
Bungee Man Third World Man : 3653.
Bunker Watch : 2355.

Bunting : 2439.
Buñuelitos : 4062.
Bureaucrat, My Love : 1431.
Burgas : 3292, 6136.
Burghers of Petty Death : 6373.
Burial at Sea : 1218.
Burial Insurance : 2993.
Buried Alive : 3780.
Buried Treasure : 452.
Burn Out : 3822.
Burn Victim : 2296.
Burned : 2451.
Burning : 484.
The Burning at Neilson's Farm : 7106.
Burning, Burning : 838.
Burning Culm : 1369.
Burning Slocan : 6999.
Burning the Garden : 899.
The Burning Tree : 5421.
Burnouts, Both : 6402.
The Bus : 4708, 5624.
Bus-Boy Secrets : 2792.
Bus Ride South : 2340.
Bus Stop Poem #2 : 5464.
Bush vs Clinton, 1992 : 2604.
A Bushwalk : 469.
The Business : 6154.
Business Trip : 442, 5804.
Busted : 7077.
Busy, Busy, Busy : 6690.
But It's a Lot Like Wearing a Raincoat : 2925.
But Look Where Sadly the Poor Wretch Comes Reading : 2032.
But Only the Captains of This Earth : 6253.
But She Had Dropped Her Crown : 1350.
But the Pecculations : 4424.
But When She Gets to Her Dream Place : 553.
But Work : 4207.
Butch Queen Strolling through the Bathhouse : 1457.
Butcher Shop, 1957 : 3121.
The Butcher Shop at Alcara li Fusi, Sicily : 4156.
Butter : 2498.
Buttercup : 6386.
Buttercup Park : 4697.
Butterflies : 2094.
Butterflies Save Me from the Cold : 6766.
Butterfly : 3690.
The Butterfly : 2646.
Butterfly Fish : 7227.
The Butterfly Hotline : 1111.
Buttons : 537.
Buying a Dozen Lemons on the Way to Heaven : 4978.
Buying Balloons — November 27, 1970 : 149.
Buying the Dildo : 3556.
Buzz Buzz : 5602.
The Buzzing in My Balls : 2943.
By a Dublin Cathedral : 1114.
By Any Other Name : 3184.
By Degrees Weary : 6238.
By Disposition of Angels : 4575.

By Five A.M. : 4275.
By Huron : 5423.
By-Laws : 6154.
By Memory : 4806.
By Now We Were Freezing : 6501.
By the Black Ships : 6299.
By the Blue Flame of 2 AM : 1930.
By the Chapel : 6299.
By the Coat Rack : 793.
By the Grand Trunk Line : 393.
By the New York Public Library : 1515.
By the number thirty-eight bus down
    Dostojevsky Lane : 2879, 6465.
By the Rising Waters : 943.
By the Score : 1259.
By the Shore : 1383.
By the Way : 100, 6415, 6465.
Byrd's Survey of the Boundary: An
    Abridgment : 1080.
Byron at Missolonghi : 4642.
Byzantium : 3224, 3619.
The Cab Driver Who Ripped Me Off : 1743.
Cables : 1036.
Caboose : 1092.
Cactus Documentary : 1292.
Caddy Tales Retold : 797.
Cadenza : 6790.
Cafe : 6444.
El Café : 2678.
Café Havana, Budapest : 5118.
Café Pamplona : 923.
Caffeine : 465.
Caffeine Ode : 744.
Cages for the Dead : 4858.
Cain : 631, 1029.
Cairene Sloth Song : 4195.
Cairns : 5256.
Caitlin in Fiesole : 4384.
Cajun Doctor : 2495.
Calcutta, for Jai : 6792.
Calendar : 4138.
Calendar Thunderhead : 2566.
California : 1611.
California Cycles : 1023.
California Immortality : 7096.
California Quail : 5378.
California Sea Lion : 6332.
California, She Replied : 1874.
The Call : 1081, 1133, 3444, 5798, 6052.
A Call to Worship : 2260.
Calle de la Amargura : 4374.
Called Up: Tinker to Evers to Chance : 372.
A Callgirl in India : 5395.
Calligraphy : 7095.
Calling : 3535.
Calling from the Gate : 1480.
Calling Him Home : 4826.
Calling on a Taoist Priest in Tai-Tien
    Mountain But Failing to See Him :
    3808, 5285.
Calling The Dead and pushing back time :
    2055.
Calling the Eagle : 2821.
Callin's Second Daughter : 910.
The Calls : 5557.

Calm : 2679.
Camano Island: Birthday Poem for My
    Brother : 2677.
Cameo : 2150.
The Camera As Infernal Machine : 5140.
Camera Obscurant : 500.
The Camera's Eye Turned to You and Then
    the Beginning of Static : 3328.
Camille Monet sur Son Lit de Mort : 7060.
Camino Real : 923.
Camp Job : 896.
Camp Tontozona : 1507.
Campaign : 3780.
The Campers : 1412.
A Campfire and Ants : 2328, 6223.
Camping in Winter : 3998.
The Camps : 979.
Camptown Races : 2425.
Can I speak : 511.
Cana : 3513.
The Canadian Girl 1937 : 6382.
The Canal : 6614.
Canal and Towpath : 2107.
Cancer Child : 5746.
Cancion : 5924.
Canción del Sencillo Amor : 371.
Candle : 3950.
A Candle Burning at the Edge of Time :
    2948.
Candle Fat : 5670, 5895.
Candlemas : 4428.
Cane : 7055.
Canning Beets : 7140.
Cannon Beach : 6123.
The Canon, A Dialogue : 5734.
Cantabile : 2215.
Cante Jondo : 143, 3786.
Canticle for a Memory : 203, 5331.
Cantico para un Recuerdo : 203.
Canto : 498, 610, 3516, 4450, 4921.
Canto XV : 1406, 5196.
Canto XLII : 3197.
Canto 72 : 5262.
Canto LXXXIV : 5262.
Canto a la Luz : 2523.
Canyon : 2799.
Canyonlands : 2977.
Canzone: Siesta Key : 6887.
Caparina : 5005.
Cape Breton's Oral Tradition : 1632.
Cape Lookout : 6123.
Cape May Point : 6300.
Capertee : 469.
Capitalism : 3782.
Capitulation : 4031.
The Captain Hurls the Ship's Log Out to Sea :
    5162.
Captain Trelawny Embellishes upon the
    Death of Byron : 1259.
Captives : 5494.
Car Men, a Play in D : 6725.
Car Plunges Off Ridge Road into Creek,
    Couple Survives : 6945.
Caracol de Sueño sobre una Cosa Que Mata :
    461.
Caravaggio: The Supper at Emmaus : 632.

Carbonation : 5509.
Cardinal : 632, 1270.
The Cardinal : 6161.
The Cardinal Detoxes: A Play in One Act :
    1592.
Cardinals : 3105.
Cardiogram : 580.
Care : 6988.
Care for a Spot of Scotch Ol' Boy? : 6975.
The Care of Things : 233, 2077, 5654.
Career Changes : 4228.
Careful of the Day : 1789, 5702, 6580.
Carlos Enriquez : 5063.
Carmen in Verona : 7175.
Carnage : 36.
Carnal Knowledge : 7273.
Carnal Pursuits : 13.
Carnality : 4532.
Carnations : 6496.
Carnival of the New Colonies : 3228.
Carnivore Currency : 6167.
The Carnivore under Glass : 1362.
Carol : 1566.
Carol called it comfort food : 1476.
Carolina (For Kelly) : 2922.
Carotid Aneurym : 6417.
Carousel : 1284.
The Carousel Club, 1957 : 1840.
Carp Lake : 4886.
Carpentry : 139.
Carrot : 807.
Carrot Colored Words : 4.
Carryover : 5419.
Cars : 4298.
Cars and Men : 3822.
Carslaw's Sequences : 6351.
Carta de Amor al Rey Tut-Ank-Amen : 3939.
Las Cartas Extranjeras : 1938.
Cartographer's Tombstone : 1662.
Cartoon : 5551.
The Carver of Masks : 2678.
Carving : 5165.
Carving Your Future : 7204.
A Casa : 143.
La Casa : 3996.
Casa del Poeta Tragico : 3899.
Casanova in Love : 6834.
The Case for Martha : 1216.
A Case for Mediocrity : 3539.
The Case of the Spurious Spouse : 3730.
Casey Dying : 4858.
Cashier's Dream, the Hunt : 6556.
Cast : 2219.
A Cast of Tens : 763.
Castaway : 5428.
Castilian Lightning : 1102.
Casting : 7290.
Casting Off : 2859.
Castle : 5436.
The Castle : 4660.
Castle Moats of New Hampshire : 7351.
Cat Deaths : 1496.
The Cat Food Factory : 1859.
Cat in an Empty Apartment : 327, 1022,
    6514.
A Cat in Love : 5081.

Cat Martha Watches CNN : 486.
Cataclysms : 7289.
The Catacombs : 4557.
Catalan Morning : 61.
Cataloguing Twelve Fenian Novels : 4245.
Catalpa in Flower : 4608.
The Catalpa Tree : 5412.
Catch & Release : 243.
Catch and Release : 1480.
Catch da Bone : 300.
A Catch in the Breath : 2737.
Catch of the Day : 981.
Catching a Porcupine : 1555, 6952.
Catching Cold from a Lover : 642.
Catching On : 3343.
Catching Time : 1791.
Catching Turtles : 337.
La Catedral : 5104.
Caterfly : 7217.
The Caterpillow : 5279.
Caterwaul : 2889.
Cathedral : 4464.
The Cathedral : 4624, 5104.
The Cathedral at Ulm : 2867.
Catholic Courtship, 1965 : 5360.
Cats : 5903.
The Cats : 986.
Cattails: A Marsh in March : 3735.
Cattle Country : 13.
Caucasians : 4739.
Causalities : 5652.
Cause and Effect : 6280.
Cause & Effect : 6346.
The Causes Tighten : 4534.
Caution: This Woman Brakes for Memories :
    4290.
Caution to Old Age : 5132.
A Caution to Us : 6876.
Caution Yellow : 3342.
Cautionary Tale for a Daughter : 5537.
Cavafy's Desires : 3903.
The Cave : 2610.
The Cave Diver : 472.
Cave Drawing : 7042.
The Cave-Drawing : 6946.
Cave Painting : 2767.
Caveat : 6862.
Caveat Scriptor : 4225.
Caving without the Shaman : 7140.
Cedar Point : 1514.
Cedarsmoke : 4285.
Cedilla : 6729.
Celebrations 1943 : 5811.
Celestial Rust : 3525.
Celia Dreaming : 6279.
Celibacy : 1733.
Cell : 761.
The Cell : 5923.
Cellar Dweller : 6138.
Cello at Barnes Lake : 7094.
Cement Running Shoes: Baton Rouge,
    Louisiana : 1259.
El Cementerio de Princeton : 4988.
The Cemetery : 4818, 6548, 7234.
Cemetery, Chapel of the Cross, Flora,
    Mississippi : 5398.

Cemetery Hickory : 177.
Cemetery in Colliure : 794, 2360.
Cemetery Nights II : 1606.
Cemetery Strike : 423.
Cenizas Quedan : 4166.
Censored : 6042.
Census and Sensibility : 3626.
The Center : 678.
Centimentality : 1689.
Central Standard Time : 7290.
Centrifuge : 7283.
The Ceration : 4428.
Ceremonial : 1599.
Cérémonie : 190.
A Ceremony : 71.
A Certain Impermeable Person : 3677.
A Certain Kind of Eden : 5731.
A Certain Light : 2975.
A Certain Poem Comes As Fear : 6836.
A Certain Slant of Light : 4782.
Certainly Not : 3311.
Certains Novembres : 1522.
Certificate : 5842.
The Cesarian : 358.
Cézanne Drawing : 6135.
Cezanne's 'Preparation for the Funeral' :
    2436.
Chaconne : 1782.
Chain : 4357.
The Chain : 2301.
Chain of Being : 339.
The Chair : 6147.
Chairman : 6319.
Chalkmarks on Stone : 4547.
The Challenge : 3004.
The Chamber : 1593.
Chamber Music : 4603.
Chamber Music Two : 1776.
Chambered Nautilus : 2898, 3333.
Champagne : 5667.
Champion : 3004.
The Champion: Neighborhood Tale : 455.
A Chance Between Things : 2269.
Chance Meeting : 5501.
Chances and Hazards : 3460.
Change : 2697, 3176, 6907.
The Change : 1181, 2114, 3677.
Change in Travel Plans : 6690.
A Change of Light : 2125.
Changeling : 7078.
The Changeling : 899.
Changes : 678.
Changes Brought About by a Baby : 6339.
Changing : 6045.
Changing Address Books : 2302.
Changing Focus : 6393.
Changing History : 3142.
Changing the World : 6750.
The Chant : 5291.
Un Chant d'Amour : 2829.
Le Chant des Serpents : 1408.
Chant Royal : 7123.
Chanukah : 6416.
Chaos Physics : 2087.
Chapter IX: Hometown (September) : 2539,
    3805.

Chapter One: Coderington : 4124.
Chapter One from the Book of Lamentations
    : 206.
Characters Around a Soriano Painting. Art in
    Miami : 6913.
Charcoal Drawing : 2717.
Chardin and the New Filoque : 1032.
Charles : 6427.
Charles I at Trial : 1786.
Charles Dilke Comments on the Engagement
    between John Keats and Fanny Brawne :
    1259.
Charles the Fifth and the Peasant : 3932.
Charleston Baskets : 6963.
Charlie Chan Solves Another Murder : 1025.
Charlie's One-eyed Loiter : 4666.
Charlotte : 3678.
Charms : 780.
Charting : 1583.
Charting Particulars : 2036.
Chartres : 5926.
Chase for One Lover Alone : 1488, 5123.
Chassé : 308.
Chassidim Dancing : 2072, 5740.
Chastity Imposes No Conditions : 1499.
Chaucer at Aldgate : 3537.
Chaucer at Park House : 3537.
CHAZ : 2939.
Cheap Gas : 2848.
Cheap Lights Cheap : 1403.
Cheap Sneakers : 5733.
Check-in at Nurnberg : 3879.
Checking the Sheep Two Mornings After the
    Glad Day : 3432.
Cheek to Cheek : 72, 1366.
A Cheer, of Sorts, for Arafat : 6690.
Cheers : 1204.
Cheese : 2588, 5667.
Cherries at Kajikawa : 793.
Cherry Trees : 6429.
Cherub : 1374.
Chess Is a Game Where Partners in Play Are
    Called Opponents : 5883.
Chess Piece : 1697.
Chest X-Ray : 6237.
The Chesterfields: A Daguerreotype : 2590.
Chez Nguyen : 2551.
Chi e Questa : 5262.
Ch'i Liang's Good Wife : 3568, 5913.
Chiaroscuro : 5420.
Chicago Green : 5535.
Chicane : 5568.
Chicano, Canto 0 8: Fangs of my puto : 186.
Chichicastenango Sestina : 7028.
The Chicken Business : 269.
Chicken Giblets : 838.
Chicken Pox : 7254.
The Chicken Tree : 2957.
Chickenology : 7306.
Chickens : 69.
Chico Wrangler : 5657.
Chief Muncie : 2461.
Chief Never Weary : 867.
The Child and the Old Man : 3538, 7371.
Child. Eight. Autistic : 5884.
The Child Is Mother of the Longing : 3470.

Child of Many Prayers : 2435.
Childfoot Visitation : 172.
Childhood : 1178, 5207, 5294, 6414, 7166.
Childhood House : 4928.
The Childhood House : 6752.
Childhood in Heidelberg : 4897.
Childhood Stories : 3343.
Childless Myth : 737.
Children : 2147, 2742, 5042.
The Children : 72, 3090.
The Children at the Shelter : 181.
The Children Beckon, Late : 4329.
Children in a Storm : 1146.
The Children of Gravity : 582.
Children with AIDS Learn to Live without
    Happily Ever After : 3822.
The Children's Corner : 4224.
Children's Games : 7180.
The Children's House : 6154.
Children's Mass in Montreal : 4075.
The Children's Tet : 674.
A Child's Bestiary : 2661.
A Child's Oval Office : 5430.
The Child's Saying : 318, 1537, 7221.
Chile During the Fifteenth Winter : 6387.
Chilka Lake : 4192, 6114, 7342.
Chilly : 2741.
Ch'in Concubine by Her Pond : 5363.
The Ch'in Envoy : 5363.
China Lesson : 6133.
Chinatown Entree : 5916.
Chinese Boxes : 339.
Chinese Cantos : 6900.
Chinese Illusions : 5519.
The Chinese New Year : 6154.
The Chinese Notebook : 37, 640, 1364, 1638,
    4781.
Chinese Restaurants : 7095.
Chipmunks Enter the World of Don McKay
    and Jan Zwicky : 653, 4070, 4997, 5060.
Chipping Some Teeth : 1384.
Ch'iu Chin, Beheaded, 1907 : 4888.
Chloral Hydrate, 500 mg May Repeat Times
    One As Needed for Sleeplessness :
    3545.
Chokecherries : 1637.
Chopper : 7178.
Chopping Garlic : 7282.
Chora : 4818, 6548.
Chorus of the Trojan Survivors : 3670, 4408.
Chowdown : 5056.
Christ : 5317.
Christ at the Apollo, 1962 : 6943.
The Christ in My Body : 6147.
Christina : 5029.
Christina Johnson: The Mother : 6876.
Christine in America : 3836.
Christmas at the Airport : 1960.
Christmas Cards : 996.
The Christmas Castle : 2943.
Christmas Day : 4578.
Christmas Days : 3673.
Christmas Eve at the Chula Vista Marina :
    1219.
Christmas Eve at the Plantation : 7055.
Christmas Guilt : 1592.

Christmas Night in Charleston Harbor : 276.
Christmas, Nineteen-fifties : 397, 4422.
Christmas Party at the German Teacher's :
    4240.
Christmas Remembrance for an Arkanasas
    House : 1972.
A Christmas Story : 6774.
Christmas This Side of the Golden Gate :
    2300.
The Christological Year : 1187.
Christopher Columbus : 2103, 3505, 4706.
Chromad : 6378.
Chromatography : 1902.
Chronic Blues : 1170.
The Chronic Liar Buys a Canary : 1767.
Chrysalis : 3093, 7357.
Church Is for Girls : 5296.
The Church Mouse's Trap : 3969.
The Church of Perivleptos : 5020.
Church Picnic : 6010.
Cicada : 6165.
Cicada of Space : 792, 6537.
Cicada Song : 387.
Cicade : 143.
Ciego de Nacimiento : 5104.
Cigarettes : 3716.
Cigars : 3462.
The Cinder : 4578.
Cinderella : 3746, 4109, 4233.
Cinderella, 1959 : 6053.
Cinderella after the Ball : 1311.
Cindy : 340.
Cinema Vérité: Jacques Derrida and God's
    Tsimtsum : 151.
Cinema Vérité: The Death of Alfred, Lord
    Tennyson : 151.
Cinema Vérité: William Makepeace
    Thackeray Follows His Bliss : 151.
The Cinnamon Bay Sonnets : 3316.
The Cinnamon Bear : 5126.
Cîntecul lui guillaume : 4219.
Cipher : 2076, 7303.
Circle : 2254, 5572.
The Circle Being Described : 5083.
Circle of Fire : 4323.
Circles : 2922, 6235, 6789.
Circling the Daughter : 3469.
Circlings : 4730.
Circulating : 6050.
Circumflex : 6729.
Circumferencia de la Palabra : 114.
Circumferencia del Recuerdo : 114.
Cistern : 985.
The Citadel : 3499.
Cita's Sister : 1651.
Citizens Committees : 3604.
The Citizen's Lobby : 3573.
City : 143, 3786, 4375.
City at Sunset : 3673.
City in Regard : 1248.
The City Is Dead : 1200, 3198.
City Limits : 3510.
The City Makes New Grass and Curbs and
    Brother Booker Blesses the Street :
    2597.
City More Than I Suspected : 5469.

City Nocturne : 318, 4035, 7221.
The City of Richmond : 4715.
The City of the Dead : 6319.
City Park : 5034.
City Sights : 6401.
City Sky Line Painted on a Blind eye : 4232.
A City State : 2837.
City-Street : 2054.
City Without Me : 203, 5331.
Ciudad sin Ti : 203.
Las Ciudades Tatuadas : 5104.
A Civil Marriage : 936.
Civil Obedience : 6172.
Civil Register : 6758.
Civilization : 6935.
A Civilized Life : 3076.
La Clairière : 612.
The Clapping : 2441.
Clare and Francis : 3984.
Clarifications : 1582.
Clarity : 924.
Claroscuro : 4166.
Class Exercise : 215.
Class Reunion : 357.
Classic Outlines : 1104.
A Classical Landscape : 5579.
Claw : 170.
Claws : 1749.
Clayton : 2469.
A Clean Page as a Snowscape : 3977.
Cleaning Day in the Garage : 2292.
Cleaning Out the Locker : 2363.
Cleaning Out the Shaker Gears, Elyria
    Foundry, Elyria, Ohio 1971 : 6988.
Cleaning Out Your Apartment : 73.
Cleaning the Book Shelf : 7055.
Cleaning the Ground : 4769.
Cleaning the Gutters : 1048.
Clear Nights : 1821.
The Clearance : 4352.
Clearing : 3478.
The Clearing : 4569, 5912.
Cleavage : 231.
Cleave a Piece of Wood, I Am There : 2607.
The Clematis Seminar : 108.
Clerihew Couple : 6091.
Clerihew: 'Dear, dear me,' purred Priscilla :
    359.
Clerihew: Despite a very large hernia, which
    hung down : 359.
Clerihew: 'Good Heavens!' cried Galileo :
    359.
Clerihew: Jacques Derrida : 6091.
Clerihew: 'The State,' said Louis Fourteen :
    359.
Clerihew: When Irene and Vernon Castle :
    3454.
Clerihew: Whenever Catherine Anne Porter :
    3454.
Clerihews : 5582.
Clerihews for the Clerisy II : 1684.
Cleritwos : 3118.
The Clerks : 5571.
Click : 4519.
Climacteric : 43, 2047.
Climate : 672.

Climbing to the Cemetery : 247.
Clinton Presides Over the Signing : 6690.
Clinton Redux : 6690.
The Cloak : 5854.
The Clock Is Cuckoo : 5505.
The Clockmaker : 4772.
The Clocks of the Dead : 6076.
Clocksville : 4680.
A Clockwork Uncle : 1401.
Cloister : 6228.
Cloistered : 5469.
Close Call : 790.
Close Quarters : 1749.
Close Reading : 466.
Close the Doors, They're Coming in the
    Windows : 2136.
Close to Me Now : 2150.
Close to Trees : 2273.
Closed Head Injury : 3352.
Closed Mill : 137.
A Closed Place : 257, 3776.
The Closed Room : 2727, 5261.
Closer to Laundry : 3710.
The Closet : 946.
Closet Relation : 3354.
Closing Scene : 2130.
The Cloth : 6893.
Clothes Make the Man : 1610.
Clotheslines : 4295.
Cloud-Play for Four Hands : 1207.
The Clouds III (Scherzo) : 7121.
Cloudy Feather : 4528.
Clown : 6558.
Clown Fish : 1122.
Clown Sees Fox in the Water's Reflection :
    2070.
Club Desire : 6055.
Club from a Deck of Concrete Cards : 4808.
Club Lido, Kansas City, 1944 : 4271.
Clutching the Known : 6442.
A Clutter of Clerihews : 5748.
Clyde Peeling's Reptiland in Allenwood,
    Pennsylvania : 7290.
Clytemnestra : 1359, 5804, 7309.
Clytemnestras : 555, 7315.
Clytie's Rattling on Again : 3345.
Coal : 1966, 4354.
Coal Chute : 2425.
The Coast of Maine : 4225.
Coastal Advisory : 6755.
Coat of Arms : 4808.
Coats : 1887, 3381.
Cobb's Barns : 982.
Coca-Cola Man : 5157.
The Cochise Tax : 2186.
Cock-a-Doodle-Doo : 1765.
Cockatoos at Dusk : 3378.
Coconut Don Fu Delight : 1815.
Coconut Island : 1734.
The Cocoon : 3759.
Code Zero : 2167.
Codicil ('Including the Cost of a Monument
    and Inscription') : 3634.
Coffee : 2939.
Coffee-Break : 2431.

Coffee Shop, 1991 (after Iraq, after Ethiopia, after Bangladesh) : 2327.
Coffee, the Cross, Change : 3586.
Coffin Lumber : 149.
Cofradia : 2488.
Coin : 1109.
Coincidental Music : 1247.
Colcothar : 6857.
Cold : 2566.
The Cold : 2558.
Cold Creek : 2856, 4404.
Cold Harbor : 620.
Cold Spell : 921.
Cold Storage : 5568.
Cold Thoughts : 4178.
Coldly : 1425, 3230.
Cole Porter Variation : 1437.
Cole Younger: Coming : 3468.
Colette's Cat : 4650.
Coleus : 6935.
Collaborators : 6004.
Collage: Murder Mystery : 6345.
Collards : 4573.
Colleagues : 5428.
Collected Sunshine : 2868.
The Collector : 1568, 6417.
The Collectors : 5970.
Colombian Priestess : 4570.
Colombo Airport : 4441.
The Colonist : 3875.
Colonus : 2441.
Color Analysis : 347.
Color Code : 5364.
Color in the Garden : 6544.
Color Merchants : 4417.
The Color of Time : 3546, 5756.
The Color of Your Eyes : 3498.
Color Struck : 2594.
Colors : 3572.
Colors from the City of White: Photographs from Bielsko-Biala : 2046.
Colors of Port-au-Prince : 2527.
Colposcopy : 328.
Coltsfoot : 6632.
Columb—I-AD : 398.
Columbia Journal : 2569.
Columbia, the Dove : 932.
Columbus, New Mexico : 7095.
Combustion : 517.
Come : 413.
Come Back from the Dead : 1439.
Come Here : 912.
Come Nandaka, let's give the lion's roar : 531.
Come Onna My House (My House) : 3134.
The Comedy of Memory : 3758.
Comentario sobre un Crimen Pasional Concretado en 1949 : 461.
The Comforts of a Bench : 1189, 5250.
Coming : 5258.
Coming and Going : 214, 4171.
Coming Back : 1223.
Coming Backstage After a Young Man's Performance : 2659.
Coming Close to Drowning : 3372.
Coming Down : 3778.

Coming Down Rain from Light : 3871.
Coming Down the Kuskokwim : 6385.
Coming Home : 6702, 7282.
Coming Home From the Circus My Son Makes Me Promise Not to Say 'Bear' : 4339.
Coming of Age : 3880.
Coming Out of the Discount Store : 1493.
Coming slowly home : 2123, 2576.
Coming to Know : 3269.
A Command of Language : 6987.
Commandments : 19.
Commemoratives : 4417.
Commencement : 4864.
Un Commencement : 1735.
Commencement Ode : 1443.
Commencement of Tai Chi : 2635.
Commercial : 436, 1076, 1968.
Commercial Street : 892.
Commission : 3821.
Common Birds : 2807.
Common Ground : 7011.
Common Knowledge : 6827.
A Common Name : 5699.
The Common One : 3535.
Common Prayer : 3910.
Commonplaces : 6268.
Communication : 496.
Communion : 17, 168, 284, 3846.
Communion at Coldwater Baptist Church : 6298.
Communique from Tithonus : 1785.
The Community : 1606.
Community Circles : 6662.
The Commuter : 5107.
Como un Río : 2352.
Compaia sul Monte Sighignola la Prima Neve o Non Compaia : 5660.
Comparative Literature : 2530, 5220.
Comparison : 498, 4716.
A Compass : 643, 4433.
Compensation : 5411.
The Complete Italian Feast : 6377.
Complete Poems : 2860, 2915.
(Complete) Shorter Stories (1992) : 3521.
Complexity and Sunburn : 5144.
Complicity : 6121.
The Composer Interviews Her Piece : 2678.
The Composer's Dream : 4882.
Composition: Vox : 1064.
Composure : 2936.
Compulsive Gambling : 4877.
The Computer Drops an e Grates : 2058.
Conan Doyle's Copper Beeches : 5214.
The Conceiving : 417.
Concentration : 83.
Conception : 2481.
Concerning Bedrooms and Bestsellers : 1643.
Concerning Classified Ads : 2086.
Concerning Fractal Geometry : 2086.
Concerning Horror Movies : 2086.
Concerning Life on the Island : 2086.
Concerning the Death of Irony : 2086.
The Concert : 6340, 7095.
Concession to Winter : 5310, 5810.
Concessione all'Inverno : 5310.

Concetta's Essay on Poetry : 5378.
Concetto Spaziale : 6518.
The Conch : 5371, 5629, 6653.
Conch Oracles on the Elders' Path : 4786.
The Concièrge Arrives in Heaven : 918.
Concorde : 4488.
A Concrete Eternity : 6894.
Concrete Shadows : 2851.
Concubine : 4050.
Condensations : 6108.
The Condition Book : 838.
The Condition of Being : 3817.
Conditions of Production : 2412.
Condolence : 2100.
Condolences : 1259.
Cone of Light : 3301.
Coney Island Beach : 7337.
Confession: After Earthquake : 1509.
Confession of Julio Gonzalez : 7084.
Confessional : 6421.
The Confessional Mode : 2875.
Confessional Type of Poem : 4532.
Confessions : 227.
Confessions II: A Killing Story : 5348.
Confessions of a Freak : 838.
Confessions of a Nude : 150.
Confessions of a Peeping Tom : 1816.
Confessions of a Steeplejack : 4496.
Confessions of One or the Other : 6982.
Confirmation : 382.
Connecting the Dots : 6785.
Connections : 1102.
Connie's Story : 3232.
Connoisseur of Consciousness : 963.
Conrad : 730.
Conscience : 2625.
Consciousness : 4130.
Consciousness Raising Revisited : 4078.
Consciousness Rising / Love Rising : 5678.
Consecration : 1047.
The Consequences of Wife-Swapping with a
    Giant : 1703.
Conservation : 5176, 5308.
Conservation Framing Co : 3222.
Conservatory : 2876.
Considering All the Moving Light, All the
    Stationary Darkness : 5606.
Consolation : 417.
Consolation of Philosophy : 6586.
The Consolation of Small Engines : 593.
Conspiracies : 3300.
The Constant : 121.
Constellation Portrait #3: Sill Life with
    Crows : 3682.
Constellations : 3234.
Construction of the Museum : 5011.
Construction Workers : 3429.
Consultation Request : 5180.
The Consumers : 690, 1932.
Containing the Color Blue : 3435.
Containing the Light : 3945.
Contemplating Roads : 5744.
Contemplatio : 3827.
Contemporary Fragment (I) : 6742.
Contempt : 3237.
Contents of a Fever : 100, 3675, 6465.

The Context of a Nectie Quilt, Silk and
    Satins, 1940s : 4357.
Continent of Mental Lapses : 1680.
The Continental Can Company at Six
    O'Clock : 7227.
Continental Divide : 3976.
Continuing Ed : 996.
Continuity : 5364, 5615.
Continuous Present : 1376.
Continuum : 5490.
Contortionists of the Free World : 3355.
The Contra : 1005.
Contradiction over and over, rolling limbs
    flailing : 286.
Contradiction This Spring : 1969.
Contrapasta Boy : 4759.
Contrary : 3238.
Contre Jour : 6235, 6745.
Contributor's Note : 3846.
Contributor's Notes : 447.
Conventional Wisdom : 1763.
Conversation : 365, 4653.
Conversation in Produce : 7037.
Conversation in Woodside : 28.
A Conversation Not to Remember : 838.
Conversation with a Dealer, about a Painting
    in Private Hands : 2535.
Conversation with a Stone : 327, 1022, 6514.
Conversation with Parnassus : 4239, 6201.
Conversation with the Sun Bittern : 169.
Conversationally : 4891.
Conversations : 5759.
Conversations: The Battle : 4349.
Conversing with an Orange : 1659.
Conversion : 6163.
The Convicted : 1290, 5666, 6196, 6234.
Conviction : 3128.
A Convoluted Red Wad of Concentric
    Circles Stuck on an Attenuated Column
    and Having an Aroma, to My Wife :
    2309.
Convoy : 6081.
Cook : 4070.
Cookie Crisis : 7125.
Cooking with Bradley : 7050.
Cook's Desire : 311.
Cool Blue Halo : 3798.
Coop : 6327.
The Coora Flower : 769.
Coping with Touch : 6773.
Copper Cliff : 3644.
Copperhead : 196.
Copying : 1726.
Coquette : 6308.
Coral Chips : 3503.
Corcovado : 6270.
The Cord : 4289.
Core : 3011.
The Corn Palace : 788.
Cornelia Street, 6. A.M. : 1112.
Corner Brook to Athens by Way of London :
    6335.
The Cornice of the Skull : 704.
Corona : 809.
Corozal : 4231.

The Corps, and the Corps, and the Corps : 3846.
The Corpse : 6315.
Corpses in Copses at the Base of Mountain : 5269.
Corpus : 3385.
Corpus Delicti : 5458.
Corpus Domini : 1121.
Corpuscles : 6029.
Corral of Flame Horses : 3920.
Corrections' Officers Certainly Predate Pyramids : 3604.
Corrections to the Saints: Transubstantial : 4643.
The Corrector Speaks : 6942.
Correspondences : 403, 2972, 7352.
Corrido de Chavez Garcia : 158.
Corrido de Ines Chavez Garcia : 1004.
Cosi Fan Tutte : 4578.
Cosmic Orpheus : 3007.
The Cosmic Significance or Rock and Roll : 5022.
Cosmology : 4328, 5091, 6649.
A Costume Straitjacket's Black Sleeve in Armoire Shadows : 1443.
A Cote d'Azur Dessert for Two : 7097.
Cottonmouth Catchers in a Night Swamp : 3425.
The Cougar : 140.
Could it be that the foot : 3431.
Could it be that the long protruding tongue : 1841, 5581.
Couldn't Get Flatter : 42, 4047.
The Council : 5145.
Councils : 5178.
Counter : 308.
The Counterfeiter's Confession : 1209.
Counterpart Wife Clementine : 3867, 5076.
Counterpoint : 6481.
Counting : 4791.
Counting Coyotes to Stay Awake : 250.
Counting Her Syllables Before They're Hatched : 4345.
Counting My Books : 6367.
Counting Potatoes : 3237.
Counting the Black Angels : 5555.
Countless Dark Bodies Are to Be Inferred Near the Sun : 2872.
Countries into Words : 1734.
Country : 2110.
Country and Western : 609, 6434.
Country and Western Torch Song : 4891.
Country Cream : 4748.
A Country Grandson, 1920 : 6228.
Country Incomplete : 6960.
Country Life : 6652.
Country Matters : 5585.
Countryside : 4474.
County Antrim Archeology : 4952.
County Night : 2185.
The Couple Inside of You : 6170.
The Couple on the Roof : 1371.
Couple Touring Black Places : 4659.
The Couple Waking Up in the Hotel Mirror : 4892.
Couplets for the Novelist : 4704.

The Courage of My Fiction : 6904.
Courtesan : 5982.
Courting the Famous Figures at the Grotto of Improbable Thought : 3348.
Courtship : 2869.
The Courtship of Whales : 1567.
Courtyard at Home, Before Autumn : 1348, 5555.
Courtyard Canary : 5121.
Cousin : 4626.
Cousin Michael and the Hognose Snake : 1523.
The Cove at Evening : 6965.
Coven Poems : 564.
Covenant : 3216, 3464.
Coventry : 214.
The Cow : 6253.
Cow Girl Madonna : 3822.
Cow Symphony : 7213.
Cowardice : 5198.
The Cowboy and the Farmer Should be Friends : 2800.
Cowboys : 7095.
Cows : 1845, 3961, 4654.
Coyoacan : 3832.
Coyote : 5744.
Coyote Lunacy : 5087.
Coyote No. 1 : 2656.
Coyote Seduces a Statue : 997.
Coyote Wind : 624.
Coyote's Citizenship : 3920.
Crab : 6156.
The Crab in 1932 : 1755.
Crabapple : 6592.
Crabapples : 5443.
Crabbing : 472, 5451.
Crabs : 427, 4717.
Crack : 3499.
Crack Baby on TV : 5549.
Craft : 4310.
Cranes : 3022.
Cranking the Louvers : 1736.
Craven Images : 336.
Crawling Between Earth and Heaven : 6994.
Crawlspace : 6770.
The Crayfish and Her Daughter : 668, 5974.
A Crazy Guy Put a Gun to Bukowski's Head Once : 2982.
Crazy Horse Mnemonic : 2812.
Crazy Jane's Return : 2332.
Crazy Louie : 1766.
Cream of Rice : 3822.
Creating Multitudes, Repeating : 1126.
Creating Transfiguration : 5606.
Creation Myth : 1636.
The Creations of Sound : 6373.
Creative Writing : 5971.
The Creative Writing Class Goes on Safari : 7045.
Creativity : 6260.
Creativity and Fire : 6500.
Creativity Returns : 4795.
Creature of God : 4032.
Creature of History: A Sequence : 1922.
Creatureliness : 6980.
Creche : 22.

Credo : 1321, 2346, 5344.
Creed : 4141.
Creeping Thyme : 5180.
Crescent : 7220.
Crescent Park : 4489.
Cricket : 7225.
Cricket: An Elegy : 3862.
Cricket crawling : 7077.
Crickets : 5451.
The Crickets : 654.
Crimes Against the Future : 702.
Criminal Intent : 5513.
Crisis : 498, 3516, 5149.
Crisp : 6510.
Cristina's Song : 2307.
Critical History : 7131.
Cro-Magnon : 4542.
Crockett in the Mountains : 6174.
Crocus : 1292.
The Crocus : 3440, 5923.
Croisett, 1853 : 3153.
Crone : 6502.
The Crone I Will Become : 2738.
Cronos and His Children : 525.
The Crooked Waters of the River Might Spell
   : 1324.
A Cross : 3981.
The Cross : 366, 4607.
Cross-Currents : 1135.
The Cross-Man : 1629.
Cross-Street : 4140.
Crossbred Driver : 5339.
Crossed : 6353.
Crossed Histories : 4849.
Crossing : 3089, 3225, 3723, 6181, 6370.
The Crossing : 4928, 5815, 6123.
Crossing Big Cypress : 573.
Crossing / Borders : 3684.
Crossing Georgia : 727.
Crossing into Urbana : 4472.
The Crossing of Orchids : 6742.
Crossing the Bridge : 5036.
Crossing the Street in the Rain : 1284.
Crossings : 2898, 3093.
Crossword : 4703.
Crouched at Lake Raven : 4282.
Crow : 226.
The Crow : 1247, 3800.
Crow Call : 2705.
Crow Light : 2706.
Crow Lore: Crow's First Lesson : 3015.
Crow Moon : 4967.
Crowdoll : 211.
A Crown of Letters to Pancho, After the Fact
   : 3508.
Crows : 625, 2890, 3103.
The Crows : 6060.
Crows Along Paradise Road : 5622.
The Crows' Calling : 3969.
Crow's Last Stand : 3015.
Las Cruces : 4023.
The Crucible : 655.
The Crucified Swimmer : 2351, 3431.
Crucifix : 2881.
The Crucifix Fish : 3918.
Crude Misunderstandings : 7013.

Cruise : 6979.
Cruise Madonna : 3822.
Cruisin the Boulevard : 969.
The Crush : 6229.
The Cry : 620.
Cry in the Night : 1848, 5581.
A Cry in the Night : 6887.
Cry of the Black Crow — and I'm the Glitter
   Easy : 4061.
Cryogenics : 4509.
Cryptic Version of Ecstasy : 448.
Cryptogram : 2126.
Crystal Madonna : 3822.
The Crystal Tree : 121.
Crystals : 621.
Csónak : 4921.
Cuando Morimos : 2678.
¿Cuándo se hizo el vino? : 162, 4170.
Cuando Yo Crezca : 4062.
El cuarto de vidrio : 6148.
Cuban Poetry : 923.
The Cuckoo : 2130, 6674.
'Cuda : 4565.
Cuddyre : 2777.
Cuentista: Story Teller : 4584.
Cul-de-sac : 1152.
Cultivating by Tractor Light : 1106.
The Culvert : 4543.
Cumbia : 4271.
Cunning Convertibles : 7215.
Cunningham Burns, Electrician : 6650.
The Cup : 1270.
Cupola : 1975.
Cups and Saucers : 107.
La Curandera : 2170.
The Curator's Lecture on Birds : 382.
The Cure : 1350.
A Cure for Back Pain : 5918.
A Cure for Smell : 3178.
The Curious : 5070, 5243.
The Curious Little Girl : 7291.
The Current Radio : 4394.
Curse : 1065, 6105, 6310, 6690, 7221.
Curse of the Cusp-Born : 1250.
Curse of the Yellow Bird : 3816.
The Curtain : 979.
The Curve : 4723, 5384.
Curved cardboard applicator : 286.
Custard of the Pawpaw : 409.
Custody : 284.
Customer Persistence : 6690.
Customs : 4842.
Cut! : 3286.
Cut Flowers : 2800.
Cut-Outs : 242.
Cutting a Finger on Obsidian : 2916.
Cutting Down a Tree Still Alive : 15.
The Cutting Garden : 3093.
Cutting Ice : 6663.
Cutting Promises : 1159.
Cutting Remarks : 2008.
Cutting the Maple : 6278.
Cutting the New Year's Firewood : 167, 456.
Cuttings : 6990.
Cuymaca Ordinary : 3160.
Cycle : 2838.

Cycling on Mayne Island : 5061.
Cyclist in Winter Air : 4041.
Cyclonic thoughts encase the rain-engines of imagination : 4835.
Cygnus Olor : 211.
Cynthia : 1590.
(Da un Testo di Zeami) : 5789.
A Da Vinci Autopsy : 1786.
Da Vinci's Man : 7119.
Dachau : 1375.
Dactyls — From Theocritus: Idyl I : 7121.
Dad : 5564.
Dad, on the Anniversary of Your Death : 2833.
Dada Nada Rama : 963.
Daddy : 2124, 6244.
Daddy Was Always Mammy : 2149.
Daddy's Home : 5848.
Daedalus : 1462, 6434.
Daedalus in Sicily : 756.
Daffodildo : 6493.
Daffodils : 4579.
The Dahlia Man : 2417.
Dahlias : 4131.
Daily Lament : 862, 4119, 6730.
Daily Offerings : 6507.
The Daily Work : 1570, 2238.
Daisy : 1122.
Dakota Abstract : 4477.
Dalai Lama : 5801.
Dali's January Moon : 2027.
Dali's Watch : 5327.
Dall'invisibile centro / from the invisible centre : 5789.
Dam Division : 469.
The Damaged Crop : 1056, 2485.
Dame's Rocket : 6285.
The Damp Hips of the Women : 2674.
Dance Coo : 107.
Dance Hall : 5169.
The Dance Has Entered the Streets : 1093.
Dance Lessons : 1395.
The Dance of Adolph and Eva : 3070.
Dance to a Primeval Air : 3046.
The Dancer : 975, 2047.
The Dancer (June 22, 1987) : 4168.
Dances with Sheep Madonna : 3822.
Dancing Alone : 4031.
The Dancing Boys : 802.
Dancing Feet : 7128.
The Dancing Girls at the Diplomat : 7055.
A Dancing Memory / or a Love from Prison : 4054.
Dancing on Water : 1038.
Dancing Static : 5781.
Dancing with Luis Buñuel : 1362.
Dandelion : 5792.
Dandelion Cross : 2716.
Danger of Falling : 2324.
Dangerous : 5933.
The Dangerous Women with Their Cellos : 6445.
The Dani : 6829.
Daniel Boone in Retirement in Femme Osage, Missouri : 1259.
Danse Winnipeg : 3322.

Dante and Virgil Descend into Hell : 4223, 5338.
La Danza Derretida : 4166.
Daphne : 2233.
Daphnia : 625.
Dare : 6242.
The Dark : 1703.
Dark Afternoon : 1028, 2009.
The Dark Back Then : 1778.
Dark City : 503.
The dark clouds are getting lower : 3256, 5638.
Dark Conceit : 5451.
Dark Flowers : 3074.
Dark Harbor : 6412.
Dark Harbour, N.B. : 3634.
Dark Ice : 627.
Dark Matter : 3347.
Dark on Dark : 5089.
Dark Palace : 6026.
The Dark Room: an Invocation : 73.
Dark Turns : 4766.
Dark Victory : 3561.
Dark White Paint : 2095.
Dark Wood : 5259.
The Darkening Green : 3014.
Darkening In : 3956.
Darkening Light : 1181.
The Darker Blue Inside : 1226.
The Darkest Leaves : 781.
The Darkness : 1070.
Darkness Familiar : 4951.
Darkness Too Is a Mirror : 3425.
Darkroom Variations : 5397.
Darksmith : 949.
Darwin and Five Gauchos : 23.
Darwinian : 1396.
Dashed Off : 7109, 7311.
The Date : 2196.
Date Night : 3880.
Daughter : 2387, 4293, 5205.
A Daughter from the Grave : 164, 5824.
Daughter in Spring : 2934.
Daughter of a Friend : 6395.
Daughter of Stockbroker, Beatrice von Guggenburg : 3822.
A Daughter's Fever : 661.
The Daughters of Lions Are Lions Too : 3461.
Daughters of Wisdom : 1292.
Davenning in the Old Age Home : 6538.
David : 3669.
David Ignatow Examines His Motives : 466.
David Johnson: The Thief : 6876.
Dawn : 2767, 3677.
The Dawn Appears with Butterflies : 2623.
Dawn, Blocker's Landing : 7231.
Dawn Heat : 899.
Dawn Kitchen : 4842.
Dawn of the Atom : 333.
Dawn of the Barn Buring : 1972.
Dawnscape : 3101.
The Day a Woman Hit a Doe : 5667.
The Day After Christmas : 3101, 4207.
Day After John Berryman's Suicide January 8, 1972 : 4276.

The Day Arrives : 1104, 4178.
A Day by Gain : 3909.
Day/Care : 1159.
The Day Has Gone : 2360, 2824, 3715.
The Day in Question : 7244.
A Day in the Life : 1343.
The day is where we never arrive : 2815.
Day Lilies : 3465.
Day Lily : 3554.
The Day My Aunt Married a White Man :
    1046.
Day Of : 4495.
A Day of Smoke and Mirrors : 3655.
Day of the Dead : 3205.
The Day of the Sick Man : 5539, 6311.
The Day Old Mermaid Traded Her Fins for
    Feet : 6113.
Day One : 1447.
The Day Speaks : 4289.
The Day the Black Man Came like an Angel :
    7324.
The Day the Leaves Came : 6042.
The Day the War Began : 7324.
The Day You Died I Thought It Would Be
    As Hard As Having to Haul All My
    Furniture into the Back Yard Then
    Sweep Up in Less Than an Hour : 5266.
Days : 1184.
Days in India : 2979.
Days of 1964 : 4411.
Days of Black and White : 824.
Days of Rules : 659.
Days with the Family Realist : 2331.
Dazzle : 5416.
De Bello Civile : 6190.
De Casibus : 6011.
De Chirico's Girl Doesn't Sleep All Night :
    4308.
De Noche : 2352.
De Planctu Naturae : 1754, 3075.
Dead : 5617.
The Dead : 917, 1514, 2818.
The Dead Are Watching Us : 1510.
Dead Baby : 6295.
Dead Dogs R I P : 7254.
The Dead Fox : 229.
Dead Horse Breeder Raises a Ruckus with a
    Beneficiary : 6020.
The Dead in Photographs : 6076.
Dead Man at the Party : 2692.
A Dead Man's Shoes : 2444.
Dead Numbers : 6524.
The Dead of Al-Julaydah, Jan. 14 : 6947.
The Dead Orchard : 3105.
Dead Pet Poem : 5730.
Dead Pig : 1816.
Dead Poets Society : 3617.
Dead Trees in the Dam : 4686.
Dead Wood : 943.
Deaf at the Beach : 4270.
Deaf-Mute : 2739.
Deafened : 6495, 7081.
Dealing with Disorder : 5597.
Dealing with the Dark : 2571.

Dealing with the Fact That My Daughter Has
    Not Slept at My House in 14 Years :
    3855.
Dealings with the Dead : 1667, 2007, 6514.
Dean, Keeping Bees in Kentucky : 4576.
Deanna Maria : 4378.
Dear Birch : 1792, 3446.
Dear Dad : 6866.
Dear Father : 4737.
Dear John, Dear Coltrane : 2636.
Dear Mama,/ I Hate Eggs : 4145.
Dear Mama,/ I Love My New Dress : 4145.
Dear Mama,/ I Think I Am Adopted : 4145.
Dear Mama,/ No One Else in the Whole
    World : 4145.
Dear Miss Angela D. : 4755.
Dear Miss Ross : 138.
Dear Mr. Chinaski : 838.
Dear Neighbor : 5021.
Dear Old Father Marzipano : 5916.
Dear Pound, I Am Leaving England : 5392.
Dear sister Now I Am Away : 2593.
The Death Album : 4869.
Death & Co : 5206.
Death and Silhouettes : 121.
Death as a Cloudless Day : 773.
Death Camp Documentary in Gray and
    White : 4483.
Death Haunts the Brave : 4370.
A Death in the Family : 4470.
Death Is Always Just : 3898.
Death Mass : 6718.
Death of a Biology Teacher : 6104.
Death of a Black Bird : 3276.
Death of a Blackman in a Holding Cell :
    3703.
Death of a Distant In-law : 6678.
Death of a Friend : 3860.
Death of a Scholar : 5315.
The Death of a Small Town : 1878.
The Death of a Swift : 5717.
The Death of All Authority : 1335.
Death of an Actress, Berlin 1937 : 4692,
    5308.
The Death of Anthony Perkins : 2741.
The Death of Audrey : 3679.
The Death of Flash-Back : 6204.
The Death of Lev : 959, 962, 2788.
The Death of Polycrates : 7315.
The Death of Reason : 622.
The Death of Sam Patch : 1743.
Death of the Blues : 4903.
Death of the Marlboro Man : 2649.
The Death of the Spectator : 232.
Death of the Woodcutter : 371, 6768.
Death Poems for My Father : 5265.
Death Says : 3907.
Death Sentence : 678.
Death Sheets : 3311.
The Death Show : 6714.
Death Sits at the Foot of My Bed : 2534,
    3687.
Death, the Last Visit : 2975.
Death to Santa Foy : 5469.
Death Vision : 5606.
Deathbed, Before : 1619.

The Deaths of Poets : 928.
La Debil Llama : 4166.
Debt : 6540.
Debut : 1135.
The Debut : 555, 7315.
Decade : 3150.
Décadence : 1408.
The Decaying Man : 1765.
Deceitful Landscapes : 6411, 6744.
December : 1635, 2332, 5144.
December 22, 1989 : 4439.
December 24, 1959 : 7212.
December 31st : 4343.
December 1909 : 3023.
December Aquarium : 6382.
December Dawn : 6123.
December Walk in Low Country : 7023.
Deception : 4202.
Deciduous : 4615.
Deciduous Desire : 3141.
A Declaration : 4672.
The Decline of the Spanish Empire : 923.
A Declining Neighborhood : 361.
The Decoyed Mistress : 4794.
Decoys : 1821.
Dedham, Seen from Langham : 636, 5804.
Dedication : 76.
Dedication (A.M.P.) : 649, 5929.
Deep and Clear : 4090, 5235.
Deep Blue Flower : 5621.
Deep Green : 3090.
Deep Night : 6218.
Deep North : 5579.
Deep Winter : 1154.
Deer-Gutting : 6958.
Deer Hunting : 1194.
Deer on the Ballfield : 4752.
Deer Park : 362, 363, 6910, 7250.
The Deer Rider : 2297.
The Deerhunter : 703.
Defeat : 1642, 7020.
Defender of the Faith : 6393.
The Defense : 5970.
Deference : 4343.
Defiance : 6154.
Defining : 7203.
Defining Life in the Sonora : 2225.
A Definition of Things : 3107.
Definitions of a Kiss : 5637.
Defoe : 5829.
Deft / Wind : 4495.
Degrazzia : 402.
Degrees of Gray at Northside : 743, 1553, 3138.
Degrees of Unsolvability : 6710.
Déjà Vu : 4325.
Le Déjeuner sur l'Herbe : 7045.
Deli Coffee : 2715.
The Delicate Thing : 2441.
The Delinquency of Winter : 4155.
Delius & Fenby : 6123.
Deliveries : 998, 1700.
Delivery Men : 813.
The Dells : 4796.
Delmar Flies Away : 3920.
Delongpre : 402.

Delphi : 7225.
Delphic : 736, 5804.
Delphine, at Twenty-Two : 2486.
Delta Blues : 4472.
Delta Winter : 4486.
Delusions of Starting Over : 983.
Demain N'Est Pas Encore : 4440.
The Demented Chauffeur : 2030.
Dementia : 6709.
Demeter to the Academic : 106.
Demeter's Lament for Her Coré : 949.
Demetrius Phalereus : 1104, 4178.
Demise of the Sun Parrot : 5869.
Democracy: Chapters in Verse : 2973.
Demolition : 7137.
A Demolition Symphony : 6117.
Demolitions IV : 5813.
Demonry (1939) : 6507.
The Demonstration : 6045.
Denial : 3968.
Denny's Restaurant, 3:00 PM : 4088.
Dental : 6070.
Denver : 755.
Denying Man : 5814, 6521.
Denying the Afternoon with Miss Mei Li : 1794.
The Department Head : 7031.
Departure : 1065, 2095, 3557, 6105, 7221.
The Departure : 3677.
Departure, Nice : 5239.
The Departure of Ceolfrith : 3942.
Departures : 1534.
Departures, Arrivals : 5724.
Dependencies Depend on These : 3358.
Depots : 3247.
Depression : 3822.
Depression Canzone : 6238.
Depression Glass : 1634.
Depression Kid : 838.
Depresssed, She : 3822.
Depuis : 75.
Deranged in the Marina Pacifica Lucky's : 1470.
Derridadaism : 3730.
Désamère : 4834.
Descant : 5134.
Descartes's Lover : 4674.
Descent : 1736, 3623.
The Descent : 2455.
Description : 1645, 2762.
Desdemona's Mother : 6055.
Desenex Every Night : 5504.
The Desert : 3228.
The Desert at Night : 5908.
A Desert Change : 6553.
Desert Flowers : 4513.
The Desert House : 5416.
Desert Love : 3204.
Desert Love, or Echo's Revenge : 2887.
Desert Night, Las Vegas : 4357.
Desert Places : 973.
Desert Poem : 2077, 4103, 5654.
Desert Romance : 2031.
Desert Space : 5792.
Desert Storm's Unknown Soldier : 570.
Desert Woman : 4540.

Deserted City : 436, 1076, 1968.
The Deserted Kingdom : 3256, 5638.
Desertion : 5872.
Desertsong : 7137.
Designs of Skin, Religion, and Trade : 6877.
Desire : 913, 944, 2099, 2202, 3850, 7338.
Desire at Work : 2281.
Desnudo / Aguafuerte : 2162, 4097.
Desperate Seeks Same : 1540.
The Desperate Series I : 30.
Despertar : 143.
Despertar del Desorden : 4147.
Destinations : 6542.
Destinations, Leaving the Map : 386.
A Destroyed Paris Theater : 793.
Destruction : 5868.
Detail from *The Garden of Earthly Delights* :
    2854.
Detail From the Large Work : 4010.
Details : 1897.
Detente : 1890.
Detention : 5831.
Detour : 2457, 4972.
Detroit Summer : 3590.
The Devaluation : 4578.
Development : 30.
The Devil : 6842.
The Devil I Don't Know : 6723.
The Devil in the House : 5828.
The Devil's Rope: Confession of an Abductee
    : 5819.
Devolution : 4132, 6512.
Devotions : 4878.
Devotions of May : 5872.
Dew Drops : 2484, 3809, 4945.
Día de los Muertos : 784.
Diabetes : 3236.
Diacoute : 4607.
Diacritic : 1568.
Dialogue Before Death (1983) : 480, 1524,
    2516.
Dialogue of Soul & Stone : 2705.
Diamond : 6607.
The Diamond Clip : 1749.
Diamond Madonna : 3822.
The Diamond Notebooks II : 5612.
The Diamond of Character : 4530, 6105,
    7221.
Diamonds : 621.
Diane Arbus, New York : 1246.
Diary Entry, 1862 : 6811.
Diary Without Dates, VIII : 189, 4363.
The Dice : 4319.
Dick Cavett : 1398.
Dickens Dickinson Melville Hardy Hugo :
    3877.
Dictation : 1686, 4688.
Dictionary : 4801.
Dictionary Love Poem : 3146.
Dictionary Sam : 5685.
Did You Think I Never Thought About It? :
    420.
Didn't I Say : 2758, 5704.
Didn't They Tell You Stories? : 3741.
Dido Was Smitten : 7347.
Diego Rivera : 4795.

A Diet of Glass : 6841.
Difference : 1645.
The Difference Between Prose and Free
    Verse : 7234.
The difference between the wrong word and
    the right : 2514.
The Differences : 1162.
A Different Landscape : 6157.
A Different Poem : 3309.
Different Porches : 6030.
Different Trains : 6932.
The Difficult Music : 6012.
Difficult Passage : 5885.
La Difunta Correa : 5182.
Digging Out : 6416.
A Digression : 7090.
The Dildo : 4780.
Dime : 1505.
The Dime : 870.
Diminished Decrepitude : 5521.
Diminishing Credo : 2542.
Diminishment : 4901.
Diminuendo : 1322, 3507, 6227.
Dining Out : 5883.
Dinner at Yonekyu : 5814, 6521.
Dinner by Candlelight : 862, 5153.
Dinner Party for One : 6048.
Dinner Table Scenes : 3631.
Dinner Theatre : 3013.
Dinosaur Country : 214.
Diogenes in Athens : 6892.
Diorama : 3499, 4177.
Diotima to Her Most Dedicated Student :
    2824, 3715, 5657.
Diplomacy : 3237.
Diplomatic Imperative : 5394.
The Diplomats : 4923.
Diptera : 3262.
Direction : 2086.
A Direction in Life : 6849.
The Direction of Light : 2898.
Directions : 3423.
Directions for Driving the Tamiami Trail :
    5719.
Directions to the House : 2279.
The Director : 6481.
The Director: Hoover, Edgar J. : 45.
Dirge : 2077, 5789.
Dirge for the New Sunrise : 6115.
Dirt Bikes : 3570.
The Dirty Talker, Boston : 7109.
Disabled Veteran : 5431.
Disaster : 5251.
Disciples Asleep at Gethsemane : 3284.
Disclaimer : 1169.
Disclosure : 3530.
Disco : 4950.
Disco Poetry : 3620.
Discourse : 1207.
A Discourse on Method : 3698.
Discoveries, Trade Names, Genitals, and
    Anciety Instruments : 5352.
Discovering Eve : 6266.
Discovery : 1124.
Discussions : 5326.
Disease : 3379.

A Disease Becoming the Hero : 685.
Disemboweled : 4304.
Disenchantments: Night Thoughts for March 1991 : 1718.
Disengagement : 7225.
The Dish of Fruit : 7121.
Disharmonies in Unpredicted Snow : 4175.
Dishes : 4312.
Dishes & Diapers : 1845.
Dishwasher's Lament : 2865.
Disillusion : 1425, 3230.
Displacement : 4869.
Dispute : 4698, 6908.
A Disquisition on 'Red' : 1807.
Disrepair : 1966.
The Dissected Bird : 1347, 4125.
Dissertation on a Wasp's Nest : 3432.
Dissolving Views : 7033.
Distance : 5099, 7358.
The Distance : 2843, 6154.
Distances : 2027.
The Distant Moon : 923.
Distemper : 4759.
Distillation, February : 125.
Disturbing Thought : 7125.
Diva Obyda : 3263, 5736.
The Diver : 46, 3809, 4945.
The Diversity University Controversy : 4525.
Divestments : 678.
Divided Continent : 5928.
Divided Touch, Divided Color : 5099.
Dividing the Dolls : 6236.
Divinations : 3526.
Divine Collaborator : 6076.
The Divine Sarah : 6218.
Divine Scripture : 1238.
Divining : 382.
Division of Worlds : 5673, 6871.
Divorce : 288, 4669, 7057.
Divorce After Many Years : 3834.
Divorce in Wellfleet, Massachusetts : 1080.
Divorce Poems : 3631.
A Divorced Father Takes His Two Small Children to McDonald's for Breakfast on Easter Morning : 1371.
Dizzy Girls from the '60s : 6242.
Django's Guitar : 5393.
DNA, or, the Legend of My Grandfather : 923.
Do Da Day : 4748.
Do-It-Yourself : 3460.
Do Not Forget in Peace Times : 745.
Do the Dead Dream of Waking? : 2765.
Do You Hear Me? : 3393.
Do You Know Where Your Children Are? : 155.
Do You Know Where Your Daughter Is? : 1264.
Do You Remember : 155.
Do You Think of Me : 3780.
Do You Want a Chicken Sandwich : 6388.
Docile in Dublin : 208.
Dock Lady : 2527.
A Dock Poem : 3120.
Docking, Midmorning : 4377.
Docteur Gachet : 5449.

Doctor : 7095.
The Doctor : 923, 3841.
The Doctor Book : 2833.
Doctor Nitty-Gritty : 2331.
The Doctor Said He Suffered a Stroke, in Those Days There Were Many Strokes : 3195.
A Doctor's Register : 10.
A Document in Madness : 6808.
Documentary : 632.
Does Anyone Ever Learn Anything? : 3877.
Does Enough Happen? : 3352.
Does he want to vanish without a trace : 3547, 5638.
Does the Lethe : 5132.
Dog : 2446, 7226.
The Dog : 4084.
Dog Before the World : 1696.
Dog Days : 332, 7125.
Dog Days of the Empire : 344.
The Dog Without Fleas : 6847.
Dogbone : 2372.
A Dog's Bark Away, Where the Cigar : 808, 2915.
A Dog's Death : 49.
A Dog's Life : 3287, 7003.
The Dog's Life : 7330.
Dogwag Bummerstead : 4274.
Doing Good : 5553.
Doing Lucretius : 864.
Doing the Right Thing : 841.
Doing the Tarantella with Lola Montez : 2173.
Doing Theory : 6231.
Il Dolce Stil Novo : 1383.
Dole : 6690.
A Doll House : 1748.
Dolls : 764.
Dolls and Rags : 1039.
The Doll's-Eye Maker : 5559.
The Doll's Talk in Translation : 6439.
Dolly : 604.
Dolly Varden : 2095.
The Dolphin : 1512.
Dolphin City, Neptune Beach : 5936.
Domestic : 5162.
Domestication : 2858.
The Domicile : 5493.
Don Antonio, at His Club, Shares a Secret : 3518.
Don Giovanni in Hell : 5015.
Don Quixote's Counsel to Poets : 3474.
Donald Duck in Danish : 2331.
Donation : 1582.
Donde Esta Tu Abuela? : 5595.
Donne : 87.
Donor : 4113.
Don't : 5434.
Don't Ask : 486.
Don't Back a Laureate : 3753.
Don't Bank on It! : 2754.
Don't Be Afraid : 2552.
Don't It Make Your Blue Eyes Cry : 5022.
Don't Leave Us, Di : 6690.
Don't Tell *Me* You Don't Like Bukowski : 7087.

Don't Wory : 741.
Doo-Bop : 6500.
The Doodler : 4411.
A Doomsday Library : 6282.
A Door : 6044.
The Door Closing : 7126.
The Door to a Wall : 4698.
Doorbell : 6063.
Doorish : 3389.
The Doors : 7227.
Doorway : 441.
The Doppler Effect : 4165.
Dora : 934.
Dora Ann : 870.
Doré II. *La Pesadilla.* The Nightmare : 5195, 5338.
Dorland : 5451.
Dormi dragostea mea : 4219.
Dorothy Later : 1563.
Los Dos Caminos : 1013.
The Dostoyevsky Face and the Other One : 5546.
A doua poveste pentru stefana : 4219.
The Double : 6111.
Double Crossers : 546.
Double Dactyl : 3624.
Double Feature : 1362.
Double Image : 127, 274, 2240.
Double Imaging : 4587.
Double Scenery : 4531, 4720, 7044.
Double Sonnet: Sunday Drive : 3210.
Double Standard : 4038, 6842.
Double Target : 1762.
Double Triolet : 789, 3146.
The Doubt : 2051, 4390.
Doubts of a Poet-Scholar : 5141.
Dover Sole : 4801.
Doves : 1073, 7266.
The Dowels : 1679.
Down by the rancid River Rockaway : 3372.
Down Front : 1534.
Down into Mill Valley : 6579.
Down the black dirt highways : 6571.
Down the Road : 1207, 7217.
Down There : 1351.
Down to Dream : 5984.
Down to Earth : 4400.
Down to Sleep : 5094.
Down to the Creek : 4616.
Downstairs : 6720.
Downstairs My Son : 5791.
Downtown, Lindberg's, Featuring the Belairs : 549.
Doxology : 417.
A Dozen Things : 3805, 7339.
Dr. Fulton : 5328.
Dr. Kenton Prepares to Run Off to the Creek Again, This Time Dead : 3216.
Draft-Dodger : 5943.
Dragon Bay : 601.
The Dragon Lady and the Nun, 1960 : 149.
Dragonflies : 2095, 6127, 6747.
Dragonfly Days : 1513.
Dragons : 1560.
The Dragons' Soirée : 6590.
Dramatis Personae : 3470.

Drapery Factory, Gulfport, Mississippi 1956 : 6688.
Drastic Measures : 7013.
Drawing Close : 1087, 1731, 6235.
Drawing the Storm : 7180.
Drawn to Water : 2854.
Dream : 172, 6382.
A Dream : 1751, 6983.
The Dream : 2465, 3022, 6386.
Dream III : 3054.
Dream 22: Sitting on a Nest of Swans : 6013.
Dream at the Center of a Seed : 5192, 6870, 7251.
Dream at the Death of James Wright : 798.
Dream Avenue : 6076.
Dream Child : 680.
Dream Cycle : 92.
Dream Factory: The Autobiography of Lana Turner : 6247.
Dream in the Abstract : 6277.
Dream Journals : 448.
The Dream-Language of Fergus : 4311.
Dream Meeting : 3162.
Dream Memorial : 411.
A Dream of Death : 5638, 7026.
Dream of Evil : 303, 6669.
The Dream of Gold : 5979.
Dream of Maria Abruzzino : 459.
A Dream of Newness : 6481.
A Dream of the Three Sisters : 1688.
A Dream of William Carlos Williams : 604.
Dream on Daddy : 5911.
The Dream Remains : 4512, 5598.
Dream Tiger : 4668.
Dream Time : 5139.
Dream Train : 141.
Dreamcats : 4291.
The Dreamer on the Stone Couch Dreams and Wakes : 3989.
The Dreaming : 3598.
Dreaming Anna Mae : 80.
Dreaming Another Verson : 3945.
Dreaming During a Lecture on How to Publish Poetry : 6613.
Dreaming Houses : 706.
Dreaming My Father's Body : 7149.
Dreaming of Baseball : 4294.
Dreaming of Crazy Horse : 4539.
Dreaming of My Wife : 2576, 7298.
Dreaming Space Awake : 4232.
Dreaming the Days : 5557.
Dreaming You Out of Honduras : 6466.
Dreams : 2337, 4512, 5968.
(Dreams) : 3686.
Dreams II : 6054.
The Dreams of Early Mammals : 6404.
Dreams of Interpretation : 1495.
Dreams of Milk and Honey : 1657.
The Dream's Restlessness : 636, 5804.
Dreiser Books Passage : 3554.
Dress : 1991.
A Dress Unknown : 7125.
Dressed to Die : 4774.
Dressed to Spill : 469.
Dressing for the Funeral : 2843.
Dressing the Wound : 2104.

The Dressmaker : 1396.
Dried Flowers in a Milk Bottle : 5061.
Dried Out Plants : 1845.
Dried Prunes : 3468.
The Drift : 6631.
Driftwood Days : 1375.
Drinking with Sparrows : 3222.
Drinks in the Town Square : 7033.
Drive Thru : 833.
The Driver Ant : 3961.
Driving : 38, 454, 2461, 4509, 6000.
Driving Back from the Hospital in the Rain : 3822.
Driving Cattle Through Washington : 2313.
Driving, Highway 15 : 1343.
Driving Independence Day : 7290.
Driving into the Unbeautiful City : 3638.
Driving Like Mad : 2614.
Driving North : 973, 4876.
Driving on Empty : 4672.
Driving, Some Used Cars : 4528.
Driving to Judgement : 3753.
Driving Up Baja California, Norte : 4377.
Driving with the Dead : 4846.
Drought : 336, 6032, 6292.
Drought in the Alps : 4428.
Drought Rain : 3145.
Droughtmonger : 3890.
Drowned Sailor 1946 : 6919.
Drug Store Trolls : 6319.
Drugstore Cowboy : 4885.
Drumology : 3126.
Drunk Talking to No One : 4467.
The Drunkard's Last Words : 5295.
The Drunkard's Prayer : 1535.
Drusilla, After Writing Her Third Letter to Her Exiled Husband, Ovid : 1259.
Dry Dream : 310.
Dry Ground : 4417.
Dry Moon : 2095.
Dry Toast : 264.
Dry Twigs : 1746.
Dryland Farmer : 7141.
Drylot : 6976.
Drzazga Mojej Wyobrazni : 5254.
Dual Vision : 3184.
Duck Eye : 2884.
Duck-Hooks and Slices: Hazards, Handicaps, Poetry : 6158.
Duckling, Swan : 1793.
The Ducks : 6356.
Ducks on Thin Ice : 4774.
Dude Descending a Staircase : 5122.
Due Direction : 154.
Los Duendes : 4990.
Duet : 1727.
Dugout : 862, 5343, 6844.
Dulcza Wielka : 6138.
The Dull Lecture : 435.
The *Dumka* : 1878.
Dundee : 863.
Dune : 214, 4171.
Dunham's Dance : 5678.
Dunlins : 1380.
Dupe University : 2800.

Durante el viento helado de anoche nevó y nevó : 4170, 7297.
Dürer's Rhinoceros : 333.
During a Calm, My Brother and I Clear the Driveway : 3467.
During Celibacy the Mind Tends to Wander : 5424.
During the Prelude : 1397.
During These Hours : 3891.
Durmiendo Junto al Río : 5689.
Dusk : 3339.
Dusk: December 10, 1991 : 1259.
Dusk in the Garden : 3658.
Dust : 352, 385, 865, 6418.
Dust Devil : 6042.
Dust on the Water : 5517.
Dusting Doll Dishes : 6734.
Dustmice Are the 1950s : 4091.
The Dwelling : 1969.
DWF, 36, Sensitive, Stunning, Petite, Sexy . . . : 5283.
Dyeing Wool : 4302.
Dying : 1952, 3266, 5624.
Dying Dog Mantra : 3019.
The Dying God : 2917.
Dying to Shout : 4630.
Dynamics : 7014.
The Dynamite Confession of Eraser Grunt : 6452.
E.J. Bellocq: Storyville Portraits, 1912 : 569.
E.S.P. : 6994.
E. W. Burns Shoe Salesman : 502.
Each Breath More Precious : 3604.
Each Leaf Individual : 3528.
Each morning i pull myself out of despair : 1149.
Each night my mouth, my cough, my sweat : 5113.
Each Sound a Bird : 4613.
Each Step : 2869.
An Eagle above Mt. Hunger : 381.
The Eagle and the Worm : 5922, 5974.
An Eagle Finer Than Truth : 1900.
The ear no longer hears the echo : 2133, 6239.
Ear Training : 4789.
Ear   virus   *(character)* • *(dementia)*virus : 511.
Early : 1428, 6864.
An Early Afterlife : 5050.
Early Daffodils : 6174.
An Early Garden : 678.
Early in the Morning : 143, 3786.
Early March in the Park : 444.
Early Morning: Ludvika, Sweden : 5408.
Early Morning Mire with Betty : 574.
Early Morning Quiet : 3972.
Early Music : 653.
Early Riser : 4257.
An Early Sequence : 7175.
Early Sonnet : 5286.
Early Spring : 540.
The Early Years : 6544.
Earrings : 1627.
Ears : 2700.
Ears, Not Knees : 5491.

Earth : 248, 1524.
Earth and Sky : 4769.
The Earth Is a Living Thing : 1149.
The Earth Worm : 3772.
Earthbound : 7120.
Earthlight : 4957.
Earthquake : 4081.
The Earthquake : 3723.
The Earthquake (1047) : 1190, 2587.
Earthward Gliding : 4067, 6799.
East Boogie Rap : 4734.
East Bronx : 3054.
East Shore, New Haven Harbor : 2428.
East Side Friday Evening : 6224.
East Texas Wild Life : 5198.
East Thirtieth Street : 2599.
Easter : 2406.
Easter 1991 : 2437.
The Easter Bunny Talks : 563.
Easter in the Campground : 7129.
Easter Morning : 1294, 6299.
Easter with the Ukrainians : 4000.
Eastlake Avenue Bar : 5082.
Eastpoint, Bill's Grocery, and Love : 472.
Easy Living : 6966.
The Easy Part : 2405.
Easy to Say, Easy to Say : 5555.
The Easy Way : 5286.
Eat That Chicken : 4198.
Eat Your Heat Out : 6377.
Eating Baby Jesus : 7241.
Eating Crabs with Bob and Jim : 5753.
Eating Death : 5606.
Eating Disorder Madonna : 3822.
Eating Smarties in the Truck : 6587.
Ebb-Tide : 4472.
Ebenezer : 6661.
Ebony : 2150.
Ecclesiastical History : 6283.
Echo : 1321, 3805, 5155, 7247.
The Echo : 5808.
Echo for an Anniversary : 288.
Echo of a Scream : 5394.
Echoes : 3866, 5778.
Echolocation : 2890.
Eclipse : 331, 3452, 3682.
The Eclipse : 4472.
Eclogue One: Honour : 5562.
Ecology : 911.
Economics : 2678, 3673.
Economies : 3114.
L'Ecrevisse et Sa Fille : 668.
Ecstasy : 448, 979.
Ecstatic : 3499.
Ed Rollins Speaks : 6690.
Edda, Will You Walk with Me Tonight? :
    1299.
Eddy : 2670.
Eddying : 6228.
Eden : 1344, 5373.
Edgar Degas (1834-1917) : 2345.
Edge : 5206.
Edge of a Field : 6335.
The Edge of Something : 2441.
Edges : 820, 3554.
Edges of Wales : 5986.

Editing the Anthology : 3822.
Editorial : 1401.
The Education : 2426.
The Education of Hawa : 4497.
Edvard Munch's Magnetic Shoes : 6954.
Edward R Murrow : 3822.
Edwardians (Old Photograph) : 1462.
Eel : 1628.
Eerie Dreams : 5638, 6651.
Effect Over Distance : 2331.
The Efficacy of Anything : 550.
Efficiency, Ecstasy : 1316, 6235.
Effie's Excursion : 7217.
Effigy : 720.
Egg Roast : 2095.
Eggplant : 6328.
Eggs are months and days too : 715, 4875.
Eggsaggeration : 2711.
Egress : 2710.
The Egypt Street : 1966.
Egyptian Cotton : 4428.
Eidolons : 2812.
Eigenheim : 3664.
Eight Months Pregnant in July, High Noon,
    Segesta : 4944.
Eight Parents : 5416.
Eight Tattoos : 3570.
Eighth Air Force : 3147.
Eighth Grade Acrostic : 2560.
Eighth Grade Science at Blessed Sacrament :
    1025.
An Eighth Grader's Prayer : 7255.
The Eighth Month : 3805, 7338.
Einstein Looking Down : 398.
Einstein's Colour : 5416.
Einstein's Curse : 409.
Einstein's Violin : 5869.
E.J. Bellocq: Storyville Portraits, 1912 : 569.
Ejaculation : 172.
El Elvis : 3279.
El — Mentido Adios : 4512.
El — Presencia : 4512.
Elation Translation for Melinda : 3298.
Elderberry-Blossom : 188, 605.
The Elderly Ladies : 6130.
Eldridge Cleaver Addresses the East Lake
    Baptist Church : 4486.
Election Day Barrel Fire : 4315.
Election Year : 511.
Elective Mutes : 752.
Electric Heart : 1051.
The Electronic Generation : 2768.
Elegance : 909.
The Elegance of a Withered Flower : 7354.
Elegia a Maurice Bishop : 4592.
Elegiac Stanzas : 632.
Elegy : 488, 4178, 5483, 5935, 6932, 7279.
Elegy: Adieu near those fields that smoke
    disembowels : 214, 4171.
An Elegy, After RMR : 4077.
Elegy and Rant for My Father : 6031.
Elegy for a Dog Larger Than Life : 1198.
Elegy for a Former Neighbor Whose Name
    I've Forgotten : 3153.
Elegy for a Log-Truck Driver : 4867.
Elegy for a Mariachi : 5118.

Elegy for Cuz : 2196.
Elegy for Empire : 7182.
Elegy for Laverne : 4683.
An Elegy for Lorraine Hansberry : 6966.
Elegy for Maurice Bishop : 1450, 4592.
Elegy for My Brother : 1688.
Elegy for Orchardist and Orchard : 5021.
Elegy for Peter : 6988.
Elegy for Rajiv : 5395.
Elegy for the Eastern League : 244.
Elegy for the Living : 1433.
Elegy for the Old Mexican Woman and Her
    Dead Child : 2507, 5790.
Elegy for William Mathias : 2182.
Elegy in Blue and White : 2425.
Elegy in March : 5463.
Elegy: No God can make my words ring free
    or clang : 7359.
Elegy: O loveliest daughter of Hsieh : 2576,
    7298.
Elegy to an Adobe Wall : 5150.
Elementary Algebra : 2466.
Elepaio : 2095.
An Elephant : 1821.
Elephant Butte, Utah : 1768.
Elephant Dream : 1176.
Elephant Meditation : 119.
Elephants : 7200.
Elisabeth : 4293.
Elixir : 3833.
Elizabeth and Sally : 351.
Elizabeth, Mother of John the Baptist : 842.
Elk : 6832.
The Elke Sommer Story : 6067.
Ella — No Es Fácil : 4512.
Ella Respira la Sombra : 461.
Ellsworth Kelly's *White Curve VIII* : 2659.
Elm Street : 1616.
Elocution Lesson : 4578.
Elocution Lessons : 385.
Eloquence : 6573.
Eloquent Lingo : 180.
Elsewhere : 865, 4836.
Elsewhere and Otherwise : 7184.
Elsie's Pearl Necklace : 6966.
Elusive Pisces : 2689.
Elves : 3078, 5241, 6235.
Elvis is *Dead*, Bubba : 1437.
Embalming : 2367.
Embarrassments : 401.
Ember : 3789.
Emblems Merge Blood, Lick Empires, Map
    Song : 6884.
The Emerald Tattooed on My Arm : 6858.
The Emergence of Flight from Aristotle's
    Mud : 2331.
Emergency : 2265, 2957.
Emerson: Concord, 1882 : 6321.
Emigration : 3053, 6235.
The Emigration : 3677.
Emily Dickinson: A Clerihew : 304.
Emily Dickinson's Answerphone : 1332.
Emily Dickinson's Writing Table in Her
    Bedroom at the Homestead, Amherst,
    Mass : 4892.
Emily Was Right : 5687.

Emily's Dreams : 5691.
Emissaries : 5606.
Emma Remembers Somethinig of the World
    Series : 4996.
Emma's Kiss, Redeemed : 4996.
Emma's Nursery Rimes : 503.
Emmet Street : 6350.
Emotional Detachment : 3457.
Empedocles' Physics : 2869.
The Emperor's Rejoinder : 6135.
Empire : 670, 5801.
Empire of Dreams : 715, 4875.
The Empire of Snow : 1226.
Employment : 2678.
Emptiness : 5371, 5731, 6653.
The Emptiness Between My Hands: Poems
    to Prove the Photographs in *The Family
    of Man* Published by the Museum of
    Modern Art : 5113.
The Empty Angel : 6791.
The Empty Bed : 2521.
Empty Cage : 118.
Empty / Day : 4495.
The Empty Dish : 5956.
Empty Hallways : 7294.
Empty Hands : 5145.
Empty House : 2576, 7298.
Empty Rooms : 3021.
En la montaña con agua clara hago casa de
    hierbas junto a la roca : 162, 4170.
En la Siesta : 4841.
En mi buhardilla : 212.
En Nueva York : 5618.
The Enchanted World of Fairytale : 2617,
    2915.
Enchantment : 872.
Encierro : 971.
The Encircling Memory : 114, 4291.
Enclosure : 2762, 3011.
Encomium : 5940.
Encounter in The Hague : 2335.
Encounter on the Street : 3557.
Encounter with an African Princess : 2054.
Encounter with La Llorna upon His Return
    from Harvard : 3914.
Encuentro : 277.
The *Encyclopaedia Britannica* Uses Down
    Syndrome to Define 'Monster' : 2950.
The End : 686, 1581, 4419.
The End and the Beginning : 327, 1022,
    6514.
The End Is an Animal : 3328.
End Notes : 4532.
The End of an Era : 4776.
The End of Black and White : 6991.
End of Run : 6458.
The End of the Affair : 150.
End of the Century : 1667, 2007, 6514.
End of the Day : 3743.
The End of the History Lesson (Professor
    Guillaume) : 955, 4219, 5236.
The End of the Pier : 6123.
The End of the Welfare State : 1760.
The End of the World : 1204, 5638, 6651.
The End of Waiting : 5724.
The End, the Beginning : 7148.

An Ending : 4983.
Endive : 4428.
Endnote : 979.
The Ends of the Earth : 149.
Endsheet : 2300.
Endurance : 7316.
The Enemy : 454.
Enero : 2796.
L'Enfant sur le Toit : 1408.
Enfin : 4578.
The Engineer : 3301.
English 123 Discusses Virginia Woolf : 1844.
English con Salsa : 6750.
English Summer, 1861 : 1910.
Englit : 921.
Engravings in the Books of the 17th Century Scientist/Mystic Athanasius Kircher : 2331.
Enigma Variations : 486.
Enisled : 2850.
Enivrey-Vous : 403.
The Enlightenment : 4565.
Enniscorthy, Virginia : 7023.
The Enormous Engine : 2441.
Enough to Make Him Howl : 1461, 1524.
Enough with This Horible War : 806, 2868.
Entelechy Just Happens : 1032.
Enter the VIRUS : 2699.
Entering Beijing : 1160.
Entering History : 6299.
Enterprise : 4036.
Entertainment Tonight : 5763.
Enthalpy : 2145.
Entire Dilemma : 848.
Entire Lives : 2331.
The Entomologist : 836.
Entomology : 5405.
Entrance to the View : 5434.
Entrenched : 694.
Entry : 4417.
Entry in a Baby Book: Two Weeks : 2655.
Envidia Does Not Translate : 3708.
The Environmentally Sound : 3386.
Environs of Tangiers 1912 : 1905.
Envy : 2208.
Epejos Negros / Los Caminos del Silencio : 4069.
Epernay : 4088.
Epic : 3807, 3810, 5885.
Epidermal Hell : 3816.
The Epigone : 5787.
Epigrams : 283, 4149.
Epileptic's Song : 7359.
Epiphanies (1993-A) : 3521.
Epiphanies of an Old-Model Hoover : 6299.
Epiphany : 6796.
Epiphany 1992 : 2228.
The Epistemology of Rescue : 1300.
Epitaph : 143, 3786.
Epitaph for a Transsexual Dead of AIDS : 784.
Epitaph for Etheridge Knight : 687.
Epitaph for J.V. Cunningham (1911-1985) : 1562.
Epitaph for Our Cook : 5916.
Epithalamion : 5991, 6217.
Epithalamium : 4685.
Építök : 4921.
Epoch : 7105.
Eppur Si Muove : 6112.
Equal Opportunity : 3946.
Equanimity : 3346.
Equations : 6834.
Equilibrium : 2821.
Equinox : 73.
Equipoise : 829.
Equity : 3632.
Era Una Vez America : 5024.
Erano Passi : 4546.
Erasure : 3596.
Eravamo a Napoli : 1887.
Erma Jacowitts Pleads Her Case : 3500.
Eros Thanatos : 143, 3786.
Erotic Thoughts As the World Prepares for War : 1129.
Errata : 548, 2220.
Errata 5uite : 5467.
The Error : 2334.
The Errors of the Mythopoetic Search : 3420.
An erudite scholar of Michelangelo : 5132.
Erudites on Campus : 794, 2360, 5470.
The Escape Artist : 3730, 7290.
Escaping : 6665.
Escaping Eden : 472.
Escucha : 3680.
Eskimos Carving : 1978.
E.S.P. : 6994.
L'Espirt de L'Escalier : 2340.
Essay: Empire Poets : 511.
Essays : 6625.
Estate Sale: The Scrabble Game of a Dead Woman : 4845.
Estella Inscrita : 6759.
Estella Thinks of Pip : 1302.
Esto es distinto : 715.
Estrangement : 7239.
Eszter's Swim : 5867.
Et in Arcadia Ego : 2396.
Etait-ce le monde et l'arc-en-ciel : 1285.
The Eternal City : 6090.
Eternity : 3354, 4472.
Eternity Blues : 979.
Eternity Suffers from Distemper : 1156.
Ethics of the Fathers : 7353.
Ethnic : 3167.
Ethnic Cleansing : 5512.
Ethnic Disturbances : 1337.
Etiquette : 5763.
Etymology: the Com- of 'Compassion' : 2331.
Eucharist : 2202.
Euphony : 1870.
Eureka : 5379.
Euridice at THE HAPPY TAP : 1724.
Europe : 2465.
Eurydice : 1550, 3952.
Eurydice Reveals Her Strength : 6302.
Eurydice Spoke to Orpheus Mostly in Prose : 230.
Eva : 3868.
Evacuees : 1750.
Evangeline : 4924.

Evaporations : 442, 3058, 5804.
Eve : 7353.
Eve Alone : 74.
Eve As a Paperdoll : 606.
Eve at the Paradise : 2437.
The Eve of Rosh Hashanah, 500 Years after the Inquisition : 1082.
Eve Out of Season : 5466.
Eve Reflecting on Her Fall from Innocence : 4507.
Eve Speaks to God : 6105, 7221.
Even at Night : 4291, 4512.
Even If the Snow Should Fall : 4427.
Even in Ruins : 143, 3786.
Even into the Night : 5673, 6871.
An Even Number : 6129.
The Even Shorter Gavin Ewart : 2137.
Even Song : 6827.
Even still perception moves : 504.
Even the Vanishing Housed : 2869.
Even Then : 1534.
Even Though I Waited : 3276.
Evening : 4346, 5792.
Evening Air : 1696.
Evening in South Africa : 1944.
The Evening is Red : 299, 843.
Evening News : 5111.
Evening Practice : 4842.
The Evening Slips Off Me : 2072, 7161.
Evening — 'So This Is My Life Now' : 4698.
Evening Song : 4495.
Evening Train : 3772.
Evening Visitor : 6076.
Evening Walk : 4334, 5539.
Evening Wind : 3285, 3479.
An Evening with the Author : 3523, 3745, 6195, 6196, 6506.
Evenings with Grandmother : 5948.
Evensong : 2369.
Event Horizon : 6307.
The Event of Her Missing Body : 3335.
Events : 5494.
Eventually : 2947.
Ever Since : 75.
Ever So Close : 6985.
Everglades Canal : 5727.
The Everlasting Yes : 6716.
Every Definitive in July : 891.
Every Future Climb : 4682.
Every Island a God : 6676.
Every Night : 6788.
Every night I dream : 5230.
Everybody's Baby : 485.
Everyday Occurrence : 693, 4942.
Everyone Will Write Poetry : 3853, 4460.
Everything Changes to Beauty : 869.
Everything Good between Men and Women : 7220.
Everything Happens to Me : 1366.
Everything in Relation to the Sky : 4864.
Everything That Rises Must Convene : 2435.
Everything Where I Left It : 2333.
Everywhere Is Out of Town : 7290.
Everywhere We Go : 5465.
Eve's Daughters : 2345.
Eve's Lament : 6505.

Evidence : 2845, 6299, 6932.
The Evidence of Miracles : 111.
The Evidence Suggests She Was Never a Slave : 6174.
The Evil Eye : 4112.
Evolution : 5678, 6468.
Evolution and Poetry : 2880.
The Evolution of the Flightless Bird : 3375.
The Evolution of the Piano : 7095.
The Ewe of the Vapors : 2051, 5017.
Ex-Brother-in-Law : 4249.
Ex-Ho : 3876.
An Examination of the Body : 5638, 6116.
The Example of the Cat : 392.
Exams : 4647.
Excathedra : 1618.
Excavations : 4741.
The Exchange : 4950.
Exchange: A Memoir : 4159.
An Exchange Between Levi Ibn Al-Tabban and Yehuda Halevi : 57, 67, 2548.
Excitement, The Need for : 5813.
Excused by the First Thing in His Mind : 1291.
Excuses 2 : 625.
Exemplary Life Above Ground : 103.
The Exhausted Bug : 604.
Exile : 829, 1968, 5891.
An Exiled Child's Letter : 1792, 3446.
The Exiled Poet Nazim Hikmet Writes a Letter to His Country from Varna, Bulgaria, a Year Before His Death in 1963 : 3289.
Exiles : 378.
Existential Moments : 6947.
The Existentialist : 6218.
Existentialists : 6970.
Exodus : 4950, 5937.
The Exorcism : 858.
Exotic : 7046.
Exotica / Babysitting / Scherzo #1 : 3668.
Expatriate Babble : 1794.
The Expatriate Returns to Dream Street : 1794.
Expect the Worst : 2394, 3035, 4438.
Expectation : 188, 1118.
Expectations : 518.
Expecting : 7.
Expecting Summer : 1172.
The Expedition : 2873.
Experiment : 182.
An Experiment : 4161, 6289.
Experiments : 7027.
The Experts, the Man in the Street, the Crowd : 2173.
Explaining a Few Things : 6076.
Explaining the Eastern Wahoo Tree to Girl Scouts : 1737.
Exploring the Dark : 343.
Exploring the Poles : 6617.
The Explosion : 740.
Explosive Decibel Journeys : 79.
Exposure : 2761.
Expressions in Cement : 5636.
Expulsion : 1492.
Extended Care Facility : 6707.

Extended Metaphor : 6599.
Exteriority : 6864.
'Extinct Moon' No. 15 : 6954.
Extinguished : 2147, 2742.
Extra Innings : 5607.
Extract from Antarctica : 469.
Extramadura : 1749.
Extraordinary References : 6373.
Extravagant : 154.
The Extravagant : 6682.
Eyat : 5750.
The Eye : 899.
Eye : Void : Matter : 5927.
The Eye and the Heart : 112.
Eye Brooch : 1109.
Eye Cannot Edit : 6008.
The Eye of the Hawk : 2759.
Eye on the Sparrow : 4209.
Eye to Eye : 1565.
Eyes : 3650, 4890.
The Eyes of the Bull : 62, 2824, 3715.
The Eyes of Travel : 6619.
Ezra Pound: Binghampton, New York,
     11/2/72 : 7188.
Ezra Pound, Ode : 1551.
The F.B.I. Involvement Rumor : 996.
The f in soft-pedal : 146.
F Stop : 713.
A Fable : 2749, 5638.
Fable du Monde : 2180, 6459, 6459.
Fabliette de la Souris : 2494.
Fabric : 3637, 3659, 4877, 6443.
Fabrics : 7144.
Façades for Theron Ware : 2294.
Face to Face : 3772, 5165.
Faces II : 6591.
Faces Imagined Rise Up : 4834.
Facets of a Name : 1640.
Facing a Stone : 2697, 3176, 4545.
Facing Both Ways : 3162.
Facing the Leopard : 511.
Facing the Music : 683.
Facing the Truth : 6447.
Fact : 4378.
Factory Sacrifice : 172.
The Facts Speak : 4451.
The Faculty Club: A Table of Truth : 6917.
Faery Ring : 6562.
Fagerfjäll, Tjörn, 1986. For Pentti : 3762,
     6230.
Faggot : 6485.
Fahrenheit 451 : 7175.
Failed Memory Exercise : 3237.
Fair Exchange : 1016, 2001.
Fairgrounds : 2615.
Fairy Tale : 6254.
Fairy Tales : 4109.
Fait Accomplis : 3196.
Faith : 329, 336, 1188, 2392, 2451, 6607.
Faith in Flight : 177.
Faith of an Old Man : 2899.
Fall : 279, 310, 1207, 1871, 3292, 5063,
     6740, 7064, 7143.
The Fall : 3881.
Fall in L.A. : 6970.
Fall in the Tuileries : 350.

Fall Turns Us Too : 5301.
Fallen Apples : 939.
Fallen Leaf : 7175.
The Fallen Nest : 4253.
The Faller : 1612.
Falling : 1423, 2902, 3429.
Falling Asleep : 2446.
Falling in Love over Dallas : 4282.
Falling in October #3 : 719.
Falling in October #4 (Possession Landscape)
     : 719.
Falling Off : 4483.
Falling Snow : 2697, 3176, 4545.
Fallingwater : 6733.
Falls : 6640.
The Falls : 5785.
Falls to the Floor, Comes to the Door : 214.
False Dawn : 6043.
The False Morel's Formula : 1314.
False Pregnancy : 6576.
False Tracks : 426, 5717.
La Familia Sagrada : 2850.
Family : 1401, 2732.
Family Fight : 1259.
Family Formicidae : 620.
Family Gathering : 7032.
Family Matters, Sex, and Other Concerns :
     1534.
Family Memoirs : 6005.
Family Outing: Yorkshire : 7041.
The Family Plot : 6154.
Family Portrait : 2386.
Family Portrait, 1963 : 6691.
Family Possessions : 2300.
Family Romance : 424, 1520.
Family Still Life : 6818.
Family Tradition : 4454.
Family Week at Oracle Ranch : 4411.
Famous Doctor : 2625.
Famous Moments : 4316.
Famous Vegetarians : 3272.
Fang : 2331.
Fans : 5706.
Fantasia of the Bride : 3237.
Fantasies of Coma : 5998.
Fantasma : 3098.
Fantasmas : 277.
Fantasy : 607, 3182.
Fantasy Poems : 4176.
Far Away from the House and the Voices, the
     Crying, the Slam of the Back Screen
     Door : 4917.
(Far Away Near) : 5011.
A Far Cry from Africa : 6859.
Far from Home : 1112.
Far-Off Atlantic Nights : 4472.
The Far-Removed Mountain Men : 979.
Far Sleep : 2428.
Farcical Eye : 93.
Farewell : 40, 6412.
The Farewell : 636, 5804.
Farewell Letter : 173, 5638.
Farewell Song for the Author : 646, 2076.
Farewell to the Sea : 4624.
The Farm : 515, 2570.

Farm Accident with Heron and Freckles : 3944.
A Farm in Kansas : 5454.
Farm Life : 5299.
Farm Stories : 5179.
The Farmboy, Before He'd Seen Paris : 4980.
The Farmer from the Mill House Door : 3216.
Farmer's Market : 5069.
The Farmer's Mistress : 6598.
Farming in Doohat : 4873.
A Farmwife and Son : 6658.
Farrier Talk : 6299.
Fascinating Four : 1056, 2485.
Fashion : 1144.
Fast : 5644.
Fast Loans : 3545.
The fast train? The express? : 389, 442, 5804.
Fat Angels : 4377.
A Fat Man Makes History at Mabel's Cafe : 433.
Fat Woman Talking : 5979.
Fate and the Future : 1777.
Fate Map : 3246.
The Fate of Women : 6536.
Father : 2027, 4881, 5187, 5211.
A Father : 5708.
Father Above : 5936.
Father and Son in 1934 Attend the Sunday Ball Game, Arriving and Leaving Separately : 1708.
The Father and the Son : 826.
Father Andrew Considers Evil : 3103.
Father Andrew's Creed : 3103.
Father Falling : 5709.
Father I Starve : 4378.
Father, Mother, Robert Henley, Who Hanged Himself in the Ninth Grade, et al : 1720.
Father Scarmark — World War I Hero — and Democracy : 7295.
Fatherhood in Middle Age : 3234.
The Fatherland : 4621.
Fathers : 4483.
Fathers and Sons : 2644.
Father's Day, 1993 : 2326.
A Father's Deafness Late in Life : 1297.
Father's Disaster Tale : 6650.
Father's Fall : 3504.
Father's Gloves : 7149.
The Father's Life, the Mother's Death : 2404.
A Father's Pain : 5651.
Father's Voices : 4987.
Fatslug and the Bumperstickers : 4577.
Faulkner at Work : 2272.
Faulkner in Hollywood : 748.
The Fault : 4076.
Faultline : 2132.
Faultlines : 2521.
Faust : 1201.
La Fauvette des Jardins : 3192.
Favorite : 5692.
Favors : 2305.
The Favour of 40 Years : 550.
The F.B.I. Involvement Rumor : 996.
Fear II : 1120, 2833.
Fear Ghazal : 3640.

Fear in a Public Place : 3611.
The Fear of Being Noticed : 5525.
Fear of Death Awakens Me : 3381.
Fear of Reconstruction : 4199.
Fear that the Bough : 942.
Fearful Moments : 1483, 2701.
A Fearful Symmetry : 1194.
Feast Day : 6076.
The Feast of Saint Joseph : 536.
Feast of San Gennaro : 6333.
The Feast of the Tangible : 2843.
The Feast Under the Clitoris-Tree : 5416.
Feather Merchant : 2095.
February : 762, 2892, 3494, 5763.
February 29 : 1025, 6887.
February '63 : 5830.
(February '92) : 5011.
February 1922: My Father's Conception : 3656.
February 1944 : 5473.
February Heat : 3353.
February Morning : 979.
February Walk Near False Creek Mouth : 108.
February's Air of Waiting : 4969.
Feed Beetles : 3216.
The Feeder : 1270.
Feeding Birds : 4033.
Feeding My Angel : 6710.
Feelers : 6842.
Feeling Old in New Chinatown : 206.
The Feet of Pilgrims : 6699.
Felina : 3914.
Feline Mediator : 6172.
Felis Domestica : 3555.
Fellini y Yo : 6218.
Female Navigation (1818) : 422.
Feminine Metaphysics : 6377.
Fence : 47.
The Fence : 4410.
Fence Mouse : 2095.
A Fence of Lights : 5592.
Fengdu Infrastructure : 2904.
Fenway Park : 4564.
Fer de Lance : 4029.
Ferns : 5265.
The Fertile Imagination : 930.
A fervor parches you sometimes : 5473.
Festival in Fishing Village No. 5 : 3479, 5027.
Festival in the Park : 6030.
Festive Snow : 1372.
Festividad del Dulcisimo Nombre : 5657.
Fetchin' Bones : 1743.
Fever : 3780.
The Fever Squeezes the House : 1666.
A Few Good Women : 6432.
A Few Moments : 1706.
Few Understand : 49.
A Few Words More : 4424.
A Few Words Were All He Needed : 2154.
The Fiction Writer : 404.
Fiddle Player Dreams of Skinks : 6018.
Field : 1512.
A Field, a Lily, a Great White Egret : 1226.
Field Report from Sodom : 3490.

Field Study: A Sestina : 6512.
Field Trip : 7290.
Field Trip to My First Time : 2629.
Field Work : 2725.
The Fields : 1458, 6060.
Fields of Buffalo : 4282.
The Fields of January : 6527.
Fields of Words : 2210.
Fierce : 5367.
A Fiery Courtship : 7125.
Fifteenth Child : 5084.
Fifth Avenue Uptown: James Baldwin, 1924 -
    1987 : 6162.
The Fifth Man : 2276, 5013, 7342.
Fifth Symphony : 4667.
The Fifth World Nation Attends Sunset on
    Wolf Creek Pass : 6746.
Fig : 4866.
The Fighter : 4191.
Fighting Society : 2287.
Fighting the Elements : 5615.
Il Figlio dell'Uomo Fa l'Aeroplano : 6754.
Figs : 43.
Figurating : 2331.
Figure : 6112.
Figure and Ground, or, Art Up to Its Neck in
    History : 725.
Figure / Ground : 388.
Figure on the Edge : 6432.
Figures Among the Fauves : 6336.
Filaments : 169.
Filial Affection : 2419.
Fill 'Er Up : 2211.
Filling in the Blanks : 5910.
Filling Out the Form : 6682.
Filling Station Poems : 6709.
The Film : 1960.
Film Noir : 303, 5809.
Final Anthropic Principle : 6120.
Final Exam : 6175.
The Final Poltergeist of Pompeii : 79.
The Final Shocker : 6690.
Final Song : 2500.
The Finale : 1624, 2697, 6907.
Finally Learning to Hate : 5063.
Finally, the Truth about Critics : 3127.
A Finding : 2532.
Finding Horse Skulls on a Day That Smelled
    Like Flowers : 2773.
Finding Myself : 3607.
Finding Oscar Wilde : 350.
Finding the Worry Stones : 4016.
Finding What's Lost : 3683.
Fine China : 5454.
Fine Lines : 5685.
Fine New Stances Toward the World : 2498.
The Fine Printing on the Label of a Bottle of
    Non-alcohol Beer : 3920.
Fingernails, Nostrils, Shoelaces : 838.
Fingerprints : 314.
Fingers in Popcorn : 676.
Fingertips : 839, 4300.
Fiona's Dream : 4136.
Fire : 493, 4122, 4859, 5801.
The Fire : 2869.
Fire and Ashes : 4427.

Fire and Flood : 7122.
Fire and Ice : 6236.
Fire and Water : 1337.
Fire Begets Village : 764.
Fire Blight : 6174.
The Fire Fetched Down : 700.
Fire Frets Uneasily on Leaf : 3528.
Fire in the Woods, Flood in Town : 6469.
Fire Not Water : 2344.
Fire Scenes : 5570.
Fire Swallower : 3956.
Fire Tender : 1527.
Fire Tower : 2404.
The Firefighter : 5985.
Fireflies and the Dry-Cleaners : 4104.
Firenze : 6143.
Fires : 6123.
Fires in November : 522, 6649.
First : 1809, 6176, 6630.
First Birthday Sonnet : 6650.
The First Brith : 3237.
First Charlotte Street Show, 1959 : 1632.
First Child : 3780, 5207.
First Communion : 298, 4281.
First Crush : 1505.
First Day Morning, Haddonfield Meeting :
    244.
First Day of the Season : 6031.
The First Days of the World (God Speaks) :
    2180, 6459.
First Epistle to Eva Hesse : 1434.
First Flight : 861.
First Frost : 3592.
First Frost in the Suburbs : 5631.
First Generation : 1479.
The First Girl I Kiss : 2675.
First Hand : 1329.
First ideas of pale and dusty death : 4740.
First Impression : 4682, 5698.
First Interrogation : 3344, 4995.
First Lecture on Poetry : 1756.
First Lesson: Winter Trees : 6943.
First Love : 1894, 2807.
First Metaphor : 460.
First Mile : 6943.
First Night : 595.
First of March : 1438.
The First of October in Tibet : 4001.
First-Order Enthymeme : 4736.
First Performance of the Rock 'n' Roll Band
    Puce Exit : 6342.
First Person Singular : 4663.
The First Photograph of Hitler : 1667, 2007,
    6514.
First Poem About My Father : 2789.
First Poem from Slovakia: A Dream in the
    Carpathians : 2273.
First Poke Your Eyes : 1571.
First Prairie Winter : 6678.
First Reading : 4255.
The First Red Place : 422.
First Ride : 2634.
First Snow : 524, 3250, 5405.
The First Snow : 1504.
First Sorrowful Mystery: The Agony in the
    Garden (Repentance) : 5459.

First Star : 2948.
First Step From the Playpen : 172.
First Step from the Playpen : 172.
First Storm Warning of the Season : 4640.
First the Uterus : 6827.
The First Thing : 4581.
The First Time : 3880, 4581, 5605, 7167.
First Turtle : 3716.
The First Tutu : 6386.
First Visit to San Michele : 5323.
First Walk : 7023.
First Week : 3705.
First Weeks : 4892.
First Words : 3239.
First Year in Gettysburg : 4535.
The Fish : 541, 2869.
The Fish Becomes a Flower : 5253.
The Fish House : 6742.
Fish Magic : 3529.
Fish Name : 2800.
Fish Story : 3197, 3298, 3943.
Fisherman : 5006.
Fisherman Blues : 4775.
Fishing : 169, 2018, 4141, 6887.
Fishing Below the Dam : 3161.
Fishing Blues : 4212.
Fishing Guides : 5584.
Fishing in Bed : 5954.
Fishing in the Keep of Silence : 2441.
Fishing Minnesota : 225.
Fishing Sonnet : 4668.
Fishing, Winter 1989 : 6929.
Fishing with Izaak Walton : 3396.
Fishing with Uncle : 527.
Fit : 3997.
Fitting in 1913 : 2419.
The Fitting Room : 7107.
Five-and-Dime, Late Thirties : 3372.
Five Attempts: No Way to Talk Around the
    Hole : 1492.
Five Characters in Search of Reality : 3421.
Five Poems : 1353.
The Five Senses of the Witness : 6151.
Five Sure Ways Toward Self-Actualization :
    3202.
Five-Thirty A.M. : 979.
(Five) Untitled Poems: Rain : 217.
Five Verse Memoirs : 498.
Five Verses : 578.
Fixed Stars 2 : 146.
Fiyeda : 1671, 2121.
Flaccus, Drive Up : 2552.
The Flag : 4675.
Flags : 3350.
Flagstaff : 4194.
Flame Dance : 5667.
Flamingo Sunset : 7185.
Flash Cards : 1621.
Flashback II : 1895.
Flashforward: Global Warming : 836.
The Flat : 6604.
A Flat One : 6196.
Flat sky going down to leaves : 1777.
Flatcar : 1159.
Flatfish : 2095.
Flaubert : 2790, 4458.

Flavius Spurius Replies : 1886, 2001.
Flaws of the Flawless : 4621.
The Flea Market at the End of History : 2437.
Fleas on the Space Shuttle Challenger : 1426.
Fleeing from Baghdad : 3215.
Fleeing Walden Pond, Italy : 36.
The Fleet : 1355.
Fleeting Snow on scarf : 636, 5804.
Fleetwood : 5185.
Flemish Beauty : 169.
Flèrida : 1848, 5581.
Flicker : 3706.
Flies in Uardere : 2847.
Flight : 1317, 3408, 5265, 6381.
Flight 1 : 5011, 5041.
The Flight into Egypt : 1349, 2824, 3715.
Flight of Gravity's Attention : 5028.
Flight of the Blind Bird : 3207.
The Flight Path : 2725.
Flight Pattern : 5787.
Flights : 4221.
Flo : 6325.
Floating : 4308.
Floating Hats : 2800.
Floating on a Kitchen Chair : 6095.
Floating Parables : 2198.
A Flock of Golden-Eyes : 4742.
A Flock of Sheep Near the Airport : 117,
    591.
Flokati : 2380.
Flood : 7023.
The Flood : 1362, 4428, 5097, 5114, 5164,
    7312.
Flood Before and After : 4207.
The Floozie Clause : 5050.
Flophouse : 5189.
Florencia : 2792.
Flores, Flores por los Muertos : 3902.
Florida Bay : 4928.
Florida Pools : 1834.
Florilegium : 5987.
Flossie : 6576.
Flossie's Clematis : 2292.
Flotation Device : 5715.
Flounder : 4267, 6688.
Flourishing Gnarled : 4731.
Flowa : 4482.
Flowering Almond Blossoms : 5501.
Flowering Judas : 5016.
Flowers : 705, 2862, 4868, 5196, 6784.
Flowers and Creatures : 2397.
The Flowers Are Screaming : 2580.
Flowers Become a Job You Can Never Finish
    : 7050.
Flowers by the Sea : 211.
The Flowers in Sinsheim : 4583.
Flowers in Winter : 7221.
The Flowers of Hell : 3851.
Flowers, Trees, Clouds : 1073, 7266.
Flowing : 6347.
Flu Song : 2331.
Flumen Tenebrarum : 7090.
Fluorescent Sorrow : 4055, 4536, 6648.
A Fly : 4026.
The Fly : 5501, 6076.
Flyfishing : 2900.

Flying at Night : 5303.
The Flying Dwarf : 521.
Flying Home in December : 5845.
Flying Home to Jersey from the Top of the
    Empire State : 2290.
Flying into Birmingham : 1421.
Flying into Memphis : 1421.
Flying into St. Louis : 979.
Flying over a River : 899.
Flying Sideways : 5685.
Flying to the Moon : 1772.
The Foam : 4254.
Focal Point : 132.
Focus : 1297.
Focus Throws : 3246.
Fog : 620, 5742, 6378, 6970.
Fogbow : 78.
The Folding Table War : 4267.
Folds : 2326, 4835.
Folk Saying : 2256.
Folk Song: On the Road Again : 979.
Folk Talk : 5344.
Follow Orders : 172.
The Following Word : 678.
Folly Bridge : 1111.
Fontanel : 4576.
Food and Lumber : 991.
Food for Thought, or Just Deserts : 2287,
    2320, 2429, 2683, 3012, 3335, 3978,
    6503, 6691.
Fool Thoughts : 546.
Foolish : 6664.
Foolishly Halved, I See You : 4010.
Fools the Eye : 2721.
The Foot : 3219.
Footage of Hitler : 1043.
Footloose : 4286.
Footloose radish : 3704.
Footnotes to a History of the Flood : 2775.
Footsoldier's Slow Drag and Breakdown :
    4788.
Footsteps : 6171, 7259, 7271.
For a Dead Cardinal Below the Window :
    1582.
For a Feminist : 4578.
For a Fiftieth Anniversay : 2518.
For a Friend : 1068, 2612.
For a Friend Who Died Three Days Before
    His Letter Came : 571.
For a Gelding : 2869.
For a Lost Scarf : 3130, 6087.
For a Modest God : 4928.
For Adrian, April 14, 1986 : 6859.
For Alice Notley : 1588.
For All I Know, In a Cleared Patch of Wood
    a Granite Rock Floats Free of Gravity
    Unseen by You or Me, Therefore : 2012.
For All Our Presence : 2663.
For All That : 4050.
For All Those Who Wait for Time to Pass :
    2507, 5790.
For All We Know : 3536.
For an inexhaustible instant I sat : 3119,
    5861.
For Andrew Wood : 1933.
For Andrzej, for Marek, for Szczepan : 6138.

For Anne Frank : 6291.
For Any Known Fact: Nude Walking Alone
    on a Beach in Moonlight : 5606.
For Cesar Vallejo : 5997.
For D.R., Dead of AIDS at age 25 : 7213.
For Darwin or the Reverend : 791.
For dear life : 4025.
For Dennis : 4537.
For each human act there's a place meant :
    5132.
For Edward Abbey : 4667.
For Emily Wilson from a Newcomer : 121.
For Erin, for Others : 5162.
For Esther — (Apoc.) : 3518.
For Etel Adnan : 4195.
For Etheridge : 6721.
For Etheridge Knight : 6573.
For Example (8): And the Fire Spread : 3682.
For Farris : 4472.
For Federico García Lorca : 5589, 6653.
For George : 2048.
For George Whitman & Wm. Shakespeare :
    1176.
For Greater Precision : 1983, 2095, 4919.
For Her Only : 5642.
For Herr Neumann, Retiring to Las Vegas :
    7131.
For Howard Nemerov : 1919.
For in Her Heart Wounds Are Driven Most
    Deepest : 832.
For Instance : 4528.
For J.L. : 1321.
For Jack Kerouac : 2124.
For Jacques-Henri Lartigue, Who as a Child
    Mourned the Death of Moments : 1861.
For James Edmundson as Willy Loman :
    4777.
For James Wright : 3158.
For Jan, with Love : 3716.
For Jean MacDonald, b. 1910 : 6606.
For Jesse Owens : 6359.
For Job at Forty : 5970.
For Joe, 20 December 1991 : 6961.
For Joe, Who Is Not at All a Coin : 5162.
For John Berryman : 20.
For Joyce Rankin : 5991.
For Judy & Richard Segasture Upon Their
    Departure for Phoenix (Keep in Touch) :
    2020.
For Julie at Tom Thumb : 5903.
For Keith Spicer : 6682.
For Kevin Ziegler : 2245.
For Kim : 6616.
For Kivi : 3278.
For Krishna's Sake : 734.
For L. : 4838.
For Leyvick Halpern : 5741.
(for Linda) : 1235.
For Lori : 3054.
For Lysa, That She May Rise Early : 4287.
For M. M. : 552.
For May Is the Month of Our Mother : 1644.
For Men : 259.
For Men Only : 3394.
For Miles : 7056.
For Miles and Miles : 1853.

For Milton's Granddaughters : 4673.
For Most of Us : 3127.
For Mutual Consent : 1984.
For My Beloved Son : 121.
For My Body : 1989.
For My Brother at a Dark Time : 415.
For My Daughter, Leaving : 7122.
For My Father : 4513, 4747.
For My Friend and Partner in Poems and
    Conspiracies: Alfredo Matías : 2792.
For My Friends, Who Complain That I Never
    Write Anything Happy : 2435.
For My Granma Souter Who Was Wrong
    About : 5433.
For My Husband Sleeping Alone : 4177.
For My Husband Who Wants to Know
    What's Going to Happen This
    Anniversary : 2472.
For My Lakota Woman : 3920.
For My Mother : 5200.
For My Oldest Child : 7246.
For My Son : 7025.
For My Son in Mariner Valley : 3216.
For My Washer and Dryer : 5124.
For My Widowed Sister : 7028.
For My Wife, on Our Son's Third Birthday :
    861.
For My Youngest Aunt : 4602.
For Northern Papa : 4472.
For Old Dog, a September Walk : 2401.
For Persephone : 7170.
For Poetry : 6060.
For Poetry, My Son : 3780.
For Robert Briscoe, the First Jewish Mayor
    of Dublin : 1259.
For Rudolf Hoess, Commandant of
    Auschwitz : 5395.
For Sale : 5896.
For Salman Rushdie, 14 February, 1992 :
    5397.
For Shawn : 3900.
For Some Strange Reason : 3464.
For Someone Gone : 6299.
For Spring : 1834.
For Suzanne : 5860.
For the Absence of Home : 1141.
For the Asthmatic : 2615.
For the Book Reviewer Who Laughed : 3225.
For the Child Stirring : 6660.
For the Cutover Woods of Dixie : 4472.
For the David Murray Octet : 6159.
For the Deer : 2759.
For the Engraver : 5089.
For the Fighting Spirit of the Walnut : 2861,
    3766.
For the Gentleman of the Waterfront (Feby.
    13, 1993) : 5228.
For the Lady Who Hates It : 838.
For the Losers of Things : 6302.
For the Love of Living Things : 414.
For the Man Who Knows He Is the Father of
    His Country and Will Not Be Named
    Here : 1420.
For the Oral : 5359.
For the Organic Farmers : 5179.
For the Recorder of Suicides : 1252.

For the Scythian Princess They Found in the
    Mud : 2445.
For the Soft God Paula : 2498.
For the Taking : 2439.
For the Woman in the Bookstore : 6178.
For the Young Woman Who Left the Room
    When I Read a Poem About Chld Abuse
    : 2316.
For They Are Beautiful, in Many Languages
    : 6065.
For Those Who Have Asked : 3247.
(for Tiger) : 1235.
For Two Daughters : 2037.
For Valerie, Seven Days Out of Detox :
    3441.
For You : 4771.
For Your Information : 6393.
For Zoe Stephens : 5265.
Forbidden Pictures : 840.
Forbidden Things : 2153.
Force of Wind Table: Land Criterion : 304.
Force of Wind Table: Sea Criterion : 304.
The Force That Drives the Tulip Drives the
    Ox : 1567.
Forced March : 2232, 5342.
Forces of Nature : 5038.
Forcing the Muse to Stay Up All Night :
    1172.
Forcing the Narcissus : 4691.
Forecast : 2435, 5239.
Forecast: New Orleans : 6228.
Forecasting : 4883.
Foreclosure : 6838.
The Foreground Is All Flowers : 625.
Foreign Field : 4555.
Foreigner : 1199.
Foreplay : 6665.
Foreplay and Entrapment : 3816.
Forerunner : 620.
Forest for the Trees : 1207.
The Forest in the Palm of My Hand Is
    Burning : 3855.
The Forest King : 5789.
A Forest Pilgrimage : 5244.
Forest Service Cabin #114 : 6970.
The Forest Summit Issue : 6690.
Foretelling : 812.
Forever Bent : 5447.
Forever Is Not as Long as You Might Think :
    6918.
Forfeit : 1334.
Forges at Conshohocken : 773.
Forgetfulness, with Ghost and Snow : 4019.
Forgetting : 855.
Forgetting the Liberty : 7047.
Forgive Me : 901.
Forgive Me That I Am Coping Badly : 4910.
Forgive Them, O Lord : 1792, 3446.
Forgiveness : 4127.
Forgiveness: Mother Learns to Talk : 2947.
Forgiving the Dead : 2046.
Forgotten Frontier : 5305.
Forgotten Infancy, Kentucky : 3145.
The Forgotten Park : 6966.
Forgotten Streams : 4417.
Forklift : 1853.

The Forlorn Hope : 2785.
Form : 863.
A Form of the Tell-Tale Heart by Edgar Allan Poe and Michael Basinski : 391.
The Formality : 4679.
The Formation of Vegetable Mould, Through the Action of Worms, with Observations on Their Habits (God to Darwin) : 1823.
The Formative Years — For a Friend — : 3144.
The Forties : 3822.
Fortress : 1290, 5666, 6196, 6234.
Fortunate : 4562.
Fortunate Traveller : 3020.
Fortune : 78.
The Fortune : 1694.
Forty-Five : 979.
Forty-Percent Chance of Rain : 3866.
Fossil : 1095.
Found by the Pool : 96, 3872.
Found Cure Nine : 3171.
Found Eye : 3654, 4060, 5901.
Found Language : 1059.
Fo(u)nd Memories : 6577.
Found Parable : 4250.
Found some space : 1820.
Founders : 4608.
Foundlings : 2435.
The Fountain of Youth : 5594.
Four : 400.
Four A.M. : 2591.
Four and Forty, the Same Wave Cresting : 1383.
Four Bathers : 2400.
Four Carolina Elegies : 1139.
Four Coffees : 549.
Four Cut Sunflowers, One Upside Down : 1645.
Four Days : 7284.
Four Drafts : 1726.
Four Endings : 2745.
Four from the Spider : 26.
Four Greek Men : 2388.
Four Hours : 1703.
The Four-Hundred Player of the Game : 1676.
Four Kinds of Water : 451.
Four-Leaf Clover : 6278.
Four Old Men : 3914.
Four Poems : 1536, 5298.
Four Reasons for Destroying a Spider's Web : 377.
Four Roses : 2824, 3715, 6815.
Four Rounds from 'Narrative: Ali' : 73.
Four Scenes with the Sea: Love and Solitude : 4602.
The Four Thousand Four Hundred & Two Faces of Dada : 2668.
Four Times the Feast : 2362.
Four Years : 4270.
Fourteen Hours to Loredo : 1221.
Fourth of July : 341.
The Fourth of July : 1259.
Fourth of July Heritage Festival : 6172.
Fourth of July in North Orange, Mass : 2182.
A Fox : 6544.

The Fox : 2935.
Fox Abandons Hope, Almost : 2070.
Fox Clownhunts in a Temple's Rock and Sand Garden : 2070.
Fox Gains in Courage : 2070.
Fox Weeps, Cured of Amnesia : 2070.
Foxes : 2404.
The Foxes : 4488.
Foxes Have Holes : 282.
Foxfire : 3880.
Foxtails : 3850, 3864.
The Foxtrot : 2928.
Frackle : 2698.
Fractions : 6365.
Fractions of a Lament for a Friend : 3344, 4995.
Fragment from a Mennonite Journal : 6457.
Fragment From the Age : 3301.
Fragment under Florescent Light : 1659.
Fragments : 1395, 5230.
Fragments after Robert Browning : 1420, 3756.
Fragments for an Elegy : 2052.
Fragments of a Progression : 2643.
Fragments of a Spanish Marriage : 2792.
Fragments of Athena : 2046.
Fragments of Rose : 5285.
Fragments on the Last Night : 4107.
Fragrances : 4928.
Frailty : 862, 4119, 6730.
Frame 323 : 2197.
Framed : 2641.
Frames : 1290, 1458, 5666, 6196, 6234.
Frames of a Coptic Funeral : 4258.
Framingham : 7047.
The Franciscan Baths : 3995, 5638.
Francois de Maynard, Poet — 1582-1645 : 4417.
Frank : 1210, 6376, 6549.
Fran's Revenge : 1785.
Franz Died : 6255.
Franz Kline : 4795.
Fraud : 2331.
Freddie's Elegy : 4768.
Frederick Douglass: the Last Day of Slavery : 4486.
Frederick: The Decision : 6876.
Frederick: The Drought : 6876.
Frederiksted, Dusk : 6859.
Free at Last : 418.
Free China Girl : 3920.
Free Enterprise, Again : 5367.
Free Fall : 1579.
Free Speech Can Be Expensive : 3877.
Free Throw : 3545.
Free to Walk : 4176.
Free Verse : 3328.
Freedom : 3529.
Freedom's Poem : 3703.
Freestone : 3992.
French : 73.
The French Expressionist Idea : 5907.
French Kissing : 5452.
The French Lesson : 4660.
Frenzied Fingers : 2118, 3805.
Fresh Air : 2339.

Fresh from a Shredding : 2716.
Fresh Notions & Co : 6076.
Fresh Salt : 2095.
Fresh Snow : 3292, 6334.
Frida Kahlo : 5397.
Friday Afternoon Before Labor Day : 1261.
Friday Morning — Amman : 4028.
Friday Night : 5980.
Friedrich Nietzsche : 3132.
Friend : 318, 4035, 7221.
Friend of the Family : 838.
A Friend of the Family : 5930.
The Friendly City : 214.
Friendly Fire : 1670.
Friends : 2147, 2742, 6985.
Friends on the Next Street : 5082.
The Frog : 5420.
The Frog in the Swimming Pool : 2437.
Frog Prince : 5955.
The Frogs : 1448.
From a Cafeteria Window : 6482.
From a Cheap Hotel at the Edge of the
    Known World : 741.
From a Child of the Provinces Who Wound
    Up Livng in a Chagall : 145, 3198.
From a Distance : 1681, 5507.
From a Family Obituary: October 8, 1887 :
    2000.
From a Picture Book : 797.
From a Prayer for the Bride : 1082.
From a Train : 2864.
From a Train Window at Night : 2153.
From a Window in Jerusalem : 4820.
From an Island : 6544.
From Assisi : 4547.
From Bakersfield : 198.
From Canto the Eighth, 'That' *Goddess* : 186.
From CODA: Echo & Variations : 1135.
From Exile : 2828.
From Here On : 214, 4171.
From His Porch in Galloway : 7265.
From July 1990 : 2130, 6674.
From Laramie : 1329.
From Lively Painful Twigs : 3601, 5254.
From Love in a Dry Land : 1245.
From Nature : 965.
From Night to Night : 3546, 5756.
(From One of Zeami's Texts) : 2077, 5789.
From Poseidon : 3329, 5539.
From Rock to Rock : 264.
From Rodin's Nightmare of Camille 1917 :
    6178.
From Second Mesa : 760.
From Small Chimes, One voice : 4200, 6230.
From Tafia : 3981.
From the Abstract to the Real : 2120.
From the Artist, Letter to Arthur Stieglitz :
    4742.
From the Bridal Book II : 3830.
From the California Beach Town : 3531.
From the cliff at the foot of Skull Mountain :
    3762, 6230.
From the Devotions : 5162.
From the Earth to the Moon : 3197.
From the Gulf : 3429.
From the Louvre to Jeu de Paume : 6314.

From the Magic Mountain : 1125.
From the Manger : 1491.
From the Pinède, Juan les Pins : 3988.
From the Prophet's Mosque : 3562.
From the River Merchant: A Letter : 2873.
From the Roof : 5185.
From the Rooftop : 6508.
From Thes Hye Hilles, As When a Spryng
    Doth Fall : 7193.
From Tombstones Back Home : 6299.
Front Porch, Listening : 2818.
Front Porch Visiting : 1025.
Frontier : 2438.
Frontier Thesis : 5787.
Frost Warning : 3651.
Fruit : 2397.
Fruit and Produce — by U.P. : 7351.
Fruit Flies to the Too Ripe Fruit : 2309.
Fruit Tramps : 3969.
Fruits So / Bunched : 4495.
Frusos : 3143, 5977.
Fu Hao : 6926.
Fuckability : 2013.
Fucking in the Spirit : 3424.
Fugitive : 7005, 7352.
Fugue : 73, 3518.
Fugues in the Gutters : 3969.
The Fulfillment of Wishes : 6495.
Full Cycle : 4675.
Full Flower Moon : 72.
Full Fridge on Bank Street : 1578.
Full Moon : 1009, 1102, 1727.
Full Moon in May : 5432.
Full Moon Madness : 4483.
Full of Rain, the Word : 1548.
Full Speed Ahead : 6842.
The Full Women : 3136, 4925.
Fullblood Girl on a Blue Horse : 3920.
Funeral : 1667, 2007, 6514.
The Funeral of My Cousin Phil Maddux:
    Tinicum, Bucks County, in the Spring :
    6128.
Funeral of Words : 3001, 4824.
Funeral Parlor, Trieste : 1112.
Funeral Pie : 2095.
Funeral Spring : 3116.
Funereal Toast : 4065, 6993, 6993.
Fünf Fantasiestücke in Harry Grahams
    Manier : 2137.
Furious Motion Blurred : 3379.
The Further Demise of Robin Hood : 3513.
The Further Travels of Marco Polo : 2437.
Further Triangulations : 2972.
A Furtive Life : 338, 1945.
Fusiles y Frijoles : 2217.
Futile : 5763.
Futile Determination : 1785.
The Future of Vaginas and Penises : 1703.
Future Tense : 6576.
G-d : 6573.
Gabriel : 5490.
Gacela of Departed Love : 4481.
Gagaku : 5504.
Gaia : 6120.
The Gaiety of Form : 604.
Gail in New York : 4869.

Gail White : 7175.
Galileo in the Snow : 2914.
The Gallery of Owls : 2914.
Galore : 2445.
Gambell, St. Lawrence Island : 6146.
Game : 5753.
The Game : 838, 1342.
Game Called : 5139.
A Game for November : 1834.
The Game Tried to Go On : 6842.
Gameday Saturday Afternoon : 6118.
Games : 4640, 6434.
Gams : 2943.
Ganga Slanga : 969.
The Ganges at Benares : 2655.
The Ganges in Flood : 4258.
The Gannet (A Sestina) : 7136.
A Gap in the Streaming : 942.
The Garage Sale As a Spiritual Exericse :
    1592.
Garbage Truck : 3538.
The Garbage Truck at 7:30 A.M. : 3958.
Garden : 4417.
The Garden : 16, 466, 1028, 2009, 3274,
    3855, 7023.
Garden by the Adriatic : 5323.
The Garden God : 302, 6411, 6822.
The Garden in the Air : 3805, 4958.
The Garden of Your Delights : 4291, 5657.
Garden Party : 4523.
Garden Tour, Autumn : 1398.
Garden Wedding : 3902.
Garden with Stone Wall and Quince Trees :
    442, 5804.
Garden without Flowers : 6769.
The Gardener : 5296.
Gardening in a Dry Year : 1332.
The Gardens of the Body : 3139.
The Gardens of Warsaw : 2679.
Gardens We Have Left : 4670.
Garter Snake : 6338.
Gaslight : 1682.
Gasoline : 1845.
The Gate : 2044, 4649, 6409.
The Gate of Paradise : 4001.
Gate of Virtue and Victory (De Sheng Men) :
    1077, 2482, 5646.
Gates : 442, 647, 3270, 5804, 7327.
The Gathasaptasati : 2546, 5932.
Gathering : 3022, 4038.
Gathering Seed : 3689.
Gatherings : 21.
Gatos Soñados : 4291.
Gauguin in Kansas : 4009.
Gawkers Block Traffica After Accident :
    3300.
Gay Chimp Falls in Love with Circus Dwarf
    : 7045.
The Gecko and the Beanie Weanies : 149.
Geckos : 6317.
Geese : 638, 654.
Gelatin Factory : 674.
Gelatin Maps : 998.
Géminis Deshabitado : 1003.
Genealogia : 6758.
Genealogy : 2300, 3499, 3970.

Genealogy of Colours : 3628.
The General : 3392, 3516, 4921, 5363.
The General Compares His Late Wife to His
    Daughter : 1259.
General Delivery : 2168.
General Italo Balbo : 4195.
General Mail Facility Night Shift Dreams :
    3419.
General Sir Harry Flashman, K.C.B. : 5524.
Generally : 5167.
The General's Daughter Remembers Her
    Mother : 1259.
The General's Opposite Number : 1259.
Generation : 7234.
Generation Epitaph : 5919.
Genes : 4877.
Genesis : 847, 4141, 6324.
Genesis Reconsidered : 5132.
Genetic Pattern : 4276.
Genetics : 6365.
Genghis Khan : 5590.
Genie : 899.
The Genius : 1593.
Genius Loci : 5512.
A Gentile's Response : 6329.
The Gentleman Bookworm : 3796.
Gentleness : 4070.
Gently, the Orange : 6609.
Genu : 6185.
Geode : 5127.
Geografía Invisible de América : 59, 2034.
Geography : 1905, 3400, 7195.
Geography IV : 6994.
Geography Lesson : 615.
The Geography Lesson : 1596.
The Geography of the Department of
    Geography : 2507, 5790.
Geology, Summer 1983 : 3785.
Geometria Emocional : 5593.
Georg Grosz : 3123.
George and the Dragon : 5156.
George Bowering : 653.
George Washington Dies : 5665.
Georgia O'Keeffe : 3822.
Georgic after an Argument : 5549.
Gerard for Unction : 789.
Gergen, Gergen : 6690.
Germany, Bavaria : 542, 3486.
Gertrude Stein : 3938.
Gesture : 2925, 3546, 5756.
Get bombed, piss'd in face : 3218.
Get the Picture : 6375.
Getting a Mosquito : 5875.
Getting Going : 6299.
Getting Happy : 2574.
Getting Inside the University of the Road :
    1794.
Getting It Right : 1534.
Getting It Together : 6842.
Getting My Children to Rub My Feet : 2343.
Getting Over There (Outside Mendocino) :
    2269.
Getting Ready for Bed : 2481.
Getting Ready for the Night : 4928.
Getting Ready to Spray Beans : 943.

Getting Ready to Take Off from Cleveland Hopkins Airport in What Feels Like a Hurricane : 6956.
Getting Something Done : 2026, 5197.
The Geyser : 498, 4716.
Ghazal of the Empty Thing : 6491.
Ghazals III : 2239.
Ghazals: Electric Lawn-Mower Cords : 3999.
Ghazals on Lake Erie in March : 3363.
Ghetto Song : 166, 3538.
Ghost : 3299, 5322.
Ghost Child : 4341.
The Ghost in My Bed : 1887.
The Ghost in the Wedding Photograph : 1313.
Ghost Pig : 6772.
A Ghost Poem : 6023.
Ghost Poem for Blacky Hix : 6023.
Ghost Riders of the Moon : 214.
Ghost Song : 5151.
Ghost Story : 6055.
A Ghost Story : 3147.
Ghost Talk : 7054.
Ghost Triptych : 4847.
Ghostbusters : 6225.
Ghosting : 562.
Ghosts : 2153, 2446, 5265.
Ghosts in Flight : 5421.
Giacometti : 122.
Giacometti on Parade: Almost Home : 5556.
Giacumbert Nau : 6706, 6839, 6840.
The Giant Panda : 4325.
Giant Sequoia : 3094.
Giant Steps : 958.
A Gift : 810.
The Gift : 1780, 3114, 3509, 4691, 6309.
Gifts : 2000, 5837.
The Giggly Girls or the Fourth Opening : 1850.
Gilbert White Street : 385.
Gilded Rule : 2711.
Gilding the Lily : 4476.
Gilgamesh: A Lament : 1079.
Gillis van Coninxloo, Landscape : 1828, 2463.
Gimme a Break : 3877.
Gina's Taste : 3360.
Ginseng : 2556.
Giraffe : 3771.
Girl at Sewing Machine : 3701.
Girl Cadaver : 128.
The Girl Calls Herself Gentle Names : 4797.
The Girl Dressed in Blue Feathers : 2080.
Girl Help : 3797.
The Girl in 301 : 3667.
Girl in a Fish Bowl : 4681.
Girl in the Doorway : 881.
A Girl Needs Something of Her Own : 4797.
The Girl of Seven Spirits : 2077, 5654, 7319.
A Girl Sings to Moravia at the World's End : 2737.
The Girl That Got Away : 4289.
The Girl, the Parrot, the Ghost : 4891.
The Girl Who Cuts Your Hair : 3036.
The Girl Who Dances in Snow : 5543.
The Girl Who Taught Time to Fly : 287.

The Girl with Purple Hair : 2290.
Girl with Sad Face : 6723.
Girl with Wood : 6772.
Girl Writing a Letter : 964.
Girlfriend : 2071, 6701.
Girlfriend's Got It Goin' On : 19.
Girls : 1488, 5123.
Girl's Bed : 5864.
The Girls' Home : 3544.
Girthia : 7217.
Gitár : 4921.
Giullian's Pool & Billiards : 3608.
Give Me Back My Man : 1315.
Give the snow a good interrogation! : 442, 5804.
Give Us This Day : 5497.
Given : 1184.
Given the Choice : 4409.
Given the Questions : 4010.
Giving Birth : 4902.
Gladiola : 5050.
The Glances : 5361.
Glancing through your letter again I see your phraise : 6493.
Glass : 121, 4535, 4743, 5016.
The Glass Cage : 3396.
Glass Goblet : 2319.
A Glass Look Over a High Hill : 4643.
A Glass of Clear Water : 4987.
The glass room : 6148, 6184.
Glass Slippers : 5731.
The Glass Tower : 2254.
Glaucoma : 3538.
Glazed : 6665.
Glazunoviana : 214.
Glen Ridge, NJ : 1030.
Glen Uig : 3017.
The Glimpse of Flabbergassment : 2331.
A Glimpse of Simon Verity : 2521.
Glimpses : 2916.
Glittering Ghost : 6841.
Global Aphasia : 6031.
Globe Street : 6790.
Glory : 5926.
The Glove : 4895.
A Glowworm, a Lemur, and Some Women : 6544.
Glukupikron : 4930.
Glynmill Inn Bar, Corner Brook, December 2, 1992 : 6897.
Glyph : 1109.
Gnashing : 1238.
Gnats : 2255.
Go-Behind : 2095.
Go Figure : 3588.
Go Fly a Kite : 2997.
Go Out Like a Real Man : 2982.
Go South, Old Man : 4471.
Go Twenty-Nine : 6296.
Go Twenty-Six : 6296.
The Goal : 7111.
Goalies Are Weird : 3662.
The Goat : 2298, 7121.
Goat's Hair : 2095.
Goatsbeard : 6501.
Gobbling : 742.

Gobi : 4818, 6548.
God : 3124.
God Alone : 5606.
God Appears to the Atheist : 751.
God at Forty : 6943.
God of the Desert Night : 2475.
God Sightings : 1979.
God went down on me in a graveyard : 6646.
Goddess : 6340.
A Goddess : 1989.
The Goddess : 3306.
The Goddess Corn Finds Her Dress in
     Disarray : 6472.
Goddess Prayers for the Twenty-first Century
     : 6281.
The Godfather : 6652.
The Godfather's last Hurrah : 4059.
Godlike Freedoms to Dream up Destiny :
     2707.
Godlines : 2704.
Gods : 5204.
God's Blood : 994.
The Gods' Picnic : 3341.
Going : 4472.
The Going : 545.
Going Away : 1506.
Going Back : 1342, 6008.
Going Back to a December Day : 1950.
Going Back to Teaching ESL : 5035.
Going Down : 3674, 3755.
Going Fishing : 4567.
Going Home : 824.
Going Home Day : 1596.
Going Home to Georgia : 417.
Going Nowhere, Fast : 1238.
Going Places : 5894.
Going Softly : 5421.
Going the Rounds: A Sort of Love Poem :
     2728.
Going Under : 2296.
A Gold Ring : 1774.
The Gold Sun : 4993.
Golden : 4387.
The Golden Age of Gay Literature : 4558.
The Golden Highway to Boipatong : 1944.
The Golden Lotus : 722.
Golden Moments of English Verse : 513.
The Golden Ring : 7362.
Golden Shades : 1736.
Golden Warriors End Year with Big Loss :
     6558.
Die Goldene Zeit : 779.
Goldenrod : 2421.
Goldfinch : 5021.
The Goldfish : 804.
Goldfish at Loring Pond : 1821.
Goldilocks : 1966.
Golf Crazed Women : 1371.
Goliath : 1635, 2332.
Gone & Gone : 7180.
Gone Bad : 1974.
Gone Out Is Part of Sanity : 1197.
Gonzalo Arango : 4596.
Good Breeding Will Out : 3877.
Good-bye : 6512.
The Good-Bye Sonnet : 5763.

A Good Cry : 5667.
The Good Day : 4894.
The Good Earth : 3529.
The Good Fortune of Others : 5664.
Good Friday in Logroño : 3442.
Good Grease : 6526.
The Good Host's Song : 1154.
Good Humor : 3247.
The Good Jew : 1082.
Good Kind Souls, May 2, 1992 : 89.
A Good Life : 7173.
Good Man Blues : 4884.
Good Morning : 5505.
Good Voices : 3145.
Goodbye, 1992 : 6743.
Goodbye Home. Hello Somewhere : 1999.
Goodbye Margo : 6445.
Goodbye Note to Debbie Fuller: Pass It On :
     1148.
Goodbye on the Wind : 5152.
Goodbye to Yorkshire : 828.
Goodguys : 6842.
Goose Egg : 2095.
Gophers : 2608, 7100.
Gore Redux : 6690.
Gorgeousness : 4254.
The Gospel According to Perse and Others :
     2131.
Gossip : 6231.
Gothic : 1908, 5712.
Gothic Fears : 5372.
Gothic Mud : 4906.
Götterdämmerung : 204, 4556.
Gouldsboro Bay : 592.
Goya : 1524, 3421.
Grace : 1463, 3215, 3297, 3586, 3848, 6419.
Grace Notes : 2325, 6932.
The Grace of Grace : 3298.
Grace Pretty Shields: Caught : 3468.
Grace Street : 6063.
Grace's Tree, II : 7013.
Gracias, Fidel : 5063.
The Grackles : 717.
Graffiti : 688, 6228.
The Grail : 1045.
Grammar and Usage : 1813.
Grammar Lesson : 5530.
The Grammar of Simultaneity : 3385.
Grammarian : 4801.
Grampa buried the cow : 2603.
Grand Canyon : 4915.
Grand Central Station : 4175.
The Grand Entrance : 4664.
Grand Jour : 662.
Grand Rapids Woman Last Seen at Motel 6 :
     3300.
Granddad : 3746.
Les Grandes Chaleurs : 3554.
Grandfather : 342, 487, 5444, 7302.
Grandfather, His Book : 6887.
Grandfather William : 3397.
Grandfather's Garden : 6354.
Grandfather's Story : 6333.
Grandma : 5101.
Grandma Came Down : 2378.
Grandma Gladys : 1489.

Grandmother : 3088, 6299, 6871, 7245.
Grandmother: An Interior Dialogue : 4611.
Grandmother Rising : 6598.
Grandmother: tries lending dogs to people : 7072.
Grandmother: warns the children NOT to play with their bellybuttons : 7072.
The Grandmothers : 1596.
Grandpa : 2696.
Granizo : 5328.
Granny : 2446.
The Grape : 5502.
The Grapes : 1295, 4178.
Graphology : 7191.
Grass : 6012.
Grass Growing from a White Pine Stump : 6180.
Grass Roots : 4582.
Grass the Fine Body Hairs of Earth : 1892.
Grasses in November : 4928.
The Grasshopper Man : 4866.
Gratia Plena : 620.
Grave Grass : 4295.
The Gravedigger : 5558.
The Gravedigger Wiping Sweat : 3425.
Graves : 979.
Graves at Quang Tri : 674.
The Graves in Estacado Canyon : 4282.
The Graves of Animals : 4844.
Gravetalk : 6502.
Graveyard Picnic : 7241.
Graveyards in the North Country : 2739.
Gravitas : 994.
Gravitation : 5333, 5402, 7004.
Gravity : 1674.
Gravity Debris Resonating : 998.
Gravity for Beginners : 5711.
Gravity, Grace : 7054.
Gravity Looms on the Other Side of the Stumbling Block : 4382.
Gravity, Ya Know : 6377.
Gray Bat : 3043.
Gray Distance : 3789.
Gray-Eyed Effie : 7217.
A Gray Matter : 2403.
The Great Alvar, Öland, Sweden : 650.
Great Blue Heron : 681.
Great Blue Heron Poems : 564.
The Great Bridge Game of Life : 214.
The Great Chain of Being : 1966.
The Great Day : 1514.
Great Egg Harbor Creek : 5345.
The Great Escape : 838.
Great Falls of Paterson : 6082.
The Great Green Lion : 54.
The Great Horned Owl : 5267.
Great Pitches : 3796.
Great South Bay : 3533.
The Great Taming Force : 1440.
The Great Wall : 1047, 4428.
The Great Wind : 2069.
Great Work Farm Elegy : 2471.
Greece : 2350, 2907.
The Greedy Man and the Envious Man : 251, 6135.
Greek Easter : 1479.

Greek Lyric Meter : 6518.
Greek Things : 189, 4363.
The Greeks Had a Word for Me : 6931.
Green : 742, 4337.
Green Acorn : 3988.
Green and Gold : 442, 3058, 5804.
Green Ash, Red Maple, Black Gum : 6943.
The Green Car : 540.
Green China Tea : 988.
Green Dodge : 6729.
The Green Grocer's Daughters : 7058.
Green Heron : 6921.
Green Light : 5150.
Green Peaches : 1768.
Green River Reservoir : 1039.
The Green Room : 3532.
Green Salsa : 1706, 4372.
Green Shade : 7239.
A Green Song : 1263.
Green Spring in the Morning : 4899.
Green Thief : 2934.
The Greenest Eye : 1241.
Greenhouse Blues : 3748.
Greeting Card Verse : 5078.
Greeting the New Year in Vancouver : 681.
Greeting the Return of the Wolf to Colorado : 5844.
Grendel's Song : 4885.
Gretchen at the Wheel : 13.
Gretel : 1205.
Gretel, Lost : 4553.
Grey, creamy slate : 286.
The Grey-headed Griffin : 3033, 5638.
Greyhound Rock : 1577.
Grief : 1534, 5817.
Grief Notes & Animal Dreams : 4668.
Grief Stages : 6771.
Griefwork : 3886.
Grieving, for Five Voices : 2158.
The Grinder's Monkey : 5610.
Gringo Ghost : 6736.
Grits : 177.
Groceries : 675.
Gros-Ilet : 6859.
Gross National Product : 1238.
Ground : 1837.
The Ground of Events : 942.
Ground Zero : 5884.
Grounded : 6524.
The Groundhog : 5004.
Grounds : 5722.
Groundwater : 6527.
Groundwork : 3825.
A Group Diary : 5170.
Grove Street Hyacinths : 4018.
Grove Workers at Frost Time : 5022.
Growing Cheese : 2095.
Growing Ordinary : 582.
Growing Up : 2565, 3571.
Growing Up Backward : 4327.
Growing up Perpendicular on the Side of a Hill : 3727.
Growing Up Short : 4626.
Growth : 4468.
The Guard : 3541.
La Guardia, the Story : 4365.

Guardian : 4038.
Guardian Angels : 846.
Guatemala : 4383.
La guerra entre los orejas cortas : 3757.
Guest Place : 3348.
Guests : 2183.
Guide : 2188.
The Guide of Tiresias : 491.
A Guide to Ancient Places : 6888.
Guide to Summer : 436, 1076, 1968.
Guidebook : 7283.
Guided Tour of a Well-Known House : 1655, 3564.
Guillaume's Song : 955, 4219, 5236.
Guillotine : 1408.
Guilt : 2427.
Guilt Like Salt : 5088.
The Guilt Trip : 5395.
Guilty : 6493.
The Guineaman : 2828.
Guitar : 3392, 3516, 4921, 5906.
Guitar Man : 4038.
Guitars and Tigers : 7013.
Gulags : 4861.
Gulf Stream Mediation : 4472.
Gulls : 4636.
Gumbo : 2790.
Gummed Reinforcements : 214.
Gus Is Gone : 6631.
The Guts : 3219.
Guy's Boast : 550.
Gwendolyn : 1503.
Gwendolyn Was Here/Is : 4053.
Gwensways : 5419.
Gynechologist : 7042.
Gypsophila : 1268, 6683.
Gypsy Child : 1735.
H.F. : 2552.
H: We sat on the cliff-head : 5011.
H: Yet the after is still a storm : 5011.
Habituation : 6238.
Hacia Ti : 2354.
Hades Welcomes His Bride : 6302.
Hagada : 2337.
Hagiographies : 4715.
Haiku : 770, 1797, 1993, 2823, 2958, 3444, 5678, 6825.
A Haiku : 2331.
Haiku: Exhausted : 4144.
Haiku: I shade myself in : 7217.
Ha'ina 'ia Mai Ana ka Puana (Let the Story Be Told) : 3672.
Hair : 5427.
Hair Grass and Spiders : 3822.
The Hair on Your Chest : 7047.
Hair Wreathes : 3822.
Haircut : 2993.
Haircut (1956) : 7213.
Haiti : 3614.
Half a Hedgehog : 2517, 2927, 7282.
A Half Inch of Blue Sky : 3974.
The Half of Life : 2907, 5640, 5855.
Half Price : 2538.
A Half-Remembered Visit : 2888.
Half-Time at a Nephew's Soccer Game : 681.
Halfway : 4999, 5987.

Hallelujah : 4400.
Halley's Comet : 649, 5929.
Halloween : 6172.
The Hallows : 6960.
Halls : 4643.
Hal's Dad Cracks Up : 4332.
Ham Spray : 2182.
Hamilton Street : 6121.
Hamlet : 4642.
Hammer : 3704.
Hammer Death : 1712.
Hammering : 6335.
Hamm's Beer Mobile : 1134.
Hand : 2302.
The Hand of Thomas Jefferson : 5770.
Hand-Picked Rose of a Fading Dream : 2605.
Handicapped : 6370.
Handkerchief : 5530.
Hands : 6080.
The Hands : 3839, 6598.
Hands and Fathers : 240.
Hands and Feet : 3255, 3850.
The Hand's Black Hymns : 6065.
Hands Surprised as Starfish : 3628.
Handy Hint : 6652.
The Hanged Man : 847.
Hanging from a maple branch : 264.
Hanging Tree : 6722.
Hangouts : 2387, 3501.
Hannah : 5808, 7041.
Hannibal : 3464.
Hannibal in the Alps on a Sunday : 6417.
Hansel and Gretel : 3640, 3892, 7318.
Hap : 7288.
Happiness : 6076.
Happy : 5550.
Happy Accidents : 6291.
Happy and Unhappy Families : 4651.
Happy Birthday : 3300.
Happy Birthday Mama : 3822.
The Happy Camper : 7095.
Happy Conspiracy : 188, 718.
Happy Marriage : 2992, 4729, 7221.
The Happy Ones : 1518.
A Happy Poem : 6852.
Harbor at Old Saybrook : 1700.
Harbor Island : 5432.
The Harbor-Master of Hong Kong : 763.
Harboring : 6228.
Hard Eyes : 4483.
Hard Sell : 1175.
Hard Times : 1743, 4376.
The Hard Way : 2000.
Hard Wired : 2271.
Hard Words : 470.
Hardie : 5924.
Hardwood : 5050.
The Hare : 467.
Hare and Hounds : 2775.
Hareton Earnshaw, 1803: 'Hareton Earnshaw, 1500' : 1683.
Harlequinode : 3337.
Harm : 5850.
Harm and Boon in the Meetings : 2271.
Harmless Hours : 4111.
Harmonica : 2331.

Harmony : 91.
Harness : 4031.
Harold Lindgrin: The Judge : 6876.
A Harp Sounds Midnight : 2883.
Harpo and the Angel : 7106.
Harry Was : 4581.
Harry's Girl : 2107.
Harvard : 1845.
Harvest : 1359, 1631, 3432, 3794.
Harvest Snow : 7351.
Harvesters of Night and Water : 2898.
Hat : 458, 3112.
Hat Face : 2806.
The Hatbox : 3444.
Hauling in the Net : 238.
The Haunting : 3197.
Haut Goût : 4808.
Havasu Falls : 6738.
Have a good day : 912.
Have Strength : 4099.
Having Begonias : 5319.
Having Come This Way : 4565.
Having Done So : 2640.
Having Gone to Glory, Nana Speaks to Me :
    3070.
Having Gotten Your Phone Number : 7186.
Having Read Hawthorne : 691.
Having Spoken Only Once : 909.
Hawaiian Archipelago : 6527.
Hawks : 3339.
Hawthorne : 2017.
Haystack at Sunset Near Giverny : 2607.
Hazard Avenue : 3513.
Haze : 2426.
He Calls Me : 706.
He Doesn't Like to Be Liked : 1637.
He hated to see his young daughter go : 2221.
He Interrupts My Regularly Scheduled
    Dreams : 3840.
He Is Dead : 4529.
He Is Not Thinking About Last Night : 2825.
He Lay There and Was a Great Lover in a
    Night Without Civilization : 2563, 5851.
He Makes the Figs Our Mouths to Meet :
    6015.
He Said I Don't Enunciate Clearly : 3822.
He Saw the Mounds of Hair Under Glass :
    2801.
He Sleeps : 826.
He was drunk, this time a little less so than
    other times : 5638, 7026.
The Head of a Girl : 5663.
Head of a White Woman Winking : 6544.
Heading Home to You : 7018.
The Headlight Through Us : 6393.
Headlights : 5995.
Headline News : 6306.
Headlines : 2446.
Heads : 4640.
Headwaters : 3195.
Heal-All : 4473.
Heal Protocol : 4682.
Healer : 3958.
Health : 5956.
A Health Care Plan Is Sent to Congress :
    6690.

The Hearing : 4356.
Hearing Aid for the Younger : 6445.
Hearing from Corinna : 3694.
Heart : 2538, 4224.
Heart: A Taunt : 5982.
The Heart and the Symbol : 3799.
The Heart As Origami : 2869.
Heart Clinic : 993.
The Heart Dances with Malinche. El
    Corazon Baila con la Malinche : 4389.
Heart Grab : 107.
Heart, Hurt : 6930.
The Heart in Its Wisdom Can Melt Stone :
    2575, 6833.
Heart of Day : 143, 3786.
The Heart of Europe Is Elegant and Dead :
    3546, 5756.
Heart Throbs : 966.
Heartbreak : 807.
Heartland : 4651.
Hearts : 407.
Heart's Companion : 1880.
Heartspace : 155.
Heartthrobs : 6164.
Heartwell : 4823.
Heartwood : 3333.
A Hearty Welcome to the Antichrist : 3406.
Heat Lightning above Lake Michigan : 3608.
Heat Wave : 247, 3191.
Heaven : 1398, 1596, 6274.
Heaven: A Definition : 7330.
The Heaven Bound : 5983.
Heaven Holds Forth a Land Mover Most of
    All : 1255.
Heaven Sonnet : 3146.
Heavenly Firebird : 862, 5153.
Heavenly Flower : 1143, 4837, 4949.
Heavens uploaded seem to chaperone the
    monsters : 4682.
Hecate at Fiftysomething : 3900.
Hector at the Plate : 5873.
Hector First Suspects : 4138.
Heft of the Afternoon : 1095.
The Heir of the Dog : 324.
Heirloom : 2383, 2446.
The Heirloom : 1620, 6935.
Held in by the ribs of the garment : 6252.
Held Over : 237, 367.
The Helicopter : 4578.
Helicopter by the Lake : 4668.
Hell Cat's Best Friend : 2877.
He'll Have to Climb : 1569.
Hell Is Wherever I Am : 4382.
Hellbender : 5379.
Hellespont : 75.
Hello Desire : 653.
Hello Stranger : 5230.
Help Me! : 179.
Help Wanted : 6697.
Helpless Fishes : 264.
Helplessness (IV) : 2153.
Hemophilia/Los Angeles : 2517, 2927, 7282.
Hemstitching : 3799.
The Hen : 448.
The Hen it is a noble beast : 4303.
Henhouse Longing : 5187.

Henrietta: Farming : 6876.
Henry Cowell Plays the Standards : 7013.
Henry Moore's *Three Motives Against a Wall* : 2659.
Henry Wiggins' Reading Matter : 7202.
Her Account of Herself : 2244.
Her Advice to the Still Life Painter : 1874.
Her Becoming : 2087.
Her Broadloom Dream : 3047.
Her cherry red lips : 4605.
Her Children, Leaping in the Atmosphere : 1171.
Her Door : 3701.
Her Ecstasy : 4632.
Her Explanation : 3360.
Her Face : 2552.
Her Family : 2147, 2742.
Her Favorite Color : 600, 1345.
Her Finest Quarter-Hour : 3877.
Her Garden : 3590.
Her Husband's Name : 2451.
Her Loneliness : 1491.
Her Loving Net : 6394.
Her Memory of the Picnic : 6332.
Her Mother's House : 7060.
Her Planet : 6027.
Her Quiet Words Let Loose : 3062, 3294.
Her Shapeless Ukraine : 6049.
Her Silence : 253.
Her skin is like a crumpled paper : 469.
Her Studio : 6743.
Her Talisman : 2196.
Her Things : 947.
Her Wallpaper : 4104.
Herald : 608.
Herbert's Pebble : 7315.
Herbstzeitlose : 596.
Herculaneum : 3477.
Herd of gray horses : 2503.
Here : 883, 4055, 4536, 4899, 5390, 5712, 6648.
Here a Different Ocean : 1479.
Here and Back Again : 970.
Here and Now : 1392, 2934.
Here and Then : 1994.
Here is the vessel from which I must drown : 1713, 2160.
Here, Now : 5785.
Here Stands the Aged Hammurabi, All Flesh and Blood : 3415.
Here there are girls with tearing breasts : 3484.
Here There Is Only One Season : 899.
Here Yet Be Dragons : 1149.
Hereafter : 4903.
Here's Me at 40 : 2934.
A Heresy : 3772.
Las Heridas del Hudson : 178, 641.
Heritage : 4726.
Hermana : 58, 6724.
Hermaphrodite : 4382.
Hermes : 4090, 5235, 5789.
Hermetic : 5493.
The Hermit : 1122, 3235.
Hermit Crab : 200.
Hermitage : 519, 7345.

Hernan Cortes Sails : 189, 4363.
Hero : 6260.
Herodotus on a Date : 4195.
Heroes : 360.
Heroes, Saints, and Neighbors : 1232.
Heroic Moment : 6076.
Heron : 994, 2257, 6923.
The Heron : 6887.
Herons : 4107, 7144.
Herrenbad : 3513.
Hershey's Cocoa : 5213.
He's Making a Movie : 4830.
Hey, Buddy : 1238.
Hey, Rube : 6976.
Hey You Sitting There Looking at This : 4271.
H.F. : 2552.
Hibernation : 5619.
Hickok and the Sign : 767.
Hidden Marriage : 5337.
Hidden Poem : 1449.
Hide & Seek : 4684.
Hide and Seek : 4770, 5532.
Hide & Seek : 5942.
Hide Away : 6078.
Hiding : 3630.
Hieroglyph : 1135.
High Court : 783.
High Mortgages : 1925.
The High Road to Taos : 1764.
The High-School Band Director Conducts 'The Grand Canyon Suite' : 1411.
High Speed : 2438.
The High Street : 1111.
High Summer on High Street : 3554.
Highline Evaluation Treatment Center : 993.
Highway 51, New Mexico : 6705.
Highway 200 : 5069.
Highway to Nowhere : 6467.
Highways : 2578.
Hijas de Mab : 1071.
Hikers : 2739.
Hiking : 6173.
Hilderic's Palace : 423, 3962.
Hildirici regis fulget mirabile factum : 3962.
Hill Country Cedar : 5566.
Hill's Curve : 3829.
A Hilltop (for Sam) : 5395.
Him : 5451.
Him — (Slash) Her : 793.
Hinglish : 6362.
Hip Replacement : 4199.
Hired Man : 1456.
His Eminence Plays the Soular System : 5419.
His Forearm Across My Mouth : 1981.
His Granddaughter Arrives : 6432.
His Horses : 4984.
His Picture : 3391.
His Secret : 4845.
His Skin the Color of This Coffee : 5020.
His Thighs Strange. Broken. Knowledgeable : 2309.
His word means nothing : 2122, 2576.
Hispaniola : 1124.

The Hiss of the Spirit as It Leaves a Woman's Body : 4864.
Histoire d'Hiver : 2038.
Historic Site : 2256.
Historical Notes : 1079.
Historically Speaking : 4874.
Histories : 2188.
History : 1496, 3829, 6004, 6869.
A History : 1270.
History As the Painter Bonnard : 2869.
History, Biography: French Series : 2115.
History Lesson : 130.
The History of a Voice : 3241.
The History of Abuse, a Language Poem : 1012.
A History of Hellas : 186.
The History of Henry Simpson : 3998.
A History of Prisoners : 4880.
The History of Shaving : 6167.
A History of Stone : 3216.
The History of the World : 4316.
The History of Uncle Botolph, or My Sainted Aunt : 1459.
A History Poem : 3714.
History's Midst : 4936.
A Histry F Censrship : 2331.
Hitchhiking : 285.
Hitchhiking Past the Drive-In : 642.
Hitching a Ride with Gold Miners in the Yukon : 175.
Hitting a Skunk at 60 Miles Per Hour : 1173.
Hivaoa : 2204.
Hoarder of Tragedy : 6076.
Hoarse Song : 143, 3786.
Hoatzin : 614.
Hog : 1895.
Hog Heaven and Bum Hell : 6069.
Hog Myth : 510.
A Hog Slaughtering Woman : 4131.
Hölderlin at the River : 4417.
Holding : 4640.
Holding Katherine : 288.
Holding On : 1148, 6394.
Holding One's Lover : 4026.
Holding Out : 547.
Holding Out the Hands : 5555.
The Holding Shed : 5896.
The Hole : 7330.
Hole Digger : 4596.
Holes in Our Speech : 604.
Holiday Season at the White House : 4381.
The Holidaymakers : 7021.
Holland: *Hungerwinter* (The War Years End) : 2947.
Holloween Costume Contest : 7125.
The Holly Bush : 680.
Hollyhocks Madonna, 1 : 3822.
Hollywood : 3237.
Hollywood Goes Too Far : 6690.
Hollywood Sidewalks : 3164.
Holocaust : 2274.
Holocaust Day : 1082.
Hologram : 3846.
Holograma : 1013.
Holy : 2183.
The Holy Bloom : 231.

Holy June : 1494, 5075, 6411.
Holy Saturday : 1166.
Holy Water : 1899.
Holy Week : 1661.
Homage : 7232.
Homage, Basho : 4700.
Homage to Derrida : 5142.
Homage to N. : 2567.
Homage to Walt Whitman : 6260.
Home : 1365, 1433, 3300, 6659.
Home After Two Weeks Away : 3689.
Home alone : 6977.
Home Boy Carvajal : 4023.
Home Farm : 863.
Home for Christmas : 1.
Home From School : 6831.
The Home-Front : 4140.
Home Girl Steps Out : 3247.
Home in October : 5771.
Home Movie : 5162.
Home on Highland Ridge : 1243.
Home Planet : 6939.
Home Thoughts from the Kimberleys, WA : 1363.
Home-Town Vignette : 5325.
Homebody : 2010.
The Homebody Goes on Tour : 7304.
Homecoming : 3683, 4538, 6940, 7217.
The Homecoming : 5107.
Homecoming Dinner, Dr. Elizabeth Riefsynder, 1914 : 1454.
Homecoming Queen : 3780.
Homecomings : 4587.
Homefires : 1269.
Homegrown Homeopathy : 3163.
Homeland : 2438.
Homeless : 363.
The Homeless : 6975.
Homeless Nixon : 6979.
Homeless Veteran : 163.
The Homely Soldier : 6861.
Homemade Guilt : 2435.
Homemade Mincemeat : 4198.
Homemade Stars : 1632.
Homer Speaks of Penelope : 1259.
Homestead, Florida : 2233.
Homestead, News from - : 6386.
Hometown : 60.
Homeward Turn : 1954.
Homicidal Domicile II: Night of the No-Par : 3476.
Homing In : 3899.
Homo Delphinus : 5395.
Homo / Latino : 252.
Honesty Is Hard to Find : 5323.
Honey and Plaster : 6211.
The Honey Tree Cut Down for Firewood : 865.
Honeycomb : 6120.
Honeymoon : 1852, 2700, 7233.
Honeysuckle : 5993.
Honeysuckles : 4526.
Honfleur : 4377.
Honky-Tonk : 6887.
Honorable Army Discharge : 6333.
An Honorary Habsburg : 2307.

Hoofbeats : 1666.
Ho'ohui'aina Pala ka Mai'a : 3277, 5188.
Hook : 494.
Hooked Bait : 532.
Hooked Ram : 7041.
Hookers Near Arbor Hill : 3822.
Hoop : 2225.
Hootenanny : 4212.
Hoover Trismegistus : 45.
Hope : 5955, 6842, 7192.
Hope Is the Thing with Feathers : 7328.
Hopeless : 2589.
The Hopelessness of the Co-op Butcher :
    664.
Una Hora Antes : 1281.
Horace : 2634.
Horal : 5738.
Horeb Revisited, or: Five Ways to Walk
    Right by a Burning Object : 3628.
Horizon : 1204.
Horizon of Gun Butts : 6500.
Horizons : 279, 3292, 5527, 6939.
Horizons and Myopia : 1001.
The Horned Rampion : 1124.
Horns : 2422.
Horns That Blow at Midnight : 4532.
The Horrible Santas : 1869.
Horrors : 3635.
Horse : 6493.
The Horse : 442, 647, 5804.
Horse Heart : 6883.
Horse Swimming : 4890.
Horseboy : 6939.
Horsecollar Is Rarely : 2552.
The Horses : 6475.
Hortatory : 3815.
Horus : 6003.
Hosanna : 5522.
Hospital : 276.
Hospital Corridors : 6016.
Hospital Room in Yellow and Green : 4041.
Hospital Visit : 2371.
Hospital Window : 2287.
Hospitality : 2195.
Hospitals : 3247.
The Host : 4377.
The Hostage Deal : 3427.
Hostile Witness : 6152.
A Hot Dog Kind of Girl : 3051.
Hot Green Pepper : 912.
Hot Pillow Poems, Remembered : 6406.
Hotel Ballrooms : 2263.
Hotel Beach / After the Hurricane : 494.
Hotel Dauphin : 214.
Hôtel de la Rêve : 211.
Hotel Laundromat : 2542.
The Hotel Miramar : 1112.
Hotel, River View : 5239.
Hounded to the Coast : 4938.
The Hour : 5926.
The Hour Before Dawn : 345.
The Hour of Misrepresentation : 100, 6415,
    6465.
An Hour with Longfellow : 4611.
Hourly : 4410, 5738.
The Hours, Keepers of Heaven : 1777.

Hours of the Cardinal : 3974.
House : 4660, 6292.
The House : 143, 733, 973, 3786, 3996,
    4512.
A House, and the Fields Beyond : 6233.
House Fable : 3300.
A House for the Son : 6525.
The House Growing : 6740.
House-Hunting : 4660.
The House in Winter : 2869.
A House Like This : 4015.
House of Anger : 3897.
The House of Hernan Cortes, Antigua,
    Veracruz : 189, 4363.
The House of Roots : 771.
The House of the Body : 490.
House of the Sun : 511.
The House on Bitterstrasse : 6695.
The House on the Borderland : 5330.
The House on the Boulevard : 4863.
The House on the Hill : 1749.
House Painters : 1775.
The House They Lived In : 1343.
House Walk Over the Mountain : 3816.
Housebroken : 3789.
Households : 3821.
The Housekeeper : 5896.
The Housekeeper and the Handyman : 1187.
Housekeeping : 2404.
The Houseparaders : 771.
Houses : 1512.
Housewarming : 5583.
The Housing Problem : 4624, 5104.
Hovingham : 6649.
How : 1399.
How a Heart Breaks : 5638, 6058.
How a Sunset Works : 815.
How Abstract, the Idea of Mulberries : 5650.
How Can I Whine? : 36.
How curious : 7357.
How Did They Recognize Autumn in the
    Dark of the City? : 3070.
How do you say tomorrow in this country? :
    214, 4171.
How Elvis Would Have Wept for the
    Children of Baghdad : 1129.
How Fur Seals Keep Warm : 2885.
How Grimly They Bare It : 585.
How He Cut Himself Shaving : 3122.
How I Became the Glorious Mr. Dot : 2445.
How I Developed a White Marigold : 6429.
How I Learned That Men and Trees Don't
    Grow in Kansas : 2597.
How Is It? : 2943.
How It Goes in This Family : 131.
How It Is in Fishing : 2529.
How Kukutis Regained His Senses : 4161,
    6290.
How Lester FallsApart Came to Believe in
    Magic After He Tripped Over a Beer
    Bottle . . . : 80.
How lonely the spirit of Erich Fromm : 302.
How Long Peace Takes : 4845.
How Many : 498, 3516, 4920.
How Might This Corner Come to Be? : 4427.
How Mountains Crumble : 1433.

How Music Fought Its Way Through : 2026, 5197.
How My Sister Loves Me : 3934.
How Odd This Landscape : 5581, 5772.
How Often I Used Silence to Mask Anger : 1324.
How Rain Arrives : 6390.
How Say : 5510.
How Seem Bedeviled Be: On the Marriage of Elsie and Wallace Stevens : 3945.
How shall I praise you, polis, as the center or the snare at the center : 4840.
How Some of It Happened : 2975.
How Sudden Dies the Blooming : 1863.
How Sweet the Bye and Bye : 2752.
How the Crazy Love : 5170.
How They Are with Each Other, the Woman, the Man : 6042.
How They Come Back to Us : 7212.
How to Commit Suicide : 1534.
How to Fire a Forklift Driver : 1447.
How to Get a Man : 6192.
How to Get in the Best Magazines : 7137.
How to Grow Young Painting Pictures : 4022.
How to Live Forever : 193.
How to Live with a Bitch : 2549.
How to Lose What You Never Had : 6515.
How to Love a Colorblind Artist : 2288.
How to Love the Dead : 2271.
How to Order Chamomile Tea : 2531.
How to Read a Poem : 1580.
How to Teach Them : 6414.
How to Tell a Bird of Prey : 455.
How Toad Improved Upon Hensel and Gretel : 3877.
How We Are Taken : 1080.
How We Grow : 3494.
How We Listen : 4031.
How White the Lilies : 4711.
Howard : 1634.
Howard Nemerov : 4795.
How's College? : 4078.
Hoyt Knuckles Down : 3969.
Hubbel Trading Post : 1768.
Hubby, Pass the Beer : 7025.
Huellas Rituales : 178.
Huevos son los meses y también los días : 715.
Huge Umber : 5650.
Human Arrangement : 6373.
Human Condition! : 2580.
Human Form : 7182.
Human Nature : 4203.
Human Remains Safely Contained : 4353.
Human Wrecks Whose Years : 1239.
Humanities Lecture : 2852.
Humdingers Kneeslappers Sidesplitters & Yuks : 2331.
Humiliation of the Aphorism : 5356.
Humility : 5042.
The Hummingbirds : 5923.
Hummingbirds, Dazzling in from the Calif Desert : 6858.
Humphrey Gilbert, Going Down : 1383.
Humpty Dumpty : 236.

The Hunchback Sits Up at His Funeral : 6831.
Hundreds of Paired and Spinning Seeds : 1313.
Hung (17° N 88° W) : 5545.
Hung Gao Liang (Red Sorghum Wine) : 2187.
Hungarian Rhapsody 66 : 2328, 3582.
Hungarian Trouble : 416.
Hunger : 4852, 5194.
Hunger, a Cookbook : 5624.
Hunger Moon : 51.
Hunger of the Lost Children : 5112.
Hunger Strike : 4532.
Hungers : 2131.
Hungry : 2371, 5592.
Hunt in Couples : 21.
The Hunter : 2390, 2812.
The Hunter and the Tiger : 251, 6135.
The Hunter, Now Butcher, Dances : 3296.
The Hunters : 2552.
Hunter's Moon : 673, 4407.
Hunting : 892.
Hunting Deer : 5067.
Hunting Horn : 4596.
Hunting Lodge, Wakullah Springs, Florida : 3902.
Hunting Wildflowers : 860.
Hurricane : 5169.
Hurricane Hazel : 1657.
Hurricane Sestina : 4514.
Hurried Night : 436, 1076, 1968.
Hurry, Get Up, There's Work to Do : 6772.
Hurt to See : 3899.
Hush & Taunt : 5540.
Husk : 2153.
Husk and Germ : 4601.
Hutterite Twins Tropical : 381.
Hybrid Magnolias in Late April : 5683.
Hydra : 6228.
Hydrogen: Lightness : 4485.
Hydroponic Madonna : 3822.
Hyena : 3435.
Hymn : 5334.
Hymn of Fire : 3153.
Hymn to Artemis : 979.
A Hymn to X. : 3805, 6227.
Hyperbole : 921.
Hyperborean Letter : 3159, 4803.
The Hyperboreans : 1112.
Hypnogogic Sonnets : 648.
The Hypocrite : 1927, 2489.
Hypothermia : 4501.
Hypothetical : 2705.
I accidentally poured this lousy coffee on myself : 3547, 5638.
I always take my own death with me when I go outside : 3547, 5638.
I Am : 362, 643.
I Am a Black : 769.
I Am Abandoning Iconoclastic Levels : 3546, 5756.
I Am America : 5764.
I Am at Vons : 1002.
I am going home now, Mama : 1138.
I Am Going to Vanish : 4328.

I Am Here for You : 5326.
I am in matters of love : 6186.
I am Judas Too : 4468.
I am living among people whose concerns are not mine : 5585.
I am Not As Philosophical About : 1324.
I am sitting by a pond : 1781.
I Am the Bodhisattva Who Saves the People on This Bus from the Smell of My Feet : 2254.
I Am the No and the Yes : 6202.
I Am the Shepherd of Water : 715, 4875.
I Am Waiting for a Boat : 6321.
I am woman she says : 2206, 7124.
I Been Fractured : 2594.
I Belong : 3996, 4512.
I Better : 5144.
I Bite the Onion : 6902.
I Bought a Yesteryear Major-league Replica Cap : 4909.
I Bought the : 4581.
I Came : 6187.
I Can Imagine the Earth : 316.
I can't drink : 3515, 5601.
I can't make her into a child : 1138.
I Chose the Law : 7098.
I Come Home : 2499.
I come to this park to train : 5113.
I Come to This World As Romance Dies : 6454.
I confess I love the ambiguity of distance : 6879.
I Could Have Danced All Night If I Hadn't Spontaneously Combusted : 483.
I Count the Beery-Lanterns : 7027.
I Did Not Request Your Song in My Dreams : 5377.
'I did what I did,' declared Id : 5132.
I Didn't Know : 4581.
I Do Hate Lollipops : 1546.
I Do No Want to Be : 4128, 5638.
I Do Not Hazard Exegesis : 3877.
I Do Not Sleep Well in This Place on the Hill : 2415.
I Do Not Understand : 1596, 5945.
I Don't Have My Homework, Cause My Uncle Ate It : 14.
I Don't Know Blues : 1496.
I Don't Know How to Sew Buttons : 2638.
I Don't Know the Local : 5865.
I Don't Know When : 2072, 7161.
I don't Know Where You Came From : 3263, 5736.
I Dont Know Who It Is, That Sings, Nor Did I, Would I Tell : 752.
I Don't Stop When I Play Bebop : 5427.
I Don't Touch My Breasts Anymore : 2753.
I Don't Understand Russian, and I Translate : 2103, 3505, 4706.
I Dreamed of You Again Last Night : 3714.
I Dreamt of Blowing Up the Dick Clark Show : 5211.
I Dreamt That Hugo Wolf Got Out of the Asylum : 5001.
I Dwell Too Often : 5902.
I.E. : 5681, 6870.

I Expect the Devil : 2846.
I Feel My Left Hand   Its Flesh   Its Bones   Its Muscles : 4328.
I Find a Rock for You : 5752.
I Found a Bird : 4930.
I Geneviève Bergeron : 6022.
I get enough : 82.
I Give You Life : 3298.
I Glance at Windows : 5460.
I Go After the Clock : 5095.
I go out at night into the garden naked : 3547, 5638.
I Got a New Bed Today : 5477.
I Got the Blues : 3748.
I Grew Two Voices : 2377, 3922.
I Had a Lot to Learn : 6842.
I Had to Pull the Car Over & Swallow Smoke : 6023.
I Have a Hunger : 3944.
I have also loved : 3900.
I Have No More Time : 862, 4057, 4517.
I Have Set My Heart on the Sparrow : 2333.
I Have Stopped Talking About the Ants : 264.
I Have This Poem. It Has No Name : 7160.
I Haven't Given Up : 7027.
I Hear Music : 1366.
I Honestly Don't Remember : 2025.
I Imagine the Gods : 2271.
I invoke you: our shyness and our courage, return : 2160, 2897, 6047.
I Just Wanna Testify : 1743.
I kneel, and in the center of the rose, amid thorns : 5222.
I knelt before my friend, unable : 4690.
I Know (I'm Losing You) : 1743.
I Know Love : 155.
I knowing I'm getting older every day : 5230.
I laugh not knowing: The wind above : 2815.
I Left a Long Time Back : 4530, 6105, 7221.
I Lie Mauve in the Courtyard : 6626.
I Like Ike : 6288.
I like to go see those old blues players : 1195.
I like to think of you naked : 5473.
I Liked Ike : 679.
I lived in a time of revolution at 18 : 4595.
I long for the mantle : 3431.
I Love How One Season Ends in the Middle of Another : 7283.
I Love Your Freedom : 4223, 5338.
I Loved It, Your Pain : 1359.
I Loved You Once But Then I Was Not I : 1080.
I.M. Reverend Lawrence Scanlan, D.D., 1843-1915, First Bishop of Salt Lake : 4826.
I made a hut : 2165.
I may be bruised : 5230.
I Never Thought About It : 4304.
I Oblige the Dean of Enrollment by Writing a Recommendation for My Daughter : 1884.
I open your letter and mouth to mouth : 5113.
I Parked That Damn Girl's Cadillac : 1324.
I peak around the corner, ask : 665, 3589.
I Picture the Rain : 5581, 5656.

I Polished My Nails for This : 6665.
I Poured Into : 6665.
I Promised My Love I Would Boil Her a
    Herring : 2625.
I Read Two Articles in the Paper This
    Morning : 6686.
I Recommend Norway : 1992.
I Remember : 4935.
I Remember Clearly : 498, 3516, 4920.
I Remember Haifa Being Lovely But : 3822.
I Remember the Desert : 4099.
I remember when I was younger and
    everybody was all one big mass of
    pulsating stuff : 3659.
I remember you : 7357.
I Rescue Del Cashin : 3727.
I rinse you in what's mine : 4682.
I roll off her — satisfied, fired, heart : 4186.
I said the forest : 2210.
I Saw Rod Scurry : 5873.
I Saw You There : 2177.
I Say a Little Prayer : 4291, 5657.
I See a Truck : 3054.
I See an Indian Girl I Used to Know Near
    Larimer Street in Denver : 3920.
I See the Future : 1368, 4060, 5901.
I Send Letters : 5344.
I set off from home to define life's way :
    6589.
(I) She Writes with Fire : 3654, 4060, 5901.
I Should Have Known : 3948.
I Should Like to Be Hanged on a Summer
    Afternoon : 5783.
I Shout Into the Phone : 826.
I sleep in your sweater : 3302, 5990.
I slept with the Singing Nun : 1399.
I sob in a deserted city : 2201.
I squashed a beetle walking across my carpet
    : 634.
I Stand and Look : 7070.
I Stared in the Mirror : 5281.
I Stopped Too Long : 2035, 4288.
I Suppose You've Noticed : 2552.
I Swim in the Golden Heat of Jazz's Pure -
    Land of Anarchy : 2254.
I Talk About You : 650, 4818.
I Tell You : 5113.
I, the Excommunicate : 1979.
I Think Continually of Those Who Went
    Truly Ape : 1579.
I Think He's Dead : 3298.
I Thought It Would Be Cold : 3831.
I. To All the Old Apollos : 2045.
I told her in case she was dying : 1138.
I Took a : 4581.
I Took the Devil Standing : 3673.
I tried to catch the evening : 3627.
I Tried to Write a Letter of Longing and Loss
    : 905.
I Turn to You Unfaithful : 4615.
I Used to Think Salt : 7027.
I.V. : 6380.
The I.V. As Control : 3822.
I Wake Her in Vain : 3853, 4460.
I Walk : 4682.
I Want the Power to Go Out : 3545.

I want these fingers to say : 5943.
I want to be somebody's hero sometime :
    5230.
I Want to Know How Rilke Did It : 6935.
I Want to Plug My Ears with Cotton : 2668.
I Want to Walk : 4854.
I was already not too happy that tuesday
    morning : 6550.
I Was Angry : 3054.
I Was Born Before Homogenized Milk :
    3877.
I Was Four in Dotted : 3822.
I Was Gullible : 4621.
I Will Die of Cancer of the Spine : 4889,
    6809.
I Will Leave You in Possession of the Field :
    5045.
I Win : 3298.
I Wish : 5883.
I Woke Up — Smiling : 3175.
I Won't Get Up : 6247.
I Worry : 1263.
I Write Short Poems : 1238.
I Write to the One I Love Who Lives on in
    My Boots : 2254.
I write with clear water   Birds singing :
    2201.
Ianeta's Dance : 6103.
Iatrogenic : 1925.
IBM Memo: Mouse Balls Available as Field
    Replacement Unit (FRU) : 7212.
Icarus : 538.
Icarus in the Garden : 5558.
Ice : 1386.
The Ice Age in Dixie : 4472.
Ice and Sun : 478.
Ice Cream in America : 214.
Ice Cube Epigrams : 4211.
The Ice Fisherman : 3161.
Ice-Fishing : 2651.
The Ice Princess : 2601.
Ice Storm : 2659, 5061.
Ice Time : 5987.
The Iceman : 3503.
Ichthys : 5475.
Icon : 5439.
Ida Goes to the Hens : 6624.
The Idea : 4039.
The Idea as Mollusk, or The Shadow of Fruit
    : 266.
The Idea of Form : 5673, 6871.
The Idea of Poetry : 1274.
The Idea of Rooks : 5586.
Ideas In and Out : 2172.
Identifiable Wings : 5144.
Identity : 2467, 5673, 6871.
Ideogram : 6512.
The Ides of April, North : 5878.
Idiom : 6204.
Idiot-Savant : 2818.
Idle Aria in Battery Park : 4662.
Idylls and Illusions : 3564.
I.E. : 5681, 6870.
If : 6921.
I(f)-55 : 4392.
If all I'd leave you be a poem : 1468.

If genius is nine-tenths tenacity : 2514.
If God Is a Diviner : 4550.
If I am living it is a sign that here nothing is in order : 5638, 5917.
If I Could Keep Her, I Would, He Says : 6473.
If I Had a Lover : 7014.
If I Have Not Trashed My Dearest Treasures : 1324.
If I held back each word, perhaps : 3866.
If I met him   if he wanted me : 2259.
If I pause for an instant this afternoon : 1138.
If I Should Die : 3235.
If Looking, Like : 4038.
If My Mother : 1614.
If Ontogeny Does Not Recapitulate Phylogeny, Then What Is Metaphor? : 2010.
If the Bicycle Is Painted Blue : 3315.
If the race wasn't lost from the start : 5132.
If the Silence Should Suddenly Return : 442, 3077, 5804.
If, Then : 6768.
If there were a sun to see you : 442, 5804.
If This Is Belgium : 1965.
If We Become Famous Lovers : 6970.
If We Can Unwind : 2063.
If we let the Greeks in, they'll betray us : 5132.
If Wishes Were Horses : 2522.
If You Just Imagine : 7354.
If You Love Something, Let It Go : 1443.
If You Were Us, What Would You Do? : 6045.
If You're Bored, Why Not Nosh on a Bit of Nash? : 5051.
If You're Waiting, You May as Well : 5516.
Igne Fifteen : 6296.
Igne Nineteen : 6296.
Igne Thirteen : 6296.
Ignis Fatuus : 5148.
Ignition : 5821.
L'Ignorant : 3100.
Ignore the Wires : 1904.
Ill Wind : 3624, 4417, 7125.
Illegals : 5813.
Illinois Fantasy : 4557.
Illiterate : 278.
Illness : 923.
Illuminated Page : 4879.
Illusion : 6278.
The illusions of youth nearly dead : 5132.
Ils on Vantüraivels : 5096, 6839, 6840.
I'm a Happy Person : 2622.
I'm a Poem : 2937.
I'm Bridges Away : 206.
I'm Dating : 1151.
Im Gewitter der Rosen : 273.
I'm Listening : 736, 5804.
I'm Mad Because of You : 294, 3685, 5962.
I'm No Poet : 1860.
I'm Not Alice : 4872.
I.M. Reverend Lawrence Scanlan, D.D., 1843-1915, First Bishop of Salt Lake : 4826.
I'm Sorry for All the Dads : 6433.

'I'm Temporarily Insane' and Permanently Blue : 5230.
I'm the same age Ted & Jack were : 3983.
I'm tortured : 610, 4450.
I'm With You, Anna Akhmatova, On the Bridge : 3151.
I'm Writing This Poem to Keep Us Alive : 3953.
Image : 127, 274, 2240.
An Image Comes : 7029.
The Image in a World of Flux : 5606.
Imagenes en Dos Tiempos : 2408.
Imagenes I : 2408.
Images : 4541.
Images I : 2408, 4512.
Images in Two Times : 2408, 4512.
Images of Father in the Cremating Heat : 5137.
Imaginary Photographs : 1971.
Imagination : 1135.
Imagine : 701, 4010.
Imagined, Not Recalled : 3642.
Imagining Cavafy : 254.
The Imagining Eye : 2095.
Imagining Their Own Hymns : 3348.
Imaginining It : 351.
Imago : 4364.
Imago 7: Elegy for the Images of Christopher Okigbo : 2237, 6539.
Imago 8: Proportions : 2237, 6539.
Imago 9: The Parchment : 2237, 6539.
Imago . . . to let bloods divide : 511.
Imagoes : 398.
Imhotep : 3499.
An Immense Hand : 957, 6235.
Immersion : 2129, 3681.
The Immigrant Voyeur : 6241.
Immigrants in Arlington : 2525.
Immortality : 7283.
The Immovable Object : 2161.
Immune : 1625.
An Imp Tale : 381.
An Impartial Answer : 7204.
The Impasse : 2426.
Impatient : 318, 4035, 7221.
Impedimenta : 5823.
Implicated : 3054.
The Importance of Angels : 1283.
Important Telephone Numbers : 6726.
Impossibilities : 1110.
The Impossible : 4474.
Impostor : 1757.
Impotence : 867.
Impoverished Land : 1215, 3172, 6235.
Impression : 378, 803.
Impressions : 1379, 6492.
Impressions from the Legends about The Twelve Constellations : 127, 274, 2240.
Imprint : 2939.
Imprints : 1259.
Impromptu Meeting in the Falklands : 110.
Improvisations : 2955.
Improvisations on a Secret Theme : 4283.
In a Bar with CNN on TV : 2256.
In a Blue Light : 5854.
In a cafe   Birds fly round our table : 2201.

In a clock's small space : 6252.
In a College Town : 5599.
In a Desert : 7.
In a Dream : 3054.
In a far-away land alone in my thoughts I live : 4068.
In a Field of Wild Flowers : 6853.
In a Fit of My Own Vividness : 3248.
In a Flat Between Pianos : 5626.
In a Letter Explaining Everything : 5296.
In a Mild Autumn : 6121.
In a Moment : 4850.
In a New Year and Old Moon : 2529.
In a Northern Country : 5050.
In a Season of Political Faction : 6718.
In a Tribal Society : 6974.
In Absence : 5448.
In Adolescence : 4795.
In Amber : 6841.
In Annus Mirabilis : 5718.
In Another World : 3556.
In April : 4834.
In Argentina : 670.
In August : 1152, 7160.
The In Between : 2706.
In Blue Gown and in Black Satin Gown : 5783.
In Both Ears, Out Some Others : 3045.
In Brooklyn : 28.
In Case of Rapture : 1148.
In Celebration of My Uterus : 5957.
In China : 1343.
In Common Ground : 4351.
In Deer Country : 5498.
In Defense of the Body : 3974.
In Defense of the Fallen Clergy : 5635.
In Disiecta Membra : 5718.
In Dubio : 5718.
In England : 1725, 2697, 3176.
In Essence : 4038.
In February : 3136, 4925.
In February, Thinking of the Gulf War : 5603.
In Fire Season: Suite for Sitar and Tabla : 1133.
In Flower : 6196.
In Frosty March : 5508.
In Gratitude : 3076.
In gray morning fog : 1702.
In Hell with Virg and Dan : 1406, 3451.
In Her Kitchen : 5981.
In Heraclitus's River : 327, 1022, 6514.
In Historic Perspective : 4213.
In History, I : 1448.
In History, II : 1448.
In Individuo : 5718.
In Ireland, Shabby Boats Move On : 3283.
In Kandinsky's Korner : 963.
In Kenyon's Fields : 6698.
In la Cabaña : 6973.
In Lacrimae : 5718.
In Lenk We Read the *Zauberberg* in German : 2910.
In Locust Weather, Speaking of Angels : 5944.
In Maine : 4306.

In March : 5385.
In March We're Going to Egypt : 4506.
In Medias Res: A Definition : 1608.
In Melville's Room : 3853.
In Memoriam : 2095, 3268, 6127, 6412, 6747.
In Memoriam: Franklin Walker III 1954 - 1988 : 4547.
In Memoriam: Howard Nemerov : 7365.
In Memoriam: Prayers for William Stafford, 1914-1993 : 5548.
In Memoriam, Virgil Fish, 1925-1977) : 4822.
In Memoriuam : 4993.
In Memory : 291.
In Memory of Abner Troop : 379.
In Memory of Angelica : 362, 643.
In Memory of Audre Lorde, Clifford Lashley and Fritz Henle: Sister of Light : 2624.
In Memory of David Hines : 3616.
In Memory of Martha : 4218.
In Memory of Patrick Kavanagh (1905-1967) : 1905.
In Memory of W. H. Auden : 7033.
In Memory of William Carlos Williams : 1828, 3771.
In Middle Age : 3076.
In Midlife : 4140.
In Mist, in Fire : 1383.
In Mourning Wise : 7236.
In Mudville, In a Time of Plague : 5332.
In My Dream : 1109, 4467.
In My Father's House : 5805.
In My Garden : 6285.
In My Insomnia I Was Advised : 454.
In My Mother's Kitchen, 1943 : 7167.
In My Old Age : 2095, 3557.
In my tree : 1532.
In My Vase : 1049.
In Neutral : 2107.
In New Orleans : 1687.
In October : 4537.
In One Version of the Shape of Things to Come : 582.
In Opere Citato : 5718.
In Order of Line : 3179.
In our identical shirts we hug ourselves hugging each other : 2613.
In Paradisum : 3967.
In Passing : 1535, 1548, 3510.
In Perfect Harmony : 1259.
In Pobiddy, Georgia : 4900.
In Pocatello : 659.
In Praise of Darkness : 3879.
In Praise of Motels : 2843.
In Progress : 6493.
In Pryor, Oklahoma : 6147.
In Quest : 7110.
In Response to Cole Porter's 'You're the Top' : 2627.
In Retreat : 3061, 3264.
In Rivera's Studio : 6743.
In Ron Bernstein's Office at the Gersh Agency : 3983.
In Sickness and in Health : 6561.
In Smoke : 204, 4556.

In Stratford Town upon the Avon : 1192.
In Thai, This Is Called : 3305.
In That Apartment, in That City : 2107.
In That Other Universe : 6059.
In the Act of Becoming Timeless : 6709.
In the Age of the Radio Telescope : 5909.
In the Attic : 3259.
In the Backyard : 1123.
In the Bamboo Hut : 3431.
In the Bathroom Mirror : 861.
In the Beginning : 2928, 3260, 6481.
In the Big Blue Buildings : 7155.
In the Big City : 1014.
In the Bindery : 174.
In the Black Forest : 6309.
In the bowling alley of egalitarian ideologies
    : 2514.
In the Buda Hills : 6890.
In the Cemetery : 4713.
In the Country of No Remorse : 3070.
In the Cross Hairs : 784.
In the Dark : 4510.
In the Darkness : 2228.
In the Descartes Mountains : 6501.
In the Desert : 4608.
In the Distance : 2293, 5515.
In the Doghouse Stag Cafe : 5557.
In the Doorway : 4417.
In the Driver's Seat : 4815.
In the Duchess : 3651.
In the English Class : 2822.
In the Ersatz-World : 5673, 6871.
In the Evening : 5490.
In the First Circle : 1406, 5196.
In the Forest : 2023.
In the Forest of Signs and Dreams : 5414.
In the frozen Bracken : 6767.
In the Garden : 6918.
In the Garden of the Tantalus Museum :
    1097.
In the Green Drawing Room at Hollins
    College : 1881.
In the Half Life : 4378.
In the Hazel Wood : 1631.
In the High Fierce West : 5022.
In the Highstreet of Tralee : 3677.
In the Hollow of an Intricate City : 2820.
In the Hospital : 2095, 6127, 6747.
In the Hotel : 2398.
In the House of the Slaves : 3673.
In the Intense Latitudes : 474.
In the Jungle : 1576.
In the Kitchen of the Bungalow : 264.
In the Land Where Ludwig Came Only in the
    Evening : 3569.
In the Last Seconds : 5516.
In the Lifting of Faces : 2717.
In the Little Church of St. Mary's : 4942,
    6778.
In the Little House at Sunset : 802.
In the Locked Room : 942.
In the long evening : 159, 2576.
In the Long Run : 2857.
In the Marsh : 428.
In the Microscope : 2927, 4498.
In the Middle of Nowhere : 2457.

In the Middle of the Tall Night in the Cobble -
    Stone City, Captain James — the Sailor
    Man — Heads for Home : 1794.
In the Middle of This Century : 117, 2509.
In the Midnight Hour : 2864.
In the Mirror : 6935.
In the Moonlight : 4612.
In the Morning : 3522, 5825.
In the Mountain View Municipal Parking Lot
    : 3081.
In the Mouthcage : 1584, 5243.
In the Museum of the Eighteenth Century :
    2437.
In the National Gallery : 10.
In the New Garden : 3343.
In the New World : 3343.
In the Night : 5368.
In the Night Kitchen on Emerson Street :
    3283.
In the Parking Lot at the Junior College on
    the Eve of a Presidential Election :
    4365.
In the Pasture of Dead Horses : 7022.
In the Pines: For Annie : 3052.
In the Pit of Crinoline Ruffles : 4640.
In the Place of the Absence of Desire : 211.
In the Rainbows : 155.
In the Reading Room of the 42nd Street
    Library : 3537.
In the Retirement Home : 4730.
In the School of Dance : 1491.
In the Shawangunks : 5128.
In the Shower Room : 4195.
In the Sorry Part : 1448.
In the Southern Hemisphere : 4095.
In the spring I am always afraid : 5132.
In the Stable : 7073.
In the Storm of Roses : 273, 5129.
In the Streets : 3161.
In the Talmud : 1958.
In the Telling : 3206.
In the Tenth Mounth, There Are Flowers :
    4551.
In the Twinkling of an Eye : 5089.
In the Valley of the Moon : 6454.
In the Viennese Style : 6031.
In the Village : 3998.
In the Virgins : 6859.
In the Waiting Room : 2445.
In the Wake of the Strafing and Bombing,
    My Sullen Silence : 4350.
In the Wasteland : 1458, 6669.
In the Weather : 6743.
In the Windbreak : 5444.
In the Window/Monk : 2382.
In the Woods : 3998.
In the Workshop : 2714.
In the World : 1700.
In There Anyone Out There in that Editor
    Suit? : 3630.
In These Days Hooked like Railway Cars :
    1829.
In these worlds, in every one : 5673, 6871.
In this Big Bed : 2589.
In This House : 4692, 5308.

In this moment, in the twilight of a cold room, thunder approaches : 1483, 4410.
In This Old Fastness : 1088.
In This Place Scented of Lilacs : 4072.
In This Room : 884.
In This Version : 3822.
In This World : 6477.
In Those Days : 3232, 4179.
In Toledo : 3198, 5749.
In Tongues : 5526.
In Touch at Last : 2580.
In Transit : 5373.
In Ultima Thule : 5718.
In Unison : 1855.
In Urbe : 5718.
In Used Light : 6980.
In Visible Light : 2298.
In Water : 4923.
In Weeds : 5102.
In Which Nothing Is As It Seems: Vizcaya : 494.
In Which the Ancient History I Learn Is Not My Own : 622.
In Your Garden : 5691.
Inca Doves : 4231.
Incan Forests : 6895.
Incarnate Eternity : 5282.
Inch-Long Baby : 6318.
Incident on the Second Floor : 1259.
InCityFrozen : 1533.
Incoming : 6233.
Incontinence : 2538.
Independence Day, 1956: A Fairy Tale : 2157.
Index of First Lines : 1579.
The Indian : 2114.
Indian Death Song : 7241.
Indian Head Tavern : 6287.
Indian Heaven : 5361.
Indian Lake : 5415.
An Indian Legend Says : 2630.
Indian Paint : 2295.
Indian Paint Brush : 3328.
Indian Statue: Pioneer Park : 7372.
Indian Summer : 4539, 5836, 6097.
Indiana Thunderstorm : 1812.
India's Increments : 5647.
Indicia of Madness : 6220.
Indifference : 2465.
Indifferent Paradise : 1499.
Indifferently, he watched her through the shadows of furniture : 1483, 4410.
Indirective : 2157.
Indra's Falls : 521.
Induction Center '71 : 1188.
Industrial Lace : 2129.
Industry : 6242.
Inevitable Meetings : 2046, 3282, 5037.
The inevitable roof with antennae : 4152.
The Infant King : 4820.
Infant of Prague : 5526.
Infantry Reunion : 7031.
Infatuation : 1222, 6474.
Inferno : 1406, 2153, 5196, 5196.
Inferno: Canto V (Paolo and Francesca) : 1406, 5196.

Inferno, Canto XIII: The Wood of the Suicides : 1406, 5196.
Inferno, Canto XXII: Among the Malebranche : 1406, 5196.
Infestation : 5483.
Infidelity : 759, 2971, 3730.
The Infinite Possibilities of Desire : 4104.
The Infirmary : 1596.
Infomred Consent : 6417.
Ing Poem for Sheila Murphy : 858.
Ingrid & Elsa : 3422.
Inheritance : 2219, 5998.
Inhuman : 360.
The Inhuman : 6495.
Initiation : 4505.
Ink : 1757.
Inland Waterways : 5709.
The Inn : 5995.
Inner : 2422.
The Inner City Exhibits : 3712.
The Inner Life : 3247.
Innocence : 585, 2095, 6234, 6781.
Innocent Bystanders : 4682.
An Inordinate Fondness for Beetles : 5955.
Inquest : 911.
Inquiry : 3247.
Insanity creeping up behind me : 4386.
Insanity Runs in the Family : 2138.
Inscribed at the Temple of Immortal Roaming : 2606, 6984.
Inscribed Stele : 6759, 7065.
Inscription : 904.
Inscription in Stone : 4894.
Insemination Tango : 6772.
Inside : 4160.
Inside a Ring : 267.
Inside and Outside Houses : 3228.
The Inside Angel : 6752.
The Inside of Cut Strawberries Is Sharp, Sexual, Pink as Bone : 4969.
Inside Out : 2454, 3219.
Inside Passage : 154.
Inside St. Paul's : 301.
Inside the Church in Lodz : 3822.
Inside the Eyelids : 4890.
Inside the Inside of the Moon : 4261.
Inside the Marvelsphere : 1135.
Inside the Sound : 3093.
Insider Trading : 6481.
Insight : 753, 3998.
Insistent : 943.
Insleave for A Hieroglyphic Key to Spiritual Mysteries: Published Posthumously in Stockholm, 1784 : 2845.
Insomnia : 56, 2076, 2538, 3198, 3910, 3958, 4512, 5598, 5749.
Insomnia After Moving : 505.
Insomnia Asylum : 12.
Insomnia at the Solstice : 3381.
The Insomnia of the Portrait : 2465.
Insomniac : 2977.
Insomniac Trains : 1343.
The Insomniac's Lexicon : 6978.
The Insomniac's Pet Shop : 4113.
Insomnio : 56, 2175, 5598.
Inspiration : 6544.

Inspired by a Rumor That Edward Abbey
    Was Spotted Last Week at a Hardware
    Store in Espanola, New Mexico : 4268.
Instability : 648.
Instances : 143, 3786.
Instant : 1927, 2697, 3176, 3603, 4545, 6453.
Instant Sleep : 1351.
Instant Systems : 7155.
Institution : 6624.
Instruction Manual : 4235.
Instructions : 7047.
Instructions on Catching a Salmon : 2511.
Instructions to Crossing the Border : 3344,
    4995.
An Instrument Also : 5469.
Integer : 1514.
Intelligence of Rhyming: Poems & Stories —
    VI : 3521.
Inter-Species : 4296.
Intercept : 4857.
Intérieur : 729.
Interior : 729, 4410.
Interior with Faded Colors : 442, 1584, 5804.
Interior with Two Women at a Linen Chest :
    4800.
Interjections V-VIII: A Poem for Lyman
    Larson : 6457.
Interlude : 350.
Intermezzo : 5239.
Internal Damnation: the Furnace of Angels :
    6003.
Internal Differences : 6916.
The International : 5265.
The Interpreter on the Santa Maria: Luis de
    Torres : 5141.
Interracial Series : 4052.
Interrogation : 94.
The Interrupted Life : 752.
Interrupted Prayers : 1924.
Interrupted Version : 1591.
Intersection : 665, 1057, 3152.
Intersection Blood : 1940.
Interstate : 6697.
Interval : 5392.
An Interval of Five Tones Being the
    Dominant : 2705.
Interview owith Carmela : 455.
Interview with the Patient in 302 : 305.
An Interwoven Man and Woman Talked :
    5783.
Intimacy Joint Ventures : 998.
The Intimacy of the Song Inverse to the Dull
    Lores : 68.
Intimate Fishing Secrets : 3387.
Intimations : 2935.
Intimations of Snowlight in Autumn : 497.
Into a Punchline : 2800.
Into Care : 1444.
Into History : 72.
Into It : 7147.
Into Mexico : 6764.
Into the Heart : 5054.
Into the Hill Country : 6518.
Into the Night : 4593.
Into the Trees : 6743.
Intone : 4293.

Intrepid : 6842.
Introdução as Canto : 143.
Introducing 'Love' : 2431.
Introduction : 4038, 6252.
An Introduction : 371, 6768.
Introduction: How to Get Your Wings : 4591.
An Introduction to Greatness : 838.
Introduction to Poetry / Rhyme : 3450.
Introduction to the Asylum : 5686.
Introduction to the Introduction to Wang Wei
    : 653, 4070, 5060.
Introduction to the Song : 143, 3786.
Intruder : 3162.
Invaded by Souls : 2150.
An Invalid : 2244.
Invariably I can't rid myself of the feeling :
    5638, 7026.
Invasion : 6934.
Invasions of Privacies : 1975.
Inventing the Filipino : 3830.
The Invention of Feedback : 2875.
The Invention of Strangers : 1968.
Inventive Story Telling : 3926.
The Inventor : 5303.
Inventory : 2727, 3651, 5261, 6213.
The Inventory of Rage : 6933.
The Inventory Queen : 3360.
Inversion : 2215.
Invert : 5440.
Invicta Carne : 2323.
Inviolata : 3967.
Invisible Dark : 3031.
Invitation : 4127, 5091.
The Invitation : 6890.
Invitation to a Voyage : 5610.
Invitation to a Wedding : 7023.
Invitation to the Dance : 956.
Invocation : 210, 767, 1242, 7153.
An Invocation : 2331.
Invocation of the Second Chance : 5650.
Iowa Blues Bar Spiritual : 2797.
L'Ipocrita : 2489.
Iraqi Eviction : 5209.
Iris : 5621.
The Iris : 2533.
Iris Is Last : 1044.
The Irish Wilderness : 1975.
Iron : 2697, 3176, 6907.
Iron Eyes Cody : 4447.
An Ironic Nocturne : 4735, 7309.
Irony : 3961.
Irrational Numbers : 3028.
Irrefutable Evidence : 3911.
Is Light : 2508.
'Is This a Feminist Statement?' She Asked,
    Dismayed : 2344.
Is This What Hemingway Meant? : 3273.
Isaac Taub Finds His Vocation as Rabbi:
    Czechoslovakia, 1791 : 1259.
Isabel : 5747, 5941, 6032.
Isla Negra: for Neruda : 811.
Island : 973, 1342, 1897, 6143.
The Island : 1458, 2552.
Island Woman : 3184.
Islands : 1045.
Islas de Canarias : 663.

Ismene : 3802, 6135.
An Isolated Piano Note : 2625.
Isotropic Mist : 783.
Issavienojums : 4652.
Issei Strawberry : 4670.
Istanbul, 1923 : 4195.
Istante : 3603.
Istehar Returning : 7353.
Isthmus Is a Particularly Difficult Word : 3460.
It : 4964, 6122.
It Begins with a Presentiment : 3945.
It Blows, Is Blowing : 3844.
It Came to Him : 4347.
It Can't Be Spring : 1534.
It Comes As No Surprise : 5661.
It Doesn't Matter Why : 862, 5343, 6844.
It Happened in the Afternoon : 498, 4920.
It Has Been Written : 4718, 5965.
! It invites direct experience : 2111.
It Is : 1725, 2697, 3176.
It Is Believing : 4392.
It Is Difficult to Remember a Name in a Lanugage You Don't Speak : 4542.
It is for you I write, hypocrite : 897, 1033.
It Is Hard to Look at What We Came to Think We'd Come to See : 2309.
It is intelligence : 5548.
It Is Sticky in the Subway : 5875.
It Isn't Because the Years Like Water Leak from My Hands : 7209.
It isn't war you fear so much as peace : 4615.
It Makes Sense That Lawrence Welk Died on a Sunday : 3888.
It moves and you're standing a stone : 511.
It Must Be Love : 3521.
It Needs Brains : 2332.
It Seemed Like Forever : 5505.
It Takes Me : 5440.
It takes more flickering, wires : 5113.
It Takes One to Know One : 3620.
It Takes Seventeen Cups of Coffee to Fuel Us from Nebraska to Kentucky and Back : 6372.
It Takes Time : 2917.
It Was a Dorm Hall : 3384.
It was a spring of cool flowers : 5222.
It was all there under my grandfather's apple tree : 5222.
It was at your funeral : 6801.
It Was Like Having : 3822.
It Was Sigmund : 2552.
It Was Toward the End of the Revolution That Tatanya Melanovna Became a Sensation in Petersburg : 2389.
It Was War : 389, 442, 5804.
It wasn't fire : 715, 4875.
It Will Wait : 5555.
It Would Only Be Right : 3135.
Italiam Non Sponde Sequor : 1678.
Italian American Home School : 3610.
Italian Smoking Piece : 5794.
The Itch and Scratch of Earth — for Rod Tullis (1960-93) : 339.
Itemized Expenses : 2507, 5790.
Itinerario del Sueño : 59.

Itinerary of Sleep : 59, 2034.
It's a Drag Just Breathing Through My Nostrils All Day Long : 838.
It's Always Getting Later : 3004.
It's Always Night : 1185.
It's an Art of Balance : 6665.
It's Basic : 1010, 4963.
It's because of flowers : 5117, 5254.
It's Been So Long : 3822.
It's Good But It Ain't Heroin : 6975.
It's in the Kitchen : 4668.
It's not the precision : 3119, 5861.
Its Origin : 3054.
It's Said He'll Die : 3298.
It's So Nice : 7040.
Its the Bottom of the Eighth, and So Far They've Knocked Every Pitcher Out of the Box : 1842.
It's the Truth : 2492.
It's Then You Begin to Burn Things : 5991.
It's This I Ask : 4839.
It's Time : 1034.
It's time — farewell to irony! : 442, 5804.
It's True He Met Her at Druxy's & His Coffee Was Cold Before She Offered Him a Seat : 6959.
It's Twenty Degrees, and It's Snowing, and I'm in My Livingroom, Idly Contemplating a Page of Grimy Erasure : 2331.
It's twilight : 3303, 4720, 7044.
It's winter in the haiku that hardly anyone believed : 4152.
I.V. : 6380.
The I.V. As Control : 3822.
I've Been Everywhere and Nowhere : 5025.
I've charged the lout next door : 4149, 4199.
I've gotten nothing for weeks : 7270.
I've Heard a Lot About You : 3662.
I've known for years I would be the one to find her : 1138.
I've lifted above to hear below : 6589.
I've Never Told : 4581.
I've Seen God Only Twice : 100, 2879, 6465.
The Ivory Novel : 2562.
Ivwri: Invoking the Warrior Spirit : 4887.
Izquierdo : 6441.
Jaap's House : 6743.
Jack : 2741, 5395.
Jack and June Laughing, 1958 : 2999.
Jack-in-the-Box : 5538.
Jackhammer in the Bakery : 678.
Jackie and Campy : 6497.
Jack's Beans: A Five-Year Diary : 6182.
Jacob : 7331.
Jacob and Esau : 1514.
Jacob's Ladder : 3379.
Jacumba : 3531.
Jade, Emerald Ad Chartreeuse [sic] Light in the Branches : 3822.
Jade Void : 4105.
Jaffrey Center Cemetery : 435.
Jalisco Exhibit 1992: To the Smiling, Seated Woman : 3018.
James : 4515.
James Joyce : 349, 643, 4433.

Jamestown : 3488.
Jan Pakarati : 3757.
Jane Is Doing Phone Sex Again : 6246.
Jane, Remember These Men and Women :
   1114.
Janet on Thin Ice : 6278.
Janis Joplin : 1356.
January : 1942, 3854, 5434, 6906.
January 7th: Two Views : 3453.
January 16, 1991, Owls's Head Park, False
   Spring : 1454.
January 23, 1991 : 1129.
January 23 — I go out / Le 23 janvier — Je
   sors : 4688.
January 25, 1993 : 1986.
January 27, 1990: P.M. : 4439.
January 1991 : 1149.
January in Indianapolis : 5518.
The Japanese: a Prose Poem : 4671.
Japanese Beetles : 3372.
The Japanese Desire : 5713.
Japanese Slump : 6690.
Japonais : 1595.
A Jar of Teeth : 6215.
Jardín : 1028.
El Jardin de Tus Delicias : 5657.
Jardin du Luxembourg : 7216.
Jardins intérieurs : 1285.
The Jaws of Factory (Graveyard Shift) : 296.
Jazz Me, Baby : 4707.
Jealousy : 6911.
Jean Garrigue: An Appreciation : 3862.
Jean Stafford : 7175.
Jeanne Marie Plouffe : 3822.
Jean's Garden, Before the Rain : 4018.
'Jeff' of 'Mutt and Jeff' Leans on Air : 2331.
Jefferson Davis, Blackhawk and the
   Emergence of the Acceptance Principle
   in Mid-19th Century America : 5377.
Jehovah's Witnesses : 4217.
Jellyfish : 339.
Jenaer Elegien : 5382.
Jesse James: Jesus Saves : 3468.
Jesus and the Cat : 6586.
Jesus As Infant in a Renaissance Painting :
   3835.
Jesus Considers the Night : 6202.
Jesus in Cape Girardeau : 2867.
Jesus the Low Rider : 1333.
Jet Flight : 2379.
Jethro Martin, Elvis Impersonator : 7175.
The Jetty : 4260, 6451.
Jeu de Boules at Sunset: Bimini : 3258.
The Jeweler : 2834.
The Jewels of Windsor : 4732.
The Jewish Cemetery in Prague — Tisha
   B'av : 6538.
Jewish Cemetery in Weissensee : 3579, 6336.
The Jews in England : 6065.
The Jews of England : 6065.
JFK and Martin Luther King : 4246.
Jiaohe : 6051.
Jigglebustation (n.) : 1559.
The Jilted Maiden : 3493, 4604.
Jim Left the Pet Cemetery with a Feeling of
   Disgust : 6544.

Jimmy : 3971.
Jimmy Swaggart : 3132.
Jinx : 1449.
The Jo-Al Beauty Shoppe : 1052.
Joan Herself : 260.
Job : 36, 1104.
Job Printing : 3464.
Job's Comforters : 6650.
Job's Punishment : 1280.
Jocasta : 2152.
Joe : 2083.
Joe Boxer : 4472.
Joey : 3971.
Joey McGraw's Desk, 1960 : 5555.
Johannes from Dresden : 6168.
Johannesburg Jacarandas : 1944.
John : 677, 2540.
John Berryman's Lost Son : 6282.
John Brehm's Latest Poem : 3592.
John Cage Collage in the Marble Hall : 1673.
John Crow Batty : 5169.
John Smith : 7216.
John Sprockett Finds Shelter for Himself and
   Sophia Starling from a Sudden
   Snowstrom, Colorado Territory, 1873 :
   1259.
John the Baptist. Two Hungers : 6772.
Johnetta Betch Cole : 1863.
Johnny and the Post-Nuclear Family : 6288.
Joining the Imperial Bourgeoisie : 5293.
The Joke : 4927.
Jonah Considers His Right Hand from His
   Left Hand : 6586.
Jordanville : 5777.
Jorge Wrote This Poem : 923.
José Carreras : 1169.
Josefa's Dream : 670.
Josephine Baker: Two Poems : 73.
Josephine Johnson: The Sister : 6876.
Joshua and Jesse : 2618.
Jouissance : 5707.
Journal Entry from an Empty Hand : 613.
Journal Entry, July 28, 1972 : 2233.
Journal from My Night Hotel : 2669.
Journey : 4667, 6004.
The Journey : 1038, 2927, 7282.
Journeys on the Highway : 1385.
J'ouvre cette orange : 1285.
Joy to the World : 1778.
Juan Angel : 206.
Juan of the Angels : 2678.
Juchitec Market Women : 6963.
Judah P. Benjamin in Exile in London, 1865 :
   1259.
Judas : 6165.
Judgment : 130.
Judgment Call : 6970.
Judgment Day : 4733.
La Judicial : 2704.
Judson Baptist Church : 2867.
Judy : 97.
Judy Garland Laughing : 5069.
Juego de Imágenes en Azul en Palabras :
   4948.
Juego de Manos : 63.
Jukebox 1946 : 6966.

Julia : 1349, 2824, 3715.
July : 2222, 2418.
July 4, 1974-1984 : 5403.
July Funeral : 611.
July, I-77 : 337.
July: Moon of Bird-listening : 6379.
Jump : 4429.
June : 7053.
June 1st : 921.
June 12, 1812: Egg Harbor : 4206.
June 21, 1989 : 6628.
June, 1987 : 2317.
Junín : 349, 643.
Junk : 5286.
Junk Cars: Mina, Nevada : 6035.
Junk Week : 5669.
Junkets on a Sad Planet: A Poetic Novel
    Based on the Life of John Keats : 1135.
Jurassic Church : 6010.
Just a Suggestion : 5617.
Just After I Knew : 2363.
Just Another Bearish Downsweep : 4153.
Just Another Faggot Poet : 6643.
Just as a Star : 4689, 6839, 6840.
Just Asking : 1274.
Just Before Curfew (Rattling Chains) : 1650.
Just Before Dawn : 2401.
Just Before December : 3642.
Just Before Ovulation : 784.
Just beside us a flock of days : 4063, 5804.
Just Cool It : 6690.
Just for Fun : 2264.
Just Grass: a Prairie Walk : 6215.
Just Married : 3398.
Just Next Door : 6577.
Just Now : 2975.
Just Off Highway 82 East : 4472.
Just Off the Bus : 3746.
Just off the ground and the mower : 5113.
Just Say : 5412.
Just the Two of Us : 5667.
Just Visiting : 1243.
Just War : 7324.
Just What's There : 214.
Just When I Thought I'd Seen It All : 6287.
Just Wonders : 1499.
Just You at the Last : 5210.
Justice, 1937 : 2153.
Justifying the Margins : 6365.
Justine Has a Few Words for the Marquis de
    Sade : 1206.
Ka Parlekt Savai Enai : 4652.
Kafka and Milena in Bed : 1918.
Kagami : 819.
Kahlo : 5963.
Kala — Seventh Grade, Me — Sixth Grade
    Sitting on Our Bikes by the Catholic
    Church : 7254.
Kaleidoscope : 3094.
Kaliyugen : 2064.
Kambuja: Stelae from the Khmer Empire :
    4092, 6539.
Kandinsky Paints the Deep South : 3257.
Kansas : 1719, 3161.
Kansas 1888 : 535.
Kansas As Metaphor : 6096.

Kansas: Stories : 2331.
Karl Shapiro : 5971.
Karol's Bridge in Prague, Watercolor : 2046,
    3282, 5037.
Kate O'Brien Weekender Meets La Leche
    Leaguers : 4873.
Kathmandu, A Canto : 708.
Katie at Twenty-One : 5265.
Katie Can't Go Out Today : 5315.
Katrina's Bedroom : 1187.
Kaua'i : 483.
Kaulana Na Pua : 6676.
Keats and Coleridge : 858.
Keats at Chichester : 1124.
Keats in Ohio : 2437.
Keats Rants About Having Been Poisoned,
    Rome, December, 1820 : 1259.
Keen Edges : 5792.
Keen to Leaky Flowers : 3017.
Keep House : 5551.
Keeping Afloat : 3634.
Keeping America Beautiful : 1653.
Keeping Books : 921.
Keeping Company : 7160.
Keeping That Cancer Letter to Myself:
    Flying to Romania : 2585.
Keeping the Books : 1399.
Keeping the Plane Up : 6876.
Keeping Time : 678, 1691.
Keeping Up with the Jones' : 54.
Keeps on Turning : 7071.
Kelly at Graveside : 5201.
Kensington Place : 2027.
Kenya : 4693.
The Kenya Rumor : 996.
Kevin : 5685.
Kevin Plays the Goldberg Variations : 2678.
Key Episodes from an Earthly Life : 7220.
A Key into the Language of America : 6871.
Key Lime Pie : 1568.
Keyholes II : 6393.
Keys : 6256, 6511, 7370.
KI som nah, Can speak : 511.
Kibitzer : 7304.
Kid Hielero : 5534.
Kid Moves Out : 2800.
Kid's Day : 4795.
Kien-Wu in a Nocturnal Storm : 1102.
Kilcoolie Fern : 6174.
Kilimanjaro's Self-Introduction : 4239, 6201.
Killer Teach : 7183.
The Killers of Everything : 2447.
The Killing Poem : 1371.
Killing Time : 1023.
Killing Youth : 2998.
Kilmeresque : 2639.
Kimberley Brief : 4686.
Kind Hands and Soft Voices : 5416.
A Kind of Ascension : 2713.
A Kind of Darkness : 6030.
A Kind of Goodbye : 3438.
A Kind of Grace : 1121.
A Kind of Loving : 6716.
Kindergarten : 3429.
The Kindergarten Way : 5119.
Kindling the Family Orchard : 5557.

Kindness : 3423.
Kinescope : 4165.
A King, a Sheik, and a Sailor Give a Flower and a Bird to a Beast : 3732.
King Kong Daddy at the Movies : 2910.
King Maggot : 6023.
King of Hearts : 5162.
The king of the fools ordered : 5638, 7026.
King Queen Jack : 5145.
King Richard's Faire : 954.
King Snake : 1188.
The Kingdom : 654.
Kingdom Come : 314.
Kinglet Banding : 4627.
Kings Road Cafe : 449.
Kiss : 672.
The Kiss : 4167, 6247.
Kiss Chase : 7296.
A Kiss in the Dark : 1800.
Kiss of the Moon : 6154.
Kiss Pressed Like a Flower : 2150.
Kisses : 4112.
Kissing : 2359.
Kissing Faulkner : 588.
Kissing the Mirror : 863.
The Kitchen : 3396.
Kitchen Study : 5308.
The Kitchen Table : 527.
Kite : 1927, 3603.
The Kite : 2570, 3238.
Klamm : 1971.
(kN) : 5011.
Kneading Bread : 141.
Knell : 7360.
The Knife : 1889, 2697, 6907.
Knight in Error : 7283.
Knights of the Round Table : 1197.
Knives for the Mushroom : 4696.
Knocking at This Door : 360.
Knotted Letter : 2150.
Knotted Webbing : 5277.
The Knowing : 4892.
Knowing the Place : 4681.
Knowing the Way : 6935.
Koan for a Friend : 2571.
A Kona : 5750.
Kong Views an Experimental Art Film at the City Library : 6697.
Kore in Bloom : 2914.
The Korean Market : 2306.
The Krazy Kat Rag : 5164.
Krell : 6512.
Krishnamurti's Journal : 530.
KRS-1 : 6306.
Kukutis' Appeal to the Alphabet : 4161, 6289.
Kukutis Beats Scholar Pliugzma's Dog : 4161, 6289.
Kukutis' Consciousness Becomes Alienated : 4161, 6289.
Kukutis Dreams up Zuveliskes Village in the Cathedral Square : 4161, 6289.
Kukutis Opens His Eyes : 4161, 6289.
Kukutis' Sermon to the Pigs : 4161, 6290.
Kukutis Wants to See His Homeland : 4161, 6290.

Kukutis' Words : 4161, 6289.
Kulaiwi: Source of Bone : 6971.
Kung Yee Fat Choy : 7229.
Künstlerroman : 3191.
Kupec Family Reunion : 1385.
The Kurds : 3578.
Kuwait Interlude : 5209.
Kwan Yin : 3612.
L.A. Cops : 6975.
L.A. on the Half Shell : 4180.
La-Z-Boy : 4325.
Lab Rats : 1015.
Laberintos : 3174.
Labor : 6647.
Labor Day : 1122, 4073.
Labor Day Nap : 1447.
The Laboratory : 6842.
Labyrinth : 470.
Labyrinth: The Shadow of the Wind : 1584, 5243.
The Lachrymose Marie d'Oignie : 894.
Lack of Leda : 3439.
A Lack of Sound : 6386.
Lackawanna : 4417.
The Ladies : 5494.
Lady Chatterly : 3985.
Lady Dorrance : 4588.
The Lady in Idaho : 6266.
Lady in Mink : 7146.
Lady Xoc : 3499.
Lady's Slippers by Deer Pond : 802.
Lágrima : 143.
The Lake : 6147.
The Lake in Winter : 5161.
Lake Nora : 5418.
Lake Snow : 4260.
Lake Under the Skull : 3765.
Lake Union, Early Spring : 4490.
Lambing, Upstate New York : 3105.
Lame Ducks, 1945 : 3783.
Lamen 'Tater : 4325.
Lament : 822, 1621, 1641, 2500, 6055, 7121.
A Lament : 5480.
Lament for a Young Son Who Fell from a Roof : 5315.
Lament for Anne : 902.
Lament for Eyak : 2660.
Lament for Frida Kahlo : 2041.
Lament for Icarus : 2659.
Lament for Marguerite : 141.
A Lament for Myself : 426, 5717.
Lament for the Death of Parsifal Hoolig : 548, 2220.
Lament for the Nape of Tom Steward's Neck : 548, 2220.
A Lament for the State of Ohio as a Lament for Ohio State : 6903.
Lamentation : 11, 2202, 4644, 6447.
Lamentation and Farewell : 350.
Laments of the Gorges : 2856, 4404.
La Lampara : 4166.
Lana Turner : 7168.
Lance and Andi: Friends Gone West : 7212.
Land Changes : 4573.
Land Lights: New Orleans : 6228.
The Land of Bears : 7235.

Land of Mud : 1983, 2095, 4919.
The Land of the Cochise Apaches : 2186.
The Land of the Knobble-Jobble Tree : 121.
The Land of the Lemon Trees : 332.
Land of the Morning : 940.
Landed Immigrants : 5439.
Landfall : 49.
A Landing Place : 7226.
Landlocked : 1313.
A Landlord Tale : 381.
Landmarks : 6743.
Landrum's Diner, Reno : 3683.
Landscape : 1109, 5088.
The Landscape : 521.
Landscape and Headache : 5416.
Landscape for a Yorkshire Woman : 1396.
A Landscape in the North Riding : 3998.
The Landscape Is Behind the Door : 214, 4171.
Landscape: January 1991 : 4602.
The Landscape of Desire : 2430.
The Landscape of the Breast : 3958.
Landscape Over Some Film of Godard's : 1690.
Landscape with Coyote and Special Effects : 5792.
Landscape with Houses : 7021.
Landscape with the Fall of Icarus : 5323.
The Landscapist : 214, 4171.
The Langlois Bridge, March 1888, Arles : 4102.
Language : 1488, 1719, 5123.
Language and Experience : 5606.
Language and Humility : 2506.
Language Barrier : 7132.
Language Burns : 4004.
Language, Cool Down : 2092.
The Language of Crows : 7158.
The Language of Flowers : 1709.
The Language of Rilke : 537.
Langueur : 6805.
Lao-Tzu : 281, 6872.
Lappland: Ammarnäs : 617.
Lapse : 5408.
Lapsed : 863.
Lara and the New World : 2261.
Lareina Silenciosa : 320.
Lark : 4417.
Larry Josephs, 34, Writer About AIDS, Dies of the Disease : 3813.
Larry's Back in Town : 3748.
The Larynx : 3219.
Laser Opera, July 3, 1991 : 4798.
Lassitude : 4578, 6805.
Last : 678.
The Last and Longest Conversation : 4183.
Last April : 1978.
The Last Argument : 5432.
Last August : 514.
Last Baskets Before Night : 5900.
The Last Belle of St. Joe's : 1266.
Last Blues : 4634.
Last Breath : 6033.
Last Call : 28, 838, 4322.
Last Campfire : 1337.
The Last Canoe Trip : 5396.

The Last Child in Hamlin : 4833.
The Last Cigarettes of Aurora Bligh : 1872.
Last Contact : 386.
The Last Corn of Summer : 4911.
The Last Dance Saved : 3269.
The Last Day at Safeway : 7175.
The Last Door's Name Is Sorrow : 4530, 6105, 7221.
Last Fight : 1534.
The Last Five Minutes of Of Mice and Men : 309.
The Last Garden : 4178.
The Last Goat in Bergen County : 5762.
The Last Good Restaurant in New York : 5225.
The Last Great Flood : 632.
Last Hunt : 4724.
The Last Image : 859.
Last Light on the Keel : 1995.
Last Meeting : 1065, 6105, 7221.
The Last Mer-Mother : 1964.
Last Mile blues : 5058.
Last Minute Instructions : 2555.
Last News of the Little Box : 3224, 5237.
The Last Night : 5786.
Last Night, After the Party : 1582.
Last Night News of an Uncle's Death Reached Me : 6393.
The Last Night of Exile : 4842.
The Last Night That Stirred : 645.
Last night very late : 4063, 5804.
Last of the Guelder Roses : 470.
Last One in Should Bring the Light : 3124.
A Last Poem : 4058.
Last Poem for Gary Eddy : 1142.
Last Poem of the Season : 4557.
Last Request : 3191.
Last Row, Last Seat : 7332.
The Last Saloon in Slaton : 4282.
Last Scene in The Prince of Toads : 7009.
The Last Sky : 1975.
The Last Song of the Reluctant Landlord : 943.
The Last Summer of America : 1521.
The Last Time I Saw My Daughter : 2949.
Last Two Jars of Pears on a Shelf : 2212.
The Last Visit : 5316.
Last Week in the Cottage : 3829.
Last Will : 6172.
Last Words : 4199, 6089.
Last Year in Capricorn : 4090, 5235.
Lasting : 3945.
Lasting Images : 4141.
Late : 4394, 6374.
Late Afternoon : 3987.
Late Anger in a Cathedral : 568.
Late Arrival : 6076.
Late Arrivals : 2292.
Late   As Budding Node : 1827.
Late at Night : 204, 4556.
Late Autumn Run : 3208.
A Late February Storm : 2581.
Late for the Sky : 4532.
Late March Night : 3847.
Late Night Caller : 7212.

Late Night During a Rainy Season : 5814, 6521.
Late of April : 2140.
Late One Night on a Car Trip to N.Y. : 6535.
The Late Perpendicular of England : 3883.
A Late Rembrandt Self-Portrait : 965.
Late Round : 28.
Late Sonata : 6595.
Late Spring : 7096.
Late Summer : 1574, 4803, 6845.
Late Summer, Chill Nights : 2015.
Late Summer Evening : 6702, 7282.
Late Summer Evening Near the Hoko River : 4786.
Late Summer Fires : 4686.
Late Summer: Harmonie du Jour : 5878.
Late Summer Heat Wave : 2894.
Late Variant : 4044.
Late Winter : 1116, 5308.
The Lateen Cross : 1977.
Lately She Has Been Dreaming : 1433.
Latin Lover : 4795.
Latina Cultura : 107.
Latitudes : 2384.
The Laugh : 4317.
A Laugh, a Bump, Potato Chips : 3833.
The Laughing Heart : 838.
Laughter : 6064.
Laundry : 3300.
Laundry Day Soliloquy : 5126.
Lava : 4655.
Lava Soap : 3490.
'Lavabo' by James McGarrell : 5251.
Lavery Hill : 698.
Law and Order : 367, 5232.
'The Law — She Is an Ass' in Sacramento : 2910.
The Lawn : 3538, 6966.
The Lawn Bowlers : 3117.
The Laws of Casuality : 6819.
The Laws of Gravity : 7046.
Laying On of Hands Vs. Laying On of Ears : 172.
Lazarus : 3846, 7126.
Lazarus Envisions His Next Accident : 4535.
Lazarus Steals a Compact Car : 4535.
Lazarus the Cat, Nineteen : 2662.
Lazarus Under the New Moon Dreaming : 4535.
Leaf Mould : 3835.
The League of Failed Poets : 1595.
Leah : 5708.
Leaning back in his leather lounge chair : 2317.
Leaning In : 3957.
Leap-Centuries : 1026, 2572.
Leap Year : 2335.
Leaping Over My Shadow : 1035, 4652.
The Learning Dungeon : 5320.
Learning How to Cry : 5284.
Learning Natural Instincts : 5555.
Learning the Drum : 3464.
Learning the Language : 3638.
Learning the Stars : 5555.
Learning to Dance : 1596.
Learning to Dance for Rain : 3890.

Learning to Drive : 6319.
Learning to Drown : 4722.
Learning to Float : 6291.
Learning to Make a Good Confession : 382.
Learning to Read : 1342, 1955.
Learning to Ride : 3736.
Learning to Swim : 2196.
Learning to Swim in Lake Adley : 6876.
Leather Bar : 131.
Leather Slippers : 3492.
Leave now all stale lack-luster : 1146.
Leave-Taking Trio : 5122.
Leave Wife : 4118.
Leaves : 6076.
Leaves and Grass and Missy Hayward's Cup of Coffee : 3032.
Leaves of an Autumn Past : 6068.
The Leaves of December : 2961.
Leaves Under Snow : 6528.
Leaving : 1344, 2139.
Leaving a Head Behind : 6393.
Leaving Atlantic City : 4679.
Leaving Autumn : 764.
Leaving Guatemala : 1343.
Leaving Home, Pittsburgh, 1966 : 917.
The Leaving of Scotland : 5056.
Leaving Port : 1215, 3172, 6235.
Leaving the Island : 6299.
Leaving the Old Gods : 4224.
Leaving the World We've Loved Speechless : 6447.
Leavings : 216, 7263.
Lebanon : 5640.
Lecture : 6668.
Lecture to Third-Year Medical Students : 6417.
Leda : 3198, 5528.
Leda 3 : 1149.
Leda and the Swans : 1724.
Lee in New Orleans : 7356.
Leeward : 214.
Left Us Talking : 1901.
Leftovers : 1191.
Lefty : 1909.
Leg Trap : 7044.
Legacy : 632, 7212.
The Legacy : 4896.
Legend : 1105, 1109, 1369, 2814.
Legends : 625.
Leggiero : 2678.
The Legs : 1355.
Leguminous : 3417.
Leipzig : 1745.
Lemmings : 2474.
The Lemon : 3917.
Leng-Tch'e (An Execution by Dismemberment, 1905) : 4715.
Length of Life : 4901.
Lengthening Light : 2678.
Lenin : 4795.
Lent : 1896.
Lent Is : 6010.
The Leonardo Improvisations : 5011.
The Leper Eye : 5314.
The Lepidopterist : 4326.
Lesbian Heaven : 3906.

Less than One-Sixth Gravity : 126.
The Lesson : 1946, 4574.
Lesson #121: Weights and Measures : 2054.
Lesson #122: Weights and Measures : 2054.
Lesson in Law : 6634.
A Lesson in Sex : 941.
The Lesson Is : 6587.
Lessons : 1343, 4787.
Lessons in Another Language : 1148.
Lessons in Cartography : 3572.
Lessons of the War, 1945 : 7202.
Lest He Put Forth His Hand : 3440.
Lester and Martha : 1260.
Let Engine Cowling : 2552.
Let Me : 259.
Let Me Die First : 6111.
Let Me Go : 7099.
Let Them Move : 1455.
Let There Be Words : 2717.
Let Us Eat : 2159.
Let Us Save : 4056.
Let's Face It, You Say, Let's Say Distance :
    1608.
Let's Not Chat About Despair : 2143.
Let's Play : 367.
Letter : 581, 3317, 3317, 3697, 4704, 5161,
    7085, 7085.
The Letter : 5967.
A Letter Beginning with *O Thirty* : 3671.
A Letter Beginning with *The Tulips* : 3671.
Letter From a Schoolfriend : 6935.
Letter from a Summer Home : 4735, 7309.
Letter from Anywhere : 5888.
Letter from Hawai'i to David Ray : 5314.
Letter from Japan : 2284.
Letter from K on a Drunken Raft : 5989.
Letter from Paris : 7206.
Letter from the Arizona Women's Prison :
    1246.
Letter from the Land of the Red Roofs. To
    Anna Maria. To Pawka Marcinkiewicz :
    2946, 3035, 5218.
Letter from the Shaman: The Rite of Fertility
    : 1122.
A Letter Home : 4561, 5581.
Letter Home, 1860 : 6876.
Letter Home from North of Saigon — 1972 :
    148.
Letter in November : 5206.
Letter Not Sent: Woods : 3376.
Letter of Inquiry : 4950.
Letter to a Bishop : 4861.
Letter to a Friend : 2227, 3772.
Letter to an Old Flame : 7359.
Letter to Dara, June : 4212.
Letter to David : 5315.
Letter to Dylan Thomas : 5908.
Letter to Flavius : 1016, 2001.
Letter to Kathy from a Frigate at Sea : 917.
Letter to Marcia : 6055.
A Letter to Marie : 5746.
Letter to My Friend in the Convent : 7054.
Letter to My Husband in Colorado : 6339.
Letter to My Mother on the Anniversary of
    Her Suicide : 1226.
Letter to My Postmaster : 2556.

Letter to My Sister : 6679.
A Letter to My Storyteller : 4093.
Letter to Nobody : 973.
Letter to Orpheus : 4893.
Letter to Paul Alpers : 5904.
Letter to Robert Lax of Patmos, Greece :
    1224.
A Letter to the Denouncers : 5613.
Letter to W. D. S. : 6713.
Letters : 742.
Letters from a Dry Island 1: Greenwich Mean
    Time : 4516.
Letters from a Dry Island 7: The Young Men
    : 4516.
Letters from Home : 6.
Letters from Marilyn : 4727.
Letters from Tucson : 6567.
Letting Go : 1891.
Letting Him Go : 6544.
Leveled : 2281.
Leveling Grain : 5267.
Levelling : 2182.
The Levitator : 1458.
Lewis Carroll Advocates Severe Discipline :
    1869.
Li Ch'ing-Chau : 7201.
Liars : 1505.
Liberation Theology : 6422.
Liberty Enlightening the World: The Statue
    Has Her Say : 2977.
The Library : 6614.
Licks : 83.
Lieutenant Colonel : 2993.
Life after Death : 3987.
Life and Death: All the Lost Accordions and
    Concertinas : 5606.
Life Before and Life After Tampico : 5546.
The Life Dance : 3054.
Life Drawing : 2015.
Life Extension : 7229.
Life Imitates Art in Abilene : 1967.
Life in a Mirror : 4934.
A Life in a Steel Mill : 6966.
Life in an Expanding Universe : 5606.
Life in the Movies : 582.
A Life in the Senate : 6690.
Life Insurance Is Not the Answer : 149.
Life Is a Bunch of Moments : 1729.
Life Is Risky, Life Is Grand : 1265.
Life: It Must Suffice Us : 3762.
The Life of Each Seed : 2324.
The Life of Literature : 2441.
The Life of Poetry : 6544.
The Life of the Body : 635.
The Life of the Party : 2552.
Life Story : 45.
Life within a Museum : 3520.
Life Without Nipples : 3709.
Life's Sporadic Turnabout : 6667.
Lifestory #3 : 508.
A Lifetime : 3098, 4291.
Lift : 386.
Light : 3479.
The Light : 2055.
Light a Middle Way : 1155.

Light Beneath the Skin (or Pronoun 2) : 2297.
Light Brigade : 2307.
Light Change : 2047.
Light in January : 3822.
Light, Near Perth : 1336, 1871.
Light Observations : 5412.
The Light of Asia : 201.
The Light of This March Day : 6709.
Light on Oil and Water : 2910.
The Light on the Door : 6607.
Light over Television Hill : 5847.
Light Singing Before the Earth : 3890.
Light Splinters : 4193.
The Light Through the Pig : 1840.
Light Turnouts : 214.
Light Under the Door : 5780.
A Light Within the Light : 2047.
Lightbulbs catch fire. The rooms are full : 52, 3302.
The Lighter Side of Shadows of Monsters : 4640.
Lighter Than Air : 6377.
The Lighting of the Candles : 5926.
The Lighting Process : 648.
Lightning : 2789.
Lightning at Night : 288.
Lightning Bolt in the Black-Out : 2739.
The Lightning Photographer : 175.
The Light's Beginning : 177.
The Lights of Marfa : 682.
Lightyears : 3156.
Like a Diver : 1259.
Like a Dog, He Hunts in Dream : 6472.
Like a God : 1511.
Like a Great Wind : 4576.
Like a Leaf : 1098, 1101, 2135.
Like a Scarf : 6544.
Like a woman I labored to change : 6545.
Like an Odysseus Doomed : 6898.
Like Any Hall of Famer : 1890.
Like Children : 724.
Like Father, Etc : 3880.
Like Glass : 1692.
Like in the Mirror : 1034.
Like Leonardo, Like a Dog : 68.
Like Miles Said : 235.
Like Most Revelations : 2972.
Like Our Bodies' Imprint : 117, 2509.
Like Remedies : 3926.
Like Sabines : 3357.
Like Sleeping on a Gymnasium Floor on an Island in a Typhoon : 3877.
Like Spikes : 4767.
Like the Titanic : 5868.
Like Them : 5763, 6989.
Likely : 1167.
The 'Likes' of Sandhill Cranes : 2878.
Lilac : 4127.
The Lilacs : 6766.
Lilacs on Brattle Street : 4220.
Lilies : 2686, 4305.
Lilith, I Don't Cut My Grass : 1389.
Lily, Crystal, Mirror : 328.
Limbo Dancer : 5201.

Limerick: Marianne, an inveterate flirt : 5132.
A Limerick Sequence : 5401.
Limerick: We know about bimbos and hunks : 5132.
Limitation : 3298.
Limits : 354, 643, 865, 4433.
The Limits of Safety : 2096.
A Line : 1400.
Line-Men : 4316.
The Line of Aridity : 6835.
Line Sketch : 3479, 4566.
Lineage : 7046.
Linens : 1943.
Lines and Photographs : 7252.
Lines for a Civic Statue : 3663.
Lines for a Driftwood Table : 3977.
Lines for Castaways : 3977.
Lines for Eudora : 5395.
Lines for My Grandmother's Grave : 6743.
Lines Imagined Translated into a Foreign Language : 3691.
Lines of Descent : 5709.
Lines of Thought : 5184.
Lines on Turning Forty : 3191.
Lines that Rely on Voice for Authenticity : 3328.
Lines to a Dead Thrush : 1573.
Lines to Restore Van Gogh's Ear : 521.
Lines Too Long for a Postcard: Love, Emma : 4996.
Lines Written After a Sleepless Night : 2203.
Lines Written Beneath a Stone : 1618.
Linesquall : 639.
The Lineup : 1806.
Lingering Reflections on a Populist Inaugural : 6690.
Linguistics : 7324.
Link : 6502.
Linkages : 5314.
Links : 5347.
The Lion Tamer's Daughter : 1853.
A Lion Turns Seventy : 7087.
Lions' Mouths : 6716.
Lipstick : 6377.
Liquid Diet : 996.
Liscomb Sanctuary : 1632.
A List of Prayers and a Gift : 1078.
Listen : 1520, 2948, 3680.
Listen Carefully : 3783.
Listen. Put on Morning : 2402.
Listen, the Children : 1548.
Listening : 2190.
Listening Again to 'Take the A Train' : 6612.
Listening to a Flute Above Deer Creek Canyon : 1133.
Listening to Brahms : 1908.
Listening to Mozart : 5002.
Listening to Oneself : 1080.
Listening to Rodrigo's Concerto for Guitar : 6447.
Listening to Spring : 6409.
Listing : 3551.
Lit. Crit : 4499.
Litany : 5045.
Litany for the Screened Women : 5482.

Literary Critic : 1055.
Lithograph : 6174.
Lithuania, After Fifty-two Years : 2679, 4500.
Little, Big : 2331.
Little Big Horn : 6305.
A Little Bit of Soap : 1743.
Little Blue Nude : 4198.
Little Boar's Head : 3178.
The Little Book of Hand Shadows : 1574.
The Little Box : 3224, 5237.
The Little Box's Admirers : 3224, 5237.
The Little Box's Prisoners : 3224, 5237.
Little Boy Lost : 2401.
The Little Chair : 5173.
Little Deaths : 7232.
Little Dove, Who Made Thee? : 3877.
Little Eva's Creation upon Her Death : 952.
A Little Extortion on Traction Ave. : 1486.
Little Falls : 1237.
The Little Goat — Jean-Bertrand Aristide : 3.
Little Jack Horner Lives : 4377.
Little Joe was a vicious drunk : 2049.
Little League : 2957.
Little Lion : 3478.
Little Man : 1916, 6405.
Little Man's Gonna Getcha : 5088.
The Little Mermaid : 3449, 6313, 6712.
Little Nanna : 2397.
A Little Nothing : 2264.
The Little Old Ladies of Camden Town : 296.
Little One of Bangladesh : 1407.
A Little Open Space : 292.
Little Owl Who Lives in the Orchard : 4900.
The Little Persian : 143, 3786.
A Little Prayer for a Barn, for a Tree : 4287.
Little Read Reading Habits : 3404.
Little Remains of Sparta : 335.
A Little Request : 1041, 1913.
A Little Singing : 5308.
A Little Speech Called Silence : 6982.
The Little Square : 736, 5804.
Little Stabs at Happiness : 1333.
The Little Street : 4230.
A Little Supper Music : 2805.
Little Tavern, Georgetown : 2158.
A Little Thing Like That : 121.
'Little Venice,' Mykonos : 4306.
Little Vessels : 2960.
A Little While : 3481.
Liu Huifang : 6966.
Live and Learn : 7125.
Lived in Nectar, Absorbed : 5047.
Lives I Remember Come Back As I Clean the Garage : 6409.
Lives of the Artists : 1620.
The Living : 5997, 7290.
The Living Fence : 1966.
Living for Two : 848.
Living in Hope : 6891.
Living in Someone Else's House : 3247.
The Living Land : 1102.
The Living Mountain : 2759.
Living Past Mozart : 457.
Living Statues : 6299.

Living with Cannibals : 5746.
Living with Opposition : 6.
Livingstone Metalwork : 6656.
Lizzie Design : 4509.
La Llamada : 5798.
Llangattock Escarpment in the Black Mirror : 5416.
The Llano : 2666.
Llano Estacado : 2225.
Llanto para Margarita : 141.
Lloreda, Llorar, Lluvia : 3540.
Lloyd Byrd's Women : 108.
Loblolly Pine : 2189.
Lobster : 2952.
Local Anesthetic: A Woman's Womb Is Opened : 6772.
Local Haole : 5920.
Local Legend : 3300.
Local Peaches : 4104.
Local Superstition : 2060.
Localization : 6871.
The Lock-Keeper of Josselin : 2586.
Locks : 4424.
Locomotion and Landscape : 4334.
Locus : 2215.
The Loess Hills : 943.
Logbook : 3933.
Logic kisses : 5775.
Logs in the Grate : 6493.
Loma Prieta : 7175.
The Lone Ranger Rides Off : 6654.
Loneliness : 4057, 4855.
Loneliness Begins : 3785.
Loneliness has chased me into strange corners : 5230.
Lonely Avenue : 5230.
The Lonely Latin Lover : 206.
The Loners : 5707.
Lonesome Ceilings : 7215.
The Long and Short of It : 2250.
Long Body of America : 3208.
The Long Distance : 4789.
Long-Distance Poem : 291.
Long Division : 3774.
The Long Haul : 1313.
A Long Island Fish Story : 2812.
Long Jump, Berlin, 1936 : 4769.
Long Lunch : 6899.
Long Shots Sheldom Come In : 2951.
The Long Slide : 903.
Long-term Misunderstanding : 5696, 7313.
Long Way Home : 5947.
A Long Way Home : 5947.
Longevity : 1725, 2697, 3176.
Longing : 417.
Longing for Summer : 4616.
A Longing for the Impossible : 3874.
The Longing Season : 7346.
Longings on a Sunday Morning : 2792.
Look Ahead — Look South : 2291.
Look at This Wound : 2672.
Look at Us : 7046.
Look Death in the Eye : 1811.
Look for Spring in Life : 5457.
Look, It's Poetry! : 2324.
Looking : 6414.

Looking Around : 1000.
Looking at Kilauea : 2932.
Looking Back : 6834.
Looking Backward : 1999.
Looking for Blues : 1095.
Looking for God at the Supermarket : 7372.
Looking for Italian Names : 5617.
Looking for Miss Gordon : 1963.
Looking into Lomans : 6600.
Looking into the Sun : 3416.
Looking through my skylight : 134, 212.
Looking up at the Moon : 3809, 4945, 6021.
Looks Like Rain : 3222.
Looks Like the Day Will Take Its Time :
    765, 5365.
Loom : 211.
Loose Faces : 5416.
The Lorca Variation : 5670.
Lord Byron in Family Therapy : 1951.
Lord, Deliver Us from This Affliction : 2655.
Lord Set My Feet on Higher Ground : 4472.
Lord Vulture Lady Pelican : 792, 6537.
Lorelei : 277.
Lorraine Motel, Memphis : 5926.
Lorrie : 6297.
Los Angeles : 6750.
Los Angeles, 1990 : 4795.
Los Angeles, April 30, 1992 : 5826.
Los Angeles, April 1992 : 5358.
The Los Angeles at Lankershim : 779.
Los Angeles: Two Chapters from the Sex
    Manual of Lamentations : 206.
Losing Eurydice, Neutrinos & Quarks : 4811.
Losing It : 1861, 4565.
Losing Memory : 6917.
Loss : 1263, 4810.
Loss, Grief, and Time : 5476.
The Loss of a Culture : 1381.
The loss of Eternity : 1837.
Loss of Soul : 5085.
Lost : 1963, 2686.
The Lost : 5492.
A Lost Art : 2972.
The Lost Bells of Heaven : 2441.
Lost Brilliance: Poems to Persephone and
    Demeter : 1656.
The Lost Child : 2316.
The Lost Country : 5881.
Lost Daughter : 7052.
Lost Dogs : 217, 7095.
Lost Exposures : 3981.
Lost in a Dream : 3145.
Lost in Austin : 4521.
Lost in the Forest Near Nacogdoches : 4732.
Lost in the Iodine of Green Kelp Seas : 4899.
Lost-lost Sister : 3644.
Lost Mona Lisa : 5814, 6521.
Lost on the Quad : 7067.
Lost Red Parrots Come Home to the Loquat
    Tree : 5062.
The Lost Son : 2649.
The Lost Song : 3677.
Lost Steps : 1337.
A Lost Street : 610, 4450.
The Lost Town : 3209.
Lot for Sale : 1900.

Lot's Wife 1 : 3820.
The Lotus Leaver : 6908.
Loudmouth Soup : 3961.
Louise : 3746.
The Lounge : 214.
The Lourdes Prayer : 4492.
Loutre Creek : 7235.
Love : 362, 665, 3222, 3589, 3865, 7248,
    7354.
Love (2) : 5135.
Love American Style: The Holocaust on
    Washington St. at the Triangle
    Shirtwaist Factory Saturday, March 25,
    1911 Approximately 5:04 PM : 5501.
Love and Beauty Saves the World : 4861.
Love and Booze : 6975.
Love and Rice : 6671.
Love and Something More : 3993, 5807.
Love at a Distance : 5574.
Love at Midlife : 1271.
Love at the Base of the Spine : 1591.
Love Canal : 1254.
Love Doesn't Come with an Order of Fries :
    5975.
Love Episode : 5638, 6651.
Love Everlasting : 6398.
The Love Hunter : 1959.
Love in Places I-X : 3873.
Love in the Time of AIDS : 5492.
Love in the Time of Cholera : 2906.
Love in the Time of Menopause : 6181.
Love in Venice : 466.
Love Is a Many Splendored Thing, in
    Brooklyn : 4419.
Love Is Not All : 4461.
Love, it left me : 2259.
Love Letter : 3391.
Love Like a Wolf : 6026.
The Love of García : 4023.
The Love of Red Soil : 5961, 7256, 7277.
The Love of the Flesh : 2924.
Love Poem : 67, 690, 783, 794, 1481, 2120,
    2374, 2548, 3965, 5696, 6616, 7313.
Love Poem for a Cook : 3833.
Love Poem for a Familiar : 3114.
Love Poem for My Grandfather : 716.
Love Poems : 3222.
Love Ravages the Tree of Life : 7204.
Love Song : 67, 1026, 1500, 2548, 4195.
Love Song After Chet Baker : 656.
Love Stamps : 3722.
A Love Story : 2244.
Love Talk : 6890.
Love, the Barber : 3816.
A Love We Have at the Start : 7265.
The Loved Ones : 6165.
Lover : 2202, 3088.
Lovers : 1095, 2590, 6495.
The Lovers : 1848, 1969, 3683, 5581, 6076.
Lovers and Other Dead Animals : 5464.
Lovers and Spoons : 1168.
Lovers Losing Lovers : 5344.
Lover's Moon : 3919.
Lovers, Union Station, Chicago : 2231.
Love's Cursive : 3412, 4239, 5767.
Love's License : 3460.

Love's Mileposts : 6172.
Love's Pavilion : 4993.
Love's Vocabulary : 573.
Loving Like the Water : 4616.
Loving Song : 220.
Loving the Angel : 2741.
Lovings Three: A Collection of Stories :
    3521.
Lovis Corinth at Walchensee : 7206.
Low Pressure : 2890.
Low Ratings : 5975.
Low Tide : 5987.
Lower Level, Room EE : 2521.
Loyal to Our Species : 4796.
Loyalty : 436, 1076, 1968.
Luanda by Night : 1745.
Lubok : 5638, 7026.
Luca: Discourse on Life and Death : 4968.
Lucia : 6174, 6464.
Lucifer Is Haunted by the Echo of His Last
    Goodbye : 6586.
Lucille : 6426.
Luck : 3111, 5994, 7212.
The Lucky One : 6012.
Lucy, Refusing to Listen to Bruckner : 4359.
Lucy Z. : 877.
Lucy's Story: Marigolds : 1133.
Ludwig Wittgenstein, 1946 : 927.
Los Lugares Adonde Voy : 1490.
Lugubrious Gondola No. 2 : 2130, 6674.
The Lukens Cache, Excavated 1981-1988 :
    5302.
Lullaby : 168, 422, 756, 4413, 4466, 6135.
A Lullaby : 2553.
Lullaby for a Bebop Baby : 919.
Lullaby for a Showgirl : 4475.
Lullaby for My Other Mother : 5513.
Lullaby for Regret : 4845.
Luminist, National Gallery : 6841.
Luminist Paintings at the National Gallery :
    2864.
The Luminosity of Sheets : 4334.
Luminous Path : 1337.
Lunalilo House : 2178.
Lunar Eclipse : 5406.
Lunar Eclipse 16th Aug 1989 : 2027.
Lunar Variations : 189, 4363.
Lunch Hour : 2782.
Lunch with My Grandparents : 6357.
Lunch with the Boss : 1706.
Lure : 4176.
Lush Survivor : 339.
Lust : 227, 5994.
Luxury : 3772.
The Luxury of Distance : 1184.
Lycidas : 1636.
Lydia Sails to Byzantium : 2968.
Lying about Money : 4305.
Lying In : 4842.
Lying in Bed Reading Robert Gray : 653.
Lying on the Water : 2329, 5388.
The Lynx : 1749.
The Lyre-Treee : 3772.
Lyrical : 5673, 6871.
Lyrics from the Song of Songs : 534, 590,
    591.

The Lyrics of Despair : 5652.
Lyrinda's Visit : 5201.
M.F.A. : 90.
M.I.A. : 4715.
M O M A : 5971.
Ma Bohème : 5529.
Ma Chandelle Est Morte : 214, 4171.
Maalaea Bay : 4356.
A Maasai in Flagstaff : 3648.
The Mabinogion : 1710.
Mace for the Child Molester : 3806.
The Machinery : 3301.
Macho-Macho-Macho-Man : 6633.
Macklin Was : 4581.
Macy's Dressing Room : 5203.
Mad Alyce in October : 823.
Mad Business : 6076.
Mad Doctor : 2745.
The Mad Girl Is Flip, Uses Words : 3822.
The Mad Girl's Mother Lives Vicariously
    Thru Her Daughters : 3822.
Mad Marge Speaks : 3426.
Mad Queers at Union Square : 3833.
Mad Song : 6649.
Mad Woman : 165, 4867.
Madame Est Servie : 4278.
Madame Thebes : 6076.
Madár : 4921.
Madera : 1102.
The Madhouse : 1654.
Madness : 5001.
Madonna Accused by an Ex-Student of
    Stealing His Poems She Can't
    Remember : 3822.
The Madonna and the Hoe : 5526.
Madonna in Rome : 934.
Madonna of the Candidate : 3822.
Madonna of the Confidences : 3822.
Madonna of the Over Reactions : 3822.
Madonna of the Provocations : 3822.
Madonna of the Spaces : 6014.
Madonna Who Lives in Terror of Taxes and
    Men : 3822.
Madonna Who Starts to Write Prose : 3822.
Madrigal : 188, 1118.
Maestro de Maestros : 6061.
The Maestro of Meadows : 730.
The Mag : 6218.
Magdalena : 2996.
Maggie, and How I Hurt Her : 4298.
Magi : 3103.
The Magi : 921.
Magic Dog Man : 2016.
The Magic Flute : 4620.
Magic Learned on Men : 4797.
Magic Word : 2568.
Magician : 4483.
The Magician of Cracow : 6153.
The Magician's Wife : 5578.
Magis : 5185.
The Magnets : 2362.
Magnitudes : 254.
Magpie : 5031, 6356.
Magus : 423, 3962.
Mahjong Party: Chinatown, New York City :
    1046.

Mahler's Shed : 1745.
Maiden Voyage : 5201.
Mail : 2620.
The Mail : 838.
The Mail Box : 3522, 5825.
Mail Call : 6939.
Mailboat : 1547.
Major Scott : 3971.
The Make-Believe : 6605.
Make Yourself Invisible : 6076.
Making a Rubbing : 839.
Making Amends : 1762.
Making Brownies : 3954.
Making Cider : 5862.
Making Do : 1133.
Making Hot Oil : 2820.
Making It Right! (for David) : 2580.
Making Love : 4808.
Making Money : 1703.
Making Movies : 771.
Making. Rain : 5488.
Making Room (for a Friend From Italy, Who
    Only Knew the Half of It) : 81.
Making Stands : 2055.
Making Tortillas : 5329.
Making Up : 3222.
La Mala del Cuento : 5593.
Malaika Waits for the Good Times : 3488.
Malaika Waits for the Good Times (Re-Mix
    Version) : 3488.
Malaiseville : 912.
Malcolm and the Fish : 1186.
Malcolm X : 769.
Malcolm X, 1964 : 4470.
Malcolm X, August 1952 : 4470.
Malcolm X, February 1965 : 4470.
Malcolmorphosis : 5678.
A Male in the Women's Locker Room : 5753.
Male Nipples : 2848.
Malespina : 6333.
Malice : 4538.
Mama : 187, 452, 3822, 5653.
Mama Ken : 384.
Mama Performs Surgery on a Chicken :
    3149.
Mamie Sharp : 4730.
Mammography Survey, Bispebjerg Hospital :
    6263.
Man : 6114, 6783, 7342.
Man About Town : 6842.
Man and His Shadow : 2277, 6537.
The Man and the Echo : 7269.
Man and Woman in Landscape : 5373.
Man Are So Shallow : 4796.
Man-at-Arms : 3804.
The Man at the Doorway : 7031.
A Man Awakens at Dawn, Steps Out of Bed,
    and Rises to the Ceiling : 2782.
Man Crying on the Sidewalk : 4453.
Man Disappears : 5269.
A Man Escaped : 6932.
A Man-Fly : 2679, 4500.
The Man. His Bowl. His Raspberries : 5373.
The Man in a Shell : 308.
The Man in the Chair : 3373.

A Man Looking at Jim Fletcher's Painting,
    'The Warrior and His Death Companion'
    : 1768.
Man of Letters : 580.
A Man of Reason : 6012.
Man of the House : 2818.
A Man on the Road : 5520.
Man on Verandah : 4072.
Man Posing As Cheerleader Sentenced :
    4305.
Man-Thing : 150.
The Man Upstairs : 3527.
A Man Wearing Blue Y Fronts, a Happy
    Lady and the World : 3042.
Man Wearing Neck Collar Entering Lawyer's
    Office : 2014.
The Man Who Became a Horse : 5501.
The Man Who Drew Days : 1622.
The Man Who Patched the Floor : 861.
The Man Who Played Bagpipes : 1502.
The Man Who Set His Son on Fire : 1693.
The Man Who Tried to Rape You : 443.
The Man Who Wears a Hat : 4483.
The Man Who Wears No Hat : 4483.
The Man with a Hole in His Heart : 5344.
The Man with Delicate Feet : 1131.
Man with Picture Frame : 7185.
The Man Without a Body : 5356.
A Man without Food : 1863.
The Man Writes, the Woman Listens : 6155.
The Management of Dolls : 4233.
Manager Fired, Managed Named : 2800.
The Manager of the Apollo Drive-In Prepares
    for Winter : 2436.
Mancha de Lluvia : 1531.
Manchester : 2124.
Mane and Skull : 498, 3288, 3516.
Maneuvers : 7184.
Mango : 2082.
Mango flesh : 5871.
Mangos : 3591.
Mangosteens : 2551.
Manhattan : 4378.
Manhattan Elegy : 73.
'Manhunter' (1986) : 231.
Mania : 2538.
Manifest Destiny : 4377.
The Manifestation of Civilization : 687.
Manifesto : 3628.
Manly Mantra Melody : 1266.
Manoa Before Dawn : 2863.
Manoeuvres : 542, 7093.
Man's Best Friend : 5357.
Man's Fate : 2570.
A Man's Wife : 3435.
The Mansion of Forgetting : 5777.
Manti High on Heaven, Manti Back on Earth
    : 2905.
Mantidae : 232.
Mantra : 4269.
Manuia : 3757.
Many : 7078.
The Many : 1514.
Many Happy Returns : 1975.
Many Rivers to Cross : 1520.
The Many Ways Not Supreme : 121.

Many Were Here, But They Left Again : 2617, 2915.
The Map : 7346.
A Map of the World : 1803.
Maple Sap : 802.
Maple Tree Suffering the County Home : 3180.
Maples : 5461.
Maps : 7039.
The Maps of Imagined Geography : 3945.
Mar en Sueño : 4512.
Marathon : 997, 5190.
Marathon House : 3704.
The Marbled Murrelet : 5317.
March : 1650, 5572.
March 4th Madonna : 3822.
March 7th : 2398.
(March '93) : 5011.
March Again : 639.
March — In the Year of the Heart : 2619.
The March Kite : 5949.
March Quest : 4257.
March Storm— Contusion : 4835.
March Wind : 5581, 5772, 6180.
Marcus Garvey : 3896.
Mardi Gras in the Dead of Summer : 6670.
Mare Glaciale : 1519.
Margaret As Windfall : 6830.
Margaret Fuller, Pregnant — December 1847 : 2748.
Margaret Mead's Refrigerator : 2730.
Margarita : 6623.
Margin of Need : 632.
Marginal : 137, 2446.
Marginalia : 6600.
Marginalia to Baudelaire : 1837.
Margueritte : 5086.
Maria of the Night : 1822, 4334.
Marian Sonnet : 222.
Maria's Skin : 4302.
Marie Antoinette Ocean : 1482.
Marimba Eroica : 2628.
A Marine's Last Leave : 317.
Marionette : 4549.
Marionettes : 836, 5528.
Marital Nirvana : 4578.
Mark Does Pipes : 4771.
Mark Rothko: Three Paintings : 4950.
The Marked Ones : 299, 843.
Markers : 3397.
The Market : 865.
Marking : 3329, 5539.
Marking Time : 2051, 4390.
Marks of Light : 6228.
Marks of Spiritual Punctuation : 1867.
Marlene Dietrich's Dead : 6417.
Marlene's Grave : 5860.
A Marriage : 5981.
Marriage, and Other Science Fiction : 2331.
Marriage Counselling : 6079.
Married : 3300.
Married Love : 5801.
Marry Me : 2019.
Mars : 6806.
Mars Hill : 1768.
Marsh House at Pointe au Chenes : 428.

Marta: Inventing Herself : 6876.
Marta: The First Year in Minnesota : 6876.
Martha and Mary : 224, 2824, 3715.
Martha's Vineyard : 4127.
Martin Luther : 3132.
Marty : 6333.
Martyr of These Miles and Hours : 1974.
A Martyr's Lament : 7217.
Maruki Bridge : 4531, 4720, 7044.
Marvel® Wonder : 4635.
Marvelous Pursuits : 2332.
Mary : 5323.
Mary Agnes : 4131.
Mary Babnick Brown's Incredible Hair : 1866.
Mary Before the Pageant : 4848.
Mary, How Does Your Garden Grow : 6267.
Mary Magdalene Thinks of Cherries : 1819.
Mary Smokes, 2 : 3222.
Maryland : 5781.
Mary's Discontent : 5611.
Mary's World : 4265.
Más Números y una Palabra : 1938.
The Mask : 2721.
Mask Series : 6197.
Masque for Paul Celan : 4639.
Mass : 1207.
The Massacre of the Innocents : 6076.
Massacre of the Innocents: Pieter Bruegel the Younger : 3327.
Mastectomy : 4950.
The Master, 1941 : 211.
Master and Man : 1236.
The Master of Bees : 2209, 4448.
Master of Winds : 1085.
The Master Stroke : 4324.
The Match : 1117, 5638, 6716.
The Matchmaker in Flight : 4730.
Material Girl : 3196.
Material Madonna : 3822.
Matériel : 4317.
Math : 3079.
Math Class is Tough : 784.
Mathemaku for John Martone : 2480.
Mathemaku No. 3 : 2480.
Mathemaku No. 10 : 2480.
A Mathematics of Breathing : 5162.
Matija Beckovic : 426, 5717.
Matin : 1782.
Matinada Catalana : 61.
Matisse in the Company of Strangers : 582.
The Matisse Network : 5747.
Matoaka : 1124.
Matreshka : 99.
Matrimonial : 2047.
Matter of Fact : 1732.
A Matter of Indifference : 550.
A Matter of Posturing : 996.
A Matter of Timing : 6377.
Mattress Cowboys : 5478.
Maturity : 4483.
Mau Hawai'i ka Lanakila : 3267, 3277.
Maugherow : 3389.
Maundy Thursday : 13.
Maurice Ravel at the Piano : 4516.
Max Ernst : 4795.

A Maxim : 2770.
Maxwell : 4297.
May : 4712, 4720, 7044.
May 8 -24 90   1 6 8 5 : 1777.
May 21-26 'The Holy Innocents Will Not
    Be Little Children in Heaven . . . .' :
    1306.
May 27 : 5050.
May 27 Ascension: 'I always see the good
    side of things. . . .' : 1306.
May Bluebells, Coed Aber Artro : 6374.
May Blues : 4634.
May Day '44 : 3846.
May Frolic : 4511.
May — There is a flue trapped in the beehive
    : 2239.
Maybe Even This Memory Is Useless : 1943,
    6106.
Maybe If : 36.
Maybe, Someday : 3329, 5539.
Maybe There's No Going Back : 2194.
Maybe You're with Me : 598.
Mayflies : 2655.
Mayflower's Yellow Rose : 1906.
The Maze : 1412.
Mazilli's Breakfast : 1043.
McGee, Doing for Himself : 4975.
McGuire, McGoo : 1882.
McGwinn and Son : 4354.
Me : 329.
Meadowing : 3455.
Mean : 4483.
The Meaning of Bones : 5958.
The Meaning of Simplicity : 3329, 5539.
The Meaningful Sun : 3050, 5514.
Meanwhile : 5792.
A Measure of the Sin : 4797.
Measurements : 2604.
Measures : 5199.
Measuring the Coastline : 3825.
Meat and Secrets : 682.
Meat Counter in Winter : 3200.
Meat Strike : 6885.
The Mechanics of Waiting : 3760.
Med-Evac : 2296.
Media : 5505.
Medias Res : 6492.
Medicine Stone : 1294.
Meditación sobre el Desconocido : 371.
Meditation at Melville Ave : 6988.
Meditation at Red Canyon : 2465.
Meditation at the Top of the Mountain :
    3038.
Meditation on a Beaver Pelt : 4983.
Meditation on a Writer's Notebook : 2153.
Meditation on the Law of Changes : 2298.
Meditation on the Unknown : 371, 6768.
The Meditation Room : 3543.
Mediterrània : 183, 5581.
Medusa : 742, 5206, 6029.
A Meeting : 5292, 7342.
The Meeting : 2812, 5154.
Meeting an Old Friend in the Supermarket :
    6299.
Meeting at the Hotel : 6357.
Meeting Ezra Pound : 2095, 2517, 2927.

Meeting in Hawaii : 7323.
Meeting Mr. Doroshenko : 6300.
The Meeting of the Weather : 598.
Meeting the Famous at the Turf Club : 838.
Meeting the Gaze of the Great Horned Owl :
    424.
Meeting the Light Completely : 2869.
Meeting with Dante in a A Narrow Street :
    6266.
Meetings : 5158.
Mein Kampf : 6299.
The Melancholic Speaks : 5.
Mele Ko'ihonua no Lili'u : 1988, 3277.
Melrose Park : 6575.
Melting : 1108.
Melting Pot : 2925.
Melville, Even, Lives Various Illusions,
    Leaves Learned Evidence : 6884.
Melville of the North Country : 6344.
Melville's Marginalia : 2976.
Mêm' Rain : 1840.
Memento : 5180.
Memorabilia : 4976.
Memorial : 3553, 4660.
Memorial Day : 1768.
Memorial Day, 1985 : 7171.
Memorial Days : 2988.
Memorial Service in Newark : 4001.
Memories in Winter time : 2563, 6056.
Memories of the Atomic Age: Richland,
    Washington : 2437.
Memorizing the Mountain : 624.
A Memory : 2853.
Memory and Flight : 6413.
Memory and Hope : 6495.
Memory and Rowboat (A Diary) : 2839.
The Memory Dance : 3162.
Memory Jog : 3196.
Memory of a Dream : 5243, 6389.
Memory of Stone : 1653.
The Memory of the Wound III : 610, 4450.
Men : 3425.
Men as Fathers : 2046.
Men at Home from the Factory : 5276.
Men at Work : 5492.
The Men Decide : 6703.
Men Deified Because of Their Cruelty :
    6076.
Men in the Sky : 1719.
Men Who Turn Back : 204, 4556.
Mendelssohn at Thirty-Eight : 6123.
Mending : 1474.
Mending Fence on Hardscrabble : 4282.
Mending Test : 6715.
Mendocino Sea Chair : 2806.
Menelaus : 6859.
Menstrual Cramps : 5554.
Mental Health Meeting : 1506.
Menteth Glen : 3243.
Meow Mix : 4701.
Mercator : 1591.
A merchant who lives on the Tyne : 1393.
A Merchant's House, West Friesland : 863.
The Mercury Climbs in Happy Valley : 3432.
Mercy : 106, 6107, 6152, 7361.
The Mercy Seat : 1688.

Mere Islands : 3284.
Meridel Le Sueur : 1711.
Merle Haggard, Two Farmers, *The End of the World* : 3216.
Mermaid : 1277.
Mermaids Invade Seacoast Town : 2411.
Merry Christmas, Happy New Year : 2055.
Merry Dancers : 1647.
The Merry-Go-Round at Hieronymus Park : 4758.
The Mesopotamian Tool Room : 7329.
Message : 516.
Message to Etheridge Knight : 4573.
Messages : 3402.
Messages They Left Behind : 4139.
Messengers : 1247.
Messiah : 6071, 7211.
The Messiah & the Bag Lady : 750.
Metabolism : 188, 1730, 7083.
Metabolism: A Letter : 521.
Metamorfosi III : 4148.
Metamorfosi Ultima : 4148.
Metamorphosen : 4222.
The Metamorphoses of Ovid : 4961, 6135.
Metamorphosis : 5614, 7033.
The Metamorphosis : 2813.
Metamorphosis III : 1305, 4100, 4148.
The Metamorphosis of the Indigenous : 158.
Metaphor : 3351, 4950.
Metaphor for Something That Plays Us / Remembering Eric Dolphy : 2269.
Metaphysical : 6414.
Metaphysics : 1302.
Metempsychosis : 2734, 5663.
The Meteor and the Deer : 6481.
Meteor Shower : 2678.
Methodists : 1462.
Methods of Hygiene : 4014.
Methylene Blue : 4922, 5810.
Metro Station VDNKH : 2033.
Metronome : 4914.
Meudon : 2277.
Meurig Dafydd to His Mistress : 10.
Mexicans and Others : 5788.
Mexico : 6743.
Mexico City : 3818.
M.F.A. : 90.
Mi Amado : 1211.
Mi Casa : 4841.
Mi Gato de Copo de Nieve : 583.
Mi padre : 3757.
Mi Vida : 1838, 3098.
M.I.A. : 4715.
Miasma fills the valley hiding the contours : 3773.
A Mica Mine : 5987.
Mice : 442, 2241, 5804.
Michael Kincaid's Kitchen : 6180.
Michael Mourning : 6400.
Michael, on the Seventh Floor : 3885.
Michelangelesque : 7013.
Michigan August : 3070.
Mickey Mouse Was a Scorpio : 5805.
Micro-stories : 100, 2879, 6465.
Mid, Mid-West : 3328.
Mid-West Scorcher : 104.

The Middle-Aged Lazy Fox Keeps on Circling : 4340.
Middle-aged Men, Learning : 6549.
Middle Lake : 6233.
The Middle Voice : 5787.
The Midget : 1749.
Midlife Lullaby : 1802.
Midnight : 509.
Midnight Blue : 3796.
The Midnight Cows of Holcombe : 4018.
Midnight, June 16th : 897, 1033.
Midnight Stroll : 2093, 4702, 5539.
The Midnight Sun : 4428.
A Midsummer Nightmare : 7003.
A Midsummer Night's Dream : 5501.
Midtown Gym, 1991 : 6972.
Midwest, Summer Storm : 6827.
A Midwestern Vocabulary : 1582.
Midwife : 1623.
Midwife: After Chernobyl : 3142.
Mientras el Hombre la Admira y la Vulnera : 2990.
A Mighty Fortress : 6818.
Mighty Tall and Handsome : 6432.
The Migrant Lovers : 5903.
Migrants : 3340.
Migrations : 4981.
Mija : 1350.
*Mijikayo : 4657.
Milan : 5395.
The Mild Day : 766.
The Mild Sorrows of Travel : 4212.
Miles Davis : 6100.
Miles from Anywhere Usual : 429.
Miles to Go : 6652.
Milestone: The Birth of an Ancestor : 5419.
Military Park : 1508.
Milk Glass : 495.
Milk in a Cup Can Be Used for Divination : 2445.
Milk Toast : 2095.
A Milkman Goes to Court : 1748.
The Milkweed Parables : 1912.
Mill Ball : 7189.
The Millennium Turning : 2631.
Miller & I Were : 4581.
A millionaire : 3647.
Millstone : 4025.
Milton's Daughters : 4563.
Mimnermos and the Motions of Hedonism : 980.
The Mimnermos Interviews : 980.
Mimnermos: the Brainsex Paintings : 980, 4503.
The Mind : 26.
The Mind Addresses Its Bone Carriage : 266.
The Mind Blows up the Moon : 814.
The Mind/Body Problem : 5854.
Mind Train : 3553.
Mind Writing Slogans : 2287.
Mindin' Your Business : 6306.
Mine : 6549.
The Mine : 2387, 2524.
Mineral Life : 847.
Minerva, Ohio : 1705.
Miniature : 3329, 5539.

Minimal Fictions : 3521.
The Minimum Circus : 1187.
Minions : 3359.
A Minister Changes Congregations : 2598.
Minneapolis Intersection : 498, 3516, 4921.
A Minnow for Morris Graves : 2914.
A Minor Resurrection : 6353.
Minority : 3488.
Minotaurs in Love : 1854.
Mint : 2725.
Minuet : 2557.
Minus 0.3 : 7046.
Minus Water : 3798.
Minute Mysteries : 2331.
The Miracel of Transubstantiation : 1179.
Miracle : 761, 3287, 6210, 7003.
A Miracle : 1375.
The Miracle : 7285.
The Miracle at Sea : 1190, 2587.
Miracle et rêve : 1285.
Miracle Fair : 1667, 2007, 6514.
Miranda : 7246.
Miras el Ala : 1531.
Mirror : 5117, 5254, 5416.
The Mirror : 4578, 4624, 5226.
Mirror Kill Drug : 3196.
Mirrors : 778, 3349.
Mirror's Edge : 6932.
Mirrors for Gold : 6564.
The Misanthrope's Afternoon Walk : 3950.
Mischa / Mischa Langdon / The Late Sixties /
   New York Town : 6392.
Misericordia : 6481.
Misfits in a Singles Bar : 3534.
Misplaced : 5565.
Miss Bea Cuts the Lights : 2456.
Miss Blue : 4732.
Miss Edda Mc Clanahan : 6766.
Miss Emily : 757.
Miss Harkins : 7292.
Miss Rose Chisolm. Lois Day. Miss Rose
   Chisolm and Lois Day : 97.
Miss Siegel's Boardinghouse : 982.
Miss Snider : 6697.
Miss X. : 3213, 4410, 5738.
The Missed Conception That Might Have
   Been Christ : 7308.
The Missiles, 1962 : 2185.
Missing : 2086.
The Missing : 3764, 6154.
Missing Entries from a Polish-English
   Dictionary : 2536.
Missing Panels from an Altarpiece : 7162.
Missing the Barque : 3551.
Missing You : 1103, 6038.
Missing You at Long John Silver's : 2435.
Mission : 2202, 4640, 6934.
Mission to Mars : 6690.
Mississippi: Bell Zone 1 : 6917.
Mississippi Dogs : 4185.
Mississippi River Poems : 3636.
Mississippi Situation : 1658.
Mist : 100, 887, 6465.
Mist, February : 3822.
Mist Net : 6174.
Mistaken Identity : 6932.

Mistakes : 1939.
Misterioso : 1921.
Mistletoe Tea : 6233.
Mixed Doubles : 2440.
Mixed Media : 5334.
Mixed Signals : 2267.
Mixmaster : 4532.
Mob Rules : 2535.
Models and Mentors : 5419.
Models and Their Painters : 3327.
Models of Instruction That Encourage
   Critical Thinking : 3490.
A Modern History of California : 1122.
Modern Jesus : 2626.
Modern Language Association Annual (Near
   Mission Dolores) : 1153.
The Modern Life of the Soul : 3328.
Modern Love : 430, 835.
Modern Marriage, Postmodern Marriage :
   1774.
Modern Medicine: Pro and Con : 1917.
A Modern Midrash : 7353.
The Modern Mistress : 2725.
Modern Times : 2902, 6501.
Modes aginst Too Much : 121.
A Modest Harvest of Stars : 6446.
Modi Tchaikovsky Names the Sixth
   Symphony : 2891.
Mojo : 7162.
Mollusc : 4686.
Molly : 1825.
The Molly D. Mine : 595.
Mom Told Me to Grow Up and Win the
   Nobel Prize : 2243.
Moment : 2722.
The Moment : 2314.
The Moment of Truth : 3730.
Moments of Old Age : 3344, 4995.
Moments of the Body Rises : 2324.
Momentum : 7320.
Mommy : 7006.
Mon Semblable : 1540.
Mona Island : 3026, 5802.
Monarchs : 2681.
Monastery, School, Cloud : 2446.
Monday Mornings on Vacation : 1126.
Monday, One P.M. : 5783.
Monday's End : 3178.
Monde Renversé : 3945.
Mondrian : 4801.
The Mondrians : 256.
The Monet Show : 5735.
Monet's Breakfast : 6457.
Monet's Olympia : 234.
The Mongolian Contortionist with Pigeons :
   1979.
Monk : 951.
The Monkey : 3624.
The Monkey's Paw : 5048.
Monoliths Near Shiprock, New Mexico :
   3403.
Monologue : 2155.
Monophobia: The Fear of Loneliness : 6713.
The Monsoon Hour : 270.
The Monster : 318, 4035, 7221.
Monsters : 206.

Monsters Playing Kissing Games : 1487.
Montage: MTV : 3499.
The Montage of All Varied Things — I Have : 1324.
Montagnard Sax Player : 54.
Montana : 3492.
Montana Prenuptials : 1283.
Montes Veneris : 6740.
Monticello 4 July 1826 : 398.
Montreal : 5395.
Monument Valley : 4915.
Monuments : 665, 3152.
Monumentum Aere : 2370.
Mood : 6488.
Mood-Swings : 2055.
Moon : 3820.
The Moon : 5624, 6059.
Moon & Snail : 6382.
Moon and Stars : 2299.
Moon Arrangement : 4598.
Moon Bath : 6622.
Moon Goddess : 3210.
Moon Over the Sangre de Cristos : 2666.
Moon Tub : 653.
Moondust : 2131.
Moonlight on the Sea : 2391, 6516.
Moonman : 6650.
The Moonraker (Rocky Pt., Pacifica) : 4835.
The Moon's Robe : 6618.
Moonshot : 2389.
Moonup : 3182.
Moose : 5004.
The Moosead : 476.
Mooz : 7088.
Moraine : 1628.
Moral : 2262.
Moralizing Prose : 524, 3250.
Morana : 4057, 5880.
Morana's Lullaby : 4057, 5880.
Moranbah : 7164.
Morandi II : 7222.
Mordana : 5097, 5114, 7312.
Mordant Greenery : 6780.
More : 1207.
More About Crocodiles : 1035, 4652.
More and More Narrow : 2727, 5261.
More Humans : 530.
More News from the Front : 337.
More or Less a Sorrow : 4474.
More Poetry : 1183.
The More Sufficient : 3329, 5539.
More Than Hemingway : 691.
More Than Watchmen for the Morning : 5450.
Moreton Island : 5366.
The Morgualos : 3143, 5977.
Morning : 1759, 1782.
Morning After : 5239.
The Morning After the Election : 749.
The Morning After the Running of the 116th Kentucky Derby : 477.
Morning Gathering : 5511.
Morning Geography : 1012.
Morning Glory : 2528, 4845.
Morning in Greece : 1238.
Morning, Merrymeeting Lake : 3974.

Morning on the River : 6702, 7282.
Morning Poem : 2778.
Morning Song : 5638, 5703.
Morning Song with Smoke : 907.
Morning Songs : 2941.
A Morning with Abby Shahn : 6966.
Mornings Like This : 1579.
Mornings on the Air at Ten : 7101.
Morpheus and the Candle-Skin : 1618.
Mortality : 6331, 6644.
Mortuary Art : 904.
The Mosaic of Creation : 2437.
Mosaico II : 6092.
Mosquito : 4610.
Mosquito / Manila Haiku : 2383.
Mosquito Net : 318, 1537, 1538, 7221.
Mosquitos & Poison Ivy : 6125.
Moss : 4046.
The Most Important : 6493.
Motel : 4080.
Moth : 442, 5804.
The Moth : 2023.
Mother : 360, 510.
Mother and Child : 2661.
The Mother-and-Child Riddle : 2117.
Mother and Daughter Swim Icy Chesapeake Bay : 3822.
Mother and Son : 2387.
The Mother at the Zoo : 2290.
Mother Day : 4510.
Mother Earth : 1426.
The Mother Explains the Father to the Son : 6552.
Mother Girthia : 7217.
Mother, I Have Broken Ribs : 2159.
Mother-in-Law : 6236.
Mother in the Kitchen : 4761.
Mother Stanzas : 5612.
Mother Talks to the Dead : 6111.
A Mother Tells : 2799.
Mother the Great Stones Got to Move : 2366.
Motherhood : 3126.
Mother's Breasts : 34.
Mother's Milk : 33.
Mother's Nerves : 5255.
The Mothers Say No : 670.
Mother's Third Husband : 4154.
Motherwish : 5652.
Moths : 2255.
The Moths : 5923.
Motionless Swaying : 5539, 6311.
Motions of the Soul : 6625.
Motivations of the Day : 1127, 5542.
The Motor : 2378.
Motor-Balancing the Untimed Snow: Ella Waking : 4835.
Motorcycle Nightmare : 502.
Mounding Potatoes : 780.
Mount Vernon : 5839.
Mountain : 1744.
The Mountain : 1895.
The Mountain Ash : 4230.
Mountain Elegy : 6960.
The Mountain Gorillas : 1749.
The Mountain Outside My Window : 6732.
Mountain Poem of Korea : 4239, 6201.

Mountain Rhyme : 2088.
Mountains on the Moon : 2193.
The Mountaintop : 5522.
A Mourner : 1877.
Mourning Cloak : 3762, 6230.
Mourning Song : 2623.
The Mouse : 2494, 5974.
Mouse Perspective : 3155.
The Mouse Whole: An Epic : 4578.
Moustache : 2531.
The Mouth : 1737, 3162.
A Mouth Filled with Earth : 299, 843.
The Mouth of Grief : 1270.
Mouthflowers : 5069.
Mouths : 2153.
Movable Rings : 1815.
Move : 278.
Movement : 1784.
The Movie Palace : 3829.
Moving : 595, 2417, 3382, 5746, 5770.
Moving Apart : 1760.
Moving, by Roads Moved : 4580.
Moving Closer : 5105.
Moving Days (A Poem in Two Parts) : 7276.
Moving Expenses : 974.
Moving Figures : 121.
Moving House : 5818.
Moving In : 6748.
Moving into Minimum Security : 3363.
A Moving Man Goes On : 4462.
Moving North : 1133.
Moving On : 5678.
Moving Parts : 3300.
The Moving Statue at Melleray : 2737.
Moving Targets : 6749.
Moving the Bed : 2945.
Moving the Frame : 3381.
Moving the Walls : 6098.
Mozart : 3788.
Mozart Variations : 4200, 5290, 6230.
Mr. and Mrs. Von Kleist : 2946, 6494.
Mr. Cleaver Explains a Contemporary Poet to
    the Beave : 546.
Mr. Crunchy : 5781.
Mr Dead and Mrs Free : 7267.
Mr. Doodle Man : 1465.
Mr. Gianelli Installing Window Screens :
    2144.
Mr. Jefferson on 63rd Street (Chicago's South
    Side) : 800.
Mr. Matson's Super Abundance : 4276.
Mr. October Came to Catawba County :
    5095.
Mr. Washington : 120.
Mr. X. : 682.
Mrs. Biswas Banishes a Female Relative :
    6792.
Mrs. Biswas Giving Advice to a
    Granddaughter : 6792.
Mrs. Johnson : 1437.
Mrs. Lincoln Winters in Nice : 3969.
Mrs. Yoshida : 1594.
Ms. Mason, your (ahem) love poetry : 4182.
Mt. Moriah Dawn : 435.
Mt. Pisgah : 3639.
Much Ado about Nothing : 4292.

Much of marriage is mastery : 5874.
Much to Be Said : 6768.
Mud Daubers : 4505.
Mud Road : 6476.
Mud, Sky, Stars, Wind : 4581.
Muerte del Leñador : 371.
La Muerte, Patron Saint of Writers : 1850.
Muette Danse : 4141.
Una Mujer : 5639.
Mulberries : 5265.
Mulberry Time : 1649.
The Mulch : 7137.
Multiple Personality : 4377.
Multitone Monotone : 3986.
Munchausen's (By Proxy) : 5494.
El Mundo del Oro : 4113.
El Mundo del Teror : 4113.
El mundo es una bola de billar : 715.
El mundo es una casa de muñecas : 715.
El mundo está en blanco : 715.
Mural from the Temple of Longing Thither :
    4944.
Murder, Inc : 3123.
The Murder of a Poet While Sleeping : 3001,
    4824.
Murder: Three Dreams : 1362.
Murmurs from the Cult of Marriage
    Counselors : 2481.
Murphy's Law : 4795.
Murray Valley : 6399.
Muscle Fetish : 220.
The Muse : 1045, 3871.
Muse & Drudge : 4658.
The Muse and the Poet : 1579.
The Muse As Recording Angel : 4377.
The Muse Behing the Laurel : 2443.
Musée : 612.
Museum : 4116.
Museum of Comparative Zoology : 4173.
Museum Pieces : 4477.
Museum Visits : 1592.
Museums of Antiquity : 7201.
Mushrooms : 1905, 2255.
Music : 4526.
Music & Guaracha When Stories Sound Too
    Tall : 1008.
Music Becoming Stone : 865.
Music Box : 5405.
Music Class, P.S. 158 : 181.
Music of the Spheres : 4601.
Musical Staff : 960.
Musicians : 7369.
The Musicians : 4697.
The Muskie : 6180.
Musky Nights after Rain Rose : 3822.
Mutation Stops : 5933.
Mutatis Mutandis : 6457.
Mutative Metaphors : 3358.
The Mute : 2857.
Mutiny : 1291, 1420, 3756.
Mutton Birds : 5453.
The Mutual Animosity of Houses : 1630.
My : 2309.
My 2¢ Worth : 6975.
My Aloneness : 4112.
My Arm and the Night : 5113.

My Black Madonna : 3109.
My Body in Summer : 6293.
My Bomb : 2333.
My breath is small game for the night wind : 1136.
My Brother Abel, the Wounded : 3782.
My Brother Fell : 2097.
My Brother in the grand Canyon : 3022.
My Brother's Ballet Dancer : 3586.
My camera kept strapped, frantic : 5113.
My Cat Snowflake : 583.
My Chinese Ring : 4945.
My Crime : 7138.
My Daughter : 3380.
My Daughter the Thief : 2304.
My Daughters Look : 1610.
My Daughter's Room : 5621.
My Days : 786.
My Dear Old Uncle Bobby : 5672.
My Dentist Defends Creationism : 3197.
My Elvis Sighting : 2899.
My Family : 2637.
My Father, After Summer Storms : 2647.
My Father and I : 2059.
My Father and I Are Alone Together : 5464.
My father flew : 6455.
My Father Mounted Me : 5773.
My Father on Paper : 332.
My Father Opened Doors for Women : 1145.
My Father, Shaking Pepper : 1105.
My Father Shaves with Occam's Razor : 1122.
My Father Teaches Me a Kind of Driving : 1602.
My Father Was a Carny Man : 4332.
My Father Was Electrocuted : 4523.
My Father'a Food : 3456.
My Father's Back : 2864.
My Father's Binoculars : 4789.
My Father's Breakfast : 6265.
My Father's Crucifix : 5207.
My Father's Death : 5621.
My Father's Ghost Hangs on My Bones : 3364.
My Father's Glass Eye : 3201.
My Father's Hands : 3022.
My Father's Landscape : 935.
My Father's Letters : 1626.
My Father's Love Letters : 3499.
My Father's Lullaby : 4989.
My Father's Mother : 6573.
My Father's Neck : 604.
My Father's Pliers : 4525.
My Father's Poker Game : 6209.
My Favorite Paperweight : 4276.
My Fifth Trip to Washington Ended in Northeast Delaware : 3916.
My Final Bread : 2402.
My First Best Friend : 7344.
My First Day Teaching in a Nursing School : 5866.
My First Duchess : 4360.
My First Kinglet : 6362.
My First Season as an Orioles' Fan Without Orsulak, Billy, and Milligan : 5999.
My Flame : 5621.

My Friend : 7099.
My Friend and I Watch Our Daughters Play on the Lawn Beside the Quaker Meeting House : 6339.
My Girl : 3780.
My Good Performance : 3196.
My Grammar School Sweetheart Came from a Broken Home : 2792.
My Grandfather in the Back Room : 3212.
My Grandmother and I Say Goodbye : 3611.
My Grandmother Did the Polka : 6110.
My Grandmother's Crystal Ball : 424.
My Grandmother's Name : 86.
My Heart Does Not Leap : 2802.
My Heart Is Not As Strong As Birds' : 7163.
My Heart Toward Evening : 2079, 6669.
My Hippo : 6266.
My Holocaust Flowers : 757.
My Inner Ear : 6417.
My Job : 5621.
My Last Door : 3902.
My Last Hustler : 2972.
My Life : 1846.
My Life as a Comic Strip : 4504.
My Life in Song : 2255.
My Life on a Distant Planet : 670.
My Little Heart at Night : 2051, 5625.
My Long-Spent Body : 2526.
My Love Is a Kayak Man from Sweden : 1770.
My Love Is Caught Descending : 6901.
My Lover's House: Night Journey : 3731.
My Masterpiece Is Four Hours Shorter Than O'Neill's : 3877.
My Methodist Grandmother Said : 4006.
My Mind : 3409, 3479.
My Morning Walk, a Lament for Eyes : 4769.
My Mother Also Ate : 3175.
My Mother and the Calendar : 3822.
My Mother Bakes Pies for the Clearwater Cafe : 352.
My Mother Growing Old : 131.
My Mother, Her Mornings : 4431.
My Mother Is Still Alive : 3615.
My Mother, Memphis, 1931 : 4858.
My Mother, on Stronger Pain Killers : 3822.
My Mother Sabotages What Could Be to the End : 3822.
My Mother Shaving Her Legs : 3822.
My Mother with Purse the Summer They Murdered the Spanish Poet : 3783.
My Mother's Cowboy : 999.
My Mother's Handkerchief : 3235.
My Mother's Incest : 3666.
My Mother's Pears : 3580.
My Mother's Poets : 2447.
My Mother's R and R : 3431.
My Mother's Story : 1721.
My Mother's Third Call on a Day of Sleet and December Falling : 3822.
My Mother's Voice : 5485.
My Mouth : 1528.
My Muse Relentless : 2939.
My Name Is Campaspe : 4120.
My Neighbor Asks My Mother : 1741.

My Nextdoor Neighbor, Mrs. Fischetti :
    6280.
My Other Son : 3893.
My Own Name : 3677.
My Own Recognizance : 7283.
My Pagan Baby : 238.
My Parents : 785.
My Parents Were Simple Folk : 6299.
My Penis : 6479.
My Perfect Androgyne : 6680.
My Personal Hercules : 4357.
My Pets : 2711.
My Poems : 6493.
My Poetry : 5814, 6521.
My Poodle Can't Swim : 4299.
My Porch : 5621.
My Prairie Grandmother : 3423.
My Prize Possession : 264.
My Problem : 192.
My Promise : 7138.
My Reaction to Life : 7111.
My Reader : 338, 1945.
My Rock at Hidden Valley : 2609.
My Room Rules : 5427.
My Seventh Winter in Shanghai : 3805,
    6227.
My Sinister : 755.
My Sister Sends Photos of Her Divorce :
    2659.
My Sister Takes the Milk to Town : 2391,
    6516.
My Sister's Garden : 3235.
My Sister's Window : 4812.
My son wakes screaming : 7284.
My Spiritual Advisor : 3584.
My Students : 3799.
My Sweetheart's Voice : 2994.
My Thought-Up Story to Cheer Up Hanged
    Kukutis : 4161, 6289.
My Thoughts : 6032.
My Tragic Opera : 3673.
My TV Doesn't Love Me Anymore : 6442.
My Two Aunts : 1399.
My View : 6641.
My Village : 5621.
My Wife : 5621.
My Wife and the Snake : 5876.
My Wife Is Contemplating Adultery : 6321.
My Wife Suffers From Excitability : 24.
My Wife the Actress : 6481.
My Wife's Shoes : 2700.
My Window : 2710.
My Woman : 651, 669.
My X : 5407.
My Zulu Warrior : 1309.
Mylady Lives Unto the World : 501.
Myrtle : 214.
Myrtle Brocee Amends *The Klondike Nugget*
    from Heaven : 554.
Mysteries : 2641, 2733, 3724.
The Mysteries of the End : 4903.
The Mysterious Maps : 6412.
The Mystery : 4519.
Mystery Kiss : 4289.
Mystery Lives Even in New Jersey : 7015.
The Mystery of Winter : 1458.

Mystic : 4472.
Myth : 5614.
The Myth of Memory : 6157.
Mythic Sorbet : 4849.
A Mythical Creature : 1365.
Mythologies of Music : 5265.
Mythonomy : 144.
Mythos : 3392, 6094.
Myths : 4418.
Myxomatosis : 6921.
The Nagging Question : 2785.
The Nail Star : 6951.
The Nailhead : 3054.
Naked : 530.
Naked Ape : 1920.
Naked Charm : 4487.
Naked Eye : 632.
Naked in the City Where I Honeymooned :
    6147.
Naked Truth : 4444, 6322.
The Nakedness of Fathers : 5207.
Nam Cuts : 7262.
Name : 4864.
The Name, the Bird : 3689.
The Nameless : 5554.
The Names : 494, 986.
Nami no Kokoro, Heart of the Wave Temple
    : 1279.
Naming : 2717.
The Naming : 6303.
Naming the Child : 2219.
Nana Knew Men Were Different : 4454.
Nancy: After Her Bath : 1024.
Nancy Drew on the Azalea Path : 1302.
Nanny : 2366.
The Nanny : 1859.
Nanosecond : 700.
Nan's Soap : 3727.
Naola Beauty Academy, New Orleans,
    Louisiana 1943 : 6688.
Napalm : 2571.
Napoleon's Snuffbox : 7214.
Napoli è Vecchia : 4471.
The Napper : 5934.
Nappy : 4293.
Narciso : 4166.
Narcissus at 60 : 5050.
Narcissus Goes Down the Third Time : 1724.
Narcissus on Echo Beach : 6012.
Nareen Singing : 4488.
The Narrator : 3794.
Narrow Gauge : 2448.
The Narrow Road to the Deep North : 1701.
Natalie : 353.
Nathaniel Hawthorne in Hell : 5864.
Nation : 4918.
National : 4813.
The National Anthem : 1774.
National Cold Storage Company : 5970.
The *National Enquirer* Headline Writer Calls
    Etheridge Knight to Interview Him
    about Gravity : 6876.
National Pastime : 2868.
National Review : 5906.
Native : 192.
Native American Barbie : 1703.

The Native American Savings & Loan : 80.
Native Fever : 7230.
Native-Made : 3407.
Nativity : 5161, 5268, 6483.
Natural Beauty : 263, 3809, 4945.
Natural Buoyancy : 6416.
Natural Habitats : 5774.
Natural History : 5337, 6154.
A Natural History of Southwestern Ontario : 1543.
The Natural History of Trees : 5128.
Natural Selection : 1567.
Natural Sequence : 3535.
The Naturalist at Large on the Delaware River : 1579.
The Naturalist's Emergency : 5389.
Naturalist's Notes : 4656.
Nature : 7212.
Nature Lessons : 1612.
Nature Lover : 5489.
Nature Lovers : 6287.
The Nature of Beauty : 4950.
Nature or Nurture : 4441.
Nature Poem : 858.
Nausicaa: The Movie : 4208.
Navajo : 2375.
Navigator : 6076.
NDE : 4999.
Nduta : 4541.
Near : 398.
Near a Wabash River levee raunchy clergymen abound : 3361.
Near Autumn : 2368.
Near Danant : 4846.
Near Death Experience : 7157.
Near Incident : 4810.
Near Kitami Station on the Odakyu Line : 3092, 4633.
Near Silk Farm Road : 3711.
Near the Paulite Church : 5555.
Near to Prayer : 7263.
The nearness of day like the fangs of a wolf : 5638, 5917.
Nebraska Wine : 5842.
The Necessary Angel : 3134.
Necessary Explanation : 2093, 5539.
Necessary Racket : 2086.
The Necessary Sting : 6191.
The Necklace : 862, 1259, 4119, 4892, 6730.
Necklace: Rich Pink Corona Round a Flashing Yellow Heart : 1341.
Necrophilia : 3499.
Ned Bowen Explains the Mystery of Shroyer Hill : 3439.
Need: A Chorale for Black Woman Voices : 3916.
The Need for Change : 3508.
The Need to Adore : 5606.
Needle's Eye : 2816.
Negation : 3696.
Negative : 6191.
Negative Paranoia : 4313.
Negev Anatomy : 133.
A Negro Church in Harlem : 5318, 7016.
Neighbor : 2665.
Neighbor Blood : 2114.

A Neighborhood Kid : 747.
The Neighborhood of Make Believe : 3961.
Neighborhood Woman : 1820.
Neighbors : 3716, 6381.
The Neighbor's Son : 4619.
Neighbour : 2446.
Neighbours : 845.
Nellie Evans : 3727.
Nelson Crocket's Pants : 1676.
The Nemunas River Today : 302.
Neo : 1502.
Neon Jesus : 6030.
Neon Leon : 1437.
Neons : 2924.
Nero's Respite : 1019, 3329, 6017.
Nervous Breakdown Blues : 2229.
The Nest : 2000, 4230.
Nest Building : 3695.
Nettle : 1055.
Neutra's Window : 5624.
Nevelson : 6135.
Never criticize a man : 776.
Never Dreaming He'd Have Two Daughters Die Before Him : 3252.
Never Say Goodbye : 1464.
Never Stop : 5615.
New Age : 836.
New Age Bear : 7140.
The New America : 3585.
New Americans in San Jose : 54.
New & Used, 1964 : 810.
New Ceremonies : 6793.
The New Chinese Fiction : 6544.
New Christian's Church, Columbia, SC : 54.
The New Country : 5959.
A New Covenant : 1592.
New David : 2939.
New Desert : 6335.
New Discovery : 362, 3865, 7340.
New England : 3780.
A New Era : 6833.
New Face : 6873.
New Folsom Prison : 4199.
A New Garden : 3343.
New Growth / New Time / No Growth / No Time : 5344.
The New Highway Song : 2153.
New House : 3209.
New House on the Market : 2435.
New Jersey Diviner : 2744.
A New Kind of Delicate : 6035.
The New Leda : 3520.
New Life : 756, 3994.
The New Love Poem : 1371.
New Love Too Soon : 3439.
New Math : 6363.
New Metafours : 7114.
A New Metropolis : 5630.
New Moon : 4638.
A New Notice of Motion: The Lover Waiting : 5606.
New Orleans, Unearthing : 7182.
The New Peace : 1102.
A New Poem : 1710.
New Poet Sleeps Beside the River : 6507.
The New Poetry : 6020.

New Republics : 3782.
The New South : 4472.
New Stone Age : 5293.
A New Style: Or Would There Be Any
  Buildings Left Standing If You Crossed
  a Post-Structuralist with a Neutron
  Bomb? : 3308.
New Tenants : 2304.
A New War : 838.
The New Woman : 5926.
New Woman in an Old Familiar Shoe : 1174.
New World : 2327, 6859.
The New World : 6261.
The New World Dictionary : 3425.
New World Dreams : 5264.
New World Island, Notre Dame Bay : 6897.
New Year : 3529, 4571, 6643.
New Year Meditation : 1286.
New Year's Eve : 2448.
New Year's Eve, 1992 : 2182.
A New Year's Trek : 2655.
New York September in Snow : 54.
The New York Times, Sunday, October 25,
  1953 : 214, 3484.
New Yorkers : 1952.
Newborn : 1816, 2508.
The Newcomers : 1350, 2080.
Newlywed : 4851.
The Newmans of Connecticut : 1973.
Newness : 5069.
News : 1184, 6171, 6300, 7089, 7259, 7271.
News, Always the Same : 2414.
News and the Rut : 29.
News form Home: Burning Water : 1343.
The News from Grunwaldstrasse : 6490.
News from the Maze Stone : 243.
News Item : 66.
News of My Death : 6111.
Newsboy, Skid Road : 144.
Newsbreak : 983.
Newspaper Columnist Dies While Snorkeling
  : 7212.
Newton : 7211.
Newton Revisited : 339.
Next Door My Neighbor Is Moving : 3822.
The Next Morning : 7040.
The Next Move : 2095.
The Next Set : 3027.
Next Time Use a Rope : 4039.
Niagara : 2017.
Niccolo's Ghost : 5839.
Nice People : 2081.
Nicholas : 3998.
Nicholas by the River : 6772.
Nickey, Turn Off the Lights : 503.
Nietzsche's Cat : 1808.
Nieuniknione Spotkania : 5037.
Night : 1927, 2234, 2542, 3321, 5175, 5587,
  6480, 7027.
The Night : 3431.
Night at Hakioawa : 2356.
A Night at Modern Prototype : 2818.
Night at the Texas Lone Star Bar : 5136.
The Night Becomes You : 625.
The Night Before Christmas : 7366.
Night beyond the Night : 1200, 3198.

Night-Blindness : 3187.
Night Blooming Cereus : 3948.
Night Brings Its Own Sadness : 4583.
Night Bus : 7205.
The Night Café : 3212.
Night Comfort : 3168.
The Night Crawlers : 3958.
Night Cry : 3165.
Night Currents : 3976.
Night Diving : 1998.
Night Drive : 1514.
Night Feeding : 1128.
Night Ferry Intimations : 6117.
Night Fields : 7079.
Night Gym : 5516.
Night Hags Over America : 1862.
The Night He Came : 5832.
The Night I Decided : 6529.
A Night in the Emergency Room : 4756.
A Night in Tunisia : 3499.
The Night Is Deep : 6569.
Night Janitor : 2960.
Night Kitchen : 336.
Night Landing in a Light Rain : 538.
The Night Left a Scent : 3062, 3294.
Night Life : 1604.
Night-Light : 32.
Night Light : 528.
Night Lights : 5987.
Night Melodies: A Cycle : 4544, 4735.
Night Mirror : 6188.
Night Neighbors : 4316.
Night News: August 1986 : 5164.
Night-Night : 5264.
The Night of Christ's Birth : 2965.
Night of the Following Day : 6310.
Night of the Hunger Moon : 5233.
Night of the Octopus : 231.
A Night on the Dead Sea : 214, 4171.
Night on the Seine : 1416.
Night Out : 3871.
A Night out of Goethe : 1117, 5638.
Night Patrol : 436, 1076, 1968.
Night Piece : 44.
Night Poem : 4403.
Night Pushing In : 345.
Night Reader : 318, 4035, 7221.
Night River : 673.
Night School: A Dream : 5719.
Night Session : 5411.
Night Shift : 6842.
Night Singing : 4417.
Night Skiing : 1990.
Night Snow : 2455, 4418.
Night Song : 3247.
Night Songs : 1375.
Night Sounds of Cave Creatures : 4564.
Night Space : 1474.
Night, St. Mark's Place : 3651.
The Night Table : 4412.
Night Temptation : 5402, 7004, 7261.
Night, the mountains, a storm. The shelter
  packed with people : 665, 4048.
The Night, These Men : 5020.
The Night They Held a Wake on the
  Southside : 643, 4433.

Night Traffic Over North Street : 7063.
The Night Unloads in Lilacs : 4114.
Night Vision : 1149.
Night Visit : 1539.
Night Voices : 6743.
Night Walk Around Green Lakes : 7221.
Night Walk at Shepherd's Landing : 2427.
Night Watch : 414.
Night Wing : 6864.
The Night You Saved the World : 5048.
Nightclub : 1204.
Nightcrossing: The Wigella of Christmas :
    6513.
Nightfall : 3499.
Nightfishing : 5000.
The Nighthawk Sanskritist : 764.
Nighthawks, Blasted from Their Customary
    Air : 2941.
The Nightingale and Death : 1450, 4592.
The Nightingale Has No Objection : 1839.
Nightingales : 3688.
Nightmare : 893.
The Nightmare of My Worst Professor :
    4294.
Nights : 571.
Nights at Londeon With Tess : 7308.
Night's Drownings and Resuscitations : 6393.
Nights in San Jose : 7175.
A Night's Sleep : 935.
Nights Without Rockets : 4282.
Nightshade Preserves : 255.
Nightshift : 109.
Nightwatch : 3583.
Nightworks : 5572.
Nijinsky's Solo : 6218.
Nijinsky's Winter Afternoon, with Faun :
    6012.
Nine Hours at the Benji Cafe in Plains,
    Montana : 5877.
Nine Skies : 1109.
Nineteen Cows in a Slow Line Walking :
    769.
Nineteen Urn-Thoughts : 6175.
Niño : 3914.
Ninstint : 1782.
Ninth Month : 495.
Nipples : 4026.
Nissiros : 2554.
Nitpicker : 4276.
No Apology, No Clarity the Waves Speak in
    Tongues : 7272.
No But About It : 69.
No censorship : 7234.
No Complaints : 4510.
No Defense : 1055.
No Dream? : 1777.
No el sol : 3757.
No Finis : 5875.
No fue el fuego : 715.
No-Good Blues : 3499.
No Heavy Lifting : 6947.
No Jive : 5058.
No Leap : 6150.
No Mindless Digging : 319.
No Mo Faith in the Stepsa Salvation : 7047.
No Mo' Fish on Maui : 4188.

No More : 1425, 3230.
No More Fires to Fight : 3080.
No More to Prophesy : 6448.
No More Words Now : 3575.
No Need for Bullets, the Heart Explodes on
    Its Own : 3302, 5990.
No, Not Victimized : 4424.
No Offense : 7290.
No One by That Name : 308.
No One Escapes from Fresno : 3949.
No Pasaran! : 5589, 6653.
No Put-Up Job : 2089.
No Quarrels Today : 2173.
No Se Permite : 6323.
No Sparrow Falls : 2768.
No Surprises : 422.
No tengo ojos : 3757.
No Thank You : 4962.
No title: In the beginning : 1544, 5682.
No title: It's high time : 1544, 5682.
No Title Required : 327, 1022, 6514.
No Weather Map But Poetry : 4936.
No Win : 838.
No Windows : 2254.
Una Nobildonna : 5938.
The noble riff-raff : 1727.
Nobody Knows : 862, 4057, 4517.
Nobody Loves the Dead Enough : 6361.
Nobody's Answering Machine : 5581, 5772.
Noche de Invierno : 4988.
La Noche Es un Mar Profundo : 2353.
Nocturne : 716, 1232, 1467, 2255, 3316,
    3529, 5787.
Nocturne for Two Voices : 143, 3786.
Nocturne of the Rose : 3173, 6814.
Nocturno de Washington : 4374.
The Noise : 5340.
Nolan Ryan : 1043.
Noli Me Tangere : 417.
Le Nombre des Ombres : 3246.
Nome Industry : 6866.
Non-Biodegradable : 4802.
None on the daffodil dish : 4698.
Nonetheless : 6393.
Noodles, Snakes and Mothers : 1107.
Noon : 6335, 6886.
Noon Sun, East Bay : 2025.
NOR : 5884.
Nora: Part One : 308.
Nora: Part Three : 308.
Norita Eldodt Meets Josef Mengele, Alias
    'Dr. Fritz Fischer,' in Bariloches, a
    Resort in the Foothills of the Andes,
    March 1960 : 1378.
Normal Heights : 192.
The Normal Man Responds : 5561.
Normal People : 3264, 5705.
Normally : 4509.
The North : 1484.
North, 1991 : 632.
North of Bridgeport, Morel Hunting : 2457.
North of San Diego : 3998.
North of Tam Ky, 1967 : 130.
North Star : 211.
The North Starts Here : 6777.
North West : 3341.

North Woods : 6675.
A Northern Setting : 749.
Northern Spotted Owl : 2151.
Norwegians at the Shetland Hotel : 2156.
Nostalgia and Complaint of the America
    Buffalo : 4714.
Not : 2526.
Not a Green Thumb : 4242.
Not a Love Story : 7149.
Not a monument have I raised in your soul :
    955, 4219, 5236.
Not About May Roses : 882.
Not About the Ocean : 735.
Not Again : 367, 4440.
Not at once did you grasp the message : 665,
    4048.
Not Calico : 2638.
Not Dancing: Sex in the 40's : 1534.
Not Dodging : 854.
Not Dreaming : 3464.
Not Far : 6588.
Not For : 1477.
Not Grace Exactly : 4916.
Not Hatred : 5613.
Not Included in This Landscape : 1923.
Not Just Shadow : 6381.
Not Knowing What Will Heal Him : 4113.
Not Like the Red Paint Peoples' Burials :
    3046.
Not Long for This World : 6842.
Not Mowing : 7367.
Not Much Singing : 838.
Not Myself Today, I Hope : 6896.
Not Only That Shattered Day : 4713.
Not Praying : 398.
Not Quitting the Choir : 3899.
A Not So Good Night in the San Pedro of the
    World : 838.
Not the Female Body : 3214.
Not the Right Way : 5224.
Not Watching the Men : 5020.
Not Wishes : 4711.
Not Yet Dead : 4082.
Not Yet Visible : 1375.
Nota Bene : 665.
Note : 651.
A Note : 4907.
Note from the Imaginary Daughter : 406.
Note from the Stratosphere : 5537.
A Note of Thanks : 5303.
Note to a Culture Vulture : 3920.
Note to a Silent Member of the Committee :
    2669.
A Note Upon the Masses : 838.
The Notebook of Uprisings : 2028.
Notes and Scraps: 18:XI:92 : 5844.
Notes Concerning the Ontogeny of Flight :
    5650.
Notes from a Cold Place : 6301.
Notes from Indian Country : 3920.
Notes from the Underground : 3004.
Notes of an Afternoon : 436, 1076, 1968.
Notes on a Disremembered Past : 6166.
Notes on Divining : 3432.
Notes on Mushrooms : 2974.
Notes on the Orgasm : 150.

Notes to Myself: Ten Lessons on Dying :
    706.
Notes Toward a Garden Undoing Itself :
    5069.
Notes Toward Creation : 3760.
The Nothing Above the Water : 308.
Nothing But Margery Kempe : 3537.
Nothing But Ourselves : 50.
Nothing disguises the rush for love : 897,
    1033.
Nothing Doing : 1207.
Nothing here which won't remember me /
    Rien, ici, qui ne se souvienne de moi :
    4688.
Nothing Is Happening : 3673.
Nothing Is Ours : 972, 3719.
Nothing Left to Chance : 2405.
Nothing, My Aging Flaccus : 2552.
Nothing Nietzsche : 4374.
Nothing remains of which one would : 3119,
    5861.
Nothing Serious : 204, 4556.
Nothing to Crow About : 6172.
Notice : 825, 838.
Notion : 1562.
Nourish the Crops : 3054.
Nourlangie Cave at Night : 4866.
Le Nouveau Temps : 3129.
Nouvelle Hantise : 5417.
A Novel about Dentists : 7095.
November : 817, 2111, 3512, 3822.
November 5, 1989 : 4439.
November 6, 1989: Morning : 4439.
November 11, 1918 : 2812.
November 16, 1988 : 1986.
November 24, 1969 : 1907.
November Birches : 3367.
November Bus Ride Between Prairie Cities :
    734.
November Digging : 3998.
November Evenings : 4951.
November First : 6076.
November or Else: An Ode : 124.
November Sun : 639.
La Novia de Lázaro : 3939.
Now : 838.
Now and Again : 6432.
Now Ezra : 838.
Now Hear This : 3707.
Now I go to live : 159, 2576.
Now I Know There Are Bored People
    Everywhere : 4172.
Now I'm Forty-five : 3269.
Now I'm New and Improved : 2120.
Now Is the Time to Love Quirks : 6947.
Now or Never : 665.
Now That I Am Forty : 5581, 5772.
Now the Fitzgerald Brothers Growing Older :
    4619.
Now Then : 498, 4920.
Now, When I Pass the Chabad House : 7027.
Now winter nights enlarge the number of
    their houres : 922.
Now You Can Study : 1774.
Nowhere More Vivid : 7013.

Nu un monument am ridicat in sufletul tau : 4219.
Nuages : 5522, 6012.
Nuclear Age : 4747.
Nude Figure Dancing in the Foreground : 3866.
Nude in the Street : 2774.
Nude on a Cincinnati Porch : 6904.
Nudes & Interiors : 4684.
Nudist Camps & Queers, 1964 : 4626.
Nuisance Grounds : 1292.
The Number Five and Blue : 7218.
Number Three : 2991.
Number Two : 2991.
Numbers : 3188.
The Nun : 5868.
A Nun Lifts the Veil : 3149.
The Nun's Antechamber : 5274, 7196.
Nurse Waking : 4042.
Nursery Rhyme : 4225.
Nursing the Hamster : 1574.
The Nurturer : 5793.
The Nutcracker Seat : 2367.
Nutty : 2003.
O : 3287, 7003, 7139.
O Britain! what glories are thine! : 5132.
O! Bury me not on the lone prairie : 3773.
O Camilla, Is It : 2552.
O come all ye faithful : 3884.
O Henry's Go-Go Cafe : 4294.
O Pequeno Persa : 143.
O, the Names : 6484.
O you in that little bark : 5011.
Oak : 2074.
Oak Alley : 4445.
The Oak Screams Out : 3061, 3264.
Oak Time : 4417.
Oaktown, CA : 3876.
Oasis : 4037.
Objects Contain the Possibility of All Situations : 2872.
Objects in This Mirror Are Closer Than They Appear : 3109.
Objet d'Art : 4294.
The Obligations of Furniture : 4377.
Obscene Silly Doggeral. The Ballad of Doc and Lulu : 5230.
Obscenity : 6472.
Observations at a Clinton Press Conference : 6690.
Obsession : 6649, 6690.
An Obsession with Curlers : 923.
Occaisonal Poem : 863.
Occasion of an Unopened Bloom : 5897.
Occupational Therapy : 6366.
Occupied City : 1104, 4178.
Occurrence : 544, 3483.
An Occurrence on Kissena Boulevard : 6353.
Ocean Cave : 6742.
Ocean Dream : 4291, 4512.
Ocean Park (I) : 1696.
Ocean Park (II) : 1696.
October : 522, 6649.
October 27th October 27th : 1591.
October Dogwood : 6072.
An October Evening : 5501.

October Lambs : 3129.
October Petunia : 6319.
October Swallows : 2156.
'October': The Brothers Limbourg : 5361.
Octopi : 1307.
Octopus : 521.
Oda a la muerte : 5618.
Oda do Wlasnego Kolana : 5037.
Odalisque 1 : 391.
Odalisque 2 : 391.
Odalisque 3 : 391.
Odalisque 4 : 391.
Odas IV al Caminante : 330.
The Odd Couple : 7175.
Odd Mercy : 6362.
Ode : 4750.
Ode for Adam : 4339.
Ode for Mrs. William Settle : 3783.
Ode Man Out : 3753.
Ode to a 60's Militant : 2792.
Ode to a Bottle of Cheap Wine : 1650.
Ode to a Fallen Idol : 5051.
Ode to a Grain of Salt : 6319.
Ode to a Node (Deja Vu) : 6003.
Ode to Clint Eastwood : 7154.
Ode to Early Work : 4357.
Ode to Maori Women / Tateni No Te Vaine Maori : 3318.
Ode to Morpheus : 6890.
Ode to My Knee : 2046, 3282, 5037.
Ode to the New California : 3471.
Odes I, V : 2944, 4862.
Odex — Scenarios for a Functionoid : 4554.
The Odor of Lemon, the Odor of Sweat Reminds Me of Love : 2103, 3505, 4706.
Odysseus at Home : 1104, 2929, 4178.
Odyssey : 4982.
Oedipus at Colonus : 2350, 2907.
Of a Display : 7013.
of all the blessings which to man kind progress doth impart : 1353.
Of Ancient Origins and War : 3348.
Of Arms : 7089.
Of Corsets, a Sonnet : 2685.
Of Icons and Roaches : 3482.
Of Lines Poetic : 2558.
Of Mice and Men : 347.
Of Painting : 1019, 6397.
Of Ray Young Bear, Des Moines Poetry Festival 1992 : 2031.
Of Rings and Roses : 895.
Of Saints Sleeping : 2012.
Of the Sea : 1104, 4178.
Of Three Polite Warnings This Is the Second : 4133.
Of 'Turning Away from the World' : 458.
Of typewritten pages and greased thumbs leafing over painted objects in a room : 4386.
Of Wars and Such : 2278.
Of Weeds : 7310.
Of Which Nothing Is Known : 643, 4433.
Off Off Off Off Broadway : 4970.
Off Season Repairs : 6154.

Off-shore, even if there was a shore, some distance from it : 4840.
Offered and Taken : 3599.
Offering : 3219, 6414.
An Offering : 2579.
Offerings : 5941.
Office des Morts : 1054.
Office Hours Ancestors and Drought : 5724.
The Office of Revels : 2628.
The Office Supply : 4680.
The Office Watch : 3799.
Official Love Story : 2441.
Officially Lent : 3233.
Ogden Nash Revisited : 1920.
Ogiwara Morie : 5814, 6521.
Ogunquit Danse Macabre : 1757.
Oh, Angel, You Skipped the Atlantic : 3315.
Oh Darkest Mother : 3419.
Oh How Can I Keep on Singing? : 2645.
Oh Lord, Oh Lord, Oh Lord : 3488.
Oh no, you have to keep the lights burning : 3218.
Oh! To Daufuskie (dah first key) : 1742.
O'Hara Sonnet : 3146.
Ohio : 4860.
Ohio Vital Statistics : 1534.
Ohioans : 2449.
Ohun Pataki : 5422.
Oil : 4986.
Oil for the Lamps of China : 2460.
Oil Men at a Jewish Cemetery : 6863.
Un Oiseau de Passage : 3421.
Oisin and the Angels : 6145.
Okay the Dream : 6864.
Okeydokey : 3460.
Oklahoma : 3161.
An Oklahoma Birth : 4904.
Oklahoma Gold : 498, 3516, 4921.
Oklahoma Prairie Fire : 714.
Old : 5763.
Old Anew : 7067.
Old as the Hills : 4400.
The Old Ball Game : 6172.
Old Bert : 2618.
Old Black Suit : 1676.
Old Boy News (Same Old Story) : 3908.
Old Cars : 4205.
Old Desires : 9.
Old Discipline : 1460, 5068.
Old Dominion Prose : 4472.
Old Faithful : 5132.
The Old Fan : 5837.
Old-fashioned Language : 5638, 5757.
The Old Flame : 3932.
Old Folsom Prison : 4199.
Old Friends : 6299.
The Old Guy : 973.
The Old Hand : 149.
Old Hat : 7061.
Old Hat in a New Wave : 7175.
The Old Indian : 3677.
The Old Literary Chitchat : 838.
Old Lovers Can Be Sighted : 4015.
Old Man : 4901.
The Old Man : 2743.

The Old Man, Bereaved, Paces Upstairs in a Jumble of Rooms : 3070.
The Old Man Talks About, Among Other Things, Fireflies : 560.
Old Man Watching the Storm : 6772.
The Old Man's Hornpipe : 5352.
The Old Men : 5494.
Old Men Going to Bed : 6853.
Old Men in Restrooms : 2886.
Old Men Playing Basketball : 1878.
The Old Men with Canes Know : 296.
The Old Neighborhood : 1288.
(Old News) Dear Cynthia : 7160.
The Old Nostalgia : 5970.
The Old Ones : 4296.
The Old Parents Blues : 5427.
An Old Play Re-enacted : 6387.
Old Poem Found on a Scrap of Paper: Penultimate Supplication : 979.
Old Question : 4417.
An Old Recipe : 1930.
Old Red : 651, 669.
Old Revolution : 1828, 2463.
Old Road : 4528.
Old Scarecrow Cowley : 2673.
The Old Stories, the Red Peppers : 547.
Old Story : 6226.
An Old Story : 4424.
The Old Story : 1824.
The Old Urge : 3386.
The Old Woman in Amsterdam : 3822.
An Old Woman Remembers : 1078.
An Old Woman's Property : 3980.
Old World Light : 4903.
An Old Wounded Cow Talks to the Mountain : 4403.
Oldest Known : 6316.
Oldtimers : 6299.
Ollie Olsen: The Accomplice : 6876.
The Olson Women and their Hair : 6236.
Olympia : 4073.
The Olympian : 3356.
Omaha : 2536, 6372.
Omega Farms : 226.
Omeros : 6859.
Omer's Gallery : 4954.
Omission : 4565.
On a Country Walk Hayden Explains to Count Apponyi the First Movement of His D Major Quartet : 767.
On a Farm in Nebraska : 5925.
On a Four-President Press Conference : 6690.
On a Gothic Ivory : 6630.
On a Greyhound Back to Base : 6280.
On a Morning When the Season Is Most like Itself : 6006.
On a Mountainside : 6853.
On a Navy Ship at Sea: For Inspection : 695.
On a Park Bench in Heaven : 780.
On a Pottery Figure of a Storyteller from the Eastern Han Dynasty (A.D. 25-220) : 3175.
On a White Horse : 214.
On a Young Man Packing Groceries : 1078.
On African-American Aesthetics : 578.
On an Almost Empty Wednesday : 3323.

On an Etching, 'Antiope,' by Dunoyer de
    Segozac : 4715.
On an Island in the Silence of the Stream :
    1568.
On an Island on an A Train : 750.
On Attempting to Comment on the First One
    Hundred Days : 6690.
On Becoming Lovers : 6594.
On Being 20 : 838.
On Being Alone: Berkeley 1969 : 1278,
    5596.
On Being Asked to Sign an Organ Donor
    Card : 3158.
On Buying a Sprig of Quince : 5830.
On Cabbages and Kings : 4325.
On Censorship : 2868.
On Certainty : 632.
On Cooking a Gourmet Dinner : 4578.
On Death : 7354.
On Earth As It Is in Heaven : 543.
On Empty Air the Orchid Feeds : 840.
On Entering the Hospice : 6964.
On Entering the Supermarket : 395.
On Eternity : 436, 1076, 1968.
On Finding a Former Lover Cut All
    Dedications to Me from Her *Selected
    Poems* : 5165.
On Forgetting a Dream : 354, 643, 4433.
On Frost's *The Gift Outright* : 1343.
On Glenn Gould's Goldberg Variations,
    Sainte-Colombe, Marais, Radnoti and
    Petrarch : 6718.
On Hearing About the Disappearance of
    Frogs : 4491.
On Hearing Celan's Son Is an Aerialist Not a
    Juggler : 4639.
On Hearing Mendelssohn's Oratotio *Elijah* :
    2515.
On Hearing Paul Celan's Son Is a Juggler :
    4639.
On Hearing That Childbirth Is Like Orgasm :
    7350.
On Hearing That the Waioli Tea Room Has
    Closed : 3803.
On Hearing That We Were All Boundless,
    Unimaginable Energy : 5555.
On Hearing the World Premiere of ——'s New
    York : 2153.
On Heat and Cold : 2095.
On *Hellas* : 3390.
On Her Head : 4371.
On Hiding : 3511.
On Jenny : 5827.
On Kitty Kelly's Book : 2409.
On Leaving the Big A : 6206.
On Leaving the Visitor's Interpretative
    Center: Rain : 5680.
On Line at the Supermarket, Wandering
    Through Entertainment and Fashion
    Magazines : 36.
On Losing My Camera Below Dead Horse
    Point : 2977.
On Matters Equestrian : 6383.
On Meeting Lesbia : 3422.
On Military Intervention : 6690.
On Moving to Illinois : 4021.

On Mowing a Lawn : 5346.
On My Fifty-First Birthday in Minneapolis :
    498, 3516, 4921.
On My Forty-fifth Birthday : 4704.
On My Way to Lake Michigan Sunrise on the
    Milwaukee Lakefront Breakwater : 172.
On My Wedding Day : 2389.
On Our Way Toward Literacy : 6280.
On Past Georgia : 4472.
On Photographs of War : 101.
On Poetry : 2220, 3838.
On Reading Certain Contemporaries : 775.
On Reading John Donne's Sermons : 7054.
On Reading *The Man in the Gray Flannel
    Suit* Some 35 Years After Publication :
    5164.
On Receiving a Contract to Translate *The
    Iliad* : 4578.
On Red Steed : 3520, 6701.
On Rising from Bed, Obliterate the Print of
    Your Body : 2872.
On Saving Art, Beauty, Spirit, Etc : 4578.
On Seeing a Collage by K. Johnson Bowles
    on Ash Wednesday : 3453.
On Seeing an Egyptian Mummy in Berlin,
    1932 : 1751.
On Skellig Michael : 1497.
On Snipers, Laughter and Death: Vietnam
    Poems : 4690.
On Snow Mountain : 572.
On Sorrow : 654.
On Speaking to the Dead : 1031.
On Standby : 6299.
On Stannard Mountain : 7367.
On Stengel Beach : 6507.
On Strike : 6800.
On tawny leaves rests the grape, the hope of
    wine : 2907, 5640, 5855.
On the 9 Train, Downtown : 231.
On the Accusation That Former Italian
    Premier Giulio Andreotti Kissed the
    Mafia's Boss of Bosses : 6690.
On the Afternoon of the Prom : 6943.
On the AIDS/Hospice Ward : 6424.
On the Allusive Pleasure of Modern Arts :
    4153.
On the Ambiguity of Injury and Pain : 6988.
On the Antalya Road : 3232.
On the Appointment of David Gergen as
    White House Communications Director
    : 6690.
On the Asphalt Road : 2177.
On the Atlantic : 5132.
On the Banks of the Chattahoochee : 396.
On the Big Rez : 4915.
On the Black Keys : 4077.
On the Blue Wire : 43.
On the Border, Three Poems : 3568, 5913.
On the Bus : 6708.
On the Chastity of Henry James : 206.
On the Death of Aldo Moro : 1999.
On the Death of Park Squirrels : 5839.
On the Disinclination to Scream : 1992.
On the Evening Road : 10.
On the Ferry, Reading the Lives of
    Astronomers : 2561.

On the First Day of Class, I Ask My Students Two Questions : 6280.
On the Flyleaf of Cavafy's *Complete Poems* : 3229.
On the Footfalls' Side : 848.
On the Forest Floor : 6853.
On the Genuine : 3767.
On the grave of my hunger : 4063, 5804.
On the Interstate : 7320.
On the Last Morning : 7150.
On the Late Massacre in Lima: June 19, 1986 : 4223, 5338.
On the Law School's Steps : 3392, 5508.
On the Loss of Lemon : 4437.
On the Morning of Our 20th Anniversary : 7140.
On the Mountain of Spices : 1512.
On the Nature of Desire : 3730.
On the Nature of Physical Law : 5438.
On the Nature of the Iconic : 6204.
On the Necessity of Surrealism : 4472.
On the Night My Brother Moved in with His Girlfriend : 2745.
On the Nomination of Ruth Bader Ginsburg : 6690.
On the Oregon Coast : 604.
On the Other Side of the Oasis : 4778.
On the Phone with My Parents : 1778.
On the Plains : 6853.
On the Question of Redemption : 3251.
On the Raritan, 1959 : 110.
On the Reservation : 3198.
On the Road : 3154.
On the Road: New Brunswick : 1105.
On the Rosebud : 2479.
On the Rue Git-le-Coeur: Mirage #9 : 1208.
On the Second Birthday of My Grandson Mikki (June 16, 1991) : 3157.
On the Second Day of Christmas : 2046, 5037.
On the Sisters : 4159.
On the 'Son of Man' by Gerry Squires : 2282.
On the Substance of Things : 2640.
On the Sunken Fish Processor, Tenyo Maru : 5131.
On the Theory of Transformation : 2504.
On the Top Floor of the Empire State : 715, 4875.
On the Untimely Death of One Beloved : 3000.
On the Way : 2046, 3282, 5037, 6867.
On the Way to Churchcamp, Mother Meets the Devil : 1150.
On the Way to Human Anatomy : 2075.
On the Way to the Gas, One Woman : 3822.
On the Wings of a Fallen Angel : 4313.
On These Days Driving : 4991.
On This Earth : 3966.
On This Hallowed Eve's Night : 3629.
On this journey, nothing we already know : 1377.
On This Side of the Canvas : 773.
On This Side of the River : 484.
On Turning Ten : 1204.
On TWA Flight 720, June 1990 : 1378.

On Watching a Friend Trying to Make Her Baby Drink from a Cup for the First Time : 3443.
On Watching Stanley Kubrick's *Spartacus* Again : 1259.
On What to Do with My Ashes : 264.
On Writing Poems Directly on a Typewriter Again After 15 Years : 2868.
On Ya 'Gin : 6711.
On Your Fiftieth Birthday : 1303.
On Zeno's Bus : 5004.
Onanism : 6997.
Once in a Blue Moon : 1262.
Once, Love, I Wanted Faith : 4999.
Once Over Lightly : 7125.
Once there was a fellow : 5638, 7026.
One : 6942.
The One : 6988.
The One Alternative / L'un Alternatif : 4688.
The One Among the Many : 3359.
One Day with Honeysuckle : 1716.
One Explanation : 4879.
One Fell Swoop : 1658.
One Flew Over the Cuckoo's Nest : 7175.
One for Alzheimer : 4476.
One Good Hand : 107.
One Hundred Hawks : 5876.
One Hundred Versions of the Peaceable Kingdom : 4619.
The One in the Other Place : 107.
One Is the Point : 2872.
One Kind Favor : 1743.
The one lapwing wheeling away from me : 360.
One Little Witness : 6299.
One Man's Biography, One Man's Autobiography : 6001.
One Man's Story : 1765.
One More for the Quilt : 1952.
One More Sunday : 4771.
One More Sunrise : 1652.
One More Time : 6474.
One night : 4998.
One of the Foolish Women : 5956.
One of the Lives : 4417.
One of the Professors : 3613.
One of Their Gods : 1019, 3329, 6017.
One of Those Moments in Life Where Nothing Is Going on But the Rent : 2982.
One Parable : 3328.
One rarely finds a bra without a catch : 2514.
One Rose : 1244.
One Skit, Then Another : 4334, 5539.
One Small Angel : 170.
One Story Contains All His Past : 1725, 2697, 3176.
One That Will Do to Swell a Progress : 2785.
One Thing : 1445.
One Thing Seen in an Other Space Burst : 1248.
One Thousand Four Hundred Fifty Two : 3460.
One Time : 4417.
One Tough Mother : 7257.
One Train May Hide Another : 3484.

The One True God : 5606.
One Tuesday in June : 1021.
One Version of the Struggle : 1572.
One Wave : 247.
One Way : 3880.
One Way Street Game, 1943 : 2718.
One Way There and One Way Back : 3990.
One Who Has Yet to Sleep with the Moon :
    713.
The One Who Won : 3753.
One Wing : 3472.
One Word : 2442.
One World, Two Voices : 1040.
One Year Sonny Stabs Himself : 4640.
Onion : 730, 4330.
Onion Enraged : 3628.
The Onion Song : 2215.
Onions : 3022.
Only Aachen : 4583.
The Only Dance There Is : 889.
Only Heaven : 5522.
Only in America : 2047.
Only Jump Up on the Table : 1917.
Only One Promise : 7166.
The Only Other Beautiful Thing : 3625.
The Only Pebble on the Beach : 2578.
The Only Photograph of Our Affair : 2884.
The Only Plaster Casting of *The Thinker*
    Rodin Made : 6581.
Only Saints May Wash Their Hands in
    Memory : 7117.
The Only Security : 3720.
Only Son : 4908.
Only the Body Recalls : 3646, 3776.
Only This Is Manageable : 1385.
Only We Can Speak of a Beauty : 5568.
Onomathesia : 1662.
An Onondaga Trades with a Woman Who
    Sings with a Mayan Tongue : 6684.
The Onset of Winter : 1336, 1871.
Ontological : 137.
Onward, Christian Soldiers : 2867.
Oolong : 6508.
Opa : 5867.
The Open Door : 4905.
Open House : 545.
Open Letter to My Friends : 2173.
Open Letters to Filipino Artists : 3605.
The Open Mic Massacre : 1486.
Open Mike: Flashback : 3445.
An Open Rose : 604.
Open Season : 3979.
The Open Season : 1237.
The Open Sleeve of Love : 4785.
Open Strings : 7369.
Open Throat : 632.
Open Windows : 4127.
Openers : 6240.
Opening : 2076, 2448, 7303.
Opening Day : 3131.
Opening Scene : 6299.
Openings : 3162.
Opera : 7013.
Opera for Two Voices : 3862.
Opera in a Closed Car : 672.
Operaciones Fundamentales : 5104.

Operations: Desert Shield, Desert Storm :
    7137.
Opinion Poll : 723.
Opinionless : 1845.
Opinions : 5151.
Opinions About Guillaume : 955, 4219,
    5236.
Opinion's Pinions : 121.
Opium : 6120.
Opthamology : 483.
L'Opticien d'Argus : 880.
Opticks : 4050.
Optics : 6174.
Options for Girls: Patience & Loathing :
    1151.
The Optometrist Worries Me About : 1609.
Opus 28, the Preludes : 486.
Or Anything Resembling It : 5011.
Or Say: While Your Old Lovers : 2552.
Oración : 1531.
Oracion Agnostica: Respuesta a Quevedo :
    1769.
The Oracle, After a Long Silence : 6439.
An Oracle for Delfi : 5670.
The Oracle of Repeated Danger : 4012.
Oral History : 2426.
The Oral Tradition : 1514.
Orange : 150, 1603, 2521.
The Orange Armchair : 454.
The Orange Cat : 4950.
Orange Free State : 5215.
Orange Nights, Cold Stars : 917.
Les Orangers : 975.
Oranges : 1024, 1090, 3327, 3418.
The Oranges, the Dog, the Wind : 3560.
Orangutan : 1635, 4024.
Orar: To Pray : 1165.
Orators Make Speeches on the Squares :
    2984, 3186.
Orbitas Transparentes : 1787.
Orbiting God : 2867.
Orchard : 2697, 3176, 4545.
The Orchard : 870, 2255.
The Orchard in August : 3805, 7247.
Orchard Story : 5279.
The Orchardist : 1418.
El Orden y los Dias : 6824.
The Order and the Days : 6824, 7012.
Order *Ephemeroptera* : 5973.
An Order for Eucharist : 6598.
The Order of Grace : 2507, 5790.
An Ordinary Madman : 3264, 5705.
Ordinary Questions : 4428.
An Ordinary Woman : 3584.
Ordination : 7047.
Oread : 4377.
Los orejas largas quisieron : 3757.
Organic : 1812.
The Organization of Space : 6309.
Organized Toward Night : 3029.
Oriel Road : 2182.
The Oriental Ballerina : 1656.
Oriental Barbie : 1703.
Orienting-Lent : 6010.
Origami : 3178, 5679.
Origami for Adults : 5502.

Origami Meatballs : 5084.
Origin : 6109, 6397.
Origin of the Constellation Called Froggey's
    New Year's Eve : 6944.
Origin of the Milky Way : 1815.
Original Basement Tapes : 1740.
The Original Tree : 6165.
Origins : 4928, 6859.
Origins of Corn : 2898.
Oriole's Nest : 6887.
Ornithology of Icarus : 6468.
Orozco : 4795.
Orpah's Song : 5648.
Orphan Spring : 1392.
Orphanesque : 4501.
Orpheus and Eurydice : 4930.
Orpheus Ascending : 2153, 2864.
Orpheus Semantic : 6204.
Orpheus: The Descent : 2864.
An Orphic Legacy : 4200, 4460, 6846.
Ortho-Novum 777 : 1703.
Oscar : 1289.
Osprey : 2752, 4407.
Ossipee Lake : 6450.
Osso Buco : 1204.
Osteon / the Atelier of Bones, Invention in
    Two Voices, D Minor : 4720, 6530,
    7044.
Other Cities : 2455.
Other Folk's Mirrors : 5425.
The Other Man : 3934.
Other Marías : 2170.
Other Nights : 2868, 3889, 6212.
The Other Side : 3490.
The Other Tiger : 643, 4433.
Other Time : 4417.
Other Times : 1460, 5068.
The Other Woman : 199.
The Other World : 2629.
Otis' Leather Jacket : 6966.
La Otra Cara : 2523.
Ouija Boards : 7173.
Our breasts reveal : 5595.
Our Curious Position : 838.
Our Dogs : 4483.
Our God, some contend, is immutable : 5132.
Our Grandmothers : 156.
Our House Was Full without Us : 6772.
Our Lady of Last Night : 5052.
Our Lady of the Fine Torso (A Vision of
    Marky Mark in Cavin Kleins) : 6680.
Our Lady of the Hubcaps : 4016.
Our Language : 1506.
Our Last Day of Freedom : 2085.
Our Lives : 2306.
Our Lives Teach Us Who We Are : 1324.
Our Living Room : 1976.
Our Mad Nest : 2943.
Our Neighbor Neil : 4276.
Our Photos of the Children : 1197.
Our So Subtle City : 2820.
Our Softball Tournament Rained Out, I Settle
    in with Some Bourbon and Watch the
    Leaves : 7212.
Our Songs Beginning with If : 5482.
Our Star : 4112.

Our Town : 264, 914, 4472.
Our Wombs : 221.
Our Wonderful Inventions : 2313.
Out Back : 6300.
Out by Dark : 3782.
Out East, Hamptonites Share Convictions
    with Faraway Bronx Neighbors, They
    Never Leave : 3931.
Out here the evening soughed : 832.
Out in the Barn : 508.
Out of Earshot : 6208.
Out of It : 4578.
Out of Nothing : 3127.
Out of Nowhere : 7237.
Out of Place : 838.
Out of the Air : 3854.
Out of the Blue : 3248.
Out of the Darkness : 2759.
Out of the Fields : 3923.
Out of These Days : 7116.
Out of This Long Waiting and Sleeping :
    3258.
Out of Time to the Music : 5164.
Out on a Limb : 6842.
Out to Tea : 51.
Outcast : 179.
Outermost : 6871.
Outhouse Blues : 4748.
Outing : 692, 2446.
Outing in October : 956.
Outlaws : 2455.
Outlets : 259.
Outlook : 639.
Outpost : 247.
Output : 3317, 7085.
Outside : 801.
Outside Language : 2385.
Outside of Delacroix : 25.
Outside tent's screen : 3189.
Outside the Blue Nile : 3499.
Outside the Medical Supply Shop : 4760.
Outside the Window : 4730.
Outside: Winter Solstice : 4169.
Outskirts of the Kingdom : 231.
Outtakes from an Interview with Malcolm X
    after Mecca : 5924.
Outtakes of Mom When Young : 1845.
Over Again : 7367.
Over All : 5332.
Over & Out : 6587.
Over Boulder : 2465.
Over Darkening Gold : 3248.
Over Dust : 5216.
Over Lunch with My Father : 7061.
Over Montana : 6299.
Over Northern Ontario : 6335.
Over-stimulated : 3395.
Over the Transom : 170.
Over the Undertaker : 7235.
Overcast : 3258.
Overcoming Anthropology : 6741.
Overdose : 897.
Overflow / Trop-Plein : 4688.
The Overgrown Cranberry Bog : 6189.
Overhaul : 4146.
Overheard at a Feminist Conference : 4578.

Overnight in the Cardiac Unit : 3910.
Overtime : 168.
Overture : 6932.
Overview : 6493.
Ovid on the Outer Cape : 2437.
Ovoviviparous : 249.
Owed to Ogden : 2452.
Owl : 3238.
The Owl : 6019.
Owl in the Winter Trees : 4900.
Owls : 3114.
The Owls of St. Anne du Beaupré : 3868.
Oyá : 1071.
Oyster : 5982.
The Oyster : 2223.
Oysters : 2361.
Ozymandias : 6002.
Π : 4601.
P. C. Compatible : 2871.
P.O. Box 11946, Fresno, Calif. 90731 : 838.
P.S. : 6994.
Pa for the Course : 7125.
Pablo Guevara's Vision : 4223, 5338.
The Paccary's Paradise : 3969.
Pace : 3114.
Pacific Composition : 4774.
Pacific Ocean Time : 1820.
Package Empire : 1396.
Packing My Bags : 70.
Packing Nana's Kitchen : 6507.
The Pact : 4287.
Paesaggio Notturno : 7222.
Page Turner for J.R. and Eddie : 2100.
Paging Isaac Watts : 3554.
Paging Through the Tavern Post and Reading
    Steve Yamamoto's Haikus Again : 7175.
La Païenne des Vallons : 5263.
Pain Killers : 6293.
Pain Merchant : 3499.
The Pain of Relativity : 678.
Painted Fishes : 5783.
The Painter at Yaddo : 796.
The Painter Pedro Moreno : 4596.
The Painters : 4836.
The Painting : 181, 5199.
Painting Elena Passacantando's Door : 4619.
Painting Is the Lightning Art : 108.
Painting the Fence : 5621.
Painting, Time, and the Music Box : 2512.
The Pair-Oared Shell : 1875.
A Pair of Bookends : 5987.
Pairs : 639.
País Portátil : 1938.
La Palabra, Meditacion Conceptual : 330.
The Pale California Moon : 6472.
A Paleolithic Fertility Fetish : 327, 1022,
    6514.
Palette : 1187, 5240.
The Palimpsest Soul : 6006.
Palimpsests : 194.
Pallbearing : 3592.
Palliative : 7270.
Palm : 1542, 6753.
Palm Reader : 3846.
Palm Sunday, Palm Springs : 385.
Palmerina : 6055.

Pamela Many Wounds: Fired : 3468.
Pan in Winter : 2665.
The Pancake Hour : 1514.
Pandare : 4481.
Pandora : 2453, 4554, 6309.
Pandora: The White Gift : 5495.
Panic : 6432.
Panis Angelicus : 3967.
Panorama Without a View : 2032.
The Pans, the Pots and the Fire in Front of
    Me : 3083, 4720, 7044.
Pantophobic : 5395.
Pants : 150.
Pantyhose : 410, 1130.
The Paolo Poems : 3203.
Papa Was a Rolling Stone : 1743.
Paper Boy Stress : 5431.
Paper Dolls Cut Out of a Newspaper : 6076.
Paper Mâché : 3136, 4925.
Paper Swans : 2042.
Paper Women : 2277, 6762.
The Paperboy's Father : 2559.
Paperweight : 1174.
Papouli : 5255.
Papyrophobia: The Fear of Paper : 6713.
Papyrus : 2908.
Par Nothing : 6772.
Para Que Te Liberes de un Viejo
    Pensamiento : 4988.
Parable : 610, 4450.
Parabola : 4964.
Paracelsus : 1914, 6839, 6840.
Parachute : 4576.
Parade : 1, 1321, 7082.
Parade at Elmina Castle : 6963.
Parade with Piccolos : 4580.
Paradise : 3883, 4224, 6842, 7283.
The Paradise Diary : 1283.
Paradise Permanently Lost : 7045.
Paradox : 3554.
Paragons in Obscurity : 3249.
Parallel Lines : 3470.
Parallel Sky-Lines : 4843.
Paranoia : 2696.
Paranormal Boot Camp : 521.
Paraphrase : 5624.
A Paraplegic's Flying Dreams : 6434.
Parasite : 4071.
The Parcel : 622.
La Pareja : 1013.
Parenthetic : 537.
Parenthood : 1137.
The Parents They Would Be : 4339.
Paris : 279, 3292.
Paris Brothel : 3364.
Paris in the Winter : 4989.
Paris Postcard : 5007.
Paris Subway Tango : 4290.
A Parisian Dinner : 6160.
The Park Keeper : 2543.
The Park of the Monsters : 409.
The Park, the Bells, the Lovers : 288.
The Park They Say Is Dead : 2235, 2680.
The Parked Car : 3338.
Parking : 1130.
Parma : 3494.

Parodia de la Especie : 4990.
Parody on E. Dickinson : 2771.
Parole del Politico : 6585.
Paros, View from the Harbor : 3496.
The Parrot House on Bruton Street, 1830 :
    4444.
Part VI From Gypsy Christ : 736, 5804.
A Part for the Part : 5968.
Part Your Lips : 2254.
The Parthenon : 6140.
Participation : 849, 6839, 6840.
Participatory Anthropic Principle : 6120.
Particularity : 979.
The Particulars : 7367.
Parting : 3292, 6136.
Parting the Collection : 6632.
Parting with a View : 327, 1022, 6514.
Partizipation : 849.
Partners : 987.
Parts : 1321, 5671.
The Parts : 3731.
Parts of the Body : 4892.
Party : 1065, 6105, 6966, 7221.
Party Flashback : 6357.
Party Talk : 7292.
Partypooper : 6842.
Pas de Deux : 3780, 4295, 4836.
Pasar Malam (Night-Market) : 3593.
Pascal's Idea : 6076.
Paseo Bolivar : 2684.
Pasquinade : 2646.
Passage : 608, 724, 2438, 5108.
The Passage : 924.
Passing : 1330, 5162.
A Passing Acquaintance with Death on the
    Desert : 2916.
Passing Along Parallels : 1600.
Passing the Frontier : 214, 4171.
Passing the Refugee Camp : 4845.
A Passing Thought on a Clear Night : 1180.
Passing Through : 4378.
Passing Through Air : 1132.
Passing Through Albuquerque : 297.
Passing Through Hometown : 3031.
Passing Through, Passing On : 5882.
Passing without Censure : 3723.
Passion : 3866, 3998.
Passion Vs. Perception : 5915.
Passion Weather : 3563.
The Passionate World : 4436.
The Past : 2724, 3054, 5420.
The Past III : 3772.
The Past: A Letter : 7151.
The Past Is Not History : 778.
The Past Master : 3899.
Past Midnight, I Soak My Feet, Ravenna,
    1317 : 7016.
Past Perfect : 2441.
Past This Ignorant Present : 3527.
Pasta Potion : 6600.
Pastel Dresses : 1606.
Pastoral : 915, 2724.
Pastoral — 1954 : 5613.
Pastoral Letter : 5537.
Pastoral Remains (Hitherto Unpublished)
    from the Rectory : 2972.

The Pastor's Wife Considers African Violets,
    the Annunciation and the Practice of
    Church Suppers : 2191.
Pasts : 3350.
Pasture : 6960.
A Pat on the Back : 102.
Patched Quilt (For Aunt Grace) : 7276.
Patchwork : 4629.
Paternalisms : 4446.
Pateros Blues : 3605.
Paterson, N.J. : 2264.
Paterson Re-Visited : 2264.
The Path Blocked by Woods : 1200, 3198.
The Path of Darkness : 2759.
A Path of wet leaves : 4277.
Pathfinder : 6808.
Pathfinders : 734.
Pathless Wanderings : 214.
Pathment : 2249.
The Pathologist's Report : 7202.
Patience : 6228, 6950.
The Patience of Bathtubs : 7106.
Patient : 2027.
The Patient : 5745.
Patients : 6577.
The Patio Light : 143, 3786.
Patriotism : 5554.
The Patron Saint of Venice : 2437.
Patti Catches a Ride, Mojave : 4915.
Paul Celan in the Seine : 1322, 3507, 6227.
Pause : 2446.
A Pause : 6417.
Pause at 47 : 43.
Pause at Delta Assembly : 4842.
Pavan: the Four Elements : 1169.
Pavane : 692.
Paysage Moralisé : 6481.
Peace Bridge, in Light : 3898.
Peace Offerings : 5056.
The Peacefull Province : 1578.
Peach Trees : 1795.
Peaches : 143, 3786, 5115.
Peaks Island, Maine : 6484.
Peanut Agglutinin : 7047.
The Pear as One Example : 5015.
The Pearl Diver : 1545.
Pearl Earrings : 3301.
Pearl's Song : 4251.
Pearly Everlasting : 6632.
Pears : 1852, 2717.
Peasant Fare: At the Museum of Fine Arts :
    674.
The Peat-Bog : 5677.
Peavine Canyon : 4508.
The Pebble : 6147.
Pecking Order : 2682.
Pedal Music : 1526.
Peddling Another Go at It : 5459.
The Pediment of Appearance : 6373.
Peekaboo : 3746.
Peeking at My Mother : 3063.
Peel the roof off Chemo's bakery and empty
    the glass case of pan dulce : 2049.
The Peevement of Achievement : 7091.
Pegasus : 2791.
Pegasus Jockey : 1135.

The Pelican : 2044.
The Pelican Girl : 1778.
The Pellet Bucket Coming : 3833.
Pelt : 4902.
The Pen As Spade : 6117.
Penance : 3544.
The Penates : 6835.
Pendant : 5572.
The pendulum is tired : 5171, 6471, 6637.
Penelope's Despair : 3329, 5539.
Penelope's Turn : 4143.
Penguins : 441.
The Penitent Peters : 6135.
Penney's, Closed Now : 5328.
Pennies from Heaven : 4220.
Pennsylvania Collection Agency : 848.
Pennsylvania Road Trip : 5694.
Pennsylvania Turnpike, West : 4769.
Penny Candy : 1399.
La Pensée : 4779.
Pension : 1428.
Penthesilea : 6141.
The Peony Background : 7028.
The People of the Other Village : 3961.
People on a Bridge : 1667, 2007, 6514.
People who read : 5804, 7309.
Pepsi Plant, Detroit : 1534.
Perceptions : 1782.
The Perche Creek Trestle : 6709.
Perching in the Midst : 827.
Percolation : 2869.
Perdida : 2146.
Los Perdidos: 'Angel' : 7043.
Perdjodohan : 7368.
Peregrine : 2136.
Perennial Ritual : 6696.
Perfect : 6012.
The Perfect American Poem : 3221.
The Perfect Couple : 1302.
The Perfect Day : 1020.
The Perfect Host : 6842.
Perfect Legs : 7068.
A Perfect Moment : 4796.
Perfect Summer Dream : 3183.
Perfecta : 1027.
Perfection : 2493, 3197, 7221.
The Perfection of War : 702.
Performance : 3714.
Performance of Music : 6238.
Perhaps It Started : 2589.
Perhaps Our Parents Made Love After All : 5446.
Peridot : 5478.
Period : 121, 3220, 6969.
The Peripheral Marathon : 1591.
Permanent Grooves : 197.
Perognathus Fallax : 3531.
The Perseid Meteors of August : 3070.
Persephone : 5466.
Persephone and Hades : 6692.
Persephone at Home : 6834.
Persephone in Nebraska : 435.
Perseus and Andromeda, As If by Emily Dickinson : 5887.
The Persian War after Marathon : 2672.
Persimmon Tree : 4785.

The Persistence of Memory : 7134.
The Persistence of Zachary : 1602.
Persistent Karma : 2652.
A person learns your name : 873.
Personal Accounts : 3657.
Personal Ad : 4578.
Personal Cult : 3599.
Personal Stamp : 1337, 4929.
A Personal System of Symbols : 3768.
Personales : 5618.
Personations : 5602.
Perspectives : 1767.
Pertenezco : 3996.
Perturbed Guitar with Boom and Bow : 4906.
Perugia : 6263.
Pesadilla : 4937.
Pesadilla No Soñada : 4062.
Peter : 6228.
Peter and Roxanne : 2177.
Peterson's Field Guide to the Beefcake Kings : 3645.
Petit Grand Mal : 2779.
La Petite Danseuse de Quatorze Ans : 2437.
Pets : 7095.
Petty Cash : 6795.
Phantom : 3098, 4291.
Phantom Love : 1979.
Phantom Pain : 5393.
Phantoms : 5106.
Phase : 3682.
Phasing Out : 5960.
A Phenomenology of Collusion : 3436.
The Phillies vs. Toronto : 6690.
Phillip Rutland : 2696.
The philosopher, who knows nothing is 'real' : 2331.
The Philosopher's Child : 5881.
Philosophical Investigations : 6299.
A Philosophical Question : 6970.
The Phoenix Myth : 5314.
Phone Call from Tempe : 1644.
Phone Call from Tucson, AZ to Lindon, NE : 2225.
Phone Log : 4199.
Phone Sex : 6939.
Phosphorescence : 985.
Phosphoros : 4166.
The Photo Exhibit* Will Be Closed Today : 313.
Photo of a Minor League Baseball Team, ca. 1952 : 4294.
Photo of Dexter Gordon, About to Solo, 1965 : 1743.
Photo of Miles Davis at Lennies-on-the - Turnpike, 1968 : 1743.
Photo: The Dump : 492.
Photograph for My Father: Kansas Settlers, 1897 : 3572.
Photograph of a Woman Falling : 4715.
A Photograph of Buchenwald : 4667.
A Photograph (Taken 1890) : 3405.
Photographed : 5428.
Photographer : 2275.
The Photographer : 5162.
Photographer's Sestina : 7025.
Photographs : 5383.

Photos of Louise Brooks : 6258.
Photosynthesis : 1675.
Phototropism and Sardines : 6612.
Phyllyp Sparrowe : 6119.
Physical Geology : 2008.
Physical Measurements in Aphasia : 4173.
Physics : 1369.
Physics for Poets : 2655.
Physics in the Family : 316.
The Physics of Dating : 5502.
The Physics of Desire, As a Milky Thing,
    Categories : 6202.
The Physiology of William Blake : 3350.
Pi See Π (Greek letter at beginning of the 'P'
    section)
The Piano Lesson : 6426.
Piano Life : 3491.
Piano Man : 1968.
Piano Passage : 6918.
The Piano Player : 1587.
Picaresque : 4195.
Picasso: Still Life with Fruit Dish and
    Mandolin : 3877.
Picayune : 6247.
The Picker : 2023.
Picking Chokeberries : 7024.
Picking Her Up at the Airport : 6970.
Picking Persimmons : 141.
Picking Ticks : 2401.
Picnic Forest Crater Rhyme : 653.
A Picnic in June : 7359.
Pictograph : 2716.
Picture : 1749, 2724.
The Picture I Didn't Take : 4586.
Picture in the Attic : 539.
A Picture of Both My Sons : 2803.
Picture on the River Cherwell : 5239.
Picture Show : 4973.
The Picture Show : 7080.
A Picture Which Magritte Deferred : 4444.
Pictures : 6932.
Pictures Drawn by Atomic Bomb Survivors :
    1202.
Pictures Not in Our Albums : 4256.
La Pie, Monet : 4089.
Pièce de Résistance : 4225.
A Piece of Lightning : 4383.
Pieces for Robert Creeley : 4254.
Pieces of Eight : 1292.
Pieces of Pangaea : 1662.
Pien River Freezing Over : 6702, 7282.
Pier : 4715.
Piero di Cosimo : 6572.
Piers : 1236.
Piers Plowman (The C-Text) : 1754, 3641.
Pieta : 579, 3053, 4173.
Pietà : 4999.
Pieta : 6235.
Pieta in Black, II, The Bearer : 195.
Pig : 6319.
Pig Tales : 6322.
Pigeon Fucking : 6474.
Pigeons : 3552, 4942.
The Pigskin's Pout : 2092.
Pigtailing the Wiring : 4955.
The Pilgrim Fathers : 27.

Pilgrim Signs : 5636.
Pilgrimage : 2300, 4218.
Pilgrimage in Question : 6445.
Pilgrims in Assisi : 7054.
Pilgrim's Progress : 6305.
The Pillars : 5469.
Pillow : 2931, 6214.
The Pillow Book of Leonard Gontarek :
    2358.
Pillow Fight at Bologna : 3859.
Pillows : 2331.
Pills for Split Seconds : 6027.
Pills, or Why We Got Up This Morning :
    5637.
Pilot : 211.
Pimps Double Back on Sprague Street :
    3661.
Pin-Up : 1204.
The Pinch Hitter in the Bottom of the Ninth :
    2857.
Pine Judgment : 6365.
Pine Rest : 6269.
Pine Tree : 1524.
Pineapples : 1480.
Pines : 2112.
El pino solitario junto al río es fuerte y recto :
    162, 4170.
Piñón : 4023.
Pins and Combs : 4344.
The Pinwheel of Fortune — Double Ninth
    Festival : 1047.
Pipe Organ : 5355.
Piping to You on Skye from Lewis : 3017.
Pirandellos' Shirt : 3235.
Pirate : 4275.
The Pirate Map : 4021.
The Pirate Ship : 7130.
Pirotecnia : 4166.
Pisces in Flight : 20.
Pishkun : 3017.
Piss : 838.
Pistachios : 5069.
Pit : 5124.
The Pit : 434.
Pit Fall : 6396.
The Pitcher : 1964.
Pitcher: A Sestina : 1917.
Pitcher Plant, Bog Pluto : 1383.
Pittsburgh : 2459.
Pity : 3794.
Pixilated Geese : 2600.
The Place : 1321, 3839.
Place Between Us : 48.
The Place Came Over You : 5065.
Place Clichy : 385.
Place des Vosges : 350.
The Place of Beautiful Trees : 3031.
The Place the Musician Became a Bear on
    the Streets of a City Meant to Kill Him :
    2623.
Place to Hide : 6063.
The Place to Vacation : 3140.
The Place Where You Live : 218.
Places : 990, 3952.
Places, Everyone : 329.
The Places I Go : 1490.

Places I've Been, Places I'm Going : 6147.
Places Left : 1598.
Places Like This : 3311.
Places You'll Never Go : 3295.
Plain Talk : 5373, 6432.
Plains Hope : 2256.
The Plaintiffs : 4648.
The Planet as the Temple's Inner Shrine :
    6520.
Planet Earth : 4993.
Planet News : 6242.
Planisféria, Map of the World, Lisbon, 1554 :
    2855.
Planked Whitefish : 5783.
Planks and Boards : 2776.
Planting : 4882.
Planting the Lion's Paw : 2943.
Planting Trees for the Walamut Paper
    Company : 175.
Plastic nostrils and everything in them :
    4386.
Plastic Surgery Madonna : 3822.
Platonism : 4016.
Play Directions for an Impromptu Creation of
    the Ideal Universe : 6791.
The Play Is Love : 6265.
Playa de las Rotas : 3113.
The Players : 2784.
Playing : 6565.
Playing Bach : 4858.
Playing Boggle in the Psych Ward : 4864.
Playing Favorites : 7324.
Playing Seven-Card Stud with the Men of
    My Wife's Family : 3910.
Playing War : 5020.
Playing with Dolls : 7301.
Playing with Tar : 4623.
Playroom a Plus : 1810.
A Plea : 544, 3483.
Pleasant Lake — Waiting for My Sister to
    Deliver : 5663.
A Pleasant Song about the Time before Items
    : 2445.
Please : 6023.
Please Send : 1615.
Please Take the Joy of It : 2307, 4079.
The Pleasure of Summer Light : 5279.
Pleasure Principle : 6871.
The Pleasure Principle : 3730.
Pleasures of a Spring Night : 5493.
The Pleasures of Reading : 6076.
The Pledge : 678.
Plegaria en Bahía : 5618.
Plenitude : 5673, 6871.
Plenty : 3300, 6883.
The Plot : 3323.
The Plot to Kill My Grandmother : 2745.
Plots : 4026.
Plovdiv : 3292, 6136.
Pluck : 394.
Plucked : 6144.
Plum : 1458.
The Plum Tree : 2935.
Plumbers of the Liquid Word, or: How to Be
    a Good Poet : 2970.
Plunge Pool : 1625.

Plunging into the River : 1852.
A Plus Madonna : 3822.
P.O. Box 11946, Fresno, Calif. 90731 : 838.
Po Hakioawa : 2356.
El Pobrecito : 4989.
Pococurante : 2156.
A Poem About Breasts : 2746.
Poem About Nothing : 1608.
Poem about Quantity : 643, 4433.
Poem After Sappho : 1016, 2001.
Poem After Solstice : 2726.
Poem: All for once I melt to like it : 150.
Poem: As I often dread the morning : 3459.
Poem before Breakfast : 3510.
Poem Beginning with a Line from Canto
    LXXXVI of Pound : 7027.
A Poem by Michelle : 2592.
A poem comes to me like night dressed in
    pyjamas : 5638, 5917.
Poem: Could it be that the foot : 3431.
Poem Ending with a Line from Dante : 4199.
Poem for a Desert City : 5074.
Poem for a Poem : 1520.
Poem for Adlai Stevenson and Yellow
    Jackets : 7282.
A Poem for Ahab : 3853.
Poem for Corn Moon Sister: What I Learned
    Among Women : 312.
Poem for Dizzy : 26.
Poem for Haruko : 3244.
Poem for Isaac Shams : 3222.
Poem for Jody B. : 5878.
A Poem for Joe : 7281.
Poem for Leonard Cohen : 5523.
Poem for Lizzy : 5133.
Poem for Mildred, Wherever You Are : 1037.
Poem for My Father : 6950.
Poem for My Friend, Nearly a Year After
    Her Death : 5641.
Poem for My Hate & Rage : 4332.
A Poem for Poetry Haters : 3127.
Poem for the All-Canadian Bookstore : 4696.
A Poem for the Blue Heron : 4900.
Poem for the Brother : 3397.
Poem for the Dead Mother : 4632.
Poem for the Fat Lady Singing : 5652.
Poem for the Revival of the Democratic Party
    : 604.
Poem for Tony : 1650.
A Poem for Two Sisters : 2215.
Poem for Valéry Larbaud : 2972, 5138.
Poem for Wendell : 4629.
A Poem: Her skin is like a crumpled paper :
    469.
Poem: Here there are girls with tearing
    breasts : 3484.
Poem: How do you say tomorrow in this
    country? : 214, 4171.
Poem: I long for the mantle : 3431.
Poem: If I held back each word, perhaps :
    3866.
Poem: I'm the same age Ted & Jack were :
    3983.
Poem in Honor of the 50th Anniversary of
    the Navajo Code-Talkers : 4113.

Poem in Jeff Beddow's Absence : 4717, 6636.
Poem in Leopardese : 5608, 6570, 6826.
Poem in November : 3317.
Poem in Parts : 67, 2548.
Poem in the Form of a Snake That Bites Its Tail : 2287.
A Poem in Three Parts About My Father : 5699.
Poem: It is intelligence : 5548.
Poem: It's twilight : 3303, 4720, 7044.
Poem: My breath is small game for the night wind : 1136.
Poem No. 8: On this journey, nothing we already know : 1377.
Poem: of all the blessings which to man kind progress doth impart : 1353.
Poem of Apology : 5866.
Poem of My Skin : 1060.
Poem of Puu Kalena, Hawaiian Mountain Goddess : 4239, 6201.
Poem of the Cid : 158, 566, 1788.
Poem on a Line by Parra : 7315.
Poem on a Trip to Ohio : 7227.
Poem on Progress : 4540.
Poem on the Quantum Mechanics of Breakfast with Haruko : 3244.
Poem to a Daughter : 6482.
Poem to My Hungry Daughter : 1428.
Poem to the Reader : 4892.
The Poem When It Comes : 3750.
Poem with a Familiar Ending : 1636.
Poem with a One-Word Title : 3343.
Poem with Prologue : 1985.
Poem Written After Contemplating the Adverb 'Primarily' : 4444.
Poem Written in the Logic of Late Capitalism : 4617.
Poem: You should remember : 2077, 5654, 7319.
Poema de la Lluvia : 277.
Un Poema por Michelle : 2592.
Poemas: a Alba Díaz : 4665.
Poemas Recurrentes / Si Puedes Quémate, Oh Baby / Poemas Californianos : 533.
Poeme Trouve : 1760.
Poèmes : 1639.
Il Poemetto : 186.
Poems : 1849.
Poems & Fables : 3920.
Poems for Seven Decades : 734.
Poems from Hana (1939) : 862, 1427, 4119.
Poems from Photographs : 5113.
Poems from the Japanese : 1825.
Poems of the Bicameral Mind : 5893.
Poems of the Mothers : 3594, 4518.
Poems of the Saddest Mother : 3594, 4518.
Poems on the Voyage : 604.
Poems, Poems, Poems : 1707.
Poemwalls : 4226.
Poet : 1378.
The Poet : 4474, 4924.
Poet & Critic: the Danger : 4796.
The Poet and the Journalist : 4709.
The Poet as Commuter and Cockroach : 5019.

Poet at a Loss : 6690.
The Poet Falls Down under Wordsworth in the Afternoon : 6266.
The Poet Finds Himself : 4578.
The Poet Gives a Reading : 3211.
The Poet Has No Privacy : 495.
Poet in a Tattered Yellow Dress : 7035.
The Poet Reports to the Dean That She, During Recent Sabbatical Leave : 4327.
Poet Whore in the 9th Circle of Hell : 5440.
Poetic Trace : 2835.
Poetic Wisdom : 4472.
Poetica : 5068.
Poetical : 1460, 5068.
Poetizing at the Med : 6060.
Poetry : 1624, 2658, 2697, 6907.
Poetry à Go-Go : 3460.
Poetry and Sleep : 858.
Poetry Class : 3429.
The Poetry Dream Dance : 7266.
Poetry in Public Places : 5120.
Poetry is no excuse : 5040.
Poetry Is Wine : 1115, 3479.
Poetry Reading : 4057, 4855.
Poetry Reading in Pisgah : 5635.
The Poetry Room : 232.
Poetry Sex Love Music Booze & Death : 6549.
Poetry Teacher : 2761.
Poetry Visits an Old Lady : 862, 5153.
The Poetry Workshop Dream : 3822.
Poetry Workshop: The Extra-Large Muse : 6942.
Poets : 862, 4119, 6074.
A Poet's Alphabet of Influences : 6412.
Poet's Chair : 2725.
The Poet's Crisis : 4294.
Poets East of the Don : 4072.
Poets' Hearts : 3372.
The Poet's Licence : 6427.
Poet's Séance: Stopping by Woods : 6677.
Poi Bowl : 7253.
Poignant Moment, Listening to 'Lakes' Played by the Pat Metheny Group, Summer, 1984 : 3855.
Point : 3329, 5539.
Point Blank : 1007.
Point Dume : 6858.
Point No Point, B.C. : 2755.
Point of No Return : 3332.
Point of Ordure, or, Two Questions, but Just One Answer : 66.
Pointe Shoes : 3822.
Pointed Hour : 2252, 2387.
The Poison : 1828, 2463.
Poison Ivy : 6887.
Pol Pot : 5926.
Poland : 1834.
Polar Bears and Rabbit Watching the Northern Lights : 5367.
The Police : 1512.
Polite Nods from the Host : 4343.
Political Correctitude : 4801.
Political Poem : 2655.
Politics : 6244.
A Politics : 5763.

The Politics of Grief : 2695.
The Politics of Three Horrors : 6551.
Polity : 5106.
Pollen : 517, 3238.
Pollen Memory : 797.
Pollok Park : 5056.
Polo : 4765.
Polonaise: A Variation : 756.
The Pomegranate : 622.
Pomegranates : 3067, 3069, 5155.
Pomp and Circumstance : 836.
The Pond : 4223, 5338.
The Pond at Twilight : 4073.
A Pond Reflection : 4391.
Ponds, in Love : 7220.
Pony Time: Metaphysical Blues on a Lakota
    Reservation : 5387.
Pooh : 7175.
Pool : 7229.
The Pool Clock : 6886.
Pools of Strong Indian Tea and Urine : 3660,
    3762.
Poor Bird : 7118.
The Poor House : 4426.
The Poor Man Naps in the Dunes : 5416.
A Poor Story : 3154.
Poor Us : 1939.
Poplar Cove : 3791.
Poplars : 5879.
Por Nada : 4672.
The Porcelain Head : 3883.
The porch the things around them, the trees :
    4840.
Pornography : 915, 5886.
Port of Call : 6616.
Portage : 5730.
Portents : 4885.
Portia : 7148.
The Portland Vase : 7041.
Portrait : 436, 1076, 1968, 2073, 2684, 4443,
    5662, 6004, 7235.
The Portrait : 3344, 4995.
Portrait by the Artist : 4866.
Portrait from the Age of Henry the Eighth :
    2134.
A Portrait from the Renaissance : 1412.
Portrait of a Gentleman with His Horse and
    Groom : 1259.
Portrait of a Lady : 6858.
A Portrait of a Woman and the Shadow of a
    Man : 2589.
Portrait of Bather : 3198, 3869.
Portrait of Hunger : 4809.
Portrait of My Father the Last Day I Saw
    Him Alive in the Nursing Home : 4579.
Portrait of the Artist : 6112.
Portrait: White on White : 4384.
Portraits in Green : 6733.
The Portuguese Uncle : 2156.
Position : 4784.
The Positions : 1355.
Positive : 1628.
Positive Negative : 6860.
Possess-possess : 2570.
The Possessed : 6932.
Possession : 1135.

Possibilities : 1667, 2007, 6514.
The Possible : 632.
Possible Companion : 2848.
Possibly : 4132.
Post : 1371.
Post-Impressions : 3731.
Post-Point (1993) : 6371.
Post-War Culture : 3308.
Post-War Days : 177.
Postal Routes : 3444.
Postcard: 'Distant View of the Forbidden
    City' : 6972.
A Postcard from Cairo : 7215.
A Postcard from Devils Tower : 3920.
Postcard from the West : 6422.
A Postcard from Wildwood : 2460.
Postcard Poem : 1263.
Postcard to Akemi Miyazawa : 2049.
Postcard to Cynthia Macdonald in Italy :
    2152.
A Postcard to John Greening : 2784.
Postcard to My Father : 1902.
A Postcard to Popeye : 214, 3484.
Postcard to the Poet from a Jilted Bridegroom
    : 3960.
Postcards from Italy : 5792.
Postcards from Paradise : 7162.
Postdiluvian : 2639.
Posterestante : 2747.
Posting the Banns : 5246.
Postman Says : 7133.
Postmodern : 7182.
Postmodern: A Definition : 3826.
The Postmodern Mariner : 5193.
Postscript : 2725.
Postscript: Devils Tower : 3920.
Potato : 3381.
The Potato Mash (More Indefinite and More
    Soluble) : 3436.
Potatoes : 1367, 4066.
Potential: Two Times : 4850.
The Potter : 3362, 3475, 4380, 6909.
The Pottery Sailboats : 5412.
Pounding : 7149.
The Poverty of Theory : 7213.
Powdered Sugar : 4542.
Powell Street Lines : 3242.
Power : 3379, 4298.
Power in Toronto : 3301.
The Power of Names : 4251.
Power Sources : 5144.
Power Surge on Hummingbird Lane : 4504.
Power — Three Lectures : 1997.
Powerhouse Mechanic, 1920 : 141.
Powers : 7367.
Pozzanghera Nera il Diciotto Aprile : 5899.
Practical Concerns Continue : 6520.
A Practical Girl : 3724.
Practice : 6300.
Practice: Father and Son : 6477.
Practicing Death Songs : 3920.
Prado Museum : 62, 5843, 6481.
Prairie Boy Waltz : 589.
A Prairie Garden : 5454.
Prairie Rattler : 3003.
Prairie Scene : 821.

Praise : 6960.
Prajna Paramita : 6686.
Pralines, Mt. Dora, a Bookmark : 917.
Prayer : 862, 1488, 3502, 4121, 4169, 5098, 5123.
Prayer Against the Curse Bomb : 3816.
Prayer Ascending, Prayer Descending : 2260.
A Prayer for the Buddha : 6754.
Prayer for Vicente : 793.
Prayer to the New Moon : 1555, 6952.
Prayers, Wishes and Other Impossibilities : 1404.
Praying for Rain : 1540.
Praying Mantis : 1492.
Pre-Echo : 7013.
The Preacher Prays Silently at the Potluck Social : 6177.
Preacher's Camp : 6327.
Precambrian Strata : 5697.
Precaution : 7164.
Precedent : 3040.
Preceding the Sudden Death of Eva Rueda, Newly Famous Spanish Gymnast, on Bouevard St. Germain, No. 133 : 6478.
Precious Little : 3981.
Precision Bomb Run, Tkyo, 1945 : 4565.
Precocity : 3730.
Preconcieved : 1350.
Predestined Instructive Brother : 6520.
Predictions : 1296.
Preemie : 4415.
Preface in Invisible Ink to Accompany the Gift of a Blank Book : 4357.
Preface to the Dictionary of the English Language : 3046.
Prefatory Nymph : 1425, 3230.
Preghiera al Buddha : 6754.
Pregnant Pos : 3196.
Prehistory : 1488, 5123.
The Prejohn : 2700.
The Prejudice Against the Past : 6373.
Prelude to a Miracle : 3178.
A Prelude to Dawn Light : 726.
Preludes : 5004.
Premiere : 6970.
Premiers Jours du Monde : 6459.
Premonition of Passage : 1760.
Premonitory : 1135.
Preoccupation : 3460.
Preparation : 6694.
Preparations for a Journey : 4726.
Preparatory Poem : 5673, 6871.
Preparing for the Hurricane : 5768.
Preparing for War : 6885.
Preparing for Winter : 3871.
Preparing the Body : 5062.
Preparing the Way : 773.
Preposterous Pets : 7054.
The Presbyterian Reads the Song of Solomon : 5311.
Prescient : 752.
A Presence : 5361.
The Presence of Absence : 4535.
The Presence of Absences : 4726.
Presence of Death in the Living Room : 2694.

The Presences : 4730, 4993.
La Presencia : 1937.
Present : 2842.
The Present : 1512.
The Present Is Like Sailcloth : 3061, 3264.
Present Tense : 1852.
Presentación : 371.
Preservation of Order : 6420.
The Preserving : 7290.
President Declares Cute Day : 1399.
The President of the United States : 4378.
President Reagan's visit to New York, October 1984 : 4199.
The Presidents of the United States of America, 1853 : 3982.
The Press Poem : 2721.
Pressing Needs : 4259.
Prestidigitation : 6273.
A Pretty Baby Girl in a da Nursery : 557.
Pretty Soon : 3038.
The pretty twins, Lottie and Lou : 5132.
Preview : 2769.
The Price of Admission : 3777.
Pride : 1906.
Primal Sympathy : 465.
Primary Season : 1636.
Primavera : 5789.
Prime the Wall That You Pass : 808, 2915.
Primer : 3411.
A Primer for Tonight's Audience : 2800.
The Priming Is a Negligee : 2129.
Primitive Renaissance : 6335.
The Prince and the Poplars : 6437.
Prince Valium and King Toot : 5230.
The Princess and the Frog : 1041, 1913.
The Principle : 4428.
The Principle of Plenitude : 2583.
Principles of Conversion : 2300.
The Prior : 3682.
Priority Mail for My Sons : 1375.
Prison Island Exile : 1537, 1538, 5399, 7221.
The Prison Poems of Ho Chi Minh : 1394, 2874.
The Prison Room : 2870.
The Prisoner : 211.
Prisoners: From a Diary by Julie H. : 3428.
Prisoners Stealing Plums : 934.
Prisons There and Not : 121.
The Privacies of Light : 5991.
Private Enterprise : 753.
Private Joy : 5667.
A Private Urge to Travel : 7355.
Private Viewing : 6014.
The Privilege : 3237.
Probability : 6242.
Probablemente al Final : 3086.
Probably : 3877.
Probation : 1189.
Probe on Occupation : 2956.
The Problem : 128.
Problem Performed by Shadows : 4365.
The Problem with the Pills : 6775.
El Problema de la Vivienda : 5104.
Problemas de Botánica : 5104.
Problems : 6682.

Problems in Painting: Spring Landscape with
    Melting Snow : 6203.
Problems of Botany : 4624, 5104.
Processes and Relationships : 3114.
Procession : 1255.
Processional : 5162.
Procrastination Is Rampant at H.U.D. : 2982.
Prodigal : 147.
The Prodigal Son's Brother : 3531.
Proem: i call it *the staple job* because
    misanthropy is paradise : 4378.
Prof with Both Hands on the Rail : 6242.
Professing That : 672.
The Profession : 2552.
A Professional Dying : 8.
The Professor : 4021.
Professor Ed : 5297.
The Professor of Strangeness Out for a Walk
    : 2331.
The Professor Stares at Salted Popcorn :
    3997.
The Professor's Wife to the College Boy :
    3487.
Progeny of Air : 1463.
Program : 7225.
Progress : 1585, 2051, 5374.
Progression : 3651.
Progressive Relaxation : 1110.
Projection : 4160.
Prologue : 5.
Prologue: The Waldorf Astoria : 613.
Prologue to the Book : 2253, 6235.
Prolonged Sonnet: When the Troops Were
    Returning from Milan : 64.
Prolonged Sonnet: Whent he Troops Were
    Returning from Milan : 5659.
The Prom Dress : 6251.
The Promise : 2975.
A Promise Renews Its Intimate Minute :
    3604.
Promised to a Dead Man : 7049.
Promoting Neurite Growth in the Mammalian
    Nervous System : 2297.
Propagation : 6085.
A Proper Blank Wall : 2694.
Prophecy : 5746.
Prophet Having Seen Jesus Perform a
    Miracle : 6885.
Prophets : 6563.
Prophets Climbing to Machu Picchu : 3425.
Prophylactic II : 6561.
Propinquity : 5112.
Proposal for an Observation : 5638, 5703.
Proposing to the Widow Dewine : 5430.
Prosas para Arturo R. : 6813.
Prose : 4065, 6993.
Prose #2 : 2112.
Prose Poem: Clair's semi-yuppie calico
    kitchen with an assertive twinge : 2965.
Prose Poem: He will come to cause mischief
    : 1138.
Prose Poem: If I can, I'll read birds : 1138.
Prose Poem: Restless before the canary :
    1138.
Prose Poem: Why can't I tell you I want you
    to press your thick fingers : 1138.

Prospect : 2325.
Prosthesis : 3064.
Protect Yourself : 6111.
Protection : 6842.
Protégé : 5230.
Proteus : 3580.
Prothalamion : 5952.
Prothalamion: Tableau Vivant : 3832.
The Prototype Bimbo, Grotesquely Preserved
    : 7223.
Proud of Myself : 3054.
Prove It : 3464.
The Provinces of Sleep : 3611.
Provincial Morning : 6539.
Proviso : 5286.
Proxy : 422.
Prudence : 1.
Pruner Speculates on Oscar Night : 653,
    4070, 4997, 5060.
Pruzzian Elegy : 605, 4366, 4367.
P.S. : 6994.
Psalm : 1127, 5542, 6076.
Psalm 118: Taking Out the Trash : 4141.
Psalm Before Sleep : 1247.
Psalm for Modernization : 39.
Psalm for the Summer Solstice : 5207.
Psalm: Let Us Think of God as a Lover :
    3145.
Psalms for the New Catechism, #17 : 39.
A Psalter : 3331.
Psyche, 6 : 5644.
Psychiatric : 2988.
Psychiatric Dreams : 6366.
Psychic's Holiday : 6742.
The Psychological Present : 2091.
The Psychology of the Sentence: Case
    Histories : 6350.
The Psychotropic Squalls : 79.
The Pterodactyl : 2474.
Ptolemy and Me : 7112.
PTSD : 6023.
The Puberty of Smell : 172.
Public Life : 2331.
Public Needs : 4111.
Public Relations : 5577.
Public School : 1264, 5950.
Public Works : 6472.
Puddles : 4244.
Puffins : 2223.
Puget Sound : 5412, 5632.
Puissant : 1350.
Pulling the mirror closer : 5113.
Pulse and Terrace : 129.
Pumpkin Lust : 2700.
Punch-Drunk : 2022.
Punishment : 4108, 5075, 5220, 6025, 6411.
Punk Flesh : 1636.
Punk Rock : 731.
Punto de Vista : 3597.
A Puppet Play : 6076.
Puppet Show : 1158.
Puppet to Puppeteer : 1158.
The Puppet's Obsession : 2978.
Pure Colors : 1603.
Purgatorio : 1406, 4417.
Purgatorio, Canto II : 1406, 4417.

Purity : 3628.
Purity, a Failure in White Robes, Goes
    Dreaming in the Far Pasture : 6658.
Purple Fighter : 3110.
Purple Hearts : 6164.
Purple Passion : 2188.
Purple Power: A Summer Dream, 1992 :
    5953.
The Purposes of Skin : 4643.
The Pursuit of Learning : 108.
A Purtian looked at his yard : 5132.
The Push-Pull of This Love : 6251.
Pushkin : 5741.
Pussy Willows : 7095.
Put These in Your Pipe : 6299.
Putting a Dog to Sleep : 5519.
Putting in a Word : 6938.
Putting Myself on the Couch: Or the Poem I
    Wrote After I Wrote the Poem : 3630.
Putting on the Stutz : 3969.
Putting the Books Back : 5301.
Putting the House in Order : 3310.
Putting William to Sleep : 667.
Puzzle : 5347.
Pylos : 6584.
Pyre Tender : 318, 4035, 7221.
Pyromancy : 4260.
Quake Fever : 6735.
The Quaker Dreams of Violence : 2804.
The Quality of Grace : 4001.
A Quality of Wind : 2948.
Quality of Wine : 979.
Quandary : 7125.
The Quarrel : 6960.
Quartet: Photo Collage : 4087.
Quasi-stellar Object : 6841.
Quaternary : 464, 3094.
Que Hora Budu Ya Là? : 3828.
Que Pretty In Tejas : 6242.
Queda el Sueño : 5598.
Queen Anne's Lace : 2914, 5234, 6632.
Queen of Hearts : 625.
The Queen of Sheba Restaurant : 344.
The Queen of Spain, Grown Old and Mad,
    Writes to the Daughter She Imagines
    She Had by Christopher Columbus :
    3698.
The Queen on the Tower : 5789.
Quelques Leçons des Tenebres : 378.
Query : 5164.
Question : 1336, 1871.
Question in Red Ink : 3484.
Questions : 1554, 3921.
Questions Asked of Women at a NYC Bus
    Stop : 4300.
Quetzalcoatl : 494.
The Queue : 1749.
The Quick : 1095.
The Quick Cave : 6472.
quick i the death of thing : 1353.
Quién Es Que Anda? : 98.
Quiet : 2256.
The Quiet Chambers : 1266.
A Quiet Life : 7213.
The Quiet Limits : 5242.
A Quiet Madman : 3264, 5705.

The Quiet Side of the Island : 6527.
The Quiet Women : 5592.
Quietness : 1135.
The Quill : 1164.
The Quilt She Started : 177.
Quince : 4417.
The Quiñero Sisters, 1968 : 1112.
Quintessence : 1424.
Quintet : 4719.
Quotas : 2404.
(R) : 6066.
R.I.P. : 2840.
R.M.I. 3 : 4554.
The Rabbi's Wife : 1082.
The Rabbit Catcher : 5206.
Rabbit Man : 5805.
The Rabbit Queen : 6664.
A Raccoon : 2057.
Race Point : 4559.
Racine Street : 4697.
Racing the Dark Language : 3305.
Racing to Istanbul : 7215.
Ración del Don : 4990.
Racists : 196.
Radiance of the Hundred Door Cast : 7027.
Radio : 6187.
The Radio : 5621.
Radio Babylon Goes Off the Air : 5500.
Radio Lady : 912.
Radio Pope : 2331.
Radio Tuning : 1373.
Radiography : 632.
Rafting down the Mississippi : 5051.
A Rag, a Bone, and a Hank of Hair : 1743.
Rag Doll Mary : 3968.
Rage : 4384.
Ragged Island : 5432.
Raid : 2136.
Raiding Party : 6499.
Railroad Bridge : 1112.
Railway Stanzas : 4928.
Railway Station : 2697, 3176, 6907.
Raimondo de Soncino, Agent of the Duke of
    Milan, to the Duke, 18 December 1497 :
    4862.
Rain : 1715, 2220, 3721, 3838, 5232, 5286,
    5943, 5995.
The Rain : 3592.
The Rain Children : 2478.
Rain Near Heart Lake : 5792.
The Rain on the Roof : 3677.
Rain Patterns : 3016.
Rain, Steam, and Speed : 1875.
Rain Two Times a Year : 4282.
Rainbow : 2387, 2524.
The Rainbow Shower : 6527.
Raindrops : 6306.
Rained Out : 2156.
Raining Fire : 3841.
The Rainman Out of Snow : 3846.
The Rain's Burden : 6798.
The Rainstick : 2725.
Rainy Day : 6544.
Rainy Day Nap : 5425.
Rainy Morning : 5432.
The Rainy Night : 308, 7248, 7341.

A Rainy Night: The Pine Barrens, N.J. : 3862.
Raisins : 3372.
Raiz Absurda : 925.
Ralph : 206.
Ralph Steiner's Photograph: 'Hanging Sheets' : 6767.
Ramen : 2903.
Rampant : 6867.
Ram'zaan : 3562.
Ranakpur : 1662.
The Rancher : 1202.
Rancor of the Empirical : 3682.
Random : 2477.
Random Events : 2818.
A Random Gospel : 2760.
The Range : 1105.
Ransom Note for Brion Gysin : 1176.
Rant : 1552.
A Rant Against Losses : 7346.
The Rape : 2050.
Rape Honey : 6174.
The Raptor : 1964.
Rapture : 3431.
The Rapture : 1703.
Raptures : 6135.
Rapunzel, Rapunzel : 1975.
A Rare Book : 3392, 6094.
A Rare Photograph Taken Somewhere in Eastern Europe, Probably in 1941 : 3327.
Rari for O'Otua : 1789, 5702, 6580.
Rari for Tahia and Piu : 1789, 5702, 6580.
The Rattlesnake : 7116.
The Rav of Berditchev : 5546.
Ravaged : 7011.
Raven : 1817.
Raven Afternoon : 2425.
The Ravens at the Tower of London : 231.
Ravine : 3300.
A Raving Madman : 3264, 5705.
Razor : 3973.
Razor Blade Woman : 3917.
Razor Roxit : 1591.
Re-Creation : 6082, 6719.
Re-Entering the Past : 1045.
The Reach : 86, 5162.
Reaching for the Latch : 3216.
Reaching Out Past Pale Illuminations : 4899.
Read This Now : 1540.
Read Your Fate : 6076.
The Reading : 3606.
Reading a Poetry Assignment on Wednesday at 11:09 p.m. : 1505.
Reading and Talking : 7364.
Reading by Christmas Light : 609.
Reading Critical Theory to My Mother Over the Phone : 4760.
Reading Early Morning (or I Could Commit Justifiable Homicide) : 7326.
Reading Frank O'Hara in the Hospital : 151.
Reading Freud : 6871.
Reading History : 6076.
Reading in a Hammock : 1204.
Reading in Fredonia : 802.
Reading in the Poetry Journals : 1466.
Reading Moby Dick Aloud to My Dead Nephew : 3662.
Reading Nietzsche in the Factory Canteen : 5997.
Reading Plato : 6921.
Reading Robert Hayden on a Quiet Morning : 2969.
Reading Sex : 900.
The Reading Seas : 2128.
Reading Stafford Late at Night : 6528.
Reading the Poem My Sister Wrote That I Hadn't : 3822.
Reading Tour : 3822.
Reading While Driving : 1371.
Reading Your Poem on Miracles : 597.
Ready-Made Bouquet : 7283.
Ready to Be Beheaded : 5814, 6521.
The Real Blues : 5755.
Real Boreal, Arboreal : 4049.
Real Estate : 4789.
A Real Event : 584.
Real Life : 3662.
Real Life, Still Life : 722.
The Real Me : 5230, 6134.
Reality : 1751.
The Reality : 623.
Reality Demands : 327, 1022, 6514.
A Realm of Probability : 864.
Reappraisal While Sliding Down a Trough Made Slick by Watery Lies and Layoffs : 2012.
Rear View : 466.
Rear-View Mirror : 36.
The Reason I Refused My X Husband's Last Name : 7160.
Reason Is a Zoning Commissioner : 6947.
The Reason of Nature : 3292, 6334.
A Reason to Live : 6842.
The Reason We Work So Hard : 172.
Rebecca's Way : 4950.
Rebirth : 2333.
Rebus Feast : 1591.
Receding Surf : 143, 3786.
Receiving a Videotape of My 36th-Year High School Reunion : 291.
Receiving the Violently Killed : 5813.
Recent Discoveries : 1253.
Recess : 7010.
Recessional : 5926, 7097.
Recidivist : 1694.
Recipe: One Artichoke : 5537.
Reckoning : 2498, 3097.
Reclaiming an Old Debt : 3920.
Reclamation : 633.
The Reclining Poet : 2400.
Recognition : 624.
Recounting the Day : 7316.
Recovery : 3197, 5549, 7243.
Recovery Notebook : 4950.
Recreation : 2877.
The Recreational Parachutist : 2977.
The rectangular distress of the city : 3119, 5861.
Recurrence in Another Tongue: Homage to Tristia and Osip Mandelstam : 7137.
Recyclables : 3608.

Recycling Relationship : 3358.
Red Bank, N.J. (1941-45) : 7066.
Red Banner's Whereabouts : 6539.
The Red Bed : 206.
Red Creek : 5580.
Red Eye : 4266.
The Red Fox : 6498.
Red Geraniums : 1606.
Red Leather Jacket : 3735.
Red-Light District : 3503.
Red Maple : 6356.
Red Oasis : 7230.
Red Orphan : 1262.
Red Overcoming : 7166.
The Red Parrot : 5668.
Red Poet : 6465.
Red Poppies : 2869.
Red Poppy : 3902.
Red Poppy — O'Keeffe, 1927 : 4682.
The red Raging Waters : 6595.
Red Reed : 417.
Red Riding Hood Buys Term Life : 784.
Red Rust in the Sunset : 1001.
Red Sea : 18.
Red Shoes : 1511.
The Red Shoes : 1575.
Red Tail Sin : 4373.
Red Tee Shirt : 7243.
Red Trails : 197.
The Red Train : 3070.
Red wine and blues : 5230.
Redding fur : 511.
Redemption : 1074.
Redemption's Wilderness : 1006.
The Redemptive Figures : 5808.
Redhead : 529.
Reds, Purples, Blues : 2321.
Reducing the Dose : 3102.
A Reed Boat : 3499.
The Reels for TR and CJ : 6486.
Reencarnación : 1071.
Reentry : 5840.
Refinement : 2331.
Reflecting : 1034, 1035, 4652.
A Reflection Across the Yard : 3986.
Reflection on El Train Glass : 5592.
Reflections : 4444, 4622, 7086, 7168.
Reflections by a Window : 6666.
Reflections on My Lesbian Body : 1485.
Reflections on Violence : 5875.
Refrain for My Sires : 3070.
The Refrain Man : 5459.
Refuge : 773, 5891.
Refugee : 1259, 2783.
Refugees : 1104, 2333, 2333, 2346, 4178.
Regarding the Investment of the Ship Owner
     Mr. Andreas Embeirkos in a Blast
     Furnace (March 1935) : 1104.
Regarding the Investment of the Ship Owner
     Mr. Andreas Embeirikos in a Blast
     Furnace (March 1935) : 4178.
Regina : 2974.
Regina Vagina : 6685.
A Region : 3332.
Regions of Restlessness : 6411, 6744.
Regions of Silence : 6411, 6744.

Registro Civil : 6758.
Règle : 5232.
Regret : 5527.
The Regret : 4416, 7138.
Regrets : 965, 1685.
Regrets Only : 4045.
Rehearsed in Oblivion : 4160.
Reinaldo Arenas : 4596.
Reincarnation : 1781, 1858, 6743.
Reincarnation of a Love Bird : 958.
Reinventing Tradition in Malawi : 3198.
Reject What Confuses You : 3961.
Rejected, Not Quite : 116.
The Rejected Suitor : 3726.
Relative Sufferings : 3819, 5172.
Relativity : 1448.
Relax, Petrarch! : 6717.
Relay : 1898.
Released through Stone : 4106.
Relics of an Ice Age : 3115.
Relieving Beethoven : 3837.
Religio Medici, 1643 : 643, 4433.
Religion : 769.
Reliquary: Trnava : 6034.
Relocation: The Building of the Dyke Levee :
     4017.
Reluctant Shipwright : 6260.
The Remains of Christmas : 3998.
Remarks on Our City : 6625.
Rembrandt Drawings : 7235.
Rembrandt's Lucretia : 271.
Remedies : 3738.
The Remedy : 3235.
Remember Home Art : 7265.
Remember the Moose : 5018.
Remember the Source : 2939.
Remembered Weather : 3145.
Remembering Dryden on the People's Road :
     5346.
Remembering I.B. Singer : 6250.
Remembering Kitchens : 4640.
Remembering Lynn : 3052.
Remembering Old Wars : 3433.
Remembering Solomon Mahlangu, Reburied
     This Week : 1885.
Remembering the Egg : 3629.
Remembering the Scholar : 1513.
Remembering What Was Said : 886.
Remembrance : 4038.
A Reminder : 7243.
Reminiscence : 1488, 5123.
Reminiscence of a Distant Exile, Or, Song of
     Houston : 2256.
Remodeling : 2709.
The Removers : 6286.
Rendered World : 4528.
Rendering : 5177.
The Rendez-Vous at Cophinou : 2207, 3514.
Le Rendez-Vous de Cophinou : 2207.
Rendezvous in Bilad-as-Sudan : 3337.
René Rilke : 6638.
Renegade Angels : 4640.
Renga : 451, 1830, 4744.
Renoir : 4801.
Rent : 6293.
Renting Videos : 6686.

The Renunciation of Poetry : 2864.
Repairs : 6335.
Reparations : 2677.
The Reparations Draft Agreement : 3344, 4995.
Repeated Sightings : 2331.
Repetitions of a Young Captain : 6373.
Reply to Sirens : 2219.
Report from the Heartland : 6299.
Report on the Mothers : 1203.
Repression : 6409.
Reprieve : 5107.
Reprinted by Permission of *Architectural Digest* : 1442.
Reprise : 5452.
The Reptile Tent : 6642.
Request for a Little Water Music from the Night : 6867.
Requested Rhetoric : 5688.
Requiem : 436, 783, 1075, 2912, 4201, 4284.
Requiem for a Teacher : 3157.
Requiem for Ray : 2811.
Requiem with Nudes : 3136, 4925.
Reruns in the Oncologist's Waiting Room : 2553.
Rescue : 4565, 5994, 6174.
Rescue: A Letter : 521.
Rescue the Dead : 3054.
Rescue Tips : 4804.
Researchers in the Human Sciences : 2604.
A Reservation Table of the Elements : 80.
Reserve : 5008.
The Reservoir : 4082.
Residential Zone : 794, 2360.
Residual : 1534.
Resilience : 3747.
Resistance : 1633.
Resolution : 5981.
Resorts : 979.
Respeto y Amor Sincero : 4062.
Response : 938.
Response to a Letter from My Ex : 6059.
Responsibilities : 290.
The Rest of the Year : 1082.
Restaurant Overlooking Lake Superior : 3161.
Restoration of a Copy of an Imaginary Painting : 6481.
Results: HIV Positive : 4026.
The Results of the Accidents of Conquest : 797.
The Resurrected : 2387, 5205.
Resurrection : 2502, 3197, 4003, 4142, 5110, 5931, 6038, 6556.
The Resurrection : 2441.
The Resurrection of the Body : 2439, 5015.
Retablo with Multiple Sclerosis and Saint : 5131.
A Retelling : 4660.
Retelling the Story : 5845.
Retief's Kloof : 5890.
Retitled 'Silent Noon' : 5517.
Retorno a la Realidad : 6657.
Retrato Doble : 3856.
Retribution : 466.
Retrograde : 3421.

Return : 1121, 5016, 6219.
The Return : 1247, 3730.
Return: Buffalo : 2898.
Return from Nepal : 3324.
Return Journey : 5890.
Return Leter : 4159.
Return to a Spring Full of Little Boys : 2026.
Return to Ellis Island : 5806.
Return to Sender? : 7221.
A Return to Simple Stories : 519, 7345.
The Return to Spain, 1992 : 5531.
Return to the Love Canal : 7202.
Return to Wang River : 362, 363, 2576, 6910, 6910, 7250.
Returning : 5993.
A Returning : 724.
Returning Back to My Body : 6498.
Returning From the Home of a Friend Along South Mountain Drive : 20.
Returning Light : 5179.
Returning to Standard Time : 2411.
Returning to the Nest : 176.
Returning to Town in Summer : 642.
Retzer Sphinx : 5349.
Reunion : 398, 545, 1199, 2434, 2765, 4799, 5786, 6598, 7217.
Reunion: August '89 : 5652.
Reunion on the Northfork : 4479.
Reunion on the Weekend of the Fourth : 5724.
Reunions : 3167.
Revalations [Revelations?] Under Oak and Stars : 4490.
Revealing German : 2376.
Revelation : 225, 1736, 2255, 5268.
Revelations : 6577.
The Revenants : 3602.
Reverberations of the Day Pheasants Flew Up : 5795.
Reverdie : 5787.
Reverence for Wood : 3933.
Reverend Billy : 6960.
Reverie : 5560.
Reverie Over and Above the Essences : 5003.
Reversing the Process : 1966.
The Revised Versions : 5330.
Revision : 3933.
The Revisionist: On Noah's Ark : 836.
Revisited : 6941.
Revisiting a Mountain Town : 1699, 6102, 7260.
Revisiting Eden : 6006.
Revival : 6089.
The Revolution : 6259.
Revolver : 2300.
The Reward of Harvest, Then : 4472.
Rewind : 7173.
Rex Jacobus Ludi : 6953.
Rhadamanthine : 3961.
Rhapsody : 3031, 3491.
Rhetoric of Senses : 783.
Rhetorical Judea : 3920.
Rheumatic : 7027.
Rhubarb : 6818.
Rhyme : 3592, 6806.
Rhyme Gone to Hell : 3753.

(Rhythm) : 6574.
The Rhythm of Work : 4178.
Riangolare gli Assi : 5789.
Rib : 6988.
Ribbon : 5906.
The Ribs : 1175.
Rich Man, Poor Man : 3780.
Riches : 3614.
Ric's Progress : 2552.
Riddance : 2487.
Riddle : 2117, 4525.
Riddle: Get the horses! Call the chief! : 6635.
Riddle: I resist the sadness of daily drudge :
    1228.
The Riddle of the Sphinx : 7215.
Riddles Wisely Expounded as Beauty Speaks
    from Sleep : 5091.
Ride : 696.
The Ride : 3334.
Rider : 5694.
Ridiculous the Waste : 816.
Riding a Hydrofoil to Budapest : 3639.
Riding Cross-Bronx Expressway : 1911.
Riding Rapunzel : 784.
Riding the Mad Mouse : 2505.
Riding What Life Handed Her : 1452.
Rien d'Autre Que le Tonnerre : 450.
Right After Breakfast : 6479.
The Right Hand : 1355.
Right Now (for Michelle) : 3937.
The Right of Opinion : 1920.
The Right Reader : 1760.
The Right Way to Be a Woman : 2344.
Rigor : 1194.
The Rigors of Death : 5723.
Rilke in the Middle Ages : 2437.
The Rim : 6030.
Rimbaud Takes the Stand : 6312.
Rimbaud's Cancer : 2553.
The Ring : 6922.
Ring-a-by : 862, 5343, 6844.
Ring of Fire : 6123.
Ring Poem : 5509.
The ringing sound when you lost your sense
    of humor : 2049.
Rio del Mar : 4494.
Rio Frio : 2177.
Rio Soy : 4512.
The Riot Police : 867.
Riot Trousers : 2889.
R.I.P. : 2840.
Rip Van Winkle : 1831, 6871.
Ripe, in fire dipped, broiled : 2907, 5640,
    5855.
Rise and Fall : 2135.
Rise 'N Shine : 3836.
Rising and Falling : 2551.
Rising Faire : 3718.
La Risurrettione de Giesu Cristo, 1708 :
    5306.
Rita : 341.
Rite of Passage : 4628.
Rite to Life : 1776.
Rites : 6998.
Rites de Passion : 2054.
Rites in the Bay : 3181.

Rites of Passage : 1247.
Rites of Wrong : 5042.
Ritmos Negros del Perú : 5797.
The Ritual : 2869.
The Ritual Quiet : 4705.
River : 768, 1519, 3300, 6597.
The River : 2378.
The River Again : 2837.
The River at Land's End : 6149.
River Blindness (Onchocerciasis) : 3961.
River Bottom : 3639.
River Colorado : 3415.
The River-Merchant's Wife: A Letter : 7123.
River Music : 674.
River Pulse : 3425.
River Travel : 337.
Riverbed : 1413.
Riverbend : 442, 2236, 4127, 5804.
Riverbottom : 4508.
Rivers : 4897.
Rivers and Seas, Harbors and Parts : 5479.
Rivers on Fire : 848.
The River's Tale : 2654.
Rivka's Dream : 3791.
Rizal's Ghost : 2318.
Rm #2 : 3751.
R.M.I. 3 : 4554.
The Road : 1321.
Road Crew : 1833.
Road Kill : 865, 1472, 3490.
The Road Not Taken : 3197.
Road of Remembrance : 286.
Road, River, Snake : 386.
Road shoulder mail boxes : 3430.
Road to Dhaka : 1045.
The Road to Giverny : 6338.
The Road to Marshfield Lake : 307.
Road Warrior : 4754.
Roadside : 5558.
Roadside Flowers : 614.
The Robed Heart : 6279.
Robert DeNiro : 80.
Robert Mapplethorpe's Photograph of Apollo
    (1988) : 3082.
The Robes of Feathers : 6520.
The Robin Moor, 1893 : 5838.
Robinson : 3995, 5638.
Robot Man : 2078.
Rock a Bye : 6207.
Rock and Relic : 3101.
Rock Bottom : 3878.
Rock Falls, Illinois : 4307.
Rock Garden & Decaffeinated Tea : 6975.
Rock Jetty : 3836.
A Rock Mulls Things Over from a Bend in
    the Wapsipinicon : 3905.
Rock-O-Plane : 3353.
A Rock Presented by a Friend from Alaska :
    6299.
Rocks My Pillow Too : 2692.
Rodeo of Blood : 206.
Rodin Exhibit on the Rooftop, Metropolitan
    Museum of Art : 4113.
Rodney King Beating: Round Three, or, A
    Pebble Dropped : 5425.
Rodney King Blues : 1743.

Roger, the Tattoo Artist : 5431.
Rogue Hydrant, August : 3440.
Rogue Transmissions : 6472.
Rogues' Codes : 4858.
Roland Barthes : 5440.
Roland of Nantes, Forced to Bring His Wife
   and Daughter on the Second Crusade :
   1259.
The Role Model : 3730.
Role Play : 6634.
Roles Rewritten : 1478.
Roling Off : 240.
Roller-Coaster : 5432.
Roller Coaster : 5726.
Rolling Thinking : 6039.
Roma : 1222.
Roman Sketchbook : 1321.
Roman Tomb : 1642.
Romance : 1135, 1512, 3683, 4668, 5091.
Romance has reached the low g's when your
   date moves down a notch : 3068.
Romance Language : 7028.
Romance Type Poem for Miz Martinez :
   4271.
Romancing Debussy : 5914.
Romanesque : 4417.
Romantic Landscape : 6076.
A Romantic Occasion : 1869.
The Romantic Subway : 554.
Romanticism, a Sequel : 5361.
Rome Beauty : 752.
Ronald : 7103.
Ronda : 5395.
Rondeau : 5238.
Rondeau at the Train Stop : 443.
Rooftops : 1867, 7040.
The Room : 6559.
The Room at Gedney Farm : 4589.
A Room of One's Own : 1327.
Room of Rooms : 4472.
A Room Without Doors : 3866.
Roomful of moonlight : 5039.
Rooms : 537.
The Root Canal : 149.
Root Song : 4573.
A Root Story : 1505.
Roots : 2056.
The Roots of Sweetness : 2690.
Rope : 6716.
The Rope : 2812.
Ropes : 537.
Rosa : 6934.
La Rosa de Ceniza : 4166.
Rosa, Maria, Lucia : 2798.
Rosamund : 5344.
Rose and Amelie : 587.
A Rose and Milton : 4433.
The Rose Bus : 4749.
The Rose Chapel : 2545.
Rose Garden : 1143, 4837, 4949.
Roseate Tern : 3043.
Rosebud : 6372.
Rosemary Ducks : 4018.
Roses : 674, 3082, 6689.
The Roses : 5486.
Rosetta : 1189.

Rostenkowski Accused : 6690.
Rotary : 3167.
Rote of Forgetfulness : 1664.
Rotten Cloth : 793.
Roué : 3389.
The Roué at the Breakfast Table, or
   Breakfast in Bloom : 6262.
Rough-Cut Head : 5385.
The rough weight of it : 1149.
Roughhousing : 1606.
Round : 1765.
Round and around it bobs and drifts : 466.
Round Face in a Little Town : 6512.
The Route : 1582.
Route 80 : 4078.
Route One Postcard : 5631.
Route Six : 3580.
Rowboat : 1360.
Roxanne : 3545.
Roy Uhde: The Sheriff : 6876.
Royal Entertainment : 3136, 4925.
Royal Poinciana : 558.
RR in Spanish = : 5595.
RSVP : 678.
Rubberneck : 139.
Rubbing Down the Horse : 1717.
Las Rubias : 2170.
Ruby Moon : 5069.
Rubyglass : 7170.
Ruby's House : 379.
Rude But Nonetheless an Awakening : 3513.
Rue : 6123.
Rue Montmartre : 5820.
Ruega por Nosotros : 4439.
Rufino Tamayo: *The Merry Drinker*, 1946 :
   3877.
The Ruiner of Lives : 6723.
The Ruins of Phylakopi : 6222.
El Ruiseñor y la Muerte : 4592.
Rule for the New Liar : 2714.
Rule Number Three : 6749.
The Rule of the North Star : 6723.
Rum Rhymes and Comic Capers : 3443.
A Ruminant : 2728.
Ruminating : 3054.
Rummage Sale, East Baldwin, Maine : 1116.
Rumor : 1109, 3064.
Rumors : 2465.
The Run of Silvers : 6042.
Runaway : 3796.
Runaway Dreamer : 3529.
The Runner : 3707.
A Runner's Quarrel : 86.
Running : 6887.
Running the Stunt Over : 170.
Running Water : 4038.
Running Wire : 2505.
Runyonesque : 1288.
Rural Development : 4225.
Rushing Back : 6300.
Rustle : 6314.
La Ruta 16 : 1531.
Ruth : 6364.
Ruth Briggs : 1043.
Ruth Stone Reading My Poem : 6852.
Ruthless as a Tibetan Monk : 6513.

The Ruts of the Oregon Trail : 435.
Rx for Modern Times : 1583.
Rybaudoure : 3146.
Rye Bread : 3753.
The Rye Field : 3319.
Sa Nafanua : 6103.
Sabang, 1964 : 2182.
The Sacral Dreams of Ramon Fernandez :
    2157.
Sacrament : 1187.
A Sacrament : 6964.
Sacramental : 3942.
Sacramento : 5474.
The Sacred Blue : 5971.
Sacrifice : 5607.
The Sacrifice : 7025.
Sad Cabin : 619.
The Sad Disruptions : 1388.
Sad Numbers : 1545.
Sad Wine : 1460, 5068.
Saddam Hussein, Saddam Hussein : 6690.
Sadie and Laura : 658.
Sadie and Maud : 769.
Safe : 2741.
Safe Familiars : 3692.
The Safe House : 5641.
Safety First : 1834.
Sage : 3067, 3069, 5155, 6123.
Sagesse : 4624, 6805.
Sagging Chests : 2696.
Sail Away : 3298.
Sailing on the broad Pacific : 1238.
Sailing on the Zuider Zee : 1238.
Sailing one day on the Black Sea : 1238.
Sailing the Stone Boat : 1106.
Saint . . . See also St. . . . (arranged as
    spelled under ST)
The Saint : 1104, 3054, 4178.
Saint Beethoven : 535.
Saint Flaubert : 3153.
Saint Lucia's First Communion : 6859.
Saint Petersburg Daze : 758.
Saint Sebastian's Widow : 4969.
Saint Wilgefortis : 1979.
Sainte-Chapelle : 200.
Saints : 7211.
The Saint's Cookbook : 4131.
Sake : 6279.
Salad : 4513.
The Sale Sale : 121.
The Salmon Has Entered Our Winter : 3070.
Salsa at Midnight : 4185.
Salt : 921, 2439, 6035.
Salt for Me : 6664.
Salt Free Talk : 6858.
Salt Marsh : 6858.
Salt Tears : 4721.
Salt Woman : 4668.
Salty Bore : 1192.
Salute — To Singing : 258, 2067.
El Salvador del Mundo : 4224.
Salvador's Ox : 2890.
Salvation Man : 5046.
Sam Cooke Would Be Sixty-One This Year :
    6012.
Samaras : 2404.

The Same Material : 425.
The Same River : 3871.
Same Sidewalk : 6975.
The Same, Yet Not the Same : 1169.
Samovar : 2095.
San Antonio, Cayo District, Belize : 3633.
San Diego in Late October : 6935.
San Francisco : 4137.
The San Gabriels : 5624.
San Miguel Sketchbook : 438.
San Sepolcro : 2398.
Sanctification : 2667.
Sanctuary : 1996, 3985.
Sanctuary of Chimayo : 4023.
Sanctum Sanctorum : 2032.
Sanctus : 478.
Sand Crabs at Lookout Point : 6408.
Sand Dance : 7351.
Sand Lake : 4662.
The Sandpiper : 4993.
Sands : 3198, 5749.
Sandwiched : 4454.
Sandy : 4123.
Sangre de Cristo, July 4 : 6650.
Sans Serif: Blue Ridge Parkway, March 1989
    : 2781.
Sans Souci : 571.
Sansevieria : 2015.
Santa Ana River Sequence : 293.
Santa Claus : 135.
Santa Fe: A Jewish Wife, 1895 : 4820.
Santa Paula : 4243.
Santa speaks : 3437.
Santiago: Five Men in the Street : 1606.
Santiago: Forestal Park : 1606.
Santiago: Plaza de Armas : 1606.
São Paulo : 6740.
Saplings : 5481.
Sappho : 716.
Sappho on the East Side : 4270.
Sara 10, Never Talks About : 3822.
Sarah: Her Sibling in the Woods : 967.
Sarah's Laughter : 2246.
Sarajevo : 2679, 4500, 5717, 7168.
Sarajevo Bear : 5069.
Sarajevo Sorrow : 6075, 6077.
The Sari Thief : 1903.
Saskia Looking Out of a Window, c. 1633-34
    : 7235.
Sat 'n Lied : 469.
Satan Owns a Boneyard : 2751.
Satin Mules : 2491.
A Satire : 5326.
Saturday During the War : 2469.
Saturday in Chinatown : 6242.
Saturday Morning : 109.
Saturday Morning 4/26/80, Huntington
    Galleries : 4328.
Saturday Night : 4950.
Saturday Night at the Pahala Theater : 7254.
Saturday Night Cafés : 4282.
Saturday's Child : 7125.
Saturn : 945, 6848.
A Saucepan for Three Planets : 2422.
Saudades : 1662.
Saul's House : 565.

Savages Sighted Wandering Aimlessly : 2395.
Savanna : 6419.
Save the Last Dance for Me : 5230.
Saved : 5914, 6716.
Saved From Lani Guinier : 6690.
Savoring the Season : 3441.
Sawhorse with a Wife Sitting Against It : 7265.
The Sawmill Road : 3716.
Say Adieu : 1266.
The Say-But-the-Word Centurion Attempts a Summary : 4686.
Say God came back : 3218.
Say *Partridgeberry* : 1383.
Say When : 2423.
Saying Goodbye : 6702, 6935, 7282.
Saying Goodbye to Sweetapple : 6045.
Saying No to a Vampire : 3697.
Says Pat, on the shore of the Irish Sea : 2474.
Scaffold : 2705.
Scaffolds Everywhere : 7046.
Scale : 921, 5381.
Scapegoat : 3590.
The Scar : 675.
A Scarcity Model for Waves : 3458.
Scarecrow : 6817.
Scarecrows : 6470.
Scared by a Leaf : 4008.
Scarifying : 4601.
Scars : 4910, 6672, 6935.
Scatter : 6819.
Scattering the Ashes : 2099.
The Scene Shifts : 3682.
Scene with Pelicans : 5888.
Scenery : 436, 1076, 1968.
Scenes for a Dying : 5362.
Scenes from a Puppet Play : 6152.
Scenes from the Black Hole : 1254.
Scenes of Male-Feminine Mystique in P - Town : 4215.
Scent : 2939.
Schatten Rosen Schatten : 273.
Schedule : 7000.
The Scholar : 3202.
School : 5006, 5541.
The School : 1426, 3187.
School — AAAA!! : 5320.
School Building : 1466.
School Days : 3253, 3812, 5541.
School Friend : 3688.
School Metaphors : 4777.
School Spirit : 5427.
Schoolteacher Raking Crimson Leaves : 1447.
Schumann: Answer to Joachim : 4516.
Schumann's Piano Concerto in A Minor : 1177.
Sciatica : 6963.
Science : 1912, 6966.
Science and Snacks : 1672.
Scientists Search Burial Vault for Seventeenth Century Air : 5239.
The Scissors of Max Ernst : 5870.
Scout : 3186, 5071.
Scratch : 2547.

A Scratch : 5009.
The Scratch : 1561.
The Scream : 1952.
Screaming in Our Hearts : 3240.
Screen : 6125.
Screwdriver : 1749.
Screwed within the Universe : 838.
Scríob : 931.
Scripture of the Heart : 3488.
Sculpt : 4025.
Scuttlebutt : 5162.
Sea : 7181.
The Sea : 978, 3339, 6493.
Sea Blouse Open : 432, 774.
Sea Change : 3197.
The Sea Chest : 5550.
Sea-Cucumber : 1957.
Sea Gull, Singer Island : 917.
The Sea in the Wind : 2493, 7221.
The Sea Mouse : 4900.
The Sea Otters : 5923.
The Sea Sprite, Hermosa Beach : 6089.
Sea Wolves : 506.
Seafarer : 4532.
Seafood : 3238.
Seagull : 2193.
The Seagulls : 3809, 4945, 7019.
Seal Beach : 6142.
Seamen Three : 5079.
Search : 3621.
The Search : 1412, 1442.
The Search for Scarlett : 6263.
Search the Darkness : 2758, 5704.
Searching for Arrowheads : 219.
Searching for Grandpa : 2401.
Searching the Doll : 3162.
Seascape with Beach Umbrellas : 6050.
Seascape with House and Stars : 1063.
Season : 4417.
A Season : 6733.
A Season for Berries : 6036.
Season of Flies : 4342.
The Season of Persimmons : 7075.
The Season of the Falling Face : 2455.
Seasonal : 4700, 6194.
Seasons : 4088.
Season's Greetings : 6807.
Season's Tickets : 6603.
Seattle : 3073.
Seaward : 1505.
Sebastopol : 4576.
Seclusion in Mexico City : 5392.
Second Birth : 787.
Second Chidren : 6266.
Second Coming : 521.
The Second Coming : 5516, 5926.
Second Comings : 757.
Second Diptych : 7267.
Second Fairy Tale for Stefana : 955, 4219, 5236.
Second Grade : 3877.
Second-Grade Angel : 5555.
Second Growth : 1883.
Second-Hand : 4596.
Second Illustrated Advertisement for Jerry's Barber Shop : 2974.

The Second Kind : 5863.
The Second King of Japan : 3803.
Second Language : 4353.
Second Language (Somalia, 1973) : 6851.
Second Lecture on Poetry : 1756.
Second Marriage : 4241.
Second-Mortgage Lovers : 6868.
Second-Order Enthymeme : 4736.
The second Presence : 2162.
Second Religion : 6672.
The Second Search : 4436.
Second Series : 2171, 2174, 5539.
Second Sight : 3245.
Second Woman and Insecurity : 257, 3776.
Seconds : 3782.
Seconds of Free Fall and Chaos : 4282.
The Secret : 3207.
Secret, Ancient Voices of the Night : 2824,
    3715, 6727.
The Secret Faith : 7054.
The Secret Fire : 7177.
The Secret Identity : 3829.
The Secret of Life : 2406.
Secret Sale : 6947.
Secret Talking : 280, 3809, 4945.
Secretly : 3054.
Los Secretos Mas Blancos : 641.
Secrets : 382, 1779.
Sed de Correr : 1124.
Seduced Again by Bukowski : 3803.
Seduced and Abandoned : 442, 5353, 5804.
Seductions : 6634.
See by my third eye : 3218.
See the Pyramids : 1969.
See, the Smell of My Son : 2018.
See Willow : 521.
Seeds : 1791.
A Seedy Story : 7125.
Seeing : 2517, 2927, 4164, 7282.
Seeing Eye Dog : 5726.
Seeing for Ourselves : 2156.
Seeing the Scar : 5752.
Seeing the thin-sliced moon : 2678.
Seeing Things : 742, 4377, 6891.
Seeing Your Face : 7044.
Seems Like an Ocean Between Us : 2004.
Seems to Me : 6300.
Seen from a Balcony on Carral Street : 7051.
Seesaw : 6842.
Segments of Spine : 4528.
Seguidillas de Santiago, Nacido en Denton :
    1558.
Seguidillas to Santiago, Born in Denton :
    874, 1558, 5010.
Seismic Events : 4827.
Seized with a disease : 390.
Selah : 6147.
Selected Orgasms : 150.
A Selection of Epigrams : 1016, 2001, 3261,
    4149.
The Self : 6044.
Self and Soul : 1514.
Self-Body-Portrait : 2799.
Self Defense : 4014.
Self-Fulfilling Prophecies : 3300.
Self Portrait : 4682.

Self-Portrait : 5135, 7222.
Self-Portrait as John Garfield : 5930.
Self-Portrait as Winter : 692.
Self-Portrait at the Embrace : 1864.
Self-Portrait : Camille Pissarro : 5127.
Self-Portrait, Collage : 2829.
Self-Portrait: October, 1991 : 6566.
Self-Portrait with Disasters : 5914.
Self-Portrait with Dying Empire : 4516.
Self Portrait with Max Beckmann : 7267.
Self Reflections: The Eve of City Clean-Up :
    3002.
Self Reliance : 2448.
Self There Then : 2562.
Selling the Farm : 3577.
Selma : 240.
Selvage : 6228.
A Semblance of Place : 5260.
Seminal Statement : 7212.
The Senate Confirms Janet Reno, 98-0 :
    6690.
Send in the Clowns : 1366.
Sending Anna Home : 5208.
Seneca Country : 2812.
Senior Question : 1818.
Senior Speicals : 689.
Senior Tax Accountant at Star Field, Inc :
    535.
The Sense of an Ending : 1481.
Sensibility Shaped by Blood : 4153.
Sentence : 7273.
Sentences : 5968.
Sententious Blather in the Boneyard : 6172.
The Sentinel : 6154.
Separate But United : 5480.
Separate Piles : 5181.
Separation : 3866.
The Separation : 646, 2076.
Separations : 4526.
Sepia : 2437.
Sept 26 91   1 6 9 7 .x x x x : 1777.
September : 1274, 2133, 2224, 3887, 6239.
September 21, 1993 : 1845.
September 30, 10:00 p.m : 4877.
(September '92) : 5011.
September, 1972 : 498, 4920, 4920.
September: An Act of Renunciation : 2418.
September Evening : 3730.
September for Joe : 7253.
September Memory: My Father When He
    Stood : 5082.
September Night : 1270, 2095, 6127, 6747.
September Song : 4452.
Septic : 153.
Septicus Interruptus : 5159.
Sequeiros : 4795.
Sequel : 1283, 6735.
The Sequel to Moby Dick : 1415.
A Serene Heart at the Movies : 4199.
Serenity of Bone : 5558.
Serial : 5395.
A Series of Failures So That I'm Sick of the
    Word : 4660.
The Serious Blues : 5170.
A Serious Feminist : 4796.
A Serious Smoker : 6842.

Sermon for the Comfort of the Masses : 392.
The Sermon of St. Franics : 1412.
Sermon to the Birds : 264.
The Serpent : 1996.
The Serpentine Is a Lovely Lake and There Is
    a Drowned Forest at the Bottom of It :
    625.
The Servant's Happiness : 6779.
The Service Charge : 4472.
Service for the Dead : 1054, 3514.
Serving Time in Wichita : 1251.
Sestina : 1354, 2810.
Sestina in Photographs : 6519.
Sestina: My Women : 7162.
Set Apart from the World : 4587.
Set Theory : 2789.
Séta : 4921.
Setting the Stage : 5305.
Seven A.M. on the East Hill : 4078.
Seven Crows : 4525.
Seven Days : 1514.
Seven Days in October : 5629.
Seven from England : 4018.
Seven from Nine : 3728.
Seven Gnomonic Measurements : 3246.
Seven Horses : 1058.
Seven Lean Cows : 586, 5386, 6235.
Seven Love Songs Which Include the
    Collected History of the United States of
    America : 80.
The Seven Sourpusses of Okolona, Illinois :
    3114.
Seventh Heaven : 2435.
Seventh Heaven Can Be Seen at First Glance
    : 442, 3280, 5804.
Severance & Cages : 6368.
Severed Moon : 648.
Séverine Between Marriages : 7097.
Severn Sketches Keats and Writes to Brown :
    4187.
Sevilla Cathedral : 1734.
Sewers (Is This How Love Dies — ?) : 4942,
    6088.
Sewing Batman's Cape After the Funeral of a
    Friend's Son : 7349.
Sewing: Nineteenth-Century Sampler : 7096.
Sex : 6472.
Sex and Drugs in the Caribbean: Ferry to
    Port Royal (1992) : 2416.
Sex Appeal : 1723.
Sex Education : 6761.
Sex Fo' Sale : 6216.
Sex Manual : 1055.
Sex Trees : 4240.
Sexism : 3730.
Sexual Ode I : 5195, 5338.
Sganarelle, or The Imaginary Cuckold :
    4548, 7090.
The Shadblow Trees : 2935.
Shade : 5924.
Shadow : 1204, 4696, 4715.
A Shadow : 4894.
The Shadow : 2869, 6279.
Shadow Dancing : 4613.
A Shadow of a Great Rock in a Weary Land :
    2911.

Shadow of Ebony : 3488.
The Shadow of Hanged Man : 2464.
The Shadow of the Crow : 2215.
A Shadow Play, Romance : 5047.
Shadow Roses Shadow : 273, 5129.
The Shadow That Trails the Body : 5450.
Shadowboxing : 95.
Shadowing Mengele: Holocaust Poems :
    1378.
Shadows : 2607.
Shadows of April and Blue Hills : 5783.
Shake : 7081.
Shaker Chair : 2655.
Shakespeare & Co : 350.
Shaking It Out of the Orient : 186.
The Shale Disparities : 5443.
Shall I Compare Thee to a Summer's Day? :
    5964.
Shall Inherit : 1294.
Shaman : 1512.
A Shaman Purpose a Minute : 4832.
The Shaman Talks to the Documentary Crew
    : 182.
Shame : 1703, 4202, 7109.
Shame the Monsters : 3237.
Shameless Light : 3444.
Shampoo : 1635, 2332.
Shana Yardena : 5883.
The Shape of a Scream : 2303.
Shape of a Whisper : 3520.
Shape of Pear : 3298.
The Shape of Saying : 4910.
The Shape of the Goddess in Homestead Park
    : 2255.
The Shapes of Things : 2302.
Shards : 931.
Sharing the Onus : 3372.
The Shark : 4260.
Shark Bait : 1100.
Sharks' Teeth : 3333.
Sharktalk : 211.
Shatter Glass / Kristallnacht : 728.
A Shattered Glass : 2161.
Shaving : 484.
Shawnee National Forest : 520.
She and I : 878.
She Can Count on Two Hands the Times
    She's Gone to a Beauty Parlor Most
    Times Sorry She Did : 5374.
She Cunsults Her Maps : 1677.
She Cuts Stars : 7027.
She Goes for the Spin-Off : 838.
She Had a Lot of Tinsel But Her Stems :
    1324.
She Had Twins and Moved to Paris : 2616.
She Has Become an Older Woman : 670.
She Has Her Palm Read : 3401.
She (In the Cleared Field) : 1658.
She Is a Woman like Glass : 5752.
She Is Privileged : 3434.
She Likes the Pace of Insects : 871.
She Lived : 1149.
She Loves Old Men : 3677.
She made me sing : 2510.
She Marvels at His Face : 406.
She Must Be Giant : 136.

'She' only wanted to get up in female attire : 3218.

She Said Poems : 6022.

She Said, 'You Are Your Own Worst Enemy' : 3268.

She Senses the Presence of a Dead Suitor in Her Room : 2244.

She Titupped along the Quai Henri Quatre : 2625.

She Told Us to Bury Her : 4401.

She Turns the Ceramic Dogs in, toward the Living Room, Meaning: My Husband Is Here : 4715.

She Wants to Hear the Man I Love : 5763.

She-Wolf : 1395.

She Writes with Fire : 3654, 4060, 5901.

She Wrote : 5833.

Sheba : 2000.

Sheep Station : 3517.

Shekinah : 2695.

Shelling Jacobs Cattle Beans : 3576.

Shelling Peas : 5892.

Sheltered Garden : 2513.

Shelters : 6182.

The Shelving Unit : 5636.

Shem Grows Impatient Aboard the Ark : 3323.

Shepherding : 1666.

Sherlock Holmes in America : 3005.

Sherwood Anderson : 5783.

Sherwood Estates : 4041.

She's a *midnight lady* in a five o'clock town : 5230.

She's Done It This Time : 6083.

She's Gone : 6968.

The Shespak Letters : 6304.

A Shift in the Wind : 4228.

Shifting the Rod : 2095.

Shiksa : 6382.

Shine : 4634, 6507.

Shining Through : 3444.

Ship of State, High Tide : 2552.

Ships : 2978.

Shipshewana : 345.

Shipwrecked : 1472.

The Shipwrecks' Cabal : 1822, 4334.

Shit Happens : 2091.

Shiva : 6207.

Shiva for Kivi : 3278.

Shiva's Prowess : 6089.

Shmelke : 10.

The Shock of the New : 3883.

Shock Therapy : 3730.

Shod and clothed I am counting the minutes : 3547, 5638.

Shoe Shop, Urbino : 5030.

A Shoebox : 4501.

Shoeshine : 5859.

Shoot-out at Sun-down : 1962.

Shoot-Up : 367, 403.

Shooting Back : 1800.

Shooting for Line : 4828.

The Shooting Lesson : 6866.

Shooting the Rapids : 1471.

The Shopper : 2812.

Shopping for the Revolution : 7028.

Shopping for Towels : 3118.

Shopping Trip : 2371.

Shore : 1516.

The Shore : 4892.

Shorebirds in Seasonal Plumage Observed Through Binoculars : 1124.

Short Fat Flicks : 4317.

A Short History of Lloyd Bentsen's Dealing with Special Interests : 6690.

A Short History of the Sybarites : 5753.

A Short History of the Vietnam War Years : 90.

Short Journey: Four Months After Diagnosis : 4738.

A Short Poem : 4562.

Short Walk : 766.

Shortchanged : 6735.

Shorter : 7133.

Shorty Rogers at the Scattering of Stan Getz's Ashes : 6463.

Shot While Playing in the Street : 6353.

Should, Should Not : 4410.

Should You Die : 6645.

Should You See Me Naked : 5685.

The Shouters : 1275.

Shoveling Coal : 1043.

Shovelling Snow with My Sons : 3717.

Shower : 4198.

Shower in A Major : 3761.

Showing My Father Through Freedom : 3431.

The Showing of the Instruments : 2829.

Shrewd is the one who hears nothing : 3119, 5861.

The Shrike : 360.

Shrimp Boats, Biloxi : 4307.

Shrine : 673.

Shrinking As They Rise, The : 5555.

Shrinking the Pacific : 3065.

Shucking : 2300.

Shunga : 2679.

Siamese Twins, Rio de Janeiro, 1907 : 702.

Siberia : 1069.

Sibling Rivalry : 3863.

Siblings : 2280.

The Sick Child: Homage to Edvard Munch : 2043.

Sick Farm : 2520.

The Sick King : 686.

The Sick Man's House : 1102.

Sick Room : 6796.

The Sickening Smile of Jesus : 6451.

Sickness : 2898.

The Sickness of the Soul, V : 5673, 6871.

Side Streets : 5452.

Sidekick : 4249.

Sideshow : 5989.

The Siege of Derry : 1481.

The Siege of Leningrad : 1688.

The Sierras : 5624.

Siesta : 3073.

Sieves : 6881.

Sifting : 2213.

Sifting Through : 2325.

Sight : 493.

Sight Words : 856.

A Sighting on the River : 3389.
Sighting the Sandhill Crane : 3204.
Sightings of a UFO : 1180.
Sigmund Freud Writes a Postcard from
    Coney Island, 1909 : 5958.
Sign : 586, 5386, 6235, 7264.
The Sign : 4599.
Sign in the London Underground : 7041.
Sign Language : 80.
Signaling : 867.
Signals : 5602.
The Signals : 1104, 4178.
A Significant Poet : 149.
Signposts : 148.
Signs : 4616.
Signs of Life : 660.
Signs of Salvation : 4357.
Silence : 442, 452, 2236, 5405, 5804, 6791.
The Silence : 150.
Silence Deep as the Bone at the Bottom of
    the Skull : 3345.
Silence Equals Death : 1199.
Silence, Listening to Silence : 4377.
The Silence of Cochise : 2186.
Silent Film : 3506.
Silent Lareina : 320.
Silent Night : 1058.
Silent Playgrounds : 4856.
Silent Rust : 6489.
Silent Scream : 4756.
Silent Voices : 6144.
Silk : 3496, 4820.
The Silk in the Sow's Ear : 6474.
Silky : 742.
The Silky Islands : 6858.
Silky Sullivan : 4168.
Silver : 206, 949, 1949.
Silver Arrows : 6858.
The Silver Cuffs : 1187.
Silver Poplars : 723.
Silver Queen : 2295.
Silver Shrine : 1512.
The Silver Streak : 6891.
Similar But Different : 5072.
Simon Turetzky Who Died at Dachau : 7213.
A Simple Design : 5692.
Simple Future Tense : 7249, 7271.
A Simple Love Story : 7061.
A Simple Man : 7353.
Simple Sentence : 2256.
A Simple Truth : 1450, 4592.
Simple Verdad : 4592.
Simplification : 6481.
Sin : 2095, 4560, 6234, 6781, 7212.
Sin Energía : 2796.
Sin in the 50's : 1534.
Sin Soars : 324.
Sin Título: Estoy amenazado de muerte, cada
    día : 4841.
Sinbad : 5610.
Since I Was Thrown Inside : 2831.
Since I've Come Inland : 1734.
Since silence links precaution : 3119, 5861.
Since You Insisted on a Modern Love Poem :
    1063.
Sinfonia for Strings : 5066.

Sing Me a Song, sister : 3126.
The Singer of Tales : 4200.
Singing for a Little Change : 7237.
Singing Like Parrots : 1093.
Single Beds : 5064.
A Single Strand Holds Us All : 1648.
Sinister Company : 6076.
Sinister Earth : 2542.
Sinking : 2392.
Sinning : 3299.
The Sins of Charity : 6329.
The Sins of the Father, the Sins of the Sons,
    and the Sins of the Nephew : 36.
Sinsora : 3915.
Siren : 7034.
Sirrah : 2650.
Sister, Aunt, Mother of Poetry Comes for a
    Visit, Brings Stars : 6495.
Sister Betty Reads the Whole You : 2904.
Sister Jupiter's Rubber Soul : 2573.
Sister, Lend Me : 4807.
Sister Mary Agnes's Prayer : 3714.
Sister Mary Appassionata Explicates a
    Graffito for the Eighth Grade Boys :
    1122.
Sister Mary Appassionata on the Nature of
    the Hero : 1122.
Sister Mary Appassionata to the Editor of
    The Columbus Dispatch : 1122.
Sister Mary Lucinda : 1534.
Sister Montego : 6001.
Sister, Morning Is a Time for Miracles :
    3916.
Sister Sukie II : 3194.
Sister (Y)our Manchild at the Close of the
    Twentieth Century : 2641.
Sisters : 2095, 5967, 6127, 6747.
The Sisters : 4950.
Sisters Die by Drowning : 5269.
Sisters in Rain : 4468.
Sisyphus in the Wartime Housing Projects :
    1724.
Sisyphus Rolls His Ball Up Mobius Hill :
    6947.
Sisyphus's Sibling : 4725.
The Site : 5078.
Sitting in a Doghouse : 2895.
Sitting in the Drake : 2672.
Sitting on an Eastern Bluff along the
    Mississippi River : 5287.
Sitting on the Back Porch the Night Before
    Our First Family Reunion in 15 Years :
    7212.
Sitting on the Front Porch of Andalusia : 963.
Sitting Shivah : 1758.
Sitting Still at the End of the Year : 3022.
Sitting Up with Thomas (Aged 2) : 4612.
Sitting with Buddhist Monks, Hue 1967 :
    6988.
Six Burnt Croissants : 1578.
Six Chinese Painters : 5665.
Six False Starts. No Stops. Getting Homesick
    : 6978.
Six-four : 6854.
Six Movements for Portraits of Erzulie :
    4357.

The Six O'Clock News : 5364.
Six o'clock news peak : 3913.
Six of Diamonds : 3239.
Six Thin Ladders : 6733.
Six Things to Know If You Love a Convict : 5821.
Six Times Stronger Than Steel : 2233.
The Six Toms : 7199.
Sixteen : 1852.
Sixteen Haikrazies From Being in Love : 3876.
Sixty-Three : 639.
The Size of the Lesion : 6417.
The Size of Things : 3759.
Size Queen, a Love Poem for 2 Strippers : 2602.
Sizing Up a Marriage : 6242.
Skake Board Man : 5142.
The Skater : 2062.
Skating out of the House : 1338.
The Skeleton in the Closet : 5875.
Skeleton Tableau : 5813.
Skeletons : 7160.
Skepticism : 100, 1096, 6465.
Sketch : 2076, 2129, 6765, 7303.
The Sketch : 5624.
A Sketch from 1844 : 2130, 6674.
Sketch: Jacquie reading Blofeld's 'Wheel of Life' in Christmas light : 2254.
Sketches : 6630.
Ski Hill : 1343.
Skin : 2435, 2898, 4455.
Skin Diver : 2106, 4184.
Skin Divers : 4436.
Skin Is Wrapping for Bones : 100, 3495, 6465.
Skinhead Heaven : 1282.
Skink : 6020.
Skipper Saves Copper Cooper : 3727.
The Skiptracer : 5212.
Skull and Crossbones : 1399.
The Skull on Its Occiput : 6481.
Skull the Apostate (On Physics) : 6951.
Skunk Talk : 2169.
Sky : 123, 4085.
The Sky : 6299.
Sky Above, Water Below : 6474.
Sky of Thorns : 648.
The Sky Opens : 1953.
The Sky Over the Seno de Reloncavi : 1226.
The Skyblue Tarp : 5716.
Skylight : 1428.
Slam, Dunk, & Hook : 3499.
Slap the shore : 7077.
Slate Mine, Wales : 1786.
Slattees : 3499.
The Slaughter : 7290.
Slaughter of the Innocents : 3899.
Slaves : 7095.
Sleep : 643, 973, 2077, 4433, 5655.
Sleep as Travel : 4655.
Sleep My Love : 955, 4219, 5236.
Sleepers in Jaipur : 3381.
Sleeping Car : 1749.
The Sleeping Horsemen : 498, 4716.

A Sleeping Man Must Be Awakened to Be Killed : 443.
Sleeping on the River Styx : 1238.
Sleeping Out : 4481.
Sleeping Pill : 1828, 2463.
Sleeping Retrospect of Desire : 5821.
Sleeping Sickness : 7120.
Sleeping with Boa : 6493.
Sleeping with Dean, 2:54 a.m. : 3888.
Sleepless : 264.
Sleepless Nights : 6143.
Sleeplessness : 665, 2095, 3152, 6127, 6747.
Sleeps : 2750.
Sleepy : 3054.
The Slide in Kindergarten : 2957.
Slides : 3470, 6393.
Slides of the Jazz Age : 5838.
Sliding Home : 5429.
Slipper Sex : 1339.
Slipping Away : 1395.
The Sliver of My Imagination : 3601, 5254.
Slope Breast : 4193.
The slope of the church roof : 4063, 5804.
The Slopping Crew : 2365.
The Sloth : 4325.
The Slow Boat to China : 6479.
Slow Dance in Kitchen : 1145.
Slow down the stair-way : 671.
The Slow Hours : 4031.
Slow Learners : 170.
Slow News from Our Place : 6299.
Slow Starter : 838.
Slow Storm : 3332.
Slow Train North : 4903.
The Slowness of Oxen : 3198, 3869.
Slug Song : 7054.
Slumber Music : 4237.
The Slush Pile : 556.
Sly and the Family Stone under the Big Tit, Atlanta, 1973 : 3233.
Small Animals : 1343.
Small Dead Girl : 2727, 5261.
Small Hours : 3673.
Small Inns and Lodges : 376.
A Small Moment : 1743.
A Small Observation : 3148.
Small Planes Near Nome : 6866.
Small Poem About Peripheral Matters : 4070.
Small Talk : 7228.
Small Town : 3571.
Small Town Story : 678.
Small Visits : 7119.
Small Worries : 4820.
Smazyna : 6138.
The Smell of Hot Metal : 3628.
The Smell of the Sea : 3503.
Smiler : 6972.
Smoke : 2446, 5381.
Smoke Smiler : 5080.
Smoker : 1805.
Smokestacks, Chicago : 4307.
Smokey : 7268.
Smuggled Pencil Stubs : 3816.
Snail : 2529.
Snail of Sleep over a Killing Thing : 461, 976.

Snail River : 521.
Snail-Shell : 1409, 6875.
Snake : 227, 2525, 4417.
The Snake : 2817.
Snake Charmer : 1840.
Snake Dance : 3822.
Snake Date : 304.
The Snake in the Garden Considers Daphne : 6848.
Snake in the Parsonage : 3139.
Snake Pit : 226.
Snakes : 4509.
Snapping Beans with the Jehovah's Witness : 4131.
Snapshot: Express to Winnipeg : 2327.
The Snapshot Never Taken : 5265.
Snapshots : 2131.
Snapshots from the Border : 4676.
Sneaking into the Stephen Hawking Lecture Then Sneaking Back Out Again : 5726.
Sneaking Out : 1541.
Snipers : 5214.
Snips & Spins : 1761.
Snow : 498, 2324, 3092, 3119, 3516, 4633, 4921, 5345, 5861, 6414, 6960, 7027, 7073.
Snow Angel : 1965.
Snow As the Rain's Father : 3961.
Snow Day : 2047.
A Snow Day : 7008.
Snow Fence : 4234.
Snow Geese : 435.
Snow in Condoland : 6723.
Snow in June : 5836.
The snow is everywhere : 3119, 5861.
Snow Showers, a Prothalamion : 5050.
Snow Tires : 3490.
Snow Wine : 594, 6739.
Snowball : 5590.
Snowfall at Children's Mercy Hospital : 5910.
Snowfall (on not giving in to government concessions) : 1642, 7020.
Snowfield with Crows : 2590.
Snowflakes : 636, 5804.
Snowing : 783.
Snowman : 3287, 7003.
Snowshoe Thoughts : 4947.
Snowshoeing Back to Camp in Gloaming : 6927.
So : 1249.
So Granpa Wouldn't Know : 6554.
So Help Us : 6439.
So I'm Not Handy : 4796.
So I've Got the Class : 5095.
So Let's Get One Thing Straight, Sweetness : 210.
So Many Poets : 7175.
So Many Roads : 141.
So Many Selves : 7239.
So Many Things Still Aching to Be Described : 7215.
So Mr. Rogers Became : 4424.
So Much for Traveling : 2387, 3501.
So Much to Show, Tell : 2939.
So, So Long : 1157.

So That I Might Be Held : 2526.
So We Hear : 1414.
So What's the Worst That Could Happen? : 1575.
So You Won't Have to Ask Why I Don't Do Criminal Law Anymore : 7098.
Soap Opera : 1595.
Soap Opera Life: Its Relentlessness : 1204.
Soap Opera Wedding : 3618.
Sobre Adoquines : 203.
The Soccer Ball, or How to Succeed in Life : 2066, 5974.
Social Notes from All Over: Mt. Olympus : 4199.
Social Security : 3880.
Socket : 2841.
Socrates : 4814, 4912.
Socrates on the Battlefield : 2984, 3186.
The Soda Fountain : 6614.
Soft Money : 232.
Soft Shoulders : 5839.
Softly : 3117.
Softly, William, Softly : 958.
Soir Bleu : 4709.
Sojourner Truth 1797-1883, If the Truth Be Told : 3104.
Solar : 424.
The Solar System : 3343.
Solar Tide : 362, 3865, 7258.
Soldier : 4814, 6679.
Soldiers on East Park : 3031.
Soledades: Berkeley 1969 : 1278.
Solicitude : 7151.
Solitary : 971, 7230.
Solitary Cheating : 1804.
Solo : 466.
Solomón : 3914.
Solstice : 2864, 3197.
The Solstice Blues : 4634.
Solving for N : 4858.
Somber Cantata : 1337, 4929.
Sombra de la Familia : 629.
Sombras Imaginarias : 6751.
Some Amatory Epigrams from the Greek Anthology : 158, 185, 937, 3677, 4388, 5168, 5701, 6062.
Some Aspects of the Real Alcazar, Sevilla : 1734.
Some Bitterness Always : 4165.
Some Blood : 10.
Some Canvases That Will Retain Their Calm Even in the Catastrophe : 5214.
Some Coins : 6242.
Some Days : 5183.
Some Effects of the Weather : 6352.
Some Feelings : 458.
Some Friends : 678.
Some Hug : 3852.
Some Impulsive Ideas : 105.
Some Keep the Sabbath Going to Church : 1564.
Some Kisses for Bill : 4232.
Some Lilac from My Mother : 1308.
Some Moments on Earth : 7166.
Some Mornings : 2173.
Some Music, Then : 678.

Some Notes in the Margin : 2470.
Some Notes on the Violin : 6299.
Some of Them : 6280.
Some Orange Juice : 348.
Some People Know : 6299.
Some Places in America Are Anonymous : 7227.
Some Thing Seen in Some Other Space : 1248.
Some Things I Wanted to Say to You : 1719.
Some Things My Father Liked : 6218.
Some Trick of Light : 2308.
Some Ways Along : 3735.
Some Wonder Why I Need Fantasy Women, or : 1324.
Some Words on a Stranger : 5265.
Somebody Stole George Washington's False Teeth : 158.
Someday : 4189.
Someone : 3344, 4995.
Someone Else : 2978.
Someone from Around Here : 2800.
Someone Speaks : 2226.
Someone Though : 7175.
Something : 1220.
Something About Not Being Safe : 1930.
Something Almost Always Drops into Place : 839.
Something Borrowed, Something Blue : 5428.
Something Dark : 1302.
Something Faithful : 900.
Something Infinite : 5434.
Something Inside You : 3769.
Something Meaner : 4864.
Something Not There : 2700.
Something to Agree On : 1259.
Something to Do with Hunted Animals : 1776.
Something's Got to Give : 6691.
Sometimes : 2441, 4581, 5050.
Sometimes a Snake Is Just a Snake : 193.
Sometimes Hope : 3139, 3199.
Sometimes, I Think We Are All Sunblasted Birds : 4899.
Sometimes I'll be drinking by myself : 1195.
Sometimes Married Guys Get Phone Calls Like This at Night from Their Unmarried Friends : 3748.
Sometimes the Coat Closet : 5312.
Sometimes the Land Can Be Shaken from Its Thin-lipped Silence : 684.
Sometimes the Obvious Is a Blessing : 4165.
Somewhere in a House Where You Are Not : 4134.
Somewhere in America : 773.
Somewhere in Georgia : 3191.
Somewhere It Still Moves : 1606.
Somewhere on the Edge of a Field and the Woods : 6233.
Somewhere within Reach, for Sarah : 4508.
Somnambulist Poet : 4795.
The Somnambulists' Hotel : 131.
The Son of Man Plays Airplane : 6754.
The Son of the Muse Plays a Maccaferri : 6217.

Sonata : 6821.
Un Soneto a lo Inalcanzable : 576.
Soneto ao Inverno : 4585.
Soneto de Londres : 4585.
Sonetto Prolungato: Quando la Gente Tornava da Milano : 64.
Song : 767, 1224, 1878, 3348, 4451, 4495, 5352, 7321.
Song Accompanied by Tuneless Whistling : 2777.
Song Against Time : 4113.
A Song Among Beds : 4634.
Song As Song : 6890.
Song Before Birth : 4873.
The Song Dropped from Opus 15 : 6436.
Song for a Small Boat Leaving Biloxi on a Night in June, 1979 : 5412.
Song for Basho : 2193.
Song for Syrinx and Pennywhistle : 1968.
A Song for the Daughter I Do Not Have : 5834.
Song for the Lizard Painted on the Plate : 2362.
Song for the Scarlet Tanager : 5784.
A Song from Yeats Country in Praise of the Great Queen : 5279.
Song of a Survivor : 862.
Song of Dying : 4013.
Song of Joy : 55.
Song of Mary, Leaking : 626.
Song of Occult Solar Riddles : 79.
Song of Rabelais : 4086.
The Song of Regrets : 4797.
A Song of Simple Love : 371, 6768.
Song of Songs : 534, 590, 591.
Song of the Andoumboulou, 17 : 4007.
The Song of the Artichoke Lover : 5417.
Song of the belt : 1592.
A Song of the Colony : 6379.
Song of the Gourd : 7220.
Song of the Just : 6700.
Song of the Outsized Asteroid : 4105.
Song of the Palace of Ch'en : 3568, 5913.
Song of the Pied Parrot : 3170.
Song of the Righteous Man : 3568, 5913.
Song of the Wasteland : 3568, 5913.
Song to a Porcupine in Mating Season : 2339.
Song While Bathing by the Open Window in the Country : 6147.
Songs for A. : 7127.
Songs from the Riverbank : 2544, 3414.
Songs of Fire : 223, 7322.
The Songs of Miriam : 4950.
Sonic Relations : 7220.
Sonnet : 5926.
Sonnet III : 346.
Sonnet 52: In every beauty lies some hidden sorrow : 462, 4208.
Sonnet About Those Who Strangled Her : 5638, 6116.
Sonnet for Constituents Not Permitted : 6352.
Sonnet for David (Horny Neighbor) : 3229.
Sonnet for Jorge Soto, Painter, b. 1947, New York, d. 1987, Vermont : 39.
Sonnet for Miss Beausoleil : 39.
A Sonnet for Philip Glass : 3262.

Sonnet for Raymond Castro : 39.
Sonnet Framing the Thoughts of a Forefather
    Before the Pequot Battle : 6885.
Sonnet from London : 1643, 4585, 5307.
Sonnet: Now the god of rainy August hangs
    his mask : 7165.
Sonnet of the Beginning and the End : 2507,
    5790.
Sonnet on a July Night in the Highlands :
    5638, 6116.
Sonnet Right Off the Bat : 4801, 6797.
Sonnet: Thanksgiving Day in England : 5257.
Sonnet: The National Game : 5517.
Sonnet: This morning I wished (once) to be a
    quiet : 73.
Sonnet to Sustenance, or, How Do I Love
    Thee, Food : 4480.
Sonnet to Winter : 1643, 4585, 5307.
Sonnet: Tompkins Square Park, October
    18th, 1989, 5:45 pm : 39.
The Sonneteer : 1204.
Sonoluminescence : 5988.
Sonoran Variegation : 4748.
Sons : 2446.
Sons of God, Daughters of Men : 841.
Soon the Sea : 3640.
Soot : 5196.
Soothe Me : 1743.
Sophia and True : 432, 774.
Sophia Tolstoy at Yasnaya Polyana : 7206.
Sophistry : 1217.
Sorrel and Tamarind Teas : 7174.
Sorrow of Matter : 2848.
The Sorrow of the World : 1294.
The Sorrow of Wood : 4112.
A Sort of City Sonnet : 4975.
A Sort of Proof : 3957.
Sortes Vergilianae : 2864.
Sorting Papers Before Leaving : 505.
Sorting Snapshots : 339.
Sorting Through Documents : 3729.
Sosnowiec Is Like a Woman : 325, 2946,
    2946.
La Souffrance : 237.
Soul : 3783, 5967.
The Soul : 442, 2164, 5804.
The Soul in Its Predicament : 1873.
Soul in Paraphrase : 2658.
The Soul Is Not Colorless : 2156.
Sound : 143, 3786.
A Sound : 3965.
Sound All Around : 5800.
Sound Bites: Early Autumn : 4129.
Sound Bites: Jets : 6355.
Sound Bites: Taste of Morning Breakfast :
    6925.
Sound Burier : 4687.
Sound Garden : 6458.
Sound Going Out : 393.
A Sound in the Night : 3510.
The Sound of Gabriel's Wings : 316.
The Sound of Grief : 294, 3685, 5962.
The Sound of Kennels : 4248.
The Sound of Leaves : 1596, 3037.
The Sound of My Father : 3489.
Sound of My Voice : 1318.

Sound/ (system) : 5381.
Sounding : 6856.
Sounding Fields : 5428.
Soundings : 3689.
Soundings: Doppler's Doppleganger : 7296.
Sounds of the Sun : 382.
Sour Acres : 4601.
Source : 993.
South : 6515.
South and North : 6218.
South Boulevard : 628.
South Central Olympics : 721.
South of Boston : 4472.
South Shore Summer : 4641.
The South Sussex Downs : 3718.
The Southern Collection : 4472.
Southlanders : 6675.
Souvenir : 78, 5349.
Soviet Joke : 4333.
Sower : 436, 1076, 1968.
Soy Jorge : 5460.
Soy una Criatura Marina : 2621.
Space : 645.
The space of my sleep : 610, 4450.
Space of No Moment : 152.
A Space Telescope : 1989.
Spaces : 1015, 2331, 3269.
Spaces in the Light Said to Be Where One/
    Comes From : 5381.
Spaces to Fill : 5098.
Spaghetti : 5522.
Spain : 653.
Spanish Guitar : 6299.
Spanish Moss : 4384.
Spanner/Wrench : 3087.
Spans : 192.
Spared : 1520.
Spark : 611.
The Spark : 2848.
Spas : 2387, 2524.
Spätlese : 2258.
Speak Softly : 862, 4057, 4517.
Speaking : 1456.
Speaking in Tongues : 6299, 7156.
Speaking into the Candles : 4311.
Speaking Mexican : 860.
Speaking of Eyes : 2051, 5625.
Speaking to Ockanickon: Talking Across
    Time : 3862.
Special Effects : 678.
Spectator Sport : 1760, 6172.
Speech : 7111.
Speech after a Spectacle : 7033.
Speed : 749.
The Speed of Light : 7232.
The Speed of the Drift : 6193.
Speed Reading : 6288.
Speer at Spandau, Remembering : 6957.
Spell : 5442.
Spell-Check : 4504.
The Spellers : 848.
Spelt from Sibyl's Leaves : 2942.
Spelunking at Brown's Cave : 291.
Spendere il Cielo : 6754.
Spending Heaven : 6754.
Sperm : 3855.

Sperm Bank: A Post-Modern Love Story : 6761.
Sphericity : 517.
Spice Island : 7041.
Spider : 3805, 6905.
The Spider : 6848.
Spider and Squirrel Nightfall Construction : 2460.
Spider Man : 5202.
Spider Naevus : 7078.
The spider on this curb : 5113.
Spider-Woman : 4053.
Spiders : 3724, 4900.
The Spiders : 4889, 6809.
The Spider's Art : 3440.
The Spider's Net : 4472.
A spike in the head during the holidays : 5638, 5917.
Spike Logic : 4345.
Spin : 530.
A Spin Around the Countryside : 2331.
Spingarn : 7175.
Spinner Sponn : 3051.
Spinners : 2110.
Spinning Jenny : 4240.
The Spiral : 2314.
Spirea : 985.
Spirit Lake and Shang-lin Park : 6429.
The Spirit of Old Matresses in Junk Heaps : 6430.
Spirit Wall : 3456.
The Spirit Yard : 3895.
Spirulae: Crossroads : 1180.
Spit : 3899.
Spleen : 2953.
Splendor Veritatis : 2824, 3715, 4932.
Splinter : 2566.
Splinters on my tongue : 4386.
Split : 7007.
Split Infinites : 6871.
Split Tractate : 2848.
Splitting Wood on My 48th Brithday : 802.
Spoiled Poem : 3392, 5508.
Sponges : 675.
The Spool : 1749.
Spoon : 2832, 4950.
A Spoon in Words, or, How Many Fathoms Deep : 1050.
A Spoon of Water : 3074.
Spoonbridge and Cherry : 749.
Spoonfed Step by Step — All Those Years : 5113.
Spore : 7230.
A Sport of Nature : 2501.
The Sports Complex : 2347.
Spotting the Goddess : 5663.
Sprigs of grass greening : 6977.
Spring : 2095, 3265, 3591, 4509, 6127, 6747.
Spring Cleaning : 5621.
Spring Comes to East Lansing : 5323.
Spring Equinox : 4214.
Spring Forward, Fall Back : 6544.
Spring Glen : 2552.
The Spring House : 6228.
Spring in the South : 6702, 7282.
Spring Light : 653.

Spring Planting : 4806.
Spring Rain : 6182.
Spring Snow : 2935.
Spring Song : 5792.
Spring Songs : 4239, 6201.
Springhill Pen, NS : 5300.
Springtime : 2077, 5789.
Springtime for Some: Expounding on a Theme of Ezra : 7092.
Spruce Hen : 3195.
Sprung : 1807.
Sputnik Measures : 6587.
Spy : 6046.
Square I : 2371.
Squaw Peak in Sepia : 4682.
Squeaky Bed : 1528.
Squeeze Play : 1749.
Squid : 2262, 3727.
Squirrels : 2498.
St. . . . See also Saint . . .
St Boniface : 5614.
St. Croix 11 : 6384.
St. Francis and the Hawk : 6885.
St. Frideswide's Chapel, Christ Church, Oxford : 5986.
St. John's Christmas 1992: Harvey Road Fire : 3731.
The St. Kitts Monkey Feuds : 3816.
St. Lawrence Winter : 4524.
St. Luke's Hospital, Duluth : 4981.
St. One : 422.
St. Patrick's Day at the Oxford Bar : 2364.
St. Paul de Vence : 1735.
St. Peter Healing the Sick with His Shadow : 6611.
St. Peter's Harbour, PEI : 5300.
St. Thomas in Heaven : 1847.
St.-Trophime 1956-Rosedale 1958 : 4870.
Stage-Fright : 1667, 2007, 6514.
The Staged Confession : 1852.
Stained Glass : 3139.
Stained Glass at Père-Lachaise : 3096.
Stair Case : 929.
Staircase : 2697, 3176, 6907.
The Stake Stabbing the Tongue Has Sprouted Leaves : 1143, 4837, 4949.
Staking Tomatoes, I Think of Angels : 678.
Stalin : 848.
Stalking : 1827.
Stamina : 2553.
The Stammer : 4820.
The Stamped : 3875.
Stamped Objects : 1949.
Standards : 6665.
Standing at an Open Window : 6278.
Standing in the World's Most Renowned Concert Hall : 4463.
Standing Room : 6720.
Standing Watch : 4755.
Standing Wave Standing Sill : 550.
Standoff : 4196, 6432.
Stanley Spencer Arriving in Heaven : 2478.
Stanley Spencer's Beatitude : 5.
Stanzas on the Snowfall : 2471.
Stanzas Written at Baba Yaga's : 3974.
Star Dust : 4132.

Star-flower : 6632.
Star of Bethlehem : 5435.
Star on High : 862, 4119, 6730.
Star Sapphires : 5125.
Star Vehicles : 3491.
Starch Bosom : 4739.
Starchild : 1800.
Starez Silouan : 6610.
Starlight Mints : 4107.
Starlight Scope Myopia : 3499.
A Starling : 3287, 7003.
Starlings : 738, 6720.
Stars : 1453, 4155.
The Stars : 3592.
Stars Falling : 5023.
The Stars in November : 1182.
Starting a Star : 5166.
Starting Over : 4494.
Starting Somewhere : 6366.
Starting Up : 5097, 5114, 7312.
Starts Out a Mouse : 170.
Starwork : 211.
The State : 5775.
State Fair : 4299.
State of Grace : 2642.
The State of Wyoming : 665.
State Street : 3930.
[Statement] : 6493.
States : 192.
The Stationary Writer : 5816.
Stationed in Somalia : 3166.
Stations of the Cross : 1669.
A Statistician to His Love : 2349.
Statues : 498, 3782, 4716.
Stay Awake : 2302.
Stay With Me, Make Me Still : 3871.
Staying Afloat : 757.
Staying Out Late : 5437.
Steak : 6199.
Stealing : 2202.
Stealing Blackberries : 1152.
Stealing Coal : 3022.
Stealing Thundaah: Out Dare and Around :
  2695.
Steam : 855.
Stearn Wharf : 7316.
Steel City Blues : 4472.
Stele for Catullus : 2095, 3557.
Stele fúr Catull : 3557.
Stenographer : 3091.
Stephanie Gorski Weeps When Her Car Is
  Towed : 1802.
Stephanie's Bees : 2671.
Stephen Hawking, Walking : 2331.
Stepped Leader : 388.
Stepping into the Night : 6335.
Steps : 983, 3108.
Steps into Spring : 6557.
Steps Were : 2868, 4546.
Stereognosis : 5623.
Stereotypes : 1617.
The Stereotypical Bear : 5116.
The Stewardess : 3541.
Stick-Figures : 1411.
Stick People : 1002.
Stickball : 341.

Stigmata Me, Baby : 3129.
Still : 5056.
Still Awake : 7243.
Still Born : 1061.
Still Life : 442, 2355, 3197, 5710, 5804,
  5823, 6111, 7044.
Still Life: Shipyard, September, 1950 : 1352.
Still Life with Dogma : 6423.
Still Life with Drive-In : 7106.
Still Life with Elements : 3341.
Still-Life, with Huidobro : 1837.
Still Life with Muscovy Ducks : 4677.
Still Life With Pear : 5664.
Still Life with Statement : 1760.
Still Trying : 1544, 5682.
Stimulating Yr Gone Relationship : 3273.
Stingers : 4621.
Stirrings : 742.
Stitched Up Madonna : 3822.
Sto Lat : 6138.
Stockholm Syndrome : 863.
Stocktaking : 6387.
Stolen : 1888.
Stolen Kisses : 5823.
A Stolen Moment : 7080.
The Stone : 1332, 4359, 4417.
Stone Crab Claws : 6887.
Stone Creek : 973.
Stone in the Shallows : 4377.
Stone Love : 6902.
Stone Mountain Man : 6386.
The Stone of Heaven : 2869.
The Stone Sleeper : 1601, 3224.
Stone Soup : 855.
A Stone Souvenir : 6527.
Stone Throwing : 3377.
Stonehenge : 4066.
Stones and Soil : 3114.
Stones: Holy Land 1988 : 4196.
The Stones of Callanish : 2156.
Stoning the Birds : 6943.
Stool Aid's Song : 3816.
Stop Me Before I Hurt Again : 1234.
Stopgap Arrangement : 498, 3516, 5149.
Stopped at Tahoe for inspection : 3624.
Store Boy : 860.
Stories a Man Keeps to Himself : 3625.
Stories on the Mountain : 2791.
Stories Told about the Natural World : 3901.
Storm : 7241.
The Storm : 2578, 3091, 4910.
The Storm and the Jar : 6135.
Storm at Night : 5752.
Storm at Point Sur : 1596.
Storm Cellar : 7152.
Storm Front: February 1991 : 6487.
Storm Lantern : 2921.
Storm on Fishing Bay : 1683.
Storm Sketch : 4343.
Storms : 6629.
Storm's Opal : 5649.
Story : 5426, 6741.
A Story : 192.
The Story : 4191.
The Story Aunt Beth Told : 106.
Story Between Two Notes : 4311.

Story from the Mountains of North Carolina : 4239, 6201.
A Story I Have to Tell You : 6299.
Story in the Style of Henry James : 6575.
Story Lines : 1312.
The Story of Bones : 908.
A Story of Hair : 702.
The Story of the Day : 2433.
The Story of the Past : 742.
The Story of Two People Picking Zucchini : 375.
Story Time : 766.
A Story Worth Repeating : 2905.
'Storya : 5475.
Storyline : 509.
Storyteller : 3429.
A Stout One : 7278.
Stoves : 4759.
The Strads : 6121.
Strand : 5933.
Strange : 4982.
The Strange Attractor : 4601.
Strange Attractors and the Failure of Simple and Complex Systems : 3177.
Strange Food : 5347.
Strange Hope : 1523.
Strange Magus : 6049.
Strange Newes from the New-found Lande : 2662.
Strange Things Happen at Night : 214.
Stranger : 3518.
A Stranger in Town : 3975.
Strangers : 780.
Strangers: An Essay : 1793.
Strangers Meeting the Course in Painted Voice : 3679.
The Stratospheric Canticles : 79.
Strawberries of Wrath : 5272.
Stray Plenum : 4946.
Strayhorn : 1196.
A Streak of Blood That Once Was a Tiny Red Spider : 3961.
Street : 4818, 4918, 6076, 6548.
Street Cleaning in November : 1080.
Street Cornor Man : 2054.
Street Gangs : 5788.
Street Girl : 6915.
Street-Lights, Leaves : 6335.
The Street of Chinese Restaurants : 1930.
The Street Plan : 6614.
Street Scenes : 2518.
Streetcorner Church II: For James Baldwin : 6414.
Stress : 893.
A Stricter Means : 2892.
The Strike Out King : 1094.
Strike Rally : 2184.
Strikebreaker : 2763.
String : 5105.
String Two : 3521.
String Up Your Idiot Kings : 231.
Strings : 2426.
Stripped Car : 6723.
Stripped Tales : 2487.
Stripper : 7147.
The Stripper : 4699.

Striptease : 5097, 5114, 7312.
Stroke : 3418.
The Stroke : 3843.
A Stroll : 3392, 3516, 4921.
The Stroller : 3381.
Strolling Down St. Dominic Hill : 6174.
Strong Anthropic Principle : 6120.
The Strong Swimmer : 352.
Strophe : 3779.
Structural Adjustment: An Introduction : 1343.
Structures : 4660.
The Struggle to Accept : 942.
Stubborn : 1087, 1731, 6235.
Stubs : 5103.
Stuck : 84, 977, 7240.
Students : 510.
Students in Line : 5363.
Studies for an Actress : 2192.
Study : 1142, 5015.
Study in Gray : 5270.
Study in Green : 5270.
Study in Orange : 5270.
Studying : 1774.
Studying Your Hands : 6882.
Stunned in the Garden of Luxembourg : 2625.
Style : 6477.
Su Color Preferido : 600.
The Subject : 2333.
A Subject of My Affections, Plus Muse and Person Loved : 6520.
Subjectivity : 2398.
Subjunctive : 812, 6087.
Submitted : 3981.
Subsequent Meeting : 5629.
Subsistence : 5043.
Substrata Errata : 3753.
Subtitles : 6996.
Subtropical Fruit : 305.
A Suburban Hotel : 3744, 6546.
Suburban Sheik : 929.
Suburbanites : 6985.
Suburbia : 1113.
Subversion : 3317.
Subway Goddess : 5733.
Subway Poem : 5670, 5895.
Subway / Underground : 2181.
Success : 1982.
'Success' and Requests : 1544, 5682.
Successful Effort : 498, 3060, 3516.
Such a State : 2446.
Sudden from Heaven : 4906.
Sudden Light : 1283.
Sudden Mendenhall Glacier : 6858.
Suddenly Everyone Beheld an Empty Sky : 1143, 4837, 4949.
Sueño de Miel : 4584.
El Sueño Que Parece Mío : 5024.
Sueños : 2337.
Suffenus : 1016, 2001.
Sufferin' from Succotash : 4325.
Sugar : 1095, 3494, 3720.
Sugar for Diabetics : 3551.
Sugar Skulls, Oaxaca : 4307.
Sui Generis : 6360.

The Suicide Kid : 838.
A Suicide Note : 7190.
Suicide on Christmas Eve : 2349.
The Suicides : 6752.
The Suicide's Picnic : 1592.
Suite : 5690.
Suite for Emily : 3020.
Suite for Kokodicholai, Sri Lanka : 3566.
A Suite of Objects : 4751.
Sullen B. : 710.
Summer : 646, 1550, 2076, 3952, 3957, 5760.
The Summer : 848.
Summer '90 : 2098.
Summer, 1987 : 2044.
Summer, & Her Painted Flowers : 2309.
Summer, and the House Finally Crumbles : 4279.
Summer As a Large, Reclining Nude : 334.
Summer at War : 7353.
The Summer Before the War : 4282.
The Summer before the War : 4282.
Summer Celestial : 1458.
Summer Cousin : 4175.
A Summer Day : 4244.
Summer Ends Tonight : 4509.
Summer evening rain : 1042.
Summer Ice : 7351.
Summer in New York : 209.
Summer in the Crumbling State : 6152.
Summer Jobs : 5588.
Summer Lilies : 6045.
Summer Marriage : 6242.
A Summer Night with Thunder : 3671.
Summer Nights in Chicago : 3882.
The Summer Nuthatch : 6858.
Summer of '82 : 3652.
Summer on Rewind : 804.
A Summer Place : 4428.
Summer Pneumonia : 899.
Summer: Silver Flashing : 3974.
Summer Solstice : 6628.
Summer Songs : 4239, 6201.
Summer Storm : 870, 3039.
The Summer Storm : 3858.
Summer Swelled, Whirred : 2755.
A Summer Swim : 7358.
The Summer the Crows Cried My Name : 1637.
The Summer Triangle : 1135.
Summer Tripe Dream and Concrete Leaves : 7295.
Summer View with Metronome : 630.
A Summer Visit : 7175.
Summer Work, 1968 : 6457.
Summer's Breath : 6890.
Summer's End : 2890.
A Summer's Night : 636, 5804.
Summersounds : 1556.
Summertime : 5978, 6300.
Summing Up : 2142, 6728.
Summoning : 6733.
Summoning a Boat : 4884.
A Summons : 1225.
Sun : 3845, 3853, 4460.
The Sun : 1501.

The Sun Drench : 3704.
Sun on the Bottom : 5520.
Sun-Room Scenario : 7125.
The Sun Workers : 3500.
Sunbathing : 2989.
Sunday : 1963, 4740, 5162, 6012, 6880.
Sunday After Thanksgiving : 4336.
Sunday Afternoon : 4328.
Sunday Afternoon at Aunt Maud's : 1325.
Sunday Afternoon Palindrome : 2433.
Sunday at the Ruins : 2437.
Sunday Before Thanksgiving : 5620.
Sunday Bells : 5430.
Sunday Best : 5247.
Sunday Drive : 3197, 3551.
Sunday Drivers : 6975.
Sunday Evening : 5787.
Sunday in a Small American Town : 498, 3516, 4921.
Sunday in Babylon : 1794.
Sunday in San Miguel : 4889.
Sunday in the Park : 4810.
Sunday Jazz : 1673.
Sunday Morning in Foster City : 4956.
Sunday Night : 545, 918.
Sunday Night at the Gyldenlove Hotel, Oslo : 3725.
Sunday Nights in the Fifties : 6319.
Sunday Outing : 5580.
Sunday Picnic : 3630.
Sunday Radio : 3683.
Sunday, Real : 1777.
Sunday Ride to Brooklyn : 5931.
Sunday School and the Promised Land : 1510.
Sunday, Thinking of What's Been Lost : 6049.
Sundays : 4467.
Sundays, Too : 80.
Sundays Were Religious Days : 7115.
Sundown : 2451.
Sunflowers : 7121.
Sunflowers Hidden Away : 6357.
Sunlight Through the Window : 6460.
Sunrise : 2479, 7070.
Sunrise Highway : 231.
Sunrise on Tisang River : 5628.
The Sun's rays come in lance over lance : 3218.
Sunscreen : 5976.
Sunset : 6517.
Sunset District: Diminished Seventh : 2433.
Sunworshippers : 6226.
Supermen : 1078.
Superstar : 858.
Superstring Theory : 4096.
Supply & Demand : 80.
Suppose Heaven : 4858.
Suppose It Were Petrarch : 5091.
Supposing That Truth Is a Woman — What Then? : 1840.
Suppressed Misfortunes : 7013.
The Supreme Moment : 6076.
The Supreme Theme : 4950.
Surcease : 7360.
Surface : 3054.

Surfer's Thighs : 1845.
Surfing as Meditation : 372.
Surgery : 296.
Surprise : 6842.
Surrealism : 979.
Surrealism: Essay and Rhapsody : 1645.
The Surrealist Learns to Fly : 4879.
Surrender : 530, 3688, 5956.
Surround : 1109.
Surveyors : 3510.
Survival : 1301, 3968.
Survival, It's a Gift : 6124.
Surviving : 6684.
Survivor : 2219, 4878, 6191.
Survivors : 378, 803, 1082, 3581, 3866.
Suspect Retrievals : 272.
Suspended : 3772.
Suspended Sentence : 1607.
Susquehanna : 4017.
Swallowing : 5985.
Swallows : 3809, 4434, 4945.
Swallowtail Light, Grand Manan Island :
    5289.
Swamp : 7195.
Swamp Light : 5506.
Swamp Roots : 3969.
The Swamp Song : 6209.
Swan : 1586, 3795.
The Swan : 403, 2521.
Swan Song (Poem for Nijinsky) : 6504.
The Swansong of J. Richard Bachman : 7073.
The Swarming Bees : 3677.
Sway : 1993.
The Swaying Lotus : 1537, 1538, 5399, 7221.
Swaying Slightly in Geoff's Hammock :
    3958.
Sweat : 4276.
A sweatband finds the fieldhand's thirst :
    6294.
The Sweater : 2526.
Sweet Afton : 3985.
Sweet Apples : 5075, 6411, 7363.
Sweet Autumn : 1946, 4574.
Sweet Briar : 852.
Sweet Citrus : 3122.
Sweet Hitchhiker : 3197.
Sweet Land of (Fabric) Woven : 3941.
Sweet Razor, My Editor : 1147.
Sweet Sleeper : 3136, 4925.
Sweet Soul Music : 3247.
Sweet-Talk : 172.
Sweet Town : 2339.
A Sweetening All Around Me As It Falls :
    2869.
Sweetie : 3421.
The Sweetness of Apples, of Figs : 2869.
The Sweetness of Frenzy : 870.
Sweets for the Dead : 5038.
Swelter : 6084.
Swept : 979.
The Swiftness of the Clouds : 636, 5804.
The Swimmer : 2455.
Swimmers : 2383, 5264.
Swimming at Night : 6784.
Swimming Pools from the Air : 3532.
Swindle : 1514.

Swine Dysentery : 2888.
Swing : 1287.
The Swing : 6990.
Swing Shift : 4001.
Swinging into Space : 1510.
Sycamore : 3442.
Sycamore Bay : 4110.
Sycamore Bridge : 2074.
Syeeda's Song Flute : 958.
A Syllabus of Errors : 3436.
Syllogism : 4165.
The Sylphe : 4894.
Sylvia : 4442.
Symbiotic : 4386.
Symbol of Sound : 463.
Symbolic Logic : 625.
Symmetrical : 530.
Sympathy : 6299.
Sympathy for the Devil : 83.
Symptoms of Drought : 1736.
Synecdoche : 5141.
Synonyms : 2002.
The System of Mellon's Hell : 4054.
T : 5381.
—T : 5381.
T-Square : 840.
T.V. : 1089.
T.V., Ghosts, and Poets Past : 1417.
Tabasco on the Table : 4115.
Tables : 4877.
Tabletop : 5857.
Tábonok : 4921.
The Taboo : 3219.
The Tacit : 3682.
Tadamori and the Oil Thief : 2262.
Tahiti Trot : 214.
Tai Chi : 3929, 5633.
Tailgating America Astride the Holy Cow :
    1045.
Tails You Lose : 5144.
Taino : 4642.
Taipei Tangle : 2562.
Tajo, tajo, tajo! tajo, my mackey massa! :
    161.
Take a Girl Flaubert Doesn't Know : 5010.
Take a Whiff It's Home : 3703.
Take, for Example / the Pristine Air : 2614.
Take me down to the MEXICAN moon :
    4595.
Take My Wings : 6247.
Take this smudged snapshot for a sign : 52,
    3302.
Take your losses and move on : 5230.
Takeoff : 6332.
Taking a Chance on Love : 1366.
Taking a Language : 347.
Taking Easter Morning Back : 3423.
Taking Heart : 4118.
Taking in Your Bookstore : 6093.
Taking My Mother to the Bathroom : 3822.
Taking My Mother's Ring : 3822.
Taking the Bus along Khayaban-e-Iqbal :
    3574.
Taking the Sun in a Carpark Beside the East
    River : 6481.
Tale : 3187.

Tale from Balzac: Bette : 6578.
The Tale of Myrrha : 4961, 6135.
The Tale of the Angel's Return : 5638, 5757.
The Tale of the Fan : 2923.
Tale of Two Heroes : 6377.
Talismán : 63.
Talk : 392, 694, 4578.
Talk about the Money : 1196.
Talk Between Women Is Stitchery : 5544.
Talk Endless as a River : 6458.
The Talk of Sailing : 1357.
Talk Radio : 5937.
Talk to Me : 6914.
Talk Too Much : 2805.
The Talker : 2099.
The Talker the Same : 3298.
Talking : 1220.
Talking 3 A.M. : 2105.
Talking Back : 7217.
Talking Barbie : 3968.
Talking to Myself at the Once in a Blue
    Moon Café : 4165.
Talking to the Tortoise : 3008.
Talking to Wendy at My Mother's Funeral :
    3922.
Talking with God : 5555.
The Tall Women : 1350.
Talus Slope : 4534.
Tamboura : 318, 4035, 7221.
Tambourine : 1800.
Tango : 5286.
The Tango : 643, 4433.
Tango of the Dragonflies : 4181.
Tantalus in May : 6012.
Tantas veces sonar, ¡tantas veces! : 933.
Tantrum Girl Responds to Death : 1151.
The Tao of Junk Mail : 2046.
Taoist Song : 1084, 6872.
Tapdancing : 2985.
The Tape of Silence : 866.
Taps : 632.
La Tarde Encendida : 4166.
Tarde Oscura : 1028.
Target Quilt : 2462.
Targeted by What Attracts : 3407.
Tatiana, Older : 6135.
Tattoo : 2894.
The Tattoo : 6593.
Tattoo #47, 'Happy Dragon' : 97.
Tattooed : 2556, 4816.
The Tattooed Cities : 4624, 5104.
Tattooed City : 6076.
Tattooed Fish : 4739.
Tattooed Man : 1161.
The Tattooed Woman in Heaven's Flower
    Shop : 231.
Tattooing My Tit / and Other Things in
    Yuppiedom on Tuesday Morning :
    5189.
Tattoos : 244, 4509, 5737, 6855.
Taunted : 7166.
Taurus : 2584.
A Taxi to the Flame : 3295.
Taxidermy : 322.
Taxing : 4701.
Taxonomy : 2425.

Taylor Moore: Queer : 3468.
Taylor's Chapel : 1597.
Te Di el Nombre de Míriam : 3059.
Tea Leaves : 337.
The Tea Light of Late September : 2869.
The Tea Party : 2647.
Tea-stained Lust : 5799.
Teacher : 205, 7140.
The Teacher : 5049.
The Teacher in Her Dress of Woe : 232.
Teacher's Pet : 3450.
Teacher's Valediction : 851.
Teaching Composition : 2634.
Teaching Dreams : 4616.
Teaching Mary Ann Mah Jong : 2383.
Teaching My Son to Ride His Bike : 3214.
Teaching Three Essay Classes in a Row :
    1371.
Tear : 143, 3786.
A Tear in Directions : 5732.
Tearing Papers : 5841.
Teatro de Sinonimos : 1013.
Technical Love #47: Inspection : 5271.
Technicians in the Capitol : 1591.
Technological Night : 5846.
Technology and Medicine : 923.
Technology Transcendent : 4578.
Ted : 1038.
Tedium Drum : 4025.
Tee-Hees / The Call to the Ark : 2331.
The Teenager : 1602.
Teeth of Garlic : 1229.
Teh Care and Treatment of Pain : 491.
Tel Aviv, 1993 : 398.
A Telegram from the Muse : 4199.
The Telephone : 3072.
Telescopic : 4141.
Televangelism : 5496.
Tell Me How Old I Am : 245.
Tell Me, Mama : 4737.
Tell Me of the Hells You Went Through :
    1324.
Tell the Truth : 2535.
Tell Them I Sent You : 6631.
Tell Them   Was Here : 6544.
Tell Us : 724.
Telling About It : 1670.
Telling Erin About Iowa on Office Time :
    3038.
Telling Less : 4845.
Telling My Sister How I Taught a Lesson on
    Child Abuse : 1231.
Telling Our Lives: Susan's Turn : 7069.
Telling Stories, The Evening Star : 2541.
Telling the Lanugage : 6326.
Telphone Poles : 4698.
Temperamental : 523.
The Temple : 318, 1537, 7221.
Temple de Las : 2505.
The Temple of Nature : 1419.
Templemore Talking : 208.
Temporary Losses : 4165.
Temporary Resurrection #408 : 4378.
Temptation : 1827.
Tempus Fugit : 5602.

The Ten Best Episodes of *The Patty Duke Show* : 6691.
Ten Day Week : 3981.
Ten Reasons Why I Never Made Love to Your Mouth : 6232.
Ten Sonnets : 3600, 3763.
Ten Years After Michael : 3227.
Tenants : 2371.
Tender death : 6186.
Tender Is the North : 4352.
Tenderly : 1606.
The Tenderness : 848.
Tending : 454.
Tending One's Garden : 665, 3152.
Tenebrae : 1026, 1929.
The Tennis Club : 4488.
Tent Meeting : 5325.
Tents : 321.
Terminology : 4328.
Terminus : 1112.
Terms of Collection : 4532.
Terra Incognita / Taino Incognito : 2242.
Terra Mara : 6802.
The Terrible Fear : 499.
Terrible Weather Conditions : 1821.
Territorial : 675.
Territory : 5973.
The Territory : 1212.
The Terrorist : 472.
A Terrorist Angel : 1826.
Terry : 5480.
Terza Rima for a Girl Stranded in White : 3355.
Tess Learns to Be Professional : 6578.
Tess of the D'Urbervilles : 4819.
The Tesserae : 2911.
The Test : 3235.
Testament Not Found in the Dead Sea Scrolls : 6379.
A Testimonial : 6259.
Testimonials from the Boarding House : 6351.
Testimony : 3344, 4995.
Testimony of the Female Serial Killer : 2560.
Testing the Aubergine : 1706.
The Testments : 5132.
Tests : 7166.
Texas (2) : 643, 4433.
Texas and Eternity : 3205.
The Texas Chainsaw Revival : 2435.
Textiles : 2997.
Thaba Nchu : 5215.
Thabong : 5215.
Thai Restaurant, Edmonton : 7046.
A Thainglish Collection of Poetry : 3936.
Thallium Poisoning : 7050.
Thank You America : 5576.
Thank you for pinstripe (cozy place to sit and wield my pen : 4682.
Thank You Note : 4332.
Thanksgiving : 1969, 2125.
Thanksgiving on Ghost Ranch : 2432.
Thasos : 1570, 2238.
That a body might sag with many weights : 4627.

That Boy from Georgia Is Coming Through Here : 2420.
That covers half the Earth with goodbye : 5113.
That Damn Painted Cave : 140.
That Day at Arnaud's Mill, Risking Poetry : 4405.
That Domestic Circle : 345.
That Empty Place : 1433.
That Evening : 3235.
That Fall: Icarus in the Exurbs : 217.
That He Will Wake : 7073.
That Hearing a Slide Projector : 672.
That It All Might Have You : 154.
That Lonely Shoe Lying on the Road : 6257.
That May There Were Alligators in Green Lake : 6231.
That Night : 303.
That Other May : 3822.
That Same, in Winter : 5491.
That Same Prayer : 2659.
That Shape : 2331.
That Slant of Light : 6076.
That Stone : 2697, 3176, 4545.
That Sun Is Gold Blood : 5403.
That Sweet Atmosphere of Tango Around Three : 2824, 3715, 6815.
That the World Was There : 5673, 6871.
That Thin Man : 6248.
That Was Some Saxaphone : 3386.
That Will Do Nicely : 1312.
That's Not in My Job Description : 421.
Thaw in the Bracken : 343.
Thawed : 2331.
The : 2434.
The The : 1728.
Theater : 2055.
The Theft : 2521.
Thefts from Italian Churches Reach All-time High : 1122.
Their Favorite Author : 5906.
Their Honeymoon Trip : 1317.
Their Stories : 6063.
Their Wedding Picture : 184.
Thel : 1149.
Thelonious Dedalus : 6125.
Them and Us : 1149.
The Theme of Power : 6481.
Theme Park : 3300.
Then : 654.
Then I Read about Eve in *Paradise Lost* : 5956.
Then I Read About Eve in Paradise Lost : 5956.
Then We Found the River : 2298.
Then You See : 3298.
Theo Didn't Smoke : 107.
A Theologian at Prayer : 5992.
The Theologian Talks Baseball : 3216.
The Theories for Ball Lightning : 1966.
The Theory and Practice of Postmodernism: A Manifesto : 171.
The Theory of Bureaucratic Digestion : 5109.
The Theory of Bureaucratic Elimination : 5109.

The Theory of Bureaucratic Locomotion :
    5109.
Theory of Departure : 3825.
The Theory of Flight : 7191.
Theory of Tables : 2882, 5011, 5011.
The Therapeutist: After Magritte : 2046.
Therapy : 3924, 6887.
There : 2330, 2331.
There Are Days : 3595.
There Are More Where That One Came
    From : 3877.
There Are Plenty of Angels, She Said in the
    LADIES : 1874.
There are snakes in the water : 511.
There Are Two Days I Remember : 2163.
There Are Two Stills : 1435.
There arrives a beast the spring : 5638, 5917.
There Be Monsters Here : 5440.
There Comes a Time : 3730.
There Is a Door : 2035, 4288.
There Is a Joyous Sound : 4899.
There Is a Place : 6278.
There Is a Snake Which Has Appeared Here.
    Come See the God! : 2023.
There Is a Sweetness in It : 2441.
There Is a Thing Called : 1283.
There Is a World: Lee Harvey Oswald and
    the Seduction of History : 702.
There Is Also a City : 2964.
There Is Failure to Ignite, As If There Were
    No Air : 2040.
There Is No Sky : 6377.
There Is No Wind in Heaven : 7009.
There Is Nothing Waiting to Emerge : 6335.
There is something in this house : 1476.
There once was a miser who hoarded : 5132.
There Shall Come No Other and Better
    World : 3062, 3294.
There There : 2836.
There Was a Time : 631, 5951.
There Was a Young Female Clerk : 2982.
There was this big great dane that ran all over
    the neighborhood biting kids : 2049.
There Will Be Another Time : 7027.
There will be other falls : 1138.
There's a Hole in the Sky : 1473.
There's a thin little man : 5230.
There's Justice : 6607.
There's Never a Never : 3677.
There's Nothing Left in Your File : 6159.
There's something about a grown man fishing
    for change : 4783.
Thesaurus : 1204.
These Are Acts of Devotion : 5052.
These Are the Sleeping Conditions : 189,
    4363.
These Are the Streets : 5970.
These Days : 4528, 4892.
These Fireflies : 4965.
These Hands Found : 3447.
These Heart Hammers, These Small
    Xylophone Joys : 296.
These leaves getting fat : 5113.
These Many Tricks : 4864.
These Minutes : 6982.
These Photographers Recede : 6541.

These Reeds : 3947.
These Things from Words : 442, 4423, 5804.
These Valleys Seem Old : 5783.
Theseus Describes the King of Hell : 2289.
They Annotated Alice : 625.
They Buried All Their Dead : 6278.
They Call Me the Barber, or, the Barber's
    Blues : 5230.
They Come : 5416.
They Dance : 7007.
They Fertilize My Welcome Mat : 3877.
They Fill the Air : 6432.
They Last : 5937.
They Obey the Same Signal : 3274.
They Polka'd Till His Shoe Broke : 550.
They Said : 2397.
They Say : 2220, 3838.
They Work Indoors : 1.
They're Closing It Down But It's Still going
    On : 6884.
They're Sleeping in a Row : 3315.
Thick With Fingers : 3927.
Thie Promise : 2318.
Thief : 3737.
The Thief : 3683.
The thief eschews the dark : 6186.
The Thief of Your Poem : 2156.
Thin Black Man with Wife and Child in the
    Polonia Restaurant, New York, 1970 :
    1080.
The Thing, 1951 : 1696.
A Thing About Bridges : 6254.
'The Thing From Another World' Frozen Fast
    and Loose : 5103.
The Thing That Waits for You : 1475.
Things : 2340, 3256, 5638.
The Things a Man Keeps : 3195.
Things As They Are : 5324.
Things Cheaply Had : 2992, 4729, 7221.
Things Even Out : 3877.
Things Have a Way of Getting Away : 1931.
Things I Can Do Listening to Music : 5273.
Things That Float in the Air : 1101, 5220.
The Things That Have Never Happened
    Before : 2724.
Things That Might Have Been : 643, 5441.
Things to Do : 3418.
Things to Read : 4682.
Think of Palermo : 5617.
Think Without Words : 3291.
Thinking about Citizenship While the
    Workmen Are Here : 6792.
Thinking About Ecstasy : 2271.
Thinking About the Past : 3259.
Thinking Bed : 1124.
Thinking Clearly : 653.
Thinking of Getting Remarried in a Time of
    Shifting Roles : 1534.
Thinking of You : 4020.
Thinning the Walnuts : 5555.
Thinning Train of Summer : 1571.
Third Eye for Etheridge : 5714.
Third Grade: Later in November 1963 : 6035.
Third-Order Enthymeme : 4736.
Third Pantoum for My Parents : 5612.
Third Series : 2171, 2174, 5539.

Third Shift : 6903.
Third Street, Nome : 6866.
The Third Visit : 1930.
Thirst : 319.
A Thirst for Work : 2943.
Thirst Song : 3772.
Thirsty Dreams : 4015.
The Thirsty Heart : 1722.
Thirteen Ways of Looking at a Memo : 1383.
The Thirteenth Floor : 3880.
Thirty Miles East of Niagara : 2319.
Thirty Years Ago, in a Suburb of Bombay :
    1549.
This : 648, 2131, 5617.
This a divergence words yellow : 6252.
This April : 3822.
This Bird : 4242.
This Bloody Thing : 1653.
This clear morning : 3621.
This Crow : 442, 4423, 5804.
This Dance : 466.
This Distance : 2936.
This Drove Me Nuts : 2664.
This Eventide Seems Spilt : 53, 3137.
This Everlasting Evening : 62, 2824, 3715.
This Fragile Sphere : 4179.
This Future : 1305, 4100, 4148.
This Girl : 2934.
This Great Weight : 7240.
This House : 1321.
This is different : 715, 4875.
This Is Important : 1956.
This Is It : 3781.
This Is My Language : 7011.
This Is No Fairmont in Deadwood : 5714.
This Is Not a Letter : 961.
This Is Not My Life, But the Life I Would
    Like : 7246.
This Is Our Address : 6205.
This Is the Body : 7302.
This Is the Box Pandora Shook : 3170.
This Is the Middle : 5959.
(This Isn't a Smile, It's a Smirk.) : 2230.
this is it! i've found it at last! nirvana, the
    Elysian fields, heaven : 712.
This Kind of Grace : 5606.
This lady who cremates the dead : 4034.
This Life : 5731.
This Life, This Word Unsaid : 2886.
This Light of Physics : 2774.
This Love : 2869.
This May's a Scorcher : 3822.
This Morning : 979.
This Morning a Strange Bird : 1387.
This morning clouds bunch : 3466.
This movie, see I wanted to take you to :
    2210.
This Night Train : 318, 1066, 7221.
This October Light : 2537.
This Pantoum Was Not On My Schedule :
    2413.
This Place in the Ways : 5702.
This Place Looking Out Upon : 4472.
This Poem Is Not About Charleston, South
    Carolina : 6321.
This Poem Is Not For You : 3239.

This rain slowly in the dark : 5113.
This ring of fire about my wrists : 5732.
This South : 3044.
This Splendor : 1310, 4098.
This Suit : 2312.
This Swallowtail : 7175.
This Table : 5683.
This Time the splinter, wedged : 5113.
This Tune : 6806.
This Unnamed Town : 732.
This watchband kept alive : 5113.
This Wawa Is Out of Applications : 3313.
This Way : 2291.
This Way Out : 1083.
This wood is bordered by dust and rot : 52,
    3302.
This World : 1942.
This Year of Floods, Riots and Earthquake :
    6341.
Thisbe Changing Her Mind : 6439.
Thomas : 4385.
Thomas More (1478-1535) : 3551.
Thomas's Birthday : 6852.
Thoreau : 3866.
The Thoreau Cane : 1966.
Thorns and Abrasion : 6335.
The Thorough Earth : 757.
Those Hours : 1058.
Those Men Who Go Thump in the Night :
    881.
Those Pelicans : 6349.
Those Stains : 4829.
Those Times I : 4581.
Those unlovely friends you drag : 4149,
    4199.
Those who cultivate their manhood : 3218.
Those Who've Survived Open-Heart Surgery
    : 4252.
Thou Art Durga : 318, 1066, 7221.
Thought by Rembrandt's Wife and Model
    During the Painting of 'Flora' : 5695.
The Thought of It : 3822.
Thought Patterns Hazy : 7263.
Thoughts of the Wise Men : 1318.
Thoughts on Filibustering : 6690.
Thoughts on the Senator from Georgia Who
    Might Have Been President : 6690.
A Thousand Petals Dry Under Sex's Flexed
    Biceps : 6057.
Thrashing : 1282.
Thread Box : 4820.
Threadleaf : 91.
Threads : 3237.
Three : 2570, 3673.
Three 1-Line Poems : 1284.
Three A.M. : 90.
Three AM : 3798.
Three Conversations : 5645.
Three Cows and the Moon : 3348.
Three Dreams : 5886.
Three Dreams in Chiang-ling : 2576, 7298.
Three Dreams: South Bronx : 4557.
Three Epigrams : 4801.
Three Figures : 6625.
Three Fragments of Pindar : 2350, 2907.
Three from the Tang Dynasty : 5245.

Three Generations (A Photo) : 5759.
Three Glimpses : 3677.
Three Horses in a Field : 3841.
Three Images : 471, 3325, 4695.
The Three Lambs : 6271.
Three mares : 442, 5804, 6410.
The Three Marias of East Third Street : 4225.
Three Months Without Electricity : 4468.
Three Paintings by Mary Pratt : 722.
Three Peas in a Pod : 4965.
Three Photographs : 6688.
Three Prayers for the First Forty Days of the Dead : 950, 1843, 4417.
Three Printers Eating Lunch : 341.
Three-Quarter Moon : 1990.
Three Questions : 6429.
Three Russias in One April : 982.
Three Short Clay Poems : 3625.
Three Stanzas : 2130, 6674.
Three Tanka Because John : 7084.
Three Together Sat on the Shore : 1261.
The Three Tortoise Secret-of-the-World Power Plant : 2324.
Three Verses on Running into the Taoist Master 'In Emptiness' : 3568, 5913.
Three Views from the Latin American Summit : 2678.
Three Views of Narrative : 4769.
Three Voices in Stone — Plus Wood : 6583.
Three Ways of Recovering a Body : 1717.
Three Weeks Back from Saigon : 502.
Three Who Passed: 1987 (Baldwin / Killens / Washington) : 2054.
Three Wishes : 1703.
Three Women : 2652, 5206.
Three Young Women on a Coal Bank : 3022.
Threesome : 453.
Threshold : 6125.
A Thrice Happy Romance : 5132.
Through a Rift in the Natural Fabric : 2978.
Through a Slit in the Tent : 3640.
Through Have Around : 3981.
Through Many Waters, Leaf-Light, the Tree : 5334.
Through the Fire : 2325.
Through the weight of this uneasy summer's air : 665, 4048.
Through the Window : 1479.
Through the Window in the Subway Station Ceiling, Angels : 4072.
Throughout the Duration of a Pulse a Heart Changes Form : 68.
The Throw : 6278.
Throwing Away Several Pages of Poetry : 3855.
Throwing China into the Sea : 5069.
Throwing the Sofa Out the Window : 1590.
Thrown : 2688.
A Thrown Stone : 1897.
Thule : 211.
Thunder, or A Place in the Sun : 3300.
Thunderstorm at Night : 5022.
Thurbers : 4532.
Thurman Munson : 6658.
Thursday : 4704, 6244.

Thursday, Across from My Work Station : 1447.
Thus I Registered : 498, 3516, 5149.
Thwarted Suitor : 6932.
Tibi cum non sit diai panis : 3962.
Ticket : 3870.
Ticks : 6165.
Tidal Basin, Washington, D.C. : 6219.
The Tide : 3772.
Tides : 5780.
Tie and Slur : 3710.
Tierra del Uomo : 211.
Ties : 6658.
The Tigerettes Are Our Monuments : 5419.
Tight Jeans : 4414.
Tijuana Haiku : 2315.
Till Death Do They Part : 2782.
Till My Teeth Rattle : 5606.
Timberland : 5700.
Timberline : 1184.
Time : 1321, 4199, 5112, 5638, 6116.
Time and Times : 204, 4556.
The time comes : 3119, 5861.
Time Enough : 6810.
Time for Zinnias : 180.
Time in a Bottle : 3245.
A Time in February : 431.
Time Machine : 2782.
The Time of Our Lives : 4199.
Time of sugaring : 6673.
The Time of Wind : 473.
Time Off : 6300.
Time Over Earth : 7343.
Time Piece : 5627.
Time Port : 3369, 3371, 4064.
Time Slides : 3209.
Time to Change the Furnace Filter : 344.
Time Was : 3284.
Timeclock : 6218.
Timeless, Twinned : 6927.
Timepieces : 157.
Time's Up : 906.
The Timetable : 6614.
Timid Family : 322.
Timon of Athens : 4292.
Timshel: Thou Mayest : 1892.
Tin Whistle : 2850.
Ting-Lotta : 3298.
Tiny Dramas : 3658.
Tiny Treaties : 80.
Tips from My Father : 1442.
Tired, Leaning on the Hills : 5171, 6471, 6637.
Tiresias and Narcissus : 4961, 6135.
Title-at-End-Poem : 6940.
Tlingit Market II : 2940.
To a Coin : 355, 643.
To a Croatian Poet : 5609.
To a Dutch Potter in Ireland : 2725.
To a Faddist : 1225.
To a Feminist Collective : 4225.
To a Formal Poet : 466.
To a Former Lover : 7328.
To a Garbage Truck : 6358.
To a High-School Sophomore Who Requested a Love Poem : 2631.

To a Lovely Old Bitch : 7121.
To a Nipple : 11.
To a Photographer : 6649.
To a Poet, from a Gardner : 5408.
To a Pulaski County Prisoner : 2556.
To a Small Light : 425.
To a Sports-Car-Owning Friend on His
    Fortieth Birthday : 5491.
To a Statue I Would Like to Know : 6936.
To a Watery Page : 5059.
To a Young Feminist Who Wants to Be Free
    : 26.
To a Young Poet : 4768.
To All the Old Apollos : 2045.
To Allen Ginsberg : 4500.
To an African Friend, After His Announcing
    His Intention to Move to the United
    States : 2764.
To an Old Black Woman, Homeless and
    Indistinct : 769.
To an Old Woman Walking : 6155.
To an Umpire : 3099.
To an Unborn Daughter : 4379.
To Artemis, Protector of the Newly Born :
    2045.
To Bakchus : 1035, 4652.
To Be a Deserter : 58, 6724.
To Be a Folder of the Creek : 6435.
To Be Continued : 3875, 4795.
To Be Opened in the Event : 7177.
To Beat the Shit Out of Someone : 6970.
To Bend the Sun : 4472.
To Butter a Bagel : 1517.
To Carlos Orchida : 5458.
To Carry On : 5442, 6491.
To Celia : 4374.
To Circumferate : 6491.
To Diotima : 2907, 5640, 5855.
To Donald Davidson in Heaven (southern
    Section) : 1451.
To Dr. Paul Mendelsohn, My Former
    Student, Killed While Jogging : 5180.
To Dream, to Sleep : 2092.
To Execute : 1119.
To Fall : 6491.
To Father Don Angelo Grillo : 6333, 6543.
To Federico with Some Violets : 2176, 2824,
    3715.
To Giuseppe in October : 522, 6649.
To Hanawa, Terayama, As Far as Nagare :
    3066, 5935.
To Harry Crosby at the Hotel des Artistes :
    1830.
To Harvey, Who Traced the Circulation :
    7227.
To Hear the Chorus Sing : 4113.
To Heather, Away : 2948.
To Heloise: Yet Another Letter : 3449, 6313,
    6712.
To Here : 2589.
To Hernandez : 656.
To His Mother Whose Name Was Maria :
    522, 6649.
To His Wife Who Works Days from Her
    Husband Who Works Nights : 2794.
To Irrevoke : 6491.

To Joey : 3983.
To John at the Summer Solstice, Before His
    Return : 5290.
To Jon : 6820.
To Kornis : 498, 3516, 5149.
To Kronos, or Words from a Drunk : 1310,
    4098.
To Lautréamont : 6154.
To Live : 1494, 5075, 6411.
To Live and Die in L.A. : 1636.
To Logan in the Grave : 448.
To Look Between Night : 5375.
To Make a Talisman : 1337, 4929.
To Make It Big : 1259.
To Marcos in the Coming Years : 3814.
To Mistranslate Saudade : 3894.
To Mothers : 4057, 4855.
To My Cousin : 2092.
To My Cousin on Star Mountain : 6277.
To My Daughter : 7017.
To My Father — Who Raped Me : 4020.
To My Husband : 4892.
To My Mother : 1396.
To My Patron and Friend Maecenas : 2558.
To My Wife : 4886.
To Nail the Evening : 3287, 7003.
To Nothingness : 1425, 3230.
To One of Her Sisters : 1714.
To One Who Died Young : 2079, 6669.
To Our Eyes the Blind Man : 2739.
To Plant : 65.
To Pope Formosus : 1208.
To Re-angle Axes : 2077, 5789.
To Remain : 3460.
To Return : 5643.
To Robert Forst: A Letter Never Sent : 2710.
To Robinson Jeffers : 362, 437, 7247.
To Ross and His Children : 610, 4450.
To Save the Innocent, Anything Possible :
    5361.
To See Far : 783.
To See If I've Really Done Anything at All :
    4969.
To See Is Only a Lanugage : 4353.
To See You Again : 6742.
To Shakespeare on the Death of His Son :
    3558.
To Silence : 2815.
To Sleep : 3328.
To Spirit : 3651.
To Spot the Centralia Mine Fire : 3550.
To start the limp you lace : 5113.
To Tell the Truth : 4616.
To the Ark : 1667, 2007, 6514.
To the Black Madonna of Chartres : 6752.
To the Black Woman on the Postcard : 4202.
To the Boy Elis : 2079, 6669.
To the Children : 1078.
To the Earth Right Now : 4200, 4460, 6846.
To the Finder : 1513.
To the Household Goddess : 6932.
To the Librarian at the Tesson Ferry Branch :
    3801.
To the Mystic River Bridge, Boston : 3312.
To the One Reading Me : 643, 4433.

To the Reader From the Heart of the Moment : 149.
To the Ski Instructor, Regarding the Paradox of Grip and Glide : 6568.
To the Soul : 1514.
To the Spider of My Hand : 1687.
To the Spirit of My Father I Address This Poem : 866.
To the Unknown Dutch Postcard-Sender (1988) : 4101.
To the Whiteness of Bone : 6863.
To Them This May Consume : 1793.
To Think About Eternity : 5171, 5484, 6637.
To Those Who Fear Explosions : 505.
To Urania : 756.
To Waken : 143, 3786.
To What You Said : 7070.
To Whatever Remains of Caedmon Wherever It's Remaining : 4365.
To William Blake : 610, 4450.
To Willie Loman: Life as a Package Deal : 5591.
To Win Deliverance : 4899.
To Wit a Very Small Gland : 6871.
To Word : 6491.
To Wordsworth : 1486.
To Writers Forbidden to Write : 3372.
To yearling place this border : 6252.
To You on Wave #10 : 5309.
Toad : 4216.
Tobekobekon : 3217.
Toboggan : 4343.
Toda Drug : 4356.
Toda la gente es tonta : 3410, 4170.
Today : 555, 3983, 7315.
Today, Accidentally : 498, 4920.
Today for Homework : 5119.
Today I Am Wearing a Suit : 3235.
'Today I Felt Like Matisse,' she Said : 3298.
Today I walk, a sandwiched event like history : 6589.
The Today Show : 5986.
Today's Visit : 1361.
Together : 635.
Together Among Monarchs : 2283.
Tokens of Living : 5321.
Tolstoy's Snowball : 2424.
Tom (d. 1990) : 6063.
Tom Singer's Bracelet : 6607.
Tomato Soup : 2849.
Tomato Worms : 899.
The Tomb of Charles Baudelaire : 4065, 6993.
The Tomb of Edgar Poe : 4065, 6993.
The Tombigbee's ugly, the Hudson's a mess : 3524.
Tomboy : 984.
A Tombstone Carved from Speech : 6086.
Tombstones : 2488.
Tomintoul : 5061.
Tomis : 7182.
Tomorrow : 1227.
Tomorrow Is a Difficult Idea : 5615.
Tomorrow We Discuss Cottonwoods : 2950.
Tondo of Hell : 2542.
Tone Deaf : 3518.

Tongue : 2812.
The Tongue : 899.
Tongue and Groove : 2740.
Tongues : 5130, 5753.
Tonight : 716.
Tonight Martial Law Was Imposed : 165, 4867.
Tonight We Bow : 5413.
El Toño Loco de la Placita de Guadalupe : 2796.
Tonto Plateau, Grand Canyon : 5792.
Tonto's Expanding Headband : 3798.
Too : 783.
Too Fast for the Eye to Hold : 645.
Too Little Care : 6707.
Too Much : 4568.
Too Soon : 2410.
Too Soon to Be True : 5178.
Tool's, Word's and People's Confusion : 4161, 6289.
The Tooth : 4755.
Tooth, Fang, Tusk : 4298.
Toothache and Australia Fantasy : 4123.
Toowoomba in the Fog : 5675.
Topography : 475.
Torn Shadow : 2848.
Tornado Alley : 5021.
The Tornado-Drawer : 1703.
Tornado Weather : 3955.
Tornadoes and Other Hassles : 3004.
Torque : 5914.
Torso : 1187.
Tortoise : 6336.
Tortoise Relocation : 6544.
Tory Wig : 5725.
The Toss : 997.
The Toss of Bones : 5025.
Total Eclipse : 654.
Total Madness : 838.
A Totally New Time, a Completely New Era : 1983, 2095, 4919.
Totem : 478, 2331, 3015, 4571, 5789.
Totem and Taboo : 7198.
The Totems : 7106.
Totenbuch : 1153.
Totes : 3124.
Touch-Me-Not : 6723.
The Touch of Lizard's Skin : 1259.
The Touch of Velvet : 6433.
Touchdown : 6720.
Touched by Frost : 4524.
The Touched, Loonies, Full Moon : 4633, 6028.
Touchers : 1398.
Touching in the Sweatshop : 6885.
Tough as a Bone : 4830.
Tough Audience : 6842.
A Tour : 6742.
A Tour of the Tomb of Guiliano De' Medici : 1233.
A Touring Man Loses His Way : 5162.
The Tourist : 5107.
The Tourist at Cadiz : 5796.
Tourist Season : 3518.
Tourists Under Glass : 5854.
Tournament of Destruction : 5600.

Tours : 7220.
Toward a Catalogue of Falling : 1241.
Toward the End of the Century : 3139.
Toward Water : 2344.
Towards a Ridge of Blue Sky : 7076.
Towards the End : 2124.
Towards the End of November : 3368.
Tower : 745.
The Tower : 6076.
Town : 7280.
A Town I Know : 6045.
Town Line Road, by Bicycle Twenty Years
    Later : 5456.
A Town Lit by the Sea : 7193.
Town Pool : 654.
The Town That Voted the Earth Flat : 2046.
Toxic Sonnets : 5401.
Toy : 6559.
The Toy Warehouse : 396.
The Toymaker Gloomy But Then Again
    Sometimes Happy : 458.
Traces : 5610.
Tracing : 463, 4910.
Track Meet : 1514.
Tracking X. : 5308.
Tracks : 1464, 1990.
Tracks and Ties : 4533.
Trade : 5729.
Trade Off : 1238.
Trade-Off : 6985.
Trade Wind : 2692.
Trading : 4357.
Trading Post : 5910.
Traditional Comforts : 3010.
Traducciones : 2796.
Traffic : 5621.
Traffic Report : 2189.
Traffic Was Stopped on P.V. Drive North :
    1505.
Train : 2179, 6200.
The Train : 5694.
Le Train Bleu : 6055.
Train Set : 2218.
Train to Chicago : 5063.
Trains : 1336, 1871, 3799.
The Tramps of Shepherd's Bush : 296.
Trance : 4985.
Tranquility : 6596.
Transcending a Prison : 5147.
Transfer : 505.
Transfigured Fall : 970, 6669.
Transform or Perish : 5416.
Transformations : 31, 625, 795.
Transience : 4142.
Transitions, 1979-1992 : 2627.
Translating : 1524.
Translation : 6439, 6481.
Translation from the Chinese : 542, 7093.
Translation of Blood Quantum : 7207.
Translations : 4377.
Transmission : 4116.
Transparencies : 4817.
Transparency : 7354.
Transparent Things : 151.
Transplant : 2044, 2538.
Trapeze in Autumn : 7126.

Trapped Light : 6621.
Trash : 1680, 7175.
Trasplantada : 6657.
Traumerei : 2435.
Travel : 6045.
The Travel Industry : 4557.
Traveler : 4429, 5085.
A Traveler Seeks to Send This to Chou
    Chung Yang : 1346, 2986.
Travelers : 2898.
The Traveler's Story : 965.
Traveling at Night in Fukushima : 4864.
The Traveling Circus : 1765.
Traveling in America : 1960.
Traveling on a Sunday Afternoon : 2934.
Traveller : 3433.
The Traveller : 3665, 5616.
The Traveller's Garment : 5469.
Travelling Over the Mountains : 1773.
Travelling with Tomas : 6242.
The Traverse : 295.
The Travertines : 4614.
Trays : 4871.
The Treacherous Hour : 4964.
Treacherously, from Behind : 2790, 4458.
Treason Would Fain Be in One So Fair :
    2030.
Treasure : 6852.
The Treasure in Books : 4616.
Treasure Island : 6113.
Treasures : 1171.
Treating the Spring Box : 7232.
Treatment : 5933.
Treblinka : 3822.
Tree : 654.
The Tree : 442, 5804, 6763, 6960, 7055.
The Tree at the Edge of the Precipice : 3809,
    4945, 7335.
Tree Fort : 7292.
A Tree Full of Fish (Nine Dreams of a Girl) :
    5356.
The Tree in the World : 2399.
Tree Limbs Letting Go of Snow : 5354.
Tree Planting : 839.
Tree, Salt, Sea : 278.
The Tree That Knowledge Is : 3866.
Trees : 498, 4716, 5750.
Trees at Night : 3193.
Trees V : 1120.
The Trek : 5482.
The Trek of the Wind : 2200, 4821, 5765,
    6757.
Trellis : 6120.
A Trellis : 2551.
Tremendous Mood Swings : 369.
Treml : 7315.
Trepidations : 6716.
Les Très Riches Heures de Paris : 2437.
Trespassers : 2157.
Trial : 2883.
Trial and Error : 5606.
Tribe : 2762.
The Tribe of Women : 3300.
Tributaries : 4334.
Tricia LeClair : 7213.
Trick Candle : 5015.

Trick of Light : 3935.
Tricked : 6985.
A Tricksy June : 6374.
Trigger Housings : 2455.
Trilce : 616, 6760, 6760.
Trilobites : 18.
Trilogía de la Maldad : 6061.
Trimmings : 812.
Trini Tabanca — Carnival 92 : 4094.
Trinity or Blackberry Stitch : 6120.
Triolet: Procrustes Is Diverted : 5146.
Triplet : 3329, 5539.
Triptych : 2205.
Tripwire to a Halo : 637.
Tristeza : 277.
The Triumph of Idleness : 746, 3198.
The Trodden Wheel of Andrew Wyeth :
	3699.
Trojan Women : 5946, 6135.
Trombone Baseball : 2957.
Trop de Vert : 1226.
Trophy : 7166.
The Trophy Wives : 3677.
The Tropic Bird of Maui / Te-Tavake-a-Maui
	: 3318.
Tropical Moment : 6007.
Troth Tryst : 5783.
Troubador : 289.
Troubadour : 2500.
Trouble in History : 3343.
Trouble, Maybe : 91.
Trouble with Consonants : 4820.
Trout Fly : 7023.
Trout Tank, Café Le Sporting : 3440.
Truce : 4377, 6160.
A Truce : 3399.
The Trucker's Head Music : 4676.
Truco : 349, 643, 4433.
True : 1620.
A True Artist #1 : 6288.
A True Confession : 1789, 5702, 6580.
The true measure of a man's mind : 2514.
True North : 6420.
True Romance : 3727.
True Stories about Color : 4684.
A True Story : 2965.
True Tales of Synchronicity : 1043.
The Truest Sight : 2148.
Truffaut : 4619.
Trumpet / Sax : 3386.
Truro : 6279.
The Truss : 1749.
Trust : 2807, 6812.
Truth : 2737.
The Truth : 1095, 1771.
The Truth about AIDS : 7095.
The Truth About God: Seventeen Poems :
	980.
The Truth about Small Towns : 288.
Truth As We Know It : 5606.
Trying the New Volvo : 7175.
Trying to Sleep, Corsica : 968.
Trying to Tell My Mother about Her
	Guardian Angel : 5555.
Tryst : 545.
Tsubuka : 7126.

Tu Ne Quaesieris : 1948.
Tu ne Quaesieris : 2944.
Tuesday : 3329, 5921.
Tuesday Afternoon, the M & M Tavern :
	3216.
Tuesday, August 13, 1912 : 3440.
Tulips : 5206, 7246.
Tullumayu : 4223, 5338.
A Tumble for Skelton : 5868.
The Tumor : 4678.
Tundra Month : 6354.
Tunnel : 511.
Tunnel Rats : 5163.
Turf : 6924.
Turn : 5288.
The Turn : 3855, 5089.
Turn on the Lights, for Christssake : 1666.
Turned Ermine : 5324.
Turner Cassity in Atlanta? I Thought He
	Was in Chicago : 870.
The Turning : 4011.
Turning Fifty : 130.
Turning In on Itself : 4529.
Turning Over the Earth : 4474.
Turning Point : 3353.
Turning the Key : 4078.
Turning the Words on Surfaces into Faces
	Without Masks : 3596.
Turning Things Out Good : 121.
Turtle : 5295.
The Turtle : 4497.
Turtle Hunter : 1816.
The Tutor (Budapest, 1936) : 7036.
T.V. : 1089.
T.V., Ghosts, and Poets Past : 1417.
The TV Responsible : 1147.
The Twain Meeting : 2972.
Twelfth Night : 4345.
Twelve-Tone Row 1 : 3521.
Twentieth Century Rant : 3854.
Twenty Facts : 2166.
The Twenty-First Century : 2695.
Twenty-four Logics in Memory of Lee
	Hickman : 5011.
Twenty Fourth Meditation: Man to Man :
	7372.
Twenty-Nine Rules About Horses : 6571.
Twenty Shores : 2766.
Twenty Years Later, to a Friend : 5255.
Twentysome : 2215.
Twilight : 261, 2106, 5322, 5405, 5432.
Twilight in Bombay : 1045.
Twilight, Poconos : 1851.
Twilight Slide : 4986.
The Twilight's Last Gleaming : 7215.
Twin : 6338.
Twins : 3136, 4925.
Twins But Not Sisters : 5000.
Twisted Cord Madonna : 3822.
Two Alarm Fire : 2818.
Two Baths : 6943.
Two Battlefields : 3733.
Two Beautiful Young Women : 3022.
Two Birds : 861, 7352.
Two Blackbirds : 3929.
Two Bowls : 422.

Two Boys Glimpsed in Late Night : 6012.
Two Brothers : 2363.
Two Burns : 43.
Two Cardinals : 1753.
The Two Churches of Chimayó : 5391.
Two Circuses : 381.
Two Climbing : 2446.
Two Colors : 4073.
Two Cousins : 4276.
Two Dolphins : 254.
Two Figures with Heat Lightning in the
    Sangre de Cristo Mountains : 4307.
Two fingers : 5191, 5472.
Two for History : 5053.
Two Friends Talking : 3022.
Two Generations After the Lynching : 5073.
Two german officers and their driver : 5012.
Two Grandmas : 342.
Two hercules swung down low over the
    marsh then on to the estuary : 360.
Two Horses : 3195.
Two Hymns : 4722.
Two in July : 4795.
Two Lessons in the Sacred : 5956.
Two Lives : 3009.
Two Lovers : 1331.
Two Loves : 4793.
Two Meditations on Chuang Tsu : 507.
Two Men in a Corner : 4977.
Two Men Swimming : 604.
Two Mentors : 5395.
Two Minutes After I Told You to Leave :
    2638.
Two Mississippis : 2247.
Two Montagnard Boys : 54.
Two Novels : 4660.
Two Nursery Rhymes : 239.
Two of a Kind : 2625.
Two or Three Wishes : 1514.
Two Pasts and a Present : 2477.
Two Poems : 617.
Two Poems of Awakening : 7048.
Two Porpoises Passed By : 6010.
Two Prayers for the Sioux : 3920.
Two Ramages for Old Masters : 604.
Two Readings : 2331.
Two Seasons : 6681.
Two Seated Women : 115.
Two Self-Portraits : 6481.
Two Sided Tape for One Track Minds : 7287.
Two Sides of the Afternoon : 1567.
Two Singers : 885, 2106.
Two Sisters Were Walking by the River :
    7286.
Two Small Poems for a Riddle and a Street :
    1585, 2051.
Two Songs : 1224.
Two Special Senses : 3352.
Two Studies : 1469.
Two Teachers at a Window : 2469.
Two Views of a Beautiful Woman in the
    Same Mirror : 582.
Two Views of Lake Placid : 6675.
Two Voices : 3054.
Two Women : 1045.
The Two Worlds : 684.

Two Young Men 23 to 24 : 5420.
Two Zen Poems : 3480, 4239.
Twos : 6630.
Tying One On at the University : 6407.
Typically Left-Handed & Oblivious : 6975.
Tyrannical Stream : 2866.
U.S. Buried Iraqi Soldiers Alive in Gulf War
    : 3772.
Uchepas : 2678.
The Ugliest Flower in the World : 5718.
Ugly Money : 947.
The Ugly Step Sister : 1703.
Ultima II True Blood Eye Shadows of the
    Past : 5327.
The Ultimate Drape : 6456.
Ultimate Metamorphosis : 1305, 4100, 4148.
Ultimate Nightingale : 5621.
Uluru Wild Fig Song : 6199.
Umatilla to Spokane : 1858.
Umberto Boccioni : 1355.
Umbra : 829.
Umbrella : 6259.
Umkupozi : 5890.
Umpteen : 4504.
Un-buh-liev-able : 3833.
Unable to Cross at Yunzhi : 6702, 7282.
Unarmed : 4598.
Unarmed Heart : 2819.
Unauthorized Autobiography : 3109.
Unborn Child to Its Parents : 289.
Unbound : 2270.
Unbrick the Night : 1390.
The Uncelebrated Birthday : 1852.
Unchaste Virgin : 2119.
Uncle : 2295.
Uncle Aaron Has Alzheimer's Disease : 6417.
Uncle Clinton's Decoy : 4033.
Uncle Dom : 2317.
Uncle Douglas and the Whirring Blades :
    4282.
Uncle Hank : 6264.
Uncle Jack : 4552.
Uncle Jim : 1534.
Uncle John Got Married : 4793.
Uncle Means Stop : 7049.
Uncle Moe : 342.
Uncle Nestor's Last Birthday Cake : 772.
Uncle Ray Shoots Craps with Elvis : 2383.
Uncle Seagram : 769.
Uncle Ted : 6095.
Uncle X Dying Alone in a Field : 1618.
Uncles : 5499.
Uncles (Who Lie Still and Perfect) : 5744.
Uncompass : 4682.
An Uncorrected Room : 2980.
The Uncrippling : 5615.
Under : 3981.
Under a Belly of Clouds : 3693.
Under a Funeral Canopy in Rockingham,
    N.C. : 813.
Under a Spell : 3248.
Under Control : 2458.
Under Four : 5097, 5114, 7312.
Under Hardscrabble Skies : 4282.
Under Heaven : 3629.
Under moonlight, & birdbath : 6186.

Under My Stornoway Hat : 2156.
Under the Best of Circumstances : 6493.
Under the Desert : 4359, 5995.
Under the Hills Near the Morava River : 6199.
Under the Influence of Autumn : 1585, 2051.
Under the Lens : 1316, 6235.
Under the Old Eyes of the Night : 3136.
Under the Overpass : 425.
Under the Same Roof : 5696, 7313.
Under the Tent : 119.
Under Three : 5097, 5114, 7312.
Under World Arrest : 1837.
Undercover Agent at Work : 2873.
Underlying Ideologist : 469.
Underneath Our Skirts : 1631.
The Understanding : 697, 7299.
Understanding Fog : 2298.
Understanding Glass : 3320.
Undertow : 1152.
Undervoicing : 95.
Undine : 1246.
Undressing : 1752.
Undulation : 1984.
Unearthing the Remains : 1005.
Unearthly Voices : 2864.
Unemployment : 6665.
Unencumbered : 2442.
The Unexplained Territories : 1230.
Unfinished Adoration : 3622.
Unfinished Ode: to a Lightbulb : 1501.
Unfinished: On the Anniversary of Loose Ends : 6321.
Unfinished Sonnets : 3949.
The Unfolding Eye : 4590.
Unfolding Flowers, Matchless Flames : 3752.
The Unfolding Mystery : 4936.
Unforgiving Joy : 1215, 3172, 6235.
Unfulfilled Desires Make Lifelong Ideals : 5357.
Unguent : 4314.
Unhinged : 812.
Unholy Desire — It Depends : 31.
Unholy Sonnet : 3145.
Uniforms : 3593.
The Unignorable Thing : 4975.
Union : 1430.
Unity : 1301.
The Universal Waste Basket : 4731.
The Universality of Experience : 4578.
The Universe Next Door : 4661.
A Universe of Broken Symmetries : 4112.
University Commencement : 498, 3516, 4921.
University of Vienna, 1876 : 3324.
The Unkindest Cut : 3796.
The Unknowable : 5548.
The Unknowing : 3100, 3514.
The Unknown Player : 2719.
Unknown Poets, Unremembered People : 1915.
Unlearning English : 4395.
Unleaving : 1405.
Unless You Think : 246.
Unlike Stars : 6858.
The Unmaking of Stalin : 2033.

Unnatural Laws : 5043.
Uno : 2786.
Unpaintable Landscape : 3901.
Unpleasantness : 1868.
Unraveling : 77, 1970.
Unravelling : 6970.
The Unreal : 4898.
The Unremembered Future : 1326.
Unrepentant Witch Burned for Adultery in 1503 : 6885.
Unrequited Love: A Slide Presentation : 7162.
Unsafe Soundings : 3981.
Unsent Letter 2 : 4694.
Unsent Message to My Brother in His Pain : 6391.
Unsigned Confession : 1043.
Unsung Hero : 1920.
The Untelling : 3682.
Until December : 6012.
Until She Returns : 6012.
Until the Shore's Dream Reappears I Hear Its Water Barrel Out from Over : 3335.
Untitled 7/23/91 : 4268.
Untitled (April '91) : 5011.
Untitled: At the front, defending the mother tongue : 436, 1076, 1968.
Untitled: Bad Boy ro mancin his lady : 3784.
Untitled: Bad Boy un practiced in the art of the interview : 3784.
Untitled: becky rosner was the only jewish girl I knew : 6627.
Untitled: Being against this large white cerebrum in my skull : 3659.
Untitled: Brought to the surface form the floor of the ocean : 5926.
Untitled: Contradiction over and over, rolling limbs flailing : 286.
Untitled Dreams : 5968.
Untitled (Far Away Near) : 5011.
Untitled (February '92) : 5011.
Untitled: God went down on me in a graveyard : 6646.
Untitled: Held in by the ribs of the garment : 6252.
Untitled: I confess I love the ambiguity of distance : 6879.
Untitled: I have also loved : 3900.
Untitled: I like to go see those old blues players : 1195.
Untitled: I remember when I was younger and everybody was all one big mass of pulsating stuff : 3659.
Untitled: I said the forest : 2210.
Untitled: I sleep in your sweater : 3302, 5990.
Untitled: I sob in a deserted city : 2201.
Untitled: I was already not too happy that tuesday morning : 6550.
Untitled: I write with clear water   Birds singing : 2201.
Untitled: If all I'd leave you be a poem : 1468.
Untitled: In a cafe   Birds fly round our table : 2201.

Untitled: Insanity creeping up behind me : 4386.

Untitled: It is for you I write, hypocrite : 897, 1033.

Untitled: It was a spring of cool flowers : 5222.

Untitled: It was all there under my grandfather's apple tree : 5222.

Untitled: It's winter in the haiku that hardly anyone believed : 4152.

Untitled: I've gotten nothing for weeks : 7270.

Untitled (kN) : 5011.

Untitled: Leave now all stale lack-luster : 1146.

Untitled: Lightbulbs catch fire. The rooms are full : 52, 3302.

Untitled: Little Joe was a vicious drunk : 2049.

Untitled (March '93) : 5011.

Untitled: Much of marriage is mastery : 5874.

Untitled: My camera kept strapped, frantic : 5113.

Untitled: Night, the mountains, a storm. The shelter packed with people : 665, 4048.

Untitled: Not at once did you grasp the message : 665, 4048.

Untitled: Nothing disguises the rush for love : 897, 1033.

Untitled Number Three : 2991.

Untitled Number Two : 2991.

Untitled: O you in that little bark : 5011.

Untitled: Of typewritten pages and greased thumbs leafing over painted objects in a room : 4386.

Untitled: Our breasts reveal : 5595.

Untitled: Out here the evening soughed : 832.

Untitled: Peel the roof off Chemo's bakery and empty the glass case of pan dulce : 2049.

Untitled Picture : 1749.

Untitled: Plastic nostrils and everything in them : 4386.

Untitled (September '92) : 5011.

Untitled: She made me sing : 2510.

Untitled: Sketch: Jacquie reading Blofeld's 'Wheel of Life' in Christmas light : 2254.

Untitled: Sometimes I'll be drinking by myself : 1195.

Untitled: Splinters on my tongue : 4386.

Untitled: Take this smudged snapshot for a sign : 52, 3302.

Untitled: That a body might sag with many weights : 4627.

Untitled: That covers half the Earth with goodbye : 5113.

Untitled: The inevitable roof with antennae : 4152.

Untitled: The one lapwing wheeling away from me : 360.

Untitled: The philosopher, who knows nothing is 'real' : 2331.

Untitled: The ringing sound when you lost your sense of humor : 2049.

Untitled: The wall needs paper or a painting : 716.

Untitled: There was this big great dane that ran all over the neighborhood biting kids : 2049.

Untitled: This movie, see I wanted to take you to : 2210.

Untitled: This ring of fire about my wrists : 5732.

Untitled: Through the weight of this uneasy summer's air : 665, 4048.

Untitled: Two fingers : 5191, 5472.

Untitled: Two hercules swung down low over the marsh then on to the estuary : 360.

Untitled: We may not have always been masters of ourselves : 6040.

Untitled: Weighed down by his bags, gray whiskers on his chin : 665, 4048.

Untitled: What's circus in a name? : 3981.

Untitled: When whole town talk bout Bad Boy : 3784.

Untitled: When you begin to stumble on the simplest of words : 2373, 5972.

Untitled: Whenever he described to me this park, this pathway : 665, 4048.

Untitled: Where does the slave woman's face : 2420.

Untitled: Who will bear witness to these times : 665, 4048.

Untitled: Why did the oxymoron cross the road? : 3118.

Untitled: Woman in a sailor suit : 4838.

Untitled Work in Progress : 3006.

Untitled: Would proof lie none sweet : 5370.

Untitled: Xiomara, she treats me well : 2049.

Untitled: You can tell a lot about a country by its Madonna : 6786.

Untitled: You drew me under yards of bad luck : 4645.

Unto You a Cube Is Given : 546.

The Untold : 5200.

Untreated Condition : 4608.

Untrue : 5874.

Unwitnessed Nightfall : 3556.

Up : 3570.

Up All Night : 6232.

Up from the Metro into Fire : 350.

Up-Helly-A : 1647.

Up-Hill : 5658.

Up in the Attic Madonna : 3822.

Up Periscope : 6225.

Up River on a Hot Summernite : 6571.

Updraft : 3676.

Uphill Battle : 2300.

Uphill Struggle : 3177.

Upon a Confessional Poet : 1055.

Upon Cobblestones : 203, 5331.

Upon Finding in a Volume of William Blake a Card Pledging Love Forever from an Ex-Lover : 7263.

Upon Hearing of My Friend's Marriage Breaking Up : 7283.

Upon Hearing of the Death of Y-Bham Enuol, a 'Fulro' Leader : 54.

Upon Looking into Sylvia Plath's Letters Home : 6740.

Upon My Mother's Death : 2521.
Upon Receiving a Fan Letter Asking Me to Explain One of My Poems : 6763.
Upon Splitting with the Last Woman : 838.
Upper Westside Commerce : 5599.
Upside Down in the Rafters : 5256.
The Upstaging of a Coastal Sunset : 489.
Upstairs at the Copernican Revolution : 2152.
Upstate : 466.
Ur-Valentine? : 160, 5971, 7104.
Urban Chivalry : 4520.
Urban Love : 2264.
An Urban Myth : 4234.
Urban Sketch : 1199.
The Urban Stream : 860.
Urinals : 4753.
U.S. Buried Iraqi Soldiers Alive in Gulf War : 3772.
Use : 72.
The Use of Wrens : 5686.
Used Books : 3247.
Used to Be : 3184.
Used to This Kind of Heat : 4238.
Uses of the Past : 1514.
Utility Pole : 4396.
V-Girls : 1496.
Vacation Bible School : 357.
Vagina Dentata : 7359.
The Vainglorious Present : 5835.
Valdosta : 4598.
Valentine : 1505, 4040, 4415, 6587.
Valentine at Fifty : 26.
Valentines : 1052.
Valentine's Day, 1991 : 5906.
Valentine's Day After Watching Too Much Television the Night Before : 6934.
Les Valeurs Personnelles : 920.
Value : 517.
Valyermo, St. Andrew's : 1207, 1871.
A Vampire Song : 3509.
Van Gogh's 'Undergrowth with Two Figures' : 7224.
Vanilla's Fragrance, Peppermint's Scent : 1143, 4837, 4949.
A Vanished House : 2350.
Vanishing Point : 908.
Vanitas : 3519.
Vanity : 1739, 3191.
Vantage Point : 3974.
Vantage Point in Light : 2109.
Variation and Centrifugue on 'No Love, No Nothin'' (or, Cole Porter, Ethel Merman, Where Are You?) : 6218.
Variation on a Theme : 1608.
Variations : 436, 1076, 1968.
Variations on a Theme by May Swenson : 1924.
Variations on a Variation by Stevens : 2909.
Variations on the First Elegy : 6481.
Variations on the Trapped Theme : 6329.
The Various Reasons of Light : 217.
Vasectomy : 6226.
Vast Problem Still Obscure : 6841.
Vathi : 4263.
Vaudeville, 1916 : 5783.
Vegetable Calendar : 2293, 5515.

Vehicle : 1660.
Vei auzi din nou: fii inima mea : 4219.
Veinna, Ohio : 4165.
Vel par Krokodiliem : 4652.
La Vela Olvidada : 4166.
Velada : 2404.
Velazquez' Venus Makes Her Position Clear : 6532.
Vellum (Ireland) : 5813.
Velvet Dips : 6555.
Vendor of Sweets : 40.
Venera : 5607.
Venetian Blinds : 5043.
Venetian Nights : 2552.
The Venetian Optician : 7321.
Venetian Way : 3293.
Vengo con el Sudor de Mis Manos : 330.
Venice : 2300, 5274, 6055, 7196.
Venice Wind-Catchers : 1857.
Venn Logic : 5663.
Il Vento Ha Fame : 3603.
Ventura's Visits : 5744.
Venus After Dark : 7242.
The Veranda : 5745.
Verbal : 766.
Verdell's Morning Constitutional : 3920.
Verisimilitudes : 5787.
Vermilion Rain : 4038.
Vermont House : 374.
Vernal Vernacular : 6003.
Vérollay : 5438.
Veronica : 3460.
Verses : 100, 1096, 6465.
Versions : 1491, 1774.
Versions of Shakespeare : 5547.
Versons (of You) : 3712.
Vertical : 7353.
Vertical City : 5813.
Vertigo : 2277, 3136, 4925, 6537.
Vertigo: A Letter from San Francisco : 2912.
Verum, Fama, tibi vultum pictura notavit : 3962.
Very : 3460.
The Very Large Telescope : 6841.
The Very Old Woman with Total Recall : 6330.
Very Red : 2757.
A Very Short Story : 4392.
Vespers : 5364.
Vesuvius : 7270.
The Veteran : 1952.
Veteran — WWII : 4301.
Vetting : 2909.
Via del Tritone : 6076.
Vice : 7142.
Vice Squad : 3870.
Victim : 4293.
The Victim : 5230.
Victorian Cemetery : 3236.
Victorian Women : 5923.
Victory Towels : 2987.
La Vida al Contado : 2337.
Video : 6937.
Viendo : 4164.
Vienna in New Orleans, 1940 : 3489.
View : 1738, 6300.

The View : 6123.
The View from Home : 7063.
The View from My Lawyer's Office : 7095.
View from the Dream House : 3947.
A View from the Highway : 1653.
A View from the Truckstop : 6709.
A View, in Lieu of Valentines : 5460.
A View of the Firmament : 6625.
A View of the Water : 3541.
Views : 129.
Vigil : 852, 921, 1852, 5746.
The Vigil : 5219.
Vigil for the Disappeared (Los Disparecidos) : 3634.
Vigil Strange : 6457.
Vigilancia : 5063.
Vigilia : 925.
Vilanelle: Procrustes Explains : 5146.
Vill-ah-nelling: thrivin' on a Riff : 958.
Villa That Made Us Clairvoyant : 5792.
Village at Dusk : 6403.
The Village Claws to Its Feet : 898.
Village: Kahuku-Mura : 2932.
Village of the Mermaids : 4158.
The Village of the Mermaids : 6055.
Village Women : 5568.
A Villanelle : 1668.
Villefranche : 3662.
Vilnius. Archaeology : 2095, 6127, 6747.
Vincent (Edna St Vincent Millay) : 3822.
Vincent's Prayer : 1535.
The Vine : 285.
Vinegar and Oil : 3092, 4633.
Vineyard : 362, 363, 2483, 4083.
Vingt-et-un : 1412.
Vinnie Died Last Night : 3740.
Vintages : 5265.
Violence : 362.
Violencia : 455.
Violent Mercy : 841.
Violet : 6262.
The Violin Mark : 6121.
Violinists in the Snow : 6513.
Vipunen's Gift : 4464.
Viral Surgery : 4173.
La Virgen de la Paz : 1226.
Virgil to Dante : 4982.
Virgin Tributaries : 709.
Virginia Murray : 4782.
Virginia Woolf : 5783.
A Virgual Incarnation : 3890.
Virsil for an Urchin : 5376.
Virtual Reality : 722.
The Virtue of Poesy : 4105.
A Virus Named AIDS : 1488, 5123.
The Visible World : 4660.
Vision : 442, 4979, 5804, 6185, 7166, 7235.
A Vision : 2268.
The Vision : 1996.
Vision in the Ice Cream Parlor : 4730.
A Vision of Two Lovers : 6357.
Vision Through a White Stone : 7372.
Visiones de San Narciso : 2534.
Visions : 721.
Visions of Marthe Bonnard : 1622.
Visions of Saint Narcissus : 2534, 2900.

Visit : 985.
A Visit : 4596.
The Visit : 1458, 1614.
A Visit from Hurricane Bob : 4986.
The Visit: November 22, 1990 : 1396.
A Visit to Qin Dynasty Terracottas : 7300.
A Visit to the Cathedral : 151.
A Visit to the Mayo Clinic : 1579.
Visit to the New York Museum of Modern Art : 5143.
Visitation : 862, 5343, 6844.
Visitations : 2972.
Visitations. Shields in the sky : 2815.
Visiting an Aunt in New York : 3379.
Visiting Edwin : 5265.
Visiting Hours : 4199.
Visiting Jonah : 4195.
Visiting My Father's Grave : 5115.
Visiting the Henry Ford Estate, July, 1991 : 1534.
A Vision : 3034.
A Visitor : 3673.
The Visitor : 3793, 4655.
Visitor from Overseas : 625.
Visitors : 1880, 3275, 5265.
The Visitors : 6439.
La Vita Nuova : 1406, 2108, 2108, 2108.
The Vital Knot : 6871.
Vital Signs : 5751.
Vivid : 5517.
Vivisection : 3305.
Vocabularies : 7013.
Vocabularies of Space : 4764.
Vocabulary Builders : 2833.
Vocabulary Lesson : 5462.
A Voice : 4053.
The Voice : 993, 3219, 5020, 6154.
Voice from the Cage : 6076.
The Voice of the Miller Cries Out : 4328.
Voice on the Train Out of Grand Central : 1214.
Voice Out of the Void : 838.
The Voice Singing in the Gardens : 3224, 3619.
Voiceover : 7177.
Voices : 375, 5814, 6521, 7273, 7317.
The Voices : 1055.
Voices of America : 2878.
Voices of the Fathers : 3212.
Voices Over the River : 3833.
Voir Dire : 5045.
Volcanic Holiday : 4411.
Volkswagen on Calle Cerra : 4175.
Voluntary on a Flight of Angels : 4018.
Volunteer : 5088.
Voodoo Sonata : 6063.
Voodoo Summer Job : 4489.
Voracities and Verities Sometimes Are Interacting : 4575.
Voracity : 5469.
Voting for Elvis : 3702.
Vows : 4377.
Voyage : 3247, 6431.
The Voyage of the *Moonlight* : 1112.
Voyager : 3206.
The Voyager : 3451.

Voyages : 26.
The Voyeur : 6198.
Voyeurism : 1135.
Vues de Près : 1530.
The Vulcan's Mirror : 1350.
The Vulgar Materialist : 4578.
Vulnerability : 442, 1961, 5804.
Vultures : 2474.
W.A.S.P., White Anglo-Saxon Protestant : 7202.
W.C.W. : 1284.
W Drodze : 5037.
W.E.B. DuBois : 4470.
Waders and Swimmers : 5214.
The Wailing of the Hundred Million : 5814, 6521.
Waimanalo : 7255.
Wait : 6687.
Wait! : 3049, 4941.
The Wait : 6495.
Waiters and Geopolitics : 5042.
Waiting : 1503, 2566, 4066, 6300.
Waiting at the Coronet : 4409.
Waiting for a Double Espresso in the King Street Coffeehouse : 5550.
Waiting for a Friend : 4936.
Waiting for a Heart : 1968.
Waiting for a Wind : 3084, 4720, 7044.
Waiting for Heraclitis : 373.
Waiting for Kafka : 3109.
Waiting for the Archduke : 3848.
Waiting for the Barbarians : 1019, 3329, 6017.
Waiting for the Breath of God : 250.
Waiting for the Bus : 2678.
Waiting for the Electric Train to Leningrad : 2808.
Waiting for the Messiah in Somerville, Mass : 1063.
Waiting for the New Madrid Earthquake : 2867.
Waiting for the Paint to Dry : 4542.
Waiting for the Palagi : 3991.
Waiting for the Phone : 868.
Waiting for the Telephone Repairman to Show : 5069.
Waiting for Tu Fu : 7222.
The Waiting Game : 3846.
Waiting in the Car for My Father at the Youngstown Sheet & Tube : 1783.
The Waitress at the Day and Night : 5726.
The Wake : 3520, 3840.
The Wake After Maxie's Funeral : 4668.
Wakefulness : 3520.
The Waker's Loss : 4361.
Waking at Night : 6429.
A Waking Call : 3367.
Waking Differently : 2222.
Waking in Intensive Care : 1133.
Waking Life : 5829.
Waking to Makaleha : 6527.
Waking to Names of the Dead : 2561.
Waking Up : 6629.
Waking Up in New Jersey : 5762.
Waley, Waley : 6960.
The Walk : 1244, 1596.

A Walk in the City : 2331.
A Walk in the Fall : 5796.
A Walk in the Woods : 6093.
A Walk on a Country Road 16 Miles Northeast of Iowa City : 2297.
A Walk on the Beach with Hitler : 2395.
Walkers : 4417.
Walking : 1355, 3054, 5898.
The Walking After the Riding After the Shouting : 6631.
Walking Around Walden Pond : 459.
Walking Back to Sackville : 6037.
Walking Basil : 1269.
Walking by the Lion's Den Adult Theater and Bookstore, Sister Mary Appassionata Experiences the Stigmata : 1122.
Walking Estero : 7208.
Walking Home : 654, 1119.
Walking in Monet's Gardens at Giverny : 1332.
Walking in the Oakland Hills After the October Fire : 1876.
Walking In, Watching You : 6232.
Walking on Hollister Avenue After the Rain : 1350.
Walking on Worms : 433.
The Walking Sun : 1258.
Walking the Alley : 2653.
Walking, thumb-sucking within fluid, the self is set against blankness : 5822.
Walking to an Eight O'Clock Class : 3114.
Walking to My Office on Easter Sunday Morning : 6528.
Walking to School : 2521.
Walking to the Pond : 1297.
Walking Trees : 3106.
Walking Until You Come Home : 4409.
Walking with Blackie : 4291, 7314.
Walking with Donna Near Del Mar : 5884.
Walking with Jeanne : 6440.
The Wall : 6626.
Wall Cycle : 5308.
The wall needs paper or a painting : 716.
The Wall of Remembrance : 2521.
Wall/paper : 625.
Wall Street : 1401.
Walled Garden : 6742.
Walls : 1019, 6397, 6917, 7358.
The Walls : 7137.
Walls Mating : 5311.
Walls of Discovery : 4959.
The Walnuts : 6309.
Walt Kuhn's *Gourds*, 1937 : 3877.
Walt Whitman, AIDS Worker : 1436.
Walt Whitman Called Today : 4827.
Walt Whitman in Hell : 3023.
Walt Whitman Mall : 1743.
Walt Whitman: 'Whispers of Heavenly Death Murmur'd I Hear!' : 1103.
Walt Whitman's Sunday with the Insane : 1371.
Walter : 5069.
Walter Anderson in Mississippi : 6174.
Walter Parmer : 7123.
A Waltz Dream : 214.
Wanderer Gone West : 2181.

Want : 3651.
Want, Part Six : 6631.
Wanting : 4668.
Wanting It : 6228.
Wanting to Be Like God : 2302.
Wanting to Enter : 6551.
War : 2578, 6434.
The War : 3490.
The War Against Irony : 6436.
War Dancing : 1399.
War Is Hell : 6169.
War Song : 5110.
War Story : 6400.
Warblers : 4900.
Warcry vs. Blowjobcry : 172.
Wariant Villanelle for Two Voices : 5132.
Warm Enough : 1924.
Warm fuzzy phrases : 7357.
Warm living room rug : 4277.
Warm Wood : 4739.
Warning : 3300, 6004.
The Warning : 5589.
Warning to the Reader : 604.
The Warning Track : 5787.
The Warrior : 4013.
The Wars of Faery : 3734.
Warsaw at Night : 6935.
Warsaw Pediatrics 1939 : 2338.
Was I Ever Welcomed? To the Womb : 1324.
A Wash : 4704.
Wash, Early Monday : 7096.
Washday : 4668.
Washerwoman's Song : 7359.
Washing Beans : 2139.
Washing Clothes : 667.
Washing My Hair in the Platte : 5752.
Washing Out Lingerie : 7008.
Washing the Dead : 3468.
Washing Windows and Writing : 4226.
Washing Your Body : 5803.
Washing Your Hair : 6369.
Washington — 6288 Ft : 6378.
Washington DC, 1990 : 1694.
The Washita : 2476.
W.A.S.P., White Anglo-Saxon Protestant :
    7202.
Wasp's Sting : 5931.
The Wastebin : 3676.
The Watch : 3633.
Watch for Deer : 6970.
The Watcher : 907.
Watcher at the Cross : 6073.
The Watchers : 645.
Watches : 7095.
Watching for Tlaloc to Cool the Sun : 1163.
Watching My Father Look at *Playboy* : 1095.
Watching Peter Arnett Report from Baghdad
    : 5010.
Watching Something Like a Documentary on
    Ed Sullivan : 3703.
Watching the Equinox Arrive in
    Charlottesville, September 1992 : 7222.
Watching the Moon with My Husband :
    7167.
Watching Them Ride the Rides : 7307.
Watchman : 3523, 3745, 6195, 6196, 6506.

Watchtower : 6449.
Water : 493, 4826, 5369, 6729.
Water, Air, Fire, Earth : 265.
Water and Light : 6242.
Water Babies : 2775.
Water Bears No Scars : 2939.
The Water Breather : 7073.
The Water Diamonds : 2869.
The Water Dog : 79.
Water Images : 4943.
The Water of Light : 1093.
Water Striders : 3367.
Water Through Rock : 2344.
The Water Tower : 4088.
Water Witch : 7119.
Watercolors : 5636.
The Watercress Gatherer : 6382.
Waterfall : 1065, 6105, 7221.
Watering Impatiens : 2737.
Watering Place : 6929.
Watering the Horses : 2657.
Waterlines : 5602.
Waterloo : 979.
The Waterman's Children : 472.
Watermeldon Tales : 4195.
Watermelons : 4016.
Watermusic : 1446, 6432.
Waterworks : 567.
The Waterworld : 4073.
Waunfawr and After / 'The Collar Work
    Begins' : 2676.
Wave & Particle : 1892.
Waves : 5231.
The Waves Roll In : 7242.
Waving Goodbye : 2948.
The Waving Lady : 3545.
Waving to Hart Crane : 25.
Waxing : 1526.
The Way : 3300.
The Way Between Them : 3301.
The Way Extends : 1548.
The Way He Breaks : 900.
The Way I Always Like It : 5555.
The Way I Do It : 6299.
The Way It Is : 6244.
The Way of All the Earth : 6107.
The Way of Examples, II : 5673, 6871.
The Way of Geese : 1024.
The Way of Stories : 5673, 6871.
The Way of the Impossible : 5673, 6871.
The Way Sun Keeps Falling Away from
    Every Window : 3822.
The way to keep your body thin : 1798.
The Way We Live : 1831, 6871.
The Way We Love : 6343.
Ways of Seeing : 5882.
Ways to Give Way : 2285.
Wayward Ballerina : 3184.
W.C.W. : 1284.
We : 3805, 4958, 6492.
We all go with the flow : 3256, 5638.
We All Knew Garbo Would One Day Die :
    231.
We Are Gathered Here : 3901.
We Are the Dinosaur : 2920.
We Assume : 2636.

We Belong Together : 3298.
We Buried the Salamander : 5580.
We Entitled : 5505.
We Gypsies : 1794.
We have here no one and you are welcome : 4025.
We honor our love in the breach : 4609.
We Lay Down Worlds : 6929.
We Left Our Work : 6444.
We may not have always been masters of ourselves : 6040.
We punted on the Hellespont : 7054.
We row the johnboat : 2736.
We Sat in Open Fields : 4227.
We, the Dangerous : 4513.
We Think the Heart Can Hold Most Anything : 4305.
We Thought of Each Other as Food : 424.
We walked on nights after work : 2577.
We Want One to Fall : 3022.
We Wear Each Other's Levis : 923.
We Who In : 4812.
Weak Anthropic Principle : 6120.
Weaknesses : 5064.
Wear and Tear : 2925.
Wearing a Human Face : 2231.
Weather : 2818, 6493.
The Weather : 4877, 7212.
Weather and Turtles : 214.
Weather Central : 3510.
The Weather in My Heart, the Articulate Region Where I live, the Map of the Rain : 6147.
The weather is fair, but to not quiver is an unravelling of all yesses : 1268, 6683.
The Weather of the Game : 4264.
Weather or Bruise : 5144.
Weather over the Lake : 5089.
Weather Report : 6927.
Weathering : 1764.
The Web : 1371.
W.E.B. DuBois : 4470.
Wedding : 805.
The Wedding : 2869.
Wedding Anniversary : 1204, 3700.
Wedding Dress : 7219.
Wedding in a Lost Republic : 1102.
Wedding Morning, September 1970 : 1293.
Wedding Photo : 4038.
Wedding Psalm : 4141.
Wedding Song : 442, 5804.
A Wedding Toast : 521.
The Wedge : 4600.
Wednesday : 2756, 3329, 5921.
Wednesdays : 847.
Wednesday's Truth : 6010.
Weed : 2298.
Weed in Drought : 1893.
Weeds Happen : 2595.
Weehawken Once : 4236.
A Week Before Christmas : 953.
The Week the Dog Went Blind : 6788.
The Weekly Loaf : 4820.
Weep : 3024.
Weeper : 6250.
The Weepers : 4732.

Weeping Waters / Vai Tangi : 3318.
Weighed down by his bags, gray whiskers on his chin : 665, 4048.
The Weighing : 2869.
Weight : 2455.
The Weight : 2441.
The Weight Guesser : 479.
The Weight of the Earth : 649, 5929.
Weimar II : 324.
Weird Sisters : 228.
Welcome : 4309, 5621.
Welcome Back : 435.
Welcome Hardings' Clocks & Music Boxes : 5207.
Welcome Home : 1309.
Welcome, President Clinton : 6690.
A Welcome Song for Laini Nzinga : 769.
Welcome to America : 2061.
Welcoming All Comers : 1067, 7342.
The Welder : 1202, 4496.
Welfare Diet : 1323.
The Well : 3270, 7327.
Well, Fame, the Painting Is : 423, 3962.
Well, Son, We Could Always Throw the Pigskin Around : 262.
We'll Understand It All By and By : 4313.
Weltschmerz : 5358.
We're All Angels Under the Skin : 505.
West End Girl : 2124.
West Oakland Somniloquy : 6470.
The West of Ireland : 5092.
West Point : 6864.
West Texas : 4282.
West Then East : 386.
The West Window : 4417.
Western Hemlock : 2023.
Western Movie : 2047.
Westwego : 5858, 6245.
Wet : 6852.
Wet Autumn Night : 3096.
Wet Basement: an Elegy : 4667.
Wet Cellar : 6629.
Wet Rocks : 88.
Wetbacks cross the Rio Grande : 7054.
Whale Watch Madonna : 3822.
The Whales : 5199.
What a Comet Is : 4759.
What a Gas It Was : 3273.
What a Hooting Glory, the Geese Alanding : 6944.
What a Kick Feels Like : 598.
What am I going to do with all the years : 5585.
What Am I to Do With : 4392.
What Amelia Taught Me : 1193.
What Are We? : 4848.
What Are Years? : 4575.
What Can Be More Useless Than Happiness? : 5164.
What Children Eat : 3423.
What City : 4212.
What Could Happen : 3683.
What Daffodils Don't Need to Hear : 4018.
What Death with Love Must Have to Do : 2202.
What Difference Does It Make? : 5753.

What Do I Say About Marriages? : 3983.
What Do Women Want? : 5770.
What Do You See There, Brother : 3263, 5736.
What Does She See in Him : 3877.
What Doesn't Happen : 2446.
What Exactly Is a Valvis? : 6763.
What Fish Signify : 6131.
What Flashes Before You : 7159.
What Follows the Death of Your Body : 6276.
What Gave Me Away? : 4796.
What Goes On : 3890.
What Happens Next : 4528.
What Hawks Know : 3976.
What He Knows : 1017.
What He Said When His Wife Asked Him to Mow the Lawn : 6850.
What I Am Saying : 1498.
What I Could Be : 2714.
What I Did : 1392.
What I did as a boy was cowboy, really : 1836.
What I Did on a Rainy Day : 6493.
What I Have Been : 5513.
What I Have Remembered : 882.
What I Hear at the Worm's Campfire: The Greybeard's Story : 3858.
What I Knew : 3442.
What I Know : 3039.
What I Mean by His Bones : 4197.
What I Missed When I Left Before Summer : 505.
What I Say, Perhaps, Isn't True : 214, 4171.
What I See : 1701.
What I Thought I Loved : 7283.
What I Used to Think About, Looking Out the Window As a Little Kid : 1309.
What I Wanted to Be to You : 7062.
What If? : 6852.
What If Lot Says, 'All Right : 6321.
What Is a Man? : 296.
What Is In a Canadian Boy's Blood : 2154.
What Is Invisible : 1342.
What Is Kept : 2441.
What Is Left to Tell : 5239.
What Is Next? : 4386.
What Is to Be Done? : 6682.
What It Comes Down To : 4483.
What It's All About : 3662.
What It's Like : 328.
What It's Like to Be an Angel : 2254.
What I've Done with Your 'Nocturne' : 5944.
What Kinds of Times Are These : 5490.
What Left : 5465.
What Might Be Called Burning : 3911.
What Morning Does He Wish for Still : 143, 3786.
What Mother's Weather : 801.
What Mr. Ambidextrine Was Told at Confession at the 31st St. Shrine : 6586.
What My Mother Left : 4966.
What My Son's Haricut Taught Me About Flying : 5955.
What Myth Is : 5162.
What Obstructs Literature : 1104, 4178.

What of This Jesus : 419.
What one hears when the soul : 3119, 5861.
What Pisses Me Off : 4854.
What Praise Escapes the Night : 20.
What Profits : 4687.
What Remains : 2050.
What Ripens Quickly : 4113.
What Scared Me As a Boy Was Not My Sex : 5912.
What She Can Control : 268.
What She Knows : 3871.
What She Tells Herself Before Dialing the Number She Never Has to Look Up : 5178.
What Should I Do? : 6247.
What Should I Write about Today? : 5069.
What Sins, Now : 5555.
What Some People Won't Do : 1148.
What Stays : 3007.
What the British Bluez Boyz Dream : 4924.
What the City Was Like : 6544.
What the Clouds, the Sky, the Sun, and the Sea Taught Me : 3253.
What the Cook Said : 5162.
What the Fast Girl Knows : 2305.
What the Lecturer Showed Us : 1966.
What the Sea Turtle Said : 3026, 5802.
What the Stars Owe Me : 6247.
What the Wastebasket Tells : 1999.
What the Water Knows : 2576.
What the Widowers Will Say When the Words Turn to Ice : 3324.
What the Window Cleaner Thought : 5942.
What There Is : 1840.
What They Don't Know : 4080, 6558.
What They Really Meant : 6377.
What They Wanted : 412.
What They've Come Up With : 2899.
What They've Let Me See : 927.
What to Do When You Can't Control Anything : 926.
What to Do with a World : 5673, 6871.
What to Listen for in Music : 1696.
What Was Indigo Then Is Kudzu Now : 3969.
What Was Lost : 4950.
What We Fear Most : 5050.
What We Forgot : 3871.
What We Made a Long While Back a Certain Acquaintance Wishes Me to Do Again : 1346, 2986.
What We Whistle While We Work : 2800.
What Wilderness Tells You : 5792.
What Woman Wants : 924.
What Would It Have Been? : 3292, 6334.
What You Do and What You Say : 4610.
What You Do Not Know : 3551.
What You Don't Need : 5229.
What You Don't See : 5848.
What You Don't See Is There : 177.
What you hear could be a mountain : 5113.
What you hear is one winter : 5113.
What You Need : 6299.
What You Remember About Natural Disasters : 505.

What You Want Means What You Can
    Afford : 633.
Whatever Happened to Cyprus? : 6690.
Whatever Hidden Drummers : 296.
Whatever It Was : 5279.
What'll You Give Me For It? : 6172.
What's a Shook Slicker Bridge? : 5642.
What's circus in a name? : 3981.
What's in a Locker? : 2611.
What's in it For Me : 3851.
What's Required Is : 6275.
What's This Love : 3302, 6249.
Wheat : 4133.
Wheel : 5011, 6078.
Wheelbarrow : 6976.
The Wheelchair : 6581.
When a Woman's Hair Catches Fire : 2583.
When big daddy Chronos : 3218.
When Bitterness Is All We Have : 6509.
When Blackbirds and Shadows Traverse the
    Night : 6639.
When Borges Dreamed : 6606.
When Death Comes : 4900.
When Dexter Ran Away : 5567.
When Did the Dream Scrotum Darken : 43.
When Earth Brings : 5468.
When Eye Was a Child : 5788.
When Fat Girls Dream : 2522.
When Girls See Me for the First Time : 5632.
When Grad Prof Swears : 2409.
When Grandfather Tours the Countryside :
    1493.
When He Was Dead : 6436.
When I Am at Uncle Buddy's Grave : 3833.
When I Come Home : 3497.
When I Consider How My Light Is Spent :
    4502.
When I Cracked His Teeth Out with a Frilly
    Victorian Lamp by the Bedside He
    Suddenly Remembered Where His
    Wallet Was : 5211.
When I Have Fears : 3326.
When I Really Dream : 6756.
When I Say the Moon Is a Boat : 699.
When I Socially Interact with All of My Sick
    Friends : 7135.
When I was a young man on the Ganges
    banks : 1192.
When I Was Young : 2552.
When in Public : 5350.
When It Happens : 1110.
When It Is Over, When It Has Gotten to Be :
    1324.
When It Rains : 1537, 1538, 5399, 7221.
When Kingship Descended from Heaven :
    536.
When Light Falls : 2059.
When Living Was a Labor Camp Called
    Montgomery : 2170.
When Louanne Gave a Haircut : 2597.
When McCorkle Is Working on the Rail :
    1276.
When Mongols crossed the River Ob : 3624.
When My Father Goes Down : 4831.
When Our Women Go Crazy : 3299.
When she is born : 3290.

When She Moves Beside Me : 4017.
When She Stitched the Flag : 4283.
When She Used to Be Pretty : 4759.
When Spring Finally Came, After a Terrible
    Winter: A Watercolor : 2254.
When That : 5572.
When that I was and a little tiny boy : 3732.
When the Angel Finally Came Down : 5555.
When the Beat Comes Back : 7128.
When the Birds Spoke Greek : 1342.
When the Body Speaks to the Heart It Says :
    7292.
When the earthquake hit : 4133.
When the Last Beatle Dies : 7176.
When the Lord God Gathered Up the Spirit
    of Virginia Woolf : 2965.
When the Moon Drifts Away : 1799.
When the Muse Is Absent : 4578.
When the Outside Gets In : 2136.
When the Snow Falls in Summer : 4289.
When the snow stopped falling : 3119, 5861.
When the strong ventriloquist crumbles :
    1476.
When the Unimaginable Becomes Easy :
    855.
When the Vision Comes : 4398.
When the Young Husband : 2552.
When There's Pause : 742.
When Things End Sometimes They Go Back
    to the Beginning : 1845.
When This Land Was Ours : 4099.
When We Discovered : 1169.
When We First Felt Our Minds : 7343.
When We Pass : 6123.
When We Were Children : 1525, 1948.
When whole town talk bout Bad Boy : 3784.
When word came about christ's return : 2389.
When you begin to stumble on the simplest
    of words : 2373, 5972.
When You Died Willie : 2983.
When You Read This Poem Out Loud,
    Someone Will Call You an Ugly Bitter
    Bitch : 5883.
When You Were Fifteen : 3311.
When Your Teenager Lacks Ambition :
    5505.
Whenever he described to me this park, this
    pathway : 665, 4048.
Where Are the Boyscouts When You Need
    Them? : 948.
Where Books Come In : 5568.
Where Divinity Begins : 1511.
Where Do You Get Your Ideas From? : 1263.
Where does the slave woman's face : 2420.
Where Does This Gladness Come From? :
    3900.
Where I Come From : 3529, 6629.
Where I Found It First : 5410.
Where I Live : 4150.
Where I Look : 3739.
Where I Pray : 2053.
Where Is Cinderella When I Need Her? :
    4259.
Where It All Began : 4425.
Where It Is and the Colorless Rainbow :
    4153.

Where It's At : 4174.
Where Last I Saw You : 4399.
Where Names Come From : 7215.
Where the Delta Ends : 4472.
Where the doctor may see a brilliant
 technique : 2514.
Where the Heron Goes : 3895.
Where the Raspberries Grow : 5199.
Where the Scars : 1383.
Where the Sky Used to Be : 2468.
Where the Stars Disintegrate : 582.
Where the Train Carries You : 7031.
Where the Wisecracks Grow : 3877.
Where time imitates a solid line : 5673, 6871.
Where Was I? : 6247.
Where When Was : 6012.
Where Would You Want the Rail? : 2058.
Wherein Wife Urges Sale of Gun : 4839.
where's Jack Was : 1353.
Where's My Money : 4229.
Wherever You Go : 2714.
Whether or Not the First Snow Appears on
 Mount Sighignola : 5660, 5810.
Whether the Thing in Nature Speaks to You
 or Not : 7148.
Which Do You Prefer : 494.
While crossing the Styx I could tell : 5126.
While Eating a Pear : 1204.
While Emily : 4992.
While He Leaves : 3780.
While the River Is Wide : 5604.
While Trading Clothes in a Rest Stop
 Bathroom : 2173.
While Unity Lasts : 100, 6428, 6465.
While Waiting to Audition for the Role of
 Ben Stone in Law and Order : 4603.
While walking softly within these walls :
 2764.
While We Watch : 2095.
While Working : 5480.
Whim : 6867.
Whirligigs : 2789.
Whirlybird Ride : 5150.
Whiskey : 3716.
Whispering Through Ice : 2787.
White : 2214, 6147.
White Birch : 1838.
White Blossoms : 3866.
White Bread : 948.
White Buffalo Calf Woman's Spirit : 4606.
The White Buildings on Shea's Hill : 1632.
The White Butterfly : 5384.
White Cabs Connect the Dots All Over Town
 : 3463.
White Cardamom : 6858.
White Christmas : 3167.
White Chrysanthemums : 2606, 6984.
White City : 926.
The White City : 6154.
White Cotton Bed Sheets : 3151.
White Crane : 7283.
The White Cup : 2962.
White duck frozen in the river's edge : 3189.
White Flower of Wild Blackberry : 4931.
White Flower, White Flower : 1294.
White Fog : 5889.

The White Helmet : 2562.
White Herons : 536.
The White Horse : 6309.
White Knight, Knave of Hearts : 5897.
White Lips : 5491.
White Lungs : 577.
The White Meal : 4820.
White Morning : 4417.
White Musk : 1383.
The White Narcissus : 211.
White Nightmare : 2632.
White Oaks Ascending : 5214.
White on White : 1305, 4100, 4148.
White Owl Flies Into and Out of the Field :
 4900.
White People : 1404.
White Picket Fence : 2712.
The White Rainbow : 5522.
White Rest : 3993, 5807.
The White Room : 4106.
A White Rose in a Blizzard : 149.
White Sale : 4002.
A White Shawl : 670.
White Sheets : 4151.
The White Ship of My Heart : 6147.
White Space : 2322.
White-Tailed Deer : 5345.
White Tiger and the Mosquitos : 3816.
White Tigers : 5518.
The White Tulips : 2072, 7161.
White Water : 6963.
Whitemarsh Graveyard : 536.
The Whiteness of Death : 299, 843.
Whiteout: The Disappearance of
 Impossibilities : 5606.
Whitman Visits the Armory Square Hospital
 : 2313.
Whitsunday in St. Nicholas' Cathedral : 3547,
 5638.
Who? : 6690.
Who Am I, Among These, She Asked, a
 One-Time Lover : 1324.
Who Burns for the Perfection of Paper :
 1838.
Who Cares for the Blind Stork : 442, 1584,
 5804.
Who could, paid : 5638, 7026.
Who Do We Have Here? : 995.
Who Fell : 1695.
Who Flies, Who Swims : 400.
Who Is She Beyond : 3593.
Who Is the Novice in This Poem and What Is
 She Doing Here? : 4168.
Who It Is : 4417.
Who Knows : 4191.
Who Knows Where It Comes From? : 3281.
Who Knows Who She Was : 188, 2381.
Who Malingers, Who Mimes : 5487.
Who Needs Men When You've Got a Fast
 Car : 6101.
Who Still Needs Find Stories? : 2984, 3186.
Who They Were : 6992.
Who We Are Now : 3620.
Who will bear witness to these times : 665,
 4048.
The Whole Idea : 4581.

The Whole Time : 1449.
Whore : 5652.
Who's There : 766.
Who's Who in the East : 2800.
Whose Eyes : 625.
Whose Move : 4314.
Whose Performance Am I Watching? : 3248.
Why : 7178.
Why? : 3677.
Why Chicken Places Give Me Nightmares :
 4202.
Why did the oxymoron cross the road? :
 3118.
Why I Became a Pacifist : 3244.
Why I Don't Drive a Car : 2792.
Why I Don't Drive a New Car : 1644.
Why I Hate Earth Day : 4179.
Why I Like to Eat Red Meat : 1747.
Why I Scrawled on the Back of This Photo
 the Words 'Late Autumn Sunfall 1979'
 — : 5720.
Why I Seldom Read Newspapers : 5431.
Why I Sometimes Sing the Songs I Hated As
 a Child : 4969.
Why I Think About Hiroshima & Nagasaki :
 1648.
Why John Sanderson Won't Go Back To
 Where He Came From or Anywhere
 Else : 7175.
Why Little Red Riding Hood Couldn't
 Happen Today : 6735.
Why Men Won't Ask for Directions : 7336.
Why, on a Bad Day, I Can Relate to the
 Manatee : 1703.
Why So Many Forms : 575, 6087.
Why There Is a Talking Sea Lion at the New
 England Aquarium : 380.
'Why,' They Asked Sir Edmund Hillary, 'Did
 You Want to Scale Mons Veneris?' :
 3877.
Why They Split : 2401.
Why We Are Truly a Nation : 4199.
Why We Bombed Hiroshima : 1534.
Why We Care About Quarks : 1966.
Why We Quit Having These Things in the
 First Place : 3846.
The Wicked Queen : 739.
Wicked Stepmother : 1847.
Wickerware : 4986.
Wide Icy River : 6042.
Widow : 4639.
Widow, 1 : 3963.
Widowed : 2371.
Widower and Son — 1926 : 4276.
The Widow's Desire : 4519.
Widow's Hole : 4420.
The Widows of Aflenz : 3364.
Widow's Walk : 1679.
Wife : 881.
The Wife in the Window, the Woman
 Bending in the Sun : 2731.
Wife of the Bath : 7305.
The Wife of the Man of Many Wiles : 6302.
Wife Poem : 979.
Wild : 2065.
Wild Apples : 6906.

Wild Blackberries : 2156.
Wild Card : 2324.
Wild Garlic : 5537.
Wild Horses : 4436.
Wild Iris and Tiger Lily : 275.
Wild Oats : 1749.
Wild Onions : 3541.
Wild Peavines : 4601.
Wild Strawberries : 1286.
Wild Strawberry Walkabout : 1320.
Wild Thing : 5805.
Wild Woman : 4406.
Wildebeest : 1392.
The Wilderness : 865.
Wildflowers : 1184.
Wilding : 1654.
Wildings, Lavenham : 2853.
Wile E. Love : 5900.
Will : 6432.
Will and Football : 981.
Will of a Rich Man : 5581, 5772.
The Will of Things in Appalachia : 5487.
Will the Circle Be Unbroken : 6432.
Will There Be No Great Thai Restaurants in
 a Hundred Years Time? : 3991.
Will Work for Food : 6927.
William McGonagall Meets Ogden Nash in
 Heaven : 4577.
William Pachner: View from a Passing Train
 : 4165.
William Wyncherly : 767.
Willie and I Discuss Myths of Sacrifice :
 4618.
Willie Two Hats Shot Down During a 7 -
 Eleven Robbery Dies : 54.
Willin' : 5227.
Willis' Fall : 5716.
Willow : 481, 482, 6272, 6731.
Willow Creek : 27.
Willow Tree : 6586.
Willow Ware : 1411.
Wind : 1, 493, 7001.
The Wind : 3591, 6159.
The Wind Is Hungry : 1927, 3603.
The Wind Picks Up : 5752.
Wind, Santa Anna : 975.
The Wind Still Breezes Your Name : 4054.
Windchime : 288.
Windfall : 1256.
Windfalls : 4816.
Window : 2978.
The Window : 2869, 5014, 5351, 5552, 7342.
Window in March : 6886.
Window in the Country, 1915 : 2400.
The Window in Wind : 3829.
Window Light : 2677.
The Window Man : 472.
Window Shopping : 5186.
The Window That Loves to Weep : 1725,
 2697, 3176.
Window with a Dozen Small Square Panes :
 3114.
Windowless Rooms : 1845.
Windows : 1765, 5621, 6284.
The Windows : 1370, 7342.
Windows facing north get no sun : 4960.

The Windows That Eyeball the Street : 1680.
Winds Becoming North : 6625.
Windsong?. Windpoem?. Whatever!!! :
     4280.
Windsurfing : 6222.
Windward : 5439.
Windy Day at Kabekona : 6180.
Wine : 214, 4171.
The Wine at Cana : 2202.
Wine Glass : 6782.
The Wing as Lever / Air as Fulcrum : 2470.
Wing Chou : 7051.
Winged Man : 3071.
Wings : 2021.
Wings & Bones, or, La Rigidité Cadavérique
     de l'Écriture — Derrida : 6253.
A Winking Eye : 6182.
Winners : 1881.
The Winners Inn : 3751.
Winning : 4483.
Winter : 1441, 1834.
Winter '65 : 2216.
Winter Afternoon : 4459.
Winter Afternoons : 2387, 5044.
Winter Berries : 2202.
Winter Break from College after My Father's
     Plane Crash : 2248.
Winter Cemetery: Annapolis : 3327.
The Winter Closet : 5953.
A Winter Evening : 1458, 6669.
The Winter Funerals : 6630.
Winter Gales in Orkney : 1647.
Winter Garden : 1383.
Winter Grapes : 3374.
Winter Ideology, 1986 : 5684, 5776.
Winter League Baseball : 644.
Winter, Leper of the World : 1892.
Winter Light : 2830, 4720, 7044.
A Winter Marriage : 1102.
Winter Morning : 7011.
Winter Night : 2521.
The Winter of No Money : 3300.
The Winter of Our Summer : 4792.
Winter on La Veta Pass : 1328.
Winter or Another Land : 4318.
A Winter Past : 1589, 5318.
Winter Rain Poem : 3319.
Winter Road : 2133, 6239.
Winter Run : 4913.
Winter sine Anno : 127, 274, 2240.
Winter Songs : 4239, 6201.
Winter Still Life : 1319.
Winter Storm : 2091.
The Winter That Succeeded : 1481.
Winter Trees : 7317.
Wintergrace : 5910.
Wintering : 571, 4950.
Winterkill : 2806.
Wipers on Full : 6463.
Wireless : 3846, 6630.
Wisdom : 4397, 4451, 6154, 7113.
The Wise : 2024.
Wise Choice : 6377.
Wise Guy : 2425.
Wisewoman : 3223.
Wishbone : 510.

Wishes : 2139.
Wisteria Floribunda : 5050.
The Witch : 686.
The Witch *Is* Dead : 6437.
The Witch's Tit : 1133.
With 28 Flavors, One Must Be Crow : 5103.
With a Baby in the Men's Locker Room :
     6343.
With a Month to Go : 3773.
With a Whimper : 1674.
With an Instinctive Certainty of the Charms
     of the Modish, 'for the Fairest' : 2829.
With Apologies to a Hitchhiker : 1375.
With Apologies to Carl Sandburg : 3968.
With Both Hands : 7096.
With Bread to Fill the Air : 3911.
With Charles and Holly at Giubbe Rosse in
     Florence : 6076.
With Eberhart at Occom : 1227.
With Grass As Their Witness : 7220.
With Heavenly Fire : 240.
With Him : 3822.
With His Things : 1402.
With It : 95.
With Lettuce : 2331.
With My Looks : 6300.
With the Cloud Formations : 5308.
With the Communist Radio Buzz Behind:
     Leaving Beijing : 1046.
With the moonlight a butterfly : 2171, 2174,
     5539.
With the Table Ready : 224, 2824, 3715.
With the Tongues of Angels : 6867.
With the Visiting Writer : 1122.
With This Ring : 1908.
With Vacations Like This, Who Needs a Job
     : 6423.
With Walt Whitman in Freiburg : 4477.
With What Is Left : 5278.
With Wings / Con Alas, Versos de Invierno
     para Hugo / Winter Lines for Hugo :
     2256.
With You : 3822.
With You in the Darkness : 6030.
With Youngest Daughter at Parents' Grave :
     2446.
Without a Net : 3835.
Without a Sequel : 6270.
Without a Sound : 6645.
Without Asking : 6682.
Without Commitments : 1635, 4024.
Without Eyes : 2759.
Without Fear : 6911.
Without my voice : 5113.
Without Regard to Autumn : 5217, 5638.
Without Translation : 5440.
Without Words : 3814, 4773, 6836.
Without You : 4535.
Witness : 275.
A Witness to the Moment : 2292.
Witnessing the Sea : 5362.
Wit's End : 779.
Wittgenstein in the Trenches, 1916 : 927.
Wizard : 3231.
Woe! : 2679, 4500.
The Wolf : 3855.

The Wolf and the Kid : 251, 6135.
The Wolf's Reply : 4486.
The Wolgan Valley : 469.
Woman Abducted from Ohio Home by
    Aliens : 2522.
Woman Alone Under the Lunar Eclipse :
    6236.
The Woman and the Soul : 3698.
Woman and Tree : 4584.
Woman at a Window : 4228.
Woman at the Door : 4435.
Woman at the Schwarzenegger Film : 5726.
Woman Bathing : 44.
A Woman Bathing in a Stream, 1654 : 2331.
Woman from the Waiting Room : 2716.
Woman Hit by Lightning : 4331.
A Woman in a Black Coat Who Could Be
    Memory : 3911.
Woman in a sailor suit : 4838.
Woman in an Attic : 5617.
Woman in an Interior : 6742.
Woman in Bathtub : 228.
The Woman in Black : 6171, 7259, 7271.
The Woman in the Closet : 2748.
Woman in the Dunes : 7145.
Woman in the Ermine Dress : 398.
Woman in the Pool : 4289.
The Woman in the Supermarket : 4362.
A Woman Is Drawing Her Mother : 2702.
A Woman Kneeling in the Big City : 2795,
    4010, 4010.
The Woman Next Door : 818.
A Woman of Parts : 4825.
Woman off Physics, November 1991 : 2599.
The Woman on Summer Street : 1768.
The Woman on the Fire Escape : 6432.
Woman on the Roof : 5140.
A Woman Playing Ball : 4981.
Woman Quilter — Woodard, Oklahoma :
    1972.
A Woman Remembers Her Ex-Husband :
    4329.
A Woman Who Liked Babies : 1644.
The Woman Who Mistook Her Life As
    Teatime : 3609.
The Woman Who Was Left at the Altar :
    1165.
Woman with a Crow : 2981.
The Woman With a Perfect Garden : 7059.
The Woman with Five Hearts : 1719.
Woman With the Flow of Blood : 842.
A Woman Without Children : 5856.
A Woman's Place : 6878.
Woman's Tongue : 3101.
A Woman's Word : 3185.
Womb Regalia : 3563.
Womb Tidings : 1361.
Women : 2220, 3838.
The Women Always Wave the Flags : 85.
Women Are People Too : 149.
Women at Fifty : 830.
Women Holding Up the Sky : 5872.
Women in My Life : 4939.
Women in Vats: Indian Summer Vinegar
    Factory : 4287.
Women of Fable : 6512.

The Women of Ravenna : 3428.
Women of the Future : 5939.
Women Talking : 7137.
The Women Who Lived in Byron's Body :
    857.
Women Who Sleep on Stones : 5131.
Women with Knives : 4478.
The Women You Are Accustomed To : 1149.
Women's Center Crisis Line : 841.
Women's Condition : 1488, 5123.
A* Wonderland Party : 7194.
The Wonderwheel at Coney Island : 7179.
Won't you celebrate with me : 1149.
Wood Mentor : 2140.
The Wood Pile : 2706.
Wood Work : 4225.
The Woodcut on the Cover of Robert Frost's
    Complete Poems : 979.
Woodland Spring : 4950.
Wood's Edge : 2136.
The Woods near Eureka, California : 1582.
Woody n Me : 1386.
Wool on a Wire : 3643.
Word : 3546, 5756.
The Word and Wondering Violent : 3760.
Word Processing : 439, 3776.
The Word Thistle : 7014.
A Word to Sylvia Plath after Seeing
    Heptonstall Cemetery : 5727.
Word Up : 6796.
Word Works : 5769.
Words : 365, 4653.
The Words : 188, 1835.
The Words   5-12-1993 : 5569.
Words and Babies: Issues of Creation : 3953.
Words Are the Only Fingers of the Soul : 4.
Words Fail Me : 858.
Words for a Friend : 2584.
Words for Ruth Miller : 8.
Words for Xn : 165, 4867.
Words Growing Wild in the Woods : 7324.
Words Instead of a Thousand Pictures : 5854.
Words into Words Won't Go : 4051.
Words I've Lost Forever : 1218.
Words of Comfort : 1752.
Words of Experience : 4578.
The Words of the White Eyes : 2186.
Words on the Moon : 2411.
Words over the Entranceway to Hell : 5164.
Words Written Thinking of Being Near the
    Surface of Water : 231.
Work : 4343, 4900, 5145.
The Work : 192.
Work in Progress : 3006.
The Work of Men's Hands : 2928.
The Work of Saints : 1502.
A Work of Spinning : 5674.
The Worker : 4190.
Working : 5779, 5782.
Working for the Future : 6111.
Working from Home : 1633.
Working Man Fashion : 881.
Working on It : 7274.
Working Out : 5361.
Working Out in the New South : 2564.

Working Overtime on the Surface of the Sun : 3447.
Works : 3435.
The World : 1187, 3460, 6076.
A World Beneath : 4519.
The World Enters : 1362.
World-Famous Sex Acts : 308.
The World from Under : 2298.
World Gone White : 6300.
A World I Never Made : 5230.
The world is a billiard ball : 715, 4875.
The world is a doll house : 715, 4875.
The world is blank : 715, 4875.
The World Is Grief : 5991.
World Light : 6752.
The World Map : 7013.
World Poetry Projections : 6652.
The World Series : 2006.
World War II : 3239.
World Without End : 6342.
Worldly Considerations : 6299.
Worldly Embraces : 206.
World's Fair : 6345.
The World's Largest Flower Is a Parasite : 6462.
Worm : 4847.
Worm Casts : 858.
Worms : 6898.
Worse Than I Thought : 6842.
Worship : 1, 2256.
Would I? : 6041.
Would proof lie none sweet : 5370.
Wounded Animals : 6794.
Wounded Knee : 1407.
Woundings Past Weather : 1383.
Wounds : 1053.
The Wrangler Kid : 4291, 5657.
Wrapping Bread : 1399.
Wrappings : 812, 2177.
Wrassler Céleste : 6215.
The Wreck of Days : 4194.
Wreckage : 435, 1153, 5687.
Wreckage 1944 : 2723.
Wrecking Ball : 1184, 6353.
The Wrecking of Old Comiskey : 1086.
Wrecks : 1801.
Wrinkled Night Magic : 5728.
Write Off : 6099.
The Writer in the Mirror : 5721.
Writer's Block : 4795.
Writer's Dream (The Wagon) : 5011.
Writer's Dream (Untitled) : 5011.
Writers in Winter : 707.
Writing : 3056.
Writing Exercises : 1756.
The Writing Life: As It Should Be : 4748.
Writing Poems Late : 26.
Writing Sonnets : 5026.
Writing with a Feather : 5386, 6235.
Written in a Copy of the Geste of Beowulf : 354, 643.
Written in the Margin : 2652.
Written in the Mountains : 3568, 5913.
The Wrong Town : 4747.
The Wrong Way Home : 6544.
Wuyi Mountain Cave : 6007.

Wyoming : 3849.
Wyoming I Do Not Own : 5621.
Wyoming Winter Sunset, Ten Miles From Nowhere : 5836.
X Rated : 5404.
Xenia : 364, 4556.
Xiomara, she treats me well : 2049.
Xmas, 1991 : 1011.
Y W H : 599.
Ya Basta / Stream of Consciousness : 5460.
Yad Vashem : 3581.
Yak : 6215.
Yale Medical Center, the Evoked Response : 4878.
Yard Sale : 3587.
Yard Work : 3122.
Yardwork : 679.
Yarn : 386.
Yarn Wig : 7254.
A Year : 4469.
Year End Monologue with Inner Space : 7372.
Year of the Bloodhound : 1999.
The Year of the Horse : 2720.
The Year of the Horse, 4688 : 2453.
Yearbook Photograph of the Crest High Future Farmers of America. Dated January, 1971 : 5379.
Years After : 6079.
Year's End : 2518.
Years Later : 4869.
Years of Apocalypse : 4596.
Yeast : 4204.
The Yellow Cat : 7030.
Yellow-eyed Grackle : 1024.
Yellow Grass : 702.
Yellow Insanity : 888.
Yellow Man : 5454.
Yellow Pitcher Plant : 2500.
The Yellow River and the Carp : 3809, 4805, 4945.
The Yellow Shirt : 7128.
The Yellow Stone : 2044.
Yellow Weeds : 673.
Yes, Bill : 7175.
Yes They Had No Tomatoes : 1122.
Yes yes : 5638, 7026.
Yesterday : 3983.
Yesterday Morning : 291.
Yesterday my sense of adventure : 1213.
Yesterday's Barn : 4527.
Yet I Must : 3392, 5508.
Yet to Be Reconciled with the Reality of the Dark (Princess Shikishi) : 2445.
Yin/Yang : 7176.
YMCA : 6147.
Yo, Man! : 5320.
Yo Moxley : 3146.
Yo-Yo : 5537.
The Yoking of the Two Modes : 2331.
Yomesan : 3057.
You : 1703, 1936, 3782.
You (II.) : 318, 4035, 7221.
You and I and Sir John Franklin : 5025.
You Are Here : 5162.
You Are Not For My Eyes : 7027.

You Ask Me a Question : 973.
You Asked About My Life. I Send You, Pei Di, These Lines : 362, 363, 6910, 7250.
You can only feel the wind here in spurts / Ici le vent ne se fait sentir que par bouffées : 4688.
You can still make out the waterfall : 5113.
You Can Take the Boy Out of the Country : 6438.
You can tell a lot about a country by its Madonna : 6786.
You Can't Drive the Same Truck Twice : 675.
You Can't Get There from Here : 3896.
You Can't Say : 7108.
You Can't Win : 5667.
You Checked Beneath Your Bed : 7241.
You Come When I Call You : 1187.
You Don't Miss Your Water : 1743.
You drew me under yards of bad luck : 4645.
You expect the noon-alarm at City Hall : 5113.
You Have to Go Through Bowlegs : 5561.
You, in Darkness : 6157.
You in the Tomb of My Eyes : 4969.
You kno, honey, it's great when ya got ya brandnew money : 3218.
You Know I Used to Work in the Sex Industry : 4179.
You Know You Are Getting Old When : 3968.
You know you've really wound up my heart : 1820.
You Leave the City : 653.
You: My Friend, My : 848.
You Never Compared Me to a Summer's Day : 2127.
You, on Settlement Day : 1072.
You Said I Should Look : 5724.
You Said Love : 3673.
You Say You Love How Unexpected, Open Fields : 307.
You see him come, always : 631, 5951.
You Should Know : 7047.
You should remember : 2077, 5654, 7319.
You, Snake : 1987.
You still don't trust seabirds : 5113.
You Truly Did Not Imagine It : 3263, 5736.
You Will Be Listening : 3731.
You Will Hear Once More: Be My Heart : 955, 4219, 5236.
You Will Never Know Me : 202.
You/ with the Hundred Tongues of Fear : 2614.
You Wouldn't Know : 5221.
You Wouldn't Listen : 2179.
You'd Never now : 6337.
Young Ahab : 7213.
Young Edgar : 2552.
Young Girl Peeling Apples : 5770.
Young Maiden : 4320.
Young Man and Sailor : 6816.
Young Man Going Uphill with a Bird : 4348.
Young Thoreau : 2095.
The Young Wife : 6859.
The Young Wilde : 191.

The Young Woman at the Window : 3541.
Youngblood : 1743.
Your Angels : 4834.
Your Anger : 3820.
Your Celebrated Summer : 1824.
Your Celia keeps company with eunuchs : 4149, 4199.
Your Coat to Somebody Colder : 2934.
Your Dream of Moose : 1748.
Your Last Illusion, or Break Up Sonnets : 5171.
Your Life Without Me : 7359.
Your Liquid Eyes : 3891.
Your milkyeyed glance : 6022.
Your Mouth Near My House : 897.
Your Name : 323, 1524.
Your Name on the AIDS Memorial Quilt : 6132.
Your Parents Get the News You Are Dead : 7325.
Your Picture on the Wall : 1299.
Your Poem: Boat to Saltaire : 4212.
Your Sacred Idiot with Me : 432, 774.
Your Secret Life : 495.
Your Thing : 6235, 6789.
Your Three Wishes : 188, 2473.
Your Voice : 3559.
Your Warmth, the Night : 3076.
Your Whole Life : 5936.
Your Words : 6582.
You're Going With Me : 5230.
You're Right : 5186.
Yours Is My Nightmare : 3767.
Youth : 7217.
Youth's Temple : 1267.
You've Just Been Told : 4010.
Yusuf-al-Durr Recalls the First Crusade, While Preparing for the Second : 1259.
Z Zywych Bolesnych Galezi : 5254.
Zai El-Hawa : 4195.
Zarzyski Curses the Burning of His Bro, Zozobra, Old Man Gloom : 7324.
Zazen : 1018, 4043.
Zen America '89 : 2331.
Zen and the Art of Marriage : 1518.
Zen Baker : 3230.
Zen Pace : 6250.
Zen Water : 6787.
Zeroes : 7308.
Zeus Returns : 3945.
Zhivago : 3855.
Zhivago's Fire : 7216.
Zig Zag : 6120.
Zinnias : 1391.
Zip Codes : 150.
The Zipper : 1529.
Zodiacal Light : 2504.
Zona Viva: Mexico City Market : 5106.
Zones of Embarkation : 545.
Zoo : 442, 5804.
The Zoo : 6243.
The Zoo in the Zodiac : 2909.
El Zoologico : 6243.
Zundel : 7172.
Zûni Fetish : 1270.
Zurück : 3664.

About the Authors

RAFAEL CATALA (B.A., M.A., Ph.D., New York University) is president of The Ometeca Institute and editor-in-chief of *The Ometeca Journal*, both dedicated to the study and encouragement of relations between the sciences and the humanities. He was born in Las Tunas, Cuba in 1942 and came to the United States in 1961. His books of poetry and literary criticism, as well as many essays and poems, have been published in the United States, Canada, Latin America, and Europe. He has taught Latin American Literature at NYU, Lafayette College, and Seton Hall University. In 1993-94 he was visiting professor at the University of Costa Rica. Catalá is a major proponent and practitioner of *cienciapoesía* (sciencepoetry), an embodiment of the integration of aesthetics, ethics, and the sciences. A new book of critical essays about Catalá's poetry and literary work was published in 1994: *Rafael Catalá: del Círculo cuadrado a la cienciapoesía — Hacia una nueva poética latinoamericana* (Ed. by Luis A. Jiménez. Kent, WA: Ventura One).

JAMES D. ANDERSON (B.A., Harvard College, M.S.L.S., D.L.S., Columbia University) is associate dean and professor of the School of Communication, Information, and Library Studies, at Rutgers the State University of New Jersey. His library career ha included service at Sheldon Jackson College, Sitka, Alaska, and the Portland (Oregon) Public Library. He taught at Columbia, St. John's, and the City University of New York before coming to Rutgers in 1977, where he specializes in the design of textual databases for information retrieval. Major projects have included the international bibliography and database of the Modern Language Association of America and the bilingual (French & English) *Bibliography of the History of Art*, sponsored by the J. Paul Getty Trust and the French Centre National de la Recherche Scientifique in Paris. At Rutgers he also chairs the President's Select Committee for Lesbian and Gay Concerns, and for the Presbyterian Church (U.S.A.), he edits and publishes the monthly journal *More Light Update*, on lesbian and gay issues within that denomination.